Stone tools as cultural markers: change, evolution and complexity

Stone tools as cultural markers:

change, evolution and complexity

EDITED BY R. V. S. WRIGHT

Prehistory and Material Culture Series No. 12

AUSTRALIAN
INSTITUTE OF
ABORIGINAL
STUDIES
Canberra
1977

HUMANITIES PRESS Inc.

New Jersey, U.S.A.
1977

*Papers presented to a symposium at the 1974 Meeting of the
Australian Institute of Aboriginal Studies*

Illustrations of artifacts, maps, figures and photographs have been
supplied by contributors. The publishers acknowledge the assistance of
the following for illustrative material they have prepared: Winifred
Mumford, Joan Goodrum and Keith Mitchell (Australian National
University); Maria Szent-Ivany (South Australian Museum); Ken Lyon
(Australian Institute of Aboriginal Studies).

Library of Congress Catalog number 77 93952

National Library of Australia card number and ISBN 0 85575 062 6 hard cover
0 85575 063 4 soft cover

U.S.A. edition ISBN 0 391 00835 8 hard cover
0 391 00836 6 soft cover

Typeset in Australia by Dudley King Pty Ltd, Melbourne
Printed in Australia by John Sands Pty Ltd, Artarmon, NSW
3000 78 3

Contents

Introduction and two studies

R. V. S. WRIGHT

Though a research worker can afford to shut the door on distracting publications which would clutter up the working space of his mind a teaching research worker should have values which welcome the publication of a wide range of work, much of which may not accord with his own scholarly temperament. So long as there is a variegated literature he can hope that his inquisitive students will see beyond his own horizons. And they may do this on pages which he has advised them to ignore.

In Australian archaeological studies we are short of the sort of published compendium which has heterogeneous contents to which we can advise the archaeologically inquisitive to turn. This volume of papers, loosely organised around the theme of stone implements, is offered with this scarcity in mind.

Many authors have substantially revised their papers since the conference in May 1974 at which they first presented them. The discussions at the conference itself were among the most instructive and entertaining I have experienced (and they are fortunately all retained on tape). I thank all those who contributed to the happy outcome of the conference. The names of many of them appear in the list of contents of this book, but two that do not are those of Peter Ucko and Jacquie Lampert of the Institute who designed the scenario and worked to ensure that we all gave a good performance.

In this introduction I have not been tempted to lay out sets of explanatory flower-beds in which I artificially cultivate the papers of individual authors. I presume that those who read this book will not want to have me breathing down their necks while they explore its contents. Furthermore we are fortunate that Glynn Isaac, after the conference, wrote a special paper which I have put first in this volume and which spins into an introductory thread many of the loose strands customarily left to a formal introduction. Therefore I shall use the rest of this introduction to enjoy two earlier pieces of research into stone implements, the styles of which catch the spirit of much of the work being described in this volume.

If I had to nominate just one fine contextual description of stone implement manufacture I would choose Skertchly's 1879 monograph *On the Manufacture of Gun-Flints* which was published as a Memoir by the British Geological Survey.

It is true that Skertchly's archaeological reconstructions are shaky—the attempt to add time depth to his study of the craft being an undistinguished imagining. What is superb is Skertchly's study in the contemporary material culture. He decided to improve on two earlier antiquarian accounts by the untried method of participatory fieldwork. Skertchly did not merely make weekend railway excursions to view the curiosities of East Anglian natives. He took a share in a flint mine and learned the craft himself. The account he then wrote was mostly written on the spot and it was revised for publication with his informants as consultants. As a final gesture to posterity Skertchly had one man make a series of specimens for a museum; in his publication he lists these according to the ethno-taxonomic categories. For each specimen Skertchly gives an account of how his informants say it deviates from the ideal; each is technically described by Skertchly in terms of lithic technology using both qualitative and quantitative variables.

The workshops sat atop the quarries. Skertchly gives the geographical distribution of these flint quarries with their stratigraphic details and the ethno-taxonomy of the strata and their various qualities of flint. He describes sequences in the manufacture of the gun-flints (together with the manufacturing artifacts used) from the extraction of the raw quarried nodule, through the process of striking flakes to the finishing of the gun-flints by secondary flaking.

Skertchly gives us figures on the rate of output of flakes per day and the number of secondarily flaked gun-flints that could be produced per minute. The finished products are tested by Skertchly who comments on the statistics of success and failure of particular gun-flints in igniting charges of powder.

Skertchly's study is tightly technical yet he also expands into information on the sociology of the craft, the economics of the international trade in gun-flints and signs of its decline. He identifies decline in what his informants tell him as well as by site-surveys of the archaeological relics of abandoned quarries and manufacturing areas.

Skertchly's decision to study the technology of gun-flints was an eccentric one, motivated by a belief that the tradition of flint flaking in East Anglia had been passed on as an unbroken craft from the Palaeolithic—the craft serving differing functions in differing eras. This theoretical bee-in-the-bonnet is off-putting but does not damage the objectivity of his technical accounts of the living culture.

Skertchly's report is neglected—one of those constantly unread memoirs held internationally by libraries of science. Though stone implements have been an archaeological obsession ever since Boucher de Perthe's work was vindicated around 1860 the fascinating ethno-archaeological work of Skertchly does not seem to have stimulated anyone to repeat the performance among natives more distant from London than the East Anglians.

In the 1920s Skertchly emigrated to Brisbane, lectured to Queensland's Royal Society on his part in glacial man's discovery and died soon after. Over forty years had passed since his Brandon study was published and nobody anywhere had been immersed to anything like the same depth in a study of living lithic technology. The topic needed an eccentric compulsion, the time and the tolerance of discomfort which we see combined again today in scholars of the mid 20th century.

There were, however, some forerunners of today's studies and debates and one of these is from Central Australia. On 6 February 1922 W. H. Gill an art dealer and connoisseur living in Melbourne, wrote the first of a series of letters to Daisy Bates at Ooldea asking her to make (what we would call) ethno-archaeological enquiries into the lithic technology of the area. The Mitchell Library holds only Bates's replies, but it is easy to work out from them the sorts of questions Gill was asking. He wanted to know about the types of stone implement that had been used by Aborigines now living at Ooldea. In particular he wanted to know about their forms, functions and names.

Bates's first reply to Gill was on 14 February. From the start she was apprehensive about those of Gill's typological assumptions which grated on her empirical observations. She seems to be forewarning him with a manifesto:

> I may say at the outset that my method of investigation of *all* customs etc. is the 'method of ignorance'—the very best method of obtaining reliable information from native races. Scientists consciously or subconsciously form theories, & half their investigations is expended in the endeavour to 'fit in' the information with this or that theory, & half their conclusions are thereby of no value to anyone but themselves—for they are not correct conclusions.[1]

She points out that those Aborigines coming into Ooldea from the north have already made a switch to the 'white man's chisel, tomahawk, penknife etc.' and that she had, for instance, seen 'a very ingenious "chisel" made from a pen-nib stuck in a piece of spinifex gum! the point being covered with gum'.

Furthermore she knows how availability of raw material affects the size of artifacts found lying around the landscape. This proper understanding allows her to negate one easy assumption (of the relationship between the size of artifacts and their archaeological antiquity) which assumes large artifacts are early ones:

> If there is plenty of material then there will be . . . plenty of *larger* flints which are said to be the earliest; but if the flint matrix or core has to be bartered from long distances then the flints will be flaked & re flaked and re-chipped down to very tiny specimens.

Ooldea, being in the sandhills, is particularly short of raw material so that:

> All around & about Ooldea Water the palaeoliths of these long vanished peoples can be picked up, all kinds & varieties but none very large, tho' now & again I came across a large flint matrix from which pieces had been flaked.

She is sending Gill a local collection of stone implements but is careful to stress that they are archaeological specimens, none being made locally.

There was, nevertheless, information to be gathered from Aborigines who had recently moved in from the north. And it is now that we see the perceptions of Bates and Gill drifting apart. Gill must have asked her to find out specific correlates of form and function. Bates suggests that this is a fruitless commission:

> No stone—except the initiation flint—can be said to be made for a definite purpose. [To this she adds the hammerstone in a later letter.]

We learn that this is not a snap judgment but the result of practical enquiry:

> I have collected many flints. . . . Often I turn them out & say to the natives—which do you groove with, scrape with, mark with etc. & not infrequently two or three sides of the same flint or a point on it with [sic] make it utilizable for all three!

---

1. Permission of the Mitchell Library to quote from these letters is gratefully acknowledged.

We see that she has perceived that the edge of a piece of stone is what is important in this technology. She has archaeological knowledge enough to perceive that her observations call into question a generalisation of European Palaeolithic prehistorians:

> Mr Reid Moir in his work speaks of the racloir or scraper as having but one *definite* use—that of scraping—but I've seen these natives use the same flint for scraping & grooving & chipping the little dents in the *handle* part of a club to give hold.

Bates implies that there is a native taxonomy, but we can see that it is not of the sort Gill had anticipated: 'They have special names for special *colored* flints', and also for meat cutting flints and the initiation flint (the latter a 'sacred word').

In her second letter to Gill, written on 9 March 1922, she gives an account of an experiment she had tried the day before on an Aboriginal newly arrived from the Western Australian border. Milyilyi,

> . . . came with his woman. I said 'make me a miro [spear-thrower]'. 'No tomahawk' said Milyilyi: (as soon as they see a tomahawk in use away goes all their own flints). 'Why not Kandi (flints) I said. 'I've got no Kandi'. So I brought my bag of flints. 'Now get those you want for cutting out the miro from the tree trunk & for shaping it & making the markings'. Milyilyi picked *three* calling them all Kandi but adding bi'duli or bi'dul to the smallest,—the *chisel* so to speak or groover—bi'dul means 'vein' making or grooving. Now I'm sending these three Kandi . . . so in these three you have a set of miro making tools. . . . If a man has a sharp flint set in the top of a miro, he will use that to remove the piece from the tree trunk, but Milyilyi has not got a miro just now.

To reinforce her contention that there is no tight association between form and function—that indeed there are no special forms—she adds:

> I asked him [Milyilyi], would not the big Kandi cut up Kooga (meat) too. Yes, he said Kandi are used for anything—that is there are not specialized Kandi.

Then she generalises:

> Now these C.A. natives use their little knives and flakes for *any* purpose. A large flake may be used to skin and cut larger meat, or a smaller sharpened & chipped flint may be used. . . . A scraper may be a gouge & so on—at times.

And then wandering away momentarily from her previously avowed empiricism she induces, '*No primitives* have a "complete set of tools".'

Mentioning again an important part of the native taxonomy she says she will send:

> a number of flints *whose colors* are differentiated in their names, but which are all Kandi. Kandi bi'am—light colored (wâ bi'am—face light colored = half caste) and so on.

This letter produced one from Gill (unseen by me) in which he seems to have politely questioned whether Daisy Bates was seeing things properly.

In his letter Gill must have apologised for his bluntness. Bates replied on 28 April 1922:

> I'm glad you *are* candid. I am not anything else & of all things I have candor, so please let me know *exactly* what you think & mean. In the collection of stones I sent you there is a representative of every working flint these natives use, but as you see they are crude and badly made.

and

> If I looked amongst every flint area (no heaps) around Ooldea I could not get a specimen similar to the one you sketched. . . . I am sorry that I shall not be able to get a perfectly chipped flint in these areas.

She refuses to be drawn on the ethnic reality of museum classification:

No I would *not* divide the flints into domestic, tools, warfare. The only domestic stones are the upper & lower millstones, the tools may be used for cutting up meat, as well as cutting off 'elbows' of trees to make clubs—there are no 'warfare' stones . . . any little stone will make . . . scars on body.

To support what she is asserting she says she will:

get the natives to pick out from my samples stones they would use for different purposes, & I'll send these to you if you like, but I think you'll find them similar to those you already have. Anyhow I shall be glad to do this when the natives come here again.

She is perfectly well aware that there are 'types' to be found elsewhere in Australia and describes geographical clines for patterned stone implements:

As one goes north . . . [and] into the Darling, Cooper's Creek—and those eastern areas—*always going north*, you'll find the shapes gradually becoming more even & well made—but not here . . . There is no 'correct form or type' here at all. The material is in plenty in the ranges—but there is no special type—each 'flaker' or 'chipper' works on his own lumps of flint core.

It seems that her technical understanding was better than Gills. He returned as broken a specimen she had sent him. She teaches him an elementary characteristic of a struck flake in a letter of 4 June:

I found a little one similar to that which you returned & it also has no pointed end. The part where you thought the point had been broken off is the flat part of the 'core' . . . from which the flint was flaked before being chipped into shape.

Gill had evidently asked several times about a special artifact of repetitively formal shape (I am not sure what it was—probably a geometric backed blade). It was by 25 July that Daisy Bates was showing some impatience with Gill's persisting belief that ethno-archaeology could shed light on the function of this implement:

I can only go by the specimens here & by what the natives say. I shall send you all we have obtained of a shape approaching the little palaeolith you returned, but none is so regular as the little one.

And on 9 August she writes reassuringly:

As you are associated in my mind with the pointed chipped flint, no matter where or when I shall come across a specimen I will remember & send it on to you.

It turned out that by the end of the following year she had found some of these flints 'chipped towards both ends' as scarce archaeological specimens and sent them on 10 October 1922 to Gill.

It seems that Gill and she then gave each other up. She wrote on 22 December 1928 but did not mention stones. The next and last letter in the collection was written 12 years after the first: on 28 January 1934 Daisy Bates wrote (and it is hard to believe it was without a wisp of irony):

Thank you for your kindly letter. I remember your interest in native flints & your desire to have some special types, which however are not made in Central areas.

So the exchanges ceased. Daisy Bates refused to be shifted from the empiricism of what was before her eyes. Gill was seeking *a priori* decided information about the catalogue of formal stone implements. Implicit in the existing paradigms of world academic archaeology were predictions about what Daisy Bates *should* be seeing in the ethno-archaeological field. To Gill these predictions seemed to convert Bates's real observations into incompetent irrelevancies or inaccuracies.

We now have hindsights based on extensive studies of the lithic technology of the Australian desert areas. I think it is proper to claim that Daisy Bates was correctly sticking to her original manifesto of the 'method of ignorance'.

Would any archaeological editor of the 1920s have thought it worth publishing the sort of misunderstandings which were taking place between Bates and Gill? I doubt it. Yet they have the familiar ring of contemporary debate. Ethno-archaeological participatory observation is no longer regarded as eccentric behaviour.

How you interpret Daisy Bates's general performances on the stage of Aboriginal studies is determined by what you are programmed to applaud in the theatre of social attitudes. She is booed as an opinionated and bossy do-gooder. She is applauded as the selfless analgesic nurse ministering to what she thought was the deathbed of a race.

It is therefore disarming to discover how explicitly hedonistic she could be when giving motives for the work she did. As early as 1913, in a letter from the harsh remoteness of Eucla on the edge of the Nullarbor Plain, she says:

Many of my friends in W.A. deplore my 'burying myself in the bush & for a lot of ungrateful blacks'. They ask, 'Is it worth while?' (as if one were doing the work for a 'worth-while'.) I'm doing it because it gives me pleasure in the same way that hockey & tennis & foxhunting gave me pleasure when I pursued them.

If we admit to hedonistic motives in our own work we can be entertained and not threatened when we realise that many of today's archaeological researches are refurbished antiques. It is true that we have a lot more information and that this information is sometimes better tailored and measured. But to see a diachronic straight line improvement in archaeology is a delusion which can persist only if we censor the published literature with our own ephemeral and restricted values— that is, filter yet again the published literature which successive generations of editors have themselves put through the changing filters of letters of rejection.

This volume of papers contains a variegation of contemporary archaeological praxis. It is intended to cater as much for our historically curious descendants as for our selectively curious individual selves.

Squeezing blood from stones

Comments on the importance of Australian data for the promotion of realism in 'Stone Age' studies. Notes towards discussion of general issues and of issues raised by contributions

GLYNN ISAAC

Expectations about what information can be derived from stone tools has mounted in a series of leaps during the century or so that they have been studied seriously. When their existence was first rediscovered by Europeans in the golden days of Tournal, Boucher de Perthes, Falconer, Evans, etc., everyone was delighted merely that they could be used as markers of man's geological antiquity. A short while later, with de Mortillet leading the field it seemed that they could be used to define the rungs of the ladder of progress of humanity. Then as studies proceeded it became apparent to workers such as Breuil, Peyrony, and Burkitt, that the story was more complicated: stone tools varied in space as well as time—and they came to be used as the markers of palaeocultural entities each with its own geographic distribution and time range. For many, stone age prehistory became like a game of chess, with techniques and cultures weaving their way through time and space, with complex interactions. This approach can be characterised as 'culture historic', and in recent years there has been a reaction against it as the predominant goal of prehistory. Other schools of researchers have become convinced that stone tools contain information not only about culture history but also about the 'activities' of particular ancient societies. Interest in this idea arose gradually in various regions: in Africa I am aware of it in the 1950s in the writings of J. D. Clark (1959) and M. R. Kleindienst (1959, 1961). But it was the Binford and Binford paper of 1966 that dramatically caused attention to be focused on it. Since that time many prehistorians have entertained the conviction, or the hope, that suitable studies of stone tools could add spectacular new dimensions to our knowledge of the stone age past through the recognition of 'task forces', seasonal rounds, patterns of exploitation, etc.[1] For ten years the feasibility of such inferences has been the cause of major debates among palaeolithic prehistorians.

If one takes a dispassionate view of the mounting demands for information that we have made from stone tools, then it is clear that the temptation towards over-interpretation is very strong. They can be used in many ways—as markers of man's antiquity, as indices of 'progress', as symptoms of cultural differentiation in time and space and as indicators of the organisation. However, we need to assess the limits to the amount of blood that can realistically be squeezed from these stones.

Fortunately, many prehistorians are now thoroughly aware that proper understanding will come not from artifacts alone but from artifacts in the context of distributions within and among sites and in relation to food refuse and other economic and ecological markers.

How are we to determine what information can realistically be obtained from stone tools and what the limits may be? Clearly this will have to be done by trial and error for each region and time period—we have to search for order and pattern among the artifacts and then see if we can find geographic, chronologic, economic, ecological, or sociological correlates of these patterns. However, when we work with the Pleistocene record we are in a way groping in the dark and herein lies the importance of Australia. It is only in this continent that we have direct observations on the lives of stone-using hunters living entirely in a world of hunters. In spite of the fact that stone tools have been a crucial agent of human adaptation for some $99\cdot8\%$ of the $2\frac{1}{2}$ million years for which we have an archaeological record, in almost all other areas peoples, whether farmers or not, became involved in associated social, economic, and technological complication. Australia is the only continent where the stone age archaeological record can be traced to the point where it merges with an ethnographic record of non-agricultured peoples dependent on stone tools. Thus while Australian prehistory has its own intrinsic interest, it also has importance as a testing ground for ideas about the role of stone tools in the lives of people. It can also be a hone for methods of study.

In saying all this, I do not wish to imply that we can simply transfer chunks of Australian pattern and apply it to the stone age elsewhere. To do so would be to preclude the discovery of original, non-Australian patterns. However, we can use it to improve our insight into function and enlarge our imagination with regard to the processes involved in making, using and discarding stone tools. From this may come more realistic hypotheses for testing against the Pleistocene record, and alternative ideas about how particular configurations may have arisen in the past. Above all, our zeal to overinterpret may be tempered with constructive realism.

In Australia one can apply all the techniques and methods that are being developed by archaeologists who have nothing but archaeological evidence—but in Australia there is the unique opportunity of looking to see how the apparent results compare with 'ethnographic information'. The papers prepared for this conference show that this process is getting under way with great vigour and enterprise.

---

1. Symptomatic of the urge for finer and finer exegesis of the record and of the concern with process has been the development of a remarkable vocabulary—our stone age hunters are now involved in 'extractive activities' and in 'procurement'. They 'maintain', 'curate' and 'utilise' their artifacts as they move about on 'maintenance' or 'monitoring' trips or as they do things at 'task specific localities' and so on. All of these terms cover concepts for which we need labels in our discussions but one also cannot help smiling at the way in which stone using men have come to sound like operators in a Rand Corporation design for Pleistocene living.

No two stone artifact assemblages are identical and it is common experience that any set of assemblages varies in a complex fashion with some distinctions being subtle and others being striking and conspicuous. In my understanding, the thrust of this conference was to discuss the interpretation of variation in stone tools as it bears on Australian data. The key questions can be paraphrased as follows: How well do stone tools work as markers of distinct cultural systems that changed, intergraded, and interacted through time and space? How sensitive are stone tools as indicators of economic and ecological relationships? Can stone tools be used as clues to the differentiation of activities (seasonal or otherwise) within an individual socio-cultural system?

The contributions prepared for the conference range from case studies to tentative syntheses and exploratory generalisations—all of which bear on these questions whether or not there is explicit treatment of them. As an outsider to the specifics of Australian research, perhaps the most useful thing for me to do is to offer some commentary on methodology. In doing so I intend to point to the use of the ethnographic information which in Australia alone is available to serve as a kind of throwing stick to knock down unrealistic interpretations that the stones by themselves might tempt one to set up as theories.

Generalisations about material-culture history or about the economic relationships of stone tools must stem from the perception of recurrent patterns amongst a set of artifact assemblages. This necessarily involves comparative studies, and it is with aspects of that operation that this post-conference commentary will mainly be concerned.

The following steps are entailed in a comparative study:

(1) Acquisition of a set of valid samples of assemblages relevant to the problem in hand;

(2) Characterisation of the assemblages (samples) in terms relevant to the questions that the enquiry seeks to answer;

(3) Analysis—the assessment of patterns of resemblance and difference, plus search for regularities and order among the variables;

(4) Projecting patterns discerned in the artifact evidence against external 'dimensions' such as time, space, habitat, site character, etc.;

(5) Interpretation.

Fig. 1 presents a flow diagram of the process, and further comments are scattered through the text that follows.

The characterisation of an assemblage   Stone artifact assemblages commonly show a range of forms that grade from specimens expressive of arbitrary, purposive design to forms that are merely determined by banal contingencies of simple stone fracturing processes. The forms showing purposive design through trimming and retouch are by convention amongst palaeolithic archaeologists termed 'tools', while the untrimmed flakes and chips are termed 'debitage' or 'waste'. This is a technical, morphological distinction that has nothing to do with recurrent judgments about whether individual objects in each series were or were not used. The two poles of the continuum intergrade through pieces in which the trimming or modification is minimal or highly irregular.

There exists also another axis of differentiation: items may display varying degrees of damage or wear resulting from use. Within an assemblage specimens will commonly range from those showing zero perceptible use damage to some showing comparatively conspicuous, intensive damage. Clearly items

showing definite use damage were 'tools' in ordinary parlance, but they are not necessarily 'tools' in the technical sense.

Now it seems necessary to spell out these distinctions because changing practice in stone artifact analysis is causing confusion. The danger is particularly acute in Australia because of abundant ethnographic evidence that non-'tools' (in the technical sense) were in fact important 'tools' (in common parlance). One has to look at the history of method in palaeolithic studies in order to understand the situation. In the early days of study in Europe it was customary only to collect and report the fancy trimmed forms which were designated as 'the tools'. Even amongst this selected series it was usual to base cultural classification of assemblages on particularly distinctive forms—*fossiles directeurs*. Now as time has gone on archaeologists have become more and more demanding with regard to the interpretation of stone tools and more and more conscientious over collecting and reporting complete assemblages. In Europe this movement culminated in the systematisations of typology and procedure that are associated with Francois Bordes (1950, 1961) and with de Sonneville-Bordes and Perrot (1954, 1955, 1956). These systems involve comprehensive reports on the technology of the assemblages including debitage, but cultural (industrial) taxonomy still depends largely on the composition of the trimmed tool series, which is commonly represented by the graphic display technique of a cumulative graph. That is to say the features of the most highly designed segment of each assemblage remain the criteria for 'cultural' classification. Questions regarding aspects of the assemblages other than 'cultural affinity' must be answered by reference to other segments of the data.

During the past decade there has been greatly expanded interest in stone artifacts as indicators of 'activities' rather than as mere markers of culture historic patterns. This has led to the sense in some quarters that pieces for which use as utensils can be demonstrated as a result of use-marks are quite as important as trimmed tools, in the technical sense. This in turn is apt to lead to mixed characterisation of assemblages and to comparative statements in which inferences based on specific 'design' elements and inferences based on potentially generalised use patterns become garbled up together.

In some regards it is regrettable that the upper Pleistocene stone artifact assemblages of Western Europe have become, through the historical accident of priority, a standard of reference for the rest of the stone age world. It appears that they are more highly patterned than is the case in many other regions and as a consequence it has been easier to recognise the distinctions between 'tools', 'utilised' and 'waste'. There has thus been too little explicit discussion of the validity and practicality of these distinctions.

Because of this legacy of confusion, I would like to advocate that clear distinctions should be made in the presentation of artifact categorisation data ('so called' typology).

These can be made to express the two axes of structure:

explicitly designed forms ↔ Opportunistic
                                                          untrimmed forms
perceptibly used items   ↔ items without traces of
                                                          use.

In my view a hierarchical layout along the following lines would promote clarity:

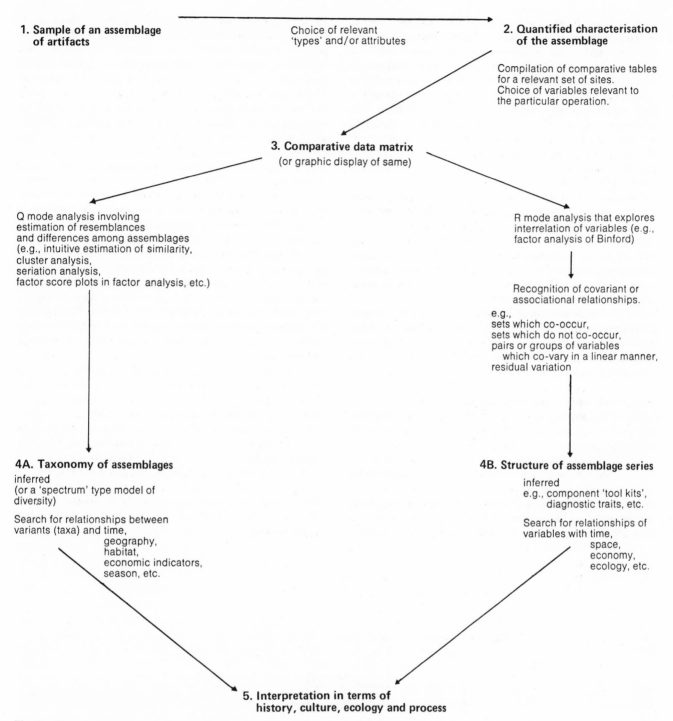

Fig. 1: Steps and procedures in the investigation of variation between assemblages.

i. Gross composition of assemblage with percentages for A-D relative to the total sample:

    A. Trimmed (designed) tools
    B. Utilised items
    C. Cores etc.
    D. Untrimmed flakes and flake fragments.

ii. Detailed breakdown of sub-categories (≃ 'types') within each of the above categories—with percentages relative to the sub-sets A, B, C, and D respectively.

iii. Technological categorisation—eg. percentage of blades, of Levallois flakes, of bipolar flakes, etc. (This may cross cut the A-D categories, with one specimen being simultaneously a 'tool' and a flake of a specific kind.)

iv. Utilisation-damage categorisation, which may cross cut A-D; i.e. if some items are simultaneously trimmed, designed 'tools' and show use damage of a kind also found on non-trimmed implements.

v. Other categorisation data—eg. raw material, fire damage, etc.

In many Australian industries, as with African and other stone industries, there is an important gradient within the trimmed 'tool' series from formalised, explicitly 'designed' forms to casually trimmed, opportunistic forms. In some instances this may justify splitting the 'tool' category between 'Formal' and 'Informal' divisions.

In addition to the categorisation data discussed above, clearly there are many other qualitative and quantitative attributes which may be determined and reported. Some of these may be suspected to have primarily 'stylistic' significance (eg. scar counts on coeval Acheulian biface assemblages) while others may be suspected of having strong functional determinants (eg. edge angles for scraper-like objects). The attributes selected for presentation should have definable relevance to questions being asked about the assemblages in question and they too should be presented in such a way as to facilitate clear thinking about implications for cultural affinity and for functional determinants.

This plea for orderliness in the gathering and presentation of data used to characterise assemblages for comparative purposes, is made in all humility. There is no region where clarity of thought and presentation is yet common practice. The interest of Australian data and the fact of ethnographic information on function, makes orderliness of added importance. Mulvaney makes a similar plea in the closing paragraphs of his contribution to this conference.

Let me leave this point by rephrasing it in metaphoric terms: presentation of a meal, as a series of discrete dishes does not prevent those who wish, from making various kinds of amalgam—but it can be very hard to separate out the components of an Irish stew!

Recognising pattern and order among assemblages Once a series of samples has been characterised in a systematic and comparable fashion it is possible to seek to discover pattern and order amongst them. Once again procedure should be explicitly related to the questions that are being asked. If one is primarily concerned with culture as an information system operating within space and time and if one wishes to measure degrees of interconnection and continuity, then most emphasis will be given to those aspects of surviving material culture that are sensitive to 'stylistic' and 'fashion' differentiation.

Experience up to now suggests that the peculiarities of the most highly 'designed' components of stone tool industries provide the best markers of idiosyncratic 'phases' and 'provinces' within the culture transmission system—and of continuity and interchange between phases and provinces. These objectives are of course closely allied to those involved in conventional 'culture historic' approaches. However such an approach can perfectly well be concerned with 'process' and 'system'—as I have tried to show in my phrasing of these comments (see also D. L. Clarke, 1968, 1972).

Alternatively one may be primarily concerned with the role of artifacts as functional parts of an adaptive, economic system. Concern with generalisations regarding this aspect may be best rewarded by weighting sections of the data in which 'style' has minimal importance—for instance attributes that directly relate to edge character and mode of usage, etc.

It should be stressed that these two alternative lines of attack are not mutually exclusive, but in my opinion they are best kept separate until the integrative, interpretative stage of the investigation (step 5 of Fig. 1). If one feeds in an uncontrolled mixture of 'stylistic' and 'functional' data, then the patterns emerging from the analysis may be liable to more contentious and subjective lines of interpretation than are really necessary.

After acquisition of data on a set of assemblages for which comparative study is appropriate (eg., a set deriving from some geographic region and from a reasonably restricted time range), and after selection of variables germane to stated palaeo-anthropological objectives, a 'data matrix' can be compiled (step 3 in Fig. 1). This is usually and most conveniently in the form of a table with the categories (types) and attributes (means, ratios, etc.) labelled down the side and the assemblage-samples labelled along the top. Each row then is comprised of all the expressions of a single 'variable' and each column is a list of the values determined for all the variables in one sample viz.:

The data matrix can often be so ordered as to facilitate direct perception of pattern. Thus if there is a question such as 'do samples from shore line locations (habitat I) differ from those on forested hilltops (habitat II)?'—then it will be sensible to group these sets in the table so as to make a first judgment possible by scanning. Alternatively the columns can be grouped by time divisions, by geographic provinces, etc. Equally the variables can be grouped in relation to their supposed significance ('style', 'technology', 'function' etc.).

The systematic analysis of a data matrix can proceed by two routes: one can compare assemblages (columns) assessing degrees of similarity and difference with regard to some or all variables. This is *Q-mode analysis* and it usually leads to a taxonomy of assemblages—or more rarely to a 'spectrum' type of ordering of assemblages as points along a continuum, as in seriation. Alternatively one may search for relationships between variables (rows)—this is *R-mode analysis* which in stone-age studies have been made known by the celebrated factor-analysis of Binford and Binford (1966). (For good general accounts of the theory behind these terms, see Sokal and Sneath, 1963, Sackett, 1966, D. L. Clarke, 1968, Hodson, 1970.)

Both Q-mode and R-mode analyses can proceed by many different techniques, details of which fall outside the scope of this commentary. At the simplest, various graphic display devices can serve well taking a few variables or a few cases at a time and projecting them. The *graphique cumulatif* of Bordes is one such technique—histograms, bivariate plots, and ternary plots are others.

Alternatively more complex computation procedures can be undertaken. *Principal Components Analysis* and the closely related technique of *Factor Analysis* are capable of revealing either Q-mode or R-mode patterns and structures—though not every individual run will yield equally interpretable Q and R results. Other techniques include some form of cluster analysis, seriation, multidimensional sealing, etc. Reviews by Cowgill (1968) and by Hodson and co-workers in *World Archaeology* provide good introductions to the application and relative merits of some of these techniques.

Multivariate techniques involve putting data into a hopper, letting them be processed in what for most of us is in some degree a 'black-box' and then getting a print out suggesting certain patterns or relationships. It cannot be stressed too often that if bad or irrelevant data are fed in, then meaningless or misleading results will come out. Once a configuration or relationship has been suggested by a multivariate analysis, its archaeological reality and nature should be carefully scrutinised. Recent re-examination by means of bivariate plots of apparent covariant relationships with high correlation values in some early factor analysis studies has shown that peculiar distribution patterns for the pairs of variables can make Pearson *r* a misleading summary of the data—and hence brings the whole proceeding into question.

In this essay I am urging that the artifact data be analysed to discover its own intrinsic patterns and order. As already stated I think that initially one should separate data relating primarily to 'design', to 'technology' and to 'function'. As patterns emerge in each analysis, the interrelationships which they may show can be explored and integrated.

Once pattern (taxonomy of assemblages) and structure (relationships between variables) have been established from the artifact data considered without regard to other non-artifact information, then these patterns and relationships should be projected against relevant external information.

One must ask certain questions: To what extent do groupings within the comparative set coincide with time periods? To what extent with geographic regions or provinces? To what extent do they show direct relations with habitat or with non-artifactual evidence of activities? By asking and answering these questions the artifact study can make its contribution to understanding cultural history, cultural process, and to interpreting ecology and economy.

Synchronic and diachronic variation Classic, culture historic approach to stone-tool archaeology is primarily concerned with change through time (diachronic variants) and differences between several regions at the same time (synchronic, allopatric variants). However, this approach makes little allowance[1] for the possibility that there could be markedly different stone tool assemblages being generated in the same region, at the same time (synchronic, sympatric variants).

Archaeological research in a number of areas has produced sets of assemblages that vary significantly, but for which the spectrum of variation may not be clearly associated either with geography or with time—within the limits of resolution of the latter. The most famous examples of this have been the patterns of variation reported in the Mousterian Complex (Bourgon, 1957; Bordes, 1961a; Bordes and de Sonneville-Bordes, 1970; Binford and Binford, 1966, 1969; Freeman, 1966; Mellars, 1970) or in the Acheulian and Oldowan complexes of Africa (Clark, 1959; Kleindienst, 1961; Isaac, 1969, 1972a; Leakey, 1971; Binford, 1972). One possible solution to the dilemma that confronts a culture historian when he meets such a situation is to develop a model involving distinct co-existent traditions ('tribes') living in overlapping/interpenetrating territories. These kinds of solutions have been explored and advocated by various scholars (Bordes, 1961b; Leakey, 1971). Another solution which has had wide appeal is to explain large parts of the observed variation as being the artifactual expression of essentially the same people doing different things in different times and places. Thus, it is argued, they generate contrasting assemblages which are none the less *sensu lato* synchronous and sympatric. This is the 'activity differentiation model' made famous by Binford and Binford (1966).

Protagonists of these positions have stated them so clearly and so dramatically that, with all due respect, the palaeolithic intellectual scene has rather come to resemble the stamping grounds of rutting male antelope. However, there are other possibilities: all of the aforementioned positions assume persistent regularity in the determinants of stone artifact morphology through time and space—either as a consequence of stable 'tribal' tradition or as a consequence of persistent functional constraints. However, it is possible that *we should not assume such tight regularity and constancy.* What if a rather wide range of forms will fulfil the basic functions of stone tools equally well? What if the norms with regard to artifacts 'drift' about within broad limits? If we then draw samples whose time relations are not known in detail from assemblages representing such floating norms, would we not expect them to show sympatric and at the low level of time-resolution, apparently synchronic variation? This is a possible way of explaining some of the bewildering variety that I have termed *stochastic* or *random-walk* patterning, and for which Francois Bordes in a letter to me used the phrase 'drunken

1. Quarry sites and shell midden sites have long been recognised as liable to significant deviants from regional-phase norms.

man' progression. In people's eagerness to find grand designs, this possibility has perhaps as yet been too little considered.

It is important to stress that the random walk idea is *not* an explanation in its own right—it is the equivalent of residual variance in an analysis of variance. We must first seek to see how much of the variation in a given archaeological situation can be associated with time, space and independent evidence of activities, but we should not assume in advance that *all* variation has to be definably associated with these. I have developed these ideas in two recent essays and will not repeat them at length here (Isaac, 1972a, 1972b).

Getting at activity differentiation Over the past decade, concern with the relationships between 'activity' and the morphology of artifacts has clearly been a vital new development in palaeolithic studies. Initially, the concepts involved were handled in part on the basis of the intuitive sense that assemblage character would necessarily express 'activities'. Many workers retained a certain sceptical reserve about the directness and simplicity of this relationship, but the objections were not often spelled out and forcefully stated. Now in the second round of studies the theoretical structure of the relationship between activity and assemblage characteristics is being explored and also practical studies are yielding evidence about cases with ethnographic control. This symposium breaks important new ground in this regard and the material and discussions have importance far beyond Australia.

Ammerman and Feldman (1974) recently presented a discussion of the processes involved. From a purely theoretical point of view they point out that an archaeological occurrence incorporating artifacts is in fact generated by a complex series of processes, amongst which the following are conveniently separated as 'steps':

(1) Manufacture of a given artifact or kit of artifacts;
(2) Use of the artifacts for one or more purposes—with possible associated modification, resharpening or damage;
(3) Discard of the artifact.

Now simple relationships between assemblage character and activity will only result from cases where usage and discard coincide spatially and temporally and in which only one activity is represented. More usually one has to recognise that each of the three component processes has its own distinct spatial distribution—and its own rate of occurrence. That is to say the total system involves complex differential mapping relationships between manufacture, use and discard. Ammerman and Feldman go on to show that such a system can generate 'correlations' between artifact forms used for different activities and mask correlation between forms used in the same activity.

This theoretical position had been formulated prior to the conference, but independently, direct observations of ethnographic situations were found at the conference to point in the same direction. The papers of Binford, Gould and Hayden constitute very important milestones in this regard. Binford introduces the verb 'to curate' to denote the carrying around of artifacts so that use occurs in many places and discard only in very few. Clearly explicit attention has to be given to this factor.

Both Gould and Hayden have provided estimates of the number of tools of each major variety made by the Aborigines of the Australian desert in the course of an average annual round of activities. This is extraordinarily valuable data of a kind that has not ever, as far as I am aware, been offered before for flaked stone tools. Lack of time prevented detailed discussion at the conference of these estimates and of discrepancies between them, but clearly the observations of the component processes involved have far more importance than the precise numerical values, which could not in any simple way be reapplied to other situations.

Gould also presents a clear account of spatial segregation between 'camp site' assemblages which occur in concentrated patches and special activity artifacts such as those for heavy wood cutting which occur dispersed over the landscape. This too is new and very important information. It immediately occurs to me that it may have relevance for the debate in African prehistory over whether the 'Sangoan' heavy duty assemblages are a 'culture' or a facies. It also establishes the importance for prehistory of studying dispersed and low density traces as well as the much more conspicuous and attractive dense patches on which attention has hitherto been focused.

A series of contributions also represents another line of attack on the important matter of the relationship between 'activity' and assemblage composition. These involve careful study of artifact assemblages from the recent past of areas for which ethnographic documentation exists. The objective in these studies is to gauge the extent of variability amongst assemblages that are reasonably regarded as deriving from the same land use system, and then to seek to match archaeological data on assemblage variation with ethnographic information on the structure of daily and seasonal tool using activities. Studies of this kind presented and discussed at the conference, were those of Lourandos, McBryde and O'Connell, and similarly oriented research is also actively under way in Western Australia though it was not reported in detail (Sylvia Hallam, personal communication and in the Annual Reports of the Australian Institute of Aboriginal Studies).

O'Connell's study, of which a brief preliminary account is offered in this conference, involves his being shown traditional camp sites by a group of Aborigines who abandoned a nomadic hunting and gathering life within living memory. The sites are identified by the informants as having been primarily used in wet or dry seasons etc. and their proximity to significant food resources and raw materials can be determined. Collections of the stone artifacts lying around on these sites are then taken as a basis for attempting to determine the relationship between ethnographically determined site function and archaeologically determined assemblage characteristics. Clearly the research design involves risks and difficulties. The surface collection samples do not derive simply from the time span of ethnographic memory, the assemblages may have accumulated over centuries, even millenia and they may incorporate items from much earlier, different material culture systems. In spite of these risks it seems possible that if a sufficient number of sites can be sampled any patterned differentiation that may have existed between artifact composition and site character will emerge. The interest of the propositions is quite sufficient to justify the continuation of O'Connell's experiment. As his paper in this volume shows, the most clear cut patterning to emerge as yet relates to the relative availability of quartzite and chert at the sites. O'Connell was kind enough to allow me to examine the pilot series of samples collected to date. My impression was that variations, other than those associated with raw material frequencies, are rather subtle—they do not have the amplitude for instance of the much debated Mousterian variants in France or the Middle Pleistocene variants in East Africa. One must await the continuation of the experiment for more definite resolution of these matters.

McBryde has been engaged over the past decade in a careful archaeological and ethno-historical study of parts of northern New South Wales. Her contribution to this conference presents in miniature excellent exemplification of many of the questions discussed in this essay. Within her study area she appears to have differentiated both between subtly distinguished material culture systems ('microcultures') each appropriate to different sub regions and she seems to have assemblage differentiations within each sub region that are associated with specific habitats and economies ('activity facies'). This impressive body of archaeological information provides important opportunities for testing some of the analytical approaches discussed earlier, and for testing the results against ethnography.

Out of the discussions of 'activity facies' a proposition emerged at the conference—perhaps in Australia the archaeological expression of activity differentiation is weak because many crucial tools were carried about and used in many places where they were not discarded. By contrast, so the argument ran, perhaps in earlier segments of the stone-age such as the 'Mousterian' or the 'Acheulian' tools were more prodigally treated, being made for an immediate need and discarded on the spot immediately after use. This is a provocative hypothesis which should be tested. The Australian data cannot be used to prove or disprove the proposition, but it does enjoin caution.

Conclusion Much of the current research reported to the conference seems likely to have a critical impact on our understanding of the relationship between stone tools and adaptation. In as much as important studies remain uncompleted one should be careful to avoid premature judgment; however, some of the outcomes seem apparent already. In Australian prehistory, marked variations in stone tool morphology and assemblage composition have complex time and space distributions. Attempts to find simple relations between the variants and economy, ecology or 'activity' do not seem likely to be successful, and prehistorians will have to continue to incorporate 'irrational' culture historic accidents in their treatment of the record. Also, if I judge the signs correctly, intra-cultural differentiation of assemblages in relation to 'activity' is detectable but it is far more subtle than many workers have supposed it would be. It seems to me that in general we are better off getting our inferences regarding 'activity', 'ecology' and 'economy' from food refuse, pollen analysis and the context of sites than from artifact studies alone.

Many facets of the information from past and present work in Australia are important for us all. Amongst the most important lessons, are a series of warnings against the dangers of over interpreting stone artifacts. It is clear that stone artifacts do provide a rich record of cultural transmission patterns ('culture-history') and that their characteristics are also related to economy and ecology. However, archaeology is not well served by unrealistic attempts to squeeze too much blood from stones alone. We need to concentrate our efforts on situations where the stones are only a part of a diverse record of mutually related traces of behaviour and adaptation.

References

Ammerman, A. J. and M. W. Feldman 1974. On the 'making' of an assemblage of stone tools. *American Antiquity*, 39: 610–16

Binford, L. R., 1972. Contemporary model building: paradigms and the current state of Palaeolithic research. In *Models in archaeology*, (ed) D. L. Clarke, pp. 109–66. London: Methuen.

—— and S. R. Binford, 1966. A preliminary analysis of functional variability in the Mousterian of Levallois facies. In *Recent studies in paleoanthropology*, (eds) J. D. Clark and F. C. Howell, pp. 238–95. *American Anthropologist*, Special Publication 68 : 2 : 2.

—— and —— 1969. Stone tools and human behaviour. *Scientific American*, 220 (4): 70-82.

Bordes, F., 1950. Principles d'une méthode d'étude des techniques de débitage et de la typologie du Paléolithique ancien et moyen. *L'Anthropologie*, 54 : 19–34.

—— 1961a. Mousterian cultures in France. *Science*, 134 : 803–10.

—— 1961b. *Typologie du Paléolithique Ancien et Moyen.* Bordeaux: Imprimeries Delmas.

—— and D. de Sonneville-Bordes, 1970. The significance of variability in palaeolithic assemblages. *World Archaeology*, 2 : 61–73.

Bourgon, M., 1957. Les Industries Moustériennes et Pré-Moustériennes du Périgord. *Archives de l'Institut de Paléontologie Humaine, Mémoire 27.*

Clark, J. D., 1959. Further excavations at Broken Hill, Northern Rhodesia. *Journal of the Royal Anthropological Institute*, 89 : 201–32.

Clarke, D. L. 1968. *Analytical archaeology.* London: Methuen.

—— (ed), 1972. *Models in archaeology.* London: Methuen.

Cowgill, G. L., 1968. Archaeological applications of factor, cluster, and proximity analysis. *American Antiquity*, 33 : 367–75.

Freeman, L. G., 1966. The nature of Mousterian facies in Cantabrian Spain. In *Recent studies in paleoanthropology*, (eds) J. D. Clark and F. C. Howell, pp. 230–37. *American Anthropologist*, Special Publication 68 : 2 : 2.

Hodson, F. R., 1970. Cluster analysis and archaeology: some new developments and applications. *World Archaeology*, 1 : 299–320.

Isaac, G. Ll., 1969. Studies of early culture in East Africa. *World Archaeology*, 1 : 1–28.

—— 1972a. Early phases of human behaviour: models in Lower Palaeolithic archaeology. In *Models in Archaeology*, (ed) D. L. Clarke, pp. 167–99. London: Methuen.

—— 1972b. Chronology and the tempo of cultural change during the Pleistocene. In *Calibration of Hominoid Evolution*, (eds) W. W. Bishop and J. A. Miller. Edinburgh: Scottish Academic Press.

—— 1972c. Some experiments in quantitative methods for characterising Acheulian assemblages. In *Congrès Panafricain de Préhistoire, Dakar 1967, Actes de 6ᵐᵉ session*, (ed) J. J. Hugot. Paris: Imprimeries Réunies de Chambéry.

Kleindienst, M. R., 1959. *Composition and significance of a Late Acheulian assemblage based on an analysis of East African occupation sites.* Dissertation submitted to the Faculty of the Division of the Social Sciences in candidacy for the degree of Doctor of Philosophy: Department of Anthropology, University of Chicago. Microfilm Thesis no. 4706. Chicago, Illinois, August 1959.

—— 1961. Variability within the late Acheulian assemblage in eastern Africa. *South African Archaeological Bulletin,* 16 : 35–52.

Leakey, M. D., 1971. *Olduvai Gorge,* (vol 3). Cambridge: Cambridge University Press.

Mellars, P., 1970. Some comments on the notion of 'functional variability' in stone tool assemblages. *World Archaeology,* 2 : 74–89.

Sackett, J. R., 1966. Quantitative analysis of upper Palaeolithic stone tools. In *Recent studies in paleoanthropology,* (eds) J. D. Clark and F. C. Howell, pp. 356–94. *American Anthropologist,* Special Publication 68 : 2 : 2.

Sokal, R. R. and P. H. A. Sneath, 1963. *Principles of numerical taxonomy.* San Francisco: W. H. Freeman and Co.

Sonneville-Bordes, D. de and J. Perrot, 1954, 1955, 1956. Lexique typologique de Paléolithique supérieur, outillage lithique. *Bulletin Société Préhistorique Française,* 51 : 327–35; 52 : 76–79, 53 : 408–12, 547–59.

Evolution of the hominid tool-making hand and forearm

DAVID ALLBROOK and LEONARD FREEDMAN

Two concepts are of particular value in discussing the evolution of the hominid tool-making hand and forearm, for they assist materially and may stimulate further research work into a critical stage of human development.

(1) The first is the concept of the *total morphological-functional pattern*, well known to modern biologists who interpret details of an organism's structure in terms of major adaptations and functions (Clark, 1955). In the topic under consideration, the function (to make tools) is related very directly to a total morphological-functional unit comprising (i) brain, neural pathways in the spinal cord and peripheral nerves, and (ii) upper limb joints, bones, muscles and skin, including all their sensory and (in muscle) their motor nerve supply.

(2) The other concept is that of '*mosaic evolution*', which implies differences in the rates of development of the various functional systems of the body, such that, for example, in the course of evolutionary change one anatomical part (or one functional system of the body) may reach a high level of development, whilst other parts may apparently not alter greatly from a somewhat basic or 'primitive' form. In the case of the tool-making 'system' just outlined it is quite evident that there has been a remarkable enlargement of the parts of the brain known as the frontal and sensori-motor neocortex in the hominids, but the structure of the upper limb—and particularly the hand—is said to have retained a somewhat generalised, basic or 'primitive' form. If this is so then a tool-making capacity would seem to have arisen by this rather curious example of 'mosaic' evolution. However, we believe the human hand to be a rather more specialised organ than is usually posited, and this is one of the themes of the present paper.

Functional morphology of the forelimb

The basic vertebrate pentadactyl limb can first be clearly recognised in the early labyrinthodont amphibians of the Devonian and Carboniferous periods of some 300–400 million years ago. The pattern, once fully evolved, has in general proved remarkably stable and versatile. There have been a number of marked specialisations in particular phyletic lines, leading to such apparently diverse structures as the bird wing, the single-toed horse limb and the whale flipper, yet in the case of the zoological order Primates the number and arrangement of bones has been relatively little changed.

In both the upper and the lower basic tetrapod limb, one finds a single proximal segment of bone (humerus, femur), followed progressively towards the limb extremity by a pair of bones (radius-ulna, and tibia-fibula), then a group of small bones (carpus and tarsus), the five hand or foot bones (metacarpus and metatarsus) and terminally the five digits, usually with three phalangeal bones in each (except the thumb and great toe which each have two).

Although there are great differences in the relative sizes of the limb bones in various vertebrates, there have been very few total bone losses or marked skeletal adaptations from this pattern in the upper limb bones of Primates. The most notable of these are the absence, or great reduction of the thumb in certain semibrachiating monkeys (eg. *Colobus* in Africa and *Ateles* in Central and South America) and the loss or vestigial nature of the 2nd digit in some lorises (eg. *Nycticebus* of Asia and *Perodicticus* of Africa). In addition, in the human, gorilla and chimpanzee carpus, the *os centrale* fuses with the scaphoid during embryological development (Clark, 1959). Flat nails are almost always present on all of the digits of the primate hand, the notable exception being the claws found on all of these digits, except the great toe, in the marmosets and tamarins (*Callithricidae*) of South and Central America.

The original pattern of vertebrate limb muscles consisted of a dorsal group of extensor muscles, to straighten the limb joints and extend the limb, and a ventral group acting on the joints to flex them. Other functional muscle groups evolved from the main extensor and flexor groups, to give the limb a comprehensive range of movements. Examples are abductors and adductors, medial and lateral rotators, pronators and supinators. There are many important differences in the number and relative sizes of muscles in the forelimb of various vertebrates. The mammalian pattern has, however, been relatively stable, although some important variations in the Primates will be described later.

With regard to other soft tissues of the hand, dermal ridges are characteristic of the palmar and plantar skin of Primates. The digital and palmar pads found on the manus of all Primates show some interesting variations, an extreme example being the apical pads of *Tarsius* from southeast Asia which are so highly developed that it is stated that the animal can actually walk up a vertical plate of glass!

The use of hands in Primates, and the primary functional concepts necessary for their description, have been outlined by Napier (1961). The movements allowed at the metacarpophalangeal joints provide the necessary basis for the observable convergence and divergence of the digits during the movements of flexion-adduction and extension-abduction of the fingers. The bone movements concerned are dependent on the shape of the reciprocal bone surfaces of the joints and also on the degree of 'cupping' of the palm (i.e. the amount of concavity, viewed from the palmar aspect, of the bones of the transverse carpal arch). When a hand, by the convergent action of its digits on the palm, can securely grip and hold an object, the hand is said to be prehensile. Manipulations without actually gripping, eg. by pushing, are said to be nonprehensile. In various Primates the degree of prehensile ability is, in general, functionally correlated with the depth of the carpal arch, which appears to have evolved primarily in relationship to the mode of locomotion. Thus the carpa arch is deeper when finger flexion is important as in brachiation and knuckle-walking.

Prehensile movements may be functionally subdivided into those involving a power grip and a precision grip (Napier, 1961). As defined for man, in the power grip an object is gripped 'between the flexed fingers and the palm, counter pressure being applied by the adducted thumb'. When a precision grip is used, the object is held 'between the palmar aspect of the terminal phalanx of the finger or fingers and the thumb'. For man the concept underlying these definitions is that it is the 'purpose' rather than the shape of the object that determines the grip used.

Opposability in man is a special form of prehension and is primarily a property of the joint at the base of the thumb and the muscles moving it. During opposition the converging thumb undergoes abduction, conjoint medial rotation and flexion at the first carpometacarpal joint, the movement ending by the thumb pad facing those of any of the other digits. The ability to make this movement depends on the saddle-like shape of the 1st carpometacarpal joint, the absence of ligaments binding together the distal ends of metacarpals I and II, and the presence of certain small muscles acting on the thumb (see later).

Use of the forelimbs and hands in non-human Primates is related to a variety of functions of which locomotion, feeding and certain social activities (such as grooming, play, fighting) are the most important. A great diversity of movements is revealed correlated with the functions performed (Bishop, 1964).

Prosimians (the most primitive Primates), do not pick up objects with the palmar surfaces of their digits even though they have flat fingernails and a pseudo-opposable thumb. Prosimians have many grips, but their prehension of small objects is limited to a single pattern involving the digital (not thumb) and the palmar pads, the action being under 'whole hand' nervous control.

The *Ceboidea* (New World monkeys) show an interesting gradation of complexity of hand function. These range from simple patterns such as those seen in the *Callithricidae* (eg. marmosets) where feeding-use involves both two-handed and one-handed prehension. Prosimian-like usage is found in *Saimiri*, the squirrel monkey and *Aotes*, a nocturnal form. At the other end of the spectrum there are species with relatively free control of complex movements, using the sides of digits 2 and 3 or gripping in the first joint of the thumb or digit 2 (eg. *Cebus*, the capuchin and *Cacajao*, the uakari).

The ceboid functional sequence of graded complexity presumably had an evolutionary parallel in the Old World Primate lineage to which man belongs. However, in the living Old World monkeys (Cercopithecoidea) one finds more uniformly rather complex behaviour patterns. These include increased interest (curiosity) about food, other objects and also themselves (eg. in grooming, play, etc.). These characteristics are all presumably correlated with cerebral evolution and one would therefore expect to find increasingly improved peripheral control. All in this group are at least able to grip

small objects between the thumb and some part of the second digit or the side of the hand; the index finger and possibly even other digits may be separately controlled (eg. in *Papio*, the baboon). For large objects, in both New and Old World monkeys the power grip is the 'transverse hold under the first interphalangeal joint of d2, d3, d4 and d5' (Bishop, 1964).

In the Pongidae (great apes) there are found some marked adaptations eg. a relatively short thumb, curved phalanges and a 'double-locking' mechanism at the metacarpophalangeal joints of digits 2–5, all said to be for brachiation (but see next paragraph). Fine prehensile patterns of movement are dissimilar to those in man and true opposition of the thumb, as previously defined, does not occur. The precision grip for small objects involves the thumb and adjacent second digit, but not in a pulp to pulp movement; in the power grip the action is either 'hook-like when the metacarpophalangeal joints are extended and the remaining joints flexed' or when all the finger joints are flexed. In neither case is the role of the thumb significant (Napier, 1961).

All living great apes can brachiate, but the African forms apparently rarely do so as adults in the wild. Smaller ancestral forms, however, may well have been habitual brachiators as the young of both forms do brachiate quite frequently. Although they do suspend themselves and swing between branches, gorillas and chimpanzees are essentially quadrupedal climbers in the trees (Schaller, 1963). Gorillas spend most of their time on the ground and chimpanzees a variable time depending on whether they are in tropical rainforests or in more open woodlands. In both species the mode of locomotion on the ground is by forelimb knuckle-walking, the body weight being transmitted to the ground via pads of friction skin over the middle phalanges (Tuttle, 1969). In these animals the large and powerful hands have strong stabilising flexor tendons, which lie enclosed in deep carpal tunnels in the palm. The effect is of a massive hand, with the fingers characteristically held in flexion, and a short small thumb inturned and adducted. Thus the special mechanisms which enable thumb opposition and the effective pinching movement of the precision grip of thumb and index to occur in the human hand are both impossible and functionally redundant in the hands of both *Pan* and *Gorilla*. Actually in these apes specialised muscles for opposition (mm. *flexor pollicis brevis* and *opponens pollicis*) are either small or absent (Day and Napier, 1963). Study of the combined morphological and electromyographic evidence concerning the function of the hand muscles and ligaments indicates a degree of specialisation in these animals quite different from that of the modern human hand (Tuttle *et al.*, 1972).

Extreme specialisation such as those seen in the gorilla and chimpanzee are most unlikely to have preceded the evolution of the modern human hand, which is unique in its proportions. Evolutionary reversals need not be imagined to explain the proportions and morphology of man's hand. Such views stem from the mistaken attempt to use the hands of living, specialised anthropoids as the model from which the hand of *Homo sapiens* is derived. Clearly, it is to a theoretical hand model of some unknown unspecialised Pliocene hominoid or known Pleistocene fossil that one needs to look, rather than to modern forms.

Structural adaptations which enable the fundamental demands of the hominid tool-making hand to be met include changes in wrist morphology, and finger and thumb structure.

An increased mobility of the wrist joint is brought about by a 'freeing' of the ulnar styloid from the joint, and the development of the intra-articular triangular meniscus. In the lower Primates ligaments tether the ulnar head to the carpal bones and thereby limit mobility of the former. But in the great apes and in some specialised brachiating monkeys, the ulnar head is no longer part of the wrist joint, nor is it tethered to carpal bones by restraining ligaments. Instead, a complex synovial joint is found in these forms which allows increased mobility of the hand and forearm. The joint contains an intra-articular meniscus which effectively excludes the ulnar styloid process from participation in the wrist joint. This meniscus allows much greater mobility of the hand and also of the ulna bone, the latter permitting an increased range of movement in pronation and supination. In the Pongidae and in man the full range of pronation and supination is about 180°, whereas in the monkeys it is usually only about 90° (Lewis, 1965).

Observations of living brachiating animals indicate that a wide range of forearm pronation-supination may be a necessary condition for true brachiation (Avis, 1962). In other words, these morphological data might tend to support the well known Keith-Gregory hypothesis that the great apes and man had a common evolutionary history of adept, suspensory, arboreal locomotion. However, the various specialised brachiation adaptations listed earlier (and several others) are not present in man and, rather than propose a series of reversals, it would seem that a possible common ancestral form was a quadrupedal arboreal climber. More important, however, from the viewpoint of this discussion is the fact that (whatever its evolutionary origin) a wide range of pronation-supination is a necessary prerequisite for an adequate tool-making hand.

Several finger and thumb adaptations in man have been noted but of special interest is the perfection of the saddle-joint at the base of the thumb. This joint facilitates the full movement of thumb opposition. Also the development of functionally efficient length proportions of thumb and fingers is necessary in order to attain both precision and power grip of the tool-making hand. Important too is the development of broad terminal phalanges and nails to allow the formation of a finger pad which increases tactile and fine grip areas. The ability to make a deep 'cupped' hand, necessary for a single hand grip of a large object, is achieved by the stability of metacarpals II and III and the mobility of metacarpals IV and V.

Tool use has been observed in a number of species of birds and mammals and recently simple tool manufacture has also been described eg. the termite 'fishing sticks' of chimpanzees (Goodall, 1963). But whatever the forearm and hand morphological requirements were for the production of stone tools, the evolution of an appropriate level of brain and peripheral nervous system development was certainly crucial.

The role of the brain

The human brain, and especially the part called the neocortex, may be taken to represent a kind of biological zenith of nerve cell organisation and increase in size, which presumably is the result of genetic selection. The organisational level of the brain was sufficiently advanced in middle and late Pleistocene man to allow the development of an entirely new kind of evolution—a stage which is absolutely characteristic of *Homo sapiens* and which is commonly termed biocultural evolution.

Basic to this phase is the development of tool-using and tool-making which must therefore be a function of brain evolution, correlated with both its motor output and sensory input from the special senses, especially the binocular eyes and also other parts of the body, notably the hands. It must also somehow be related to the ability to abstract ideas, and to create new concepts. The human brain possesses the motor skill to give these concepts physical form, for example the manufacture of wooden, bone and stone tools and other cultural objects.

A clear appreciation of the attributes of the hominid brain can only be obtained through an understanding of the processes and trends underlying its evolution. Such information comes mainly from palaeoneurology and comparative neuroanatomy. The former uses endocranial casts of fossil material to reconstruct brain topology—and the limitations of such a crude method are obvious. Comparative neuroanatomy, though using more valid neurological data, suffers from the crippling disability that one is forced to use a model of an extant form to predicate an evolutionary process occurring in the long past.

Comparison of brain cytoarchitectonics of man and anthropoids, however, is an important area of study which still remains to be fully explored. In particular data are needed on the absolute and relative size of cerebral cortical motor areas controlling hand movements, and the associated extrapyramidal neural control areas. Another study of great importance would be one to quantify the numbers of spinal nerve cells in the eighth cervical and first thoracic spinal cord segments, for these parts house the nerve cells which are motor to the small hand muscles. The numbers might be expected to be absolutely and comparatively more in the human spinal cord when compared with the anthropoid, if 'neural capacity' was a significant determining factor in the development of tool-making skills. Quantification of this kind of data is now possible using modern counting-scanning and computer techniques, coupled to modern neuroanatomical methods of study.

Numerous studies of non-human Primate behaviour in the field and under laboratory conditions have been reported in the last decade and are still being continued actively (eg. DeVore, 1965; Rowell, 1972). These, too, are basic studies in unravelling the processes involved in the evolution of the hominid brain.

The significance of peripheral connections of the nervous system

Motor peripheral nerves end in muscle. Microscopically nerve filaments terminate at myoneural junctions on individual muscle fibres. A single spinal cord nerve cell may control contraction of a variable number of fibres—from 20 to say 200. Clearly the precision of nerve control of a muscle depends on the smallness of numbers of fibres controlled. A nerve cell which controls 20 fibres will control movement more exactly than one that controls several hundred. Thus muscle fibre numbers related to nerve supply give an indication of the precision with which a muscle can be used. Not only would the retention of the individual long flexor muscle to the thumb and the increase in size of the thenar muscles in man be important, but also the actual size of motor units in individual muscles used in fine control of the hands. If control is more accurate the controlling nerve cell should motivate fewer fibres. Thus differences may be postulated between man and say the great apes. No such work has yet been reported to our knowledge, but it would be a significant contribution to Primate studies.

Evidence from palaeontology

Unfortunately, even despite the large number of Pleistocene hominid excavations performed in recent decades, the evidence from fossil material of hominid hand and forearm evolution is still very meagre and confusingly contradictory.

Hand and upper limb bones are scarce and it is difficult to correlate these with skull material on which affinities must necessarily be based. This is especially so in the East African remains where the gracile and robust australopithecines and also specimens that appear to represent *Homo* are all found in the same deposit and are not clearly separated in time. The relationship of the discovered fossil remains to early stone tools likewise becomes problematical. This is even the case where only one form of australopithecine is found with stone artifacts. Stone tools are so frequently found without associated human skeletal material that one cannot consider the association of australopithecine and stone tools as necessarily being of 'maker and product' relationship.

There is a small number of hand bone fossils described from lower Pleistocene beds in Africa. This appears to be a critical time zone for the earliest development of the hominid tool-making hand. A list would include the following fossils: SKW 14147, found at Swartkrans, is a fifth metacarpal almost identical to that of *Homo sapiens* (Day and Scheuer, 1973). SK 84 and SK 85 are first and·fourth metacarpals respectively found at Swartkrans (Napier, 1959). This material is discussed at length by Robinson (1972) who concludes, in agreement with Napier, that the fourth metacarpal resembles that of modern man, but that the first (thumb) metacarpal differs markedly from that of man, more closely resembling what might be expected in a form assigned to the genus *Paranthropus*. TM 1517, from Kromdraai, consists of most of a ? second left digit metacarpal, a ? second left digit proximal phalanx and a ? fifth digit proximal phalanx (Broom and Schepers, 1946). The specimens were associated with the type skull of *Paranthropus* though their assignment to this genus by association has been questioned (Robinson, 1972). From Sterkfontein comes a capitate and a ? proximal end of a first phalanx (Broom and Schepers, 1946). The capitate has a morphology similar to that of man, and the authors suggest that this implies a carpal mobility in excess of the gorilla or chimpanzee but less than that of modern man. The matter is discussed in some detail by Robinson (1972).

From Bed I at Olduvai comes a number of specimens (Napier, 1962). Juvenile specimens found include a middle phalanx, two terminal phalanges and a terminal thumb phalanx. Also present are two adult proximal phalanges and, of uncertain maturity, one each of the following: trapezium, scaphoid, capitate, base of the second metacarpal, and two middle phalanges. The taxonomic assignment of this material has produced a good deal of debate, for cases have been made for its inclusion in *Paranthropus*, *Homo habilis*, and *Australopithecus africanus*. For our purpose the following features are significant. The terminal phalanges are spatulate as in modern man. The middle phalanges are strong and curved and show obvious markings for strong tendons and powerful muscles. The carpal bones (scaphoid, trapezium and capitate) are damaged, though the trapezium has the saddle-shaped joint needed for an opposable thumb. The terminal phalanges and trapezium suggest that they could have come from a hominid hand. However the hand must have been short and powerful, with curved digits, and a massive power and precision grip. The possibilities of knuckle-walking and brachiation are thus indicated. But most important for this discussion—could this hand and the brain behind it have made the Oldowan stone tool culture? Unfortunately there is no direct evidence, but if the answer is in the affirmative then the implication is that tool-making was established before the modern hominid hand and brain existed. These are fascinating questions ready for debate but with as yet no conclusive evidence available.

The earliest tool-makers

The earliest generally accepted stone artifacts were recovered from the East Rudolf formations and have been dated as 2.6 million years BP (R. E. F. Leakey, 1970). Evidence as to the first tool users and makers is however, suggestive but also inconclusive. Thus Oldowan choppers have been recovered from early Pleistocene deposits at Sterkfontein and Swartkrans in South Africa, and from the lower levels of Olduvai in Tanzania (M. D. Leakey, 1970). These sites have yielded the fossil remains of *Australopithecus* and/or *Paranthropus* but *Homo erectus* is also present at the latter two sites. Further, although *Australopithecus* fossil material has been recovered from the type site (lower breccia) and extension site (middle breccia) at Sterkfontein, artifacts have only been found at the extension site (Robinson, 1962). From Makapan, which has yielded *Australopithecus*, no evidence of stone tools has been found, even though an exceptionally thorough search has been made. The use of bone, teeth and horns (the osteodontokeratic culture) has been postulated for *Australopithecus* at Makapan (Dart, 1957) but doubt has been repeatedly expressed about this concept.

Other evidence for the manufacture of primitive stone tools by *Homo erectus* is also indirect. The Trinil (Java) and Chou Kou Tien (China) sites give no conclusive evidence, though in both, fossil remains are found at the same stratigraphic level with non-associated primitive tools. Similar suggestive evidence, this time that *H. erectus* was responsible for the handaxe culture, comes from Ternifine in Algeria and Olduvai. The Ternifine mandibles and skull fragments attributable to *H. erectus* were stratigraphically associated with many handaxes, and, in Bed II and Bed IV at Olduvai, there was a similar association.

Thus, though it seems that tool-making by hominids may have occurred 2.6 million years ago, the evidence as to the maker is incomplete, and until more is forthcoming it is not possible to dogmatise as to which hominid population, *Australopithecus africanus*, *Paranthropus robustus*, *Homo habilis*, *Homo erectus*, early *Homo sapiens* (or some unnamed population between them) was responsible for manufacturing the tools we currently have available for study.

Conclusion

Man's tool-making hand and forearm are the result of a long and complex evolution. The flexibility, suppleness, proportions and sensitivity of the hand make it a considerably more highly specialised organ than is generally conceded. In addition the human hand must be viewed as having evolved in concert with the brain, sense organs and peripheral nervous system, probably after its emancipation from locomotor functions. Neither fossil evidence nor apparent association with implements are presently very helpful in enabling one to decide definitively when an evolving hominid was first able to construct implements to a pattern—a capability that heralded man's entrance into the bio-cultural evolutionary era.

References

Avis, V., 1962. Brachiation: the crucial issue for man's ancestry. *Southwestern Journal of Anthropology*, 18 : 119–48.

Bishop, A., 1964. Use of the hand in lower primates. *In* J. Buettner-Janusch (ed.) *Evolutionary and genetic biology of Primates*, vol. 2, pp. 133–225. New York: Academic Press.

Broom, R. and G. W. H. Schepers, 1946. *The South African fossil ape-men, the Australopithecinae*. Transvaal Museum Memoirs No. 2, Pretoria.

Clark, W. E. LeG., 1955. *The fossil evidence for human evolution*. Chicago: University of Chicago Press.

—— 1959. *The antecedents of man*. Edinburgh: Edinburgh University Press.

Dart, R. A., 1957. *The Osteodontokeratic culture of Australopithecus prometheus*. Transvaal Museum Memoirs No. 10, Pretoria.

Day, M. H. and J. R. Napier, 1963. The functional significance of the deep head of flexor pollicis brevis in primates. *Folia primatologica*, 1 : 122–34.

—— and J. L. Scheuer, 1973. SKW1417, A new hominid metacarpal from Swartkrans. *Journal of Human Evolution*, 2 : 429–38.

De Vore, I. (ed.), 1965. *Primate behaviour*. London: Holt, Rinehart & Winston.

Goodall, J., 1963. Feeding behaviour of wild chimpanzees. *Symposium of the Zoological Society, London*, No. 10 : 39–48.

Leakey, M. D., 1970. Stone artefacts from Swartkrans. *Nature*, 225 : 1222–25.

Leakey, R. E. F., 1970. New hominid fossil remains and early artefacts from Northern Kenya. *Nature*, 226 : 223–24.

Lewis, O. J., 1965. Evolutionary changes in the primate wrist and inferior radio-ulnar joints. *Anatomical Record*, 151 : 275–286.

Napier, J. R., 1959. Fossil metacarpals from Swartkrans. *Fossil Mammals of Africa*, No. 17. London: British Museum (Natural History).

—— 1961. Prehensility and opposability in the hands of primates. *Symposium Zoological Society London*, No. 5: 115–32.

—— 1962. Fossil hand bones from Olduvai Gorge. *Nature*, 196 : 409–11.

Robinson, J. T., 1962. Australopithecines and artefacts at Sterkfontein. Part I: Sterkfontein stratigraphy and the significance of the extension site. *South African Archaeological Bulletin*, 17 : 87–107.

—— 1972. *Early hominid posture and locomotion*. Chicago: University of Chicago Press.

Rowell, T., 1972. *Social behaviour of monkeys*. Harmondsworth: Penguin Books.

Schaller, G. B., 1963. *The mountain gorilla*. Chicago : University of Chicago Press.

Tuttle, R. H., 1969. Knuckle-walking and the evolution of hominoid hands. *American Journal of Physical Anthropology*, 26 : 171–206.

—— J. V. Basmajian, E. Gegenos and G. Shine, 1972. Electromyography of knuckle walking. *American Journal of Physical Anthropology*, 37 : 255–66.

Masticatory and non-masticatory uses of teeth

M. J. BARRETT [1]

Molnar (1972) has given an account of various masticatory and non-masticatory uses of teeth in a recent review article on tooth wear and culture. He suggested that the records of activities of the masticatory apparatus which are retained on the teeth in the form of dental attrition and abrasion marks should provide evidence of the food and eating habits of prehistoric human populations and the practice of crafts involving the use of teeth as tools. Molnar drew attention to the paucity of information on the dynamics of human tooth wear and the relation of tooth wear to culture. He emphasised the need for continuing investigations of tooth wear by the collection and analysis of data from skeletal collections and from groups of people living under conditions which lead to tooth wear as a normal concomitant of masticatory function. He also referred to the need for further ethnographic studies of the use of teeth as tools in manufacturing processes.

Molnar's article has stimulated the present paper which aims to provide some background information on a few of the relevant features of the human masticatory system and a brief account of masticatory and non-masticatory uses of teeth as observed in Aborigines living at Yuendumu in the Northern Territory of Australia. The examples cited are mainly from personal observations and from descriptive accounts given by informants at Yuendumu. Various kinds of tooth wear will be described and the possibility of distinguishing between masticatory and non-masticatory tooth wear will be discussed.

The masticatory system

Main components of the masticatory system are the teeth and associated gingival tissues, the periodontal ligaments suspending the teeth and providing alveolar attachment, the maxilla and the mandible, the temporomandibular joints, the muscles attached to the mandible, the muscles of the lips, cheeks and tongue, various glands, the blood supply, and the nerve centres and pathways concerned with these tissues. (Posselt, 1968; Ramfjord and Ash, 1971; Sicher, 1966; Sicher and Du Brul, 1970).

Teeth consist of four main tissues: enamel, dentine, dental pulp and cementum.

Tooth enamel, mainly inorganic material (96% by weight), is the hardest tissue in the body. It provides a protective covering of variable thickness over the tooth crown surface. The hardness and the structure of enamel make it brittle, especially when unsupported by dentine. This occurs when there is defective dentine formation or an advanced stage of dental caries or dental attrition.

Dentine is a vital tissue making up the bulk of the tooth and it mainly consists of organic material, about 70% by weight. It is much softer than enamel but a little harder than bone which it resembles in its physical and chemical properties. Odontoblasts are the cells of dentine. Their bodies are located in the dental pulp, forming a layer on the pulpal surface of the dentine, and their processes extend in dentinal tubules through the dentine to the junction of dentine and enamel. The formation of secondary or reparative dentine on the pulpal surface of the dentine may continue throughout life.

The dental pulp occupies pulp chambers and root canals of teeth. Its main functions are the formation and nourishment of dentine. With progressive formation of secondary dentine the size of pulp chambers is reduced.

Cementum is the softest of the dental hard tissues, containing about 50% inorganic material. It covers the root surfaces of the tooth and provides attachment for the periodontal fibres which bind the tooth to the alveolar bone. Cementum deposition may continue throughout life through the action of specialised cells derived from connective tissue cells of the periodontal ligament.

The periodontal ligament attaches the tooth to the alveolar process of the jaw and provides support for the tooth in its masticatory displacements. The ligament has a formative function in that it provides the cells which make cementum, bone, and the fibres of the ligament.

Nerves and blood vessels serve sensory and nutritive functions. The periodontal ligament is continuous with the connective tissues of the gingiva surrounding the tooth at its neck.

The alveolar processes of the maxilla and mandible form the sockets of the teeth which give attachment to fibres of the periodontal ligaments. Forces applied to the teeth are transmitted to the alveolar bone via the ligaments. Alveolar bone is a plastic tissue which adapts to functional forces. Resorption of alveolar bone follows tooth loss and, in some instances, dietary disturbances.

The maxilla and its embedded teeth form the passive component of the masticatory mechanism and the mandible with its teeth the active component. The mandible is joined to the cranium through bilateral temporomandibular joints and it is suspended and activated by a sling of muscles. Articulation of the mandible involves three surfaces—the articular surfaces of the two condyles and the masticatory surfaces of the teeth.

The elevator and depressor muscles attached to the mandible act in coordination to effect opening and closing movements, protrusive, retrusive, and lateral movements. Forces that can be applied through the teeth range from gentle tapping and delicate biting to powerful crushing and

---

1. It was with regret that I learned of the death of Dr M. J. Barrett before this paper went to press.   RVSW

grinding. Muscles of the lips, cheeks and tongue play an essential part in mastication by placing and keeping the food between the teeth.

Masticatory movements are conditioned reflexes guided by proprioceptors located in the periodontal ligaments, the joints and the muscles. The pattern of movements developed in infancy is subject to continual modification throughout life. Mastication involves a complex series of lateral and combined lateral and protrusive movements of the jaw in the application of cutting, crushing and grinding forces which lead to comminution of the food and mixing of the food with saliva ready for swallowing. The integrated jaw movements and muscular activity of lips, cheeks and tongue in mastication are determined by the size of the morsel, its texture and state of comminution as well as the shape, number, position and state of health of the teeth.

The system is involved in speech and respiration as well as mastication and swallowing.

Masticatory uses of teeth

Many accounts have been written of the food and eating habits of Australian Aborigines living under native conditions. These have been summarised by Campbell (1939) and illustrated in a documentary produced from movie film sequences obtained at Yuendumu (Campbell and Simpson, 1953).

Aborigines used very simple methods to prepare their food for eating and they consumed their food without the aid of eating implements. When hunting and food gathering or travelling from one place to another the Aborigines took every opportunity of eating small items of food collected while on the move. Usually they had their cooked meals while seated on the ground near a fire.

Fruit and other vegetable foods were often eaten in their fresh raw state. Sometimes they were cooked in ashes. Grass seeds were ground between flat stones and water added to form a mixture which was baked in ashes at the edge of a fire on the ground. The resultant loaf was rough in texture and gritty.

Flesh foods were cooked by covering with ashes, embers and hot sandy earth from the edge or the centre of a low fire. In cooking large animals or birds a crude oven was made by digging a hole in the ground and lighting a fire in it. The skin of the animal or bird was scorched in the fire. When the earth oven was well heated the fire was raked out and the carcass placed in position and covered with hot earth and ashes. The cooked meat was chopped and cut into portions with the use of hand-held or hafted cutting tools or the sharp end of a boomerang. Bones were cracked with stone pounders or with the teeth to get at the marrow inside.

The fibrous texture and toughness of native foods was not reduced to any great extent by the simple methods used by Aborigines in their preparation of foods for eating. Vigorous mastication was required for comminution of the foods prior to swallowing. This vigorous mastication, together with the abrasive materials such as sand, grit, ashes and bone fragments which were incorporated in the foods during gathering, cooking and eating, resulted in wear of the teeth during use.

Movie films have been obtained at Yuendumu for analyses of masticatory movements (Barrett, 1956). They show that in chewing meat a portion is torn off a lump held in the hand by gripping a piece firmly between the incisor teeth and pulling the remainder of the lump forwards and sideways. Head and neck muscles resist the pulling action of arm and shoulder muscles. As the meat is torn and a small piece finally severed the head often jerks backwards.

The separated morsel is then moved to the back of the mouth and positioned between the molar teeth by the lips, cheeks and tongue. Chewing movements proceed with machine-like regularity until the bolus is ready for swallowing. Lip, cheek and tongue muscles are active in holding the meat portion as the teeth are brought together in the closing or crushing and grinding phase of the masticatory cycle. The same groups of muscles collect the crushed meat during the opening phase of the cycle and rapidly position the reshaped bolus between the teeth.

Slow motion film sequences taken with the lips separated by retractors illustrate the speed, precision and integration of muscle activity. Effective mastication proceeds in spite of the forceful separation of the lips. The tongue and cheeks can be seen in a continuous state of activity in control of the position of the food bolus in the mouth.

The movie film records show that Aborigines use wide lateral excursions of the mandible when chewing meat and that with a full complement of teeth there is alternating use of teeth on one side of the mouth and then the other. The meat is chewed on one side for a few strokes and then the mouthful is shifted to the other side for a few strokes, and so on, until ready for swallowing.

The vigor of mastication is uninhibited by social convention. Often the lips are parted during mastication and not brought together until swallowing takes place.

The teeth are subjected to hard usage in mastication. Mention has already been made of the use of teeth to crack open bones. A similar use is to crack open small galls found on bloodwood trees to get at the edible contents. In gnawing bones the teeth are used to peel and strip off all remnants of meat and other tissues. Bone fragments are often included in the food and these contribute to fracturing of tooth enamel and wear of the teeth.

Masticatory tooth wear

Tooth wear is the most obvious but not the only effect of heavy demands on the dentition. Vigorous masticatory use of the teeth induces functional and morphological changes which tend to improve performance capacity and the ability to cope with the demands. Muscle power is developed and an efficient pattern of mastication. Heavy demands also lead to solid but resilient periodontal and alveolar support for the teeth and a bone structure adapted to the functional demands.

Tooth wear begins in infancy as soon as the deciduous teeth emerge into functional occlusal contact with their antagonists and are engaged in mastication of solid foods; and it continues in the mixed dentition and in the permanent dentition progressively throughout life.

Enamel wear of the incisal edges of anterior teeth and the occlusal surfaces of posterior teeth is followed eventually by exposure and differential wear of the softer dentine. The dental pulp responds to tooth wear by the reparative laying down of secondary dentine on the roof of the pulp chamber at the site of odontoblasts damaged by the wear process.

Incisal wear and occlusal wear lead to changes in the shape and area of the tooth surfaces and reduction in crown height. In the permanent first and second molar regions where the lower dental arch is usually somewhat narrower than the upper arch the occlusal wear is almost always greater on the buccal aspect of the lower teeth and on the palatal aspect of the upper teeth. In the third molar region where the lower arch is usually as wide as the upper arch, or sometimes wider, the inclination of the worn occlusal surfaces is often horizontal and sometimes reversed in comparison with the first molar region.

Eventually all traces of cuspal eminences are obliterated by the wear process and the cuspal interdigitation characteristic of the occlusion at an earlier age is replaced by broad occluding surfaces in helicoidal configuration. The occlusal surfaces of the worn posterior teeth often have depressions where there were cusps previously. Sometimes with extreme wear the severely affected incisal and occlusal surfaces of the lower teeth all incline labially or buccally and the occlusal surfaces of the upper teeth all incline palatally. In this situation the functional occlusal relations of the lower to the upper teeth are strikingly similar to the relations of a pestle working in a mortar.

Proximal surfaces of teeth in contact with neighbouring teeth are also involved in the wear process. The shape of these surfaces continually changes as well as the area of proximal contact. There is progressive reduction in the mesiodistal crown size of individual teeth. Changes in the position of teeth within the dental arches by a mesial drift maintain proximal contact and lead to a reduction of the dental arch perimeter

The pattern of mastication continually changes in response to progressive changes in the shape and size of teeth and the mode of tooth occlusion. Chewing movements in early life are constrained by cuspal eminences and the incisor overbite. In later life the mandibular excursions in mastication are wider because such movements are needed for efficient chewing with flatter occlusal surfaces. Biting function is modified by the acquisition of an edge-to-edge incisor relation.

These sequelae and many others are natural concomitants of vigorous masticatory function under environmental conditions demanding vigorous use of teeth and jaws. The rate at which they occur depends mainly on the physical nature of the food, especially its abrasive qualities. Tooth wear in its early stages may be considered as a normal physiological accompaniment of aging. However, in its later stages it may become pathogenic.

Continued heavy functional demands on the dentition may result in breakdown of the mechanism. Adverse changes affect the teeth, their supporting structures, the temporomandibular joints and the muscles.

Continued loss of tooth substance by the wear process leads to exposure of secondary dentine and eventually to exposure of pulp chambers when the reparative deposition of secondary dentine is overtaken by the wear. The teeth may be worn down to gum level. In this event there is loss of proximal contact with adjacent teeth. Individual teeth may be dislocated by masticatory forces as their bony support becomes less secure. These misplaced teeth are subject to abnormal wear. With multi-rooted teeth the wear may extend so far that root fragments are all that remain of the teeth. The exfoliating root fragments are often tipped laterally and they sometimes show wear facets along the entire exposed root surfaces to the apex.

Infection of the exposed dental pulps results in periapical and alveolar pathologies. The chewing pattern is disturbed by the avoidance of painful teeth or, when teeth are lost, by the abnormal use of those remaining. The tooth occlusion is deranged and the temporomandibular joints and muscles are affected. Degenerative changes in the articular surfaces of the temporomandibular joints are often seen in association with severe tooth wear.

Non-masticatory uses of teeth

The teeth and jaws serve for various grasping, biting, piercing, cutting, tearing, shredding, crushing and grinding uses not associated with mastication and they provide a ready means of holding objects or materials when the hands are otherwise engaged.

Some of the non-dietary uses of teeth observed at Yuendumu involve chewing in much the same manner as in mastication but the material chewed is not swallowed. The most commonly seen example is the chewing of tobacco. Leaves of the native tobacco plants are preferred but if a supply is not available the Aborigines are satisfied with plug tobacco purchased from the store. The teeth are used to bite off a portion of tobacco. The quid of tobacco is chewed and held in the mouth for long periods and it is dipped in ashes from time to time. The ashes may be freshly prepared by burning leaves over a spearthrower or shield to be used as a mixing dish or they may be old ashes stored in a tobacco tin. As well as having a mild narcotic effect the chewing of tobacco stimulates saliva flow.

Dried kangaroo or emu sinew is chewed and insalivated to soften it in preparation for use as a binding material when making or mending a spear and when attaching a wooden peg to the end of a spearthrower during its manufacture (Campbell and Barrett, 1958). One end of the softened sinew is held between the teeth while a string of the desired thickness is split off using both hands to separate the fibres. While the separated string is being used in the binding process the remainder of the sinew is returned to the mouth for temporary storage. Saliva secretion is also stimulated by the chewing of sinew.

Material which acts as a sialogogue is chewed when a supply of fluid is required in the manufacture and handling of spinifex gum (Campbell and Barrett, 1963a). A strip of bark obtained from a witchetty bush or an ironwood tree is chewed for up to ten minutes or so to release the substances which stimulate saliva flow and to give time for the accumulation of a sufficient quantity of saliva in the mouth. A copious supply of thick, ropy saliva is produced for incorporation in the spinifex gum during its manufacture and to cool the hands and to prevent the gum sticking to them as it is being formed into a cake. Saliva produced in the same way is also used to make a paste of ochre when decorating the body in preparation for a ceremony or when coating wooden implements or ceremonial objects.

The teeth are used for various peeling, stripping and gripping tasks when making a spear or digging stick (Campbell and Barrett, 1963b). A tree branch or long root of a tree cut for the purpose is passed through the warm ashes of a fire to soften or loosen the bark. The teeth are then used to strip off some of the bark as a preliminary to final smoothing and removal of irregularities with the aid of a stone or metal tool mounted with spinifex gum on the end of a curved wooden handle or a spearthrower. In the final stages of straightening the shaft it is warmed in the ashes to increase its pliability and then gripped between the teeth which serve as a vice or clamp to hold the shaft firmly while both hands are used to apply the straightening forces.

The teeth are used in a similar fashion to peel the bark off a freshly cut small branch of a bush when making the spindle-bobbin to be used as a tool in the manufacture of hair string

(Campbell and Barrett, 1963c). The cross arms of the tool are made of equal length by biting off and trimming a small stick from the same bush to the desired length and then splitting it longitudinally with the teeth. The two halves of the stick are split or pierced in their centres, using the teeth, and then slid into position on the spindle shaft to form the completed assembly.

The teeth are used for sharpening tools. When a knife or axe is not available a spear or digging stick may be sharpened by nibbling away small slivers of wood from the blade. The teeth are also used to form ends on small wooden tools for various purposes. A pointed stick may be required or one with a blunt, roughened end. In the tooth evulsion operation, for example, a pointed bone or sharpened stick is used to strip the gum away from the neck of the tooth to be removed (Fry and Tindale, 1933; Cleland and Gray, 1934). The point on the stick may be formed by the operator using his teeth. At a later stage of the operation a stick with a broad blunt end is required for placement on the tooth so that the evulsion force can be applied by hitting the other end of the stick with a stone held in the hand. The operator shapes the stick with use of his teeth.

In days gone by the teeth were used to sharpen stone tools by pressure flaking (Barrett, 1960; Gould, 1968).

The teeth and jaws provide a convenient 'third hand' for holding things. When playing string games children may hold a loop of the string between the teeth while the thumbs and fingers of both hands are engaged in manipulating the complicated design (Campbell and Barrett, 1963c). The teeth are often used to hold the end of a piece of string which is being used in a binding or a coiling process—when tying up a parcel in paper bark, binding the hair, applying a tourniquet to the upper arm in blood-letting, when making hair-string belts and shoulder straps, pubic tassles, and ceremonial objects using hair string.

The use of the teeth to hold a stone axe when the hands are engaged during tree climbing has been reported (Mitchell, 1959). A spear may be held between the teeth when stalking a kangaroo by creeping up to the animal on hands and knees. The blade end of the spear trails behind the hunter. A stone knife may be held between the teeth during a fight when both hands are taken up with holding spears and shield. In the manufacture of wooden implements the teeth are occasionally used to stabilise the work piece or to temporarily hold parts of an assembly. Decorated wooden sticks and other objects are held between the teeth by performers in ceremonies.

Teeth are occasionally used in fighting. Women are reported to use their teeth for this purpose more often than men. The arms of an opponent are main targets for biting attacks. In a recent fight between two men at Yuendumu one of them had a piece of his nose bitten off in the affray.

A medicine man may bite the skin of his patient as part of the treatment. The skin is not penetrated but sufficient force is applied to leave tooth marks on the skin.

In summary it may be said that Aborigines use their teeth and jaws for many purposes not associated with the mastication and swallowing of food. A wide variety of tasks can be conveniently carried out with the aid of the teeth as tools or as a holding device.

Non-masticatory tooth wear

Toothbrush abrasion is one of several types of mechanical injury to teeth which are seen in modern communities (Pind-borg, 1970). Horizontal brushing, using an abrasive paste or powder on the brush, results in wedge-shaped notches in the neck region of the labial surfaces of upper incisors, canines and premolars. Usually the left side teeth of a right-handed person are more affected than the right side teeth, and vice versa. The abrasion cavities mainly involve dentine of root surfaces exposed by gum recession.

Toothpick abrasion is another type of tooth injury associated with mouth toilet. This leads to notches in the dentine of proximal tooth surfaces. Campbell (1925) has described cavities on the proximal surfaces of premolars and molars in Aboriginal skull specimens which are similar to those caused by toothpick abrasion.

A pipe smoker who habitually holds the stem of his pipe between the teeth in one region of the mouth may show marked notching of the upper and lower teeth due to abrasion. The incisal edges of several teeth may be involved. Pipe-stem abrasion of teeth was more frequently seen in days gone by when clay pipes were used. In the skull collection of the South Australian Museum there are several specimens which show what appears to be pipe-stem abrasion.

A woman who regularly opens hair pins with her teeth may abrade the incisal edge of an upper central incisor, forming a notch. A tailor or seamstress who repeatedly bites off thread or holds needles between the teeth may show notching of incisal edges of anterior teeth. A shoemaker or carpet-layer may hold a supply of nails or tacks in the mouth. These may be dispensed individually by manipulation between the teeth, tongue and lips, leading to abrasion notches. Players of wind instruments may show abrasion marks on incisor teeth.

All of the above examples of tooth abrasions seen in modern communities require the development of habitual or occupational abuses confining injury to single teeth or a few teeth in the front part of the mouth. Furthermore, they all require repeated applications of the abrasive forces over considerable periods of time for their effects to become apparent. Very few tooth abrasions of similar nature have been documented for Aboriginal communities. Therefore the remainder of this section has to be speculative and suggestive of areas for future investigation.

Tobacco chewing for long periods each day would lead to the abrasion of premolar and molar teeth and the effect would be more noticeable if the habit was restricted to one side of the mouth. The abrasive effect of ashes and grit incorporated in the quid would tend to wear the occlusal surfaces of the teeth. In older persons who have lost most or all of the enamel from the occlusal surfaces it is likely that the dentine would be cupped out on corresponding upper and lower teeth in the region where the tobacco is chewed. The buccal rim of enamel is likely to be rounded rather than sharp because of the tobacco mass squashing out towards the cheek where it would be frequently collected by the tongue and cheek and squeezed against the buccal surfaces of the clenched teeth by contraction of the cheek muscles to extract the juices. In dental examinations of older Aborigines at Yuendumu it is not uncommon to find a quid of chewing tobacco in the vestibule of the mouth, 'parked' alongside the lower first molar. Records have not been kept of the side of the mouth where the tobacco was found in these instances or of the nature of the tooth wear—whether the dentine was markedly cupped out or whether there was a side difference in the degree of occlusal wear.

The chewing of sinew to soften it and the chewing of bark for the production of saliva would have an abrasive effect on teeth similar to that of tobacco chewing. However, these practices would have much less effect because they are not carried out as frequently or for such long periods as tobacco chewing.

Stripping bark with the use of teeth may be an incision task in its initial stages but it mainly involves gripping of the bark between the front teeth while the branch is rolled away or pulled away from the mouth with use of the hands. The outer surface of bark is drier and usually rougher than the inner surface and it would have adherent grit and ashes from its preliminary warming in the fire. If a person developed a preference for engaging the outer surface of the bark with the lower incisors while the corresponding upper teeth were used to make the initial incisions and later to engage the inner surface of the bark in a gripping action, it is likely that the lower teeth would be subjected to greater abrasion than the upper teeth. The labial surfaces of the lower teeth would be worn as well as the incisal edges and this would be more noticeable if the anterior teeth were opposable only in an edge-to-edge relation. Repeated use of the teeth for stripping bark in this manner over a period of years would have a discernable effect.

Sharpening a spear or digging stick with use of the teeth is usually performed in the canine or premolar region. The blade is carefully positioned on the lower teeth and steadied with the hands held against the lower jaw. A gentle nibbling movement of the jaw engages an upper tooth in a planing or splintering action. Sharpening a stone tool by pressure flaking with the teeth would be carried out in a similar manner. Tooth damage from these practices is unlikely to be as great as might be imagined at first sight because of occlusal sense and the ability to exercise delicate control over the position of the jaw and the direction and magnitude of the forces applied through the teeth. However, some minor chipping or flaking of tooth enamel could be expected if these practices were repeated often.

Severing hair string with use of the teeth and holding string between the teeth would have a noticeable effect only if practised frequently over a long period of time. Enamel and dentine would be abraded by the hair fibres and adherent grit, particularly if there was a tearing or pulling action causing the string to slide between the tooth surfaces.

Holding a spear shaft between the teeth for straightening and holding other objects for various purposes is likely to cause damage by chipping or flaking of tooth enamel. The occlusal surfaces of molar teeth are rarely horizontal when viewed from the front. Masticatory tooth wear in the first molar region leads to greater loss of tooth substance on the buccal aspect of lower teeth and the lingual aspect of upper teeth. Gripping a spear shaft between these teeth is likely to chip enamel from the lingual marginal ridges of the lower teeth and the buccal marginal ridges of the upper teeth. Holding any hard object of irregular shape between the teeth is liable to cause chipping of sharp edges of unsupported enamel on the labio-incisal and bucco-occlusal margins of upper teeth and the linguo-incisal and linguo-occlusal margins of lower teeth.

The use of teeth for biting attacks in fighting or by the medicine man when biting the skin of his patient is unlikely to damage the teeth. There would be greater injury to the bitten than the biter.

Discussion

At present there is insufficient detailed knowledge of tooth wear and its variability in Australian Aborigines to enable confident distinction between different wear patterns which might be associated with dissimilarities in food and eating habits. Regional differences could be expected, for example, between the type and degree of tooth wear shown by Aborigines living in the tropical north, the arid and semi-arid centre, and temperate regions of Australia. Further study of tooth wear is needed in relation to foods available in different regions, various methods used to prepare foods for eating, and differences in eating habits. The associations of food and eating habits with sex differences in tooth wear also need further study.

The biophysics of tooth wear in all its forms is not well understood. At present there is insufficient knowledge of the precise nature of the various wear processes to differentiate between masticatory and non-masticatory tooth wear with any degree of certainty. Unless the craft uses or other non-masticatory uses of teeth by an individual had been restricted to a particular segment of the dental arches and carried out repeatedly over a long period of time they would be difficult to distinguish. Abrasive wear and enamel chipping which seem to be inconsistent with masticatory tooth wear can be seen in the teeth of Aborigines at Yuendumu and in the Aboriginal skulls housed in the South Australian Museum. These lesions need systematic study.

Future studies of tooth wear should be carefully planned and they should employ standardised methods of data collection. It is important that they should be based on modern concepts of the masticatory system and not confined to teeth alone. Although it would be necessary to study the detail of wear on each tooth of a specimen or subject—the degree of wear, the location and inclinations of wear facets, the involvement of dentine, the nature of enamel chipping, and so on—the final analysis for each individual would need consideration of these data in relation to the functioning of the masticatory system as a whole. Assessments would also require other features to be taken into account—the positions of individual teeth and their within-arch relations, the state of health of each tooth and its supporting structures, the relations of the upper and lower arches in various mandibular positions, the effects of malposed, diseased or missing teeth on the pattern of mandibular movements, and the state of health and the relations of components of the temporo-mandibular joints.

Further investigations of the patterns of tooth wear conducted in this manner and further ethnographic studies of the non-masticatory uses of teeth by Australian Aborigines are needed before the evidence of dental attrition and abrasion marks can be interpreted with confidence in their relations to food and eating habits and the practice of crafts. Molnar's article referred to in the introduction of this paper is a timely reminder that much more research is required.

Summary

The masticatory system is a highly coordinated assembly of tissues serving the prime function of preparing food for swallowing and digestion. Because of the wide variety of activities developed for this function the system is also suited to tasks unconnected with mastication. Australian Aborigines living under native conditions show tooth wear resulting from vigorous mastication of tough abrasive foods and from various non-masticatory uses of teeth. At present there is insufficient detailed knowledge of tooth wear patterns to allow confident distinction between these two sources of tooth wear.

References

Barrett, M. J., 1956. *Mastication—a dynamic process*. Teaching film, Department of Restorative Dentistry, University of Adelaide.

—— 1960. Parafunctions and tooth attrition. In *Parafunctions of the masticatory system (bruxism)*, (eds) D. Lipke and U. Posselt. Journal of the Western Society of Periodontology, 8 : 133.

Campbell, T. D., 1925. *Dentition and palate of the Australian Aboriginal*. Adelaide: Hassell Press.

—— 1939. Food, food values and food habits of the Australian aborigines in relation to their dental conditions. *Australian Dental Journal*, 34 : 1; 45; 73; 141; 177.

Campbell, T. D. and M. J. Barrett, 1958. *The woomera*. Documentary film, Board for Anthropological Research, University of Adelaide.

—— and —— 1963a. *Palya-prepared spinifex gum*. Documentary film, Board for Anthropological Research, University of Adelaide.

—— and —— 1963b. *Aboriginal spears*. Documentary film, Board for Anthropological Research, University of Adelaide.

—— and —— 1963c. *Aboriginal hair string*. Documentary film, Board for Anthropological Research, University of Adelaide.

Campbell, T. D. and J. M. Simpson, 1953. *So they did eat*. Documentary film, Board for Anthropological Research, University of Adelaide.

Cleland, J. B. and J. H. Gray, 1934. Pathological lesions met with amongst Aborigines in the Musgrave Ranges, South Australia. *Journal of Tropical Medicine and Hygiene*, 37 : 305.

Fry, H. K. and N. B. Tindale, 1933. *A Jankundjadjara tooth evulsion rite*. Documentary film, Board for Anthropological Research, University of Adelaide.

Gould, R. A., 1968. Chipping stones in the outback. *Natural History*, 77 : 42.

Mitchell, S., 1959. The woodworking tools of the Australian Aborigines. *Journal of the Royal Anthropological Institute*, 89 : 191.

Molnar, S., 1972. Tooth wear and culture: a survey of tooth functions among some prehistoric populations. *Current Anthropology*, 13 : 511.

Pindborg, J. J., 1970. *Pathology of the dental hard tissues*. Copenhagen: Munksgaard.

Posselt, U., 1968. *Physiology of occlusion and rehabilitation*. 2nd ed. Oxford: Blackwell Scientific Publications.

Ramfjord, S. P. and M. Ash, 1971. *Occlusion*. 2nd ed. Philadelphia: W. B. Saunders Company.

Sicher, H. (ed), 1966. *Orban's oral histology and embryology*. 6th ed. Saint Louis: C. V. Mosby Company.

—— and E. L. Du Brul, 1970. *Oral anatomy*. 5th ed. Saint Louis: C. V. Mosby Company.

Forty-seven trips

A case study in the character of archaeological formation processes

LEWIS R. BINFORD

One of my motives for initiating ethno-archaeological work among the contemporary Nunamiut Eskimos was the recognition that they were one of the few remaining groups of people still largely dependent upon hunting for their subsistence. It was possible to study the dynamics of an ongoing technological system in the context of an essentially self-sufficient subsistence economy. To many, the Nunamiut may appear uninteresting since most of the tools currently in use are no longer manufactured locally, but are purchased through mail order houses or obtained through a variety of other commercial means. These conditions fascinated me. If archaeology is to achieve the status of a science it must seek to establish law-like propositions. If law-like, such propositions should cover contemporary as well as past organisational situations. Too long have anthropologists sought the unique, or singled out as 'exceptional' specific features of a case as justification for abandoning the goal of law-like propositions.

The purpose of this paper is to examine the dynamics of behaviour in the context of which archaeological remains are generated: the aim being the specification of some behavioural characteristics which may regularly condition the content and forms of patterning observed by the archaeologist.

The data to be discussed is derived primarily from observations of 47 trips made by Eskimo males out of the village of Anaktuvuk between 4 and 17 April 1971. The following information was obtained regarding each trip: (a) the time of departure, (b) the composition of the party leaving the village, (c) the expressed purpose of the trip, (d) the anticipated destination, (e) an inventory of all gear carried by the party members, and (f) the mode of transportation to be used. When the party returned (or in some cases when I was on the trip and could make a journal) the following information was obtained: (a) the route travelled, (b) the location of all stops, (c) the activities performed at each stop, (d) the duration of each stop, (e) the total distance travelled, (f) the duration of the trip, and (g) an inventory of all gear returned to the village. Subsequently, interviews were conducted with the participants of the trips regarding their ideas and cognitive organisation of the gear used.

Information was sought regarding the reasons for discrepancies between the list of gear leaving the village and that which returned. No attempt was made to inventory the items carried in pockets. Cigarettes, sun glasses, a wad of toilet paper, a small screwdriver for adjusting gun sights, and a sharpening stone are the items which most hunters have on their person at any time, and these items can generally be assumed on all of the trips.

Table 1 presents the 47 trips arranged left to right in order of decreasing round trip distances from the village at Anaktuvuk. The inventory of items is grouped into three major categories. Group I is all items which are specific to the use of the snow-mobile for transport. Group II is all items which might be termed the hunter's basic spring equipment, arranged in a descending order of occurrence on the trips inventoried. Group III is items considered 'optional' by the hunters, and represents items carried more frequently on longer trips.

Group I (The snow-mobile) There is a perfect association between the presence of Group I items and the use of the snow-mobile for transport. The use of the snow-mobile by the Nunimiut is interesting in terms of its recent introduction. The first snow-mobile to be purchased was delivered to the village during the winter of 1967–68. It was bought by Simon Paneack. Quickly most families worked toward the purchase of a snow-mobile, and by the spring of 1971 there were 23 functional (running) snow-mobiles in the village and 5 working dog teams, averaging 7.2 dogs per team. By 1971, snow-mobiles represented 82.1% of the operational winter and spring transportation means. Interviews on the use of the snow-mobile and its advantages over the dog team brought forth a number of comments. Almost universally, the response of the hunters was that the speed of the snow-mobile made it possible to range further without the need for extended overnight camping. In addition, they claimed that the snow-mobile permitted the pursuit hunting of wolves, which they saw as a clear advantage. 'It is fast enough to run them right down.' The disadvantages were clearly recognised to be of two types: (a) frequent breakdown in the field, and (b) difficulty in maintenance due to lack of parts, expense of spare parts, and difficulty in repairing the machines in cold weather.

Of the 33 snow-mobile trips recorded in Table 1, 6 were 'breakdown' trips on which the hunters either had to walk back to the village or spend the night in the field awaiting the arrival of other monitors to take them home. This amounts to an impressive 18.1% of the total trips made by snow-mobile. Of the dog team trips recorded, none were 'breakdown' trips. This difference in reliability is fully realised by the hunters, although the risk is tolerated for the added advantage of speed, and the fact that short trips can be made for packing even when the snow is poor or gone.

Although 82.1% of the operational transport means during winter and spring were snow-mobile, only 70.2% of the recorded trips were made with these vehicles. The difference in proportion reflects, to some extent, differences among the active hunters in their willingness to take the risk of breakdown. For instance, during the spring of 1971 I was a member of two parties which experienced snow-mobile breakdowns in the field. The hunter had killed his dogs the previous fall, keeping only three large ones for summer packing. During the summer of 1971 he was very anxious to get puppies to begin training as a team, since he was 'fed up' with snow-mobile breakdowns during winter. I anticipate a slight increase in the number of functional dog teams among the active hunters during the next several years.

Group II (Hunters' basic equipment) The items listed as Group II, Table 1, make up the basic 'trip gear' inventory of the hunters. Most of these items have functional counterparts in the traditional technology of the Nunamiut.

The axe is the most characteristic item which distinguishes the winter and spring equipment from that of summer and autumn. The axe is used for a variety of tasks during the months of freezing weather. Its most common use is to chop out the meat from frozen caches, and to complete any butchering tasks that may be considered necessary at the time of loading meat from caches. In addition, it may be used in cutting down large willows for transport back to the village, and as an ice chisel while in the field if ice fishing is attempted. In case of mishap it may be used to breach the hard crust of the packed snow for making an emergency snow house. I have also observed it being used as a hammer, particularly during attempted snow-mobile or sled repairs, and the handle being used as an expedient snow probe when one is not handy. In extreme cold the axe is frequently used to butcher even unfrozen animals, since the use of the knife generally ensures that the hunter's hands will become covered with blood and therefore more subject to freezing and general discomfort.

The metal axe was one of the first items to be adopted enthusiastically into the traditional Nunamiut technology, once trade with Russian and Euro-American sources was opened up in the last half of the 19th century. However, it was not the first item selected if a maximising choice had to be made. Interestingly, the saw was given selective preference over the axe because 'it could be cut into men's knives and ulus when it was worn out'; the implication being that it was difficult to do much with a broken or worn out axe. In the early trading days the saw was used for many of the tasks for which the axe is used today. The saw was used for secondary and primary winter butchering of frozen meat, and was also used in gathering winter firewood. Traditional ice chisels, generally hafted on the end of a snow probe, spear, or ice shovel, continued to be used for many of the ice chopping and chipping tasks which today are usually performed with the axe.

Prior to the Russian-European trade, highly valued axes were made from Alaskan 'jade'. Although the living informants can remember seeing these items in their youth, they were heirlooms largely used by shamans. By that time metal items obtained in trade had already become an integral part of their technology. Questions directed to the older men regarding the form of the stone axes drew a variety of responses. Most agreed that the 'oldtimers' axes' were not hafted like modern metal ones. Instead, they were hafted with the blade transverse to the handle, which would render the item an adze in our terminology. In addition, they agreed that Alaskan 'jade' was not the only material used for the production of the blade. One informant said he had seen them made with flint blades, and offered the interpretation that one of the steeply retouched 'sidescrapers' which I recovered

archaeologically in 1971 was like the flint blades hafted in the oldtimers' axes. They all agreed that the blades were hafted into an antler sleeve which was then lashed to a handle. Items recently described by Hall (1971 : 41) as adzes fit very nicely the descriptions of the informants regarding the 'oldtimers' axes'. In addition, one 'sidescraper' pictured by Hall (1971 : 90) appears identical to the item which informants identified as a flint axe blade. Informants related that the 'oldtimers' axes were used in cutting up frozen meat, working wood, and chopping antler. They suggested that those with flint blades were better for fine work on wood. I was unable to obtain information from the informants regarding the frequency of jade axes in the past, and the degree that they were consistently used for winter butchering and cache removal tasks as the metal axe is used today. All informants agreed that 'it must have been used that way', since all recognised as a difficult winter task the coping with frozen meat. For this job a knife is considered of little value.

Axes are owned today by each household, and most have more than one. They are rarely stored inside the house, generally being found standing up inside a pile of firewood next to the house, or lying on top of a partially unloaded sled. It is important to note that on every trip made outside of the village during the spring period an axe was included in the equipment.

Matches are today the other item which is considered as essential as the axe in winter and spring field equipment. They have only a single function, unlike the axe. Matches were known through trade as early as the 1890s, but they did not replace the earlier flint and steel set until they were consistently available around 1915. As late as 1946 some old men were still carrying flint and steel sets as part of their regular field equipment. The latter were manufactured from files obtained in trade and a combination of gun flints or locally obtained flints.

Informants, when queried regarding the methods of making fire prior to the availability of trade files, said that the bow drill was used in a wooden hearth. Willow cotton rubbed in charcoal was the preferred tinder. This technique has been used in recent times by hunters with either wet matches or otherwise caught without modern fire making equipment. The young hunters are familiar with the technique and most admit to having used it under emergency conditions sometimes during their lifetime.

Today each hunter has anywhere from two to four rifles, generally varying in size and power. Reloading of spent shells is still common, and new shells are not purchased regularly. Rifles and shells are generally stored in the houses and are rarely left outside. In the field they are carried in a rifle case made of either caribou skin or canvas. The case is sewn so that the rifle is extracted from the butt end. The case is slung over both shoulders so that it hangs across the back with the barrel tip pointing down. Ammunition is generally carried in a small pouch especially made for the purpose, and worn so that it hangs on the right side just above the belt. Sometimes the rifle is packed on the sled, rolled in the 'sled skin' so that the jarring of the sled will not damage the rifle. Nunamiut hunters are not extremely meticulous in the care of their guns. However, I have never seen a hunter load his rifle until game is sighted or he is following very fresh tracks or spoor. Rifles are never stored loaded.

The rifle was first known to the Nunamiut during the time of the great-grandfathers of the old men living today. The first guns were flintlock rifles obtained in trade. There are

Table 1   Gear carried by hunters on 47 trips

Trip	28	27	26	25	41	40	42	39	36*	24	23*	35	43*	33	38	21*	32	34	46	47
Kilometres (Round trip)	274	274	274	274	203	183	183	183	179	163	158	158	76	76	69	68	63	63	60	60
Group I																				
Pliers	•	•	•	•	•	•	•	•		•		•	•	•		•	•	•	•	•
Screwdriver	•	•	•	•	•	•	•	•		•		•	•	•		•	•	•	•	•
Wrench	•	•	•	•	•	•	•	•		•		•	•	•		•	•	•	•	•
Spark plug	•	•	•	•	•	•	•	•		•		•	•	•		•	•	•	•	•
Extra gas	•	•	•	•	•	•	•	•		•		•	•		•		•		•	•
Oil	•	•	•	•	•	•	•	•		•		•	•						•	
Wire	•	•	•	•	•	•	•	•		•			•	•			•		•	
Extra chain	•		•				•	•		•					•					
Hammer	•	•					•	•	•	•										
Group II																				
1 Axe	•	•	•	•	•	•	•	•	•	•	•	•	•	•	•	•	•	•	•	•
2 Sled skin	•	•	•	•	•	•	•	•	•	•	•	•	•	•	•	•	•	•	•	•
3 Matches	•	•	•	•	•	•	•	•	•	•	•	•	•	•	•	•	•	•	•	•
4 Rifle	•	•	•	•	•	•	•	•	•	•	•	•	•	•	•	•	•	•	•	•
5 Ammunition	•	•	•	•	•	•	•	•	•	•	•	•	•	•	•	•	•	•	•	•
6 Pilot bread	•	•	•	•	•	•	•	•	•	•	•	•	•	•	•	•	•	•	•	•
7 Snow probe	•	•	•	•	•	•	•	•	•	•	•	•	•	•	•	•	•	•	•	•
8 Sugar	•	•			•	•	•	•	•	•	•	•	•	•	•	•	•		•	•
9 Coffee	•	•			•	•	•	•	•	•	•	•	•	•	•	•	•	•	•	•
10 Knife	•	•	•	•	•	•	•	•	•	•	•	•	•	•	•	•	•	•	•	•
11 Cup	•	•	•	•	•	•	•	•	•	•	•	•	•	•	•	•	•	•	•	•
12 Coffee can	•	•			•	•	•	•	•	•	•	•	•	•	•	•	•		•	•
13 Extra mukluks	•	•	•	•	•	•	•	•	•	•	•	•	•	•	•	•			•	•
14 Extra socks	•	•	•	•	•	•	•	•	•	•	•	•	•	•	•				•	•
15 Extra line	•	•	•	•	•	•	•	•	•	•	•	•	•	•		•				
16 Extra skin	•	•	•	•	•	•	•	•	•	•	•	•	•	•	•	•		•	•	•
17 Glass	•	•	•	•	•	•	•	•	•	•	•	•	•	•	•		•			
18 Big knife	•	•	•	•	•	•	•	•	•	•	•	•	•	•		•				
19 Extra parka	•	•	•	•	•	•	•	•	•	•	•	•								
20 Corn meal	•		•		•	•	•	•	•	•	•	•								
Group III																				
21 Snow shoes	•	•	•	•	•	•	•	•		•			•			•	•			
22 Dry meat							•	•		•			•				•	•		
23 Needle and skin	•		•			•							•	•						•
24 Rib slab	•		•	•	•			•	•	•		•								
25 Scapula			•			•				•		•								
26 Steel traps					•	•				•										
27 Sardines		•		•	•		•			•		•		•	•					
28 .22 pistol		•	•				•													
29 .22 rifle			•			•			•											
30 Peanut butter		•		•	•		•													
Gear carried by hunters and not returned																				
Peanut butter jar		•		•	•		•													
Sardine can		•		•	•		•			•		•		•	•					
.22 shells		•	•	•			•	•												
Steel traps					•	•			•											
Ribs	•		•	•	•	•	•	•	•	•										
Scapula			•				•			•		•								
Cup			•		•					•										
Coffee can			•		•		•			•				•			•			
Knife	•																			
Snow probe					•															
Rifle shell cases					•															
Axe													•							
Skin					•															
Line									•											

* Indicates use of dog team on the trip

29	30	20	2*	6*	18*	15	5	44*	31*	12	4	17	19*	37	9*	46	11*	13*	45	14	3	22	10	7	8	1
55	55	50	48	43	42	37	35	34	27	27	27	26	23	21	21	19	19	19	19	19	19	18	18	18	14	8

many stories which the old men heard from their fathers about the novelty of this gun. Most of the stories relate humorous facts about their exploding, failure to fire, or other inefficiencies. Although such pieces were known and owned by Nunamiut during the last half of the 19th century, they were never numerous or reliable enough to replace the conventional hunting gear, and seem to have had little effect on the traditional hunting practices.

Beginning in the 1890s, rifles obtained from the coast (largely 30–30s) became rather numerous in the interior, and by 1900 had generally replaced the conventional hunting gear, although this was sporadically used until as late as 1946. The combination of the increase of trading activity with the coast and the adoption of the gun somewhat modified the traditional pattern of life in the interior, and had, of course, profound effects on the character of the technology.

The skinning knife, big knife and snow probe all had counterparts in the traditional technology. Today, the most common skinning knife is a small pocket knife. Younger men tend to have larger knives, and the older men comment on how they behave like 'sheep hunters', having a big fancy knife, but not knowing how to use it. Clearly, the small knife is preferred by the skilled hunters. Traditionally, all men carried a 'man's knife', worn in a sheath tied transversely to the belt, directly above the 'belly button'. These knives generally had an additional lashing hole through the antler handle, enabling them to be tied to the belt as insurance against slipping from the sheath. The vertical sheath worn at the hip is an innovation of the late forties, in the mountains, when sheathed knives became available. Prior to that time, most knives were purchased without sheaths, and a sheath was manufactured from the leg skin of caribou.

The big knife is today a large butcher knife, generally of poor quality. Traditionally, these were made of antler, ivory, or whale bone, and were the typical snow knife of earlier ethnography. Today, the big knife is used in several different ways. It is carried as a snow knife, 'in case something happens and you have to build a little snow house'. A more common use is in the preparation of peeled willow sticks for starting fires, or as a small bolo knife for cutting firewood. The back of the blade is also used frequently by the men in the field as a hammer for breaking marrow bones.

The snow probe is used for testing for dangerous overflow waters under snow, or secondarily for locating buried objects. Almost any convenient stick about one metre long can be utilised. Today, men are frequently seen carving a suitable dry willow stick during the summer, which may also be used occasionally as a walking stick in the snowless months. During winter, these will be carried on sled trips and used to test the snow, particularly around lakes and streams that may have overflow water periodically during the winter. These sticks can always be used in an emergency as firewood or as good fuel for starting fires of wet willows or animal bones. The older hunters will rarely go out without such a stick tucked under the sled skin. When dog teams were more prevalent, these sticks were also a source of material for replacing the harness spreader which is a frequent casualty on dog team trips.

Field glasses are common today, and were one of the items sought during the early days of trade, both from Russian sources and the later American sources. Long telescopes of the naval variety were obtained during the early trading years. Field glasses are more recent, and were rare before 1950. There were no functionally equivalent items in traditional technology.

The items remaining in Group II are sugar, coffee, pilot bread, corn meal, coffee can, cup, extra socks, mukluks, skin, parka, and line.

Clothing is generally traditional in design and manufacture except socks, which today are purchased, but formerly were made from caribou fawn skin. The food items are interesting. Customarily, there are three basic kinds of trail foods: dried meats, akutuk, and marrow bones. Hunters generally preferred dried meat which had bones, such as dried rib slabs or a scapula. This preference is directly related to the versatility of bone use. Once the meat had been consumed, the bones could be used as fuel, or pounded up into small chips and boiled to yield a 'bone juice'. This was the only drink besides pure water which hunters customarily consumed in the field. akutuk was carried as small cakes. These were manufactured by the women from bone marrow and rendered bone grease, sometimes with berries mixed into the marrow, or small strips of dry meat. Akutuk cakes are still occasionally carried by the men, but its manufacture has dropped off considerably since commercial grease has been readily available (since 1953). Marrow bones were carried for the same reason that dried meat containing bones was preferred. They were a ready source of fat, and once the marrow was consumed the bones could be pounded up to produce 'bone juice', or used as fuel.

Statistics accumulated over a four year period from both observation and interview regarding the frequency with which different anatomical parts were carried as trail food are very revealing. Table 2 presents the actual frequency of parts carried into the field by members of parties ranging from one to four men, for a total of 111 trips on which either dry meat or marrow bones were packed.

Table 2 Frequency of dry meat and marrow bones packed by hunters on 111 trips

Anatomical part	Dry meat	Marrow bones
Rib slab	68	
Scapula	47	
Belly sheet	27	
Tenderloin	23	
Pelvis	13	
Tibia		73
Metatarsal		57
Radio-cubitus		13
Femur		9
Metacarpal		4

The preferences demonstrated for dry meat is clearly in favour of rib slabs and scapula; next come tenderloins and belly sheets (both parts containing no bones). Least desirable for these purposes is the pelvis. The preferences are not absolute and are relative to season, anticipated activities on the trip, and the regular attrition through a year in the parts remaining in storage.

Tables 3A and 3B present the breakdown of meat and bone parts carried on trips during different seasons.

It is clear that during summer and autumn the boneless dry parts are carried more frequently when fuel is more readily available. Similarly, marrow bones are never carried during summer when marrow spoilage is high and emergency fuels are not a major concern. Another interesting fact is that the

Table 3A Frequency distribution of dry meat parts carried by season

Anatomical part	Spring[1] %	Summer %	Autumn %	Winter %	Total
Rib slab	13 37.14	6 16.66	20 38.46	19 42.22	68
Scapula	11 31.32	0 0.00	14 26.92	22 48.88	47
Belly sheet	0 0.00	19 52.77	8 15.38	0 0.00	27
Tenderloin	2 5.71	11 30.55	10 19.23	0 0.00	23
Pelvis	0 25.71	0 0.00	0 0.00	4 8.88	13

Number of trips on which dry meat was carried:

	17	24	23	22	86

Number of items:

	35	36	52	45	168

Mean per trip:

	2.05	1.50	2.26	2.04	

Table 3B Frequency distribution of marrow bones carried by season

Anatomical part	Spring[1] %	Summer %	Autumn %	Winter %	Total
Tibia	3 10.00	0 0.00	19 59.37	51 54.25	73
Metatarsal	10 33.33	0 0.00	13 40.62	34 36.17	57
Radio-cubitus	8 26.66	0 0.00	0 0.00	5 5.31	13
Femur	5 16.66	0 0.00	0 0.00	4 4.25	9
Metacarpal	4 13.33	0 0.00	0 0.00	0 0.00	4
Total items	30	0	32	94	156
No. of trips	10	0	21	30	61
Mean per trip	3.0	0.0	1.52	3.13	

1. Data tabulated here is independent of the data tabulated in Table 1. At the time of collecting the data in Table 1 I did not keep records on marrow bones.

femur and metacarpal are more commonly carried during spring when stores are apt to be low. These are the least desirable of the marrow bones listed, the marrow cavities

being smaller and the marrow of the femur less fatty than the marrow of the tibia.

Table 4 shows the seasonal breakdown of the trips recorded with regard to the relative incidence of packing dry meat versus marrow bones.

Table 4 Number of trips on which dry meat, marrow bones, or both were carried by season

Season	Both	Dry meat only	Marrow bones only	Total
Spring	3	14	7	24
Summer	0	24	0	24
Autumn	14	9	7	30
Winter	19	3	11	33
Total	36	50	25	111

The clear tendency for increased use of marrow bones during the colder months is obvious. Similarly checking this information against Table 2, it is evident that dry meat with bones is more commonly carried in the cold months. Both of these trends reflect the relevance of alternative uses for bones as both fuel and additional nourishment in the form of 'bone juice'.

Group III The items listed here need little discussion. Today the snowshoes are still manufactured locally in traditional styles. The needle and skin are clothing repair items: mail order steel needles and small scraps of worked caribou skin. Steel traps are purchased by mail order, as are the .22 pistols, rifles, sardines and peanut butter.

Types of trips and the gear carried

Data obtained from the Eskimos regarding the purpose of the trip fall into two broad categories: (1) maintenance trips made for the purpose of recovering meat from caches, and/or trips made for procuring firewood, and (2) monitoring trips made for the purpose of searching for game, frequently coupled with checking traps. Data on distances covered are summarised in Fig. 1.

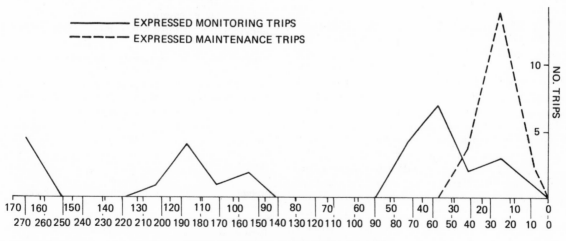

Fig. 1: Distances covered in monitoring and maintenance trips.

The distances which hunters covered on trips exhibit an interesting distribution. Of the 20 trips made for the expressed purpose of recovering cached meat or obtaining firewood, the mean round trip distance covered was 23.7 km, with a range between 43.5 km and 8 km. On the other hand, trips made for monitoring purposes exhibited a tri-modal distribution. The cluster accounting for 55.5% of the monitoring trips exhibited a mean round trip distance of 53.5 km. This means that the hunters reached an average distance from the village of 26.7 km, or roughly a five to seven hour walk back in the event of mishap. This is a distance that could be covered on the same day the trip was made, depending, of course, on wind and weather conditions. No trips were recorded which were between 76 km and 158 km round trip distance. Eight trips clustered between 203 and 158 km round trip, for a mean trip distance of 192.5 km. Hunters on such trips reached an average distance from the village of 96.2 km. If mishaps occurred, or much time was spent in hunting, an overnight stay would be almost imperative, since the walk home would require upwards of 20 hours. Trips of this distance can, however, be easily made in a single day, barring mishap, since the snow-mobiles can average just slightly under 16 km per hour. A dog team is slower, averaging only about 9.5 km per hour on such a trip (this figure assumes a good trail as is generally present by spring). Hunters using dog teams normally prepare for an overnight stop, while snow-mobile drivers make such preparations but plan to return the same day, barring mishap. Hunters making trips of this distance follow two strategies. The first is for two men to arrange to go out on sequential days along the same general route. This ensures that in case of mishap, aid and transport back to the village will be available. The other strategy is to go out in a party of two or more men. All trips of this distance were handled in this manner, while trips averaging 53 km were all made by single individuals, except for one on which two men went together. The trips recorded which exceed 203 km were made by a monitoring party, and they clearly anticipated staying overnight. We might summarise the monitoring trips as (a) one day trips regardless of mishap, (b) one day trips with provision for overnight camping in case of mishap, and (c) two or more day trips.

Relationship between distance anticipated and the quantity of gear carried

Since the trip distance shows a multi-modal distribution along one dimension-monitoring and a single normal distribution for the maintenance trips, we might anticipate some correlation between the trip distances and the quantity and kinds of gear carried. Upon investigation, a clear relationship is demonstrable, but it is not a linear correlation with distance. Fig. 2 plots the mean number of items carried exclusive of Group I (snow-mobile gear) for trips falling into 16 km round trip distance intervals up to 80 km, and then the means for the trip distance clusters up to 274 km round trip. A curvilinear relationship exists in which there is a rapid and regular increase in the numbers of items carried until a 80 km round trip distance is reached; then the graph levels off with only a slight increase in numbers of items out to trips of a mean round trip distance of 274 km. This particular pattern is to be understood in terms of the hunters' anticipation of possibly having to remain in the field overnight. As the anticipated round trip distance increases between 16 and 80 km the possibility of returning to the village in

case of mishap regularly decreases; therefore, the men tend to carry more emergency gear as a direct function of the anticipated distance. After the overnight threshold is passed, however, few items are added to the gear inventory in anticipation of greater distances.

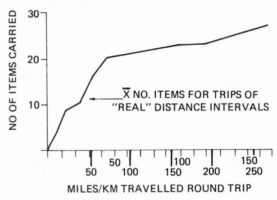

Fig. 2: Number of items carried compared with the distance of trips.

The hunters' conception of the gear

Many archaeologists continue to insist that patterning observed in the archaeological record is a direct reflection of the shared ideas and values of a group of people (Rouse, 1972 : 164–68; Dunnell, 1971 : 123). I was interested in investigating the nature of the relationship between the way hunters thought about their gear and what, in fact, they did with it. I interviewed seven hunters regarding their ways of viewing the items on the total inventory list of the items carried on the 47 trips. The procedure was to make up a pile of gear representing all the items on the list exclusive of Group I and ask the informants to divide the pile into separate piles in terms of the way they thought about the gear when they were anticipating a trip. Items listed in Group II, Table 1, were all singled out by the seven men as constituting the basic inventory of field items which hunters carried. This is the 'trip gear'. Items listed in Group III of Table 1 were all singled out as 'optional gear'. Within the inventory list of 'trip gear' the hunters consistently recognised three categories: (1) 'tools and things', (2) food, and (3) clothing. Table 5 presents the inventories of the items segregated by the hunters into their three categories.

Table 5 Hunters' categorisation of the 'basic trip' gear

Group II A Things — tools	Group II B Food	Group II C Clothes
Dog team or ski-doo	Sugar	Big knife
Axe	Coffee	Extra line
Sled skin	Cup	Socks
Matches	Pilot bread	Mukluks
Rifle	Coffee can	Extra skin
Ammunition	Corn meal	Parka
Skinning knife		
Field glasses		
Snow probe		
(9 items or 42.8% of the list)	(6 items or 28.5% of the list)	(6 items or 28.5% of the list)

The archaeologist will immediately recognise that this categorisation is inconsistent. Items which we would include under the heading of 'tools and things', such as the coffee cup or the big knife, are listed under 'food' and 'clothes' respectively. Repeated questions, and queries aimed at pointing out alternative categorisations, including those likely to be employed by archaeologists, resulted in the gradual recognition of the cognitive principles standing behind the way the Nunamiut viewed their gear. For instance, when queried about the cup and coffee can as being 'tools and things', the following response was common. 'Yes, but I carry them when I think about myself and how I will feel, not when I think about what I may have to do out there.' The inclusion of extra line and big knife under 'clothes' brought forth the following explanation: 'They are in that pile because I'm thinking about what may happen to me out there; suppose the dog team lead broke or I had to build a snow shelter'. Quite clearly, the three categories represent three cognitive dimensions of contingency planning: (1) what I will have to do in terms of the goals of the expedition, (2) how I may feel in terms of hunger, and (3) what may happen to me in terms of mishaps. The Nunamiut, in this context, think of their gear in terms of the analogous functions of the items in regard to their dimension of contingency planning, and not in terms of analogous formal properties of the items themselves.

I turn now to an examination of the three recognised categories of gear as they relate to one another. Do they represent independent dimensions in terms of actual association and variation? The frequencies of items falling in the three Nunamiut categories have been arranged according to the four types of recognised trips. These data are presented in Table 6.

The above data permits us to examine the degree that these three categories actually represent independent dimensions in terms of behavioural dynamics. The summary percentages in each column for each class of gear express the relative proportions of each class of gear taken on trips of varying distances. These relationships are summarised in Fig. 3.

Each of the three categories seemingly behaves somewhat independently of one another. 'Tools and things' and 'food' appear as inverse parabolic curves, while 'clothes' represents a low sigmoid curve. Nevertheless, it is clear that 'clothes' and 'food' are strongly correlated and this is, of course, what we would expect since 'how I may feel' and 'what may happen to me' are not necessarily independent. As expected, these interact in a closely correlated manner. We might summarise the situation as follows: (1) when gear is being assembled for each of the recognised cognitive categories, different consequences of sometimes similar contingencies are being considered; (2) this situation ensures that there will be strong correlations between components of the different cognitive categories; and (3) there are slightly different thresholds for the consideration of varying consequences, correlated with anticipated distance to be travelled, eg. a mishap within return walking distance eliminates the consequence of having to stay overnight, but not the consequence that I may get hungry. These facts ensure that there will not be a perfect correlation, and that there will be some partial independence between the categories as is indicated on Fig. 3.

I turn now to a more complicated problem, changing our perspective, and assuming that of the archaeologist beginning the analysis of four samples of gear (the four trip distance samples) as if these were four assemblages remaining from

Table 6 Frequency of items in three Nunamiut categories arranged according to recognised trips

Gear categories			Trip categories					
					Monitoring trips			
	Maintenance		Short		Medium		Long	
Class I.	#	%	#	%	#	%	#	%
Tools and things								
Axe	20	15.5	15	7.0	8	5.0	4	5.4
Sled skin	20	15.5	15	7.0	8	5.0	4	5.4
Matches	20	15.5	15	7.0	8	5.0	4	5.4
Rifle	11	8.5	15	7.0	8	5.0	4	5.4
Ammunition	11	8.5	15	7.0	8	5.0	4	5.4
Skinning knife	4	3.1	13	6.1	8	5.0	4	5.4
Field glasses	0	0.0	7	3.3	8	5.0	4	5.4
Snow probe	8	6.2	13	6.1	8	5.0	4	5.4
Total	94	72.8	112	52.8	64	40.0	32	43.2
Class II.								
Food								
Sugar	8	6.2	14	6.6	8	5.0	2	2.7
Coffee	8	6.2	14	6.6	8	5.0	2	2.7
Pilot bread	8	6.2	14	6.6	8	5.0	4	5.4
Corn meal	0	0.0	0	0.0	8	5.0	3	4.1
Cup	3	2.3	13	6.1	8	5.0	4	5.4
Coffee can	2	1.5	12	5.6	8	5.0	2	2.7
Total	29	22.4	67	31.6	48	30.0	17	23.0
Class III.								
Clothes								
Socks	1	0.8	9	4.2	8	5.0	4	5.4
Mukluks	1	0.8	10	4.7	8	5.0	4	5.4
Extra skin	0	0.0	6	2.8	8	5.0	4	5.4
Parka	0	0.0	0	0.0	8	5.0	4	5.4
Line	4	3.1	8	3.7	8	5.0	4	5.4
Big knife	0	0.0	4	1.8	8	5.0	4	5.4
Total	6	4.7	37	17.4	48	30.0	24	32.4
Grand total :	129		212		160		73	

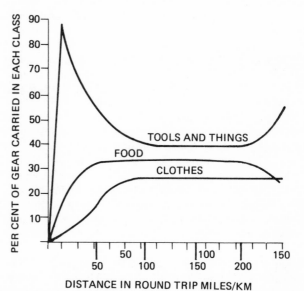

Fig. 3: Percentage of classes of gear carried compared with distance of trips.

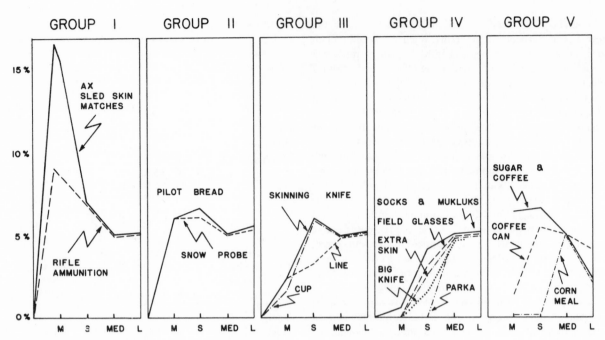

Fig. 4: Covariation of items carried according to nature of trip.

different sites. The analytical task would be to isolate those patterns of association and co-variation characteristic of the items represented in the four samples. In concrete situations, one might elect to perform some 'data reducing' operation such as factor analysis or cluster analysis. This would permit the recognition of sets of items which exhibited strong patterns of co–variation among themselves and analogous patterns with respect to all other items. (See, for instance, Binford and Binford, 1966, and Binford, 1972). The number of cases is too small for the actual performance of such an analysis; however, some hint as to the likely results can be obtained from a graphic display of the percentage relationships between items across the four samples. This display is presented in Fig. 4.

Items depicted in Group I, Fig. 4, are highly intercorrelated. These are the axe, sled skin, matches, rifle, and ammunition; all items listed by the Nunamiut as 'tools and things'. Group II consists of pilot bread (food) and a snow probe (tools and things). It is quite likely that sugar and coffee displayed in Group V would exhibit a lower but dominant correlation with Graph II items, the latter being listed as 'food' by the Nunamiut. Here we observe an interesting situation. Items from two of the Nunamiuts' cognitive categories are apparently strongly related co-variantly. Why? The answer is very clear behaviourally. The Nunamiut tend to have various items cached in regularly utilised sites all around their village. These are the normal stopping places for the preparation of field snacks. Sugar, coffee and pilot bread are the normal contents of such snacks, and they can anticipate cups and coffee cans being cached at such locations. Nevertheless, they must find the cached items in the snow—hence the correlation with the snow probe. These correlations reflect contigencies considered by the Nunamiut not made explicit in his cognitive categories. They reflect the actual dynamics of behaviour under a specific set of conditions. Group III is even more interesting in this regard. Extra line (clothes), cup (food), skinning knife (tools and things) make up the highly inter-correlated items with the possible addition of the coffee can from Group V. Here we find a set of correlations between

items in all three of the cognitive categories. Why? Once again, in terms of the real behaviour or organised dynamics of gear use, these correlations all make a great deal of sense. The cup and the coffee can are items carried when a stop is anticipated at a place not normally used. Extra line is carried when some mishap is anticipated or feared. Mishaps normally occur at locations not systematically used for the preparation of food— on the trail. The skinning knife is the most versatile item used in repairing dog harness, obtaining firewood from low or minimal willow growth, carving from the snow probe another harness spreader, etc. Thus our correlations group together the gear actually used in case of a mishap. It is, of course, used in conjunction with the sugar, coffee and pilot bread, but those may be used in other situations in the absence of these items. These are the items actually used in the specific and immediate context of a breakdown.

Group V includes socks, mukluk, extra skin, big knife and extra parka, all items listed as clothes, together with field glasses, listed as tools and things, and probably corn meal displayed in Group V. Once again we have a mixed assemblage with regard to the cognitive categories of the Nunamiut. Why? If the previous grouping of items can be summarised as the 'breakdown-stop' assemblage, this represents the 'overnight-stop' assemblage which may or may not be correlated with a breakdown or trail mishap, but may be correlated with a personal mishap such as falling through ice or getting wet in an overflow near a spring, etc. The presence of field glasses and possibly the addition of corn meal is understandable in terms of this type of concrete situation. Corn meal is a more substantial food, and field glasses would aid in locating or spotting a rescue party or emergency game, as well as generally used on long trips.

In summary, from the perspective of the archaeologist, the correlations would betray something of the actual behavioural context of gear use, while the cognitive categories are a convenient planning convention. The contingencies considered in planning, how I will feed, what may happen, and what I have to do, are not in reality independent. What may happen may clearly condition how I may feel, etc. *Thus the archaeo-*

logist's analysis would not yield direct information relative to the Nunamiut cognitive categories, but would rather faithfully reflect the concrete dynamics of the hunters' behaviour in the field.

Optional gear

The third category recognised by the informants was optional gear which they systematically divided into two sub-categories: 'young men's gear' and 'old men's gear'. The items in the two sub-categories are listed below (Table 7) together with the mean ages of the hunters carrying each item.

Table 7 Two categories of optional gear divided according to age

Young men's gear	Age of hunters	Old men's gear	Age of hunters
.22 pistol	33.4	Dry meat	34.9
.22 rifle	33.7	Snow shoes	35.6
Sardines	33.8	Needle and skin	36.4
Peanut butter	27.0	Steel traps	35.3
		Rib slab	35.5
	31.9 years		35.5 years

The reader will immediately note that the items categorised as young men's gear represent largely 'store bought' items, while old men's gear includes more traditional items with the exception of steel traps. As is shown, there is a difference between the mean ages of the hunters carrying the two types of gear, although there is not as much as one might anticipate from informants' conversation. It is interesting to note that the range of ages represented by hunters carrying the two categories of gear are identical, the oldest being 43 and the youngest being 26. It is quite clear that there is no neat correlation between the age of the hunter and the type of optional gear he carried. The distinction is not really one of age but one of traditional versus modern orientation of the hunters, and these persuasions are not necessarily a reliable predictor of age.

What conclusions can be drawn regarding the proposition that archaeologically observed patterning reflects the ideas and values or the cognitive characteristics of a culture? The first conclusion which I drew from my interviewing was that Nunamiut have many ways of cognitively structuring their gear, depending upon the behavioural context specified. This observation leads to the suspected proposition that cognitive categorisations vary in terms of the behavioural context specified. We all know this to be true. If asked about my cousins in the context of maternal versus paternal relationship, I will differentiate one way; if asked in terms of how often I interact with them I will differentiate another way. If asked in the context of who I like, I would differentiate still another way, and *ad infinitum*.

Cognition is not a static-formal system, but a dynamic system whose form is partially dependent upon the behavioural or interactive context of discrimination. Such contexts are complicated as in the case of the Nunamiut deciding which gear he will carry. It is convenient for him to think dimensionally in terms of what he will do, how he will feel, and what may happen. In reality, these are not necessarily independent, hence the strong intercorrelation between items

considered dimensionally distinct at the cognitive level of trip planning. Based on these data as well as on a general knowledge of behaviour, I must insist that assemblage patterning observed in the archaeological record derives from the dynamics of organised behaviour. In the case of the Nunamiuts' 'assemblages' on trips of different distances, there is no necessary or direct relationship to the cognitive or formal classificatory devices of the people.

The archaeological record of the trips

We turn now to a very interesting body of data, the tabulation and relative frequencies of the items which were not returned to the village by the hunters. Table 7 presents the data on non-food items not returned, arranged according to the same format as Table 1, increasing trip distances from right to left. Initially, it is necessary to place the items listed in Table 7 in some kind of context. There were 647 trip items carried; regardless of quantity, each unit is counted as a single trip item. Of these, 99 are items which are totally consumed in the course of their use. Most such items are foods: pilot bread, sugar, etc., all items which yield no by-product. Ninety-one of the 99 items were consumed on the trips and not returned to the village. Five hundred and forty-eight of the trip items carried were visible in that there were tangible by-products from their use, or no destruction occurred during their use. Of these items, 53 or only 9.67% of the total visible items were not returned to the village, the items listed in Table 7. Of these 53 trip items, 36 are items which are disposable by-products in the context of use, including the peanut butter jar, sardine can, shell cases, ribs from dry meat slabs, scapula from dry meat slabs and rifle shell cases. This is not to say that all of these items could not be reused or recycled, but that in the contemporary setting they are not, and are immediately disposable by-products of use or consumption. Of the remaining 18 items not returned to the village, 14 or 26.3% of the total were cached in the field for future use. Of the remaining four items, three were unintentionally lost on the trail, and *only one was discarded, broken, at the location where it was used.* This is not, however, the only item broken during the course of the 47 trips. Twelve additional items were broken, but were returned to the village for repair. We may summarise that 91.9% of the food carried was consumed, leaving no tangible by-products. Of the 548 items exclusive of food not leaving tangible by-products, only 53 items remained in the field. Of these, 36 were tangible by-products of consumption or use, and only 18 were actual items of gear. Of those 18 items, 14 were cached in the field for future use, leaving only four items lost (three) or discarded (one) in the context of the activities. During this time, however, 12 additional items were broken but returned to the village for repair or recycling into other items.

For the archaeologist who approaches the archaeological record with the expectation that there is necessarily some direct relationship between the importance of the item in the cultural system and importance in the assemblage, and anticipates a neat structure of spatial associations reflecting the behavioural context of use for the items recovered, this is a very grim picture. Let us examine the situation further. From one perspective, the formation processes are one aspect of the organised dynamics in terms of which material items are integrated into a cultural system. All such dynamics must include some organised strategy of procurement, and most archaeologists have given time and thought to this aspect of technological organisation. Equally important is the variability in the organised properties of discharge or entropy. What are the organised ways in which items are discharged or lost to the system? In order to consider systems from the perspective of their efficiency, there must be some balance between these two sides of the dynamics coin. Increases in efficiency may be achieved at either end or in terms of both. For instance, if it takes twenty minutes to manufacture a projectile point, and from that investment of labour I can use the projectile point reliably for four months, this is more efficient than if from the same labour investment I only find the product good for two months' use. I may find that by the additional investment of maintenance and curatorial labour I can increase the life expectancy of an item, and I may, in turn, increase the efficiency of the technology. Thus, maintenance and curatorial investments of labour may achieve increases in the total efficiency of the technological system and, in turn, increase the life expectancies or utilisation time of items. Similarly, by various means of recycling, or using the materials in worn out items for the fabrication of other items, I may substantially cut down on procurement labour investments. *The Nunamiut are a classic case of a system in which the technology is highly organised curatorially, and is frequently characterised by recycling.* For the archaeologist, this means that we cannot expect to find butchering tools at butchering locations, or wood cutting tools at wood collecting locations. Such items are curated, transported, and, if broken in the context of use, frequently transported to residential locations where they may be recycled or repaired for future use.

I recently made a survey of eleven of the more popular books treating the subject of archaeological methods and was unable to find any reference to the organisation of a technology with regard to maintenance and curation of items. Most authors mentioned procuring and manufacturing sequences, but no one mentioned the possible differences between cultural systems in their degrees of maintenance investment or curation of the technology.

Let us consider for a moment the relationships between the relative importance of items in the ongoing technology of the Nunamiut as measured by the frequency with which they were carried on trips, versus the frequency of items remaining as potential archaeological remains at the locations where activities were conducted. The cumulative graphs in Fig. 5 display these relationships. *It is quite clear that there is an inverse relationship between the importance of the item as measured by the frequency with which it is carried, and its occurrence as an item remaining in the field.* Stated another way, 69.0% of the assemblage remaining in the field is composed of trip items which represent only 5.82% of the trip items carried into the field. In contrast, 58.2% of the trip items carried into the field are represented by only 5.76% of trip items remaining in the field. This points out very clearly the character of a curated assemblage. *Important items are maintained and curated, thus their entry into the archaeological record, in terms of frequency, is inversely proportional to the level of maintenance and hence their technological importance, other things being equal.*

This observation coupled with the observation that 67.9% of the items remaining in the field were items that were the immediate by-products of consumption, such as bones from dry meat or shell cases from firing guns, provides us with a valuable clue. It tells us that working out analytical means

for treating archaeological remains of the immediate by-products of either work or consumption is the most important task. This class of archaeological remains will yield information regarding the tasks performed at varying locations.

Such a suggestion is certainly at variance with general archaeological practice where features when treated comparatively are generally considered secondary to tool assemblages. Similarly, when faunal remains are given analytical attention it is generally in the context of environmental reconstruction, or as a means to evaluating the character of diet rather than the activities of food procurement. Recently, some attention has been given to patterns of bone breakage, but not with an eye to understanding the activities performed, except as the authors believe them to be related to tool production, and hence as a means to tool recognition. (See Sadek-Kooros, 1972). We need to give more analytical attention to the relationships between features, and mundane remains such as fire-cracked rock, bone fragments, chipping debris, and garbage, not as a means to categorical types of generalisation about diet, etc., but as a means to understanding the behavioural context in terms of which the site was produced.

The items remaining in the field which were not the immediate by-products of consumption or work totalled 18 items. Seventeen of these (94.4%) remained as unbroken items either cached for future use, or unintentionally lost during the course of the trip. Only 5.6% remained in the field as broken or discarded items. Nevertheless, 12 additional items were broken but were returned to the village for repair or recycling.

These observations suggest that we might anticipate certain regular contrasts between archaeological assemblages deriving from highly organised, curated technologies, versus those that are poorly organised and tend toward the expedient manufacture, use, and abandonment of instrumental items in the immediate context of use.

We may now speculate on some of the possible archaeological consequences of cultural systems differing in their degrees of technological organisation on a scale from completely expedient manufacture, use and abandonment of tools, versus a curated and maintained technology:

Several major points of contrast stand behind the development of arguments regarding expected forms of patterning in the archaeological record. Most important is the recognition that in non-curated technologies, replacement rates are directly proportional to the frequency of participation in activities in which tools were used. In curated assemblages, replacement rates are directly proportional to the life span or utility of the tool under maintenance care, and may bear no direct relationship to the frequency of activity performance involving tool use.

The second major point of contrast is related to the locational or associational relationships anticipated under the two types of organisation. In non-curated assemblages, the debris from manufacture, and the by-products of the activities in which tools were used should be spatially associated. However, in curated assemblages, where tools are transported and returned to a residential location for repair (as in the case of the Nunamiut), we can expect there to be no necessary regular relationship between the by-products of activities in which tools were used and the numbers of tools themselves. Similarly, we can expect that tool manufacturing debris will only regularly be associated with broken or discarded parts of tools, and not vary with the numbers of tools manufactured 'from scratch' which would have been removed from the location.

We are now in a position to deduce certain expected archaeological consequences of differences in the organisation of a technology.

I. *Relationships between debris and instrumental items*

A. Under conditions of expedient manufacture and use of tools, other things being equal, we can expect:
  (1) A regular inverse set of relationships between the number of broken and worn out tools and the number of unbroken unworn tools present.
  (2) A regular proportional set of direct relationships between the number of tools present, regardless of condition, and the quantity of debris remaining from tool manufacture.
  (3) A regular proportional set of direct relationships between the quantity of debris remaining from food consumption and both the quantity of tools and the quantity of tool-making debris.

B. *Discussion:* The qualification that other things are equal is very important to these propositions. For instance, in intersite comparisons we might anticipate that quantities of food by-products remaining on a site would vary with the character of the diet represented. An obvious example is variability in the relative dependence upon plants versus animal foods. Such factors would tend to reduce the observed regularities between numbers of tools and the amount of food debris observable archaeologically under normal conditions of preservation. Another consideration is the character of the organisation of the food procurement strategy itself. For instance, if consumers are moved to resources, then we can anticipate the predicted relationship to hold very well; however, if foods are transported to consumers, then we can expect an attrition along the logistics route which may not be proportional to the numbers of persons present, or the intensity of tool using activities performed.

The same caution holds for the predicted relationship between manufacturing debris and tools, since variability in the character and efficiency of manufacturing techniques would tend to introduce variability in the expected relationships between quantities of debris and numbers of tools.

Some clarification may be necessary to the first proposition offered. Under conditions of expedient manufacture and use of tools, the numbers of worn or broken tools should relate to the duration and intensity of the activity in which tools were used. Thus, the number of tools in unbroken-unworn condition should be inversely proportional to the number of tools in 'mint' condition.

C. Under conditions of curated, maintained and portable technological organisation, other things being equal, we can expect:
  (1) Proportions of broken to unbroken tools to vary independently of one another.
  (2) A regular proportion set of direct relationships between the numbers of broken and worn out tools and tool manufacturing debris.
  (3) A low but regular proportional set of inverse

relationships between the numbers of unbroken or unworn tools and tool manufacturing debris.
  (4) High variability approaching randomness between the total numbers of tools and the quantity of tool manufacturing debris among random site samples. Inverse relationships will dominate comparisons between special purpose locations such as hunting camps, quarries, kill sites, etc., and a tendency toward direct relationships will pervade comparisons between base camps or residential locations, where repairs are more apt to be made.
  (5) High variability in the relationship between the quantity of debris from food sources and the quantity of debris from tool production or repair among random site samples. Inverse relationships will pervade comparisons between special purpose locations, while low but direct relationships may be anticipated in comparisons between base camp or residential locations.

D. *Discussion:* As previously mentioned, the qualification 'other things being equal' is very important. For instance, I have not considered differences in food procurement strategy. It should be clear that a logistics strategy in which foods are moved to consumers may be expected to be correlated with increases in curation and maintenance of tools, since both are organisational responses to conditions in which increasing efficiency would pay off. Given this expectation, we can anticipate differences in archaeological patterning between tools, tool making debris, and the by-products of food sources. All should vary as a function of the degree that a logistics strategy is correlated with a curatorial technological strategy. Similarly, we may anticipate that composite tools might be expected to occur more commonly in curated assemblages. The degree that this is true may condition the expected relationships between tools used directly in subsistence tasks and tools used in tool making tasks. Both may well vary in their levels of curation and maintenance, introducing an added complication with regard to debris relationships.

II. *Relationships between different types of tools*

A. Under conditions of expedient manufacture and use of tools, other things being equal, we can expect:
  (1) Relative frequencies of tool types observed among a sample of site locations will vary directly with the quantities of immediate by-products deriving from the activities in which tools were used.
  (2) Intersite variability in relative tool frequencies to be high and to vary directly with the seasonal and situational differentiation in the locus of task performance.

B. *Discussion:* These propositions should be clear in that they are the consequences of a technology in which tool use and tool disposal are coincident.

C. Under conditions of curated and maintained technologies, other things being equal, we can expect:
  (1) Relative frequencies of tool types, observed among a sample of site locations, will vary independently of the quantities of immediate by-products deriving from different activities in which tools were used.
  (2) Intersite variability in relative tool frequencies to be relatively low and to vary independently of the

seasonal and situational differentiation in the locus of task performance.

D. *Discussion:* The contrasts indicated in the above propositions derive from the fact that in non-curated assemblages relative frequencies derive directly from the relative size of the task force and the intensity of the activity involving tool use. On the other hand, in curated assemblages relative frequencies derive directly from the relative life expectancies of a tool under continuous maintenance. In the latter situation we cannot regularly anticipate an association between the tool and the task in which it is used. Associations among tools derive from relative life expectancies in the context of localised maintenance activities.

III. *Implications for temporal patterning*

A. Under conditions of expedient manufacture and use of tools, other things being equal, we can expect:
(1) Changing frequencies to vary directly with the importance of the activity in which the tool was used.

B. Under conditions of a curated and maintained technology, other things being equal, we can expect:
(1) Decreasing relative frequencies through time to *vary inversely* with the importance of the item in the technology. In short, as curation increases, the relative frequency of technologically important items will decrease.

C. *Discussion:* These propositions are important. For instance, if we observe a decreasing relative frequency for a particular class of item, it may well reflect:
(1) Increasing curation and maintenance of the item class.
(2) Its prominence in the technology. Remember, in curated assemblages, relative frequencies refer directly to replacement rates and not to incidences of use as in non-curated assemblages. Important items may well be expected to have lower replacement rates than less important items because of the greater utility derived from higher levels of maintenance. This view of the potential significance of frequency trends is directly at variance with the prevailing traditionalists' ideas of the significance attributed to temporal trends in relative frequency. To the traditionalist, decreasing trends mean decreasing popularity, while increasing trends refer to increasing popularity.

In this contrast we see clearly the differences between an approach which has a series of conventions for translating observations into interpretations, rather than attempting to investigate the processes responsible for the observed relationships.

Summary conclusions

Given the data from the Nunamiut hunters, several conclusions seem warranted: (1) Regardless of the degree of curation and maintenance of the tool assemblage, we can anticipate variability in the immediate by-products of work or consumption to relate to seasonal or situational variation in the activities performed—witness the seasonal variability in the anatomical parts carried by the hunters for food. (This latter point will be demonstrated more forcefully at a later date through the analysis of faunal remains and intersite structure of contemporary Nunamiut sites.) (2) The cognitive categories of the Nunamiut hunters at the assemblage level generally have reference to contingency planning which is treated as if the real world was dimensionally independent. In fact, such dimensional independence is not evident, thus the actual patterns of co-variation among gear items derive from the actions performed in the context of various contingencies, and bear little relationship to the cognitive categories used by the hunters for organising their gear. These data demonstrate nicely that archaeological remains refer directly to the organisation of behaviour itself, and not to the cognitive conventions in terms of which behaviour may be expressed or anticipated. (3) The distribution, association between, and relative frequencies of tools are greatly affected by the character of the technological organisation. No simple equation between tool and task, or frequency and popularity is possible. Before one can make meaningful statements as to the significance of patterns of observed variability in the archaeological record, he must consider the causal determinants of the patterning. Processes vary as organisations vary, forms of patterning vary as processes vary. Organisational variability is one of the major characteristics of cultural variation in general. Investigation of the organisational properties of systems and their processual consequences, archaeologically, is the first step toward an accurate attribution of meaning to observed patterning. This must be accomplished through the trial specification and testing of law-like proposition. Implied here is the further investigation of the conditioning relationships implied by the statement 'other things being equal'. I have offered a number of such trial law-like statements. The testing of their validity may take us a long way toward a more accurate understanding of observed forms of patterning in the archaeological record.

I hope this paper serves to prompt greater attention to the formation processes of the archaeological record, for only against such an understanding can we begin to reliably attribute meaning to observed forms of archaeological patterning.

Acknowledgement This research was partially financed by a grant from The Wenner-Gren Foundation for Anthropological Research, and by a grant from the National Science Foundation. I am most grateful to both granting agencies.

References

Binford, L. R., 1972. Model Building-Paradigms, and the current state of Paleolithic Research. *In* R. Binford (ed.), *An archaeological perspective*, pp. 244–94. New York: Seminar Press.
—— and S. R. Binford, 1966. A preliminary analysis of functional variability in the Mousterian of Levallois facies. *In* J. Desmond Clark and F. Clark Howell (eds), *Recent studies in Paleoanthropology*, American Anthropologist, (special publication) 68, No. 2, Part 2, pp. 238–95.

Dunnell, C., 1971. *Systematics in prehistory.* New York: The Free Press.
Hall, S., 1971. Kangiguksuk: A cultural reconstruction of a sixteenth century eskimo site in Northern Alaska. *Arctic Anthropology*, viii (1) : 1–101.
Rouse, I., 1972. *Introduction to prehistory: A systematic approach.* New York: McGraw-Hill.
Sadek-Kooros, H., 1972. Primitive bone fracturing: A method of research. *American Antiquity*, 37(3) : 369–82.

Time and space limits of the Mousterian

FRANCOIS BORDES

Abstract

The Mousterian is a cross-section made by the human mind for reasons of convenience through the continuous evolution of Palaeolithic material cultures. This cross-section slants through time, so it is impossible to define the temporal and spatial limits of the Mousterian. What is possible is to define a Mousterian stage of evolution.

The term 'Mousterian' (*Moustiérien* first in 1872, *Moustérien* later) was created by G. de Mortillet for the material remains of a culture found in the upper rock shelter at le Moustier (Dordogne district, France). It was extended later to any assemblage showing the same general features: flakes, side-scrapers, points, sometimes handaxes, even though, when handaxes occurred, they were often considered as Acheulian.

With the progress of Palaeolithic research, similar assemblages were found outside France, in Europe, the Near East, North Africa, and the similarity was considered good enough for the same word to apply. The difficulties came when one had to deal with north-east Asia or Africa south of the Sahara Desert. In these parts there are assemblages that have sometimes been called 'Mousteroid', such as many of the aspects of African middle Stone Age, or sites like Shoei Tong Keou in China or Teshik Tash in Uzbekistan.

Also, long before the Mousterian people lived during the last glaciation, pre-Neanderthal men made assemblages which are sometimes very similar to the Würmian Mousterian. Is it valid to call these industries Mousterian? Then, some sub-modern people too have been said to have a 'Mousteroid' tool-kit, for instance the Tasmanians. And it is true that at least a good number of Tasmanian implements could easily be lost among a Mousterian collection.

So, one is a little at a loss how to define the Mousterian, even in Europe. We can try a chronological approach and say that the Mousterian represents the cultures that flourished during the first half of the last glaciation. But then we would have to include the Micoquian, and to exclude such industries as the inter-glacial one from Ehringsdorf (East Germany), the Rissian one from Rigabe (Provence, France) or the one from layer 4 at la Micoque, all of which, found outside a stratigraphy, would unhesitatingly have been called Mousterian. Can we take cultures posterior to the Acheulian, and anterior to the upper Palaeolithic? Some Mousterian assemblages are contemporary with the Acheulian, and others with the beginning of the upper Palaeolithic.

A typological approach is a little better, but the old definition: Mousterian = flakes + side-scrapers + points + (sometimes) handaxes may also apply to assemblages south of the Sahara. One can try an anthropological approach and say that the Mousterian is the material culture of Neanderthal man and his equivalents, but (alas) the Jebel Qafzeh skeletons

in Israel belong to *Homo sapiens sapiens*, even if nobody will contest the Mousterian character of the tools found with them! (Vandermeersch, 1969).

Recent research shows that the Mousterian presents a wide range of variation even in Western Europe where we could try, as a beginning, to define it. There seems to be more than one kind of Mousterian. Whatever the explanation for this, be it cultural as we think it is for the most part (Bordes and Sonneville-Bordes, 1970) or a matter of different activities, as Lew Binford tried to demonstrate (Binford and Binford, 1969), we classify, as Mousterian, assemblages as widely different as layer 13 at Combe-Grenal, in Dordogne (Denticulate Mousterian) and layer 24 of the same site (Quina Mousterian). However, in the former site side-scrapers, rather degenerate, amount to 4.2% and the same types of tools, often magnificently made, count for 80.7% in the latter. To complicate things a little more, some Mousterians used the Levallois technique intensively, whilst others frowned on it. Percentages of Levallois debitage (the Levallois Index) can vary between 0.6 (layer 20 at Combe-Grenal) and 28.9 (layer 7 at the same site).[1] And the percentage in the tool-kit of such Levallois flakes left unretouched (Typological Levallois Index) may vary from 1.04 in layer 20 at Combe-Grenal to 73.6 in layer J3 at Pech de l'Azé IV (Dordogne).

Is the Mousterian purely a flake culture? Some Mousterian assemblages have up to 30% or even 40% of blades, sometimes of a strikingly good quality, which is probably as much as some upper Palaeolithic cultures can boast. But even if we accept the Mousterian as a 'flake culture', not all flake cultures are Mousterian. Clactonian, for instance, has a lot of flake tools. It has also choppers and chopping-tools, but so does the Mousterian when these types have been recognised and picked up by the excavators. And it would probably be stretching it too far to call all the flake cultures of the middle Stone Age of Africa Mousterian.

In our study of European, North African and Middle Eastern assemblages, we have found several recurrent types of Mousterian, more or less well represented in these different regions. Each of these types may or may not use the Levallois technique.[2] These are the Mousterian of Acheulian tradition

---

1. When the Levallois index is greater than 30 or 35, this means a selection has been made among the flakes and tools made on flakes, either by the excavator or by the Palaeolithic men themselves. For instance, the site of Oissel, near Rouen, has a Levallois index of 79.5. Only one core has been found with the assemblage. The flaking was done elsewhere, not necessarily far away.

2. In truth, there are practically no assemblages after the late lower Acheulian in which one cannot find at least one Levallois flake. But when the Levallois Index is lower than 4 or 5, we consider that these Levallois flakes may well be accidental. As a rule, we consider that when between 5 and 16, the Levallois Index indicates a 'non-Levallois culture'.

(MAT), the Quina-Ferrassie type (Q–F), the Denticulate Mousterian (D) and the Typical Mousterian (T). Typical Mousterian and Quina-Ferrassie types can extend from the Riss glaciation to upper Palaeolithic times.

Mousterian of Acheulian Tradition (MAT) is characterised by (a) the presence of handaxes different from Acheulian ones (even if some Acheulian types can remain in it), numerous in subtype A (5% to 40%), much less so in subtype B, (down to 2%); (b) by backed knives (mainly in subtype B); (c) by a medium to low percentage of side-scrapers; (d) by a considerable number of upper Palaeolithic types of tools (end scrapers, burins, borers, truncated flakes and blades); and (e) by a considerable number also of denticulated flakes. Probably it is no more than the continuation, during Würmian times, of late Acheulian. Its relationship with the partly contemporary Micoquian, probably another continuation of the Acheulian, is not quite clear. They may represent the end of two different branches of the Acheulian. MAT may use the Levallois technique lavishly, or almost ignore it, as do the other types of Mousterian.

Quina Mousterian is characterised by a great number of side-scrapers (50% to 80%), usually very well made. Some of the subtypes of side-scrapers are rare or non-existent in the other Mousterian cultures: for instance, the 'Quina' type scraper (thick, often with a very convex edge, with scalariform retouch) and its variant, the bifacial Quina scraper which, at one extreme, is sometimes difficult to tell apart from a true handaxe. Transverse scrapers are numerous, and flakes are mostly thick and short, with a wide and more or less oblique striking platform ('Clactonian-like'). Quina-like scrapers do exist in the Acheulian, when it is of non-Levallois facies (for instance at Et Tabun, in Israel) and in low percentage in some other Mousterian assemblages. Rare bifacial Quina scrapers exist also in the MAT, but their appearance may be a case of convergence, and they may really represent some kind of bifacial, but unilateral handaxe. The Quina Mousterian has no backed knives as a rule, but may have some rather special handaxes.

The Ferrassie Mousterian is the Levallois aspect of the Quina type, with fewer Quina scrapers (Levallois flakes are usually thin) and fewer transversal scrapers (Levallois flakes are usually elongated).

Denticulate Mousterian is characterised by (a) a paucity of scrapers, habitually of a mediocre quality (25%); (b) the absence of points, backed knives and handaxes (there may be some nucleiform ones); and (c) the great development of notches and denticulated flakes (up to 50% or more), which together may comprise 80% of the total tool-kit. The debitage may or not be Levallois.

Typical Mousterian is the most variable, and may represent,

in the present state of our knowledge, a kind of 'rag bag' in which are put all the assemblages which are neither MAT, nor Q–F or D. The percentage of side-scrapers varies from 25% to 55%, Quina scrapers are rare or absent, there are usually neither handaxes nor true backed knives, the proportion of notches and denticulates is moderate, and there is often, but not always, a rather high percentage of Mousterian points. There are clear differences between Typical Mousterian in Würm I and Würm II, differences that may correspond to an evolution or to something else. It may be that part of the Typical Mousterian corresponds to special activities of the MAT (subtype A) or of the Ferrassie Mousterian, with less of Quina scrapers, but it is by no means proved.

As we have said, in all these kinds of Mousterian the percentage of unretouched Levallois flakes may vary widely. Table 1 summarises the range of variation of the principal features of the Mousterian in the sites of Combe-Grenal and Pech de l'Azé.

All this shows very clearly that *the* Mousterian does not exist, even in Western Europe. What exists is a very wide range of variation in a series of assemblages that are called Mousterian for convenience, but may represent different cultures and/or (up to a point) different activities. This is not the place to argue why we do not accept Binford's point of view that *all* the variation observed can be explained by considering it as the mere result of different activities of the same basic culture (see Bordes and Sonneville-Bordes, 1970; Binford and Binford, 1966).

Anyway, it is now clear that the search for the time and space limits of the 'Mousterian' as a whole is a hopeless quest. The variation becomes even greater if we take into account assemblages from outside Western Europe. Tata in Hungary is a case in point. Here we have an assemblage that, at first glance, seems to relate closely to the Quina Mousterian, but there are many differences; among them a great development of bifacial scrapers (but only 1/6 of them are Quina-like). On the other hand, Erd, also in Hungary, looks very much like true Quina. The *Blattspitzen* Mousterian of Central Europe seems to have some features of the MAT, but also many special ones, notably the presence of numerous bifacial foliate tools. The Russian Mousterian may approximate the Typical, as in Moldova, but may be also very different from any Western kind (Volgograd, Staroselie, etc.). In the Near East, Jabrud in Syria, has given equivalents of the Quina (Jabrudian), Typical, MAT and Denticulate, but with special traits and that holds also for other sites of the same regions: for instance elongated Levallois points, rare in Western Europe, play a great role here.

So, if one tries to give a definition of a 'Mousterian culture',

Table 1   Range of variation of the principal features of the Mousterian at Combe-Grenal and Pech de l'Azé

Levallois Index	28.9	(Combe-Grenal, layer 7)	0.6	(Combe-Grenal, layer 20)
Scraper Index	80.7	(Combe-Grenal, layer 24)	4.2	(Combe-Grenal, layer 13)
Quina Index*	27.1	(Combe-Grenal, layer 25)	0	(many layers)
Handaxe Index	15.3	(Pech de l'Azé I, lower layer)	0	(many layers)
Backed knives	11.5	(Pech de l'Azé I, upper layer)	0	(many layers)
Upper Palaeolithic types	17.8	(Pech de l'Azé I, upper layer)	2.9	(Combe-Grenal, layer 35)
Denticulates	46.7	(Combe-Grenal, layer 14)	1.9	(Combe-Grenal, layer 24)
Typological Levallois Index	73.6	(Pech de l'Azé IV, layer J3)	1.04	(Combe-Grenal, layer 20)

* The Quina index is the percentage of Quina-type scrapers inside the category of scrapers.

this definition has to be so broad as to be meaningless. What can be attempted is to define a Mousterian stage of evolution.

For that, we have to distinguish between flake tools and handaxes. The flake tool component of the upper Acheulian (after Riss II) is so close to the MAT (type A) in typology and proportions as to be practically identical. The flake tools of layers 56 to 60 in Combe-Grenal, found in another stratigraphical context, would be classified as MAT. However, the handaxes *are* Acheulian. The same is true of the Acheulian at Bouheben (Riss III also, in the Landes district). So, we can say that the Mousterian level of evolution for flake tools has already been attained in Riss III times. For cultures other than the Acheulian, it may even be earlier. Layer 4 at la Micoque (Dordogne), probably Riss II, and even layer 3, probably Riss I, are good examples. In Rigabe (Provence) the assemblage (without handaxes) is already 'Mousterian', while belonging to Riss III. Contrariwise, there may be industries which are later than Würm II, in Africa for instance, that were still at the Mousterian level. How can we define this level?

The main component will be flakes, either Levallois or not, blades being a minor part, albeit sometimes not negligible as we have seen. These flakes will be retouched in part to make side-scrapers, notches and denticulates, these three types, in variable proportions, being the major part of the assemblage (Table 2). Points, either Mousterian or Levallois, may be an important, but secondary component: some 'Mousterians' have no points. Upper Palaeolithic types of tools also play a secondary role. Miscellaneous tools make up the remaining part.

To this flake tool-kit, characterising a 'generalised' Mousterian level of evolution are added the typical tools that give more specificity to the assemblages: handaxes for the Acheulian, Micoquian and MAT, backed knives for the same cultures (mainly for MAT, type B), tanged tools for the Aterian, elongated Levallois points for the Near Eastern Mousterian, foliate bifacial tools for the *Blattspitzen* Mousterian of Central Europe, for the Stillbay of Africa, and also for the Russian Mousterian etc. Sometimes it is only the proliferation of one type of tool which highlights the individuality of the assemblage: side-scrapers (ordinary and Quina) for the Quina-Ferrassie, denticulates and notches for the Denticulate Mousterian, upper Palaeolithic types of tools both for the MAT (type B) (together with backed knives), and for the 'Mousterian' of Choei Tong Keou in China.

Subtypes of Mousterian exist too: the Jabrudian, basically a Quina type, is characterised by a higher than usual percentage of canted convergent scrapers (*racloirs déjetés*) (Bordes, 1968 : 99).

So, in Europe, North Africa and the Near East, one should speak of a Mousterian Complex (as we have done long ago) (Bordes and Bourgon, 1951) for the culture of the first half of the last glaciation or its temporal equivalents, but NOT of a Mousterian culture. The cultures without handaxes

Table 2   Total percentage* of side-scrapers, notches and denticulates in different layers at Combe-Grenal and Pech de l'Azé I and IV

Denticulate Mousterian Combe-Grenal		Typical Mousterian Combe-Grenal		Quina Mousterian Combe-Grenal	
Layer 5	68.4%	Layer 6	62.8%	Layer 17	74.1%
8	63.7	7	71.7	18	81.1
11	67.8	28	75.0	19	81.5
12	66.4	29	71.6	22	84.5
13	70.9	30	63.4	23	83.1
14	77.1	31	77.3	24	85.2
15	64.2	40	59.3	25	85.8
38	60.8	42	65.8	26	87.3
		50 A	68.4		
		50	77.5		
		52	72.4		
		54	70.7		

Ferrassie Mousterian Combe-Grenal		Mousterian of Acheulian tradition			
		Pech de l'Azé I		Pech de l'Azé IV	
Layer 27	80.2	Layer 7	44.6	Layer F1	33.7
32	75.9	6	41.4	F2	36.8
33	80.5	5	50.0	F3	52.6
35	85.1	4	63.9	F4	66.2

Acheulian Combe-Grenal	
Layer 56	66.6
57	73.6
58	70.1
59	74.1
60	75.6

* All percentages are given as counts where the Levallois flakes are not included. There is some kind of gradual decrease in the series Acheulian-Mousterian of Acheulian tradition type A (Layer 5 at Pech I, F4 at Pech IV), type AB (Layer 5 at Pech I, F3 at Pech IV) and type B (Layers 6 and 7 at Pech I, F1 and F2 at Pech IV). This may be significant and announce the passage to lower Perigordian, the first upper Palaeolithic culture in this area.

between Riss I and Würm could be considered as a pre-Mousterian Complex, probably polygenetic. During the same time there also existed an Acheulian at a Mousterian level of evolution as far as the flake tools are concerned. Outside this zone, it would be better to speak only of Mousteroid cultures or complexes, or of cultures with Mousteroid features. Some may be pretty close to one or the other type of the Mousterian Complex, others have only the basic traits in common with them, and some only part of these basic traits. As ever, reality is more complicated than was thought at the beginning, and classifications are a kind of corset which she is somewhat reluctant to wear.

References

Binford, L. F. and S. R. Binford, 1966. A preliminary analysis of functional variability in the Mousterian of Levallois facies. *American Anthropologist*, 68(2) : 238–95.

Bordes, F., 1968. *The old Stone Age.* London: Weidenfeld and Nicholson.

—— and M. Bourgon, 1951. Le complexe moustérien. *L'Anthropologie*, 55 : 1–23.

—— and D. de Sonneville-Bordes, 1970. The significance of variability in Palaeolithic assemblages. *World Archaeology*, 2(1) : 61–73.

Vandermeersch, B., 1969. Les nouveaux squelettes moustériens découverts à Qafzeh (Israel) et leur signification. *Comptes rendus de l'Académie des Sciences de Paris*, 268 : 2562–65.

Waisted blades and axes

A functional interpretation of some early stone tools from Papua New Guinea

SUSAN BULMER

In this paper I discuss assemblages of waisted blades and axe-like tools from three early sites in Papua New Guinea in an attempt to interpret their technological and economic significance. The time period covered by these assemblages, based on radiocarbon dates from two of the sites, is from about 25 000 years ago until about 6000 years ago. During the earlier part of this period the peoples of Papua New Guinea must have engaged in hunting and collecting for their livelihood, but some time during the later part of this period a transformation from an economy based totally on hunting and collecting to one based partly on agriculture took place. This transformation has not yet been documented archaeologically; although a number of excavated sites were occupied during this period, we have not yet focused on the evidence for the transformation. In any case, by about 5000 years ago the mountain forest of Papua New Guinea had been extensively cleared of trees (Powell, 1970), pig-husbandry had begun, quarrying and trading in fine-quality polished stone axe/adzes had commenced, and a transformation in stone technology was taking place, i.e. the replacement of the late Pleistocene assemblage (S. Bulmer, 1973, 1974).

The general interest in the stone tools of the early period, then, is to assist in the understanding of the way of life of the early peoples, and to search for evidence of the evolution of the economic base. Although it cannot, of course, be assumed that there will necessarily be a close correlation between stone technology and the general character of economy, stone tools provide most of the evidence available at present. There will also eventually be evidence from faunal collections from one of the early sites, Yuku, which are currently being studied at the University of Papua New Guinea by Geraldine Fenner and J. I. Menzies. These data will provide direct evidence of the hunting and animal husbandry aspect of the economy of one early montane settlement.

The study of the waisted blade perhaps needs no further justification than that it is the most numerous large artifact form in the three assemblages pertaining to the early period. Readily identified on the basis of a single feature, i.e. the presence of a 'waist' or reduction of the sides of the butt, waisted blades have attracted considerable general comment. The 'waist' has been interpreted as a device to assist in hafting the tools as an axe or adze (Bulmer and Bulmer, 1964 : 66; Golson, 1972 : 544–48; Allen, 1972 : 183). This interpretation has led to comparisons with axe-like tools with butt modification outside Papua New Guinea, particularly the early ground axes from Northern Australia (C. White, 1967, 1971; Golson, 1972). It has been suggested that the flaked waisted blade evolved into a polished waisted axe during the final period of its use at one site in the Western Highlands Province (S. Bulmer, 1966 : 129–31), in the face of new trade in fine-

quality axe/adzes from the quarries of the Wahgi and Jimi valleys (Chappell, 1966). Golson (1968 : 6–7) has suggested that the polished axes of New Britain and Bougainville, which include a variety of butt modification, are similarly technological descendants of the earlier flaked form.

However, these tools have previously not received much detailed attention, and this paper is intended both as a contribution to the record of waisted blades, and also as an attempt to answer certain questions about them, particularly whether or not they were indeed axes, whether they were hafted, and what the economic or ecological circumstances might have been in which they were made and used.

My paper falls into three sections:

(1) I review the conditions of montane hunting and collecting in Papua New Guinea and the range of artifacts relevant to these;

(2) I examine the assemblages of waisted blades and axe/adzes from three early sites in terms of some features that are thought to be functional rather than cultural or stylistic. I hypothesise that these implements can be interpreted as 'tools of extraction' (Binford and Binford, 1969 : 3) on the basis of the features they possess and ethnographic data, and that they pertain specifically to the context of arboreal hunting and collecting;

(3) I consider other implements with butt modification, within and outside Papua New Guinea, and discuss the possible significance of the distribution of waisted blades.

Hunting and collecting in montane Papua New Guinea

In order to interpret the early artifact assemblages and the sites from which they come, some understanding of the particular conditions of hunting and collecting in this region is needed. The environmental conditions of early human settlement in montane Papua New Guinea have been discussed in detail (Hope and Hope, 1976: 29–55) so I will not do so here. However, the general period considered in this study is that of the glaciation of Mt Wilhelm and other high altitude regions, from about 22 000 to about 14 000 years ago, the subsequent period of the melting of the glaciers, returning to the general state of modern climate at about 5000 years ago (G. Hope, 1973). The glaciation would have affected human habitation by causing the forest zones to compress downhill. The upper treeline retreated down to about 2500 m and the general snowline advanced down to about 3500 m, with tongues of snow down to about 3000 m in places. Following the melting of the glaciers, the treeline moved up to slightly higher than its present level, before returning to about 3500 m (G. Hope, 1973 : 222–25).

Although early hunters and collectors would have exploited the resources of the upper mountain *Nothofagus* and mixed broadleaf forest above 2000 m, and of the alpine grassland above 3500 m, they may have dwelt mainly below about 2000 m making periodic visits to the upper mountain zones. The lower altitude zones would have been more favourable for living in terms of general comfort, but it is possible that the mid-mountain forest contained a wider range and greater density of resources. Unfortunately so much of the mid- and lower mountain forest has been ecologically transformed by the activities of more recent agriculturalists that its former condition can only be extrapolated. However, it is apparent that there is a marked contrast between the biogeographical character of the forest above 1200–1500 m and that below about 1200 m, and the former would have provided a rich ecological niche for hunter-collectors. Schodde and Calaby (1972 : 293) consider that this montane province supports the core of the Australo-Papuan bird and mammal fauna with a greater density and variety of species.

J. and G. Hope, in a paper in this conference (Hope and Hope, 1976), explore the possibility that early man in Papua New Guinea may have primarily exploited the alpine savannah and scrub zone in preference to the mid-mountain forest, rather than used it for seasonal or periodic hunting as I suggest below. While a recent finding cited by them of fossil bone in the Southern Highlands dated to about 40 000 years

ago sets the stage for alpine woodland hunters in the upper mountains of New Guinea, there is no direct archaeological evidence of this as yet. On the contrary, the analysis of the bone collections from Yuku indicates the exploitation of a wide variety of species of the mid- and upper-mountain forest and grassland back to about 15 000 years ago. Two other arguments should be mentioned against permanent habitation in the upper mountain grasslands. The first is that the conditions of living in the high altitude zone would be considerably less comfortable and for this reason alone it might be expected that early man would have normally lived at lower altitudes and ventured up the mountain only seasonally. It is also the case that the alpine grass and scrub land lacks edible wild plants in any abundance, in contrast to the mid- and upper-mountain forest (R. Bulmer, 1964). As I argue below, montane hunters should be expected to have exploited a variety of ecological and altitudinal zones.

There is no detailed ethnography of a montane hunting and collecting people in Papua New Guinea, and in this respect archaeologists of that country are less assisted than Australian colleagues. However, there is a fair amount of general information about these activities among recent agricultural groups (Anell, 1960; R. Bulmer, 1968), particularly the Kalam of the Bismarck-Schrader Mountains (R. Bulmer, 1964, 1968, 1974; Bulmer and Menzies, 1972–3). This is of assistance in considering the specific activities of hunting and collecting in an archaeological context and the range of artifacts involved, although recent peoples in some respects have used a different range of implements than their prehistoric predecessors. As well, the recent hunters are exploiting mainly the higher altitude zones, as their gardens occupy the mid-mountain zones.

Hunting and killing The only big-game animals in Papua New Guinea are feral pig (*Sus scrofa*), and three species of cassowary (*Casuarius*). Pig is thought to have been introduced by man to Papua New Guinea in post-Pleistocene times, but it possibly was self-introduced to lowland forest areas at an earlier time (S. Bulmer, 1974b). In some parts of Papua New Guinea wallabies are the most numerous terrestrial game of any size, but their distribution is very uneven. Other terrestrial mammals hunted by man include bandicoots (Peramelidae), echidnas, and a wide variety of rodents.

Forests at all altitudes would have been rich in arboreal mammals, as is relatively undisturbed forest today. These include tree-kangaroos (*Dendrolagus* spp.), cuscuses (*Phalanger* spp.), ringtail possums (*Pseudocheirus* spp.), giant rats (such as *Mallomys rothschildi*) and a wide variety of smaller marsupials and rodents. Large fruit bats are common in forests up to about 2000 m, as are many species of small bats. The bird fauna of the Papua New Guinea forest is particularly rich, but the bulk of bird game in prehistoric times as today may have consisted of relatively small fruit- and blossom-feeding birds, such as doves, honey eaters and lorikeets.

No recent Papua New Guinea people to my knowledge made stone implements specifically for hunting and killing game, although the recent polished axe/adze was much used in the course of hunting, as is described below under 'Wood chopping'. Hunting is accomplished with the use of wooden spears, bows and arrows, pit traps, springes, dead-falls, sticks, stones, and bare hands (R. Bulmer, 1968). It is of interest that no prehistoric stone implements have yet been excavated in Papua New Guinea that have been interpreted as hunting weapons, in contrast to Australia and Southeast Asia.

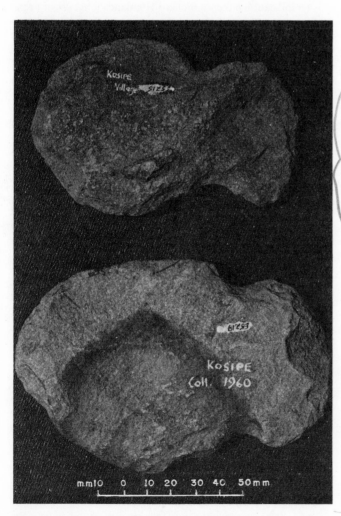

Plate 1: Waisted blades from Kosipe, Central Papua (Papua New Guinea Museum).

Undated surface collections do contain a small number of pointed implements which could possibly be spear points, but I think it reasonable to assume that the prehistoric hunters of the montane areas used wooden implements. It could be argued that this may be related to the absence of large or dangerous game, prior to the introduction of the pig.

Digging Hunting and collecting in the montane forest and grassland requires a considerable amount of digging. Edible roots (including a wild *Dioscorea* sp. and the introduced feral *Pueraria*) are now collected with the assistance of a wooden digging stick. Several kinds of subterranean animals, including small rodents, skink's eggs, and ant larvae, are obtained with a considerable amount of earth moving. The digging of pit traps is an activity that would have been facilitated by a stone-headed digging tool.

Wood chopping Wood chopping occurs in montane hunting and collecting in four main activities: arboreal hunting; collecting of tree fruits and nuts; construction of shelters; and obtaining larvae from timber.

Cutting and chopping branches, saplings and light timber is a common part of hunting in the Papua New Guinea montane forest. This includes cutting of climbing and bridging poles, building platforms, hides, and springes, and clearing of foliage for a number of purposes, including to isolate an animal in a tree. The height and character of the mountain forest and its arboreal fauna require hunters also to be arboreal. Likewise, collecting tree fruit and nuts, and raw materials, such as leaves and vines, commonly involves climbing, cutting and chopping.

The range of edible wild foods exploited in recent times has been reviewed by R. Bulmer (1964; S. and R. Bulmer, 1966 : 48–49). In general they include a range of plants that would not require stone implements other than pounding stones to smash kernels of hard nuts and possibly mortars to grind some of them for processing. However, exploitation of tree nuts and fruits would have been facilitated, like arboreal hunting, by axe/adze-like tools for wood chopping and cutting.

The most distinct foods of the Papua New Guinea forest are the nuts and fruits of *Pandanus* spp.; the main nut-bearing species (*P. julianettii* and *P. brosimos* are only in the upper mountain forest from about 1800 m to about 3300 m, while the fruiting species (*P. conoideus*) is found in the mid-mountain zone up to about 1600 m, but only as a cultivated plant. Other trees bearing edible nuts and seeds include *Elaeocarpus* (several species), *Castanopsis*, *Sloanea*, *Finschia*, and *Sterculia*. *Quercus* s.l. acorns could have been utilised, although they would have required leaching. Two other trees providing important food resources are the cultivated seed-bearing breadfruit (*Artocarpus* sp.) and the semi-cultivated sago (*Metroxylon* sp.). This breadfruit grows wild below about 1000 m and is now gathered by agricultural people living at higher altitudes, but its wild distribution in primary forest is not known. Sago was used only by lowland people, although some trees occur up to 1200 m. This may reflect attempted cultivation of sago at this altitude, which is much higher than its natural distribution, although there is no record of it having been used at this altitude.

Other edible wild foods in the mountain forest include cucurbits, edible fungi, and the foliage of a wide range of trees, shrubs, and ferns.

Although forest hunting and collecting could have been served by hand-held axes or choppers, a haft or at least a handle would have been of great benefit, and many of the larger tools, even if used unhafted might have been hard to carry and hold onto in the tree tops without an attachment. In these activities, an edge-ground implement would have been of more assistance than a tool with a flaked cutting edge.

In the Papua New Guinea mountains, where rock shelters are found only in certain localities, and where rainfall is high and almost daily, hunters and collectors must have built at least temporary shelters, and possibly more substantial dwellings at some camps. Modern Highlanders build temporary bush houses of saplings, leaves and foliage, a 'bee-hive' hut form which is thought to be an ancient dwelling form on the basis of its pan-tropic distribution (Aufenanger, 1965; Vicedom and Tischner, 1943(I): 176). Obviously, some sort of axe-like tool would have been of assistance in this activity.

Another chopping and wood cutting activity is that of extracting larvae from timber, often dead timber. These larvae are a delicacy and a valuable source of fat for modern Highlanders, and their collection in prehistoric times would have been greatly facilitated by a stone axe-like tool. Modern Highlanders also fell suitable soft-wood trees, leave them for the larvae and return later to 'harvest' them; this would not be practicable without an axe-like tool.

Skinning and cutting game Although implements thought to have been used for these purposes are common in stone assemblages of early hunters in other parts of the world, there is no indication either in modern Highlands practices or in the stone assemblages so far excavated for implements for skinning and slaughtering game.

All Highlands game, except feral pig and possibly cassowary, is usually cooked whole, although birds and animals of any size are gutted first. Pigs can be (and are) slaughtered and prepared for cooking with a wooden club, heavy pebbles for smashing large bone joints, and a bamboo knife for cutting. Skins are not used for clothing in the Highlands, although some fur and bird skins are used in head-dresses and other ornaments. In the latter case, the skinning is done with the bamboo knife and the hands.

The fashioning of bamboo knives requires a sharp cutting tool, although the knife is subsequently resharpened by stripping the edge with the teeth. Therefore, a flake or flaked stone tool could be expected in association with the bamboo knife, and if such a flake was repeatedly used it might show silica polish on the cutting edge.

There is no evidence yet of the antiquity of bamboo suitable for knives in Papua New Guinea, though some species concerned are thought to have been introduced by man. Therefore, it is possible that flake knives would have been used as a part of the early stone assemblages, to the limited extent these were required on the relatively small-sized game.

Processing seeds and nuts Indented nut cracker stones and mortars for grinding seeds and nuts can be expected to be an early part of the stone assemblage of hunter-collectors. One stratified indented anvil stone (on the face of an axe/adze) was excavated at Kosipe (J. P. White *et al.*, 1970 : 134, Fig. 24a), and a number of mortars was found at the same site in uncertain, but certainly prehistoric, context. A mortar was found in the excavations at Niobe, but this is also undated although possibly associated with early deposits. R. Bulmer (1964) has reviewed the possible uses of stone mortars in Papua New Guinea.

Grass and leaf cutting A sharp knife would have been necessary, or at least highly desirable, in obtaining grass and leaves as raw materials for thatching, mats, and other domestic items. Bamboo could have served these purposes, as it did in recent times in the large bamboo grass knife, but if they lacked suitable bamboo the prehistoric Highlands collectors would have needed a sharp stone implement. It may be that the use-polished flakes found at several sites (S. Bulmer, 1966a : 114; J. P. White 1972 : 98, 136) were used in this way.

Processing bark, fibre, cane and leaves These materials were processed by recent Highlanders in the manufacture of clothing, containers, ornaments, and miscellaneous domestic items. String clothing and carrying bags, as well as string and rope for utilitarian purposes, are made from wood bast and plant fibre. This processing of string fibre includes the scraping of the plant flesh from twigs to extract a residue of fibre, and the shredding of the fibre. I have argued previously (S. Bulmer 1966 : 148) that small convex flake scrapers and highback cores with irregular steep edges would have been useful in this work, although bone and wooden tools could also have been used.

Cane for woven ornaments and artifacts, bamboo fire thongs, and bamboo bow strings require planing and shredding. Bark cloth, made from wood bast, is processed with the use of wooden, stone, or pig bone pounders. The outer bark of certain trees is used for belts and housing material, and for cooking and storage containers. Rough pebble tools would have been adequate for the task of obtaining bark, but convex planing tools could also have been employed in processing the bark.

Manufacture of wood and bone artifacts Digging sticks, and perhaps hunting weapons and axe/adze hafts would possibly have been a part of the early hunting-collecting tool kit. In the manufacture of digging sticks, a simple unretouched flake could have sufficed for scraping, as it did in recent times, but retouched concave scrapers are present in hunting-collecting sites from the earliest layers (S. Bulmer, 1966 : 142).

There is no evidence yet for the antiquity of either the spear or the bow and arrow, but the concave scraper, and a variety of other small stone implements could have been employed in the making of these artifacts, as well as in the manufacture of spatulate and pointed bone implements that are also a part of the early excavated assemblage (S. Bulmer, 1966).

In general, montane hunter-collectors in Papua New Guinea would inevitably have been involved in arboreal activities, and is was probably difficult, if not impossible, to exploit this montane forest environment without relatively large artifacts made of reasonable quality rock and capable of fairly heavy wood chopping and cutting. For this reason it can be expected that hunting-collecting domains in the mountains would have been located with respect to access to rock sources, and that the settlement of areas lacking in good quality rock would have depended upon trade.

The assemblages

The stone implements discussed in this paper come from two excavated assemblages from montane sites, Yuku and Kosipe, and a surface collection from a series of sites at Passismanua, southern New Britain. Four other excavated montane sites, Kiowa, Kafiavan, Niobe, and Batari, also contain stone artifacts from part of the same period of time as Yuku and Kosipe. However, none has sufficient complete implements, either waisted blades or axe/adzes, to provide an adequate sample for comparison here.

KOSIPE This is the earliest dated human settlement site in Papua New Guinea (White *et al.*, 1970), located on a sloping flat-topped ridge extending into a 28 km² permanent swamp at Kosipe, Central Province. The site is about 2000 m a.s.l. and the habitation remains consisted of stone artifacts and charcoal lumps stratified in a series of volcanic ashes. These are identified as ashes from eruptions of Mt Lamington in the Northern District. A total of 134 m² was excavated at this site during 1964 and 1967 by J. Peter White. Six radiocarbon dates have been obtained from charcoal samples from different layers of the 80–100 cm of deposit, ranging from about 4000 years to over 25 000 years.

Because it is close to the permanent Kosipe swamp, the occupation at the site is interpreted as probably representing seasonal occupation during the collecting of *Pandanus* nuts at the swamp (White *et al.*, 1970 : 168). A variety of stone tools was excavated, including 11 waisted blades, 10 axe/adzes, 15 flakes and 5 other stone artifacts (White *et al.*, 1970 : 163). A wider range of artifacts was found during the construction of mission buildings at Kosipe, including stone mortars and planlateral-sectioned polished axe/adzes, but their stratigraphic origins are not certain. In some calculations below I include 4 waisted and 10 unwaisted end-edged tools from unstratified collections from Kosipe, but on the whole I limit my discussion to the stratified implements from the excavations.

The deposits at Kosipe included a second buried soil profile in Levels 4–6, thought to be a humus soil formed during a cessation of ash showers and dated to some time between about 9000 and 16 000 years ago. There was little contrast in the artifact types found in the two soils, the only difference being the presence of a polished axe/adze in the upper soil, with no polished axe/adzes occurring in the lower soil.

YUKU This is a small rockshelter with about 21 m² of protected ground, near the junction of the Lanim and Yuem rivers, the former being a tributary of the Lae River in the Western Highlands Province. Yuku is located at about 1280 m a.s.l., deep in a river gorge facing north in a protected and sunny position, on the northwestern slopes of Mt Hagen. During October to December 1959 the author excavated about 9·5 m² of deposit at Yuku, to a maximum depth of 360 cm below the ground surface.

Seven radiocarbon dates have been obtained from samples from Yuku (S. Bulmer, 1974), ranging from 4500 and 7000 years in Layer 3 to about 12 000 years in Layer 5, with 150 cm of deposit lying below this date. The stone assemblage discussed in this paper comes from Layers 3–7 and is thought to reflect the general habitation of 'broad-spectrum' unspecialised hunter-collectors. A wide range of large and small stone tools made of local rock and the bone refuse of cooking reflect general site use. A variety of forest and grassland animal species was represented in all layers, including egg shell of brush turkey and cassowary.

In the most recent layer of the early occupation of Yuku, the first flakes of polished axe/adze are present, as well as pig bone and marine shell. The larger of the two polished fragments is of a lenticular-sectioned axe/adze. In the same layer all waisted blades are ground, possibly in response to the imported axe/adzes from the Wahgi and Jimi quarries. This assemblage is interpreted to reflect a period of economic change.

There is then a break in the occupation of Yuku, during which three burials were placed in the shelter. The site then appears to have been used mainly as a cooking site, with a number of oven pits present. This cooking is likely to have been in association with a nearby open settlement, as is still the case; Yuku was most recently used for the ritual cooking of game and pigs.

The assemblage of stone artifacts from Layers 3–7 at Yuku includes 230 implements, 2 waste cores (multi-directional flaking), and 713 waste flakes (S. Bulmer, 1966 : 129). In spite of White's criticism that the ratio of waste to implements is not sufficiently high for this to be a stoneworking site (White, 1972 : 146), the waste flakes include the same range of rock types used for artifacts, all of which are available in the nearby river. The shelter is small, only about 360 cm deep from rock face to drip line, and in the circumstances some of the refuse of living would have spilt outside the sheltered area. When originally occupied Yuku was at the riverside, although now that the river has cut a deep gorge some distance from the shelter the site faces onto gardens.

Of the 240 implements from the early layers at Yuku there are 149 retouched tools, 74 utilised flakes, 8 other stone artifacts and 9 pebbles.

Retouched tools:
2 fragments of polished axe/adze
7 bifacially retouched unwaisted tools
23 waisted blades (8 unifacially flaked, 11 bifacially flaked and 4 ground)
8 pebble tools (6·3–12·6 cm in length)
10 large retouched flake tools (side-edged) (3·9–6·0 cm in length)
39 small flake tools (7 with one or more straight retouched edges, 32 with one or more convex retouched edges)
51 'highback' cores—single platform, flaked at about 90° (1·2–5·8 cm in length)
9 concave scrapers (steeply trimmed thick blades or cores)

Utilised (unretouched) tools:
5 large flakes (10·0–15·2 cm in length)
69 small flakes (1·0–7·3 cm in length)

Miscellaneous:
5 worn fragments of red pigment
1 flake used as grinder
1 grindstone (anvil)
1 hammerstone (pebble hammer)
9 pebbles (raw material or oven stones)

This assemblage includes artifact types not yet reported from other archaeological sites in Papua New Guinea, particularly hand axe-like pointed bifaces and large retouched side-edged flake tools. Three of the bifaces are end-edged tools, so they are included in the discussion of end-edged implements below. The retouched large flake tools are very similar to some Australian 'Elouera' arthy(McC, 1967 : 24–26; Mulvaney, 1969 : 81–83).

PASSISMANUA COLLECTION A surface collection of over 400 stone artifacts, 342 of which are discussed in this paper, was made in 1962–4 by Ann Chowning and Jane Goodale. The collection was made in an area stretching from about 16 to 32 km inland from the southern New Britain coast east of

Kandrian, at about 120 to 450 m a.s.l. The artifacts occur in a district where flint is available as stream pebbles, but the implements appear to be eroding from some sort of habitation deposit, not from waterlain layers, as they show practically no signs of rolling or secondary breakage. Their age is unknown, but some of them could well be of late Pleistocene age, although others may be much more recent. Many appear to have been in the ground a very long time on the basis of their heavy patina, and local residents do not recognise any but polished axes as artifacts.

A description of part of this collection was published by Shutler and Kess (1969), but the remainder are here described for the first time, other than in an introductory unpublished paper (S. Bulmer, 1971) and in preliminary accounts of the collection by its discoverers (Chowning and Goodale, 1966; Goodale, 1966). Shutler and Kess described the implements they studied as follows: 8 waisted blades; 6 lanceolates (possibly knives); 7 flake scrapers (of a variety of forms, including 2 blades); 4 bifacial core ovates; 3 core adzes; unifacial flake axe and adze; 1 borer; and 1 probable projectile point.

Of the 342 artifacts discussed here, 333 are implements (including the 32 described by Shutler and Kess) and 9 are waste flakes and cores. The implements include 119 waisted blades (including 13 lacking end-edges), 78 unwaisted flaked axe/adzes and 3 polished axe/adzes, 22 waisted or unwaisted tools broken in mid-section (= 'short axes' in the Southeast Asian context, e.g. Heekeren and Knuth, 1967 : 37), and 120 other implements. I have divided the tools into those with end-edges and those without; as the object of this paper is primarily to consider axes or axe-like implements, only end-edged tools are considered in detail.

The tools in the Passismanua collection that lack end-edges include:

Retouched tools:
13 implements with concave side-edges
7 implements with straight side-edges
3 hammers (oval cores, flaked all over, with percussion marks)
6 single platform cores: 'horsehoof' and 'keeled'
25 bifacially flaked disc cores (oval or round)
23 flakes with unifacially retouched convex or irregular edges
5 flakes with bifacially retouched convex or irregular edges

Utilised tools (unretouched):
8 amorphous cores
28 large blade, or near-blade, flakes
22 amorphous flakes

Most of these will not be discussed further in this paper. It is of interest, however, that the only implement types in this collection not also present in the Yuku early assemblage are the bifacially flaked disc cores and the flaked hammerstones. The Passismanua collection, on the other hand, lacks only the pebble tools and the Elouera-like large flake implements of the Yuku assemblage.

OTHER SITES Waisted blades have also been found at two sites near Chuave Government Station, Chimbu Province. Three specimens were excavated from Layers 2, 3 and 5 at Kiowa, with another possible example in Layer 2 (S. Bulmer, 1966 : 109). The most recent of these was a partly finished example in Layer 2 made from a broken polished axe/adze.

The other two are flaked examples from layers dated to between 5000 and 6000 years. At Niobe, about 3·8 km south of Kiowa, two waisted blades were found (White, 1972 : 132, Fig. 23d) in the lower horizon, one with a ground edge. The stratigraphy of this site was partly disturbed, and White did not date the deposits. Further excavations at Niobe by Mary-Jane Mountain have uncovered other waisted blades and areas of undisturbed stratigraphy (Mountain, pers. comm. 1972).

Although these specimens are too few to be used as a comparative sample for this study, they are of interest in light of a group of 21 axe/adze-like tools in unstratified collections from Chuave. These implements have unground blunted edges as if they were used for gardening or digging, and when I purchased two examples from a local resident which were still in his possession, I was told they were used for clearing grass. These tools all lack butt modification.

Another assemblage of direct relevance to this study is from Kafiavana rockshelter in the Eastern Highlands, about 34 km southeast of Kiowa and Niobe. No waisted blades were found at this site, but 3 complete axe/adzes and 51 fragments of axe/adze were excavated throughout all layers of deposit, the deepest layer being over 11 000 years ago (White, 1972 : 95). Some of the specimens in each layer showed signs of grinding. The early layers at Kafiavana, at least from Layer VI to IX, and possibly Layers III to V as well, fall within the period considered in this study, but unfortunately there still is too small an assemblage to provide an adequate comparative sample for this study.

White argues that the absence of waisted blades from Kafiavana and from his two other excavations in the Eastern Highlands at Aibura and Batari may reflect a technological contrast between the stone-working in the eastern and western regions. The absence from Aibura is not surprising in light of the fact that it was only occupied in the last 4000 years (White, 1972 : 20), beginning later than any of the dated examples of waisted blades elsewhere. At Batari the stone assemblage reflected up to 8000 years of occupation, but included only 3 unstratified axe/adzes and one stratified axe/adze chip in a layer dated to between 4000 and 8000 years (White, 1972 : 57). At Kafiavana only an estimated one-tenth of the habitation deposit has been excavated (White, 1972 : 83), and in light of the fact that at Yuku all waisted blades were found in less than one-third of the habitation area, I do not think it should be discounted that waisted blades may be found in future excavations at earlier sites in the Eastern Highlands.

Description of stone tools

The assemblages that will be considered here are not only few but relatively small in size. There are 29 waisted blades and axe/adzes from Kosipe, a total of 41 stone artifacts from layers spanning about 20 000 years. At Yuku, 25 waisted blades and axe/adzes, out of a total of 240 implements, are present in layers covering possibly 10 000 years. It may be that we will never find relatively large sites of the early occupation of Papua New Guinea, but until further early rockshelters are excavated and early open settlements located and excavated, little can be said about the character of this early settlement.

As well, caution needs to be paid to treating the site assemblages as assemblages in the sense of the tool kit of an actual group of people. With about 23 implements per 1000 years at Yuku and 2 per 1000 years at Kosipe, this must inevitably be considered an insufficient sample. I had hoped

that the Passismanua collection might have provided a sample which could supply expected frequencies for an analysis of the other collections, but considering the variation between this collection and the total excavated sample, I do not think it justified to use it in this way here.

There remains some ambiguity about the precise definition of waisted blade and axe/adze, in order to separate them from all other stone artifacts in the assemblages. The implements discussed below consist of all tools with a working edge on one end, with flaking to shape the implement on the sides, whether or not it has butt modification. I acknowledge that there are two respects in which they are not entirely separate from the other artifacts. Some end-edged pebble tools also have working edges on the sides. Some end- and end-and-side-edged implements are small versions of the large tools discussed here. Although I think these ambiguities can be resolved, I will not go into this further, as it would involve detailed consideration of the total assemblages. In any case there are very small numbers of ambiguous implements in this sense.

The following features will be discussed:

(1) *Size and shape*. The tools are described according to maximum length, maximum width, width of butt and blade if waisted or tanged, and maximum thickness. A measure of general robustness is given in an index of width/thickness $\left(\dfrac{\text{thickness}}{\text{width}} \times 100\right)$ to suggest whether it is plausible that the implements were intended to be used for heavy or percussive work.

(2) *Working edges*. The tools were inspected under a microscope, under both low and high magnification to learn where working edges were present; microscopic 'chattering', smoothing, blunting, and step-flaking were taken as evidence of use-wear, although heavy smoothing in the waist was considered to be possible wear from hafting. The tools were sub-divided according to Fig. 1:

(a) Presence or absence of working edges of sides and butt;

(b) Shape of each working edge in plan (concave, pointed, or convex), irregularly convex edges were included with convex edges;

(c) Character of bevelling of end-edge (symmetrical or asymmetrical), this was judged on the basis of the actual shape of the bevel, not unifacial or bifacial flaking or retouch.

The tools were also studied according to the finish of their working edges (ground, retouched, natural flake edge), but this was not used as a criterion for sub-dividing in this study.

(3) *Treatment of butt*. This overlaps somewhat with (2), but was intended to assist in the consideration of the hafting of the tools. The following were used as criteria for sub-dividing the implements:

(a) Presence or absence of working edge on butt,

(b) Presence or absence of waisting and tanging.

Consideration was given to whether the waist or tanged concavities were used as working edges. A high proportion of the implements are ambiguous in this respect.

An index of tanging $\left(\dfrac{\text{maximum width of butt}}{\text{maximum width of blade}} \times 100\right)$ was calculated in order to attempt to sub-divide the tools into waisted and tanged tools, and to consider this variant in light of other features. This was attempted because the distribution

Table 1   Sub-groups of end-edged implements from Yuku, Kosipe, and Passismanua

	End-edge								
	Symmetrically bevelled				Asymmetrically bevelled				Total
	Convex		Pointed		Convex		Pointed		
	n	%	n	%	n	%	n	%	n	%
Yuku										
Waisted:										
Butt-edge pointed	1	(4.4)	—	—	—	—	—	—	1	(4.4)
Butt-edge convex	4	(17.4)	—	—	1	(4.4)	—	—	5	(21.8)
Butt not edged	11	(47.8)	—	—	2	(8.7)	—	—	13	(56.5)
Unwaisted:										
Butt-edge pointed	1	(4.3)	—	—	—	—	—	—	1	(4.3)
Butt-edge convex	1	(4.3)	—	—	—	—	—	—	1	(4.3)
Butt not edged	1	(4.3)	1	(4.4)	—	—	—	—	2	(8.7)
Total	19	(82.5)	1	(4.4)	3	(13.1)	—	—	23	(100.0)
Kosipe										
Waisted:										
Butt-edge pointed	—	—	—	—	—	—	1	(3.5)	1	(3.5)
Butt-edge convex	7	(24.1)	—	—	—	—	—	—	7	(24.1)
Butt not edged	5	(17.2)	—	—	1	(3.5)	—	—	6	(20.7)
Unwaisted:										
Butt-edge pointed	—	—	—	—	1	(3.5)	—	—	1	(3.5)
Butt-edge convex	3	(10.3)	—	—	—	—	—	—	3	(10.3)
Butt not edged	11	(37.9)	—	—	—	—	—	—	11	(37.9)
Total	26	(89.5)	—	—	2	(7.0)	1	(3.5)	29	(100.0)
Passismanua										
Waisted:										
Butt-edge pointed	—	—	—	—	3	(1.7)	—	—	3	(1.7)
Butt-edge convex	10	(5.4)	—	—	13	(7.1)	—	—	23	(12.5)
Butt not edged	25	(13.6)	—	—	54	(29.4)	1	(0.5)	80	(43.5)
Unwaisted:										
Butt-edge pointed	8	(4.4)	—	—	6	(3.1)	—	—	14	(7.6)
Butt-edge convex	12	(6.5)	—	—	5	(2.7)	—	—	17	(9.2)
Butt not edged	27	(14.7)	1	(0.5)	13	(7.1)	6	(3.3)	47	(25.5)
Total	82	(44.6)	1	(0.5)	94	(51.1)	7	(3.8)	184	(100.0)

and frequencies of waisted and tanged implements in Southeast and East Asian collections vary a great deal.

The features above are ones that I think are possibly related to the functions of the tools, rather than to cultural or stylistic patterns. For this reason I have specifically not considered details of, for instance, techniques of manufacture or shape. I will sub-divide them according to functional features, but do not intend to imply that what I report as sub-groups are functional types of tool in any absolute sense. My main intention is to consider more closely certain basic questions about the tools, and the sub-division and cross-tabulations of the features and metrical traits is to assist in this. I will try to examine the tools to find evidence about whether or not they were hafted, whether or not they are a plausible size, shape and robustness to be interpreted as axe/adzes, whether they have been used as hand implements, or whether some or all of them appear to have been used only as end-edged, percussive, wood-working tools.

Sub-grouping of end-edged tools   Before considering particular features in detail, I will sub-divide the implements from

three assemblages into homogeneous sub-groups hierarchically, by cross-tabulating four variables. The assemblages discussed here comprise 23 tools from Yuku, 29 from Kosipe and 184 from Passismanua (Table 1).[1]

The hierarchical presentation is based on a twenty-four fold table, cross-tabulating nine variants of four variables recorded: waisting; symmetry of end-edge bevel; shape of butt-edge; and shape of end-edge. These variants are illustrated in Fig. 1. Of the 24 possible sub-groups, seven do not occur in these assemblages. The frequencies of these sub-groups are presented in Table 1 and the percentage frequencies of sub-groups in the three assemblages are illustrated in Fig. 2.

It appears that the smaller range of variation in the Yuku and Kosipe assemblages may possibly be due to the small size of the samples; Yuku and Kosipe have only 9 and 7 sub-groups represented, while the much more numerous Passis-

1. There are minor differences in total number of implements between the various calculations in this study. This is because I used the maximum number of measurable implements in each case, rather than reducing the total to all those on which all measurements could be taken.

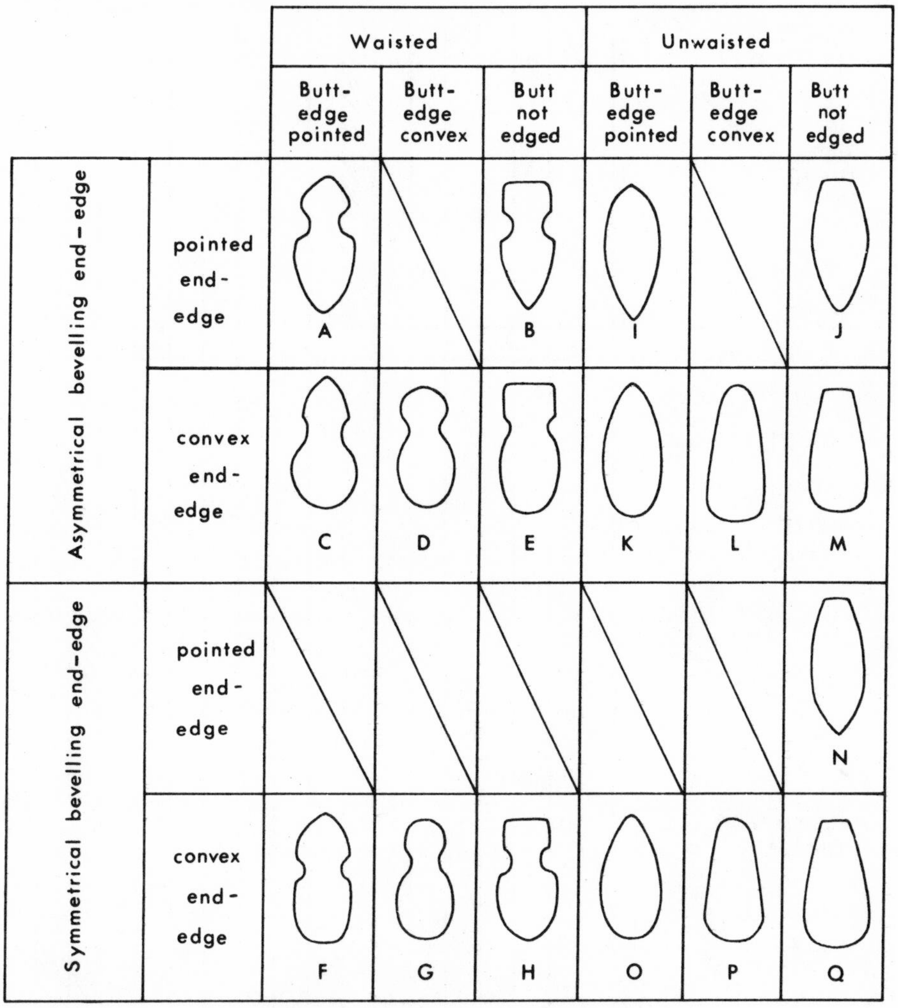

		Waisted			Unwaisted		
		Butt-edge pointed	Butt-edge convex	Butt not edged	Butt-edge pointed	Butt-edge convex	Butt not edged
Asymmetrical bevelling end-edge	pointed end-edge	A		B	I		J
	convex end-edge	C	D	E	K	L	M
Symmetrical bevelling end-edge	pointed end-edge						N
	convex end-edge	F	G	H	O	P	Q

Fig. 1: Sub-groups of end-edged implements from early Montane sites in Papua New Guinea.

manua collection includes 14 sub-groups. One consistency between the assemblages is the rarity of pointed implements, either end pointed or butt pointed. This is notable because some of the pointed implements present are very carefully flaked and not accidental. As well, the collectors did not consciously select for any particular shape or variety of implement (A. Chowning, pers. comm.), so the rarity of this form may possibly reflect its true infrequency in the tool-kit of its makers or alternatively that other explanations such as chronological differences or insufficient site-sampling should be considered.

Another consistency between assemblages is the sharing of some of the commonest sub-groups. Yuku and Kosipe share three of their four most common sub-groups (Yuku: E, G, H, and Q; Kosipe: G, H, P, and Q). The Passismanua collection has all five of these among its commonest sub-groups, while having a substantial number of D and M as well. I would suspect the absence of B, C, K, and M from Yuku and Kosipe is due to insufficiency of numbers in the assemblages.

Although the small assemblages at Yuku and Kosipe mean that it is very likely that these samples are unrepresentative of the true range of variation in the tool-kits of the groups who live there, nevertheless it is notable that there is little contrast between the two sites in the range of sub-groups present. Kosipe was interpreted to be a site of specialised function, as a seasonal high altitude collecting camp, while Yuku was interpreted to be a site of general 'broad-spectrum' hunting and collecting, but Kosipe seems to have a similarly wide range of end-edged implements, although it should be noted that it did not contain a small stone-tool assemblage (see above). Another interesting consistency is the similarity in general proportion of waisted implements in the three assemblages: 48·3% at Kosipe, 56·4% at Yuku, and 57·7% at Passismanua.

Although there are differences between the assemblages in occurrence of sub-groups, I would place little confidence in the significance of these differences until further site assemblages are available for comparison.

Chronology of sub-groups In Table 2, I present the stratigraphy and radiocarbon chronology of the sub-groups at Yuku and Kosipe. This is given here mainly for its negative information, that is, to show that on present evidence there is no marked patterning in the chronology of the sub-groups. Because of the sample size in the assemblages it would not be justified at this time to place any confidence in the differences of distribution of the sub-groups over time at the two sites.

Size and shape Fig. 3 gives the percentage distributions of maximum length of end-edged implements from the three assemblages (sub-divided by waisting and shape of bevelling of end-edge). The tools from Yuku range from 8·6 to 21·5 cm

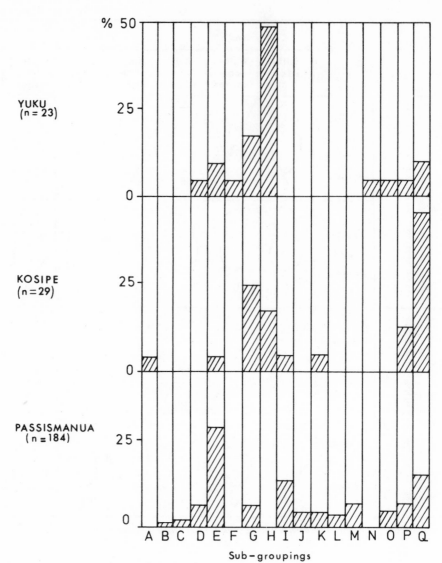

Fig. 2: Percentage frequencies of sub-groups of end-edged tools.

in length, with a mean length of 12·2 cm and a standard deviation of 3·4 cm. Kosipe implements range from 8·3 to 22·0 cm in length, with a mean of 12·9 cm and a standard deviation of 3·8 cm. The Passismanua tools are on the average smaller, measuring from 4·2 to 15·0 cm in length, with a mean of 8·8 cm and a standard deviation of 1·6 cm (see Tables 3-6).

I think the relatively smaller size of the Passismanua tools may be due to the small size of the nodules of flint from which the tools were made. The raw material at Passismanua seems to have been deeply weathered pebbles, and it is apparent from the assemblage that tools on which the weathered cortex was not completely removed tended to break. Amongst the broken implements are some examples that would have been larger than any of the complete tools but apparently broke during manufacture.

In general the size range of these tools is a plausible one for axe/adzes, if the size range of recent Highlands implements can be taken as a comparison (S. Bulmer, 1966 : 45–54; Lampert, 1972 : 8). The polished axe/adzes made and used in recent times in montane Papua New Guinea range from 4·5 to about 30·0 cm in length, and Lampert gives a mean of 10·9 for

Wahgi Valley axe/adzes, for example. This is similar in central tendency but of a wider range than the 8–12 cm given by Semenov (1970 : 130) for medium-sized flaked axes in Europe and elsewhere. In the Papua New Guinea Highlands the size range of any given local assemblage varies particularly according to the distance of the locality from the rock quarries from which the axe/adzes derive. In general, the greater the distance from the quarry of origin, the smaller the average length of the axe/adzes, both because smaller tools tended to be traded to those lacking direct access to rock sources, and also because broken tools would be refashioned into smaller polished blades. However, from ethnographic accounts, the smaller axe/adzes were used for only certain kinds of wood-working, such as splitting firewood, while the larger tools were all-purpose axe/adzes. It is not clear how large a tool needed to be employed as an all-purpose axe/adze. The largest of the end-edged tools from these three assemblages must have been used for heavy work.

Fig. 3 shows that the assemblages contrast in size range if sub-divided according to presence of waisting, shape of bevelling, and shape of end-edge. However, the specific contrasts are not consistent between sites. I think the differ-

Table 2 Chronology of sub-groups of end-edged implements at Yuku and Kosipe (cf. Fig. 1)

Level	C-14*	D	E	F	G	H	I	O	P	Q	Total
Kosipe											
2	4–9000	—	—	—	2	—	—	—	—	1	3
3	undated	—	—	—	1	—	—	—	1	—	2
4		—	—	—	1	1	1	1	1	1	6
5	16–27 000	—	1	—	1	2	—	—	—	1	5
6		—	—	—	—	1	—	—	—	1	2
Total		—	1	—	5	4	1	1	2	4	18
Yuku											
3A–B	4500–6000	—	—	—	1	—	—	—	—	—	1
3C–D	undated	—	—	—	—	3	—	—	—	—	3
4A	undated	—	—	—	—	—	—	—	—	—	0
4B	undated	—	—	1	—	—	—	—	—	—	1
4C–E	7–10 000	—	2	—	1	5	—	1	—	—	9
5A	undated	1	—	—	1	2	—	—	—	—	4
5B	12 000	—	—	—	—	—	—	—	—	—	0
6	undated	—	—	—	—	—	—	—	—	—	0
7	undated	—	—	—	—	1	—	—	1	—	2
Crevice	undated	1	—	—	—	1	—	—	—	—	2
Total		2	2	1	3	12	0	1	1	0	22

* Approximate radiocarbon ages in years. For details of dating these sites, *see* S. Bulmer 1974

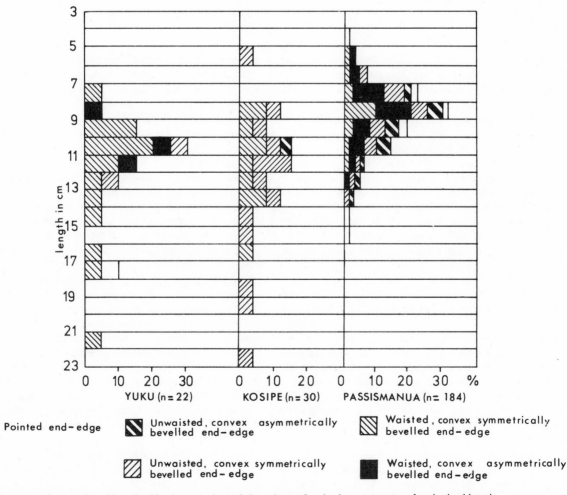

Fig. 3: Percentage frequencies of length of implements, by waisting, shape of end-edge, asymmetry of end-edged bevel.

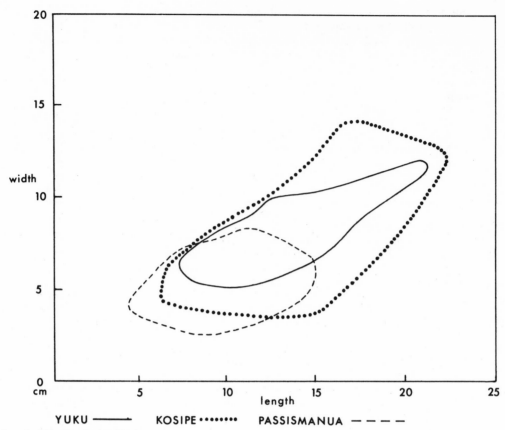

YUKU ———   KOSIPE ••••••••   PASSISMANUA — — — —

Fig. 4a: Length and width of end-edged tools.

ences should be attributed to the small size of the assemblages, as the most numerous group in each assemblage has the widest size range, and therefore it should be suspected that the more numerous a group is, the wider its size range would be. Each assemblage has a relatively normal unimodal distribution of maximum lengths.

Fig. 4 shows graphs of length-width distributions of end-edged tools in the three assemblages. The only contrast apparent is in the tendency at Kosipe for waisted implements to be rather broader than unwaisted implements. This is similar to the relative widths of digging tools and axe/adzes in the surface collections from Chuave (S. Bulmer, 1966 : 50). The Chuave digging tools were all at least half as broad as they were long, and were relatively much broader than polished and ground axe/adzes in the same collection.

Fig. 4 also shows that there is in general a simple linear relationship between length and width in all assemblages, and a relatively normal unimodal distribution of lengths and widths.

Fig. 5 reports the percentage frequencies of the index of width-thickness in the three assemblages. This measure may not necessarily be relevant to polished axe/adzes made of very hard or tough rock, which would be serviceable for percussive work even if relatively thin. However, the index was calculated as a measure of the general robustness of the implements in these assemblages, some of which are made of rather un-promising rock. Some of the waisted blades seem to me to be relatively too thin and fragile to be used as striking implements, which is why the term 'waisted blade' was used in the first place. Kosipe tools range from 11 to 57 in index of width-thickness, with a mean of 26 and a standard deviation

of 13. Yuku tools range from 14 to 68 in this index, with a mean of 30 and a standard deviation of 12. Passismanua tools are relatively thicker, ranging from 13 to 80, with a mean of 46 and a standard deviation of 14. Unwaisted tools are relatively thicker than waisted at both Kosipe and Passismanua. There were so few unwaisted tools in the Yuku assemblage that I calculated only the combined index.

In reference to width-thickness, the waisted blades from the Kiowa excavations should be mentioned. These have been labelled 'so-called' waisted blades (Golson, 1971 : 131), presumably for their unimpressive proportions. Four waisted blades were excavated at Kiowa: two unpolished examples from Layers 3 and 5, one definite and one probable example from Layer 2. The Layer 2 implements are partly polished, one being refashioned from a broken polished axe/adze blade. These are all relatively small tools: one is broken, one 12·0 cm in length, and two 8·9 cm in length. They have indices of width-thickness of 12, 16, 22, and 36. Therefore the Kiowa waisted blades are not outside the general range from other sites in either length or relative thickness.

There is no separate thin group apparent from measurements or from index of width-thickness, so I have selected here those implements from the three sites with an index of width-thickness of less than 20 for consideration as possible non-percussive tools. The question to be answered if possible is whether there is any consistency of features to suggest a distinct thin or non-axe-like group of implements. In general these thin tools are nearly all waisted convex end-edged tools, although they range a great deal in length and they vary in bevelling of end-edge.

There are only six implements in the Passismanua collection

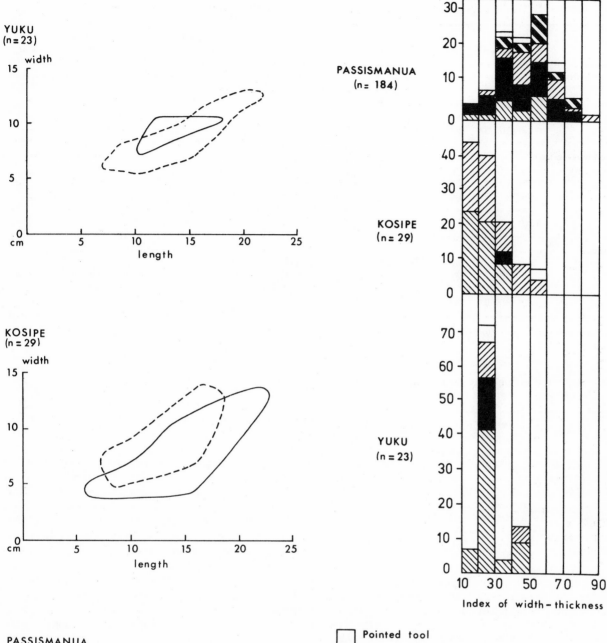

YUKU
(n = 23)

KOSIPE
(n = 29)

PASSISMANUA
(n = 184)

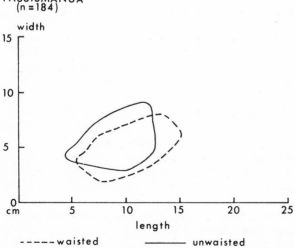

- - - - waisted   ———— unwaisted

Fig. 4b: Length and width of waisted and unwaisted implements.

PASSISMANUA
(n = 184)

KOSIPE
(n = 29)

YUKU
(n = 23)

Index of width – thickness

☐ Pointed tool

◨ Unwaisted, convex   ◨ Unwaisted convex
    asymmetrical bevel   symmetrical bevel

◨ Waisted convex   ■ Waisted convex
    symmetrical bevel   asymmetrical bevel

Fig. 5: Percentage frequencies of index of width—thickness, by waisting, shape of end-edge and symmetry of bevelling.

with a width-thickness index of less than 20. They are all waisted, one is symmetrically bevelled and the rest asymmetrically bevelled, and all have a convex end-edge. They range in length from 4·2 to 8·6 cm.

In the Kosipe collection there are four stratified and seven unstratified tools with a width-thickness index of less than 20. Two of the stratified and four of the unstratified tools are waisted. All are symmetrically bevelled and all are convex in end-edge, but four are not edged on the butt and seven have convex butt-edges. These tools range in length from 5·8 to 13·3 cm.

Table 3 Frequency and percentage of presence and absence of waisting, by other non-metrical features*

	Waisted		Unwaisted		Total	
	n	%	n	%	n	%
Shape of end-edge:						
Pointed	2	(1.4)	8	(8.2)	10	(4.2)
Convex	137	(98.6)	89	(91.8)	226	(95.8)
Total	139	(100.0)	97	(100.0)	236	(100.0)
Shape of butt-edge:						
Pointed	5	(3.6)	16	(16.5)	21	(8.9)
Convex	35	(25.2)	21	(21.7)	56	(23.7)
Butt not edged	99	(71.2)	60	(61.9)	159	(67.4)
Total	139	(100.0)	97	(100.0)	236	(100.0)
Bevelling:						
Symmetrical	63	(45.3)	66	(68.0)	129	(54.7)
Asymmetrical	76	(54.7)	31	(32.0)	107	(45.3)
Total	139	(100.0)	97	(100.0)	236	(100.0)

* The three assemblages from Yuku, Kosipe, and Passismanua are combined in Tables 3–6.

Table 4 Frequency and percentage of shape of end-edge, by other non-metrical features

	Shape of end-edge					
	Pointed		Convex		Total	
	n	%	n	%	n	%
Waisting:						
Waisted	2	(20.0)	137	(60.6)	139	(58.9)
Unwaisted	8	(80.0)	89	(39.4)	97	(41.1)
Total	10	(100.0)	226	(100.0)	236	(100.0)
Shape of butt-edge:						
Pointed	1	(10.0)	20	(8.9)	21	(8.9)
Convex	0	(0.0)	56	(24.8)	5	(23.7)
Butt not edged	9	(90.0)	150	(66.3)	159	(67.4)
Total	10	(100.0)	226	(100.0)	236	(100.0)
Shape of bevelling:						
Symmetrical	8	(80.0)	99	(43.8)	107	(43.3)
Asymmetrical	2	(20.0)	127	(56.2)	129	(54.7)
Total	10	(100.0)	226	(100.0)	236	(100.0)

There are only two end-edged tools in the Yuku assemblage with a width-thickness index of less than 20. Both are waisted, with symmetrically bevelled convex end-edges, and they are 7·3 and 10·3 cm in length.

For comparison, I calculated an index of width-thickness for 20 tools in the Passismanua collection which are similar to the end-edged tools in general appearance and have straight or concave side-edges, but which lack end-edges. They range in width-thickness index from 18 to 74, with a mean of 52, suggesting that in general relative thinness is not a helpful measure for distinguishing striking from non-striking tools.

Table 5 Frequency and percentage of symmetrical and asymmetrical bevelling of end-edge, by other non-metrical features

	Symmetrical bevelling		Asymmetrical bevelling		Total	
	n	%	n	%	n	%
Shape of end-edge:						
Pointed	8	(7.5)	2	(1.6)	10	(4.2)
Convex	99	(92.5)	127	(98.4)	226	(95.8)
Total	107	(100.0)	129	(100.0)	236	(100.0)
Shape of butt-edge:						
Pointed	10	(7.8)	11	(10.3)	21	(8.9)
Convex	37	(28.7)	19	(17.8)	56	(23.7)
Butt not edged	82	(63.6)	77	(71.9)	159	(67.4)
Total	129	(100.0)	107	(100.0)	236	(100.0)
Waisting:						
Waisted	63	(48.8)	76	(71.0)	139	(58.9)
Unwaisted	66	(51.2)	31	(29.0)	97	(40.1)
Total	129	(100.0)	107	(100.0)	236	(100.0)

Non-metrical features In order to consider any possible correlation between non-metrical features, or differences in measurements according to non-metrical features, I have combined the three assemblages and cross-tabulated the various features. I have not been able to find any positive or negative correlations in these data, so I present them here primarily as descriptive tables. With the three assemblages combined, nearly all (95·8%) have convex end-edges. They are nearly equally divided between symmetrically bevelled (54·7%) and asymmetrically bevelled (45·3%) tools, while 58·7% are waisted and 41·1% are unwaisted. Less than one-third of the tools have a working edge on the butt (32·6%).

In the cross-tabulation of features, there is only one marked positive correlation apparent, between pointed edge on butt and absence of waisting (see Table 6). In view of the very small number of implements with pointed edge on the butt, this correlation may possibly be due to bias in the small sample, and therefore cannot be taken as significant in terms of the present assemblages.

I think the general lack of correlation of variants of these non-metric features is a quite interesting, if negative, finding. It supports perhaps the consideration of the entire series of end-edged tools as a single implement group, as the data here do not suggest any kind of sub-division.

The object of this study is not only to describe the artifacts, but to try to cast some light on certain functional questions. I would now like to turn to some of these:

Do there appear to be contrasts between tools that might be axes, as against adzes, or should they be considered a single group?

What is the nature of the 'waist'? Is it a hafting device or a working edge, and is there any apparent sub-division between waisted and tanged tools?

Which of the implements are likely to have been hafted? Is there any indication of the character of the haft?

Table 6 Frequency and percentage of shape of edge on butt, by other non-metrical features

| | Shape of butt-edge | | | | | | Butt not | | | | |
| | Pointed | | Convex | | edged | | | | Total | | |
	n	%	n	%	n	%		n	%		
Waisting:											
Waisted	5	(23.8)	35	(62.5)	99	(62.3)		139	(58.9)		
Unwaisted	16	(76.2)	21	(37.5)	60	(37.7)		97	(31.1)		
Total	21	(100.0)	56	(100.0)	159	(100.0)		236	(100.0)		
Shape of end-edge:											
Pointed	1	(4.8)	0	(0.0)	9	(5.7)		10	(4.2)		
Convex	20	(95.2)	56	(100.0)	150	(94.3)		226	(95.8)		
Total	21	(100.0)	56	(100.0)	159	(100.0)		236	(100.0)		
Symmetry of bevelling:											
Symmetrical	10	(47.6)	37	(66.1)	82	(51.6)		129	(54.7)		
Asymmetrical	11	(52.4)	19	(33.9)	77	(48.4)		107	(45.3)		
Total	21	(100.0)	56	(100.0)	159	(100.0)		236	(100.0)		

Axes, adzes, or axe/adzes? The assemblages considered in this study comprise all those tools that possess working edges on their ends, the presence of the working edge being established on the basis of the presence of smoothing, chipping, and 'chattering'. I have not yet been able to study striations from use-wear, and whether there are contrasts between tools used as adzes and as axes (Semenov, 1970 : 123–25). Semenov points to the fact that axes are not nearly as common as adzes in Neolithic context, whereas the adze, although presumably an ancient tool form, is only documented as early as the Mesolithic.

The tools in these assemblages from Papua New Guinea contrast markedly in the bevelling of the end-edge, and I have considered the possible contrasts in other features between those with markedly asymmetrical bevelling to those with symmetrical bevelling. Bevelling here, as mentioned above, is taken to be the actual shape of the bevel, rather than unifacial or bifacial flaking. Although the asymmetrical bevelling is often rendered through the unifacial flaking of the edge, in some cases it is not, and since the object of the study of the feature was to attempt to relate it to asymmetrical adze bevelling, the actual shape was taken.

The use of the term axe/adze in reference to Papua New Guinea Highlands polished tools is a result of a lack of correlation between the form of hafting and function, and the fact that nearly all Highlands axe/adzes were symmetrically bevelled. In the Highlands in recent times a few relatively small stone axe/adze blades were hafted adze-fashion, that is, with the line of the cutting edge at right angles to the line of the haft handle, but most were hafted at only a slight angle to the handle, at about 10° or rarely up to about 45°. This tool was used both for adzing and for axing, although some Highlands groups also used a swivel-socket haft, rotating the blade for the two kinds of use.

There are very few recent Highlands blades with markedly asymmetrical bevelling. Although Lampert (1972 : 10) in a study of Wahgi Valley tools found more than half of his sample of 180 had asymmetrical bevelling, he included the small sharpening bevel on one face, which is common on the recent fully polished blades, together with the general bevelling

of the working edge. I excluded the sharpening bevel from earlier calculations on polished axe/adzes from the Kaironk Valley and Baiyer River (S. Bulmer, 1966 : 41–54), as the general bevelling on these tools is usually symmetrical. Excluding the short sharpening bevel, all of a sample of 75 axe/adze blades from the Kaironk Valley were symmetrically bevelled, and 447 of 466 Baiyer axe/adzes were symmetrically bevelled. I refer to bevelling as 'markedly asymmetrical' or 'symmetrical', including the asymmetrical sharpening with whichever category is relevant to the general bevelling of a tool.

Only one of the four polished axe/adzes in the Kiowa excavations, in levels dated to between 3000 and 6000 years ago, was symmetrically bevelled; the others were markedly asymmetrical. However, White (1972 : 6, 95) found no asymmetry in the bevelling on the axe/adzes at Kafiavana. These assemblages are too small to be an adequate sample, but it appears that there may be differences in bevelling on earlier axe/adzes.

Table 7 gives frequencies and percentage of the total assemblage of symmetrically and asymmetrically bevelled implements, cross-tabulated with other non-metrical features. In all, the symmetrically and asymmetrically bevelled tools share a range of other features, and do not appear to form exclusive groups of tools in any sense measured in this study.

From data presented in Table 1 above, there is a contrast apparent between the percentages of symmetrical and asymmetrical bevelling at the three sites. Yuku had 87·0% of tools symmetrically bevelled and Kosipe had 89·7% symmetrically bevelled, in contrast to the Passismanua collection which had only 45·1% symmetrically bevelled. I would offer two comments on this contrast. Firstly, the Passismanua collection may contain implements from much more recent stone-working at the same sites, so the much greater proportion of asymmetrically bevelled tools may relate to a different period of occupation.

However, I also suspect the contrast may be due to differences in available rock and its flaking quality, rather than to functional contrasts between the assemblages. The stone-workers at Yuku and Kosipe apparently did not have access

Table 7 Frequency and percentage of total assemblage of symmetrical and asymmetrical bevelling, by other non-metrical features

| | Shape of end-edge bevel | | | | | |
| | Symmetrical | | Asymmetrical | | Total | |
	n	%	n	%	n	%
Shape of end-edge:						
Pointed	2	(0.9)	8	(3.4)	10	(4.3)
Convex	127	(53.8)	99	(41.9)	226	(95.7)
Total	129	(54.7)	107	(45.3)	236	(100.0)
Presence of butt-edge:						
Butt edged	47	(19.9)	29	(12.7)	77	(32.6)
Butt not edged	82	(34.8)	77	(32.6)	159	(67.4)
Total	129	(54.7)	107	(45.3)	236	(100.0)
Waisting:						
Waisted	63	(26.7)	76	(32.2)	139	(58.9)
Unwaisted	66	(28.0)	31	(13.1)	97	(41.1)
Total	129	(54.7)	107	(45.3)	236	(100.0)

Table 8 Frequency and percentage of edge on butt by waisting on end-edged implements from Yuku, Kosipe, and Passismanua

| | Butt edged | | Butt not edged | | Total | |
	n	%	n	%	n	%
Yuku						
Waisted	6	(31.6)	13	(68.4)	19	(100.0)
Unwaisted	2	(50.0)	2	(50.0)	4	(100.0)
Total	8	(34.8)	15	(65.2)	23	(100.0)
Kosipe						
Waisted	8	(57.1)	6	(42.9)	14	(100.0)
Unwaisted	4	(26.7)	11	(73.3)	15	(100.0)
Total	12	(41.4)	17	(58.6)	29	(100.0)
Passismanua						
Waisted	26	(24.5)	80	(75.5)	106	(100.0)
Unwaisted	31	(39.7)	47	(60.3)	78	(100.0)
Total	57	(31.0)	127	(69.0)	184	(100.0)
Combined Collections						
Waisted	40	(28.8)	99	(71.2)	139	(100.0)
Unwaisted	37	(38.1)	60	(61.9)	97	(100.0)
Total	77	(32.6)	159	(67.3)	236	(100.0)

Table 9 Frequency and percentage of total assemblage of edge on butt, by other non-metric features

| | Butt edged | | Butt not edged | | Total | |
	n	%	n	%	n	%
Waisting:						
Waisted	40	(16.9)	99	(41.9)	139	(58.9)
Unwaisted	37	(15.7)	60	(25.4)	97	(41.1)
Total	77	(32.6)	159	(67.4)	236	(100.0)
Shape of end-edge:						
Pointed	1	(0.4)	9	(3.8)	10	(4.2)
Convex	76	(32.2)	150	(63.6)	226	(95.8)
Total	77	(32.6)	159	(67.4)	236	(100.0)
Symmetry of bevelling:						
Symmetrical	47	(19.9)	82	(34.8)	129	(54.7)
Asymmetrical	29	(12.7)	77	(32.6)	107	(45.3)
Total	77	(32.6)	159	(67.4)	236	(100.0)

to flint for stoneworking implements, and they used rather coarse-grained and less flakable rock available locally. They achieved a symmetrically bevelled curved end-edge on some implements by using the natural curvature of a waterworn pebble from which a very large primary flake was removed, but did not retouch this edge. It may be that the asymmetrically bevelled edge required edge-retouching which was not possible on most of the rock available.

Hand or hafted tools? Two kinds of data are presented here in order to consider whether these tools were hafted or not. Firstly, I discuss evidence for the waisting having been a hafting device, and secondly I consider the working edges on the sides and butts of the implements, and whether these are related to hafting. It is, of course, well known that waisted implements in Australia (McCarthy, 1967 : 59, Fig. 36) and in other parts of Papua New Guinea were definitely hafted in recent times for use as axes, but all of these are at least edge-ground tools, and nearly all are ground and polished in general.

Unfortunately, the character of the wear in the concave 'waist' edges on the tools is, in my opinion, ambiguous. Some of the concave waists have undercut, step-flaked edges, just like concave scrapers that lack end-edges, but others of the waists are heavily smoothed as if worn by the rubbing of a haft. I think it is the case that some waisted blades definitely have been used as concave scrapers in the waists (12 of 21 tools at Yuku, for example, have use-wear), and a small number has very heavy smoothing that I would attribute to hafting. Although being hafted does not necessarily preclude also having been used at times as a concave scraper, a minority of the tools in these assemblages does not appear to have been used at all in the concave edges. In between these definite examples are the majority of implements, the evidence for wear on which is indefinite.

There is also evidence for use wear on edges on the butts of many implements in the assemblages. Of the total of 139 waisted blades in the three collections, 40 (28·8%) have a working edge on the butt. Of the 97 unwaisted tools, 37 (38·1%) have a working edge on the butt. Table 8 gives the frequency and percentage of working edges on the butt on waisted and unwaisted implements at the three sites and for the total collection. Although the Kosipe assemblage shows a positive relationship between waisting and presence of edge on butt, this is not apparent in the other two assemblages.

It could be, of course, that waisted or unwaisted blades were hafted somewhat like the Australian 'kodj' axe (Mulvaney,

Table 10 Frequency and percentage of total combined collections of waisting, by other non-metric features

	Waisted		Unwaisted		Total	
	n	*%*	*n*	*%*	*n*	*%*
Shape of end-edge:						
Pointed	2	(0.8)	8	(3.4)	10	(4.2)
Convex	137	(58.1)	89	(37.7)	226	(95.8)
Total	139	(58.9)	97	(41.1)	236	(100.0)
Symmetry of bevelling:						
Symmetrical	63	(26.7)	66	(28.0)	129	(54.7)
Asymmetrical	76	(32.2)	31	(13.1)	107	(45.3)
Total	139	(58.9)	97	(41.1)	236	(100.0)
Edge on butt:						
Butt edged	40	(16.9)	37	(15.7)	77	(32.6)
Butt not edged	99	(42.0)	60	(25.4)	159	(67.4)
Total	139	(58.9)	97	(41.1)	236	(100.0)

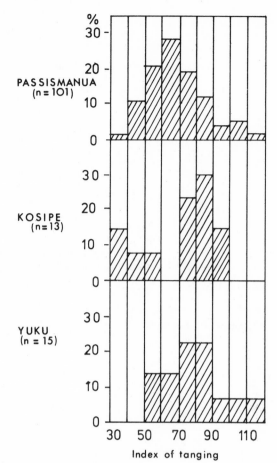

Fig. 6: Percentage frequencies of index of tanging.

1969 : 92–93), so that working edges at both ends could be used alternately. However, it is also possible that some waisted blades were only fitted with a carrying handle, with which to hold onto them in the course of arboreal hunting and collecting, rather than being hafted for use as a striking implement. On the other hand, a few of the larger waisted blades are implausibly large for hand tools, and one of the largest shows the heaviest wear in the waist which I would attribute to haft-wear. I am aware of the very large size of some palaeolithic hand axes from other parts of the world, and can only suggest that if the largest of the assemblages considered here were hand tools, they must have been used primarily on the ground, rather than in trees.

Whatever the interpretation, it appears that a markedly smaller proportion of waisted implements was provided with a working edge on the butt, than unwaisted tools. On this basis it could be argued that a certain proportion of waisted blades were probably normally hafted (or handled), without proposing that even a majority of them were.

Waisting and tanging Because there were no obvious immediate contrasts between waisted and tanged implements, these were combined in most of the calculations and cross-tabulations. However, tanged implements have a very different distribution outside Papua New Guinea than do waisted implements, so I considered further whether there was any evidence in these assemblages for sub-dividing them into waisted and tanged groups. Although this feature could also be considered one of style, I present it here on the grounds that it might also be related to different forms of hafting and/or function.

Fig. 6 shows the percentage frequencies of the index of tanging for the three sites. The index expresses the proportion of the width of the butt to the width of the rest of the tool $\left(\frac{\text{width of butt}}{\text{width of blade}} \times 100\right)$. It appears that this index ranges widely at all three sites, although the Yuku and Kosipe tools are slightly broader in general than those in the Passismanua collection. This might conceivably be related to the more careful secondary flaking on many of the Passismanua tools, which might have removed a slightly greater proportion of the butt in fashioning the tool. However, the differences here, even if significant, are not helpful in sub-dividing the implements.

The only possible separate group of implements in Fig. 6 is the four tanged tools with an index of less than 60 in the Kosipe assemblage. These four tools also fall at the thinner end of the width-thickness index range (22, 14, 12 and 23 respectively), and are all convex-ended, symmetrically bevelled tools (3 of sub-group G and 1 of sub-group H). They all come from Levels 4 and 5 at Kosipe. These are too few in number to place any confidence in the validity or reliability of the sample, but they indicate the kind of patterning that might be searched for in a larger sample or in future site assemblages.

Figs 7 and 8 record frequencies of index of tanging, sub-divided by symmetry of bevelling and shape of butt-edge. In both cases the variants show nearly normal unimodal curves of frequency, and do not exhibit differences that could be considered to be significant.

Comparisons

In this final section I will briefly discuss other waisted and tanged implements in Papua New Guinea and in the Pacific in general.

Papua New Guinea There is a variety of waisted and tanged tools in Papua New Guinea, nearly all of which are accidental finds and undated. Already mentioned in the introduction are the polished axe/adzes of New Britain and Bougainville,

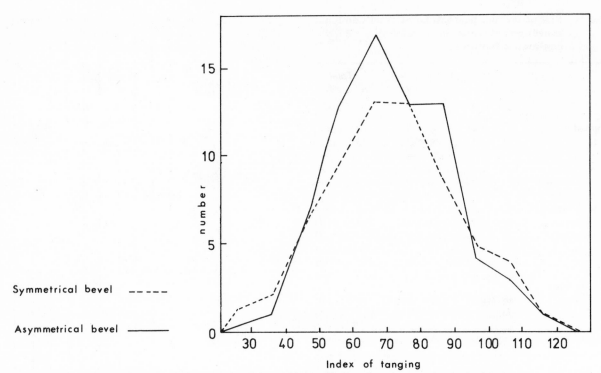

Symmetrical bevel ─ ─ ─ ─

Asymmetrical bevel ─────

Fig. 7: Frequencies of index of tanging of 135 waisted tools in combined collections, by symmetry of end-edge bevel.

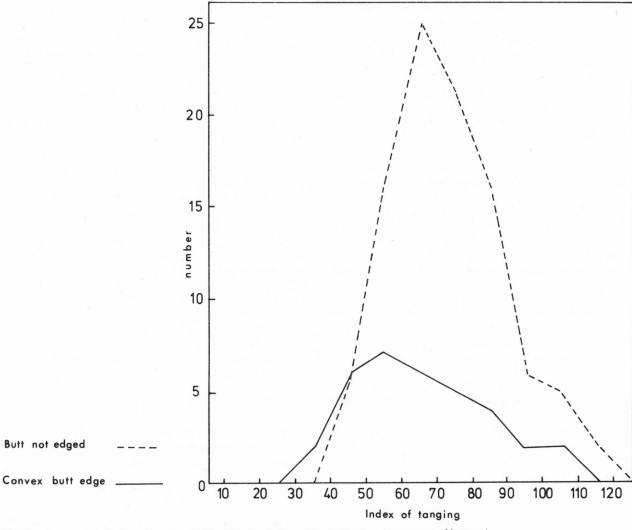

Butt not edged ─ ─ ─ ─

Convex butt edge ─────

Fig. 8: Frequencies of index of tanging of 133 waisted tools in combined collections by presence of butt-end.

(Parkinson, 1907 : Abb. 80, 81) made and used in the historic period and thought possibly to be the technological 'descendants' of the earlier flaked waisted blade. To my knowledge this is the only area where waisted and tanged tools were used in recent times, although there is a variety of scattered undated finds from many parts of the country, some of which are likely to be relatively recent. Also worth noting are the flaked implements recorded by Nash and Mitchell (1973) from southwestern Bougainville which seem very similar to the implements of the Passismanua collection.

An archaeological assemblage of tanged tools has been excavated by the author at an open habitation site, Wañlek, at about 1700 m a.s.l. in the Shrader Mountains on the northern fringe of the Highlands. Dated to between about 5500 and 3000 years ago, this site is interpreted as a settlement of agriculturists. The artifact assemblage also includes lenticular polished axe/adzes, small flaked tools, and small polished wood-carving chisels. The tanged tools are thought to be some sort of digging tool, although not necessarily used in cultivations (S. Bulmer, 1974). Another of these tanged tools was found in unstratified position in one of the swamp cultivation sites in the Wahgi Valley (Allen, 1970). These tanged tools are characterised by carefully flaked, smoothed tangs, with very wide convex or pointed end-edges. It is not possible to say whether or not these tanged tools are technologically related to earlier flaked implements in montane Papua New Guinea, as there are no waisted blades at Wañlek and no other tanged implements have yet been excavated.

Another assemblage of implements with some similarity to the end-edged tools from the early sites is the series of digging tools from Chuave. These tools are broad flaked axe/adze-like implements, lacking edge-grinding but with heavily worn and blunted end-edges in some cases. They have roughly convex or straight end-edges, but have no butt modification. On the basis of the wear on their edges, these seem likely candidates for the category of 'hoe' (Semenov, 1970 : 129), although there is no ethnographic record of the hoe, as such, in Papua New Guinea, in the sense of a cultivating tool (S. Bulmer, 1973 : 19). However, one Chuave man who sold me two of these flaked implements in 1960 said he used them for clearing grass, and there are wooden and stone implements in the Goroka Museum, Eastern Highlands Province, registered as grass-clearing tools (S. Bulmer, 1973 : Fig. 6). The Chuave tools range in length from 8·3 to 25·5 cm, with a mean of 12·0 cm, and a standard deviation of 3·0. In index of width-thickness they range from 10 to 56, with a mean of 28, and a standard deviation of 12. They are all at least half as broad as they are long.

There is a variety of other tanged implements in undated collections from Papua New Guinea. These include, for instance: the Bomai axe, from the Eastern Highlands District (Bulmer and Tomasetti, 1970), interpreted to be a replica of a bronze axe; elaborate 'winged' axes from New Britain (e.g. Casey, 1939); and tanged tools found in burial caves in the Trobriand Islands (R. Bulmer, pers. comm.). I think most of these artifacts can be interpreted as ceremonial spear heads, but their cultural context and chronological position are not known.

Pacific and eastern Asia The distribution in the western Pacific and eastern Asia of waisting, tanging, grooving, and other forms of butt modification on axe/adzes has recently been reviewed (Golson, 1972). In spite of the fact that tanged polished 'shouldered' implements are among the most distinctive of tools in the Southeast Asian 'Neolithic', the unpolished waisted and tanged tools are conspicuously absent in the earlier archaeological assemblages from Southeast Asia (Gorman, 1971, 1972; Heekeren and Knuth, 1967). There are a few tools in Hoabinhian assemblages with very slight waisting, but I do not find those at all convincing as 'waisted blades'. However, there seems to be some similarity in other of the large flaked tools in the Hoabinhian sites with those of the early Papua New Guinea assemblage. Even if the waisted tools are comparable, the fact that they are so unusual in the early Southeast Asian assemblages contrasts with their high frequency in Papua New Guinea assemblages. In more recent Southeast Asian sites, 'necked' axes are common, but there is no similar implement in the Papua New Guinea assemblages of the same general period.[1]

As far as I am aware, the Papua New Guinea assemblages contain the only waisted blades dated to the Pleistocene period. However, waisted blades are common in Japan in early post-Pleistocene contexts (Munro, 1911 : 95, Fig. 25; Kidder, 1959 : 55), and there are a number of undated finds from several regions in Eastern Asia (Golson, 1972), particularly in the upper Yangtze River area in China (Cheng, 1959 : 60). They have also been found in what appears to be relatively recent use on Botel Tobago Island (Leach, 1938).

Waisted axe/adze-like implements have been found in widely scattered localities throughout the Pacific, suggesting that they were possibly a part of the tool-kit of post-Pleistocene agricultural groups. One explanation for their absence from reports from many islands in the Pacific might be that they were often rendered in wood or bone, rather than stone. Waisted tools have been reported from Botel Tobago, near Formosa (Leach, 1938), where they were said to formerly have been hafted as adzes and used for digging the soil. A few waisted tools have been found on Easter Island (Heyerdahl, 1962 : 155, Fig. 42), where they are labelled 'digging tools', and one example was found in New Zealand (Scott, 1970 : Fig. 7b). Waisted and tanged flaked tools are common in unstratified museum collections in Southeast Asia, as are a variety of polished adzes with butt modification (Duff, 1970). These facts make the issue of the waisted blade in post-Pleistocene context very complicated; its elucidation will depend upon a great deal more archaeological research in both Melanesia and Southeast Asia.

Australia The other area where waisted tools have been found in Pleistocene context is northern Australia, where a series of assemblages was excavated, dated to over 20 000 years ago (C. White, 1967, 1971). Waisting is only a minor element in these tools; only five axes of a total of 47 have butt modification. These include one waisted, one tanged, and two grooved implements. This indicates that butt modification was not a late development in Australian axes, but was present at an early date. These northern Australian axes also differ from the montane Papua New Guinea waisted blades of the same period in the presence of grinding. Although only one example from Yuku in a pre-10 000 year old level has some grinding on it, 34 of the Australian implements are edge-ground and the rest have grinding elsewhere. They are in fact much closer to historic Australian Aboriginal axes than to their Highlands Papua New Guinea contemporaries. However,

---

1. There is a small number of unground waisted implements in the Passismanua collection that may be comparable, but they comprise a very small proportion of the total assemblage.

they are of similar size and proportions: they range in length from 7·0 to 16·5 cm, with a mean of 9·3 cm and a standard deviation of 2·2 cm. Their index of width-thickness ranges from 24 to 118, with a mean of 43 and a standard deviation of 17, making them of similar proportions particularly to the Passismanua implements.

Edge-ground axes of Pleistocene age have only so far been reported from northern Australia (Mulvaney; 1969 : 110, 112), while elsewhere in Australia the evidence so far indicates ground axes only within the past 5000 years, although they were ultimately very widespread in occurrence. Although I will not for the purposes of this paper review the substantial literature on Australian ground axes, McCarthy summarises them as follows, reporting that they range in length from about 3·8 to 48·0 cm and weigh up to 4·2 kg.

> The universal method of hafting was by bending a strip of split vine or cane, bark or wood cut from a sapling or branch, round the axe head, and sealing the joint with gum cement. In some areas a binding of twine is set in the gum. The handle is bound with twine at several points but in northeastern Queensland the cane is bound all the way down with a split cane. Axe heads were not always hafted but were sometimes used in the hand. They served as wedges, and the hafted axes were used for cutting toe holds, chopping out bees' nests and possums' nests, trenching around sheets of bark for containers and canoes, and for adzing and cutting wood. (1967 : 43)

Some of these collecting activities for which the Aborigines used the axe are similar to some of the arboreal activities described in montane Papua New Guinea.

The relationship between butt modification and the form of hafting in Australia is of direct relevance to the interpretation of the montane implements from Papua New Guinea. Even though a majority of the Australian axes have no butt modification, these features were geographically widespread and early in time, and the only haft with which they are associated is the split cane or wood haft. I think this offers an answer to Allen's comment (1972 : 185) about the waisted blade: '. . . why, with the exception of an echo in northern Australia, this implement failed to penetrate the great land to the south?'. It did not fail to, indeed, it was universal by historic times; it just was not normally waisted.

Relatively large unifacially and bifacially flaked implements found in Australia include tools that appear to be similar to the end-edged implements from montane Papua New Guinea, except that there is no sign of waisting on the flaked unground form in Australia, except on Kangaroo Island (Cooper, 1968; R. Lampert, pers. comm. 1974). It seems that we may have begun to find some clues to the connection between the late Pleistocene peoples of Papua New Guinea and Australia.

Conclusions

(1) Waisted blades are not an exclusive group on grounds of either metrical or non-metrical features as measured in this study. Rather, waisted blades share with un-waisted end-edged tools a range of functional features. However, waisted tools make up about half of the end-edged tools in the early montane Papua New Guinea assemblages.

(2) Waisting and tanging appear to form a continuum, and do not seem to contrast markedly in either metrical or non-metrical features. Waisting is a complex of features, and includes concave working edges as well as notches for hafting.

(3) The majority of waisted blades was probably used as hand implements at some time in their careers, but a minority shows no signs of use in the waists and was possibly always used hafted. A large proportion of both waisted and unwaisted tools has working edges on the butt; this suggests that most of these tools were never or only sometimes hafted, or were hafted in such a way that both ends could be used alternately.

(4) The waisted blades were most likely hafted in a split cane type of haft, but some or all of the waists could also be a device for attaching a handle, rather than a haft, for convenience in arboreal activity.

(5) Ethnographic information from the hunting and collecting among predominantly agricultural groups in recent times indicates that the early montane peoples would have needed to engage in a great deal of arboreal hunting and collecting in order to win a livelihood from the mid- and upper-montane forest. The variety of wood chopping and cutting required in this economy suggests that the waisted and unwaisted end-edged tools of the early assemblages probably constituted the primary tools of extraction for these peoples. The Australian axe is put to similar uses.

(6) Different interpretations of site function at the two early sites, Yuku and Kosipe, are not reflected in differences in the variety or range of end-edged tools. As a high-altitude seasonal collecting camp, Kosipe has as wide a range of these tools as does Yuku, a mid-mountain site of general habitation.

(7) Grinding was present on some implements at both Yuku and Kafiavana over 10 000 years ago, although it was not as common as on early northern Australian axes. However, the montane waisted blade assemblage terminated in a phase when waisted blades were completely ground, contemporary with the importation of polished axe/adzes from Highlands quarries. This suggests that the early montane tool assemblage was discontinued in the face of competition from more efficient implements of similar function—and/or of new functions such as the substantial clearance of forest for gardens.

(8) Waisted blades in association with edge-ground axe/adzes were on present evidence characteristic of Japan and the upper Yangtze in the early Holocene, and presumably in the late Pleistocene, periods, but they are not apparently characteristic of Southeast Asia. An hypothesis to explain this distribution might be that it reflects primarily the settlement of groups exploiting forest regions substantially for their arboreal, and not merely terrestrial, resources.

Acknowledgements I am very grateful to Ann Chowning, Jack Golson and Ralph Bulmer for reading and helpfully commenting on an earlier draft of this paper. I would also particularly like to thank Ronald Lampert for drawing my attention to the waisted blades that have been found on Kangaroo Island, including some unpublished examples of his own discovery. Karel Peters has redrawn the figures and graphs for publication, and I am very grateful for his assistance.

References

Allen, F. J., 1970. Prehistoric agricultural systems in the Wahgi valley—a further note. *Mankind* 7(3) : 177–83.

—— 1972. The first decade in New Guinea archaeology. *Antiquity* 46 : 180–90.

Anell, B., 1960. *Hunting and trapping methods in Australia and Oceania.* Stuia ethnographica Upsaliensia 18.

Aufenanger, H., 1965. Aus der kultur der Simbai-pygmäen im Schradergebirge Neu-Guineas. *Ethnos* 3–4 : 141–74.

Binford, S. R. and L. R. Binford, 1969. Stone tools and human behaviour. *Scientific American* 220(4) : 70–84.

Bulmer, R. N. H., 1964. Edible seeds and prehistoric stone mortars in the Highlands of East New Guinea. *Man* 64(183) : 147–50.

—— 1968. The strategies of hunting in New Guinea. *Oceania* 38(4) : 302–18.

—— 1974. Selectivity in hunting and in disposal of animal bone by the Kalam of the New Guinea Highlands. *In* Sieveking, G. de G. (ed.), *Problems in social and economic archaeology.*

—— and J. I. Menzies, 1972–3. Karam classification of marsupials and rodents. *Journal of the Polynesian Society* 81(4) : 472–99; 82(1) : 86–107.

Bulmer, S., 1964a. Prehistoric stone implements from the New Guinea Highlands. *Oceania* 34(2) : 246–68.

—— 1964b. Radiocarbon dates from New Guinea. *Journal of the Polynesian Society* 73(3) : 327–78.

—— 1966. *The prehistory of the Australian New Guinea Highlands. A discussion of archaeological field survey and excavations, 1959–1960.* Unpublished MA thesis, University of Auckland, New Zealand.

—— 1971. Early stone industries in New Guinea. Paper presented to the Far Eastern Prehistory Association, Canberra, January. Ts. 29pp.

—— 1973. *Notes on 1972 excavations at Wañlek, an open settlement site in the Kaironk Valley, Papua New Guinea.* Working paper in archaeology No. 29. Department of Anthropology, University of Auckland.

—— 1974. *Settlement and economy in prehistoric Papua New Guinea: a review of the archaeological evidence.* Working paper in archaeology No. 30. Department of Anthropology, University of Auckland.

—— and R. Bulmer, 1966. The prehistory of the Australian New Guinea Highlands. *American Anthropologist* 66(4), Part 2 : 39–76.

—— and W. E. Tomasetti, 1970. A stone replica of a bronze socketed axe from the Chimbu District of Australian New Guinea. *Records of the Papua New Guinea Museum* 1(1) : 38–41.

Casey, D. A., 1939. Some prehistoric artifacts from the Territory of New Guinea. *Victoria, National Museum, Memoirs* 11 : 143–50.

Chappell, J. M. A., 1966. Stone axe factories in the Highlands of New Guinea. *Proceedings of the Prehistoric Society* (ns) 32 : 96–121.

Cheng, T., 1957. *Archaeological studies in Szechwan.* Cambridge University Press.

Chowning, A. and J. C. Goodale, 1966. A flint industry from south-west New Britain, T.P.N.G. *Asian Perspectives* 9 : 150–3.

Cooper, H. C., 1968. A further description of large stone implements from South Australia. *Records of the South Australian Museum* 15(4) : 581–603.

Duff, R., 1970. *Stone adzes of Southeast Asia.* Canterbury Museum Bulletin No. 3, Christchurch.

Golson, J., 1968. Archaeological prospects for Melanesia. Pp. 3–14 *In* I. Yawata and Y. K. Sinoto (eds), *Prehistoric culture in Oceania.* B. P. Bishop Museum, Honolulu.

—— 1971. Both sides of the Wallace Line: Australia, New Guinea, and Asian prehistory. *Archaeology and Physical Anthropology in Oceania* 6(2) : 124–44.

—— 1972. Both sides of the Wallace Line: New Guinea, Australia, Island Melanesia and Asian prehistory. *In* N. Barnard (ed.), *Early Chinese art and its possible influence in the Pacific basin*, pp. 533–96. Intercultural Arts Press, New York.

Goodale, J. C., 1966. Imlohe and the mysteries of the Passismanua (Southwest New Britain). *Expedition* 8(3) : 20–31.

Gorman, C., 1971. The Hoabinhian and after: subsistence patterns in Southeast Asia during the late Pleistocene and early Recent periods. *World Archaeology* 2(3) : 300–320.

—— 1972. Excavations at Spirit Cave, North Thailand: some interim interpretations. *Asian Perspectives* 13(1970) : 79–108.

Groot, G. I. and Y. H. Sinoto, 1952. *The shell mound of Ubayama.* The Archaeological Institute of Japan. Konodai, Itikawa City, Japan.

Heekeren, H. R. van and E. Knuth, 1967. *Archaeological excavations in Thailand. Volume I, Saiyok.* Munksgaard, Copenhagen.

Heyerdahl, T. (ed.), 1962. *Reports of the Norwegian archaeological expedition to Easter Island and the eastern Pacific.* Allen and Unwin, London.

Hope, G. S., 1973. *The vegetation history of Mt. Wilhelm, Papua New Guinea.* PhD thesis, Australian National University, Canberra.

Hope, J. H. and G. S., 1976. Palaeoenvironments for Man in New Guinea. *In* Kirk, R. L. and A. G. Thorne (eds), *The origin of the Australians*, pp. 29–55. Australian Institute of Aboriginal Studies, Canberra.

Kidder, J. E., 1959. *Japan.* Thames and Hudson, London.

Lampert, R. J., 1972. Hagen axes. Mimeographed, 34 pp., Department of Prehistory, Australian National University, Canberra.

McCarthy, F. D., 1967. *Australian Aboriginal stone implements.* The Australian Museum, Sydney.

Metraux, A., 1940. *Ethnology of Easter Island.* B. P. Bishop Museum Bulletin Number 160, Honolulu.

Mulvaney, D. J., 1969. *The prehistory of Australia.* Thames and Hudson, London.

Munro, N. G., 1911. *Prehistoric Japan.* Yokohama.

Nash, J. and D. D. Mitchell, 1973. A note on some chipped stone objects from South Bougainville. *Journal of the Polynesian Society* 82(2) : 209–12.

Parkinson, R., 1907. *Dreissig Jahre in der südsee.* Stuttgart, Strecher und Schröder.

Powell, J. M., 1970. The history of agriculture in the New Guinea Highlands. *Search* 1(5) : 199–200.

Scott, S. D., 1970. Excavations at the 'Sunde Site', N38/24, Motutapu Island, New Zealand. *Records of the Auckland Institute and Museum*, 7 : 13–30.

Seligman, C. G. and T. A. Joyce, 1907. On prehistoric objects in British New Guinea. *In* Rivers, W. H. R. *et al.* (eds), *Anthropological essays presented to Edward Burnett Tylor*, pp. 325–41. Clarendon Press, Oxford.

Semenov, S. A., 1970. *Prehistoric technology.* Adams and Dart, Bath.

Shutler, R. Jnr. and C. A. Kess, 1969. A lithic industry from New Britain, Territory of New Guinea, with possible areal and chronological relationships. *Bulletin of the Institute of Ethnology, Academia Sinica* 27 : 129–40.

Tweedie, M. W. F., 1957. *Prehistoric Malaya.* Background to Malaya series, Number 6, Donald Moore, Singapore.

Vicedom, G. F. and H. Tischner, 1943–48. *Die Mbowamb: die kultur der Hagenberg stämme in Östlichen Zentral-Neuguinea.* 3 volumes. Hamburg, de Gruyter.

White, J. P., 1969. Typologies for some prehistoric flaked stone artefacts of the Australian New Guinea Highlands. *Archaeology and Physical Anthropology in Oceania* 4 : 18–46.

—— 1972. *Ol tumbuna.* Terra Australis 2. Department of Prehistory, Australian National University, Canberra.

——, K. A. W. Crook and B. P. Buxton, 1970. Kosipe: a late Pleistocene site in the Papuan Highlands. *Proceedings of the Prehistoric Society* (ns) 36 : 142–70.

White, C., 1967. *Plateau and plain: prehistoric investigations in Arnhem Land, Northern Territory.* PhD thesis, Australian National University, Canberra.

—— 1971. Man and environment in Northwest Arnhem Land. *In* Mulvaney, D. J. and J. Golson (eds), *Aboriginal Man and environment in Australia*, pp. 141–157. Australian National University Press, Canberra.

The four dimensions of artifactual variation

J. K. CLEGG

What causes variation in artifacts?[1]

1. *Personality of artisan.* If different people are given the same task, under similar physical conditions and using similar materials, results of their activities are distinguishable. One artifact is neat and tidy but may not work; another is poorly made, but of some use; a third is very good all-round. Think of the variation between essays written by various students, essays all on the same topic, and using the same bibliography.

2. The *medium*—the materials used, and the techniques which manipulated them. A plastic-handled nail-brush is different from a wooden-handle one, as a result of the materials in use; yet there are also differences which are not simply differences of material, as would be demonstrated if an accurate plaster cast were made of each; the wooden handle has a form different from the plastic one.

3. *Function* A wooden-handled wire brush is different from a wooden-handled iron frypan even if they are both made by the same person using similar materials and methods—because one is for cleaning paintwork, the other is for frying bacon.

4. *Culture.* Chinese, I believe, use plastic chopsticks for eating with; Americans use plastic forks. They may both be eating the local fried chicken or chop suey, they may both have very similar personalities, yet the artifacts in question are different though made by the same means from the same material, and for the same function.

We have four things which influence the production of variant artifacts. These four things are not necessarily independent, as personality is of course partly a function of culture, and vice-versa. All four are probably interlinked.

Neither are the four things unities; they are galaxies of causes, they are dimensions. Within the dimension culture, there are many cultures, as there are many mediums, personalities and functions.

So far I have presented a simple model which contains information that I imagine most of my readers have known since the year dot. I put it forward as an aid to the work of archaeologists. How may it be used to help that work?

If we want to know which of our students is the most capable, we subject them all to the same environment, then give them all the same test, and some of us believe that the results of marking that test convey information about the relative capacities of the students. But if we were to subject student Bloggs to a driving course in Winnipeg taught for three years by a megalomanic dwarf, then test Bloggs in his ability to weld aluminium, how revealing would the results of that test be when compared with the test of Smith, who has had a two-week typing course in Katmandu, which is tested by asking Smith to cook a hamburger? I think we would be mad if we were to assert that the results of those examinations tell us about the relative capacities of Bloggs and Smith to ride an elephant.

If we want to know about cultural differences, we should look at artifacts made in the same medium, for the same function, by people of the same personality, but from *different* cultures, thus examining the effects of one variable at a time. Similarly if we want to know about functional differences (some might call them adaptive) we need similar materials, similar personalities, similar cultures—and the differences we get tell us something about function. A 1974 Australian metal car made by a machine is different from a 1974 Australian machine-made metal stove because one is a car, the other a stove. If three of the dimensions are controlled, the variation can be assigned to the fourth.

How can the dimension be controlled in archaeology? Culture could be controlled by the assumption that people living in one place at one time are of the same culture.

Medium can be at least partly controlled because the material of the artifact is known (or may be ascertained) if the artifact is extant, and an analysis of its surface tells us a certain amount about how it was made.

Function can be partially controlled, at least sometimes, by direct assumption (food remains are the remains of food), sometimes by association and guesswork (a barbed hook often found with fish remains and never with remains far from any source of fish just might be a fish-hook).

Personality would be difficult to control, but may be treated as 'noise'—assumed to cancel itself out—if the sample is large enough.

Perhaps I can illustrate the use of this model by showing how a rather pedestrian site report can be made to yield extra information of archaeological interest.

The site report I have chosen to use as an example was written by me in 1964, and circulated to Australian archaeologists. It refers to the stone material excavated from various spits of 'layers' in two trenches in Cathedral Cave, Carnarvon Gorge, Queensland.

The relevant statistics are shown on Table 1.

Page 6 of the report says:

From a glance at Table 1, it would appear that there are distinctions to be made between the artifacts from three groups of layers.

---

1. This model was developed from Fine Arts theory, and expounded, in a paper entitled 'A method of resolving problems which arise from style in art' (Clegg, in press).

Table 1   Cathedral Cave artifact frequencies

Spits	1A	1B	1	2	3	3	4	5	5C	5D	5–8	6	7	7	8	8	9	9	10	10	11	11	12	12
Ground axe fragments	2																							
Cores		2			3		2			1	3		2											
Elouera				1								1												
S Side	2	4	2	2	9		4	1		1			1		1		1		3					
C Side and end		2	1		2								1											
R 2 sides	3		1	1			1																	
A 2 sides and end		1	2																					
P Discoid			1		1																			
E Distal end	3	3	1	4	9		2						2				2				1			
R Butt-end					1												2		1					
S Double end			1																					
Concave side	1		1	1	1																			
Burins A S Normal tulas	3	1			2						2				1									
D L Double tulas	3	1			2																			
Z U Butt-end tulas	2		2		2																			
E G S Tula-burins			2																					
Microliths									1			2	4	2	2	2	1		1		1			
Ochre	present in every spit																							
Scratched ochre					1		2			1		1	1		1				1		1			
Hammer stones	9	3	2		1		2		2	2		1											1	
Miscellaneous retouch				1	2					1		1	3				1							
Complete waste flakes	210	252	225	84	549	107	80	16	5	148	?	72	29	119	65	22	22	40	68	40	66	13	16	6

Table 2 Occurrence of vertebrate species in holes 1 and 2, Cathedral Cave excavations

Determinations	Layers Hole 1																			Layers Hole 2									
	1A	1B	2A	2B	3	3B+	3C	4	5	5A	5C	5D	6	7B	8	9	10	11	12	1	2B	3	4	7	8	9	10	11	12
Mammalia																													
Rodentia																													
Muridae																													
Indet. rodent fragments					r																								
Carnirora																													
Canidae																													
Canis familiaris dingo				r	r																								
Marsupialia																													
Dasyuridae																													
Satanellus halluctus																													
Peramelidae																													
Isoodon macrourus	r			r	r																			r					
Indet. peramelid fragments		r		r	r											r		r						r					
Phascolomidae																													
Indet. phascolomid fragments																										r			
Phalangeridae																													
Trichosurus vulpecula		r		r	c	r		r						r	r	r	r		r								r		
Pseudocheirus peregrinus					r													r											
Indet. phalangerid fragments												r																	
Macropodidae																													
Potorous tridactylus		r		r	r									r								r	r	r					
Bettongia sp.	r			r	r																r								
Aepyprymnus rufescens												r															r		
Petrogale penicillata	a	r		c	a	a		a	a	c	r	c		r	r	r	r		r	c		c	r	a	a	r	r	r	
Macropus parryi	r			r	r				r		r																		
Macropus robustus																													
Reptilia																													
Squamata																													
Indet. ophidian fragments	r													r								r		r					
Amphibolurus c.f. *A. barbatus*		r		r	r																		r	r					
Tiliqua sp.																	r										r		
Varanus sp.	r																r						r				r		
Indet. lacertilian fragments	r																			r					r		r		
Chelonia																													
Indet. chelonian fragments	c					r		r	r				r						r	r					r				r
Osteichthyes																													
Teleostei																													
Plotosidae																													
Tandanus tandanus	r																												
Indet. teleost fragments	c	r			r			r	r					r					r			r	r						r

r = rare (1–4)   c = common (5–9)   a = abundant (10+)

Layers 1-5, where tula slugs, ground axe fragments, and many scrapers occur, but microliths are absent.

Layers 5C-7, characterised by microliths, but few scrapers, and no tulas.

Layers 7 (hole 2)-12, where a tula slug, ground axe fragments, and scrapers are found with the microliths.

I found this tripartite division interesting, but unconvincing, based as it was on small numbers of implements. There was, however, more information available, in the form of measurements made on complete flakes. The length/breadth ratio of all the complete flakes from each layer-group was measured, and the mean calculated and expressed as the proportion of breadth to a unit length of 10. (Clegg, 1964:10):

Layers	1-5C	5D-6	7-12
Mean ratio	10:0.679	10:7.839	10:8.690
Total numbers	1548	274	475

These results were taken to indicate that the divisions postulated from the implements were valid. Sullivan (1973:5.6) conducted some less naïve statistical tests on the figures from Cathedral Cave L:B ratios, and confirmed that there are differences as Clegg thought.

The report speculates on the significance of the changes between layer-groups, suggesting changes in diet or environment on the one hand, or changes in the tradition of implement manufacture on the other, as possible causes. There was no means then available to me to go beyond the stage of speculation.

Page 15 of the report says:

I looked also for a change in the raw material used for the flakes. This search was also unrewarded, it being clear that Billy (Quartzite) was the preferred material throughout, and that any other suitable raw material found in the stream bed was used occasionally.

This is here interpreted as indicating that there are no significant differences in material. If that assumption is made, then we may take material to be homogeneous throughout the site. Personality, also, we assume to be homogeneous.

Since the report was written, Alan Bartholomai has kindly provided a description of the fauna from the excavation, which is shown on Table 2.

Tables 1 and 2 contain the data which will be used with the model in an attempt to discover the significance of the changes.

It is possible that there is some sort of functional connection between stone tools and bone remains—a fairly indirect connection through economics. Such connections should be reflected in a fairly high or low correlation between stone and bone types, whereas the types which do not relate strongly to anything else must be (we assume) more culturally than economically conditioned. So we look for close relationships between stone and bone types.

So far we have been looking at the Tables in order to compare spits, and we have made this comparison in terms of which objects are found in each spit. But we could equally well compare the various sorts of bone and stone with each other, using for the comparison which spits they occur in. The simplest way of doing this, is to count the number of times the objects occur in the same spit, and the number of times they fail to occur in the same spit. This simple technique is described and discussed in Sokal and Sneath (1963), and the results of the comparison are shown in the matrix of Table 3.

A little explanation is necessary.

Whole flakes occur in most spits. The average is 75.1 per spit. Whole flakes were counted when more than 75.1 of them occurred in a spit.

Total implements were counted when more than 6.6 of them occurred in a spit.

$\dfrac{Implements \times 10}{Whole\ flakes}$ was counted when the index was greater than 0.88.

Bone total was calculated by counting r as 1, c as 2, a as 3, adding them for each spit. More than 4.2 counted as bone total present.

$\dfrac{Bone \times 10}{Stone}$ was counted present when there were more than .074 bones for each stone in the spit.

High *negative* correlations between two tool types would suggest that one type was replacing the other, but only if there is no change in economics, for which, in this case we only have the bone information.

High *positive* correlations between tool types would suggest that they are both part of the same culture, possibly because their functions are inter-linked, like, shall we say, bottles of ink and blotting-paper, or road maps and sparking plugs.

Sokal and Sneath discuss various ways of measuring association (1963:123 ff.). No attempt has been made here to choose the most suitable, only the easiest to manipulate.[2] For each pair of categories, the number of matching occurrences was observed and is shown to the top right of the diagonal line.

In the diagonal line are the numbers of positive occurrences. Below and to the left of the diagonal is the coefficient of resemblance, which was derived as follows:

a is the total number of spits—in this case, 30.

x is the number of positive occurrences for one attribute.

y is the number for the other attribute. x is less than or equal to y.

Then the maximum possible score is a+(x−y).

The minimum possible score is a−(x+y).

o is the observed number of matching occurrences.

The coefficient of resemblance is

$$\frac{o-min.}{max.} \quad i.e. \quad \frac{o-a+x+y}{a+x-y}$$

giving a possible variation between 1 and 0.

A coefficient of 0 shows a high, but negative relation, and the least related are those nearest 0.5

The coefficient of resemblance makes all the numbers comparable; they are all on a scale from 0-1. The device of making them comparable seemed necessary, because the number of matching occurrences—the raw numbers to the top and right of the diagonal—are necessarily high if both rows being compared have a high or low number of positive occurrences. Similarly the raw numbers are low if there is great discrepancy.

The upper left square compares stone/stone, lower right compares bone/bone, lower left bone/stone.

So, to find out which stone types are most closely related to

---

2. McBurney (1968, 1971, 1973 and 1974 in press) has been developing relevant and more sophisticated techniques.

Table 3 Matrix comparing occurrences of stones and bones in Cathedral Cave

	ground axe frags	cores	side	side and end	double side	double side and end	discoidal	Distal end	Butt end	Concave side	Tula, normal	Double tula	butt Tula	microliths	scratched ochres	hammerstone	miscellaneous retouch	whole flakes	total implements	imps/w. flakes, X10	Isoodon	Peramelidae frags	T. vulpecula	P. peregrinus	Indeterminate	Potorous	Bettongia	Petrogale	Wallaby	M. Robustus	Lacertilian	Chelonia	Teleostei	total bone	bone/stone
ground axe frags	**5**	17	18	23	23	24	24	23	24	25	23	27	24	16	22	22	21	22	23	16	23	23	21	23	22	27	23	12	20	24	22	19	21	19	19
cores	0	**8**	19	24	22	23	23	22	21	20	18	20	21	19	17	23	20	23	22	18	22	20	18	25	21	20	20	11	19	21	19	22	18	18	16
side	·8	·75	**15**	19	19	18	18	25	18	19	21	19	18	14	16	18	23	24	25	21	19	21	17	18	16	17	17	18	14	18	16	17	16	21	12
side and end	·25	·75	1	**4**	24	27	27	24	25	24	24	26	25	17	19	23	22	25	24	16	26	24	22	29	23	26	24	1·	23	27	23	22	24	22	20
double side	·25	·5	1	·25	**4**	25	25	24	23	28	22	24	29	15	19	23	22	25	24	20	26	22	24	25	23	22	26	11	19	23	21	22	20	22	18
double side and end	·33	·67	1	·67	·33	**3**	26	23	24	25	23	25	26	18	20	22	19	22	21	17	23	23	21	26	24	25	23	8	20	26	22	21	21	19	19
discoidal	·33	·67	1	·67	·33	·33	**3**	23	26	27	23	27	26	16	22	26	21	24	23	17	25	21	21	28	24	23	25	10	22	26	20	19	21	19	19
Distal end	·8	·63	1	1	1	1	1	**10**	21	24	20	24	23	13	17	21	26	27	28	20	24	26	22	23	17	22	25	15	17	21	19	20	20	22	14
Butt end	·33	·33	1	·33	0	0	·33	·67	**3**	23	23	25	24	18	24	24	19	20	21	17	25	23	21	26	26	25	25	10	22	26	22	17	21	19	19
Concave side	·5	·25	1	25	·75	·33	·17	1	0	**4**	22	26	29	15	21	22	25	24	19	26	22	22	25	23	22	24	11	19	23	21	20	20	20	18
Tula, normal	·4	·17	1	·5	·25	·37	·33	·5	·33	·25	**6**	26	23	15	18	21	19	21	20	16	24	22	22	23	21	22	24	12	21	27	21	20	24	24	18
Double tula	·75	·25	1	·5	·25	·33	·67	1	·33	·5	·75	**4**	25	15	22	25	22	25	24	18	26	24	24	25	23	24	26	11	21	27	23	20	24	22	18
butt Tula	·30	·0	1	·33	1	·38	·33	1	0	1	·33	·33	**3**	16	20	22	21	24	23	19	26	23	23	26	24	23	27	10	20	24	22	21	21	21	19
microliths	·20	·5	·45	·25	0	·33	0	·20	·33	0	·16	0	0	**11**	22	18	13	14	13	21	17	17	13	18	22	19	15	18	22	16	16	15	15	13	21
scratched ochres	·4	·14	·43	0	0	0	·33	·29	·67	·25	·08	·37	0	·71	**7**	22	19	18	19	21	19	19	17	20	26	21	19	12	20	20	18	17	17	15	19
hammerstone	·20	0	·8	·25	·25	0	·67	·6	·13	·20	·5	0	·40	·40	**5**	23	24	23	21	23	19	21	24	24	21	23	12	20	20	18	17	19	19	19
miscellaneous retouch	·33	·62	·83	1	1	·67	1	·90	·67	1	·58	1	1	·27	·57	·80	**12**	27	28	18	22	22	22	21	19	20	20	17	15	19	19	22	20	20	14
whole flakes	·60	·62	1	1	1	·67	1	·89	·33	1	·5	1	1	·22	·23	·80	1	**9**	29	21	25	23	23	24	20	21	23	16	19	22	20	21	21	23	15
total implements	·80	·2	1	1	1	·67	1	·90	·67	1	·5	1	1	·20	·43	·80	1	1	**10**	20	24	24	22	23	19	22	22	13	17	21	19	20	20	22	14
imps/w. flakes, X10	·30	·5	·75	·25	·75	·33	·33	·60	·33	·62	·33	·5	·67	·64	·71	·80	·22	·66	·60	**12**	20	20	16	17	19	16	18	15	17	15	17	16	16	20	20
Isoodon fags	·25	·5	1	·5	·5	0	·33	1	·33	·5	·5	·5	·5	·25	0	·25	1	1	1	·75	**4**	26	24	27	23	24	28	11	23	25	23	20	24	24	20
Peramelidae	·60	·37	·87	·75	·5	·67	·33	·87	·67	·5	·75	·67	·37	·29	·20	·75	·62	·75	·62	1	**8**	22	23	19	24	24	13	21	23	21	18	24	22	18
T. vulpecula	·40	·25	·63	·5	·75	·33	·33	·63	·33	·5	·5	·75	·67	·13	·14	·40	·75	·62	·62	·37	·75	·5	**8**	21	21	20	24	13	19	23	19	22	20	24	14
P. peregrinus	·17	1	1	1	·33	·33	·67	1	·33	·33	·33	·33	·33	0	·33	1	1	1	·33	·67	·67	·33	**3**	24	25	25	10	24	26	22	21	23	21	21
Indeterminate	0	·33	·67	0	0	0	0	0	·33	0	0	0	0	1	1	·33	·67	·33	·33	·67	0	0	·33	0	**3**	23	23	8	20	24	22	19	19	17	19
Potorous	·75	·25	·25	·5	0	·33	0	·75	·33	0	·25	·25	0	·5	·25	0	·75	·25	·75	·25	·25	·75	·25	·33	0	**4**	22	11	23	25	23	20	22	22	22
Bettongia	·25	·25	·75	·25	·5	0	·33	·75	·33	·25	·5	·5	·67	0	0	·25	·75	·75	·75	·5	·75	·75	·75	·33	0	0	**4**	11	22	25	21	18	22	22	18
Petrogale	1	·71	·71	1	1	·67	1	·5	1	1	·92	1	1	1	·85	1	·85	1	·71	·71	1	·86	·86	1	·67	1	1	**23**	14	10	12	15	13	15	11
Wallaby	·20	·28	·43	·5	0	0	·33	·5	·33	0	·33	·25	0	·71	·28	·20	·28	·36	·29	·43	·5	·43	·28	·67	0	·5	·37	1	**7**	22	18	17	21	19	23
M. Robustus	·33	·33	1	·67	0	·33	·33	·67	·33	0	1	·67	0	0	·33	·67	·67	·67	0	·33	·33	1	·33	1	·33	·33	1	·33	3	**3**	22	21	25	23	19
Lacertilian	·40	·28	·57	·5	·25	·33	0	·43	·33	·25	·33	·5	·33	·28	·14	0	·57	·42	·43	·43	·5	·43	·29	·33	·33	·5	·25	·86	·14	·33	**7**	23	25	19	21
Chelonia	·40	·63	·60	·75	·75	·67	·33	·5	0	·5	·5	·5	·67	·30	·29	·20	·7	·56	·5	·40	·5	·38	·63	·1	·33	·5	·25	·86	·29	·67	·71	**10**	22	24	18
Teleostei	·40	·25	·56	·75	·25	·33	·33	·5	·33	·25	·67	·75	·33	·25	·14	·20	·63	·5	·5	·37	·75	·63	·38	·67	0	·5	·5	·86	·43	1	·71	·63	**8**	22	22
total bone	·40	·38	·80	·75	·5	0	·33	·60	·33	·5	·83	·75	·67	·20	·14	·40	·60	·67	·60	·60	1	·62	·75	·67	0	·5	·75	·86	·43	1	·43	·70	·62	**10**	18
bone/stone	·20	·13	·31	·25	0	0	·13	0	0	·63	·29	·25	·25	·25	·20	0	·12	·12	·62	·25	·25	0	·33	0	·5	0	·71	·57	0	·13	·37	·5	·37	**8**

Note: To the right of the diagonal the figures are the number of matches that is the number of spits which have both or neither of the attributes being compared. If only one attribute is present in a spit a match is not counted. The bold figures on the diagonal are the number of spits which contain one or more occurrences of the attribute in question. To the left of the diagonal the figures represent the coefficient of resemblance (see p. 63).

Table 4 'Mainly cultural' artifacts as distributed in spits

Layer	1a	1b	1	2	3	3	4	5	5c	5d	5–8	6	7	7	8	8	9	9	10	10	11	11	12	12
Hole	1	1	2	1	1	2	1	2	1	1	1	1	1	2	1	2	1	2	1	2	1	2	1	2
Tulas	•							•							•									
Whole flakes	•	•	•	•	•	•	•			•			•											
Implements	•	•	•	•	•	•	•			•			•	•										
Distal end scrapers	•	•	•	•	•	•							•	•			•				•			
Implements/waste flakes	•					•	•	•		•		•	•			•			•		•			
Cores	•		•			•	•			•	•		•								•			

Table 5 'Mainly functional' artifacts as distributed in spits

Layer	1a	1b	1	2	3	3	4	5	5c	5d	5–8	6	7	7	8	8	9	9	10	10	11	11	12	12
Hole	1	1	2	1	1	2	1	2	1	1	1	1	1	2	1	2	1	2	1	2	1	2	1	2
Butt tulas	•	•																						
Double side scrapers	•	•	•	•																				
Double side and end scrapers		•	•																					
Discoidal scrapers				•	•	•	•																	
Hammer stones					•	•	•		•	•		•	•	•	•	•	•	•	•		•			
Scratched ochre										•	•	•	•	•	•	•	•		•					
Microliths									•	•									•		•			

bones, and which are least related to bones, we must add the deviation from 0.5 of each of the columns in the lower left rectangle of the matrix, excluding the bottom row, which contains information about both bone and stone material.

The stones with the highest totals are most closely related to the bones, these with the lowest totals are least closely related to bones. In this paper it is assumed that those stones which are most closely related to the bones have the highest content of function in their distribution.

The totals are set out below:

Implement	Score	Order	Diagnosis
ground axe fragment	3.15	12	
cores	2.87	15	C
side scrapers	3.48	9	
side and end scrapers	2.92	14	C
double side Ss	3.67	7	F
double side and end Ss	4.03	2	F
discoidal Ss	3.7	6	F
distal end Ss	2.74	17	C
butt end Ss	3.04	13	
concave side Ss	3.42	10	
tula, normal	2.68	18	C
double tula	3.59	8	
butt tula	3.88	5	F
microliths	4.1	3	F
scratched ochre	5.18	1	F
hammerstones	3.9	4	F
misc. retouch	3.4	11	
whole flakes	2.78	16	C
total implements	1.36	20	C
imps/w. flakes, $\times$ 10	1.88	19	C

We are now in a position to ask again our original question: What happened at Cathedral Cave? Was there a cultural change, or a functional one, or some combination?

On Table 4, the occurrence of 'mainly cultural' stone artifacts is plotted against the spits.

On Table 5, the stones whose distribution related most closely to function are plotted against the sequence.

From Table 4, it appears that there was a gradual change in culture throughout the sequence.

Table 5, indicates a stable period up to layer 5, followed by a fairly rapid functional change.

What had been thought of as a 3-stage sequence is now revealed as a gradual change in culture throughout, combined with a late but relatively rapid change in function.

Could this insight have been achieved without going through the arithmetic rigmarole in which I have been indulging? Presumably the functional business could have been discovered through a detailed analysis of Table 2, but the stone material would still be the result of both cultural and functional vectors, and would fail to show the cultural situation as clearly as does Table 3.

Note: This example has been worked to show the advantages of using the model. To keep this aim clear, the arithmetic has been of the simplest sort, and there has been no discussion of significance or reliability limits. For this reason (and others— see Clegg, 1964) it should not be taken as indicating my belief in rigid conclusions about what occurred in Cathedral Cave in prehistoric times. But the conclusions reached in this paper could be used as hypotheses to be tested through further excavation at the site, which is very large and probably 95% undisturbed.

References

Clegg, J.K., 1965. *A preliminary report on the stone artifacts from Cathedral Cave*. Department of Psychology, University of Queensland.
——(in press) A method resolving problems which arise from style in art. *In* P. J. Ucko (ed.) *Form in indigenous art: schematisation in the art of Australia and prehistoric Europe*. Canberra: Australian Institute of Aboriginal Studies.
McBurney, C.B.M., 1968. The cave of Ali Tappeh and the Epi-Palaeolithic of N.E. Iran. *Proceedings of the Prehistoric Society*, 34:368-84.
—— 1971. The Cambridge excavation at la Cotte de St. Bre-

lade, Jersey—A preliminary report. *Proceedings of the Prehistoric Society*, 37:167-207.
—— 1973. Measurable long term variations in some old stone age sequences. pp. 305-17. *In* C. Renfrew (ed.) *The explanation of culture change; models in prehistory*. London: Duckworth.
—— (in press) *Proceedings of the Prehistoric Society*.
Sokal, R.R. *and* P.H.A. Sneath., 1965. *Principles of numerical taxonomy*. San Francisco and London: W.H. Freeman.
Sullivan, K.M., 1973. *The archaeology of Mangat*. B.A. (Hons) thesis, Department of Anthropology, University of Sydney.

Green timber and Polynesian adzes and axes

An experimental approach

P. J. F. COUTTS

Introduction

Pacific and Australian archaeologists are frequently confronted with the problem of examining adze and axe-like stone artifacts. The usual procedure is to designate them axes or adzes and then classify them according to some well established schema (e.g. Duff, 1970; McCarthy, 1967). While this procedure may be useful for purposes of description and determining the chronological associations of these tools it does not elucidate their functional aspects. Indeed there is a serious void in the published literature on the subject of axe and adze functions. Discussions are largely speculative, centring on questions of how they were manufactured and hafted. Clearly, such questions are important, but others no less; why were the tools discarded, how efficient were they, what materials were they used on, how were they used, and for what purpose?

It is commonly accepted that adzes and axes were used primarily on timber, though timber remains are normally rare in archaeological contents. However, they later occur quite frequently in ethnographic collections and, like adze/axe studies, when published data are available, the technological details are normally absent and at best speculative. Besides a detailed description of wooden artifacts (including the types of timber used), and their probable functions, it seems logical to try and discover the types of tools used to produce them, what materials the tools were made from, their method of manufacture, why particular timbers were chosen and whether they were green or dry at the time of manufacture.

The object of the present paper is to describe various exploratory techniques which may help to diminish speculation in these areas and to test some widely accepted assumptions linked with the topics of adze-functions and timber technology. Six archaeological sites situated in the neighbourhood of Southport, a small harbour inside Chalky Inlet, Fiordland, New Zealand and which had both prehistoric and European/Maori contact occupation horizons, yielded an unusual variety of well preserved organic materials including thousands of wood-chips, finished, semi-finished and broken wooden artifacts as well as broken and discarded stone tools (Coutts, 1972). These data afford a unique opportunity for studying adze function and timber technology in juxtaposition and are discussed in this paper.

Materials and methods

The presence of wood working industries at the specified sites raised a number of questions which invited investigations. What varieties of timbers were used and were they obtained locally? Were there specific wood working areas at the sites? What sort of tools were used and were they stone and/or steel, axes and/or adzes? How many tools were used and what were their characteristics? What sort of artifacts were being manufactured? Unfortunately, there were few relevant studies available for consultation (see McEwan, 1946; Knapp, 1928; Semenov, 1964; Keller, 1966; Sonnenfeld, 1962; Jorgensen, 1953; Gould *et al.*, 1971; Moir, 1926) and an appropriate research strategy was adopted to explore these problems.

The wood working areas at the various sites were located from wood-weight contour plots and the two timbers most frequently used were identified as rimu (*Dacrydium cupressinum*) and totara (*Podocarpus totara*).

Questions of wood technology were investigated by examining the morphological characteristics of wood chips freshly cut with newly hafted prehistoric and more recent adzes under controlled conditions. Fourteen adzes of various types and materials (Table 1) including four steel adzes, one piece of hoop iron, and one serpentine adze specially manufactured for this study were hafted and used to cut batches of green totara and rimu wood chips. The hafts were made from manuka (*Leptospermum scoparium*) branches specially chosen to suit each adze and the home-made adze was completely ground and polished and given the sharpest edge possible. The working edges of all the adzes were photographed through a microscope before and after use and one of the fourteen sets of photographs is reproduced here (Figs. 1 and 2). Green timber was chosen after it was found that stone tools would not cut dry or semi-dry totara or rimu. Each tool was used for approximately two hours and the wood chips were not cut until some expertise had been developed in handling the adzes. At the outset it must be recognised that this approach has at least two weaknesses, in that qualified assumptions have been made about the hafting methods and modes of use (see Sonnenfeld, 1962 : 59).

A random selection of wood chips cut by each adze was measured and described. Measurements included the mean lengths, breadths, lengths of adze cuts and thicknesses at the points of maximum adze penetration. The penetration or impact angle of the adze was calculated by utilising the approximate relationships:

$$D = O \times P \text{ (arc = radius} \times \text{penetration angle)}$$

where D = the thickness of wood chip at the point of maximum penetration

O = penetration or impact angle

P = length of cut.

The shapes of the struck ends of the wood chips were described as random, square or asymmetrical and the numbers of wood chips exhibiting tool marks were counted. Tests on the continuous data showed them to be significantly skewed but

Table 1 Details of steel and stone adzes used in the woodchip experiments.
Comparisons of cutting edge angles predicted from woodchip measurements and the actual cutting edge angles

Tool No.	Type after Duff, 1956	Material	Otago Museum catalogue no.	Weight (gm)	Working	Cutting edge angle	Predicted cutting edge angle	Thickness at chin (cm)	Max. thickness (cm)	Max. length (cm)	Shape of cutting edge	State of edge	Width of cutting edge (cm)
1	1?	Serpentine	Home made	600	CP	60	61	2.1	2.2	23.6		Good	6.0
2	1?	Quartzite?	D62.302	940	SP and HD	78	68	3.2	4.4	20.6		F. sharp and s. damaged	6.5
3	2?	Bowenite	D40.128	148	CP and sawn	69	74	1.5	1.9	12.3		Blunt and damaged	3.6
4	1?	Argillite	D25.495	99	SP and HD	70	76	1.7	1.8	9.4		F. sharp s. damaged	3.3
5		Steel	D29.800	135*		40	71	0.3	0.5	?		F. sharp damaged	4.4
6		Steel	D24.778	250*		18	26	4.3		?		V. sharp s. damaged	6.1
7	2A	Rodingite	D18.294	36	CP	48	87	0.6	0.8	6.7		Sharp damaged	3.1
8	2?	Riverton argillite	D25.2253	246	SP and HD	72	43	2.5	2.6	14.9		F. sharp s. damaged	2.1
9	1?	Nephrite or rodingite	D40.30	970*	CP and sawn	65	61	2.3	2.7	27.7		F. sharp s. damaged	7.0
10		Modern adze		760*		40	38	3.2				F. sharp	8.0
11		Modern adze		760*		43	44	2.5				F. sharp	4.2
12		Hoop iron		126*		35	41	3.5				F. sharp damaged	3.9
13	2B	?	D41.35	365	SP and HD	85	64	2.6	3.0	13.3		F. sharp s. damaged	5.5
14	4A	Argillite?	D52.719	1760	MP and HD	82	59	6.9	6.9	29.0		F. sharp s. damaged	2.2

A = shape of cutting edge looking down on adze. B = shape looking into cutting edge at eye level.

* estimated weight.   SP = semi-polished.   MP = mostly polished.   CP = completely polished.   HD = hammer dressed.   F = fairly.   s = slightly.   V = very.

Table 2 Concise summary of results of the D² analysis.
Layers with reasonable numbers of woodchips in one or more squares

Site	SP/1	SP/5 1A				SP/9	SP/10			SP/11			CH/1
Layer	2	Spoil	2+	4+	2-	2-	2	4	5	3	4	6	2B
Adze No.													
4	•	•	•	•	•		•	•	•	•	•	•	•
6	•	•	•			•	•	•		•	•	•	
7		•	•	•	•	•	•	•	•	•		•	•
10						•						•	
11	•		•			•	•				•	•	
12	•	•	•	•	•	•	•	•	•	•	•	•	

this situation was rectified by fitting the data to log-normal distributions.

The mean values of the log-transformed variable were correlated with the non-transformed adze data. The analysis resulted in statistically significant correlations[1] between the widths of the cutting edges of the adzes and the mean widths of the wood chips (t = 2.731) as well as the cutting edge angles of the adzes (A) and the mean impact/penetration angles of the wood chips (t = 2.959). Partial correlation analysis indicated that an important relationship existed between the cutting edge angle (A) and the mean lengths of the cut (P) of the form.

$$A = 86.8 - 105.8 \, \text{Log} \, P$$

where the multiple correlation coefficient is

$$0.74 \, (t = 3.89 \text{ and } Z_{0.955} = 3.25)$$

which is significant. A comparison of actual and predicted values of cutting edge angles showed that nine of the predicted values are good, two are fair and the remaining three are poor. A number of factors could account for the poor predictions, including the weights of the adze and helves and the condition and sharpness of the cutting edges.

In general, the results of these correlation studies indicate that there are strong relationships between the adze and wood chip parameters.

It follows that if wood chips derived from archaeological contexts can be sorted into appropriate batches there is promise that some of the characteristics of the adzes used to produce the wood chips can be deduced.

The Mahalanobis D² technique (Rao, 1952; Leach, 1969) was used to group the archaeological wood chips. D² statistics were calculated for the 14 reference groups of modern totara wood chips using six variables and each archaeological wood chip was then assigned to one of these groups with a specified probability.

The D² analysis followed the procedure adopted by Leach (1969). The six selected variables had non-normal, skewed distributions which were greatly improved when log transformed. Using the transformed data, the D² statistics were calculated for the 14 reference groups of modern wood chips. The individual chips in each of the reference groups were then re-allocated to one of these groups with a specified probability in order to test the discriminating powers of D². The analysis of the re-allocated wood chip distributions (see Fig. 3) indicated that too few primary variables have been used and it was concluded that the D² values are not powerful enough to

clearly discriminate between wood chips from the different batches. Nevertheless, it is still a useful, though not entirely satisfactory means of classifying the archaeological wood chips. Again there is a strong possibility that these D² statistics will discriminate between stone and steel cut wood chips.

Two further techniques were used to distinguish them. One of these methods also provides criteria for discriminating between axed and adzed timber.

The first method is based on the qualified premise that chips cut with steel will have a greater proportion of square tops and recognisably marked surfaces than those cut with stone. The respective percentages for each of the reference groups of modern wood chips are set out in Table 3 from which the following criteria have been extracted:

	Percentage number of wood chips with square tops	*Percentage number of wood chips with clearly discernible tool marks*
Steel tools	greater than 30	greater than 50
Stone tools	less than 15	less than 25

The interpretative reliability of these criteria are increased in situations where either steel or stone cut wood chips predominate.

The second method is based on the results of an examination of the type of marks left on the surface of timber with different types of tools (Figs. 4–6). In general, it was found that the sharper the tool the smoother the cut wood surface; the marks on the surfaces of the timbers are mirrors of the edge damage on the tools that produced them; the marks left by stone tools tended to be broad, fairly irregular, ill-defined and in relief; marks left by steel tools were often very fine, regular, well defined, close together and incised as well as in relief; marks left by both steel and stone adzes were always parallel to the direction of the striking blade, a fact which enabled axed and adzed timbers to be distinguished. A greater percentage of asymmetrical or lopsided wood chips, as opposed to square topped chips, are produced when timbers are axed.

The experimental adze studies were initially conducted on green totara, but since rimu is just as important in the archaeological assemblages, a restricted number of studies were duplicated using rimu to determine whether or not comparable results could be obtained. Although the absolute values of continuous parameters and D² values were generally different the same trends were noted for both timbers, and it is therefore considered reasonable to apply the results of the more extensive analysis to mixed assemblages of totara and rimu wood chips.

---

1. Student's test $Z_{0.005} = 2.98$
$Z_{0.05} = 1.76$ for N = 14

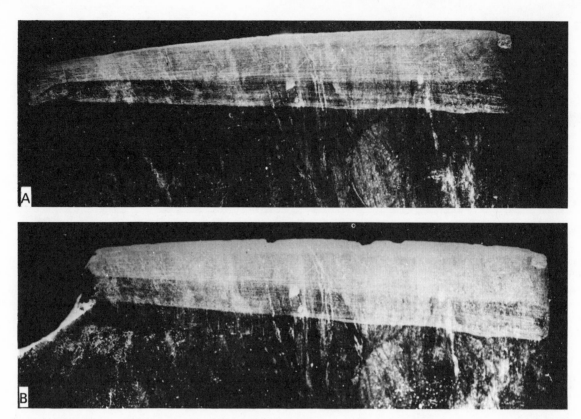

Fig. 1:   Serpentine stone adze no. 1, surface opposite bevel A—before use, B—after use. Magnification approx. 2:1.

Fig. 2:   Serpentine stone adze no. 1, surface with bevel A—before use, B—after use. Magnification approx. 2:1.

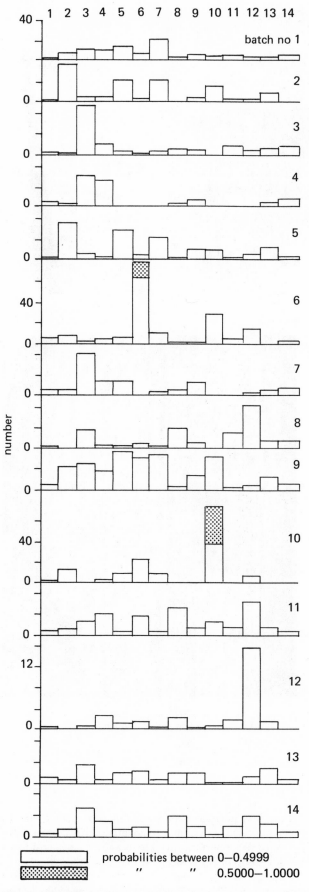

Fig. 3: Mahalanobis D² analysis of modern woodchips. Percentage re-allocation of batches of woodchips with specified probabilities greater or less than 0.5.

probabilities between 0–0.4999
″ ″ 0.5000–1.0000

Finally, it is instructive to compare the photographs of the tool edges before and after use (Figs. 1 and 2, following Semenov, 1964). Two sets of lines were distinguished. Firstly, there were randomly positioned scratches, often at right angles to the cutting edge but not always starting at the edge. Several new scratches appeared, presumably caused by the wood working. Secondly, there were a series of regular, close spaced scratches, usually extending from the cutting edge at an oblique angle which are almost certainly honing marks. In some cases they diminished in clarity following the period of wood working.

With the exception of the steel tools all cutting edges were damaged through use (cf. Keller, 1966 : 503). The nephrite tools sustained least damage, the home-made serpentine tool the most (Fig. 1). Cross-grain working was found to increase the edge damage. Edge damage was generally manifested in one or a combination of three forms—blunting of the tool edges, fracturing of parts of the working edges, or removal of small flakes from the working margins, usually on the faces opposite the bevels. It is interesting to observe that Gould *et al.* (1971 : 159–60) has also observed this last category of edge damage on Australian adzes following periods of use.

Grab samples, comprising about 25% of the total numbers of wood chips in each square of each archaeological layer, were analysed. Each wood chip was measured and described in the same way as the reference samples. Burnt wood chips were also noted. The copious results of the D² analysis, relevant percentages of square topped, asymmetrical and burnt chips for each square in each of the excavations are given in detail in Coutts (1972).

The wooden artifacts were allocated to functional categories wherever possible and technological features, such as the methods of making holes in and cutting timber, have also been classified (Table 4).

Results of the analysis

Wood technology The living areas of all six sites were constituted from similar ranges of organic materials and though the densities varied from site to site, totara (*Podocarpus totara*) and/or rimu (*Dacrydium cupressinum*) were the most common timbers represented.

Adzes and chisels were the predominant types of cutting artifact used though there are examples of woodchips that could have been cut with side-hafted tools (Table 4).

The results of the D² analysis suggest the presence of steel cut woodchips in most layers, with group or adze numbers 4, 7 and 12 predominating and pointing to the presence of both broad and narrow blade widths at all sites. Analysis of the other quantitative data (% square topped and % marked chips) indicates that stone tools were used in layer 2B of CH/1, layers 2 and 4 of SP/5, layers 2, 4 and 5 of SP/10 and steel tools in layer 4 of SP/5 and layer 6 of SP/11. The data from SP/1 suggest that there were no predominant accumulations of steel and stone worked timbers.

Many wood chips could not be classed as steel or stone cut because the qualitative criteria are not precise enough for decision making. Indeed, when Banks (in Best, 1912 : 125) observed wood being worked with stone tools, he concluded that 'it would often puzzle a man to say whether the wood they have shaped was or was not with an iron hatchet'. His remarks are particularly apt.

The qualitative evidence for use of steel and stone tools at the various sites is summarised in Table 4 and documented

Fig. 4: Green totara cut with sharp stone adze no. 1. (1) and (2) are back and front views of the same wood chip. Note the wide, rough relief lines on (2) which mirror the edge damage on the tool; (3) and (4) are the faces of two further woodchips; (5) shows the surface of a rough trimmed totara branch.

more fully elsewhere (Coutts, 1972). The use of extremely sharp tools at SP/11 is a notable feature of that site. Measurements of blade impressions in the timbers confirm the hypothesis arising from the D^2 analysis, that a number of adzes with different blade widths were used at the various sites (Table 4). There are also several examples of timbers that have been cut or gouged with narrow width cutting implements, chisels or pieces of hoop iron. Steel saws were used at SP/1, SP/5, SP/10 and SP/11.

While it is possible that hoop iron was used to cut the timber allocated to group 12, no qualitative evidence was discovered to support this hypothesis and it seems most likely that this group of chips was produced with stone chisels.

A number of technological features are manifested in the timber remains (Table 4, Figs. 7–9). Firstly, the methods used to cut branches or roughed timber are very distinctive and may be due to technical limitations imposed by the adzes themselves. Timber was cut by chopping a 'V' shaped section

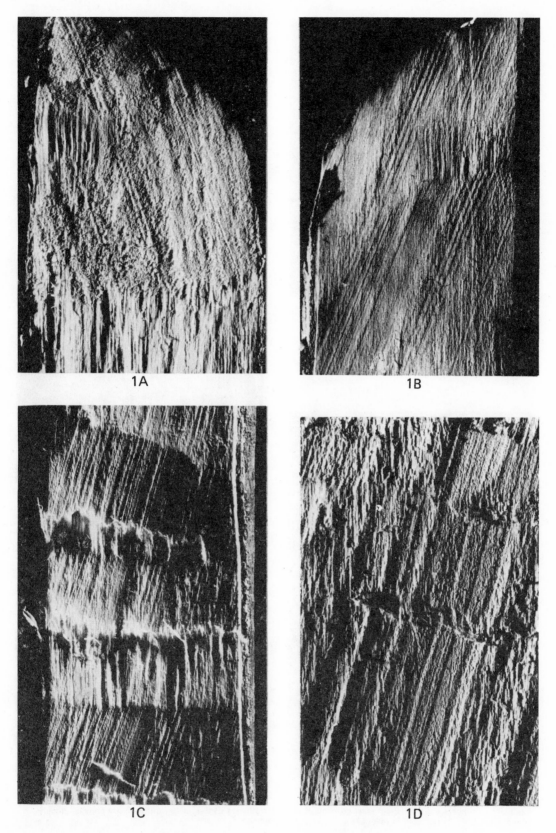

Fig. 5: Four examples of timbers cut with a steel axe. The edge damage patterns, as reflected by the markings left in the timber are similar to those produced with steel adzes, but are angled to the longitudinal axis of the woodchips.

Fig. 6: Five examples of timbers cut with sharp steel adze no. 6. The smoothness of the finish, and the very precise, closely spaced, well formed lines, both incised and in relief are suitable characteristics.

Table 3 Percentage numbers of woodchips with square tops and with clearly discernible tool marks for each reference batch of woodchips

Adze No.	% no. of wood chips with square tops	% no. of wood chips with clearly visible marks on their surfaces	Timber	Sample No.
1	15	28	totara	160
2	9	7	totara	140
3	4	6	totara	140
4	1	6	totara	140
5	23	55	totara	140
5	26	26	rimu	154
6	25	96	totara	208
6	27	91	rimu	158
7	4	40	totara	159
8	1	0	totara	140
9	19	7	totara	298
9	19	13	rimu	116
10	31	100	totara	140
11	25	92	totara	160
12	1	94	totara	168
13	53	0	totara	140
14	4	0	totara	100

around the circumference of the branch or on both faces of a plank and snapping it into two pieces (Fig. 7; 'chop around and snap method'). Secondly, holes were made in timber by adzing from both sides with a chisel or by drilling a number of holes with fine drills approximately 2 mm in diameter and forcing the centre plugs out. Other holes were drilled directly with larger drill pieces from both sides. Thirdly, timber appears to have been rough dressed at the sites, with broad bladed tools, leaving the surface rough and 'wavy'. Most of the rough dressing follows the grain of the wood, though there are examples of cross-grain working. The fine dressing was conducted with smaller cutting tools, probably chisels and generally crossgrain. The same distinctive patterns of cross-grain herringbone dressing (Fig. 9) occurred on timbers from SP/5 and SP/11 (cf. Best, 1912 : 135).

No drill pieces were found at the site, but a number of badly preserved supplejack fragments were recovered which may have derived from traditional drill wheels. Several methods are known to have been used by post-contact Maori to drill wood: pieces of metal such as files (Best, 1912 : 60), drill wheels with wooden or stone points (*op: cit.:* 63, 73, 82; Steel, 1930: 187; Shortland, 1851 : 37, 118) and awls or augers consisting of wooden handles with stone or shark tooth points (Best, 1912 : 73, 81–82).

Within each relevant archaeological layer the spatial distribution of woodchips cut by the various tools (as seen through the results of the D² analysis) were similar. This suggests that there were no localised areas in any layers which were linked exclusively with particular types of adzes or wood technology.

There are significant numbers of charred woodchips and many fragments of burnt bark. Most of the woodchips are blackened on one side, often at one end only. This suggests that fire was used during woodworking as was the established practice during the early European–Maori contact era (Firth, 1925 : 285; Smith, 1893 : 451). Another possibility is that the original timber was felled with the aid of fire—a common practice in the North Island (see Best, 1925) and that the burnt woodchips derived from areas of the timber affected by fire during felling.

Wooden artifacts A wide variety of wooden artifacts was recovered from these sites. They included pointed implements or pegs (?) and half round lengths of dressed timber from most sites. They were either made from timber or from twigs or branches. These pegs may have had many functions: for drying seal skins (Chapman, 1893 : 450), securing canoe timbers or for making fish spears.

One of the larger half round artifacts from SP/5 (layer 1A), 60 cm long, 3 cm wide and 2.2 cm thick would have made a suitable crossbar for a canoe as its dimensions and shape compare favourably with those observed in museum collections. Artifacts with established ethnographic parallels include portion of a canoe washboard from CH/1 (layer 1B), part of a god stick (?) from SP/5 (layer 3), fire sticks (see Best, 1912 : 115) from SP/10 (layer 4) and CH/1 (layer 2B), and a broken adze haft (?) suitable for a small adze from SP/10 (layer 2). The chisel hafts comprise cylindrical pieces of timber with longitudinal grooves at one end to accommodate the butt end of the chisels which were kept in place by some sort of binding. There are also several recognisable items of fishing gear—spreaders, net floats, fishing line winders, barracouta lure shanks in various stages of manufacture and parts of multi-pronged (?) combs.

Woodworking tools Having considered the woodworking industry through its waste materials it has been possible to predict some of the characteristics of the woodworking tools. Hence it is appropriate to complement this approach by examining the surviving (and presumed) woodworking tools, drawing on the results of the wear pattern studies.

Stone tools were rare from all sites, though this may not have been the case originally, since all sites have been disturbed and tools could have been removed (Table 5). However, the rarity of flake tools, waste flakes and general evidence of stone working activities, and the fact that the archaeological layers are mostly post European–Maori contact in date argues against the proliferation of stone tools at these sites.

The remains of two chisels and several adzes were excavated and most of these tools are made from local raw materials. The latter are utilitarian with ground cutting edges. Where cutting edges have survived for study, honing and use-wear marks are clearly visible under the microscope, the bevels have many more scratches than the blades, and the blade edges tend to have most of the edge damage. One tool (from SP/11, layer 6A) has two very large flakes missing from the blade edge effectively removing most of its surface. The evidence suggests that the tools were used as adzes or chisels and were hafted in the traditional manner.

In addition to adzes and chisels, several hammerstones were excavated and although they could have been used as mallets for chiselling, it is more likely they were used to manufacture the stone tools.

Summary and conclusion

In this paper it has been shown that it is possible to frame reliable quantitative and qualitative criteria to distinguish between adzed (including chiselled) and axe cut wood and steel and stone cut timbers. These findings are important for several reasons.

Firstly, in situations where the archaeologist is confronted with numbers of archaeologically derived wood chips and wooden artifacts with no associated time-markers or no obvious evidence of the technology employed, these criteria

Table 4   Wood technological features manifested at the Southport sites   • evidence present in layer.

Item	SP/1	SP/5				SP/9
Site						
Layer	2	1A Spoil	2⁻	2	4	2⁻
Evidence for use of stone tools						
Woodchips, back or front	• several squares	• •	•	• • cross grain	• •	• •
Rough dressed timber			• cross grain			
Fine dressed timber	Some examples	• herringbone pattern				
Adze cuts, depth of penetration and fineness of cut	•	•				Evidence doubtful
Evidence for use of steel tools						
Woodchips, back or front	• several squares	•	?	•		
Rough dressed timber	•	?		• •	• • •	
Fine dressed timber		? ?				
Adze cuts, depth of penetration and fineness of cut	•	•	? vertical distance 1.3 cm			
Evidence for use of chisels Probably stone				• cross grain		
Evidence for use of saws Probably steel		•	•	•		•
Evidence for use of the same tool from matching tool patterns	•	•	•	•		•
Technique of cutting branches 'Chop around and snap method'	•		•	•		•
Technique of cutting prepared timber 'Chop around and snap method'		•	•	•	•	•
Techniques of making holes in timber						
Drilling several holes and removing plug	•	• •	• several examples drilled from one side only, holes incomplete	• Half drilled		•
Drilling and adzing from both sides	•	•				
Drilling using wide drill from both sides						
Adzing from both sides	•	•	•	•		
Direct evidence of adze and/or chisel widths at cutting edge	• very blunt	•	•	• P/2 •	•	•
Evidence of adze bounce						
Evidence of cross grain working	•	•	•	•	• •	
Evidence of woodchips stained with red ochre		•			•	
Evidence of no. of tools used based on tool marks	• at least 2 tools		• at least 2 tools	• at least 3 tools	•	at least 2 tools
Evidence for use of side hafted tools		•		• mechanical	• possibly cut with …	
Method working timber unknown						

Item	Site SP/10			SP/11					CH/1
Layer	2	4	5	2	3	3A	4	6	2B
Evidence for use of stone tools									
Woodchips, back or front	●	●			●			●	●
Rough dressed timber	●	●			●		●	●	
Fine dressed timber					●		●	●	
Adze cuts, depth of penetration and fineness of cut									
Evidence for use of steel tools									
Woodchips, back or front	●	●	●	●	●	●	●	●	●
Rough dressed timber									
Fine dressed timber									
Adze cuts, depth of penetration and fineness of cut									
Evidence for use of chisels									
Probably stone	●			●	●	●		●	●
Evidence for use of saws									
Probably steel	●	●		●	●	●		●	
Evidence for use of the same tool from matching tool patterns		●			●			●	●
Technique of cutting branches									
'Chop around and snap method'		●	●					●	●
Technique of cutting prepared timber									
'Chop around and snap method'		●	●					●	●
Techniques of making holes in timber									
Drilling several holes and removing plug		●						●	
Drilling and adzing from both sides					●			●	
Drilling using wide drill from both sides			Drilled one side only		●		●	● drilled from one side	
Adzing from both sides	●	●	●						
Direct evidence of adze and-or chisel widths at cutting edge		●			●		●	●	●
Evidence of adze bounce					●		●	●	●
Evidence of cross grain working						●		●	
Evidence of woodchips stained with red ochre	●	●	●	●	●	●		●	
Evidence of no. of tools used based on tool marks									
Evidence for use of side hafted tools									
Method working timber unknown									

Table 5 Stone artifacts: adzes and chisels from the Southport sites

Site	Layer	Square	Tool description	Material	Probable origin of material	Weight (gm)	Max. length (cm)	Max. width (cm)	Width of cutting edge (cm)	Cutting edge angle	Technology
SP/1	2	1/3	Adze/chisel broken	Schist/quartzite*	Local				3.5	70	Cutting edge ground and polished
		G/3	Chisel	Bowenite	Anita Bay	14	3.8	1.8	1.8	40	Sawn and CP
SP/4	2	C and D/3	Adze	Green argillite	Southland	106	11.7	3.3	3.4	60	S. fl, HD and SP
		G and H/3	Broken adze, re-worked(?)	Green argillite	Southland possibly Riverton						S. fl, HD and SP
		C/2	Hinge flake from adze	Green argillite	Southland						HD with polish
		E/2	Adze/chisel	Nephrite	West coast	42	6.2	3.0	3.2	60	Sawn, HD and CP
SP/5	1A	Spoil	Adze/chisel broken	Schist/quartzite*	Local						S. fl
	2	0/1	Butt of adze	Schist/quartzite*	Local						S. fl
		0/—1	Adze/chisel broken	Green argillite	Southland						S. fl, HD and SP
	2⁻	1/—5	Adze flake	Fine grained sedimentary	Imported						CP on one side
SP/10	2	K/2	Adze	Quartzite*	Local	170	11.7	4.9	3.5	89	S. fl, HD, SP
		J/3	Adze frag.	Quartzite*	Local wwp.						S.fl, HD
SP/11	6	A/—1	Chisel	Probably quartzite*	Local wwp.	21	8.4	1.5	1.0	23	Cutting edge ground
		A/—1	Adze/chisel broken	Schist/quartzite*	Local	28	6.2	3.1	3.1	?	One side of cutting edge ground and polished
		A/2	Chisel broken	Nephrite	West coast			0.7	0.4	45	Sawn, CP

* abbreviation for meta-quartzite.
wwp—water worn pebble.
S. fl =step flaked, CP = completely polished, HD = hammer dressed, SP = semi-polished and ground.

may be used with effect. Take CH/1 for example, a suspected late prehistoric site. It yielded few artifacts and a number of wood chips which were analysed. The results indicated that they were cut with stone and not steel tools. Later, C[14] dates confirmed the age of the site. Again site SP/9 yielded no European material, but radiocarbon dates suggested that it was post European–Maori contact in age and analysis of the wood chip data indicated that some at least of the wood chips had been cut with steel tools.

Secondly, these criteria may be helpful in deciding whether or not controversial ethnographic wooden artifacts are post European–Maori contact in age. In the past, decisions of this type have been made on the basis of subjective data and great weight has been attached to the authority rather than to the criteria used. However, it is necessary to point out that the methods advocated here will not always be applicable, as in cases where the tool marks have been obliterated by weathering or sanding.

Thirdly, the criteria have application to materials other than wood. Thus excavations at Southport yielded several pieces of whale-bone that had been adzed and the stone tool impressions were clearly visible.

Lastly, these criteria with further refinements may be used to resolve more specific problems. For example, whether or not the prehistoric Maori used side-hafted stone tools.[1]

The fact that axe-adze like tools leave their special imprint on timber or bone can be used sometimes to identify the range and extent of their use at a site or on a particular artifact (see Fig. 8). At SP/1 for example, wood chips with the same tool imprints were found over several square metres of the living area suggesting that there were no specialised wood working areas at the site. Again at the same site, examination of the tool mark patterns on wood chips clearly indicated that at least two tools were used.

Measurements of the widths of the tool imprints and the D^2 results enable reasonable estimates to be made of the tool widths. Moreover, if the angle of impact and/or the lengths of cuts can be measured it may be possible to estimate the cutting edge angles of the adzes producing them, using formulae of the type derived above.

1. Unfortunately no side-hafted stone tools were included in the experiments. However, examinations of the edge damage and use-wear patterns produced by such implements plus intensive studies of ethnographic specimens (Australian stone axes for example) should yield the necessary criteria to resolve such intriguing questions.

Fig. 7: Wood Technology seen in archaeological timbers
(1) Chisel impressions, SP/5 M/1 layer 4, rimu.
(2) 'Chop around technique', SP/5 P/1 layer 2+.
(3) Stone chisel impressions, SP/5 P/1 layer 2+.
(4) Stone chisel impressions, SP/5 P/2 layer 2+.
(5) 'Chop around technique', SP/5 L/2 layer 2+.

1A

1B

1C

Fig. 8: Wood technology seen in archaeological timbers: Examples of matching edge damage patterns, SP/10 M/—2 layer 4.

It has been suggested that consistent patterns of edge-damage and to a lesser extent use-wear are produced when stone adzes are used to work timber. This gives rise to criteria which allow the helving orientations of archaeological specimens to be deduced. Observations of edge damage and use-wear patterns on chisels indicate that they are identical to those produced on hafted adzes and it is concluded that they were hafted with their bevels orientated similarly. In practice no clear criteria have been worked out to distinguish adze-cut as opposed to chisel-cut timbers; to date the only bases for

discrimination are the widths and rounding of the tool imprints.

Other findings of some interest are that the sharpness of stone tools diminishes rapidly with use, particularly on hard or dry timbers or when used cross-grain. Again it was found that tools made from nephrite tend to hold their cutting edges far more effectively than adzes made from other stone materials, supporting ethnographic traditions that nephrite tools are superior. However, these results also underscore one of the disadvantages of stone adzes. It is clear that constant

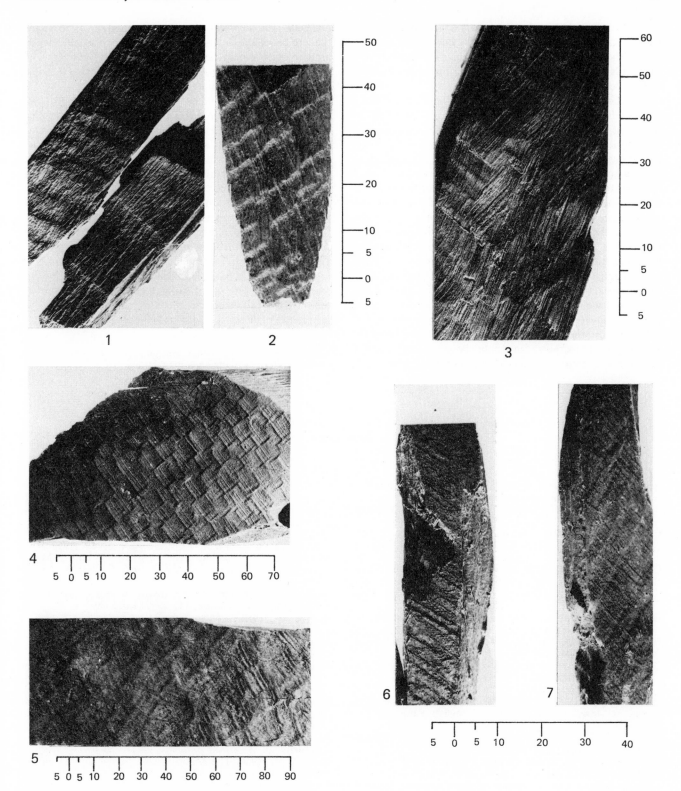

Fig. 9: Wood technology seen in archaeological timbers
(1) Timber rough dressed with a stone tool, SP/5 layer 1A.
(2) Timber rough dressed with a stone tool, SP/5 0/3 layer 2+.
(3) Timber, possibly dressed with hoop iron or stone tool, SP/5 layer 1A.
(4) Fine herringbone dressing with stone tool, cross-grain, SP/5 L/2 layer 2+.
(5) Fine herringbone dressing with stone tool, cross-grain, SP/5 layer 1A.
(6) Method of dressing unknown, SP/5 0/2 layer 2+.
(7) Fine dressing with stone tool, cross-grain, SP/5 0/2 layer 2+.

resharpening would have been necessary (cf. Shortland (1851) who noted a constant preoccupation with this activity amongst the southern Maori) which no doubt helps to explain why steel tools were so much sought after during the early period of European–Maori contact.

Nor should the potential importance of this type of study for illuminating culture-history of an area be forgotten. In respect of the Southport sites, it was found, for example, that prehistoric and European–Maori contact wood technologies shared much in common; totara as a raw material, methods of making holes in wood, methods of cutting timber, the use of fire in woodworking, multiple tool kits including stone chisels with wooden hafts, tools with cutting edges of similar widths, manufacture of half round rods, net float blanks (?) and two piece bait-hook shanks. However, some differences were apparent; a greater variety of working tools, including steel tools and the presence of pattern dressed timbers and stone tools manufactured from local materials from the European–Maori contact levels; use of exclusively imported adzes and chisels and the absence of short or pointed artifacts from the prehistoric layers.

Specifically where stone tools occur, they may assume the role of cultural markers; but it must be remembered, and it has been illustrated here, that they are not always found in archaeological deposits, nor in such numbers as to enable them to be reliably interpreted. Hence it is important that the archaeologist remains alert to the possibility of recognising secondary manifestations of stone and other tools as they may well turn out to be useful cultural markers.

In conclusion, it should be remembered that today there are thousands of Polynesian adzes and chisels in museum collections which continue to gather dust. Scholars have a habit of merely using them to speculate on their place in artifact typologies, geographical contexts or chronological horizons (often of course, with important results). It is surely time that more effort is expended on elucidating their functional aspects as well. There are still many widely held assumptions about these tools which need to be questioned and verified, indeed the very words adze, axe and chisel are functional terms. Although lack of time has precluded an exhaustive study of all such assumptions and ramifications, enough has been done to suggest that it is possible to test some of them in a fruitful, reasonably scientific way. Finally, there is little need to point out that the problems and methods outlined here are not unique to Polynesia.

Acknowledgements The author gratefully acknowledges the Myer Foundation for generously supporting this research.

References

Best, E., 1912. *Stone implements of the Maori*. Wellington: Dominion Museum Bulletin No. 4.

—— 1925. *The Maori canoe*. Wellington: Dominion Museum Bulletin No. 7.

Chapman, F. R., 1893. Notes on the depletion of the fur seal in the Southern Seas. *Canadian Record of Science*, (October): 446–59.

Coutts, P. J. F., 1972. *The emergence of the Foveaux Strait Maori from prehistory: a study of culture contact*. Unpublished Ph.D. thesis, University of Otago, Dunedin, New Zealand.

Duff, R., 1970. *Stone adzes of south-east Asia*. Christchurch: Canterbury Museum, Bulletin No. 3.

Firth, W. R., 1925. The Maori Carver. *Journal of the Polynesian Society*, 34 : 277–91.

Gould, R. A., D. Koster and A. H. L. Sontz, 1971. The lithic assemblage of the western desert Aborigines of Australia. *American Antiquity*, 36 : 149–69.

Jorgensen, S., 1953. Skovrydning Med Flintokse. *Fra Nationalmuseets Arbejdsmark*, pp. 36–43. English Summary pp. 109–10.

Keller, C. M., 1966. The development of edge damage patterns on stone tools. *Man*, 1(4) : 501–12.

Knapp, F. V., 1928. Maori scrapers. *Journal of the Polynesian Society*, 37 : 113–24.

—— 1941. Maori saws. *Journal of the Polynesian Society*, 50 : 1–9.

Leach, B. F., 1969. *The concept of similarity in prehistoric studies*. Studies in Prehistoric Anthropology, Vol. 1. Anthropology Department, University of Otago, Dunedin, New Zealand.

McCarthy, F. D., 1967. *Australian stone implements*. Sydney: Australian Museum.

McEwan, J. M., 1946. An experiment with primitive Maori carving tools. *Journal of the Polynesian Society*, 55(2) : 111–15.

Moir, J. R., 1926. Experiments in the shaping of wood with flint implements. *Nature*, 117(2949) : 655–56.

Rao, C. R., 1952. *Advanced statistical methods in biometric research*. London: John Wiley.

Semenov, S. A., 1964. *Prehistoric technology*. Translated by M. W. Thompson. London: Cory, Adams and Mackay.

Shortland, E., 1851. *The southern districts of New Zealand. A journal with passing notices of the customs of the aborigines*. London: Longman, Brown, Green and Longman.

Smith, T. H., 1893. Maori implements and weapons. *Transactions and Proceedings of the New Zealand Institute*, 26 : 423–52.

Sonnenfeld, J., 1962. Interpreting the function of primitive implements. *American Antiquity*, 28(1) : 56–65.

Steel, R. H., 1930. The Maori sewing needle. *Journal of the Polynesian Society*, 39 : 310–14.

An archaeologically oriented classification of ethnographic material culture

ELEANOR CROSBY

This paper describes a solution to problems of classification encountered while describing morphological variation within a class of artifacts represented in ethnographic collections from Melanesia. The study is an attempt to describe the artifacts in archaeologically useful morphological terms, and then to evaluate the various ways in which artifacts may be grouped morphologically against environmental and cultural factors suspected of direct or indirect effects upon artifact forms and their distributions.

A major task was, therefore, to achieve a method to produce replicable groups of artifacts which would be as efficient as possible in permitting the relatively rapid production of several sets of analyses for comparison both with each other and with environmental and cultural (i.e. ethnographic) information. The paper presents a solution in terms of an artifact group in which is represented one variant of each aspect of variation considered, and in which all artifacts have the same combination of variants. This group can then be considered by itself on the basis of its unique combination of variants, or it may be considered in combination with other groups sharing one or more variants.

The solution is adapted from the methods and techniques of population biology, and the resulting artifact classification may be said to stand in much the same relationship to prehistoric archaeology as does zoology to palaeontology. If successfully tested the method should be of considerable interest wherever the prehistory of an ethnographic situation is under investigation.

Artifact class and setting

The study was set in Melanesia (Map 1), and included artifacts in Australasian collections or reported in the literature. The study was restricted to artifacts known to have been collected during the early years of European contact.

Following the lead of Durrans (1972) the class was defined in mechanical terms. The implements have been termed *percussive cutting implements*. This is adopted from Leroi-Gourhan's 1945 study *L'Homme et la Matière*. Leroi-Gourhan terms the class *percussions lancées linéaires* (1945 : 187–95). Hinderling, in his 1949 study of Oceanic cutting implements terms them *schwunghafter Schnitt* (1949 : 13). These implements are all used with a chopping motion and are swung with percussive force to strike a blow with a cutting edge. Most of the implements within this class are axes or adzes, but the well-known Melanesian habit of hafting edge-tool blades having either axe or adze bevel conformations at any angle precludes the use of the terms axe and adze except in reference to hafted implements. I have preferred to call their loose blades edge-tool blades. However, not all implements within

the class can be described as edge-tools for a number of more specialised implements, such as, for example sago pith choppers, do not absolutely require sharp edged blades.

All Melanesian percussive cutting implements encountered are hafted, having a blade, handle, and lashings. Some have additional hafting features such as a separate socket to hold the blade. The top of the separate socket is attached to the handle.

Melanesian percussive cutting implements are assembled in a restricted number of ways, and a restricted range of tasks is assigned to them ethnographically. Only complete hafted implements were recorded. Together with provenance, these factors are used to provide the controls for the study of morphology.

One reason for the choice of percussive cutting implements is the near universality of the class within Melanesia. Only Frederick Hendrick Island, or Kolepom, is apparently without percussive cutting implements of some kind. By virtue of their relatively indestructible materials of stone, shell or bone the blades are relatively common in archaeological sites. Analysis of their ethnographic counterparts, with the advantage of information about their ethnographic manufacture and use, should provide useful data for prehistoric interpretation.

However, serious deficiencies in the ethnographic literature about ethno-technology were emphasised by this study. It is also disappointing to note that both the distribution and numbers of artifacts which were actually recorded for this study, are deficient for all areas, except parts of Papua and the New Guinea Highlands. The numerical deficiency was perhaps the factor having most effect on the classification method followed.

Methods of classification

Nineteenth century typologies, of which modern clustering techniques are the linear descendants began the process of establishing a classification by examining the morphological variation perceived within a group of artifacts. These artifacts were then sorted and re-sorted into groups until the final groups reached were both identifiable morphologically, and coincident with some perceived archaeological unit, such as a stratum of a site, a time horizon, or a region. Modern clustering techniques, depending on more refined attribute discriminations, and far more complex in their ability to handle a multitude of attributes, still operate in this manner. These clustering strategies (e.g. Lance and Williams, 1967a; 1967b; 1967c; 1968; Lance, Milne and Williams, 1968) have one point in common—they are all very time consuming and consequently financially expensive. Moreover, if they are to be used it is important that the objects submitted (a) be

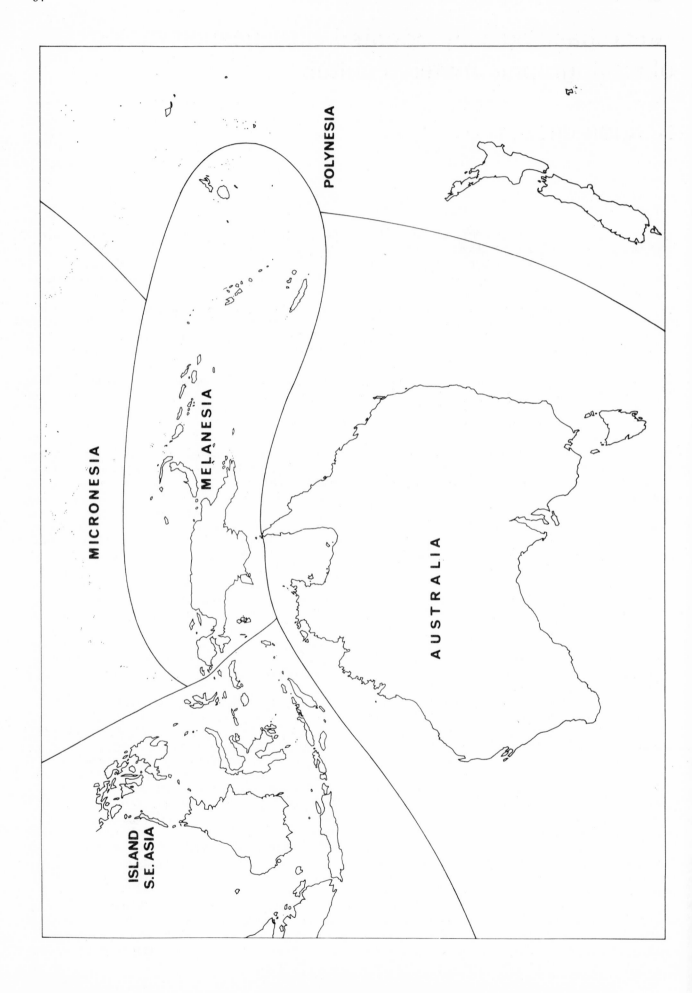

POLYNESIA

MICRONESIA

MELANESIA

AUSTRALIA

ISLAND
S.E. ASIA

sufficiently numerous to enable the formation of clusters which can be evaluated as statistically sound; and (b) be numerous enough to enable the clusters which are formed to reflect the known facts of the distributions with which the clusters are expected to be coincident.

My initial approach to classification was an exploration of such clustering strategies. After discussion with Dr Williams and others at the Division of Computing Research, CSIRO, Canberra, I decided that a straight application of clustering techniques to the material was inappropriate. The material was too sparse, and the number of attributes too large for it to be likely that any easy cluster solution to the description of artifact variance would emerge. In discussion with Dr Williams it was pointed out that if a method of grouping artifacts without employing clustering techniques could be discovered, then it would be a relatively simple task to test first the statistical soundness of the groups and secondly their inter-relationships.

I therefore began to examine possible criteria associated with the artifacts themselves, and to examine the basis of modern biological systematics, that is numerical taxonomy or population biology. Much of my understanding is derived from a text called *Quantitative Zoology* by Simpson, Roe and Lewontin (1960).

Population biology is a method of describing intra-species variation by selecting groups of animals or plants so that all the non-genetic factors which may affect variation are controlled. These aspects of heterogeneity are identified for animals as the variants which may be observed of date (i.e. contemporaneity), place (i.e. same area), environment (i.e. ecological unity), age (i.e. animals of approximately the same age), and sex (Simpson, Roe and Lewontin, 1960 : 103). Each population is selected so that a single variant of each of these aspects of heterogeneity is represented. The population is thus homogeneous and able to be described by a single statistical statement of its morphological homogeneity. Because each aspect of heterogeneity is under control, the effect of any one can be studied by testing the morphological variance which is apparent when populations similar in all but the heterogeneity under scrutiny are compared.

Decisions about what constitutes population homogeneity must be made anew for each study. The concept of population homogeneity constitutes an important difference between typological systematics and population systematics when applied to artifacts. In artifact typology the initial selection of the basic groups is made from observed morphology and validated by the goodness of fit with other perceived archaeological units. In artifact population systematics the initial selection of groups is through what Simpson, Roe and Lewontin call 'collection data' (1960 : 103), and these are validated by appeal to morphological homogeneity.

A question arises about how artifact population homogeneity might be verified. The zoologist can say that, after all the non-genetic factors which affect intra-species heterogeneity have been controlled, the morphological variance represents the genetic variance and that the sum of all the population variances is the variance which defines the species. So far as I am aware no archaeologist has considered the problems in terms of the morphological variance which might be allowable in an artifact population. To allow testing it might be suggested that if population samples are correctly constituted for the factors affecting or reflecting variance then the variance should be restricted to a particular range. Whether or not this range might be comparable to the ranges perceived by the zoologists

it should indicate the stylistic variations permissible in artifact populations. These artifact populations are the maximum group in which all artifacts have the same combination of variants of aspects of variation. They are thus the smallest groups represented within the study and are the basis for all further analyses, by themselves or in combination.

Whatever the process by which the smallest groups used in a study are reached, once they are verified they can be used in all subsequent operations. This is shown diagrammatically in Fig. 1. This figure is designed to show that the smallest groups resulting from classification methods must be verifiable from both morphological and external corroborative evidence. In population systematics the statistical tests of morphological homogeneity allow replicable groups to be selected, regardless of what cultural or environmental significance is later assigned to the groups. In Fig. 1 this stage, and the succeeding one of presenting the interpretation in the form of a classification is portrayed as common to both methods.

Techniques

1. Artifact measurement A population approach to artifact systematics is clearly as much dependent upon the skill with which the morphological variations are described as is a typological study. Therefore a first concern is the selection of features which encompass as much of the variation as possible while attempting to strike a balance between the usually vast possible number of variants which could be recorded, the physical limitations of time and the statistical techniques available. This is often a tedious process of recording and simplification. In the study of Melanesian percussive cutting implements two sets of features were used, measured on different scales. One set of features describes shapes in terms of the approximation of features of the blade to a set of designated shapes (Fig. 2). These designated shapes are termed attributes and are measured on a nominal or classifying scale. The other set of features (Fig. 3) measures sizes and proportions of the implements in terms of true ratio scale measurements. The distinction is necessary because each scale is more powerful when used in particular statistics (Siegel, 1956). These features were used to provide descriptions of sample variance, and to test their homogeneity.

2. Homogeneity requirements As a first step towards grouping a population study requires that a decision be made about what aspects of heterogeneity in the collection data it is possible to control. We must therefore attempt to clarify the factors affecting artifact variance. These include the following:

(1) differences between artifact classes arising from the different mechanical functions required for the achievement of different general purposes;

(2) major differences in manufacturing methods;

(3) differences between artifacts handled by different specific methods and used for different specific tasks;

(4) differences between implements made of different materials, arising from environmental differences;

(5) differences of style (which is here defined as the agreed range of variation permitted by a group of craftsmen) between artifacts from different communities at different temporal and/or spatial locations;

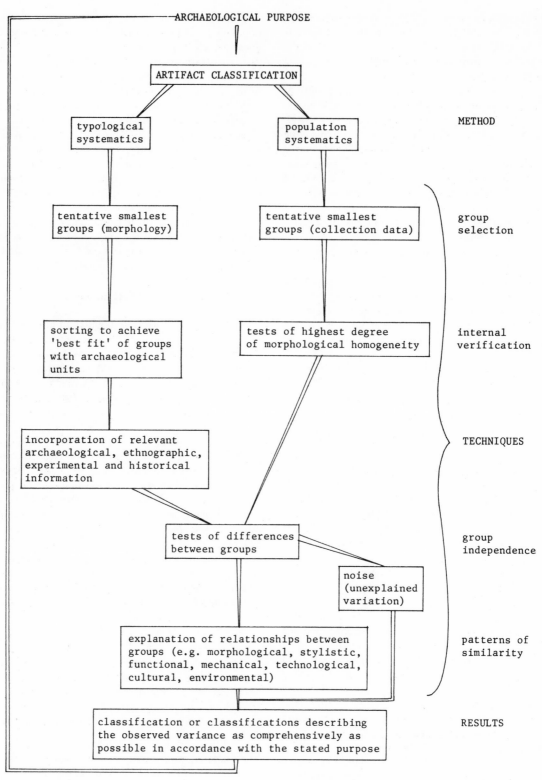

Fig. 1: Artifact classification.

(6) differences between individual artisans arising from the exercise of individual preferences and skills within the bounds of a particular style.

Regardless of cause all these differences can be given a geographic and chronological expression, though in this ethnographic study where time is so tightly controlled the geographic dimension of this framework is the more important. This also relates to the question of population homogeneity,

for the group of artifacts nominated as the population sample will be the largest which satisfies all the criteria of homogeneity decided upon. In effect this is controlled by the aspect of heterogeneity which has the largest number of variants; in this case style.

Because the collection data associated with Melanesian percussive cutting implements very rarely give attribution to individuals, be they owners or makers, the geographic expression of style which is the next smallest is that offered by those morphological features by which the percussive cutting implements of one community may be distinguished from those of their neighbours. The nature of artifact provenances determine the extent of the groups, with which such a study may be endowed. In this study provenances in general relate to districts such as 'Hood Bay' or as denoted by 'Motu tribe'. By a fortunate coincidence these districts are closely similar to those which form the ethnic context for many ethnographies.

Given the information associated with the implements in museum records (mainly date and place of collection, occasionally owner, maker, uses, and methods of manufacture), and attested in ethnographic records (chiefly of a general nature), it was decided that a reasonable degree of control could be attained over time, geographic districts, hafting methods and artifact use.

Hafting methods distinguished are based upon the methods of assembling the parts of the implements into a whole. Four major groups were isolated (Fig. 4):

(1) T1, having footed (elbow-shaped) handles with the blade set directly against the foot and held by lashings, with or without a wooden cover over the outer or right face of the blade, and set on the front or the side of the foot.

(2) T2, having footed handles with the blade held in a wooden separate socket (tang), the upper end of which is lashed to the foot of the handle;

(3) T3, having straight handles in which the blade is set directly within a hole or slot or prongs in the proximal end of the handle;

(4) T4, having straight handles in which the blade, set in a separate socket, is held in a hole or slot or prongs in the proximal end of the handle.

Handle attributes are feature A, blade holding attributes feature B of Fig. 5.

These major hafting methods are widespread within Melanesia and when mapped are seen to have very large and continuous distributions. They rarely occur contemporaneously in any area and in those places where an overlap is recorded, implements having different hafting methods are never reported as having been used for the same tasks. The four hafting methods are called manufacturing traditions T1–T4 largely because their distributions cross-cut other geographic and cultural subdivisions of Melanesia and thus suggest long histories.

The elucidation of variants of artifact use proved to be the most difficult of all the aspects of artifact heterogeneity studied. One approach lies through experimental replication of uses, and studies of the results of such use on the blades in particular. Some work on edge-ground blades by Semenov (1964) appears to discriminate certain kinds of woodworking uses, notably use-wear resulting from the cross-cutting of timber grain as in hollowing activities. However, from my examination of use-wear it appears that the development of recognisable wear patterns depends upon the nature of the blade material and upon how long a blade is in use without requiring the obliteration of the evidence through resharpening. Thus the presence of a particular use-wear is an indication of a concomitant manner of use having a high probability of correctness, but the absence of a particular use-wear by no means precludes a particular manner of use. It is also a fact that in Melanesia most of the percussive cutting implements may be described as multipurpose.

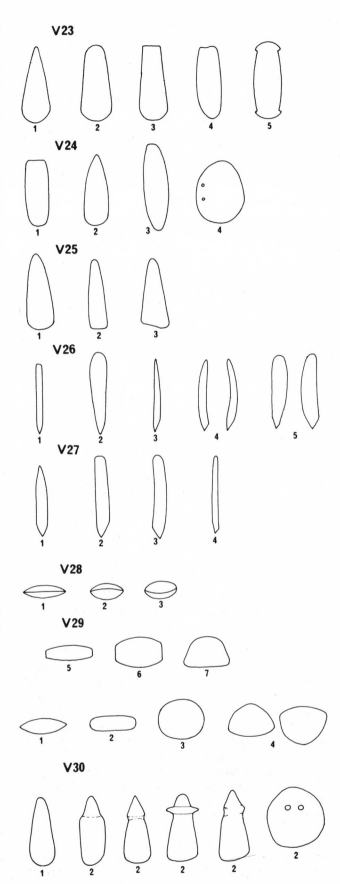

Fig. 2: Nominal scale attributes used to describe blade features.

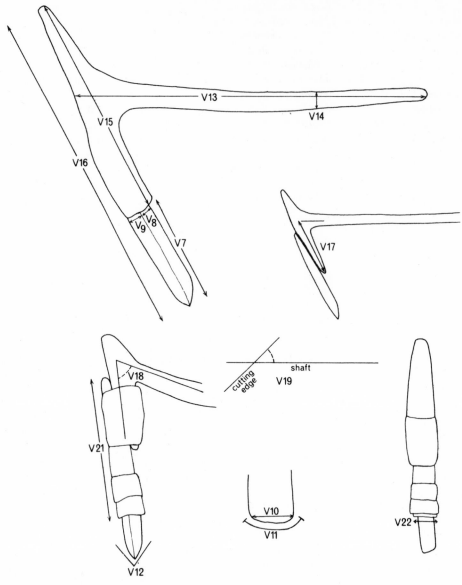

Fig. 3: Position of measurements used in description of complete Melanesian percussive cutting implements.

Durrans (1972) has recently proposed that artifact functions be studied according to variations in how artifacts were used. This results in a series of broad mechanical divisions having clearly defined morphological features which identify them. Durrans argues that the discovery by archaeologists of mechanical functions is more susceptible to empirical testing than is the determination of actual uses.

The argument that generalisations about the concomitance of use and morphology may better be made in terms of mechanical functions than in terms of actual uses seems to be worth testing, but in order to do this it is necessary to determine the range of tasks within which the mechanical functions must operate. Therefore, at the outset of this project a study of percussive cutting implement uses was directed towards associating artifacts with the uses reported ethnographically. Thus it was made a tenet of population selection that a sample should be represented by artifacts reported as having one use or a defined range of uses. Because the ethnographic evidence is deficient for many areas, the major exceptions being offered by studies of single communities (e.g. Blackwood, 1950 for the

Ekuti Kukukuku; Malinowski, 1934 for the Trobriands; and Firth, 1959 for Tikopia), many samples do not have directly associated testimony of function. In these cases if, after application of the other selection procedures, all the implements in a group had similar looking blades, then they were assumed for the purpose of preliminary testing to have satisfied similar ranges of tasks.

The resolution of the various kinds of geographic locations into discrete districts was achieved through the application of a simple typology to the collections. Four features which in combination were represented on every recorded artifact and which reflected restrictions to such districts were selected. Two of these features were the handle form (*a*) and hafting modification (*b*) already discussed for the manufacturing traditions. Within the major groups established by these means two further features, details of blade attachment (feature *c* having 29 attributes) and lashing or form of proximal end of the head (feature *d* having 35 attributes) were incorporated. The attributes are depicted in Fig. 5. It may be noted that as few features as possible were used in this typology, and that in

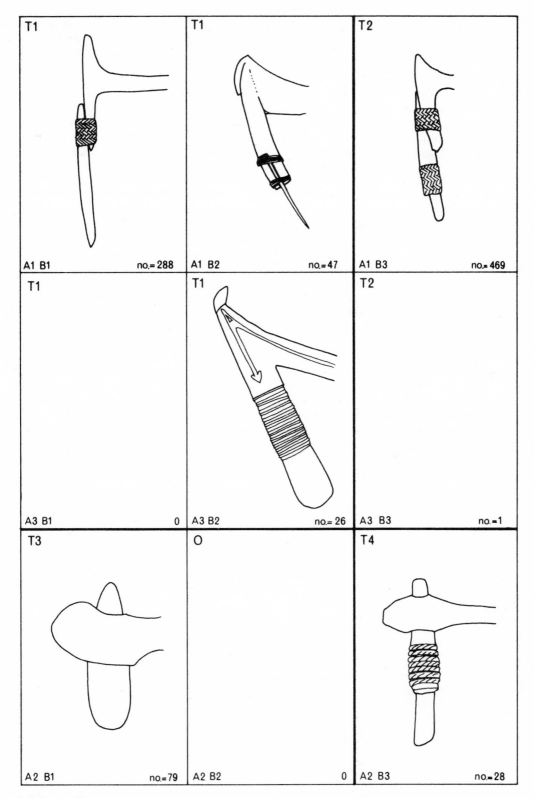

Fig. 4: Manufacturing traditions.

particular features of the blade were excluded so that the description of these archaeologically significant parts of the artifacts could be directly compared with descriptions of excavated materials. These four features contribute to the stylistic description of a population but are only a part of the stylistic characterisation of it.

When listed with the *a* and *b* attributes 118 four attribute combinations were distinguished on the 938 implements recorded. As more than 2000 combinations could theoretically occur this is further confirmation that we are dealing with a technologically and culturally restricted class of artifacts. Eighty-five of these 118 combinations, or 73%, proved to be restricted to a single geographic district. Two combinations occurred in areas where geographic subdivision into districts was not possible because of a lack of internal localisation but where on other ethnographic grounds such a subdivision might be expected (Fiji, part of south New Guinea). One combination occurred in neighbouring districts and in this case alone was provenance the sole basis of district separation. Two other combinations occurred in neighbouring districts but here the distinction was made on grounds of blade differentiation as well as by geographic differentiation. The remaining 28 combinations, occurring in from two to seven districts, all widely separated, were distinguished on the form of the heel (if footed handles were in question) or on the form of the head (if straight handles were in question) as well as upon geographic grounds. Though uncoded in studies to date this feature (e) will be described in nominal scale attributes in any future study. It may be noted that it is in the resolution of such problems that the nature of the attribute discrimination becomes important. For example, all the occurrences of attributes of features c and d in widely separated districts are recognisable as coming from a particular district, but the discrimination of attributes to meet this degree of differentiation could easily be pursued to the point where individual artifacts have unique combinations. The problem is one which must be resolved for each study.

The restriction of an a–d attribute combination to a single district does not mean that it is necessarily the only combination found in artifacts from the district. In particular the variation in lashing pattern is one where individual choice might be expected to play a part. Lashing material, however, is usually restricted within a particular district or group of neighbouring districts. As a test of the effect of lashing

patterns on geographic districts an area, northeast Papua, was selected. Here all implements belong to the same manufacturing tradition, were used for the same tasks as nearly as could be ascertained, and were collected mainly within the period 1890–1898. The 142 implements were divided into samples rigorously according to their a–d combination, tested for internal homogeneity, and compared for differences. No internal differences were revealed within two sets of three groups, but a few appeared between those in one set and those in the other. Thus only two groups were involved. These differences were marked by the differences between the two sorts of separate socket involved ($c13$ and $c14$) regardless of the lashing patterns present ($d13$, $d14$, $d16$). As additional confirmation the two groups marked by separate socket differences occur in more northern and more southern areas of the general region respectively.

3. Resolution into population samples The combination of the variants of the four aspects of heterogeneity—manufacturing tradition, use, time and district—resulted in 138 population samples being recognised among the 938 recorded artifacts.

An advantage of this approach is that it allows the incorporation of items mentioned in the literature despite the impossibility of measuring their other features. A further 108 populations were recognised from the literature, while one putative sago felling population was allowed a number, making 247 in all. Because of the gaps in the literature and among the collections available for study it is likely that many more populations remain to be distinguished.

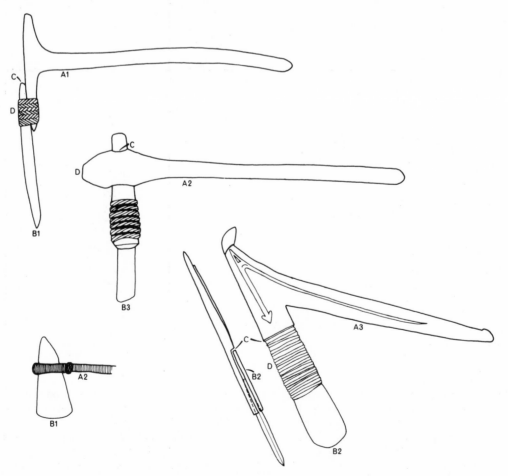

Fig. 5: Hafting features and attributes used in describing Melanesian percussive cutting implements.

Fig. 5 continued

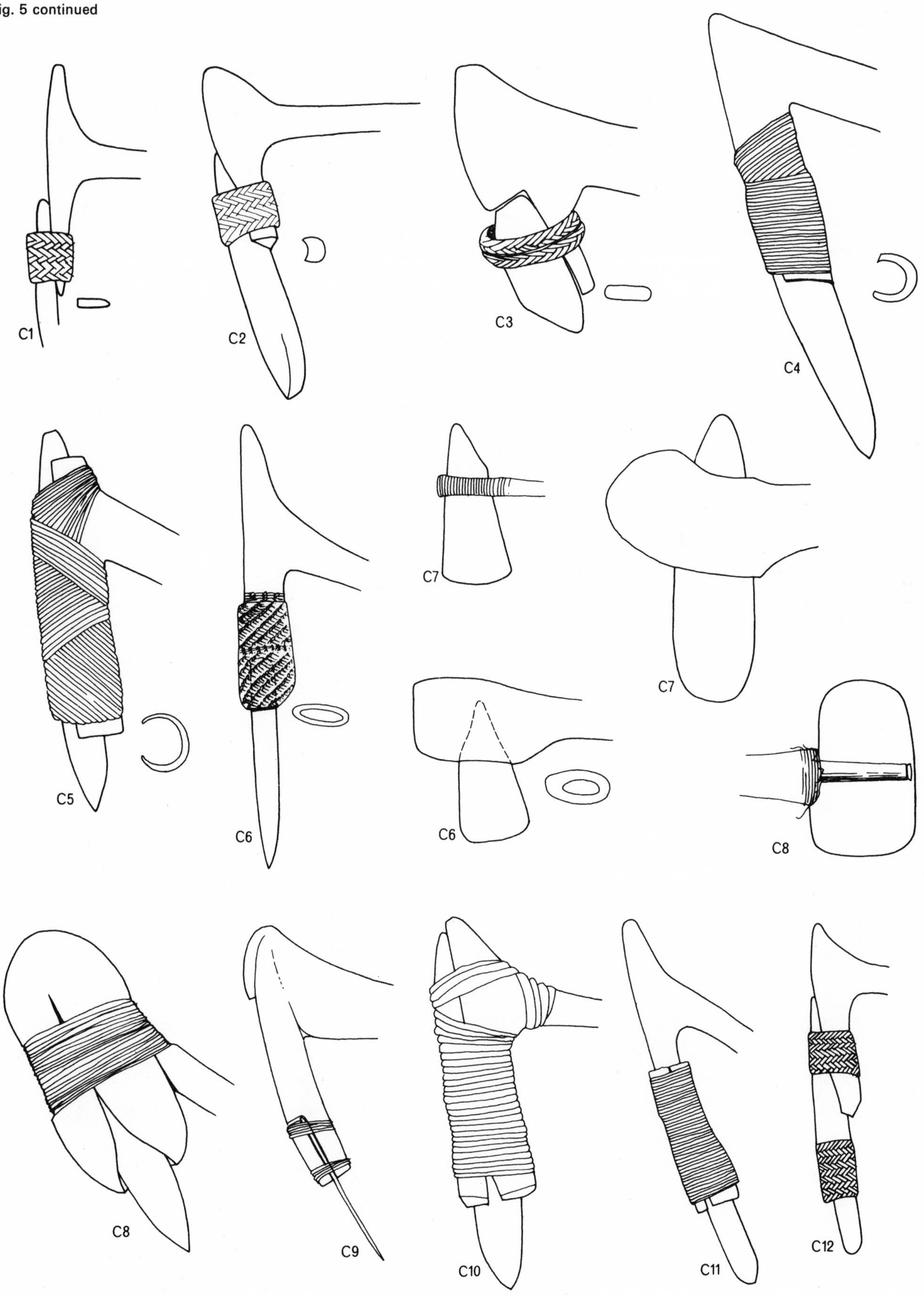

C1

C2

C3

C4

C5

C6

C7

C7

C6

C8

C8

C9

C10

C11

C12

Fig. 5 continued

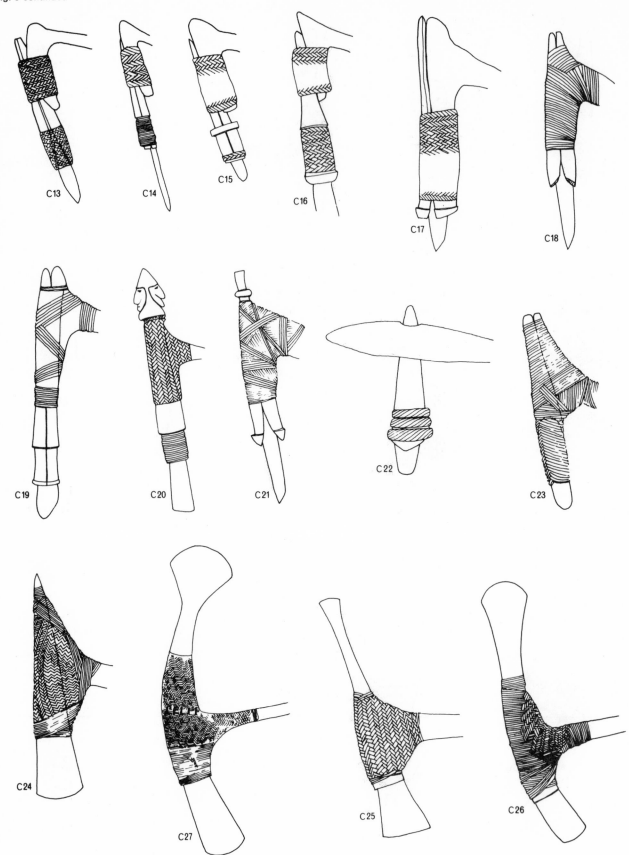

Fig. 5 continued

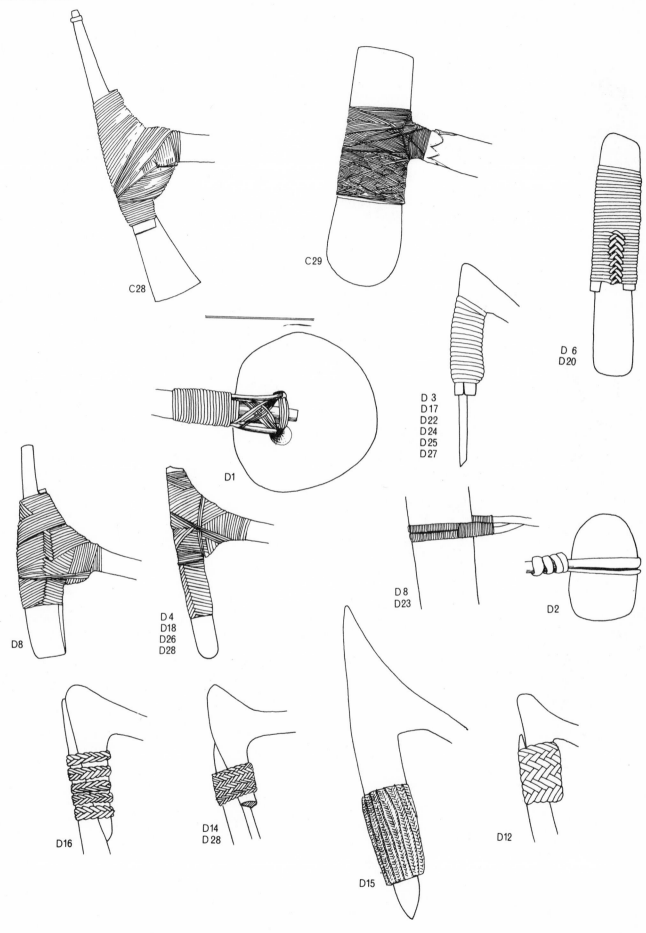

Fig. 5 continued

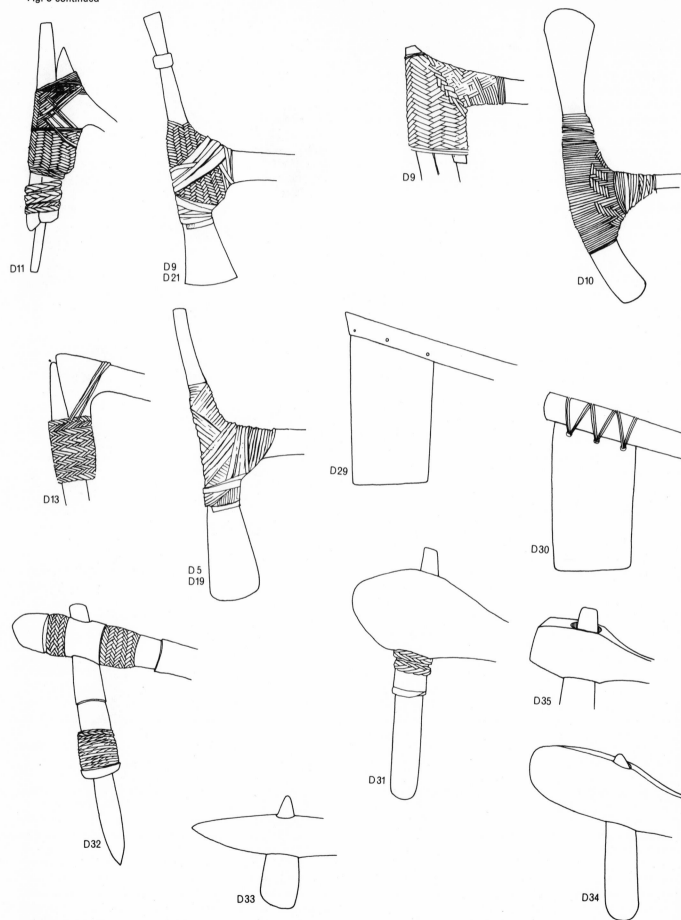

D11

D9
D21

D9

D10

D13

D5
D19

D29

D30

D32

D31

D35

D33

D34

4. Testing samples The verification of whether the samples are soundly chosen lies in tests of their morphological homogeneity. If a sample can be characterised as stylistically homogeneous then the homogeneity can be presented visually, verbally or statistically. Because the populations are represented by samples, if discussion of the populations is desired, then the reasoning from sample to population is statistical (Simpson, Roe and Lewontin, 1960 : v). Moreover, statistical descriptions are a concise technique for expressing variation within a sample, and further, the use of statistics requires that the steps in the process be clearly expressed.

Unfortunately, statistics are limited by the morphological measurements made, so the measurements used must comprehend as much as possible of the variance, and any other observations of morphological differences must be expressed verbally. Statistics are also limited by the number of objects within a sample. Of the 247 populations recognised 138 are represented by actual samples of recorded implements but only 40 samples are large enough for statistical tests to have any applicability. Seventeen of these samples have between 6 and 13 members, twenty-three from 14 to 75 members. Because of the two measurement scales employed two sorts of tests to verify homogeneity were needed.

For ratio scale measurements the closer a distribution approached a normal curve the more homogeneous it was taken to be. Tests of the shape of a curve are skewness, which is the degree to which the sample median is separated from the sample mean, and kurtosis which measures whether the curve is more peaked or flatter than normal. Preliminary tests showed that samples tended to conform to normal distributions. This is not only extremely interesting in itself, but considering future testing, it means that the samples have variances quite comparable to zoological samples. In the absence of any consensus of the permissible variance range for artifact samples I was therefore able to use those established for zoology. Sample homogeneity was considered to fall within the bounds of $+1$ and -1 for skewness, and down to -1 for kurtosis (Simpson, Roe and Lewontin, 1960 : 143–47). A high positive score for kurtosis was considered acceptable because it indicated an increased concentration around the sample mean and hence variation towards a smaller range. Each of the 16 ratio scale measurements was described for each large sample according to the numbers present, the mean, standard deviation, minimum and maximum reading, and the amount of skew and kurtosis.

Tests of morphological homogeneity for nominally scaled attributes lie in the frequency and percentage distributions. The 11 features measured were described by a total of 55 attributes. Each artifact has a combination of 11 of these. The more homogeneous a sample the fewer attributes should be represented on its constituent artifacts. A homogeneous sample was taken as one in which at least one attribute of each of the 11 features was represented on at least 50% of the artifacts in the sample.

Having thus described the samples and ascertained that they were as nearly as possible homogeneous the next step was to determine that they did, as hypothesised, belong to different populations. For ratio scale measurements the means and standard deviations were used in *t*-tests. To be different, pairs of samples had to have at least one highly significant difference ($\alpha = 0.001$) among the 16 measurements compared. For the nominal scale measurements supplied with percentage distributions a development by L. M. Groube of Robinson's 1951 similarity statistic, which was used by Groube to test differences between assemblages of Oceanic adze-blades (Groube and Chappell, 1973), was employed.

These tests were conducted on the 20 largest samples from New Guinea. In all cases but those of two large samples from northeast Papua already commented on, all samples were markedly different from each other.

By these means the samples were established as acceptable. The stage was then set for tests of variance attributable to various causes. Four comparative studies were undertaken. One of the degrees of similarity between the 18 large populations as independent groups using all the measurements by themselves, a second comparing different uses, a third comparing different manufacturing traditions, and a fourth examining similarities within possible regional units. These last three analyses employed all the available information.

Discussion

The method of selecting artifact groups described raises several important questions.

One of the most interesting of these is the fact that artifact populations, selected as they were in accordance with the imprecise collection data available, should in fact be morphologically homogeneous within the bounds accepted by zoologists. It is a tenet that artifact similarity has a cultural significance but in the case under discussion it is anything but clear what kind of group is represented by the populations into which the collections have been resolved. In at least some instances the population coincides quite well with language family distribution, for example population EI 4 and the Mountain Koiari Family (Dutton, 1969), but in other cases, for example the lower Sepik, population SEP 4 cross-cuts a wide range of unrelated linguistic groups (D. Laycock, unpublished map). This aspect of the study has been incompletely surveyed to date but it is apparent that percussive cutting implement populations but rarely coincide with ethnic or linguistic distributions despite the hope that the selection procedures would result in such coincidences. It is also apparent that single populations only rarely (in such situations as on small islands) coincide with subdivisions of the natural environment.

The question therefore arises, what effects these cross-cutting distributions have upon the acceptance of populations as representing styles established and maintained through inter-communication between groups of craftsmen. If we continue to recognise the populations in stylistically as well as in statistically homogeneous terms then we assert that the social controls postulated over style can in some cases extend beyond ethnic boundaries. It is also possible that the agreed range of variation which constitutes a style might vary from group to group of craftsmen. Reasons for particular geographic and morphological restrictions of range might lie in factors particular to the society in which the artifacts are made. This is not to say, given collection data in enough detail, that single communities might not be discovered to produce identifiable artifacts; nevertheless in this study the equation *morphologically homogeneous population = style = community of a single kind* cannot be resolved.

However, the study has produced groups of artifacts which are statistically homogeneous and unique. These groups can be used as standards against which archaeological finds can be tested, as palaeontologists test their fossils against zoological standards (Simpson, Roe and Lewontin, 1960 : 205–12).

A further difficulty is the problem of including shapes measured on nominal scales in the same tests with sizes and proportions measured on ratio scales. This becomes particularly important when making comparisons between samples in multivariate terms, that is in terms of the contribution of all the measurements to the characterisation of the whole sample as summed up in a single numerical statement. At present it is necessary to deal with such comparisons in terms of different kinds of statistics. In this study the two sets of multivariate comparisons were compared by ranking the 20 large samples according to the average similarity of each with the 19 others. A test of the resulting ranks showed that the ratio scale multivariate statistic used and the nominal scale multivariate statistic used produced unrelated patterns of similarity. While this conclusion acts as a warning that no test of similarity necessarily produces better patterns of relationship than any other, it also points up the need for mixed-data programmes. Computer botanists have been examining this problem for some time (e.g. Lance and Williams; Lance, Milne and Williams, *op. cit.*) but are no closer to a solution of the problem of information loss sustained when ratio scale information is submitted to the less powerful non-parametric tests appropriate to nominal scale measurements.

The application of population systematics to artifacts has resulted in artifact groups which no more closely reflect some recognisable kind of 'social reality' than do artifact groups produced by other classification methods, though as Dunnell (1971) points out there is no reason why archaeologists should necessarily aim for social reality. Nevertheless the population method has proved successful in this study and leads me to suggest that the method may be more widely applicable. Remembering that its contrast with typological systematics lies in the information used as a first stage in selecting the smallest units in the analysis—population systematics using collection data, artifact typology morphology—it must also be remembered that the concept *population* has no general content, only a content specific to a particular study. Simpson, Roe and Lewontin (1960 : v) can say for zoology, 'There are still some typological systematists, but it is today widely admitted that all zoological problems without exception relate to populations'. Will this one day be paraphrased to read 'all artifact problems without exception relate to populations'?

References

Blackwood, E., 1950. *The technology of a modern stone age people in New Guinea.* Oxford: Pitt Rivers Museum, Occasional Papers in Technology No. 1.

Crosby, E., 1973. *A comparative study of Melanesian hafted edge tools and other percussive cutting implements.* Canberra, unpublished Ph.D. thesis.

Dunnell, R. C., 1971. *Systematics in Prehistory.* New York: Free Press.

Durrans, B., 1972. *A morphological-functional analysis of some types of Oceanic canoes.* London: University College, unpublished Ph.D. thesis.

Dutton, T. E., 1969. *The Koiarian languages of Central Papua: an historical and descriptive linguistic study.* Canberra: A.N.U., unpublished Ph.D. thesis.

Firth, R., 1959. Ritual adzes in Tikopia. *In* D. Freeman and W. R. Geddes (eds.) *Anthropology in the South Seas,* pp. 149–50. New Zealand: Thomas Avery.

Groube, L. M. and J. Chappell, 1973. Measuring the difference between archaeological assemblages. *In* C. Renfrew (ed.), *The explanation of culture change; models in prehistory* pp. 167–84. London: Duckworth.

Hinderling, P., 1949. *Uber Steinzeitliche Beile der Südsee.* Aarau.

Lance, G. N. and W. T. Williams, 1967a. A general theory of classificatory sorting strategies: I. Hierarchical systems. *Computer Journal;* 373–80.

—— and —— 1967b. A general theory of classificatory sorting strategies: II. Clustering systems. *Computer Journal* 10: 271–79.

—— and —— 1967c. Mixed-data classificatory programs: I. Agglomerative systems. *Australian Computer Journal* 1 : 15–20.

—— and —— 1968. Mixed-data classificatory programs: II. Divisive systems. *Australian Computer Journal* 1 : 82–5.

——, P. W. Milne and W. T. Williams, 1968. Mixed-data classificatory programs: III. Diagnostic systems. *Australian Computer Journal* 1 : 178–81.

Leroi-Gourhan, A., 1945–1949. Evolution et techniques, Vol. 1. *L'homme et la matière,* Vol. 2. *Milieu et techniques.* Paris: A. Michel.

Malinowski, B., 1943. Stone implements in eastern New Guinea. *In* E. E. Evans-Pritchard (ed.), *Essays presented to C. G. Seligman,* pp. 189–96. London: Kegan Paul.

Semenov, S. A., 1964. *Prehistoric Technology.* Bath: Adams and Dart.

Siegel, S., 1956. *Non-parametric statistics for the behavioural sciences.* New York: McGraw-Hill.

Simpson, C. G., A. Roe and R. Lewontin, 1960. *Duatnitative Zoology.* New York: Harcourt, Brace and World.

Quartz flaking

F. P. DICKSON

Abstract

An account of experiments in flaking quartz from archaeological sites in the A.C.T. and N.S.W. to assess its working properties and its productivity for flakes of specified sizes.
Information was obtained about the formation of bipolar
cores and the techniques of working the material in the hand
and between hammer and anvil. Bipolar cores appear to be
simply residuals and not implements. Selection effects relating to the choice of material were explored and several
criteria for working quality were found.

Silica in one form or another is an ubiquitous mineral and
stones consisting almost wholly of amorphous silica have
been the principal materials for making flaked stone tools all
over the world. The properties which have made them so
generally used are their hardness, isotropic structure and conchoidal fracture, so well displayed in flint, obsidian and chalcedony and in varying degrees in stones like chert, silcrete and
quartzite. With all these man learned to make finely wrought
and finished tools.

One of the commonest forms of silica, quartz, stands out as
an exception, seldom used for fine secondary work though it
served for coarser implements. Clear crystalline quartz has all
the desired properties, including mechanical isotropy, unusual
in a crystalline rock, but is so scarce as a surface mineral that
it has seldom been used. The common forms of quartz found
as rounded pebbles eroded from sedimentary rocks or as
massive angular lumps of vein quartz are plentiful enough in
Australia but were little used where other siliceous stone could
be had. Of their nature these forms of quartz may be generally
similar in working properties though usually tougher and more
cohesive than flint or silcrete. Compared with those materials
quartz sounds 'dead' when struck. In practice quartz of desirable quality is not often found because of its geological
history, having frequently been subjected to great pressures
and heat which induce in it strains and incipient fractures.
Quartz pebbles are particularly subject to internal fractures
because the processes which made them from angular lumps
can almost be guaranteed to damage their structure. In consequence quartz often breaks upon working into chunky
pieces and short flakes of little value. Normally the fracture
edges are very sharp even when obtuse and primary flakes
have keen edges. Good conchoidal fracture is rarely seen and
even when best developed is rather flat.

Nonetheless, quartz of good quality can be satisfactorily
worked. In his excavations in the Hunter River valley Moore
found quartz artifacts in several sites (Moore, 1970). As shown
in his Table 7 for the Bobadeen site it is clear that quartz was
less often worked than the chert, jasper and quartzite available

in the area. At this site some of the quartz was in the clear
crystalline form which made very well finished artifacts,
otherwise milky quartz was used and there was a variation in
the artifacts from very fine to crude and lumpy.

At Kurnell some quartz in the form of pebbles eroded
from the Hawkesbury sandstone was worked, leaving waste
in the form of irregular bits. Secondarily worked quartz
implements were rare and crudely shaped. The toolmakers
had a preference for silcrete, chert, rhyolite and silicified
wood, all of which had to be procured from considerable
distance. There was no sign of crystalline quartz (Dickson.
1973 : 7).

Despite its rather unattractive properties quartz will of
necessity be used in areas where more desirable stones cannot
be found locally or acquired by trade. If it is of poor quality,
as pebble quartz often is, the artifacts will tend to be poor. If
some better quality quartz is available, as from large exposed
veins, it will produce better artifacts and the industry will be
less impoverished and will reflect the characteristics of the
material. Thus on a coastal bondaian workshop site we usually
find a great number of waste flakes, many of which could, if
necessary, have been secondarily worked. In addition there
are numerous quite small polygonal cores. In contrast to chert
or silcrete, quartz does not lend itself to forming polygonal
cores because of its toughness and modes of fracture and these
would not be found in a quartz industry. Nor would there be
cortical flakes produced in stripping off weathered parts of the
cortex because quartz does not produce such a cortex. Apart
from the cores one could expect to find other evidence of
differing techniques used for working quartz. Unmodified
flakes, though numerous, would be outweighed by other forms
of quartz debris.

The occasion for the experimental work on quartz described
in this paper was a recent study by Josephine Flood of the
Australian National University of contemporary quartz using
industries at four sites which contained bondaian elements
in the Australian Capital Territory and nearby in New South
Wales. The experiments were undertaken at her request and
the results made available for her thesis (1973). Later (1973)
these results were also used by Katherine Sullivan of the
University of Sydney.

In my work much interest attached to bipolar or scalar cores
with battered opposing ends, as described by White (1965 :
665). Artifacts of this kind had previously been observed at
Sassafras, one of the four sites involved (Hume, 1965 : 20).
Bipolar cores, otherwise known as fabricators, are artifacts of
dubious status and have been the subject of much discussion
and of a number of papers. This status has been analysed by
White who concluded that, at least in Australia and New
Guinea, fabricators are residual cores and the end product of

flaking down larger pieces (White, 1968 : 664). Because of the evidence from Currarong and Burrill Lake Lampert agreed with White's view that bipolars are residual cores from the production of small flakes but considered that they may also have been used as implements in their own right (Lampert, 1971 : 47).

My experiments had no direct concern with possible uses for bipolars, only with their production, and were restricted to quartz specimens. As had previously been observed (Breuil and Lantier, 1965:63), the bipoplar method is the only way to reduce a lump of quartz. It soon appeared that unless they collapsed at the last moment, bipolar cores were certain to be the end product. Some account of this production of bipolars seems warranted.

When a piece of quartz has a surface which can be used as a striking platform the hammer blows can be positioned and angled in the usual way to secure long flakes but this is ineffective because of the toughness of the material and its difficult fracture. The platform is crushed rapidly into fine debris and so develops a rounded contour from which a hammer blow tends to glance with reduced transfer of energy. The only remedy then is to strike further towards the centre and attempt to remove a comparatively thick chip. Quite soon the platform becomes pillow-shaped and further blows produce a battered but fairly straight central ridge. At this stage one reverses the core to work on the opposite end which, as the reaction of the anvil is wider spread, has suffered less. Sooner or later a typically bipolar form is produced, unless the core is broken, when repetition of the same processes yields smaller bipolars. The rounding of the cores results in considerable quantities of fine debris. In recording the experiments the very fine debris was collected and weighed as particles smaller than 1mm, fine debris was particles between 1 and 4 mm.

While it is easy to show that bipolars are the normal products of flaking lumps of quartz, this does not exclude the possibility that they may have been used as tools, as implied by the name fabricator which has been in use for a good many years. It is natural for me to look at tools like these with the eyes of an engineer and to handle them with an engineer's tactile feelings for tools and materials. I have been told that as the product of a vastly different culture it is naughty of me to attribute any such feelings to ancient stoneworkers but I still think it is permissible. Indeed I think that pure technique can remain invariant under cultural transformations. This does not imply anything so mathematically definable as the Lorentz invariance I am accustomed to use in another field of science, but an invariance upon which I can usefully rely. There is only a finite and indeed small number of ways to make some particular implement out of a piece of stone. It goes further than that for there is ample evidence that a user of stone tools would pick up some piece which would serve his immediate purpose and not modify it unless he had to. One does just that today. Perhaps some piece of material has to be turned to a specific shape. If one of the bits of tool steel in the workshop will serve, for that task it is a tool; if not one has to modify a piece. The work to be done, the shape to be formed, is the primary problem—what tool will serve is a secondary matter. It need not be specialised.

A statement by Michael Polyani seems very appropriate here:

Take for example the identification of a thing as a tool. It implies that a useful purpose can be served by handling the thing as an instrument for that purpose. I cannot identify the thing as a tool if I do not know what it is for—or if,

knowing its supposed purpose, I believe it is useless for that purpose. (1962 : 56)

Now I am unwilling to identify bipolars as tools on both of Polyani's counts. I do not know what purpose they would serve and no one has told me a convincing story about how to use them. On the second count, to the prejudiced engineer's eye, bipolars seem unsuitable as tools. The uses for them that have been suggested to me resemble those for a cold chisel such as is used for chipping cast iron. Cold chisels have numerous other uses but I nominate chipping cast iron because it has a brittle fracture like stone. I quite often use a chunk of quartz as a hammer driven chisel to remove some undesired bulge from an axe blank or to form a hafting groove. It works well and is remarkably durable. I do not need it to be bipolar, sharp at both ends, as it works much better when the hammered end is blunt, preferably even dome shaped. After a fair amount of use the blunt end will become so broken away that the chisel becomes more or less bipolar and when this process has reached the limit it is time to discard it. It has then arrived at the stage where its structual integrity has been impaired to such an extent that it is likely to collapse under the next moderate blow and give me a couple of painfully bruised fingers. This is another way to make bipolars but I would not in that case admit them as tools; they are only the useless remnants of what have been tools.

In this argument I am not trying to prove a negative, that it is impossible to use a bipolar as a tool, as a 'fabricator'. I might even use one if nothing else were available but it would be very much a last resort. It is just not a tool user's tool, not the sort of thing one would deliberately set out to make and I think that the probability of it really being a tool is infinitesimal.

A further matter of investigation was that on three of the four sites there was evidence that the quartz was worked down to bipolar cores between hammer and anvil. However this did not appear to be the case at the fourth site where there was no evidence of bipolar working though large numbers of quartz flakes were present, perhaps indicating that the material used there permitted the production of flakes in some other way. There also seemed to be evidence that where bipolars occurred each was accompanied by some thirty flakes very nearly as long as the bipolar, typically 18–19 mm flakes from a 20 mm core.

One of the purposes of the experiments was to learn something about the productivity of the material for making flakes. A known use for quartz flakes was arming death spears and it appears that these flakes were of small size. Lampert (1971 : 46) refers to them as small and quotes a length of 10 mm found by Eylmann, Mulvaney (1969 : 91) describes them as 'minute' and 'tiny'. However, on Flood's sites, considerable numbers of flakes of 18 and 19 mm were found indicating that flakes larger than 5 to 10 mm were desired, perhaps for other uses. As Bordaz has shown, long flakes can always be subdivided, as for making geometric microliths (1970 : 94). Since it was desired to test the material also for the production of bondi points and geometric microliths a wider specification was adopted covering flakes 10–35 mm long and 10-25 mm wide and with fairly straight but very sharp edges. While arbitrary (in that it admits only the largest size used for death spears) this specification provided a practical working basis.

Apart from these specific matters the experiments were expected to yield other interesting information and this proved to be the case. Two sets of experiments were made using two lots of samples, identified by the site names and the designations Series 1 and Series 2. This doubling was the consequence of a preliminary visual examination of Series 1 material and is, in itself, a result of some interest. Inspection and handling of the material suggested that most of it would not be suitable for the experiment intended. There appeared to be a selection bias in that the pieces of quartz had been collected essentially on the basis of ready availability in the vicinities of the sites. An experienced stoneworker, however, would have selected pieces which appeared to him most promising for the production of usable artifacts. Accordingly the pieces comprising Series 2 were taken from material excavated from the actual sites on the assumption that they had been deliberately selected and taken there to be worked. The importance of these selection effects was sufficiently demonstrated in the experiments.

Before starting the two sets of experiments it seemed proper to improve on a modest experience in working quartz obtained several years ago during a study of bondi points, so a preliminary run was made with a number of large quartz pebbles from various localities. Although it was not deliberately intended and in fact some attempt was made to form polygonal cores, these pebbles all reduced to bipolars.

The preliminary run also gave the opportunity to test a fine mesh cage erected over and around the working position. Its purpose was to prevent the loss of material during flaking due to the tendency of bits to fly away at high velocities. This is especially the case with quartz, which has to be hit rather hard to dislodge flakes. The cage proved effective enough to keep the loss of material below 0.5% by weight and to particles smaller than 1mm.

During this run it was observed that indirect percussion methods are unrewarding with quartz. My earlier impression that quartz is a rather unpleasant material for concentrated working was confirmed by diffuse bleeding at the fingers due to microscopically small but sharp particles penetrating the skin at high speeds.

Because of the suggestion that hammer and anvil working might not have been used at one of the sites, Nardoo, attention was paid to the dynamics of flaking quartz. It is well known that a large core can be flaked while held in the hand but there are limits to this. The main factor is the inertia of the core, determined by its mass. Other factors are the shape and texture. Obviously the most unfavourable shape is spheroidal, hence the normal practice of making a striking platform. The most unfavourable texture is tough and cohesive as is the case with good quartz. With it my limit for a core held in the hand appears to be between 60 and 90 g. A piece below this limiting mass cannot be held firmly enough without the reaction, due to its low inertia, being too painful to continue using blows strong enough to drive off useful pieces. Light blows remove only very small fragments from quartz, thus rounding the core and increasing the difficulty. Presumably other operators would find somewhat differing limits depending on the size and strength of the hand and the extent to which stone working is regularly practised. The use of some form of padding between the hand and core will help to reduce the discomfort but does nothing to prevent the hand and arm moving under the impact, thus reducing the energy transferred to the core.

Below the limit for satisfactory hand holding some form of support for the core is needed, commonly but not necessarily, a stone anvil. A slab of hard wood can also be used as an anvil for working quartz and there is no infallible way to tell from the worked material whether the anvil was wood or stone. The operator naturally reverses a quartz core from time to time and the result with a wooden anvil is just as bipolar as one that came off a stone anvil. Wood, however, is not resistant enough for sustained work and a bipolar may be driven deeply into it.

The main quality for an anvil is also inertia; it ought not to move when the core is struck. If it does move then once again too much of the kinetic energy of the hammer is lost. The anvil may have large inertia from its own mass or indirectly through firm support on the ground or other large mass. Naturally, one chooses, where possible, an anvil of tough stone without brittle fracture and preferably at least twice the weight of the core. The anvil used in these experiments was a piece of fine grained basalt originally collected for an axe blank. It weighed 810 g and after flaking some 3 kg of quartz on it, 14 g had been eroded from the anvil, leaving a roughly conical pit surrounded by a pecked area.

There are several qualities to consider in selecting a hammer. It should be of a hard, tough stone which will not easily fracture in use. It is most irritating to have one's hammer break in the middle of a job and it takes a while to feel at ease with a substitute. There is much more to the use of a hammer than merely hitting; it must be carefully directed and the force of impact regulated. As is common with all craftsmen, one can become attached to a favourite tool and do better work with it than with another. A waterworn pebble makes a good hammer as it provides useful contours and is unlikely to have easy fracture planes. For working quartz it should be heavy compared with the minimum sized core that can be held in the hand. Its function is to provide the kinetic energy for breaking pieces off the core, by virtue of both its mass and its velocity at the instant of impact.

Even though the same energy results from a light hammer moving fast and a heavier one moving more slowly, these are not just simple alternatives. If the hammer is very light it will be difficult to move it fast enough and still more difficult to have adequate control over the point and angle of impact. Too massive a hammer, however, will be clumsy to handle and equally hard to control. During the preliminary run a variety of hammers ranging from 165 g to 1100 g was tried with the result that one in the range 300 to 400 g appeared most satisfactory.

For the experiments on Series 1 and 2 material a new hammer of 325 g was chosen and proved very satisfactory. It was an oval pebble blank 110 mm long, 70 mm wide and 33 mm thick, dimensions which made it pleasing to handle and not tiring to hold in sustained use. From flaking the 3 kg of quartz it lost 12 g, all in the form of small particles by wear. The hammer remains good enough to work another such quantity.

The pattern of wear on a hammer varies with its application, its shape and the way in which the operator handles it. Both the actual ends and the sides close to the ends may be worn. A nearly cylindrical hammer is largely used end-on and to a lesser degree side-on for heavy swinging blows. The oval shape of the hammer used in these experiments became more worn at the sides than on the ends. The tips of the broader sides were effective in the initial dislodgement of broad flakes from angular work pieces while the narrow sides were more worn at later stages. The concentrated impact from the narrow sides was good for working very intractable material because it seemed to give better control. It was also good for neat splitting of oversize rounded bipolars.

During the experiments the massive initial lumps that could be flaked were brought down to bipolars, each lump yielding a number of bipolars. That bipolars outnumber lumps appears to be a consequence of the properties of the material. An initially angular piece offers natural striking platforms but the cohesion and virtually non-conchoidal fracture of quartz, shown by the lack of percussion bulbing, results in the platforms becoming too rounded for effective flaking. As a new platform cannot be made just by knocking off the rounded part, more drastic treatment is needed. One simply splits the core with a hard blow, thus providing two secondary cores to work and restoring the desired angularity for platforms. Several repetitions of this procedure result in a plurality of bipolars from the original core. The ultimate length of bipolars is determined by the thickness of one's forefinger and thumb, principally the latter. One becomes acutely aware of this end point.

During the working some thought was given to the matter of obtaining flakes similar in length to their bipolar cores. As with other materials, it is possible to get somewhat longer flakes by holding the core very tightly with strong thumb pressure on the face where the flake is to be detached. White (1968:661) describes a method of binding cores which enables longer flakes to be made and this was tried in my preliminary experiments. With the quartz available the gain appeared to be only marginal and the method was not continued.

On further consideration of the flakes that were almost as long as the bipolars as found by Flood, it seemed that they had been obtained before the core was reduced to its final length. Such a core necessarily tends to a pillow shape and the probability of getting a full length flake off it, short of completely splitting it, must be low.

It is apparent that in these experiments there are a number of subjective elements, ranging from the choice of pieces to be worked and the way they were treated, to the determination of the end points. In experiments where one is trying to take the place of one of the original stone workers this seems quite legitimate and, indeed to some extent, unavoidable. Experience in working with stone generates a kind of awareness which, with a modicum of additional experience in a new kind of stone, can soon be applied to it and quartz is no exception. While some information can be gained from its appearance, more and better information comes from feeling and handling it. Thus it is known from engineering practice that, in assessing texture, a sensitive fingertip can detect surface irregularities as small as 2.5 microns which may be difficult to see without optical aids. Irregularities of 10 microns are easy to feel.

Subjective judgments based on experience are often borne out. It is probably more than coincidence that in these experiments a big bipolar core from Tidbindilla Series 2 was judged useless before taking the hammer to it. Another core from Gudgenby in Series 2, starting at 85 g was abandoned as too intractable at 53 g although it had yielded some good flakes. At the time of writing it was brought out and worked again. Though carefully worked it yielded only one instead of the 10 or 12 flakes that might have been expected on *a priori* grounds, probably because of internal fractures induced by hammering. Decisions as to what looks promising cannot be other than subjective.

In the sections that follow, details of the experiments are set out for both Series 1 and Series 2. In describing the products, pieces struck off are called flakes only where they meet the usual specifications. As much of the material seemed to have multiple intersecting planes of fracture, pieces were checked by soaking them in a strong solution of Crystal Violet or Brilliant Cresyl Blue stain. On washing the stain from the surface it was seen that it had penetrated otherwise invisible fractures, throwing them into strong contrast. Secondary working to convert flakes into backed blades was done by the chimbling process as successfully used on other kinds of stone (Dickson, 1973:13). It proved successful with quartz. Obviously the shape and size of the resulting bondi must be related to the flake used. The quality of the finished product depends on the small scale fracture of the material. Generally, where there is freedom from flaws, the glossier and more translucent material produces more shapely and better finished points.

We now come to the flaking experiments with the samples identified as Series 1, the first of which came from Tidbinbilla. This material was massive vein quartz in roughly triangular prisms. It was patchy grey-red and white, opaque and without lustre. Few planes of fracture could be seen; it appeared very tough and cohesive.

A large lump weighing 384 g, held in the hand, failed to give substantial fragments in any orientation when struck hard. It finally broke into three pieces of 200, 134 and 50 g. The 200 g piece was reduced in the hand to 112 g. The 88 g removed contained several large irregular bits but no flakes. The four largest bits were worked down to bipolars yielding chips but no flakes. Similarly the 112 g piece reduced on the anvil resulted in six bipolars but no flakes.

As the 134 g and 50 g pieces could be expected to behave similarly these were not reduced. The material was wholly unsuited for flaking.

The sample from Gudgenby was also massive vein quartz but in rectangular prism, grey, opaque and lustreless, with brown stained surfaces. Transverse fracture planes were visible. Working with a lump of 345 g in the hand 62 g had come off as chips when it broke into two pieces 141 g and 130 g with a few spalls amounting to 12 g.

The 130 g piece was reduced to 87 g and transferred to the anvil where it formed a large pillow shaped bipolar $45 \times 31 \times 24$ mm weighing 44 g. It did not seem worth further work.

The 141 g piece yielded a number of pieces which seemed more homogeneous. These were worked on the anvil into six bipolars. In the process one large flake weighing 8g was obtained. It had a good edge and was made into a backed blade $40 \times 21 \times 10$ mm. A smaller flake made a bondi $23 \times 12 \times 7$ mm. A third which had an edge 25 mm long was $29 \times 15 \times 9$ mm; it was made into a small elouera. There were several other flakes too small to meet the specification. The three artifacts together weighed 14 g, representing 10% by weight of the core.

The Sassafras sample contained several round quartz pebbles stained black on the outside but they were translucent grey inside and about 20 mm in diameter. One of these collapsed into small fragments when hit on the anvil. There were also two larger somewhat rounded lumps 101 g and 99 g, opaque dull white. Multiple fracturing made them coarsely granular in appearance with a grain size of 6-8 mm. They broke randomly into irregular bits.

Nardoo material was the most varied in sizes and textures. The biggest piece, 140 g was a fawn colour and promised to break into irregular chips. It did so break. The 97 g lump was even worse, with the appearance of having been fired. It collapsed into crumbs when lightly struck.

A piece weighing 52 g was translucent grey with a shiny fracture and it broke readily into pieces after three moderate blows. Four of these pieces seemed fairly cohesive and were reduced to bipolars. In forming these, three flakes of usable size were obtained but they seemed fragile. Two broke while backing but the third made a bondi $19 \times 17 \times 5$ mm.

One of the pieces weighing 27 g was itself a flake. It was

translucent, almost glassy, with the flat bulb usual with glassy quartz. Examined at 8 × magnification after staining it showed no flaws. On being worked it produced flakes rather than chips. Five were of specification size and a sixth made a bondi. The lengths ranged from 13.2 to 21.6 mm. The weight of these products was 11 g, representing 40.7% of the core. Coarse debris as undersize flakes was 8 g, fine waste 5 g and very fine 3 g.

This was the only really good piece in the whole series and was clearly of Aboriginal selection.

The samples from all these sites included numerous small pieces which were worked for test purposes before trying the bigger ones but the results were not recorded.

As remarked earlier the samples in Series 2 were generally superior and the results of working them are set out below taking the sites in the same order as before. In the Tidbinbilla sample there were no large pieces and none resembling the grey-red lumps of Series 1. The biggest piece of 64 g was pinkish white, opaque, dull and may have been fired. It shattered into crumbs. The next largest piece, 21 g, off-white in colour and lustrous was itself a bipolar 40 × 29 × 18 mm, evidently worked down from a larger core. It looked like a discard and appeared unrewarding for further work despite its lustrous quality; upon working it yielded only under-size flakes and proved to have numerous flaws.

The Gudgenby sample contained three sizeable lumps, 97 g, 74 g and 65 g. The 97 g and 74 g lumps had been fired and shattered into crumbs. The 65 g piece was translucent grey and had fracture planes that made it yield long slender flakes especially suitable for bondi points. Its geological past had evidently induced strains resulting in a preferred direction of fracture. Nine satisfactory flakes were obtained (Table 1). These flakes, after backing, weighed 7 g or 10.8% of the core. In their production the core was reduced to four small bipolars between 19 mm and 20 mm long. Their weight was 8 g or 12.3%. Coarse debris was 40 g, fine 6 g and very fine 4 g.

Additional material from Gudgenby, identified as Rendezvous Creek, contained two lumps. One, of 85 g, was translucent grey, lustrous and uniform. It proved extremely tough and cohesive requiring unusually heavy hammering. After reduction to 53 g, when its size was 35 × 32 × 26 mm, it was abandoned as too intractable. It had yielded eight acceptable flakes (Table 2). The last two of these were made into bondis. The eight flakes weighed 13 g, 15% of the core and 40.6% of the material removed, 32 g. In the debris there were 8 g of coarse fragments, 7 g of fine and 4 g of very fine. This high proportion of fine material is consistent with the toughness of the material.

The 58 g lump was grey, poorly translucent and had rough fracture surfaces indicating a coarse texture. It flaked fairly well and was worked down to a bipolar 23 × 20 × 14 mm weighing 6 g or 10.3% of the core. It yielded nine flakes of acceptable size of which one was suitable for a bondi. The others had very ragged edges. Their dimensions are in Table 3. The flakes weighed 17 g or 29.3%. Coarse debris was 24 g, fine 12 g and very fine 5 g.

Two small pieces which had been worked by Aborigines were tested and flaked well but were too small to give large enough flakes.

The pieces from Sassafras were too small for full scale working. One was a thick translucent flake with a rudimentary bulb. It was 29.8 × 25.8 × 9 mm and readily split to give five flakes (Table 4). Two of these were made into bondis and one into a geometrical microlith.

With this sample was included a flat pebble with the query whether it might have been a small anvil. It weighed 95 g and

Table 1 Material from Gudgenby, Series 2

Length mm	Breadth mm	Thickness mm
21·5	8·0	4·8
18·9	9·2	6·9
18·6	8·5	3·3
18·2	9·3	4·4
20·5	5·4	4·3
21·2	10·0	8·0
17·2	8·9	4·6
17·6	7·5	3·6
16·5	5·4	4·8

Table 2 Flakes from Gudgenby (Rendez-vous Creek), Series 2, 85 g lump

Length mm	Breadth mm	Thickness mm
18·1	13·4	5·0
16·2	11·7	5·1
15·7	12·7	3·2
15·1	11·1	6·0
17·8	10·5	4·0
19·2	13·8	8·0
30·9	15·0	8·3
27·4	11·6	5·1

Table 3 Flakes from Gudgenby (Rendez-vous Creek), Series 2, 58 g lump

Length mm	Breadth mm	Thickness mm
29·2	18·1	6·3
23·0	14·2	7·1
27·9	12·4	5·8
24·8	18·2	5·2
21·5	14·8	6·2
20·5	14·2	9·3
18·0	11·4	3·1
15·5	13·8	2·6
23·2	10·5	6·9
		(bondi)

Table 4 Flakes from Sassafras, Series 2

Length mm	Breadth mm	Thickness mm
21·1	13·4	5·0
23·0	10·6	7·4
24·3	12·0	4·8
21·6	4·8	3·6
17·4	5·6	3·6

was $60 \times 44 \times 21$ mm in size. Both the fairly flat faces showed pitting which suggested use as an anvil. The nearest similar pebble in my material weighed 135 g and was $62 \times 44 \times 30$ mm. Working down two pieces of quartz amounting to 17 g produced similar though somewhat deeper pitting. Such a small anvil, if well supported, would serve for working small pieces but could not be expected to withstand the loading of large cores, especially tough material like the Rendez-vous Creek specimen.

The Nardoo sample contained two big lumps, one of medium size and some small ones of which two were flakes of 25 g and 22 g.

The big lump was spherical in shape, apparently rounded by human action. It was good to hold and at 414 g was of suitable weight for a pounder. It was white and lustrous and seemed very cohesive. A test was made though it was probably an implement and not a core to be worked. Continued hammering removed only 36 g in small crumbs and it resisted heavy blows with the 1100 g hammer.

The other big piece, 356 g, was also glossy white except for one rounded side which was dull and looked almost like a cortex. Sizeable pieces came away when worked in the hand until it was reduced to 75 g. Ultimately it was completely reduced. Forty-four specific flakes were obtained. These weighed 52 g or 14.6%. Five bondis and a microlith were produced from them (Table 5). There was a total of eleven bipolars (Table 6). These weighed 31 g or 8.7%. The coarse debris was 161 g, fine 72 g and very fine 40 g.

The 97 g lump was also lustrous white and of very angular shape though the edges were blunt compared with new fractures. Worked on the anvil it produced numerous flakes but flaws made most of them too brittle. In all seven good flakes were obtained of which three were made into bondis which were 18.7 mm, 19.9 mm and 21.0 mm long. These flakes weighed 13 g which was 13.4%, coarse debris 40 g, fine 23 g and very fine 12 g. No bipolars were produced, presumably because of the unusually brittle fracture which also resulted in much fine debris.

The 25 g piece, grey and translucent, which was itself a large flake, yielded three acceptable flakes.

The other piece of 22 g was also a flake of similar material and likewise split to give three secondary flakes one of which was made into a point.

As in Series 1, small pieces from all sites were also worked for test purposes, largely to check visual assessment of quality. As was to be expected, pieces which were already flakes made by the Aborigines were of good quality like those described above. Many of the small unworked pieces were quite unproductive.

In Series 2, counting only the primary cores which were worked down, the results can be expressed in average values based on cores with an average weight of 132 g as set out in Table 7.

Some conclusions may be drawn from these quartz flaking experiments. Although the material came from a geographically restricted area the variety of samples exhibited a range of physical properties which makes it reasonably representative of quartz from most parts of Australia and from other areas. Accordingly the results obtained may be widely applicable.

The most important visual indication of quality for flaking in quartz is its translucence. The working properties improve with increasing translucence towards the limit in transparent

Table 5   Bondi points and a microlith produced from Nardoo material, Series 2

Length mm	Breadth mm	Thickness mm
22·2	9·3	5·8
21·2	9·0	4·9
24·6	11·2	5·0
19·4	8·2	3·5
20·9	12·0	3·6
15·8	7·6	3·6
		(microlith)

Table 6   Bipolars from Nardoo material, Series 2

Length mm	Breadth mm	Thickness mm
23·3	13·4	6·0
21·9	15·5	9·2
20·3	16·5	11·7
22·4	13·4	8·6
19·7	16·6	9·0
21·5	15·3	8·6
20·5	14·5	9·3
19·0	12·1	9·4
22·0	13·1	9·1
28·8	9·3	8·0
18·1	11·5	7·9

Table 7   Averaged results from Series 2

Product	Number	Weight	Percent of core weight
Flakes	16	1·35	15·4
Bipolars	4	3·00	14·8
Coarse debris	—	65·6	49·6
Fine debris	—	24·0	18·2
Very fine debris	—	13·0	9·82

glassy quartz. Connected with this is the lustre of a fresh surface. Of two pieces with the same translucence the more lustrous will probably be the better to work.

Strong colour and opacity are negative indications; thus a red colour suggests the presence of ferritic iron compounds isomorphic with quartz but making it unworkable like the Series 1 sample from Tidbinbilla. Opaque white and lustreless quartz commonly has had its structure damaged by thermal shock and can be expected to break into irregular chips without yielding flakes. Internal fractures in translucent pebble quartz are of mechanical origin and while flakes may be obtained they tend to be fragile.

Because of its tough cohesive nature quartz of workable quality calls for some specialisation of technique. It is best worked with a heavy hammer delivering heavy blows in direct percussion. Cores lighter than about 100 g have to be worked upon an anvil to obtain flakes.

The need to work in this way results, as others have observed, in the formation of bipolar cores. Bipolars are also formed when using wedge-like pieces of quartz as stoneworking chisels, the process being essentially similar.

There seems to be no convincing evidence that bipolars were deliberately made for use as tools and that their sizes are determined not by design but by the size of the operator's fingers. They are thus residual cores from flaking or the unusable remnants of tools, in which case as F. D. McCarthy suggested in discussion that they might be classed as slugs. Also in discussion Professor Bordes suggested that bipolars might have been used as wedges for splitting pieces of wood. This is possible but it seems to me a variety of unmodified pieces of stone might also have been used in that way and that one would normally make the effort of shaping a bipolar for that purpose.

There appears to be general agreement between my experimentally based conclusions about bipolar cores and the observationally based conclusions reached by R. Vanderwal in 'The "fabricator" of Australia and New Guinea' (this volume).

References

Bordaz, J., 1970. *Tools of the old and new Stone Age*. New York: Natural History Press.

Breuil H. and R. Lantier, 1965. *The men of the old Stone Age*. London: Harrap.

Dickson, F. P., 1973. Backed blades and points. *Mankind*, 9(1):7-14.

Flood, J., 1973. *The Moth Hunters*. Ph.D. thesis, Australian National University.

Hume, S. H. R., 1965. *The analysis of a stone assembly to determine change*. B.A. thesis, University of Sydney.

Lampert, R. J., 1971. *Burrill Lake and Currarong*. Terra Australis, 1. Canberra: Australian National University.

Moore, D. R., 1970. Results of an archaeological survey of the Hunter River Valley. *Records of the Australian Museum*, 28(2):25-64.

Mulvaney, D. J., 1969. *The Prehistory of Australia*. London: Thames and Hudson.

Polyani, M., 1962. *Personal knowledge*. London: Routledge and Kegan Paul.

Sullivan, K. M., 1973. *The archaeology of Mangat*. B.A. thesis, University of Sydney.

White, J. P., 1968. Fabricators, outils écaillés or scalar cores? *Mankind*, 6(12):658-66.

Early and late stone industrial phases in western Australia

C. E. DORTCH

Introduction

This paper surveys the archaeological sequences of two regions in western Australia (Fig. 1). The first of these, the Ord valley in east Kimberley, is dealt with in some detail since it is an area which until recently was very poorly known archaeologically but for which some new data are available. The second region is the lower south-west where in 1973 I began a survey of archaeological sites.

Here 'stone industrial phase' refers to a particular stone industry or industrial complex which for a period of time continued in use over a given area (cf. Willey and Phillips, 1958.: 22). The concept is useful because available archaeological data from western Australia consist very largely of stone artifacts, and at present it is through dated stone artifact assemblages that regional archaeological sequences can most conveniently be ordered, and the archaeological evidence from various regions or periods most easily compared. In both the Ord valley and the lower south-west earlier and later stone industrial phases have been identified.

I am concerned here only with the description of archaeological material relating to prehistoric or traditional times. European settlement in western Australia resulted in profound and aberrant changes in Aboriginal technology, economy and tribal distributions, and these are to some extent reflected in the composition and distribution of artifact assemblages and tool types dating to the historic period. For example, in the late 19th century Kimberley men convicted of misdemeanours such as cattle killing were imprisoned on Rottnest Island near Perth (Figs 1, 10) some two thousand kilometres to the south. There they manufactured numbers of Kimberley-type pressure or percussion flaked bifacial points of bottle glass (Serventy, 1967). To include Rottnest bifacially flaked points in any study would not show the traditional distribution of this tool type, and to indicate Aboriginal artifacts on the island would not reflect traditional occupation patterns.

Gardner (1944 : xxx) divides western Australia into three main climatic zones based on differences in rainfall and temperature which, together with edaphic factors, determine the nature of the regional vegetation. He distinguishes these zones as: 'a northern area of summer rainfall of a monsoonal character, with a cool dry season; a south-western area of winter rainfall with a period of summer drought; and a vast central area of low and unreliable rainfall of no marked periodicity, depending entirely upon extensions of the climatic systems which dominate the northern and southern areas'.

According to Gardner the northern province comprises a major region, Kimberley, and a minor, marginal one extending over the northern part of the Pilbara district (Fig. 1). Both are distinguished not only for their rainfall pattern and subtropical temperature range but also by their flora which includes a number of Indo-Malaysian forms. The Kimberley region itself, which forms the north-west corner of the continent, is basically a massive, dissected plateau bounded by the Fitzroy valley to the south and the Ord-Victoria drainage system to the east.

The second region, the south-west, is characterised by its eucalypt forests and woodland formations and its extensive coastal dunes, sand plains and swamps. Gardner delineates it as a 'triangular-crescentic area' occurring south and west of a line 'extending from Shark Bay to Israelite Bay' (1944 : xxxvi).

The central arid zone extends from about latitude 18–20°S to about latitude 30–33°S. The geology, climate, topography and flora are relatively uniform for a region this size, and in broadest terms it is characterised by wide plateaux carrying arid to semi-arid steppe vegetation including spinifex grasslands, acacia scrub and eucalypt woodland. The limestone Nullarbor Plain with its very low rainfall and scrub vegetation is included in this central province.

Present evidence shows that regional stone industries from western Australia can partly be subdivided along the lines of the three climatic zones listed above. It is advantageous to use these occurrences here where the evidence is being discussed on a regional basis, and because there is important recent archaeological evidence from each region. However the significance of this partial coincidence of climatic zones and regional industries is not entirely clear.

The Ord valley industrial sequence

Background At present the only comprehensive data available for Kimberley prehistory are from the Ord valley to the east where in 1971 and 1972 a number of riverside or flood-plain rock shelter sites were excavated and numbers of open sites and upland shelter sites were surface sampled in a salvage programme carried out by Western Australian Museum staff and sponsored by the Australian Institute of Aboriginal Studies and the Western Australian Museum (Dortch, 1972a).

Most of the work of the survey has been carried out in the Lake Argyle-Kununurra district (Fig. 2). This area, covering some 7000 square km, has undergone intensive agricultural development though most of the district is still under pastoral lease. The construction of the Ord River dam, which was the reason for the Ord valley archaeological salvage and survey programme, has resulted in the formation of the Ord reservoir, now called Lake Argyle, intended to provide water for the irrigated fields of the Kununurra district.

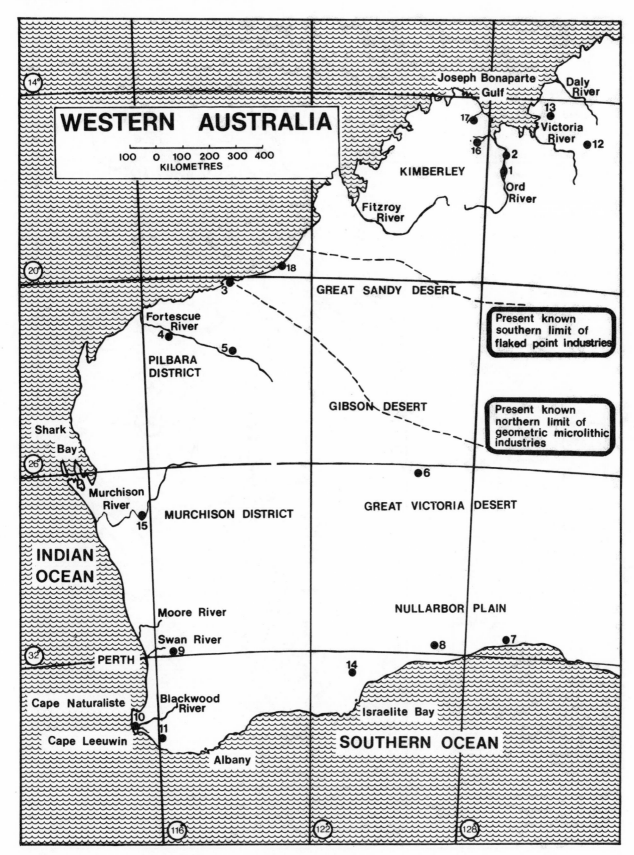

Fig. 1: Map of western Australia showing sites and areas mentioned in the text.
1 Lake Argyle; 2 Kununurra; 3 Pardoo Station; 4 Millstream Station; 5 Chichester Range; 6 Puntutjarpa Shelter; 7 Koonalda Cave; 8 Horseshoe Cave; 9 Frieze Cave; 10 Devil's Lair; 11 Northcliffe; 12 Ingaladdi Shelter; 13 Yarar Shelter; 14 Balladonia Station; 15 Billabalong Station; 16 Forrest and King Rivers; 17 Berkeley River; 18 Eighty Mile Beach.

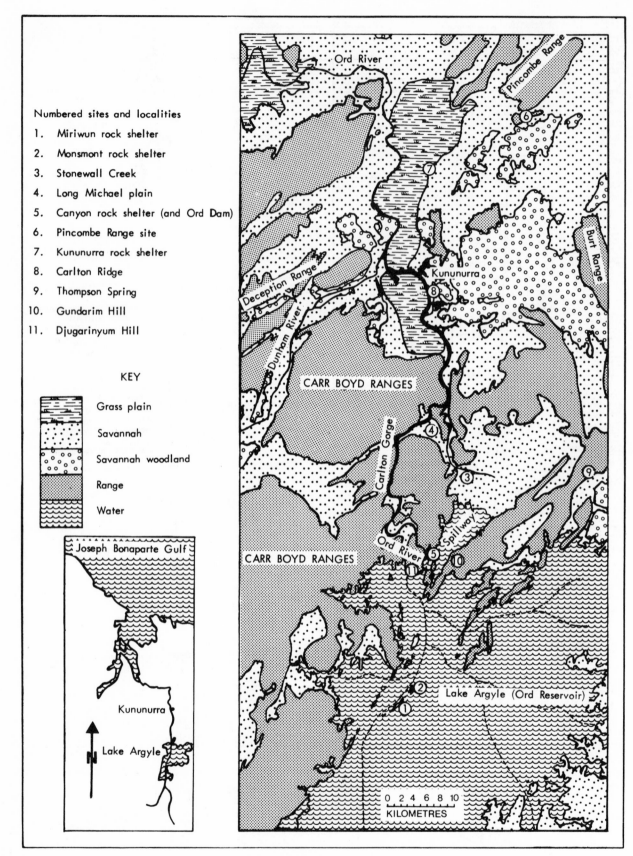

Numbered sites and localities

1. Miriwun rock shelter
2. Monsmont rock shelter
3. Stonewall Creek
4. Long Michael plain
5. Canyon rock shelter (and Ord Dam)
6. Pincombe Range site
7. Kununurra rock shelter
8. Carlton Ridge
9. Thompson Spring
10. Gundarim Hill
11. Djugarinyum Hill

KEY

Grass plain
Savannah
Savannah woodland
Range
Water

Fig. 2:   Map of Lake Argyle–Kununurra district, Ord valley, east Kimberley.

The greater part of the area generally referred to as east Kimberley lies within the Ord-Victoria drainage system to the east of the central Kimberley plateau. It is a semi-arid, sparsely populated region of rugged ranges, undulating plateaux and erosional or alluvial plains extending from the northern fringes of the central desert region at about latitude 19°S to Joseph Bonaparte Gulf, a part of the Timor Sea, at latitude 15°S. Most of east Kimberley is cut off from north-west and central Kimberley by a series of north-south trending ranges, but to the east and south lies the more open country of the Ord-Victoria basin.

The climate of east Kimberley is dry monsoonal and hot with a long dry season from April through November and a somewhat variable wet season beginning in December. Over most of the area mean annual rainfall is about 60–70 cm, but it ranges from 45 cm at Halls Creek in the south to about 90 cm along the coast. The rivers flow only for a few months during the wet season but they and their tributaries often contain large pools throughout the dry season. Except for the grasslands and scrub of the lowest rainfall areas to the south, the vegetation of east Kimberley is characterised by savannah woodland. (For detailed description see Stewart *et al.*, 1970.)

The chief topographical features of the Lake Argyle-Kununurra district (Fig. 2) are the massive Carr Boyd Ranges to the north and west of Lake Argyle, the alluvial plains north of Kununurra and in the area now inundated by Lake Argyle, the sand plains and sandstone residuals to the north and east of Kununurra, and the dry, rolling basaltic plains to the east and south of Lake Argyle. Interspersed throughout the district are ridges and rocky outcrops.

The major vegetation zones consist of the short grass formations of the alluvial plains, the eucalypt savannah woodland with tall grass (*Sorghum* sp.) understorey of the sand plains, the open savannah and tussock grassland of the basaltic plains, and the sparse eucalypt and spinifex (*Triodia* sp.) cover of the ridges and dry, upland valleys. Other important formations are gallery forests along the river and larger streams; and small patches of subtropical forest (*Melaleuca* sp., *Pandanus* sp., etc.) found in the vicinity of springs and pools, and occurring typically in small canyons and other sheltered areas.

Except for open camps beside or in the beds of water-courses which would have been flooded in the wet season, and shelters and open camps high up in the hills, which would have been waterless in the dry seasons, most Ord valley archaeological sites could have been occupied any time of year. Most sites are located within easy reach of water and different kinds of habitats. The marked differences in topography over short distances, such as is found in the northwest corner of the Lake Argyle area, and in a number of other localities, provide a number of closely situated contrasting habitats. It is in these localities that the most numerous as well as the richest archaeological sites have been found.

Ethnographical data (i.e. Kaberry, 1935, 1938, 1939), archaeological survey and the information given by local Aborigines suggest that the areas most favoured by the Aborigines of traditional times were the alluvial grass plains and the basaltic plains with their variety of edible grasses, roots, animals and birds; the rivers, streams, lagoons and billabongs, which were a varying but constant source of birds, plants, fish, molluscs and reptiles; and the small patches of subtropical forest and freshwater swamps which contain palms

with edible fruit, various other fruits and roots, and are a reliable source of water and shade.

For the purposes of this paper I am using the term 'Ord valley' to refer to the middle reaches of the Ord River and its tributaries as distinct from the more elevated and more arid country of the upper Ord, and the marshlands and higher rainfall areas of the lower Ord. The use of the term in reference to only the middle part of the river system is felt to be justified for two reasons. First, with the important exception of the estuarine marshes at the mouth of the Ord, the country along the middle reaches includes most of the vegetation zones and topographical features found along either the upper or lower parts of the river. Second, as far as can be determined from the available ethnographic evidence (i.e. Kaberry, 1938, 1939), Aboriginal hunting-gathering adaptation was much the same throughout the greater part of the valley, with the probable exception of the estuarine environment at the river's mouth and in the lowlands which extend to the coastline.

Sites, dates, subsistence and survey The best evidence for the Ord valley industrial sequence comes from the rock shelters of Miriwun and Monsmont, both of which are now inundated by Lake Argyle (Fig. 2). These riverside sites are located at the foot of a steep quartzite ridge which runs for several kilometres immediately along the former east bank of the Ord River (Plate 1). The archaeological sequence at each site can be divided between an earlier and a later phase based on a number of marked technological and typological differences in the stone industries recovered from different layers or depths (Table 1).

Monsmont is not strictly speaking a shelter but is an open space at the foot of an overhanging quartzite cliff. The occupation deposit is approximately 40 m long and about 6 to 10 m wide, and in the sampled part extended to a depth of 3 m. The Monsmont deposit is probably largely alluvial in origin. This is suggested by the site's location on a part of the river where both banks consist of high terraces of silty earth similar to that of the deposit itself. The presence in the deposit of tiny molluscs of a riverine variety is regarded as further evidence of an alluvial origin as is the fact that some of the stone artifacts when excavated were found lying on edge or on end, suggesting that they were shifted slightly by water currents. These assumptions are substantiated by information given by engineers of the Western Australian Department of Public Works who maintained a water gauging station 100 m downstream from Monsmont for nearly 20 years. The gauging station, the surface of the Monsmont deposit and the extensive alluvial terraces in the vicinity are all very much the same elevation. Water level records from the station indicate that the Ord flash flooded these terraces, the station itself, and thus the Monsmont deposit on at least two occasions during the time records were kept. It is probable then that much of the deposit is the alluvium of infrequent high water levels.

The high water levels must have caused very little disturbance as artifacts, stones, bones, shells and other material of greatly varying sizes were bedded side by side in the matrix of silty earth. Nor were there any river pebbles in the deposit, aside from those brought into the site to be used as hammer-stones, etc., and none of the stone artifacts has rolled or battered edges.

Further evidence of the undisturbed nature of the deposit

Plate 1: View of Miriwun rock shelter, Ord valley, east Kimberley from the south. The dry bed of the Ord River is seen in the middle left distance. In the left background are silt terraces on the west bank of the river, and in the far distance can be seen the Carr Boyd Ranges. Monsmont rock shelter is located 1400 m further north, but is not shown here.

is provided by the presence of an occupation floor occurring 8 cm below the surface (Plate 2). The floor consists of stone artifacts and chips, animal bones and two small piles of edible gastropods, *Notopala* sp., (Kendrick, 1973 and personal communication) lying on the surface of a 10 cm thick ashy grey horizon thought to be a hearth.

The occupation floor and the 10 cm thick ashy layer were the only units taken out as separate layers. The rest of the deposit, in which no stratification was visible, was dug in 10 cm arbitrary levels. Except for the ashy layer and a band of carbonate concretions occurring at about 150 cm the whole of the excavated part of the Monsmont deposit consisted of a buff coloured silty earth. Artifacts and faunal remains were scattered throughout the upper 2 m of the deposit, and virtually disappeared at a depth of 3 m. Work was discontinued at this level because of an accumulation of large carbonate encrusted stone fragments and many carbonate concretions.

The change between the earlier and later stone industries occurs at a depth of about 220 cm in the Monsmont deposit but is not accompanied by any differences in stratigraphy. Three radiocarbon dates ranging between about 1400 and about 1700 years BP (Tables 1, 3) were received for charcoal samples taken from a depth of 65 to 130 cm in the middle of the late phase industrial sequence.

Miriwun is a smaller shelter located 1400 m upstream from Monsmont. It occurs in the face of the quartzite ridge about 35 m above the former bed of the river (Plate 1), and is over 10 m higher in elevation than Monsmont. The floor of Miriwun is over 20 m long and is 5 to 7 m wide (Fig. 3). The deposit is shallow and rocky except in the southeast corner where it has a depth of about 120 cm (Plate 3, Fig. 4). It consists mainly of layers of silty earth, much of which may have been blown into the shelter from the extensive terraces on the other side of the river or from the river itself during dry seasons (Plate 1). This possibility was suggested to us during the 1971 excavation when strong cyclonic winds blowing down the dry river bed and across the terraces on the west bank created dense clouds of dust. Only a few afternoons of blowing dust resulted in an appreciable amount of sedimentation in the sheltered south corner of Miriwun. The deposit also contains much quartzite roof collapse and rubble fallen from the cliff above the shelter.

The upper part of the deposit (Fig. 4) is designated 'surface complex'. This consists of bands of silty earth containing much paperbark and leaves, two presumed animal burrows (one is shown) and a large hearth. Surface complex overlies a thick homogeneous layer called 'light brown silty earth'. Surface complex and light brown silty earth contain assemblages of the late Ord valley stone industrial phase. Light

Table 1   Radiocarbon dates and stone industries, Ord valley, east Kimberley

Ord valley (radiocarbon dates in years BP)

	Sites				
Late Ord valley stone industry	Kununurra	Pincombe range*	Monsmont	Canyon	Miriwun
Tools	end of traditional times *c.* 1900 A.D.				
Prismatic blade					
Levallois point					
Bifacial point	SUA 54				
Unifacial point	1030±80			SUA 58	
Backed point				680±75	
Adze flake					
Thick notched flake	SUA 55		SUA 57		SUA 141
Denticulated piece	1940±80		1730±80		1675±185
Notched piece			ANU 1130		
Levallois flake			1420±70		
Burin on concave truncation					
Edge-ground axe			ANU 1129		
Grindstone			1480±90		Early Ord valley stone industry (Miriwun only)
Flake from discoidal core		GaK 1767			
Retouched flake		3560±100			
Small utilised flake					
Core tool	SUA 56	GaK 1768			tools
Pebble tool	3110±85	2660±90			
					SUA 142
					2980±95 — small blade, adze flake, thick notched flake, denticulated piece, notched piece, pecked and grooved axe, flake from discoidal core, retouched flake
					ANU 1008 — small utilised flake, core tool
					$17\,980\,^{+1370}_{-1170}$ — pebble tool

* I. M. Crawford excavation

brown silty earth is dated to about 1700 years BP (Fig. 4) though the sample was taken from the middle of the layer, and it is probable that its base is older.

In several trenches light brown silty earth rested on a thin patch of carbonate, the significance of which is not yet clear. A small group of tools found lying on the surface of the patch belongs to the late stone industrial phase. None of the stone artifact assemblages below this, including a small assemblage excavated from earthy sediments between the pair of 'grey indurated bands' seen in the east section of Trench 2 (Fig. 4) can be related to the late phase.

Below light brown silty earth and separated from it in part by the carbonate deposit and in part by rock fall (not shown) is a layer named 'dark silty earth'. Archaeological material excavated from the light coloured patch below the indurated bands (Fig. 4) was included with that from dark silty earth. A radiocarbon date of 2980±95 years BP (SUA 142) was obtained from a charcoal sample taken from dark silty earth in Trench 9, and its approximate position in the east section of Trench 6 is shown in Fig. 4. The charcoal was found 20 cm from the edge of a pit or burrow (not shown) and care was taken to ensure that the charcoal was not contaminated by the more recent pit fill. However, an age of about 3000 years BP was not expected for the early phase stone industry occurring in the dark silty earth, and the date

does not agree with another one from the Ord valley (see below). Unfortunately there is no way to check this radiocarbon date as no other charcoal was found in dark silty earth and the site is now submerged.

Several features including a sandy lens, a scatter of carbonate nodules and a second light coloured patch of silty earth occur between dark silty earth and a strikingly homogeneous layer called 'dark brown silty earth' (Plate 3, Fig. 4). Dark brown silty earth contains a relatively rich early phase stone industry and more diverse mammalian remains than the layers above. A charcoal sample taken from the lower part of the layer was dated at $17\,980\,^{+1370}_{-1170}$ years BP (ANU 1008).

The base of dark brown silty earth rests on a rubbly layer which contains much silty sediment as well as stone artifacts and some bone. This rubbly layer continues to the quartzitic base rock of the shelter. Several problems relating to probable variations in the mode of deposition at Miriwun and to apparent post-depositional alterations, eg. partial deflation or erosion and weathering, in some of the layers await detailed analysis.

According to the Miriwun radiocarbon dates the transition between the early and late phases occurred less than 3000 years ago. This evidence is somewhat inconsistent with two other Ord valley dated sequences which are associated with

Plate 2: Occupation floor 8 cm below surface of deposit at Monsmont rock shelter, Ord valley, east Kimberley. The rear wall of the shelter can be seen in upper left hand corner. The range pole segments are 50 cm long.

late phase industries. The first, GaK 1767, 3560±100 years BP, was obtained from a charcoal sample collected in a test excavation done in 1962 by I. M. Crawford in a rock shelter in a series of sandstone outcrops near the Pincombe Range, about 20 km east of the Ord River and 75 km north of Miriwun and Monsmont (Fig. 2). This sample occurred above another sample (GaK 1768) dated at 2660±90 years BP. No early phase material was found at this site, and both dates are associated with late phase stone industries. Therefore, despite the inversion, the older date should be treated as a correct age tentatively for an early part of the Ord valley late industrial phase.

The second date, SUA 56, provides an age of 3110±85 years BP for the lower part of a very rich late phase industrial sequence at Kununurra rock shelter on the east edge of the Ord River floodplain about 60 km north of Monsmont and Miriwun (Fig. 2). This is the only Ord valley site I test excavated which was not part of the salvage programme. SUA 56 (Table 1) is the oldest of a series of three self consistent radiocarbon dates received for charcoal samples taken from a very dark silty to sandy deposit containing quantities of massive rock fall in its lower part and overlying light coloured sand at a depth of about 2.5 m.

Unfortunately the Kununurra excavation had to be abandoned when I was unable to remove numbers of large

rock fragments fallen from the roof of the shelter, some of which weighed over 100 kg. Before filling in the trench I dug a small test pit in the northeast corner and in 40 cm of light coloured sand found several flakes and chips. It is possible that SUA 56 dates the early part of late phase occupation at Kununurra rock shelter, and that the light coloured sand contains an earlier phase assemblage.

The only other available Ord valley radiocarbon date, SUA 58 : 680±75 years BP, when first received was thought to be anomalous. The date was obtained from a charcoal sample collected at a depth of about 60 cm in the silty deposit of Canyon rock shelter, now submerged under the spillway basin at Lake Argyle (Fig. 2). The sample occurred 20 cm below a clearly identifiable late phase horizon and was associated with a sparse assemblage of stone artifacts which included several very small, thick flake scrapers and thick notched flakes, a few small atypical blades and many rough, apparently utilised flakes. All of the tool types found in the assemblage are common to both early and late Ord valley stone industrial phases. It is possible then that the date is in order, and the associated industry may relate to the late industrial phase.

Available radiocarbon dates provide somewhat equivocal evidence for the beginning of late phase industries in the Ord valley. The statistically similar dates provided by SUA 142

Table 2　Tentative check list of faunal remains, Trench 10, Miriwun rock shelter, Ord valley, east Kimberley

	depth in cm ± datum		murids	mar-supials	reptiles	fish	bird (egg shell)	fresh-water mollusc
Modern period *c.* 1900 A.D.	10–3	surface to top of grey brown silty earth	•	•	•	•	•	•
	3–6	grey brown silty earth		•	•	•		•
Surface complex	6–27	grey brown silty earth	•	•	•	•	•	•
	6–27	hearth		•	•	•	•	•
Light brown silty earth	27–35	light brown silty earth	•	•	•	•	•	•
SUA 141　　1675±185	35–45	light brown silty earth	•	•	•	•	•	•
	45–55	light brown silty earth	•	•	•	•	•	•
Late Ord valley industries	55–60	light brown silty earth ?	•	•	•	•	•	•
Poorly defined stone assemblage under review	60–65	light brown silty earth ?	•	•	•	•	•	•
Early Ord valley industries	65–70	dark silty earth	•	•		•	•	•
Dark silty earth	70–73	dark silty earth	•	•	•			•
	73–74	indurated surface						
Dark brown silty earth	74–75	dark brown silty earth	•	•	•	•	•	•
ANU 1008　　17980$^{+1370}_{-1170}$	75–80	dark brown silty earth	•	•		•	•	•
	80–90	dark brown silty earth	•	•	•	•	•	•
	90– base	dark brown silty earth mixed with basal rubble	•	•	•			

(2980±95 years BP) for the upper part of the early phase sequence at Miriwun, and SUA 56 (3110±85 years BP) for the lower part of the late phase sequence at Kununurra rock shelter suggest that this transition may have occurred about 3000 years ago. However the inverted dates from Crawford's excavation near the Pincombe Range suggest an older age for the early part of the Ord valley late phase. This problem will remain unsolved until further radiocarbon dates can be obtained for the period of transition.

Faunal remains from Miriwun and Monsmont indicate that the human occupants exploited a variety of aquatic and terrestrial habitats all of which occur within a few 100 m of each site. None of the fauna has been analysed but preliminary findings indicate that the same range of animal foods persists throughout the archaeological sequences of both sites (Tables 2, 3). These include terrestrial animals such as wallabies, possums, bandicoots, lizards and rodents and a number of lacustrine and riverine forms including molluscs, reptiles, catfish and goose eggs. At neither site does the change from the later to the earlier industrial phase appear to be accompanied by significant changes in the kinds of animals eaten. The uniformity and continuity of these animal foods from each layer or each arbitrary level in the deposits of both sites suggest that human subsistence in the locality may have undergone few changes for about 18 000 years, according to the lowermost radiocarbon date obtained from the Miriwun deposit.

In the Ord valley, as in other parts of northern Australia, human economic activities and movements were divided between wet season and dry season patterns of adaptation (Kaberry, 1935, 1938, 1939). Although dry season occupation cannot be discounted, extensive wet season occupation of Miriwun and Monsmont over thousands of years is indicated by the presence of numerous eggshell fragments of pied or semi-palmated goose (*Anseranas semipalmata*) occurring throughout the archaeological sequences. These birds breed only during the wet season from January through March (G. M. Storr, personal communication), and their nests of six to eight large eggs would have been readily available in the marshy areas around Argyle Lagoon, about 3 km south of Miriwun.

Argyle Lagoon, which until the recent inundation of the area was an important breeding ground for pied geese, was also a source of other animal foods including fish, reptiles, edible molluscs (Kendrick, 1973) and birds, the remains of all of which have been found in the Miriwun and Monsmont deposits. No plant remains have yet been recovered from sediment samples taken from the sites but none of the fauna is inconsistent with the evidence for wet season occupation. Because of its presumed infrequency and short duration the flooding which probably accounts for the formation of much of the Monsmont deposit is not likely to have seriously affected regular wet season occupation of this site.

Only very small amounts of fauna were found in the excavation of other Ord valley occupation deposits. The presence of a few catfish otoliths at Kununurra rock shelter indicates that its occupants were collecting fish from the Ord River or from pools or lagoons in its flood-plain. A few fragments of baler shell (*Melo* sp.) (G. W. Kendrick, personal communication) in the deposit at Canyon rock shelter indicate some form of contact between Ord valley people and coastal tribes.

Most of the archaeological survey carried out so far in the Ord valley has been in the Lake Argyle area though numbers of other sites have been examined along the river downstream

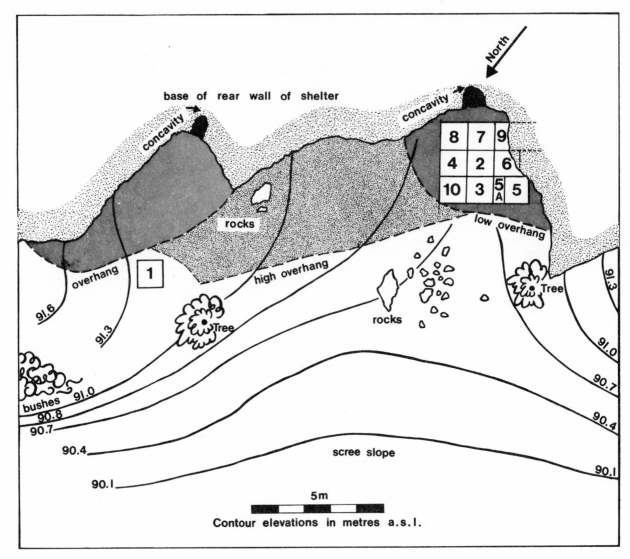

Fig. 3: Plan of Miriwun rock shelter, Ord valley, east Kimberley.

from the Ord dam and in areas further away from the river. The more important of these sites or areas are noted on the map in Fig. 2. The largest and richest occupation sites so far recorded in the Ord valley are open camping grounds or rock shelters on the Ord River and open camps on its tributaries.

Extensive open camps occur on the alluvial terraces all along the course of the river. Artifact assemblages which may relate to both Ord valley stone industrial phases are associated with successive alluvial deposits on Stonewall Creek, a tributary of the Ord River. Here pecked and grooved axes and other possible early phase stone artifacts rest on the eroded surface of a truncated 'fossil' soil. The truncated soil is partly overlain by a more recent deposit which has a typical late phase stone tool assemblage lying on its surface. Two of the three grooved axes from the truncated soil are carbonate encrusted, and one was partly imbedded within it. It is likely that the two axes and some of the other artifacts were buried by the more recent deposit, and that the carbonate encrustations result from subsequent weathering.

A series of rock shelters and open sites are situated on Long Michael Plain and below the cliffs on the opposite side of the river. There are also important series of occupation sites in the spillway area of the reservoir, along the east face of Carlton Ridge, in the north part of the Deception Range, and in sandstone outcrops near Kununurra and the Pincombe Range. Rock shelter occupation sites with extensive wall paintings are located on Djugarinyum and Gundarim, high ridges on the northern edge of the reservoir. The shelters on Djugarinyum hill were probably occupied during the wet season as the steep hillside and summit are completely waterless in the dry season, and the shelters are about 150 m above the river.

One of the most promising rock shelter occupation sites in the Ord valley is near Thompson Spring 25 km east of the Ord River. The shelter is 70 m wide and extends over 30 m into the quartzite cliff face. Paintings and wooden artifacts are found in the shelter, and earthy deposits occurring in parts of its rocky floor appear to be undisturbed. Permanent water exists a short distance away at Thompson Spring, and it is possible that the large shelter was a dry season occupation site.

Although in my survey of areas away from the river I have found no certain evidence of dry season occupation I have recorded a few large open sites on watercourses which could be dry season sites, including some on the basalt plains east

Table 3 Tentative check list of faunal remains, Monsmont rock shelter, Ord valley, east Kimberley

Monsmont rock shelter, Trench 3, faunal remains

	depth in cm	murids	marsupials	reptiles	fish	bird (egg shell)	freshwater molluscs
Modern period	0–20	•	•	•	•	•	•
c. 1900 A.D.	20–30	•	•	•	•	•	•
	30–40	•	•	•	•	•	•
	40–50	•	•	•	•	•	•
	50–70	•	•	•	•	•	•
	70–90	•	•	•	•	•	•
ANU 1130 1420±70	90–110	•	•	•	•	•	•
ANU 1129 1480±90	110–130	•	•	•	•	•	•
	130–140	•	•	•	•	•	•
	140–160	•	•	•	•	•	•
	160–180	•	•	•	•	•	•
Late Ord valley	180–200		•	•	•	•	
industries	200–220		•	•	•	•	•
Early Ord valley	220–240	•	•	•	•	•	•
industries	240–250					•	
	250–265		•	•	•	•	•
	265–275		•	•	•	•	•
	275–285	•	•	•	•	•	•

of Lake Argyle. It is significant that several of these last centre on large stands of pandanus palms, the fruits of which were eaten only during the late dry season.

Most of these presumed dry season sites contain artifacts belonging to the later Ord valley industrial phase. Stonewall Creek, which is also thought to be a predominantly dry season site, is significant in that it includes artifact assemblages possibly relating to both industrial phases. Whether this is so, the probable considerable age of the early Stonewall Creek tool assemblage helps to substantiate the evidence for uniformity in occupation patterns of Ord valley huntergatherers over a long period.

In north-east Kimberley few areas are more than 20 km away from either the Ord River, one of its major tributaries or one of the neighbouring rivers. In summary it seems correct to designate the inland east Kimberley tribes as river people who may have always lived within a few hours' journey of one of the larger streams.

Ord valley stone industries The archaeological material from the Ord valley sites is still under analysis, but enough is known about the stone artifact assemblages from Monsmont and Miriwun to outline the early to late phase industrial sequences. The stone industries at both sites are rich and varied, the material from the Monsmont late phase particularly so.

The two main kinds of stone material used in both early and late Ord valley industrial phases were pebbles taken from numerous gravel beds in the Ord River, and stone quarried from cliff faces and outcrops. The rock types include cherts, fine grained quartzites, quartz, dolerite and metasediments all occurring as river pebbles, and rough quartzite and basaltic rock found as pebbles or in quarried fragments.

(i) LATE PHASE ASSEMBLAGES Ord valley late phase assemblages are most easily identified by their blade and point component which includes a number of distinctive forms, the most diverse being the bifacially and unifacially flaked points. These can be subdivided into a number of types or styles based on differences in technique of manufacture, size, proportions, and nature or extent of retouch. However, all are characterised by the feature of invasive flaking either on both faces or on the dorsal face only. Invasive flaking is simply scalar or flat retouch which encroaches more or less on the face of the piece, as distinct from edge trimming (light retouch) or backing (abrupt retouch). Flaking appears to have been done by percussion with a hammerstone or piece of wood or bone, or by pressure using a wood or bone retoucher, or in some cases by a combination of the two techniques.

Serrated or denticulated edges are common among bifacially flaked points (Fig. 5 : 1), and some specimens have relatively large elaborately flaked notches on both edges (Fig. 5 : 2). A number of denticulated or notched points are not invasively flaked. Some of these are made on leilira blades or points (see below), and another group consists of those made on very small, thin flakes (Fig. 5 : 4).

There are many variations in outline in the bifacial points though simple leaf shapes or elongated triangular forms with rounded or squared bases are common (Figs. 5 : 3, 19). A number of these forms resemble some of the points analysed by Flood (1970) from Yarar rock shelter in the Port Keats district some 250 km north-east of the Ord valley.

Some of the unifacially flaked points are very similar to the pirri point defined by Campbell (1960) and McCarthy (1967). Intermediate between the bifacially and unifacially flaked forms are points which are only partly flaked on the bulbar face. The most distinctive of these is one in which the proximal end of the bulbar face has been invasively flaked in order to remove or reduce the bulb of percussion and to help remove the butt (Fig. 5 : 5). Campbell (1960) includes these in the pirri category and McCarthy (1967) and Flood (1970) appear to do so as well.

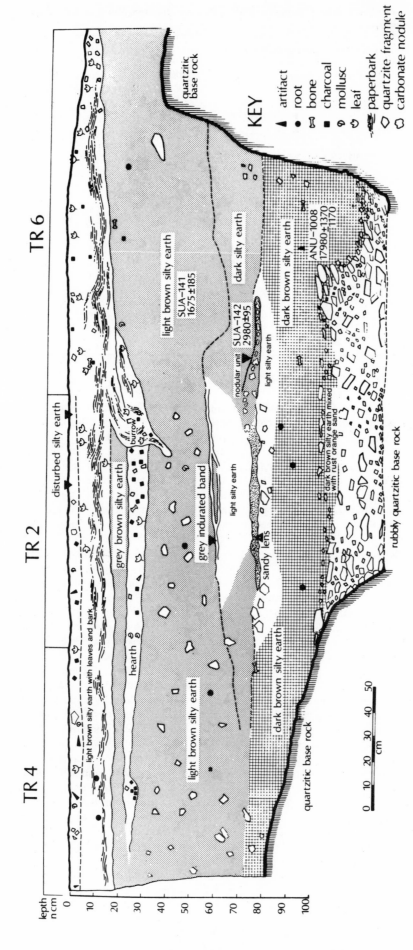

Fig. 4: East section of Trenches 4, 2, and 6, Miriwun rock shelter, Ord Valley, east Kimberley.

Plate 3: Miriwun rock shelter, Ord valley, east Kimberley. Trench 2, east section. The dark layer opposite the lower white segment of the range pole is dark brown silty earth. The range pole segments are 50 cm long.

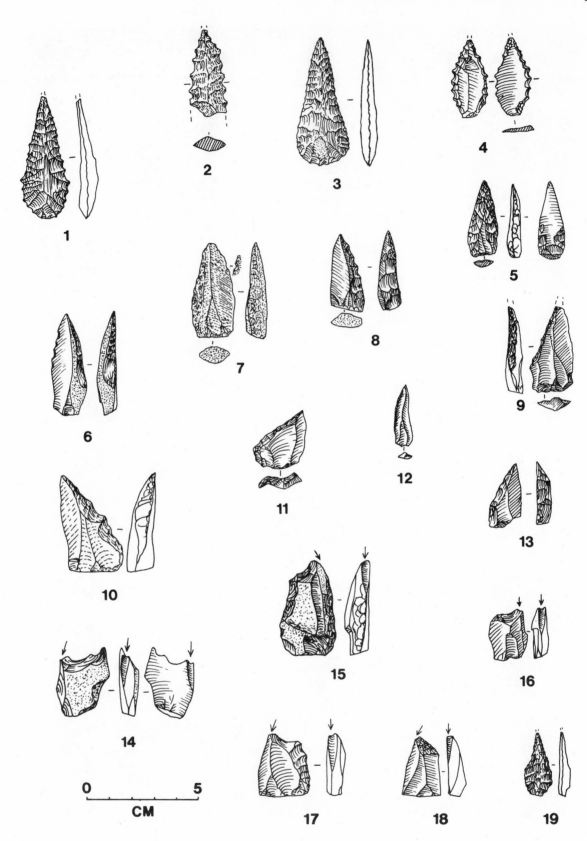

Fig. 5: Invasively flaked points, backed points and burins, Ord valley, east Kimberley.

A number of unifacially flaked points are made on thick pieces, and the retouched edges of some of these appear to have been used in wood working. Davidson (1935 : 159–60) reported that stone points similar to the pirri had been used by people of the Wardaman tribe in north-west Northern Territory for various types of wood working including both scraping and engraving. Flood (1970 : 49), accepting Davidson's observation, concludes 'that the small unifacial points in the Yarar deposit were used as general purpose adze-points or as spearpoints'. Mulvaney (1969 : 115) states that 'pointed adze-flakes' were excavated at Ingaladdi.

Backed points occur commonly in Ord valley late phase assemblages (Fig. 5 : 6–10, 12, 13). Most of these pieces are larger and much thicker and broader than bondi and other microlithic backed points, and they differ considerably in style. In most cases the retouched back is heavily notched or lightly denticulated (Fig. 5 : 8, 10), and in all cases the backing has been produced by direct percussion and not by bipolar percussion as is sometimes the case with microlithic backed points. The backing also differs from that of microlithic backed points in that it is generally semi-abrupt instead of abrupt, and does not extend around the proximal end of the piece thus leaving the butt intact. An exceptional specimen in which the butt has been removed is illustrated in Fig. 5 : 13.

Although further analysis of these tools is needed I suggest that they be referred to as 'Kimberley backed points' to distinguish them from microlithic backed points ('bondi points'). At the same time it must be made clear that several of these pieces resemble large geometric microliths (Fig. 5:13) or bondi points (Fig. 5 : 6, 12).

Some of the backed points (eg. Fig. 5 : 9) have marked crushing or undercutting along the proximal edge of the abruptly retouched back which is very similar to that found on the working edges of ethnographically known adze flakes. There seems little doubt that some were used as adzes, just as were some of the unifacially flaked points.

Obliquely truncated pieces (Fig. 5 : 11) are common in Ord valley late phase assemblages. There is an apparent gradation in form between these and backed points (eg. Fig. 5 : 9, 10, 13).

Most of the unifacially and bifacially flaked points and some of the backed points are made on blades of leilira type (Spencer and Gillen, 1904; McCarthy, 1967; Mulvaney, 1969). The leilira category, as found in Miriwun, Monsmont and many other Ord valley sites, comprises a technological range extending from prismatic blades, pointed or not, to classic Levallois points.

Bordes (1967) was the first to note that some pointed leilira blades are technologically the same as elongated Levallois points, and Dortch (1972b) has briefly described Levallois forms occurring in a point and blade assemblage from a site in the Chichester Range, Western Australia. Other writers record the use of 'prepared core techniques' (Allchin, 1966; Glover, 1967 : 423; McCarthy, 1967) but none is explicit. McCarthy (1964 : 240) mentions the Levallois technique, though in reference only to the faceting of the butts of flakes, a feature which is not diagnostic (see Bordes, 1961 : 14).

Levallois points (Fig. 6 : 1–14), as defined by Bordes (1961), are more or less elongated triangular flakes whose forms have been predetermined by preparatory flaking of the flaking faces of special cores. In all cases the axis of percussion bisects the distal extremity of the piece though the configuration of the flake scar facets on the dorsal faces of these points is variable. Some Levallois points have blade-like proportions but they differ from Levallois blades by their triangular form and converging edges. In the Ord valley typical Levallois points often have three principal flake scar facets on their dorsal faces, the last produced of which removes the proximal part of the central ridge formed by the adjacent flake scar facets of the two initial preparatory flakes. Most Ord valley Levallois points are of the elongated form (Bordes, 1961), and most have plain butts though faceted butts are not uncommon.

Many Ord valley Levallois points as well as some prismatic blades, in addition to the invasively flaked and backed forms above, have been retouched. This often consists of light trimming of the lateral edges or one or both edges of the distal extremity. Occasionally the distal retouch is abrupt, its purpose appearing to have been to strengthen and sharpen the tip of the point. Other points and blades have notched or denticulated edges, and some have abrupt retouch extending the length of both lateral edges.

A number of typical Levallois point cores have been recovered from Ord valley sites (Fig. 7 : 1–3, 5, 7, 8). Though there is no doubt that they have been used in the systematic production of Levallois points, some aspects of the technique require clarification. The main problem with the identification of the Levallois point technique is that pointed blades resembling Levallois points can sometimes be obtained from other kinds of blade or point cores, and a range of such cores occurs in the Ord valley. These include a few prismatic cores of pyramidal form, prismatic cores with single or opposed striking platforms and some Levallois blade cores. Present data show that intermediate forms exist between each of these and Levallois point cores. Perhaps the most common form is one intermediate between Levallois point cores and prismatic blade cores (Fig. 7 : 4). These have flaking faces which are often flat and generally triangular in plan with flake scar configuration suggesting that blades as well as points, which were probably indistinguishable from Levallois points, have been removed. Some of these have opposed striking platforms.

The same problem of intermediate forms between Levallois point cores, prismatic and other cores is known from other contexts where the Levallois point technique was used. One of these is in the earliest upper Palaeolithic horizons in the shelter of Ksar Akil near Beirut (I. Azoury, personal communication), and another occurrence is in the Mousterian layers at the site of Abou Sif in Jordan (Neuville, 1951).

In the Ord valley there is also evidence to suggest that typical Levallois point cores were flaked after the principal Levallois point or points had been removed. This is borne out by the configuration of the flake scar facets of several Levallois point cores and is clearly demonstrated in the specimen illustrated in Fig. 7 : 1. Fig. 7 : 1a shows the core as it was found, and in Fig. 7 : 1b it is illustrated with one of the flakes struck from it replaced. The replacement of the flake reveals a central flake scar facet which forms the outline of an elongated Levallois point. The parts of the outline of this principal flake scar indicated by dotted lines show (1) where the replaced flake had been notched after being removed, (2) where a flake was mis-struck after the principal point had been removed, and (3) where a small triangular flake was struck off from the other end of the core subsequent to the removal of the principal point but prior to the removal of the flake shown replaced.

The core, the flake and a small number of other flaked pieces of the same stone, a fine grained quartzite, including

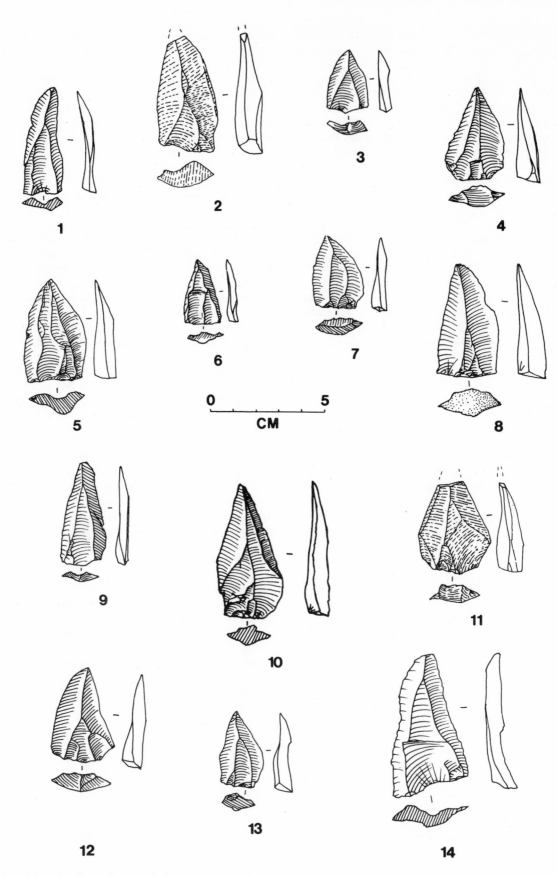

Fig. 6: Levallois points, Ord valley, east Kimberley.

a worked down or exhausted core, two Levallois points, a pointed blade of prismatic type as well as a hammerstone were found together on bare ground on the Ord floodplain. This small site, measuring 30 × 50 cm, is presumably the remains of a resting place or temporary camp where a stone worker, on ethnographical evidence probably a man, produced some stone points. Unfortunately the principal point produced on the core could not be found, though it is speculative that this was the piece which fitted the man's idea of the perfect pointed blade and thus was the one he took with him. The single pointed blade of prismatic type from the site could have been produced from the core in Fig. 7 : 1 at an earlier stage in its flaking, or could have been produced on the other worked down core.

The best evidence so far recovered for the use of the prismatic blade technique in the region comes from a quartzite quarry and factory high above the river a few hundred metres downstream from the Ord dam. Here occur numbers of typical prismatic cores, prismatic blades with parallel sides and many unretouched blades of trihedral section struck off to prepare the angular flaking faces of the cores for the removal of a succession of blades.

Numbers of pointed blades and some elongated Levallois points occur at the factory. Some of the cores on which these points were produced are intermediate in form between Levallois point and prismatic blade cores (Fig. 7 : 4). Only a few Levallois point cores have been identified. The prismatic cores include a variety of forms, some with single platforms, others with opposed or multiple platforms, and others which are similar to Levallois blade cores. More detailed analysis of the cores and blanks from this site will provide essential data for delineating the gradation between the different types of blade and point cores occurring in the Ord valley.

The different aspects of point and blade manufacture outlined here could be resolved easily by simply combining the different kinds of points, blades, point cores and blade cores under the general heading of the 'leilira' group. However to do this would mask the presence of Levallois and prismatic blade manufacturing techniques, cultural traits which are likely to be significant in relating Australian and Indonesian stone industries.

The discoidal core technique was much used in Ord valley late phase industries and many discoidal cores (Fig. 8 : 16, 17) as well as numbers of flakes apparently struck from discoidal cores have been recovered. Numbers of Levallois flakes (Fig. 8 : 6–13, 15, 18) and several Levallois blades (Fig. 8 : 14) have been identified, as well as Levallois flake cores (Fig. 8 : 1–3, 5) and a few typical Levallois blade cores (Figs 7 : 6; 8 : 4). The relative scarcity of Levallois flake cores compared with the numbers of Levallois flakes may be because many struck cores were further flaked as discoidal cores. Bordes (1961 : 72–73) discusses the occurrence of this practice in Mousterian industries, and there is no reason to think that Ord valley Levallois flake cores were not worked in similar fashion.

Trimming flakes from the manufacture of bifacial axes or points are common in late phase assemblages, and their dorsal flake scar configurations are similar to those of Levallois flakes. Breuil and Kelly (1956) describe biface trimming flakes in the Acheulean of the Somme valley and show that these flakes can be distinguished from Levallois flakes by their thinness and curvature and by their very thin or irregular butts.

Most of the Levallois flake cores and some of the Levallois point cores are made on small chert pebbles. The result is that many Ord valley Levallois flakes and points are quite small with maximum dimensions of about 3–4 cm.

Stratigraphical evidence shows that these Levallois techniques of point, blade and flake manufacture were in use after the time of European contact. Inquiries among Aborigines with traditional knowledge have so far failed to produce any information on the techniques. However early ethnographers in central and northern Australia (eg. Spencer and Gillen, 1904) recorded the functions and to some extent the technique of manufacturing leilira points and blades. A number of other core types have been identified in late phase assemblages from the region. These include some small bipolar cores, large pebble cores of various forms and some single platform flake cores of horsehoof type. These last are sometimes made on very large and thick flakes, with the bulbar faces serving as striking platforms. Some cores of all kinds have flaking or crushing along the proximal edges of their flaking faces, and in some cases this appears to be the result of use. Other cores have been deliberately retouched, presumably to be used as tools. For example the upper end of the core in Fig. 7 : 6 has been retouched as a scraper.

In shelter sites the native rock of the walls was often used as a source of raw material. The Miriwun deposit contains many quartzite flakes struck from the walls or from fragments fallen from the roof.

Bifacially flaked, edge-ground axes occur commonly in Ord valley late phase tool assemblages from open sites although only three have been found in excavated deposits. One of these, a broken specimen from Kununurra rock shelter, occurred 10 cm below a charcoal sample dated 1940±80 years BP (SUA 55); and another, from Monsmont, was found 10 cm below a charcoal sample dated 1730±80 years BP (SUA 57).

Numbers of burins on concave truncation (Fig. 5 : 14–17) and a few burins on transverse or oblique truncation (Fig. 5 : 18) occur in the late phase horizons of Miriwun and Monsmont. The association of some with objects of European origin (eg. bottle glass) indicates that burins were being used until after the time of European contact. I have not been able to obtain information on their function from local Aborigines.

Late phase assemblages contain a variety of other small retouched pieces including a few tula adze flakes (McCarthy, 1967 : 27–28; Mulvaney, 1969 : 70, 72), numerous adze flakes of other forms, thick notched or dentated flakes, retouched flakes and many very small flakes with chipped edges which in some cases have resulted from use. Pebble tools (choppers and chopping tools), grindstones and anvils are present in most late phase assemblages.

Denticulated and notched pieces are some of the most common kinds of retouched tools in the Ord valley late industrial phase. It is not easy to classify them according to size or shape but most are made on flat flakes or fragments with maximum dimensions of about 3–5 cm. It is possible that many of the denticulated pieces were used as knives whereas some of the notched pieces may have been used as spokeshaves.

No detailed quantitative data are presently available for the Ord valley stone industries. However the combined tentative findings from several trenches in Miriwun are tabulated (Table 4) to give some idea of the relative frequencies of the major tool forms in the late phase assemblages. These are divided into two main stratigraphical units, surface complex and light brown silty earth (Fig. 4). Small, possibly

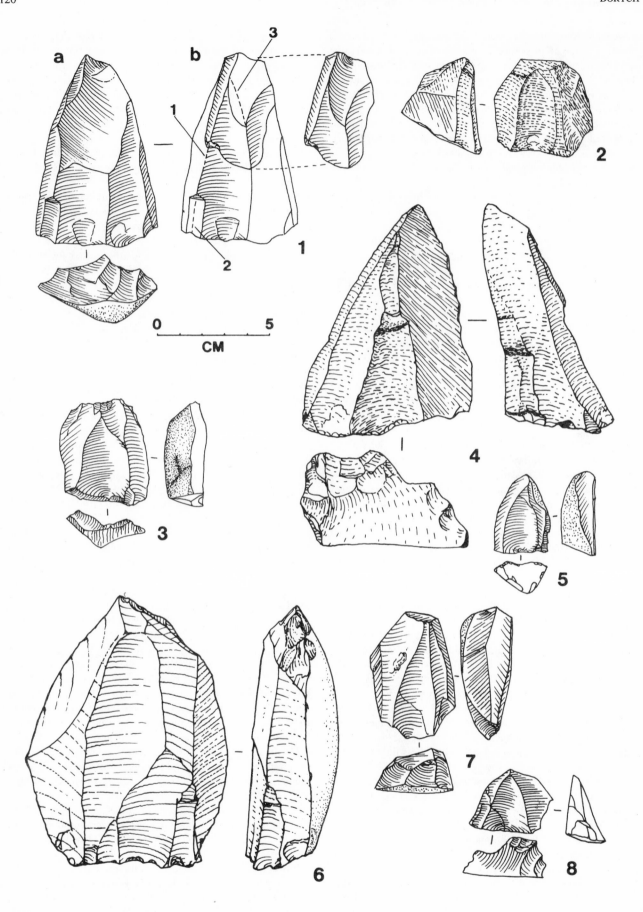

Fig. 7: Levallois point and blade cores, Ord valley, east Kimberley.

utilised flakes are numerous in these layers but are not computed here. The category 'other tools' includes pebble tools and core scrapers. The columns of percentages show that the two tool assemblages are similar. Each is characterised by high percentages of prismatic blades, Levallois points, denticulated and notched pieces, and retouched flakes. Unifacially flaked points are poorly represented in each. For the sake of convenience I regard these as point and blade assemblages even though denticulated and notched pieces and retouched flakes make up about half of the tools in each. It seems correct to do this as the range of points and blades gives these and all other Ord valley late phase assemblages their special character.

Table 4 Tentative relative frequencies of major tool forms, Miriwun

Tool type	Surface complex		Light brown silty earth	
	Count	Approx. %	Count	Approx. %
Prismatic blade	31	10.2	12	6.3
Levallois point	30	9.9	20	10.5
Bifacial point	20	6.6	8	4.2
Unifacial point	1	0.3	3	1.6
Backed point	7	2.3	7	3.7
Adze flake	3	1.0	3	1.6
Thick notched flake	5	1.7	3	1.6
Denticulated piece	59	19.5	42	22.0
Notched piece	52	17.2	43	22.6
Levallois flake	9	3.0	4	2.1
Burin on concave truncation	16	5.3	4	2.1
Flake struck from discoidal core	16	5.3	8	4.2
Retouched flake	34	11.2	19	9.9
Grindstone fragment	8	2.6	4	2.1
Other tools	12	4.1	11	5.8
Total	303		191	

(ii) EARLY PHASE ASSEMBLAGES The stone artifact assemblages from dark silty earth and dark brown silty earth (Fig. 4), which represent the early industrial phase at Miriwun, are both characterised by the small size of most of the retouched tools. Present analysis of these assemblages shows that thick flake tools, denticulated or notched flakes and retouched or utilised flakes comprise the great majority of all the tools occurring in the Miriwun early phase. Most of these are very small with maximum dimensions of between 1 and 3 cm. The other tools include a few core scrapers and pebble tools, some small blades most of which are very irregular (Fig. 9 : 2, 3), and a single pecked and grooved edge-ground axe (Fig. 9 : 1). The rest of the stone industry consists of flakes and chips, some cores and utilised pebbles, pieces of red ochre and a few quartzite fragments which may be parts of grindstones or anvils.

The first group, thick flake tools, includes two forms: thick notched flakes (Fig. 9 : 4, 5) and adze flakes (Fig. 9 : 6, 8). Both types are characterised by their very small size, their relative thickness and the nature of their working edges. The thick notched flakes include both broadly notched and denticulated forms. The adze flakes are defined by their upright working edges which have undercutting, overlapping flake scars and crushing similar to that seen on ethno-

graphic adze flakes. Some resemble the 'micro-adzes' from Puntutjarpa (Gould, 1971, 1973). The adze flake in Fig. 9 : 6 shows characteristic adze wear on both lateral edges. It is likely that this piece was used hafted, and it may have been rehafted in the course of its use. Both illustrated specimens occurred in the lower part of the dark brown silty earth layer and are late Pleistocene in age (Fig. 4, Table 1).

Denticulated and notched pieces are the most numerous group of tools in the Miriwun early phase assemblages. Many of these are delicately flaked specimens made on very small flakes or fragments. Numbers of very small bladelets or flakes with trihedral sections occur in the Miriwun early assemblages, and some of these have denticulated or notched edges. Often however it is impossible to be certain if the retouching had been done after the piece was produced, or whether the piece had been struck from the denticulated or notched edge of a larger flake. The bladelet in Fig. 9 : 12 appears to have been struck from the notched edge of a larger piece. The small trihedral flake in Fig. 9 : 11 has been notched after being produced.

Most of the retouched flakes in these horizons are very small. There are also many other very small flakes with fine edge chipping. In some cases the chipping may be use wear as it seems too regular and too marked to have come from the pieces being trodden on by people or animals, or from their being damaged by rock falls. It is possible that some of these flakes were used as hand held knives or scrapers, or as cutting edges in composite tools.

The axe in Fig. 9 : 1 comes from the upper part of dark silty earth a few centimetres above the position of charcoal sample ANU 142 (2980±95 years BP). The piece is fully pecked or hammer dressed; it has a bifacially ground cutting edge and a deeply pecked groove around its centre section. Similar axes excavated from Arnhem Land sites date to the late Pleistocene (Kamminga and Allen, 1973; White, 1967, 1971). Although no pecked or ground axes were recovered from the late Pleistocene horizon at Miriwun, a single flake from the lower part of dark brown silty earth has smoothing and clear striations on its dorsal face which suggest that it was struck from the face of a partly ground, flaked axe.

The small number of cores recovered from the Miriwun early phase layers give some idea of the stone working techniques used in these assemblages. Most of the cores are amorphous and a number have been worked down to a very small size. Some of these last are block-like or globular with multiple striking platforms, and it is possible that most of the very small flakes and bladelets of trihedral section noted above were struck from the angular edges of these cores. Small cores such as the two illustrated in Fig. 9 : 7, 9 show that the early phase stone workers were purposely manufacturing very small flakes, and this supports the view that the very small, apparently utilised flakes are small tools and not just trodden on *débitage*.

A number of flakes appear to have been produced on discoidal cores, and a single discoidal core (Fig. 9 : 10) was excavated in the rubbly basal layer of the deposit. No Levallois cores of any kind have been identified from the Miriwun early phase and only a few flakes resemble those struck from Levallois cores. A few very small bipolar or 'scalar' cores (White, 1968) also occur in these layers. The regular appearance of a small number of blades and bladelets (Fig. 9 : 2, 3) from the Miriwun early phase assemblages suggests that these pieces have been manufactured by a form of blade technique. However no blade cores were recovered

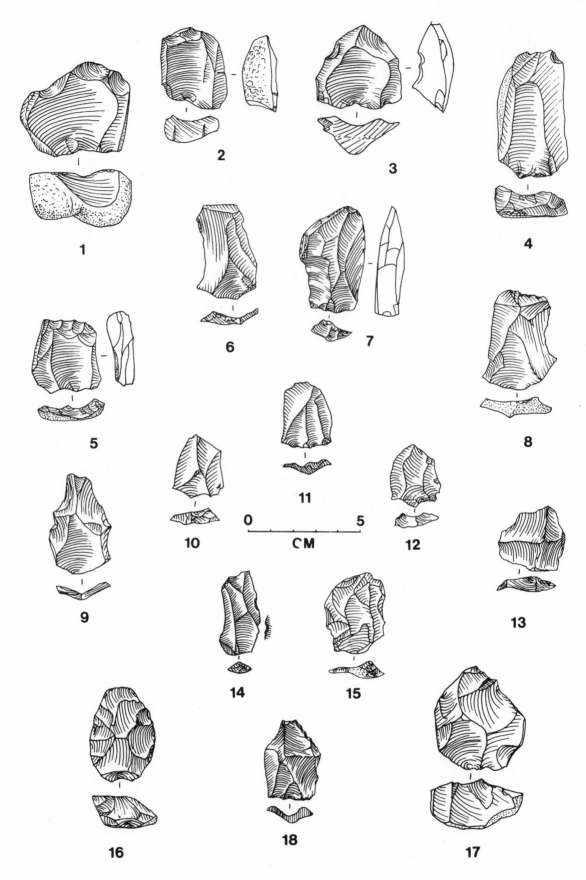

Fig. 8: Levallois flakes and cores, and discoidal cores, Ord valley, east Kimberley.

from these layers, and thus the possibility that the blades were produced fortuitously cannot be dismissed.

Finally, two flakes recovered from dark brown earthy layer at a depth below that of charcoal sample ANU 1008 ($17\,980\,{}^{+1370}_{-1170}$ years BP) have been identified as pieces struck from australites (W. H. Cleverly, personal communication). Australites are not thought to occur naturally in the Ord valley or any part of northern Australia (Baker, 1959 : Fig. 4). If so their presence in Miriwun demonstrates that some contact took place, perhaps in the form of long range trade, between the late Pleistocene hunter-gatherers of northern and southern Australia.

Discussion   It is clear that a whole series of new stone working techniques and tool types came into use in the Ord valley about three or more thousand years ago and continued in use until the end of traditional times. The apparent paucity if not lack in the early phase horizons at Miriwun and Monsmont of such distinctive late phase features as the Levallois techniques of point and flake manufacture, the prismatic blade technique, the techniques of invasive flaking by percussion and pressure, as well as the absence of distinctive late phase tool types including burins on truncation, tula adzes and backed points, shows that the industrial sequence of neither site is a direct evolutionary development of an older stone industry into a newer form.

At the same time early phase tool forms such as thick notched flakes, adze flakes, core scrapers, pebble tools, denticulated and notched pieces and small retouched flakes continue in use throughout the later phase. Although most of these are the basic cutting, scraping and chopping tools made on flakes and fragments (the 'maintenance tools' of Binford and Binford, 1969) which occur in many stone age cultures, their apparently similar and possibly coextensive range of size, form and technique between earlier and later phases suggests a certain degree of continuity. This is further suggested by the presence in both phases of the discoidal and bipolar core techniques and the practice of bifacially grinding the cutting edges of axes.

The continuity of some tool types and techniques is paralleled by the recurrence of the same range of animal foods throughout the Miriwun and Monsmont archaeological sequences (Tables 2, 3). However the continuity of subsistence patterns in a single locality has no bearing on the industrial change which takes place in that it is probable that most hunter-gatherers would have eaten most of the locally available animal foods. What is suggested by the continuity of not only subsistence, but also by continued occupation of the same sites, is that the transition which occurred between earlier and later stone industries may not have been accompanied by any great changes in adaptation.

The Miriwun and Monsmont evidence suggests that some form of diffusion and not local invention was the basic factor in the change which took place in the Ord valley industrial sequence. Whether this suggested diffusion resulted from an influx of new ideas or from movement of people is an open question. However there is ample ethnographic evidence showing that diffusion of goods and ideas over wide areas in northern Australia occurred not through movements of large tribal groups but through elaborate trading systems (Berndt, 1951; Berndt and Berndt, 1964; Kaberry, 1939; McCarthy, 1939) made possible by the bridging mechanism of local group, family and individual movement. There is no reason to think that similar processes did not take place three or four thousand years ago. If so they could account for the spread of many tool forms and techniques over wide distances.

Present evidence suggests that the Ord valley industrial sequence is a case of direct continuity with wholesale received traits. These wholesale received traits, and I am referring mainly to the range of flaked and backed points, burins and the Levallois point, Levallois flake and perhaps the prismatic blade manufacturing techniques which characterise the later phase, may have diffused from Arnhem Land where similar industries date back over six thousand years (White, 1967, 1971). Or, a western, northwestern or immediately northern source is possible as similar point and blade industries occur over the whole of Kimberley. As for the ultimate origin of the Ord valley late stone industries I can only say that counterparts to Ord valley Levallois points, leaf-shaped bifacial points, serrated or notched points, backed points, dentated backed points, obliquely truncated pieces and prismatic blades exist in the so called Toalian industries of Sulawesi (Glover, 1973; van Heekeren, 1957, Plates 28, 29 and 45; McCarthy, 1940; Mulvaney, 1969 : 165; Mulvaney and Soejono, 1970).

Archaeology in the south-west of western Australia

Stone industries   An earlier and a later series of stone industries have been identified in the southern part of western Australia. The earlier material has been described from only three sites, Devil's Lair (Dortch and Merrilees, 1971, 1973; Dortch, 1974), Puntutjarpa (Gould, 1968, 1971, 1973) and Koonalda (Wright (ed.), 1971). Late phase stone industries are known largely through Gould's descriptions of the more recent Puntutjarpa artifact assemblages and through a number of other papers dealing with the distribution, morphology and function of various tool types (Akerman, 1969, 1973; Butler, 1958; Davidson and McCarthy, 1957; Gould and Quilter, 1972; Gould *et al.*, 1971; Hayden, 1973; McCarthy, 1967; Mulvaney, 1969; Noone, 1943; Pearce, 1973; and Ride, 1958). In addition Glover (1967) described a tool assemblage from Millstream, a rich open site in the Pilbara, which is very similar to southern late phase assemblages (Fig. 1). Since then a number of other Pilbara sites containing the same kind of assemblages have been recorded.

The late phase assemblages from the southern regions, the Pilbara and the central arid zone are typified by a number of diverse tool forms including a range of geometric microliths and microlithic backed points and bladelets, a variety of adze flakes including a high proportion of tula form, various axe types but notably bifacially flaked, edge-ground axes, horsehoof cores and thick flake scrapers, denticulated or notched pieces, pebble tools, and grindstones and mortars. Burins are not commonly found and tools resembling eloueras (Mulvaney, 1969 : 81–83; McCarthy, 1967 : 26) are known from only a few sites (eg. Millstream : Glover, 1967). Prismatic blades and blade cores occur in all districts but the evidence for blade manufacture is not nearly so great as that for the production of flakes from single and multi-platform flake cores and bipolar cores. Discoidal cores and flakes presumably struck from discoidal cores occur in most districts, but very few flakes, blades or points similar to those made by Levallois techniques have been collected in the southern region. Pilbara late phase assemblages, however,

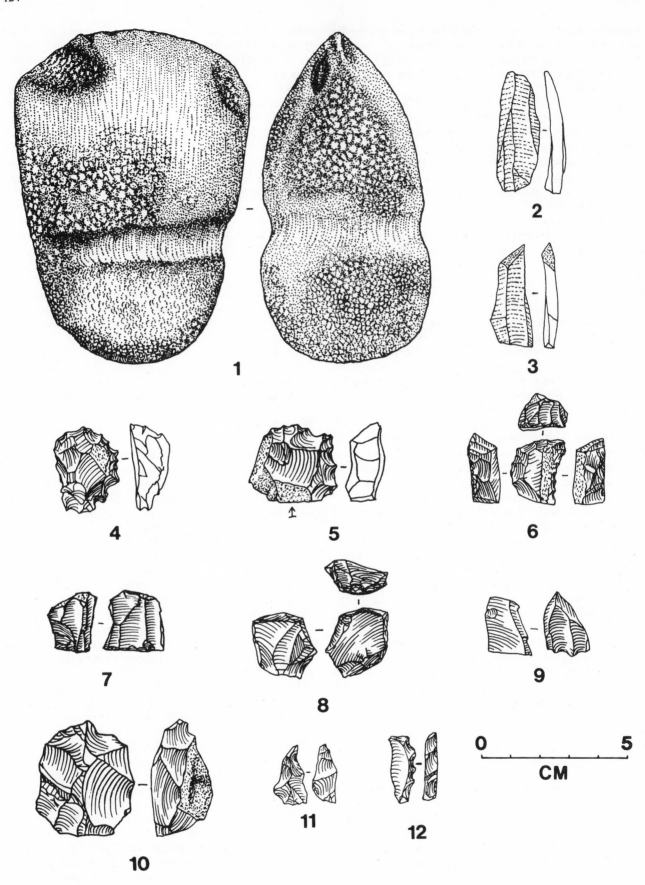

Fig. 9: Early phase stone artifacts, Miriwun rock shelter, Ord Valley, east Kimberley.

include Levallois points and large prismatic blades (Dortch, 1972b).

Area studies At present systematic survey of prehistoric occupation and subsistence patterns has been carried out in three districts in the southern two thirds of western Australia. The first of these is in the Gibson and Great Victoria deserts to the east (the 'western desert' of anthropological literature) where Gould has conducted a classic area study based on the excavation and sampling of occupation sites and on ethnographic studies among desert Aborigines, some of whom had only a short time previously ceased to live a traditional life (Gould, 1968, 1971, 1973). Gould's main excavation was at Puntutjarpa rock shelter (Fig. 1) where he recorded an archaeological sequence covering the past 10 000 years. The oldest assemblages containing geometric microliths and other late phase tool types at Puntutjarpa date to about 4000 years BP though the use of small, presumably hafted adze flakes extends to the earliest occupation of the site.

The second area is the Nullarbor Plain in the extreme south-east where a group from the University of Sydney was until recently engaged in a programme of field research. Here also Gallus and Wright (Wright (ed.), 1971) carried out detailed investigations at Koonalda Cave (Fig. 1) where the earliest archaeological horizons are about 22 000 years old. Another Nullarbor site, Horseshoe Cave, also has an archaeological sequence and diverse faunal remains radiocarbon dated to as old as the late Pleistocene (M. Archer, personal communication).

In the third area, the south-west, Hallam and Dortch are conducting separate but complementary area studies of adjacent districts. Merrilees *et al.* (1973) provide a useful summary of the present state of archaeological research in the south-west.

Hallam (1972) has recorded a number of diverse sites in her survey of the Perth basin and areas east of the Darling Range (Fig. 10). Her excavations at Frieze Cave in the Avon valley near York have provided radiocarbon dates for geometric microliths ranging from more than 3000 years BP to Modern times (Hallam, 1972 : 16–17). Open dune sites near the Moore River investigated by her (Merrilees *et al.*, 1973) appear to relate to an earlier industrial phase. Hallam has made much use of ethnohistorical data in her research and in this way and through area survey has compiled a comprehensive record of Aboriginal land use in the south-west (1972; 1971).

The lower south-west In 1973 I began an area study in the lower south-west as part of the research centring on the key late Pleistocene site of Devil's Lair, a limestone cave about 20 km north of Cape Leeuwin (Fig. 10) (Dortch and Merrilees, 1971, 1973; Dortch, 1974). More recently this study was expanded to join with Gardner's survey of sites in the Northcliffe district further east along the south coast.

For the purposes of this paper the lower or extreme south-west is the area south and west of a line drawn between Cape Naturaliste on the west coast and Point d'Entrecasteaux on the south coast (Fig. 10). Following Gardner's classifications (1944) the area can be roughly divided into two main vegetation zones. The first is the mosaic of eucalypt forests and woodlands formed by the distribution of three major species, jarrah (*Eucalyptus marginata*), marri (*E. calophylla*) and karri (*E. diversicolor*). The most widespread of these is the jarrah forest which is characteristic of lateritic soils but is typically

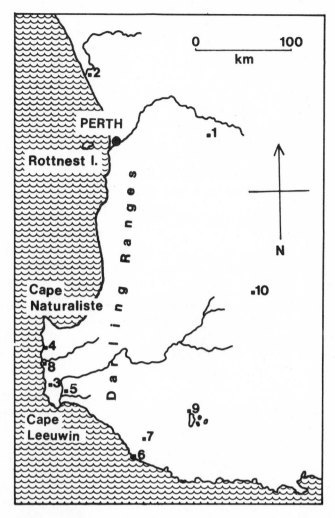

Fig. 10: Map of the south-west, western Australia showing sites and areas mentioned in the text.
1 Frieze Cave; 2 Moore River; 3 Devil's Lair; 4 Cowaramup Point · 5 Blackwood River; 6 Point d'Entrecasteaux; 7 Northcliffe; 8 Mouth of the Margaret River; 9 Lake Muir; 10 Lake Wagin.

in association with marri on alluvial soils in valleys and in areas of sandy loam. The karri forest is confined to the higher rainfall areas and is characteristic of soils derived from gneissic or granitic rocks. Karri also may be associated with marri in areas of alluvial soil. The understoreys of these forests vary widely and include a number of species which were of economic value to the Aborigines.

The second zone comprises the complex of low open woodland, scrub, heathland, sedgeland and swamp which extends over the coastal dunes and sand plains of this district. Archaeological sites occur in both zones, and most have been found in sheltered valleys in the jarrah-marri forests and in the woodlands, swamps and sedgelands of the coast. The sites usually consist of a scatter of stone artifacts. They are often situated on sandy ground and typically in the vicinity of streams and swamps. The richest and largest are located in areas of contrasting vegetation formations and topography.

Scatters of marine shell of edible species and stone artifacts, including a few geometric microliths, have been collected at dune sites on the coast between Capes Leeuwin and Naturaliste. One of these is at Cowaramup Point 32 km north of Devil's Lair. A series of partly deflated dune soil horizons occur at this site and test excavations show that two of these contain

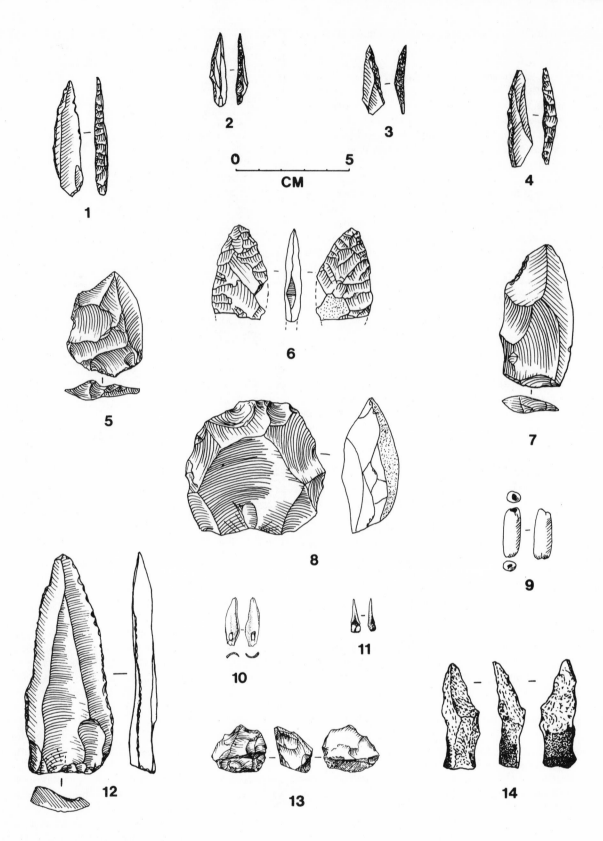

Fig. 11 : Stone and bone artifacts from western Australia.

stone artifacts. A number of stone artifacts and other archaeological material are cemented to a massive band of calcrete upon which the succession of dune soils rests. So far it has not been possible to collect sufficient charcoal from these soils for radiocarbon dating. Other coastal sites containing geometric microliths and some marine shells have been located by Gardner in the vicinity of Point d'Entrecasteaux on the south coast (Fig. 10). The finds from these sites suggest that south-west Aborigines were using shellfish as food in late phase times, evidence which is contrary to first hand observations made at the period of European contact (e.g. Grey, 1841) which indicate that these animals were not eaten by the Aborigines.

Finds of geometric microliths, bladelets and a few prismatic cores show that some of these recently recorded sites in the lower south-west and almost all of those found by Gardner around Northcliffe and Point d'Entrecasteaux relate to the later industrial phase. There is stratigraphical, typological and petrological evidence to suggest that a few sites may date to an earlier period.

The most notable of the presumed early sites occur in a series of old red dunes exposed in road cuttings a few kilometres south of Devil's Lair (Fig. 10). The dunes are located on the present eastern edge of the karri forest near Cape Leeuwin and are densely vegetated. They overlook a series of freshwater swamps, and it is probable, during times in the past when drainage patterns and quantity of rainfall were much as at present, that the people who occupied the dunes exploited various edible plants and animals found in the swamps. The age of the dunes is unknown, but they are in part overlain by massive moving dunes of unconsolidated calcareous sand. Thus it appears that the old red dunes relate to an earlier aeolian episode and possibly are early Recent or late Pleistocene in age.

The archaeological evidence consists of stone artifacts, many of which are made of the same kind of distinctive chert as that found in artifact assemblages from Devil's Lair (see below). Artifacts are found scattered in the face of the dunes at various depths. No occupational features such as hearths have been identified in the sections examined, and the artifacts do not appear to be laterally oriented in bands or clusters.

The artifacts from the old red dunes are very similar to those from Devil's Lair which date to the late Pleistocene. They include several small thick flake scrapers resembling adze flakes, bipolar cores, various notched or denticulated pieces and a few flakes probably struck from discoidal cores. No blades, geometric microliths or other typical later phase artifacts have been seen at the dunes. The main objective of the excavations planned there will be to determine whether the archaeological material is contemporaneous with occupation at Devil's Lair, and to recover biological remains which may show the probable function of these sites.

One of the most interesting aspects of recent research in the south-west is the study of the different kinds of stone used during prehistoric times. Glover (Glover and Cockbain, 1971) and Hallam (1972) have located a number of sites in the Perth basin which contain quantities of artifacts made of a distinctive kind of Eocene fossiliferous chert. No west coast sources of this stone are known, though it occurs abundantly on the south coast some 450 km south-east of Perth. Glover (1974) recently examined all of the chert artifacts so far recovered from Devil's Lair and found that all were made of the distinctive fossiliferous kind. His identification supports Hallam's postulate (1972; in Merrilees

et al., 1973) that the chert was used extensively in the earlier but only to a very limited degree during the later industrial phase.

It is possible that the chert artifacts from Devil's Lair and from the old red dunes immediately to the south are made from stone quarried from outcrops on the south coast to the east. Gardner has located the westernmost known outcrop of Eocene fossiliferous chert 14 km east of Northcliffe and 110 km south-east of Devil's Lair, and he thinks it is possible that other outcrops occur further west (personal communication).

Gardner found another deposit of stone near Northcliffe (Fig. 10) which is of significance to south-west prehistory (Dortch, 1975). This is an outcrop of silcrete (J. E. Glover, personal communication) which is overlain by dune sands developed into an iron humus podzol (W. M. McArthur, personal communication). Gardner interpreted the site as a quarry and as the source of numerous silcrete artifacts found in the Northcliffe-Windy Harbour area. A recent test excavation (Trench 1) at a bulldozer cutting in the sandy soil yielded quantities of silcrete artifacts, not only quarrying debris but also geometric microliths (Fig. 12 : 1, 2), bladelets and very many tiny chips indicating that the quarry was also a factory where geometric microliths and other tools had been manufactured in quantity.

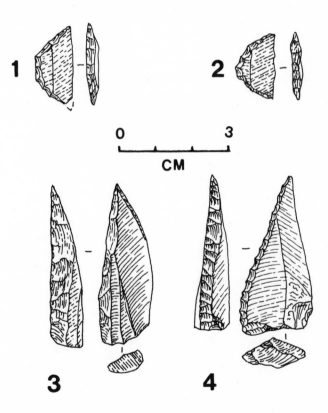

Fig. 12: Geometric microliths from the Northcliffe quarry-factory, south western Australia, and backed points from the Berkeley and King Rivers, north eastern Kimberley.

The richest part of the stone industrial succession occurs in the pallid zone or A_2 horizon of the soil profile (Dortch, 1975 : Fig. 2). A radiocarbon date of 3080±75 years BP (ANU 1131) was obtained from a charcoal sample taken in the upper part of the pallid zone, and a second charcoal sample collected from the lower part of the pallid zone yielded a date of 6780±120 years BP (SUA 379). The uppermost geometric microliths in the soil profile occur 3 to 7 cm below the position of ANU 1131; the lowermost geometric microlith (Fig. 12 : 2) was found 1 to 3 cm above the upper part of the 10 cm thick horizon from which charcoal for SUA 379 was collected. These two radiocarbon dates thus show that geometric microliths were manufactured here between three and about six thousand years ago.

These radiocarbon dates from the Northcliffe quarry-factory and the four radiocarbon dates ranging from 3090± 240 years BP (ANU 830) to 110±70 years BP (ANU 827) which are associated with a succession of microlithic assemblages from Frieze Cave near York (Fig. 10 : Hallam, 1972) indicate that the microlithic tradition in southwestern Australia extended from about 6000 years BP until Modern times, this being the longest duration for industries containing geometric microliths yet recorded for Australia.

A radiocarbon date of 6490±145 years BP (SUA 364) has recently been obtained from a charcoal sample collected from layer G, Trench 7, Devil's Lair (Dortch, 1974 : Fig. 3). The layer is stratigraphically the uppermost which contains archaeological material which is believed to be *in situ*. Unfortunately there are no artifacts of great diagnostic value from this layer, the archaeological material consisting only of a quartz flake, some possible bone artifacts, some fragments of mussel shell and animal bones. SUA 364 is the same radiocarbon age as the lowermost Northcliffe date (SUA 379) described above. It is speculative that the former date represents the end of early phase occupation at Devil's Lair and that SUA 379 represents the beginning of late phase quarrying and tool manufacture at the Northcliffe quarry factory. It is thus possible that the early—late phase transition in the extreme south-west took place about 6500 years ago.

The analysis of pollen samples taken from Trench 1, Northcliffe (B. E. Balme, personal communication) shows that three eucalypts, *Eucalyptus marginata*, *E. diversicolor* and *E. calophylla*, species still dominant in the Northcliffe area, were present here prior to about 6780 years ago (SUA 379) and at times since. The occurrence of these three major species over thousands of years suggests that on the south coast climate was at times during the mid-Holocene much the same as at present.

Many late phase tools made of silcrete very similar to that from the Northcliffe quarry occur in an open site on the Scott River about 80 km west of the Northcliffe quarry-factory site and 20 km south-east of Devil's Lair (Fig. 10). A few silcrete artifacts have been found along with quartz geometric microliths at open sites in the Cape Leeuwin-Cape Naturaliste area. No outcrops of this stone are known in the capes area, and it is probable that the silcrete artifacts came from a south coast source, possibly from the Northcliffe quarry-factory. No silcrete artifacts have been recovered in the Devil's Lair excavation, and only two specimens have been collected from the area of the old red dunes a few kilometres to the south.

Thus present findings from the lower south-west suggest marked differences in the kind of stone used in the earlier and late phases. The hypothesis can be tested further by excavation of stratified deposits containing late phase assemblages in the capes area. Such sites may exist in the series of shelters at the foot of limestone cliffs at the mouth of the Margaret River, 20 km north of Devil's Lair and along Turner Brook, about halfway between Devil's Lair and Cape

Leeuwin (Fig. 10). Devil's Lair continues to be the most important site under investigation in western Australia (Dortch and Merrilees, 1971, 1973; Dortch, 1974). Archaeological assemblages from there contain a variety of mammal, bird and reptile species, mussel and emu shell, a number of different kinds of stone artifacts and a range of diverse bone tools including points made on the fibulae of macropods, small awls (Fig. 11 : 11), two very small perforated pieces one of which is probably a bodkin (Fig. 11 : 10) and the other clearly a bead (Fig. 11 : 9). Among the stone artifacts are a few flakes in part covered with a dark resinous substance which is thought to be hafting gum (Fig. 11 : 14), as well as a few small adze flakes (Fig. 11 : 13). The use of the bipolar flaking technique by Devil's Lair stone workers is indicated not only by bipolar or scalar cores (White, 1968) but also by flakes whose small size, bipolar flake scar configuration and irregular, thin butts suggest that they have been produced by bipolar percussion (see Hayden, 1973).

The radiocarbon dates noted above from Northcliffe and Devil's Lair (R. Gillespie, personal communication; Dortch and Merrilees, 1973 : Table 1); and the uppermost date from Frieze Cave (ANU 827 : 110±70 years BP; Hallam 1972) provide a radiocarbon dating sequence for southwestern prehistory which extends from the modern period to about 31 800 years BP.

Western Australian Museum catalogue numbers of artifacts illustrated in Figures 5-9, 11, 12

Figure 5

1. B2543	6. B20	11. B2047	16. B920
2. B918	7. B67	12. B937	17. B890
3. B131	8. B890	13. B941	18. B890
4. B18	9. B392	14. B223	19. B889
5. B224	10. B23	15. B2040	

Figure 6

1. B927	5. B24	9. B940	13. B918
2. B24	6. B930	10. B24	14. B55
3. B890	7. B399	11. B24	
4. B24	8. B24	12. B24	

Figure 7

1. B2187	3. B2188	5. B2563	7. B33
2. B2123	4. B2155	6. B2502	8. B8A

Figure 8

1. B2150	6. B2221	11. B390	16. B930
2. B2556	7. B2544	12. B2188	17. B2502
3. B934	8. B203	13. B92	18. B214
4. B33	9. B937	14. B204	
5. B2556	10. B224	15. B930	

Figure 9

1. B2085	4. B211	7. B2138	10. B2139
2. B211	5. B219	8. B209	11. B2138
3. B212	6. B219	9. B249	12. B2137

Figure 11

1. B2331	5. B169	9. B1556	13. B1514
2. A14083	6. B2332	10. A22028	14. B1576
3. A14083	7. B2381	11. B1538	
4. A14083	8. A17214	12. B1001	

Figure 12

1. B2410	3. B2291
2. B2414	4. B2244

Other research A number of other sites from the southern third of western Australia provide considerable potential for archaeological and geomorphological research. Some of the most important of these occur in the lunettes on the shores of the salt lakes in the interior of the south-west. Bowler has recently surveyed some of these lunettes, and at one site, a lunette on the east side of Lake Wagin (Fig. 10) he found a stone artifact in a horizon which by comparison with radiocarbon dates from other lunettes in the region is probably at least 15 000 and perhaps as much as 17 000 years old (J. Bowler, personal communication).

Recently stone artifacts are reported to come from commercial working of peat deposits at a freshwater swamp near Lake Muir (Fig. 10). I have, in two attempts, been unable to locate artifacts *in situ* in the peat, though they are present in the section of a lunette on the south-east shore of the swamp, and on the shelving edge of the north-west side of the swamp. Several geometric microliths have been collected but no other distinctive types.

In the 1960s Churchill (1968) carried out pollen studies in the peat deposits of a number of freshwater swamps in the south-west including one of the swamps near Lake Muir. He determined that *Eucalyptus marginata*, *E. diversicolor* and *E. calophylla* were present in the south-west over the past 9000 years, evidence which is in part confirmed by the pollen identified from the Northcliffe excavation. Ashy horizons and abundant charcoal occurred in some of the peat beds, and at Weld swamp, south of Lake Muir, Churchill found charcoal throughout the deposit indicating that 'periodic fires have occurred [there] for more than 5000 years' (1968 : 145). It is possible that these ashy horizons are the remains of periodic burning by Aborigines (for detailed discussion see Hallam, 1975). Churchill's data, the archaeological material from Lake Muir and Hallam's findings in the Perth area suggest that freshwater swamps in the south-west were being exploited for their plant and animal foods by prehistoric hunter-gatherers just as they were by the southwestern Aborigines at the time of European invasion (Grey, 1841).

Merrilees (1968) found stone artifacts and the remains of extinct marsupials including *Thylacoleo* and *Phascolonus* in a formation of paraconglomerate near Balladonia homestead to the south-east (Fig. 1). He also records the probable association of bones of *Sthenurus* and stone implements in a sandstone deposit at Balladonia, as well as the occurrence of a stone artifact and a *Zygomaturus* mandible in the same geological formation at Billabalong Station on the Murchison River (Fig. 1).

Discussion

The concept of stone industrial phases used here is not an explicit hypothetical model but is simply a convenient device for the ordering of new data from different regions. While it is true that the concept is empirical it is also consistent with Mulvaney's interpretation of the Australian archaeological sequence. The early and late stone industrial phases in western Australia broadly correspond to Mulvaney's early 'core and flake-tool' phase (1969 : 164) and to his later 'inventive' phase (1969 : 107). However the western Australian two phase regional sequences outlined in this paper are not based on any assumption of technological progress but are defined simply on technological and morphological differences between the stone industries which have so far been identified.

Here I have regarded the Puntutjarpa industrial sequence as having earlier and later phases based on the appearance of geometric microliths, tula adze flakes and other stone tools typical of the later industries in the southern part of western Australia. This is contrary to Gould's interpretation (1971 : 151) which places the whole of the Puntutjarpa sequence within Mulvaney's 'hafted' (or 'inventive') phase (1969 : 107, 110). Gould emphasises the continuity in subsistence and technology which exists at Puntutjarpa and postulates that the whole of the 10 000 year archaeological sequence should be called the 'Australian desert culture' (1971 : 174; 1973 : 15). Thus in his argument for cultural continuity Gould restricts the importance of the introduction of late phase tool types such as geometric microliths and tula adze flakes.

It is possible that in several regions including the 'western desert' the events represented by the introduction of the characteristic later phase tool forms into the archaeological record were not of any great significance to the people actually living at the time, other than the adoption of a new method of working stone or of using a new kind of stone tool in traditional activities. However this change or series of changes which takes place is by no means unimportant in the ordering of archaeological data and the correlation of regional industrial sequences. Until now it is virtually the only major event in western Australian prehistory for which there is any evidence. It would be quite wrong to depreciate its occurrence in the Ord valley or the south-west where very marked differences exist between the tool assemblages of the earlier and later industries. Whatever the degree of its local or regional cultural significance the fact remains that the transition or change did take place, and that it is certainly of considerable value in making archaeological comparisons within Australia and in attempting to understand past connections between Australia and the rest of the Old World. I feel then that it is not unrealistic to regard the Puntutjarpa industrial sequence as having an earlier and a later phase corresponding to those outlined for the south-west, and to those which have been identified in other parts of Australia.

No attempt is made here to correlate the western Australian industrial sequences with those described for eastern Australia (eg. Lampert, 1971). However broad similarities exist between the later stone tool assemblages from many areas in Australia (Mulvaney, 1969), and across the continent these industries can be roughly divided between northern and southern variants, the apparent boundary being along the northern edge of the central arid zone. Industries containing geometric microliths and microlithic backed points seem confined to the deserts and southern regions (Mulvaney, 1969 : Fig. 28), whereas the northern industries are characterised by a range of invasively flaked points. A significant exception to this division is in the distribution of unifacially flaked points of pirri form (Campbell, 1960; McCarthy, 1967) which occur over most of the area between northern Australia and the south coast of South Australia (Mulvaney, 1969 : 116–22). However very few tools resembling pirri points have been collected from the Nullarbor Plain or the desert areas of western Australia.

At this time it is very difficult to distinguish early phase from late phase assemblages collected from unstratified open sites in western Australia. This is due to the apparent narrow range of early phase tool forms and the continuance of most of these into the later phase, and also because of the lack of a large amount of early phase material from stratified sites which can be used for comparison. Present distributional data of stone artifacts in western Australia then are almost entirely confined to assemblages or individual specimens known to be characteristic of the later phase. Data based on the archaeological collections at the Western Australian Museum are by no means complete but some aspects of late phase stone artifact distribution seem clear.

The most outstanding feature is the marked difference already noted between the northern (or Kimberley) industries characterised by various kinds of invasively flaked points and the southern industries containing geometric microliths and microlithic backed points (Fig. 1). However the Kimberley and southern industries share a sufficient number of tool forms to show that it is better to think of them as regional variants within a single industrial complex rather than as two rigidly defined and separate provinces.

These shared tool forms include not only such generalised tools as core scrapers, grindstones, pebble tools, flake scrapers, denticulated and notched pieces but also more distinctive types such as bifacially flaked, edge-ground axes and tula adzes. Prismatic blades or bladelets are present in late phase assemblages in all districts, and single or multi-platform flake cores, bipolar cores, prismatic cores and discoidal cores occur in varying relative frequencies in most assemblages.

For some years the most northwesterly known tool assemblege containing geometric microliths, microlithic backed points and tula adze flakes was from Millstream in the Fortescue valley, Pilbara (Fig. 1) (Glover, 1967). Recently Dix collected a typical microlithic backed point (Figure 11:1), an atypical geometric microlith and other late phase material including some tula adze flakes and blades in an open campsite on Pardoo Station some 300 km north-east of Millstream (Fig. 1). At another late phase open site on Pardoo Dix found a broken bifacially flaked point (Fig. 11 : 6). This piece and a number of other stone artifacts from the site are heavily and similarly patinated and appear to be of the same age. Thus the Pardoo material comprises not only the most northerly find of geometric microliths and microlithic backed points but also includes an apparently associated bifacially flaked point. I regard these finds as evidence that the Eighty Mile Beach area (Fig. 1) was an access route between the Kimberley and Pilbara districts during late phase times.

Definite evidence of north-south contact is provided by finds of Kimberley pearl shell in the southern regions of western Australia (McCarthy, 1939; Map 14; Mulvaney, 1969 : Fig. 19), and possibly the australite flakes from the bottom of the Miriwun deposit also indicate contact. No dates are available for any of the pearl shell found in the southern regions, but the australite flakes from Miriwun suggest that contact took place between northern and southern groups as much as 18 000 years ago.

The classic question concerning the later Australian industries is that of the significance of the differences between the northern and southern variants. Several authors (eg. Mulvaney, 1969 : 164–65) have noted that most of the different kinds of late phase tools which characterise both northern and southern regional industries also occur in southern Asia or Indonesia. Mulvaney states: 'It is a speculative hypothesis that both point and microlithic blade industries had differentiated before reaching Australia, although diversification continued here, and that while Arnhem Land was the likely beachhead for the former technology, north-western Australia was the possible entry area for the latter' (1969 : 127).

It is possible to accept the first part of Mulvaney's hypothesis, assuming that Indonesia is the source of the characteristic late phase tool forms. However northwestern Australia (i.e. the Pilbara and northwestern Kimberley) does not seem to be a more likely point of entry for the microlithic industries than does the Joseph Bonaparte Gulf area (Fig. 1) or Arnhem Land. Although no one has identified microlithic tool assemblages in any of these areas there is some evidence to suggest that such material may exist in one of the latter.

Some years ago R. M. Berndt collected three typical microlithic backed points on the Daly River to the west of Arnhem Land (Figs. 1; 11 : 2–4). Berndt (personal communication) has stated that these points were not made locally but had been traded from the country of the Nangiomeri people north of the Victoria River. Unlike the Kimberley backed points these specimens are typical of microlithic backed points found in southern Australia. Their occurrence in the tropics of northern Australia may be evidence of trade from the south or even from Indonesia. Or they may represent an hitherto unknown type in the tool kit of this part of northern Australia.

More recently Western Australian Museum staff have carried out a preliminary archaeological reconnaissance in the Berkeley, King and Forrest River districts in northeastern Kimberley. Here we identified stone tool assemblages in surface sites which are very similar to the Ord valley late phase industry. These assemblages contain backed points similar to those from the Ord valley (Fig. 5 : 6–10, 12, 13) including some which resemble microlithic backed points (Fig. 12 : 3, 4). Further investigations should indicate whether microlithic backed points were ever a significant part of the stone industries of northeastern Kimberley, the Ord valley and adjacent districts to the east.

It seems likely that the differences between the northern and southern late phase industries result from a combination of geographical and cultural factors. I have here regarded the coast along Eighty Mile Beach as an access route, even so the physical barrier of the Great Sandy Desert is likely to have greatly hampered communication between the Kimberley and Pilbara regions. The second factor is as suggested by Mulvaney (1969 : 127) 'that both point and microlithic industries had differentiated before reaching Australia'. This hypothesis can adequately explain the differences between the Kimberley and southern industries, though if true it is very surprising that no microlithic assemblages have been identified in tropical Australia. I feel that the idea of microlithic tool manufacture was once known in tropical Australia even if it never became established, and conceivably an as yet undiscovered microlithic sub-phase exists within one of the northern regional industrial sequences.

The best data for the Levallois techniques in western Australia come from east Kimberley and the Pilbara district. Glover (1967 : Fig. 3 : 191, 4758) illustrates pointed blades from Millstream which are very similar to elongated Levallois points (Fig. 11 : 12) from a large collection made at a probable late phase site in the Chichester Range about 190 km to the east (Dortch, 1972a). Most of the east Kimberley Levallois material comes from the Ord valley. Other specimens include the Levallois flake core in Fig. 11 : 8, collected by Butler on Bedford Downs, a station 200 km south-west of Lake Argyle, and the Levallois flake in Fig. 11 : 5, which comes from near Hall's Creek about 300 km south of Lake Argyle. Both these specimens are surface finds collected with other late phase material.

As already noted very few flakes, blades or points resembling those produced on Levallois cores have been recovered in the southern third of western Australia. This may in part be due to the scarcity of suitable raw material in most areas. The flake in Fig. 11 : 7 is one of the very few specimens from the south-west which is of Levallois form. The specimen is interesting because it is made of the kind of Eocene chert used for artifacts at Devil's Lair and other early or presumed early sites. It comes from the Blackwood River about 20 km east of Devil's Lair (Fig. 10), and it may be of considerable age as it was brought up in a post hole boring 50 cm deep in an undisturbed sandy soil.

There is no certain evidence for the use of Levallois techniques in western Australian early phase assemblages. The presence of obvious Levallois points in some of the stone industries from Sulawesi (van Heekeren, 1957; Plates 28, 45) suggests that the Levallois point technique may have been introduced from Indonesia within the past few thousand years.

Detailed comparisons have not yet been made between the early phase industries from Miriwun, Puntutjarpa, and Devil's Lair. Small adze flakes occur in the early phase at all three sites (Fig. 9 : 6, 8; Gould, 1971, 1973; Dortch, 1974; Dortch and Merrilees, 1973). At Devil's Lair and particularly at Miriwun the early assemblages contain a variety of very small retouched tools made on flakes (Fig. 9 : 11; Dortch and Merrilees, 1973). The presence of some small blades and bladelets (Fig. 9 : 2, 3) in the early phase horizons at Miriwun suggests that blade making techniques are not confined to more recent stone industries in Australia.

Regional stone industrial sequences in western Australia are still very poorly defined. It is not yet possible to say whether the Ord valley industrial sequence is typical of the whole of Kimberley, though it has close similarities with the stone industrial sequences of the Victoria River area (Flood, 1970; Mulvaney, 1969) and western Arnhem Land (Kamminga and Allen, 1973; White, 1967, 1971). The present south western archaeological sequence, based though it is on a very small sample, is consistent with developments in other parts of southern Australia. The prehistoric stone industries of other districts, including northern Kimberley, the north-east desert region, the Pilbara and the Murchison district, are represented almost entirely by surface collections of artifacts, most of which have no supplementary information. There are virtually no data available for several districts including the Great Sandy Desert, most parts of the east central desert and many districts in Kimberley, the Pilbara and the south-east. It is possible that stone industrial sequences different from those described here exist in these districts where there has been little or no investigation. It is also possible that earlier or intermediate phases exist in Kimberley, the 'western desert' and the south-west. Only detailed analysis and further field investigations will determine whether regional industrial sequences in western Australia can continue to be divided simply into earlier and later phases.

Acknowledgements The following Western Australian Museum staff helped in the preparation of this paper. J. Balme, K. Cannon and R. Henderson prepared the maps and site plans. A. Muller and M. Thompson drew some of the artifact illustrations, and V. Mackaay printed the photographs. G. Handley, with great patience, typed the penultimate draft and the final version. G. W. Kendrick and D. Merrilees advised on faunal and other matters, and H. Powell helped compile the faunal lists. I. M. Crawford and W. C. Dix allowed me to use unpublished field data collected by them in east Kimberley and the Pilbara.

A number of people took part in the field investigations in the Ord valley or the south-west, 1971–1974. They include E. Archer, J. Balme. P. Colombera, W. C. Dix, D. Merrilees, J. K. Porter, H. Powell. J. Stewart, S. Sofoulis and M. Thompson all of the Western Australian Museum; M. Archer, A. Baynes, A. McConnell and R. Pearce of the University of Western Australia; W. M. McArthur of the Land Resources Management of the CSIRO; G. Gardner of Northcliffe, W. A. and D. Jones of Kununurra, W.A.

I wish to express my gratitude to all of the above people for their help and co-operation. I also thank those people from the Division of Natural Science, Western Australian Museum, the CSIRO, the Queensland Museum, the University of London, the Australian National University and the University of Western Australia who have given personal communications, and I acknowledge with sincere thanks the information which G. Gardner of Northcliffe, W.A. has allowed me to use.

I am very grateful to the administration and the Prehistory Advisory Committee of the Australian Institute of Aboriginal Studies for their financial aid in the Ord valley salvage programme and for the sponsoring of 15 radiocarbon dating assays. Finally I thank D. J. Mulvaney of the Australian National University for his continued close support of prehistoric research in Western Australia, and my wife for her help in the field, with the illustration of artifacts, and for reading the manuscript.

References

Akerman, K., 1969. Walyunga: an Aboriginal site near Perth, Western Australia. *Ilchinkinja*, 3 : 12–16. (Western Australian Anthropological Students' Association.)
—— 1973. Further evidence of the manufacture and use of ground-edged axes in south western Australia. *The Western Australian Naturalist*, 12 : 107–11.
Allchin, B., 1966. *The stone-tipped arrow—late stone-age hunters of the tropical old world.* London: Phoenix House.
Baker, G., 1959. *Tektites.* National Museum of Victoria, Memoir, 23. Melbourne.

Berndt, R. M., 1951. Ceremonial exchange in western Arnhem Land. *Southwestern Journal of Anthropology*, 7 : 156–76.
—— and C. H. Berndt, 1964. *The world of the first Australians*: an introduction to the traditional life of the Australian Aborigines. Sydney: Ure Smith.
Binford, S. R. and L. R. Binford, 1969. Stone tools and human behaviour. *Scientific American*, 220 : 70–84.

Bordes, F., 1961. *Typologie du paléolithique ancien et moyen.* 2 vols., Institut de Préhistoire, Université de Bordeaux, Mémoire, 1. Bordeaux.
—— 1967. Considerations sur la typologie et les techniques dans le paléolithique. *Qüartar*, 18 : 25–55.
Breuil, H. and H. Kelly, 1956. Les éclats acheuléens à plan de frappe à facettes de Cagny-la-Garenne (Somme). *Bulletin de la Société Préhistorique Française*, 53 : 174–91.
Butler, W. H., 1958. Some previously unrecorded Aboriginal artifact sites near Perth, Western Australia. *The Western Australian Naturalist*, 6 : 133–36.
Campbell, T. D., 1960. The pirri—an interesting Australian Aboriginal implement. *Records of the South Australian Museum*, 13 : 509–24.
Churchill, D. M., 1968. The distribution and prehistory of *Eucalyptus diversicolor* F. Muell. *E. marginata* Donn ex Sm. and *E. calophylla* R. Br. in relation to rainfall. *The Australian Journal of Botany*, 16 : 125–51.

Davidson, D. S., 1935. Archaeological problems of northern Australia. *Journal of the Royal Anthropological Institute of Great Britain and Ireland*, 65 : 145–83.

—— and F. D. McCarthy, 1957. The distribution and chronology of some important types of stone implements in Western Australia. *Anthropos*, 52 : 390–458.

Dortch, C. E., 1972a. Archaeological work in the Ord reservoir area, east Kimberley. *Australian Institute of Aboriginal Studies Newsletter*, 3(4) : 13–18.

—— 1972b. An archaeological site in the Chichester Range, Western Australia: preliminary account. *Journal of the Royal Society of Western Australia*, 55 : 65–72.

—— 1974. A twelve thousand year old occupation floor in Devil's Lair, Western Australia. *Mankind*, 9 : 195–205.

—— 1975. Geometric microliths from a dated archaeological deposit near Northcliffe, Western Australia. *Journal of the Royal Society of Western Australia*, 58 : 59–63.

—— and D. Merrilees, 1971. A salvage excavation in Devil's Lair, Western Australia. *Journal of the Royal Society of Western Australia*, 54 : 103–13.

—— and —— 1973. Human occupation of Devil's Lair, Western Australia, during the Pleistocene. *Archaeology and Physical Anthropology in Oceania*, 8 : 89–115.

Flood, J. M., 1970. A point assemblage from the Northern Territory. *Archaeology and Physical Anthropology in Oceania*, 5 : 27–52.

Gardner, C. A., 1944. The vegetation of Western Australia with particular reference to the climate and soils. *Journal of the Royal Society of Western Australia*, 28 : xi–lxxxvii.

Glover, J. E., 1974. Petrology of chert artefacts from Devil's Lair. *Journal of the Royal Society of Western Australia*, 57 : 51–53.

—— and A. E. Cockbain, 1971. Transported Aboriginal artefact material, Perth Basin, Western Australia. *Nature*, 234 : 545–46.

Glover, I. C., 1967. Stone implements from Millstream Station, Western Australia: Newall's collection re-analysed. *Mankind*, 6 : 415–25.

—— 1973. Late stone age traditions in south-east Asia. *In* N. Hammond (ed.) *South Asian archaeology*, pp. 51–65. London: Duckworth.

Gould, R. A., 1968. Preliminary report on excavations at Puntutjarpa rockshelter, near the Warburton Ranges, Western Australia. *Archaeology and Physical Anthropology in Oceania*, 3 : 161–85.

—— 1971. The archaeologist as ethnographer: a case from the Western Desert of Australia. *World Archaeology*, 3(2) : 143–77.

—— 1973. *Australian archaeology in ecological and ethnographic perspective*. Andover, Mss.: Warner Modular Publication, Module 7.

——, D. A. Koster and A. H. Sontz, 1971. The lithic assemblage of the Western Desert Aborigines of Australia. *American Antiquity*, 36 : 149–69.

—— and J. Quilter, 1972. Flat adzes—a class of flaked stone tools from southwestern Australia. *American Museum Novitates*, no. 2502 : 1–14.

Grey, G., 1841. *Journals of two expeditions of discovery in north-west and western Australia during the years 1837, 38 and 39*. 2 vols. London: Boone. (Reprinted Adelaide, Libraries Board of South Australia 1964.)

Hallam, S. J., 1972. An archaeological survey of the Perth area, Western Australia: a progress report on art and artefacts, dates and demography. *Australian Institute of Aboriginal Studies Newsletter*, 3(5) : 11–19.

—— 1975. *Fire and hearth: a study of Aboriginal usage and European usurpation in south-western Australia*. Canberra: Australian Institute of Aboriginal Studies.

Hayden, B., 1973. Analysis of a 'taap' composite knife. *Archaeology and Physical Anthropology in Oceania*, 8 : 116–26.

Heekeren, H. R. van, 1957. *The stone age of Indonesia*. The Hague: Martinus Nijhoff.

Kaberry, P. M., 1935. The Forrest River and Lyne River tribes of north-west Australia. *Oceania*, 5 : 408–36.

—— 1938. Totemism in east and south Kimberley, north-west Australia. *Oceania*, 8 : 265–88.

—— 1939. *Aboriginal woman: sacred and profane*. London: Routledge.

Kamminga, J. and H. R. Allen, 1973. Alligator Rivers environmental fact-finding study: report of the archaeological survey. (Darwin) Mimeographed report.

Kendrick, G. W., 1973. Molluscs from archaeological excavations at Miriwun rock shelter, Ord River valley, Western Australia. *The Western Australian Naturalist*, 12 : 111–13.

Lampert, R. J., 1971. *Burrill Lake and Currarong: coastal sites in southern New South Wales*. Research School of Pacific Studies, Australian National University, Canberra. (Terra Australis I.)

McCarthy, F. D., 1939. 'Trade' in Aboriginal Australia, and 'Trade' relationships with Torres Strait, New Guinea and Malaya. *Oceania*, 9 : 405–38; 10 : 80–104, 171–95.

—— 1940. Comparison of the prehistory of Australia with that of Indo-China, the Malay Peninsular, and the Netherlands East Indies. *In* Report of the Third Congress of Prehistorians of the Far East, Singapore 1938, pp. 30–50.

—— 1964. The archaeology of the Capertee Valley, New South Wales. *Records of the Australian Museum*, 26 : 197–246.

—— 1967. *Australian Aboriginal stone implements*. Sydney: Australian Museum.

Merrilees, D., 1968. Man the destroyer: late Quaternary changes in the Australian marsupial fauna. *Journal of the Royal Society of Western Australia*, 51 : 1–24.

——, W. C. Dix, S. J. Hallam, W. H. Douglas and R. M. Berndt, 1973. Aboriginal man in southwestern Australia. *Journal of the Royal Society of Western Australia*, 56 : 44–55.

Mulvaney, D. J., 1969. *The prehistory of Australia*. London: Thames and Hudson.

—— and R. P. Soejono, 1970. Archaeology in Sulawesi, Indonesia. *Antiquity*, 45 : 26–33.

Neuville, R., 1951. *La paléolithique et le mésolithique du desert de Judée*. Archives de L'Institut de páleontologie humaine, Mémoire, 24. Paris.

Noone, H. V. V., 1943. Some aboriginal stone implements of Western Australia. *Records of the South Australian Museum*, 7 : 271–80.

Pearce, R. H., 1973. Uniformity of the Australian backed blade tradition. *Mankind*, 9 : 89–95.

Ride, W. D. L., 1958. The edge-ground axes of south-western Australia. *The Western Australian Naturalist*, 6 : 162–79.

Serventy, P. E., 1967. Aboriginal artifacts on Rottnest Island. *The Western Australian Naturalist*, 10 : 123–24.

Spencer, W. and F. J. Gillen, 1904. *The northern tribes of central Australia*. London: Macmillan.

Stewart, G. A. (*et al.*), 1970. *Lands of the Ord-Victoria area, W.A. and N.T.* Commonwealth Scientific and Industrial Research Organization (Australia), Land Research Series no. 28.

White, C., 1967. Early stone axes in Arnhem Land. *Antiquity*, 41 : 149–52.

—— 1971. Man and environment in northwest Arnhem Land. *In* D. J. Mulvaney and J. Golson (eds.) *Aboriginal man and environment in Australia*, pp. 141–58. Canberra: ANU Press.

White, J. P., 1968. Fabricators, outils écaillés or scalar cores? *Mankind*, 6 : 658–66.

Willey, G. R. and P. Phillips, 1958. *Method and theory in American archaeology*. Chicago: University of Chicago.

Wright, R. V. S., 1971. *Archaeology of the Gallus Site, Koonalda Cave*. Canberra: Australian Institute of Aboriginal Studies.

Organic typology

The interdependence of form, function (technology) and toolmaking

A. GALLUS

Introduction

Two approaches to prehistoric archaeology must be distinguished (Gallus 1963):
  (a) The formal or object morphological approach (documentation).
  (b) The humanistic or culture-morphological approach, including diachrony (history, evolution).

At the A.I.A.S. Conference, 1974, during discussions on the analysis of Australian rock art, Brandl emphasised the same two levels of analysis:
  (a) Aspect of form (eg. Ucko's morphological-typological reality);
  (b) Aspect of content and meaning.

On level (b) we can only risk inferences. Biebuyck added (and Brandl agreed), that on level (a) all interpretation must cease.

Brandl's example was that the picture (image) of a 'bison' appears on level (a) as the representation of the natural object 'bison'; however on level (b) it must be left open whether or not it is something else, eg. the representation of a concept symbolised by a bison.

In a similar way when it comes to human artifacts such as tools 'morphological-typological reality' (in other words the prehistoric objects themselves) must be distinguished from culture-morphological reality, which these objects likewise represent.

On level (a) the artifacts are only objects which have shape, form and exactly observable and quantifiable properties—bulb, ripples, striking platform, extension of worked surface, secondary work, edge etc. One can fabricate mathematical indexes. Categories of types can be artificially created (by multivariate analysis and computer if you wish). Data can be statistically handled and cumulative diagrams and histograms can be made. Materials used can be studied.

However, there exists also level (b), *the human aspect*. The artifactual character includes use, purpose, function. What was the need they satisfied? It is the same humanistic level as in rock art, involving 'meaning' and 'content'.

(a) The object-morphological approach It is only logical that archaeologists who endeavour to remain on a strictly morphological (formal-typological) level in their classification on stone tools omit the use of the concept of *culture*.

The conceptualisation of culture originates from usage in ethnology and cultural anthropology and its basis of reference is on our level (b).

Here much confusion has been caused by authors who use the term 'culture', when obviously only the objects themselves are meant.

Several systems of classification have been constructed on a strictly object-bound level of which perhaps Bishop and Clark's 1967 discussion on use of terms (pp. 824–75) and recommendations for terminology (pp. 893–98) might be regarded as the most successful one.

In Australia classificatory systems remained mainly object-oriented [level (a)] though function appears to be considered because some of the types could be observed in ethnographic use (Mulvaney, this volume). Wright (1963) has described a scheme of classification which remained strictly on the object-level.

Bishop and Clark (1967) offer the following general terminology:
  i. *Occurrence* the point of contact with stratigraphy or the archaeological material in its context.
  ii. *Industry* 'All the known objects that a group of prehistoric people manufactured in one area over some span of time'.
  iii. *Phase* a unit within an industry. An industry may comprise a series of successive (or in some cases contemporaneous) distinct and discrete groups. Members of such successive groups are called *phases*. In the latter case the term has the meaning of a *facies*.
  iv. *Industrial Complex* grouping of industries considered to represent parts of the same whole.

(b) The culture-morphological approach Mead (1953) states that the model situation on which the 'anthropological concept of culture is based is that of the total, learned, shared behaviour of a functionally autonomous society that has manifested its existence through a sufficient number of generations so that each stage of the lifespan of an individual is included within this system'.

I would like to add that I include under 'total behaviour' also behaviour (drives) which derives genetically. Mead (1953) has not specified the actual size and organisation of a 'functionally autonomous society'. I prefer to regard as the largest, homogeneous, natural, human, social unit an 'ethnic group' as defined in ethnology and ethnography.

Oakley (1948) has made the following distinctions:
  i. The sum total that a particular society practises, produces and thinks, may be called its culture.
  ii. Sets of artifacts of the same material which are evidently the work of a single group or of related groups . . . constitute an industry.

It is hardly possible to fully distinguish the two categories (a) and (b). Nevertheless a clear theoretical distinction can be kept, and it must be clear on which level one is working.

A pertinent error likely to occur is to mistake object-morphology (especially technology) for culture-morphologically all-important criteria, and to employ units of analysis, which obviously have meaning on the object-morphologic level only, for the construction of units whose meaning and basis of reference are on a completely different level of analysis.

A good example is the reappraisal by Bordes (1950–51) of the term 'Levalloisian', which was used by Abbé Breuil as a 'culture', Bordes proved that it refers to a technique of flake production only, which as such has found its way into many different human communities. It is also very instructive to study the problems Bordes (this volume) has to face in confronting the term 'Mousterian'.

Transmuting the general terminology of Bishop and Clark (1967) into the language of culture-morphology we arrive at the following possible parallelisation:

    i. Observable remains of human activity at one particular 'occurrence'.

ii-iii. Observable remains of the activity of a human, social unit in space and time. In most cases the stage of social organisation will not clearly be distinguishable—*ethnic group* or *subgroup; culture*.

   iv. An appropriate, large grouping was attempted by the Vienna school of *Kulturkreislehre*. Culture-morphologically this grouping might be regarded as a *civilisation* (by its technology and science) as distinct from *culture* (Gallus, 1972a : 555; 1974 : 98).

In the culture-morphological aspect prehistory is concerned with the nature, behaviour and history of man, whose evolutionary position does not yet include written records. Artifacts are *documents* which have to be interpreted to reach prehistoric man himself. Conceptualisations must be distinguished from those in object-morphology by employing a different terminology.

The basis of references is the *human individual* within an ethnic group (culture), whose psychic processes and activity have caused the presence of the prehistoric evidence. Inferences have to be made from 'material to non-material' (cf. Rouse, 1953 : 61–62).

General remarks

A tool-complex forms only a minimal part of human manifestations, and one which is not even the most importantly ethnospecific one as it refers *prima facie* only to technology.

Solely through inferences and assumptions of different kinds, during which strict certainty is necessarily lost, can we reach deeper, historical and cultural reality. Prehistory involves reconstruction, and reconstruction can never attain strict infallibility. However loss in certainty does not justify the attitude of object bound purists, who stop timidly at the object level or its nearest derivative *ecology*.

Typological analysis

Margenau (1950 : 72) states: '. . . experience in becoming complete and integrated, moves from the sensory and spontaneous to the rational and reflective. By this transition the elements of the given take on *orderly* traits, and allow reason to take hold of them' (italics mine).

The human brain, when confronted with the great variety of perceptions in its environment, takes notice of the repeated occurrence of a certain number of identical or similar perceptions. Instinctively it forms cognitive units or engrammes (Margenau, 1950 : 58–61; Lancaster, 1965 : 75, 'naming'; Gallus, 1972a : 543–44, 547).

The formation of engrammes is a function of the human explanatory 'apparatus' (Geertz, 1966 : 15) and is performed subconsciously by the central nervous system. It is the same process as the formation of 'general nouns' in language.

There is no change in the basic neuronal process of typifying even if it is performed on an extended conscious level with statistical practices and multivariate factor and cluster analysis, etc. The information fed into these artificial systems remains in the same way subjectively established by the brain as before. There is no escape from that.

Such mechanisation might even detract from the efficiency of typological analysis. The human brain has evolved, under selective pressures, exactly in the direction of being able efficiently to reduce to order the variety of recurrent sense perceptions. It can continuously correct itself during functioning, which mechanised practices cannot once they have been programmed (Cahen *et al.*, 1971; Miller *et al.*, 1972; Collins, 1970 : 19–20).

The aim of typological analysis is to establish *tool-types*. Assuming that 'science' wants to be objective (in the sense that engrammes formed in the brain of the researcher should approximate as closely as possible to 'reality'), we have to ask first, what 'reality' do we want to know?

There is a modern tendency to base typology on objects alone. Artifact types are no longer 'considered as implements made and used by man, but as mere objects' (Cahen *et al.*, 1971 : 211). A case in point is Bishop and Clark (1967). In order to distinguish clearly I call the results of object bound morphology *artifact types* and restrict the use of the term *tool-type* to organic typological classification alone.

In organic typology the concept of a *tool-type*, which a prehistorian has formed in his mind, should match as closely as possible the idea formed by the prehistoric artisan himself (Cowgill, 1967 : 236, 'alien system of cognition'; Chang, 1967a : 228, 'cognitive system of the makers'; Chang, 1967b, 'real' or 'cognitive, folk taxonomy'; Gallus, 1968: 453; 1970a : 6; 1970b : 6; 1971a : 88).

A *tool-type*, then, is much more than a simple, material object (cf. Hodson, 1970 and Dobzhansky, 1965 : 65).

A *tool-type* at its inception was the concept of a prehistoric artisan, externalised in the form of an actual tool, in order to serve a *need*. The tool had been made to perform a *task* which serves the fulfilment of this need. Every single artifact is the solution of the problem of how to perform a task in order to attain a goal (to satisfy a need).

I fully agree with Northorp (1953 : 316) when he warns that: 'You understand the facts you find in a given culture objectively only when you find the concepts used by the people in that culture to conceptualise the facts'.

The *conceptual model* (Müller-Beck, 1969) in the mind of the prehistoric artisan is the unique property of a unique mind, a cultural and *historical* phenomenon, like our own concept about it.

Our awareness of a particular concept in the mind of a particular individual restores historicity and rescues prehistory from remaining object-bound and shallow. It also steers clear of creating pseudo-agencies, like the influence of the 'environment' or of another culture, etc. It connects typology to need, function, use and performance, which all are included in a tool-idea in the mind of the artisan and of the particular tool user.

Though the majority of Africanists congregated at Burg Wartenstein (Bishop and Clark, 1967) opted for object based morphology there were notable exceptions. Mason (1967 : 739–43) came near organic typology by enlarging his interests with:

i. The determination of activity variants as reflected in the artifact assemblages. (See also Binford and Binford, 1966, 1969; Binford, 1968; Mellars, 1970; Isaac, 1969 : 12)

ii. Regarding use-damage as a valid criterion for classifying a 'tool'.

iii. Taking function as a basis for classification.

Inskeep (1967b : 816) has argued that there sometimes comes a point when classification must be combined with function.

Clark rightly declared (1967 : 820) that there is often a considerable variation in shape and attributes in tools which had been nevertheless made for the same main functional purpose. These various differences must be distinguished in classification, otherwise we loose our basis for the comparison of industries. I do not see any difficulty in distinguishing such idiosyncratic differences as artifact types within one *tool-type*.

Isaac has also stated (1969 : 12–19) that without knowledge of function our understanding of observed variants in the morphology of types will remain severely limited. 'Types' as used today in archaeological typological method are only 'arbitrary' segments of complex multi-attribute modalities with large variances.

Lévi-Strauss (1953) also considered that tool use and function must be established when classifying tools. There is a kind of correlation between the term 'use' in the field of technology and the term 'meaning' in the field of language (cf. also introduction to this essay). One has to explore the complete function, the intellectual and spiritual level as well as the practical one, of the technical form under consideration (see also Pradel, 1966 : 603, 605; 1974 : 752–53).

On the other extreme Tixier (1967a : 815) did go so far as to declare that he defines as a 'tool' that which we ourselves call one, and not what prehistoric man might have regarded as such. That is dehumanised prehistory indeed. With our modern conceptualisations and mathematical techniques we surely are in danger of arriving at historically anachronistic results.

Need, function and performance

A human need is an important biofunctional factor in human behaviour. It is a psychic urge (drive) or energy which aims at the satisfaction (fulfilment) of a necessity. Needs appear during the evolution of life as determined by biological requirements of a given living form in a given environment and in a given time period.

With man we have the immensely enlarged category of cultural, social and spiritual necessities. A *need* is a basic entity of human existence which is a *basic unit of cultural analysis* and can be studied historically in its development.

The problem of how new needs arise is ultimately a biological one, and in man also a psychological one which relates to creative activity. New needs arise as a historical process, as a reformulation of human necessities according to a continuous development of man's behaviour and of his control over the environment (cf. Renfrew, 1969). Human behaviour continuously creates a new environment to which man has continuously to adapt himself. This is a feedback system which constantly creates new situations.

A *tool-type* is the externalisation of a *tool-idea*, for the fulfilment of a task. A task is a specific and practical goal to be attained. Variations of form belong to the same tool type as long as all the variations perform the same function in the fulfilment of the same task.

The temporary satisfaction of a need is attained by using the tool, i.e. by its *functioning and performance*. Function is defined here as *performance in the carrying out of a goal directed activity*.

The degree of satisfaction can be measured according to a simple energy rule—best result attained through the smallest expenditure in energy and time (best in relation to the fulfilment of a task).

The contents of a *tool-type* we may analyse as follows:

(a) in the subconscious of the toolmaker—need;

(b) in the long term memory of the toolmaker—task, form, function and performance;

(c) in the consciousness of the toolmaker—need experienced as an urge;

(d) creative activity and logico-rational behaviour of the toolmakers—externalisation of the *tool-idea;* ordered kinesic sequence performed—toolmaking (Durbin, 1971 : 399);

(e) object reality—the actual tool collected by the archaeologist; documentary material.

During scientific analysis this sequence of *realities* has to be reconstructed in order to arrive at an acceptable result from the point of view of organic typology.

Prehistorians might feel that by burdening themselves with behaviouristic sciences (and with psychology in particular) subjective elements are being introduced into a so called exact, scientific enquiry. However the subjective element is present in any historical process, and in any scientific enquiry and consequently cannot be eliminated. The individual and the particular are part of human, creative behaviour, and their omission would lead to a severe distortion of historical reality.

During the discussions at this AIAS symposium Binford observed that there is no typology which can claim general validity. There are only typologies made by archaeologists for specific tasks. There is no general typology. There is no objective science.

I agree in so far that there exists a general element of necessary subjectivity in human cognition shared by all scientific observers, caused by the intervening matrix of our senses and of the central nervous system, and by the necessary egocentric position of every observer (Gallus, 1972a : 557–58).

However *in a historically oriented analysis*, after having granted this general level of uncertainty, the acceptance of the individual product as the smallest methodical unit of enquiry establishes the only possible claim for a general validity of its results.

Every tool is the result of individual activity whether the result of imitative learning or of a new creation. The personal, psychic element is an essential part of our understanding of human behaviour and cannot be neglected.

Function defines form and without specific needs and correlated function there is no differentiation of toolforms. Change in form can only be understood as the result of *dissatisfaction* with the performance of a particular toolform (Gallus, 1971a : 88), except of course in aesthetically or otherwise determined nonfunctional variability. New toolforms arise during the process of satisfying new needs.

Objective criteria for the reconstruction of function (Gallus, 1970b)

(1) *Broken parts.* A tool would break either during fabrication (when deductions can be made as to technology of tool-making) or during use, in which case breaking relates to that part of the tool which receives most stress or punishment during performance.

    If breaking occurs consistently at the same spot, deductions as to use are possible (Gallus, 1971b : 9).

(2) *Traces of use and wear.* Consult Semenov, 1964 (for other examples see Kamminga, this volume; White, 1967; Gallus, 1971a : 101, 102, 107, 114, 124, 126, 129).

(3) *Reconstruction of hand grip or of hafting.* The body of a tool consists of human alterations to its surface which are purposeful. Every alteration has a reason why it was made. Particulars which can be observed are form and bulk; sharpening or dulling of the edges (secondary retouch). Sharpening points out functional parts. Dulling points to a situation within the palm, or coverage by hafting, or may be a finger-rest for added pressure.

There may be flakes removed from the bulk of the tool or some other constructional detail which makes sense only if it is assumed to accommodate a handgrip or to facilitate hafting (Gallus, 1971a : 102, 106, 107).

The correlation of measurements of certain constructional features of a tool and of anatomical measurements of the human hand is also of interest, when those features are suspected to accommodate hand grip.

(4) *In situ position.* cf. Gallus, 1971a : 112, 114; 1972b: 17–18, Fig. 204; Pradel, 1973 : 17–19.

(5) *Practical test* by handling the tool oneself. Often one will find that there is only one way to hold a tool in a functionally satisfactory position, without damage to the hand or without unease.

(6) *Consistent reappearance of constructional features* on specimens of the same tool-type.

(7) *Analysis of consistent change* of the same part of a tool, within the *typological series* (see later) of a tool-type.

(8) *Association between tool-types and activity units,* Binford and Binford, 1966, 1969; Binford, 1968; Mellars, 1970. The idea was criticised by Bordes and de Sonneville Bordes, 1970. It was discussed at the Congress of Africanists (Cole, 1967 : 873; Inskeep, 1967a : 874; Mason, 1967 : 759–60; see also Isaac, 1969 : 12; Clark and Haynes, 1970. Chang, 1967a : 232 recommends us to 'structure ... types around a series of activity systems').

(9) Ethnological parallels and study of traces of use of ethnological specimens (cf. White, 1967).

(10) *Experimentation.*

(11) All deductions from the above considerations must lead to end results which are not in contradiction with each other.

It must be kept in mind however that one tool can perform several functions and thus can accommodate several different hand-grips. The position of one grip might cover up functional parts of the other (Gallus, 1970b : 7).

The methodological position of attribute cluster analysis

Once a tool-type has been defined according to need, task, function, performance and form, attribute cluster analysis can be employed to define artifact-type sub-categories. These categories will be on level (a) (object-morphological typology).

In this way we arrive at a series of conceptualisations ascending towards the reconstruction of a particular engramme in the maker's mind. Actual single objects form an artifact type, several of these form a tool-type, which is the externalisation of a tool-idea, in so many concrete forms. Attribute cluster analysis was pioneered by Spaulding (1953, 1960), Sackett (1966), Movius *et al.* (1968), Binford and Binford (1969). The levels of abstraction involved in the conceptualisations are of interest to us (Gallus, 1970a : 5–7).

Attribute signifies a property or quality of an object or of an event which includes position in time and space: 'Tools are thus considered analytically as clusters, and the definition of types proceeds from the discovery of non-random attribute clustering' (Movius *et al.*, 1968 : 2).

According to Sackett (1966) attributes result from an analytic codification of the actually existing dimensions of variation. Type is a cluster of quantifiable attribute units. Measurement being established as a morphological variable, *type* appears defined by a number of measurements which all fall within the same *limit.* The limit itself is judged by the scholar.

Sackett calls such a bundle of measurements an 'attribute set'. A number of sets, which characterise a tool, he calls an 'attribute system'. Each set in a system codifies a different 'morphological variable'. The term attribute is used for the one concrete measurement which falls within a morphological variable. Several 'attributes' describe *one concrete tool.* Movius has accepted the term 'attribute' but he defines it in the sense of Sackett's 'attribute set'.

The above system includes two important points: the inclusion of 'position in time and space' (Movius) and the clear distinction between the individual tool and theoretical conceptions of the scholar (Sackett).

It must be stressed however that an 'attribute' *is not* 'one of the possible concrete expressions of an attribute set' (Sackett). The prehistoric artisan when he gave 'concrete expression' to his tool, did not have an 'attribute set' or 'attribute system' in mind when he made a tool, but a tool-idea, the contents of which are much more complex than measured form. It is not likely that he measured his tools.

An 'attribute set' is a conceptual tool of the scholar, a theoretical conception, which helps him to bring order into the variety of concrete objects before him. It is only *his* construct, present in *his own* mind.

A prehistoric artisan cannot make exact copies of already known and presently used specimens. But he has to keep his own, personal externalisations of his tool-idea within certain limits, if he wants to apply his tool effectively to the concrete task which is contained in his tool-idea. Too much aberration from a form which has already been proved to be efficient would spoil performance.

The phenomenon of 'morphological limit', which is essential for attribute-cluster analysis, is actually the function of a *tool-idea* in the mind of an individual artisan, and without it it cannot be understood.

Only by retaining the concrete basis of our abstractions

(the living human individual) can we keep prehistoric archaeology alive as an anthropological historic and humanistic discipline.

Summary

i. An attribute (Movius, but 'attribute set' in Sackett) is a theoretical concept which determines the limitations within which a concrete measurement can still be regarded as a characteristic of the same artifact-type.

An attribute system (Sackett) is a theoretical concept which determines all concrete measurements which can be accepted as characterising the same artifact-type.

ii. A category (Movius but 'attribute' in Sackett) is the concrete measurement of a single trait of a single object (quantitative description).

All measurements add up to specify one single object (the concrete artifact as measured, described and determined).

The methodological position of ecological analysis

When identifying tool-types one must naturally be aware of the environment and the economic system of its exploitation in time and space.

Such awareness will lead to a determination of 'systems of activity' as mentioned above. Technology is clearly in relation with the possibilities the environment can offer for subsistence.

However ecological argument, in order to be manageable, is often based on simplified assumptions. The determining force of 'stimuli' received from the environment becomes overstressed and the stochastic nature of human decision making (Gallus, 1974 : 95–97; in press) becomes underrated.

Man is able to impose his own will onto the environment. How far a presumed determining force of the environment can be regarded as a quantifiable variable in economic enquiry regarding prehistoric man has not yet been established with precision.

Until it is, it is better to argue that the environment is not a determining force but only a limit within which human creative activity explores positive, possible action. Otherwise environment will appear in the role of a personified pseudo-agency which 'influences' human behaviour.

When reconstructing human economic activity the primary source of documentation must be sought in the available remnants of human activity itself. If a reconstruction of prehistoric environment receives equal or more emphasis there is the danger that, in reconstructing economic activity, it will subconsciously influence assumptions about possible artifact categories and their function.

Binford (1972 : 175–76) has argued that part of people's 'culture' allows them to discriminate between the stimuli received from the environment and decide which are the appropriate responses in terms of the recognised contingencies. Insofar as the archaeological record is a by-product of human behaviour it is 'equally' a by-product of the character of the stimuli which humans were receiving, as well as a repertoire of appropriate responses, which they may have elected to perform in the context of those stimuli.

Therefore variability in the archaeological record itself may be 'equally' referable to different distribution of stimuli. In this way behaviour becomes a differential expression of a cultural repertoire that I may bring to a whole series of stimuli. The archaeological record is a reflection of human behaviour

which 'inevitably' involves the interraction between learned responses and the particular character of the stimuli.

One cannot, argues Binford, take 'measured differences' in the archaeological record as an exclusive measure of differences in the character of the cultural repertoire which people brought to the behavioural situations: it might 'equally well' refer to differences in the distribution of environmental stimuli which 'prompted' a certain kind of behaviour.

The mechanistic terminology of Binford's argument and assumptions clearly derives from ethology. However ethology treats much less plastic animal behaviour circuits than those which prehistoric man had already acquired during biological evolution.

Binford's extremely simplified conceptualisation about the 'equality' of 'stimuli' which 'prompt responses', and about human cultural repertoire makes an equally simple picture of their 'inevitable interaction' possible. This results finally in a static formula in which human behaviour emerges as the 'differential expression' of a richer cultural repertoire, (eg. stimuli + human cultural repertoire = human behaviour).

In this equation the stimuli actually reduce a given richer human behavioural potential to a more restricted actuality. The formula establishes a kind of human slot-machine. The outcome depends on the fact, into which one of the slots a stimulus penny can or will actually fall. How the given factors which are present in the equation have come about is no concern to this kind of simplified, neoprimitive thinking.

There is an acute danger in neoprimitive neoarchaeological thinking of ending up with a restricted scope of enquiry which adapts itself to easily accessible and easily controllable data, which also lend themselves to quantification and mathematical treatment (becoming 'scientific'). The danger of distorting human reality can hardly be avoided in statements like:

'This idea of the grandeur of man, that his religious and spiritual life is more important than his technology is a Victorian concept'. In this sentence 'Victorian' is used in the popular pejorative sense (Renfrew, 1972a : 70).

'. . . new archaeology is going completely away from history' (Renfrew, 1972a : 68).

'Prehistory is now shifting towards economic and social history' (Renfrew, 1972b : 104).

This of course does not mean that the discovery of Renfrew and Binford and others of the 'deductive' method cannot be used with gain in archaeology. It only means that archaeology as a holistic and humanistically oriented discipline cannot be abandoned in our quest for an understanding of the phenomenon man.

However when thinking leads into the direction of a simplified methodology which conceives mankind not as composed of individuals but as a congregation of nearly identical particles in which the discrete units appear interchangeable and replaceable (like molecules in a volume of gas) and thus lend themselves without qualification to mathematical treatment, then we have arrived in a world of conceptualisations where sharp and logical formulations are possible, but reference to human reality is lost and confusion begins (cf. Clarke, 1972).

Classification of material

Artifact type A single implement which is used for different purposes is to be classified as a *complex tool-type*. Morphologically different artifacts which are used for the same purpose, are to be classified as *artifact types*, but should be listed under the same *tool-type*.

This classification of artifact types as a subsystem of a tool-type typology, actually takes notice of Mason's (1967 : 79) criticism of the Bordes's method. Mason maintained that Bordes's classification is based on an overfine subdivision of artifact morphology. He charges that 'class-status' is given to 'attribute groups', which can be regarded as being within the range of a natural variation of classes. His criticism is legitimate and Bordes's system is far from establishing tool types which can be regarded fully as the equivalent or the approximation of tool-ideas of the prehistoric artisan himself.

Bordes's system is a good analytical tool for establishing morphological differences between tool-assemblages but it cannot be profitably used for culture-morphological analysis, its conceptualisations being on another level.

However it is perhaps of interest to note that Bordes's system is the result of conscious planning. At the discussion of artifact typology during this symposium Bordes came up strongly with the view that there is no possibility of bringing together morphology and function in one typological system. Thus we have to regard Bordes's system as the most successful object-morphologic typological approach at present in use [Level (a)].

We might still mention Mellars in this context, who stated (1970 : 79–80) that one encounters large morphological variations which are without any functional significance, and which might be termed 'stylistic'. Our suggested system can take care of that too.

Tool manufacture Balout (1967 : 717) wants to establish 'une morphologie dynamique' which would be based on a clear determination of tool making techniques. This can be done by experimenting oneself with tool making and retouch. 'Les formes et les types sont définis par leur méthode de fabrication, qui correspond à *la conception que l'artisan préhistorique se faisait* de l'outil à fabriquer' (italics mine).

It must be accepted that some basic template forms or blanks are defined by the toolmaking technique, but if our aim is the reconstruction of the tool-idea which the pre-historic artisan had in mind a more complicated creative activity has to be considered. With the exception of a simple way of toolmaking, to be discussed later, technology is defined by the tool-idea and not the other way round. Technology is a means to an end. The idea comes first and how to externalise it comes second.

The process of toolmaking needs special tools (hammerstone etc.) and produces intermediate forms (modified raw material). At a higher stage, modified raw material is produced in the form of sophisticated nuclei which might be regarded as tools for making tools.

Classification of toolmaking must include *everything* which has been produced during toolmaking activity, from tools to waste. This principle has often been neglected in the past.

Nondescript flakes, untrimmed flakes and waste material The views of Africanists, during their congress in 1967, varied. Isaac (1967 : 768) thought that unretouched flakes are 'taxonomically irrelevant'. M. D. Leakey (1967a : 768–69) agreed. This is a grave mistake. Howell (1967 : 768–69) rightly answered that one of our main tasks is to distinguish that which is 'consistently distinguishable'. For instance so called Levallois flakes which bear no retouch (but share the

same form and pattern with retouched flakes) might have well been tools; others might have been only blanks.

Cole (1967 : 769) remarked that by analysing flakes one can determine that a certain portion of them was made deliberately as flakes, rather than being the result of artifact manufacture. Isaac (1967 : 769) agreed.

Tixier (1967b : 767) proposed an analysis of industries under three different heads:

i. Intentionally retouched tools;
ii. Pieces with use-retouch;
iii. The Levallois tools and the debitage of trimmed and untrimmed flakes and cores.

Isaac agreed again and added the important remark that what we have been calling 'waste' was probably not regarded as such by the toolmakers and that *we should find another term* (italics mine).

During discussions at this symposium Isaac put forward a modified scheme:

i. Designed forms (tools);
ii. Utilised pieces;
iii. Special technological markers.

He suggested that we should be aware that there is a big difference between carefully made and kept material, and casually made, easily discarded material. This tallies with Binford's proposal of 'curated' artifacts (see under).

Mason (1967 : 740–43, 759) regards the· proportion of trimmed, utilised and untrimmed flakes as a 'broad feature' of his 'analytical procedure'. He wants to distinguish the following groups to be used for a 'preliminary comparison of artifacts'.

(a) *Carefully trimmed.* Always in lowest minority;
(b) Flakes *morphologically identical* to those with careful trimming but either with no trimming at all or only small scars, presumed to be use-damages. These are regarded as tools;
(c) *Flakes* of a type not represented in groups (a)–(b). Not for comparison. Waste;
(d) *Broken* artifacts;
(e) Stone objects showing signs of *utilisation* (pounding, grinding);
(f) *Cores;*
(g) Unmodified *raw material;*
(h) Artifacts of bone, wood or shell.

This classification is acceptable, however I cannot go along with him when, for a detailed comparison between tool complexes, he wants only to employ categories (a), (b), and (e). I would argue that all the material as classified must be used for comparison.

Mason (1967) rightly criticises Bordes for excluding the bulk· of untrimmed flakes from comparison. Untrimmed flakes can be regarded as *reservoirs* of artifacts, either for immediate use or for trimming into artifacts of other form. They are not waste product or debitage. 'Incomplete analysis of this flake element *eliminates an artifact class* comprising the bulk of all earlier, middle and late Stone Age industries we have studied' (italics mine). Leakey too distinguishes (1967b : 423–25) 'utilised material', as a separate class for analysis (compare Dickson, 1968; Crosby, 1969). My own analysis of the occupation floors of Koonalda Cave led to similar observations, where rough, quadrangularly formed chalcedony blocks were broken down by blows, directed downwards from the upper surface at the edges. Thus the flakes were broken down, from along the sides of the blocks. The block stood on the ground (when flat) or was placed with a pointed lower part firmly into the ground. The block was not 'flaked' but simply hammered, broken or shattered (quartered). Large heaps of material were found intact, neatly heaped on the floors (Gallus, 1971a : 111, 119, 125).

A similar breaking and shattering technique and subsequent selection from the breakage was described by White (1967 : 661) in Papua New Guinea.

The material recoverable from Koonalda shows not only true flakes but also a large number of amorphous looking pieces. Given the above technique this result seems obvious enough. It can be inferred that the resulting heaps of material were used for picking out suitable flakes or broken pieces for immediate use (razor sharp edges) or as blanks for toolmaking.

Elsewhere (Gallus, in press) I have argued that the cave was not a simple quarry as opined by Wright (1971 : 56) (on the evidence of a single excavated trench which covered only a small area) but an important place where artisan activity was continuously exercised in connection with the observance of ritual practices. Thus material was kept in place to serve as a 'reservoir' in the sense of Mason, and also reverentially handled.

Chalcedony is brittle, like glass, and extremely hard to flake. Often enough shaping was done not by flaking, but by a carefully controlled and efficient technique, which was a sort of guided breaking of the material. This often resulted in splitting the material along natural planes of breaking, a technique which does not produce any signs of a bulb or ripples, so dear to the heart of purists. Pressure flaking was successful.

Though resisting analysis on 'classical' lines, the material is classifiable with the organic method. White's remarks are also extremely helpful when he calls attention to the relative unimportance of 'formal patterning' (1967 : 412) and the desirability of treating each tool as a 'series of edges', and of taking the implement 'as a whole only in relation to a particular edge'.

So called 'nondescript flakes' can be classified as results of toolmaking (flaking, chips), or variously as breaking down stone material, as blanks for toolmaking (cf. Mason's 'reservoir') and/or utilisation. Traces of use can be observed on completely formless pieces in this context.

This category can be analysed in order to recognise toolmaking techniques, in which case they are 'technological markers' of the first order. A reservoir of blanks for toolmaking is characteristic of a particular approach towards toolmaking and tool use and needs our attention as such. The 'utilised' category contains artifacts which, from the point of view of classification, must be regarded as tools.

Binford has lately created an important classifactory unit, by distinguishing what he calls *curated implements* (1972 : 176; 1976). These are implements which are constantly 'kept for', 'kept valued', i.e. maintained in good order and used over a long time. These tools need an investment of 'maintenance and care'.

It must be added however that 'curated' implements are not especially a clearly defined object-technological phenomenon. They merge into the area of human cultural behaviour where logico-rational object technology and tool use become integrated into mythic symbolling, into man's framework of cognitive thinking (Gallus, 1974 : 98).

Binford maintained that curated implements are not left simply where they are used. However when elaborating on this idea, during this symposium, it was quickly pointed out by Australian anthropologists that whereas Australian Aboriginal culture knows 'curated' implements, they are, nevertheless, left at particular places where they are used. When the same group (or another group for that matter) arrives at the place of use, the objects (fish traps, grinding stones) are employed again. Thus the objects are linked with important localities in the environment and not in the possession of individuals.

Formal analysis of change

The psychology of toolmaking We have isolated two important contents in the human mind in connection with toolmaking:

i. Need;
ii. Tool-idea.

On the process of toolmaking itself the following conceptualisations can be attempted, quoting Durbin (1971 : 399). Toolmaking is 'kinesic behaviour' with hierarchically ordered activity features. It is biologically akin to the mechanistic, instinctive action circuits of animals, only much more plastic.

It entails, according to Durbin (1971 : 399, note 4) the retention and manipulation of cognitive 'subcategories' like, 'Type of material to be used for certain tools, the location of the raw materials, the fracturing qualities of the different materials, the physiological subcategories required to flake each material properly, as well as the subcategorial techniques required to use the finished product'.

Categories depend originally on memory complexes which are not necessarily abstract, but retain a large amount of sensory material. It seems reasonable to suggest that such engrammes are more primordial than those involving language symbolling and could well have been formed before language symbolling became possible.

Toolmaking involves only associations of sense impressions like surface texture, colour and type of fracturing of stones etc. (Durbin, 1971 : 399, note 5). Toolmaking relates and leads to the satisfaction of a need which appears in concrete form as a particular task and as the attainment of a particular goal. As a result the artisan experiences satisfaction in attaining his goal and gratifying his need.

The psychology of change in tool-forms and the typological series Montelius pioneered relative chronology based on a series of conceptualisations relating to the evolution of tool forms. His ideas derived from a large body of empirical facts which he and his pupil Åberg collected in their monumental works on the Bronze Age of Italy and northern Europe (Montelius, 1903; 1895–1910; 1912; Åberg, 1929; 1930–31). Their formulations became assimilated into thinking about pre-history, though few today take the trouble to read them anew.

Consecutive externalisations of the same *tool-idea* when placed into diachronic order form a linear series, the typological series. In this series any single member or link both follows and precedes another single member.

When analysing such a series closely one soon becomes aware that the form of an immediately following single member is based on that of the immediately preceding one, except for a small change. Thus *its presence depends on the existence of an immediately preceding form*. As we are dealing with human activity we must assume that the formal link between the two members is a *causal* one.

Every member of the chain has a double role:

i. it is the result of a minor, formal alteration of an earlier externalisation;

ii. it may become the basis for a further change when the same tool idea becomes again externalised.

We should note that there will, of course, always be a certain time period during which the same externalisation becomes copied or the changes might be ornamental and 'stylistic' only.

This continuous and structured change of tool forms refers to human *creative activity*. The basic unit of reference, here as well as in 'organic typology', is not the tool object itself, but the creative individual who has manufactured the tool. Without him we simply cannot explain such a consistent change of tool forms, and especially why tool forms should change at all.

Keeping this in mind Montelius's observations can be summarised as follows (Montelius, 1903; Gallus, 1942 : 22–24).

(a) Any link in the chain of a series is scarcely different when compared with another one. Two immediately following links are often so similar that an untrained eye cannot observe the difference. The first and last members of a series, however, are generally so unlike that at first sight their relationship cannot be recognised. It can nevertheless be shown, when studying the whole series, that the most recent form has derived from the oldest one through small intervening modifications which might have lasted several hundred years.

(b) One should never forget that a series might often branch out so that one link in the chain is the starting point for several different series.

(c) The works of man are subject to the laws of evolution. Is it necessary for us too to progress step by step? Evolution might speed up or remain slow, but when man creates new forms the same laws of evolution which are observed in nature become effective.

These formulations were further elaborated by Åberg (1929):

(d) We find that a Typological Series of toolforms which has a solely practical function will at once stop changing when the best solution for the task to be performed has been found. In other series, where artistic considerations play a main part, the movement of the series may be maintained for a long time.

(e) Evolution might remain slow for a long time, might gain impetus, and from time to time the energy of change might operate during such a short period that development becomes abrupt and might be likened in some sense to a biologic "mutation". This last phenomenon can be observed mainly when a particular type changes over into a new environment.

(f) According to biologic law when a part of the body, an organ or a faculty can no more develop further in a useful way, it degenerates until it disappears. This lawlike principle can also be found in the Typological Series of prehistory.

(g) Some Typological Series are so natural and simple that they might be spontaneously recreated at different localities and during different time periods.

Based on this pioneering analysis (and on archaeological documentary material in general) I have developed the following propositions and their consequences in connection with the movement in time of typological series of artifacts (Gallus, 1942 : 24–36):

(a) *A tool-idea when first externalised*, and for some time after, is never the best possible and practical solution for the performance of the task envisaged.

It is only relatively best, meaning that it is 'best possible' only in relation to a particular position in time and space in which the toolmaker finds himself at the moment of his activity. The toolmaker finds himself restricted by the particular stage of human development and especially by his own knowledge, insight and skill.

This 'particular' solution does not yet fully conform to the energy-formula already mentioned: maximum usefulness with the least expenditure of energy and time. However it lies *within* the possibilities (potential) offered by a *tool-idea* without as yet realising its ultimate, full potential. This realisation can come only with time. Thus the potential itself of a tool-idea is always greater (and consequently still unknown to the toolmaker) than its restricted, first, particular externalisation in space and time.

As a result it is within the grasp of man to improve somewhat a version which has been created earlier, and which he has inherited from his forefathers or seen elsewhere. 'Improve' is relative to the energy-formula and the task to be performed. Man can create a new version which is somewhat better adapted to the task (compare also Gallus, 1974 : 96–97).

This proposition is a commonplace which can be observed in every instance when human creativeness comes into play. It is also the consequence of the restricted (finite) contents of human knowledge according to space, time and individualness, and also of the even more restricted capacity of conscious attention—of being aware of cognitive material in a synchronous situation. This situation can only be overcome or remedied by successive, sequential and creative events.

A prehistorian observes that some change has occurred. It must be obvious to him that such change cannot be understood and the reasons for a change cannot be grasped unless he knows something about the psychic process at the root of the change: *tool-idea* in conjunction with function and performance, the task to be performed and the goal to be attained with the operation of the tool, and the *need* to be satisfied as the constant psychic energy or drive behind the process.

Change is directly connected with function and performance. It is *dissatisfaction* with performance (i.e. with the current level of efficiency) which prompts an artisan to change his tool. A toolform does not change. It is changed.

(b) *If a toolform is improved* the improvement takes the form of a small modification which affects some functional part of the tool. That is why an analysis of subsequent changes can be used to define the functional parts and thus the function of a tool.

(c) *Tool externalisations will show consistent improvement* until the best performance which is potentially present in the original tool-idea has been attained.

When this form has been externalised the typological series stops. The typological series thus produced is a *Simple Typological Series*. A simple example is the form of the sewing needle invented in the Magdalenian.

The energy formula of best performance definitely establishes the presence of the individual decision-maker (the creator-craftsman) as the basic unit and ultimate mover of the typological series. It is an unrealistic simplification to omit the original human element from typology and classification.

Strickon (1969 : 92–93), discussing economic theory,

argued that human behaviour is inseparable from decision making and choice. Both are directed towards attaining '*some form of maximum return*' (maximising). This 'assumption' is 'intellectually and theoretically useful'. 'If a theory were . . . raised upon any other assumption about the nature of individual motivation, the result would be intellectual chaos or, at best, a social science very different from that which we now have'. In this way Strickon singles out in his economic theory the '*individual maximising decision maker*' (italics mine) as a 'variable'. And so do we!

We thus can regard a *tool-idea* as a psychic complex ('engramme') whose full potential according to its contents becomes externalised through a series of sequential changes which form the simple typological series.

(d) *When an energetically final solution has been reached*, according to the contents of a tool-idea, no further modifications are possible, unless the tool-idea itself becomes creatively modified.

Taking the evolution of the axe (an example used by Montelius) it was first conceived as an implement flaked in stone. The tool-idea, which contained the technology of flaking, produced either rather sturdy or very brittle edges. The sharpening of edges could not be improved any more after secondary retouch was applied to it. Subsequently the original tool-idea was creatively modified into a new tool-idea which contained the theory of grinding. The ground edge axe, made of extra hard stone, has been invented presumably in Australia. The change also contained the use of different and harder material, which previously was not suitable for flaking. The edges became perhaps not sharper but rather more durable and less brittle than before.

(e) *The creation of a new tool-idea* is closely connected to the first one through the permanence of both the original need and the original task to be performed. Consequently the modification does not result in the creation of a totally different new form.

The old form is still (until the particular moment of creation of the new) the then known best, most efficient, practical solution which is attainable for the same task which will be performed by the new tool. It is still the perfect model extant, relative to the position in time and space of the maker.

Accordingly the new tool form, when externalised according to the new idea, will copy the last externalisation known (and still used) of the old tool-idea. The full potential of the new tool-idea (the 'mutation') is still unknown and hidden (for examples see Gallus, 1942 : 25–32).

(f) *The new idea contains a new potential*, a latent energy, which triggers a new movement of a new simple typological series during which changes occur towards a full realisation of the potential inherent in the new idea. The new simple typological series proceeds through continuous and consistent small modifications until the best solution (according to the energy rule and according to the possibilities contained in the new idea) is again reached.

In the case of the evolution of the axe, the new idea begins in the form of a chipped or hammered axe with a polished edge and the series proceeds until the full axe is polished. Its body becomes thinner. However the series must again stop with the exhaustion of the new potential conveyed by the new idea. The next mutational modification involves the use of copper. Copper does not break like stone, the body of the axe can become thinner still and the edge can become more acute.

It is well known that the first copper axes appear in the form of the old polished axes, only made (hammered) in copper. This soon changes until new forms are attained which utilise the full potential of the new material, including casting. Then, because copper is soft, a new mutation involves the creation of a harder metal, an alloy (bronze) and the development of casting technology. And so on to steel. The present form of a common shaft-hole axe was invented during the Bronze Age.

(g) *A Complex Typological Series can be defined* as a series of simple typological series, which are linked together by the same human need and the same task to be performed. They progress by constant creative modifications of the underlying tool idea.

When the potential of a tool-idea has been fully exhausted by reaching the best solution possible the movement of the series stops, the last form used remains stagnant and change can only occur again when a creative modification of the tool-idea itself (not just simple improvements effected according to the potential of a tool-idea) becomes conceived.

This is a historical 'if . . . then' situation, a stochastic event, which is never bound or determined to happen, and cannot be predicted. It can only be stated that *if* such a creative innovation happens *then* a new simple typological series begins again.

Because of this the analysis of typological series in prehistoric archaeology is a potent mental tool for historical analysis. It is unfortunately fully ignored at present (compare Gallus, 1942 : 36–46).

We have stated that the essence of the new mutation is not discoverable in its first manifestation. It exists only as a potential. The best solution according to the new potential cannot be externalised (invented) because:

  i. There is the authoritative presence of the last, efficient solution of the same need and task; this is copied because no better solution is known.
  ii. The full extent of the consequences of the innovation (its full contents) necessarily eludes human knowledge. Human consciousness is narrow and fleeting and can focus on restricted issues only, one at a time.
  iii. *The new idea or deed is larger in its consequences than human consciousness can fully grasp.*
  iv. The modification of the old idea is done within a limited, narrow, restricted focus only, according to a particular level of human knowledge and awareness (as present in the mind of an individual thinker). The full potential of the new idea can only be grasped at the end of a sequence, during which subsequent historical developments have created a new, enriched cognitive situation ('summation', see under).
  v. Only when the new possibilities opened up by the new idea, or new ideas, are grasped can further modifications be effected (compare Gallus, 1974 : 96–97).

The first copper axes were hammered; the possibility of casting was, at the moment of the first use of copper axes, unknown. Bleriot wanted only to cross the Channel; it surpassed his cognitive restrictions to think of streamlining or of regular flights between continents, not to speak of supersonic aircraft; the full realisation of the potential of propelled flights needed a long series of subsequent 'focusing' until it became exhausted and replaced by the new idea of rocket power. Only the immediate first advantage of a new idea can be conceived.

This observation is of course not only valid in connection with the creation of new ideas in general, wherever this happens, but has its roots in and refers to a general cosmic *reality*. The cosmos exists in particular entities (quantas) which exclude the existence of another quantum at the same moment in 'time' and in the same place.

Change can only occur as a sequence. This is the real meaning of 'time', as distinct from measured, physical or clock-time, which appears in mathematical equations (Gallus, 1968). Measured or clock-time is not *reality* but an ultimately misleading *abstraction* for the sake of a mathematical description of processes.

In this aspect the typological series is a process which appears as a particular instance of the *structure* of Time. Indeed it must be regarded as a manifestation of the cosmic *Reality:* Time. The nearest we can come to a definition of the cosmic Reality: Time is *sequential change*. In other words the real essence of time is not its quantified abstraction as used in the physical sciences, but the conception of time as it appears in the historical sciences from the simple notion of *date* to the more complicated conceptualisations of *structured change*.

(h) *Every change is bound to happen in a particular situation within a particular Typological Series*. Typological Series are basic units of change and of evolution in general and are an essentially historical phenomenon. They do not turn back. Every member of a series takes up a unique position between a previous and a following chain link. Thus every externalisation of a tool-idea appears in a particular context of a particular typological series, occupying within it a particular situation as to space and time. That is why Montelius and Åberg were able to use the analysis of typological series as a conceptual tool for the establishment of relative chronology.

This simple statement has wide ranging consequences, which can be logically deduced; their validity can be assumed while they are not clearly contradicted by observation.

(i) *The situation within an evolving Series* determines and limits the possibilities (potential) of creative activity. As every possible improvement within a simple typological series is based on the already existing form (state of perfection) of a preceding member of a series, improvement appears limited to those particular modifications which can actually be based on this existing form.

There is only a certain latitude of possible improvements potentially present in every particular situation within a particular series. Human creative activity is limited not only by the narrowness of human awareness but also by the particular situation within a particular typological series in which a human individual finds himself involved (the cognitive stage of its evolution).

Improvements out of range of what is here and now possible cannot be externalised. This impossibility is not by necessity absolute, only relative. What is not possible here and now can be possible elsewhere or, through subsequent externalisations, made possible later (eg. by becoming a sequence).

The development of a complex typological series can also be defined as a *continuous creation of new potential*, to make possible what was impossible before (Gallus, 1974 : 96–97).

To put it simply and crudely: the iron axe could not have been invented in the Neolithic. Nobody can build a second storey before the first has been built. Improvements can be based only on what is known here and now.

A 'mutation' at the end of a simple typological series (when the modification of an old tool idea is conceived) can be understood as the formation of an engramme with a much larger scope than simple modifications. The mental energy of such a jump during the development of human insight

into 'Reality' might be generated by the stress of the impasse, due to an awareness of the exhaustion of the old idea within which no further useful modifications are possible.

(j) *Every link in a Typological Series contains the sum of all previous externalisations* which happened in the Series before it (a quintessence or end result of past developments).

I have called this phenomenon *summation*, and the continuously appearing single and new end results *summa*. A series develops from one summa to the next. Every summa is unique, has a different content and a different position in a series (eg. in space and time) (Gallus, 1972a : 556–57; 1974 : 96, and 96 note 5).

(k) *Every externalisation is the result of human decision making, in a unique Series Situation*. Every modification creates a new summa and a new potential for further improvements. In short a new *Series Situation* is created. The created potential is small after a simple modification, but exceptionally large after the modification of a tool-idea itself and largest on the creation of another new tool-idea. In every new series situation further improvements become possible, which in a previous situation were not yet possible.

I have at length analysed the historical role of human decision making as it appears embedded in a typological series (Gallus 1974 : 95–97) and came to the conclusion that the potential in a series situation for decision making is not restricted to the one particular decision or choice which actually has been made, as theorists of mechanical cultural evolution would claim (cf. White, 1949).

I recapitulate those propositions which are relevant here:

(1) *The determination of human choices, decisions and innovations* refers to a field of potential within which uncertainty reigns as to which of the possible decisions will be made:

    i. All possible decisions in a given series situation are *equally* possible;

    ii. The actual decision is unpredictable;

    iii. Whether any decisions etc. will in fact be made is also unpredictable.

I have called this 'field of potential', within which free choices can be made, a *spatium*. In the case of the typological series of toolforms every spatium contains a restricted range of possible improvements based on the last known best (*hic et nunc*) solution of a task—a spatium based, in other words, on the summa.

An artisan may or may not arrive at one particular possible externalisation and improvement which is individually available to him within his spatium, but *if* a decision and externalisation is made *then* it must lie within the spatium, that is it is *determined only by the extent of the spatium*.

(m) *A decision or choice once made prevents the actualisation* (substantialisation) of any other equally possible alternative by the same individual in the same historical moment. This proposition establishes that a typological series, as it progresses through the idea in formation of individuals, has a definite *direction*, and that it is not reversible.

However the direction is not predetermined. It depends on the stochastic decision-making (conceptualisations) of individuals in previous creative events (within a spatium).

The direction of a typological series is further made distinct and definite by the fact that decisions and choices, once made, discard or annihilate those parts of a potential spatium which have not been substantiated.

The above proposition does not exclude (it even presupposes) the possibility, which is easily observable, that in the same spatium-situation two or several creative individuals might come to the same or to two or several different conceptualisations and actualisations.

Man, by decision-making within a 'spatium', creates the *direction* of a typological series and through this achieves his eventual success or failure in the exploration of the unknown and in the adaptation to, and exploitation and domination of, this environment.

(n) *In the same series situation, within the same spatium, different actualisations (choices, decisions) can be made by different individuals.* Montelius himself observed that one link in a typological series might become the starting point for several different series. In this way different typological series can be started which lead in different directions.

This is the same proposition as the one which was made by Brandl and Gallus during discussion of the papers on 'Symboling', at another A.I.A.S. Symposium, stating that 'schematisation' is a sequential process, during which 'subsidiary processes' are generated (Gallus, in press).

Two or more typological series starting in different directions will eventually lead to different human situations, whose evolutionary position and potential are radically different. Radically different spatiums will have opened up and different potentialities will have become extinct or unexplored for them. The process of summation has led to different end results. Thus from the point of view of the analysis of typological series, *what their evolution has not realised* is also extremely important (Gallus, 1974a : 97).

It has also to be realised that the contents of a summa depend on the actual history of the typological series which precedes it, and on the whole series of idea-formations and externalisations in the past.

We can now formulate our last proposition:

(o) *In order to arrive independently at the invention of the same tool type* (convergence) or at any other link within a typological series, it is necessary to reproduce the same series situation. In other words the whole typological series preceding this situation (i.e. the summa) must be independently reproduced. This proposition is nothing else but a repetition of the well known biogenetic law (biogenetisches Grundgesetz) of Heckel, which refers to the development of the embryo.

Propositions (k)–(n) give a satisfactory theoretical basis for an explanation and understanding of the great variety of human communities existing today on the earth from hunter-gatherer societies to the affluent societies of the highest developed city civilisations.

At this stage we can also introduce the concept of the *state of maturity* of a typological series, meaning how much change has occurred up to the particular chain link we are analysing.

We must regard the ordered sequence of typological series as a *basic structural phenomenon* of the cosmos in general and of the process of human creative activity in particular.

The analysis of the typological series cannot be neglected if we want to gain insight into 'how to place cultural groups into an evolutionary scale' (as asked by the organisers of the A.I.A.S. symposiums).

The typological series and the evolution of cultural groups

I regard the largest, natural and homogeneous human community to be an 'ethnic group' in the sense of anthropology. I would be inclined to use the term 'cultural group' in the same sense; however because of the sparsity of documentation which can be regarded as ethnospecific, such identification in prehistory is extremely difficult, though possible (cf. Gallus, 1947).

Therefore we have to distinguish:

i. *Culture* (cultural group). An assemblage of objects and observable manifestations or traits in the sense of anthropology, which according to form and expression (observable externalisation) can be regarded as different (disparate) from any other such assemblage of traits.

ii. *Ethnic group.* A 'culture' where enough documentation exists to discern ethnospecific objects and traits, which warrant identification as the largest, still homogeneous, social unit or community in the sense of anthropology (people or tribe). See also the definition of 'culture' by Mead (1953) as quoted in the introduction to this essay.

Every human externalisation in every culture is part of a typological series, within which it occupies a particular series situation (propositions (h)–(i) above).

The objects and traits, which document for us a culture, are *the synchronic end result* (*summas*) *of typological series* in a particular time period and of course *in different stages of maturity* of their development.

In order to understand the presence of a cultural group (or culture) we have to reconstruct the typological series, whose different stages represent the totality of its past history.

Technology (stone tools) is only one (often not even distinctly ethnospecific) part of this history. Consequently stone typology must be studied in the full context of all available documentation. Nevertheless we can isolate toolmaking and tool use within such an assemblage of data and we can restore the position of every item within its typological series (series situation, see proposition (h)–(i) above).

It is deplorable that the typological series was fully abandoned a generation ago owing to confusion about the meaning of *evolution* (compare Closs, 1956, which is an extremely enlightening study).

Only after the reconstruction of the typological series has been attempted, with greater or lesser success, can the assessment of a particular 'culture' on an evolutionary scale be attempted.

Two lines of research are open for us:

i. The definition of tool-types, a synchronic classification according to *organic typology* and within an assemblage of traits we can call *culture* or *cultural group*.

ii. Reconstruction of the typological series of these tool types; a diachronic analysis of tool types as the summa of past typological series.

Typological series of tool types (and especially complex typological series) will extend more often than not over several cultures or cultural groups in space and time.

Such a placement of a tool type within a typological series gives us an added certainty that a tool type, as registered by a prehistorian, is really equivalent to a tool type which was in the mind of a prehistoric artisan. Its persistence through time and constancy of change furnish an added clue.

Summary of argument

Organic typology defines a tool type as the externalisation of a tool idea which satisfies a specific task within a specific need.

Form relates to function, and function relates to a need (task), and to a simple energy rule of performance.

A tool type might contain morphologically different variants which can be classified on the level of object bound typology (artifact types).

Organic typology classifies and distinguishes tool types according to need, function, performance and task. Form is a derivative of these.

Dissatisfaction with the level of functioning (according to the energy rule) or the creation of new needs leads to changes in tool form or to the creation of new tools.

A short, first résumé of organic typology, and a rather unsatisfactory exemplification with the aid of empirical material (unsatisfactory because of restrictions in time and space available) was attempted in Gallus (1971b).

The basic unit of organic typology is a tool-idea in the mind of a particular prehistoric artisan, which appears as an element within the context of the evolution of a typological series. The typological series in this aspect is a structural unit of human creative activity.

The placement of cultures (ethnic groups) and cultural groups on an evolutionary scale requires two approaches:

i. *Synchronic.* Tool-ideas and any other ideas behind other externalisations are regarded as being externalised within a particular series situation, which externalisations form an assemblage of traits within a particular culture or cultural group.

ii. *Diachronic.* Externalisations as found within a particular culture or cultural group are placed within their particular typological series and these series are analysed as they develop in space and time (historical aspect).

Propositions about the regularities of a typological series have been formulated, which propositions relate to human creative activity in general.

The presence of a restricted field (spatium) determined in its limitations by the series situation (summa), within which unpredictable, free, stochastic decisions can be made, has been suggested and established.

Recent neglect of evolutionary analysis is deplored. Without it the time factor (change) cannot be explored. The concept of the typological series is the only available mental tool which is able to explain change as an ordered (structured) historical sequence.

Glossary

Engramme: A complex of neuronal pathways, whether genetically fixed or acquired by learning. On the level of consciousness it can be evoked or formulated as an idea or a concept.

Externalisation. The creative representation of psychic contents in materials of the object world or by means of activity, so that it becomes perceptible through the senses.

Plasticity of behaviour. The extent of possible change in behaviour when facing unexpected or unfamiliar situations in the environment.

Reality. The being of the cosmos as it is, or exists in itself, independently of human observation.

Stochastic. Unpredictable. Anomic. ('Random').

References

Aberg, N., 1929. Typologie (Die Typologische Methode). *In* M. Ebert (ed.) *Reallexikon der Vorgeschichte*, 13:518-26. Berlin: Walter de Gruyter.

—— 1930-31. *Bronezeitliche und früheisenzeitliche Chronologie* I-II Stockholm: Verlag der Akademie.

Balout, L., 1967. Procédés d'analyse et questions de terminologie dans l'étude des ensembles industriels du paléolithique inférieur en Afrique du Nord. *In* W.W. Bishop and J.D. Clark (eds) *Background to evolution in Africa*, pp. 701-35. Chicago: University of Chicago Press.

Binford, L.R., 1972. The new archaeology. *The Listener*, 2237:174-76.

—— and S.R. Binford., 1966. A preliminary analysis of functional variability in the Mousterian of Levallois facies. *In* J.D. Clark and F.C. Howell. Recent studies in paleoanthropology (Special Publication). *American Anthropologist*, 69(2, part 2):238-95.

Binford S.R., 1968. Variability and change in the Near Eastern Mousterian of the Levallois facies. *In* S.R. Binford and L.R. Binford (eds) *New perspectives in archaeology*, pp. 49-60. Chicago: Aldine.

—— *and* L.R. Binford, 1969. Stone tools and human behaviour. *Scientific American*, April: 70-84.

Bishop, W.W. and J.D. Clark., 1967. *Background to evolution in Africa*, Chicago: University of Chicago Press.

Bordes, F., 1950-51. Principes d'une méthode d'étude des techniques de débitage et de la typologie du paléolithique ancien et moyen. *L'Anthropologie*, 54:19-34; 55:393-420.

—— *and* D. de Sonneville-Bordes, 1970. The significance of variability in palaeolithic assemblages. *World Archaeology*, 2(1):61-73.

Cahen, D.F., F. van Noten, F. Bordes and D.S. Brose, 1971. Stone age typology: another approach. *Current Anthropology* 12:211-15.

Chang, K.C., 1967a. Major aspects of the interrelationship of archaeology and ethnology. *Current Anthropology*, 8:227-43.

—— 1967b. *Rethinking archaeology*, New York: Random House.

Clark, J.D., 1967. Discussion of Tixier, J., Procédés d'analyse et questions de terminologie concernant l'étude des ensembles industriels du Paléolithique récent et de l'Epipléolithique dans l'Afrique du Nord-Ouest. *In* W.W. Bishop and J.D. Clark (eds) *Background to evolution in Africa*, pp. 815, 820. Chicago: University of Chicago Press.

—— *and* C.V. Haynes Jr., 1970. An elephant butchery site at Mwanganda's village, Karonga Malawi, and its relevance for palaeolithic archaeology. *World Archaeology*, 1(3):390-411.

Clarke, D.L., 1972. Book review: Watson P.J., St. A. Le Blank and Ch. L. Redman, 1971 *Explanation in archaeology*. Columbia University Press, New York and London. *Antiquity*, 46:237-38.

Closs, A., 1956. Kulturhistorie und Evolution. *Mitteilungen der Anthropologischen Gesellschaft in Wien*, 86:1-47.

Cole, S.M., 1967. Discussion of Mason, R.J. *Analytical procedures in the Earlier and Middle Stone Age cultures in Southern Africa;* and discussion on terminology. *In* W.W. Bishop and J.D. Clark (eds) *Background to evolution in Africa*, pp. 769, 873-74. Chicago: University of Chicago Press.

Collins, D., 1970. Stone artefact analysis and the recognition of culture tradition. *World Archaeology*, 2(1):17-27.

Cowgill, G.L., 1967. Comments on Chang, Major aspects of the interrelationship of archaeology and ethnology. *Current Anthropology*, 8:236-37.

Crosby, E., 1969. Review of Dickson F.P. *Aboriginal technology, some evidence from Kurnell Peninsula, Botany Bay*. Department of Industrial Art Monographs, University of New South Wales, 1(1). Sydney. *Mankind*, 7(1):71-72.

Dickson, F.P., 1968. *Aboriginal technology, some evidence from Kurnell Peninsula, Botany Bay*. Department of Industrial Art Monographs, University of New South Wales, 1(1). Sydney.

Dobzhansky, Th., 1965. Religion, death and evolutionary adaptation. *In* M.E. Spiro (ed.) *Content and meaning in cultural anthropology*. London: The Free Press, New York and Collier Macmillan.

Durbin, M., 1971 More on culture a human domain. *Current Anthropology*, 12:297-403.

Gallus, A., 1942. Prolegomènes à la typologie (les lois et le rôle de la série typologique). *Archaeologiai Ertesitö*, (1-2): 1-46.

—— 1947. Uber die Grundlagen der vorgeschichtlichen Methodik. *Anales de Arqueologia Y Ettnologia* 8:127-75

—— 1963. *Comments on papers submitted to the conference on nomenclature or implements and culture.* Typescript. Australian Institute of Aboriginal Studies. Canberra.

—— 1968. On the interrelationship of archaeology and ethnology. *Current Anthropology*, 9:452-53.

—— 1970a. General theory and method of typological analysis. *The Artefact*, 17 (February):5-7.

—— 1970b. General theory and method of typological analysis. *The Artefact*, 17 (May): 1-10.

—— 1971a. Results of the exploration of Koonalda Cave, 1956-68. *In* R.V.S. Wright (ed.) *Archaeology of the Gallus Site, Koonalda Cave*, pp. 81-133. Canberra: Australian Institute of Aboriginal Studies.

—— 1971b. Excavations at Keilor, report No. 1. *The Artefact*, 24:1-12.

—— 1972a. A biofunctional theory of religion. *Current Anthropology*, 13:543-68.

—— 1972b. Excavations at Keilor, report No. 2. *The Artefact*, 17:9-19.

—— 1974. Reply to I.A. Kryvelev: on Gallus's biofunctional theory of religion. *Current Anthropology*, 15:95-99.

——(in press). Schematisation and symboling. *In* P.J. Ucko (ed.) *Form in indigenous art.* . . . Canberra: Australian Institute of Aboriginal Studies.

Geertz, C., 1966. Religion as a cultural system. *In* M. Banton (ed.) *Anthropological approaches to the study of religion*, pp. 1-46. London: Tavistock.

Hodson, F.R., 1970. Cluster analysis and archaeology: some new developments and applications. *World Archaeology*, 1(3):299-320.

Howell, F.C., 1967. Discussion of Mason, R.J., Analytical procedures in the Earlier and Middle Stone Age cultures in Southern Africa. *In* W.W. Bishop *and* J.D. Clark (eds) *Background to evolution in Africa.* p. 768. Chicago: University of Chicago Press.

Inskeep, R., 1967a. Discussion on terminology. *In* W.W. Bishop, *and* J.D. Clark (eds.) *Background to evolution in Africa*, p. 874. Chicago: University of Chicago Press.

—— 1967b. Discussion of Tixier J., Procédés d'analyse et questions de terminologie concernant l'étude des ensembles industriels du Paléolithique récent et de l'Epipaleolithique dans l'Afrique du Nord-Ouest. *In* W.W. Bishop *and* J.D. Clark (eds) *Background to evolution in Africa*, p. 816. Chicago: University of Chicago Press.

Isaac, G.L., 1967. Discussion of Mason, J.J., Analytical procedures in the Earlier and Middle Stone Age cultures in Southern Africa. *In* W.W. Bishop *and* J.D. Clark (eds) *Background to evolution in Africa*, pp. 767-69. Chicago: University of Chicago Press.

—— 1969. Studies of early culture in East Africa. *World Archaeology*. 1(1):1-23.

Lancaster, J.B., 1965. Language and communication. *In* P.L. De Vore (ed.) *The Origin of man: a symposium*, pp. 75-78. New York: Wenner Gren Foundation.

Leakey, M.D., 1967a. Discussion of Mason, R.J., Analytical procedures in the Earlier and Middle Stone Age cultures in Southern Africa. *In* W.W. Bishop *and* J.D. Clark (eds) *Background to evolution in Africa*, pp. 767-69. Chicago: University of Chicago Press.

—— 1967b. Preliminary survey of the cultural material from Bed I and II, Olduvai Gorge, Tanzania. *In* W.W. Bishop *and* J.D. Clark (eds) *Background to evolution in Africa*, pp. 417-46. Chicago: University of Chicago Press.

Lévi-Strauss, C., 1953. Minimum units in various aspects of culture. Discussion. *In* S. Tax *et al.* (eds) *An appraisal of anthropology today*, pp. 293-96. Chicago: University of Chicago Press.

Margenau, H., 1950. *The nature of physical reality.* New York, Toronto: McGraw-Hill.

Mason, R.J., 1967. Analytical procedures in the Earlier and Middle Stone Age cultures in Southern Africa. *In* W.W.

Bishop *and* J.D. Clark (eds) *Background to evolution in Africa*, pp. 737-64. Chicago: University of Chicago Press.

Mead, M., 1953. The study of culture at a distance, *In* M. Mead *and* R. Métraux (eds) *The study of culture at a distance*, pp. 3-53. Chicago: University of Chicago Press.

Mellars, P., 1970. Some comments on the notion of functional variability in stone assemblages. *World Archaeology*, 2(1): 74-89.

Miller, S.F., F. Bordes *and* L. Cotter, 1972. On old and new concepts of typology. *Current Anthropology*, 13:139-41.

Montelius, O., 1903 *Die Älteren Kulturperioden im Orient und in Europa. I. Die Methode.*

—— 1895-1910 *La civilisation primitive en Italie.*

—— 1912 *Die vorklassische Chronologie Italiens.*

Movius, H.L., Jnr., N.C. David, H.M. Bricker *and* R.P. Clay 1968. The analysis of certain major classes of upper palaeolithic tools. *American School of Prehistoric Research, Peabody Museum, Harvard University, Bulletin*, 26:1-58.

Müller-Back, H., 1969. Comments on O. Collins, Culture tradition and early man. *Current Anthropology*, 10:308.

Northorp, F.S.C., 1953. Discussion about "Pattern". *In* S. Tax *et al.* (eds) *An appraisal of anthropology today*, p. 316. Chicago: University of Chicago Press.

Oakley, K.P., 1948. *Man the toolmaker.* London: British Museum.

Pradel, L., 1966. Quelques précisions sur la pointe moustérienne et la pointe des Cottes. *L'Anthropologie*, 70:602-05.

—— 1973. Sur la préhension et l'emmanchement de l'outillage préhistorique. *Bull. Amis du Grand-Pressigny*, 24:17-19.

—— 1974. Recherches D'histoire et D'archaeologie Chinonaise. Une série industrielle du Moustérien a bifaces de Fontmaure, commune de Velléches (Vienne) et considérations sur forme et fonction de l'outillage. *Bull. Soc. Amis Vx Chinon*, VII, 8:747-53.

Renfrew, C., 1969. Trade and culture process in European prehistory. *Current Anthropology*, 10:151-69.

—— 1972a. The new archaeology. *The Listener*, 87(2234):68-70.

—— 1972b. The new archaeology. *The Listener*, 87(2235): 104-106.

Rouse, L., 1953. The Strategy of culture history. *In* A.L. Kroeber (ed.) *Anthropology today*, pp. 57-72. Chicago: University of Chicago Press.

Sackett, J.R., 1966. Quantitative analysis of upper palaeolithic stone tools. *American Anthropologist*, 68 (2 part 2): 356-94.

Semenov, S.A., 1967. *Prehistoric technology.* London: Cory Adams and Mackay.

Spaulding, A.C., 1953. Statistical techniques for the discovery of artefact types. *American Antiquity*, 18(4):305-13.

—— 1960. Statistical description and comparison of artefact assemblages. *In* A.F. Heizer *and* S.F. Cook (eds) *The application of quantitative method in archaeology*, pp. 60-83. Viking Fund Publications. New York: Wenner Gren Foundation.

Strickon, A., 1969. Comments on Dalton, Theoretical issues in economic anthropology. *Current Anthropology*, 10:91-93.

Tixier, J., 1967a. Procédés d'analyse et questions de terminologie concernant l'étude des ensembles industriels du Paléolithique récent et de l'Epipaléolithique dans l'Afrique du Nord-Ouest. *In* W.W. Bishop *and* J.D. Clark (eds) *Background to evolution in Africa*, pp. 771-95. Discussion; pp. 795-820. Chicago: University of Chicago Press.

—— 1967b. Discussion of Mason, R.J., Analytical procedures in the Earlier and Middle Stone Age cultures in Southern Africa. *In* W.W. Bishop *and* J.D. Clark (eds) *Background to evolution in Africa*, p. 767. Chicago: University of Chicago Press.

White, L.A., 1949. *The science of culture.* New York: Farrar, Strauss and Co.

White, J.P., 1967. Ethnoarchaeology in New Guinea: two examples. *Mankind*, 6(9):409-14.

Wright, R.V.S., 1963. *The typolology of stone artefacts in the old world.* Paper presented at the Conference on Nomenclature of Implements and Cultures. Typescript, Institute of Aboriginal Studies, Canberra.

—— 1971. The flints. *In* R.V.S. Wright (ed.) *Archaeology of the Gallus Site, Koonalda Cave*, pp. 48-58. Canberra: Australian Institute of Aboriginal Studies.

The framing out and significance of a typological model for stone tools

ASOK K. GHOSH

There has been a good deal of controversy in recent years on the definition of *culture* when sub-human primates (especially the chimpanzee) are found to make and use tools for specific functions and when tool-making and using behaviours are handed down to the next generation through the learning process (Goodall, 1963, 1965; Jones and Sabater Pi, 1969; Nishida, 1973; Struhsaker and Hunkeler, 1971; Suzuki, 1966). The basis for such a controversy lies mainly in the level of improper definition. Unlike non-human primates or even other animals, human culture is characterised by continuous development, not mere change as induced by adaptation to environment. The idea of development, as necessary in the perspective of culture, has been explained by Steward (1973 : 5) and he is worth quoting:

> 'Cultural development ... must be conceptualized not only as a matter of increasing complexity but also as one of the emergence of successive *levels of sociocultural integration*'.

On the other hand non-human culture (when there is any which accords with the conventional definition), is a product of secondary adaptation and adjustment in an initially unfavourable ecological situation. The reactions are behavioural responses and there is perhaps a basic similarity between this process and the emergence of human culture. But with all non-human animals behaviour is devoid of progressive development—which may be due to biological limitation (Ghosh, 1971a : 92–93) predetermined by genetics.

Nevertheless it may be conceded that an emendation is indeed essential to re-define culture, that is human culture, in the light of recent advances in the ethology of both man and other primates. This task appears to be urgent in the context of human evolution, in drawing (if possible) the line of demarcation between man and sub-human groups. This crucial problem is really beyond solution from a mere palaeontological point of view, as Le Gros Clark (1950) pointed out:

> 'Probably the differentiation of man from ape will ultimately have to rest on a functional rather than anatomical basis, the criterion of humanity being the ability to speak and to make tools'.

What we have achieved to date in this direction is still an open question. Studies in prehistory over more than a century have mostly supplied us with information on the distribution of prehistoric sites or areas, where the sites have been attributed to arbitrary cultural stages simply based on the occurrence of types and the techniques used. In fact, there are very few areas where archaeological levels have been correlated with geological stratigraphy.

On the whole the overall aim is to reconstruct and understand prehistoric culture. The culture of contemporary *man* being the objective—how much attention has been paid to him? The direct answer is little; or to be more straight forward the answer should be nothing. Man, the maker of the culture, is always kept in his place as an assumed conventional background.

The direct physical evidences of early man are really very meagre in comparison with the enormous amount of his cultural materials. But taken on their own the skeletal finds are not insignificant. Almost all the study on early man is concentrated on anatomical and morphological examinations, identification of the finds in terms of taxonomy, comparisons and placement in the evolutionary scheme of phylogeny. However in certain instances there has been speculation about cultural capabilities. There is still an unexplored area of research on the correlation between man and his culture, or, to put it in another way, between culture and its maker. The correlation may be somewhat tentative in the formative stage of culture, and to begin with the most important sites are those which have yielded associations of both early man and his culture from the same geological stratum of known relative dating. As my general area of research is concerned with south and southeast Asia of the Pleistocene epoch, the ideal specific area for the undertaking is Indonesia, more specifically Java.

In southeast Asia the middle Pleistocene sites with fossil hominids are restricted to Java, which also possesses the credit of yielding the oldest remains of fossil man from the orient. The hominid material from the Djetis bed comprises *Meganthropus*, *Pithecanthropus* and *Homo modjokertensis*. It is interesting to note that the history of Pleistocene fauna in Indonesia shows the invasion of contemporary fauna from India and China. Above the Djetis bed the overlying Trinil bed also yielded *Pithecanthropus* finds and in addition cultural materials. The Trinil bed has been dated approximately between 600 000 and 700 000 years BP (Weidenreich, 1945; von Koenigswald, 1936; Sartono, 1961; 1964; Jacob, 1964, 1966, 1967; von Koenigswald and Ghosh, 1973).

Outside Indonesia there are a good many areas in southeast Asia which are yielding more or less similar finds of palaeoliths; Anyathian of Burma, Fingnoian of Thailand, Tampanian of Malaya should be mentioned. Comparable industries have also been found in Vietnam, Philippines, etc. Further northwest from southeast Asia, the Indian sub-continent is also immensely rich with Palaeolithic materials. But all these areas are still devoid of any skeletal remains of early man.

Further to the south of Indonesia, the whole land mass of Australia had not been considered as an area of importance in the context of early man. Stone implements having the morphology of palaeoliths were thought to be of later date. But with the discovery of fossil evidences from datable contexts, this area is gaining due importance as the dates of finds are constantly being pushed back, and the early migration of people and culture in Australia might have some relationship with southeast Asia. An intimate connection is assumed between the Australian materials on the one hand, and the Wadjak and Solo materials from Java, on the other (Poirier, 1973 : 203–04).

Stone tools as cultural traits

In this article the emphasis is on stone tools of the Palaeolithic period which is attributed to the Pleistocene epoch in terms of geological scale. The tools and their assemblages point to a number of important factors and facets of prehistoric man and his culture. Attempts will be made to explain the identity, evolution and complexity of culture in terms of stone tools, and to see whether it is possible to construct a model on the typology of stone tools.

Man emerged with his ability to make and use tools. Simultaneously, a number of anatomical and morphological factors characterise the earliest phase of hominid/pongid divergence in the process of evolution. Whether organic evolution, along with ecological shift (Mann, 1972), obliged man to make and use tools, or whether culture which evolved as a form of survival gave rise to biological evolution in the way of adaptive radiation, are major questions to be settled. Whatever the case, the direct relationship between man and his culture is not hampered in any way.

It is obvious that stone as well as other materials, such as wood, bone etc., were used by early man for producing tools. Stones are convenient tool-making materials because of their availability and physical properties. Above all, only stone tools readily survive natural decomposition so that scholars can understand the contemporary technology, types and probable functions for which the types were fashioned.

Stone tools are provided with diagnostic features by which they may be distinguished from the natural stone fragments and pseudo-tools. Tools of stone may be identified as the products of human workmanship, and the main points to be included are: general size, specific and standardised shape, technological features, functional implications (?), defined working area, traces of utilisation, etc. These features are helpful for identification of individual tools. In the case of a tool assemblage, the problem of identification turns out to be relatively simpler. In fact, the presence of an isolated stone tool may not indicate the presence of the maker in the locality concerned, because the chance of drifting is high. An assemblage, however, clearly points out the presence of contemporary man in the area. In this context the observation of the present author on the occurrence of sites with single finds and numerous finds is relevant.

During research on the Palaeolithic industries in Singhbhum (Ghosh, 1970) a factory site, Nimdih, was discovered which contained finished tools, blanks, raw materials, waste flakes, hammer stones and anvils. Within a radius of about two kilometres sporadic finds were discovered, and the number of finds thinned down from the centre to periphery. On the basis of above evidence it may probably be concluded that the factory site was located in an area where the natural resources were sufficient. Based on the factory site the prehistoric people used to cover a wider region in quest of food. The sporadic finds in the wider area resemble the finds of the central factory site. It may also be assumed that the duration of stay as well as the number of people were greater centrally than in the peripheral area. Under such circumstances it is not unreasonable to make inferences about the presence of man in the (greater) area concerned.

The occurrence of stone tools confirms the presence of man, even if the direct evidences of man are lacking. In the case of a group living during the prehistoric time period, the limiting of space and time is indeed necessary to indicate the distribution and duration of cultural tradition. The task itself is undoubtedly difficult as well as time consuming. The necessary methodology requires making distribution maps of sites and finds and compiling relative micro-chronology in terms of stratigraphy. Most of the major Palaeolithic traditions survived for considerable periods of time, which are enormous with respect to geological time span. As a matter of fact, a single specific tradition sets forth in one level, and as a result of spread with time the same tradition (or its variation) is found in the overlying levels in other areas. The variance in time dimension increases with the distance between the centre of emergence and area of spread. The centre in its own way will also give rise to modification or progress of the existing tradition, and for such change there might not be any alteration of the prevailing environment. Culture itself is inherently dynamic in nature. In the process of integration of cultural development along with the spread of greater area with time— the resultant outcome appears to be initially ambiguous. After a considerable period of time the culture centre and other region(s) within the culture area reveal two different sets of tradition. In the general process of development in an area the successive stages of development are genetically connected. With respect to spatial distribution and diffusion, the connection may be established through genesis.

As evidence of this process, stone tools are the only available and relevant data. In most cases it is not the tools as such which are utilised for the purpose of analyses but the types. The major problem lies in the classification of stone tools; each class is designed on the basis of the clustering of a number of attributes—and the emerging class is considered as a type. The type in its turn may be divided into sub-types.

Problems in typological standardisation

The problem of typology has been mentioned in detail with specific reference to south and southeast Asia (Ghosh, 1973a). Here it is necessary to give a brief review of this together with later developments. It is unnecessary to point out as ridiculous the situation of typological nomenclature often encountered with the Palaeolithic of south and southeast Asia. There is a conventional set pattern of nomenclature, but the nomenclature has been used carelessly resulting in chaotic typology. The main difficulty of such a disorderly situation lies in the absence of defined characters as well as the parameters of standard forms. Until this basic necessity is solved, the problem of communication on typology will be retained. Under the prevailing circumstances it is hardly possible to give proper importance to stone tool typology for any purpose.

How can the standardisation be achieved? To begin with, separate inventories of types should be prepared for different areas, and each type should be provided with elaborate characters which have been considered in the area. It is always essential to give sketches, photographs and metrical characters or variables. After this ground work, the analyses of characters of all the so called types are made and on the basis of clustering of characters arbitrary nomenclatures are coined to designate the type without any bias towards existing functional typology. After the completion of this exercise it is to be expected that the number of major typological classes will be appreciably reduced. From the results it will be seen that sometimes identical types were named in different ways, hampering the logical parity. Again, it is not unlikely that identical names were used to designate different unrelated types.

In spite of the differences of opinion among some scholars, it is true that there is a classical nomenclature on Palaeolithic typology. Instead of coining new terms, which is a risky business, it would be helpful if we could stick to earlier classical terms as far as possible and practicable. For such a purpose (which would be really international in character) it is advisable to set up a body of typologists for the purpose of formulating a typological nomenclature which will include both the major classes and minor classes or sub-classes. This basic work is absolutely essential for meaningful understanding of prehistoric cultures over a wide area and their interpretations at the levels of evolution, migration, diffusion and even cultural isolation. In other words the above methodology will really help the discipline towards a scientific orientation.

The criteria of standardisation are indeed many and only the major will be touched on here. To start with one can focus on the shape of the tool. Shape is customarily expressed in broad terms devoid of any precision. As a result, two different shapes are sometimes included in one shape or similar shapes are described as two different shapes. This is often met with in objects of identical shape but of different size. To denote shape, linear, curvilinear and angular measurements are to be taken into consideration, and for general uniformity of shape form the standard units should be maintained. In the author's work on the shape factor of hand axes (Ghosh, 1971b) all the forms have been converted to a unit length of 10 cm, and thereby the relative distortion of shape due to size variation was eliminated. It is true that the probability of getting tools of identical shape is remote. Therefore the relationships of shape are taken within ranges of variation, and the groups formed accordingly.

Size of tools, which has been eliminated from the shape factor, should be considered separately. Most of the tool types can be simply classified on the basis of size. Although the functions attributed to palaeoliths appear to be far from reality, even in the case of speculative function, size has an important role where the weight of the tool is automatically implied, for example with tool types like choppers or hand axes. Though the shape is the same in the case of both bigger and smaller forms the functions must have been different, at least in the nature of heavy duty and light duty tools. Nevertheless, it is hard to agree with Movius (1948 : 350) who made the distinction between the chopper and the scraper only on the basis of the difference in size. The other differences between the types are in raw material, technological manifestations and the nature of the cutting edge (Ghosh, 1974a).

Technology is actually part and parcel of typology. Their close relationship is evidenced in the realm of typological development. The level of technological observation in the context of typology is mainly two-fold. First, there is gross technology in terms of free flaking or controlled flaking where the process of flaking technique and its outfits are considered (eg. stone anvil or hammer and cylinder hammer). Secondly, there is intensive study of the flaking where the process of flaking and its outcome are investigated. Here the area, concentration, arrangement, number and proportion of different forms of flake scars are included. A detailed study of flake scars indicates the utility of flaking whether it was for general shaping, convenient grip, retouching the working area for the purpose of sharpening, pointing, serrating, etc. In technological mani-

festation, there is often found a broad pattern of resemblance in the assemblages of a specific industry irrespective of types. If the scale of technological attributes is better prepared, the course of technological spread as a part of culture can be identified to a considerable extent. An example in support of the above hypothesis may be shown from the Palaeolithic industries of India. Any type of the earlier part of the Palaeolithic period, i.e. of pebble-core element, has a close general uniformity, if found from any area of the peninsular of India. The closeness of the sites is directly related to the amount of resemblances. On the other hand some are of the opinion that lower Palaeolithic hand axes from south Africa and south India are so identical that it is difficult to distinguish the south African hand axes from the south Indian ones. But the similarity is simply of types, not of the tradition of technological workmanship. At least the author has this impression from a study of hand axes of south Africa and south India which are stored in the Department of Anthropology of the University of Calcutta. This is again confirmed by the author's study of Palaeolithic materials from Europe, Africa, the whole of southeast Asia and even of Australia. It may be mentioned that the Australian horse-hoofed scrapers are comparable with Indian steep core scrapers but from a close examination major differences can be pointed out. Of course, the differences of traditional elements are better identified in tools with relatively greater technological workmanship. In the case of choppers with fewer technological manifestations the differences are less and the task of discrimination is more difficult.

Very little attention is paid to the form of raw material out of which the tool is made—pebble, core, flake, blade-like flake and blade. In the majority of the instances only the form has been mentioned without stating the implications involved both in typology and technology. In the Palaeolithic culture of India the form of raw material is found to follow the chronological ordering, and the main elemental stages are: pebble-core, flake and flake-blade (Ghosh, 1969). Specific technology was applied for fabricating the form of raw material which is an essential task in flake and flake blade elements. Moreover, some new types appeared during flake-blade element, as burin or denticulate (Ghosh, 1974b), which can only be manufactured on a blade.

In the priority list of characters for identifying the types, the most important attribute is the working area. This is not only helpful for typological classification but also for making subclasses. This character is of real empirical relevance if worked out properly. The main basis of typological classification indirectly and unconsciously lies on speculative function. The nature, form and orientation of working area are direct in nature and their variations point to the fact of working with the tool. The complex working area in hand axes is indicative of complex (multi) functions whereas the working area in a scraper is without complication—the functional purpose being simple. However, the working areas of scrapers do differ in form and on the basis of them more explicit functions may be pointed out.

Tools of primary level of emergence

Stone tools of the Palaeolithic period, in the form of generalised types, emerged through a continuous process of basic operational stages which included, perhaps, the use of natural and convenient objects as artifacts, and the making as well as use of *ad-hoc* tools. The outcome of basic tool types may be considered as the result of cumulative products of technology and skill of the preceding stages.

Like the earliest stages of human evolution the primary levels of emergence of tools are enigmatic. The main difficulty lies in the transition(s), where the differentiation of tools or other artifacts from other objects is the crucial task. There was a universal stage when the progenitor of man did not make and use tools—a lack of culture, at least in its material manifestation. What sort of background led him to start culture? This important issue is still to be answered, and what we know (rather think) is mostly speculative assumption. Despite this there is a logic behind this enquiry, which sets forth the problem of crises and their overcoming. The crises triggered the guiding forces of cultural norms which resulted in the overcoming of critical circumstances. The crises were mainly of survival at the level of primary necessity which cannot be tackled only with simply biological adaptation; and superorganic adaptation became essential.

Therefore, it is not unlikely that the forerunners of man, belonging to the Hominidae, might have used tools. The suggestion of Simons (1964) and Simons and Pilbeam (1965) accords with the argument set forth. According to them *Ramapithecus punjabicus*, who lived *c.* 15 million years ago, had 'several anatomical, behavioural and cultural elements' with the possession of 'an increasing use of tools'. Also, Napier (1963) thinks:

> ... normal cultural tool making must have been preceded by a lengthy ad hoc tool making, and even earlier of tool making ... Cultural tool making must be looked upon as a culminating event in a continuum of manual activity commencing perhaps as early as Miocene ...

This kind of attempt to correlate man and his culture is seldom met with in the study of fossil and cultural materials of Java where they are found almost in association.

At the outset two main hindrances make it difficult to standardise *ad hoc* tools: one hindrance is their recognition, and the other is the absence of any set pattern. Most of the *ad hoc* tools had perhaps a 'use and throw' principle. If the *ad hoc* tools were found to be functionally suitable, any fabrication on them was avoided. When functionally suitable pieces were absent, minimum production energy was applied for the required shaping. With a view to understanding and examining *ad hoc* tools, signs of utilisation, in the form of battering marks or wear and tear, should be intensively observed. Once the presence of utilisation marks is confirmed the primeval technology can be investigated. As pointed out earlier, the standardisation of *ad hoc* tools is perhaps impracticable. In spite of this the arrangement and ordering of *ad hoc* tools from different areas, more especially where they are found with the fossil remains of their supposed makers, may serve as an index inventory and the guide lines may be formulated for tentative standardisation. Further, the tentative scale of *ad hoc* tools may be rectified by comparison with the standard form of tools. This is one of the ways of knowing the common functional need as well as the development of types. Practically no attempts, however, have been made along this line, even in theoretical research.

Palaeolithic types in south and southeast Asia

The Palaeolithic industrial sites are found over almost all south and southeast Asia. It is necessary to point out the salient features of some specific industries. A more comprehensive summary has been published by the present author (Ghosh, 1971c and 1973b).

There is a considerable amount of diversity in the Palaeolithic culture of India, and at least two main Palaeolithic traditions are differentiated, one in the peninsular part dominated by a bifacial complex (known as Madrasian) and the other in the extra peninsular region where the chief typological constituents are choppers and the complex has been attributed to Soan (de Terra and Paterson, 1939; Movius, 1948 and 1949). Later researches in these two major areas were probably directed by this preconceived idea of two distinctly separate culture areas and the results are in most of the cases homological in nature (Sen, 1955; Lal, 1956). To explain the intermediate region lying in between these two cultural areas, a third area was proposed as an overlapping zone or the meeting ground; it covers a big area between northeast India (Krishnaswami and Soundararajan, 1951) and central India (de Chardin, 1953). This again supports the idea of a predetermined layout of culture area. Subsequent researches in the centres of the major culture areas, viz. in the areas of Soan culture complex (Paterson and Drummond, 1962; Graziosi, 1964) and Madrasian tradition (Ghosh, 1973c) have not been able to approve the idea of two main culture areas. The concept of a meeting ground of two separate cultural traditions could not be substantiated in the area of transition (Sen and Ghosh, 1963). As a matter of fact, it appears that there is an appreciable amount of industrial or cultural unity against other kinds of diversity. The author's work in the sub-continent of India has revealed that there are three chrono-cultural stages in the Palaeolithic culture complex of this vast region and they are: Pebble-Core element, Flake element and Flake-Blade element. It is true of course that some amount of variability is observed in different geographical areas within the region, but the overall pattern of industrial sequence is more or less similar everywhere. Each element may again be subdivided into smaller units on the basis of techno-morphological characters of the content, substantiated with geological stratigraphy. For example, the Pebble-Core element has two substages in the main, and they are Indian Abbevellian and Acheulian. The Acheulian, again in its turn has three subunits, as Acheulian I, II and III. Appearance, survival, extinction and reappearance of technological manifestations and typological morphology have also been indicated and explained.

Palaeolithic materials from southeast Asia have never been compiled and treated in an integrated way, except for the pioneering attempt made by Movius (1955). His data were given earlier and the amount was relatively meagre compared with its present state. It is already high time to pursue Movius's line of investigation on a larger scale and with intensive studies.

The present state of Palaeolithic research in Thailand is perhaps still ambiguous. On the one hand stratigraphic information is scarce, and on the other the techno-typological interpretation is not very convincing. In earlier works (Sarasin, 1933a and 1933b; Heider, 1957a and 1957b; Sorensen, 1962) there are only reports on the occurrence of so called Palaeolithic types, mainly choppers and some hand axes, but it appears to be insufficient to confirm the types as palaeoliths *sensu stricto*. Very recent work in the same region by Maleipan (1972) uses again the typological basis of van Heekern (1947a, 1947b and 1948) and others. But is the typology alone sufficient to discriminate these assumed Palaeolithic materials from the Hoabinhian? Probably not. There is a similar problem with Assam materials, where Neolithic debris has been reported as Palaeolithic tools, ignoring all the contexts of occurrence, assemblage, technology and even critical typology. The Palaeolithic industry of Burma which is known as Anyathian, has an important bearing on the contemporary culture area of southeast Asia. Works of Morris (1932, 1935, 1936 and 1937) were very preliminary in nature, but were compensated for later by Movius (1943). Related work in Vietnam by Boriskovsky (1968, 1968-1969, 1969a and 1969b) is very interesting for the occurrence of simultaneous assemblages of choppers, hand axes and cleavers.

The position of the Tampanian industry of Malaya is really chaotic, and it is already high time to reclassify the whole material to understand the *real* typology instead of the highly distorted classification made by Sieveking (1958; in Walker and Sieveking, 1962). About the chronology of palaeolithic culture in Malaya, as proposed by Walker (1956 and in Walker and Sieveking, 1962), there is a considerable amount of disagreement (Ibrahim, 1973).

In the whole of south and southeast Asia, Indonesia is still considered to be the most important area for its enormous materials of fossil man (a recent comprehensive account is given by Jacob, 1973) and contemporary culture, known as Patjitanian discovered by von Koenigswald (1936). A brief report of the above collection was made by Movius (1949). The conspicuous contradictions in typological nomenclature between von Koenigswald and Movius has been pointed out by the present author (Ghosh, 1973b). Scholars interested in Pleistocene stratigraphy, environment, culture and fossil man, are impatient for fuller reports on Patjitanian collections. A similar set of data, collected by von Koenigswald, has been worked over very recently (von Koenigswald and Ghosh, 1973) and the materials are from the Trinil beds of Sangiran.

Other works on Indonesian artifactual finds (Harrison, 1959; Soejono, 1961) are mostly based on an earlier framework. Slight confusion on the typology of the Patjitanian was probably made by van Heekeren (1955, 1972). Bartstra (1973) in his report of a new research on the Patjitanian culture has furnished very preliminary observations on the geomorphology of the region, stratigraphy and spread of artifacts. His *new* ideas are perhaps much too novel and are hitherto unknown in the usual concept of culture: this is evidenced by his suggestion to revise the accepted statement: 'Patjitanian as a single, uniform culture'. It is obvious that in 'a single, uniform culture' the development of techno-typological traits are not at all unlikely. The report of the presence of hand axes in the Patjitanian culture is not new. However, the application of modern methodology in such an area is really welcome, and his additional observations and results, where satisfactory, will of course be appreciated.

The amount of work, carried out in the Philippines, within a limited time span, is really interesting. Moreover the integrated methodology of the work is directed correctly. The ground work of Palaeolithic research in this part of southeast Asia is indeed meaningful, and a typological taxonomy is being sought for the Cabalwanian industry (Fox and Peralta, 1972; Fox, 1973). With changes in the concept of culture and its diffusion, it appears to be necessary to make an intensive comparative study of tool types and technology between south and southeast Asia on the one hand, and Australia on the other It may be frankly conceded that the author's information on Australian materials is limited and he hardly wishes to intrude in this domain. In passing, the present author does not know how much White's remark (1974) is data-based.

More importantly they [the stone artifacts from Australia, New Guinea Highlands and Tasmania] are within the same general tradition as the southeast Asian 'chopper-chopping-tool' industries which persisted in that area from the time of Java man until the post-Pleistocene.

The stretching of geographical areas of research both from Asia to Australia and from Australia to Asia may be interesting in connection with the migration of early man and diffusion of stone age cultures.

Model for stone tool typology

In designing the model the structural parts are most important. The major constituents of the proposed model are: geographical area, chronology, broad typology in the macro level, and intensive typology in the micro level. Besides these, there are other points which will eventually emerge in course of discussion of the broad headings.

Location of geographical area indicates the spatial distribution of culture, or in other words the area of a specific culture which can be demarcated. In all circumstances, within the culture area there will be a centre of origin from which the culture spread through the process of diffusion. In general the movement of culture is more or less uniform, but the occurrence of hinderances on its way is not unlikely. Primary obstacles met with are natural barriers and if counteracted by cultural forces and the need of the recipient area—the natural hurdles are overcome in the flow of culture. Culture itself sometimes acts as a barrier in two main ways. In one, the culture (being isolated and somewhat conservative) does not make any kind of penetration into areas of other culture. In the other one the culture, being highly sensitive, makes obstruction for other cultural contact. In spite of these negations, cultural contacts are not rare. This is perhaps due to the fact that early man, the bearer of Palaeolithic culture, was nomadic in his economic pursuits. And it is not unlikely that he ventured in other territory and accepted and assimilated the culture of a new region. Besides this, at times the environmental shifts brought about quite different climatic régimes, and early man, like his animal contemporary, failing adjustment for survival was forced to another area.

In most cases maps on cultural diffusion are misleading as they are set flat on two dimensions, and consideration of time depth is neglected. In a wide culture area, having a number of sites in datable context, the diagrammatic representation will be self explanatory showing the direction of diffusion. Moreover, data on palaeo-environment and its change through time, if available, will be of much help to account for the movement of culture. In palaeo-anthropology the concepts on cultural change and cultural development are not well-defined. In fact culture, in its trait complexes, changes with the overall alteration of the setting in the perspective of ecology. Change is brought about by force or pressure and its sources may be one or more. Cultural development, however, is innate modification directed towards betterment.

Very unfortunately, geomorphological studies in the vast area under consideration are very scarce. Location of sites in two areas, wide apart, in different chronographic frameworks are not sufficient to draw conclusions about diffusion. It is still to be discovered whether migration during the Pleistocene epoch was possible between the two regions or whether it was hampered by natural boundaries, not only impassable hills or dividing drainage but also thick forest or other such separating zone.

Unlike geographical area, chronology has always been emphasised in Pleistocene study, which is itself mainly directed towards chronology, primarily in terms of geological dating. In its development chronology highlighted other kinds of relative dating, including typological dating. It was slightly odd when the dating of the Pleistocene was made in terms of Palaeolithic typology, while the typologists were seeking to date the types with other chronological methods. Palaeontology is one of the methods for determining chronology, at least in a relative way; human palaeontology offered a tentative chronology. Tool types were perhaps assumed by chronologists to be the fossilised remains of human behaviour and treated like organic fossils. But this is a speculative assumption. Culture, being super-organic, considerably deviates from biological or organic processes and above all some amount of social and psychological factors is involved in the matrix of culture.

An appreciable amount of error in chronology has been compensated for by chronometric dating devices. Simultaneously an arbitrary scale can be computed on the basis of fossil man from Java. A study on cultural chronology may be set forth with the geological dating of the main periods within the Pleistocene (eg. lower, middle and upper) and then fixing the sub-period within the main period (eg. lower part of the middle Pleistocene). With the help of data available from absolute dating, this chronographic framework may be verified. Finally the industrial assemblages from datable contexts may be calibrated with the above mentioned chronological structure. The data on chronology and cultural assemblage from different areas, when plotted over a wider area, offers a meaningful picture. The course of study may be extended further for finding out the iso-chron. In such circumstances the expected chronology may be deduced for data on cultural or fossil remains of man otherwise without chronological information. The typo-technological characters of cultural content help in confirming the date by comparison with remains which possess chronological information. This method, if applied intensively, may give rise to the broad scaling of cultural chronology.

The typology of stone tools may be expressed as a system of classification in which the structual and functional characters of tools are properly examined for the purpose of splitting the groups as well as lumping together individual specimens to form distinct classes or groups. The structural forms of classes are arranged on the bases of chronological ordering and techno-morphological evolution. In such circumstances we can expect to understand the emergence of types, their survival, time spectrum, process of development and transformation of typological range.

The main purpose in making a tool type lies in specific function(s) and a necessary technology is implied for achieving the maximum result. Functional inferences about palaeoliths are speculative. But why were different types made? The main differences are to be seen in the working edge around which the general morphology was arranged. As a matter of fact, barring speculation on functional need, typology itself can be arranged in a functional scheme.

The structural-functional approach may be elaborated with the help of typological data. Three main types, viz. choppers, hand axes and cleavers, have a sequential arrangement in the perspective of chronology. Choppers, in most cases, are the earliest type and went on developing through time. The next type, the hand axe, came later and has some amount of resemblance to, as well as difference from, the initial type—the

chopper. Difference is mainly of orientation of working area, to better serve the specific purpose. Accordingly, other differences came into being and they are shape, morphology, arrangement and concentration of flake scars, etc. On the other hand, despite these differences the resemblances between hand axes and choppers are still there and this can be conspicuously shown during the process of manufacture. At one stage, in the process of making a hand axe, the unfinished product is more like a chopper. It would not really be impractical to assume that one of the ways for the transformation of types from chopper to hand axe is perhaps by the route of modification which ultimately gave rise to a specific type. The author holds the same idea in the case of the hand adze (Ghosh, 1972). Cleavers, which are characteristic of the Asiatic Palaeolithic complex, might have emerged from the hand adze which is also conspicuous by its presence. In the context of the first appearance of cleaver in the Olduvai Gorge, Leakey (1951) reported the occurrence of a hand axe broken at its anterior part, and he thinks that this ultimately created the idea of the new type. Such a suggestion is far from reality, because a hand axe with anterior breakage does not serve the purpose of a cleaver in any way at all.

The micro-level of examination of typological features has gained importance in recent years with the application of attribute analysis. This method has rarely been used with lower Palaeolithic tool types, and in the context of south and southeast Asia its use is virtually absent. Attribute analysis in the micro-level would be useful in two main ways. First, checking on typological structure which is formulated on the macro-level, and secondly, finding out the differential characters of type classes with the help of clustering of attributes which again in its turn is the way of making the sub-classes. The whole integrated methodology boils down to the meaningful understanding of classification of types in material and abstract levels.

As stated earlier, in building up the model of typology of stone tools the major constituent factors are time, space and tool assemblages. If all the factors were considered simultaneously, in an integrated way, the typology would emerge and the explanation of related agents would be easier.

The process of integration starts at the basic level of geographical distribution of sites which are yielding the fossil skeletal or cultural materials within the greater area of coverage. The distribution map is first contained within a circle, and inside the boundary circle a number of concentric circles are drawn. The circles should be drawn in such a way that any site may be marked on the circumference of a circle.

To represent the horizontal distribution in time depth it is necessary to prepare a two dimensional diagram with two axes, for time and space. The time scale is a vertical one, and in accordance with this type of map and location of sites similar concentric circles are placed horizontally. The distribution of sites will now lie on the bases of two parameters, time and space. This dimensional set up represents the relative chronology of a specific site. Proper interpretation of such a diagram will lead to tentative assessments on migration of early man or distance and direction of culture diffusion.

With the application of this process one can try to get further detail. The distribution map in this case would be more comprehensive. It is based not merely on geographical distribution, but on corroboration of other information which has already been gathered and analysed. The map is a multifaceted one and the main points of consideration are: geographical distribution, chronology in terms of both relative and absolute dating methods (as far as available) and finally the sorting of assemblages which comprise fossil finds of early man expressed in terms of relevant anatomical and morphological features, as well as cultural materials with broad typology.

The redistribution of this composite data in the Pleistocene scale, with broad divisible units, will present a clearer picture on the development of fossil man as well as his culture. The assemblages of cultural materials from different regions or sites, if arranged chronologically, show the process of cumulation of cultural traits tending towards development. It is also expected that the number of sites increases with time and the cultural materials are better in form and perhaps in function. On the basis of the same it may not be unjustified to indicate population increase.

Cultural materials, when found in a stratigraphic context, are indicative of environmental condition. This is another line of investigation for understanding the process of ecological adjustment. Differences in cultural traits in the form of tool types in different ecological niches may be accounted for with the help of this exercise. Why do certain specific types, especially highly modified or new ones, emerge at a certain period? If the answer is need, need brought about by climatic change, that too may be sought with the aid of this scheme.

Finally, the problem of explicit typology is described here. For all practical purposes, especially to eliminate the bias from the conventional ambiguous classification, it is always better to start with an assemblage, preferably of a larger tool population found in a datable context. Each specimen should be examined on the basis of a number of relevant attributes of physical, technological, morphological and functional nature. This level may be considered as the basis level (I. *specimen level*) of examination. After a thorough investigation sub-types, unifacial and bifacial; hand axes with a number of primary classes of tools can be recognised. In each class the major attributes and their cluster are common, of course

within a range of variation. The group or class formed in this way of accumulation is considered at a different level, known as II. *population level*. The groups formed at the population level are in fact the assortment of initial classes, and one class is separated from the other. The range of variation of each attribute for specific class should be considered to find the mean. Means of all the broad attributes under consideration have been put together to make the type class (the range of variation for each attribute should also be stated). Analysis on this level may be expressed as III. *type level*.

The typological model may further be extended to IV. *subtype level*. In the type level, a number of type classes will come out. The specimens within a type class have some amount of similarity, on the basis of which the class is formulated. But it is also found that there are some differences among the constituent specimens, and another set of attributes is responsible for this difference. Obviously, these attributes were not considered in the type level analysis. Significant attributes may be selected from the second set of attributes, and on the basis of the same the type may be sub-classified into a number of minor classes. Examples of sub-types are choppers with sub-types, unifacial and bifacial; hand axes with a number of sub-types on the basis of shape; the sub-types of cleavers are made according to shape or form of the cutting edge. These examples state that the criteria are not uniform throughout, but depend on the type and its character of variability.

This is not the right place to discuss further the classification of fossil man. But it would be most relevant if the organic stages of human evolution could be equated with the cultural stages. The limitations are greater for the latter, but a broad formulation may be possible in which the above scheme of classification would be useful. The rate of progress in cultural development is more than the biological one. A conjunctive approach on the evolution of man and his culture may open up a vista of interaction between the two. Their mutual relationship possibly enhanced man for survival and progress.

References

Bartstra, G.J., 1973. The Patjitan culture. *Paper svbmitted to Conference on the Early Palaeolithic of East Asia*, Montreal (xeroxed).

Boriskovsky, P.I., 1968. Vietnam in primeval times, part 1. *Soviet Anthropology and Archaeology*, 7(2) : 14–32.

—— 1968–69. Vietnam in primeval times, part II. *Soviet Anthropology and Archaeology*, 7(3) : 3–19.

—— 1969a. Vietnam in primeval times, part III. *Soviet Anthropology and Archaeology*, 8(1) : 70–95.

—— 1969b. Basic problems of the prehistoric archaeology of Vietnam. *Asian Perspectives*, 9 : 83–85.

De Chardin, T., 1953. The idea of fossil man. *In* A.L. Kroeber (ed.) *Anthropology today*, pp. 93-100. Chicago: Chicago University Press.

De Terra, H. and T.T. Peterson, 1939. *Studies on the ice age in India and associated human culture*. Washington: Carnegie Institute.

Fox, R., 1973. The Philippines palaeolithic. *Paper submitted to Conference on the Early Palaeolithic of East Asia*, Montreal (xeroxed).

—— and J.T. Peralta., 1972. Preliminary report on the palaeolithic archaeology of the Cagayan valley, Philippines, and the Cabalwanian industry. *Seminar on Southeast Asian Prehistory and Archaeology*, 1:1-39.

Ghosh, A.K., 1969. Developmental pattern of palaeolithic

culture in India. *In* M. Ters (ed.) *Etudes sur le Quaternaire dans le Monde*, pp. 1033-38. Paris: VIII Congres INQUA.

—— 1970. The paleolithic culture of Singhbhum. *Transactions of the American Philosophical Society*, 60:1-68.

—— 1971a India and the evolution of man. *In* V.V. Novotny (ed.) *Proceedings of the Anthropological Congress dedicated to Ales Hrdlicka*, pp. 89-100. Prague: Academia.

—— 1971b The study of handaxe shapes. *Proceedings of the the VII Pan African Congress of Prehistory and Quaternary Studies*, Addis Ababa, Section 1 (in press).

—— 1971c Ordering of lower palaeolithic traditions in south and southeast Asia. *Archaeology and Physical Anthropology in Oceania*, 6(2):87-101.

—— 1972 Hand adzes in the palaeolithic culture of India. *Asian Perspectives*, 15:158-66

—— 1973a The palaeolithic typology in south and southeast Asia. *Paper submitted to Conference on the early Palaeolithic of East Asia*. Montreal (xeroxed).

—— 1973b Chopper/chopping and bifacial traditions in south and southeast Asia—a reappraisal. *Proceedings of IX International Congress of Anthropological and Ethnological Sciences*, Chicago (in press).

—— 1973c Emendation of Madrasian industry. *In* Graga Novak (ed.) *Proceedings of VII International Congress of Prehistoric and Protohistoric Sciences*, pp. 38–49. Belgrade.

—— 1974a Concept of chopper/chopping tools complex in India. *In* A.K. Ghosh (ed.) *Perspectives in Palaeoanthropology*, pp. 221-34. Calcutta: Firma K.L. Mukhopadhyay.

—— 1974b Denticulates in India—examination of a type concept. *Journal of the Hong Kong Archaeological Society*, 5 : 47–56.

Goodall J., 1963. The feeding behaviour of chimpanzee—a preliminary report. *Symposia of the Zoological Society of London*, 10:39-47.

—— 1965. Chimpanzee of the Goombe stream reserve. *In* I. De Vore (ed.) *Primate behaviour—field studies of monkeys and apes*, pp. 425-73. New York: Holt, Rinehart and Winston.

Graziosi, P., 1964. *Prehistoric research in northwestern Punjab*. Leiden: E.J. Brill.

Harrison, T., 1959. Archaeological and ethnological results from Niah Caves, Sarawak. *Man* 59(2):1-8

—— 1970. The prehistory of Borneo. *Asian Perspectives*, 13:17-45

—— 1973. Present status and problem for palaeolithic studies in Borneo and adjacent islands. *Paper submitted to Conference on the Early Palaeolithic of East Asia*, Montreal (xeroxed).

Heider, K.G., 1957a New archaeological discoveries in Kanchanburi Journal of the Siam Society, 45:62-70.

—— 1957b A brief summary of the work in Thailand. *Asian Perspectives*, 1:61-63.

Ibrahim, Al Rashid, Bin Mohd, 1973. Malaysian prehistory—an analysis. *In* D.P. Agrawal and A. Ghosh (eds.) *Radiocarbon and Indian Archaeology*, Bombay: Tata Institute of Fundamental Research.

Jacob, T., 1964. A new Hominid skull cap from Pleistocene Sangiran. *Anthropologica*, 6:97-104.

—— 1966. The sixth skull cap of *Pithecanthropus Erectus*. *American Journal of Physical Anthropology*, 25(3):243-60.

—— 1967. Recent *Pithecanthropus* finds in Indonesia. *Current Anthropology*, 8(5):501-04.

—— 1973. Palaeoanthropological discoveries in Indonesia with special reference to the finds of the last two decades. *Journal of Human Evolution*, 2(6):473-85.

Jones, C. and J. Sabater Pl., 1969. Sticks used by chimpanzee in Rio Muni, West Africa. *Nature* (London), 223:100-01.

Krishnaswami, V.D. and K.V. Soundararajan, 1951. The lithic tool-industries of the Singrauli basin. *Ancient India*, 7:40-65.

Lal, B.B., 1956. Palaeoliths from the Beas and Banganga valleys. *Ancient India*, 12:58-92.

Leakey, L.S.B. 1951. *Olduvai gorge—a report on the evolution of the handaxe culture in beds I-IV*. Cambridge: Cambridge University Press.

Le Gros Clark, W.E., 1950. *History of the primates*, 2nd ed. London: British Museum.

Maleipan, V., 1972. Old stone age tools at Chieng Saen. *Journal of the Faculty of Archaeology, Silpakorn University*, 4(1):42-43.

Mann, A., 1972. Hominid and cultural origins. *Man*, 7(5):379-96.

Morris, T.O., 1932. A palaeolith from upper Burma. *Journal of Burma Research Society*, 22:19-20.

—— 1935. The prehistoric stone implements of Burma. *Journal of Burma Research Society*, 25:1-39.

—— 1936. A Palaeolith from Yenangyaung. *Journal of Burma Research Society*, 26:119-21.

—— 1937. Prehistoric stone implements from the Knobyinbyint of the Irrawady and Paunglaung rivers. *Journal of Burma Research Society*, 27:74.

Movius, H.L. Jr., 1943. The stone age of Burma. *Transactions of the American Philosophical Society*, 32:431-93.

—— 1948. The lower palaeolithic cultures of southern and eastern Asia. *Transactions of the American Philosophical Society*, 38(4):329-40.

—— 1949. Lower palaeolithic archaeology in southern Asia and far east. *Papers of the Peabody Museum of American Archaeology and Ethnology*, 19(3).

—— 1955. Palaeolithic archaeology in southern and eastern Asia, exclusive of India. *Journal of World History*, 2(2):257-82; (3):520-53.

Napier, J.R., 1963. The locomotor functions of hominids. *In* S.L. Washburn (ed.) *Classification and Human evolution*, pp. 178-84. Chicago: Aldine.

Nishida, T., 1973. The ant-gathering behaviour by the use of tools among wild chimpanzee of the Mahali mountains. *Journal of Human Evolution*, 2(5):357-70.

Paterson, T.T. and H.J.H. Drummond, 1962. *Soan the palaeolithic of Pakistan*. Karachi: Dept. of Archaeology, Govt. of Pakistan.

Poirier, F.E., 1973. *Fossil men—an evolutionary journey*. Saint Louis: C.V. Mosby.

Sarasin, F., 1933a Recherches prehistoriques au Siam. *L'Anthropologie*, 42:1-40.

—— 1933b Prehistoric researches in Siam. *Journal of the Siam Society*, 26:171-202.

Sartono, S., 1961. Note on a new find of *Pithecanthropus mandible*. *Publikasi Teknik Seri Paleontologi*, 2:1-51.

—— 1964. On a new find of another Pithecanthropus skull—an announcement. *Bulletin of the Geological Survey of Indonesia* 1(1):2-5.

Sen, D., 1955. Nalagarh palaeolithic culture. *Man in India*, 35(3):176-84.

—— and A.K. Ghosh, 1963. Lithic culture-complex in the Pleistocene sequence of the Narmada valley, central India. *Rivista di Scienze Preistoriche*, 18:1-23.

Sieveking, A. de G., 1958. The palaeolithic industry of Kota Tampan, Perak, northwestern Malaya. *Asian Perspectives*, 2:91-102.

Simons, E.L., 1964. On the mandible of *Ramapithecus*. *Proceedings of the National Academy of Sciences*, 51:528-35.

—— and D.R. Pilbeam, 1965. Preliminary revision of the *Dryopithecinae*. *Folia Primatologia*, 3:81-152.

Soejono, R.P., 1961. Preliminary notes on new finds of lower palaeolithic implements from Indonesia. *Asian Perspectives*, 5(2):217-32.

Sorensen, P., 1962. *The Thai-Danish expedition*. Copenhagen: Munksgaard.

Steward, J.H., 1973. 2nd printing. *Theory of culture change—the methodology of multilinear evolution*. Urbana: University of Illinois Press.

Struhsker, T.T. and P. Hunkeler., 1971. Evidence of tool-using by chimpanzee in the Ivory coast. *Folia Primatologia*, 15:212-19.

Suzuki, A., 1966. On the insect eating habits among wild chimpanzees living in the savanna woodland of western Tanzania. *Primates*, 7(4):481-87.

van Heekeren, H.R., 1947a Stone age discoveries in Siam. *Chronica* Natural, 103-12.

—— 1947b Stone Axes from the railway of death. *Illustrated London News*, 210:359.

—— 1948. Prehistoric discoveries in Siam 1943-44. *Proceedings of the Prehistoric Society*, 14:24-32.

—— 1955. New investigations on the lower palaeolithic Patjitan culture in Java. *Berita Dinas Purbakala*, 1.

—— 1972. *The stone age of Indonesia*, 2nd Ed. 's-Gravenhage: Verh. Kon. Inst. Taal.

von Koenigswald, G.H., 1936. Early palaeolithic stone implements from Java. *Bulletin of the Raffle Museum*, 1 (series-B):52-60.

—— and A.K. Ghosh, 1973. Stone implements from the Trinil beds of Sangiran, central Java, I-II. *Konikl. Nederl. Akademie van Wetenschappen*, Series-B 76(1):1-34.

Walker, D., 1956. Studies in the Quaternary of Malaya Peninsula. *Federation Museum Journal*, 1-2:19-39.

—— and A. de G. Sieveking., 1962. The palaeolithic industry of Kota Tampan, Perak, Malaya. *Proceedings of the Prehistoric Society*, 28:103-39.

Weidenreich, F., 1945. *Giant early man from Java and south China*. Anthropological papers of the American Museum of Natural History, no. 40, Pt. 1.

White, J.P., 1974. Man in Australia—present and past. *Newsletter of the Far Eastern Prehistory Association*, 3:13-27.

Simple tools and complex technology

Agriculture and agricultural implements in the New Guinea Highlands

JACK GOLSON

The Australasian region now has, in Timor (eg. Glover, 1971) and the Central Highlands of Papua New Guinea (eg. White, 1972 : 142–48), archaeological sequences from the late Pleistocene to historic times which give no hint in their stone technologies of basic changes in subsistence, from hunting and gathering to agriculture and within the agricultural regime itself, which they are presumed or known to have encompassed (Glover, 1971 : 178; White, 1972 : 144–47). The basic tool kit remains and no new tools appear that unequivocally mark the changes inferred on other evidence. A similar situation has been remarked for Old World contexts (eg. Higgs and Jarman, 1972 : 9–10).

For the New Guinea Highlands White has argued (1971a : 190–91) on the one hand that since the sequence is based on finds at rockshelters, it may not adequately reflect the total range of the technology of the agricultural phase and on the other that flaked stone tools, which constitute the bulk of the evidence at the excavated sites, have, when ethnographically observed in New Guinea, been used almost exclusively for woodworking and are not therefore likely to reflect the economic changes under discussion (cf. L. R. and S. R. Binford, 1966 : 291 on the distinction between 'maintenance' and 'extractive' tools). At the same time 'neolithic' ground stone axes and/or adzes (see S. and R. Bulmer, 1964 : 53 on terminology) appear to go back beyond 10 000 years, a date which White remarks (1971b : 48) need cause no surprise in view of the presence of edge-ground axes in earlier contexts in northern Australia. A date in the region of 6500–5000 BP has been accepted (eg. White, 1972 : 147–48) for the practice of agriculture in the Highlands, on the basis of palynological evidence for the progressive replacement of forest by non-forest vegetation and inferentially of the archaeological presence of the pig, an animal not native to New Guinea and today by far the most important domesticated one. Direct evidence of agriculture comes in the form of drainage of the upper Wahgi swamps for cultivation, the earliest date for which until recently was about 2300 BP.

I

The belief that changes in tools are concomitant with economic and other changes in human societies is deeply rooted in the theoretical foundations of evolutionary anthropology and prehistorians have been its most faithful latter-day adherents for the obvious reason that tools provide the bulk of their surviving evidence. The most intelligent archaeological expositor was Childe who struggled manfully over the years to make the instrumental evidence of his discipline speak in wider terms relevant to the other anthropological and historical sciences (see amongst many possible references Childe's illuminating article of 1944).

Of recent years new theoretical and methodological approaches in archaeology have tended to spread around the interpretative burden traditionally loaded on the artifact and at times to reduce it to irrelevance. Of particular interest have been the discussions of population pressure as a determining factor in economic and technological change, as exemplified by Binford's (1968) propositions about the origins of food production and Boserup's (1965) about the evolutionary development of agricultural systems. The essence of the Boserup hypothesis is that under the stimulus of population growth agricultural communities intensify their exploitation of the land through progressive shortening of the periods of fallow along a continuum from the most extensive swiddening at one end of the scale to multi-cropping at the other. The progression calls for changes in agricultural technology to ensure the productivity of the more intensively cultivated land and the changes are not adopted voluntarily because they require higher labour inputs and yield lower outputs per man-hour. The direct archaeological relevance of the Boserup model rests in its symbolisation of the agricultural technologies involved in three tools of cultivation said to give place to each other as more intensive land use replaces forest by grassland: the so-called digging stick, planting stick or dibble, proper to long-fallow systems in forest; the hoe, designed to cope with situations where a grass cover begins to invade the plots as forest regrowth is inhibited by decreased fallowing; and the plough, where thick-rooted grassland takes over altogether. Smith and Young, finding virtue in the argument and satisfaction in the implication that 'the presence of certain implements in archaeological deposits can provide valuable clues as to the type (or types) of agriculture practised' (1972 : 20), have applied the Boserup model to the archaeology of agricultural development in Greater Mesopotamia.

The New Guinea Highlands provide a useful context for students of agricultural systems to discuss Boserup's general propositions (eg. Clarke, 1966; Brookfield with Hart, 1971: 89–92), for it contains a number of societies practising agriculture of medium to high intensity enmeshed in systems of low intensity (eg. Brookfield with Hart, 1971 : 92–124). It is the aim of this paper to use the information we have about Highlands agriculture to consider the particular proposition about the relationship of implements to agricultural land use of which Smith and Young have made archaeological application.

II

It is necessary first to take a general look at the intensive systems with whose agricultural tools we shall be concerned: at the Paniai (formerly Wissel) Lakes and the Baliem Valley in Irian Jaya and through a large block of country from the Southern to the Eastern Highlands of Papua New Guinea.

They are all high altitude systems, at 1500 m and above, characterised by labour-intensive cultivation of the sweet potato and its common physical separation from less intensively worked mixed gardens containing the other crops. There is much variation in these arrangements, but they have in common an agricultural technology designed to allow frequent and some times nigh continuous use of the same ground in a predominantly grassland environment that demands tillage to eradicate grass roots and aerate the soil if it is to be productive at all (Clarke, 1971 : 192–3; Clarke and Street, 1967).

A variety of techniques has been developed, from intimate experience of topography, soils, climate and the necessities of the plants (eg. Brookfield, 1964 : 34–37), to meet the requirements of particular situations (eg. Brookfield with Hart, 1971 : 111–14): complete tillage to pulverise the soil and conserve moisture in drier regions, with planting in ridged beds formed between groove drains or in small mounds; grid-iron ditching to lower the water table in wetter regions, with the spoil from the ditches spread over the surface of the intervening plots to serve as tilth; fertilisation by burning of grass, digging it in or burying it beneath added top soil; control of fallow by conservation and planting of trees; large mounding with mulching which not only enriches the soil but allows cultivation at higher altitudes by raising temperatures on top of and inside the mounds. Other techniques allow the spread of these practices on to more difficult ground, such as steep hillsides through slope retention with logs, fences or walls, and swamps through drainage. Brookfield (Brookfield with Hart, 1971 : 114) marks out the Dani of the Baliem Valley as applying the widest range of techniques in modification of the natural environment: on the swampy river flats systems of regional drainage carry the outflow of whole drainage districts to controlled points on the river and water is retained during dry periods by the use of cross dams; on the steep rocky hillsides dry-stonewalling serves both for fences and for permanent slope-retention.

These agricultural procedures support large populations with densities of 100–300 per square mile (38–115 per square km) of cultivated land and locally (as in areas of the Paniai Lakes, the Baliem and upper Chimbu) up to 500 (192) (Brookfield, 1962 : 245, 251), living in essentially man-managed landscapes and maintaining big herds of pigs.

III

The tools with which these complex and productive agricultural systems were traditionally maintained were few, simple and mainly of wood. They are, unfortunately, well described for only a few areas and their study is increasingly a matter of ethnographic reconstruction and archaeological recovery.

1. Stone-bladed axes or adzes were probably, as in swidden systems, universally employed for clearing woody growth in garden preparation, though the number of explicit statements is surprisingly small. Pospisil (1963 : 91–92) describes the role of the axe in clearing trees in Kapauku hill-slope gardening, in which classic swiddening techniques are used. Amongst the Baliem Dani (Heider, 1970 : 36, 39) similarly worked hill-slope gardens are cleared with the adze (1970 : 272–79), which is also employed (1970 : 40) in cutting trees and bushes that have grown during fallowing on the more intensively cultivated valley bottom. Strathern (1969 : 315) describes the axe as an essential tool in traditional upper Wahgi agriculture for cutting the robust grasses as well as trees and shrubs in garden preparation. Vicedom (Vicedom and Tischner 1943–8(I) :

185) specifically mentions the true adze as the tool used for cutting down the grasses.

All gardens, whether sweet potato or mixed, intensively or extensively worked, are fenced as a protection against pigs and the axe or adze is employed in making the posts. In the upper Wahgi swamps fence lines and the stone blades with which they were made and other tasks doubtless performed are occasional finds, as well as the grinding stones kept handy for their sharpening.

2. Stone knives of two types are mentioned by Pospisil as having been in use amongst the Kapauku. One Pospisil (1963 : 91) calls a stone machete because it performed the function of the steel-bladed machete today: cutting scrubby ground cover in preparing bush gardens and, inferentially (Pospisil, 1963 : 104, 123), reeds and shrubs in preparing valley-bottom gardens. About 20 cm long, it was of hard stone, polished on its surface and sharpened on its edge, and was held in the hand. The other, called simply a stone knife by Pospisil but not described (a drawing—Pospisil, 1963 : 278, fig. 48d—has no scale), was held in the same way as the stone machete for cutting during planting and harvesting in mixed gardens on the valley floor (Pospisil, 1963 : 109, 110, 111, 112, 117, 118, 119).

Allen (1970 : 179, 180) mentions the discovery of two stone 'knives' during initial drainage operations at the Kuk swamp in the upper Wahgi, a reed and swamp-grass environment. Though he gives no dimensions, he describes them as of ground stone, leaf-shaped, pointed at both ends and ground to a fine edge on both margins. He suggests that they would have functioned well for cutting, chopping or splitting and compares them to two examples published as possible stone copies of bronze spear or dagger heads (Bulmer and Clarke, 1970), which were collected from gardens in the northern Bismarcks, outside the Highlands proper and where grasslands are much less common. In size these compare well with Pospisil's stone machete, being 17½ cm and 19½ cm in length. Both are ground all over, but only the smaller example, with a distinct midrib on both faces, is specifically described as having a sharp edge, which it has all round, however, a disadvantage one would have though for hand use. The longer example has at one end a distinctly oval cross-section which could have served as a butt; the rest of the implement has a lenticular section.

3. Grass-cutting implements of various forms have been reported on other testimony than that of direct observation.

(i) A BAMBOO GRASS-KNIFE is described and figured by Watson (1967 : 97) as a traditional implement now replaced by the steel machete. Two examples were made for him. Over 76 cm long, they were manufactured from a longitudinal section of bamboo, both edges being sharpened except near one end which was roughly shaped to form a handle. Informants said implements of this type were used to cut grass to dry for firing a new garden plot.

(ii) TWO WOODEN IMPLEMENTS from the Eastern Highlands in the Goroka museum, labelled as having been used for grass-clearing in cultivation, are figured by Bulmer (1973 : 19 and fig. 6). Though cut out of the solid, they have two parts, a long handle and a splayed triangular blade, the apex of which appears as though inserted like a tang in the end of the handle.

(iii) STONE BLADES with wide cutting edges and sides converging somewhat to the poll are noted by Bulmer (1964 : 252–53) as forming part of a collection of stone implements made by her in east central Chimbu. One informant reported that such blades were used within living memory for cutting cane grass, though whether in the preparation of gardens is not specified.

4. The pointed digging stick was as basic a tool of Highlands agriculture as of less evolved systems elsewhere but has rarely been adequately described as regards form and function. There seems to have been a widespread, if not universal distinction between a heavy, larger-diameter, essentially men's digging stick and a light, smaller-diameter, essentially women's one, as reported by Pospisil (1963 : 96, 101, 108, 109, 110, 117) for the Paniai Lakes, Heider (1970 : 40, 279) for the Baliem Valley, Nilles (1942–5 : 208–9) for Chimbu, Vicedom and Tischner (1943–8(I) : 185, 186, 187, 224–25) for upper Wahgi (cf. Lerche and Steensberg, 1973 : 89, 101–2; Powell, 1974) (inferentially) Freund (1968 : 3–4) for Enga.

(i) THE HEAVIER DIGGING STICK, commonly described as up to 2 m in length and 4–8 cm in diameter, had main agricultural functions as a lever to break up and turn over the sod in grassland tillage for sweet potato and as a planting stick in the shifting sector of the agricultural system where mixed planting often takes place. At the Paniai Lakes and in the Wahgi valley where grid-iron ditching characterises intensive cultivation, the ground is not turned over. The plots are cleared by pulling and cutting the grass and reeds and covering them with the spoil from ditch digging. In this sector of the system the heavy digging stick has no role at the Paniai Lakes (Pospisil, 1963 : 122–24) and in the Wahgi valley it was used to dig out patches of tenacious roots (Vicedom and Tischner, 1943–8(I) : 185). Nilles (1942–5 : 208) also reports it as a ditch digging tool in Chimbu. Some examples have been turned up during modern drainage of old swamp gardening land in the upper Wahgi (Powell, 1974).

Like axes and adzes, the heavy digging stick finds employment outside the agricultural context, for example for digging cooking pits and post holes (eg. Nilles, 1942–5 : 208; Lerche and Steensberg, 1973 : 89).

(ii) THE LIGHTER DIGGING STICK, for which reported sizes vary from area to area, from 1 m down to 30 cm in length and from 2 to 4 cm in diameter, is generally a planting, weeding and tuber-harvesting tool, used in skilful co-ordination with the hand. The last two functions it performs both in the intensively and extensively cultivated sectors of the various systems, except that at the Paniai Lakes a special tool is used for all weeding (Pospisil, 1963 : 98, 99) (see **5** (iii) below), another tool for harvesting in the intensive sweet potato plots (Pospisil, 1963 : 125) (see **5** (i) below) and no tool at all for planting the sweet potato vines there (Pospisil, 1963 : 125). In general the reports suggest that the light digging stick is only used as a planting tool where the soil has been tilled but that it is the only planting tool used there. However, a remark by Vicedom (Vicedom and Tischner, 1943–8(I) : 187) suggests that the heavier digging stick may have been employed as a planting tool in turned earth in the upper Wahgi, while the lighter digging stick is certainly used for planting *Amaranthus* in both untilled and tilled gardens amongst the Kapauku (Pospisil 1963 : 111, 125).

The light digging stick is a fairly common find during drainage of the upper Wahgi swamps and one excavated specimen has been dated to about 2300 BP (Golson *et al.*, 1967; Lampert, 1967).

5. Wooden tools with expanded blade, called spatulae, spatulate spades or paddle-shaped spades, are widely reported, if inadequately described, in Highlands ethnographic literature.

From these reports it appears that they served mainly as trenching tools and earth-working spades.

(i) TRENCHING TOOLS Pospisil (1963 : 105–6, 123–24) describes the use and figures the paddle-shaped blade of a so-called 'earth knife' 80–100 cm in overall length, employed by the Kapauku in digging the drainage ditches of their valley-bottom swidden and intensive gardens. With it the mud is sliced into blocks. In the case of the swidden gardens these are thrown out by hand to form a low wall around the garden into which fence stakes are later set (Pospisil, 1963 : 105). In the case of the intensive gardens the ditch spoil is distributed on top of fresh and decomposed plant material strewn as fertiliser over the garden surface, but how this earth is spread is not described (Pospisil, 1963 : 124). The 'earth knife' is also used by women to open up the ground of the intensive gardens as the first step in sweep potato harvesting (Pospisil, 1963 : 125).

Heider (1970 : 40, 279) refers to a similar tool being used in the drained valley-bottom gardens of the Baliem Dani. Described as a paddle-shaped digging stick 150–200 cm in overall length with expanded blade 10–15 cm wide, it is said to be employed exclusively for slicing ditch mud into chunks which are lifted out by hand on to the bank and spread out evenly over the gardens as fertiliser with the feet (see also Gardner and Heider, 1968 : 47–48). Presumably the tool was used also for digging the ditches in the first place.

Nilles (1942–5 : 209–10) describes and figures a paddle-bladed implement 200 cm long with handle 4 cm in diameter and expanded blade of elliptical cross-section 15 cm wide and 3 cm thick. This was used by the Kuman of central Chimbu (lower Chimbu and adjacent Wahgi valleys) in digging the trenches of their grid-iron field systems, the loosened earth being thrown out by hand on to the surfaces of the garden plots. Nilles (1942–5 : 207, 208 and fn 9) says the tool was not known to the upper Chimbu, who did not ditch their gardens except on swampier ground. He also mentions its use in non-agricultural tasks like post-hole digging (Nilles, 1942–5 : 210).

For the upper Wahgi where a similar grid-iron garden pattern is employed, Vicedom (Vicedom and Tischner, 1943–8(I) : 186, 225) describes the use of a 'wooden spade' for trenching and illustrates two examples of its expanded blade. It appears from Vicedom that the implement was employed for removing as well as loosening the ground, for he says (1943–8 (I) : 186) that when the gardeners could remove no more soil with it, they used their hands. As in central Chimbu the spoil was spread over the garden beds.

In 1963 Watson (1967 : 95–96) collected two old 'spatulae' in the Kainantu area of the Eastern Highlands and had two more examples made for him. All are characterised by an unusual 'hilt' between blade and handle and their dimensions are fairly uniform, ranging from 103–115 cm in total length, 57–76 cm in blade length, 9–11 cm in blade width and 3·8–4·8 cm in handle diameter. Watson had the use of the tool demonstrated for him in loosening soil and detaching sod and his description of it being stabbed vertically into the ground and levered backwards and forwards is reminiscent of Pospisil (1963 : 105) on the use of the 'earth knife' by the Kapauku. Watson comments that the implement was evidently the tool with which the garden trenches were dug, the spoil being removed by hand or some other means, but he also says that it was used for breaking soil in the garden proper.

(ii) TILLING SPADE According to Freund (1968 : 3, 4) the Enga of the highland districts west of Mt Hagen heaped up the soil of their characteristic mounds, 1·5–4·5 m in diameter and

45–120 cm in height, and dug drains in the garden area with a 'paddle-shaped *yati*' (digging stick) which could be up to 15 cm wide. Meggitt (1958 : 305) says women used hands and paddle-shaped digging sticks to break up the clods mounded up by the men. Lerche and Steensberg (1973 : 92–101) had two paddle-shaped spades made for them in the upper Kaugel Valley southwest of Mt Hagen. The two spades were 128 and 121·5 cm long, with blades 6·5 and 8·8 cm wide, 2·4 and 2 cm thick and *c.* 30 and *c.* 35 cm long. They report that their informants had difficulty in trenching with these short and light implements which, however, were admirably suited to the work of opening up and remaking the sweet potato mounds, for which they were used in both a standing and kneeling position.

We have already quoted Watson on the use of the Kainantu spatulae for breaking soil as well as for trenching. Of the same area Clarke (1966 : 354) says that a paddle-shaped spade was used in pre-European times to turn the garden soil and heap it into the (small) mounds in which the sweet potato vines are planted, but this implement is not further described.

(iii) WEEDING TOOL Pospisil (1963 : 98–99, fig. 11, 125) describes the use by women of a small (16–20 cm long) paddle-shaped tool during weeding in all phases of the Kapauku agricultural system.

Paddle-shaped implements have been rescued during large-scale drainage of the upper Wahgi swamps over the past decade in greater numbers than simple digging sticks, partly because of the attraction of their more elaborate form. As a result they are more prominent in the recent literature. A collection recovered by the Department of Forestry during drainage at Kindeng consists of long, heavy trenching implements, whose use Lerche and Steensberg (1973 : 87–92) had demonstrated for them. The seven implements range in overall length from 2·52 m down to 1·47 m, or possibly 1·75 m, since the two shortest may be incomplete. Powell (1974) records a more diversified collection, with nine long-handled, relatively narrow-bladed examples (which she subdivides into seven 'large spatulate spades' and two 'small paddle-shaped spades') and two short-handled, relatively broad-bladed 'hastate spades'. The former implements range from 1·22 m to over 2·44 m in length, the latter group has a complete implement 93 cm in length and a broken one 69 cm long. An informant explained and demonstrated the use of the large spade for cutting and lifting material from ditches and that of the hastate spade for marking out plot lines, cutting the surface turf and shaping and lifting earth out of small holes.

6. Hoe Nilles (1942–5 : 210–11) describes and illustrates an adze-like tool of wood consisting of an elbow-haft and separate blade, used, like the paddle-shaped trenching tool, by the Kuman of central Chimbu and not by those of upper Chimbu. It was apparently not employed for breaking up new ground but for loosening the ground dug for garden trenches, for shaping the trenches themselves, for breaking up hard clods turned up by the digging tools—a function alternatively served here, as elsewhere, by digging sticks and bare hands—and for weeding.

7. Undescribed Vicedom (Vicedom and Tischner, 1943–8 (I): 186) mentions but does not describe a small digging stick used for cutting the walls of the agricultural ditches of the upper Wahgi absolutely vertical, and apparently squaring the bottoms as well.

The preceding review has pointed up gross deficiencies in our knowledge of the actual nature and use of agricultural tools employed in earlier life by Highlands farmers still alive, despite the attention paid to New Guinea agricultural systems over the past 15 years. It has, however, isolated two categories of implement apparently adapted to the particular character of Highlands agriculture—intensive cultivation in a grassland environment—and potentially therefore markers of its evolution. These are the various kinds of grass-cutting implement and the paddle-shaped earth-working spades (cf. Watson, 1967 : 97).

GRASS-CUTTING IMPLEMENTS These do not figure prominently or widely in the ethnograpic record and perhaps only the Eastern Highlands examples emerge as specialised grass-cutting tools. Against Bulmer's testimony for Chimbu (II3(iii) above), we must place that of Nilles who saw Chimbu agriculture in traditional operation and does not mention specialised implements for this purpose, though Bulmer's information came from further east than Nilles' observations. The stone knives of the Kapauku are used for other purposes besides grass cutting and for grass clearing are only an occasional supplement to hands (eg. Pospisil, 1963 : 104). Nor do they belong exclusively to the intensive sector of that system, where indeed because of prolonged use it may be sufficient to bury the grass growing between plantings under the soil dug out of the surrounding ditches (Pospisil, 1963 : 123). In the Wahgi systems where soil is similarly spread over the plot surface, grass was pulled by hand and tenacious roots uprooted with adzes (Vicedom and Tischner, 1943–8(I) : 184–85). In the Baliem (Heider, 1970 : 40) the heavy men's digging stick is used to cut the grass at the roots and dig out trees and bushes previously chopped by adzes. The same practice seems to have been typical of the Enga when re-establishing their sweet potato mounds (Freund, 1968 : 3, 4). Grass clearance by digging stick is also described for Chimbu and districts east (Brookfield and Brown, 1963 : 44), in preparation for complete tillage. It may be noted that where employed, fire is rarely used as a preliminary agent of clearance but for burning the distributed products of previous clearance for purposes of fertilisation (eg. Brookfield and Brown, 1963 : 45, 165).

PADDLE-SHAPED IMPLEMENTS It appears that these implements occupy a range somewhat specialised at both ends. At one end are the long, relatively narrow-bladed implements used for trenching. They are evidently the tools by which the swamps of the Paniai Lakes, the Baliem and the upper Wahgi were brought into and maintained in productive agriculture. They are also the trenching tools of the dry-land, grid-iron systems of central Chimbu and the Wahgi and apparently, from Watson's (1967 : 96) testimony, of the less elaborate trenching of agriculture further east.

It is unclear how far these tools performed agricultural functions other than trenching. In the Baliem explicitly (Heider, 1970 : 279) and at the Paniai Lakes by implication (Pospisil, 1963 : 105–6, 123–25) they did not. By the evidence of Vicedom (Vicedom and Tischner 1943–8(I) : 186) and Powell (1974 : 22) they were used in the upper Wahgi not only for cutting trenches but lifting spoil out of them. Watson (1967 : 96) suggests that his Kainantu trenching tools were also used for tillage and if Clarke (1966 : 354) is speaking of the same implements, they would have been used for mounding also.

Interestingly enough the Kainantu paddles recorded by Watson are, at 103–115 cm, somewhat shorter than trenching tools in other areas (*c.* 150+cm in the upper Wahgi) and blade width tends to be somewhat greater in proportion to blade length. In these characteristics, though not in others, they resemble the two tools made for Lerche and Steensberg (1973 : 92–93) and used in breaking open and turning the earth of the large sweet potato mounds typical of the districts west of Mt Hagen. This is possibly the best authenticated use of a paddle-shaped implement for soil tillage but Lerche and Steensberg's experiments (1973 : 93–94) suggest that even here it doubled as a trenching tool (cf. Freund, 1968 : 4). On present information the function of the short-handled, broad-bladed implements recorded by Powell (1974 : 22) seems to have been subsidiary to the long paddle-shaped tools in trenching.

The data for upper Chimbu show, however, that no new types of tool at all need be involved in intensive grassland agricultural regimes, for here ground clearance and soil tillage are accomplished with the same type of heavy digging stick used as a dibble in bush fallow systems. In other Highlands environments certain adaptations have been made, alone and in combination—draining, trenching, mounding, mulching, terracing—some of which are associated with other tools, predominantly varieties of paddle-shaped implement. In view of the likely need for ditching in other contexts, it seems improbable that as a trenching tool the type originated in response to the requirements of intensive agriculture. In the forms adapted for use as spading tools, paddle-shaped implements are widely distributed throughout the Pacific wherever there is need for soil tillage (eg. Barrau, 1958 : 9, 19–24; Best, 1925 : 21–32). As such, their archaeological discovery may well indicate the presence of more intensive forms of agriculture and almost certainly of agriculture itself, though their absence does not signify the absence of either.

This is as far as the evidence from the New Guinea Highlands allows us to go in this context in inferring forms of land use from the tools of subsistence activity. We may note the absence from this tool kit of the hoe, which figures so prominently in Boserup's scheme and in Smith and Young's application of it.

IV

Being made of wood, the implements under discussion are, however, only likely to be recovered in archaeological circumstances much more decisive for conclusions as to the nature and intensity of land use than the tools themselves. There is widespread ethnographic evidence in the New Guinea Highlands for the caching of paddle-shaped implements—and digging sticks—in garden ditches to prevent them drying out and becoming brittle (Watson, 1967 : 95–96; Lerche and Steensberg, 1973 : 87–88) and to weight them for use (Freund, 1968 : 4; Heider, 1970 : 279) and the archaeological finds in the upper Wahgi have been made in this context. It is the extent and organisation of the containing ditches which constitute the important evidence for significant interpretation.

This is not the place to describe in detail how current work in the upper Wahgi at Kuk Tea Research Station is using structural indications of this kind, in association with botanical evidence, to interpret the nature of agricultural operations in swampland and through this reconstruct the history of agricultural development in the region as a whole. It is enough to say that three phases of swamp drainage for agriculture have been identified at Kuk and interpreted on the basis of the patterns of drains that characterise them as follows:

1. *Phase I*: beginning before and possibly ending by 6000 years ago; unsystematised drainage articulated with through-flowing streams, interpreted as adventitious exploitation of a manageable environment for moisture-tolerant plants, for example taro. Activity ceased, it is thought, when insilting of the creeks required a level of labour input for swamp management judged undesirable and unnecessary at the prevailing ratio of land to population overall. This interpretation is consistent with a view that the phase falls early in the agricultural period, for which, as we have seen, a beginning date between 6500 and 5000 BP has been proposed.

2. *Phase II*: ending about 1200 years ago and not of very long duration; systematic drainage articulated with natural drainage channels, interpreted as labour-intensive cultivation of taro. This is equivalent to an agricultural system beginning about 2300 BP discovered at the Manton site in the upper Wahgi and already reported (Golson et al., 1967; Lampert, 1967), commented on (Brookfield and White, 1968; Brookfield with Hart, 1971 : 81, 84) and partially reinterpreted in the light of the Kuk evidence (Golson, 1977). The phase is thought to begin under deteriorating ratios of land to population and to end with the appearance of the South American sweet potato in the Highlands and its ready acceptance because of its higher yields, quicker maturation and greater edaphic tolerance than existing crops (Clarke, 1973). This proposition, for which the evidence, archaeological and palynological, will be presented elsewhere, runs counter to prevailing opinion which favours an arrival of the sweet potato in New Guinea within the last 400 or so years and an entry from island Southeast Asia following its introduction there by Europeans (e.g. Brookfield with Hart, 1971 : 83–84). It is worth noting that the new hypothesis implies that the plant would have entered New Guinea from a Pacific Island source, as has recently been argued on other, more general grounds by O'Brien (1972).

3. *Phase III*: beginning about 300 BP and ending between 75 and 100 years ago; elaborate drainage very much on the Kapauku pattern designed to adapt the swamp to the requirements of sweet potato cultivation. This adaptation and its vicissitudes have been described by Golson (1977) in a preliminary statement which is partly out of date. It now appears that this system was established in the Kuk swamp when natural drainage had completely ceased and that the nature of drainage organisation required came close to that of the Baliem drainage districts. It is thought to have operated as the labour-intensive phase of a dual system with less intensively worked mixed gardens on surrounding slopes and to have been a response to renewed pressures of population on land. This labour-intensive swampland regime had been abandoned throughout the upper Wahgi by the time Europeans entered the district in 1933, for reasons which are as yet obscure but may be related to the vulnerability of the system to natural and political upset. Agriculture became restricted to the drier land and the more manageable of the wetter places.

The question has been debated over the past decade as to how far the intensive techniques of modern Highlands agriculture are specific to the sweet potato in whose cultivation they are characteristically employed, and therefore of recent development in the Highlands, whatever the exact date of sweet potato introduction may have been (see review in Golson, 1977). Watson (1967 : 97) explicitly refers to the tools of cultivation in this connection when he says that while the spatulate spade and bamboo knife recorded by him may indicate agriculture specialised to the use of grassland, there are 'no clear implications, however, with regard to complete *v* other forms of tillage, and no specialisation on behalf of particular root crops seems reflected in the known tool inventory'.

Though that tool inventory is well represented amongst the finds made during recent large-scale drainage of the upper Wahgi swamps, a very small proportion of the implements has been recovered in secure stratigraphic position in terms of the three-phase agricultural sequence described above and no parallel sequence for the tools of agriculture can be proposed. Virtually all the well provenanced artifacts provided by the Kuk investigations so far belong to Phase III of the sequence there, the sweet potato phase, and amongst them the women's digging stick is prominent and paddle-shaped tools are present to the virtual exclusion of the heavy men's digging stick. A women's digging stick was found in a drain at the Manton site in a pre-sweet potato context (Golson *et al.*, 1967; Lampert, 1967). The marks of cultivation in a widespread layer of volcanic ash marking an early stage of the Phase II ditch system at Kuk, a pre-sweet potato phase thought to represent systematised swamp growing of taro, suggest planting with the heavy digging stick. The slot-type drains characteristic of this phase (Golson, 1974 : pl. 4), 30–50 cm deep and 20–40 cm wide at the top, look likely to have been made with the same implement. Tools of paddle shape, if present at this time, could have been used in the dry-land cultivation of yam. Watson (1967 : 91, 95) describes the ceremonially and technically elaborate cultivation of yam today in the Kainantu region of the Eastern Highlands, involving tillage. In New Caledonia the highly developed indigenous agricultural system was based on wet cultivation of taro by women, often in tiers of irrigated hillside terraces, and dry cultivation of yam by men in raised beds of thoroughly turned-over soil (Brookfield with Hart, 1971: 115; cf. Barrau, 1965). In a number of widely scattered Highlands localities yam, though economically unimportant, is a plant of significance for which men take major responsibility. To Watson's Kainantu example mentioned above we may add Enga (Freund, 1968 : 6; Waddell, 1972 : 51) and the Paniai Lakes (Pospisil, 1963 : 114). Taro seems to have no firm sexual associations, except at Kainantu where it definitely belongs to the male sphere (Watson, 1967 : 90–91). It is possible to conceive of it having once been the female crop in Highlands agricultural organisation, subsequently displaced by the sweet potato (cf. Watson, 1967 : 92).

V

One implement recovered during drainage of the Kuk swamps that is absent from the ethnographic repertoire of tools is a tanged and shouldered flaked 'slate' blade which Allen (1970 : 180, 181; 1972 : 187) has called a hoe and says, whether hafted to a straight or an elbow handle, would have served excellently for straightening ditch walls or for general agricultural purposes. In a provisional statement about her work at the important Wañlek site in the Kaironk Valley, Bismarck Range, on the northern fringe of the Highlands, Bulmer (1973) describes the excavation of a range of tanged slate tools in association with flake tools and axe/adze blades of lenticular cross-section in a buried soil. Structural evidence within this soil is dated around 2850 BP and charcoal from its base around 5500 BP.

While explicitly eschewing the use of the term 'hoe' in order to avoid specific attributions of function, Bulmer (1973 : 14) is nevertheless inclined to interpret some of the slate tools as digging or horticultural implements. She also suggests (1973 : 19) that the two Eastern Highlands wooden grass-clearing tools mentioned in **III3**(ii) above may indicate how some of the tanged blades were hafted. She notes (1973 : 15) the presence of more than one variety of working edge on the tanged tools, including a wide, curving type, which she compares to that of a modern grass-edging tool, and possibly the more pointed type found on the Kuk 'hoe'. Bulmer also mentions (1973 : 17) a small number of unpublished finds of tanged stone implements near Kainantu in the Eastern Highlands and in the Trobriands (cf. Allen, 1970 : 180).

It is precisely when we come to consider the distributional aspect in this way, however, that the data become uncontrolled. As both Bulmer (1973 : 17–18) and Allen (1970 : 180) appreciate, the tanged blades from Wañlek and the tanged 'hoe' from Kuk require consideration of the previously reported waisted-blade complex (eg. Golson, 1971 : 131–35, 138). This complex includes implements with a range of working-edge forms, from narrower pointed to wider curved, and a variety of hafting modifications, including tangs. Both the Papuan site of Kosipe (White *et al.*, 1970) and Bulmer's Western Highlands site of Yuku (Allen, 1972 : 184) show that the tradition had its beginnings well back in the late Pleistocene, in a presumably pre-agricultural context. Bulmer's contribution to this conference reviews the whole question.

It is furthermore difficult, when discussing tanged implements, to ignore the tanged mudstone blade from Gumine in lower Chimbu, published, by virtue of the up-turned terminals to its wide, flatly curving cutting edge, as a stone replica of a bronze socketed axe of the type found at Lake Sentani in Irian Jaya (Bulmer and Tomasetti, 1970). The reinterpretation of this piece as a tanged stone implement in its own right is reinforced by the character of a tanged slate blade recently found during garden preparation at Wurup near Kuk and brought to my attention by O. A. Christensen. This example, with wide sweeping cutting edge, offset tang and rounded asymmetrical shoulders that make one side of the tang longer than the other, might be easily compared with certain forms of Dong-son socketed bronze axe (eg. Riesenfeld, 1955 : 225, fig. 50; cf. fig. 58), did not its provenance, material, manufacture and offset tang more reasonably associate it with the Kuk 'hoe'. But what are we to say of the tanged Yodda 'axe' of obsidian (Seligmann and Joyce, 1907 : 327), with which the Gumine artifact has been compared (Bulmer and Tomasetti 1970) and which in its turn has been compared not only to a few other examples in New Guinea but to a small group of tanged artifacts widely distributed through eastern Australia as well (eg. Casey, 1934; Riesenfeld, 1955 : 242–43)?

Obviously we can say nothing profitable, though Bulmer's conference paper suggests a valuable new viewpoint in their regard. We therefore return to the implements with which we began, those from Wañlek and Kuk, to which we may add the Wurup specimen. We may note that these are made of slate and that this must be by design since other types of stone are found and were used in the region. Slate does not form a tough tool, but it can produce a thin one, and thinness is a characteristic of the implements now under discussion and may mark them off as performing specific functions. The Wañlek dates fall within the agricultural phase but before the appearance of the sweet potato. It may be that the tanged slate blades—or some of them—had a role within the earlier agricultural regime.

Best (1925 : 25–26) describes thin, tanged blades of wood of spade-like form lashed to long straight handles as tools of traditional New Zealand Maori agriculture. Typical dimensions seem to be 17 cm width and 19 cm length, which is close to the size of the Kuk 'hoe'. According to Best, the spades were not used for digging or other heavy work but were the equivalent of the modern Dutch or scuffle hoe, pushed away from the operator in weeding and soil loosening. Phillipps and Jury (1959)—a reference which I thank E. Crosby for bringing to my attention—record a spade end of similar type made of greenstone and said to be used ceremonially to open the season for sweet potato planting amongst a particular Maori group in the southern part of the North Island. If these New Zealand implements have any relevance for the interpretation of tanged slate blades in the New Guinea Highlands, the latter might have included tools for tilling the soil, possibly used in yam cultivation.

On the other hand, remembering Powell's (1974 : 22) report of the wooden hastate spade of the upper Wahgi being used for cutting turf and having regard to the long, curved cutting edge of some specimens of tanged blade, one might look upon these as representing tools of agriculture in grassland. It may not be accidental that there are resemblances in shape between the slate blades—and indeed some of the wooden paddle-shaped implements discussed earlier—and tools developed in the oceanic fringe of northwestern Europe to deal with the cultivation of wet grasslands (eg. Gailey and Fenton, 1970). Especially interesting in this connection is Evans's (1970 : 5) reference to Irish experiments in notching sward with polished stone axes, for which those with slanted cutting-edge were found to be particularly suited, for such edges are not uncommon on ground stone blades in the New Guinea Highlands.

If any of these propositions about the agricultural use of tanged slate implements is to be seriously entertained, it is necessary to ask why they are so few in Highlands stone collections, why they should not have persisted longer in the repertoire of agricultural implements and why slate was used instead of wood, but no answer to these questions can even be hazarded on present information.

VI

Future work may show whether within the tanged implements of New Guinea any can be recognised that performed specific agricultural functions and what those functions might have been. The general survey presented here of the known tools of New Guinea Highlands agriculture has revealed none that is indispensable to any form, from the simplest to the most complex, of Highlands agricultural practice, except the stone axe or adze and the digging stick which are not only common to all but also serviceable in other than agricultural contexts. Paddle-shaped implements are found as trenching tools where substantial ditching is necessary and may be present as tilling spades where earth mounding is practised.

In lowland New Guinea the most elaborate agricultural systems do not exhibit even this simple level of implement differentiation. The highly sophisticated island-garden agriculture of seasonally flooded Kolepom (Fredrik-Hendrik Island) was traditionally carried out with little more than a sharp piece of sago bark and a digging stick (Serpenti, 1965 : 21–46). The digging stick is the only real tool employed in the Abelam gardens where immense expertise is employed to produce long yams for ceremonial exchange (eg. Lea, 1966). Malinowski (1935(I) : 61–62, 132–34) notes that the technical efficiency of Trobriands agriculture is great and the more remarkable because of the rudimentary nature of the tools employed, a digging stick, an axe, an adze and the human hand.

All these descriptions of New Guinea agriculture serve as a footnote to the thesis, as recently phrased by Sahlins (1972 : 81), that 'for the greater part of human history, labor has been more significant than tools, the intelligent efforts of the producer more decisive than his simple equipment'.

Acknowledgement I wish to thank Susan Bulmer for comments on an earlier draft of this paper which has been revised in their light.

Addendum The summary of the archaeological finds from Kuk given in the above was based on two seasons' work. Three subsequent seasons have changed the picture radically: see J. Golson, No room at the top: agricultural intensification in the New Guinea Highlands. In *Sunda and Sahul: prehistoric studies in Island Southeast Asia, Melanesia and Australia*, J. Allen, J. Golson and R. Jones (eds.). London: Academic Press, in press.

References

Allen, J., 1970. Prehistoric agricultural systems in the Wahgi valley—a further note. *Mankind*, 7 : 177–83.
—— 1972. The first decade in New Guinea archaeology. *Antiquity*, 46 : 180–90.
Barrau, J., 1958. *Subsistence agriculture in Melanesia*. Honolulu: Bernice P. Bishop Museum, Bulletins, 219.
——, 1965. L'humide et le sec. *Journal of the Polynesian Society*, 74 : 329–46.
Best, E., 1925. *Maori Agriculture*. Wellington: Dominion Museum, Bulletins, 9.
Binford, L. R., 1968. Post-Pleistocene adaptations. In *New perspectives in archaeology*, (eds) S. R. and L. R. Binford, pp. 313–41. Chicago: Aldine.
—— and S. R. Binford (eds), 1966. A preliminary analysis of functional variability in the Mousterian of Levallois facies. *American Anthropologist (Special Publication)*, 68(2 : 2) : 238–95.

Boserup, E., 1965. *The conditions of agricultural growth*. London: George Allen and Unwin.
Brookfield, H. C., 1962. Local study and comparative method: an example from central New Guinea. *Annals of the Association of American Geographers*, 52 : 242–54.
—— 1964. The ecology of Highland settlement: some suggestions. *American Anthropologist (Special Publication)*, 66 (4 : 2) : 20–38.
—— and P. Brown, 1963. *Struggle for land: agriculture and group territories among the Chimbu of the New Guinea Highlands*. Melbourne: Oxford University Press.
—— with D. Hart, 1971. *Melanesia: a geographical interpretation of an island world*. London: Methuen.
—— and J. P. White, 1968. Revolution or evolution in the prehistory of the New Guinea Highlands: a seminar report. *Ethnology*, 7 : 43–52.

Bulmer, S., 1964. Prehistoric stone implements from the New Guinea Highlands. *Oceania*, 34 : 246–68.

—— 1973. *Notes on 1972 excavations at Wañlek, an open settlement site in the Kaironk valley, Papua New Guinea.* Working Paper No. 29, Department of Anthropology, University of Auckland, Auckland.

—— and R. Bulmer, 1964. The prehistory of the Australian New Guinea Highlands. *American Anthropologist (Special Publications)*, 66 (4 : 2) : 39–76.

—— and W. C. Clarke, 1970. Two stone spear or dagger heads from the Bismarck Mountains, New Guinea. *Records of the Papua and New Guinea Museum*, 1(1) : 42–45.

—— and W. Tomasetti, 1970. A stone replica of a bronze socketed axe from the Chimbu District of Australia New Guinea. *Records of the Papua and New Guinea Museum*, 1(1) : 38–41.

Casey, D. A., 1934. An uncommon type of stone implement from Australia and New Guinea. *Memoirs of the National Museum, Melbourne*, 8 : 94–99.

Childe, V. G., 1944. Archaeological ages as technological stages. *Journal of the Royal Anthropological Institute of Great Britain and Ireland*, 74 : 7–24.

Clarke, W. C., 1966. From extensive to intensive shifting cultivation: a succession from New Guinea. *Ethnology*, 5 : 347–59.

—— 1971. *Place and people: an ecology of a New Guinea community.* Berkeley and Los Angeles: University of California Press and Canberra: Australian National University Press.

—— 1973. *A change of subsistence staple in prehistoric New Guinea.* Paper read at the third International Symposium on Tropical Root Crops, Ibadan.

—— and J. M. Street, 1967. Soil fertility and cultivation practices in New Guinea. *Journal of Tropical Geography*, 24 : 7–11.

Evans, E. E., 1970. Introduction. In *The spade in Northern and Atlantic Europe*, (eds) A. Gailey and A. Fenton, pp. 1–9. Belfast: Ulster Folk Museum, Institute of Irish Studies, Queen's University.

Freund, R., 1968. Agriculture then and now. In *Anthropological Study Conference (Amapyaka)*. New Guinea Lutheran Mission, Wabag.

Gailey, A. and A. Fenton (eds) 1970. *The spade in Northern and Atlantic Europe*. Belfast: Ulster Folk Museum, Institute of Irish Studies, Queen's University.

Gardner, R. and K. G. Heider, 1968. *Gardens of war: life and death in the New Guinea Stone Age.* New York: Random House.

Glover, I. C., 1971. Prehistoric research in Timor. In *Aboriginal man and environment in Australia*, (eds) D. J. Mulvaney and J. Golson, pp. 158–81. Canberra: Australian National University Press.

Golson, J., 1971. Both sides of the Wallace Line: Australia, New Guinea, and Asian prehistory. *Archaeology and Physical Anthropology in Oceania*, 6 : 124–44.

—— 1977. Archaeology and agricultural history in the New Guinea Highlands. In *Economic and social archaeology: essays in honour of Graham Clark*, (eds) I. Longworth and G. de G. Sieveking. London: Duckworth.

——, R. J. Lampert, J. M. Wheeler and W. R. Ambrose, 1967. A note on carbon dates for horticulture in the New Guinea Highlands. *Journal of the Polynesian Society*, 76 : 369–71.

Heider, K. G., 1970. *The Dugum Dani: a Papuan culture in the Highlands of West New Guinea.* New York: Wenner-Gren Foundation for Anthropological Research, Viking Fund Publications in Anthropology, No. 49.

Higgs, E. S. and M. R. Jarman, 1972. The origins of animal and plant husbandry. In *Papers in economic prehistory*, (ed) E. S. Higgs, pp. 3–13. Cambridge: Cambridge University Press.

Lampert, R. J., 1967. Horticulture in the New Guinea Highlands—C14 dating. *Antiquity*, 41 : 307–9.

Lea, D. A. M., 1966. Yam growing in the Maprik area. *The Papua and New Guinea Agricultural Journal*, 18 : 5–16.

Lerche, G. and A. Steensberg, 1973. Observations on spade-cultivation in the New Guinea Highlands. *Tools and Tillage*, 2 : 87–104, 118.

Malinowski, B., 1935. *Coral gardens and their magic*, 2 vols. London: George Allen and Unwin.

Meggitt, M. J., 1958. The Enga of the New Guinea Highlands: some preliminary observations. *Oceania*, 28 : 253–330.

Mulvaney, D. J., and J. Golson (eds) 1971. *Aboriginal man and environment in Australia.* Canberra: Australian National University Press.

Nilles, J., 1942–5. Digging-sticks, spades, hoes, axes and adzes of the Kuman people in the Bismarck Mountains of east-central New Guinea. *Anthropos*, 37–40 : 205–12.

O'Brien, P. J., 1972. The sweet potato: its origin and dispersal. *American Anthropologist*, 74 : 342–65.

Phillipps, W. J. and J. M. Jury, 1959. A greenstone talisman, Kau-o-te-Rangi, Glendowie, Masterton. *Journal of the Polynesian Society*, 68 : 142–3.

Pospisil, L., 1963. *Kapauku Papuan economy.* New Haven: Yale University, Department of Anthropology, Yale University Publications in Anthropology, Number 67.

Powell, J. M., 1974. A note on wooden gardening implements of the Mt Hagen region, New Guinea. *Records of the Papua New Guinea Museum*, 4 : 21–8.

Riesenfeld, A., 1955. Bronze-Age influence in the Pacific. *International Archives of Ethnography*, 47 : 215–55.

Sahlins, M., 1972. *Stone Age economics.* Chicago and New York: Aldine-Atherton.

Seligmann, C. G. and T. A. Joyce, 1907. On prehistoric objects in British New Guinea. In *Anthropological essays presented to Edward Burnett Tylor*, (eds), W. H. R. Rivers, R. R. Marett and N. W. Thomas, pp. 325–41. Oxford: Clarendon Press.

Serpenti, L. M., 1965. *Cultivators in the swamps: social structure and horticulture in a New Guinea society.* Assen: van Gorcum.

Smith, P. E. L. and T. C. Young, Jr., 1972. The evolution of early agriculture and culture in Greater Mesopotamia: a trial model. In *Population growth: anthropological implications*, (ed) B. Spooner, pp. 1–59. Cambridge: Massachusetts Institute of Technology Press.

Strathern, M., 1969. Stone axes and flake tools: evaluations from two New Guinea Highlands societies. *Proceedings of the Prehistoric Society*, 35 : 311–29.

Vicedom, G. F. and H. Tischner, 1943–8. *Die Mbowamb: die Kultur der Hagenberg-Stämme im Östlichen Zentral-Neuguinea*, 3 vols. Hamburg: Hamburgischen Museum für Völkerkunde, Monographien zur Völkerkunde, Nr. 1.

Waddell, E., 1972. *The mound builders: agricultural practices, environment, and society in the Central Highlands of New Guinea.* The American Ethnological Society, Monographs, 53. Seattle and London: University of Washington Press.

Watson, J. B., 1967. Horticultural traditions of the eastern New Guinea Highlands. *Oceania*, 38 : 81–98.

White, J. P., 1971a. New Guinea and Australian prehistory: the 'neolithic problem'. In *Aboriginal man and environment in Australia*, (eds) D. J. Mulvaney and J. Golson, pp. 182–95. Canberra: Australian National University Press.

—— 1971b. New Guinea: the first phase in Oceanic settlement. In *Studies in Oceanic culture history*, (eds) R. C. Green and M. Kelly, pp. 45–52. Honolulu: Bernice P. Bishop Museum, Department of Anthropology, Pacific Anthropological Records, No. 12.

—— 1972. *Ol tumbuna: archaeological excavations in the eastern Central Highlands, Papua New Guinea.* Canberra: The Australian National University, Research School of Pacific Studies, Department of Prehistory, *Terra Australis* 2.

——, K. A. W. Crook and B. P. Ruxton, 1970. Kosipe: a late Pleistocene site in the Papuan highlands. *Proceedings of the Prehistoric Society*, 36 : 152–70.

Ethno-archaeology; or, where do models come from?

A closer look at Australian Aboriginal lithic technology

R. A. GOULD

A time-machine would be the perfect tool for studying processes of prehistoric human behaviour. Since time-machines belong in the realms of science fiction, we must still rely on archaeology. As we all know, archaeology is an imperfect tool for studying past human behaviour, subject to limitations of preservation, sampling, and other obvious problems. The whole history of archaeology has been one of overcoming or at least controlling these problems. The future importance of scientific archaeology depends largely on whether its practitioners are willing to ask questions of an anthropological nature which challenge them to find ways of improving their approaches. Specifically, can ways be found in which practising archaeologists can relate their findings of the past in a reliable way to ethnographic observations and issues? Success in relating the past and present in this way will assure the future of archaeology.

Ethno-archaeology and the 'new archaeology'

About ten years ago serious discussion began toward a new approach in archaeology which would, some hoped, revitalise the discipline. Much of this discussion echoed the earlier ideas of Walter Taylor, when he called for a 'conjunctive approach' (1948) which would turn archaeology into a kind of pre-historic ethnography by applying anthropological concepts to archaeological data. Today opinion within the profession is divided as to whether or not these ideas have actually made a substantial difference to the present nature of archaeology. While Leone (1971 : 222) can argue that, 'suddenly the new archaeology is everybody's archaeology', Zubrow (1972 : 205) maintains after a review of the literature that:

> If a new paradigm exists . . ., one may only conclude that it has not permeated the discipline sufficiently to have a major literary influence.

Surely just about everyone doing serious archaeology today is aware of the ideas and approaches proposed by Binford, Longacre, Hill, and other advocates of the so-called 'new archaeology' and is able to debate these ideas with his colleagues. In this sense Leone is correct—that is, everyone is talking about the new archaeology. But Zubrow is closer to the truth in his observation that discussion of these ideas among archaeologists generally has led to qualified acceptance at best and in many instances has resulted in outright rejection. This relative failure of the new archaeology to permeate the discipline requires some kind of explanation, for in such an explanation may lie the basis for improvements in the approach.

It would be presumptuous of me to suggest that, here and now, I am going to tear the whole of the new archaeology apart and put it back together again. For one thing, the new archaeology is, in fact, many new archaeologies, each with its own emphasis and unique characteristics. No single critique could do justice to this variety of approaches. So my comments here will focus on a few particular aspects of the new archaeology which seem to me to be especially important. In this regard, there are three interrelated criticisms which can be brought to bear:

(1) Emphasis on formal theory without corresponding regard for the applicability or utility of these theories in actual archaeological situations;

(2) A general shortage of detailed demonstrations which use anthropological ideas to interpret site data. Hill's work at Broken K Pueblo (1970) and Longacre's report on the Carter Ranch Site (1970) come closer to this kind of reporting than anything else so far, but they continue to stand as relatively isolated examples;

(3) Uncritical acceptance of ethnographic evidence in developing archaeologically testable hypotheses.

Many archaeologists, while sympathetic, have found the ideas of the new archaeology to be unreal for the interpretation of their own site data. In this paper I shall argue that the dual problems of obtaining reliable ethnographic observations and applying them successfully to the interpretation of archaeological patterning in both sites and regions can be solved by ethno-archaeological approaches which should, ultimately, render the new archaeology more acceptable to a wider range of archaeologists.

What is ethno-archaeology?

Here let me distinguish between ethno-archaeology in the general sense and what I have elsewhere referred to as 'living archaeology' (Gould, 1968). Living archaeology is the actual effort made by an archaeologist or ethnographer to do field-work in living human societies with special reference to the 'archaeological' patterning of behaviour in these societies. This is akin to the 'action archaeology' approach suggested by Kleindienst and Watson (1956). Ethno-archaeology, as I see it, refers to a much broader framework for comparing ethnographic and archaeological patterning, with special reference to excavated materials. In this latter case the ethno-archaeologist may rely entirely upon published and archival sources, augmented by experimental results (use and manu-facture of pottery, stone tools, etc.) for his comparisons without having to do the actual ethnographic field work himself. Thus ethno-archaeology may include studies of 'living' or 'action' archaeology along with other approaches.

The role of ethno-archaeology

Perhaps the most sweeping criticism of the 'new archaeology' has come in a recent review by Stanislawski (1973) of Longacre's Carter Ranch report. The critique focuses on Longacre's uncritical acceptance of the ethnographic literature on the historic Pueblos. Stanislawski notes that the actual patterning of Pueblo Indian behaviour with respect to such archaeologically relevant matters as pottery making and architecture differs markedly from the patterns used by Longacre in his ethnographic model. Whatever one may think of Stanislawski's arguments, the discrepancy between what the archaeologist thought the ethnographic pattern was and what it turned out to be when examined empirically can be matched by other cases as well, despite constant cautionary admonitions by ethnographers like Heider (1967) who studied the Dugum Dani of New Guinea, and Bonnichsen (1973) who attempted to study activity areas in a Cree Indian camp. In Stanislawski's view, not only do archaeological reconstructions often oversimplify living situations but such reconstructions cannot arise in a vacuum. Even when the reconstructions involve techniques like computer simulation, as is currently being tried by Thomas in the Great Basin of North America (1973), these must at some point be based on ethnographic models—in Thomas' case the Paiute Indians as studied by Steward. The usefulness of these comparisons rests largely upon the accuracy and completeness of the ethnographic evidence on which they are based. It is the primary task of the ethno-archaeologist to supply both specific descriptions of behaviour and general principles of behaviour; the former to flesh out models of past cultural systems, and the latter to render those models archaeologically testable. Stanislawski concludes:

> . . . non-archaeological models (for example, ethnographic ones) will always be used in archaeology, or else purely ethnocentric, subjective inferences are the result. The data, whether single artifacts or clusters, never speaks for themselves. We always explain them by a general cross-cultural or direct-historical analogy model. (1973 : 118)

If one accepts this view, then the next question is: How should ethno-archaeologists proceed in obtaining this evidence? In the past, my answer to this question—in common with many of my colleagues—has tended toward a rather unstructured reply which described various procedures that can yield archaeologically usable evidence. For example, careful site mapping, observations of manufacture and use of different artifacts, such as stone tools and pottery which might survive archaeologically, notes on patterning of activity areas and architectural remains, and the like. However useful these items may be, such a 'laundry list' approach cannot be expected to provide a holistic picture of the cultural and natural systems involved—in other words, to provide a model. For this something more is needed; something in the way of an approach which is focused and methodical yet at the same time workable in terms of the problems actually encountered by archaeologists in their excavations and analysis. At this point I would like to turn to some Australian data on lithic technology in order to demonstrate how ethnographic observations can be of use in developing a model which can be examined archaeologically.

Australian Aboriginal stone tools as 'durable elements' in an ethnographic model

Most archaeologists—and not only the 'new archaeologists'—have stressed the importance of viewing artifacts and other patterned archaeological remains as more than just objects left behind by ancient man. Perhaps the most frequently quoted statement of this point of view comes from Binford:

> The loss, breakage, and abandonment of implements and facilities at different locations, where groups of variable structure performed different tasks, leaves a 'fossil' record of the actual operations of an extinct society. (1964 : 425)

While there is general agreement with this point of view, operationalising it has sometimes proved difficult. To overcome some of these difficulties Schiffer (1972) has recently proposed a set of formal definitions and approaches which are helpful to the archaeologist in visualising the flow of artifacts, food, fuel, structures, and other items through a cultural system.

Schiffer's scheme proposes a dual set of flow models which trace the life cycle of two kinds of elements which, together, make up a complete inventory of a cultural system. These elements are classified into *durables* ('. . . tools, machines and facilities—in short, as transformers and preservers of energy') and *consumables* ('. . . foods, fuels, and other similar elements whose consumption results in the liberation of energy.') (Schiffer, 1972 : 157). Stone artifacts fit under the heading of durable elements and can be treated in terms of the flow model for these items, and this is how I propose to treat the stone tools of the ethnographic Western Desert Aborigines of Australia.

During life within the living cultural system a durable element such as a stone tool is seen as reflecting five *processes*: procurement, manufacture, use, maintenance, and discard. After its discard, a durable element leaves the living cultural system and enters the realm of archaeological context. By analysing the life-cycle of durable elements such as stone tools in an ethnographic culture and observing their final disposal in what would be their ultimate archaeological context we can systematise observations which provide general principles whose use will lead to archaeological predictions—in this case related to technology.

Procurement

At the outset it is important to distinguish between stone materials gathered by the desert Aborigines from definite quarries, that is specific localities where usable stone is available known to the Aborigines and revisited by them, and non-quarried stone, which is obtained from the surface of the ground at or near the spot where it is needed for a particular task. In this latter case, the stone comes from a non-localised source which may be visited only once. As a background comment I should mention that the entire Western Desert of Australia lies on an enormous pre-Cambrian plateau or shield formation which averages between 300 and 450 m elevation above sea level. This plateau is covered with ancient outcrops of resistant rock—white Australians term these formations 'reefs'—often surrounded by extensive flats covered with chunks of rock eroded from these reefs. When the original reef formation has eroded completely away these flats of pebbles and detritus—termed 'gibbers' by white Australians—sometimes form a pavement of hard rocks over wide areas. The Aborigines obtain usable stone both from localised outcrops or exposures (the quarries referred to earlier) and at large from the surface of the gibbers. In general one can expect to find hard rocks of manageable size and a reasonable degree of isotropism distributed widely over the surface of many parts of the Western and Central Deserts of Australia. Most quarry sites are not named by the Aborigines unless they have specific mythological associations and/or a watersource nearby, but these provisos do apply to some Western Desert quarries. Generalised surface occurrences of usable stone are not named, but they, like unnamed quarry sources, can always be located with reference to visible, named landmarks with sacred associations.

Behaviour at these different kinds of procurement sites follows consistent, differing patterns. At quarry sites one sees Aborigines obtaining flakes and small lumps or cores which are carried away and further trimmed for specific uses. In most cases these flakes were unifacially retouched and hafted as adzes, that is scrapers for shaping hardwoods like mulga (*Acacia aneura*), although a few exceptional instances were seen when flakes taken away to be used later as circumcision knives. At more generalised non-quarry localities, however, stones were used for immediate tasks on the spot. Sometimes this might be a unifacial handaxe for removing a slab of wood from a mulga tree to make into a spearthrower, or it might be a unifacial scraper-plane for performing the heavy shaping and trimming of a spearthrower blank. In cases like these the tool is usually retouched unifacially to sharpen the working edge, but I have seen a few occasions when a naturally sharp stone was used without any application of intentional retouch. For the sake of simplicity I shall refer to tools of this general kind as 'chopper planes'. This term implies that one tool may serve both functions and also avoids confusion with the kind of bifacial retouch and ovate form we generally associate with stone handaxes from the Old World. Aborigines, both male and female, may also pick up and use sharp flakes when roasting and butchering a kangaroo or other game. In every case observed the Aborigines always disposed of the tools that were manufactured and used at non-quarry locations at these same places. They were never observed to carry the tools away to a habitation camp or some other locality for further retouch and/or use.

Quarry sites, while not always spectacular, tend to possess a high degree of archaeological visibility. Chipping stations at large quarry sites generally consist of small circular or oval-shaped patches of ground swept clear of surface rocks and debris with occasional hammerstones lying nearby. These small clearings are mainly used when men are engaged in percussion-trimming flakes from cores with prepared striking platforms as opposed to the much heavier work of obtaining flakes by means of block-on-block percussion applied to natural outcrops and large boulders at the site. Thus most of the waste flakes one finds around and on such clearings tend generally to be smaller than those found over the site as a whole. Although surface indications of chipping-stations at quarry sites are rather faint, they tend to be permanent and not highly subject to the effects of surface erosion.

Factors other than the workability or sharpness of the stone may determine specific choices of quarry locations. As mentioned earlier, some quarries occur at or near sacred sites—that is, totemic 'dreaming' places. People who believe themselves to be descended patrilineally from the particular totemic being at one of these sites will make special trips to the quarry to secure the stone there. A man places a high value on stone from a site of his dreamtime totem. Stone like this is often transported over long distances (as much as 500 km) and is given to distant kinsmen of the same totemic patrilineage. This same attitude governs the occasional tendency to pick up ancient stone tools and refashion them for new uses. Because of his patrilineal relationship to the site, a man sees the stone as part of his own being—a fact which motivates him to carry the stone to other, distant sites, even when functionally better stone is already present at these places.

I found it impossible to make accurate calculations of the time spent by individuals in obtaining lithic raw materials at quarries, mainly because this behaviour was combined with other activities such as hunting and visits to sacred sites. Nevertheless, efforts to obtain suitable raw materials for certain classes of stone tools far exceeded any other aspect of stone toolmaking in terms of labour and time expended.

Manufacture, use and maintenance

As suggested earlier, stone tools used 'on the spot' are given the minimum amount of retouch needed to accomplish the particular task at hand. Direct percussion by means of a hammerstone (also picked up in the immediate area) to obtain a needed flake or to form a unifacial working edge for a 'chopper-plane' is the only technique employed upon these occasions. These processes of manufacture occur at or near the task locality and can result in characteristic although rather ephemeral archaeological associations. For example, one may find a few waste flakes and flake-knives near an earth-oven used to roast large game.

For tools made from quarried stone the processes are more complex. As mentioned earlier, these items are transported to the habitation campsite where they are further worked nto finished tools. Since it is inconvenient to carry large pieces of stone over long distances on foot, the Aborigines tend to remove selected flakes and cores which are small and in some cases have a basic shape close to what they intend for the finished tool. The principal tool type produced under these circumstances is the hafted adze,[1] an artifact widely reported and described from the Western and Central Deserts of Australia (Horne and Aiston, 1924; Mountford, 1941; Thomson, 1964; Tindale, 1965; Gould et al., 1971).

Initial retouch of adze flakes is always by direct percussion with a hammerstone to form a working edge with a mean angle at mid-section of 67°. On rare occasions I have seen unretouched flakes hafted for this kind of use, but in these cases the edge generally requires some retouch very soon after it has been used. Once a usable working edge is present, the adze flake is hafted to the handle of a club or spearthrower and is used as a scraper for shaping hardwoods (mulga in nearly every case observed). At this point Schiffer's process of 'maintenance' applies, since adzes are used until the working edges become dulled—then are resharpened and used again; and this process may be repeated over 20 times for a single adze before the tool is worn down to an unusable slug. Schiffer's use of the term 'lateral recycling', describes something which occasionally happens to Aboriginal stone adzes. Lateral recycling, '. . . describes the termination of an element's use . . . in one set of activities and its resumption

---

1. The term, adze, is not descriptively appropriate for this type of tool, but it has attained the level of conventional usage in Australian archaeology and thus is retained in this paper. The term, chisel, would be better.

in another' (Schiffer, 1972 : 159). There are certain, rather uncommon cases where the resultant adze slug has been laterally recycled into use as an endscraper, with one or both narrow ends being retouched and used for fine wood-scraping.

In most cases adze resharpening is performed with the stone tool remaining in its haft, and it is done by means of direct percussion using a wooden striker or by pressure-flaking with the teeth. Detailed descriptions of these techniques appear elsewhere (Gould *et al.*, 1971 : 157–60). Sometimes an adze flake is extracted from its haft and turned around or repositioned with more working edge exposed for use, and on these occasions one usually sees direct percussion with a hammerstone used for resharpening. Ultimately the adze flake becomes too narrow from repeated re-use and resharpening to be held by the haft, and this end-point is generally referred to by Australian archaeologists as the slug. Adze slugs are perhaps the most common and distinctive class of stone artifacts found on post Pleistocene age sites in the Australian desert.

Hand-held flakescrapers are also used by Aborigines for woodworking purposes, though less often than hafted adzes. Sometimes a man may forget to take his spearthrower with him, and he finds he needs to resharpen a wooden speartip or perhaps to shape a ceremonial object of wood. Irregularly shaped but fairly thick stone flakes are then unifacially retouched by direct percussion for use as scrapers, or, if a spearshaft needs trimming, a simple, unretouched flake may be used as a spokeshave. Such tools may be made either of quarried materials or of stone which is lying about in the immediate vicinity, whichever happens to be more readily available. These tools are usually not saved or recycled in any way. Tools like these are often produced, as needed, in or near habitation campsites, but they also may be made at task-specific localities—for example to sharpen a speartip while sitting in a hunting blind awaiting the arrival of game.

Processes of manufacture, use, and maintenance of stone tools also have a quantitative aspect which is essential if one is to see clearly the patterns of flow through a cultural system. Here one must review various tasks performed by Aborigines when using stone tools in an effort to arrive at calculations or at least good estimates of the amounts of isotropic stone which would be used by an Aboriginal man in the course of a normal year under traditional circumstances to perform these tasks. All of the retouched stone tools made by the Australian desert Aborigines can be classed, in Binford's terminology, as 'maintenance tools'—that is, as tools for making or maintaining other tools (Binford and Binford, 1969 : 71).

On the average, an adult Aboriginal man replaces his spearthrower about once every two years, and he replaces his club at the same rate. Throwing-sticks are replaced about once every year. Spearshaft wood tends to dry out and become brittle rather quickly, so spearshafts must be replaced about every three weeks. Speartips generally need to be resharpened at least once every other day. Wooden bowls used for digging are replaced about once a year, but fine carrying-bowls tend to be kept and used for long periods—perhaps as much as ten years. Digging-sticks, despite hard use, tend to last fairly long and need replacing only about twice a year.

How much isotropic stone does an Aboriginal man need in an average year to accomplish these tasks? To answer this question we must first know the rate at which different stone tools wear in terms of each task. On the basis of both labor-atory experiments and ethnographic observations I estimate that one adze flake is good for an average of 3058 useful strokes of scraping hard wood like mulga. This is an overall average which takes into account variations in lithic raw materials observed in use. Looked at in another way, this works out to an average of 20 resharpenings in the useful life of a single stone adze flake. An adze must be resharpened once every time it is used for resharpening a mulga wood speartip, which works out to about 182 uses per year or 9.1 adzes per man per year. Similarly, a man will need to replace an average of 17.3 spearshafts per year, and he will be able to shape two spearshafts with a single adze flake, thus needing an average of 8.7 adze flakes each year for this task. One adze flake is sufficient for shaping two clubs, and, similarly, one adze flake will suffice for shaping two throwing-sticks. One adze flake is generally adequate to do the final shaping on one wooden spearthrower. My data on wooden digging-sticks and carrying-bowls is less reliable, since I observed few cases and can offer only a rough estimate. Adzes are used in the final finishing of these implements and probably require about as much effort as a spearthrower—that is, one adze flake per bowl. Adzes are not used at all in shaping digging-sticks. These figures do not attempt to separate out occasional substitutions of hand-held flake scrapers and/or spokeshaves for adzes when these tasks are actually performed. The average number of adze flakes (including the equivalent unhafted stone flake-scrapers and spokeshaves if any were used) is summarised below:

Table 1

Tasks	Average No. of adze flakes used per man per year
Resharpening speartips	9.1
Replacing spearshafts	8.7
Replacing spearthrowers	0.5
Replacing clubs	0.25
Replacing throwing-sticks	0.5
Replacing wooden bowls	1.0
Total	20.05

In addition to these basic utilitarian tasks there are uses applied to the manufacture of sacred boards and other ritual paraphernalia. These are hard to estimate, since they take place at irregular intervals and at variable ràtes. Nevertheless on some ritual occasions, woodworking activity may be considerable. As a general estimate I would add another three adze flakes to the annual inventory, bringing the total now to 23.05. I regard this as a realistic estimate of the average number of adze flakes and other retouched tools of quarried stone needed by an Aboriginal man in a year.

In the case of stone obtained as needed for making 'chopper-planes' and flake knives, the average number of tools required is not much different from that for quarried tools. 'Chopper-planes' are used in making the 'V' shaped cut in the tree trunk when preparing to detach a slab of mulga wood for making into a spearthrower or sacred board. They are used also in cutting stalks, roots, or branches for spearshafts and in the initial shaping of every kind of wooden artifact, including digging-sticks. These implements are fashioned as the wood-working need arises and are discarded immediately after use; hence, one use = one tool. The case of unretouched flake knives is more problematical. Since these are used mainly for cutting meat and sinew, and since successful hunts in the Western Desert are rather rare events which occur at irregular intervals, it is hard to offer an accurate estimate of the rate at which these tools are used. In most cases flake knives are made of non-quarried stone, usually without any retouch. Sometimes naturally sharp flakes found lying on the ground are picked up and used as flake knives. My best general estimate would be that approximately 20 of these flake knives are used by one person each year. Of course, women use these as much as men, and I might add here that women sometimes take a hand in the final finishing of wooden bowls, too. Thus I am being arbitrary in referring to use of stone tools as male tasks, and I think it best to say so. To summarise, here are the average numbers of 'chopper-planes' used per man per year:

Table 2

Tasks	Average No. of 'chopper-planes used per man per year
Replacing spearshafts	17.3
Replacing spearthrowers	0.5
Replacing clubs	0.5
Replacing throwing-sticks	1.0
Replacing digging-sticks	2.0
Total	21.3

Here again, we must also consider tools required in making sacred boards and other ritual objects. My minimum estimate would be two per year, bringing the total to 23.3.

Now these figures can be combined with weights of individual tool types. I weighed only nine ethnographic adze flakes before they were hafted and put to use, and I obtained a mean weight of 41.4 g for these. I regard this as an inadequate sample, however, and suspect that the true mean should be lower. 'Chopper-planes' are more variable in weight (not surprising considering their *ad hoc* nature), ranging from 4700 g to 97.0 g, with a mean weight of 809.2 g. Ethnographic flake knives had a mean weight of 40 g. The total weights for these different artifact classes can now be summarised:

Table 3

Artifact classes	Total amounts of lithic raw material needed per man per year
Non-quarried	
'Chopper-planes'	17.234 kg
Flake knives	800 g
Quarried	
Adze flakes (and	
equivalent flakescrapers)	954 g

These results mean that about 18·9 times more non-quarried stone passes through the Aboriginal cultural system in a year than stone derived from quarry sources. It also means that about 99·95% of the total lithic material is used by the Aborigines in task-specific localities which are relatively ephemeral and dispersed, while only about 0·05% sees use in habitation campsites. This latter figure may vary, of course, depending mainly upon how many flake knives are used in

the context of task-specific sites and how many are used in main habitation campsites. But even if all 800 g of flake knife material were used in the habitation area it would still not really affect the magnitude of the relationship.

Discard

Heider (1967 : 62) and Stanislawski (1969) have both correctly emphasised the importance of studying patterns of disposal of artifact and material remains in living cultures as a way of understanding patterns which are likely to occur in archaeological sites. In looking at disposal of lithic materials the case of the desert Aborigines reveals several patterns worth noting.

As the preceding quantitative analysis shows, much more quarried than non-quarried raw material appears in habitation campsites, despite the fact that quarried stone represents only a minute fraction of stone used in the total cultural system. The only exception to this is when surface scatters of stone are found occurring naturally near the campsite (as, in fact, has been the case on several occasions in the Western Desert).

Waste flakes resulting from manufacture abound at quarry sites, where the initial shaping of certain tools is performed. Waste flakes from these same quarry sites occur in habitation campsites, but general observations indicate that they are much smaller in size and represent a second stage in manufacture closer to the final finishing of the tools involved. I do not have measurements to demonstrate this, but useful studies could be carried out to document shifts in flake size from quarry sites to habitation campsites.

Adze flakes and adze slugs tend to be common in habitation sites, where they are most often manufactured, used, maintained, and replaced. Along with these one may also expect to find some hand-held flakescrapers and spokeshaves. Within ethnographic habitation campsites, no special area was seen being used specifically for stone tool-making activities. Rather, all quarried stone tools were made and used by each man according to his needs in and around the immediate vicinity of his windbreak or shelter, and disposal of these tools occurred there, too.

'Chopper-planes' are left where they were used and can generally be found lying near the base of any mulga tree which shows a scar on its trunk to indicate removal of a slab of wood. Sometimes this happens to be near a habitation site but more often these task-specific localities are low on the scale of archaeological visibility and are widely dispersed over certain parts of the landscape.

Flake knives are also left where they were used, most often in close proximity to earth ovens, where they were used in butchering and dividing meat after a successful hunt. These roasting sites are low in potential archaeological visibility, although such activities can also occur in the main habitation camps when game happens to have been caught nearby. These latter situations can be recognised as activity areas within a habitation site.

Conclusions

The flow of lithic materials throughout the ethnographic Australian desert Aboriginal cultural system is summarised in the flow chart (adapted from Schiffer, 1972). This chart, together with the observations described so far, enables us to see patterns of behaviour in Aboriginal lithic technology more clearly, in the form of a model from which specific

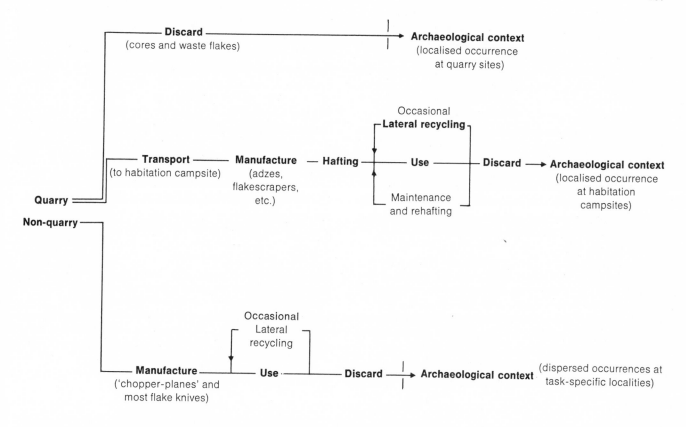

Fig. 1:   Flow-chart of Australian Desert Aboriginal stone artifacts (adapted from Schiffer, 1972).

predictions which are archaeologically testable can be derived. These are:

(1) Stone materials derived from quarry sources will tend to occur in localised associations with hearths, butchered faunal remains, living surfaces, seed-grinders, and other material remains and features characteristic of ethnographic habitation campsites.

(2) Adzes, adze slugs, flakescrapers, and spokeshaves will tend to be made from quarried stones. These classes of artifacts will occur more commonly in association with habitation campsites than with any other kind of site in the Western Desert of Australia.

(3) Artifacts of non-quarried stone will tend to be absent or to occur in low frequencies in habitation contexts unless there happen to be surface sources of such lithic material nearby.

(4) Non-quarried stone artifacts will tend to occur in dispersed contexts in connection with various task-specific sites (roasting hearths, woodworking trees, etc.).

(5) 'Chopper-planes' and flake knives will tend to be made of non-quarried stone. These tools will tend to be characteristically large, with weights of a total magnitude of over 18 times that of quarried stone artifacts.

(6) Few, if any, finished stone tools will be found at quarry sites.

(7) Waste flakes and discarded cores may be found at both quarry and habitation sites, but those found in habitation contexts will represent a narrower size range, on the whole, than waste materials found at quarries, with the means tending toward considerably reduced sizes.

(8) Some artifacts of quarried stone may be expected to occur archaeologically in localities far removed from the original source—sometimes as far as 500 km. But

there should still be a general tendency for usable lithic materials to occur in abundance in habitation campsites not far removed from the quarry (i.e. within a radius of about 40 km).

(9) Stone tools from quarried sources may not always be made of material which is ideally suited for their intended tasks. For example, one may expect occasionally to find adzes or adze slugs of white opaline, a decidedly inferior stone for any wood scraping purposes.

(10) Occasionally, too, one may expect to find stone tools of both quarried and non-quarried materials which have been laterally recycled. Choppers, for example, may be recycled into scraper-planes, and adze slugs are sometimes refashioned as endscrapers.

One may also draw specific negative or cautionary conclusions:

(1) The amount of lithic raw material represented by stone tools from quarried sources (tending as they do to occur in habitation sites which have a fairly high degree of archaeological visibility) will represent only a tiny fraction of the total amount of lithic material used within the cultural system.

(2) Flake knives will always be a problem for the archaeologist, since they are rarely ever retouched intentionally or used enough to acquire extensive edge-damage or use-wear to be identifiable as tools or distinguishable from certain waste flakes.

(3) In the case of both quarried and non-quarried stone materials, tools are made, used, maintained, and discarded in the context of one place. In the case of the former this is the habitation campsite; in the case of the latter it is the task-specific locality. Since they

are thus compressed, it may not be possible for archaeologists to separate out these processes in terms of what he finds in or upon the ground.

Finally, one may offer a few generalisations based on this data which could serve as genuine cross-cultural principles, subject to other tests:

(1) Lithic raw materials which are labour-expensive to procure and/or manufacture will be used in tools that have relatively long use-lives.

(2) Provided quarry sites were used exclusively for the procurement of lithic raw materials, few, if any, finished stone tools will be found at them.

(3) The widest variety of stone tool types and raw materials in a particular lithic assemblage will tend to occur in the context of habitation campsites.

Such general principles as these can be examined through ethno-archaeological studies in other societies and may ultimately prove useful in interpreting the archaeological patterning of lithic materials in situations as remote from Australia as Olduvai Gorge.

The Australian desert Aborigines possess a relatively simple and unspecialised stone technology. Yet it has patterning which an ethno-archaeological model (based on Schiffer's concept of artifacts as durable elements in a cultural system) reveals in such a way as to provide archaeologically testable predictions of both a specific and general nature. Unlike Stanislawski, who tends to see ethno-archaeology in opposition to the 'new archaeology', I am arguing that ethno-archaeology, by answering the crucial question: Where do models come from? fulfills rather than replaces the goals of the 'new archaeology'.

Acknowledgements Special thanks go to Dr David Tuggle, Dr Michael Schiffer, and Dr Barbara Luedtke for their patient reading and criticism of earlier versions of the manuscript, and to Dr Robert Whallon and Mr Don E. Crabtree for their advice on specific problems discussed in the paper. However, I accept full responsibility for the statements and interpretations presented here. Data for this paper was gathered during three field trips to the Australian desert, supported by the Social Science Research Council (1966–67), the Voss Fund for Anthropological Research of the American Museum of Natural History (1969–70), and the National Science Foundation, Research Grant No. GS-37105 (1973–74). Additional support in the form of a Landrover was furnished by the Australian Institute of Aboriginal Studies in 1966–67 and 1969–70. Special services, including typing were furnished by the Social Science and Linguistic Institute, University of Hawaii.

References

Binford, L. R., 1964. A consideration of archaeological research design. *American Antiquity*, 29 : 425–41.

Binford, S. R. and L. R. Binford, 1969. Stone tools and human behavior. *Scientific American*, 220(4) : 70–83.

Bonnichsen, R., 1973. Millie's camp: An experiment in archaeology. *World Archaeology*, 4 : 277–91.

Gould, R. A., 1968. Living archaeology: the Ngatatjara of Western Australia. *Southwestern Journal of Anthropology*, 24 : 101–22.

—— D. A. Koster and A. H. L. Sontz, 1971. The lithic assemblage of the Western Desert Aborigines of Australia. *American Antiquity*, 36 : 149–69.

Heider, K. G. 1967. Archaeological assumptions and ethnographical facts: A cautionary tale from New Guinea. *Southwestern Journal of Anthropology*, 23 : 52–64.

Hill, J. N., 1970. Broken K Pueblo: Prehistoric social organization in the American Southwest. *Anthropological Papers of the University of Arizona*, 18.

Horne, G. and G. Aiston, 1924. *Savage life in Central Australia*. London: Macmillan.

Kleindienst, M. R. and P. J. Watson, 1956. Action archaeology: The archaeological inventory of a living community. *Anthropology Tomorrow*, 5(1) : 75–78.

Leone, M. P., 1971. Review of S. R. and L. R. Binford (eds), *New Perspectives in Archaeology. American Antiquity*, 36 : 220–22.

Longacre, W. A., 1970. Archaeology as anthropology: A case study. *Anthropological Papers of the University of Arizona*, 17.

Mountford, C. P., 1941. An unrecorded method of manufacturing wooden implements by simple stone tools. *Transactions of the Royal Society of South Australia*, 65 : 312–16.

Schiffer, M. B., 1972. Archaeological context and systemic context. *American Antiquity*, 37 : 156–65.

Stanislawski, M. B., 1969. What good is a broken pot? an experiment in Hopi-Tewa ethno-archaeology. *Southwestern Lore*, 35(1) : 11–18.

—— 1973. Review of W. A. Longacre, *Archaeology as anthropology: A case study. American Antiquity*, 38 : 117–22.

Taylor, W. W., 1948. A study of archaeology. *American Anthropologist Memoir*, 69.

Thomas, D. H., 1973. An empirical test for Steward's model of Great Basin settlement patterns. *American Antiquity*, 38 : 155–76.

Thomson, D. F., 1964. Some wood and stone implements of the Bindibu Tribe of Central Western Australia. *Proceedings of the Prehistoric Society for 1964*, n.s. 30 : 400–22.

Tindale, N. B., 1965. Stone implement making among the Nakako, Ngadadjara and Pitjandjara of the Great Western Desert. *Records of the South Australia Museum*, 15(1) : 131–64.

Zubrow, E. B. W., 1972. Environment, subsistence, and society: The changing archaeological perspective. *Annual Review of Anthropology*, 1 : 179–206.

Topographic archaeology and artifactual evidence

SYLVIA J. HALLAM

Introduction

First I shall ask whether archaeologists, as such, *can* write prehistory. Can the directly artifactual data which are our prime professional concern be so manipulated as to generate and test models which are of wider than artifactual significance?

Second, I shall suggest that one answer lies in a spatial approach—old-fashioned distribution studies and field archaeology, but more rigorously and totally concerned with all aspects of regional usage, interpreting the word 'artifact' in the widest possible sense.

As an example of this approach I shall examine a static interpretation of the relationship of population and resources in Australia; and show that this is inadequate. Archaeological data, spatially approached, suggest an alternative dynamic model. Such a model requires testing in specific regional studies. We may thus hope to construct and test significant occupance prehistory from the topographic study of artifactual, archaeological, data.

The problem

We have a rich picture of Aboriginal life on the coastal plain around the estuary of the Swan River as it was at European contact. The picture is not due to archaeology. It is due to the learned and lively English gentlemen, and others, who explored the environs of the Swan in the years leading up to and immediately succeeding the establishment of the Swan River colony in 1829. Can the archaeologist compete? Can he, *qua* archaeologist, do the things he claims he wants to do? His professional concern is with artifacts, in the main with horrid little bits of stone, and the way they are *now* organised in space. When he goes beyond this, is he not drawing on the work, and trespassing on the preserves, of others?

Even to say when some of his flakes, chips, flaked pieces and occasional formal implements reached their present locations, and so to convert a purely spatial distribution to a space/time distribution, he must rest his argument primarily on the work of physicists, geomorphologists and biologists. To deduce anything about subsistence, the excavator depends on analyses of fauna and flora which, even if he carries them out himself, are not his distinguishing concern. For range of group movement or trade contacts he again turns *from* archaeology to lithology (for instance—Glover and Cockbain, 1971; Binns and McBryde, 1969, 1972) or, it may be, in other contexts, to the chemistry of metallic ores or beads. To trace even the actual areas of land available for occupance archaeologists must view their own data in the light of studies already carried out by botanists and geomorphologists, or directly

enlist their aid. Clark's work in the Fenland, in the 1930s onward, rested heavily on that of the Godwins (Clark, Godwin, Godwin and Macfadyen 1933; Clark and Clifford, 1935; Clark and Godwin, 1962; Godwin and Clifford, 1939; Godwin, 1940). In the 1950s archaeological field data indicating extensive settlement round the Wash in Roman times (Hallam, 1964, 1970) brought in question Godwin's conclusion that the silts on which that settlement was found was post- or late Roman; but the dilemma was resolved not so much by archaeological work (though that suggested what the answer might be and where the data should be sought) as by botanical and stratigraphic studies (Churchill, 1970; Smith, 1970a). It was again Churchill (1959, 1960) who delineated the differing extents of the Swan coastal plain through time and so showed how much can, and cannot, be deduced from archaeological distributions on the existing plain. In claiming to carry out palaeoecological studies, archaeologists are already going beyond their brief, even if they mean only that they need to know about gross zonations and changes of the physical and biological environment.

Where prehistory is concerned with the more subtle interaction of human and other populations yet more non-archaeological effort is needed. Jennings, a geomorphologist, has discussed man's effect on geomorphology (Jennings, 1965). Vita-Finzi (1969) has demonstrated the actual mass removal and buildup of Mediterranean soils, as late as Classical times and beyond. Significant studies by botanists include Iversen's work on the role of early agriculturalists in shaping the post-glacial vegetation sequence of Denmark (Iversen, 1941); or Godwin's on the effect of agriculturalists not merely on Breckland vegetation but, irreversibly, on Breckland soils and potentiality for occupance (Godwin, 1944); Dimbleby's further analyses of the effects of human occupance on pedology (Dimbleby, 1961, 1962); and Smith's demonstration that even small and apparently insignificant bands of hunters and gatherers could, by frequenting and firing, totally alter a whole landscape—vegetation, soils, and geomorphology (Smith 1970b). Robbins (1972) gives us a picture of the advance of human impact on the wooded terrain of New Guinea, leaving behind areas of open grassland and radically changed eco-systems which would no longer support the way of life which had initiated them, 'uninhabited and relatively unused'. Martin (1973) draws a fauna-based picture of a bow-wave of population advancing across the Americas, leaving behind an expanding zone of animal extinction and lowered capacity for carrying human populations. Right or wrong they are writing prehistory. Not one is an archaeologist.

But now the archaeologist must claim not merely a crude concern with environment as the changing backdrop to human action on the stage; not even or only to be presenting an updated dramatic performance in which the shadows at the back of the stage advance and become part of the action; but to interpret a yet more subtle scenario, a psychological drama where the players construct the scenery, and what matters is the way they see and give substance to the scene, the play, the other players, and themselves. Once we enter a world in which only 'the environment as the people themselves construe it' (Frake, 1962) is real, and people are part of the environment, then we are out of the competence not only of the archaeologist himself, but also of those natural scientists to whom he has traditionally turned; and within the domain of the social scientists. Is it not at this point that we, as archaeologists, must admit that a cognitive prehistory is beyond our competence, and retire to our own brain-games with artifacts in all their total triviality? Must we not leave ethnographers and ethnohistorians to delineate what it meant to view the world through non-Europeanised eyes, to make a living in that world, and to sustain in it 'the good life' (Clark, 1970)?

One illustration can make my point better than any piling up of generalities. In 1838, the explorer Grey, shipwrecked 200 miles north of Perth, staggered southward exhausted and near starving. To him and his companions this coastal plain was an unproductive and hostile terrain. His countryman Stokes was to dismiss it in one memorable phrase—'You might run it through an hour-glass in a day'. Grey rebuffed the wish of some of his men to live Aboriginal-fashion off the land, making instead a desperate dash to reach Perth on what little European food they could carry. They encountered natives near Lake Joondalup, about fifteen miles from the centre of Perth, and now becoming included in its northern suburbs.

> The natives no sooner heard the gun, and saw me approaching than they came running to me. Presently Kaiber called out to me, 'Mr. Grey, Mr. Grey, I am going to them; you sit here a little;'—and he then, with his long thin ungainly legs, bounded by me like a deer. 'Imbat, friend,' I heard him cry out, as a young man came running up to him. I grew giddy; I knew Imbat by name, and felt assured that at all events the lives of a great portion of my party were safe.
>
> The women were soon called up, bark baskets of frogs opened for us, by-yu nuts roasted, and as a special delicacy, I obtained a small fresh-water tortoise. 'Now, friend, sleep whilst I cook,' said Imbat, and lighting a fire he made me lie down and try to slumber, whilst he roasted some frogs and the turtle for me. I was not over well pleased at the skill he chose to exhibit in his cookery, for he thereby delayed me for a longer time than was agreeable—but we were all soon regaling on this native fare. (Grey, 1841, vol. 2: 91-92)

Later Grey and Imbat converse:

> I however lit a fire, and laid down, Imbat again beginning to cook—and then chattering: 'What for do you who have plenty to eat, and much money, walk so far away in the bush?' I felt amazingly annoyed at this question, and therefore did not answer him. 'You are thin,' said he, 'your shanks are long, your belly is small—you had plenty to eat at home, why did you not stop there?' I was vexed at his personalities, besides which it is impossible to make a native understand our love of travel—I therefore replied—'Imbat, you comprehend nothing—you know nothing.'—'I know nothing!' answered he; 'I know how to keep myself fat; the young women look at me and say, Imbat is very handsome—he is fat—they will look at you and say, He not good long legs—what do you know? where is your fat? what for do you know so much, if you can't keep fat? I know how to stay at home, and not walk too far in the bush—where is your fat?' 'You know how to talk;—long tongue;' was my reply; upon which Imbat, forgetting his anger, burst into a roar of laughter, and saying, 'and I know how to make you fat,'—began stuffing me with frogs, barde, and by-yu nuts. (*Ibid.*: 93)

I have quoted from Grey at length because of the importance of the picture he draws, both in its particular application to the study of the prehistory of Aborigines of this continent; and in its general application to the problem of *how* archaeologists can construct valid prehistory.

On the first level we have a salutary picture of the abundance which the swamps and lakes and their surrounds, worthless in European eyes, would yield at the very end of the dry season, the toughest time of the whole year, to those who valued supplies of water, turtles, frogs, barde, by-yu nuts and, a little later, the reed-roots which were to form a staple until the new rains should bring abundance of grass and game and watering spots, and allow the large groups aggregated about the lakes to scatter into the inland. It was an abundance available to those who *knew* their countryside, what they could rely on, where to go at which times, how to husband their resources, how so to use them as not only to ensure but to enhance future supplies; for instance by burning the swamps at the end of the growing season. These 'kangaroo pastoralists' also kept the Swan alluvium open by burning, encouraging a new 'crop' of young grass for the kangaroos. They were, in Flannery's words, no scruffy nomads, but practised and ingenious lay botanists (Flannery, 1968), skilled and competent ecologists. (See Hallam, 1972a, 1972b, 1973a, 1973b, 1974.)

The ties which linked them to their land were not those of subsistence alone. Closely interwoven with the patterning of exploitative usage was that of ceremonial usage. Their grasp was symbolic as well as economic. Not only did ceremonies follow the opportunity, and the necessity, for gathering together in the summer (dictated by the few permanent sources of water, and the need for large groups for burning-off and fire drives); ceremonies maintained the cohesion between the smaller groups which used the more scattered water and game resources of the winter, and maintained also the time patterning of aggregation and scattering, movement and activities. The evidence from the Swan–Murray–Leschenault Estuary area (eg., Bunbury, 1930) would be consistent with a schedule like that in Mrs Hassell's explicit account (Hassell and Davidson, 1936) of the area east of Albany, where the '*man carl*' ceremony at the end of the summer was the occasion for a large gathering which was to turn immediately afterwards to fire drives.

Cognitive patterning subsumes ecological *and* symbolic lore, economic *and* ritual usage. The strong links between knowledge of and impact on terrain, familiarity and proprietorship, may be summarised in the definitions George Fletcher Moore (1842) gives for those words which literally mean fire, and metaphorically something of our notion 'hearth and home', but with the added implication of complex and thorough knowledge:

> *Kalla* —Fire; a fire; (figuratively) an individual's district; a property in land; temporary resting place.
> *Kallip*—Denoting a knowledge of localities; familiar acquaintance with a range of country, . . . also used to express property in land. . . .

On the second level the quotation from Grey brings us back to the question of how the archaeologist, *qua* archaeologist, can construct valid and meaningful prehistory. Many disciplines can contribute to a picture of pre-European Aboriginal life which takes in subsistence, ecological, symbolic and cognitive patterns. Has archaeology a special contribution?

To quote David Clarke's awful pun 'the only facts in archaeology are artifacts'. He retracts somewhat in allowing them spatial, temporal and contextual attributes. But the investigation of context, and even time in any absolute sense, is not the proper concern of the archaeologist as a man with a particular expertise. If 'geography is what geographers do' then archaeology is what archaeologists do, and our particular disciplinary skill lies in the analysis and description of artifact assemblages. How does one bridge from assemblage analyses in all their complex and dull detail to the richness of Aboriginal life and lore as depicted by Grey and by Moore?

Towards a topographic archaeology

The answer lies, I believe, in a spatial approach or set of approaches to artifact studies (cf. Spaulding, 1960), incorporating much that has been labelled settlement archaeology, ecological and systems studies, demographic archaeology, site catchment analysis, ethnoarchaeology and regional studies.

Although I have been from 1949 involved in studies of settlement patterns (Hallam, 1964, 1970) of the type which have since been called 'settlement studies' (Willey, 1958; Trigger, 1968; Chang, 1968; Ucko, Tringham and Dimbleby, 1972) I do not consider the term, or the concepts it usually enshrines, adequate to describe the necessary range of archaeological space studies.

Settlement studies on agricultural populations have their own difficulties—as in determining what degree of concentration or scatter of homesteads shall be taken to comprise any single settlement—but for non-agriculturalists these difficulties are so compounded that new approaches and a new name are needed.

'Settlement' implies *settled* habitation, and while that is appropriate to the Roman Fenland or Iron Age Britain, Mesopotamia or Mesoamerica, the term and the concept become increasingly strained when applied to mobile groups— anywhere in time and space from Mesolithic Britain (Coles, 1971; Clark, 1972) to Plio-Pleistocene Africa (Isaac, 1969, 1971).

The term *habitation archaeology* could well be used in preference to settlement archaeology; even better would be *occupance archaeology*, because this could cover *all* the space aspects of the usage of an area—habitation, subsistence and other exploitative activities, movement, dispersal and aggregation, and the scheduling of movement to be in the right place at the right time and in the right numbers (Flannery, 1968)—plus ceremonial usage. One good reason for preferring the word 'occupance' is that it echoes the famous dictum of the geographer Whittlesey, a systems analyst before his time: 'Human occupance of area, like other biotic phenomena, carries within itself the seeds of its own transformation'. Already in 1929 Whittlesey was including human populations within the ecological concept of succession—of communities of biological populations so interacting through time as to change the characteristics of the whole system over time (for instance, through various stages from open water through reed fen to fen woodland communities). Where human populations formed part of such an ongoing nexus of interactions not only did their activities make a particularly strong impact on the system, but their potentiality for rapid cultural rather than slow genetic change enabled them to react in turn to changes in total equilibrium, adapting their behaviour to maintain a place within the system.

The importance of the socio-demographic structure of human populations to their effect on, and reaction to, shifts in system equilibrium have been stressed (e.g. Binford, 1968). Population rise did not *follow* the beginnings of agriculture, as Childe had supposed (in, for instance, *Progress and Archaeology*, 1944), but the necessity for change in subsistence patterning may well have arisen out of stresses and disequilibrium between already increasing populations and inflexible or variously deteriorating environments (as in New Guinea—W. C. Clark, 1966). For each area of the globe we need studies of change in population, and change in the organisation of populations, over time, some turning from the 'original affluence' of hunter-gatherers to the chores of farming, others not. Demographic estimates can be based only on space studies. It is perfectly possible, for settled societies, to arrive at useful estimates of the order of magnitude of population densities and also to compare and contrast the spacings and groupings by which such densities are achieved (eg., Hallam, 1964, 1970). For mobile societies the attempt has greater difficulties. They have been discussed and attempts to surmount them have been made, for instance by Schwarz and by Heizer and Baumhoff and other contributors to *Prehistoric Settlement Patterns in the New World*, edited in 1956 by Gordon Willey; or by various of the contributors to the 1970 symposium on *Man, Settlement and Urbanism* (Ucko *et al.*, 1972). The last word lies with those ethnographers who point out that not only do mobile groups refuse to be pinned down to an equation of one group = one settlement, but that the group itself may be a miasma which does not exist (e.g. Yellen and Harpending, 1972)—a statistical concept, the greatest or most frequent degree of commonality in composition in the flux of alternately aggregated and dispersed families ranging mostly around the same sets of nodes as each other over a span of years.

Site catchment analysis, though fashionable, is an inadequate and incomplete way of tackling man-land relationships in hunter-gatherer societies. It is not sufficient to analyse the environs of one or a few sites in an area (e.g., Vita-Finzi and Higgs, 1970) without considering the extent to which these sites represent, sample, or stand out from the totality of artifact assemblages in that area, or represent the totality of activities of the community. The range of site functions from the multifarious activities at much- and long-frequented base camps to the few at ephemeral overnight stops, kill sites, etc., has been widely discussed elsewhere (eg., Hole and Flannery, 1967–8; Butzer, 1971, 401–12; Isaac, 1969, 1971; Thomas, 1973; etc.).

It is obviously important to view, if not individual sites, certainly the totality of sites for one time-span, in relation to the ecological zones in which they occur, or do not occur, or occur in lesser or greater concentrations than might be expected on the basis of the overall density of sites for the total area which includes these ecological subzones (Spaulding, 1960; Thomas, 1973).

It is just this type of study of the occurrence, variety, and distribution of sites, and the quantities and characteristics of the artifact assemblages concentrated or scattered upon them as indicators of intensity of frequenting and variety of activities, which constitutes the most specifically archaeological, and at the same time most historically important type of investigation within space archaeology.

The flow of transformations of prehistoric societies and the archaeological data they generate can be cross-sectioned at any point, including that point in the near-past which we call the present, or the point slightly further back labelled for convenience the ethnographic present. At this point of intersection of the flow of archaeological data with the view of literate observers we can attempt an equation between artifactual and ethnohistorical material. Such a collation of archaeology, in the strict sense, and ethnohistory must be essayed within each particular region. The area studied must include, and extend beyond, the normal range of movement of the members of one specific Aboriginal community at contact.

Archaeological studies which use a regional frame and investigate the space- and (inferentially) time-relations of artifacts within it (mainly from, literally, superficial evidence) draw most directly on the traditions of their own discipline. The British topographic tradition stems back to, and beyond, eighteenth century archaeologists such as William Stukeley, and leads through nineteenth century stalwarts such as William Cunningham, to its twentieth century exponents—Crawford, Fox, Grinsell, Charles Thomas, Fowler (Fowler, 1972) and Cunliffe (1973), taking in local historians such as Hoskins, Finberg, Herbert Hallam, Beresford, Hurst and the Deserted Medieval Villages group. Richard Green (1967) acknowledged this firmly entrenched British tradition in suggesting that 'topographic archaeology' would be a very proper designation for field studies embracing and including settlement archaeology, and stretching beyond to space studies of 'whole areas of prehistoric activity' (Thomas, 1972). I have suggested 'occupance archaeology' as a possible term. But Green's term not only carries traditional over-tones, but also denotes the relationship of populations, and artifacts, to landscape, without putting undue weight on any one aspect of that relationship. It can embrace not only the social-habitation and purely economic aspects but also the symbolic and cognitive aspects of a group's grasp of, attachment to, and impact upon, their terrain (Hallam, 1972b, 1974).

Many Australian archaeologists are engaged in topographical archaeological studies of various parts of the Greater Australian landmass—detailed investigations of the interaction of landed groups and peopled terrain, from the advent of human populations as new input disturbing a previous biotic equilibrium, through to European contact when Aboriginal activity-patterns were major factors in maintaining the resource-balance of each region, and of the continent as a whole. The centre of concern is with populations in relation to resources and resource development (White, 1967; Hope and Coutts, 1971; Lampert and Sanders, 1973; Jones, 1968, 1969; Hallam, 1972a, 1972b, 1973a, 1973b; Gould, 1973).

Phillip Smith (1972) has suggested a 'band wagon' effect in current archaeological studies of population, which he sees as part of a wider concern in the community as a whole with population pressures, environment, resources—the 'space-ship earth' syndrome. But this particular wagon was well under way before the band climbed aboard. Grahame Clark's Cambridge students from the 1930s on were initiated into a tradition of archaeology which in its concern with the 'ecos', the home, the nexus of the particular locality, stemmed back to Fox and Crawford, Pitt-Rivers, Stukeley and Aubrey. The Antipodean tradition has its roots here, though it took on other grafts. Thus the Antipodes greeted and welcomed with no particular surprise those approaches to the relationship of habitat and population which in the still typologically oriented America of the sixties seemed so fresh and refreshing that the New World proclaimed the New Archaeology.

Australian archaeologists are at a particular advantage in looking at populations and terrain over time. They can focus down more closely on one 'still' from the sequence of cross-sections across the flow from the past into the future, the cross-section we call the ethnographic present. Because, for some areas, a very detailed picture can be built up and because *continuity* of flow may be demonstrated (as by Gould, 1971; Gould, Koster and Sontz, 1971; etc.) the ethnohistorical sources can provide a useful and valid baseline from which to triangulate back into adjacent, and further, stretches of the Australian past.

An Australian example: static and dynamic models

Static models of population-patterning across the Australian continent begin with Tindale's quite unexceptionable observation (1940), based on his tribal map, that there is in general a marked inverse relationship between size of tribal *area* and rainfall. Birdsell in 1953, in an attempt at elaborate quantification, transmuted this statement into an hypothesis of direct proportionality between population *density* and rainfall. This transformation rests on the assumption that the numerical size of 'tribes' is for all practical purposes constant. Birdsell has continued to maintain this assumption (e.g. Birdsell, 1973) but has never produced adequate evidence for it. Indeed, he cut down the number of tribes to be considered in his quantitative formulation by the simple process of excluding some which could be shown *not* to comply with his assumption (Birdsell, 1953 : 178)—plus all those in areas such as the coastal plain which did not help a demonstration of proportionality. Furthermore, he proposed to calculate tribal numbers differing from 500 on the basis of the ratio between the area which the tribe actually *did* occupy and that which it would be expected to occupy on the basis of a rainfall : numbers formula which had been calculated on the assumption that no tribal numbers *did* differ significantly from 500. Finally, he proposed that population densities could be calculated for the Pleistocene, even for areas now under the sea, provided the rainfall were known. The relationship of population to climate and vegetation was assumed to be unchanging.

Birdsell's essentially static model, stripped of its baseless mathematical elaboration, passed into the accepted canon in the modified and moderate formulation which formed the fifth and last part of Stanner's classic (1965) article on Aboriginal territorial organisation. Although Stanner (1965 : 4) realised that present patterns were the outcome of millenia of development he none the less accepted that 'rainfall and tribal expanse were correlated inversely'. He presented, for verification or disverification, a complex and subtle, and not invalidly over-quantified, set of ideas. The rainfall that mattered, for instance, would not be total rainfall, but effective rainfall (excess of precipitation over evaporation). He envisaged more variables than Birdsell and realised that, with few of these controlled, complex statistical techniques would be inappropriate.

None the less Stanner presented for consideration and probable validation a model of population-patterning across the continent which was still essentially static rather than dynamic—briefly low population densities over the arid centre, higher population densities at the moister margins (or much of the margins) of the Australian landmass, population as a function of precipitation. More abundant rainfall was taken to imply more abundant resources.

The general picture, while broadly true, is in detail wrong. A regional examination of the ways in which the static model is wrong shows this detailed wrongness is not trivial but basic, hinging on a misconstruction of the relationship of populations and environment which can be corrected only by taking a dynamic instead of a static view.

Birdsell himself demonstrated (1953, eg., p. 190) that while proportionality of population density to rainfall may be a general trend it does not hold in detail. He cited, for instance, the low densities of parts of the south coast of Western Australia. In this stretch karri forest on granitic hills comes close to the sea, with only a narrow and intermittent coastal plain. By contrast, Birdsell remarked on the unexpectedly high densities along the continuous and wide lower west coastal plain, even in its very arid sections.

Certainly in general recent population-density figures for the margin contrast with those for the centre. Tasmania with about 20 persons to a hundred square miles [259 km²] (Jones, 1971), the Kimberleys with about 16 (Meggitt, 1962), or the entire southwest of Western Australia with around 12 to a hundred square miles contrast with something nearer three to the hundred square miles for parts of the centre (Meggitt, 1962).

But the overall figures for the southwestern Australia, for instance, are averaged over a very large area with major contrasts within it. Both the ethnographic and archaeological data demonstrate extremely high densities on the coastal plain at contact—the figure may be as high as 50 to the hundred square miles for the Swan–Murray–Leschenault Estuary zone —with, on the other hand, very little usage of the bulk of the forested triangle east of the Darling Scarp, and moderate densities in the open, park-like countryside inland of the forest belt. The jarrah forest and, above all, the tall karri forests of the south, support only a low herbivore biomass, and were frequented and used only around their margins, and in belts of movement along streams, kept open by burning (eg., along the Donnelly). Within Tasmania population very obviously was *not* a function of precipitation, the open east carrying a higher relative density than the wet and wooded west.

It was not rainfall as such, but specific resources, such as the fish, fowl, other animal and plant life in and around estuaries, rivers, lakes and swamps, which supported the highest populations. And within general areas of relatively high population-potential the impact of Aboriginal usage on vegetation had been such as to produce a landscape which was *more* habitable —more open woodland, offering freer movement to man and richer pasture to marsupials (or cattle)—than that which replaced it when its Aboriginal developers were removed. Rainforest took over from sclerophyll woodland in north-west Tasmania once it was no longer controlled by Aboriginal burning. The alluvium along the Swan, the Canning, and the Murray would support jarrah, and from the great trees scattered individually and in clumps the first European settlers built their houses. But the European exploitation of these rich and coveted soils (the Swan valley vineyards of today, or the rich pastures around Pinjarrah) was initially possible without prohibitive labour because exploitation, frequenting, and consequent frequent burning by the Aborigines had kept them open and park-like.

Much of the damp margins, then, carried high Aboriginal populations not because of, but despite, their dampness; and those populations were related to resources which would have been less or lacking in some respects if the Aborigines were not there. High Aboriginal populations—and, in large part, the resources which supported them—were the result of long interactions over time, not of purely climatic and geomorphic factors; just as in New Guinea Bulmer (1968) says that 'much hunting is of creatures which man's activities had enabled to thrive'. The continent appeared to its first European prospectors not as God had made it, but as the Aborigines had made it. To understand the relationship between Aboriginal populations and their terrain it is not enough then to take the terrain as given—a complex of geology, geomorphology, soils, climate, and natural flora and fauna, fixed throughout time.

Stanner of course did not miss the point that the resources of an area are, as Grey shows, what their inhabitants know

them to be. They depend on Aboriginal knowledge and lore. He advocated detailed studies of the territorial structure of particular regions, to include distinctive habitats recognised by the Aborigines, named places and localities, ceremonial grounds, deposits of raw materials, tool manufactures, networks of pads, fords, crossing places, fish weirs, places where contiguous groups clustered for survival in bad times and celebration in good.

Such could well be the blueprint for the proximal end of an ethnoarchaeological investigation. Chang (1968) has advocated the replacement of the study of artifacts by the study of settlement. Charles Thomas (1972), David Thomas (1973) and Cunliffe (1974) advocate the study of entire countrysides. We need rather to extend our concept of artifact to include not only assemblages of stone tools and debris but the areas from which they come, often for instance the only blowout within an area of geologically similar sands, or the one stretch of mobile dunes along several miles of estuary; not only fish weirs but fords, wells, and the tracks between them, 'like cattle tracks and just as plain' (Hammond, 1933); belts of easy movement kept clear by much frequenting and consequent burning; the nodes where several routes converged (as at Perth itself); or whole stretches of countryside kept open and park-like by Aboriginal pasture improvement, the 'burning of the grass . . . to provide a new crop of sweeter grass' (Eyre, 1845 : II, 299). We need to consider not only habitation sites, but art and stone arrangements, and even those striking natural features—caves and underground streams and balanced rocks—which, on the evidence of postcontact accounts or names, were apprehended as significant. However difficult it may be to derive cognitive patterns from archaeological data, lore from localities, we must not ignore anything which can elucidate the social mechanics of grouping, spacing, territorial attachment and the scheduling of the ceremonial and economic year. It is by no means impossible to find in the symbolic field, as in the technological, recurrent groupings of significant features, with continuity through to contact. Caves, dark crevices, gullies, fire, crystals, red slashes, blades suitable for cicatrice-cutting, serpentine shapes—form a complex as significant as the association of a certain shape of flake, a certain type of edge-wear, and a certain edge angle in indicating a functional form persistent over time, and capable of more assured interpretation because of European observation at the near end of the continuum. An insistence on the full use of all archaeological data must not rob us of the advantage of having ethnographic data to use where they are relevant.

Even the purely ethnohistorical investigation of Stanner's proposed model has attracted relatively little demographic attention, and certainly no systematic testing (controversy has centred rather on the semantics of the terms to be used for various types of population groupings holding and using land). Mobility and group fluctuation, already discussed, would make it difficult to use archaeological data to push such investigations back through time. A possible line of approach is through the *ratios* between population density at contact and population in preceding phases, as indexed by numbers of sites for the latest phase in relation to the number of sites for previous phases, taking into account the duration of each phase, and assuming no drastic changes in the average number of sites visited by groups over comparable spells of time.

For the Swan River area of Western Australia the western coastal plain shows great numbers of late surface assemblages, characterised by a high proportion of quartz, a high proportion of quartz chips, and large numbers of 'scalar cores' or 'fabricators'. There are relatively few early-type assemblages in which steep-edge scrapers predominate. Backed blade assemblages are intermediate in date and quantity. From east of the relatively empty jarrah belt, on the other hand, come great quantities of heavy-duty steep-edge scrapers, mostly from assemblages with no material to indicate any but an early date; and relatively little bulk of late scatters, rich in quartz and chips, or the amorphous assemblages which denote final sites (eg., those known to have been occupied at European contact, or including European material, such as clay pipes and worked glass); nor indeed are there many assemblages which include backed blade material. The contrast in trends between the two areas, agrees with the relatively high densities ethnographically attested on the coastal plain at contact, and the lower densities inland of the jarrah belt. Taking these last figures, and the ratios between the numbers of sites of each phase in each broad area, it would appear that the initial densities cannot have differed greatly east of the jarrah forest and on the coastal plain; and rose in comparable fashion in both areas by the time of regular backed blade use. The rise later accelerated steeply among coastal plain populations, but apparently reached a ceiling and levelled off in the inland.

It is the contrast in trends which is particularly interesting—relatively more *late* material towards the damper margin of the continent—in general accord with Stanner's static model; but relatively more *early* material towards the relatively, and fluctuating (Churchill, 1968), arid margins of the always arid centre—suggesting an early situation in total contrast to the Stanner model, and a change over time. The dense population of the margin was, then, not a necessary function of climate, but a function, more probably, of preceding occupance and its effects, in conjunction with the increasing, and fluctuating, aridity of the post-Pleistocene.

The picture for the Perth area seems consonant with similar evidence for the rest of the continent, though everywhere the propositions I shall advance require quantitative testing. Areas in the semi-arid annulus around the arid centre appear frequently to have supported numbers in the late Pleistocene which they did not improve on, or even retain, later. The margins of the Pleistocene lakes along distributaries of the Murray system carry great numbers of early assemblages to one later scatter. The dry creek-bed between Warburton Mission and Puntutjarpa is lined with large quantities of 'horsehoofs' where later populations were sparse in the extreme. A high *late* population density would seem to characterise situations with particular favourable localised resources—the Murray valley, or some coastal, estuarine and swamp situations, rather than following any simple overall pattern. Must we envisage for Australia, as Martin (1973) does for the Americas, a Pleistocene 'bow-wave' of population? And why does later demographic history show such striking regional variety?

Any dynamic continental overview must now stretch back to the Pleistocene, and so start with a Greater Australia which stretches from the equator to 45°S, and embraces what are now New Guinea and Tasmania. In this view Australia becomes an appendage separated by relatively narrow seas, but seas which have a long continuous geological history (Walker, 1972), from a long and broad peninsula of Southeast Asia, embracing the present region south from China, through the Malay Peninsula, into Borneo and Java. In this view, the major contrast lies not so much between a forested margin and an arid interior to the Australian continent, but between an extensive and mainly tropical forested region extending through the whole of a wider and amalgamated Southeast-Asia-with-Indonesia and with slight, but significant, interruption (for Wallace's and Weber's line represent important biotic boundaries) into the north of Greater Australia (New Guinea and Arnhem Land); and, in contrast, to the south of this, the more open scrub, savannah, semi-desert and desert interior of Australia, with only minor cooler forest areas in the southwest and southeast (including Tasmania).

The overall picture for the entire region, then, is of forest towards the equator and more open lands further away. In the final Pleistocene the ecological boundary probably lay roughly where the Torres Strait is now (Walker, 1972). The ecological line may well have been more important than the later water line in delimiting the circum-central, characteristically Australian, savannah to semi-arid interior from the forested north. Such a simple, and over-simplified, picture may be compared with Alford's simple model for America (Alford, 1970). He contrasts the specialised hunting areas in the grass plains of the less forested parts of North America with the areas nearer the equator negatively characterised by their *lack* of open grassland, *lack* of herd herbivores, *lack* of specialised hunters, with instead generalised hunter-gatherers, using 'archaic', unspecialised, stone assemblages, amongst whose diversified minor strategies of resource utilisation arose those intensifications of plant utilisation which led towards agriculture.

The Asian–Australian overall picture might be seen as analogous for the final Pleistocene—'archaic' unspecialised (Hoabinhian) cultures with diversified subsistence across the Southeast Asian peninsula forming the substratum for developments towards horticulture (Gorman, 1969–70, 1971; Solheim, 1972; but see Harlan and de Wet, 1973); while around the Australian centre were not relatively heavy Pleistocene populations initially oriented towards stress on the pursuit of large game? Even though they lack the specific *stone* evidence of projectiles, it is significant that a major component of the stone assemblages comprises steep-edge scrapers, suitable for wood-working, including a great variety of convex *and* concave edges, suitable for working spears and spear-throwers. This steep-edge scraper tradition goes back to the thirty thousands (Barbetti and Allen, 1972; Bowler et al., 1972) and probably back behind that. A flake version of a steep-edge scraper, with the same type of edge-use and a similar edge angle, equals an adze flake, and such hafted wood-working tools, with their probable implications of spears and spear-throwers, are now attested back to 25 000 years ago (Dortch and Merrilees, 1973). The hunters of the 30 000s were hunting a modern-type fauna, but it seems inescapable that their yet earlier predecessors in the same general area must have encountered, and made their impact on, a wider range of game including the Australian megafauna, as is attested by charred bone in the Menindee hearths.

I would suggest, then, an initial Australian settlement phase in which the ecological situation in the discontinuous stretch of land from Southeast Asia through to South Australia paralleled that in the Americas; with generalised subsistence patterns emphasising the plant component in the diet towards the equator and more specialised, hunting cultures over the more open lands further from the equator (in a wide annulus around the most arid and least used areas of the heart). Whether, as has been suggested for the New World, the initial impact of these savannah hunters on large Pleistocene herbivores was catastrophic, for hunted and hunters, within a very short time-span (Martin, 1973); or whether slower and more subtle stages led to a relative decline in the resources and populations of the centre (Merrilees, 1968; Jones, 1968), either process would have led to a widening and intensification of the plant and small animal components of subsistence throughout the continent, and a relative recrudescence in the more varied and widely-based economies of the margins. Early grinding equipment shows that the plant element became significant within the Pleistocene (Jones, 1973; Allen, 1974).

Aboriginal firing, like European clearance, could be expected to lead to increased soil salinity, and consequent vegetational, faunal, economic and demographic trends, particularly under semi-arid conditions, and particularly under conditions of naturally *increasing* aridity, as during the post-Pleistocene (Churchill, 1968. See Hole and Flannery, 1967–8 for the results of similar environmental manipulation in Iran). Aboriginal legends in southwestern Australia tell of once fresh water becoming salty.

But while inland areas which initially offered the most abundant grazing and livelihood may have proved in the long or the short run liable to *degradation* rather than improvement under human impact; similar processes of frequenting and usage, including firing, may have opened up and *improved* the grazing in the initially unattractive, because heavily wooded, margins of the continent, particularly in the southwest and the southeast (including Tasmania). In the southwest the line of demarcation between coastal and inland-oriented groups would seem to have shifted inland with rise of sea level by about 3000 BC. In the yet drier phase which ensued from before 2000 BC it seems that the inland margin of the forest zone proved incapable of supporting as steep a rise in population as the coastal zone, being more sensitive to increased aridity, and possibly increased salinity and nitrogen depletion as a result of deforestation. Burning would, however, continue to develop rather than deplete the grazing resources of the better-watered alluvial zone immediately west of the Darling Scarp, which Stirling was to find open and park-like in 1829; while the varied fish, fowl, reptile, small mammal, root and water resources of the estuaries, inlets, lakes and swamps of the remainder of the coastal plain continued to support steeply increased usage and populations up to European contact and encounters such as Grey's.

Thus the general picture would be that, while the relatively open land around the centre probably was capable of supporting a high density of herbivores—and so of Aboriginal newcomers—*ab initio*, it was the *impact* of Aborigines and Aboriginal firing on the outer margins which improved the grazing there, initially for marsupial herbivores and their graziers, and later for European stock. The improvement went on right up to European contact at the moist periphery, as on the Swan coastal plain; but was more than balanced by deterioration relatively early at the centre; and struck a roughly even balance along the zone between. (See Jones, 1969; Hallam, 1973a, 1973b, n.d.)

The population relationships which Tindale, Birdsell and Stanner sought to delineate were thus not determined by the adjustment of population to static, given, resources; but by dynamic interactions and mutual adjustments within a total ecosystem, in which human populations were just one, though a dominant and active rather than merely reactive, component. Their adjustments showed flexibility in grouping and spacing, territorial attachment, technology, economy, skills, lore, myth, ritual, and socio-demographic organisation.

The future tasks of regional archaeologists within the continent—and the general Australian picture can emerge only from the regional studies in which we are properly engrossed (eg., McBryde, 1964, 1975; Dortch, 1972; Hallam, 1972a, 1973b, n.d.)—must include detailed investigation of such dynamic processes over time, by surface investigations of wide areas, systematically sampled, to obtain ratios between intensity of usage for different zones (as for instance, the inland margin of the jarrah forest and the coastal plain) in different phases, and from these to deduce relative figures for population densities, using the contact situation as a base-line; looking also at the relative usage of different sub-zones (for example—alluvium, swampy sand-plain, limestone soils, and coastal dunes) and so, by implication, at the relative usage of different types of resources within the range; examining significant differences in the proportions of site-types within each zone; and summoning also all available evidence, both archaeological and ethnographic, for the symbolic–cognitive aspects of the linkage of landed groups and peopled landscape.

Coda

'Recovering', in Clarke's words, 'unobservable hominid behaviour from indirect traces in bad samples'—is the task of the topographic archaeologist. He must be systematic without being uninspired; numerate without ceasing to be literate; know how to test hypotheses, but dare to explore sufficiently to generate new ones; concern himself with both the regularities and the particularities of his material; with scientific explanation of behaviour and its products in terms of mechanism and function; and with historical explication of continuity of structure and change through time. He must appraise continuity as essential to change, movement as essential to settlement, ritual and symbolic activity as maintaining *ecological* patterning; ecological 'niche-carving' as achieved with *cultural* tools, and as remoulding not only biotic communities, but also shaping those tools, the group's cultural knowledge and equipment, themselves. His statistical analyses will lead back to territorial groups within a populated landscape, adjusting their behaviour to the changing potentialities of themselves and the landscape through time, to achieve as far as possible 'the good life'.

References

Alford, J. L., 1970. Extinction as a possible factor in the invention of New Word agriculture. *Professional Geographer*, 22 : 120–3.

Allen, H., 1974. The Bagundji of the Darling Basin: cereal gatherers in an uncertain environment. *World Archaeology*, 5 : 309–22.

Bowler, J. M., A. G. Thorne and H. A. Polach, 1972. Pleistocene Man in Australia: age and significance of the Mungo skeleton. *Nature*, 240 : 48–50.

Barbetti, M. and H. Allen, 1972. Prehistoric man at Lake Mungo by 32 000 years B.P. *Nature*, 240 : 46–48.

Binford, L. R., 1968. Archaeological perspectives. *In* S. and L. R. Binford (eds), *New perspectives in archaeology*, pp. 5–32. Chicago: Aldine Publishing.

Binns, R. A. and I. McBryde, 1969. Preliminary report on a petrological study of ground-edge artifacts from North-Eastern New South Wales, Australia. *Proceedings of the Prehistoric Society*, 35 : 229–35.

—— and —— 1972. *Petrological analysis of ground-edge artifacts from Northern New South Wales*. Canberra: Australian Institute of Aboriginal Studies.

Birdsell, J. B., 1953. Some environmental and cultural factors influencing the structuring of Australian Aboriginal populations. *The American Naturalist*, 87 : 171–207.

—— 1973. A basic demographic unit. *Current Anthropology*, 14 : 337–56.

Bulmer, R., 1968. Strategies of hunting in New Guinea. *Oceania*, 38 : 302–18.

Bunbury, H. W., 1930. *Early days in Western Australia*. London: Oxford University Press.

Butzer, K., 1971. *Environment and Archaeology: an ecological approach to prehistory*. (2nd ed.) London: Methuen.

Chang, K. C., 1968. Towards a science of prehistoric archaeology. *In* Chang, K. C. (ed.) *Settlement archaeology*, pp. 1–9. Mayfield: Palto Alto.

Childe, V. G., 1944. *Progress and Archaeology*. London: Watts and Co., Thinkers Library, no. 102.

Churchill, D. M., 1959. Late Quaternary eustatic changes in the Swan River district. *Journal & Proceedings of the Royal Society of Western Australia*, 42 : 53–55.

—— 1960. Late Quaternary changes in the vegetation on Rottnest Island. *Western Australian Naturalist*, 7 : 1960–66.

—— 1968. The distribution and prehistory of *Eucalyptus diversicolor . . ., E. marginata . . .,* and *E. calophylla . . .* in relation to rainfall. *The Australian Journal of Botany*, 16 : 125–51.

—— 1970. Post-Neolithic to Romano-British sedimentation in the Southern Fenlands of Cambridgeshire and Norfolk. *In* P. Salway, S. J. Hallam and A. Bromwich (eds) *The Fenland in Roman times*, pp. 132–46. New York: Royal Geographic Society Research series No. 5.

Clark, J. G. D., 1970. *Aspects of Prehistory*. New York: Berkeley.

—— 1972. *Star Carr: a case study in bioarchaeology*. McCaleb Module in Anthropology, no. 10.

—— and M. E. Godwin and W. A. Macfadyen, 1933. Report on an Early Bronze Age site in the South-eastern Fens. *Antiquaries Journal*, 13 : 266–96.

—— and M. H. Clifford, 1935. Report on recent excavations in Peacock's Farm, Shippea Hill, Cambridgeshire. *Antiquaries Journal*, 15 : 284–319.

—— and H. Godwin, 1962. The Neolithic in the Cambridgeshire Fens. *Antiquity*, 36 : 10–23.

Clarke, W. C., 1966. From extensive to intensive shifting agriculture: a succession from New Guinea. *Ethnology*, 5(4) : 347–59.

Coles, J. M., 1971. The early settlement of Scotland: excavations at Morton, Fife. *Proceedings of the Prehistoric Society*, 37(2) : 284–366.

Cunliffe, B., 1973. Chalton, Hants: the evolution of a landscape. *The Antiquaries Journal*, 53 : 174–90.

Dimbleby, G. W., 1961. The ancient forest of Blackamore. *Antiquity*, 35 : 123–28.

—— 1962. *The development of British heathlands and their soils*. Oxford: Clarendon Press.

Dortch, C. E., 1972. Archaeological work in the Ord Reservoir area, East Kimberley. *Australian Institute of Aboriginal Studies Newsletter*, 3(4) : 13–18.

—— and D. Merrilees, 1973. Human occupation of Devil's Lair, Western Australia, during the Pleistocene. *Archaeology and Physical Anthropology in Oceania*, 8(2) : 89–115.

Eyre, E. J., 1845. *Journals of expeditions of discovery into Central Australia, and overland from Adelaide to King George Sound, in the years 1840–1. . . . including an account of the manners and customs of the aborigines and the state of their relations with Europeans*. London: T. and W. Boone. (Reprinted 1964 Australiana Facsimile Edition, No. 7, Adelaide).

Flannery, K. V., 1968. Archaeological systems theory and early Mesoamerica. *In* Meggers B. (ed.) *Anthropological Archaeology in the Americas*, pp. 67–87. Washington, D.C.: Anthropological Society of Washington. Reprinted 1971, pp. 344–64, in *Man's imprint from the past; readings in the methods of archaeology*, J. Deetz (ed.). Boston: Little, Brown and Co.

Fowler, P. J. (ed.), 1972. *Archaeology and landscape: Essays for L. V. Grinsell*. London: John Baker.

Frake, C. O., 1962. Cultural ecology and ethnography. *American Anthropologist*, 64 : 53–59.

Glover, J. E. and A. Cockbain, 1971. Transported Aboriginal artifact material, Perth Basin, Western Australia. *Nature*, 234 : 545–46.

Godwin, H., 1940. Studies in the post-glacial history of British vegetation. III. Fenland pollen diagrams. IV. Post-glacial changes of relative land- and sea-levels in the English Fenland. *Philosophical Transactions of the Royal Society*, 230B : 239–303.

—— 1944. Age and origin of the Breckland heaths of East Anglia. *Nature*, 154 : 6–7.

—— and M. H. Clifford, 1939. Studies in the post-glacial history of British vegetation: I. Origin and stratigraphy of Fenland deposits near Wood Walton, Hunts.; II. Origin and stratigraphy of deposits in southern Fenland. *Philosophical Transactions of the Royal Society*, 229B : 323–406.

Gorman, C., 1969/70. Hoabinhian: a pebble-tool complex with early plant associations in South-East Asia. *Proceedings of the Prehistoric Society*, 35 : 355–58.

—— 1971. The Hoabinhian and after: subsistence patterns in Southeast Asia during the late Pleistocene and early Recent periods. *World Archaeology*, 2 : 300–20.

Gould, R. A., 1971. The archaeologist as ethnographer: a case from the Western Desert of Australia. *World Archaeology*, 3 : 143–77.

——, D. Koster and A. H. L. Sontz, 1971. The lithic assemblage of the Western Desert Aborigines of Australia. *American Antiquity*, 36(2) : 149–69.

Green, R. C., 1967. Settlement patterns: four case studies from Polynesia. *In* W. G. Solheim (ed.) *Archaeology in the Eleventh Pacific Science Congress*, pp. 101–32. Honolulu: University of Hawaii, Social Science Research Institute.

Grey, Sir G., 1841. *Journals of two expeditions in northwestern and western Australia during the years 1837, 1838 and 1839*. 2 vols. London. (Reprinted 1964, Australian Facsimile Edition, No. 8, Adelaide.)

Hallam, S. J., 1964. Villages in Roman Britain: some evidence. *Antiquaries Journal*, 44 : 19–32.

—— 1970. Settlement round the Wash. *In* P. Salway, S. J. Hallam and A. Bromwick (eds) *The Fenland in Roman Times*, pp. 22–113.

—— 1972a. An archaeological survey of the Perth area, Western Australia: a progress report on art and artifacts, dates and demography. *Australian Institute of Aboriginal Studies*, Newsletter, 3(5) : 11–19.

—— 1972b. Comment on A. Marshack 'Cognitive aspects of Upper Palaeolithic engraving'. *Current Anthropology*, 13 : 464–65.

—— 1973a. Comment on J. R. Harlan and J. M. J. de Wet 'On the quality of evidence for origin and dispersal of cultivated plants'. *Current Anthropology*, 14 : 57–58.

—— 1973b. Ecology and demography in south-western Australia. *Journal of the Royal Society of Western Australia*, 56 : 46–48.

—— 1974. *Fire and hearth; a study of Aboriginal usage and European usurpation in south-western Australia*. Canberra: Australian Institute of Aboriginal Studies.

—— n.d. Recent archaeological research in Western Australia. *Australian Archaeology*, forthcoming.

Hammond, J. E. (ed. P. Hasluck) (1933). *Winjan's people: the story of the south-west Australian Aborigines*. Perth: Imperial Printing Co.

Harlan, J. R. and J. M. J. de Wet, 1973. On the quality of evidence for origin and dispersal of cultivated plants. *Current Anthropology*, 14 : 51–55.

Hassell, E. and D. S. Davidson, 1936. Ethnology of the Wheelman tribe of south-western Australia. *Anthropos*, 31 : 676–711.

Hole, F. and K. V. Flannery, 1967/68. The prehistory of Southwestern Iran: a preliminary report. *Proceedings of the Prehistoric Society*, 33 : 147–206.

Hope, G. S. and P. J. F. Coutts, 1971. Past and present food resources at Wilson's Promontory, Victoria. *Mankind*, 8 : 104–14.

Isaac, G., 1969. Studies of early culture in East Africa. *World Archaeology*, 1 : 1–28.

—— 1971. The diet of early man: aspects of archaeological evidence from lower and middle Pleistocene sites in Africa. *World Archaeology*, 2 : 278–99.

Iversen, J., 1941. *Landnam in Danmarks Stanalder* (*Land Occupation in Denmark's Stone Age*.) *Danmarks Geologiske Undersogelse*. Series 2, No. 66. Copenhagen.

Jennings, J. N., 1965. Man as a geological agent. *Australian Journal of Science*, 20 : 150–56.

Jones, R., 1968. The geographical background to the arrival of man in Australia and Tasmania. *Archaeology & Physical Anthropology in Oceania*, 3 : 186–215.

—— 1969. Fire-stick farming. *Australian Natural History*, 16 : 224–28.

—— 1971. The demography of hunters and farmers in Tasmania. *In* D. J. Mulvaney and J. Golson (eds) *Aboriginal Man and Environment in Australia*, pp. 270–87. Canberra: Australian National University Press.

—— 1973. The emerging picture of Pleistocene Australians. *Nature*, 246 : 278–81.

Lampert, R. J. and F. Sanders, 1973. Plants and men on the Beecroft Peninsula, New South Wales. *Mankind*, 9 : 96–108.

Martin, P. S., 1973. The discovery of America. *Science*, 179 : 969–74.

McBryde, I., 1964. Archaeological field survey work in northern New South Wales. *Oceania*, 33 : 12–17.

—— 1975. *Aboriginal prehistory in New England. An archaeological survey in northeastern New South Wales*. Sydney: Sydney University Press.

Meggitt, M. J., 1962. *Desert people : a study of the Walbiri Aborigines of Central Australia*. Sydney: Angus and Robertson.

Merrilees, D., 1968. Man the destroyer: late Quaternary changes in the Australian marsupial fauna. *Journal of the Royal Society of Western Australia*, 51 : 1–24.

Moore, G. F., 1842. *A Descriptive Vocabulary of the Language in Common Use amongst the Aborigines of Western Australia: with copious meanings embodying much interesting information regarding the habits, manners and customs of the natives and the Natural History of the country*. Reprinted in 1884, in the same covers as his *Diary*, paginated separately.

Robbins, R. G., 1972. Vegetation and man in the South-west Pacific and New Guinea. *In* R. G. Ward (ed.) *Man in the Pacific Islands*, pp. 74–90. London: Oxford University Press.

Salway, P., S. J. Hallam and J. I. A. Bromwich, 1970. *The Fenland in Roman Times: studies of a major area of peasant colonization with a Gazetteer covering all known sites and finds*. (ed. C. W. Phillips) Royal Geographical Society Research Series No. 5.

Smith, A. G., 1970a. The stratigraphy of Northern Fenland. *In* P. Salway, S. J. Hallam and A. Bromwich (eds.) *The Fenland in Roman times*, pp. 147–64.

—— 1970b. The influence of Mesolithic and Neolithic man on British vegetation: a discussion. *In* D. Walker and R. G. West (eds.) *Studies in the vegetational history of the British Isles: Essays in honour of Harry Goodwin*, pp. 81–96. London: Cambridge University Press.

Smith, P. E. L., 1972. Changes in population pressure in archaeological explanation. *World Archaeology*, 4 : 6–18.

Solheim, W. G., 1972. An earlier agricultural revolution. *Scientific American*, 226(4) : 34–41.

Spaulding, A. C., 1960. The dimensions of archaeology. *In* G. E. Dale and R. L. Carneiro (eds) *Essays in the science of culture in honour of Leslie A White*, pp. 437–56. New York: Thomas Y. Crowell Co. Reprinted 1971, pp. 22–39 in *Man's imprint from the past: readings in the methods of archaeology*, J. Deetz (ed.). Boston: Little, Brown and Co.

Stanner, W. E. H., 1965. Aboriginal territorial organisation: estate, range, domain and regime. *Oceania*, 36 : 1–26.

Thomas, C., 1972. The present significance of fieldwork in the light of the Cornish parochial check-list survey. *In* P. J. Fowler (ed.) *Archaeology and landscape*, pp. 72–95. London: John Baker.

Thomas, D. H., 1973. An empirical test for Steward's model of Great Basin settlement patterns. *American Antiquity*, 38 : 155–76.

Tindale, N. B., 1940. Distribution of Australian Aboriginal tribes: a field survey. *Transactions of the Royal Society of South Australia*, 64(1) : 140–231.

Trigger, B. G., 1968. The determinants of settlement patterns. *In* K. Chang (ed.) *Settlement archaeology*, pp. 53–78. Mayfield: Palo Alto.

Ucko, P. J., R. Tringham and G. W. Dimbleby (eds.), 1972. *Man, settlement and urbanism*. London: Duckworth.

Vita-Finzi, C., 1969. *The Mediterranean Valleys: geological changes in historical times*. London: Cambridge University Press.

—— and E. S. Higgs, 1970. Prehistoric economy in the Mount Carmel area of Palestine: site catchment analysis. *Proceedings of the Prehistoric Society*, 36 : 1–37.

Walker, D. (ed.), 1972. *Bridge and barrier: the natural and cultural history of the Torres Strait*. Canberra: Research School of Pacific Studies, Dept. of Biogeography and Geomorphology, Australian National University.

White, C., 1967. The prehistory of the Kakadu people. *Mankind*, 6 : 426–31.

Willey, G. R., 1958. *Prehistoric settlement patterns in the New World*. Viking Fund Publication in Anthropology, No. 23.

Yellen, J. and H. Harpending, 1972. Hunter-gatherer populations and archaeological inference. *World Archaeology*, 4 : 244–53.

Stone tool functions in the Western Desert

BRIAN HAYDEN

Introduction

For relatively obscure reasons, chipped stone tools seem to have always fascinated at least some individuals in agricultural and industrial societies. Recognition of the special status of prehistoric stone artifacts has occurred among uneducated peasants, ignorant of the functions of these 'thunderstones', as well as among modern prehistorians and avid collectors who spend lives and fortunes on stones of the past. What lies behind this fascination? The totally alien nature of these objects to many modern men who wonder how such forms could have been fashioned out of rock and what they could have been used for may be one reason for the unusual attention given stone tools. Perhaps the fascination lies in the exotic shapes and curious forms; 'flat-irons', 'willow leaves', 'laurel leaves', 'sumatraliths', 'short axes', 'tortoise cores', 'horsehoof cores', 'pounds of butter' and others. Perhaps the unusual nature and aesthetic qualities of cryptocrystalline rocks are major factors. And perhaps it is simply the fact that they are virtually all that remains of an unknown and mysterious era of man's history. Such outlooks and values are, of course, those of relatively contemporary Occidental men.

Whatever the cause—and there may be more than are hinted at here (see Harris, 1968 : 676)—one of the principal results has been the mystification of stone tools, and the treating of them as semi-sacred relics. Archaeology has only recently begun to rid itself of this set of values. For the first century of archaeology most analysts were content to sit back and indulge themselves in aesthetic and emotional mysteries of the past, and the successive transformations of those mysteries. What the tools were used for and how they were used was for the most part unfathomable, or pure reverie. And, in many respects it made little difference to the archaeology of the day. People were concerned with tracing the movements of past peoples, the succession of cultures, the cultural history of artifacts, and the spiritual or aesthetic progression of mankind. For this, all that was required was the recording of changes in styles and types, and the improvements in craftsmanship.

I would maintain that it has been this mystification and relegation to the semi-sacred which are largely responsible for the otherwise unaccountable lack of first hand research effort by archaeologists in the area of ethnographic use of stone tools (indeed, up until recently there almost appeared to be an avoidance relationship!).[1] The same factors are probably responsible for the still pervasive and subjective feelings among

archaeologists that stone tools could not simply have been used in a totally profane or simple minded fashion. Although this is a subjective evaluation I think that most archaeologists, somewhere in the seat of their limbic systems, *feel* that most stone tools were carefully crafted, and that the stone tool maker was doing his best to make a tool worthy of his ancestors, or himself, or his group, or something else. Perhaps more importantly, archaeologists expected that prehistoric men were striving after the particular form that they crafted, and that all else was waste, or 'debitage'.

This attitude is apparent in a number of European site reports. For instance, de Lumley (1969 : 47, 50) observes that:

> Some of the tools found at Terra Amata were probably made on the spot. The hut floors show evidence of tool manufacturing . . . The toolmaker's place inside the huts is easily recognized: a patch of living floor is surrounded by the litter of tool manufacture.

Later, he applies Jullian's remarks to Terra Amata:

> The toolmaker's seat is where one man carefully pursues a work that is useful to many.

The explicit implication is that stone tools were carefully made, and that considerable skill was necessary in their manufacture, without which the group would be in troubled straits.

In 1971, I was interested in finding out what use fully traditional, fully stone-using hunter–gatherers made of stone tools. Although there is probably no one who still uses the full complement of traditional stone tools today in Australia due to the wide availability of metal, there are men and women in contact with Occidental institutions who have used most of the traditional tools earlier in their lives. I went to Cundeelee mission (Western Australia) and Papunya government settlement (Northern Territory) and worked with older men and women who had used stone tools in their youth, and who could still make and use nearly the full range of traditional chipped stone tools. The people I worked with were from the Pintupi, Yankuntjara, and 'Wangkayi' dialect areas. Because of my Occidental cultural and archaeological background, I was to experience many surprises. This paper is a presentation of some of the more important of those surprises concerning the functions and uses of stone tools. The insights which result from this study will hopefully help to reorient prehistorians' attitudes and interpretations of what they are dealing with in their study of lithic remains from the past.

Because the hafted adze has been dealt with rather extensively by previous writers (W. Roth, 1904; Thomson, 1964;

---

1. This is not to imply that no interest was taken in the use and manufacture of stone tools, although such observations are surprisingly rare. In Australia valuable data were recorded by Roth (1904), Spencer and Gillen (1899, 1912), Aiston (1928; Horne and Aiston, 1914), Basedow (1925), Love (1942), Mountford (1941), Tindale

(1941, 1965), Thomson (1964), and Gould (Gould, Koster and Sontz, 1971). These observations are invaluable; but almost invariably, except for Gould, none of these observers was an archaeologist by training, and with the further exception of Tindale, none was involved in archaeology in any professional way.

Tindale, 1965; Gould *et al.*, 1971), it will not generally be considered in the following discussion. Rather, the less well documented and less well known hand-held tools will be the primary focus of this paper.

Surprises

Values I was certainly not the first to make the observation that stone tools were used in almost an entirely profane manner by Western Desert Aboriginals (Gould, 1969 : 81–83; Gould *et al.*, 1971 : 163), and the idea is perhaps easily accepted intellectually; however, it still came as an emotional disappointment to actually see stone tools being used in traditional ways. The feeling of 'is that all there is to it?' was uncomfortable. I was unsure of exactly what was missing, but I felt that there ought to be more to using and making stone tools.

There were a number of factors which led to this feeling of 'is that what I came all this way to see?' Probably, the most immediately influential was the attitude of the Aboriginals themselves. They seemed uninterested in the stone they were using to the point of ignoring it except when the stone no longer was suited for continued use; they were predominantly interested in the work they were doing with the stone, such as making spears. A good analogy might be drawn between the amount of interest a contemporary Occidental person takes in the pencil he uses in writing the draft of a paper as opposed to the ideas and sentences of the paper. This lack of interest in stone was my first surprise.

Another surprise was the discovery that there were no master craftsmen of stone tool making (this may not have been strictly true of the Warramunga or Walbiri where prismatic blade knives were produced for trade). No one was capable of controlling the stone medium to anywhere near the degree attained by the renowned stone knappers in the Occident, such as Bordes. Instead, there was only a moderate degree of control over the stone medium; suitable flakes for work were often picked out of almost random flakes. However, the flakes that were obtained were perfectly adequate to the technological needs of all task activities. A similar lack of detailed control was noted among the Nakako and Pitjantjatjara by Tindale (1965 : 140, 160) and the Ngatatjara by Gould (Gould *et al.*, 1971 : 160) where 'cores' were often hurled at the ground or otherwise 'smashed' or flakes 'randomly' detached with a hammerstone. Suitable flakes were then chosen from the debris. Similar procedures were also used in the Kimberley area (Hardman, 1888 : 59) and in Tasmania as well (H. Ling Roth, 1899 : 151; Hambly, 1931 : 91). In an analogous vein, Thomson (1964 : 407) remarks on the variability in craftsmanship between individuals in making wooden bowls, indicating frequent modest control over the working medium.

Rarity of 'tools' But perhaps the biggest surprise, and 'disappointment', was the unbelievable lack, or rarity, or fabrication of what the archaeologist calls 'tools'. At first, I saw Aboriginals using only unretouched primary flakes for shaving and scraping wood, and unmodified blocks of stone for chopping wood. None of these would have been recognised archaeologically as 'tools'. I wondered if the tradition or knowledge of how to make retouched tools had been lost due to some epi-culture contact phenomenon. That was not the case. Some of the earlier observations on traditional uses of stone tools had described the same lack of retouched tools (Mountford, 1941 : 316; 1948; Tindale, 1941; Gould, 1969 :

81–83; Gould *et al.*, 1971 : 163), and it was even proposed that the Pitjantjatjara possessed one of the world's most primitive technologies, since they did not have retouched tools, but only used naturally occurring forms (with the exception of the hafted adze).

What became apparent to me after considerable field observation, was that retouched tools were indeed being produced, but relatively rarely. The reason for this may be explained in part by referring back to an axiom that Bordes has verbally expressed: namely that a stone flake is sharpest right after it has been removed from the core; any secondary retouch will only make it duller. Basedow (1925 : 365) implied a similar notion. Thus, only in special cases were flakes retouched. Instead of retouching primary flakes, the more common reaction of all informants was to look over other primary flakes that had been struck from the core, for a more suitable flake for the work at hand, or to remove several more flakes from the core until a suitable one was knocked off. Often several primary flakes might be tried out before one was found with a good working edge. Horne and Aiston (1924 : 91) noted earlier a similar behaviour pattern for groups around Lake Eyre:

> Casual stones are any that have a sharp edge. They are used for scraping. Directly they are blunt they are thrown away and another picked up. Sometimes they are chipped if the stone will keep its edge long enough to warrant chipping, but usually they are not kept.

This provides important substantiation for the observations made among Western Desert groups. It might also be added that the effectiveness of working edges was sometimes difficult to gauge by superficial visual inspection due to occasional small and subtle variations of the stone surfaces forming the working edge. Pieces were selected and tried out, and sometimes discarded immediately. Of course, preliminary choice of possibly suitable pieces was done by visual inspection.

It was difficult to determine what the criteria for deciding to retouch or discard any given flake were. One criterion, I am sure, was a subjective evaluation as to how suitable the edge would be if the flake was retouched. The probability of the 'resharpening' turning out satisfactorily might also have been weighed against the relatively minor trouble it would take to remove more primary flakes from the core. But when one is seated, and getting the core means getting up because it is out of reach, this seemingly minor trouble may be a decisive factor. Moreover, some of the pieces which were retouched were discarded almost immediately because the retouch had created an unsuitable working edge. At other times, resharpened pieces would continue to be satisfactorily used. It should be emphasised that this secondary retouch was done with the aim of 'resharpening' or rejuvenating a dulled working edge into a more suitable one. There was no indication of any overall morphological ideal type, 'classic' form, or 'perfect' specimen, as collectors are wont to say, and as archaeologists often tacitly accept in conversation. Rather, the traditional attributes of importance in the Western Desert were: effective edges (which were surprisingly variable in morphological expression), and a suitable size for holding in the hand and exerting pressure. These attributes might become more patterned by habit and tradition than one would expect, but this is only an impression. I lack quantitative data on this aspect.

Others have experienced similar surprises as well. Mountford (1941, 1948) saw stone using activities for only a short time period and concluded that except for the hafted adze, the Pitjantjatjara might vanish and no trace of them would be left

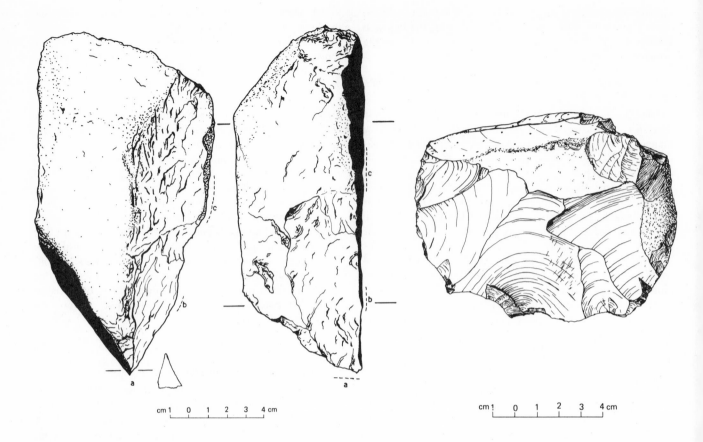

cm 1 0 1 2 3 4 cm   cm 1 0 1 2 3 4 cm

Fig. 1: Chopping implement made from local stone.   **Fig. 2:** Flaked chopping implement made of Wilson's Bluff flint.

behind. In New Guinea, Peter White (1967 : 409) was similarly 'surprised' by traditional stone tool behaviour, and originated the observation that the suitability of the edge in hand held tools is the important variable for stone tool manufacturers and users. His excellent observations have been supported by Strathern (1969).

One other factor which may influence the frequency with which primary flakes, used as tools, are retouched, is the availability of raw material. There was always spare raw material in the technological projects which I asked Western Desert individuals to work on. In traditional situations where raw material might be scarce, one could reasonably expect more primary flakes to exhibit retouch modifications. On the other hand, there was an abundance of flakes and a number of cores at most of the campsites I visited (also see Basedow, 1925 : 364; Thomson, 1964 : 406). In addition Aboriginals are known to have carried primary flakes around with them, as well as blocks of raw material (Thomson, 1964 : 405, plate 34; Basedow, 1925 : 364; Hayden, in press).

The type of raw material also appears to have an effect on the percentage of used implements which are modified. Where hard metamorphic or igneous rocks occur with naturally acute edges, I found that such rocks would be used for chopping wood, but were only modified intentionally less than 20% of the time (Figs. 1, 3). On the other hand, opal or flint nodules do not have naturally occurring acute, sharp angles as a rule, and thus flakes must often be removed from them in order to obtain a cutting edge (Figs. 2, 4). Therefore, about 90% of the flint and opal used in chopping wood had been modified by flake removal.

In dealing with primary flakes, sharp edges are present by definition. Of the flakes I saw used for 'scraping', or shaving (a more accurate descriptive term) wood, less than 25% were secondarily retouched or otherwise modified. These modified pieces did *not* always exhibit 'scraper' retouch (see below). It is tempting to conclude that retouched tools were made only when no suitable naturally occurring sharp edged rocks were immediately available (or in the case of primary flakes, only when primary flakes with suitable edges were not present). However, this would be an extreme position. There is little more, if any, effort involved in resharpening, or retouching, a tool in hand than in casting around for a better replacement, and there may well be some subtle reasons which I did not perceive, for choosing to retouch stones in particular circumstances.

Obviously, adzes were nearly always retouched, if merely because unhafting and rehafting are time consuming, and once a piece is in the haft it is in self interest to get as much use from it as possible. Nevertheless, hafted adzes are sometimes removed without being retouched, either because of breakage, unsuitability, or poor resharpening potential.

It thus appears that there is a basic dichotomy in the modes of stone tool use which has implications for behavioural patterns of resharpening and retouching stone tools. On one side of the dichotomy are hand-held tools which are less frequently retouched because procurement of other tools is relatively effortless (these tools are selected according to the criteria of edge effectiveness and grip); on the other side are hafted tools which are much more frequently retouched, rejuvenated or resharpened. This is because of increased

Fig. 3: Using the implement illustrated in Fig. 1.

Fig. 4: Using the chopping tool illustrated in Fig. 2.

replacement effort, and hafting requirements may strongly influence not only the size of the tool and attempts to reduce flakes to appropriate sizes, but also position of retouch on edges other than the working edge. This theoretical dichotomy may or may not turn out to have useful practical applications in archaeology. Certainly, hand-held tools generally seem to correspond to Binford's non-curated artifact class, and hafted tools correspond well to his curated artifact class (see p. 34). Caution should be exercised in making a one-to-one equivalence, however, since the transport and curation of unhafted flakes and 'scrapers' in bags, etc. are abundantly documented (W. Roth, 1904 : 20; Horne and Aiston, 1924 : 109; Spencer and Gillen, 1927 : 26).

To give some idea of the magnitude of retouched tool production under traditional conditions, I have attempted to calculate the number of *retouched* tools which a simple Western Desert nuclear family might fabricate in the course of a year. Although the estimate is inherently risky, at least it gives some idea of the magnitude of the problem with which archaeologists have to deal.

Table 1 gives my estimation (based on Pintupi statements and my own estimation) of the probable number of items which would have to be replaced in a nuclear family's material repertoire per year. The group on which this is based (formerly located just south of Lake Macdonald) had a limited variety of wooden tools, but many of the estimates are probably on the generous side, especially the replacement of spearthrowers, women's hardwood bowls, and 25 spears, on a yearly basis. I have calculated the number of archaeologically recognisable tools which would result from these maintenance tasks on the basis of actual retouched tools produced in their manufacture at Papunya settlement. If unmodified hand-held flake tools were incorporated those totals would have to be at least doubled. I have been liberal with the chopping implements and assumed that they were all modified; this is undoubtedly unrealistic for most cases.

As a cross-check, I also calculated the number of retouched 'tools' produced per person, per week at campsites occupied by informants when they were using stone tools exclusively, some 30 years or more ago. These rates were 2.5 to 10 flake tools per week per person (Hayden: in press), which gives

130–520 tools per person per year. This is in very good agreement with the above estimate when one realises that one of the sites was adjacent to a quarry, so that old adzes were probably discarded there, and at the other site, several spearthrowers were manufactured by young men, thereby inflating the number of tools used and produced over a short period of time. Thus, these estimates can be considered to be on the high side. For a basic husband and wife pair with non-producing children and elder parents, it seems reasonable to think of the average rate of retouched tool production as being around 150 per year (± 50), with about 40 (± 10) chopping implements being fashioned assuming almost all chopping implements were modified. Many of these tools will of course be scattered over the landscape at various locations, and it should be re-emphasised that lack of raw material may deflate these estimates considerably in some cases.

As should be apparent from the preceding discussion, many of these archaeological tools will be little more than superficially modified. Many of the functional choppers may have but one flake removed, while others may be 'used up' and be considered closer to the 'classic' type by some archaeologists (eg. Fig. 2). Western Desert archaeological tools are not generally predetermined forms, but rather mechanical results of having to create or resharpen a cutting edge one or more times. What determines the stage at which any given piece is discarded (unmodified, single flake removals, single resharpenings, or multiple resharpenings) is the nature of the material, the suitability of the individual piece for potential resharpening, availability of raw material, and the point at which the particular task at hand terminates. Thus, archaeological 'tools' are formed because of rejuvenation attempts, and pass through several stages. It is worth restating that habit or tradition may be an important factor in determining which pieces are perceived to have most resharpening potential as well as the mode of resharpening most frequently used.

Functions This leads to discussion of another surprise, or series of surprises, that I encountered during the technological projects. In the first place, I found that nearly all retouched stone tools were used in woodworking activities. This corresponds well with Long's (1971 : 269) observations of Pintupi life: 'certainly the main use of stone here was for shaping and maintaining wooden tools and weapons'. An occasional retouched piece may have been used or even made for other activities such as cutting meat or skins, but there is little doubt that the vast majority were used for woodworking. This is based on information from older Pintupi individuals, as well as the lack of manufacture of such retouched tools in any other technological projects that were undertaken, such as plant food procurement and processing. The Western Desert groups with whom I worked did not traditionally use skins for any purpose, so that in a wider Australian context, skin processing may have been another important activity for which retouched tools were produced. Recourse to other Australian and world-wide ethnographic observations of hunting–gathering groups using stone tools largely supports this impression of the dominating influence of woodworking in retouched stone tool waste. For Australia, I could only find four references which indicate the use of chipped stone tools in gathering or processing plant food:

(1) A reference by Jackson (1939) to chopping up fern roots with a unifacial implement. According to research done recently by Kamminga, this is almost certainly unreliable and incorrect (personal communication; see

Table 1 Estimate of retouched tools used yearly by an economically active nuclear family in subsistence related activities

	Stone tools needed in woodworking		
	Chopping Implements	Adzes	Hand-held Flake tools
Estimated yearly replacement of wood tools:			
1 spearthrower	5	14	1
3 throwing or adzing sticks	6	—	3
25 spears	12	50	25
spear resharpening	—	9*	10
1 woman's bowl (hardwood)	5	—	—
4 digging sticks	12	4	—
	40	77	39
			Total : 156

* from Gould (see this volume)

Bancroft, 1894; W. Roth, 1901 : 10);

(2) Tindale's observation (1941 : 37) that Western Desert chopping implements might be used to aid in digging holes for roots. This is a unique observation, digging sticks being the implement ubiquitously preferred. It seems highly likely that this was a fortuitous occurrence, or that the detachment of roots (a woodworking function) with chopping implements was confused with the actual act of excavating;

(3) Tindale's observation of using a crude hand chopper to cut off the husks of Pandanus fruit (Hale and Tindale 1933 : 114, 1934 : 131) is also ambiguous. It is not clear whether the implement was fashioned specifically for this purpose, or whether any stone would have served, and the use of a chopper was only a matter of convenience;

(4) O'Connell's recording of the former use of retouched blades as 'spoons' for eating tubers (see this volume).

I know of no definite statement from other parts of the world to indicate that chipped stone was used for procuring or processing plant foods. While there have been notable archaeological exceptions, such as cultures using sickles, there are certainly no grounds for assertions that pebble tools of Palaeolithic age were almost invariably used for chopping up plant food (Deevey, 1968 : 286). On the whole, I think that the generalisation that retouched hand-held tools were used for woodworking (and possibly skin working) is a profitable starting point in analysis. Obviously, microliths are excluded from consideration here.

As to butchering, the axiom that the sharpest flake is an unretouched one would be particularly significant since sharpness is of great importance in cutting, whereas it is not necessarily important in woodworking. In practice, any waste flake is habitually used for gutting and breaking the skin in butchering. This has been amply documented by others. Such flakes seem to be rarely retouched among the Pintupi,[1] as among the Ngatatjara. Gould (Gould *et al.*, 1971 : 156) observed that:

> These knives are discarded after only a few uses, and no effort is made to resharpen them. Thus they rarely show much in the way of secondary trimming and could be difficult for an archaeologist to recognize once the gum handle has decomposed.

For the Pitjantjara Tindale illustrates and describes the manufacture of several retouched 'knives' (1965 : 114–19). Consideration of the representativeness of these examples is rendered difficult because of several factors: (1) the larger flakes were never actually seen in use and no specific use for them is given, whereas the smaller 'knives' are described as having been primarily used to incise lines in wooden implements, and (2) the original observations were made in 1933, and the 1965 article was entirely reconstructed from field notes and memory. Indeed, the retouching of these 'knives' before they were even used is rather puzzling from a functional point of view. Of further interest is Tindale's (1965 : 141) implication that these knives often had one 'blunt, thick margin and a sharper, somewhat more arcuate one opposite'. These pieces, even though they are retouched in a similar fashion to scrapers and little used adzes, may well be morphologically distinguishable.

---

1. In Africa, MacCalman and Grobbelaar (1965) observed a group of stone using Ova-Tjimba. The parallels to the Australian situation in terms of retouching stone tools are striking. For instance, in the butchering of an ungulate, only unmodified flakes were selected from core knappings and used.

Aside from these instances of using unmodified flakes for butchering, every major ethnographic description of chipped stone tool use in Australia has mentioned woodworking of one sort or another much more frequently than any other activity. This is corroborated in Tasmania as well.

Morphology. *Choppers* For the time being, the unretouched flakes will be put aside. What did the retouched tools look like that were used in the manufacture of wooden spears, throwing sticks, spearthrowers, digging sticks, bowls, and other items? The choppers used for doing rough work were predominantly unifacial, although bifacial work was also present. Modification of the edges ranged from a single flake removal to flakes removed around the periphery, to good bifacial chopping tools (Fig. 2), and included large flake specimens. These are more fully illustrated elsewhere (Hayden: in press). They are not substantially different from the chopping implements found throughout the Western Desert on abandoned campsites today, and are generally not too different in size and weight from the Kartan heavy duty implements (Bauer, 1970). They are used for procuring wood for all wood implements, and are often used in finishing hardwood bowls, chopping out the interior of spearthrowers, thinning fighting spears, trimming branches off spear shafts, starting nocks for spear barbs, and initial shaping of spear points (eg. Figs. 3, 4). Such tools seem to be most often simply left at the site where the work was done after the task has been finished, an observation that Mountford also made (1941). Often they are fashioned out of quartzites and other non-cryptocrystalline rocks found locally. When good quality cryptocrystalline rocks were used they appeared to have been carried around and used as a source of raw material as well as a chopping implement, probably until the piece was exhausted (see Thomson, 1964 : 405; Hayden: in press). Interestingly, among both the dialectical groups with which I worked most, there was a separate name for cryptocrystalline and non-cryptocrystalline raw material suitable for making tools (*kanti* vs. *pilari* in Pintupi, and *kanti* vs. *kaltjiliri* in Yankuntjara), and on several occasions I witnessed fine grained opal material refused in favour of coarser grained metamorphics and quartzites. Contrary to what I expected, it did not at all seem as though the finer the grain of the material the more desirable it was for using. Instead of pitying the poor craftsmen who had only metamorphics to work with for core tools, as is done from time to time (Stockton, 1972 : 22), perhaps one should really pity the poor craftsmen who had only cryptocrystallines to work with. The latter may be more aesthetically appealing, and have better flaking properties, but edges on cryptocrystallines also tend to shatter more easily and become dulled more quickly when chopping hard woods. Perhaps the graininess of the metamorphics bites more into the grain of wood and is more effective in wood separation and detachment. Crabtree and Davis (1968 : 428) have indicated such results from their experiments.

Among the Yankuntjara people that I worked with, it appeared that there was a prohibition against women using cryptocrystalline rocks. One of the women I worked with said that she had never used '*kanti*' (flint, chert, opal, etc.), but had used *kaltjiliri*; whereas the men regularly used *kanti* for adze stones. A similar prohibition was recorded in Central Australia by Spencer and Gillen (1912 : 373, 376). Pintupi women also showed a preference for using *pilari*, or non-cryptocrystalline rocks, and for using choppers, as opposed to adzes, in all their woodwork. Where a man would use an adze to hollow out or thin down hardwood, a woman would use a

Fig. 5: Shaving the point of a spear with a notched flake.

Fig. 6: Using a flake shaving implement in smoothing down the shaft of a spear. Note the denticulated form of resharpening along the working edge.

chopper. When women did attempt to use adzes, they were inevitably more clumsy than males. Women also employed grinding for finishing their digging sticks, sharpening the blades, and smoothing the surfaces of bowls and fighting sticks. They said that they always used a *tjiwa* (small sandstone pounding slab) for such purposes. This was first recorded in the Western Desert by Basedow (1925 : 362), and later substantiated by Finlayson (1943 : 79) and Thomson (1964). It was probably a relatively widespread alternative method of working wood throughout Australia (see also Horne and Aiston, 1924 : 93) and was also employed in parts of Tasmania. I never saw any men use grinding on their wood implements.

Thus, in terms of chipped stone tools, grainy chopping implements were used by men and women, although women tended to use such tools to the exclusion of other types. It seems that women only occasionally used hafted adzes, whether by proscription or simple preference, and used grinding to sharpen or finish many of their tools. Edge angles on these heavy duty stone chopping implements were generally high; the mode of the edge angle was 75°.

One of the implications of the above is that women do not seem to use or make any type of chipped stone tool which is unique to their sex in the Western Desert. Females will be very difficult to see archaeologically, unless via the small flat slabs and hammerstones on which lizards were pounded and leaves for pitchuri (a species of *Nicotina*) ash burned, although even here single males use the same articles. If grinding stones are present, they are probably the best indicator, although absence of grinders is poor negative evidence for the absence of women.

Flake tools As for the morphology of the retouched hand-held flake tools, here again there was a surprise. I rather expected that if the primary flakes being used to shave (not really 'scrape') down the spear shafts were to be retouched, or sharpened, that the form of the retouch would be of the 'scraper' type. In fact, only about one half of the instances turned out this way. What I did not expect was that there could be alternative ways of achieving the same goal. For instance, a single flake might be removed from the edge, thereby creating an archaeologist's 'notch' (I am not referring here to minute denticulations, but to the larger types). These pieces are used exactly in the same way as the original flake, except that there is a new edge to cut with, which is sometimes more effective than the former edge (Figs. 5, 6). Such modifications when repeated, yield denticulates. There was even one instance where a flake was first resharpened with a notch and then flaked back into a scraper. With my limited sample, it was difficult to be sure, but I could detect no regular patterning in decisions to use either notch or scraper retouch. They appeared to occur in free variation. Even more astonishing was the finding of a very small burin in one of the ethnographic excavations, which Ngayuwa, an older Pintupi man, claimed to have made and used some 30 years before. What had he used it for? He said that he had used it for shaving down his spears. His tone seemed to question whether anyone would think of using hand held flakes for anything else. In this case, it was the side edge of the burin which was used. True burins are occasionally found in Australia (Mulvaney, 1969). Ngayuwa said that he had not learned how to make them from anyone, but that he had just thought of how to do it himself; it was about the only one he had ever made. The credibility of this story is difficult to assess; however it should be pointed out that at the settlement, Ngayuwa,

while in the process of knapping flakes for finishing spears had picked out a flake with a broken edge, which had a cross section much like a burin-blow edge. He examined the piece carefully, and placed it aside, saying that it was a good one, and he used it later as a flake shaver, and an effective one at that. Ngayuwa did not single out any other flake in such a fashion. Moreover, many of the primary flakes used at Cundeelee and Papunya had working edges close to a right angle (Fig. 7). Up until this point, the extensive use of such flakes seemed a disappointing enigma. They were obviously unsuited for retouching, and never were retouched. According to my background, hunter–gatherers should have been using real 'tools' for woodworking, not broken edges of flakes or accidental right angled edges.

Regardless of the reliability of Ngayuwa's story about the excavated burin, it did provide credible insights into possibly the major function of burins as a broad class. The slightly less than right angled edges, strongly buttressed by the body of the flake, provide excellent shaving edges which dull slowly and are very efficient as well. This has been recognised experimentally by Crabtree and Davis (1968 : 46). Many flakes with right angle breaks or edges, present the same burin cross-sectional characteristics; these are recognised and used by Western Desert Aborigines. In short, it seems as though the scraper, notch, denticulate, and burin, may well be stylistic variants of a single functional type. All of these can be used for shaving down and sharpening the ends of wooden shaft implements, particularly spears, throwing sticks, digging sticks, adze shafts, and even parts of Western Desert spear-throwers. There is the possibility that these differing types of retouch may have been used more differentially in various specialised contexts; for instance, notches might be used especially for sharpening the ends of spears, or notches might not be used on thick shafted implements, such as throwing sticks. However there is no ethnographic evidence for such assertions at this point; the occurrence of hand-held retouched tools was simply too infrequent for me to be able to arrive at any meaningful statements of preference or frequency.

I also observed flakes being used in a sawing motion for the fabrication of barbs on a particular type of Pintupi spear (the *karimpa*; Fig. 8). These saw-flakes were changed frequently, and only three out of a total of seventeen were retouched: two with notches and one with scraper retouch. One notch, near the end of a flake, was used primarily in severing cross-grain wood fibres in the barb nocks, and was not actually used in a sawing motion. The other was never used. In addition, Tindale (1965 : 147) notes that small (*c*. 3 cm long) resin-backed 'knives', which have slightly serrated edges make effective saws for incising decorative lines. A surprisingly high percentage of the saws I observed in use carried an abrupt, often cortex covered, edge opposite the working edge. Tindale implies the same characteristics for his 'knives'.

Vertically oriented rocks One of the more intriguing observations on the non-retouched artifacts concerned relatively large, flatish rocks which were embedded vertically in the sand. I saw this phenomenon twice: once in the technological projects and once in the context of an ethnographic excavation. The use was the same in both cases. The vertical slab served as a fulcrum, or pressure point, for the straightening of spears. One's hands about a metre apart would firmly grasp the spear with the part to be straightened in the middle. The centre section was then placed on the apex of the slab and force applied downward (after heating the shaft in ashes). At

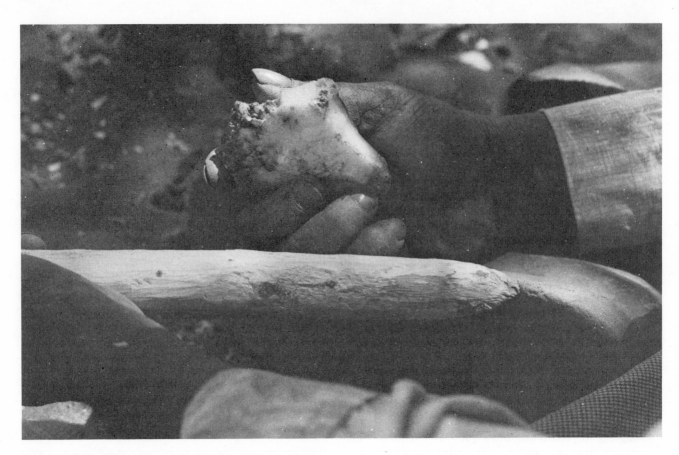

Fig. 7: Using an obtuse angled cutting edge to shave a spear shaft.

Fig. 8: Using an unmodified flake saw to undercut the sides of the *karimpa* spear barbs.

the settlement, this was done using a slab of flat cinder block: at the former campsite, a slab of iron rich metamorphic was used; it was about 20 cm in length, and more or less like a scalene triangle in cross-section. Elsewhere in the Western Desert, wooden blocks or 'Y' uprights have been observed to serve the same function (Ackerman, 1974). One of the interesting aspects of this observation is that at Isimila, Howell (1961 : 121) has reported a number of handaxes set on their sides vertically in the ground. Howell was puzzled by the enigmatically positioned artifacts. On the basis of the above observation, I would argue that there is a strong probability that the vertically oriented handaxes were used as fulcrums for straightening spears.

Wear patterns

Since a primary concern was the archaeological identification of functions of stone tools, the wear pattern on all tools was examined. Here lay yet another surprise. One might ordinarily expect hard woods to abrade stone to the greatest extent, and soft woods to leave little trace of wear at all. Whereas, in reality, stone tools used to work hard woods traditionally used by Western Desert groups, showed little trace of any distinctive or diagnostic micro edge wear; while stone used to carve out the exceptionally soft and light wood of the bean tree (*Erythrina vespertilio*) for shields and bowls seemed to dissolve the edge of the stone tools in very short time. In this latter case, a very high frequency of gloss and striations occurred. These findings are more fully presented by Hayden and Kamminga (1973).

Discussion

The above results are fundamentally empirical in nature, however, it would be a mistake to let theoretical and interpretational implications go unrecognised. I would argue that in the first place, these observations set up a more viable model of the importance and role of stone tools in generalised hunter–gatherer societies of the Australian Western Desert than the more traditional models and expectations derived from Occidental archaeology. It was in fact the extremeness of Occidental archaeological assumptions, based on no more than subjective feelings of empathy with the unknown past, which led to reluctance in accepting a traditional situation as real when actually encountered. Binford (1972) has termed such discrepancies, 'surprises', and the term is particularly appropriate to my own field experience. Others have previously made some of these same observations (Basedow, 1925; Mountford, 1941; Tindale, 1941; Gould *et al.*, 1971). I would like to help articulate the importance of these observations for archaeology. Moreover, with the same basic types of morphological tools found in large numbers elsewhere in the world, it may well be that insights derived from the Western Desert of Australia will have a wider application. Certainly, many of the possibilities which have been raised can be tested rather directly with archaeological techniques. For instance, when wear patterns are present on burins used for shaving shaft implements, edge damage and wear should be found on the sides, not on the point, which is often assumed to be the functional part (as the name implies). Similarly, if wear is found on notches or denticulates, or scrapers used for shaving shafts of wood implements, the wear should be found predominantly on the ventral face of the edge, and only slightly,

if at all on the retouched face of the edge. Also, if scrapers and notches and denticulates (and burins) are really stylistic variants of the same functional tool, then spatial distributional analysis of these different types on living floors should yield high spatial intercorrelations. Such applications might be particularly profitable with early Australian assemblages where one can probably assume that chopping implements and hand-held tools functionally replace the hafted adze.

Retouching behaviour has been divided into two types with differing determining factors: retouch on hand-held tools (possibly analogous to non-curated tools) and retouch on hafted tools (analogous to curated tools). Further, the influence of raw material on assemblages has been shown to be an important factor, and perhaps should be examined more carefully by prehistorians dealing with interassemblage variability. Indeed, it is doubtful whether the entire question of the effects of raw material on assemblages has ever been satisfactorily resolved.

Except for their grinding stones, and at burials, women seem to be exceptionally elusive in terms of archaeological visibility. With contemporary ethnological attention turning more and more toward the theoretical importance of women in hunting–gathering cultures, perhaps archaeologists should concern themselves with the nuances in material culture which may reflect their presence.

Perhaps most fundamentally, I hope to have provided what I believe is a more realistic model of the types of activities which stone tool debris represents. And even if the model is not viable for some areas, initial parameters (wear patterns, patterns of association, etc.) have been set out by which the model can be validated or invalidated. The data also make one look questioningly at some of the functional interpretations of Mousterian 'factor IV' tools—denticulates, notches, abrupt edge side scrapers, raclettes, and truncations—as representing plant food processing activities. In face, chipped stone tools appear to be used very rarely for gathering or processing plant foods among hunter–gatherers.

Finally, the realisation that many archaeological types, formerly considered very different and distinct, may actually be variants of the same functional tool, brings into question the entire problem of defining 'style' and recognising stylistic variants in archaeological contexts. I doubt that this issue has ever been dealt with directly or adequately by archaeologists, or that anyone has yet expressed the notion that stylistic variants can occur at several different levels of abstraction. It seems that in terms of contemporary aims and goals of archaeology, this would be one of the more critical conceptual areas to deal with. Perhaps this presentation of ethnographic and detailed lithic morphological data will help crystallise concepts and approaches to the problem. The issue of style is much too broad to deal with here, but hopefully the present study will have advanced the formulation of the questions in profitable forms.

Acknowledgement I wish to thank all the Pintupi and Yankuntjara individuals for their understanding and help, and for helping me to understand. The Australian Institute of Aboriginal Studies financed the basic research, the Department of Anthropology at the University of Sydney provided laboratory space and facilities, the Australian–American Educational Foundation provided transportation. I owe special debts to Peter White, Robert Edwards, John Mulvaney, Maxine Kleindienst, Jo Kamminga, and Jim O'Connell for their generous hospitality and provoking conversation.

References

Ackerman, K., 1974. Spear making sites in the Western Desert, Western Australia, *Mankind*, 9 : 310–14.

Aiston, G., 1928. *Chipped stone tools of the Aboriginal tribes east and north-east of Lake Eyre, South Australia.* Papers and Proceedings, Royal Society of Tasmania.

Bancroft, T. L., 1894. Note on Bungwal, (*Blechnum serralatum*, Rich), an Aboriginal food. *Linnean Society of New South Wales, Proceedings*, 1 : 25–26.

Basedow, H., 1925. *The Australian Aboriginal.* Adelaide: Preece.

Bauer, F. H., 1970. The Kartans of Kangaroo Island, South Australia: a puzzle in extinction. *In* A. Pilling and R. Waterman (eds) *Diprotodon to detribalisation*, pp. 198–216. East Lansing: Michigan State University Press.

Binford, L., 1972. Model building-paradigms, and the current state of Paleolithic research. *In* L. R. Binford (ed.) *An archaeological perspective*, pp. 244–94. New York: Seminar Press.

Crabtree, D. and E. L. Davis, 1968. Experimental manufacture of wooden implements with tools of flaked stone. *Science*, 159 : 426–68.

Deevey, E. Jr., 1968. Discussion. In R. Lee and L. Devore (eds) *Man the hunter*, p. 286. Chicago: Aldine.

Finlayson, H. H., 1943. *The red centre: man and beast in the heart of Australia.* Sydney: Angus and Robertson.

Gould, R. A., D. A. Koster and A. H. L. Sontz, 1971. *The lithic assemblage of the Western Desert Aborigines of Australia.* American Antiquity, 36 : 149–69.

Hale, H. and N. Tindale, 1933–34. Aborigines of Princess Charlotte Bay, North Queensland. *Records, South Australian Museum*, 5 : 63–116, 117–72.

Hambly, W. D., 1931. Types of 'tronattas,' or stone implements used by the Aborigines of Tasmania. *American Anthropologist*, 33 : 88–91.

Hardman, E. T., 1888. Notes on the collection of native weapons and implements from tropical Western Australia (Kimberley District). *Royal Australian Irish Academy, Proceedings* 1(1) : 57–69.

Harris, M., 1968. *The rise of anthropological theory.* New York: Crowell.

Hayden, B., n.d. *Lithic technology and ethnographic excavations in the Western Desert.* Australian Institute of Aboriginal Studies. In press.

—— and J. Kamminga, 1973. Gould, Koster and Sontz on 'microwear': a critical review. *Newsletter of lithic technology*, 2 : 3–14.

Horne, G. and G. Aiston, 1924. *Savage life in Central Australia.* London: Macmillan.

Howell, F., 1961. Isimila: a Paleolithic site in Africa. *Scientific American*, 205 : 118–29.

Jackson, G. K., 1939. Aboriginal middens of the Point Cartwright district. *Memoirs, Queensland Museum*, 11 : 289–95.

Long, J. P. M., 1971. Arid region Aborigines: the Pintubi. *In* D. J. Mulvaney and J. Golson (eds) *Aboriginal man and environment in Australia.* Canberra: Australian National University Press.

Love, J., 1942. A primitive method of making a wooden dish by native women of the Musgrave Ranges, South Australia. *Transactions, Royal Society of South Australia*, 66 : 215–17.

de Lumley, H., 1969. A Paleolithic camp at Nice. *Scientific American*, 220 : 42–50.

MacCalman, H. R. and B. J. Grobbelaar, 1965. Preliminary report of two stone-working Ova Tjimba groups in the northern Kaokoveld of South West Africa. *Cimbebasia*, 13.

Mountford, C. P., 1941. An unrecorded method of manufacturing wooden implements by simple stone tools. *Transactions, Royal Society of South Australia.* 65 : 312–16.

—— 1948. *Brown men and red sand.* Sydney: Angus and Robertson.

Mulvaney, D. J., 1969. *The prehistory of Australia.* London: Thames & Hudson.

Roth, H. L., 1899. *The Aborigines of Tasmania.* Halifax: F. King & Sons.

Roth, W. E., 1901. *Food: its search, capture, and preparation.* North Queensland Ethnography: Bulletin No. 3. Brisbane: Government Printer.

—— 1904. *Domestic implements, arts and manufacture.* North Queensland Ethnography: Bulletin No. 7. Brisbane: Government Printer.

Spencer, W. B. and F. J. Gillen, 1899. *The native tribes of Central Australia.* London: Macmillan.

—— and —— 1912. *Across Australia.* London: Macmillan.

—— and —— 1927. *The Arunta.* London: Macmillan.

Stockton, E., 1972. A central coast survey. *Australian Institute of Aboriginal Studies, Newsletter*, 3 : 20–24.

Strathern, M., 1969. Stone axes and flake tools: evaluations from two New Guinea Highlands societies. *Proceedings, Prehistoric Society*, 35 : 311–29.

Thomson, D., 1964. Some wood and stone implements of the Bindibu tribes of central western Australia. *Proceedings, Prehistoric Society*, 30 : 400–22.

Tindale, N. B., 1941. The hand axe used in the Western Desert of Australia. *Mankind*, 3 : 37–41.

—— 1965. Stone implement making among the Nakako Ngadadjara, and Pitjantjara of the Great Western Desert *South Australian Museum, Records*, 15 : 131–64.

White, J. P., 1967. Ethno-archaeology in New Guinea: two examples. *Mankind*, 6 : 409–14.

The Tasmanian paradox

RHYS JONES

This paper is about the causes of technological change, or rather, it is about a paradox which has emerged when a preconception as to the relative efficiency of two sets of technologies was tested against the evidence of ethnographic observation, or failing that, perhaps it is about an aberration that seemingly does not conform to general laws of human behaviour, an aberration only to be expected in such a bizarre part of the world as the Antipodes, and of no relevance to more normal places found on the proper, or upper side of most schoolboy atlases.

A parable

Leaving aside such polemics, let us consider what explanation would be offered for the following archaeological manifestation. Imagine over an entire continent and throughout a period of several tens of thousands of years, that all flaked stone assemblages consisted of scrapers of a few types, comparable in shape with say some of those of the Mousterian, together with core tools and pebble choppers (Fig. 1b). Then imagine a complex of new stone industries making a sudden appearance in the record, probably as additions to elements of the previous technology. The new industries contained variously, geometric backed microliths of various types suggestive of the Maglemosian, lanceolate unifacial and bifacial points like those of the Solutrean, tiny flake chisels as bits for composite tools and many other types (Fig. 1a). In this second phase, there was great spacial and temporal diversity, giving an impression of dynamism and flux compared with the conservatism of the previous millennia. Surely, if we were confronted by such a sequence, we would have argued that the tools of the second complex of industries were more sophisticated than those of the first, requiring greater skill and effort in their manufacture, and being more task specific. More importantly, we might have explained the adoption of the second kit or kits in terms of greater efficiency of use and perhaps in the deployment of new economic tasks beyond the capacity of the older one. The new technology would have given its users a powerful selective advantage in energy extraction, resulting in a radically greater population density, perhaps with associated reorganisation of society into larger or more numerous units. If we were not content to allow such assertions to masquerade as theories, we might try to test our explanations by looking for evidence in the archaeological record for the economic, demographic or organisational changes inferred above.

Supposing however, that by some ingenuity of imagination we were to place a large and ecologically diverse island, say the size of Ireland or Ceylon off-shore from our continent, and on this, isolate a population using the first tool kit, from all contact with the social forces which brought about the adoption of the second one on the adjacent mainland. We would now have a perfect laboratory situation, whereby the island society becomes the 'standard' against which social changes on the mainland can be measured.

Before we set about this task, let us be kind to ourselves, and like Eisenstein in the film *Ivan the Terrible*, suddenly enrich the black and white of mere stone tools with the technicolour array of the entire technology—bone, wood, basket work, feathers, gum and blood. We find that all the tentative inferences which we had made as to the relative complexities of island and mainland technologies are confirmed and enhanced five fold. Then the societies themselves are revealed to us, frozen in their camps and bands, smoke rising from fires, men poised to spear game, old women asleep. It is only a still photograph and it rapidly fades, but in the meantime we can count the people, observe their social groups, analyse their economic activities. To our stunned surprise, no significant differences can be observed in the adaptive success or demographic structure of both groups. Our hypothesis seems to be refuted. Given that 'Man does not continue to use less efficient tools when newer and better ones are readily available' (S. Binford, 1968 : 57), why then was the second technology adopted on the mainland? Is our model of 'efficiency' adequate when dealing with societies having a radically different ethos of living from our own? What do we mean by 'adaptive success' when dealing with hunters? Is a single refutation sufficient to negate 'Slob's Law' 'that nobody does anything without a good reason'? This then is the paradox of the Tasmanians.

An outline of the technological prehistory of Australia

With over 100 sites so far excavated, over 20 of which extending back into the Pleistocene and representing most ecological zones (Mulvaney, 1975; Jones, 1973, 1975), outlines of Australian prehistoric sequences are beginning to emerge. Stone tool assemblages older than 5000 years, back to at least 30 000 years ago seem to belong to a single technological tradition for which the term 'Australian core tool and scraper tradition' has been proposed (Jones and Allen in Bowler *et al.*, 1970 : 52; Jones, 1973; Mulvaney, 1975 : 172–97). These assemblages are characterised by a series of scraper types, especially steep edge scrapers, and concave and nosed varieties, together with robust, domed shaped, heavily flaked 'horsehoof' core scrapers and pebble choppers. A unity for these assemblages has long been sensed (eg. Tindale, 1937; Mulvaney and Joyce, 1965, 1969 : 50, 139, 150) but it is only in the last few years, with the development of statistical handling of attributes, particularly those of the worked

Some tools of European Upper Palaeolithic
(after Bordes)

a

Oldowan

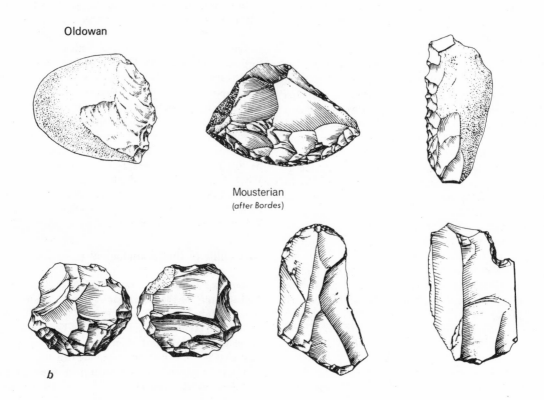

Mousterian
(after Bordes)

b

Fig. 1:   Tools of the European parable.

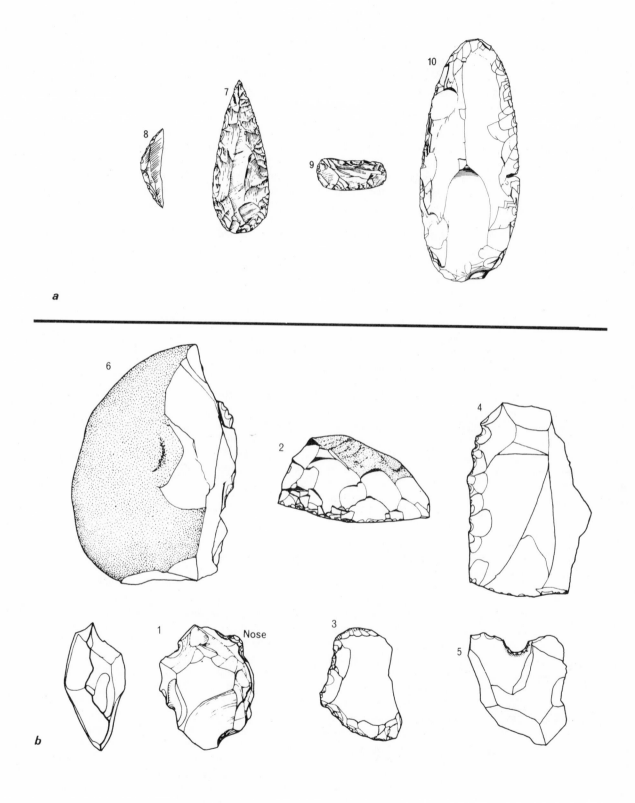

Fig. 2: Recent Australian (*after* Mulvaney *and* O'Connell) and Tasmanian toolkits compared.

edges, that the implements themselves have been adequately described for comparative purposes. Detailed statistical descriptions of excavated assemblages of this tradition have been commenced (eg. Mulvaney, 1965; Lampert, 1971; White, 1972; Jones and Allen, unpublished; Jones, 1971; Allen, 1972; Flood, 1974) leading the way for analyses of its regional and temporal structure.

A single glimpse of the wooden technology associated with, and probably made by such scrapers, is given at the 10 000 year old level at Wyrie Swamp in South Australia, where the excavated wooden tools include boomerangs, a barbed 'javelin' head and digging sticks (Luebbers, 1975 and pers. comm.). At least in tropical Australia, edge ground axes were an integral part of the technology, and analogous waisted blades, together with flaked, and later, ground axe/adzes are found in Highland New Guinea, with scrapers and core tools which are similar to their Australian contemporaries (C. White, 1971; J. P. White, 1972; J. Allen, 1972). Grinding stones are found at least as far back as 15 000 to 18 000 years ago (H. Allen, 1972; Kamminga and Allen, pers. comm.), and bone points with polish indicating possible use as awls and reamers go back to 20 000 years (Dortch and Merrilees, 1973; Flood, 1974; Lampert, 1972, and this volume; Bowdler, 1974a and 1974b). Other aspects of the culture maintained by this technological tradition, including burial customs, art, and palimpsests of the economic base are referred to elsewhere (Jones, 1973 and 1975; Hiatt, 1969; Edwards and Ucko, 1973; Mulvaney, 1975, 279–83). Broad regional provinces are already discernible, and in some areas, stylistic trends can be seen to operate over very long periods, one of the best documented being Allen's sequence in western NSW where the only significant typological changes in the scrapers and core tools over a span of some 25 000 years was a steady and progressive diminution in size as time progressed (H. Allen, 1972).

Compared with the unity of the previous 25 000 years, the next 5 or 6000 years of Australian prehistory was one of bewildering diversity (eg. Gould, 1973 : 18–22). It was a period says John Mulvaney, when 'The tempo of technological innovation had quickened and transformed Australian Society' (1969 : 153). New industrial elements made a sudden appearance in almost all the mainland sites spanning the relevant period so far excavated, though the dating of the innovations varies considerably regionally. Most of the new types were probably armatures of composite tools, heralding the introduction, or at least proliferation, of sophisticated hafting techniques (Mulvaney and Joyce, 1965, 1969 : 110).

A perplexing feature of the new developments is that there appears to have been several complexes or traditions, each characterised by a distinctive set of stone tools, and that these tended to be deployed differentially over the continent. Across the southern half of the continent are found the backed blade (or flakelet) assemblages, characterised by geometric microliths (Fig. 2 : 8) and assymetrically backed bondi points, with regional differences in the relative frequencies of these two polar 'types' (Glover, 1969; Pearce, 1973; Wright, 1974). Running north and south through the central region are assemblages containing tula adze flakes, often worked back into slugs (Fig. 2 : 9), unifacial pirri points (Fig. 2 : 7), and large pointed leilira blades (Mulvaney, 1975 : 224–25). In northern Queensland, there are side worked burren adze slugs but no tulas; in Arnhem Land, there are unifacial and bifacial pressure flaked points, together with pointed and relatively unworked large flakes or blades;

in the Kimberley region of northwest Australia there are beautiful pressure flaked bifacial points with carefully worked serrated edges and so on. Other tools included the backed, orange segment shaped elouras, simple burins, Yilugwa scraper-spoons (Fig. 2: 10) (O'Connell, 1974), edge ground axes of various types and many kinds of bone and shell tools.

In some places, distribution of these tool suites overlapped. Add the diversifying factors of raw materials (eg. Mitchell, 1949; O'Connell, this volume), sexual and other social divisions in the use of tools, the place of particular sites within the total economy or the seasonal round (eg. Thomson, 1939; C. White and Peterson, 1969), the pervasive effects of long range trading cycles (McCarthy, 1939; Thomson, 1949; Mulvaney, 1976), and we can perhaps understand the reason for the highly complex pattern of association of various tool types which characterises these later Australian assemblages. Over time too, there was diversity, with diachronism of types in some sites, yet with contemporaneity of the same types in others. Some implement suites appeared and faded at different times in adjacent areas, as can be seen by looking at the backed blade industries of coastal and inland New South Wales. The problem that all these factors posed to archaeologists working in a 'traditional' mode, where tool assemblages tended to be seen as synonymous with 'cultures', is exemplified by McCarthy and Setzler's conclusion (1960 : 286) that 'At Oenpelli, we obtained a mixed industry consisting of Bondaian, Elouran, Kimberleyan, Pirrian, Mudukian and Murundian elements'. Representatives of practically the whole gamut of late Australian industries all together in the same layers of the same sites.

Despite the sudden appearance of the new tools and their subsequent chronological and geographical pirouettes, it seems that the new technology was superimposed onto, rather than replaced the older one of scrapers and core tools. This was stated clearly by Mulvaney for Kenniff Cave that the 'striking feature' of the new phase 'was the continuance of older tool traditions within the newer complex' (1969 : 107), and further confirmation comes from more recent excavations and under more sophisticated analyses. Perhaps the persistence of the older scraper tradition can best be demonstrated in the central desert and semi-arid regions of Australia (Gould, 1971, 1973; H. Allen, 1972). Even in coastal New South Wales, where there were additions of prominent backed microlith and other elements, Lampert (1971) has shown that the scraper and core-tool component remained unchanged, both morphologically and metrically from older layers, which date back to 20 000 years ago; and a similar picture of addition of hafted elements may also have occurred within the bone tool elements of the technology (Lampert, 1971; Jones, 1971b : 158–24).

While admitting the probability of some new people associated with the new ideas—indeed the arrival of the dingo necessitates the successful landfall of at least one Charon with canine companion(s), most Australian archaeologists nowadays see these technological changes partly in terms of independent invention (eg. for tulas and perhaps other flaked adzes—F. D. McCarthy and S. R. Mitchell see Mulvaney, 1969 : 115; Gould, 1973; Dortch and Merrilees, 1973), and partly in terms of the diffusion of ideas from external sources (eg. for the geometric microliths—Glover, 1967; J. P. White, 1971). There is no evidence in Australia for a massive influx or change of population in post glacial times, indeed the vector of archaeological research points to a basically homogeneous 'Australian' economic way of life, implying its establishment and continuity over a very long period indeed, perhaps even back to the time when people collected mussels and fished for golden perch from the sandy banks of Lake Mungo those distant, thirty millennia ago (Bowler *et al.*, 1971; Jones, 1973, 1975 : 22–23, 28). The Wyrie Swamp boomerangs now add powerful new support to the view that some important items of contemporary Aboriginal technology are the legacy of a tradition pre-dating the accretion of the new 'small tools', and that despite the diversity of the past five thousand years, there has also been an unbroken strand of cultural information connecting modern Aborigines to their presumed late Pleistocene forebears.

The final stage of Australian prehistory is of course bisected by the 'ethnographic present' and the stone, bone and wooden finds of our excavations can be keyed into the totality of a technology and of a society. Thus tula slugs are seen as adze or chisel bits, mounted on the end of stout handles or spear-throwers and used to scrape and to smooth wooden implements; tiny unretouched flakes lie embedded in gum as barbs on the sides of spears; edge ground axe heads, held in pliable withy handles are used as chisels to remove sheets of bark for a coming shower of rain; fusiform bone points, the tips of multi-pronged fish leisters are impaled to their hilts in the thrashing silver flanks of fish.

Yet also, the clarity of the vision gives us some room for puzzlement given a utilitarian point of view. A stout, fire hardened wooden spear point can penetrate an animal just as easily as a stone tipped one, and it does not shatter on impact with the ground if the shot is missed (see also Peterson, 1971). On the coastal clay plains of central northern Arnhem Land, stone does not occur naturally and the Aborigines there had only one major use for flaked stone, namely as tips for spears used as status symbols to carry to ceremonies, or for duelling and punishment; the tips themselves being valued items, wrapped in paper bark sheaths and traded as nests of packed tips from stone-country quarries several languages away. For their mundane cutting and wood scraping purposes before the arrival of Macassan and European metals, these people used several species of marine mollusc shell, picked up casually from the middens around their camps, yet their material culture is probably as rich as any in Australia and they have one of the highest Aboriginal population densities (Warner, 1937; Meehan, in press; B. Meehan and R. Jones personal observation). Stone spear points from the Kimberleys, blunted after a thousand miles of exchange and travel, are used to circumcise boys in the desert; while throwing boomerangs of the northern desert tribes, become pairs of clap sticks for men's secret rituals on the Arnhem Land coast. In both cases the implement itself travels, but its use becomes transformed from the economic and secular into the non-productive and religious spheres of society.

Moving to a wider canvas, the tool kit suites of recent archaeological assemblages can in some cases broadly be related to ecological zones and 'culture areas'. Thus a good argument can be made that the tula adzes and associated tools belong to the central Australian groups of tribes (Gould, 1973 : 14–15), the most easterly occurrence of the tulas being along the eastern flank of the Darling River basin, where the semi-arid plains meet the wooded slopes of the Great Dividing Range (F. D. McCarthy, pers. comm.; H. Allen, 1972). On the other hand, similar correspondences cannot be made for most of the other major tool kits. Indeed,

the distribution of some, positively cut across major ecological zones, and bear no relation to known major 'culture areas'. For example, although conscientious attempts have been made to show how bondi backed points can be seen as successful adaptations to the economic problems of the south coast of New South Wales, the question which really needs to be asked is, why were geometric microliths/bondi points so successful here and also on the arid salt deserts near Lake Eyre, and in the sclerophyll woodland of Western Australia, and yet were not used on the coast of Queensland nor on the Barkly Tablelands nor in the Kimberleys? Why were unifacial and bifacial points so adaptive to southern Arnhem Land Peninsula and not to Cape York Peninsula? Why, if tula adzes were so effective in manufacturing the wooden boomerangs of the desert Dieri, were they not also used for the boomerangs of the south coastal Kurnai? It is not so much the presence of a tool type that needs explaining—this can often be fobbed off by some bland rubric—but rather its *absence* in an ecologically equivalent and adjacent zone, especially when we have evidence of contact between the inhabitants of both regions. What does it mean for the inhabitants of Burke's Cave in the Barrier Range, west of the Darling River, 1500 years ago, to be using both geometric microliths and tula adze slugs? (H. Allen, 1972). People do not just sit with distribution maps intersecting their brains. Binford's musings (1972 : 287) about the strange association of stone tool categories from a series of late Acheulean sites in Africa strike an evocative note, and I remember similar ideas being explored by Jack Golson in non-mathematical terms in a Sydney seminar in 1963.

Somehow in the grey shadow behind the dancing, hafted small tools, we see a woman patiently digging up lily roots with her digging stick—a young man throws a lump of wood at a goanna—women return from shell beds carrying their hauls in pandanus frond dilly bags, their nails worn back to the quick, calloused from impacted mud and sand—a man sits scraping the charred bark and knots off his straightened spear shaft, with the sturdy edge of his quartzite flake, almost hidden in the crook of his hand—a baby is born and has its mouth filled with sand to smother it to death. Here, there is no dancing, man and land are in tight embrace. It is time to turn to Tasmania.

The Tasmanian sequence

Tasmania is a mountainous island of 65 000 sq km, lying 250 km to the south of the Australian continent. It is highly varied ecologically with a cool oceanic west coast, a sub-alpine mountain core and a dry temperate eastern half, with a hint of continentality in small areas of the midlands. Its flora and fauna are predominantly Australian and show the pauperation of species, though high numbers of individuals, characteristic of island communities. Circum-Antarctic elements are present, particularly on the west coast and highlands. All major ecological zones can be matched with those from the adjacent mainland, particularly the mountains and coast of southern New South Wales and Victoria. More than 12 000 years ago, Tasmania was part of the mainland, and it was across the Bassian land bridge that the ancestors of the Tasmanian Aborigines walked, bearing with them the cultural inheritance of late Pleistocene Australia (Jones, 1968, 1971b, 1973; Bowdler, 1974a, 1974b). Since that time, due to the post glacial sea level rise, Tasmania has been an island, and the archaeological record over the past 8000 years, shows the continuity of a single technological tradition untouched by any of the cultural influences which so transformed the shape of mainland stone tool assemblages. There is not a single example of the new 'small tools' and there were no dogs. Demographically and culturally, Tasmania was a closed system. Indeed it will become the classic example of such a system, for no other human society, which survived until modern times, had been isolated so completely and for so long.

Rocky Cape and the north west   These conclusions are based on excavations at a series of open and cave midden sites in north west Tasmania (Jones, 1966, 1971b; Bowdler 1974a and 1974b), and coastal and inland sites in the south east (Lourandos, 1968, 1970). From two caves at Rocky Cape, a continuous sequence was obtained, spanning the past 8000 years. Flaked stone tools were found at all levels, and these were subjected to an attribute analysis whereby I used various statistical techniques including cluster analyses of significant inter-correlations of variables to test whether or not intuitively proposed 'types' could be justified according to objective mathematical criteria. I paid especial attention to the attributes of the worked edges and to the relationships of these to the blanks on which they were fashioned. I found that I could justify the separate identity of five types of scraper. These were:

(1) Steep edged scrapers—with steep, often right angled, heavily step-flaked robust edges, probably used as hand planes for working wood (Fig. 2 : 2).

(2) Round edged scrapers—small convex curved edges with carefully flaked, fluted retouch and edge angles about 60°, could have been used for pressure cutting, or as scraper knives for fine scraping and whittling (Fig. 2:3).

(3) Flat, straight edged scrapers, with long lightly retouched, denticulate edges along the sides of flat flakes, could have been used for a variety of general cutting and ripping tasks, from flesh and sinew to vegetable fibre and bark or wood (Fig. 2 : 4).

(4) Notched scrapers—highly standardised, concave, steep edged notches on a wide variety of blanks. Almost certainly used as spokeshaves for scraping and smoothing spear shafts (Fig. 2 : 5).

(5) Concave and nosed scrapers—the minimum definition of which being two carefully flaked concave notches on both sides of a projecting snout or nose. Usually there are a series of concavities and noses along the worked edges of these tools. The concavities could have been used for the same purpose as the notched scrapers, and the noses are either fortuitous or could have been used as delicate scraper-knives to gouge shallow grooves in wood (Fig. 2 : 1).

In addition to these scraper types, there were large unifacial and bifacial pebble choppers for heavy duty percussion cutting (Fig. 2 : 6), and many of the unretouched flakes showed microscopic wear along their sharp edges showing that they had been used for cutting.

The tasks inferred for these tools are based on a consideration of their shape, their use wear and the use of stone tools within the technology of ethnographically recorded Tasmanians (see Jones, 1971b). Overwhelmingly, the Tasmanians used their flaked stone tools for cutting and for manufacturing and maintaining wooden tools, especially spears. Sometimes, shells were used for the same purposes. Among the few 'extractive' uses of flaked stone were when women used large scraper/choppers to chop and prise toe holds in

the bark of Eucalypts in order to facilitate climbing up the trunk to get possums; and holes were also cut into the bark of *Eucalyptus gunnii* trees to tap the sweet sap which flowed within. All stone tools were held in the hand without the aid of any hafting technique, and no edge ground axes have ever been found in an authentic context in Tasmania. Simple though it was, this technology of hand held scrapers and choppers was sufficiently efficient to propel Tasmanian society through at least ten millennia.

The relative frequencies of these tool types within the seven 'analytical units' comprising the Rocky Cape sequence, are shown in Fig. 3 (from Jones, 1971b). Two main conclusions emerge. Firstly, we have evidence for the continuation of a single technological tradition. No tool type at the end of the sequence is not present at its base, and the converse is almost true, with only the flat, straight edged scrapers failing to appear in the top two units. This impression of unity of technology is also gained from the study of the unretouched flakes and of the cores, the latter consisting of both bi-pyramidal disc (Fig. 2 : 1), and single platform types.

Secondly, there was a trend towards greater efficiency in the use of raw materials, manifested in several inter-related ways. Within the steep edged scrapers, the parameters of the edges themselves tended to remain constant, but the blanks on which they were made, became smaller and more standardised. Round edge scrapers and small, sharp, slightly retouched flakes replaced the straight edged scrapers and large rough retouched flakes. Concave and nosed scrapers replaced the functionally analogous notched scrapers. All of these changes occurred gradually and systematically.

In the oldest levels, all the raw material, consisting of quartzites and indurated shales and argillites could have come from the mother rock and the beaches of the cape itself, and the ratios of cores and flakes to retouched implements showed that these were manufactured locally on the site. In higher levels, especially from 4000 years BP onwards, there was a steady and increasing introduction of high quality exotic raw materials such as cherts, siliceous breccias, and spongolites brought in as ready made tools, or at least as blanks, from quarries at 50 and up to 100 km away. The higher performance of the better raw materials made it worth while to carry them over long distances, but this extra investment of labour and of planning necessitated greater efficiency of use, which is reflected in the formal typology of the tools themselves.

These changes were only one aspect of a series of adjustments which the prehistoric inhabitants of north west Tasmania made, following the dislocation of their late Pleistocene economic system by the post-glacial rising sea. They themselves were pressed back as the sea drowned the old coast-lines of the Bassian Plain, and inland of them, the highland ice sheets finally melted, and the trees marched a thousand metres uphill. For several thousand years, pressed against their new coastline of quartzite cliffs by the tangle of wet scrub inland, the people who first inhabited Rocky Cape, gained almost 100% of their meat from the sea shore, mostly in the form of seals, rocky coast shellfish and scale fish, the latter contributing about 20% of the non-molluscan flesh weight. It was only several thousand years later, that a significant though still modest terrestrial component, mostly in the form of wallabies, was added to the meat diet.

Elsewhere, I have argued that these changes in diet and stone tool manufacture both reflected the response of pre-

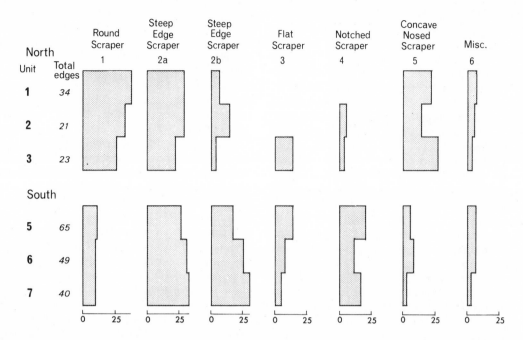

Fig. 3: Sequence at Rocky Cape Tasmania, from 400 BP at top of unit 1 to 8000 BP at base of unit 7, showing evolution of the stone tool technology (*from* Jones 1971b).

historic Tasmanian society to the opportunities offered them by the adjustment of the environment to non-glacial conditions. Thus 'natural' ecological factors such as climate and the local effects of exposure and salt spray on the new coastline, would have combined with the fire pressure of the Aborigines themselves, to open up the country into the mosaic of coastal heaths, small grassy plains and the succession from wet sclerophyll scrub to *Nothofagus* rainforest that is found in north west Tasmania today, and which is partially reverting to pure rainforest now that the Aborigines and their fire sticks are gone (Jackson, 1965, 1968; Jones, 1968, 1975 : 26–28). In mid Recent times, Tasmanian society managed to assert, or perhaps re-assert, a regionally coordinated economic system in the north west. The articulation of this system relative both to environment and to neighbouring groups is documented in Jones, 1971b and 1974.

East Tasmania In south eastern Tasmania, with its drier climate, sheltered coastline, Eucalypt dominated woodlands and tussocky grasslands, the natural barriers to easy movement were not formidable, and as a consequence, society was organised in a more 'areal' fashion rather than the 'linear' one of the north west (see also Lourandos, 1968, 1970; Jones, 1974). During full glacial conditions, eastern Tasmania was cold and dry, with a climate rather like that of the Patagonian pampas or eastern Tierra del Fuego today (McPhail, 1975). It is highly likely that evidence of Pleistocene occupation will be found in the numerous lake edge lunettes and sand sheet deposits of the Midland Valley and the south east, but so far, the eastern archaeological sequence only goes back to 8700 years. As far as stone tools were concerned, Lourandos could find no systematic morphological changes over the 6000 years of his sequence. Typologically, the south eastern assemblages are similar to the ones described above, with all the types being represented, though in different proportions. In general, south eastern assemblages are characterised by smooth, carefully flaked, convex-curved edges, placed on large flat

flakes; concave and nosed scrapers; and more formalised steep edged scrapers than was the case at Rocky Cape. Some of these differences may have reflected the abundance of high quality, easily flaked indurated hornfels, obtained from many quarries in the region (Sutherland, 1972). I also feel that there are stylistic provinces within Tasmanian stone assemblages, whose regional idiosyncrasies were maintained over the entire span of its recorded prehistory. One can distinguish between a western and an eastern province, and according to Kemp (1963) a central highland one too. These provinces can, I think, be related to social groups analogous to 'tribes' or linguistic units (terms defined in Jones, 1971a, 1971b, 1974), stone tools being only one of several artifacts and customs that had a discontinuous distribution in Tasmania during the ethnographic present.

Lourandos has been able to show much greater lateral variation in site use than was the case in my western sites (1968, 1970). Thus the big shell middens at Little Swanport were probably dumps from oyster processing activities carried out by women, the domestic camps being located in the open Eucalypt savannah around the shores of the bay. Only a few kilometres inland, is the lake side site of Crown Lagoon, where macropod hunting and the manufacture and maintenance of hunting gear were carried out and so on. The stone tool assemblages at these and other sites in the south east, reflect the specialised activities carried out at them.

Anyone wishing to draw a simple analogy from Tasmania to explain lateral variation in contemporary stone assemblages, would be sorely disappointed. On the one hand, such differences can be shown to reflect 'functional' factors such as site use, proximity to quarries, and seasonal occupation; and on the other hand to 'cultural historical' factors such as the establishment and continuity of regionally differentiated societies, practising slightly different technologies. In Tasmania, it is not a matter of Bordes *or* Binford, but Bordes *and* Binford—Tasmania is probably not unique in this regard!

Simplification Perhaps the most fascinating aspect of the prehistoric sequence in Tasmania is the hint that one gets of simplification both in technology and in the range of foods eaten, as time went on. Seven thousand years ago at Rocky Cape, people were using one bone implement for every two or three stone ones. Furthermore, analysis of the species of animals from which the blanks had been obtained, compared with those represented in the food debris, shows that many of the bone tools must have been brought into the cave from another district, contrasting with the stone tools, which had probably all been flaked from locally obtained rocks. Three thousand years later, the ratio of bone to stone tools had declined to only one in fifteen, and by three and a half thousand years ago, bone tools had dropped out of the technology entirely. Paralleling this decline in numbers, there was also a constriction in the range of tool types. In the lowest levels, bone tools included wallaby fibulae fashioned into stout, rounded-tipped points or awls, smaller needle-like points and spatulae, together with split slivers of bone made into a variety of broad uni-points. As time proceeded, this range of types became restricted to the large fibula points only (Jones, 1971b : 488–502). Confirmatory evidence for a rich bone tool technology becoming discontinued about three thousand years ago, comes from several other sites in both eastern and north-western Tasmania (Jones, 1971b : 502–13; Lourandos, 1970). The recent discovery of beautifully polished points identical to some of the best Rocky Cape ones, from Cave Bay Cave on Hunter Island, north west Tasmania, the oldest being dated to eighteen and a half thousand years ago (Bowdler, 1974b), firmly links this old Tasmanian bone technology to parallel late Pleistocene finds on the Australian mainland (Dortch and Merrilees, 1973; Jones, 1973; Mulvaney, 1975 : 151).

In the Tasmanian ethnographic record, there is not a single reliable account of the use of bone tools, wood being used for such tools as skewers and spatulae-wedges which were often made from bone on the adjacent mainland (Jones, 1971b : 515–17). Thus we now have a consistent picture of a rich bone technology stemming from a late Pleistocene Australian cultural matrix, but after some thousands of years of isolation in Tasmania, becoming progressively attenuated both in range of tools and in absolute numbers, eventually to be totally discontinued for the terminal three thousand years of Tasmanian prehistory. Elsewhere, I have argued on the basis of morphological and use-wear evidence, together with analogy from identical tools used ethnographically on the north shore of Bass Strait, that the bone points and possibly also the spatulae at Rocky Cape, were used as awls and reamers in the manufacture of skin cloaks (Jones, 1971b : 518–24). Thus not only the bone tools themselves, but also the articles manufactured with them may also have been discontinued. One looks with sharpened interest at the contrast between the Victorian Aborigines wrapped up snugly in their big possum skin rugs, compared with the Tasmanians with only rough *ad hoc* mantles of wallaby skin, slung over the shoulder and held in place with tied bits of skin.

As stated earlier, when Rocky Cape was first occupied, 8000 years ago, bony fish, as represented overwhelmingly by wrasses ('parrot fish') (*Pseudolabrus* sp) probably contributed about 20% of the non-molluscan meat, by weight. This fraction was maintained until some time between 3800 and 3500 BP when suddenly, fish completely disappeared from the diet, and this state of affairs continued until the ethnographic present. To gain a better impression of the magnitude of this break in archaeological terms, we can note that the oldest three units of my excavations yielded approximately 3000 fish bones, representing a minimum number of 480 individuals, so that ten fish were eaten for every single mammal and bird combined. Yet in the upper three units, out of a total of 1800 bone fragments, representing a minimum number of 46 mammals and birds, only one fish bone was found (Jones, 1971b : 525–54). The odds that this disparity is just due to chance is a figure fifty digits long to one against (Jones, 1971b : 553).

The dropping of fish from Tasmanian diet sometime about three or four thousand years ago is now confirmed from other sites, both in the north west and the south east of the island (Jones, 1968, 1971b; Lourandos, 1970; Bowdler, 1974a and pers. comm.). Again the archaeological evidence gains support from the ethnographic record, for there is not a single reliable eye witness account of the Tasmanians eating bony or cartilaginous fish (Hiatt, 1967 : 113–14). Indeed, there are many comments specifically stating the opposite, from descriptions of the Tasmanians refusing fish offered to them by Captain Cook, or the ethno-archaeological observations of camp rubbish dumps by Captain Bligh, to the specific statements of George Augustus Robinson (Hiatt, 1967 : 113). Thus not only do we have the strange spectacle of a coastal hunting people not utilising a major food resource; even more extraordinarily, we see them at a certain point in their history, actually dropping it from their diet. No convincing ecological explanation can be offered for this reduction, especially since identical species of fish swim lazily amongst the kelp around Rocky Cape nowadays. The explanation must lie within the realm of cultural prohibition (Jones, 1971b : 619–20). With this abnegation, part of the economic heritage of early Tasmanians slipped away. An intellectual event caused a contraction in their ecological space (for a longer discussion, see Jones, in press).

Only a few years ago, there was a tendency to view Tasmanian material culture as a fossilised version of its Pleistocene Australian parent, but the archaeological record, on both the mainland and island, shows that this can no longer be presumed. Somewhere on the long road from the tropical Greater Australia of twenty thousand years ago to the Tasmania of 1800 AD, edge-ground axes and presumably some elementary hafting techniques became lost. Whether this occurred when their makers occupied the temperate zones of Australia, or whether within the context of the Bassian isolation is not yet known. Finally the boomerangs and barbed spear heads of Wyrie, found at the very door step to Tasmania and dated to just about the time when the trap was snapped shut, may mean that these implements too were part of the cultural baggage jettisoned by the Tasmanians during their long stay within their closed world.

The simplest tool kit in the world

Stone tools form only a segment of an entire technology, and through the eyes of ethnographers we can move from the cave wall to the dazzling sunshine outside. The outstanding feature of Tasmanian technology, was its simplicity.

To hunt, men used one piece spears, between 4.5 and 6 m long made from pliable stems of *Leptospermum* tea trees, sharpened and fire hardened at their thickest ends. The long, thin, pliable tails of these spears provided a whiplash effect to give them longitudinal spin, which though thrown directly by hand without the aid of any 'machine', had a maximum 'sporting' range of almost 100 m, with 50–60 m sometimes being achieved in the field under hunting or fighting conditions (see Jones, 1971b). A stout, straight or fusiform stick, about 0.6 m long, with a roughened hand grip on one end and a blunt bevel on the other, was used both as a throwing stick to knock possums out of trees, and as a club to dispatch game which had been wounded or bailed up by other means. Small spherical pebbles were also part of the projectile armoury, thrown accurately in volleys by several men.

Women had a combination digging stick-club-chisel which was used for a variety of purposes from digging up vegetable roots, ochre and killing game, to prising bark off trees, the latter being done with the aid of a stone as hammer. Possums were caught and thrown to the ground by women climbing up the trunks of eucalypts often more than 30 m high. This usually involved the use of a short rope made from rolled grass or strips of animal fur, toe holds being made as described above. Rocky coast shellfish were obtained by diving, the women carrying in their hand a small wooden spatula or wedge, placing their catch into a deep bowl-shaped, two-ply tight weave dilly bag, suspended from their necks. Vegetable food such as bracken fern rhizomes were softened by battering with a stone pestle and mortar, also used to break long bones for marrow.

Fire was carried, usually by men, in smouldering slow burning fire-sticks, but the Tasmanians did not know how to make it (Plomley, 1962), having to go to their neighbours for a re-light if their own sticks went out. To document the total Tasmanian inventory, we need add only two hut types; water-craft made from rolls of bark and propelled by poles; kelp buckets for carrying water; possum-skin pouch bags for carrying valuables such as stone tools, ochre, and ashes of the dead; abalone shells and perhaps skulls as drinking vessels; kangaroo skins tied onto the shoulder for warmth; shell necklaces; and the impedimenta of art, such as ochre and cicatrizing flakes.

There in its stark simplicity of about two dozen items, is the entire corpus of Tasmanian technology. No simpler technology has ever been recorded in the world's ethnographic literature, and for this reason alone, the relationship of Tasmanian Aborigines to their environment has immense theoretical interest, for it documents the extreme case of 'extra-somatic adaptation' of biologically modern man.

North of Bass Strait, within the material culture of the coastal and inland tribes of south eastern Australia, we find almost all of the items used by the Tasmanians, but there is also a multitude of other tools absent on the island. These tools include spearthrowers, boomerangs, various composite tools involving a variety of hafting techniques such as edge ground axes, mounted adzes, multi-pronged and barbed fish spears, barbed game spears; fish hooks, various nets for fish, birds, wallabies and other small game; fish and eel traps made from many materials; mats, string bags, baskets and dilly bags of several types; bone awls, points and spatulae; possum skin sewn capes, shields, wooden bowls, huts of various types, sewn bark canoes, paddles; the paraphernalia of ritual and art; and also the companionship and use of the dingo. An excellent visual impression of the richness and diversity of the mainland coastal material culture, compared with the simplicity of the Tasmanian one, can be gained by comparing one of George French Angas's (1850) ethnographic prints of technological items of the coastal tribes of south eastern South Australia (Fig. 4) with Lesueur's plate (1807/11) of most of the portable items of Tasmanian

technology (Fig. 5). In the former case, we are dazzled by the minutiae, in the latter, stunned by the austerity of the five tools arranged with classic symmetry upon the page.

The proposition

We are now in a position to summarise the elements of the testable proposition. On both sides of Bass Strait, living in similar environments, we had at the point of European contact, two distantly related hunting cultures. On the island, people made their living through the medium of a technology, so simple in the number and elaboration of elements as to stagger the imagination. Let us call this 'technology A'. On the mainland, most elements of technology A, were also present, but embedded within the matrix of another 'technology B'. This latter consisted of about five times as many elements as A. Many of these were morphologically complex, having a high technical performance and were applied to a range of specialised uses. Archaeological evidence suggests, and in the case of stone and bone tools shows, that technology B was added onto A during the past five or six thousand years, probably by a process of adoption and invention, rather than by replacement of population. It can also be shown and inferred that technology A is a pauperate version of an ancestral one, common to both island and mainland, when they formed one land, the elements lost during the island sojourn, being maintained on the mainland. The propositions are that:

(1) Technology B, having numerous elements, being morphologically complex, and containing many task specific tools was more efficient than A in extracting energy from the environment—in other words it was a better hunting kit, providing more food from most sources which were exploited by A, and diversifying the economy by tapping sources beyond the reach of A.

(2) It was precisely because of this extractive superiority, that B was adopted and added onto a rump of A, or alternatively that people using B were able to usurp the place of those using A. By reference to the 'Principle of the fittest economy', the very fact of this replacement, is proof of the superior performance of B over A. These are not capricious arguments, for such assumptions are at the very core of theories about the march of technological progress and a glance again at Figs. 1 and 2, reminds one that the morphological difference in the stone tools being discussed, are hardly trivial ones.

Increased extractive efficiency can be translated into its practical effects—which allows us to test the propositions set out above. It means more food, different food, or more time; let us take each in turn.

More food?

The total Aboriginal population of Tasmania was of the order of 3000 to 5000 people,[1] giving an average density for the whole island of about twelve to twenty square km per person. Another, perhaps more meaningful index, when we consider the importance of coastal resources in the diet, would be to calculate the density as being about one or two people per

---

1. The ethnographic and geographical data upon which these calculations are based are discussed and documented in detail in Plomley (1966 : 968–76), Jones (1971a, 1971b Appendix A, and 1974).

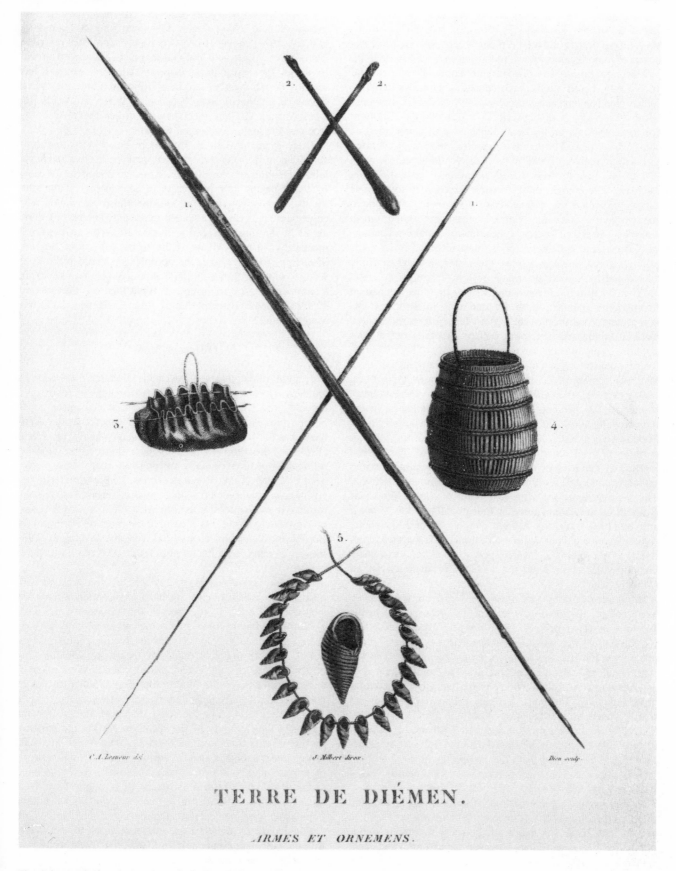

TERRE DE DIÉMEN.

ARMES ET ORNEMENS.

Fig. 4 (opposite): A plate from G. F. Angas' *'Savage life and scenes in Australia and New Zealand'* showing some of the technology of the Aborigines from coastal south-eastern Australia.

Fig. 5 (above): C. A. Lesueur's plate from *'Voyage de découvertes aux Terres Australia . . .'* showing almost the entire corpus of the Tasmanian technology.

km of coastline. The latter is measured 'crudely' so as to smooth out minor indentations and reefs, but includes the coasts of major islands known to have been visited seasonally.

This population was divided into about 80 named and territorially based bands, each consisting typically of 30 to 50 people. The core areas occupied by these bands measured some 500 sq km, with between 25 and 100 km of seashore for those abutting on the coast, depending on the richness of the environment. The bands themselves were agglomerated into larger regional social units usually numbering between 300 to 500 people, who shared all cultural traits including language. These larger units or 'tribes', accounted for regions ranging in area from 2500 to 8000 sq km, there being nine in the whole of Tasmania. Bands themselves carried out a complex pattern of seasonal movements to take advantage of seasonal and ephemeral foods, most recorded movements taking place within tribal areas, those outside being carefully sanctioned by mutual agreement with host groups.

When we turn to the mainland, we find that this Tasmanian demographic picture, both in size and in structure fits completely. Firstly, let us take crude density. Figures for well watered inland areas of south eastern Australia range from about one person per seven to one per twenty sq km. The rich Sydney coastal region supported 1500 Aborigines with a coastline density of 2.5 people per km of coast (Lawrence, 1968 : 187). H. Allen (1972) calculated that the Darling basin supported 0.6 persons per km of river, the figure being increased to about 2.5 per km for the much richer lower Murray (Eyre, 1845, II : 372). Along the Coorong, coastal densities of the Tasmanian figures were achieved. The highest Australian densities of all are found at especially favoured estuarine and coral reef coasts of tropical northern Australia. The average figure for all communities of the Gidjingali of Arnhem Land is about three or four people per km of coast and estuarine river, the Anbara community of 130 people, scoring about eight per km in their especially favoured locality (Hiatt, 1965; Jones and Meehan pers. obs.). Similar extremely high densities come from the Kaiadilt of Bentinck Island (Tindale, 1962).

If we were to rank Australian densities from the last two examples at 10 down to those of the Aborigines of the Western Desert (1 per 85–250 sq km) at 1, then I guess that the Tasmanian figures would be equivalent to about 7; thus not only within the Australian range but comfortably at the higher end of the scale, and the same as coastal figures of south eastern Australia, which is ecologically the country most similar to Tasmania. Perhaps the situation was most clearly stated by George Bass, who with Flinders, was the first white man to set foot on northern Tasmania. He said of it that 'This country is inhabited by men; and, if any judgement could be formed from the number of huts which (we) met, in about the same proportion as in New South Wales' (Bass re-written by Collins 1802, vol. 2 : 168).

In the size and structure of social groups, and in the land areas each occupied, the Tasmanian data are also in excellent accord with those for mainland groups with similar population densities. Australian linguistic tribes numbered from 150 to about 1000 people, most centring at about 250–500, and Birdsell has shown that there is a strong tendency for this central figure to be maintained, so that it is tribal area and not population which varies inversely with resources (1953, 1971).

Comparison of Tindale's map of south east Australian tribal areas with the Tasmanian data, shows the two sets to be broadly similar where similar ecological zones are compared (Tindale 1974; Jones, 1974). One night, soon after returning home from a year with the Gidjingali, I had a vivid dream, in which the entire population structure of which I had recently been a member had been transposed onto the coastal landscape of north west Tasmania. When I awoke, the transposition was not incongruous, rather the reverse was true and the image has stayed with me.

There is no need to go into more detail, we can simply state that in no sense whatsoever, neither in absolute population densities, nor in the size, structure and areas occupied by local groups, nor in density of archaeological remains, do the Tasmanian data fall outside those for ecologically equivalent areas on the adjacent mainland. The more I think about it, the more staggering this result seems to be, for it means that in terms of its ability to extract a total amount of energy from the land, the complex mainland technology was not superior to the simple Tasmanian one at least within a temperate coastal environment. What then was the function of those apparently superfluous items, and why had they been adopted?

Different foods?

We might investigate the possibility that the new technology(ies) allowed exploitation of a wider range of foods than the old, and thus enabled occupation of ecological zones beyond the reach of the users of the first one. Such an argument has in fact been advanced independently by Flood (1973) and Stockton (1974) to explain why the first intensive occupation of the mountains of the south east seems to have been achieved during Bondaian times. Lampert and Hughes (1974) have also argued convincingly that the last 3–4000 years resulted in more intensive use of rock shelter sites on the coast of New South Wales, as measured by rates of attrition and subsequent deposition of material from the cave walls. They see this as reflecting a higher population level during the later period.

However, in both cases, ecological factors associated with post-glacial re-adjustments are hard to disentangle from the technological ones. In the case of the mountains, the post-glacial warming resulted in ecological zones and perhaps associated specialised foods such as Bogong moths moving uphill. The Tasmanians managed to occupy the highland central plateau of their island, with a climate as montane as anything in New South Wales; the population densities of both areas, at twenty sq km per person, being similar (Flood, 1973; Jones, 1974). For the coast, Lampert argued that the relatively long stability of the sea shore during the past few thousand years following the previous rapid rise from glacial levels, had resulted in aggradation of sand bars, colonisation of mature rock platform communities etc., resulting in an absolutely higher littoral bio-mass than might have been the case earlier, this being reflected in the higher human population predating on it (Lampert and Hughes, 1974).

A converse example to the ones presented above, where the human population level in the late Pleistocene was certainly higher than during the later 'small tool' phase, can be seen in the Willandra Lakes area of western New South Wales. Again ecological factors associated with the end of the 'Ice Age' were involved. This time, the drying of the big lake systems, resulted in almost total depopulation of the local region (Bowler et al., 1970; H. Allen, 1972).

While dealing with the diversity of ecological zones theory, we must also remember that in the south west coast of their island the Tasmanians managed to deal with their own special environment, slightly outside the range of any encountered on the mainland. While one might concede population growth or colonisation of new areas following the introduction of the new technological elements on a local level, no systematic case has, so far, been made for such a process on a broad front—as seems for example, to have occurred in the tundra zone of northern Eurasia, following the introduction of upper Palaeolithic technology.

More time?

We are left with our last criterion for 'technological efficiency', namely not more food, but more time. The poverty of the historical records on both sides of Bass Strait makes it almost impossible to make meaningful quantitative statements about such matters as the length of time spent foraging, the rhythm of the chase, and the amount of leisure. We have only impressions. Tasmanian division of labour was similar to that on the mainland, with the women doing most of the gathering, small game foraging, carrying and other mundane tasks, the men sporadically hunting large game, fighting and relaxing. From the journals of Labillardière and Robinson, one gets a similar impression of the pattern of the days and of the chase as one does for mainland groups. In Tasmanian society, there was time for sky-larking, for gossiping, for fighting, for story-telling and dancing, for mourning the dead, for getting ochre, for making shell necklaces and as the rock carvings at Mount Cameron West and other west coast sites show us—for art.

However, there was one difference between mainland and Tasmanian social life which the more I think about it, the more significant it seems. From the very first historical accounts of mainland Australian Aborigines, observers were struck by the richness of their religious life, especially as expressed in great ritual occasions involving the participation of hundreds of people to carry out the required complex and lengthy ceremonies. Thus, for example one of the First Fleet artists depicted a large religious ceremony in Port Stephens, with about a hundred men decorated and dancing. Collins (1798) and other early scientific visitors, devoted major sections of their accounts of the Sydney Aborigines by describing and illustrating complex initiation and other rituals, involving scores of men participating in them over periods of several weeks. Even when the south eastern coastal tribes had been almost obliterated in the 1860s, Howitt recorded (and partly organised) a major initiation ceremony of the Kurnai, involving several hundred people congregated together from a radius of more than a hundred miles, the ceremonies themselves taking several weeks to fulfil the ordained ritual permutations (Mulvaney, 1970).

There are no such records for Tasmania. True, large seasonal aggregations of 300 or 400 people were observed, but these seemed to have been transitory social events exploiting seasonally abundant foods, and not welded together in a religious superstructure of obligatory behaviour. There is one settler's account of what might have been a 'ritual ground' on a small plain near Bothwell in the central east, and the Tasmanians did indeed practise religious ceremonies when disposing of their dead, and they carried out dances depicting mythical or historical themes. Even with these caveats, the fact remains that large scale religious events, such as are described for mainland society, were not part of

Tasmanian cultural behaviour. I am sure that had they been, they would have been recorded, even in an attenuated relic form in Robinson's many journals.

To say that ritual and religious life is important in mainland Aboriginal culture is an understatement. Fulfilling ritual obligations dominates it. The role of ritual as an intellectual force relating man to nature; as a social one, re-inforcing the prescribed pattern of kinship relationships and enlarging the network of social relations; and as an artistic one involving the integration of myth, art, music and dance has been well documented in the anthropological literature. The economic consequences of the great ceremonies have however been less stressed, perhaps because so few have been observed, whose logistic support came from foraged food. In 1972–73 the Gidjingali organised amongst minor rituals, two major *Kunapipi* ceremonies, whose climaxes brought together two to 300 people. An investment of some 400 man weeks was made in carrying these out (Meehan and Jones per. obs.). Elsewhere, I have shown that this much labour might have erected a small hill fort (Jones, 1975 : 32), cleared many acres of ground or written two and a half Ph.D. theses, had these been the aims of the society. Visiting the great camp of Ngaladjebama, three months after the religious climax there, all we saw was the wind, whirling red dust over midden debris, and strips of paperbark rattling against bleached poles of collapsed hut structures. The investment had been made into the intellectual and not the material sphere of life.

Homeostasy

To find a solution to the paradox we may need to shift our attention away from man and onto land, following the lead of Shawcross (1970, 1972) who has faced similar problems in the neighbouring archaeological field of New Zealand. Men, like all living organisms, live by extracting energy from the environment, technology being used to enhance the process. The ultimate source of this energy is of course solar radiation, which is captured and redistributed by the network of living forms which can, in a simplified way, be thought of as a pyramid, with the flow of energy moving from the base to the apex, energy transfer being effected by predation of one life form on another. At each stratum of redistribution, energy is leaked away from the system, but higher up the pyramid, although total amount of energy is less, it is available in a more refined or concentrated form. The relationships of life forms within such ecosystems are of course complicated, and are not adequately understood except in the cases of exceptionally simple ones. We can however, simplify the problem by looking at the relation of each life form to the whole system, pretending for a moment that it lies outside it.

A useful concept derived from farming is that of 'culling' or rather 'maximum culling rate' which can be thought of as the maximum rate of energy extraction that can be levied against a particular level (or in the case of a complex hunting and gathering economy—levels) of a life-form pyramid in a unit area, without causing a pauperation of the total resource. Theoretically, such a culling rate ought to equal the rate of energy flowing up into that particular level, but in practice it is of course much less, for there are no ecosystems outside a laboratory bell jar, where man has the capacity to siphon off all of the energy coming up to his extractive threshold. In this sense, hunting man, like the shepherd with his wolf and the orchardist with his fruit fly, is in competition with other predators.

If such a culling rate is exceeded, then only a short term advantage is achieved, for sooner or later the total resource is reduced, often dramatically. North American bison had been predated upon by the Plains Indians for over ten thousand years, yet the millions of beasts wandering the prairies in the mid eighteen hundreds were reduced to the pitiful remnants of today. Their hunters deployed against them four new items of technology—namely the horse, the Winchester repeater rifle, a food support system which included such items as tinned bully beef that did not rely on the vagaries of seasonal flux, and the railroad which could articulate the wastefully gained products of the chase into a wider economic system.

To get to the isolated sealing rocks of Bass Strait, clinker built long boats and schooners were much more efficient than the paper bark canoe-rafts of the Tasmanians. But under the new onslaught by European sealers against its breeding fastnesses, a seal population which had given substantial sustenance to several thousand people for at least eight thousand years, collapsed almost to extinction within fifteen years. Both these vignettes illustrate competition between two groups of hunters for the same resources, the white hunters in both cases having a superior technology to either red or black hunters. Yet had the whites been truly professional, their very glut-ridden success might swiftly have led to disaster as may indeed have happened when man first entered the continent and islands of Australia and New Zealand, before an eventual selection occurred towards economies more in balance with their respective environments (eg. Jones, 1975).

One of the most important results from the study of Aboriginal demography, has been to show that Aboriginal population levels were *proportional to resources and not to technology*. The implications being that throughout the continent, including Tasmania, the various technologies employed were all sufficiently efficient to achieve close to this hypothetic maximum culling rate. We must not confuse the elaboration or complexity of a tool with its efficiency in the chase. The combination of a high powered, telescopic lensed rifle with a spot light might seem a more effective killer than a digging stick, yet when deployed against rabbits this is not necessarily so.

Aboriginal women digging out burrows with their sticks, gain not only a more reliable yield, but also a higher one than the hunter taking pot shots from a hundred metres away. The only disadvantage of digging is that it requires greater investment of labour. Brush or stone weirs spanning streams are such efficient fish catchers that they have to be banned by most modern fish management ordinances, whether in Wales or in the Northern Territory, in order to give a fair go to the sporting fisherman with his fibre-glass rod, nylon cord and a swarm of plastic flies.

Throughout Australia, most of the important extractive tasks could have been, and were, carried out by the use of the same basic, simple and versatile tool kit, of which digging stick, throwing stick, spear, carrying devices, grinding/pounding stones, string, fire stick and trapping devices were important items. Such an inventory brings to mind the Tasmanian tool kit, perhaps the irreducible minimum for the long term survival of a human society in Australian conditions. Perhaps we can call this the basic Australian tool kit.

To proceed further, we must consider homeostasy, the balance between man and land which is so deeply embedded

within Aboriginal behaviour and lore, and which was the prime feature of his prehistory for three hundred centuries. Invention of a new tool can be seen as the cultural analogue of mutation, presenting new possibilities for society to choose or to discard. In Australia, the choice was towards more time and not more food. Sharp (1952) documented the incorporation of the steel hatchet into the economy of the Yir Yiront of Cape York, noting that this caused a re-organisation of many tasks within the society and that many were done much easier and quicker than with the old methods. Nevertheless, this did not result in the extraction of more food, but rather in the tasks being completed quicker. Bowdler's study (1970) of the introduction of shell fish hooks into the coastal economy of southern New South Wales about a thousand years ago, shows that rather than adding to the total fish diet, the fish hooks caused a change in the species of fish eaten, and almost certainly in the section of society doing the work. Previously, bone tipped fish spears, wielded by men, had obtained rock dwelling species, but with the arrival of the new technology, these activities were greatly reduced and the women took over, dangling their hooks for snapper from bark canoes as shown in the ethnographic drawings, thus further freeing the men for non-productive activities.

No one sector of the economy can be divorced from the full interlocking system. There would be no advantage in increasing the yield from one food resource if commensurate increases could not also be gained from other foods, at other times in the year, and during other seasons. It was the lack of water, drying up in the clay pans, and not the lack of *panicum* grass seeds that limited the stay of Aborigines in the scrub lands away from the Darling and similar rivers of semi-arid western New South Wales and central Australia (H. Allen, 1972; J. O'Connell, pers. comm.). It was the shortage of food in mid winter that controlled the population level of the west coast of Tasmania, not the abundance of mutton birds and their eggs in the balmy summer months (Jones, 1974). The siphoning off of the man hours gained by the deployment of a new technology into non-productive activities can, in this context, be seen as a powerful homeostatic mechanism, ensuring that the labour thus released is not invested into some positive feed back system, whose result might at best be anarchic to the social order and, at worse, disastrous for the long term balance of the community to its resources.

Australia is a capricious continent, and men who live there have to contend with the vagaries of abundance and of disaster, which even-out only over long spans of time. A society whose population level is geared to these long term trends, and whose available labour in good seasons has such a high proportion held in reserve, is well insured against the bad times. Perhaps it is no coincidence that these ecological matters—the continuance of plants and animals, the relationship of men to their lands, the extension of social links and reciprocal obligations—these form the main themes of the great ceremonies. Like the Di Medicis of Florence, the Aborigines, intellectual aristocrats of the savage world (Lévi-Strauss, 1966 : 89), their sustenance ensured by a basic technology, invested the advantages of new tools into the realms of the ego, the mind and the soul.

Let us end with Tasmania and consider the trauma which the severance of the Bassian bridge delivered to the society isolated there. Like a blow above the heart, it took a long time to take effect, but slowly but surely there was a simplification in the tool kit, a diminution in the range of foods eaten, perhaps a squeezing of intellectuality (see Jones, 1971b). The world's longest isolation, the world's simplest technology. Were 4000 people enough to propel forever the cultural inheritance of Late Pleistocene Australia? Even if

Abel Tasman had not sailed the winds of the Roaring Forties in 1642, were they in fact doomed—doomed to a slow strangulation of the mind?

References

Allen, H., 1972. *Where the crow flies backwards: man and land in the Darling Basin.* Unpublished Ph.D. thesis, Australian National University, Canberra.

Allen, J., 1972. The first decade in New Guinea archaeology. *Antiquity,* 46 : 180–90.

Angas, G. F., 1850. *Savage Life and Scenes in Australia and New Zealand.* London: Smith, Elder & Co.

Binford, L. R., 1972. *An Archaeological Perspective.* New York: Academic Press.

Binford, S. R., 1968. Variability and change in the Near Eastern Mousterian of Levallois facies. *In* S. R. Binford and L. R. Binford (eds) *New perspectives in Archaeology,* pp. 49–60. Chicago: Aldine.

Birdsell, J. B., 1953. Some environmental and cultural factors influencing the structuring of Australian Aboriginal populations. *American Naturalist,* 87 : 171–207.

—— 1971. Ecology, spacing mechanisms and adaptive behaviour in Aboriginal land tenure. *In* R. Crocombe (ed.) *Land tenure in the Pacific,* pp. 334–61. Melbourne: Oxford University Press.

Bowdler, S., 1970. *Bass Point: the excavation of a south-east Australian shell midden showing cultural and economic change.* Unpublished B.A. (Hons) thesis, University of Sydney.

—— 1974a. An account of an archaeological reconnaissance of Hunter's Isles, north west Tasmania, 1973/74. *Records of the Queen Victoria Museum Launceston,* ns. no. 54.

—— 1974b. Pleistocene date for man in Tasmania. *Nature,* 252 : 697–98.

Bowler, J. M., R. Jones, H. R. Allen and A. G. Thorne, 1970. Pleistocene human remains from Australia: a living site and human cremation from Lake Mungo, Western New South Wales. *World Archaeology,* 2 : 39–59.

Collins, D., 1798/1802. *An Account of the English Colony in New South Wales . . .* 2 vols, London: T. Cadell & Co. Davies. [Republished 1975 by A. H. Reed, Sydney].

Edwards, R. and P. J. Ucko, 1973. Rock art in Australia. *Nature,* 246, no. 5430 : 274–77.

Eyre, E. J., 1845. *Journal of Expeditions of Discovery into Central Australia . . . 1840–41.* 2 vols, London T. & W. Boone. Facsimile. Adelaide, Libraries Board of South Australia, 1964.

Flood, J., 1973. *The moth hunters. Investigations towards a prehistory of the south-eastern highlands of Australia.* Unpublished Ph.D. thesis, Australian National University, Canberra.

—— 1974. Pleistocene man at Cloggs Cave: his tool kit and environment. *Mankind,* 9 : 175–88.

Glover, I. C., 1969. The use of factor analysis for the discovery of artefact types. *Mankind,* 7 : 36–47.

Gould, R. A., 1971. The archaeologist as ethnographer: a case from the Western Desert of Australia. *World Archaeology,* 3 : 143–77.

—— 1973. Australian archaeology in ecological and ethnographic perspective. Andover, Mass.: *Warner Modular.* Module 7.

Hiatt, B. (see Meehan, B.) 1967/68. The food quest and the economy of the Tasmanian Aborigines. *Oceania,* 38 : 99–133, 190–219.

—— 1969. Cremation in Aboriginal Australia. *Mankind,* 7 : 104–19.

Hiatt, L. R., 1965. *Kinship and conflict: a study of an Aboriginal community in Northern Arnhem Land.* Canberra: Australian National University Press.

Jackson, W. D., 1965. Vegetation. *In* J. L. Davies (ed.), *Atlas of Tasmania.* pp. 30–37. Hobart: Lands and Surveys Department.

—— 1968. Fire, air, water and earth: an elemental ecology of Tasmania. *Proceedings of the Ecological Society of Australia,* 3 : 9–16.

Jones, R., 1966. A speculative archaeological sequence for north west Tasmania. *Records of the Queen Victoria Museum, Launceston,* 25.

—— 1968. The geographical background to the arrival of man in Australia and Tasmania. *Archaeology and Physical Anthropology in Oceania,* 3 : 186–215.

—— 1971a. The demography of hunters and farmers in Tasmania. *In* D. J. Mulvaney and J. Golson (eds.) *Aboriginal man and environment in Australia,* pp. 271–87. Canberra: Australian National University Press.

—— 1971b. *Rocky Cape and the problem of the Tasmanians.* Unpublished Ph.D. thesis, University of Sydney.

—— 1973. Emerging picture of Pleistocene Australians. *Nature,* 246 : 278–81.

—— 1974. Tasmanian Tribes. Appendix to N. B. Tindale, *Aboriginal Tribes of Australia,* pp. 317–54. San Francisco: UCLA Press.

—— 1975. The neolithic, palaeolithic and the hunting gardeners: man and land in the Antipodes. *In* R. P. Suggate and M. M. Cresswell (eds) *Quaternary Studies,* pp. 21–34. Wellington: Royal Society of New Zealand.

—— (in press). Why did the Tasmanians stop eating fish? To be published in R. Gould (ed.) *Explorations in ethnoarchaeology.* University of New Mexico Press Alberqueque School of American Research, Santa Fe.

Kemp, T. B., 1963. The prehistory of the Tasmanian Aborigines. *Australian Natural History,* 14 : 242–47.

Lampert, R. J., 1971. *Burrill Lake and Currarong: coastal sites in southern New South Wales.* Terra Australis, no. 1, Department of Prehistory, ANU Canberra.

—— 1972. A carbon date for the Aboriginal occupation of Kangaroo Island, South Australia. *Mankind,* 8 : 223–34.

—— and P. J. Hughes, 1974. Sea level change and Aboriginal coastal adaptation in southern New South Wales. *Archaeology and Physical Anthropology in Oceania,* 9 : 226–35

Lawrence, R., 1968. *Aboriginal habitat and economy.* Occ. Pap. no. 6, Department of Geography, School of General Studies, ANU, Canberra.

Lesueur, C. A. and N. Petit, 1807/1811. Atlas with F. Péron and L. Freycinet, *Voyage de découvertes aux Terres Australes . . .* Paris: de l'Imprimerie Imperiale.

Lévi-Strauss, C., 1966. *The savage mind.* London: Weidenfeld and Nicolson.

Lourandos, H., 1968. Dispersal of activities: the east Tasmanian Aboriginal sites. *Papers and Proceedings of the Royal Society of Tasmania.* 102 : 41–46.

—— 1970. *Coast and hinterland: the archaeological sites of eastern Tasmania.* Unpublished M.A. thesis, ANU, Canberra.

Luebbers, R., 1975. Ancient boomerangs discovered in South Australia. *Nature,* no. 5486, 253 : 39.

McCarthy, F. D., 1939. 'Trade' in Aboriginal Australia and 'trade' relationships with Torres Strait, New Guinea and Malaya. *Oceania,* 9 : 405–38; 10 : 80–104, 171–95.

—— and F. M. Setzler, 1960. The archaeology of Arnhem Land. *In* C. P. Mountford (ed.), *Records of the American-Australian Expedition to Arnhem Land . . .* vol. 2 : 215–95. Melbourne: Melbourne University Press.

Macphail, M., 1975. Late Pleistocene environments in Tasmania. *Search*, 6 : 295–300.

Meehan, B. (see Hiatt, B.), (in press). Hunters by the sea shore. *Journal of Human Evolution.*

Mitchell, S. A., 1949. *Stone age craftsmen: stone tools and camping places of the Australian Aborigines.* Melbourne: Tait Book Co.

Mulvaney, D. J., 1969. *The prehistory of Australia.* 1st ed., London: Thames & Hudson.

—— 1970. The anthropologist as tribal elder. *Mankind*, 7 : 205–17.

—— 1975. *The prehistory of Australia.* 2nd ed., Victoria: Penguin Books.

—— 1976. The chain of connection: the material evidence. *In* N. Peterson (ed.), *Tribes and Boundaries in Australia*, pp. 72–94. Australian Institute of Aboriginal Studies, Canberra.

—— and E. B. Joyce, 1965. Archaeological and geomorphological investigations on Mt Moffat Station, Queensland, Australia. *Proceedings of the Prehistory Society*, 31 : 147–212.

O'Connell, J. F., 1974. Spoons, knives and scrapers: the function of Yilugwa in Central Australia. *Mankind*, 9 : 189–94.

Pearce, R. H., 1973. Uniformity of the Australian backed blade tradition. *Mankind*, 9 : 89–95.

Peterson, N., 1971. Open sites and the ethnographic approach to the archaeology of hunter-gatherers. *In* D. J. Mulvaney and J. Golson (eds.), *Aboriginal man and environment in Australia*, pp. 239–48. Canberra: Australian National University Press.

Plomley, N. J. B., 1962. A list of Tasmanian Aboriginal material in collections in Europe. *Records of Queen Victoria Museum Launceston*, n.s. 15.

—— 1966. *Friendly Mission. The Tasmanian journals and papers of George Augustus Robinson, 1829–1834.* Hobart: Tasmanian Historical Research Association.

Sharp, L., 1952. Steel axes for stone age Australians. *In* E. H. Spicer (ed.), *Human problems in technological change*, pp. 69–90. New York: Russel Sage Foundation.

Shawcross, W., 1970. Ethnographic economics and the study of population in prehistoric New Zealand: viewed through archaeology. *Mankind*, 7 : 279–91.

—— 1972. Energy and ecology: thermodynamic models in archaeology. *In* D. L. Clarke (ed.), *Models in archaeology*, pp. 577–622. London: Methuen.

Stockton, E. D. and W. Holland, 1974. Cultural sites and their environment in the Blue Mountains. *Archaeology and Physical Anthropology in Oceania*, 9 : 36–65.

Sutherland, F. L., 1972. The classification, distribution, analysis and sources of material in flaked stone implements of Tasmanian Aborigines. *Records of Queen Victoria Museum Launceston*, n.s. 42.

Thomson, D. F., 1939. The seasonal factor in human culture: illustrated from the life of a contemporary nomadic group. *Proceedings of the Prehistoric Society*, 5 : 209–221.

—— 1949. *Economic structure and the ceremonial exchange cycle in Arnhem Land.* Melbourne: Macmillan.

Tindale, N. B., 1937. Relationship of the extinct Kangaroo Island culture with cultures of Australia, Tasmania and Malaya. *Records of the South Australian Museum*, 6 : 39–60.

—— 1962. Some population changes among the Kaiadilt people of Bentinck Island, Queensland. *Records of the South Australian Museum*, 14 : 297–336.

—— 1974. *Aboriginal Tribes of Australia.* San Francisco: UCLA Press.

Warner, W. L., 1937. *A Black Civilization: a social study of an Australian tribe.* New York: Harper & Bros.

White, C., 1971. Man and environment in north west Arnhem Land. *In* D. J. Mulvaney and J. Golson (eds.) *Aboriginal man and environment in Australia*, pp. 141–57, Canberra: Australian National University Press.

—— and N. Peterson, 1969. Ethnographic interpretations of the prehistory of western Arnhem Land. *Southwestern Journal of Anthropology*, 25 : 45–67.

White, J. P., 1971. New Guinea and Australian prehistory: the 'Neolithic problem'. *In* D. J. Mulvaney and J. Golson (eds), *Aboriginal man and environment in Australia*, pp.185–95. Canberra: Australian National University Press.

—— 1972. *Ol Tumbuna:* archaeological excavations in the Eastern Central Highlands, Papua. *Terra Australis* no. 2. Canberra: Department of Prehistory, ANU.

Wright, R. V. S., 1974. Significance tests and archaeological importance, *Mankind*, 9 : 169–74.

A functional study of use-polished eloueras

JOHAN KAMMINGA

One of the avenues by which archaeologists can reconstruct the subsistence behaviour of prehistoric hunter-gatherer man is through the study of stone tool functions. Prehistorians, especially during the past decade, have concentrated more on stone tool classification in pursuit of new and useful information relating to economic activities. Although many prehistorians have expressed the wish to see function used as a major criterion for classifying stone tools, this has not yet been done on any significant scale.

During the late nineteenth and early twentieth century stone tools were classified to a large extent by assumed function as well as their overall morphology and technique of manufacture (eg. Burkitt, 1925; Evans, 1872; Macalister, 1921). Functions were attributed by analogy, firstly with tools used by existing and documented hunter-gatherer groups, and secondly with the metal tools of more technologically advanced societies. This approach can occasionally still be identified in the recent archaeological literature (eg. Allen, 1972; Ponosov, n.d.; Shutler and Kess, 1969; Sieveking, 1958).

Stimulated by observations of Australian Aborigines actually using stone tools, ethnographers and prehistorians also incorporated function as a fundamental criterion in defining stone tool classes. This approach is more successful when direct analogies are used, or when the classifications encompass ethnographically documented stone tools (Gould, 1971; Gould, Koster and Sontz, 1971; Tindale, 1965). However, more often function is not explicitly stated in the ethnography but is inferred from broad comparative analogies. Classifications which rely on unverified assumed function or broad analogies are inappropriate as the designations of use remain highly speculative and there is no basis on which useful comparisons between tool classes can be made.

At this stage in the development of prehistoric research in Australia it is essential that stone function and the correlation between functional and formal classes be more fully investigated. By doing this we may gain a better understanding of the technology and economy of prehistoric man in Australia. To this end studies have already begun; notably those of Gould *et al.* (1971), Lampert (1971), McBryde (1974:217 and Carmel White (1967). Some of these studies relied on the work of Semenov (1964) who dealt with use-wear on European middle and upper Palaeolithic tools. However, caution is needed in applying *in toto* Semenov's interpretations of wear patterns to Australian stone tools. Significant cultural, economic and environmental differences do exist between the two regions which must be taken into account. Furthermore, Semenov only rarely attempted to test his inferences by experimental replication of tool use and consequently there does remain some doubt about the accuracy of his conclusions (Bordes, 1967:37-38; Keller, 1966:510).

For the purposes of aiding in the interpretation of use-wear on Australian stone tools, replicating tool use operations were conducted with the assistance of undergraduate students from the University of Sydney. The aim of this work was not to obtain identical use-wear to that observed on prehistoric tools but to gather together a corpus of wear patterns, so that the variables which might determine or influence the form of wear might be isolated and their significance assessed.

The total number of individual operations was as follows:

Woodworking	sawing	11
	adzing	21
	scraping	43
	chopping	11
	combined adzing and scraping	1
	whittling	3
Scraping skin		3
Sawing bone		9
	Total	102

In these experimental operations several variables, thought to have some significance, were controlled.

(a) Stone artifact material. Two varieties of chert, three varieties of quartzite, and one variety each of chalcedony, siltstone and flint.

(b) Material being worked. For the woodworking operations two timber species were selected according to their relatively high and low densities. The density of nearly all Australian timbers is highly correlated with other mechanically measured properties, such as tensile, compressive and shearing strength and impact resistance. The two species selected were a soft wood, *Eucalyptus viminalis* (density 34.7 lbs/ft^3) 556 kg/m^3 and a hard wood, *Eucalyptus paniculata* (density 56.0 lbs/ft^3) 897 kg/m^3. Both timbers were newly felled and in a 'green' condition. A freshly fleeced sheepskin and fresh ungulate bones were used in the remaining operations.

(c) Implement edge angle. Three categories were created to provide a discontinuous range from acute to obtuse edge angles. These categories were 25°–35°; 45°–55°, and 65°–75°. The angles were measured with a bevelled protractor at mid-section of the working edge.

(d) Angle of the tool to the material being worked. In some of the chopping and scraping operations, and all of the sawing operations, the stone tool was oriented at an angle of 90° to the wood being worked. Adzing was done at angles between 40°–45° and the remaining scraping operations at angles between 20°–25°.

(e) Mode of use. The operations were planned so as to incorporate most of the ethnographically documented
methods of wood removal with flaked tools. The modes
selected are listed above.

(f) Adaption of a wooden haft as opposed to the hand-held
use of tools.

(g) The introduction of sand, as an abrasive agent, on the
material being worked.

The tool use operations were concluded, with few exceptions,
when the working edge could no longer function efficiently.
Only in one case was the operation terminated because the
tool remained effective after prolonged continuous use.[1]

As previously stated, the variables which were controlled in
the operations were hypothetically considered the most significant in determining the form and pattern of use-wear. Planning of a revised series of more rigidly controlled experiments
is now in progress and it is envisaged that these will provide
more accurate and detailed information on use-wear determinants and patterns than was obtained from the 1971 series.

Comparison of use-polished stone artifacts from New South Wales and western Arnhem Land

1. Eloueras and polished flakes from New South Wales The
elouera, a recent phase tool type—dating from around 4000
years ago to possibly the early contact period—has been collected from archaeological sites scattered throughout south-
east Australia, and as far north as Laura on the Cape York
peninsula. Mulvaney (1969 : 81) descriptively defines the
elouera as: '. . . a triangular sectioned flake or blade resembling an orange segment, normally with bi-directional blunting
retouch or step flaking on the thick back.' He remarks that
along the acute edge or chord, there may be '. . . varying
degrees of use-fracture, trimming or use-polish.'

The obvious appearance of this use-polish, use-flaking and
retouch on the acute edges of many eloueras has stimulated a
great deal of speculation about their possible function. Among
the early investigators, Towle (1935) proposed a scraping
function, while Turner (1931 : 30) suggested that these tools
were held in the hand, serving as backed knives. Noone (1943 :
278) regarded the elouera as a form of 'specialised tula' or adze
flake, but is ambiguous as to whether the blunt retouched
edge or the acute edge was the working end of the tool
McCarthy suggested that eloueras had a wide range of uses
(McCarthy and Davidson, 1943 : 293). Relying on Hunter's
observation (1793 : 49) that the Port Jackson Aborigines hafted
stone flakes as woodworking tools, McCarthy (1948 : 31;
Davidson and McCarthy, 1957 : 408) later proposed that the
elouera was in fact an adze flake. McCarthy (1967 : 24, 26)
subsequently reiterated his initial belief that the elouera had a
wide range of uses, including woodworking, and describes it as
a hafted chisel. More recently, Lampert (1971 : 49) concluded,
after microscopically examining the heavily worn working
edges of eloueras he recovered from excavations at Burrill
Lake and Currarong, that these implements were originally
end-hafted as chisels, mainly for woodworking.

With the aim of investigating these propositions, eloueras
and polished flakes from a range of archaeological sites were
examined. A total of 30 were selected from the archaeological
sites of Curracurrang, Capertee, Sandy Hollow, Burrill Lake

(Thorpe's excavation) and Kurnell. Of this sample 11 artifacts
were quartzite and 19 were chert.

Four distinct forms of use-wear were discernible on these
artifacts: edge rounding, polishing and smoothing, edge
flaking and striation. These forms of wear are not mutually
exclusive and often, when the surface of the tool was prominently polished, it was also striated and the working edge
rounded by wear. Ten eloueras were striated at various angles
to the working edge; eight at 90°; one at 80°, and another at
intersecting angles, mostly between 75°–90°. In many cases the
striation was subparallel. Striations were more prominent on
the cherts, and this seems to be a function of artifact material.

Experimental tool use demonstrated that, in general, the
more soft and fine grained an artifact material is, the greater
the likelihood that it will be susceptible to modification in the
form of polish and striation (Kamminga 1971:73).

Of 13 chert tools used in the experimental woodworking,
skin-scraping and bone-cutting operations, in which sand was
introduced as an abrasive agent, only one tool remained un-
striated. Materials such as quartz, chalcedony, flint and a tough
quartzite did not striate nearly as readily as the chert.

The extent of polish, or its invasiveness, on the dorsal and
ventral faces of the tools, did not appear to differ although
some difficulty was encountered in defining exactly where the
polish faded out. The difference between the extent of polish
on the two lateral faces on each of the remaining eloueras was
2, 5, 10, 11 and 12 mm.

With reference to the frequency of flake scars, two eloueras
did not have scars along either margin of the acute edge; two
had scars on one margin only, and eight had scars along both
margins. On six eloueras the scars were worn, polished and
striated, subsequent to the detachment of the flakes. One
elouera with an edge angle of 26° sustained edge fracturing
which was identical to edge damage resulting from experimental
scraping or adzing soft and hard wood (*Eucalyptus viminalis*
and *E. paniculata*) with the hafted chert, quartzite, siltstone,
flint and chalcedony flakes having edge angles within the 25°–
35° range. An elouera with similar edge damage, also within
this edge angle range, is depicted by Lampert (1971:19), who
describes the edge modification as light retouch.

Wear on the polished flakes in my sample was strikingly
similar to that observed on the polished eloueras. All seven
were polished on both the lateral faces, the invasiveness of the
polish on these surfaces on four of the flakes being roughly
equal and differing no more than 2 mm on the remainder.
Concomitant with this polish was striation oriented at right
angles to the edge (see Fig. 1). On one flake striations at this
angle were accompanied by others aligned at 75° to the edge.

Use-fracturing along the working edge was not a common
wear trait, only three flakes having irregularly spaced scars on
one margin, and one flake having scars on both margins of the
acute working edge. On one flake from Sandy Hollow the
margins opposite the acute polished edge were steeply retouched, though possibly not for the purpose of blunting.
Striations at 90° to the edge and use-polish were visible on both
margins of the retouched edge, extending 6 mm inward on the
lateral faces. The edge was retouched after the formation of
polish and striation, suggesting that the flake was reversed
during use and both acute edges employed, one worn edge
being obliterated by retouch.

*Comparison of sample with Lampert's use-polished eloueras and
flakes* Lampert (1971 : 48) reports use-polish occurring on
the acute margins of 25 stone tools from Currarong and Burrill

---

1. A more complete discussion of the variables and experimental
procedure is presented in Kamminga, 1971: 38–52.

Fig. 1: Rounded edge and heavy striation on a use-polished chert flake from Gymea. ×12 (G.B. 109.D. A14-8).

Lake. Comparison of the wear patterns on the polished flakes with those on the eloueras suggested that these two groups were functionally equivalent. This proposition was further tested by a comparison of formal characteristics (1971 : 49, table 23). In three variables tabulated (length, breadth and the length/breadth ratio), there was no significant difference between the two groups—although both differed significantly from the corresponding flakes and eloueras without use-polish.

Both Lampert's and my own polished flake and elouera samples did not differ significantly in respect of wear patterns, either within or between the groups. However, Lampert does point out that the striations on his artifacts were angled between 75°–85° to the edge, and that no striations intersected. This discrepancy between our observations may well be attributed to the difference in artifact material. Subparallel and intersecting striations, when they occurred in my sample, were only observed on chert, whereas Lampert's polished artifacts were of quartzite—a material which does not easily sustain heavy striation; thus making observation more difficult.

Lampert proposes that the use-polished eloueras and flakes which he examined were end-hafted in spearthrowers and used as woodworking tools. The existence of end-hafted stone adze-scrapers in the Port Jackson area has been documented by Hunter (1793:49) who reported that: 'The throwing-stick had a piece of hard stone fused in gum instead of the shell which is commonly used by the natives who live on the sea coast: it is with these stones, which they bring to a very sharp edge, that the natives make their spears'.

Lieutenant Bradley also describes a hafted stone adze used by the Aborigines inhabiting the environs of Port Jackson, but in this case the adze was secured on the butt end of a stick (Bradley, 1788:129-30). Particularly significant is Bradley's observation that this form of hafted adze was often seen used, in conjunction with edge ground axes and stone wedges, to manfacture bark shields and canoes.

The experimental replicative tool-use operations which were carried out in 1971 support Lampert's proposal that use-polished flakes and eloueras were hafted as woodworking tools. Adzing soft wood resulted in considerable wear in the form of flake scars, polish on the ventral face extending up to 5 mm from the edge, occasional limited dorsal polish, striations angled at 75°–90° to the edge, and edge rounding. Hayden reports more extreme polish on common opal adzes used on a particularly soft wood, *Erythrina vespertilio* (density 17 lbs/ft³ (272 kg/m³)), (Hayden and Kamminga, 1973 : 4). Experimental hafted adzing and scraping of a moderately hard wood produced a restricted polish along the ventral margin of the working edge of some flint and chert tools. Edge rounding was also common and striation did occur when sand was introduced onto the surface of the wood, and flake scars appeared on the edge (Kamminga, 1971:76-80).

Of 53 flint and opal adzes used by Western Desert Aborigines to work an extremely hard wood, *Acacia aneura* (density 68 lbs/ft³ (1089 kg/m³)), only 8 % had even the most infinitesimal polish on the ventral margins of their edges (Hayden and Kamminga, 1973:6).

The variation in the degree of polish on both the ethnographic Western Desert adzes and the experimental hafted adzes and scrapers appears to be largely controlled by the properties of the timbers being worked: the more extreme the softness or resilience of the wood, the more extreme the polish on the tools used to work them.

Experimental scraping of fresh sheep skin resulted in edge-rounding and polish on the ventral margin of flint and chert flakes. However, this was by no means very pronounced, and no wear at all occurred on a quartzite used in this way. Wear patterns resulting from scraping fresh skins could not be confused with the use-wear observed on the polished flakes and eloueras examined by Lampert and myself.

The experimental operations using hafted and unhafted stone flakes support Lampert's contention that the use-polished flakes and eloueras from his south coast sites were originally hafted. There is also some further verification of this proposition. Stockton (1970:298) describes two eloueras (polished?) with specks of gum adhering to the retouched surfaces, from sites in the Blue Mountains. Two use-polished flakes from Curracurrang also have remains of gum on the surfaces which remain unpolished (Kamminga, 1971:02), and no doubt more of these artifacts with traces of gum will be recovered from excavations in future years.

Conclusions The polished flakes and eloueras examined by Lampert and myself were probably used to scrape and/or adze an extremely soft wood or bark. Experimental bark scraping and adzing were not undertaken as part of the project but will be carried out in a future series of tool use operations.

It is important to point out at this stage that polish and striation are not the most common forms of wear found on eloueras from east coast sites. Lampert reports unifacial flaking (termed chattering) on the acute edges of some of the eloueras he examined. Other eloueras which I studied have both unifacial and bifacial flaking along their working edges, sometimes associated with edge rounding. Not uncommonly, the latter was the only form of wear observed on the eloueras which were examined.

Mulvaney (1969:83) believes that 'use-polish must have been produced by action different from that which fractured the working edge', but initial examination of eloueras displaying edge fracture and rounding suggested similarities with wear resulting from hard wood adzing and scraping. Unfortunately, this sort of usage does not produce wear which can be said to be 'distinctive' or 'diagnostic'. Much more experimental work needs to be done before anything definite can be said about the distinctiveness of wear resulting from scraping and adzing hard woods.

Further research may demonstrate that use-wear on eloueras from east coast sites reflects the range of timbers and bark which were used by the Aborigines to manufacture a variety of artifacts. This could be envisaged as a continuum, with very hard wood at one end resulting in edge fracturing and/or rounding; in the centre, timbers of intermediate hardness, resulting in edge fracturing, rounding and a modest use-polish restricted to the working edge; and at the other end, very soft wood and bark resulting in extensive polish, edge rounding and probably also striation. If this interpretation can be demonstrated to be substantially correct, the wide variation of wear forms observed on east coast eloueras will be more intelligible.

2. Use-polished eloueras and flakes from Western Arnhem Land In 1960 McCarthy and Setzler published a report on their 1948 excavations at Oenpelli. Twelve rock shelters were excavated on two hills, Inyaluk and Arguluk, both plateau outliers near the mission settlement at Oenpelli. One of the more significant results of their investigations was the recovery of numerous use-polished eloueras and flakes. They remark that the ' . . . eloueras proved to be a dominant specialised type of knapped implement in the Oenpelli rockshelters that we excavated and many of the eloueras removed bear a pronounced use-polished working edge or sheen on the chord. In shape, fashioning and variety they correspond exactly with those from South East Australia' (1960 : 278).

Since then, Carmel White has recovered more of these use-polished artifacts on the alluvial plain sites of Barribarri and Nawamun, and at the plateau sites of Djimerri I and II (White, 1967). Recently I observed similar artifacts on seasonally inundated, exposed surface sites in the Woolwonga Reserve, some 35 km south-west of White's major sites.

McCarthy and Setzler's classification of many of these use-polished tools as eloueras is disputed by White, who re-examined 91 of the implements now housed in The Australian Museum (1967:235; reiterated by Lampert, 1971:49, and Mulvaney, 1969:82). White's first objection is that many of the flakes classified as eloueras do not fulfil all the necessary requisites for inclusion in this class. She states that 'few of them conform to the formal definition of an elouera, since they show a wide variety of shapes and sizes and contain varying degrees of retouch' (1967 : 235). Her second point is that the distinctive use-polish constitutes the tools as a functional rather than a formal one. She suggests that since the definition of the elouera is based in form, one should avoid this label and classify the Oenpelli artifacts as 'scrapers and utilised flakes' (1967 : 236).

I examined a group of 47 use-polished stone tools from Oenpelli and Nawamun and identified 15 as being morphologically identical to the east coast specimens, in that they were triangular sectioned flakes, shaped like an orange segment and with blunting retouch on the thick margin. These eloueras, as do the east coast eloueras, form a distinctive tool class which can be defined by formal traits, but at the same time also belong to a broader functional class. I do not wish to impute a necessary cultural connection between the two regions, but stress the integrity of western Arnhem Land eloueras as members of the formal tool class elouera, as it is presently defined.

The dating of the polished eloueras and flakes from Arnhem Land is not altogether clear. Most of them were recovered from the upper levels of shallow deposits excavated by McCarthy and Setzler, while others were found lying on shelter floors. Similar artifacts were recovered from exposed open sites on the plain and these are associated with later phase technology indicating that they are less than 7000 years

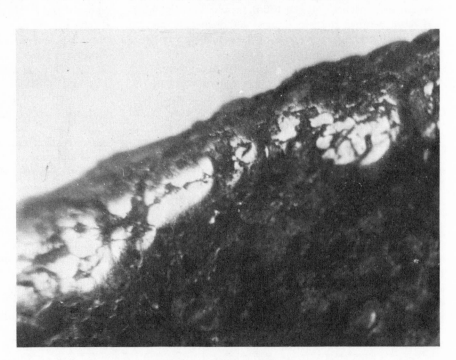

Fig. 2: Rounded edge of a use-polished flake from Oenpelli. The smoothed and polished quartz grains are clearly visible. ×15.

old (Kamminga and Allen, 1973 : 17).In fact, some of these sites were abandoned by the Aborigines as recently as just prior to the Second World War. However, there are no accounts of these implements in the ethnography, nor do the Aborigines recall their use.

Various functions have been ascribed to these tools. McCarthy and Setzler (1960 : 280) questioned the local Aborigines who, although confessing ignorance, suggested that they might have been used for woodworking, or to cut out bee's nests. Not being satisfied with these explanations, McCarthy and Setzler speculated about other possible functions, proposing such tasks as dressing skins, cleaning off outer bark, smoothing the surface of wooden shields, spear-throwers and sacred objects, and cutting the stems of wild rice, *Oryza satava*—a probable Macassan introduction. Tindale (1951 : 374)suggested that these tools were used to carve spear barbs on hard wood spears, while White (1967 : 169) believed that the polish on the flakes from Barribarri resulted from scraping skins in a uni-directional movement. She adds though, that they could also have served to scrape soft wood.

For the purpose of examining the use-wear on these artifacts, a total of 49–47 from Inyaluk and Arguluk hills and two from Nawamun—were selected from the collections housed in The Australian Museum. Four forms of wear were identified and these are discussed under separate headings.

Polish All the implements were polished along the acute working edge, light reflection often being more intense on one or other of the lateral faces or margins. Generally, the polish is more striking than polish on the New South Wales eloueras, but this phenomenon appears to be related to the properties of the stone material. Brightness or lustre is a quality conditioned by the smoothness and regularity of the microtopography of the stone's surface. Microscopic observation of the intensely polished surfaces revealed that the originally rough surface was worn very smooth (Fig. 3). The material of most artifacts is a granular red quartzite consisting of about 97% quartz in the form of large well rounded grains. Once these grains are smoothed as a result of the use of the tool these large grains reflect an intense light, exactly like the reflection of a clear quartz crystal. The non-reflective quality of the unsmoothed surface is, to some degree, due to a red iron oxide film (part of the bonding material) which coats the quartz grains. This bonding material forms less than 3% of the total composition of the stone.

Microscopic observation of both lateral faces of one of the use-polished eloueras revealed that the surface which had a dull polish was not worn to the same degree as the opposing highly reflective face. The quartz grains were not completely smoothed and the distinction between the large quartz grains and the interstitial areas of fine-grained cementing material was vague.

To compare this form of polish with the frequently reported polish on Near Eastern sickles I examined chert and flint blades from the Neolithic sites of Teleilat Ghassul and Beidha. With the aid of the scanning electron microscope it was observed that the polished surfaces on these blades could not be resolved at magnifications of up to ×3000, suggesting that quite a different polishing process had occurred from that inferred for the Oenpelli polished artifacts. Frictional heat and pressure resulting in the creation of an isotropic surface layer may be an explanation for this phenomenon but not enough is known about the polishing process to definitely establish this. Comet-shaped depressions, aligned with stri-

ations angled parallel to the working edge, were also observed at magnifications up to ×200. These striations were not in the form of surface scratches (unlike those on the Oenpelli polished artifacts [see Figs. 3 and 4]) but appeared to be 'plastic' deformations of the surface. This suggests that the surface was hydrolised and not brittle when the striations formed (Joos, 1957). Similar wear patterns on sickle blades were reported by Semenov (1964:115) and Witthoft (1967). The polish on the Oenpelli artifacts is thus quite distinctively different from the superficially similar polish resulting from sickle use.

As a proportion of the use-polished artifacts examined, 82% had intense polish on one face and comparatively dull polish on the opposite face; 13% had intense polish on both lateral faces, and 5% had dull polish on both faces. On both faces the polish did not fade along the length of the working edge but did fade along the width axis. The difference between the invasion of the polish on the dorsal and ventral faces was as follows:

0-5 mm	76%
6-15 mm	19%
16-30 mm	5%

Polish sometimes extended over slight depressions when they occurred near the edge. In such cases these concavities were not smoothed within.

Striation In nearly all cases striations were visible within the polished area on the lateral faces, only occasionally extending further up the face towards the distal end of the tool. The angle of striations to the working edge varied between 75°–90°, but on most tools in the sample striations were slightly inclined at angles less than 90°. In all cases the orientation of the angle of striation on both faces of the tool agreed.

Edge rounding and bevelling The edges of all the tools examined were blunted and rounded (Fig. 2), the width of these rounded edges never exceeding more than 2 mm. In 24 cases the edges were bevelled, the bias on all but 8 specimens being on the highly polished margin. Only 11 tools did not have a bevelled edge yet displayed differential degrees of light reflection off the lateral faces and margins.

Edge fracturing Thirty five of the sample did not sustain edge damage in the form of flake scars; 7 had one or more flake scars (never more than 4) on the margin of the face with the less intensive polish, the origin of impact being on the opposite margin. Only one tool had a flake scar on the margin of the highly polished face.

In general, the use-polished eloueras and flakes did not have obtuse working edges. The edge angles range between 20°–30°, as measured at the midpoint of the working edge (see Fig. 5). In 1948 McCarthy and Setzler recovered a hafted quartzite flake which they identified as an elouera (1960 : 269). This implement which is side-hafted has use-polish along both lateral faces and is indistinguishable from comparable eloueras in my sample. Also recovered at this time was a use-polished flake with a considerable portion of disintegrating gum still adhering to it (1960 : 270). I identified probable gum staining on a further three eloueras from the Oenpelli excavations of 1948, while White (1967 : 110) mentions a use-polished flake with traces of gum from Barribarri. In the light of this evidence it appears very likely that the use-polished flakes and eloueras were all originally hafted, the degree of wear on the tools also

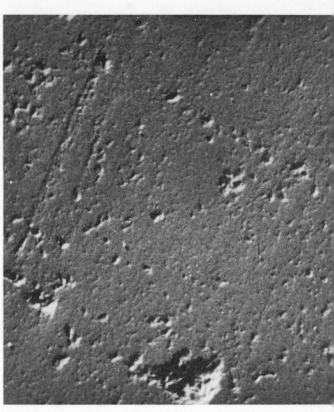

Fig. 3 (left): Use-polished surface of a fine-grained chert flake from Goose Camp 4, Woolwonga Reserve, western Arnhem Land. Back-scattered electron image. Gold coated. ×60.

Fig. 4 (above): Detail of pitting and striation on the polished surface observed in the upper right of Fig. 3. Note that the pits are the remnants of the depressions on the original unpolished surface. ×120.

Fig. 5 (below): Edge angles of polished flakes and eloueras from western Arnhem Land. N=47.

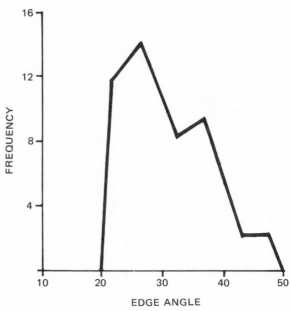

suggesting this. It may be that the side-hafted elouera demonstrates the original hafting position of the use-polished artifacts: if so it would necessitate a chopping motion, as the elouera is hafted at right angles to the handle and the stroke is consequently directed from the side.

The extreme degree of edge rounding and extent of polish on the faces of the tools indicate that a soft material was worked. The apparent lack of strength of the artifact material compared with other rock types used by Aborigines, the acute edge angles and infrequency of flake scars occuring along the working edge, all support this conclusion. The evidence of edge bevelling is not unequivocal, but might also be considered as supporting this deduction. The presence of edge bevelling, as well as the agreement in the angle and orientation of striations on the two lateral faces and margins of every tool indicates that the tools penetrated into the material being worked, causing comparatively greater wear on the ventral or lower face (Semenov, 1964 : 109). That the worked material was also fibrous in nature is indicated by the fact that shallow depressions in the surface of the stone were not smoothed or polished although polish extended beyond them across the face of the tool. These depressions were up to 1 cm wide and 3 or 4 mm deep.

It has already been demonstrated that the use-polished flakes and eloueras do not display wear typical of sickle usage or skin scraping. In some respects the wear observed on these tools does appear similar to wear produced experimentally by scraping and adzing soft wood. However, the degree and extent of the polish, edge rounding and bevelling indicates that the wood would have had to be very much softer than that used in the experiments. Unfortunately, very little is known about the mechanical properties of timbers in the Arnhem Land region. None of the timbers used by the Aborigines in this region for which we know the densities, are sufficiently soft to have caused the wear described. Bark is certainly a possibility, if not a probability. Numerous bark artifacts were manufactured by the Aborigines of this region in post-contact times, especially the bark from *Eucalyptus tetrodonta* (Spencer, 1914 : 379, 386–87; Mountford, 1956 : 8, 13; Specht, 1958 : 497; Tindale, 1925–6 : 101, 103; Warner, 1937 : 490, 504–05). Spencer (1914 : 386–87) records that the bark for manufacturing baskets was '. . . first of all carefully scraped over to remove the outer, rough surface'. This treatment was also necessary when preparing bark for painting. At the present time Aboriginal bark painters in Arnhem Land use steel axes in an adzing motion to remove the outer layers of large sheets of *Eucalyptus tetrodonta* bark before decorating them (Edwards and Guerin, 1969).

Conclusions   Polished eloueras from western Arnhem Land and south-east Australia display wear patterns which, on the evidence available, strongly suggest that they were used as hafted adzes and/or scrapers to work soft wood or bark. As well as belonging to a tool class defined by formal attributes, use-polished eloueras in both areas also qualify for membership in a functional class which includes unretouched and scantily retouched use-polished flakes.

Acknowledgements   I am indebted to the Electron Microscope Unit at the University of Sydney for making available the Scanning Electron Microscope and to Dr C. E. Nockolds of that unit for his advice and beneficial assistance. The trustees of the Australian Museum, Mr David Moore, Professor J. B. Hennessy and Professor J. V. S. Megaw made available to me the various stone tool collections which I examined and I am most grateful to them for this courtesy. Funds for the experimental work were granted by the Carlyle Greenwell Bequest, University of Sydney.

References

Allen, J., 1972. Nebira 4: an early Austronesian site in Central Papua. *Archaeology and Physical Anthropology in Oceania* 7 : 92–124.

Bordes, F., 1967. Considérations sur la typologie et les techniques dans le Paléolithique. *Quarter* 18 : 25–55.

Bradley, W., 1786–1792. *Journal 1786–92, including a voyage to New South Wales in H.M.S. Sirius and the return in the Waakaamheydt Transport.* Mitchell Library Ms. A3631.

Burkitt, M. C., 1925. *Prehistory. A study of early cultures in Europe and the Mediterranean Basin.* Cambridge: Cambridge University Press.

Davidson, D. S. and F. D. McCarthy, 1957. The distribution and chronology of some important types of stone implements in Western Australia. *Anthropos* 52 : 390–458.

Edwards, R. and B. Guerin, 1969. *Aboriginal bark paintings.* Adelaide: Rigby.

Evans, J., 1872. *The ancient stone implements, weapons and ornaments of Great Britain.* London: Longmans, Green, Reader and Dyer.

Gould, R. A., 1971. The archaeologist as ethnographer: a case from the Western Desert Aborigines of Australia. *World Archaeology* 3 : 143–72.

D. A. Koster and A. H. L. Sontz, 1971. The lithic assemblage of the Western Desert Aborigines of Australia. *American Antiquity* 36 : 149–69.

Hayden, B. and J. Kamminga, 1973. Gould, Koster and Sontz on 'microwear': a critical review. *Newsletter of Lithic Technology* 2(2) : 3–8.

Hunter, J., 1793. *An historical journal of the transactions at Port Jackson and Norfolk Island.* London: Stockdale.

Joos, P., 1957. The microhardness of the surface of glass. *Zeitschrift für angewandte Physik*, 9 : 556.

Kamminga, J., 1971. *Microscopic and experimental study of Australian Aboriginal stone tools.* Unpublished B.A. honours thesis, University of Sydney.

—— and H. R. Allen, 1973. Report of the archaeological survey. In *Alligator Rivers Environmental Fact-Finding Study.*

Keller, C. M., 1966. The development of edge damage patterns on stone tools. *Man* 4 : 501–11.

Lampert, R. J., 1971. *Burrill Lake and Currarong.* Terra Australis 1. Department of Prehistory, Research School of Pacific Studies, Australian National University, Canberra.

Macalister, R. A. S., 1921. *A text-book of European archaeology.* 2 volumes. Cambridge: Cambridge University Press.

McBryde, I., 1974. *Aboriginal prehistory in New England.* Sydney: Sydney University Press.

McCarthy, F. D., 1948. The Lapstone Creek excavation. *Records of the Australian Museum* 22 : 1–34.

—— 1967. *Australian Aboriginal stone implements.* Sydney: The Australian Museum.

—— and F. A. Davidson, 1943. The elouera industry of Singleton, Hunter Valley, N.S.W. *Records of the Australian Museum* 21 : 210–30.

—— and F. M. Setzler, 1960. The archaeology of Arnhem Land. In *Records of the American-Australian Scientific*

Expedition to Arnhem Land. Vol. 2, Anthropology and Nutrition, pp. 215–95, C. P. Mountford (ed.). Melbourne: Melbourne University Press.

Mountford, C. P., 1956. Art, mythology and symbolism. *In Records of the American-Australian Scientific Expedition to Arnhem Land.* Vol. 1. Melbourne: Melbourne University Press.

Mulvaney, D. J., 1969. *The prehistory of Australia.* London: Thames and Hudson.

Noone, H. V. V., 1943. Some Aboriginal implements of Western Australia. *Records of the South Australian Museum* 7 : 271–80.

Ponosov, V. V. (n.d.) *Results of an archaeological survey of the southern region of Morton Bay and of Morton Bay Island (1963–64).* Department of Psychology, University of Queensland.

Semenov, S. A., 1964. *Prehistoric technology.* Translated by M. W. Thompson. London: Cory, Adams and Mackay.

Shutler, R. and C. A. Kess, 1969. A lithic industry from New Britain, Territory of New Guinea, with possible areal and chronological relationships. *Bulletin of the Institute of Ethnology, Academia Sinica* 27 : 129–40.

Sieveking, A., 1958. The palaeolithic industry of Kota Tampan, Perak, Northwestern Malaya. *Asian Perspectives.* 2(2) : 91–102.

Specht, R. L., 1958. An introduction to the ethno-botany of Arnhem Land. In *Records of the American-Australian Scientific Expedition to Arnhem Land,* Vol. 3, Botany and Plant Ecology, R. L. Specht and C. P. Mountford (eds) pp. 479–503. Melbourne: Melbourne University Press.

Spencer, W. B., 1914. Native tribes of the Northern Territory of Australia. London: Macmillan.

Stockton, E. D., 1970. An archaeological survey of the Blue Mountains. *Mankind* 7 : 295–301.

Tindale, N. B., 1925–1926. Natives of Groote Eylandt and of the west coast of the Gulf of Carpentaria. *Records of the South Australian Museum* 3 : 61–102, 103–34.

—— 1951. Palaeolithic Kodj axe of the Aborigines. Further notes. *Records of the South Australian Museum* 9 : 34–37.

—— 1965. Stone implement making among the Nakako, Ngadadjara and Pitjandjara of the Great Western Desert. *Records of the South Australian Museum* 15 : 131–64.

Towle, C. C., 1935. Stone scrapers: an enquiry concerning a certain conventionalized type found along the coast of New South Wales. *Journal of the Royal Society of New South Wales* 68 : 117–43.

Turner, R., 1931. An enquiry into the methods of using the elouera. *Mankind* 6 : 30–35.

Warner, W. L., 1937. *A black civilisation.* New York: Harper and Bros.

Witthoft, J., 1967. Glazed polish on flint tools. *American Antiquity* 32 : 385–88.

White, C., 1967. *Plateau and plain: prehistoric investigations in Arnhem Land, Northern Territory.* Unpublished doctoral thesis, Australian National University, Canberra.

Kangaroo Island and the antiquity
of Australians

R. J. LAMPERT

Introduction

Kangaroo Island, some 4400 sq km in area, lies 14.5 km from the coast of mainland South Australia (Fig. 1). Early European explorers saw no signs of human occupants, and, noting also the extraordinary tameness of seals and kangaroos, concluded that the island was completely uninhabited. For almost exactly a century after its discovery Kangaroo Island was thought never to have been occupied by people other than the Europeans who settled there. However, a stone industry of large core tools, found in 1902 (Howchin, 1903) as the land was being cleared by agricultural man, showed that the island had once harboured another human population.

From 1931 onwards, Kangaroo Island was visited several times by the archaeologists N. B. Tindale and H. M. Cooper, both based at the South Australian Museum. Their field investigations were concerned largely with collecting stone implements from the numerous surface sites that had been discovered. Tindale (1937) also examined a clay bed in which tools were found stratified, and reconnoitred several of the island's limestone caves in search of occupation deposits, but at no site were tools found in useful stratigraphic association either as an assemblage or with charcoal or with faunal remains. However, the large core tools, unvarying in type at all the sites investigated, were thought to be ancient, at least predating the separation of Kangaroo Island from the mainland by rising post-glacial seas. Similar stone tools found at surface sites on the South Australian mainland were thought to be part of the same industrial tradition. It was named the 'Kartan' industry by Tindale who saw it as earlier than the industrial succession evidenced by stratigraphic excavations at the Devon Downs rock shelter site in the lower Murray Valley, South Australia (Tindale, 1937, 1957).

The Kartan industry as represented on Kangaroo Island is made up almost entirely of large quartzite core tools, pebbles being the most common source of raw material. Of tool types within the industry (Fig. 2), pebble choppers are the most common, making up over 50% of the implements in a newly-discovered site I investigated. Horsehoof type core-scrapers and hammer stones are also represented in significant numbers, but scrapers made on flakes, as distinct from cores, are uncommon. As tool types, pebble choppers and horsehoof cores have been found in a number of Australian industries widely distributed in space and time, but are usually well outnumbered by other tools, particularly scrapers made on flakes. The Kartan industry is unique in that core tools make up the majority of flaked stone artifacts. Another distinguishing characteristic is the massiveness of Kartan implements: the mean weight of the pebble choppers from a typical Kangaroo Island collection is 900 g, while horsehoof cores are similarly massive. Implement size seems well outside the range for other Australian industries, even if core tools only are selected for comparison.

Despite these differences the Kartan is typically Australian, having its closest affinities with the widely distributed 'core-tool and scraper tradition' (Bowler et al., 1970), the earliest industry that has been securely dated so far. Since later Australian industries are less like the Kartan, typological evidence alone suggests that it is ancient.

The presence of so many pebble choppers on Kangaroo Island suggested affinities with the early industries of south-east Asia (Tindale, 1937) but a metrical comparison by Matthews's (1966) of Kangaroo Island and typical Hoabinhian pebble tools showed no significant relationship. However, Matthews' study did show a close relationship between Kangaroo Island tools and those from Kartan sites on the adjacent South Australian mainland, supporting Tindale's view that the same industrial tradition was represented throughout the region. The only difference recognised was a greater proportion of pebble choppers to horsehoof cores on Kangaroo Island than on the nearby mainland, eg.,

	Horsehoof cores	Pebble choppers
Kangaroo Island collections	61	951
Mainland collections	220	47

(after Bauer, 1959)

Tindale (1957), Bauer (1959) and Cooper (1960) all thought this disparity arose from differences in cultural development that occurred after Kangaroo Island was separated from the mainland.

The hypotheses most favoured by these authors explain the settlement and later depopulation of Kangaroo Island through the following series of events:

(1) People with Kartan technology arrived on Kangaroo Island when it was joined to the mainland during the last glaciation. Although travel to the island by watercraft at a later date was not entirely ruled out, it was considered a less likely means of colonisation;

(2) Rising post-glacial seas isolated the Kangaroo Island population, whose technology—and, inferentially, other aspects of culture—took a lone path of development;

(3) The Kangaroo Island population eventually died out for one or more catastrophic reasons, those suggested being:
  (a) bush fire,
  (b) drought,
  (c) trace element deficiency,
  (d) population too small to be viable, either genetically or culturally,
  (e) disease.

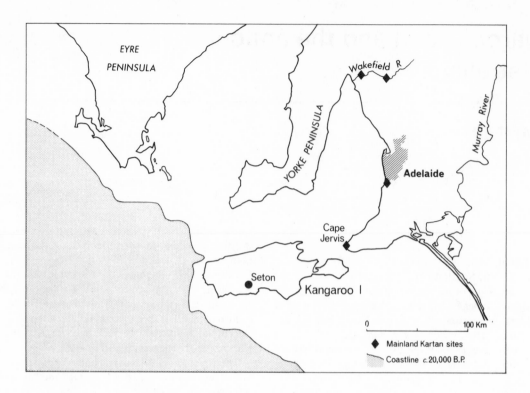

Fig. 1: Relationship of Kangaroo Island to mainland South Australia, both at present and at about 20 000 BP.

The Seton Site

Only by examining the Kartan industry within a stratified context did it seem possible that substantially more could be said about its antiquity and other associations. In 1972 I reconnoitred all limestone caves on Kangaroo Island that were known to local spelaeologists, looking specifically for floor deposits containing evidence for human occupation. Excavation appeared practical only at the Seton Site, a small cave beside a freshwater lagoon some 8 km inland from the south coast. During two short seasons in 1971 and 1973, a trench was excavated to bedrock, 1.5 m below the surface. Analysis of the excavated materials is not yet complete, but the following history of occupation seems apparent.

A little more than 16 000 years ago (ANU—1221 : 16 100± 1000 BP) men first visited the cave. Although this visit was too brief to provide a broad record of their economic activities, we know that they knapped flint into small scrapers at the site, and their diet possibly included the now totally extinct kangaroo *Sthenurus* sp., remains of which were found in stratigraphic association with the earliest tools. For several thousand years after this early occupation, the site was visited very infrequently, only a few lone, small stone flakes serving to record human activity.

Around 11 000 years ago (ANU—925 : 10 940±160 BP) there was a period of intensive occupation. Men worked stone at the site, knapping flint into small scrapers and flaking quartz by the bipolar method. Some quartz flakes were retouched to form scrapers. Bone awls were made from kangaroo fibulae. The people who occupied the site at this time pursued a varied subsistence with the modern grey kangaroo (*Macropus fuliginosus fuliginosus*) featuring prominently in their diet.

After this brief period of intensive occupation, visits to the cave by people ceased entirely.

Discussion The evidence from the Seton Site raises a number of implications.

(1) Abandonment of the site took place shortly after 11 000 years ago, that is at about the time that the island was being separated from the mainland. Jennings (1971) suggests *c.* 10 000 BP for the final submergence of the land bridge. A total lack of evidence for human activity after this date would seem to have as its best explanation the deliberate abandonment of Kangaroo Island by people who chose not to be isolated. Although geomorphologists describe the most recent transgression by the sea as 'rapid', in fact it was rising at a rate of little more than a metre per century, making it extremely unlikely that people would have been cut off without warning. Tidal fluctuations, both diurnal and seasonal, would have produced intermittent breaks of slowly increasing duration that served as indicators of impending isolation. For nomadic hunter-gatherers, one part of the territory over which they roamed was becoming increasingly difficult to reach, it became less popular and was finally abandoned. There is no need for us to invoke isolation and catastrophic extinction of the people who occupied the Seton Site to explain the absence of Aborigines on Kangaroo Island in modern times.

(2) The stone industry from the Seton Site is clearly not Kartan. Not one of the large quartzite core tools which predominate on surface sites was found at the cave. Even the specific type of stone used for these tools was entirely absent; of some 5000 small pieces of flaked stone recovered by excavation, only one is quartzite and this appears to be from a source other than that used for the Kartan core tools. However, implement size is the most obvious difference between the two industries. The mean weight of all secondarily retouched pieces of stone

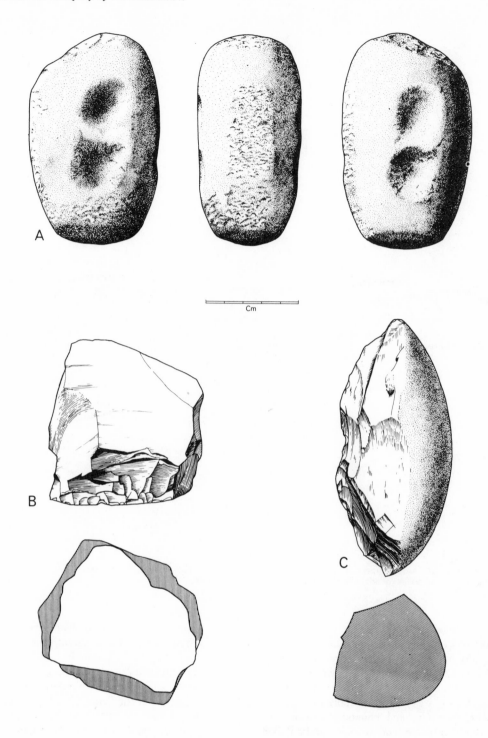

Fig. 2: Typical Kartan tools: A. hammer/anvil stone with double anvil pits; B. horsehoof core; C. pebble chopper.

from the cave is only 9 g, whereas the corresponding figure for a Kartan site from which I collected all visible stone is 900 g.

A few small scrapers, mostly of reef quartz, were found on some of the Kartan surface sites investigated by Cooper who expressed doubts about their cultural association with the Kartan (Cooper, 1960 : 486–88). Of the half dozen Kartan sites I have looked at closely, only on one did flaked reef quartz accompany the large core tools, while the others had no small flaked tools whatsoever. Obviously the question merits closer field investigation, but the evidence at hand is against any direct association between the type of stone industry found at the Seton Site and the Kartan.

The assemblages are too dissimilar to be seen as two aspects of the same industrial tradition, as, for example, in situations where marked seasonal differences necessitated different technologies and exploitative strategies among the same group of people (eg. Thomson, 1939). Today's climate in the area is 'Mediterranean', with hot dry summers and mild moist winters, but no difference in seasonal activity large enough to produce entirely

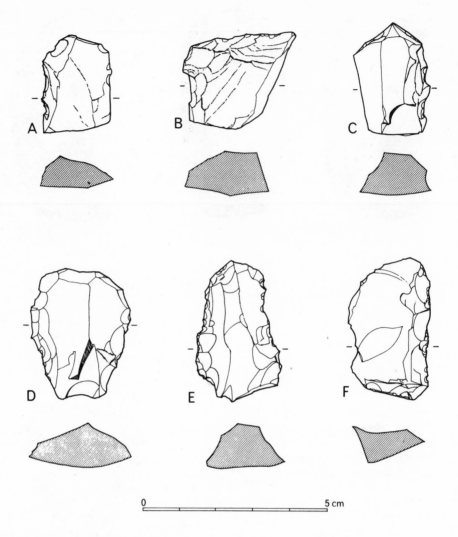

Fig. 3: Tools from Seton Site: A–C. scrapers of quartz from the more recent occupation level; D. scraper of flint from the earlier occupation level; E, F. scrapers (or adzes?) of flint from the more recent level.

different technologies was observed among recent hunter-gatherers on the adjacent mainland. Ecological differences do not appear to have been responsible, because Kartan tools are found in large numbers on surface sites with the same lagoon-side setting as the Seton Site. In any case, both assemblages consist of basic cutting, scraping and chopping implements— *maintenance* rather than *extractive* tools—and not likely therefore to be highly sensitive to environmental differences. Thus, in this situation, such great dissimilarity in size, style, technique of manufacture of implements, and in choice of raw material, suggests that two different groups of people were involved.

(3) What was the relationship between these two groups of people; did they co-exist, or did they occupy Kangaroo Island at different times? Co-existence seems most unlikely for two reasons: the same localities on the island would have been inhabited by both groups at the same time; and the boundary between the two industries would have been far sharper than any other boundary in material culture known for Aboriginal Australia, from either archaeological or ethnographic evidence. A more acceptable explanation is that the two industries represent occupation of Kangaroo Island by different groups of people at different times.

Although the Kartan has yet to be directly dated, clues to its antiquity can be gained by considering its most likely chronological relationship with the industry unearthed at the Seton Site. This site was occupied by people making small scrapers from quartz and flint right up until the time that Kangaroo Island was separated. The Kartan cannot have been developed more recently than that time—in isolation that is—because it is present also on the adjacent mainland. Therefore, it must be older.

(4) Because the industry at Seton Site has an antiquity of at least 16 000 years the Kartan must be older than that date. Without direct evidence for its antiquity, how much older than 16 000 BP must be a matter for conjecture, but I submit that it is likely to be considerably older for the following reasons.

At several southeastern Australian sites, that have long stratified histories of development, the lower industries show a persistent but very slow trend towards reduction of implement size (Lampert, 1971; Jones, 1971; Flood, 1974; Allen, 1972). Even after 20 000 years at Burrill Lake the decrease in tool size was far less marked than that seen for Kangaroo Island. Factors other than cultural change may have hastened technological development on Kangaroo Island, such as the right sort of quartzite pebbles becoming unavailable through geological change—though such change itself would suggest a considerable passage of time—but there was nevertheless an industrial change of such a magnitude that even a temporal difference between the two industries of 20 000 years could indicate a rapidity of technological development unparalleled at other early Australian sites.

The abruptness of change between the Kangaroo Island industries is as significant as the magnitude of the difference. Among the 100 or more Kartan surface sites that are known there is remarkable consistency, none showing a stage intermediate between the Kartan and later industries. Such a situation could be adequately explained through an earlier period of isolation brought about by a rise in sea level before the most recent transgression.

Isolation by high seas of the last interglacial *alone* would not be a useful explanation, even if we are prepared to accept 140 000 BP as a credible antiquity for the Kartan, because under this hypothesis a relatively brief period of isolation centring on 120 000 BP would have been followed by a longer period of contact with mainland influences. However it is possible that the island was isolated by interstadial rises of sea level, of particular interest being a transgression that may have begun about 50 000 years ago and have finished about 30 000 years ago. There is considerable controversy among geomorphologists about this, despite the publication of some 200 radiocarbon dates and several uranium series dates to support a rise in sea level at that time (Thom, 1972). Some (eg. Langford-Smith, 1973) see good evidence for a level slightly above today's, others (eg. Chappell, 1974) think the sea rose to reach a level not much higher than 50 m below today's, while others (in Thom, 1972) do not believe in interstadial high seas at all. For Kangaroo Island the critical point dividing contact from isolation would have been a rise to about 30 m below the present level; Tasmania, on the other hand would have been separated from the mainland by a rise to within 50 m of present level.

Such a separation of Kangaroo Island would allow better sense to be made of the archaeological evidence. Under this hypothesis, the Kartan industry reached Kangaroo Island some 50 000 years ago or earlier, when the sea level was lower. Faced by a rising sea level and isolation the practitioners of the industry either left the island just as recent Aborigines did, or stayed on either to become extinct or to remain in isolation until the island was re-joined to the mainland many thousand years later, in which case their culture would have been swamped by the developments that had been taking place on the mainland during the time of their isolation. Thus we may be seeing in the two totally different Kangaroo Island industries, samples drawn from the early industrial tradition in Australia at widely separated times in its development. If this is so, the Kartan or very similar industries would have been the earliest throughout much of Australia, as indeed Tindale (1957) has claimed. No such basal industry has been found in a stratified cave site, but, on the other hand, no cave site with the antiquity postulated here has yet come to light.

The implication this hypothesis, of interstadial isolation of human populations on Kangaroo Island and Tasmania, has for the physiological development of early Australians is also of interest. To explain the morphological disparity between

the crania of Kow Swamp and Lake Mungo populations, Thorne (1971; Thorne and Macumber, 1972) sees the need both for greater antiquity of man in Australia than has been found so far, and for the genetic isolation of human populations. Both of these conditions are met under the hypothesis proposed.

Perhaps men heavily endowed with *Homo erectus* physical traits and having a Kartan-like stone industry spread across Australia more than 50 000 years ago to reach Kangaroo Island and Tasmania. On these islands they were isolated by interstadial high seas, preserving their ancient physical characteristics and technology while new populations and industrial developments spread through mainland Australia.

Some after thoughts The paper above is substantially as presented at the conference. In it I have developed one line of argument and pursued it into the realm of speculation, deliberately, in the hope of stimulating useful comment from other participants. Critics rightly point out that the suggestion of great antiquity I make for Kartan tools depends entirely on my claim that they are not an aspect of the industry found in the Seton Site. No stone industry in the world, they argue, consists almost solely of large core tools, and the assemblage unearthed at the cave could be the smaller, flake tool component of the Kartan. While I accept as probable the view that the Kartan had many more tools made on flakes than the few that have been found so far on surface sites (assuming that even these were associated), I am not convinced that a relationship between Kartan and Seton is thereby demonstrated. On the contrary, the complete absence from the cave of any of the core tools, or even of a single piece of the right kind of quartzite among some 5000 pieces of flaked stone, I see as being a compelling argument against any claim for the excavated assemblage being the small tool component of the Kartan.

However, the view that the Kartan, as defined by Tindale, Cooper and me, is not a complete industry is well supported by the absence of a full range of industrial waste from the surface sites. At the site where I made a comprehensive collection of stone from the surface, the only quartzite flakes present had been struck off to trim the working edges of the heavy tools; there was none of the debitage normally associated with tool manufacture. As far as I can tell, this holds for the other Kartan sites on record, which is perhaps not wholly surprising because the sites are situated some distance away from the pebble beaches which were a likely source of raw material. However, a thorough examination of many more sites is required before I can be sure that the sites I have seen so far are truly representative.

Although in this paper I have to some extent been conjectural, I think I have also presented hypotheses that are testable through further research. It is to this end that my next field season on Kangaroo Island will be directed.

Acknowledgements I thank all participants who contributed to discussion following the presentation of this paper. Particularly useful comments were made by Professors G. Isaac, F. Bordes and L. Binford, who examined artifact collections from Kangaroo Island after the session. The illustrations were prepared by our departmental illustrator, W. Mumford, while faunal remains from the Seton Site were identified by Dr J. Hope (also of this department), who is carrying out palaeo-environmental research on the island to complement my work. I wish to acknowledge also the support given to me by both the Research School of Pacific Studies, ANU, and the South Australian Museum, Adelaide.

References

Allen, H., 1972. *Where the crow flies backwards; man and land in the Darling Basin.* Canberra: Ph.D. thesis (unpublished), Australian National University.

Bauer, F. H., 1959. *The regional geography of Kangaroo Island, South Australia.* Canberra: Ph.D. thesis (unpublished), Australian National University.

Bowler, J. M., R. Jones, H. Allen and A. G. Thorne, 1970. Pleistocene human remains from Australia: a living site and human cremation from Lake Mungo, western New South Wales. *World Archaeology,* 2(1) : 39–60.

Chappell, J. M. A., 1974. Geology of coral terraces, Huon Peninsula, New Guinea: a study of Quaternary tectonic movements and sea-level changes. *Geological Society of America Bulletin,* 85 : 553–70.

Cooper, H. M., 1960. The Archaeology of Kangaroo Island, South Australia. *Records of the South Australian Museum,* 13(4) : 481–503.

Flood, J. M., 1974. Pleistocene man at Cloggs Cave: his tool kit and environment. *Mankind,* 9 : 175–88.

Howchin, W., 1903. Aboriginal occupation of Kangaroo Island. *Transcripts of the Royal Society of South Australia,* 27(1) : 90.

Jennings, J. N., 1971. Sea level changes and land links. *In* Mulvaney, D. J. and Golson, J. (eds), *Aboriginal man and environment in Australia,* pp. 1–13. Canberra: Australian National University Press.

Jones, R. M., 1971. *Rocky Cape and the problem of the Tasmanians.* Sydney: Ph.D. thesis (unpublished), Department of Anthropology, University of Sydney.

Lampert, R. J., 1971. Burrill Lake and Currarong. *Terra Australis* 1. Canberra: Department of Prehistory, Research School of Pacific Studies, Australian National University.

Langford-Smith, T., 1973. Evidence for a Late Pleistocene interstadial from the north coast of New South Wales and the south coast of Queensland. Paper read at IX INQUA Congress, Christchurch.

Matthews, J. M., 1966. The Hoabinhian affinities of some Australian assemblages. *Archaeology and Physical Anthropology in Oceania,* 1(1) : 5–22.

Thom, B. G., 1972. The dilemma of high interstadial sea levels during the last glaciation. *In* Board, C., *et al., Progress in geography: international reviews of current research,* pp. 170–246, V. 5. London: Edward Arnold.

Thomson, D. F., 1939. The seasonal factor in human culture. *Proceedings of the Prehistoric Society,* 5(2) : 209–21.

Thorne, A. G., 1971. Mungo and Kow Swamp: morphological variation in Pleistocene Australians. *Mankind,* 8(2) : 85–89.

—— and P. G. Macumber, 1972. Discoveries of Late Pleistocene man at Kow Swamp, Australia. *Nature,* 238 (5363) : 316–19.

Tindale, N. B., 1937. Relationship of the extinct Kangaroo Island culture with cultures of Australia, Tasmania and Malaya. *Records of the South Australian Museum,* 6(1) : 39–60.

—— 1957. Culture succession in south-eastern Australia from Late Pleistocene to the present. *Records of the South Australian Museum,* 13 : 1–49.

—— and B. G. Maegraith, 1931. Traces of an extinct Aboriginal population on Kangaroo Island. *Records of the South Australian Museum,* 4(3) : 275–289.

Stone tools, settlement, adaptation

A Tasmanian example

HARRY LOURANDOS

Introduction

For the Australian prehistorian stone tools have served in the main to establish regional cultural sequences and as indicators of culture change. The study outlined in this paper sets out to examine stone assemblages as indicators of independent site function, and to describe assemblage variability between sites in functional terms (Binford and Binford, 1966; Wilkinson, 1972). Other contributors to this conference have adopted comparable approaches (O'Connell, 1977; McBryde, 1977).

The study example outlined is from my own research in Tasmania (Lourandos, 1970). The analysis of flaked stone assemblages has been combined within the frame of a settlement study (Chang, 1968; Rouse, 1972; Streuver, 1968). The aim was to construct behavioural models at contrasting sites, and to employ these models in establishing hypotheses demonstrating local and regional environmental adaptations.

This approach allowed for a wide range of comparative data to be incorporated, and for the relationship between sites, assemblages and environment to be interpreted functionally.

In this case we are dealing with a hunter-gatherer culture when attempting to reconstruct strategies of site location and subsistence organisation. Therefore the underlying assumption is that 'individual sites are part of a wider system composed of interrelated specialised activity sites'. It is towards an understanding of this system that all such studies as these ultimately are oriented; to isolate its key elements and so gain a greater awareness of how it functions through time.

The example

The field work outlined here was carried out during 1967–68. As most of the material has appeared elsewhere (Lourandos 1968, 1970). I will concentrate my discussion on the flaked stone assemblages.

The study region The temperate and mountainous island of Tasmania broadly consists of two ecological provinces, east and west. High rainfalls occur in the mountainous western half of the island whose interior is composed predominantly of inhospitable temperate rainforest. As a result Aboriginal occupation was restricted to a narrow corridor of rich heathland in the north-west and to areas of poorer sedgeland in the south-west. In contrast, the eastern half, isolated by mountains and rainforests from the west, is in a distinct rainshadow area. Rugged but in the main composed of open sclerophyll forests with savannah grasslands in the hinterland

it was here in the east that the bulk of the Tasmanian population resided. Its complex mosaic of dry and wet sclerophyll forms, vast stretches of icy lakes and moorlands at the island's centre, and extensive coast of secluded bays and estuaries to the south-east, provided the eastern tribes with an extremely varied environment.

I centred my research around the problem of relating Aboriginal settlement and subsistence to this major environmental division and testing to see whether the division was reflected culturally. It seemed reasonable to link Aboriginal settlement with the major environmental zones of the island. It was therefore proposed that the greatest Aboriginal population concentrations could be expected in the richer habitats of sclerophyll forest and grasslands (eastern Tasmania) and coastal heathland (north-west and north-east Tasmania). It was thought also that this basic occupation pattern would have been further influenced by factors such as access to water resources (abundant in the inland) and more so by access to rich and vast coastal resources (including offshore islands).

As a study area I concentrated on south eastern Tasmania and drew comparative material from the north western corner of the island (Jones, 1966, 1971). The object was to construct behavioural models of settlement and subsistence from both excavation and surface archaeological data in the two study areas.

The south-east The field work included a wide surface coverage of the south eastern and eastern areas followed by the selection of two south eastern sites for excavation. As comparative material a general classification (in settlement terms) was made of the vast surface site data which included that of earlier observers (Lourandos, 1970).

Two contrasting archaeological sites were chosen which represented typical forms in terms of the surface classification. Each was located in a separate micro-environment; one an estuarine shell midden (Little Swanport), the other an open inland site (Crown Lagoon). Both were connected by the Little Swanport River system at a distance of about twenty miles from each other.

Analysis of material Analysis was undertaken of the total flaked stone assemblages from both sites. This also included what is generally classified as 'waste' and often given no further consideration. The assumption underlying this was that a total assemblage will in some way have functional significance and as a unit will reflect the function flaked stone served at a particular site. As already mentioned above differences between total assemblages from separate sites

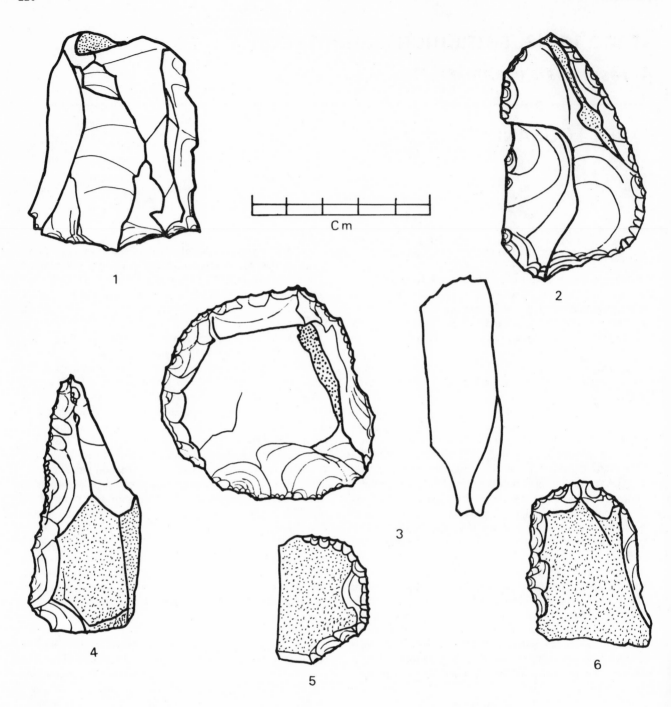

Fig. 1: Flaked stone tools from Little Swanport and Crown Lagoon. Retouched flakes (2, 3, 4, 5, 6), retouched core (1).

could be seen as representing functional rather than cultural differences (cf. Binford, 1972 : 132). If one argued along these lines then arbitrary selection of parts of assemblages (eg. retouched pieces) for comparison to the exclusion of the whole, could result in serious bias.

The total flaked stone assemblages were compared with all other identifiable trait assemblages from each site (eg. faunal, structural etc.) in order to construct site activity models. A complete analysis along these lines would lead to a comparison between sites in terms of their ratios of trait frequencies. Instead the procedure followed here was to compare sites and areas in terms of site and area activity models.

Analysis of total flaked stone assemblages also allowed for statements to be made on the possible production, maintenance and utilisation of flaked stone at individual sites. Further, it allowed for general treatment of the problem of relating form of tools to function.

Site 1 (Little Swanport—L.S.II) The site was selected because of its key position. The Little Swanport estuary is one of the largest in eastern Tasmania, and is acknowledged as having perhaps the greatest known concentrations of shell midden in this region, if not the whole island. The excavated site had a basal radiocarbon date of ANU-356, 4490±120 BP, and its occupation continued until recent times.

The faunal composition of the site consisted predominantly of estuarine shellfish with associated small quantities of land fauna (including bird)—all sclerophyll forest forms. No evidence existed to imply other than short occupations; the chief structural features being small ashy hearths. This basic pattern showed little change through time.

Table 1 Frequency of flaked stone, Little Swanport

	Re-touched		Edge-damaged		Remainder, product of utilisation	Fre-quency	
	no.	%	no.	%	no.	no.	%
> ½ inch/12.5 mm (total 164)							
Retouched flake	67	77.9	67	41.0		67	40.9
Retouched core	8	9.3	8	4.9		8	4.9
Flake	4	4.7	63	38.7		63	38.4
Naturally produced core	1	1.2	5	3.0		5	3.0
Rejuvenation flake	2	2.3	15	9.2	2	15	9.1
Broken retouched flake	4	4.7	3	1.8	1	4	2.4
Miscellaneous	?		2	1.2		2	1.2
Total	86	100.0	163	100.0	3	164	100.0
< ½ inch/12.5mm (total 12)							
Small broken pieces					12/15*	12/176	

* Total product of utilisation is 15, i.e. 8.5% of 176.

The flaked stone assemblage In Table 1 the total flaked stone assemblage has been divided into two groups of above and below half inch (13 mm) size. The group above half inch in size has been divided into seven classes: retouched flake, retouched core, flake, naturally produced core, rejuvenation flake, broken retouched flake, and miscellaneous. Rejuvenation flakes are discussed below. In Table 3 the total assemblage has been divided into three basic functional classes: retouched, edge-damaged, and waste. The class 'edge-damage' included all those pieces with some modification which (although it is difficult to classify) can be generally described as light retouch, edge-damage and/or wear. This was determined mainly through macroscopic analysis and is not to be confused with the analysis of microwear. Factors contributing to the last class would be complex and include; use, wear and tear, misuse, deposition, etc. For this reason I will use this classification in a descriptive sense only. 'Products of use' refers to flakes apparently broken or discarded on the site.

Results This was an assemblage of small size with a low density of flaked stone. It was distributed evenly throughout the site and seldom clustered. Neither flaking floors nor small secondary waste flakes—the products of manufacture and use—were detected. The assemblage consisted of: a large percentage of retouched pieces (52.4%), a low 8.5% of waste, and 99.3% edge-damaged. The edge-damaged forms could be grouped into three classes: retouched flake (40.9%), flake (38.4%) and retouched core (4.9%).

The low frequency and even distribution of flaked stone is striking, and it should be noted that evidence of shell fishing activities predominates. It would in any case seem more plausible to link stone flaking with the frequency of land fauna (and bird) which has a comparable low frequency. There is strong supporting evidence, both recent Australian and Tasmanian ethnographic, to link flaked stone assemblages with the production of wooden tools and the hunt (Gould, 1968; Lourandos, 1970 : 46; Jones, 1971).

A behavioural model to explain these features of the Little Swanport site includes a temporary, primarily estuarine shell fishing camp, with which the hunting of forest mammals (and birds) was less frequently associated, and to which (perhaps in a way related to the latter activity) flaked stone tools were brought already fashioned, and where no trimming or rejuvenation took place.

Site 2 (Crown Lagoon—C.L.) The site is situated in open dry sclerophyll forest on a high tableland, in the region of the Eastern Marshes. The cultural deposit is stratified in the upper layers of a lunette which was formed around the eastern bank of Crown Lagoon. Two radiocarbon dates were obtained which approximately date the upper and lower limits of the cultural deposit: ANU-279, 4170 ± 80 BP, and ANU-278, 4860 ± 96 BP. The main features of the site's composition were of dual activity areas of small temporary hearths and flaking floors. Associated throughout was animal bone, generally poorly preserved but identifiable as sclerophyll forest forms.

Table 2 Frequency of flaked stone, Crown Lagoon

	Re-touched		Edge-damaged		Remainder, product of utilisation	Fre-quency	
	no.	%	no.	%	no.	no.	%
> ½ inch/12.5 mm (total 743)							
Retouched flake	32	37.6	32	16.4		32	4.3
Retouched core	12	14.1	12	6.2		12	1.6
Core		0	3	1.5		3	0.4
Flake	9	10.6	41	21.0	96	137	18.4
Naturally produced core	2	2.4	3	1.5	2	5	0.7
Edge-rejuvenation flake	14	16.5	82	42.1	303	385	51.8
Rejuvenation (b) flake		0	11	5.6	131	142	19.1
Broken re-touched flake	16	18.8	7	3.6	9	16	2.2
Miscellaneous		0	4	2.1	7	11	1.5
Total	85	100.0	195	100.0	548	743	100.0
Percentage	11.4		26.2		73.8	100.0	
< ½inch/12.5 mm (total 7,059)							

The flaked stone assemblage In Table 2 the total assemblage has been divided into two groups of below and above half inch size. The latter group has been further divided into nine classes: retouched flake, retouched core, core, flake, naturally produced core, edge-rejuvenation flake, rejuvenation (b) flake, broken retouched flake, and miscellaneous.

Because of their high frequency it proved necessary to distinguish between two basic forms of rejuvenation flake. The class 'edge-rejuvenation flake' included flakes which clearly showed that part of the heavily and steeply retouched working edge (of the implement) had been removed so as to provide a fresh striking platform. The class 'rejuvenation (b)–flake' included flakes bearing signs that they had been struck from any other modified face of a flake or core. The purpose of this classification was to set up a functional division between:

   (i) flakes bearing signs of the removal of the utilised or blunted working edge (class 'edge-rejuvenation')

   (ii) flakes bearing secondary flake scars produced at the time of initial manufacture or retrimming of the implement (class 'rejuvenation (b)')

Results The following can be deduced from a comparison of the flaked stone assemblages from both sites. There appears to be a marked dissimilarity between the composition of the two total assemblages. At C.L. 73.7% (of the above half inch) was classified as waste (or by-products of utilisation), as compared to 1.8% at L.S.II. Inclusion of the below half inch size from C.L. would increase the difference further. At C.L. there is a low 11.4% of retouch as compared to 52.4% at L.S.II.

To explain these differences I propose that we have here a functional division between two activity patterns: workshop features at Crown Lagoon, displaying characteristics of manufacture, utilisation and rejuvenation; at Little Swanport, the importation of retouched forms, negligible evidence for on the spot production, retouch and rejuvenation, and no flaking floors. Morphologically the retouched forms at both sites were similar.

At C.L. 51.8% (the most populous class) was of edge-rejuvenation flakes, indicating two possible explanations:

   (i) that the predominant stone tool activity of the site was associated with the resharpening of utilised pieces

   (ii) that steep retouch and edge blunting were products of the way such forms were employed at the site (i.e. rejuvenation).

Added to this were other aspects of production, utilisation and rejuvenation: the 19.1% rejuvenation (b) class, and the 18.4% of flakes of which 29% bear edge-damage signs, as compared with L.S.II where all bore such signs.

At C.L. nuclei cores have a low frequency of 0.4%. These are absent at L.S.II, and suggest that there was a low incidence of primary production occurring at C.L. This in turn strengthens the interpretation of the site being associated chiefly with the utilisation and rejuvenation of flaked stone.

Certain observations can be made about the form of stone tools employed at both sites. At L.S.II there was a high incidence of retouched flakes (40.9%) while at C.L. their frequency was only 4.3%. Added to this at L.S.II was the sizeable frequency of edge-damaged flakes (51.8%).

The characteristic edge of the edge-rejuvenation flake (steeply retouched and blunted) is common not only to the morphology of both C.L. and L.S.II assemblages (eg. certain retouched flakes and cores) but also to the whole Tasmanian flaked stone tradition. It is interesting to note, as I have already pointed out, that its form appears related to its function at the site (i.e. the removal of steeply retouched and blunted edge flakes to provide fresh striking platforms). This latter process then can be related to the form of the tools which bear such characteristics. The frequency of these edge-

rejuvenation flakes perhaps points to the magnitude of the edge-form's utilisation.

This aspect of production was absent at L.S.II, indicating the functional division between the two assemblages. This difference can generally be seen as the utilisation of retouched flakes at L.S.II, and of steeply retouched and blunted edge-forms at C.L.

Table 3 Functional classes of flaked stone, Little Swanport (LS II), Crown Lagoon (CL)

Product of utilisation	LS11 %	CL %
> ½ inch/12.5 mm		
Retouched	52.4	11.4
Edge-damaged	99.3	26.2
Waste	1.8	73.7
< ½ inch/12.5 mm		
Calculated as a percentage of the total assemblage	6.8	90.5

Interpretation How can these differences between the two assemblages be best explained? I have already drawn a relationship between the use of flaked stone tools at L.S.II and the activity of the hunt. Although this relationship cannot stand as proof of the association it is consistent with the supporting ethnographic evidence.

On these grounds I think it is reasonable to propose the following generalised model to explain these differences: the Crown Lagoon assemblage, together with the supporting faunal and structural evidence, suggest that the site consisted of a series of temporary camps oriented chiefly around the maintenance and utilisation of flaked stone tools used to manufacture and maintain wooden implements which were themselves associated with the hunting of forest animals. In contrast the Little Swanport assemblage in form and frequency indicates both the less frequent and less complex nature of such activities at a site whose main orientation was towards the waters of the estuary.

The main points that have been brought out are:

   (i) That variation has been distinguished between two flaked stone assemblages, belonging to the same basic tradition, and that these differences can be explained functionally.

   (ii) That this variation was detected by analysing total assemblages including what is generally classed as 'waste'.

   (iii) The analysis of certain 'waste' elements (eg. rejuvenation flakes) provided meaningful evidence relating to the function of the assemblage and to the form of individual tools.

   (iv) A functional interpretation allowed for the construction of activity models and for inter-site comparisons.

Summary

This concluding section provides a brief outline of the remainder of the study. Area activity models are constructed and compared, regional hypotheses are formed in terms of behaviour and environment, and the observed cultural processes through time are discussed.

The activity models reconstructed at Little Swanport and Crown Lagoon were integrated with the surface data to construct an area model for the south east. Although only two sites had been excavated they appeared to be in no way atypical of the general surface results. The broader conclusions of the survey are of a pattern incorporating three independent site forms: (1) shell middens, predominantly reflecting the exploitation of marine resources and to a far lesser extent associated with the hunting of terrestrial game and the production and use of flaked stone, (2) open inland sites, temporary in structure, associated with varied flaked stone assemblages indicating production, maintenance and use, and sometimes associated with faunal remains and (3) stone quarries associated with the primary production of flaked stone.

The activity model advanced to explain this distribution is of a subsistence strategy oriented around the seasonal exploitation of two dominant environments—an extensive coastline, and a vast hinterland of varied sclerophyll forest— and incorporating a series of temporary, limited-activity stations associated with specific micro-environments.

It might be objected that the amount of excavation is inadequate for the conclusions, but I would answer such a criticism by saying that a great quantity of surface data has been analysed. As a further control I employed: (a) archaeological data from the contrasting environment of the north-west corner of Tasmania and (b) a study of Aboriginal subsistence activities from Tasmanian ethnographic sources.

I will not attempt to outline the details of either of these two studies but will merely summarise the results.

My study of the north-west corner used on existing material the methods described for the south eastern study.

The results of this indicated that settlement followed a closely coastal pattern being restricted in most of the area by the inhospitable rainforest inland. The most numerous site types discovered have been coastal bases (quite unlike those of the south-east) with complex activity patterns of joint marine—terrestrial exploitation (eg. Rocky Cape – Jones, 1966, 1971). The most complex examples are situated on the west coast (eg. West Point – Jones, 1966) which include extra traits of varied flaked stone assemblages, and semi-permanent structures such as pit-depressions. The latter correspond to ethnographically recorded clusters of well-built huts found only on the west coast (Lourandos, 1968, 1970). The model I advanced for this area was of a restricted coastal occupation incorporating a series of coastal bases for joint marine-terrestrial exploitation, which under optimum conditions served as semi-sedentary centres (eg. West Point), balanced by dispersion of population and activities when these conditions were not operating.

The ethnographic study (Lourandos, 1970) tended to support the archaeological deductions of a separation between eastern and western activity patterns, and the general conclusions reached on their nature. The most extreme patterns appear to have existed in the south-east and the north-west. In the south-east there seems to have existed a division between the specialised reaping of marine resources (shellfish, crustacea, seaweeds) and terrestrial hunting. All evidence indicates that these two major subsistence activities were practised separately. No coastal bases were detected and in contrast the largest concentrations of people have been recorded from the open grasslands of the midlands. On the coast a range of hut structures existed, all ephemeral in nature.

The inland hunting zone extended up as far as the farthest lakes of the high moorlands of the Central Plateau. There is strong evidence for major seasonal movement occurring in spring and autumn with population concentrations in coastal areas in the cold months and inland in the warmer months (Lourandos, 1970; pers. comm., Lyndall Ryan). This accords well with the evidence for large seasonal gatherings for the egging season (spring).

As a contrast in the north-west Aboriginal habitation was restricted to a rich, narrow coastal strip of heathland. Here were set up semi-permanent coastal bases in the form of clusters of large, well built, domed huts. From these bases exploitation of both land and sea resources was carried out simultaneously. Large seasonal gatherings were organised during the sealing, egging and mutton birding seasons (spring-summer) including expeditions to offshore islands.

Discussion

Two separate behavioural patterns have been described in terms of the stone assemblages, site forms and surface evidence, and seem to be associated with the two-fold environmental division of Tasmania. Such a division can be further expressed in terms of the constituent vegetation zones. Presented in this form the models provide hypotheses which can be tested by further research. More support is given to these reconstructions by the introduction of independent bodies of data (archaeological evidence from two related areas, and ethnographic evidence).

Chronologically the models can be related to two distinct cultural sequences: the terrestrial-coastal south eastern sequence firmly dated to *c.* 5000 BP (and plausibly to *c.* 7000 BP Lourandos, 1970 : 120); the coastally oriented north western dated to *c.* 8000 BP (Jones, 1966, 1971). The south eastern sequence, associated with the area of sclerophyll vegetation, I relate to the forestation of inner Tasmania with the upward extension of the tree zone on the retreat of Pleistocene climatic conditions (Lourandos, 1970). In contrast the north western sequence, associated with coastal heaths, has been related to the coastally restricted nature of the region which in general has persisted throughout the post Pleistocene. For the whole of post-Pleistocene Tasmania the process could be seen as one of independent cultural adaptation to separate environments. As such I tend to view this vegetational division as one of the controlling factors of the whole of Tasmanian prehistory.

Late Pleistocene south eastern Tasmania, flanked by the cold regions of the western ranges (the area of greatest glaciation) would have experienced climatic conditions perhaps closer to today's montane moorlands of the Tasmanian Central Plateau (see Bowler, 1974). As the sclerophyll forest provided one of the richest environments for later Aboriginal Tasmanians, we must envisage a far less favourable interior in this early phase. Such conditions would have restricted the bulk of the population to the forested coastal fringes. At this time the densest occupation would have been on the wide plains that stretched out across present day Bass Strait to the lowlands of southern Victoria. Around the mountainous, cold landmass of Tasmania, with a coastline comparably close to today's (see Jennings, 1971), the Aboriginal population would have been restricted to a more coastally oriented settlement. The vegetation zones they occupied could be envisaged as similar in range to those of the present which remain, together with their related faunal populations, as remnants of a past landscape. This restricted coastal occup-

ation can be expected to have lessened as the most intense period of glaciation passed and the sea level began to rise drowning the Bassian Plains (*c.* 15 000–12 000 BP).

References

Binford, L. R., 1972. Contemporary model building: paradigms and the current state of Paleolithic research. *In* D. L. Clark (ed.) *Models in Archaeology*, pp. 109–66. London: Methuen.

—— and S. R. Binford, 1966. A preliminary analysis of functional variability in the Mousterian of Levallois facies. *American Anthropologist*, 68, 2, (2) : 238–95.

Bowler, J. M., 1976. Recent developments in reconstructing late Quaternary environments in Australia. *In* R. L. Kirk and A. G. Thorne (eds) *The Origin of the Australians*, pp. 55–77. Canberra: Australian Institute of Aboriginal Studies.

Chang, K. C. ed., 1968. *Settlement archaeology*. New Haven: Mayfield Publishing Co.

Clark, J. G. D., 1954. *Excavations at Star Carr*. Cambridge: Cambridge University Press.

Clark, D. L., 1968. *Analytical archaeology*. London: Methuen.

—— 1972. *Models in archaeology*. London: Methuen.

Gould, R. A., 1968. Chipping stones in the outback. *Natural History*, 77(2) : 42–48.

Hiatt, B., 1967–68. The food quest and economy of the Tasmanian Aborigines. *Oceania*, 38 : 99–133, 190–219.

Jennings, J. N., 1971. Sea level changes and land links. *In* D. J. Mulvaney and J. Golson (eds) *Aboriginal man and environment in Australia*. Canberra: Australian National University Press.

Jones, R., 1966. A speculative archaeological sequence for north west Tasmania. *Records of the Queen Victoria Museum Launceston*, 25 : 1–12.

—— 1968. The geographical background to the arrival of man in Australia and Tasmania. *Archaeology and Physical Anthropology in Oceania*, 3 : 186–215.

—— 1971. *Rocky Cape and the problem of the Tasmanians*. Ph.D. thesis. University of Sydney.

Lourandos, H., 1968. Dispersal of activities—the east Tasmanian Aboriginal sites. *Papers of the Proceedings of the Royal Society of Tasmania*, 2 : 41–46.

—— 1969. The study of the Tasmanian Aborigine. *Tasmanian Year Book 3, Hobart*: 69–72.

—— 1970a. *Coast and hinterland: the archaeological sites of eastern Tasmania*. M. A. (Hons.) thesis. Australian National University.

—— 1970b. A description of the Aboriginal archaeological sites in Tasmania. *In* F. D. McCarthy (ed.) *Aboriginal antiquities in Australia*, pp. 35–38. Canberra: Australian Institute of Aboriginal Studies.

O'Connell, J. F., 1977. Aspects of variation in central Australian lithic assemblages. *In* R. V. S. Wright (ed.) *Stone tools as cultural markers*, pp. 269–81. Canberra: Australian Institute of Aboriginal Studies.

McBryde, I., 1977. Environment, subsistence economies, site activities, and cultural tradition as determinants of assemblage variation in New England prehistory. *In* R. V. S. Wright (ed.) *Stone tools as cultural markers*, pp. 225–50. Canberra: Australian Institute of Aboriginal Studies.

Rouse, I., 1972. Settlement patterns in archaeology. *In* P. J. Ucko, R. Tringham and G. W. Dimbleby (eds) *Man, settlement and urbanism*, pp. 95–108. London: Duckworth.

Streuver, S., 1968. Woodland subsistence—settlement systems in the Lower Illinois Valley. *In* S. R. Binford and L. R. Binford (eds) *New Perspectives in archaeology*, pp. 285–312. Chicago: Aldine.

Wilkinson, P. F., 1972. Ecosystem models and demographic hypotheses: predation and prehistory in North America. *In* D. L. Clarke (ed.) *Models in archaeology*, pp. 543–76. London: Methuen.

Ucko, P. J., R. Tringham and G. W. Dimbleby (eds), 1972. *Man, settlement and urbanism*. London: Duckworth.

Determinants of assemblage variation in New England prehistory

Environment, subsistence economies, site activities, or cultural tradition?

ISABEL McBRYDE

In recent years assumptions and procedures basic to the prehistorian concerning the definition and interpretation of artifact assemblages have been questioned. Debate first centred on the validity of the concept of the archaeological culture as defined by Childe, and its usefulness in distinguishing 'peoples in prehistory'. It was argued that the distinct associations of artifacts thought to be the material traces of distinct societies could be interpreted also as reflecting certain patterns of economic activity, or of behaviour. In addition, though few would question that the archaeological record itself directly results from human behaviour in the past (Binford, 1973: 229), they might not agree on its mirror-like qualities. We need to know not only those factors which conditioned the patterns of behaviour in the past, but also those which determine the disposal, survival, and recovery of its material traces. Consideration of these aspects created debate on the significance of assemblage variation within related cultural assemblages, such as the intriguing succession of Mousterian industries from sites in south-western France, (Bordes and Bordes, 1970; Binford and Binford, 1966; Binford, 1973; Bordes, 1973). Examination of such situations has led the student of Palaeolithic cultures to question his own assumptions on the meaning of assemblage patterning in terms of the human past, also his own ability to understand and recreate that past using the evidence available to him (see Isaac, 1972). It is vital to our understanding of the past that such variations be explained, that we *can* determine whether they reflect cultural traditions and distinct societies, or whether they reflect patterns of behaviour which may be common to many such societies, recurring in the archaeological record as often as do these activities in the life of the group, irrespective of its social and technological traditions. Environment, subsistence economy, site usage, and activities, are all factors relevant to the interpretation of such variations: their effects should be examined. Practical problems, and the limitations of archaeological evidence, may make this a difficult task. Yet the prehistorian is somewhat in the position of Job, that 'he must find God, or go mad'—he must devise procedures which allow him to answer these fundamental questions, or he must lose confidence in his discipline, its basic assumptions, and its ultimate value.

Until the last few years the problems posed by Australian prehistory were largely those of establishing the broad outlines of cultural sequence and chronology over extensive areas; there is concern now to re-interpret these in their ecological context, and in the light of ethnographic evidence. For few parts of the continent have there been sufficiently detailed regional research programmes to allow the study of minor variations in the archaeological record which might hint at problems of the kind encountered by scholars of the European

Mousterian. In this paper I wish to examine the assemblages from a number of sites investigated in the New England region of north-eastern New South Wales, and the variability which seems to exist between them. They offer excellent test cases for the discussion of the theoretical problems involved since the time span concerned is relatively short, and they are located in distinct environmental zones within the one region. The sites to be discussed are listed in Table 1 and their locations shown in Map 1.

The documented assemblage variation

The sites investigated include rock shelters, middens, and open sites in the Clarence valley, the Northern Tablelands, and the slopes of the plateau, so sampling a transect across the region under study. They were all studied as part of a regional programme under the writer's direction while at the University of New England. All sites belong to the last 9000 years, a relatively short time span, during which we have as yet no evidence for major climatic or vegetational changes in the region except those wrought during the last century by clearance of the dense coastal rain forests and the impact of grazing on the forests and grasslands of the Tablelands.

Within the 9000 years documented in the excavated deposits changes have occurred in the cultural assemblages, witnessing to changes over time in man's response to his environment, or to the impact of technological innovation. These changes are most clearly demonstrated in the sequence from the Seelands rock shelter on the Clarence River upstream from Grafton (see McBryde, 1966). However I do not wish to discuss here the nature of these changes, nor their possible interpretation, but to concentrate on the problems of the explanation of assemblage variation between contemporary artifact assemblages from these deposits.

The maps illustrating the distribution of certain artifact types within the region show the outlines of the problem in crudest form, by isolating the artifact types which have exclusive distribution patterns (see Maps 2, 3 and 5). These include the unifacially flaked pebble tools whose occurrence is confined to the coastal strip and to the river valleys east of the Great Dividing Range (Map 5) also the use-polished working edge with similar distribution (Map 2) while the sandstone grinding slabs used for the preparation of seed foods are found only on the western slopes of the tablelands (Map 3). These are artefact types which either reflect functions and behaviour patterns characteristic of distinct environmental zones, or 'cultural preferences'. This latter argument relating to 'cultural preferences' could only be sustained for the uniface pebble tool. Both the use-polished edge and the grinding

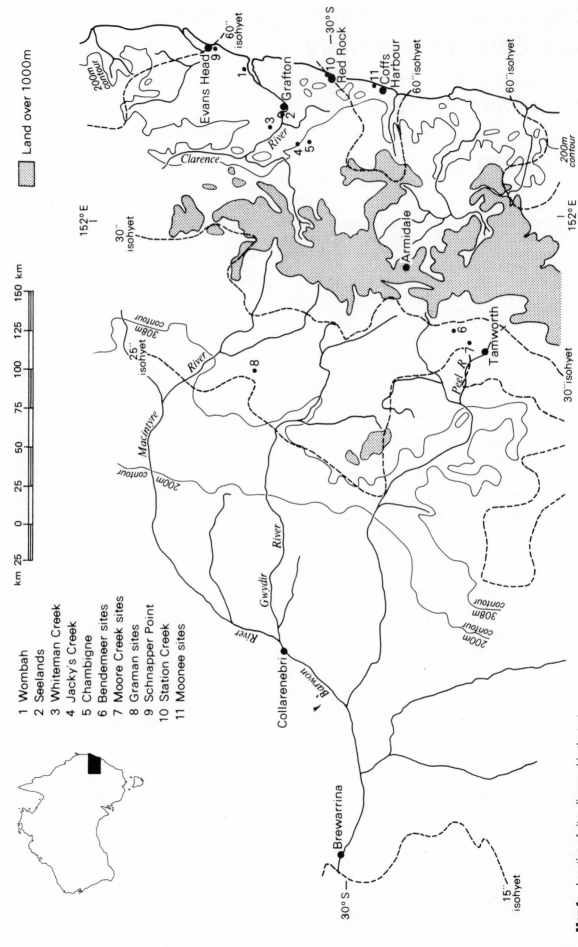

Map 1: Location of sites discussed in the text.

1 Wombah
2 Seelands
3 Whiteman Creek
4 Jacky's Creek
5 Chambigne
6 Bendemeer sites
7 Moore Creek sites
8 Graman sites
9 Schnapper Point
10 Station Creek
11 Moonee sites

Land over 1000m

Table 1 Sites discussed in the text

Site	Location	Type of site	Rock art	Chronology of deposits
Schnapper Point	Coastal dunes—Evans Head	Open working area in eroded dunes	—	—
Station Creek	Coastal dune systems, north of Red Rock	Eroded midden and working area in dunes	—	—
Moonee 1 and 2	Coastal dune systems, north of Coffs Harbour	Eroded middens and working area in dunes	—	At site 1 radio carbon dates of first and second millennia AD for associated eroded deposits
Wombah 1	Clarence estuary (north bank)	Open midden	—	Second millennium BC to first millennium AD
Seelands	Riverine, near Grafton	Rock shelter	Linear engravings	c. 6400 BP to c. 300 BP
Jacky's Creek	Foothills of Clarence valley	Rock shelter	One hand stencil, red and black drawings	First millennium AD
Chambigne	Foothills of Clarence valley	Rock shelter	Hand stencils	First millennium AD
Whiteman Creek	Foothills of Clarence valley	Rock shelter	—	First and second millennia AD
Bendemeer 1	Tablelands	Rock shelter	Paintings in red (extensive site—variety of motifs including large human figures)	First to second millennium AD
Bendemeer 2	Tablelands	Rock shelter	Paintings in red (bird tracks, parallel lines)	Third millennium BC to first millennium AD
Moore Creek 4	Tablelands/w. slopes boundary	Rock shelter	Painting in red (one bird track)	Second millennium BC to first millennium AD
Moore Creek 6	Tablelands/w. slopes boundary	Rock shelter	Paintings in red	First and second millennia BC
Graman B.1 Graman B.4	Western slopes Western slopes	Rock shelter Rock shelter	Some engravings (bird and kangaroo tracks) Some paintings in red (bird tracks)	c. 5400 BP to c. 2000 BP Second millennium BC to first millennium AD
Graman A.1 Graman A.2	Western slopes Western slopes	Open site quartzite quarry Rock shelter	Paintings in red (bird tracks)	— c. 9000 BP to c. 3000 BP (backed blade industry second and third millennia BC)
Graman A.7	Western slopes	Rock shelter	Some engravings (bird and kangaroo tracks). Both A.2 and A.7 are occupation sites in a complex of rock art sites along one gully. A.7 is adjacent to a site with mutilated hand stencils	First and second millennia BC

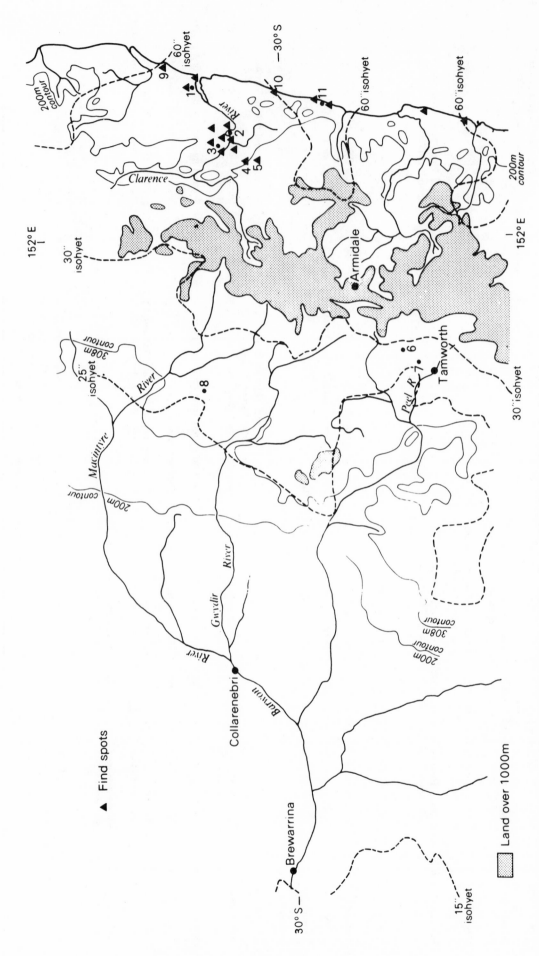

Map 2: Use-polished edges: distribution of assemblages including these (on uniface pebble tools and re-juvenation flakes).

slab are functionally defined types, so surely reflect differences in activity only. The grinding slabs may be related to aspects of the subsistence economy themselves environmentally determined, in the occurrence of suitable seed-bearing grasses. However further variations of a more significant kind emerge if we plot the distribution of assemblage types, looking at the artifact collections as a whole and the varying proportions of their individual components (see Maps 4 and 5 and Tables 2 and 3 for detailed presentation of these data). Amongst elements for which we have no exclusive distribution patterns there are yet variations in their proportional representation in the total assemblage. If we compare contemporary assemblages, we find on the western slopes and tablelands an assemblage which combines backed blades, ground-edge artifacts, burins, scrapers, utilised flakes and blades, plus bipolar pieces (fabricators), with some use of bone (see Table 2 and Map 4). Of these assemblages the backed blade class comprises 40% to 70%. The Graman sites (see Table 2), together with surface sites on the north-western slopes, suggest a minor variation to this pattern in the addition of grinding slabs, items not found on the plateau sites such as Bendemeer. The backed blade assemblage from level II of Site B1 at Graman is one of the earliest from Australia as a whole, with a radiocarbon age of 5450±100 BP (GaK 806). At nearby site Graman A2 such an industry is well established at 4960±200 BP (ANU-1353). Basal occupation at this site dates to *c.* 9000 BP (ANU-1354). Artifact assemblages from coastal sites contain the same components (if we exclude the uniface pebble tool and the use-polished edge) but their relative frequencies differ. The backed blades form a minor element, never more than 14% of the total assemblages, bipolar pieces (fabricators) are more important than on the plateau, burins less so (see Table 3 and Map 5). (Compare contemporary level assemblages from the Bendemeer sites and Seelands in Tables 2 and 3.) The tablelands and western slopes assemblages could be described as 'Bondaian' as defined by McCarthy in his work on the Capertee valley sites (McCarthy, 1964) and have close affinities with those of the Bondaian sites excavated by Moore in the upper Hunter valley (Moore, 1970). Both groups of sites are in environmental situations similar to those of the New England Tablelands. The coastal sites may share certain components of the typical Bondaian assemblage, but could hardly be said to be 'Bondaian'.

Within this coastal group of sites whose assemblages are characterised by the combination of uniface pebble tools with flake and blade tools including backed blades, scrapers and bipolar pieces ('fabricators'), further variation may be observed. This involves the frequencies of ground-edge artifacts, use-polished edges, backed blades, scrapers, and bipolar pieces (see Table 3). These variations do stand up to statistical tests of significant difference (see McBryde, 1974); they seem to be clues to the impact of a rather different set of determinants from those controlling the distinction between coastal and tableland assemblages. Geographically these eastern sites belong to coastal, estuarine, riverine, and foothill locations. Sites on the immediate coast, such as Schnapper Point and Station Creek, have a less diversified assemblage than do the others, also than do similarly situated sites elsewhere in New South Wales. The absence of backed blades (except elouera) is in contrast to coastal dune sites in the Sydney district (as at Kurnell) and on the south coast (such as Murramurrang).

Another point of contrast between sites on the north coast and those to the south is the absence of specialised fishing gear in the coastal assemblages of the recent past. Bone points

are relatively rare, while the shell fish hook, the stone fish hook file, and the multi-pronged fishing spear, are not recorded north of the Macleay and Bellenger rivers (see Map 6—qualifying Massola, 1965). The far north coast of New South Wales seems to have been isolated from the changes that brought the fish hook to the south and central coast in the early centuries of the second millennium AD (Bowdler, 1970:112). Unless one argued strongly, (as one could on the basis of the habits of the fish species available and the nature of the north coast beaches and shallow estuaries) that the fish hook, and therefore line-fishing, were not appropriate methods in the region, then this distribution pattern does seem to suggest a cultural preference among the fishers of the north coast for spear and net fishing rather than the use of hook and line. Certainly after European settlement they acquired the latter technique and used it extensively.

So in the prehistory of northern New South Wales over the last nine thousand years, where we can compare contemporary artifact assemblages in distinct environmental zones within a narrow geographical compass, there is definite evidence for patterning in the proportional frequency with which certain components occur. This patterning seems to fall into two classes, a major variation involving some distinct and exclusive distributions and variation of a finer kind involving minor alterations in the proportions of certain types. The first may be observed between sites on coast and tableland, the other between sites in different situations within one or other of the major environmental divisions. This division is comparable to that defined by Mellars as between 'inter-group variability' and 'inter-locational variability', when discussing functional variability in stone tool assemblages (Mellars, 1970: 75). Interpretation of this patterning is vital to an understanding of prehistory in the area, and of human adaptation to the opportunities and demands of its ecology. Did the steep escarpment, and the harsh environment of the tablelands form a barrier, on either side of which developed two separate 'culture-provinces', perhaps sharing some common origin in the past? This would explain the elements common to both. Or do we have the development of distinct cultural assemblages or tool kits as responses to the requirements of subsistence in the distinct environments, a 'coastal adaptation', and an 'upland adaptation', by people whose cultures were otherwise similar? The hypotheses that we have two distinct 'culture-provinces', or two styles of adaptation in the prehistory of northern New South Wales must be tested. I intend to examine possible explanations of the observed patterning in the assemblages, for the application of slightly differing approaches may indicate which hypothesis better fits the available evidence. In effect this involves applying different models to the interpretation of the evidence; those to be applied here include:

(1) the impact of environmental factors;

(2) a functional interpretation in terms of subsistence economies, site activities, site usage, and available raw material for tool making;

(3) interpretation in terms of cultural traditions;

(4) interpretation in terms of the effects of the methods adopted by the investigating archaeologist in recovering and analysing the basic data.

Table 2 Assemblages from upland sites

ENVIRONMENT	TABLELAND SITES															
Assemblages/Components	Moore Creek Site 4 Level I Spits 1–8		Moore Creek Site 6 Level I Spits 1–12		Bendemeer—Site 1 Levels I–II		Level IIIA		Level IIIB		Bendemeer Site 2 Level III		Graman Area B Site 11 Level I Trench 1		Level II Trench 2	
	N	%	N	%	N	%	N	%	N	%	N	%	N	%	N	%
A. DESIGNED TOOLS AND UTILISED																
(i) Ground artifacts																
ground-edge artifacts	1	2·2									3	1·0				
flakes from ground-edge artifacts			1	1·6			6	2·8	2	0·6			1	0·7		
grinding slabs			1	1·6									1	0·7	5	16·1
pieces with grinding grooves																
bifacially flaked 'axe blanks'	2	4·4	1	1·6					1	0·13						
(ii) Retouched artifacts																
backed blades	25	55·5	27	44·2	50	57·4	130	61·3	204	69·6	164	54·4	80	56·3	16	51·6
elouera	1		3		4		9		13		11		2		1	
geometric microliths	12		13		25		88		128		86		69		13	
Bondi points (microlithic	10		11		21		53		63		66		9		2	
Woakwine points (points																
points																
backed pieces	2										1					
adze flakes					1	1·1	1	0·4	2	0·6						
burins	3	6·6	14	22·9	6	6·8	11	5·1	12	4·0	27	8·9	9	6·3		
burin-scrapers	1	2·2														
scrapers	7	15·5	4	6·5	8	9·1	14	6·6	23	7·8	20	6·6	12	8·4	2	6·4
bipolar pieces	4	8·8	1	1·6	3	3·4	20	9·4	3	1·0	9	2·9	1	0·7		
uniface pebble tools																
(iii) Utilised																
utilised cores	2	4·4														
utilised flakes			13	21·2	19	21·8	30	14·1	43	14·6	81	26·9	38	26·7	8	25·8
use polished edges																
Total designed tools and utilised	45		61		38		212		293		301		142		31	
B. CORES, MODIFIED PIECES AND WASTE																
flaked pebbles																
cores	4		23		42		168		96		108		132		21	
flaked pieces																
core trimming and rejuvenation flakes	6						9		4		8					
waste flakes and blades,	1376		530		2810		6600		6832		2088		3361		1002	
chips																
Total 'waste'	1386		553		2852		6777		6932		2204		3493		1023	
Total stone artifacts	1431		614		2939		6989		7225		2505		3635		1054	
Implements as % of total	3·14		9·9		2·9		3·1		4·1		12·1		3·9		2·9	
'waste' as % of total	96·8		90·1		97·1		96·9		95·9		87·9		96·1		97·1	
C. ORNAMENTS–PENDANTS																
stone													2			
shell																
D. BONE ARTIFACTS																
bone points					1		2		2				1			
modified pieces			1				1		2				6			
E. PIGMENT {red, yellow, white}			present (Spit 7)		present		present		present		present		present		present	

Explanatory hypotheses

1. Environmental factors In sub-tropical latitudes (see Map 1) north-eastern New South Wales enjoys a variety of sub-tropical climatic régimes; diversity is imposed by the existence of the high, rugged plateau country of 900 m to over 1500 m, its steep escarpment on the east separating it from the coastal river valleys. On the west the tablelands grade gently to the plains country of the Darling Basin. The tablelands have also influenced the rainfall patterns of the region, for though all districts have a sub-tropical summer maximum there is a marked decline in annual average from east to west (see Map 1). These range from 1270 mm to 2030 mm on the coastal strip in the Clarence valley, to 760 mm on the plateau, dropping to 660 mm on the western slopes. Summers in the coastal zone are hot and humid, winters dry and mild, while the tablelands have lower summer temperatures and very severe winters of heavy frosts, snowfalls, and great daily extremes of temperature. Vegetation varies according to soils, rainfall, temperature,

and aspect. There is marked contrast between the dry sclerophyll forest and woodland of the western slopes, the dry sclerophyll forests and tussock grasslands of the tablelands (where the severity of the winters dominates vegetation development) and the wet sclerophyll forests, rain forests, and coastal swamps of the east coast. Thus the region as a whole offers ideal opportunities for studying various cultural adaptations to differing environments, and for testing their impact on artifact assemblage patterning.

To separate environmental factors from those relating to the subsistence economy may not be easy. It is hard to envisage the environment in itself influencing the distribution or composition of artifact assemblages, except in so far as it determines the economy, or imposes certain conditions of living, as in some particularly harsh or difficult regions. It could also necessitate mobility, or seasonal migration for effective exploitation of available resources. Yet even here cultural factors are relevant, conditioning a people's response to the environment, and the extent to which its opportunities are

WESTERN FALL OF THE TABLELANDS

Graman Area B Site 4						Graman Area A Site 2						Graman Area A Site 7					
Level I		Level II		Level III		Level I		Level II Spits 1–2		Total		Level I (Spits 1–18)		Level II (Spits 19–25)		Total	
N	%	N	%	N	%	N	%	N	%	N	%	N	%	N	%	N	%
2	3·0	1	0·1														
13	19·6	10	1·6	1	1·2	4	4·2			4	3·3	2	1·8			2	1·7
1	1·5	16	2·6	2	2·9							1	0·8			1	0·8
1	1·5	2	0·3	1	1·2							2	1·8			2	1·7
18	27·2	402	65·7	35	45·4	65	68·4	20	80·0	85	70·8	64	59·2	3		7	56·8
1		19										2				2	
13		246		29		41		12		53		35		3		38	
4		137		6		17		6		23		11				3	
												3				11	
												3				3	
						7		2		9		10				10	
1	1·5	2	0·3														
1	1·5	22	3·6	1	1·2	4	4·2	1		5	4·1	9	8·3	1	1	10	8·5
						3	3·1			3	2·5	1	0·9			2	1·7
11	16·6	55	9·0	19	24·6	4	4·2			4	3·3	6	5·5			6	5·0
2	3·0	12	1·9	1	1·2	1	1·0			1	0·8	3	2·7			3	2·5
												3	2·7	1		4	3·4
26	39·3	90	14·7	17	22·0	14	14·7	4		18	15·0	17	15·7	4		21	17·8
76		611		77		95		25		120		108		10		118	
33		234		59		4		3		7		2				2	
10		127		14		10				10		5		2		7	
						25		2		27		5		1		6	
NA		NA		NA		1556		470		2026		1495		135		1630	
2		20		3		59		29		88		14		3		17	
						1654		504		2158		1521		141		1662	
						1749		529		2278		1626		151		1780	
							5·5		4·7		5·3		6·6		6·6		6·6
NA		NA		NA			94·5		95·3		94·7		93·4		93·4		93·4
19		14		1								3				3	
												8				8	
	present		present		present		present		present		present		present		present		present
									present		present		present				
															present		

utilised. Environment could also exert a vital control over population densities and distribution, in relation to the carrying capacity of available resources, again subject to the cultural and technological resources of the peoples concerned. It could also determine patterns of isolation or contact between peoples, by the accidents of topography or stream flow. In northern New South Wales relevant aspects are the dividing range and its steep eastern escarpment, and the westward flowing rivers of the western slopes, all ultimately joining the Darling River system, in contrast to the series of parallel river valleys on the coast each divided from the next by low ranges of hills. At the time of European settlement the Aboriginal population in north-eastern New South Wales seems to have been concentrated to the east and to the west of the dividing range, with particularly high densities on the coast and its river valleys (Pierce, 1971; Belshaw, in press). Compared with the coast and the western slopes the tableland itself was sparsely peopled. This population distribution directly reflects the comparative richness of the regions as resource zones for hunter-gatherer societies. The distribution of archaeological sites suggests that this pattern may have had a long history.

In terms of resource zones the region divides into coastal and estuarine areas, riverine, foothill, tableland, and western slopes. Of these the tablelands would be the poorest, with less variety of plant and animal life, and a harsh climate in winter. The coastal valleys would offer abundant and varied resources as well as access to those of the coast itself in shellfish and marine life, while the western slopes in their forest and woodlands would support a large marsupial population and in addition were rich in grasses with edible seeds, such as the species of *Panicum*. They are also crossed by large river systems which would provide fish, shellfish and crustacea.

As well as determining the relevant densities of population within these environmental zones, the general topography of the area, and the pattern of its stream flow, may have had their impact on the region's prehistory in creating physical barriers to contact and the diffusion of ideas and technologies, so encouraging the development of slightly different cultural

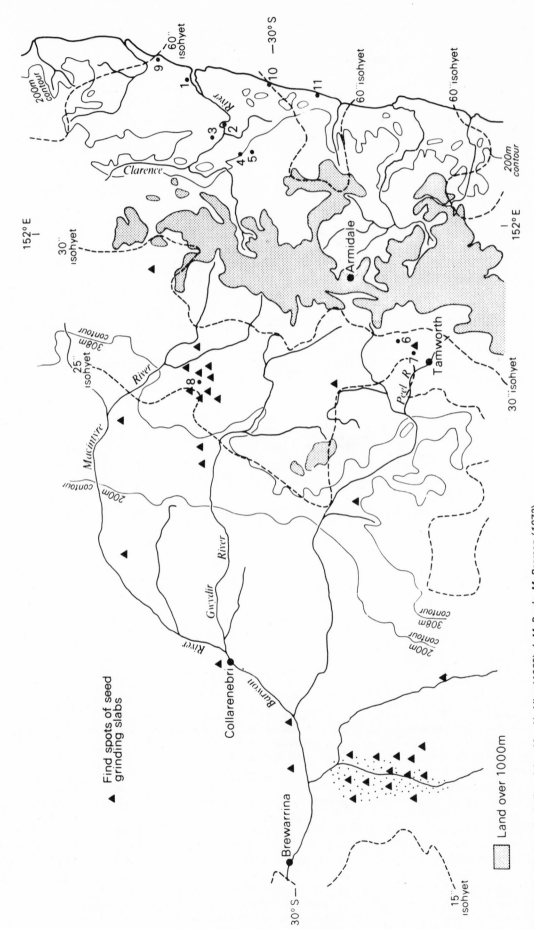

Map 3: Distribution of grinding slabs. *After H. Allen (1969). I. McBryde, M. Pearson (1973).*

adaptations. The escarpment with its steep slopes, dense rain forest, and formidable gorge country may well be a relevant factor in determining the coast—tableland dichotomy. Access to the highlands from the west, by contrast, is easy; this may explain the pattern of dispersal seen in axe lithologies in the north. Evidence for trade and contact from the southern tablelands to the west is clear and abundant, whereas the valleys of the Clarence and Richmond remain isolated from the resources of the plateau (see Binns and McBryde, 1972).

2. Subsistence economies To view the artifact assemblages against environment without considering the subsistence economy does not advance the argument beyond the question of population densities, and the creation of areas of isolation or ease of contact. These by themselves seem insufficient to explain the observed variation in the assemblages. If we adopt a functional interpretation of such variations, taking the differing frequencies of their components as a reflection of differing activity patterns imposed by the demands of different subsistence economies, can we gain more insight into their cause? To consider first the coastal situation. The economy documented in the deposits of the Wombah midden on the Clarence estuary is one almost entirely dependent on the gathering of shellfish (over 90% of which are oyster) supplemented by some hunting and a little fishing. It is a specialised economy exploiting to the full only one of the available resource zones of the estuary. Such an economy would not require a specialised tool kit, a factor reflected in the relatively meagre artifact collection from the site (see Table 3) with its uniface pebble tools, ground-edge artifacts, backed blades, bipolar pieces ('fabricators') and scrapers. A comparative poverty, and lack of diversity, distinguishes this assemblage from that of contemporary levels at Seelands, for they have components in common and both reflect the same general trends of change over time, for example in the relative frequencies of backed blades. One could argue that the differences are such as could be explained by functional rather than cultural determinants, by seasonal patterns of adaptation and exploitation of the valley's resources.

At Seelands the artifact assemblage is more diverse; it is also represented in greater quantity, with considerable evidence for the manufacture and maintenance of stone tools, which is minimal at Wombah (see Table 3). The subsistence economy at Seelands as represented by the biological remains (unfortunately only preserved in the upper levels and level IV) seems to have been a broadly-based one. It shows a wide variety of resources culled from a number of micro-environments readily available in this part of the valley with its broad river, sclerophyll forests, and patches of rain forests bordering the river (see Fig. 1). We have archaeological evidence for contact between this part of the river and its estuary at both the Seelands and Wombah sites. While evidence for winter occupation may be seen in the emu egg shell at Seelands, the dependence on oysters at Wombah (on analogy with the practices of modern oyster farmers in the area) would suggest occupation there in late spring and summer. Such a pattern of seasonal exploitation of the valley's resources is documented in the ethnohistorical literature, early summer spent on the coast, winter inland hunting (McBryde, 1974: 10, 266, 270, 337-38). It seems to offer a consistent explanation for the assemblage patterning at the two sites.

The assemblages from Schnapper Point, Moonee 1 and 2, and Station Creek offer another coastal variant, with their absence of the backed blades and Bondi points, and high proportions of uniface pebble tools. Unfortunately, as they are surface collections from eroded dune sites, we have little associated occupation evidence, though midden deposits had once been present at Moonee and Station Creek. From the foothills country west of Seelands the assemblages of rock shelters at Jacky's Creek, Chambigne, and Whiteman Creek show distinct variation from those of Seelands. They have higher frequencies for use-polished edges (on pebble tools and on flakes—presumably struck from these in re-trimming working edges) edge-ground tools and for bipolar pieces ('fabricators') (see Table 3). At Jacky's Creek, backed blades of geometric form are barely represented, at Whiteman Creek in level VI (dated to the fourth century AD) not at all, in an assemblage 70% of which is made up of uniface pebble tools.

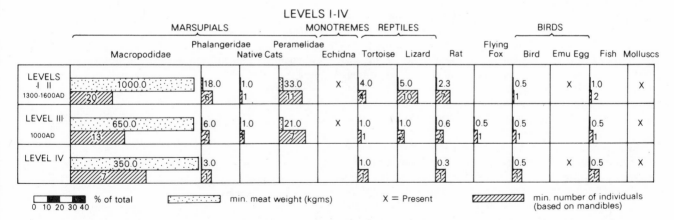

Fig. 1: Seelands Rock Shelter—meat components of diet.

Note: In Figs 1, 2 and 3 the minimum number of individuals has been calculated on the basis of mandibular and cranial pieces among the bone finds. The majority of the bone material on all sites was badly fragmented and unidentifiable, so the figures here present only a portion of the total meat food represented by the bone in the occupation debris.
To calculate meat weight, arbitrary figures had to be taken for each group which could introduce an element of distortion, especially in the macropodidae group. In other groups there would be less variation between individual species. The weights used are: Macropodidae: 50 kg; Phalangeridae: 3 kg; Native Cats: 1 kg; Peramelidae: 3 kg; Tortoise: 1 kg; Lizard: 0.5 kg; Rat: 0.3 kg; Flying Fox: 0.5 kg.

(Whiteman Creek has not been included in the main tables because of the small size of its cultural assemblages.) The implement assemblage from Chambigne again shows the high proportions of use-polished edges, ground tools, bipolar pieces and scrapers, but it also contains a considerable number (17%) of backed blades for a coastal site (see Table 3).

Unfortunately the analysis of the faunal material from these foothill sites is not yet available, so we lack the clues it might provide towards explaining this intriguing variation amongst sites so close to one another in both time and space. The high proportion of use-polished edges certainly hints at distinct activities which may be associated with the location and local resources of the site. However it is still uncertain whether those would be part of food preparation or other camp activity. Kamminga's micro-wear studies of use-polished edges on uniface pebble tools and rejuvenation flakes from Jacky's Creek have led him to suggest chopping of wood or soft bark at a low angle as their function. He feels that the high number of rejuvenation flakes bearing such edges from the shelter deposit indicates that the activity was carried out on the site.

For sites on the tablelands and western slopes we have analyses of the biological evidence for Bendemeer Site I in the high country (see Fig. 2) and Site B4 in the Ottley valley at Graman on the western slopes (see Fig. 3). Evidence for intense occupation (in terms of food refuse) is not present at Bendemeer, though its artifact collection was quite large. This would be in accord with the harsh local environment, and its comparatively limited range of resources; it could also reflect other features of the site such as its rock art. This shelter is the richest of a complex of painted sites and so may not have been used as a 'base camp'. The bone remains are predominantly marsupial, with over 90% of the meat weight represented in all levels provided by macropodids (see Fig. 2). The implement assemblage is dominated by backed blades, even in levels dating to the mid-second millennium AD. They are associated with ground-edge tools, burins, scrapers, utilised flakes, some bipolar pieces, and a few bone artifacts (see Table 2). Backed blades constitute 69% of the assemblage in level IIIB; similarly high frequencies were found in the assemblages excavated from a nearby rock shelter (Bendemeer Site 2) (see Table 2). Unfortunately the report on the bone material from this site is not yet available.

It would be tempting to invoke a functional model here, to see correlation between the high proportion of macropodid bones and the high frequency of backed blades in the tool kit. The correlation becomes even more attractive if one interprets the backed blades as spear barbs (for which we have evidence in the specimens from Graman still retaining traces of hafting gum (see McBryde, 1968)). In the open sclerophyll forest of the plateau kangaroos and wallabies could be hunted with spear, though we have ethnographic evidence also for the use of standing nets on the tablelands (Gardner, 1842-1854, I: 34). Further confirmation of this hypothesis seems to come from the cultural and biological evidence of Site B4 at Graman. Artifact assemblages from this site show a drop in the proportion of backed blades from 65.7% in level II to 27.2% in level I, associated with a rise in the relative proportions of ground-edge tools, scrapers, and utilised flakes (see Table 2). Examination of the bone material indicates that these changes coincided with a decline in representation of macropodid in the food refuse (see Fig. 3) and a rise in that of phalangeridae.

This decline could reflect either changes in dietary preference, or a local depletion of the kangaroo population from

Table 3   Assemblages from coastal sites

Environment:	Coastal dunes			
Assemblages—Components	Schnapper Point		Station Creek	
A. DESIGNED TOOLS AND UTILISED				
(I) Ground artifacts	N	%	N	%
Ground-edge artifacts	2	1·8	5	3·7
Flakes from ground-edge artifacts				
Grinding slabs				
Pieces with grinding grooves	6	5·5		
Hammerstones	2	1·8	11	8·2
(II) Retouched artifacts				
Backed blades	2	1·8		
Elouera	2			
Geometric microliths				
Bondi points microlith				
Woakwine points points				
Backed pieces				
Adze flakes				
Burins	6	5·5		
Burin-scrapers				
Scrapers	13	12·0		
Bipolar pieces (fabricators)	10	9·2	5	3·7
Uniface pebble tools	59	54·6	95	67·8
Biface pebble tools			16	11·9
(III) Utilised				
Utilised cores				
Utilised flakes	6	5·5	1	0·7
Use polished edges	2	1·8	5	3·7
Total Designed Tools and Utilised	108		138	
B. CORES, MODIFIED PIECES AND WASTE				
Flaked Pebbles	983		110	
Cores	46		72	
Flaked pieces				
Core trimming and rejuvenation flakes	1			
Waste flakes and blades	318		399	
Chips	701			
Total 'waste'	2049		581	
Total stone artifacts	2157		715	
[Unmodified Pebbles]	3850			
Designed and utilised as % of total		5·1		18·7
Waste as % of total		94·9		81·3
C. ORNAMENTS/PENDANTS				
stone				
shell				
D. BONE ARTIFACTS				
bone points				
modified pieces				
E. PIGMENT { red yellow white				

	Estuarine				Riverine						Foothills			
Wombah Middens Site I Levels I and II		Wombah Middens Levels IIA VII, VIII		Seelands Upper Levels		Seelands Level IIIA		Seelands IVA+2V		Seelands VA+2VI		Jacky's Creek Levels II+IIA		Chambigne All Levels	
N	%	N	%	N	%	N	%	N	%	N	%	N	%	N	%
		1	5·0	8	2·8			3	5·2			7	11·2		
1	1·9			28	10.0	4	3·0							1	0·7
2	3·9	5	25·0	11	4·0	12	9·0	6	10·5			1	1·6	25	17·8
												1}	1·6	4 16} 5	
1	1·9														
2	3·9	1	5·0	1	0·3	1	0·7							8	5·7
2	3·9	3	15·0	47	17·0	10	7·5	2	3·5			5	8·0	28	20·0
15	29·4	4	20·0	35	12·7	13	9·8	1	1·7			6	9·6	20	14·2
5	9·8	2	10·0	52	18·9	62	46·9	36	63·1	13		10	16·1	23	16·4
15	29·4	3	15·0	59	21·4	23	17·4	6	10·5	1		9	14·5	15	10·7
4	7·8	1	5·0	38	13·8	7	5·3	3	5·2			24	38·7	20	14·2
47		20		279		132		57		14		62		140	
1												9		15	
6		1		15		14		12		10		57		47	
1															
659		209		18044		8374		1958		177		2622		1902	
5															
672		210		18419		8388		1970		187		2688		1964	
723		230		18694		8520		2027		201		2750		2104	
	7·0		8·6		1·5		1·5		2·8		6·9		2·3		6·7
	93·0		91·4		98·5		98·5		97·2		93·1		97·7		93·3
				1											
4		1		10								2		2	

Present

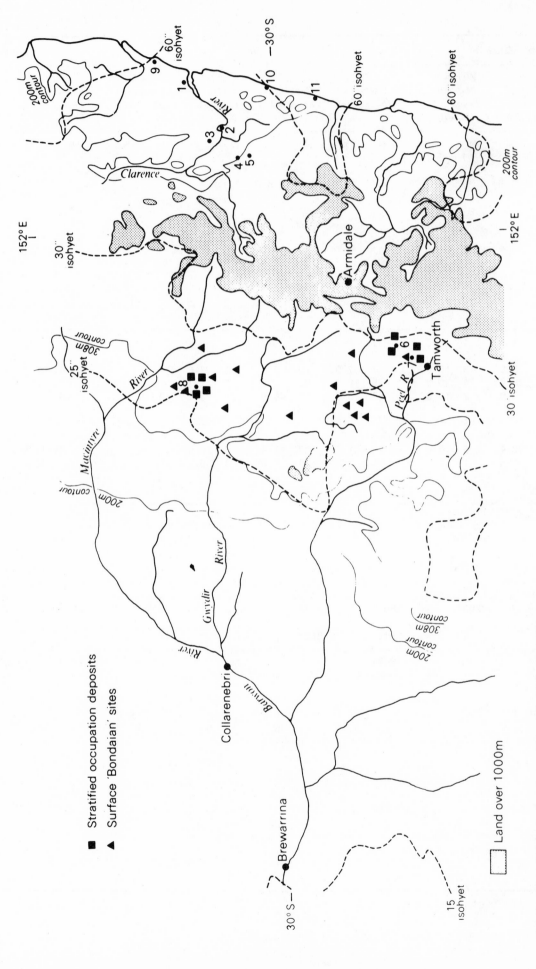

Map 4: Backed blade dominated assemblages: 'Bondaian assemblages.

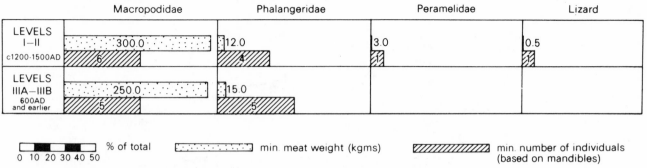

	Macropodidae	Phalangeridae	Peramelidae	Lizard
LEVELS I–II c1200-1500AD	300.0 / 6	12.0 / 4	3.0	0.5
LEVELS IIIA–IIIB 600AD and earlier	250.0 / 5	15.0 / 5		

% of total   min. meat weight (kgms)   min. number of individuals (based on mandibles)
0 10 20 30 40 50

Fig. 2: Bendemeer Site 1—meat components of diet.

'overkill'. In level I, possum dominates the meat weight represented by the bone material, which could be related to the higher frequencies of axes and tool types suitable for wood working, relevant to the capture by hand and club of a small nocturnal animal living in hollow trees. In the ethnohistorical literature for the area our sources stress that in the recent past possum was the meat staple of the local diet (A Lady [Mrs McPherson], 1860 : 207-10; Cunningham, 1828 : 171; Gardner, 1842-1854, I : 257; Greenway, 1910 : 15-16; Ridley, 1875 : 151; Wyndham, 1972 : letter 4).

The questions raised by these correlations are important; the validity of the correlations must be rigorously tested. This I intend to follow up with tests of correlation and co-variance on the New England data, and examination of the faunal and artifactual material from other Bondaian sites in upland situations.

The grinding slabs from the Graman sites are new elements in an assemblage otherwise very similar to those of the Bendemeer and Moore Creek sites. Economic activities may be reflected—the preparation of seed foods in an area which is rich in stands of various edible grasses, especially the *Panicum* species which favour the heavy alluvial soils of the valleys in the district. There is both ethnohistorical and archaeological evidence for dependence on seeds in the subsistence economy of the western slopes (see McBryde, 1968). The archaeological evidence includes seeds recovered by froth flotation from the soils of sites GA7, GB1, GB4. Some of these are crushed

and associated with fragments of starch, so bear witness to the grinding process. These Graman sites on the north-western slopes seem to represent the most easterly occurrence of economies found over wide areas of western New South Wales, and in central Australia, which have a high seasonal dependence on seed foods. Otherwise the dietary remains on the sites suggest an economy which exploits a wide range of resources, some perhaps seasonal like the grass seeds, but all available within a restricted geographical range in an environment offering abundant and diverse opportunities. There is no evidence for seasonal occupation of the sites in the Ottley valley; the seasonal indicators we do have suggest year-round use. So the Graman sites offer evidence for assemblage variation over time which can be explained in terms of changes in the subsistence economy, while the differences between recent assemblages at Graman and at Bendemeer 1 can also be related to economic factors, to the exploitation of seed foods on the slopes and the capture of possums for meat rather than the hunting by spear of kangaroos. The ultimate cause of the economic difference may be environmental, or a matter of cultural preference. If the change to possum capture was enforced by a depletion of the kangaroo population, then we have an environmental determinant of assemblage variation. Similarly, if Bendemeer Site 1 was occupied only in the winter months, the non-toxic *Panicum* grasses which do grow on the tablelands could not have been harvested. If occupation was during the summer months (far more likely from the site's

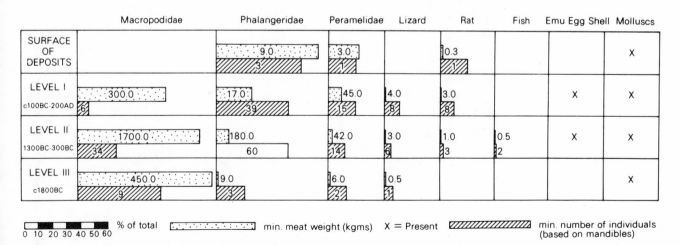

	Macropodidae	Phalangeridae	Peramelidae	Lizard	Rat	Fish	Emu Egg Shell	Molluscs
SURFACE OF DEPOSITS		9.0 / 3	3.0		0.3			X
LEVEL I c100BC-200AD	300.0 / 6	17.0 / 39	45.0 / 15	4.0 / 8	3.0 / 8		X	X
LEVEL II 1300BC-300BC	1700.0 / 34	180.0 / 60	42.0 / 14	3.0 / 6	1.0 / 3	0.5 / 2	X	X
LEVEL III c1800BC	450.0 / 9	9.0 / 3	6.0 / 2	0.5 / 1				X

% of total   min. meat weight (kgms)   X = Present   min. number of individuals (based on mandibles)
0 10 20 30 40 50 60

Fig. 3: Graman Site GB.4—components of diet (non vegetable).

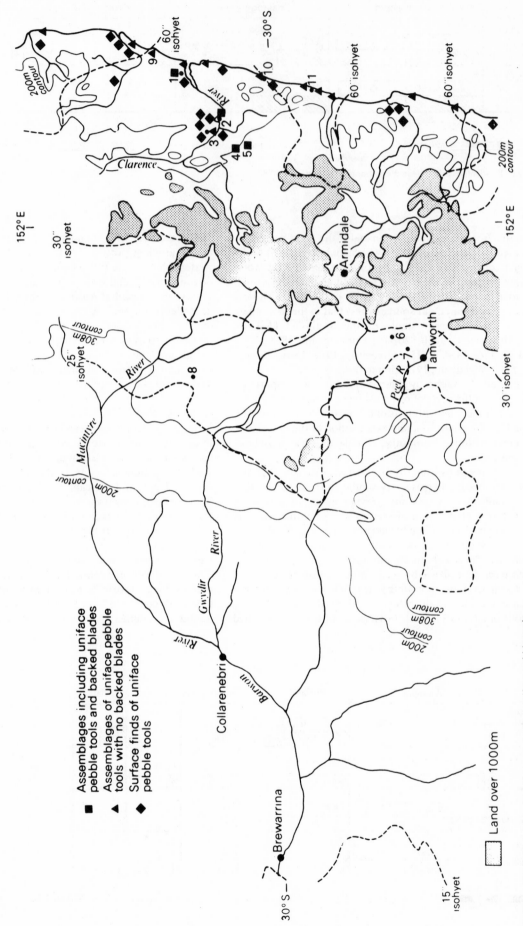

Map 5: Distribution of assemblages containing uniface pebble tools.

Assemblages including uniface
pebble tools and backed blades

Assemblages of uniface pebble
tools with no backed blades

Surface finds of uniface
pebble tools

Land over 1000m

bleak setting), then one may well ask why these resources of the tablelands were ignored, and suggest an answer in terms of cultural preferences. An alternative explanation could be offered if one regarded the site and its rock art as primarily associated with ritual and used briefly by male artists. However the absence of grinding slabs and other evidence for preparation of seed foods is not confined to the Bendemeer sites; it is general throughout the Northern Tablelands. So it would be difficult to sustain the argument of occupation by the male non-gatherers of the local population.

The distribution of assemblages similar to those of the Bendemeer site (where we have an apparent correlation between high proportions of macropodid bones and high frequencies of backed blades in the tool kit) is one largely of upland and western slopes, the areas of open dry sclerophyll forest and savannah woodland in which hunting of kangaroos and wallabies by spear would be effective (see Map 4). All sites are found above the 308 m contour line. To the south, similar assemblages are found in the upper Hunter valley and Capertee valley; it would be interesting to know the range of faunal remains recovered with these assemblages.

3. Activities Activities, in the sense of seasonal migration of groups to take advantage of certain short-lived resources, have already been suggested as likely explanations of some of the patterning observed in the artifact assemblages from the Clarence valley. Other types of activity also may be relevant. For example, were all the investigated sites comparable in their site usage? Could some perhaps have served as long term 'base camps', others as transit, or hunting camps, or have been reserved for some specific activity, which might explain the differences in the artifactual record? Here one might think of workshop or quarry sites, or sites at which intensive occupation might not be expected for ritual reasons, such as art or ceremonial sites (see the comments on Bendemeer 1, p.234).

In the excavation programme in New England certainly the rock shelter sites have predominated (see Table 1), but this has been more a matter of accident and survival of the evidence than of deliberate policy. Unfortunately most of the promising open camp sites located have been damaged, either by erosion or agricultural activities. In recent field work at Graman some likely areas were located, and they will be investigated in the future. We have large surface collections from open sites both on the coast and tableland, but most of these are from sites already disturbed, so unlikely to provide the range of evidence necessary for adequate and full comparison with the rock shelter sites.

If the rock art sites were centres for ceremonial, and traditionally sacred, one might expect either an avoidance of them for home base camps, or evidence of sporadic and non-intense occupation. The majority of the sites excavated showed some form of art (see Table 1), either paintings or engravings, ranging from the sites like Bendemeer 1 which might be termed a 'gallery' (with its range of impressive figures representing three periods of painting) to Moore Creek 4 with one very faded small red bird track on the roof of the shelter. Such variations must reflect functional differences in the art itself, so the fact that all sites show art need not put them all into the same category. There is also the question of the contemporaneity of art and occupation; in few instances can the stratified assemblages be related chronologically to the art. At Bendemeer 1 and at Graman Sites A2 and A7 the occupation evidence is not intense, nor are the artifact assem-

blages large compared with other nearby sites; one could invoke the association with art to explain these characteristics.

Arguing from evidence of either intense occupation, or use of a site over long periods of time, then Seelands, Graman B1 and Graman B4, seem to be sites differing in kind from Chambigne, Jacky's Creek, and Moore Creek 4 and 6, which appear to have been occupied less intensely, either by smaller groups of people or for short periods of time. One would think of the Moore Creek sites as transit, seasonal or wet weather shelters. The main base camps seem to be open sites down in the valley below, near permanent water. They may be associated with use of the ceremonial grounds there and the large stone quarry at Mt Daruka (Binns and McBryde, 1972). The midden at Wombah, though its total occupation is long-lived presumably records only seasonal use for limited periods.

Some clearer, quantifiable, reflection of the activities associated with these sites might be gained by dividing their assemblages into 'extractive' or 'maintenance' tool kits. If the discarded debris on an archaeological site reflects that site's usage, then this approach should give a clearer idea of which are the 'home base camps' and which the transit, hunting, or 'task specific' sites than does the rather impressionistic approach used above. It also allows the sorting of the cultural material along rather different lines from those based on typological features adopted previously; from this, new information may emerge. However, the sorting itself seems to involve making decisions based on presumed functions of the tools; these could be just as unreal as those based on morphological features or the techniques of manufacture.

In the divisions made below only those artifacts classed as 'implements' in the main tables are included, assuming that the retouched and use-fractured working-edges denote their status as tools; this ignores the possible use of unretouched flakes or cores. The by-products of stone tool manufacture (cores and waste flakes) are not included, as being by definition 'maintenance' items for both types of tool-kit. Once one goes beyond assigning the ground-edge artifacts (as axes) and the backed blades (as likely spear barbs) to an 'extractive' category, and scrapers, bipolar pieces, adze-flakes, burins and grinding slabs to a 'maintenance' tool-kit, difficulties arise. So much of the division is based on a subjective assumption of function that it begins to lose purpose. Assigning the uniface pebble tools and the use-polished edges to either category involves assumptions not only on their presumed function, but also on whether this took place at the camp or in the bush. Was the uniface pebble tool, admirable for chopping and digging, employed at the camp in preparing food, or in the field acquiring material for these activities, or both? Likewise, was the use-polished edge these tools exhibit acquired at the site or beyond? (See page 234 for use-wear evidence.) If these use-polished edges are found on the uniface pebble tools, and rejuvenation flakes (presumably struck from these in resharpening their working edges), does one prejudice the figures by including both the pebble tools and all polished edges? For these reasons the figures given below have been calculated to show results both including and excluding the uniface pebble tools and the use-polished edges. Such calculations could also be misleading in comparing the numbers of ground-edge tools and backed blades, if the latter represent elements in a composite tool such as a barbed spear. The presence of the backed blades themselves may represent a 'maintenance' activity, the repair of a barbed spear, just as the flakes with use-polished edges denote the 'repair' of the working edge of a pebble tool. One could also envisage the uniface

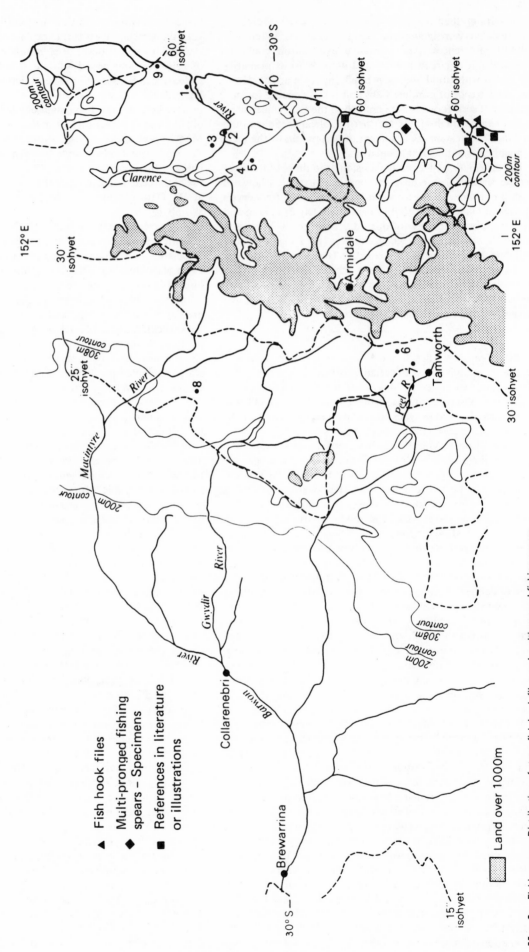

Map 6: Fishing gear: Distribution of stone fish hook files and multipronged fishing spears.

pebble tool serving both 'extractive 'and 'maintenance' functions, as a multi-purpose tool. Would one classify the wooden spearthrower with hafted chisel as an 'extractive' or 'maintenance' item? In applying this classification to a group of stone artifacts we must remember the lesson of recent ethnography in Australia, that the bulk of the 'extractive' tool kit was made from wood and other perishable materials. The qualifications here seem such as to suggest that this approach is not particularly helpful at this stage in comparing assemblages of this kind. The results are listed below in Table 4.

From this Table we see that of the upland sites only Moore Creek 6, level II of Graman site A7, and Graman site B4 (levels III and I) have an assemblage with over 50% 'maintenance' tools, though all the coastal sites achieve this. However, if we exclude the uniface pebble tools from the 'maintenance' items, only Wombah, the upper levels at Seelands, Jacky's Creek and Chambigne, fall into this category. Graman site A1 (the quartzite quarry site) (see Table 5) would have an assemblage of over 90% 'maintenance' tools, but was not included here as the bulk of its assemblage is waste, and its retouched items do not fall into categories comparable to those from the excavated sites. There does not seem to be any consistent pattern between this grouping of the sites and their rock art.

Table 4 Categorising implement assemblages into 'extractive' and 'maintenance' tool-kits

Sites	Percentage of implements classed as 'maintenance'		
Coastal regions			
Schnapper Point	96·2	(40·7)	[94·4]
Station Creek	66·2	(16·4)	[92·5]
Wombah Midden Levels I–II	94·0	(84·0)	[86·0]
Wombah Midden Levels IIA–VIII	70·0	(60·0)	[65·0]
Seelands Upper Levels	84·3	(65·4)	[70·5]
Seelands Level IIIA	87·8	(40·9)	[82·5]
Seelands Levels IVA & 2.V	82·4	(19·2)	[77·1]
Seelands Levels VA & 2.VI	100	(7·2)	—
Jacky's Creek Levels II/IIA	87·0	(70·9)	[48·3]
Chambigne All Levels	81·4	(65·0)	[67·1]

Tablelands Region and Western Slopes	
Graman Site B1 Level I	43·0
Graman Site B1 Level II	48·4
Graman Site B4 Level I	50·0
Graman Site B4 Level II	43·5
Graman Site B4 Level III	63·3
Graman Site A2	25·9
Graman Site A7 Level I	40·0
Graman Site A7 Level II	70·0
Bendemeer Site 1 Levels I–II	42·6
Bendemeer Site 1 Level IIIA	35·9
Bendemeer Site 1 Level IIIB	28·4
Bendemeer Site 2 Level III	45·6
Moore Creek Site 4	37·9
Moore Creek Site 6	51·0

Notes: ( ) % excluding uniface pebble tools
[ ] % excluding use-polished edges

The impact of differing activities within the individual site should also be considered, but its existence would not be revealed in a test excavation or exploration of only one part of the total area of a site's deposits. To gain information of this kind, extensive horizontal exposure is required, or total excavation of small sites, procedures which most archaeologists employ with reluctance. Among the sites discussed, this pattern of differential use of parts of a rock shelter is most clearly demonstrated at Graman Site B4. Here the deposits in zones (a), (b), and (c) contained food refuse, hearth remains, and quantities of plant material (predominantly *Dianella* (Blue Lily, Flax Lily); stone tools were present, but not in large quantities (for a plan of this site, see McBryde, 1974:324). Zones (e) and (f), located further away from the deepest part of the overhang, were investigated in the following season. Food refuse was still present in quantities, but there were no definite hearths, and none of the straw-like plant material though conditions for its preservation still obtained. Stone artifacts showed the same general pattern of association, but were recovered in far greater numbers, especially the backed blades, cores and waste flakes (with a total of 672 cores for the two squares in level II [compared with 41 in (a), (b) and (c)] and 5293 waste flakes in square (e) alone). Such a distribution of finds would seem to indicate the separation of areas in the shelter for cooking and sleeping from those for tool repair and manufacture.

The assemblage from Graman Site A1 is presented separately from the other collections (see Table 5). It differs so markedly from them it is hardly amenable to classification into comparable categories. The site is a working area based on a quartzite outcrop, and the collection is largely quarry waste, with the by-products of preparing useful cores. Of the other sites Schnapper Point and Station Creek would seem to offer assemblages most comparable to that of the Graman quarry, but even these include a greater frequency of classifiable retouched pieces. The Schnapper Point site is a working area based on a Pleistocene pebble beach stratified in the dune systems, and so in these terms has affinity with the Graman site.

Table 5 Graman Area A, Site 1 (quartzite quarry site)

Assemblage
Total collection from 15 of the 25 squares (10′ x 10′) over which material was collected.

N = 7593

Retouched	Flakes and blades with some retouched edges but not falling into any of the definable typological categories distinguished in the assemblages of the Graman occupation sites: 861 (11·3%)
Cores	262 (3·4%)
Core trimming flakes	21 (0·2%)
Flaked pieces	1089 (14·3%)
Flakes	1766 (23·2%)
Blades	410 (5·3%)
Chips	3184 (41·9%)

4. Cultural traditions While still considering variability arising from the behaviour, activities or preferences of the creators of these assemblages, the impact of their own tra-

Table 6 Bipolar pieces ('fabricators') from New England sites
No significant differences in variables tested by χ^2 tests.

Sites	Wombah Level II	Seelands Upper	Seelands Level IIIA	Chambigne All Levels	Bendemeer I All Levels
Wombah Level II		Length Thickness Working-edges	Length Thickness Working-edges	Thickness Working-edges Length/Breadth ratio	Length/thickness Working-edges Length/Breadth ratio
Seelands Upper Levels			Length Width Thickness Working-edges	Length Width Thickness Length/Breadth ratio Working-edges	Thickness Working-Edges Length/Breadth Ratio
Seelands Level IIIA				Length Width Thickness Working-edges Length/Breadth ratio	Length Width Thickness Working-edges Length/Breadth ratio
Chambigne All Levels					Thickness Working-edges Length/Breadth ratio

ditions in craftsmanship and technological experience, and their external contacts, cannot be ignored. To deny these factors relevance would seem to deny the humanity of the craftsmen, who surely must have been influenced by tradition and fashion, the socially accepted norms, and the work of their peers, as are all artists and craftsmen. To test the impact of these factors in isolation from the effects of such determinants as environment, economy, and activity patterns, may prove difficult given our evidence. In addition certain aspects of these (in subsistence economy and activity patterns) may themselves be individual responses to the environment, culturally determined for that society. The adaptive situation which we study through its reflection in the material remains is the result of a complex interplay of behaviour, cultural traditions and environments; granted the nature of that material evidence we may not be able to isolate the entities in the interplay and quantify their impact. However we may be able to isolate the operation of certain cultural preferences in the field of tool production by looking at the attributes of certain components of the full assemblage, such as ground-edge axes, backed blades, scrapers and the heavy pebble choppers. Unfortunately, our two most important types in terms of their dominance of certain assemblages (the backed blades and the uniface pebble tools), provide us in the first instance such a small sample from coastal sites to compare with the tablelands examples that the analysis would hardly have statistical validity, whatever its trends, while for the second we have no examples from the tablelands and no obvious functional equivalent (see pp. 225–29). Inter-site comparisons are being made for the backed blades from tablelands sites, and for the uniface pebble tools on the coast, as well as for the scrapers. Bipolar pieces ('fabricators'), which do occur on all sites (though only as a minor element in the tableland assemblages) showed considerable consistency from coast to tableland when compared on the variables of length, width, thickness, length-breadth ratio, and number and position of working edges. Application of χ^2 test to these results gave a null result for most attributes for most sites (see Table 6). Full discussion of the bipolar pieces from New

England sites and their relevance for the debate on these artifacts (often referred to as scalar cores or scaled pieces) is given in the excavation report for the Wombah site (prepared in 1972). These particular artifacts however are not a suitable type to choose for arguments of the present kind because of the debate over their classification and function.

The distribution of axe typologies in northern New South Wales does show regional patterns. Unfortunately as yet these cannot be related closely to dated archaeological assemblages. The discussion which follows is based on the sample used in study of axe petrology made by the writer and R. A. Binns, which was composed mainly of museum specimens, surface finds with little archaeological context (see Binns and McBryde 1972). Across northern New South Wales the pebble axe was found in all regions, but in greatest numbers on the coast, while the unifacially flaked pebble axes had a distinct coastal distribution. This is in accord with the distribution of unifacially flaked pebble choppers. Unifacially and bifacially flaked flake and blade axes were more common in tablelands locations than on the coast, while the hammer dressing and grooving techniques were rarely found on the coast, but had a westerly distribution pattern. For both shaping techniques and lithologies the escarpment seemed to form a distinct barrier to movement.

Lithologies suitable for all techniques of modification exist in all regions (except perhaps the far west of the state) so cultural preferences must be reflected in these distribution patterns. Some lithologies lend themselves more readily to certain techniques than to others (flaking or hammer dressing for example); obviously the prehistoric craftsman would be aware of this, and make appropriate choice of material and method of manufacture. However the nature of the raw material cannot be invoked to explain the distribution of unifacial flaking as against bifacial on blade and pebble axes, nor the presence or absence of grooves on the blade of the axe.

The nature of raw material available for tool-making should also perhaps be considered as a possible determinant of assemblage variation in the excavated collections. Is the dominance of pebble tools in coastal sites merely the result of the vast quantities of cobbles available in beach and river deposits? Are the microlithic industries of the tablelands a response to scarcity of raw material or an abundance of fine grained silicious material suitable for the production of bladelets? These extreme forms of the argument cannot be sustained, in view of the distribution of suitable lithologies in the geology of the region in sufficient quantities to support either type of industry, and the abundant river cobbles available on the tablelands and slopes. There may however, be some factors relevant to our main argument, especially if we are concerned to isolate the influences attributable to fashion and cultural traditions alone.

In the excavated deposits of the Clarence valley two distinct ranges of raw material are exploited in the two main components of the assemblages, the flake and blade tools being made in cherts and chalcedonies, the pebble tools in greywackes obtained from the pebble beds of the major streams such as the Clarence. At Seelands the pebble tools of the earlier levels were made in a distinct range of mudstones and siltstones also available in the nearby gravel beds of the Clarence; but the change in level IIIA to the use of the greywackes did not produce any clear typological impact (see McBryde, 1974:247-48). The flake and blade tools of the upper series of levels at Seelands were made of banded chert imported from north of the Richmond River, yet this access to fine grained material did not lessen the dominance of the pebble tool in the assemblage, nor the decline in the importance of the backed blades (see Table 3).

For the small-tool dominated assemblages of the tablelands the fine grained cherts available in the region are obviously important, offering scope for the development of blade technologies, but in the granite areas the less amenable vein quartz is used, and at Graman an industry similar to that of Bendemeer is maintained in quartzite, with some use of locally available chalcedonies. That quartzite (less suitable for the production of backed blades than the fine cherts and chalcedonies) is the dominant raw material at these sites would seem to argue against interpreting such backed blade industries as the result of the craftsman putting local material to its most effective and economical use. At Graman Site A2 of the retouched pieces 60.1% are made of quartzite, 27.3% chalcedony, 5.4% quartz and 7.0% in other lithologies, while of the cores 66.6% are quartzite, 22.0% chalcedony. For Graman Site A7 a similar pattern prevails. Of retouched pieces 71.9% are quartzite, 17.5% chalcedony, 7.0% quartz and 3.5% other lithologies, while of the cores 66.6% are quartzite, 16.6% quartz and the same proportion also in chalcedony.

Another cultural factor relevant to assemblage patterning is the attitude of the people themselves to their tool-kits. Binford has discussed this on the basis of his work with a Nunamiut Eskimo group (Binford 1973:141-2), who took particular care of their tool-kits, maintaining them for future use, (even if this involved travel over long distances) especially those on which much care had been lavished in manufacture. The more 'fashionable' an item, the less likely was it to be discarded at a camp site. So camp site artifactual debris would reflect those tools considered expendable, not the activities or full cultural assemblages of the people using the site. The significance of such attitudes need not be laboured. They could also prove undetectable on archaeological evidence alone. In areas of Aboriginal Australia where raw materials were scarce, or multi-purpose tools used, one could envisage a similar impact on the resulting archaeological assemblages. Certainly complete ground-edge axes are rare in the assemblages being considered here; waste flakes with ground surfaces are often the only indication of their use and manufacture.

5. Archaeological investigation The factors discussed so far have all been concerned with the prehistoric peoples themselves, their environment, subsistence economy, activities and cultural traditions. One should also consider the 'human filter' through which the uncommitted archaeological evidence passes in both investigation, collection and interpretation. The choice of sites for investigation (particularly by excavation), the methods adopted, and the collecting techniques applied to the surface sites could all have an impact on the evidence recovered. So also could the placing of excavation trenches or test squares within the site, determining the nature of the sample recovered (cf. discussion of Graman Site B4, page 241). Assemblage variation between sites for which we have only limited samples based on test excavation could easily reflect this factor alone. To test the impact of varying activities within an individual site one could well argue that total excavation and full horizontal exposure of living floors is essential, a method rarely adopted by archaeologists with a care for the conservation of deposits for future investigation.

In the analysis of artifact collections the taxonomy employed may mask or reveal relationships between assemblages. That adopted here, primarily based on technological factors but also distinguishing on morphology, with some functional categories, is unsatisfactory for this very reason, and not internally consistent. The broader technological categories adopted by Clark (Clark 1964) and Kleindienst (Kleindienst 1961) in their studies of Acheulian assemblages are clear and consistent, and so appeal, but would not seem appropriate to the more highly patterned industries being considered here. We have already seen the problems facing the user of a purely functional classification, and the assumptions involved, unless there are the independent checks of micro-wear studies and experiment.

Statistical analysis

The discussion so far has offered comparison, and interpretations of similarity and difference between assemblages on archaeological grounds. These may often be largely intuitive involving a high degree of subjective judgment at all levels of the study and classification of the data. Some testing of these comparisons and interpretations, therefore, using statistical procedures for measuring similarity and difference, seemed advisable. Indeed it was advised by Professor Isaac in discussions at the conference, though one should remember here that statistical and archaeological significance need not be identical (cf. Wright 1974). Using the data given in Tables 2 and 3, Dr Dale, statistican of CSIRO Division of Tropical Agriculture, devised a series of programmes combining a classification based on the Canberra metric matrix of similarity, and ordination (also based on Canberra metric) which further examines the clustering of units derived from the classification and brings out its determinants. For comments on the Canberra metric and its features which make it highly appropriate for the study of archaeological assemblages see Sokal and Sneath (1973 : 125–26); for description of the procedures see Hartigan (1975, ch. 11.2). The 25 archaeological assemblages were matched against their components in two series of tests, one using

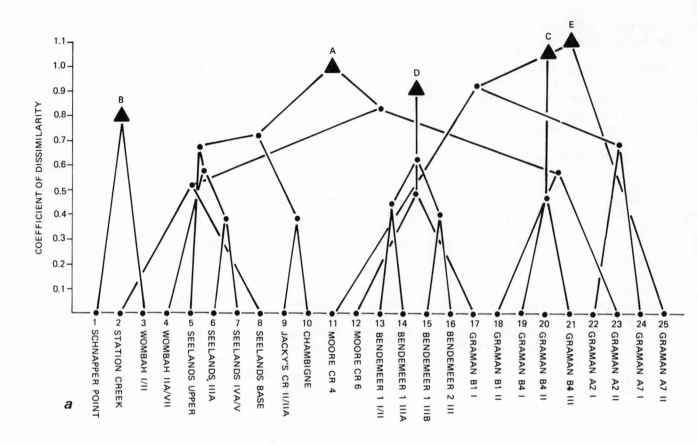

a

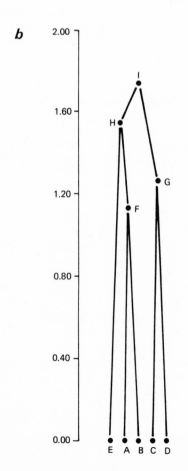

b

Fig. 4: Classification of assemblages using Canberra metric applied to the designed tools and utilised components only. The hierarchy of assemblages is created by matching pairs of most similar assemblages. The coefficient of dissimilarity is shown on the left. In Fig. 4b the five units established in Fig. 4a are further classified until they fuse into a hypothetical 'New England assemblage of the last 6000 years'.

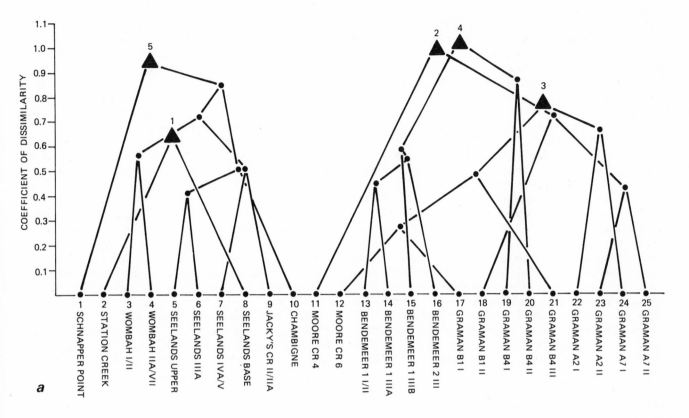

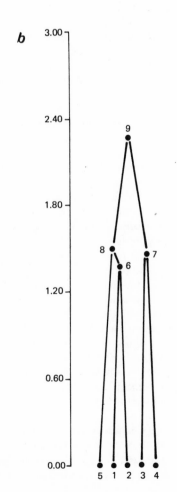

Fig. 5: Classification of assemblages using Canberra metric: in these two figures the same analyses are displayed as in Figs 4a and 4b, but applied to all components of the assemblages.

the designed tools and utilised elements in the assemblage, the other all elements. To these last were added, where applicable, data on the percentage of macropodid meat in the total meat weight represented by identifiable bone material. Traditionally, most comparisons of stone artifact assemblages are based purely on the morphologically distinct, typologically classifiable, elements of the assemblages, as are most 'cultural analyses' and tests of affiliation such as Bordes's use of cumulative percentage graphs.

It could be interesting to compare the ordering of the material that emerged from studies of the total artefact assemblages as well as of their more patterned elements. On the whole the major clusterings remained constant, but some interesting variations did emerge (compare Figs 4a and 4b with 5a and 5b).

Fig. 4a shows the classification of assemblages using the designed tool and utilised components. Classification was set at an arbitrary grouping into five units (1–5) building up a hierarchy of assemblages through a process of matching pairs of most similar assemblages using the Canberra metric. The scale at the left shows the dissimilarity level at the point of fusion of distinct sets to form a new unit. In Fig. 4b the further fusion of these clusters is shown, to the point at which they finally join into a hypothetical 'New England assemblage of the last 6000 years'.

Fig. 4a in its hierarchy of assemblages based on implement components, shows a clear division (similar to that argued on archaeological grounds, see pp. 225–29) between coastal and upland sites. Within these it forms two sets for coastal assemblages and three for the upland ones. Within the coastal assemblages the division is basal Seelands and Station Creek versus the rest. This linking of Station Creek and the lowest levels of Seelands is of interest, especially in relation to arguments on the importance of site function as against cultural change over time as determinants of variability between archaeological assemblages. In discussing the difference between the material from basal Seelands and that from the more recent levels of the site earlier in the paper I interpreted this as reflecting cultural change over time. The basal levels were seen as belonging to traditions pre-dating the impact of the introduction of the small tool tradition. The differences between the Seelands assemblages and that of Station Creek were seen as variability induced as the result of specific site function. The close linking of basal Seelands and Station Creek as a distinct sub-set on assessment of components by computer analysis makes re-argument of this position necessary. Could the undated Station Creek assemblages (derived from eroded dune deposits) be contemporaneous with those of base levels at Seelands—the similarity reflecting cultural affinities? On archaeological grounds the presence of ground-edge artifacts could be used as evidence for dates of post 4000 BP in this area of New England, though ground-edge tools have a high antiquity in other parts of Australia. The location of the site on dunes of the beach fore-dune system could also be used to support arguments for an age more recent than 6000 BP, the time at which the present coastline and its sea levels seem to have stabilised. The absence of backed blades in an assemblage of the age suggested is perhaps curious, yet backed blades are not dominant features in any coastal assemblage, and become less so in more modern sites; they are entirely absent also from the Moonee collections, even though one of these sites has dated remnant midden deposits contemporaneous with other coastal assemblages containing backed blades (see Table 1). For

these reasons I would prefer to interpret the similarity brought out so strongly in the statistical classification in terms of the impact of site function on assemblage composition rather than as betokening contemporaneity expressed in cultural affinity. It may be significant that the assemblage from Schnapper Point, another stone working site located in coastal dunes, only joins the other coastal assemblages at a relatively high level of dissimilarity (see Fig. 4a).

In the hierarchy of upland assemblages shown in Fig. 4a the grouping seems to reflect chronological status. As the linkages match roughly contemporaneous assemblages, and distinguish level sets within individual sites over time, I would interpret this as reflecting the operation of factors affecting most sites in the uplands, so suggesting little discrimination in site function within this group as a whole. Interestingly, in Fig. 4b we see one of the upland groups (2) fusing with a major coastal group (1) rather than with the other two upland sets.

In Fig. 5a classification of the assemblages based on all components is displayed; it shows less clear discrimination, together with a fusion of the upland and coastal sets at a lower level of dissimilarity. Within the coastal assemblages it is those from Schnapper Point and the upper levels of Wombah which form the distinct sub-set (B). Those from basal Seelands and Station Creek still match as a pair, but are subsumed in a larger set with the other coastal units. To these are joined (as A) assemblages from the lower levels of Graman B1 and Graman A2 (early upland assemblages— lower proportions of backed blades relevant?) The remaining upland assemblages form three distinct units (C, D, E) one of which (D) comprises the two Bendemeer sites (nos 13–16) plus Moore Creek 6 and level I of Graman B1—units that are all roughly contemporaneous. The three level units of Graman site B4 (19–21) form a distinct sub-set (C). That total assemblage analysis will not create a hierarchy identical to that based on the retouched and utilised elements of those assemblages is perhaps predictable. However, the correspondence is sufficiently close to suggest that analysis based on designed tools and utilised pieces when applied to relatively standardised assemblages such as those discussed here will create valid, sustainable distinctions. Whether the same could be said for less highly patterned industries is open to question.

The two groupings derived from the classification procedure (1–5 and A–E) were then subjected to ordination using all components of the total assemblage. The ordination is also derived from the Canberra metric and the procedure is numerically identical to a principal components analysis. It further examines the grouping, tests it, and gives an indication of its determinants. In Figs 6 and 7 the groups (1–5) according to classification on implement components are plotted on pairs of axes for vectors 1 and 2 and 1 and 3. This analysis sustains the distinctions of the classification and in the correlations between components and the major vectors (there were seven in all) picks out those which discriminate between assemblages. Figs 8 and 9 show the same plots for the groupings (A–E) derived from classification using total assemblages. In the ordination of assemblages grouped using designed tools and utilised elements the calculation of latent roots showed that vector 1 accounted for at least 25% of the variability. Correlations of the components with this axis indicate the following to be significant discriminators (they are listed in rank order of absolute values for the first ten from a correlation figure of 0.6269 to 0.3299): uniface pebble tools, use-polished edges, flakes from ground-edge tools,

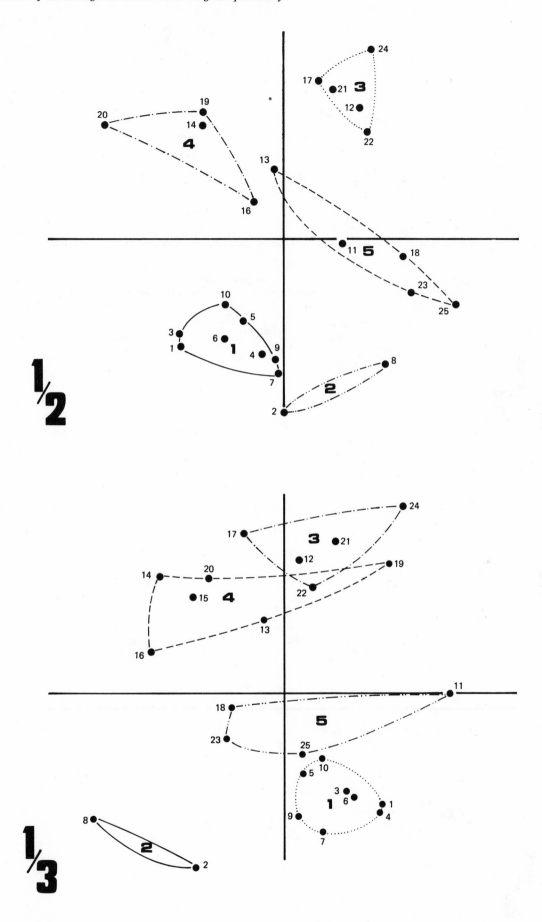

Figs 6 and 7: Ordination of assemblages: groups of assemblages (1–5—that is those units derived from classification using the designed tools and utilised components) are plotted on axes for vectors 1 and 2 and 1 and 3.

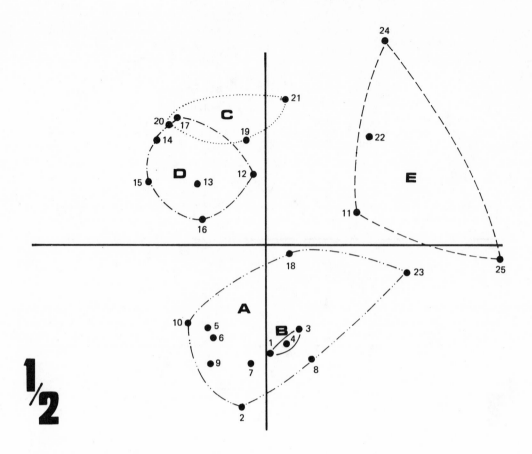

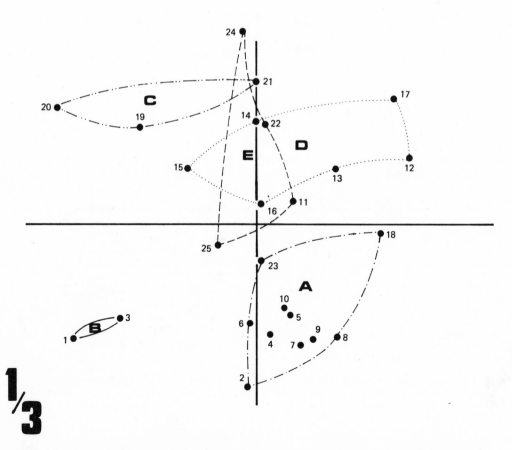

Figs 8 and 9: Ordination of assemblages: groups of assemblages (A–E—that is those units derived from classification using all components) are plotted on axes for vectors 1 and 2 and 1 and 3.

burins, backed blades, utilised flakes, cores, adze flakes, hammerstones, and core trimming flakes.

In the ordination of assemblage groupings derived from classification based on all components (A–E), vector 1 accounted for 17% of variability, and vector 2 for 12%. The ordination of assemblages plotted on the axes of vector 1. and 2, and 1 and 3 are shown in Figs 8 and 9. The attributes which correlate highly with vector 1 in this analysis (the top ten listed in decreasing absolute order from 0.6505 to 0.3552) are: uniface pebble tools, use-polished edges, flakes from ground-edge tools, backed blades, burins, utilised flakes, hammerstones, core trimming flakes, modified bone and cores.

In both sets of analyses the components which correlate most highly with the major determining axis include those which one would have selected on archaeological grounds as significant, indeed those stressed in earlier discussion. These are the uniface pebble tools, use-polished edges, backed blades, and edge-ground items. Others in the list might not have seemed so important without statistical analysis of this kind— modified bone, utilised flakes, core trimming flakes. The importance of burins, common elements in upland assemblages but not of coastal ones, is re-inforced by this study. In both sets of ordination the major determinants show little variation and are primarily found in the patterned elements of the assemblage. However this may be the result of masking induced by the lack of categorisation within the large group of the 'waste' elements of the total assemblage.

Conclusion

The fact of assemblage variation in northern New South Wales is clear, in the exclusive distribution patterns of some artifact types and in the variation of the relative frequency with which certain components are represented in assemblages as a whole. In this paper the data have been considered very simply in comparison of the differing proportion within assemblages as a whole. Further interesting variations might come from application of tests of co-variance and correlation (see Isaac 1972). Such analysis could well also hint at new explanatory hypotheses to be explored.

The variation documented so far in my analysis has two forms, a major variation in the nature of the complete assemblage which conforms to the major environmental dichotomy in the region between coast and tableland; within each region there are further variations of a less substantial kind, but none the less of statistical validity. To understand the prehistory of the region these variations must be explained; in this paper various possible hypotheses have been matched against the available evidence. For none have we found a complete 'fit', though those based on environmental and economic factors seemed the more satisfactory. However this area is one in which the prehistorian may most clearly define and test his hypotheses; the impact of the less tangible factors of the craftsman's traditions and preferences, and tribal lore, may be less amenable to either proof or disproof. We seem to have two major adaptive situations corresponding to two major environmental regions, each with its sub-strata of economic adaptation, for example the seasonality in the subsistence economy of the Clarence valley, and the extensive gathering of seed food in the Graman area of the upland zone. These economic adaptations are reflected in the artifact assemblages. However in any adaptive situation the resulting response is created of the interplay of environmental and economic factors with cultural ones, in the traditions, preferences and capacities of the human societies involved. The first group of factors may be the more clearly documented and their impact, quantified and tested against archaeological evidence, but the other, though intangible and having its impact on the human mind, should not therefore be discounted. The two major assemblage types share many elements, and it would perhaps be inappropriate to refer to them as two 'culture-provinces' when the ethnographic record shows that we are concerned with two groups of the same 'people'. Yet the distinctions are none the less substantial, and are found in aspects of the region's culture other than artifact assemblages, such as rock art and language. The development of two such distinct adaptations in adjacent regions should probably be interpreted in environmental terms, the steep escarpment of the plateau on the east and its stretch of relatively poor high country, encouraging the isolation of the two populations in the richer areas to east and west.

Acknowledgements Many institutions supported the programme of archaeological research discussed in this paper, and I have pleasure in acknowledging my debt to the Australian Institute of Aboriginal Studies, the Australian Social Science Research Council, the Nuffield Foundation, the Australian Research Grants Committee, the University of New England and the Australian National University. Thanks are due to Dr M. Dale of CSIRO for conducting the statistical analyses presented here and to Dr. Chant of the Australian National University.

References

A Lady (Mrs McPherson), 1860. *My experiences in Australia*. London: J.F. Hope.

Allen, H.R., 1968. Western plain and eastern hill. B.A. thesis, University of Sydney.

Belshaw, J. (in press). Aboriginal population in northern New South Wales: distribution, density and seasonal movement. In *Records of times past*, I. McBryde (ed.). Canberra: Australian Institute of Aboriginal Studies.

Binford, L.R., 1972. Contemporary model building: paradigms and the current state of Palaeolithic research. In *Models in archaeology*, D.L. Clarke (ed.) pp. 109-66. London: Methuen.

——1973. Interassemblage variability—the Mousterian and the 'functional' argument. In *The explanation of culture change*, C. Renfrew (ed.) pp. 227-54. London: Duckworth.

——and S. R. Binford, 1966. A preliminary analysis of functional variability in the Mousterian of Lavallois facies. In *Recent studies in palaeoanthropology*, Special publication *American Anthropologist*, 68(2): 238-95.

Binns, R.A. and I. McBryde, 1972. *A petrological analysis of ground-edge artefacts from northern New South Wales*. Canberra: Australian Institute of Aboriginal Studies.

Bordes, F., 1973. On the chronology and contemporaneity of different palaeolithic cultures in France. In *The explanation of culture change*, C. Renfrew (ed.), pp. 217-26. London: Duckworth.

—— and D. de Sonneville-Bordes, 1970. The significance of variability in Palaeolithic assemblages. *World Archaeology*, 2(1):61-73.

Bowdler, S., 1970. *Bass Point: the excavation of a south-east Australian shell-midden showing cultural and economic change*. B.A. (Hons) thesis, University of Sydney.

Clark, J.D., 1964. The influence of environment in inducing culture change at the Kalambo Falls prehistoric site. *South African Archaeological Bulletin*, 19(76): 93-101.

Clarke, D.L., 1972. *Models in archaeology*. London: Methuen.

Cunningham, A. 1828. The late tour of Allan Cunningham, esq. *Australian Quarterly Journal*, April:65-85, 151-189.

Gardner, W. 1842-1854. *Productions and resources of the northern and western districts of New South Wales*. Two volume manuscript in the Mitchell Library, Sydney.

Greenway, C.C., 1910. Kamilari Tribes. *Science of Man*, XII(1):15-16.

Hartigan, J. A., 1975. *Clustering algorithms*. New York: J. Wiley and Sons.

Isaac, G.L., 1972. Early phases of human behaviour: models in Lower Palaeolithic archaeology. In *Models in archaeology*, D.L. Clarke (ed.), pp. 167-99. London: Methuen.

Kamminga, J., 1974. Report on the edge wear on stone tools from the Clarence River sites. In *Aboriginal prehistory in New England*, I. McBryde. Sydney: Sydney University Press.

Kleindienst, M.R., 1961. Variability within the Late Acheulian assemblage in eastern Africa. *South African Archaeological Bulletin*, 16:35-52.

McBryde, I., 1966. Radiocarbon dates for northern New South Wales. *Antiquity*, XL:285-92.

—— 1968. Archaeological investigations in the Graman District. *Archaeology and Physical·Anthropology in Oceania*, III(2):77-93.

—— 1974. *Aboriginal prehistory in New England*. Sydney: Sydney University Press.

—— (ed.) (in press). *Records of times past*. Canberra: Australian Institute of Aboriginal Studies.

McCarthy, F.D., 1964. The archaeology of the Capertee Valley, New South Wales. *Records of the Australian Museum*, 26:197-246.

Massola, A., 1965. Australian fish hooks and their distribution *Memoirs of the National Museum of Victoria*, 22(1):1-16.

Mellars, P., 1970. Some comments on the notion of 'functional variability' in stone-tool assemblages. *World Archaeology*, 2(1):74-98.

Moore, D.R., 1970. Results of an archaeological survey of the Hunter River valley, New South Wales. *Records of the Australian Museum*, 28(2):25-64.

Pearson, M., 1973. *The Macintyre Valley: field archaeology and ethnohistory*. B.A. thesis, University of New England.

Pierce, R.G., 1971. *The effects of aquatic foods on the diet and economy of the Aborigines on the North Coast of New South Wales at the time of first settlement*. B.A. thesis, University of New England.

Renfrew, C., (ed.) 1973. *The explanation of culture change*. London: Duckworth.

Ridley, W., 1875. *Kamilaroi and other Australian languages*. Sydney: T. Richards, Government Printer.

Sokal, R. and P.H.A. Sneath, 1973. *Numerical taxonomy*. San Francisco and London: W. H. Freeman.

Wright, R.V.S., 1974. Significance tests and archaeological importance. *Mankind*, 9(3) : 169-74.

Wyndham, W.T., 1972. Letters in *Tide of Time*. Inverell: Inverell Historical Society.

The use of stone tools to map patterns of diffusion

FREDERICK D. McCARTHY

Any attempt to map patterns of diffusion in Australia based on the distribution of stone implements is handicapped by the lack of several vital kinds of data such as distribution maps of all Aboriginal culture traits, gaps in our knowledge of barter and gift exchange routes in many areas, insufficient data from excavations, and too few or no radiocarbon dates from vast regions of the continent. The areas of local variation that I distinguished (1940b : 250–54), and also the art regions (McCarthy, 1938; Davidson, 1937b : 133–37; Elkin, 1964 : 263–74) must remain approximations until deeper analysis based upon adequate distributional data is available. In this paper I shall discuss and reconsider much of what I have written in earlier papers on the diffusion of stone implements into and within Australia, and the part played by them both as separate items and as an ingredient of culture diffusion patterns. In this exploratory paper I shall deal also with the diffusion of the material culture, social, religious and other items into Australia only where it is relevant to stone implements, as the conference is not concerned with diffusion generally. A pertinent aspect of the subject, however, is the relationship of excavated assemblages of stone (bone and shell) implements to the local environment and to the regional culture of the locality.

In this study we are not concerned with the wider implications of topographical archaeology stressed by Hallam (1972). We are confined here to diffusion of stone implements, separately or in assemblages, still a speculative field in which trends of thought and opinion need to change as more precise data become available. Matthews's study (1966) of uniface pebble implements brought to the fore the importance of the statistical factor in the spatial relationship of stone implements, and Mulvaney (1971b : 242) pointed out that facile typological comparisons can raise more problems than they solve without supporting metrical or other quantitative studies of the tools concerned. A proper understanding of diffusion, just as of environmental determinism, parallelism and invention, is essential to the unravelling of the history and development of Aboriginal culture as a whole. For this reason, its review and further exploration are justified from time to time, and a flexibility of mind is needed to keep abreast of the evidence.

Three key matters in the study of diffusion are relevant to Australia. One is local elaboration of a trait—now generally recognised as a common feature of Aboriginal culture well demonstrated by rock paintings—the use of pecking to shape stone implements, and the complexity of linear art designs in central and south-eastern Australia. Another factor of vital importance in Australia is barter and gift exchange, and the exchange of ideas at social and ritual gatherings of Aborigines, all of which facilitate the spread of new techniques, artifacts and beliefs.

A third one is the use of distributional maps whose value was demonstrated by Davidson (1933–57), but faulty use of them was also revealed in his rigid interpretation of the geographical distribution theory. This and other criticisms of distribution maps can be overcome by an intelligent and accurate interpretation of the data. Davidson's maps (1937b) of art motifs revealed a situation common in Aboriginal culture, that of the overlapping of their distribution, indicating that there had been a considerable shifting of design boundaries in the past, resulting in the breaking up of the continuous distribution of some motifs by the spread of others, a situation characteristic also of stone implements in Australia.

Through the aid of radiocarbon dating, various excavations have shown that a long period of human adaptation and spatial expansion took place in Australia from approximately 40 000 to 6500–7000 years ago, although the latter date varies by a thousand years or so in different localities. Associated with this early era were ground-edge axes in northern Australia at least (C. White, 1967; J. P. White, 1971). It was a comparatively static period culturally, characterised by the Australian Core and Flake Tradition, an extension of the chopper-chopping tool zone of Southeast Asia (Allchin, 1966 : 166; J. P. White, 1971 : 8). Our knowledge of this colonising period is as yet too limited to discuss patterns of diffusion.

Writers in the past have advanced a varying range of ideas about diffusion into Australia, mostly from New Guinea via Cape York, with the fishermen and gatherers of the Torres Strait islands acting as the intermediate transmitters. These writers include Graebner (1905, 1913) who defined strata or levels of culture and claimed that traits from western Papua formed an ancient diffusion into the extreme west of the continent followed by a later group from eastern Papua. Elliot-Smith (1930 : 128; 1933 : 129) contended that the Aborigines received practically every element of their culture from abroad in relatively recent times. Rivers (1926) believed that similarities between the methods of disposing of the dead in Australia and Melanesia were the result of diffusion from Melanesia. A number of other writers who have discussed various aspects of this subject and itemised introduced traits include Frobenius (1901), Haddon (1920, 1935), Hamlyn-Harris (1915, 1917), Thorpe (1924) and Thomson (1933, 1952). Stone implements were not dealt with specifically in any of these studies. Mulvaney (1961 : 100) stated that:

> The pattern of Australian contact with the outside world was a constant one from the Pleistocene epoch to the age of the Dutch explorers, with Indonesia and New Guinea probably providing the corridors of entry in every instance. Each succeeding wave of migrants, or visitors, probably contributed something to Aboriginal social and material culture. But the relatively insignificant permanent manifestations of Macassan and Dutch visitations are probably a true reflection of the conservatism of tribal society.

This view I believe, underestimates the results of contact, as the dugout canoe (with sail) and the harpoon derived from the Macassans in Arnhem Land, and from the Torres Strait islanders in Cape York, are outstanding permanent additions among other traits added to the culture of the Aborigines in these regions.

Davidson was one of the few culture historians who carried out fieldwork among the Aborigines in Australia. In his long series of papers, from 1933 to 1957, he had two aims in view: to reveal links between Australian, Melanesian and Indonesian cultures, and at the same time to demonstrate the importance of local development and variation of traits in Australia. In my own studies (1940a, 1949, 1953, 1957, 1974) I have stressed a wide range of factors involved in the development of Aboriginal culture as we know it today—local variation or elaboration, invention, material, conservatism, traditional preference, substitution, environmental resources, trade and diffusion—and I regard diffusion as a factor of vital importance, both into and within Australia, in this development. Tindale (1957, 1967) linked certain stone implement types with the separate migrations of the Negritic Barrineans, Murrayians and Carpentarians into Australia, and his lower Murray River assemblages with waves of migratory Aborigines.

Stone implement assemblages and other aspects of culture

Most of the contemporary writing on Aboriginal culture development has been in the ethno-archaeology field. The linguists have found little or nothing outside Australia with which to link Aboriginal languages, but a great deal of intriguing material has come to light on dialect and language development, interaction and relationship within Australia. There was a constant spreading from group to group of sections and sub-sections (Elkin, 1938 : 421 map), and of initiation ordeals, corroborees and songs independent of stone implements. An aspect of diffusion not yet explored is the importance of ancestral spirit beings as a factor. Thus the Little Hawk Men introduced the stone knife for circumcision into central Australia, the Mungan Brothers from Bagadjimbiri likewise into north-western Australia (McCarthy, 1962), the Mother-goddess, Waramurugundji, into Arnhem Land (Berndt and Berndt, 1964 : 210) and many more of these spirit beings could probably be listed in the spreading of the use of a stone knife for circumcision and subincision. The Berndts (1964 : 207–14) have described the travels of a number of these beings in Arnhem Land: the Kunapipi cult spread into and through some 35 tribal groups in the Northern Territory and Arnhem Land region from the Roper River; Waramuru-gundji came over the sea from the northwest, from the direction of Indonesia, into western Arnhem Land and, in some versions of the myth, disappeared eastward; the Djunggawul Sisters and their brother came across the Gulf of Carpentaria from the north-east, pausing on Bralgu Island, following the path of the rising sun until they landed on the east coast of Arnhem Land between Yirrkala and Port Bradshaw; the Wawalag Sisters journeyed from the Roper River into northern Arnhem Land. A number of writers have described the journeys of the numerous ancestral beings and clan spirits in central Australia and the Western Desert, among whom Wadi Gudjara wandered across the whole of the Gibson and Western deserts, passing through dozens of local group territories and covering possibly some 25–30 dialect or language units (Berndt and Berndt, 1964 : 200). Ngurunderi

in his bark canoe chased a huge cod fish down the Darling River to the lower Murray River, Sara travelled down the west coast of Cape York, and some of the Wondjina in the northern Kimberleys came out of the sea. The Berndts' succinct summary (1964 : 201) of their functions is worth quoting:

> The majority of religious myths have as their framework the wanderings and activities of various beings. Usually such characters are not confined to one area. From the point of view of any one group of people, most of them came from somewhere else, or went off somewhere else, or both. They moved along the waterhole routes or rivers or across country from one place to the next, performing such actions at each place: putting water there, meeting other spirits, creating people or other living things, making natural features such as rocks or hollows, naming them, instituting rites, singing songs, and so on. These 'Dreaming' tracks stretch in all directions. If the situation we find in such places as the Great Victoria Desert and Western Desert, through the mountainous core of Central Australia and up the Canning Stock Route to the Eastern Kimberleys, in the Victoria River area and across the Northern Territory to Arnhem Land is any guide, hundreds of such tracks criss-crossed one another right throughout the continent, representing, at least potentially, a network of communication.

The importance of the latter point is emphasised when it is considered that persons who belong to one track are normally friendly to one another, and are free and safe when travelling along the path of their totemic hero and heroes (Elkin, 1934 : 174).

Insofar as stone implements are concerned the most relevant functions of these spirit beings were to spread the customs of circumcision and subincision with a stone knife, and to establish quarries for axes, grindstones and other implements. A detailed analysis of their myths, and plotting of their journeys, might uncover associations with various types of implements but data on their journeys and activities are not available from many parts of the continent. It is probable that the functions of many of these beings, especially the clan spirits, were limited and not added to over time, and their journeys do not always indicate patterns of diffusion, but the routes of some of the greater beings with more generalised functions might now form the basis of these patterns. There is no creator hero known to me who travelled from Arnhem Land or Cape York to the south coast of Australia carrying a major culture complex. There is a great sky hero, Baiami, in south-eastern Australia who created the Aborigines and the whole of their world, but he appears to represent a concept (because he has so many different names and lived in the sky world) rather than a migrating spirit being.

The practice of bands of natives following the sacred path of an ancestral spirit being to a stone quarry or ochre deposit, thus establishing a regular trade route, is a feature of Aboriginal economic life. Detailed studies of quarries and the distribution of stone implements derived from them, combined with petrological analysis, on the lines of Binns and McBryde's study (1972) should reveal to what extent they have become the basis of patterns of diffusion.

Art and prehistoric assemblages

There is of course the possibility of some correlation between stone implement assemblages and art, but the situation generally is confusing. In coastal New South Wales there are three phases in the Eastern Regional Sequence, four in the rock paintings, and one in the rock engravings; there is also a linear decorative art on the wooden shields and lil-lil clubs, and on the carved trees (west of the mountains) which differs from the rock art. It is important to note that the Bondaian phase extends right through southern Australia up into north-western Australia, and that the same type of outline engravings also occur in the latter region. Whether any correlation exists between the concentric circle and U art complex, and the tula phase of the Inland Regional Sequence is uncertain, but excavations in the central and western Australian regions in the future may throw light on this problem; there is a close relationship between these two traits today in central Australia, at least, but their origins may or may not have been linked. In the Kimberleys two phases of rock paintings are known but both the later Wondjina and symmetrical unifacial and bifacial points belong to the living culture, and their association in origin cannot be disregarded. Arnhem Land, also, has had several phases of rock paintings, and two phases (Oenpellian I and II) in its prehistory, with an added and comparatively recent superimposition of Macassan and European influences in both the art and its prehistory; there are, too, notable local variations in the art between western and eastern Arnhem Land and the adjacent islands. The correlation of art and prehistoric assemblages is too complex to discuss here, and much more data is required to elucidate its various aspects.

The ritual and ceremonial gatherings of Aborigines, and feasts such as the Bunya Bunya pine seeds in Queensland and the Bogong moth in New South Wales offered excellent opportunities for culture diffusion, but unfortunately precise information about who attended them is not available and it is not possible to work out any patterns. It is interesting to note that the medicine-men in south-eastern Australia actually demonstrated their methods to one another during ceremonial gatherings, especially those of the Bora type, and other techniques and customs were no doubt discussed and passed on on these occasions.

Stone implements and trade

Trade or barter and gift exchange routes are generally recognised as avenues of diffusion. They were often well defined and named. Items traditionally made or supplied by a group, or received by them from elsewhere, were bartered or given in gift exchange between the trading groups. In evaluating the *merbok* gift exchange system Stanner (1933) said that cultural influences of many kinds spread from tribe to tribe through such linkages as those formed by *merbok*, which is *par excellence* the medium of material culture transmission; all sorts of artifacts of foreign manufacture and materials of foreign origin come in *merbok* to each tribe, and they are the highroads of culture influence in myth and ceremonial life. A new kinship system and an associated matrilineal sub-section system came to one Daly River tribe in recent years, he said, along one route. Kaberry (1939) recorded a similar two-way gift exchange organisation between groups in the eastern Kimberleys. Out of six named ceremonial trading expeditions focused on Oenpelli described by the Berndts (1964 : 116, fig. 9) stone implements were exchanged in three of them.

I have extracted the following data on stone implements from my monograph on Aboriginal trade, and though it is not complete I would point out that data of this kind is surprisingly scanty in the literature (McCarthy, 1939–40).

Ground-edge axes In Victoria stone from the Mt William quarries was used in an extensive region of the state, west to the lower Murray River and north into New South Wales (p. 407); the Wudjubalug obtained stone from a quarry on Charlotte Plains (p. 407), and another quarry existed in the Kilmore district (p. 407). In New South Wales the Nepean River at Castlereagh was a source of pebbles for axes eastward to the coast (p. 409); porphyry blanks from Mts Harris and Foster travelled up to 100 miles north to Brewarrina and east to the Bogan River, stone from the Barrier Ranges was traded to Menindee and elsewhere, and axes passed down the Paroo River to Wilcannia (p. 409); Binns and McBryde have since (1972) recorded the spread of axes hundreds of miles westward into far western New South Wales from north-eastern New South Wales, and their wide distribution in the latter region from local quarries. In South Australia Horne and Aiston (1942) said that axe-heads either from Queensland beyond Cloncurry, or from the coastal tribes in the south, were traded at Kopperamanna to the Lake Eyre tribes; they were oval or circular in shape, carefully pitted in part or all over, and came from Queensland. After a flood in the Diamantina River, the blacks would travel south to meet the tribes from the lower Diamantina and Cooper's Creek (pp. 423–25); axes from the Mt Isa–Cloncurry area in Queensland were traded southward through south-western Queensland into north-eastern South Australia on a major trunk route along which many other items travelled north or south, the principal ones being Parachilna red ochre from the south and *pitjuri* from the Mulligan River in the north. Tindale said that axes were brought down from the north in exchange for red ochre from Parachilna Gorge, but they also occasionally came along a well defined route from Lake Hindmarsh north-east through the Pinnaroo country to the vicinity of Mannum and Tailem Bend, and stone axes from Victoria travelled north-west from the Glenelg River to the Coorong (p. 427); Basedow (1932) stated that the Dieri, Nangganguru, Ngamini and other Cooper's Creek tribes obtain all their stone axe-heads from New South Wales, while the Luridja, Guyani, Arabana and Gugada were regularly supplied from the Macdonell Ranges and from Queensland through Aranda agency (p. 430). Axes were included in the Daly River exchange system of *merbok* (p. 431); Elkin said the eastern Nyul Nyul natives went to an axe stone quarry at Mangil, trading pearl shell, shell beads, boomerangs and hardwood spears for axes, spearheads, ochre, and bamboo spears (p. 435); axes from the lower Drysdale River were passed along a regular route to the Forrest River (p. 436).

Grindstones In western New South Wales the Darling River natives traded stone slabs southwards to the Mara Mara in Victoria (p. 407); in Queensland the slabs from Walaya and the Toko ranges were traded through Carandotta to tribes in and north of the Leichhardt-Selwyn Ranges, and through Roxburgh down the Georgina River, branching off at Glenormiston for Carlo and the upper Mulligan River, and at Herbert Downs for Boulia, Springvale, and the middle Diamantina River; they reached the Bida-bida, Janda, Majula, Galgadung, Maidhargari and other tribes in the Georgina-Daimantina rivers area (pp. 415–16); and were bartered between the Flinders and Endeavour rivers tribes in north-eastern Queensland (p. 418). In south Australia the Jandruwunda passed on stone slabs which they obtained from the south to their neighbours higher up Cooper's Creek (p. 423); tribesmen from the south and west, and from the Flinders Ranges, took grindstones to the trading centre at Kopperamanna (pp. 423–25); Howitt reported that the Jandruwunda travelled 300 miles to get these grindstones and red ochre from Parachilna (p. 87) and Aiston said men from the William Creek trade route carried slabs on their heads.

Leilira blade In western Queensland Roth said quarries for these blades existed along the heads of the Burke and Wills River, Lawn Hills, headwaters of the Georgina River and in the ranges east and west of the latter; from the upper Georgina and Selwyn Ranges the completed knife was bartered and exchanged (a) across to Cloncurry and upper Flinders River, (b) to the middle Diamantina River via Noranside, Boulia and Marion Downs, or via Springvale, and (c) to the upper Diamantina via Kynuna; they reached the Bida-bida, Janda, Majula, Galgadun, Maidhargari and other tribes in the Diamantina–Georgina area (pp. 415–16). The Jaroinga of the upper Georgina district obtained stone knives from the Wagaja at Lake Nash, Austral Downs and Camooweal which they passed on to the Andagerebina of the Toko Ranges, and to the Galgadung and other tribes. Roth also said there was a large import of knives with decorated wooden handles from the Northern Territory southwards into Queensland (pp. 421–22). In the Northern Territory Spencer said the knives were traded widely by the Naramanga, Bingongina and other northern tribes among whom a stone-headed spear was occasionally seen (p. 430). Stone knives formed part of the Daly River *merbok* exchange system; Thomson (1949) has since recorded an extensive trade in them from the quarry on the upper Walker River in eastern Arnhem Land, and even today parcels of them pass from one mission group to another.

Another type of knife, called *Jeemari*, used in initiation, was obtained from a quarry at Lake Way, east of Meekatharra, and traded to the south and north in Western Australia, according to Daisy Bates.

Spearheads In Queensland quartz-tipped spears were bartered by the Maidhargari to the Galgadung in the Grenada district, according to Roth (p. 411); they were also traded by groups in the area between the Flinders and Endeavour Rivers (p. 418); stone-tipped spears seen at Camooweal came from the north and west (p. 411). In north-eastern Arnhem Land the Ridarngu and Djinba traded stone spearheads to the sea coast tribes. In the Kimberleys the eastern Nyul Nyul obtained them from a group at Mangil, the route passing through Yeeda and the lower Fitzroy River (p. 435).

General

Daisy Bates recorded that in drought times hundreds of Aborigines gathered at Ooldea Water, South Australia, some from afar, who offered their flints etc. for the right to share the water and live (p. 167); Roth observed that boomerangs, stone knives, unhafted adzes or pot-lid flakes, shields and spears were common objects of barter, whilst hafted adzes and clubs were not bartered (p. 173); the prepared pot-lids ready for fixation in the hafted gouge, he said, were always being traded, one line being from Camooweal to the Georgina River (p. 414). The Gan-ganda on the Stewart River, Cape York, obtained stone from Coen, 40 miles away, as there was none in their country.

Several important points are revealed in this scanty data. One is the vast distances over which stone implements, even the heavy grindstones, were traded; another is the comparative rapidity with which artifacts could travel, and a third is the systematic organisation of the barter and exchange systems along traditional routes and between traditional groups and individuals. The trade in parcels of pot-lid tulas in Queensland, and of leilira blades in Arnhem Land, partly explains the

occurrence of such large numbers of specialised implements on surface sites throughout Australia; the bartering of Kimberley bifacial points is well known, and one could suggest a similar trade in parcels of Bondi points and geometric microliths when they were in use. Another query raised is the need for and frequency of invention when artifacts were available on a regular basis from other sources by trade.

Diffusion of cultural units

The Archaic culture brought here by the ancestors of the Aborigines when they arrived on Sahul Land 40 000 or more years ago is the only example known at present of the introduction of a total culture into Australia. It is generally believed to have been somewhat similar to that of the Tasmanians. In its archaeological aspect, the Australian core and flake tool tradition, it varies considerably in different parts of Australia, various facies of it having been revealed in a number of excavations, but the pattern of its spread on the continent has not yet been worked out.

Australian small tool and symmetrical point traditions

A second example, but a disputed one, of a culture complex coming into Australia, is that of the Australian small tool tradition, now thought by a number of contemporary archaeologists to have been brought by sea from Indonesia some 7000 years ago to north-western Australia whence it spread widely over the continent (McCarthy, 1940b, 1974; Casey, 1940 : 29; Allchin, 1966 : 170; Glover, 1967 : 425; Jones, 1968 : 190; Golson, 1971a, b). Various traits have been linked with it. Macintosh (1971 : 57) stated that 'there is evidence to suggest that a whole series of innovations in Aboriginal Australia may have been linked items in a new cultural complex, of which the rapid diffusion of a revolution in stone technology is the only item objectively identified by stratigraphy and radiocarbon dating as having its beginning as early as 7000 years ago and certainly by 5000 years ago. This period saw the inclusion of the dingo into Aboriginal mythology, introduction of pecking technique in rock engravings and of subincision as an addition to circumcision, ritual tooth avulsion as a possible alternative to ritual subincision, cult heroes replacing sky gods, and *pari passu* with innovations a phasing out of more archaic items such as mythology and ritual related to Sarcophilus'. Golson associated the introduction of the spearthrower and dingo with this tradition, and I linked the linear design rock engravings with it.

Davidson (1938) rejected claims for the introduction on the north-western coast of the pressure flaked stone spear points, meander art design, Wondjina cave paintings, bark buckets and decorated pearl shells as outstanding culture traits of this region, although he subsequently admitted diffusion from Indonesia of the meander art design and the thread cross (1951) into this region. He stated that as yet we have no specific evidence to demonstrate that non-Australians have ever settled in the north-western portion of Australia or exerted any noticeable cultural influence upon the Aborigines there. He described three foreign polished stone adze blades found in Western Australia which he presumed to have come from Indonesia by chance historic or prehistoric contacts (1938b : 44, fig. 3). Noone (1943 : 280; 1950 : 2) believed that the Australian small tool tradition is indigenous in Australia. On the other hand, Mulvaney (1969 : 127), and Mulvaney and

Soejono (1970 : 29, 32) expressed caution in arriving at a decision in this matter, on the grounds that it could have originated in more than one place of which Australia was one, and on the basis of the Indonesian occurrences 'it is premature to leap from morphological comparison to diffusionist inference'. But Mulvaney (1969 : 164) admitted the possibility of diffusion when he stated that

> Prehistorians of Australia must look toward south-east Asia for the origins of their people and culture. The differential components of industries at Kenniff, Kangaroo island and Ingaladdi might be explained by ideas (or prototypes) transmitted from different points of origin (Sulawesi? Java?), by people at a basically similar technological level. Is it coincidence that parallels for many inventive phase tools occur in later prehistoric Indonesia? Is it significant that it was only in the last few thousand years that implements (and ideas) diffused on an almost global scale?

Thus the origin of the Australian small tool tradition so far as Australia is concerned is a lively controversy. Points and geometric microliths are widespread on the continent and form diagnostic assemblages in many recent excavations. As two point types are involved, the matter is worthy of further consideration here. Mulvaney (1969 : 116–19) has already drawn attention to the varied distributions of the Bondi point, unifacial and bifacial points, and the geometric microliths. On present evidence, sadly deficient in an adequate knowledge of Western Australian implements in this context, the backed blade-geometric microlith complex occurs further to the west in Western Australia than the symmetrical unifacial and bifacial points of the Kimberley–Arnhem Land region, where to my knowledge backed blades do not occur. The two traditions appear to be separated in the north-west by the desert, which extends to the coast, and they need to be separated in origin. We do not know with which tradition, if either, the dingo (with a supposed antiquity at Mt Burr, South Australia, of 8000 years) or any of the other traits mentioned above were associated, and probably never will as so few of them can be dated by radiocarbon. It is of interest, therefore, to outline briefly one's ideas about the spread of these two implement series in Australia.

The backed blade series, constituting the Australian small tool tradition, was collected on Millstream Station, on the Fortescue River, by Newall (Glover, 1967), at several widely scattered sites in the interior of Western Australia, and in south-western Australia (Butler, 1958; Hallam, 1972), but has not been found north of the 20°S parallel. The implements occur in their greatest density in the eastern half of New South Wales, and in Victoria and South Australia. The vast gaps in this distribution pattern are obvious, and form a weakness in the diffusionists' case at present. Mulvaney (1969 : 124) thought that these implements form a cultural continuum stretching from the north-west of the continent across to Lake Eyre and the south-east. The assemblage is radiocarbon dated from recent times back to almost 6000 years in New South Wales and Victoria. According to Hallam (1972 : 17) dates from south-western Australia show a backed blade tradition extant before 1000 BC, continuing with relatively little change right up to European contact; the dates, in her opinion, neither confirm nor controvert the possibility that the 'small tool' cultures might have been initiated much earlier by contact on the western side of the continent, and she suggested that her early middle phase, when backed blades appear, started perhaps as early as 5000 BC. There are no dates as yet for them from north-western Australia, a crucial region if a chain or pattern of diffusion from India to south-eastern Australia is to be confirmed.

Backed blades have been recorded in south-west Sulawesi and west Java in Indonesia (Sarasin, 1905, pl. 1; McCarthy, 1940b : 39–40; Mulvaney and Soejono 1970 : 27–28, 31), but not in the Timor archipelago, New Guinea or south-east Asia (Golson, 1971b : 9). They occur in great abundance, with elouera, in India and Ceylon. Golson (1971b : 9) believes that there is no evidence in Australia for the gestation of this new technology within the womb of the old (industries), and we may conclude that if the prototypes of the tradition were brought by sea from outside, the number of immigrants must have been very small; further, that we must think of its widespread adoption in Australia as a matter of the diffusion of an idea adding to the existing stock and not one of replacement of populations. Mulvaney and Joyce (1965 : 209–10) suggested migration, diffusion and local invention as possible causes of the origin of this technology in Australia. J. P. White (1971) drew attention to the reasonably long-term and casual contact between north-western Australia and the northern agricultural regions, and suggested that bearers of the root-crop type of agriculture during the early phases of its spread into the island world north of Australia touched upon parts of the north-western Australian coast, where they failed to establish their new economy for various reasons but left two important additions to Aboriginal culture, microliths and the dingo. The important point is of course that watercraft were probably comparatively well developed in this island world by 7000 years ago, as Aborigines had travelled over the sea to reach Australia some 40 000 years ago.

The abundant small tool industries in India and Ceylon are worthy of more attention by Australian prehistorians although they raise the problem of discontinuous distribution between India and Australia. The range of Bondi points and geometric microliths is identical in both countries, and the elouera occurs with them. The collection made on one of the Indian sites by Dr Judy Birmingham some years ago could have been dropped on any of our south-eastern coastal sites and not distinguished from the local specimens in the same materials. Allchin's description (1966) of the late Stone Age backed blade industries of India and Ceylon also revealed that they are commonly associated with paintings in rock shelters in central India and Ceylon. Their use continued until the fourth century BC, possibly later when the Iron Age was well advanced. The sites occur commonly on high ground overlooking plains and valleys where the people could observe game, enjoy the cool air and avoid mosquitoes, but sites also occur on plains, and along the coast and banks of streams in a great variety of climates and environments. The industries, in Dr Birmingham's opinion, belong to a hunter-gatherer people, who used the bow and arrow, of Veddoid or Proto-Australoid type, the basic ethnic type throughout India. They used digging-sticks, woodworking tools, mats and baskets. A wide range of stone materials was used, the industry reaching its peak and highest perfection in western-central India where semi-precious stones like carnelian and agate produced gem-like implements. Middle Stone Age elements survived into the late Stone Age. She thought the latter industry was probably introduced from the north-west into India, and that it came into Australia either from the north and crossed the continent, or reached the south coast by sea. On the other hand, she pointed out that it is not clear whether the origin of the industry was due to independent evolution of similar features in similar surroundings or to diffusion. This is precisely the situation in Australia as McBryde stated (1967) when she said that the carliest examples of blade tool industries for castern Australia come from Seelands near Grafton, Graman on the western slopes of the mountains, Wilson's Promontory and Mt Burr, suggesting either a technical revolution within the Australian cultures themselves during the fourth century BC, or the arrival of new migrants bringing with them a new range of tools.

Opinion thus varies in linking the small tool tradition with hunter-gatherers and early cultivators, but it is associated with the former in India and Ceylon. It is also clear that there is close agreement in the range of sizes and varieties of backed blades in India, Indonesia and Australia, but their ultimate age in India and Indonesia has yet to be clarified. A matter of critical importance in the origin of this delicately fashioned series of implements is whether or not they were used for the same purposes everywhere, including Africa, Europe and Asia, within a comparable time range; if they were, it implies that the whole complex developed and diffused from one place. Adding the industry to a culture probably meant a change in material culture, and more than a fleeting contact was necessary for this purpose.

We should not however, dismiss Mulvaney's statement (1970 : 29) that 'Diffusionist and evolutionary hypotheses are implicit in considering possible prehistoric parallels between Sulawesi and Australia, with the inbuilt preconception that nothing significant developed locally and that as far as Australian contacts were concerned traffic was one way; Australia absorbed traits but exported nothing in return'. Thus should the oldest dates occur in south-eastern Australia, a diffusion westward and north-westward would have to be considered, or parallel developments at different places on the continent. We are, it appears, no closer to a solution of the problem of the origin of the small tool tradition inside or outside Australia than when Mulvaney discussed it in 1969, but consensus of opinion appears to favour the idea that it represents a pattern of diffusion from the north-west to the south-east of Australia.

Symmetrical points

The unifacial and bifacial points tradition appears to have had a different history. Davidson (1938 : 69) and Mitchell (1949 : 5) both believed that pressure flaking and these points are indigenous in Australia. Allchin (1966 : 140) said that the bifacial point occurred in south-eastern India and Ceylon, and nowhere else in India, and also in Indonesia, and may have had its origin in the Arctic cultures of north-eastern Asia, as such connections as there are lie in Japan, and among the islands and promontories of the eastern seaboard of Asia, thence possibly via the Philippines to Indonesia and north-western Australia by sea. Hollow-based bifacial points occur in the Sampung industry in a number of caves in Java, and with serrated points in the Toalian industry of Sulawesi, in Indonesia.

The unifacial pirri point occurs in association with the Bondi point in the obsidian industry of western Java, according to Bandi (1951 : 137–53), and in a number of sites in Sulawesi (Van Heekeren, 1957) in the Middle Toalian (Mulvaney and Soejono, 1970 : 29). Single and bipointed bone muduk occur in both Sulawesi and Australia. Allchin (1966 : 146) and Mulvaney and Soejono, (1970 : 29–32) point out that the Toalian serrated points, superficially, suggest a comparison with the Kimberley bifacial and dentated points. The former author thinks they belong to a different tradition and the latter authors stated that on their sites in Sulawesi they

could not infer that the hollow-based points or bone tools are late intrusions. Thus the affinities of the Kimberley bifacial point are very obscure. They differ in important respects from the hollow-based Toalian serrated point, resemble the Sampung biface much more closely, but here again we face the problem of discontinuous distribution from Java to north-western Australia. Mulvaney (1969 : 127) proposed a speculative hypothesis that both point and microlithic blade industries had differentiated before reaching Australia, although differentiation continued here, and that while Arnhem Land was the likely beach head for the former technology, north-western Australia was the possible entry area for the latter. One would expect the northern Kimberleys to have been the entry point for the symmetrical points as this is the area in which they reached their highest development.

In Australia the unifacial point has a much wider distribution than the bifacial one. Both points are associated in excavations dating back to 6500 BP (C. White and Peterson, 1969 : 54) previously reported as 7110 ± 130 BP (C. White, 1967), in the Northern Territory, and in the same region more recently at Yarar (Flood, 1970) and Ingaladdi (Mulvaney, 1969 : 116). They occur together throughout the Kimberley district and the Top End of the Northern Territory, and the former region has always been regarded as their basic area. General opinion now appears to be that they were introduced into north-western Australia together and that the uniface did not give rise to the biface. The unifacial pirri point spread southward into the desert region of Western Australia, into the Northern Territory, Queensland and western New South Wales, and presumably through central Australia, with the lower Murray River forming the limit of its southward movement. Although there are gaps in this distribution pattern, there is every reason to believe that it is continuous from north to south. The pirri linked up with the tula chisel and the geometrical microliths in the southern part of its distribution. The bifacial point, on the other hand, remained within the Kimberley–Top End region but traded specimens have been found some distance to the south in Western Australia.

The distributions of the Bondi, pirri and biface points, and of the geometric microliths, illustrate a very important principle in Australian culture development, that of differential movement over time of individual traits, often dissociated from the complex or regional culture to which they belong. This appears to be true for the whole of the continent west of the Great Dividing Range, where the terrain, including the deserts, offered no insurmountable barriers to intermittent or regular barter, gift-exchange, social and ritual gatherings. It is tempting to link the symmetrical point diffusion with the rock paintings of the Kimberley district, but there is no data to associate them in origin with either phase of the rock art—the Bradshaw human figures or the later Wondjina art. In Arnhem Land these points are found in localities where the rock art differs from that of the Kimberleys, and again such a contrast appears where the points occur in the Macarthur River area of the Northern Territory. While it is possible for the Bradshaw and Arnhem Land stick figures to have originated from a common source, there is no evidence to link them with the symmetrical point tradition. There is a fertility basis to the religion of both regions, and many of the great culture heroes and heroines came out of the sea, but the language situation is the most confused one in Australia, with no less than some two dozen language families in existence. To the south different languages and religions are in force. There is also an advanced type of polished axe, lenticular in section and ovate in shape, which is limited in distribution to the Kimberley district and western Arnhem Land. The pearl-shell pendant spread from the Kimberley coast over an enormous part of Australia along the traditional barter and gift-exchange routes (McCarthy, 1939 : 96–98, map 14), accompanied in Western Australia by the bifacial point for use as a ritual knife in some localities. Elkin (1964 : 131) was of the opinion that from the Kimberleys the division of the tribe into four sections, circumcision and exposure of the dead on a platform, with subsequent inquest and final disposal of the bones, had spread southward into vast areas of the continent, while the division of the tribe into eight sub-sections diffused from the south-eastern Kimberley district north toward Wyndham, west to the Fitzroy River, and north-east into Arnhem Land in comparatively recent times, and that it had also travelled far southward to the northern Aranda. There is thus some justification for believing that a pattern of diffusion existed westward and southward and also eastward into Arnhem Land, from the Kimberley district, of which the symmetrical points, and the ovate lenticular axe, form an integral part.

Arnhem Land diffusion pattern

Apart from the symmetrical points and lenticular axe mentioned above as part of a Kimberley and Arnhem Land diffusion, no other stone implements appear to be diffusing from Arnhem Land itself. The Macassan cultural influence during 300 or 800 years introduced iron tools which replaced stone axes, choppers, scraping and cutting tools, and with European contact wire-pronged fishing spears and iron-bladed hunting spears appeared.

Central Australian regional culture

Another example of multiple diffusion is that of the central Australia–lower Northern Territory region from which a cluster of culture traits has been diffusing in all directions into Western and South Australia, Queensland and to a lesser degree into Arnhem Land. It is probable that they were not diffusing as a unit; instead they were spreading differentially over distance and time. It is probable, too, that the tremendous vitality of the central Australian regional culture, as exemplified by the Aranda, was exerting pressure in contiguous areas. Among these traits the fluted non-returning boomerang, with its diverse range of uses, apparently ousted the returning type in this region and was pushing it back in the east and the west; it spread into the non-boomerang using Arnhem Land as a clapstick. The fluted and hooked types travelled by trade to the east Kimberley area, and one of the latter is shown as a fully pecked engraving at Port Hedland (McCarthy, 1962 : pl.xvⅰh). Tjurunga and bullroarers bearing concentric circle and U designs spread northward to Port Keats where they were reproduced in a local style, to the Wardaman in the north, eastward into western Queensland and westward into Western Australia (Davidson, 1937b : 111–13). The spear-thrower with a tula chisel mounted on the grip end was also spreading in many directions, probably accompanied by the fluted wooden container. The tula chisel had a much wider distribution on wooden handles (Davidson and McCarthy, 1957 : 405–6). In the latter paper Davidson drew attention to the interesting sequence of steps in its diffusion into Western Australia as the recipients gradually learned the full process of manufacturing and hafting over time; the spearthrowers and throwing-sticks first had a blob of gum moulded on to their end, to be followed by an unspecialised type of flake set in the gum, and finally by the specialised tula chisel. Admittedly, the precise area of origin of the tula is not known, and we must await the results of excavations and radiocarbon dates in the future for the answer.

Similar remarks apply to the leilira blade, used as a knife, spearhead and fighting pick. Its distribution extends from Arnhem Land down through the Northern Territory into central Australia and western Queensland. There is a quarry for these blades in the north-western corner of New South Wales. Davidson (1935 : 176) thought this blade was made in the Northern Territory and spread into Arnhem Land, but there are quarries where it was made in the Oenpelli, upper Walker River, and other areas in Arnhem Land of which he was not aware. The use of this blade was most diverse in the Northern Territory and it formed part of a pattern of diffusion from there into western Queensland, together with bull-roarers, pearl-shell pendants, and other items, as mentioned above. Stratigraphically, the leilira blade was later than the Kimberley points in the sites excavated by Davidson (1935a) at Delamere and Willeroo. Data from these sites, and from the distribution of this blade, led him to the conclusion that as a spearhead it was invading areas of spears with barbs cut in the solid shaft in its eastward and northward diffusion, and that the symmetrical unifacial and bifacial points from the Kimberleys were in turn invading areas where the leilira was in use as a spearhead.

Subincision diffused into eastern Arnhem Land, north as far as the Rose River, with the Kunapipi, and the circumcision and subincision myths and ideology spread into western Arnhem Land with this cult also Berndt and Berndt, 1964 : 139–46: fig. 10).

Davidson (1937b : 111) and others have commented on the fact that the Top End of the Northern Territory is an area of general resistance to diffusion from the south. It is a region with a religious system based on the rhythm of the tropical wet and dry seasons, and on cults of ancestral spirit beings who came out of the sea and brought traditional art motifs with them. These cults have proved to be too strongly entrenched to be penetrated by the southern type of totemic clan increase rituals linked to travelling bands of ancestral spirits who came out of and went into the ground and had a different range of art designs.

Cape York diffusion pattern

Cape York, together with Arnhem Land and the north-western coast, is one of the three entry points through which injections or streams of culture diffused into Australia. It has been regarded as the source of a wide range and large number of traits in all aspects of Aboriginal culture, as claimed by the writers quoted elsewhere in this paper, which have diffused in varying degrees, some no further than Cape York, others in a fan-like manner over extensive regions of the Australian continent.

Among the traits relevant to this discussion that I listed as part of this pattern of diffusion were the pecking technique, transverse groove for hafting axes, and the pecked round axe, as part of a progressive refinement and development of axe types common to Australia and Oceania. Since then, of course, C. White (1967) has unearthed several axes, grooved on one side by rubbing, among her ancient series at Oenpelli, Northern Territory. Whether or not my supposition is correct it cannot be claimed that stone implements were a very important element of this pattern of diffusion.

There are two interesting similarities between Queensland and Papua worth mentioning. The discoid-lenticular axe (pecked and polished) of north-west central Queensland is identical (apart from the hole to hold the club head) with the discoid stone club head of New Guinea and Torres Strait islands, but Cape York forms an area of discontinuous distribution between them which renders suspect any claim that diffusion from New Guinea explains the presence of this axe type in Queensland; it could well represent a variation of the ovate-lenticular axe of the Kimberley–Arnhem Land region. A similar problem of discontinuous distribution is applicable to the art motif of an oval with a bar engraved in the Carnarvon district caves in eastern Queensland, and painted in caves in the Sogeri district of Papua. Is parallelism, or local development, sufficient to explain the origin of two such important traits, or are they examples of a diffusion whose nature we cannot as yet explain?

East coast of Australia

The east coast would appear to be a promising avenue for the diffusion of units or groups of culture traits, as opposed to single elements, and this is true to a certain extent. The barb-less shell or bone fish hook, together with the stone file for smoothing it, the bark canoe and paddle, nets, multi-pronged spear, and the bone *muduk* point, all part of a fishing culture, spread southward along the coast from Cape York to Victoria, most probably separately and not as a group. No specialised stone implement apart from the file appears to have formed part of this diffusion. The stone implement assemblages along this coast have revealed that the Eastern Regional Sequence prevails along the New South Wales portion, but how far north of New South Wales this sequence extends is not precisely known; there is a slightly different sequence in Victoria. The social organisation varies considerably along this coast (Berndt and Berndt, 1964 : fig. 6), and there appears to have been an intrusion of the four section system from the west rather than a diffusion of any systems from the north. The Bora religion characterised by sky heroes, outline engravings, huge ground figures and tree trunk engravings extended from Victoria to southern Queensland, but there is no evidence available to link it in origin with any of the excavated assemblages or with the above fishing traits. It is interesting to note, however, that the boundary of the Bora religion is only a little further west than that of the Bondaian backed blade assemblage in central New South Wales. We do not know, however, whether sky gods were linked with this assemblage in prehistoric times elsewhere in Australia, or whether the sky gods of south-eastern Australia belonged to the Archaic culture of the colonising period. The religion of Cape York is of a different kind with Papuan hero cults replacing the indigenous type on the east coast, and wooden sculptures forming the central feature of west coast ceremonies.

Uniface pebble implements and ground-edge axe sequence

Two other important items should be mentioned in connection with discontinuous distribution. One is the Hoabinhien uni-face pebble implements and the Bacsonien ground-edge sequence so well known in south-east Asia and Indonesia. In

1938 after examining these implements in Java and Singapore I claimed (1940b : 46) that the sequence had diffused from this region into Australia, and Tindale (1937 : 55) suggested that his Kartan assemblage from Kangaroo Island, of which the uniface pebble implements are typical, had connections with the upper Palaeolithic of Malaya. Matthews's (1966) study of unifaces was critical of the diffusionist hypothesis and distributional evidence supports his views. Unifaces occur in Tasmania, Victoria, eastern New South Wales, south-east Queensland, and south and central Australia; they have not to my knowledge been reported in Western Australia, Arnhem Land or the greater part of Queensland, the Northern Territory or western New South Wales. Until we know whether the uniface aspect (and better still both aspects of the sequence together) occur in Western Australia or Arnhem Land in particular, and more continuous distributional links are established, claims for their diffusion into Australia must be suspect. A pebble implement was dated back to 12 550 ± 185 BP at Noola, New South Wales, but the unifaces do not appear stratigraphically beyond 6500 years ago elsewhere in Australia. Golson (1971a : 130) stated that 'on the faunal and archaeological evidence reviewed a late Pleistocene date might be proposed in place of a post-Pleistocene one for the earliest edge-ground artifacts of south-east Asia and for the industries both in which and after which they appear; such a backdating of the Hoabinhien and Bacsonien would eliminate the archaeological blank that at present exists in the upper Pleistocene of the region south and east of the Upper Irrawaddy and north of Java.' He also postulated that 'Whatever the specific period of its birth the cradle of Indo-Oceanian horticulture lies in the area occupied at the appropriate time by communities of Hoabinhien–Bacsonien and allied type; their culture inventory as preserved comprises grinders and pounders appropriate to the exploitation of vegetable foods and lacks anything in the nature of specialised hunting gear'. It might be mentioned here that Australian Aboriginal hunter-gatherers possessed grinders and pounders which, found archaeologically, do not denote an agricultural people. It is tempting to believe in the diffusion of the uniface pebble assemblage, but an indigenous origin has equally favourable claims at present. It is not a question of pebble supplies because these are abundant in many parts of Australia where the unifaces are unrepresented. The similarity of a whole range of tool types, climaxed by the Sumatra-type and inclusive of such a variety as the hache courte, favours the diffusionists' claim but distributional evidence opposes it, and the problem is one for the future to decide. The occurrence of similar grindstones and mortars, mullers and pestles, in Australia, south-east Asia and Indonesia has also to be considered but their place in the archaeological context of each of these regions has yet to be clarified and correlated.

Cylindro-conical stones

A similar situation exists in regard to the cylindro-conical stones, or cylcons, the symbol of a cult centred in the central Darling River area of western New South Wales, though specimens have been found in eastern South Australia, southern Queensland and central New South Wales. No information about their function or significance has been obtained from Aborigines. Their decoration with abraded grooves and linear motifs, and their shaping by flaking, pecking and polishing, indicate that they were in use over a considerable period of time, and is the only evidence extant about their antiquity. Similar artifacts, lacking the incised motifs of the New South Wales examples, occur in the Adelaide River area of the Northern Territory, where one of their functions was sorcery. In India and Indonesia the plain cylcon functioned as a male phallic emblem, *lingam*, a symbol of Siva, the divine embodiment of the eternal reproductive power of Nature, in Hindu religion. We cannot however on the basis of such a discontinuous distribution link these occurrences simply because the artifacts are of a similar shape.

Axes and techniques

I held the view that a late introduction (1953 : 250) of the round axe took place in Cape York because axes had not appeared in excavations in Australia prior to some 7000 years ago; Mulvaney and Joyce (1965 : 73) also claimed that edge-grinding, hammer-dressing or pecking, and grooving processes, in view of the lenticular shape of most axes, had diffused into Australia from New Guinea or other islands to the north. As the antiquity of axe types and techniques is pushed further and further back, however, diffusion from abroad via Cape York, for example, is being eliminated for more and more traits. Since the excavation of ancient axes of which pebble, biface coroid and grooved types date back to 22 900±1000 BP at Oenpelli, Northern Territory, Carmel White (1971) has shown that broken basalt pebble fragments with ground surfaces occur in the base level at Laura, Cape York, and throughout the deposit going back to 16 000 years at Kenniff in Queensland, the antiquity of which fills in the time lag between the Oenpelli and other sites in which axes have been excavated. Edge-grinding in Australia is thus obviously older than the Hoabinhien–Bacsonien sequence of south-east Asia and Indonesia and cannot have been derived from it. In view of the late Pleistocene antiquity of edge-grinding in New Guinea and elsewhere north of Australia, there is no longer a problem of diffusion from Indonesia or New Guinea involved; Australia was then joined to New Guinea and southern Indonesia, and the diffusion took place within the northern portion of one continent and did not reach Tasmania.

A similar situation applies to the round axe but to a lesser degree. J. P. White's excavation at Kafiavana demonstrated its antiquity there as some 10 000 years and at this time Australia was still joined to New Guinea. The round axe was an important and widespread type in Australia, and its distribution could have been continuous with New Guinea and other northern regions. A detailed typological and distributional study of axe types in Australia is needed to provide a definition of the round axe and other types, and to ascertain whether the flattish, oval sectioned variations should be distinguished from the cylindrical forms.

Inherent in and inseparable from the development of the wide range of axe types in Australia are the shaping techniques. A succession of flaking, pecking and polishing is the general rule in Oceania, except on brittle stone materials where pecking was eliminated and the polishing took place over much finer flaking than on coarser stones. The polished ovate-lenticular axes of the Kimberleys are of the latter kind, while the discoid-lenticular axes of Queensland were shaped by the three techniques. There was an immense elaboration in the use of pecking to shape implements in eastern Australia— axes (round and lenticular sections), cylcons and *Bogan* picks (round), *Yodda*-type (lenticular), millstones (most highly advanced type is lenticular), mullers and mortars—as were

the encircling groove on axes, phallic stones in the Kimberleys and a tjurunga in central Australia, as the rounded surfaces were most efficiently shaped with this technique.

On the basis of shapes and techniques being similar, a Melanesian origin has been advocated for the above succession of techniques, and I attributed pecking to early Neolithic culture-bearers spreading into Indonesia and Melanesia (1940b : 42), but stratigraphic data is now pushing back the antiquity of pecking to the era of lower sea levels and the extension of the Australian continent to New Guinea and elsewhere in the north, thus eliminating the New Guinea–Torres Strait islands–Cape York concept. On the other hand, the major distribution of pecked rock engravings is from north-western Australia south-eastward through central Australia to Queensland, New South Wales, South Australia and north-western Tasmania, and it is difficult to decide whether the spread of the technique was from the north-west or from the north-east. Analysis of the subjects in the Port Hedland fully pecked engravings indicates that it came from the inland. The greatest development of fully pecked engravings is undoubtedly in north-western Australia, and it is consistently superimposed over abraded grooves and linear designs from the north-west to western New South Wales, a sequence of art and techniques which has suggested a diffusion from the former to the latter. On the other hand, the extensive use of pecking to shape a variety of stone implements in far western New South Wales and Queensland may be a local elaboration or development in craftsmanship. The absence of pecking in southern South Australia and southern Western Australia indicates a westward diffusion. It is interesting to note that pecked implements are rare in the coastal areas east of the Great Dividing Range, and that the technique was in general use west of the range. There may, of course, have been primary and secondary diffusions of pecking in Australia, but the pattern of diffusion of the technique cannot be defined on data available at present.

Prehistoric assemblages and regional environments

The relationship of the diagnosed prehistoric assemblages to regional environments should also be discussed within the context of this paper, as it is in many ways a denial of patterns of diffusion. The Archaic core and flake tradition was carried all over the continent as it was occupied by the expansion of the population during the colonising period, and its composition became varied in different local areas due to the nature of the material culture, methods in exploiting the environment, the stone technology of the people and in part to the stone materials available. To what degree coastal, forest, desert and other environments caused this variation, or promoted invention of new kinds of implements or even assemblages amongst the hunter-gatherers of Australia is a problem upon which much archaeological research is concentrated today, but it is not as yet clearly understood.

The Australian small tool tradition sites occur in fertile coastal, forest and tableland environments in south-eastern and south-western Australia, in climatic conditions probably similar to those when it was in use up to 6000 to 7000 years ago in these regions in which rainfall varied from 11 mm on the coast to 3 mm elsewhere per annum. It also occurs in the interior of Western Australia, and Gould (1969) excavated it in the desert region of this State, where the climate was apparently similar when it was in use to that of today. It is also worth pointing out that the small tool tradition sites occur in a great variety of habitats in other parts of the world. According to Allchin (1966 : 181) these industries are found in intermediate rainfall zones of approximately 4 to 10 mm per annum in India. In Australia the succeeding post-Bondaian or Eloueran phase has been identified in coastal and forest areas in eastern New South Wales. The major area of distribution of the bifacial points is in the sub-tropical north of Australia but it could be used as an arrow or spearhead in any environment. In similar forest and coastal regions elsewhere in Australia there are different implement assemblages.

It would, of course, be of great interest to know whether changes took place in the material culture when the backed blades, which were hafted for use, were added to the tool kit of the Aborigines, and when they dropped out of it, in the various regions in which they form a part of the sequence of prehistoric industries, especially in eastern New South Wales. According to Moore's excavations (1970) in the Hunter River valley, New South Wales, and Hallam's (1972) in south-west Australia, the Bondaian phase continued in use until European occupation. Neither is an outstanding area in material culture and woodworking, and south-west Australia, culturally, is one of the most backward regions on the mainland. The uniformity and consistency of motifs in the outline rock engravings in the region between the George's and Hunter River valleys indicate little or no change in the material culture over a long period. The Bondi point is essentially a spearhead and barb, possibly also a surgical knife, and the geometric microliths are composite cutting tools. As Bondi points occur separately from the geometrics at Lapstone Creek (McCarthy, 1948) New South Wales, and in Sulawesi (Mulvaney and Soejono, 1970 : 31), even in neighbouring sites, it is evident that they were not always, if at all, part of the one composite tool. It appears to me, therefore, that this group of small implements simply added more efficient spears and cutting tools to the Aborigines rather than a revolution in the material culture.

The tula-geometric microlith aspect of the inland regional sequence is associated with arid and desert environments in an extensive region of South and Western Australia, New South Wales and Queensland, but it is also associated with a riverine habitat on the lower Murray and Darling Rivers and with a mountainous one at Kenniff. The geometrics do not occur with the other types in the tropical north of Australia, and all of them are absent from the later Murundian aspect. Mulvaney (1960 : 75–78) accounts for the change from the pirri-microliths to the tula chisel, and the degeneration of stone technology in the lower Murray area on the basis of a change in the material culture with a new emphasis on woodworking, and a more complex exploitation of the resources of the valley; further (Mulvaney et al., 1964 : 492) the basic continuity of cultural tradition and changes in the industry were due to environmental adaptation. Again (Mulvaney, 1962) he concluded that the contrast between a rich bone industry and a meagre stone implement one at Glen Aire in Victoria demonstrated the reality of local adaptation and changing habits in the material culture. Allchin (1966 : 170) suggested that the various adze blades, their re-sharpening technique and the composite tools of which they form part might represent a response to increasing desiccation, and the necessities of desert life, due to the demands these factors made upon the ingenuity of the hunter and gatherer. On the other hand, the disappearance of the backed blades in eastern New South Wales was followed by an increase in elouera, fabricators and especially ground-edge axes and chisels, which also points toward an emphasis on woodworking.

This problem of accounting for such developments in our sequences of industries according to local adaptation, an emphasis on woodworking and incised decorative art, a more complex exploitation of resources, or by diffusion and invention, is a critical one in deciding basically whether patterns of diffusion exist. I believe that the major changes from the Archaic to both the Australian small tool and the symmetrical point traditions in Australia were due to the diffusion of new techniques and forms of stone technology, introducing more efficient spears and cutting tools, and that a more efficient and wider exploitation of the environment followed in its wake. I am of the opinion, also, that specialised and seasonal exploitation of the environment exerted a considerable influence on the kinds or range of specialised implements used at a site, as at Durras and other places. Middens in some rock shelters that I have tested in the Sydney–Hawkesbury region contained no implements at all, as they were simply camping places beside sources of food in areas where no suitable stone for implements was available.

Golson (1971b : 135) has postulated an alternative explanation for some of the major changes in Australian stone technology when he drew attention to the early presence in south-east Asia, New Guinea and Australia of a variety of hafting devices that I discussed in 1940; the similarities, he said, between these various kinds of hafted axe-like implements in a large area extending from Asia to Australia may perhaps be more realistically explained as parallels within the same technology rather than successive migrations distributing individual items. Mulvaney had expressed a somewhat similar viewpoint about the Australian small tool tradition when he stated (1971 : 12) that the process of idea-migration-invention-diffusion occurred at more than one place of which Australia was one. Discontinuous distribution of a trait undoubtedly supports such an interpretation which in itself contradicts the idea of stone implements acting as a medium for mapping patterns of diffusion. Parallel development, due to adaptation, changes in material culture and invention, has now been postulated as an explanation of the presence in Australia and regions to the north of (1) the Australian small tool tradition, (2) uniface pebble implements, and (3) hafted axe-like implements. One might question here whether parallel development in this sense means that it happened in one place and then diffused within Australia, or whether it took place in many localities on the continent. Quite long intervals of time could be expected for parallel development of a specialised type or technique in Australia, Indonesia and south-east Asia. Thus it might be said that we are back to square one, independent invention or evolution versus diffusion.

Invention, too, must not be forgotten. Quoting Childe's conclusion (1942 : 32) that the upper Palaeolithic was a time of inventiveness because new techniques spread rapidly, and local variation was evident, after the appearance of modern man enormously better equipped than any group before him, Mulvaney and Joyce (1965 : 12) interpreted the new technology—which I presume to be the Australian small tool tradition—as a relatively sudden phenomenon which diffused rapidly, resulting in a considerable variety of response with respect to working particular types, such as points, and they asked whether innovation is characteristic of other aspects of culture. There is not a great deal of evidence to support invention as a prominent principle of Aboriginal culture, as Davidson has pointed out in his various papers, while the vital importance of diffusion within Australia has been proved beyond doubt. The ease with which artifacts could be obtained by barter and gift exchange militated somewhat against a cultural climate in which invention was necessary or actively encouraged.

To sum up, I believe that some of these problems may be solved when more distributional and dating information is available, others will always be open to discussion. I believe that stone implements formed part of several major patterns of diffusion comprising (1) the Australian small tool tradition from northern Western Australia; (2) the symmetrical point tradition from the Kimberley–Arnhem Land region; (3) New Guinea–Torres Strait islands–Cape York; (4) Northern Territory to north-western Queensland; (5) north-western Queensland to north-eastern South Australia; (6) central Australian cultural diffusion; and (7) stone axe, millstone and leilira blade quarries in many parts of the continent. Stone implements and other items traded between local groups also formed minor patterns of diffusion, but it is impossible to ascertain the full ramifications of this trade owing to a lack of information in many regions of the continent. Barter and gift exchange routes aided the diffusion of stone implements, and for this reason diffusion within Australia must rank as a vital factor in changes and advancement in all aspects of Aboriginal culture. The need and stimulus for invention in

Aboriginal life was mitigated by the ease with which traits could be obtained by trade. As the antiquity of edge-grinding and axe-shaping techniques such as pecking is pushed further and further back it is apparent that their diffusion took place within the greater continent of Sahul Land rather than from across the seas to the present Australian continent. The problem of discontinuous distributions forces the culture historian to leave open the question of the origin of the uniface pebble implements, discoid-lenticular axe and cylcons at present; it also creates difficulty in linking the occurrences of the Australian small tool tradition in India, Indonesia and Australia.

The elements of regional religions in Australia need detailed distributional analysis to enable us to detect their complex relationships. The lack of accurate distributional studies in the whole field of social anthropology, which covers a considerable portion of Aboriginal culture, is one of the greatest stumbling blocks with which the culture historian has to contend. In point of fact the mapping of every trait in Aboriginal culture is needed to clarify our understanding of regional cultures, trait distributions and associations, and the interrelationships of the social, ethnographic and archaeological aspects of culture as a whole.

References

Allchin, B., 1966. *The stone-tipped arrow*. London: Phoenix House.
—— 1957. Australian stone industries, past and present. *Royal Anthropological Institute of Great Britain and Ireland, Journal*, 87 : 115–36.
Berndt, R. M., 1951. *Kunapipi*. Melbourne: Cheshire.
—— and C. H. Berndt, 1964. *The world of the first Australians*. Sydney: Ure Smith.
Bandi, H. G., 1951. Die obsidian industrie der umbergung von Bandung in West Java. In *Sudseestudien*. Basel.
Binns, R. A. and I. McBryde, 1972. *A petrological analysis of ground-edge artifacts from northern New South Wales*. Canberra: Australian Institute of Aboriginal Studies.
Butler, W. H., 1958. Some previously unrecorded Aboriginal sites near Perth. *Western Australian Naturalist*, 6 : 133–36.
Casey, D. A., 1934. An uncommon type of stone implement from Australia and New Guinea. *National Museum of Victoria, Memoirs*, 8 : 94–99.
—— 1940. The present state of our knowledge of the archaeology of Australia. *Third Congress of the Prehistorians of the Far East, Singapore, 1938, Proceedings*, 22–29.
Childe, V. G., 1942. *What happened in history*. Harmondsworth: Penguin.
Davidson, D. S., 1933. Australian netting and basketry techniques. *Polynesian Society, Journal*, 42 : 257–99.
—— 1934. Australian spear-traits and their derivations. *Polynesian Society, Journal*, 43 : 41–72, 143–62.
—— 1935a. Archaeological problems of northern Australia. *Royal Anthropological Institute of Great Britain and Ireland, Journal*, 65 : 145–84.
—— 1935b. The chronology of Australian watercraft. *Polynesian Society, Journal*, 44 : 1–16, 69–84, 137–52, 193–207.
—— 1935c. Is the boomerang Oriental? *American Oriental Society, Journal*, 55 : 163–81.
—— 1936a. Australian throwing-sticks, throwing-clubs, and boomerangs. *American Anthropologist*, 38 : 76–98.
—— 1936b. The spearthrower in Australia. *American Philosophical Society, Proceedings*, 76 : 445–83.
—— 1936c. *Aboriginal Australian and Tasmanian rock engravings and paintings*. Memoirs, American Philosophical Society, 5.
—— 1937a. Transport and receptacles in Aboriginal Australia. *Polynesian Society, Journal*, 4 : 175–205.

—— 1937b. *A preliminary consideration of Aboriginal Australian decorative art*. Memoirs, American Philosophical Society, 9.
—— 1938a. Stone axes of Western Australia. *American Anthropologist*, 40 : 38–48.
—— 1938b. Northwestern Australia and the question of influence from the East Indies. *American Oriental Society, Journal*, 58 : 61–80.
—— 1941. Aboriginal string figures. *American Philosophical Society, Proceedings*, 84 : 763–904.
—— 1952. Notes on the pictographs and petroglyphs of Western Australia. *American Philosophical Society, Proceedings*, 96 : 78–117.
—— and F. D. McCarthy, 1957. The distribution and chronology of some important types of stone implements in Western Australia. *Anthropos*, 52 : 390–458.
Dortch, C. E., 1972. Report on archaeological work carried out in the Ord reservoir area, east Kimberley. *Australian Institute of Aboriginal Studies, Newsletter*, 3(4) : 3–18.
Elkin, A. P., 1934. Cult totemism and mythology in northern South Australia. *Oceania*, 5 : 171–92.
—— 1940. Kinship in South Australia. *Oceania*, 8 : 419–52.
—— 1964. *The Australian Aborigines: how to understand them*. 4th ed. Sydney: Angus & Robertson.
Flood, J. M., 1970. A point assemblage from the Northern Territory. *Archaeology and Physical Anthropology in Oceania*, 5 : 27–52.
Frobenius, L., 1901. Die kulturformen Ozeaniens. *Petermann's Mitteilungen*, 46.
Glover, I. C., 1967. Stone implements from Millstream Station, Western Australia: Newall's collection re-analysed. *Mankind*, 6 : 415–25.
Golson, J., 1971a. Both sides of the Wallace Line: Australian, New Guinea and Asian prehistory. *Archaeology and Physical Anthropology in Oceania*, 6 : 124–44.
—— 1971b. The remarkable history of Indo-Pacific man: missing chapters from every world prehistory. Mimeo.
—— 1971c. Australian Aboriginal food plants: some ecological and cultural implications. *In* Mulvaney, D. J. and J. Golson (eds) *Aboriginal man and environment in Australia*, pp. 196–232. Canberra: Australian National University Press.

Gould, R. A., 1969. Preliminary report on the excavation of Puntutjarpa rock-shelter, near the Warburton ranges, Western Australia. *Archaeology and Physical Anthropology in Oceania*, 3 : 161–85.

—— 1971. The archaeologist as ethnographer: a case from the Western Desert of Western Australia. *World Archaeology*, 3 : 143–77.

——, D. A. Koster and A. H. Sontz, 1971. The lithic assemblage of the Western Desert Aborigines of Australia. *American Antiquity*, 36 : 149–69.

Graebner, E., 1905. Kulturkreize in Ozeanien. *Zeitschrift für Ethnologie*, 28 : 25–83.

—— 1913. Melanische kultur in nord-Australien. *Ethnologica*, 2 : 15–24.

Haddon, A. C., 1920. The migrations of culture in New Guinea. *Royal Anthropological Institute of Great Britain and Ireland, Journal*, 50 : 237–80.

—— 1935. Reports of the Cambridge anthropological expedition to Torres Strait. 1. London: *General Ethnography*.

Hallam, S. J., 1972. An archaeological survey of the Perth area, Western Australia. *Australian Institute of Aboriginal Studies, Newsletter*, 3(5) : 11–19.

Harris, R. Hamlyn, 1915. Some evidence of Papuan culture in Cape York Peninsula. *Queensland Museum, Memoirs*, 3 : 10–13.

—— 1917. Some anthropological considerations of Queensland. *Royal Society of Queensland, Proceedings*, 29 : 1–44.

Heekeren, H. R. van, 1957. *The stone age of Indonesia*. The Hague.

Jones, R., 1968. The geographical background to the arrival of man in Australia and Tasmania. *Archaeology and Physical Anthropology in Oceania*, 3 : 187–215.

Kaberry, P. M., 1939. *Aboriginal woman, sacred and profane*. Celebes: Routledge.

McBryde, I., 1967. The antiquity of man in Australia. *University of New England External Studies Gazette*, 11(6) : 1–4.

McCarthy, F. D., 1936. The geographical distribution theory and Australian material culture. *Mankind*, 2 : 12–16.

—— 1938. *Australian Aboriginal decorative art*. 1st ed. (8th ed. 1974). Sydney: Australian Museum.

—— 1939–40. 'Trade' in Aboriginal Australia, and 'trade' relationships with Torres Strait, New Guinea and Malaysia. *Oceania*, 9 : 405–39; 10 : 80–104, 171–95.

—— 1940a. Australian Aboriginal material culture; causative factors in its composition. *Mankind*, 2 : 241–69, 294–320.

—— 1940b. A comparison of the prehistory of Australia with that of Indo-China, the Malay peninsula and archipelago. *Third Congress of Prehistorians of the Far East, Singapore, 1938, Proceedings* : 1–30.

—— 1940c. The bone point known as *muduk* in eastern Australia. *Australian Museum, Records*, 20 : 314–19.

—— 1948. The Lapstone creek excavation: two culture periods revealed in eastern New South Wales. *Australian Museum, Records*, 22 : 1–34.

—— 1949. The prehistoric cultures of Australia. *Oceania*, 19 : 305–19.

—— 1957. *Australia's Aborigines; their life and culture*. Melbourne: Colorgravure Publications.

—— 1962. *The rock engravings of Port Hedland*. Kroeber Anthropological Society, Papers, 26, Berkeley.

—— 1967a. *Australian Aboriginal rock art*. 3rd ed. Sydney: Australian Museum.

—— 1967b. *Australian Aboriginal stone implements*. Sydney: Australian Museum.

—— 1974. Relationships of Australian Aboriginal material culture with that of South-East Asia and Melanesia. *In* Elkin, A. P. and N. W. G. Macintosh (eds), *Grafton Elliot Smith; the man and his work*, pp. 210–26. Sydney: Sydney University Press.

Macintosh, N. W. G., 1971. An analysis of an Aboriginal skeleton and a pierced tooth necklace from Lake Nitchie, Australia. *Anthropologie*, 9 : 49–62.

Matthews, J. M., 1966. The Hoabinhien affinities of some Australian assemblages. *Archaeology & Physical Anthropology in Oceania*, 1 : 5–22.

Mitchell, S. R., 1949. *Stone age craftsmen*. Melbourne: Bread & Cheese Club.

Moore, D. R., 1970. Results of an archaeological survey of the Hunter river valley, N.S.W. Pt. 1. The Bondaian Industry of the upper Hunter and Goulburn river valleys. *Australian Museum, Records*, 28 : 25–64.

Mulvaney, D. J., 1960. Archaeological excavations at Fromm's Landing, on lower Murray river, South Australia. *Royal Society of Victoria, Proceedings*, 72 : 53–85.

—— 1961. The stone age of Australia. *Prehistoric Society, Proceedings*, 27 : 56–107.

—— 1962. Archaeological excavations on the Aire river, Otway peninsula, Victoria. *Royal Society of Victoria, Proceedings*, 72 : 53–85.

—— 1969. *The prehistory of Australia*. London: Thames & Hudson.

—— 1971a. Aboriginal social evolution: a retrospective view. *In* Mulvaney, D. J. and J. Golson (eds), *Aboriginal man and environment in Australia*, pp. 368–80. Canberra: Australian National University Press.

—— 1971b. Prehistory from Antipodean perspectives. *Antiquity*, 37 : 228–52.

—— and E. B. Joyce, 1965. Archaeological and geomorphological investigations on Mt. Moffatt station, Queensland. *Prehistoric Society, Proceedings*, 31 : 147–212.

——, G. H. Lawton and C. R. Twidale, 1964. Archaeological excavation of rock shelter No. 6, Fromm's Landing, South Australia. *Royal Society of Victoria, Proceedings*, 77 : 479–516.

—— and R. P. Soejono, 1970. Archaeology in Sulawesi. *Antiquity*, 45 : 26–33.

Noone, H. V. V., 1943. Some Aboriginal stone implements of Western Australia. *South Australian Museum, Records*, 7 : 271–80.

Rivers, W. H. R., 1926. *Psychology and ethnology*. London: Kegan Paul.

Sarasin, P. and F., 1905. *Versuch einer anthropologie der insel Celebes: die Toalahohlen von Lamontjong*. Wiesbaden.

Smith, Sir G. Elliot, 1930. *Human History*. London: Cape.

—— 1933. *The diffusion of culture*. London.

Spencer, Sir W. B., 1921. The Aborigines of Australia. *Australian Association for the Advancement of Science, Report*, 15 : LVII–LXXIX.

—— and F. J. Gillen, 1927. *The Arunta*. 1–2. London: Macmillan.

Stanner, W. E. H., 1933–34. Ceremonial economics of the Mulluk Mulluk and Malngella tribes of the Daly river, north Australia. *Oceania*, 4 : 156–75, 458–71.

Thomson, D., 1933. The hero cult, initiation and totemism in Cape York. *Royal Anthropological Institute of Great Britain and Ireland, Journal*, 63 : 453–538.

—— 1949. *Economic structure and the ceremonial exchange cycle in Arnhem Land*. Melbourne: Macmillan.

—— 1952. Notes on some primitive watercraft. *Man*, 52.

Thorpe, W. W., 1924. Some New Guinea cultural influences found amongst the Aborigines of Australia. *Australian Association for the Advancement of Science, Report*, 17 : 484–90.

Tindale, N. B., 1937. Relationship of the extinct Kangaroo Island culture with cultures of Australia, Tasmania and Malaya. *South Australian Museum, Records*, 6 : 39–60.

—— 1957. Cultural succession in south-eastern Australia from late Pleistocene to the present. *South Australian Museum, Records*, 13 : 1–49.

—— 1967. Peopling of the lands south-east of Asia. *Colorado Quarterly*, 15 : 339–54.

Towle, C. C., 1939. Stone arrangements and other relics of the Aborigines found on the lower Macquarie river, N.S.W., at and near Mt. Foster and Mt. Harris. *Mankind*, 2 : 200–209.

White, C., 1967. Early stone axes in Arnhem Land. *Antiquity*, 41 : 149–52.

—— 1971. Man and environment in northwest Arnhem Land. *In* Mulvaney, D. J. and J. Golson (eds), *Aboriginal man and environment in Australia*, pp. 141–57. Canberra: Australian National University Press.

—— and N. Peterson, 1969. Ethnographic interpretations of the prehistory of Arnhem Land. *Southwest Journal of Anthropology*, 25 : 45–67.

White, J. P., 1971. New Guinea and Australian Prehistory: the neolithic problem. *In* Mulvaney, D. J. and J. Golson (eds) *Aboriginal man and environment in Australia*, pp. 182–95. Canberra: Australian National University Press.

Classification and typology in Australia

The first 340 years

D. J. MULVANEY

Australia's earliest ethnographer shot or kidnapped his 'informants: Jan Carstensz (Heeres, 1899 : 36–42) also set a philosophical norm with his observation that the Aborigines 'are the most wretched and poorest creatures that I have ever seen in my age or time', sentiments which had repercussions upon many subsequent artifactual classificatory schemes. 'In their wretched huts on the beach', he observed on Cape York in 1623, 'we found nothing but a square-cut assagay, two or three small pebbles, and some human bones, which they use in constructing their weapons and scraping the same; we also found a quantity of black resin . . .' Carstensz therefore combined an African ethnographic analogy with actual observation of functional use of wooden implements (described elsewhere): vagueness characterised his stone tool categorisation, and in this too, he had many imitators.

An historical survey of classification and typology until the last decade points up several morals of current relevance. One is that there is no substitute for detailed artifactual description. Another is the intellectual isolation which distinguished most 'authorities', who studiously avoided reference to other workers, while their own models were distorted by preconceived dogmatism. Prehistory may ignore national frontiers, but not so its typologists. Over many decades, stone tool classificatory schemes differed significantly between Adelaide, Melbourne and Sydney. Perhaps Darwin or Alice Springs had more to offer as being closer to tool users, but in many cases, an inverse ratio existed between ethnographic observation of stone tool use (function) and typological or classificatory precision (form).

Although Cook, Collins and Flinders described material culture in some detail, possibly the best early precise account of stone tools was provided by the observant P. P. King. Based upon a sound functional knowledge of the implements, his rough sketches and succinct descriptions allow comprehension of the stone components of tools from Port Essington (King, 1827, I : 86) and Albany (II : 137–40). Significantly, he illustrated and described a serrated, bifacial Kimberley point from Hanover Bay (I : 68), accompanied by a full scale drawing (15 cms), which depicts realistically both serrations and percussion waves and provides an associated cross section.

Two other relevant objective beginnings merit notice from the 1850s. In 1854, W. von Blandowski (1855 : 57–58) sought and found the Mount William axe quarry, evidently questioned Aborigines on its use, described the site and its geology and provided a chemical analysis of the stone and its fracturing properties. Artist T. Baines, on the Victoria River exploration led by A. C. Gregory in 1856, provided a long, objective account of stone flaking (Baines, 1866 : CIII–CIV) and portrayed Aborigines in several sketches. Yet, to judge from Gregory's own journal (1884), in which no close contact with

the Aborigines is indicated, Baines may have described the technique from first principles rather than from ethnographic experience.

A less objective but more pervading influence was represented by J. Y. Akerman (1852 : 171) in his lecture on European prehistory to the Society of Antiquaries in 1851. To illustrate prehistoric axe technology he displayed two Australian artifacts (a ground axe and a Kodj chopper). Remarkable for a colony in its rude, seventeenth year, the Melbourne *Argus* (23 September 1851, p. 2) reported Akerman's distant lecture. It observed that the tools 'were remarkable as being identical in character with the European axe and hammer heads of the primeval period'. So commenced a trend towards comparative ethnography, where general parallels were sought and detailed comparisons often avoided. It was employed by John Evans in *Ancient stone implements* (1872) to shed light on European prehistoric material culture, and by J. Lubbock and E. B. Tylor from the 1860s to illumine prehistoric social systems, on the assumption that modern 'primitive' evidence represented an unchanged 'survival' from the past. Its climax was Tylor's essay (1893) 'On the Tasmanians as representatives of Palaeolithic Man', in which he described Tasmanian stone tools. The theme was continued by W. J. Sollas in *Ancient hunters and their modern representatives* (1911). The social theorists found receptive minds amongst those who, like A. W. Howitt and L. Fison, were themselves chiefly concerned with kinship and other social systems. It is interesting, however, to observe their adverse impact on students of material culture, particularly stone tools. This is evident in R. Brough Smyth, who produced the first detailed, systematic stone tool classification in 1876. However, Smyth's *Aborigines of Victoria* largely originated with the earlier work of Aboriginal Protector, William Thomas, whose notes and collections were handed over to Smyth in 1861 (Thomas, 1859; author's knowledge of Mitchell Library sources). It is understandable that Thomas, who lived extensively with Aborigines, employed functional terms to describe Aboriginal weapons and Smyth followed him. His classification (1876, I : 358) divided stone implements into eleven functional categories (and the terms are his): hatchets, knives, adzes, chips for jagged spears, chips for cutting and scraping, pounding stones, sharpening (grinding) stones, stones for fishing, basket making and pigments, sacred stones.

Smyth (I:LV, LVII) was worried about the implications of Lubbock's evolutionary model. In the first place, he did not believe that Australia had been occupied during Pleistocene times (I : LVI, 364), and hence 'survivals' from the Drift period were not a reality. Secondly, Lubbock's newly coined terminology based on a stadial concept was erroneous: 'if . . . all the stone implements . . . of the Australians be examined, one set might be put apart and classed as the equivalents of those of the Palaeolithic period of Europe, and another . . . set . . . the Neolithic period'.

The Melbourne school of pragmatic typologists owed much to Smyth, who concluded (I : LV), that the facts 'press strongly against the theories of Sir John Lubbock'. Unfortunately, this set against European model builders encouraged a bleak nationalism, wherein 'Australian made' was virtuously pronounced unique and pragmatical—'in all discussions . . . into primitive man's history as revealed to us by the artifacts left behind him, the inquirer finds himself hampered, to a distressing extent, by the evil influence of the European archaeologist', chanted Kenyon, Mahony and Mann (1924 : 467), whose stone collections were hoarded in the vaults of the National Museum of Victoria. This was not an atmosphere in which to nurture prehistoric research.

By the time that the Australian states federated, their colonial museums appear to have adopted individual stances on implement typology. It is appropriate to first discuss Victoria. The twentieth century opened with an ambitious pseudo-scientific schema to embrace all stone artifacts. Kenyon and Stirling (1900 : 193) discovered tool types unknown to Brough Smyth, but whose function was lost. Because they were forced to abandon observed function as the sole criterion they concluded that it was evidently 'in some cases, dependent upon the apparent mode of preparation or manufacture'. Even so, there was a likely confusion between *observed* and *assumed* function, and this lack of clear definition characterises most later work also. A complex table, using numerals, the alphabet and Greek characters and categories ranging down from groups, through divisions, sub-divisions, sections and classes to sub-classes, was used to classify tools. Groups, divisions and sub-divisions depended upon function, the rest upon form (some subjectively inferred). As an example, C B 1 a 2 B, Codified a Cutting implement, ground edge, axe grooved for hafting, ovate with circular cutting edge. The seven groups designated allowed for 66 further sub-divisions. Possibly, for 1974, a system usefully designed for punch cards, in 1900 it must have seemed excessively abstruse and even Kenyon later implicitly contradicted part of it (Kenyon and Mahony, 1914 : 7). Yet the programme has a remarkably contemporary look, with even the working on tool edges recorded.

It was Baldwin Spencer who communicated the Kenyon and Stirling paper to the Royal Society of Victoria; and, as Honorary Director of the National Museum of Victoria, he enshrined their classification in the newly arranged museum display and in modified form wrote it into his *Guide to the Australian Ethnographical Collection* (1901, 1923: 78). Spencer is an interesting and influential figure in Australian typology. Trained at Oxford by E. B. Tylor, he and Henry Balfour assisted Tylor move and arrange the Pitt-Rivers ethnographic collection during 1885, into the newly constructed appendage to the University Museum. His 1901 *Guide* reflected his mentor: 'The Australian aborigine may be regarded as a relic of the early childhood of mankind left stranded . . .'; Tasmanians were 'living representatives of palaeolithic man' (Spencer, 1923 : 12, 8).

Yet, as a practical fieldworker at Alice Springs, he hinted at the difficulties of armchair typology. Spencer and Gillen (1899 : 591) observed that simple and complex stone tools co-existed, and offered an explanation which was to become a dogma. 'To a certain extent the matter is simply one concerned with the nature of the material, the quartzite being pre-

eminently adapted for chipping and flaking, and the diorite for grinding down, and with both materials at hand the manufacture of both ground, chipped and flaked implements has been carried on side by side'. Spencer said much the same in his *Guide* (1923 : 78), adding specifically that tools typical of the Palaeolithic and Neolithic periods were contemporaneous.

At the British Association Australian Meeting in 1914, Spencer (1914 : 76–77) still emphasised that 'this constant mixture of implements, usually regarded as belonging to different levels of culture, . . . forms the most striking feature of the present stone age in Australia. The nature and form of the implements is not a question of the stage of culture, but depends primarily upon the material available'. He added Eolithic to the cultural mix of Palaeolithic and Neolithic. Kenyon and Mahony went further, when arranging a special museum exhibit of 10 000 stone tools for the Association visitors. Their implement classification was based on function, but it was a subjectively deduced function in most cases. Kenyon and Mahony (1914 : 6–7) rejected form as a helpful criterion, while flaking technique was also ignored—tools were simply dependent upon the quality and quantity of available raw material. Obviously stone supply is a determining factor, but this was caricature. Microliths ('pigmy types') were exhibited—'we may state that we consider them to be the result of scarcity and consequent value of good, suitable stone'; axe shape was 'dependent on the stone used'. Typology had become a sterile variant of geological antiquarianism.

There was a more outward-looking atmosphere at the Australian Museum, Sydney, despite the colonial nationalism implicit in its institutional name. R. Etheridge (1890, 1891) began a systematic classification of stone tools, and although he dealt with spear points and axes, he evidently failed to complete a task which was eventually achieved by his later successor at the Museum, F. D. McCarthy (1946).

Etheridge (1891 : 35) dealt with a group of eleven bifacial (Kimberley) points and provided a table with length, breadth and thickness measurements and form (shape). In another article (1890 : 63) he examined seven serrated points and supplied the same measurements and the rock type. He divided them into three classes, based upon morphology. The terms were descriptive—elongate lanceolate; almost triangular and flattened; foliate, on both faces—and despite their Victorian prolixity, they represented the most objective approach yet attempted to Australian stone tools. He followed it (1891 : 357–88) with a long essay on axe classification, based upon morphological features. Unfortunately his sage advice (1891 : 702) went unheeded, that someone should 'undertake a systematic description of the Aboriginal wood weapons . . . district by district, when, I am sure, much useful and instructive information would be forthcoming'.

In 1899, Etheridge's colleague, Whitelegge, discovered extensive areas of eroded midden at Bondi Beach. Together they recovered numerous implements and described them clearly, classified them, but in illustrating specimens they set an unfortunate trend towards cramming which has marred many publications of their Museum during the first half of this century (189 photographed artifacts on a single plate must constitute a record). Several characteristics stand out in their report, which is marked by its objectivity, although numbers of each type are not listed (probably they illustrated every artifact); but only general measurements were provided (Etheridge and Whitelegge, 1907 : 239, 250). They emphasised the great variety of stone sources used for making a single implement type (ibid.) and grasped the fact that the site was prehistoric 'from which the workers may have disappeared hundreds of years ago' (235). Implicit is the conclusion that prehistoric and European contact tool types may have differed. All these observations contrast markedly with Melbourne pronouncements, but Sydney and Melbourne protagonists evidently chose mutually to ignore the existence of the other party. It is relevant that Whitelegge identified the site because of his earlier experience of flint tool sites in northern England (234). They classified their material under eleven major categories, largely functional, but admittedly 'speculative', and also subjectively distinguished by close inspection 'in the order of importance as exhibiting flaking, chipping, or skill in manipulation' (237); again, therefore, human free will is implicit in their schema. They emphasised at some length that the most abundant artifacts were small primary flakes and described them, following Brough Smyth's lead closely in this, and citing further ethnographic parallels for their possible use as spear barbs (244–48).

This is the *locus classicus* for Bondi points (actually termed 'chipped back surgical knives' in their report). These microlithic, asymmetric backed blades were hitherto unknown in Australia (239), and indeed, although backed blades of any form must have been in private collections by this date, all varieties were formally unknown. Following a verbal description of their morphology and a careful drawing of an example (two views and a cross section), they sought an archaeological parallel in India and a functional ethnographic analogy in America (238–41). Such internationalism must have shocked Melbourne readers.

The tradition of interest in stone tool classification centred on the Australian Museum during the first half of this century culminated in *The stone implements of Australia* (McCarthy, Bramell and Noone, 1946), which reviewed earlier typological classifications and presented a comprehensive descriptive typology. It was preceded by many papers by McCarthy and others, including an unsuccessful typological essay on scrapers by Towle (1934). Elsewhere, I have deplored much of the weekend excursion digging which provided some of these collectors with their specimens (Mulvaney, 1961 : 88). McCarthy and his associates (1946 : 2) adopted a broad spectrum of criteria to evaluate stone tools—processes, function, form, size, cross section, material, and a recognition that prehistoric and recent tools were being lumped together because of contemporary inadequate archaeological knowledge. Many Aboriginal names were adopted as terms, as was Tindale's practice in South Australia. Unlike Tindale, however, few of these terms resulted from direct contact with the Aborigines. McCarthy's most extensive contact with tribal Aborigines occurred later, in 1948, during the Arnhem Land expedition in which he participated. Perhaps as a consequence, McCarthy's emphasis was more on formal characteristics than upon function; Aboriginal terms were derived from the ethnographic literature. Although they never met, the line of succession from Etheridge to McCarthy appears very direct. Both were systematists drawing upon experience of classifying and cataloguing museum collections, in geology and zoology, respectively.

Walter Howchin (1893; 1934) was a friend of the barrow digger Canon Greenwell and had published on north British stone tools before his arrival in Adelaide in 1881. His systematics of the stone implements of the Adelaide area is probably the earliest South Australian typology. Presented to the A.A.A.S. meeting of 1893, it was only published in elaborated form in 1934. Yet the South Australian tradition of interest in material culture and technology extends back even to the 1840s with Eyre, Grey, Angas and Cawthorne, all men who had close contact with the Aborigines. South Australia sent rich collections of Aboriginal material to the Philadelphia Centennial Exhibition of 1876 (Knight, 1879 : 268). These included hafted stone spearheads from Melville Island (the Overland Telegraph was completed in 1872 and South Australians had obvious opportunities to collect ethnography).

A concern with field observation of the functional use of tools characterises South Australian typology from Howchin to N. B. Tindale. As early as 1887, Howchin (1934 : 51) sought the advice of Adelaide area Aborigines (unsuccessfully) on the purpose of 'a number of locally collected implements, including several varieties of what might be considered typical scrapers, according to European classification'. He extended his enquiries while on geological fieldwork in Central Australia (1934 : 69), where Aborigines flaked tools for him. Significantly, he commented on the resulting use wear produced and its implications for specimen identification (1921, 1934 : 71). In 1887, again, he studied a collection of tula adze-flakes, compared their working edges with hafted museum specimens, and on the supposition that 'something may be learnt concerning these tools from the tool marks left on the wooden articles that were shaped by their use', he described the wear patterns on four wooden containers and thirty boomerangs (Howchin, 1934 : 44–46).

Howchin also used the ethnographic data collected by Horne and Aiston (1924) in the Lake Eyre region. (This latter study, together with the W. E. Roth memoirs are possibly the most detailed published attempts at typology or technology field observation before the present generation. Indeed, Horne and Aiston's study is basic reading for any approach to stone.) Howchin (1934 : 35) also compared Australian artifacts with collections available to him from India—'in some forms identical', but he supplied no details.

Although a geologist, Howchin did not stress the identification of stone, and was free from dogmatism in describing the raw materials available to Aborigines. Unlike Kenyon, he observed (1934 : 22), that 'the aborigines showed excellent judgment in choosing the direction which the stone could best be worked to suit their purpose'. The determinant emphasised by Howchin was not the nature of the raw material, but simply the limited range of tools needed by any hunter-gatherer society, particularly one with preference for multi-purpose tools (1934 : 22, 51). That is, demand and not supply controlled typological variety.

Howchin's weakness was a failure to provide detailed analysis of his tool types. His search for functional ethnographic parallels—and an assumed identity of function—and his functional categories resulted in a blurring of morphological description; dimensions or other data were not given. Tindale (1968 : 616) has observed that Howchin, like the Victorian typologists, presented a monocultural pattern, by lumping artifacts together from every time period. This is correct, but he was also aware that great chronological depth existed. Admittedly, this was partly inspired by his slack criteria of artificial as opposed to natural fracture: Howchin (1934 : 90) firmly believed in a desert eolithic culture.

T. D. Campbell was partly responsible for refuting his eolithic claims (Jones and Campbell, 1925). He subsequently wrote many papers on typology, which drew heavily upon Aboriginal experience of tool use, but stressed morphological traits as the essential criteria. In the late 1930s H. V. V. Noone visited Australia, and influenced both Campbell and F. D.

McCarthy with his detailed knowledge of European stone typology and (presumably) his emphasis upon objective description. An attempt at such objectivity was Tindale and Noone's analysis (1941) of a hoard of knapped flint which described technological aspects and recorded striking platform angles.

In an important joint study with Noone, Campbell drew up a detailed typology of microlithic artifacts in which the importance of *distinctive* tool types as cultural markers was stressed. Campbell and Noone (1943 : 284) deplored current lax nomenclature and decided against using any assumed functions in their classification, believing 'it preferable to use terms which make familiar form and method of production . . . and when pertinent, the size'. They formulated a criterion which, though it seriously underestimated Aboriginal behavioural norms, did pose the problem facing any subjective classificatory scheme (1943 : 284).

'As the aboriginal was not dominated by any such thing as classification, but instead by his opportunist idea of what he required for his purpose, pieces are found on the borderland, between two varieties or types differentiated by us; as also some showing more than one kind of working edge. For purposes of the present classification we have had recourse to making what seemed the main use of the implement its major feature.'

'Borderland pieces', amorphous trimming, or the primary flakelets which concerned Brough Smyth and Etheridge were ignored in such schemes. How serious is the omission? As Campbell and Noone observed (1943 : 284), certain European tool types 'were so significant and distinctive that they supplied a reliable guide to differentiation of the successive cultures'. Should the archaeologist be equally concerned with the totality of his stone material? In an ethnographic situation, Horne and Aiston (1924) suggested a difference in classification of stone implements between Ideal and Casual. (In an attempt to classify surface site flake tools, Towle (1934 : 118) separated them into Conventionalised and Unconventionalised types, but his observations were superficial.)

When analysing the Kenniff Cave material, I was acutely aware of the above issues. To cover one pitfall I included a category—'utilised flakes'. To negotiate the numerous gradations and anomalies of Scraper classification (cf. McCarthy *et al.*, 1946 : 24), I attempted metrical definition (Mulvaney and Joyce, 1965 : 182). My solutions satisfied few, for utilised flakes were as numerous as the retouched flake tools which I measured. Yet was my omission as serious as some imply? As for my histograms which looked so objective in 1965, modern technology outdated those techniques almost immediately. At that time however, except for Tugby's exercise in matrix analysis (see below), it was the most 'objective' attempt on the problem, paralleling work on New Zealand flaked stone tools by Wilfred Shawcross (1964).

T. D. Campbell also merits record for his early attempt at statistical definition. His study of variant pirri points (1960) is, however, circular in argument. As collector and typologist, Campbell supplied the specimens to be measured; as statistician he found that the tests confirmed the typological reality of the principles under which they were selected. His paper also ignored possible change through time as a basic parameter; and this in the face of the Fromm's Landing excavation results then available.

Campbell later elaborated his morphological systematics to apply to the full range of South Australian stone typology (Campbell and Edwards, 1966). It is descriptive, with associated type specimens clearly illustrated, but is lacking in quantitative data, though ethnographic analogies abound. This study, together with McCarthy's more comprehensive typology (1946), still constitutes the basic typologies and it is unfortunate that they are less referred to by some younger workers than should be the case.

A more sophisticated innovatory approach was taken by D. J. Tugby (1958), using a matrix analysis of a group of stone axes from southeast Australia. This was a succinct but seminal study, although its author has not followed it by further Australian applications. In 1937, Tindale (1937 : 47, 57) presented metrical data in graphic form (length-breadth index and weight of tools), and also devised a formula ('pirri index') to show the proportion of pirri points in a total tool assemblage. Presumably, these were the earliest moves towards quantification.

My concentration upon classificatory origins up to about a decade ago has, I trust, demonstrated that different typological orientations developed between Australian research centres. Although the influence may not be absolute, the two leading protagonists of typology over the past generation, McCarthy and Tindale, were heirs to different 'cultures', quite aside from their personal research. I do not intend to retrace my own published observations on the past seventeen years, particularly my strictures on Tindale's practice (1961). Besides, Rhys Jones (1971, ch. 18) has written such a discerning critique of Tasmanian typological studies, that there is nothing to add on Tasmania. I will conclude with some general observations.

Rather than overseas typological knowledge inhibiting Australian research, as the Melbourne school proclaimed, it has given it direction. The arrival of H. V. V. Noone stimulated considerable writing and he was co-author of the best classificatory essays on Western and South Australian tools, in addition to assisting with McCarthy's memoir (1946). Dermot A. Casey has provided a stabilising influence on Victorian research since his arrival there from Britain around 1934. Conversely, the overseas study tours by Tindale and McCarthy between 1936 and 1938 obviously had profound effects in adding to their experience.

Tindale and McCarthy both added considerably to terminological and classificatory aspects of prehistoric research. Both of them introduced the concept of cultural succession based on time depth; they both named and defined new implement types; both showed a preference for Aboriginal names, applied to cultures and stone tool types by Tindale and to the latter by McCarthy; both used presumed diagnostic marker tool types to synthesise wide provinces or periods of Australian prehistory. The present generation of archaeologists concentrates more upon regional or local problems. It is more rigorous in examining the data or in seeking definitions. Problems in defining the prehistory of a continent from the vision and research of two persons are legion and reappraisals must be expected. Some of these issues were examined at an AIAS Conference composed of the then small band of prehistorians and colleagues, in Sydney during 1963. It was an invaluable experience and inaugurated a new phase of increasing objectivity and quantification, as witness a subsequent report of the Stone Implement Committee which the Conference appointed (Casey, Crawford and Wright, 1967).

Tindale (1968 : 628–29) has rightly emphasised the obligation of researchers to record all aspects of Aboriginal tool manufacture, use, and Aboriginal concepts and terms. He also correctly demands the freedom of the individual to define and describe his material as he finds it, and not 'force his observations into archaeological terms'. Yet, he also seeks 'a fixed nomenclature for archaeological implements' possibly based upon principles of scientific priority, comparable to those pertaining to zoological nomenclature. Such a concept seems unduly restrictive today. It also assumes that the unique ethnographic observation of the 'type tool' can be generalised in space and time to apply to all morphologically similar tools. This seems but a variant of the monolithic, monocultural concept which Tindale has attacked rightly so often. Biological behaviour and human choice are not analogous and to insist on inflexibility takes research back to the attitudes of Tylor, and denigrates the creativity of Aboriginal society.

I suggest that there are aspects of prehistoric research for which the establishment of ethnographic function is not the only purpose of studying the artifact in question. At a time when so much care is lavished upon microscopic use-wear study, laboratory analysis, and ethnographic observations, it is worth remembering that while it may assist our reconstruction of man the toolmaker, or *homo economicus*, it may not explain his cultural preference to fashion the tool in that particular way, rather than an equally adaptable alternative. That is why I believe that traditional typology fulfills a function that some more sophisticated analyses overlook. For example, backed blades (geometric microliths) and small primary flakes may both have functioned equally efficiently as death-spear barbs, as some have urged. But the fact that geometrics were adopted, widely used and then became less fashionable, in possible competition with the simpler flake, must have more than a functional explanation. Neither do distributional studies suggest economic or geographic differentials. The solution may rest in emotional rather than economic motives, and it is difficult to apply significance tests to 'keeping up with the Jones'.

Perhaps too, enthusiasm for a new approach masks the fact that systematic typological analysis may achieve the same end. Rhys Jones (1971 : 314) pays tribute to Balfour's analysis of Tasmanian stone tools (1925). Indeed, sitting in the remoteness of the Pitt-Rivers Museum and analysing material subjectively collected by others, Balfour deduced (and illustrated superb 'typical' specimens) almost all the categories which Jones obtained from his edge-analysis and computer processing. Jones' strength is that he also carried out a traditional typological analysis. Some prehistorians are virtually by-passing this stage, by invoking the name of function. If history teaches anything, it is that man is more than his diet and his implements; why expect prehistoric Aborigines to be any different?

Over a decade later, Spencer repeated almost verbatim, his sentiments first voiced during Victoria's reign (Spencer and Gillen, 1927, II : 536). Kenyon and his associates took their initial cue from Spencer but diverted to denigrate other typologists and the Aboriginal artisans who provided the stuff of which their cabinet collections consisted. For, if form was simply a reflection of stone type, and function largely a matter of low mentality and tradition, typology became a pointless exercise and the nature of cultural and technological processes obscured. The following quotations reduce the issue to one of geology alone, with a racist overlay. 'We are faced with the fact that the classifications, so confidently relied upon by the European archaeologist, are quite inapplicable and that the use of terms implying a geological age as well as a stage of culture cannot be sustained' (Kenyon, Mahony and Mann, 1924 : 464–65).

'Any local "culture" . . . can be shown to be due to local causes' (ibid.).

'In all consideration of the aboriginal one must endeavour . . . to view matters from the standpoint of the youth of 10 to 12 years of age. The schoolboy organization . . . is on all fours with that of the tribe' (ibid.).

'It is to be feared that our black brother was not troubled about these departures from type. He was a poor, primitive creature, who allowed the material available to govern him, and did not attempt the impossible'. (Kenyon, 1927 : 282.)

It may be significant that in his initial typology essay with Stirling in 1900, Kenyon was concerned basically with function and form, and not with the local raw material. His later obsession evidently originated with Baldwin Spencer, biologist before he was an anthropologist. Therefore the Victorian school's negation of cultural factors may be his: 'Australia is the present home and refuge of creatures, often crude and quaint, that have elsewhere passed away and given place to higher forms. This applies equally to the aboriginal as the platypus and kangaroo.' (Spencer and Gillen, 1927 : I : VII.)

In Spencer's evolutionary deterministic approach cultural isolationism was promoted. As ANZAAS President in 1921, he emphasised (Spencer, 1921 : LXXXIX) that biological polygenesis 'led, without any outside influence, to the development . . . of mammalian forms . . . but controlled by some factor . . . that has determined the retention of their marsupiality. On the other, it had led to the independent development of a race of human beings along lines parallel to those pursued by other early races . . . but always again controlled by some factor . . . that has prevented them from developing into anything higher than men of the stone age'.

Further, because of his philosophical preconceptions, Spencer observed and described Aborigines meticulously, but along narrow lines. It renders his records of many material matters less detailed and less insightful than those of his Oxford classmate, W. E. Roth. Spencer thought Roth was lacking in adequate theory, but Roth possibly understood the Aborigines better than he. Compare Roth's strictures on abstract typology, in the course of his own functionally based descriptive classification of stone tools. Roth (1904 : 18–19) indeed, was advocating ethnoclassification, a concept which passed Spencer by.

'. . . the savage most certainly does not recognise the fine distinctions embodied on the labels . . . (of axes) in an ethnological museum. In the absence of actual observation, is any one competent, for instance, to give a definite opinion as to which of such implements the special use . . . most particularly conforms to ?'

'. . . it seems to me futile to base any rational classification on shape.'

'. . . from a systematic point of view, neither does the material of construction prove of much value, rocks of similar origin undergoing not only varying methods of manufacture, but developing alterations of contour upon completion.'

Perhaps the last great collector and typologist in the Victorian tradition was S. R. Mitchell, whose *Stone-Age Craftsmen* is crammed with useful factual data—camp site locations, tool types and literature references to tool use. Mitchell travelled widely throughout Australia collecting stone tools; yet the Aborigines themselves are missing from his pages, either as informants or people. There is a familiar note in his comment (1949 : 22), that Palaeolithic, Mesolithic and Neolithic industries 'can all be matched in Australia', and in his comprehensive classification of types which combined raw material, form and function—or assumed function (1949 : 27). Tugby (1958 : 31) makes a useful comparison between Mitchell's categories and those of McCarthy, Bramell and Noone (1946) and shows that Mitchell's classes are not all logically discrete. Mitchell's stress upon function, which presupposes a realistic grasp of edge trimming, is shown in its true hypothetical futility by his improbable reconstruction of how geometric microliths were used (1949 : 56). It is relevant

to add a personal note: some collectors who hailed Kenyon as mentor, indulged in extremes of rivalry and secrecy in their field forays; once I was informed of a likely archaeological site, whose locality would be disclosed once it had been exhaustively collected over. Two other respected collectors selected their finest specimens and disposed of unwanted finds down a disused mine shaft.

References

Akerman, J. Y., 1852. On some weapons of the Celtic and Teutonic races. *Archaeologia*, 34 : 171–89.

Baines, T., 1866. On certain implements and articles of dress from South Africa (sic!). *Anthropological Review*, IV : CII–CVIII.

Balfour, H., 1925. The status of the Tasmanians among the stone-age peoples. *Prehistoric Society of East Anglia*, 5 : 1–15.

Blandowski, W. von, 1855. Personal observations in Victoria. *Transcripts, Philosophical Society of Victoria*, 1 : 50–74.

Campbell, T. D., 1960. The pirri. *Records of the South Australian Museum*, 13 : 509–24.

—— and R. Edwards, 1966. Stone implements. *In* Cotton, B. C. (ed.) *Aboriginal Man in South and Central Australia*, Pt. 1. Adelaide: Government Printer.

—— and H. V. V. Noone, 1943. South Australian microlithic stone implements. *Records of the South Australian Museum*, 7 : 281–307.

Casey, D. A., I. M. Crawford and R. V. S. Wright, 1967. The recognition, description, classification and nomenclature of Australian stone implements. Reprinted in, Mulvaney, D. J. (ed.), *Australian Archaeology*, Australian Institute of Aboriginal Studies, (Canberra, 1972, ch. 10).

Etheridge, R., 1890. On some beautifully formed stone spearheads from Kimberley. *Records of the N.S.W. Geological Survey*, 11 : 61–65.

—— 1891. Notes on Australian Aboriginal stone weapons and implements. *Proceedings, Linnean Society of N.S.W.*, 16 : 31–48, 357–88, 699–704.

—— and T. Whitelegge, 1907. Aboriginal workshops on the coast of N.S.W. and their contents. *Records of the Australian Museum*, 6 : 233–50.

Gregory, A. C. and F. T. Gregory, 1884. *Journals of Australian explorations*. Brisbane: Government Printer.

Heeres, J. E. (ed.), 1899. *The part borne by the Dutch in the discovery of Australia*. London: Luzac.

Horne, G. and G. Aiston, 1924. *Savage life in central Australia*. London: Macmillan.

Howchin, W., 1893. The stone implements of the Aboriginal tribes of the seaboard of South Australia. *Australian and New Zealand Association for the Advancement of Science*, 5 : 522.

—— 1921. On the methods adopted by the Aborigines of Australia in making of stone implements based on actual observations. *Transactions, Royal Society of South Australia*, 45 : 280–81.

—— 1934. *The stone implements of the Adelaide tribe of Aborigines now extinct*. Adelaide: Gillingham.

Jones, F. W. and T. D. Campbell, 1925. A contribution to the study of eoliths. *Journal of the Royal Anthropological Institute*, 55 : 115–22.

Jones, R. M., 1971. *Rocky Cape and the problem of the Tasmanians*. Ph.D. thesis, University of Sydney.

Kenyon, A. S., 1927. Stone implements on Aboriginal camping grounds. *Victorian Naturalist*, 43.

—— and D. J. Mahony, 1914. Stone implements of the Australian Aborigine. *Guide*, Melbourne: British Association for the Advancement of Science.

——, D. J. Mahony and S. F. Mann, 1924. Evidence of outside culture inoculations. *Australasian Association for the Advancement of Science*, 17 : 464–67.

—— and D. L. Stirling, 1900. Australian Aboriginal stone implements. A suggested classification. *Proceedings, Royal Society of Victoria*, 13 : 191–97.

King, P. P., 1827. *A survey of the intertropical and western coasts of Australia . . . 1818–1822*, 2 vols. London: Murray.

Knight, E. H., 1879. A study of the savage weapons at the Centennial exhibition, Philadelphia, 1876. *Report . . . Smithsonian Institution*, pp. 213–97.

McCarthy, F. D., E. Bramell and H. V. V. Noone, 1946. The stone implements of Australia. *Memoirs Australian Museum*, IX.

Mitchell, S. R., 1949. *Stone Age craftsmen*. Melbourne: Tait.

Mulvaney, D. J., 1961. The stone age of Australia. *Proceedings, Prehistoric Society*, 27 : 56–107.

—— and E. B. Joyce, 1965. Archaeological and geomorphological investigations on Mt. Moffatt Station, Queensland. *Proceedings, Prehistoric Society*, 31 : 147–212.

Noone, H. V. V., 1943. Some Aboriginal stone implements of Western Australia. *Records of the South Australian Museum*, 7 : 271–80.

Roth, W. E., 1904. Domestic implements, arts and manufactures. *North Queensland Ethnography Bulletin 7*.

Shawcross, F. W., 1964. Stone flake industries in New Zealand. *Journal of the Polynesian Society*, 73 : 7–25.

Spencer, W. B., 1914. 'The Aborigines of Australia' in *Federal Handbook of the British Association . . . Australia*, Melbourne.

—— 1921. Presidential Address: The Aborigines of Australia, *Australian and New Zealand Association for the Advancement of Science*, 15 : LIII–LXXXIX.

—— 1923. *Guide to the Australian Ethnographical Collection in the National Museum of Victoria*. Melbourne: Government Printer. (First published 1901.)

—— and F. J. Gillen, 1899. *Native tribes of central Australia*. London: Macmillan.

—— and —— 1927. *The Arunta*, 2 vols. London: Macmillan.

Thomas, W., 1859. *Brief remarks on the Aborigines of Victoria 1838* (MSS Latrobe Library, Melbourne).

Tindale, N. B., 1937. Relationship of the extinct Kangaroo Island culture with Cultures of Australia, Tasmania and Malaya. *Records of the South Australian Museum*, VI : 39–60.

—— 1968. Nomenclature of archaeological cultures and associated implements in Australia. *Records of the South Australian Museum*, 15 : 615–40.

—— and H. V. V. Noone, 1941. Analysis of an Australian Aboriginal's hoard of knopped flint. *Transactions, Royal Society of South Australia*, 65 : 116–22.

Towle, C. C., 1934. Stone scrapers. *Journal, Proceedings, Royal Society of N.S.W.* 68 : 117–43.

Tugby, D. J., 1958. A typological analysis of axes and choppers from southeast Australia. *American Antiquity*, 24 : 24–33.

Tylor, E. B., 1893. On the Tasmanians as representatives of Palaeolithic Man. *Journal of the Anthropological Institute*, 23 : 141–52.

Aspects of variation in central Australian lithic assemblages

JAMES F. O'CONNELL

Introduction

Recent ethno-archaeological reconnaissance in the Sandover River area of central Australia has revealed the existence of significant intersite differences in the composition of stone tool assemblages. This paper describes these differences in brief and examines some of the factors that may be responsible for them. Its preliminary conclusion is that most are a function of differences in site location in relation to lithic and biotic resources. Although seasonal variations in regional settlement and subsistence patterns are documented ethnographically, they do not seem to be reflected in the stone tool assemblages.

Background

The Sandover Basin is a broad, low plain bounded on the south by the Harts Range, an extension of the MacDonnell Range system, and on the north by the Davenport Range. It varies in elevation from 300–600 m above sea level, the principle relief provided by a series of low, heavily dissected sandstone ridges which trend across the region from southeast to northwest. The major streams are the Sandover River and its several tributaries, including Bundey, Frazer, and Waite creeks. These carry surface water only during rainy periods, but retain important reserves of sub-surface moisture in their sandy beds for many months.

The climate of the region is warm and dry (Slatyer, 1962). Rainfall averages less than 300 mm annually and is highly variable in amount from year to year. Most of the annual total falls in the hot summer months, from December through March. Winter rains are generally light and widely scattered.

The predominant vegetation is mulga (*Acacia aneura*) woodland, interspersed with open grassland (Perry and Lazarides, 1962). In the extensive dune fields which cover the northern and central part of the region, these plants give way to spinifex (*Triodia* and *Plechtrachne* spp.), mallee eucalypt, and various species of sandhill acacia (predominantly *A. Kempeana*, *dichtophleba*, and *Maitlandii*). Hills and ridges throughout the area are generally barren or covered with low grasses. River channels are lined by tall stands of red gum (*Eucalyptus camaldulensis*), while adjacent flood plains support narrow but ecologically important strips of pasture-like grassland.

Prior to the advent of Europeans, the area was occupied by the Aljawara, Anmatjera and eastern Aranda (Tindale, 1940; Yallop, 1969), all of whom pursued a traditional hunting and gathering life until the establishment of local cattle stations in the late 1920s and early 1930s. Members of these groups are now largely settled around the stations, where they are employed as casual labourers and from which they draw support in the form of government supplied rations. Kangaroo hunting still provides a substantial portion of their diet, but plant collecting, while a common pursuit at some stations, adds little more than variety.

There is scant information on pre-European life in the Sandover Basin, but we can suggest a tentative model of the annual round on the basis of evidence from neighbouring areas occupied by the better known Walbiri (Meggitt, 1962), Aranda (Spencer and Gillen, 1899, 1927; Strehlow, 1965) and Waramanga (Spencer and Gillen, 1904). During the dry winter months, Aborigines were probably dispersed in small groups camped near permanent sources of water, mainly along the larger stream channels. Subsistence was based primarily on vegetable foods, including both roots and seeds. Acacia seeds were perhaps particularly important, since they first appear toward the end of the dry season, when other plant foods may have been nearly exhausted. Lizards and other small animals may have comprised the bulk of the meat diet, but kangaroos were probably also important since they were concentrated near permanent forage and water in this season (Frith and Calaby, 1969 : 93–97) and hence readily taken by stalking and ambush.

Early in the wet season, Aborigines were probably dispersed even more widely than in the dry as families moved out to ephemeral waters to exploit permanent or near permanent, but otherwise inaccessible resources, such as *Ipomoea* roots or sedentary animal populations. Later in the wet, they collected seasonal foods, especially fruits and a variety of seeds, notably those of several genera of grasses. Hunting probably contributed little to the diet at this time, since kangaroo and other large animals were widely scattered and hence less readily taken by small groups of hunters. If the season were a relatively good one, Aborigines came together in fairly large groups, taking advantage of the abundance of resources to perform ceremonies and meet various social obligations. Meggitt (1962 : 49) suggests that among the Walbiri such gatherings took place most often in the autumn or early winter, that is at the end of the wet season or the beginning of the dry (see also Spencer, 1928 : 420).

There is little doubt that this pattern varied substantially in any given area from year to year, depending on the amount and distribution of local rainfall. Nevertheless, it is not unlike that reported for hunter-gatherer populations in other arid areas of the world, including south and east Africa (Lee, 1969; Woodburn, 1968), western North America (Steward, 1938), and highland Mexico (Flannery, 1968). It is similar in many respects to the pattern described by Gould (1969b, 1970) for the Gibson Desert, though the cycle there is less annual in character because of the extremely erratic pattern of rainfall distribution.

Recent research

During the winter of 1973, L. Major and I carried out a preliminary archaeological and ethnographic reconnaissance of the central Sandover River area near MacDonald Downs Homestead, about 200 km northeast of Alice Springs. The purpose of the work was twofold. First, we wanted to learn if enough knowledge of traditional life still existed among local Aborigines to provide the basis for a more comprehensive model of pre-European ecology. Second, we wanted to establish whether archaeological resources in the area were sufficient both to test the model and to determine how long it may have been operative. One approach to these problems was to visit pre-European camps with older Aborigines who were able to discuss various aspects of the occupation of each site as they remembered it, including the season in which it was inhabited, the size and character of the resident group, the range of resources exploited, and so forth. In the course of these visits, we observed that there were substantial intersite differences in the composition of stone tool assemblages, involving both the range of tools represented and their relative importance. At least two factors seemed likely to account for these differences. The first and most obvious was the place of the site in the seasonal round, i.e. whether it was occupied mainly in wet or dry times of the year. A second factor was the character of local resources, both lithic and biotic. Some sites, for example, were situated in areas where seed resources were abundant all year round, while others were in settings where seeds were either uncommon or seasonally limited in occurrence. Such differences might be expected to affect the presence of seed grinding tools in assemblages. Similarly, some categories of tools were made exclusively of particular kinds of stone, so that their relative importance at sites might vary in relation to the distance to certain stone sources.

In order to learn more about this situation, we collected small samples of the surface refuse at seven sites identified by Aljawara informants as having been occupied in pre-European times, but within living memory. The sites were selected because they represent a broad range of variation in terms of the factors thought likely to affect the composition of stone tool assemblages (Fig. 1). Three of them were said to have been used only in the wet season, the other four primarily in the dry.

Although we cannot yet specify the full range of potential plant and animal resources available at these sites, it seems likely that differences can be assessed in a general way by reference to the nature of the surrounding plant community. Three of the dry time camps are on riverine floodplains. Local vegetation is primarily open grassland, though dense stands of mulga woodland are found within a short distance of each site, usually at the margin of the floodplain. Mulga woodland is the dominant community at two sites, one occupied mainly in the dry, the other in the wet. The other two wet time camps lie at the base of a barren sandstone ridge, overlooking spinifex covered sandhills.

Nearly all chipped stone tools found at sites in the Sandover Basin are made either of fine grained cherts and chalcedonies or coarse, granular quartzites.[1] The seven sites in the sample can be divided into two groups based on their proximity to these materials. Four sites are adjacent to sandy stream beds that contain large quantities of chert in the form of small, well rolled cobbles. All four (with the possible exception of site 36) are more than 5 km away from the nearest quartzite source. Conversely, three sites are within 2 km of quartzite outcrops, but not less than 6 km from sources of chert.

At each of the seven sites, we collected all the implements found on the surface in one or more limited areas, which varied in size depending upon the density of the refuse. The chipped stone tools recovered were then presented to groups of Aljawara men familiar with the manufacture and use of stone tools for comments on taxonomy and function. (Initial attempts to follow the same procedure for ground stone tools were abandoned when it became apparent that the information gained was not worth the extraordinary cost in time spent sorting through the fragments.) Subsequent analysis of the material has been directed toward a statement of the principles which govern Aljawara taxonomy, the development of an independent, archaeologically operational taxonomy, and an assessment of the significance of variation in stone tool assemblages as measured by the latter. The results of this work are still incomplete, but sufficient information is now on hand to support preliminary statements.

Description of implements

Eleven implement categories have been recognised so far. Eight of these are made up of chipped stone tools and are defined in part on the basis of variation in overall form, but with particular emphasis on the characteristics of working edges, including length, shape, character and angle of retouch and use, and type of microscopic damage visible under low power magnification. This approach parallels that recently employed in the analysis of tools from other parts of Australia and New Guinea (eg. Allen, 1972; Jones, 1971; White, 1969). The three ground stone tool categories are defined on the basis of overall form and type of functional surface. Each category can be described in brief.

---

1. Analysis of the relationship between ground stone tool distribution and the location of stone sources is not yet complete.

Site Number	5	13	14	38	36	4	10
Season of occupation		Dry				Wet	
Biotic setting	Riverine floodplain			Mulga woodland		Spinifex sandhill	
Nearest stone source		Chert		Quartzite	Chert	Quartzite	

Fig. 1: Characteristics of sites in sample.

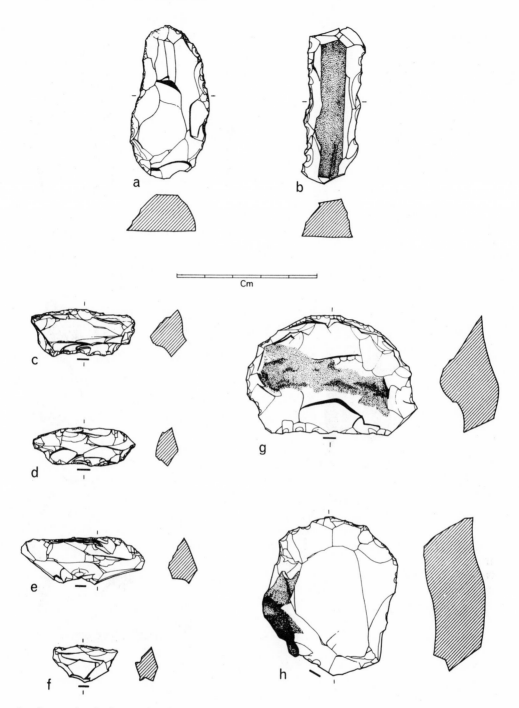

Fig. 2: a–b: burren adze slugs; c–f: tula slugs; g–h: tula adzes.

Adzes These are small to medium sized scrapers, which are highly variable in overall form. Edges are unifacially retouched, generally straight to convex in shape, and have retouch angles in excess of 50°. Nearly all edges are marked by macroscopic step flaking and microscopic step crushing or 'chattering' (White, 1969). Four sub-categories are distinguished:

BURREN ADZES AND SLUGS (Fig. 2a–b) are relatively long narrow blades or flakes with retouch along one or both lateral edges. Striking platforms are perpendicular to the long axis of the edge. On about 35% of burren slugs, the end of the flake opposite the striking platform has also been retouched

or damaged through use. These secondary edges are consistently shorter in length, but similar in shape and retouch angle to the long edges. (Gould in this volume reports that the use of short axis edges on adze slugs is relatively uncommon in the Western Desert, but the situation is clearly different in the Sandover area). About half these implements are quartzite, the rest are chert.

TULA SLUGS (Fig. 2c–f) differ from burren slugs in that they have striking platforms that are parallel rather than perpendicular to their principle working edges. More than 60% have a short secondary working edge on one or both narrow ends. More than 90% are made of chert, the rest of quartzite.

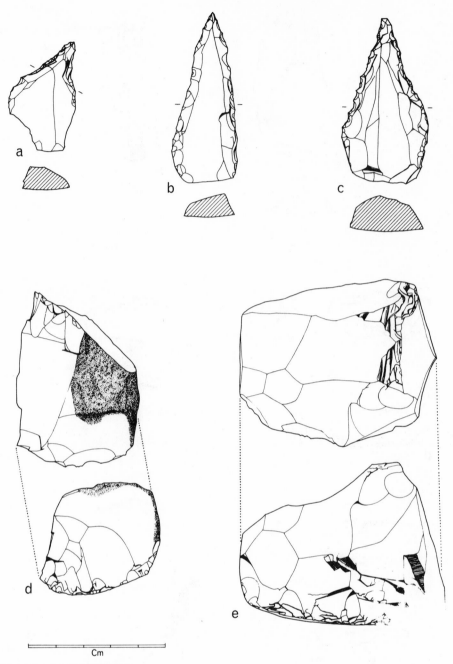

Fig. 3: a–c: unifacial points; d–e: large scrapers.

TULA ADZES (Fig. 2g–h) are thick, semi-discoidal scrapers with striking platforms parallel to the centre section of the working edge. It is commonly held that individual tula adzes gradually change in form over time through continuous sharpening, ultimately becoming tula slugs (eg. Campbell and Edwards, 1965). Examination of the edges of these specimens indicates that the pattern of use and retouch is less consistent than previously thought. In fact, if the pattern established on some were continued, it would more likely result in a burren slug. This observation is consistent with the fact that most tula adzes are made of quartzite, while the majority of tula slugs are chert (see also Gould *et al.*, 1971 : 153–54).

MISCELLANEOUS ADZES AND SLUGS lack striking platforms and hence cannot be assigned to any of the preceding categories. Nearly all have short secondary edges like those noted on tula and burren slugs. More than 90% of the pieces in this category are chert.

Unifacial points (Fig. 3a–c) These are small to medium quartzite flakes, bilaterally retouched and triangular in shape. At least two sub-categories are present. One includes long, relatively narrow, flat specimens which are trimmed along both lateral edges and resemble 'pirri' points (Campbell, 1959). Pieces in the second category are similar to these but the proximal sections of their lateral edges are untrimmed and flaring. Nearly all specimens display lateral and distal edge damage in the form of microscopic step crushing.

Large steep edged scrapers (Fig. 3d–e) These are medium to large core scrapers with short, high angled, unifacially re-

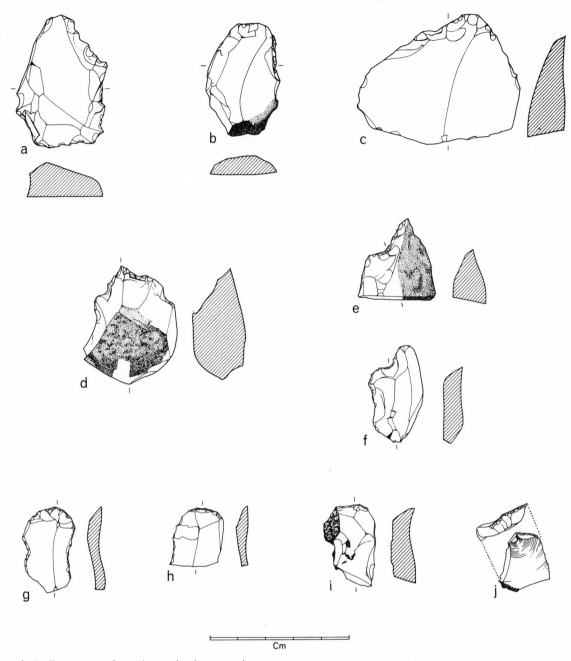

Fig. 4:   a–d : small scrapers ; e–f : notches ; g–j : micro-retouch scrapers.

touched or use damaged edges. Most are highly irregular in shape and have working edges in more than one plane. A few are distinguished from the others by their domed appearance and may be termed horsehoof cores. More than 60% are chert, the rest quartzite.

Small steep edged scrapers and utilised flakes (Fig. 4a–d) These are small, irregularly shaped pieces with one or more straight or slightly convex working edges. More than 60% of all edges are retouched but few display the step flaking characteristically found on adzes. About 80% of these specimens are quartzite, the rest are chert.

Small flake scrapers with 'micro retouch' (Fig. 4g–j) (After Gould, 1969a). These are small, thin flakes or blade sections

with short lengths of fine, unifacial retouch or edge damage. Examination of the damage under 30 × magnification reveals that it is nearly always step crushing, though fine edge abrasion and perpendicular striations were noted on a few pieces. These tools are distinguished from those in the preceding category by their smaller size and shorter retouched or utilised edge length, as well as by the fact that more than 75% are made of chert.

Notches (Fig. 4e–f)   These are small flakes or chunks with one or more steep, very concave edges. Specimens made of quartzite are more common than those of chert.

Sharp edged utilised blades or flakes (Fig. 5a–d)   These are blades or long flakes with one or more edges damaged by

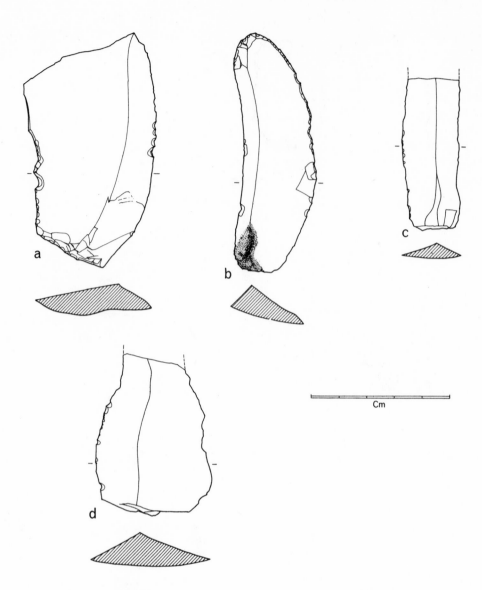

Fig. 5: Unretouched, utilised blades and flakes.

macroscopic nicking or nibbling but otherwise essentially unretouched. Nearly all are quartzite. These tools are almost certainly underrepresented in the sample, since visible edge damage does not inevitably result from the uses to which they are put (primarily meat cutting, see below), and one cannot therefore distinguish utilised but undamaged pieces from chipping debris (cf. Spencer and Gillen, 1904 : 655; Gould, this volume, for similar observations).

Retouched blades (Fig. 6a–f) These are medium to large, parallel sided quartzite blades, all of which have extensive unifacial retouch on both lateral and distal edges. Continuous lengths of microscopic step crushing are visible on about 30% of all lateral edges.

Flat or bevelled handstones (Fig. 7a–b) These are thin, hand held grinding tools which vary from circular to sub-rectangular in outline and from plano-convex to bi-convex in section. Some grinding faces are flat, while others have a marked median keel which apparently divides the surface into two distinct working facets. Edges on most pieces are thin, and often damaged by battering.

Domed handstones (Fig. 7c) These are fist-sized cobbles, roughly circular or ovoid in outline, domed in section. Basal grinding surfaces are flat or slightly convex, and often have a small, circular pecked depression in their centres. Edges are often heavily pecked and battered.

Grinding slabs (Fig. 7d) All specimens recovered are fragmentary, but examination of complete pieces found in other contexts indicates that they were originally thin, flat surfaced slabs with one or more long, shallow grooves worn in the grinding face(s). The sides of these grooves are often longitudinally scored or scratched. On bifacially worked pieces, the reverse surface may be either grooved or ground flat.

Relationship with ethnographic taxonomy

Nearly all the adzes and the greater percentage of notched pieces, small steep-edged scrapers and utilised flakes, and 'micro-retouch' flake scrapers were identified by Aljawara men as *yilbila*. I infer from discussions that the term may be applied to any steep-edged scraping tool, but most often refers to small or medium sized pieces with cutting edges parallel to

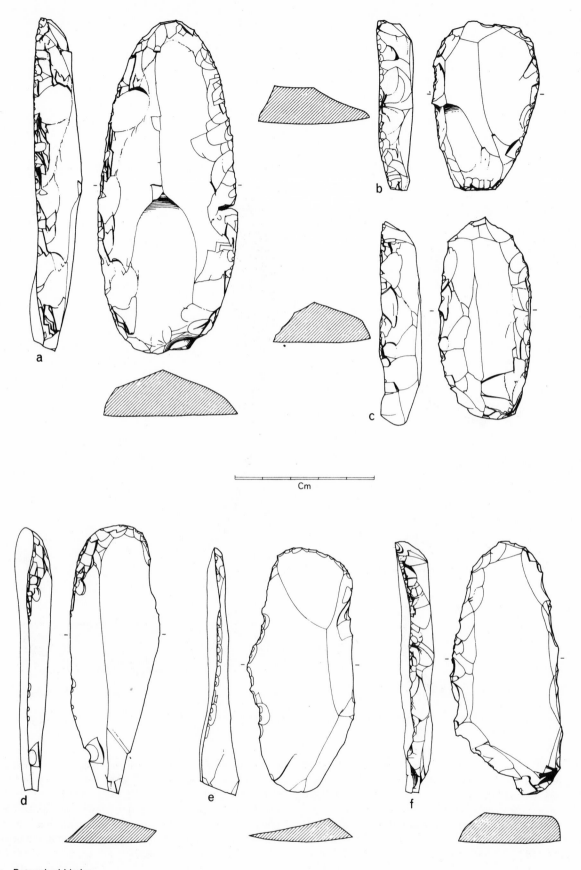

Fig. 6: Retouched blades.

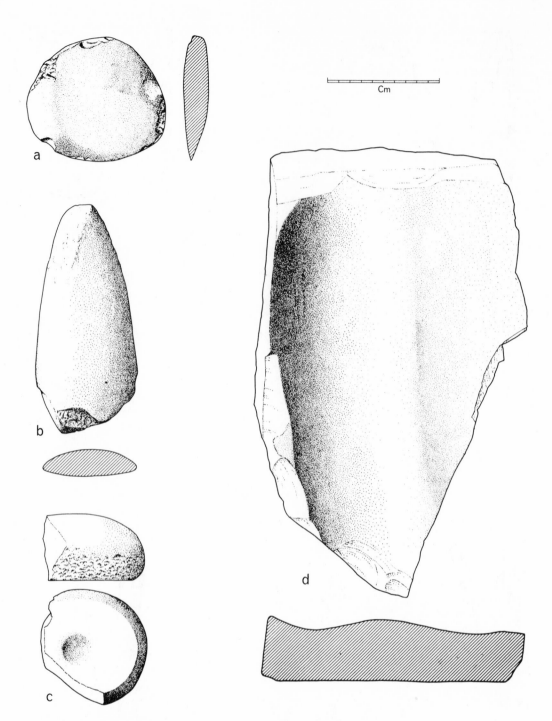

Cm

Fig. 7:   a–b: flat or bevelled handstones; c: domed handstone; d: grinding slab.

their long axes. The Aljawara say these tools may either be mounted on the ends of sticks or spear throwers or hand held, and that they are used in a variety of tasks, particularly those involving wood working. Tools comparable in form and function have been described from several areas of central Australia, including the MacDonnell Ranges (Spencer and Gillen, 1899 : 583), the Lake Eyre region (Horne and Aiston, 1924 : 89, cf. *tuhla*), and the Western Desert (Gould *et al.*, 1971 : 149*ff.*; Tindale, 1965 : 133–39, cf. *purpuna*).

Some of the adze slugs and most of the unifacial points were called *algunya*, a term applied to relatively short, steep working edges perpendicular to the long axis of an implement. When asked about the assignment of adze slugs to this category, informants indicated that they were referring to the short edges on the ends of slugs rather than those which paralleled the long axis. These tools were hafted on the ends of adze sticks, often at the end opposite a *yilbila*, and used for gouging and engraving wood. The longitudinal grooves in wooden bowls and dishes and the complex incised designs on sacred boards and other objects are examples of the kind of work done with *algunya*. Similar tools are reported for the Aranda, Kaididj and Waramanga by Spencer and Gillen (1904 : 638–40; Spencer, 1928 : 500*ff.*) and for Western Desert groups by Gould *et al.* (1971 : 155, cf. *pitjuru-pitjuru*).

Most of the large steep edged scrapers and horsehoof cores were identified either as *yilbila* or *uldunda*, the latter term roughly translatable as 'core'. As one might expect, they were used as heavy duty chopping or cutting tools, primarily in working wood, and as cores.[2]

Sharp edged blades or flakes were called *ngwardia*, a word the Aljawara translate as 'stone knife'. They were hand held or equipped with a simple, spinifex gum haft or wooden handle and served primarily as cutting and butchering implements. Western Desert groups refer to similar implements as *tjimari* (Gould *et al.*, 1971 : 149–57; Tindale, 1965 : 132), while those from the Lake Eyre region call them *yutchawunta* (Horne and Aiston, 1924 : 87).

Retouched quartzite blades were identified as *yilugwa* and were said to be used for a number of purposes, including cutting, wood scraping, and as spoons in the consumption of cooked roots and tubers. In an earlier discussion of these tools (O'Connell, 1974), I followed Spencer and Gillen, Roth, and Tindale in suggesting that they were used primarily by women. However, subsequent fieldwork indicates that this may not have been the case, at least among the Aljawara. Older men claim that the tool was widely used by men as well as women and examples have been observed recently in the possession of members of both sexes.

Bevelled handstones and grinding slabs were called *tjunga* and *aturra* respectively. These implements are used primarily to grind seeds, but may occasionally serve as hammer and anvil to pulverise lizards and other small animals. Domed handstones, termed *alyara*, were employed as multipurpose hammerstones and mullers, but were said to be particularly useful in crushing and grinding hard seeds or nuts, like those of the kurrajong (*Brachychiton* spp.) and several species of acacia.

Interassemblage variability

The following discussion is based on two important assumptions. First, I take it that assemblages on the sites we sampled represent the operation of a single settlement-subsistence system and that their composition is unaffected either by long term changes in style or technology, or by ecological shifts which might alter either the regional pattern of man–land relationship or the place of a particular site in terms of the seasonal round or in relationship to local resources. The idea of long term continuity in central Australian material culture is supported by the recent work of Gould (1969a, 1971) and Stockton (1971), who show that there is little evidence of stylistic or technological variation in the area during the past 10 000 years. Those changes which are apparent involve categories of tools not represented in the samples under discussion. Since the possibility of local or regional ecological change over the same period cannot be controlled on the basis of available data, I am forced to assume for the sake of discussion that it has not been significant.

The second guiding assumption is that the samples collected adequately represent the range of assemblage variation at the sites from which they were drawn and that they are unaffected by intrasite differences in artifact distribution as a function of spatial segregation of certain activities. In fact, such differences do exist, particularly in samples which are small or which were drawn from limited areas (i.e. less than 100 m²).

For the purposes of this preliminary paper, I have chosen to combine samples from two pairs of sites, MD/13 and 14 and MD/4 and 10, in order to reduce the effect of this aspect of variation. As Fig. 1 indicates, these sites are similar in all critical respects, so that such consolidation should have no serious effect on the discussion or conclusions.

The frequency of various implement categories at each site or pair of sites is presented in Table 1 and summarised graphically in Fig. 8. The pattern of variation is clearly complex, involving significant intersite differences in the relative frequency of every category, with the exception of large, steep edged scrapers. Nevertheless, most if not all of these differences can be accounted for by site location, either in relation to stone sources or to plant communities. We can consider each of these factors in brief.

Differences in access to stone affect the ratio of chert to quartzite tools in all categories, as well as the relative importance of tools made exclusively or almost exclusively of quartzite. Sites near quartzite sources are marked by high ratios of quartzite to chert tools and relatively high frequencies of sharp edged utilised blades and flakes, retouched blades and unifacial points. Conversely, sites near chert sources are marked by low quartzite to chert ratios and the absence or low frequency of the latter three categories. While the overall pattern may not be surprising, it is interesting to note that there is no apparent complementary increase in the frequency of functionally similar chert tools to offset the decline in these three particular categories at sites near chert sources. This may mean simply that the activities with which these tools were connected were more often carried out near quartzite sources, but this seems unlikely. A more plausible explanation, at least in terms of both the utilised and retouched blades, is that chert pieces used for the same range of functions were less often recognised as distinctive implements.

Adzes as a group are somewhat less sensitive to differences in proximity to various stone sources than are other tools. This is partly a function of the fact that the Aljawara prefer to make adzes out of chert, regarding those made of quartzite as too brittle. Older men say that particularly valued cherts were often traded over distances in excess of 160 km. Moreover, since adzes were hafted to spear-throwers and adze handles, they were more likely to be carried along when people moved about, further dampening the degree of intersite variation in this category.

Nevertheless, there are significant differences in the particular kinds or types of adzes represented at various sites, and it seems likely that these are a function of local stone resources. As indicated above, nearly all tula slugs are chert, but barely more than half of all burrens are made of this material. Table 2 shows that the ratio of tula slugs to burrens is much greater at site 5, located near chert, than at site 38, near quartzite. A Fisher Exact Test (Siegal, 1956 : 96–104) indicates that the probability that these samples were drawn from similar populations is of the order of 0.001, and that the difference is therefore highly significant. It is tempting to suggest that this difference results from the fact that flakes struck from chert cores are consistently shorter than those struck from quartzite, and are thus less likely to sustain the lateral edge use necessary to reduce them to burren slugs. With the longer quartzite flakes, the situation might be the opposite. Alternatively it may simply be that chert cores available along the river channels are smaller than the quartzite cores produced and worked at outcrops and that this factor rather than differences in the properties of the materials

---

2. Fieldwork done since this paper was written indicates that the term *uldunda* refers primarily to cherts in a variety of forms and contexts rather than to a pan-material, functional category such as 'core'.

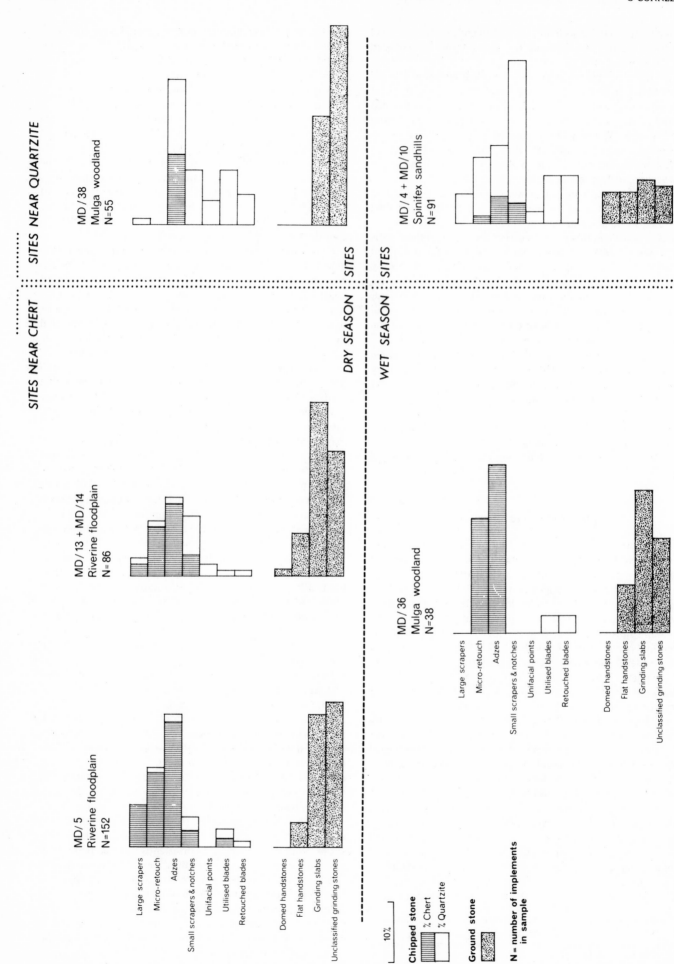

Fig. 8: Relative importance of implements by site.

Table 1   Frequency of implements by site

Q = number made of quartzite, *C* = number made of chert, *T* = total implements in category.
% = percentage of total assemblage represented by all implements in that category

Site	5				13/14				38				36				4/10			
	Q	C	T	%	Q	C	T	%	Q	C	T	%	Q	C	T	%	Q	C	T	%
Adzes																				
Tulas	1	1	2	01	—	—	—	—	—	—	—	—	—	—	—	—	4	—	4	04
Tula slugs	1	23	24	16	—	6	6	07	—	2	2	4	—	5	5	13	2	3	5	05
Burrens	—	2	2	01	1	2	3	04	5	1	6	11	—	2	2	05	1	1	2	02
Misc. adzes	—	6	6	04	—	3	3	04	2	3	5	09	—	4	4	11	1	—	1	01
Total adzes	2	32	34	22	1	11	12	14	7	6	13	24	—	11	11	29	8	4	12	13
Unifacial points	—	—	—	—	2	—	2	02	2	—	2	04	—	—	—	—	2	—	2	02
Large, steep edged scrapers	—	10	10	07	1	2	3	04	1	—	1	02	—	—	—	—	5	—	5	05
Notches	—	2	2	01	1	1	2	02	1	—	1	02	—	—	—	—	5	1	6	06
Small, steep edged scrapers	3	2	5	03	5	2	7	08	3	—	3	05	—	—	—	—	17	2	19	21
Micro-retouch scrapers	1	18	19	13	1	7	8	09	—	—	—	—	—	7	7	18	9	1	10	11
Utilised blades	2	3	5	03	1	—	1	01	4	—	4	07	1	—	1	03	7	—	7	08
Retouched blades	2	—	2	01	1	—	1	01	3	—	3	05	1	—	1	03	7	—	7	08
Chipped stone sub-total	10	67	77	51	13	23	36	42	21	6	27	49	2	18	20	53	60	8	68	75
Flat handstones	—	—	6	04	—	—	6	07	—	—	—	—	—	—	3	08	—	—	5	05
Domed handstones	—	—	—	—	—	—	1	01	—	—	—	—	—	—	—	—	—	—	5	05
Grinding slabs	—	—	33	22	—	—	26	30	—	—	10	18	—	—	9	24	—	—	7	08
Unclass. frags.	—	—	36	24	—	—	17	20	—	—	18	33	—	—	6	13	—	—	6	06
Ground stone sub-total	—	—	75	49	—	—	50	58	—	—	28	51	—	—	18	47	—	—	23	25
Total implements		152				86				55				38				91		

themselves is responsible for variation in flake size and adze type.

Variation in the frequency of adze types may also account for the apparent absence of a functional correlate for unifacial points at sites near chert, or rather, remote from quartzite. Specifically, one might argue that burren adzes and unifacial points form a functional pair or set of woodworking tools whose distribution varies inversely with tula slugs as a function of proximity to chert. The absence of unifacial points at sites where tula slugs were common might be offset by more frequent use of the short, retouched distal edges which appear on about 60% of the latter. The fact that the Aljawara apply the same name (*algunya*) to both short axis adze edges and unifacial point tips is consistent with this suggestion. If this were so, one might predict that (1) the frequency of short retouched edges on adzes and adze slugs should be significantly greater at sites close to chert sources, but that (2) there should be no significant difference in the frequency of the total number of implements with such edges (i.e. adzes with short edges plus unifacial points) regardless of proximity to different stone sources, all other factors being equal. Data relevant to

these propositions are summarised in Table 3. A Chi square test indicates that the first proposition is not supported by the available data. It is not necessarily disproved, however, and should be kept in mind for further consideration in light of a larger sample. The second proposition is supported by the data.

Table 3   Frequency of implements with short, steep retouched edges (*algunya*) at sites 5 and 38

Site number	5	38	
Adzes with one or more short secondary edges (*algunya*)	20	8	28
Adzes without short secondary edges	13	5	18
	33	13	

$\chi^2 = 0.0042$
Samples not significantly different.

	5	38	
Total implements with short *algunya* edges	20	8	28
Other chipped stone implements	57	19	76
	77	27	104

$\chi^2 = 0.1243$
Samples not significantly different.

Table 2   Frequency of tula slugs and burrin adzes at sites 5 and 38

Site number	5	38	
Tula slugs	24	2	26
Burren adzes	2	6	8
	26	8	34

Differences in site location in relation to biotic communities appear to account for variation in the ratio of chipped to ground stone tools and in the relative frequency of particular types of ground stone tools. Sites on flood plains and in mulga woodland have assemblages which include relatively large numbers of seed grinding tools, but a low proportion of domed handstones (Table 1). Conversely, sites in spinifex sandhills have relatively few seed grinding tools, but a greater percentage of domed handstones. These differences may reflect the character of local seed resources. Both mulga woodland and riverine floodplain communities produce substantial crops of economically important grass seeds, most of which are classified by the Aljawara as 'soft' and which they process primarily with bevelled handstones and grooved grinding slabs. I am less certain about the nature of seed resources in spinifex sandhills, but I suspect that they were less abundant than in other communities and that they may have included a greater proportion of 'hard' seeds (esp. kurrajong and certain species of acacia) which are generally prepared with the domed handstone. If the differences in local seed resources are as I have indicated, they would account for the observed variation in grinding tools.

Other aspects of interassemblage variation, particularly in the relative importance of adzes (as a group), small steep edged scrapers and utilised flakes, notched pieces and 'micro retouch' flake scrapers are less readily explained. Nevertheless, at least two hypotheses might be considered. First, since the adzes appear to vary inversely with small scrapers and notches, and since they are identified by the same Aljawara term (*yilbila*), one might argue that they are functionally equivalent, and that the differences in overall form, edge shape, and edge damage which distinguish them are the result of such factors as degree of use wear or the expression of use damage in different material (adzes being primarily chert, the other pieces largely quartzite). If this were so, one might predict that if the categories were combined they would represent roughly the same proportion of the chipped stone sample at all sites. This expectation is reasonably well fulfilled. However, the argument seems less than completely satisfactory in that it fails to account for differences in the relative importance of these categories at sites which have similar stone resources (eg. site 5 *v.* 13–14 or site 4–10 *v.* 38).

As an alternative, one might suggest that there are significant differences in the context in which these tools are used. Specifically, the frequency of adzes at sites in mulga woodland or on floodplains is higher than at sites in dunefields, while the latter boast relatively greater numbers of small scrapers and notches. It is tempting to suggest that these differences are a function of the kinds of wood being worked or the variety of wooden tools being made. Unfortunately there are no data available on which to base such an evaluation and the matter remains unresolved. Both hypotheses will be tested in the course of future work.

Implications

Although the analysis presented here is quite preliminary, it raises two important points about interassemblage variability. One involves the apparent lack of evidence in the lithic material for the seasonal differences in settlement and subsistence which prevailed in the Sandover River area in pre-European times. In terms of the chipped stone material, the reason for this is simple: most of these artifacts are connected with maintenance activities rather than directly with subsistence and are therefore unlikely to reflect seasonal variations of the kind suggested. On the other hand, the ground stone tools should vary according to the overall proportion of seeds in the diet or in terms of the relative importance of particular kinds of seeds (eg. 'hard' *v.* 'soft').

The sites which offer the best basis for comparison on this point are MD/36 and MD/38, both located in mulga woodland, but occupied at different seasons—MD/36 in the wet, MD/38 in the dry. As Table 1 and Fig. 8 indicate, there are no significant differences in overall importance of ground stone tools or in the relative frequency of particular types of tools at these sites. At least two factors may be involved here. First, the seasonal differences in plant food diet, especially seeds, may not have been as great as I have implied. For example, ants collect the seeds of certain species of grass (e.g. *Panicum* sp.) shortly after they fall to the ground and store them in piles or mounds, so that the seeds constitute a permanent or near permanent resource, particularly in mulga country or on floodplains. Clearly, if the same resource is available and exploited at both wet and dry camps, it should not lead to differences in the tool kit. Alternatively, one can argue that hunters generally collect seasonal foods whenever available, rather than permanent ones, and that wet season diets are therefore more likely to be based on fruits and seasonal seeds. However, even if this is the case, such differences in diet are unlikely to be reflected in the ground stone assemblage, either because the foods in question require no preparation, or because those that do are prepared with the same set of general purpose seed grinders used at the dry time camps.

Although I am reluctant to generalise on the basis of such a small sample, the obvious implication of this is that seasonal systems, insofar as they exist in central Australia, are unlikely to be reconstructed or verified on the basis of lithic material. Direct evidence of diet in the form of plant and animal remains will be essential to achieve these objectives.

The second point raised by this discussion pertains to the interpretation of interassemblage variation in Australia at large. It seems fair to say that where such variation is recognised, it is generally seen either as *functional*, that is, as resulting from differences in the range of activities carried out at particular sites, or *stylistic*, reflecting certain traditional standards applied in the manufacture of artifacts. There is no doubt that such interpretations are often quite correct. Nevertheless, the data presented here indicate that a substantial amount of interassemblage variation may be the result of differences in access to material used in the manufacture of tools and of the particular characteristics of these materials as they affect the form of implements. Specifically, I have suggested that the occurrence of two varieties of adzes commonly taken as indicators of separate 'cultural traditions' (eg. Glover and Lampert, 1969 : 244; McCarthy *et al.*, 1946 : 29–30; Mulvaney, 1969 : 113–16) is controlled in at least one area of Australia by the character of local stone sources. It also seems likely that the same factor governs the distribution of unifacial points, and that moreover, the functional equivalents of the latter may not even be separate implements, but are instead represented by auxiliary edges on adze slugs. Given these kinds of differences, reconstructions of site activities and/or the identification of cultural traditions on the basis of variations in implement frequencies alone are likely to be misleading.

The data on which these observations are based are clearly quite limited, but are sufficient to support the contention that both access to and the mechanical characteristics of lithic material need to be considered in defining implement categories and in assessing the significance of variation in the frequency of those categories between assemblages. Jones (1971), Lampert (1972) and others have made the same point, but it deserves far broader consideration.

Acknowledgement The research reported in this paper was supported by the Department of Prehistory, Research School of Pacific Studies, Australian National University. Mr and Mrs Mac Chalmers and members of the Aboriginal community at MacDonald Downs Station provided both the opportunity and the assistance necessary to carry out the field-work. Jack Golson, Rhys Jones, Glynn Isaac, Ron Lampert, Laura Major, John Mulvaney, Nic Peterson, and Peter White contributed to ideas expressed here. Winifred Mumford prepared Fig. 2; Gennesse Winch and Peggy Cole typed the manuscript. I gratefully acknowledge their help. All errors are my own.

References

Allen, H., 1972. *Where the crow flies backwards: man and land in the Darling Basin.* Ph.D. thesis, Department of Prehistory, Australian National University, Canberra.

Campbell, T. D., 1959. The Pirri—an interesting Australian Aboriginal implement. *Records of the South Australian Museum*, 13(4).

—— and R. Edwards, 1965. Stone implements. *In* Cotton, B. C. (ed.), *Aboriginal man in south and central Australia* (pt. 1), pp. 159–220. Adelaide: University of Adelaide.

Flannery, K. V., 1968. Archaeological systems theory and early Mesoamerica. *In* Meggars, B. (ed.), *Anthropological archaeology in the Americas*, pp. 67–87. Washington: The Anthropological Society of Washington.

Frith, H. J. and J. Calaby, 1969. *Kangaroos.* Melbourne: Cheshire.

Glover, I. and R. Lampert, 1969. Puntutjarpa rockshelter excavations by R. A. Gould: a critical review. *Archaeology and Physical Anthropology in Oceania*, 4 : 222–28.

Gould, R. A., 1969a. Preliminary report on excavations of Puntutjarpa rockshelter, near the Warburton Ranges, Western Australia. *Archaeology and Physical Anthropology in Oceania*, 3 : 161–85.

——, 1969b. Subsistence behaviour among the western desert Aborigines of Australia. *Oceania*, 39 : 252–74.

——, 1970. A journey to Pulykara. *Natural History*, 79(10) : 56–67.

——, 1971. The archaeologist as ethnographer: a case from the western desert of Australia. *World Archaeology*, 3 : 143–77.

——, D. Koster and A. H. L. Sontz, 1971. The lithic assemblage of the western desert Aborigines of Australia. *American Antiquity*, 36 : 149–69.

Horne, G. and G. Aiston, 1924. *Savage life in central Australia.* London: Macmillan.

Jones, R., 1971. *Rocky Cape and the problem of the Tasmanians.* Ph.D. thesis, Department of Anthropology, University of Sydney, Sydney.

Lampert, R. J., 1972. Hagen axes: a pilot study of axe typology in the central highlands of New Guinea. Unpublished Ms. on file, Department of Prehistory, The Australian National University, Canberra.

Lee, R., 1969. !Kung bushman subsistence: an input-output analysis. *In* Vayda, A. P. (ed.), *Environment and cultural behavior*, pp. 47–79. Garden City: Natural History Press.

McCarthy, F. D., E. Bramell and H. V. V. Noone, 1946. *The stone implements of Australia.* Australian Museum, Memoir 9, Sydney.

Meggitt, M. J., 1962. *Desert people.* Sydney: Angus and Robertson.

Mulvaney, D. J., 1969. *The prehistory of Australia.* London: Thames and Hudson.

O'Connell, J. F., 1974. Spoons, knives and scrapers: the function of Yilugwa in central Australia. *Mankind*, 9 : 189–94.

Perry, R. A. and M. Lazarides, 1962. Vegetation of the Alice Springs area. *CSIRO Land Resources Series*, 6 : 208–36.

Siegel, S., 1956. *Nonparametric statistics for the behavioral sciences.* Kogakusha: McGraw-Hill.

Slatyer, R. O., 1962. Climate of the Alice Springs area. *CSIRO Land Resources Series*, 6 : 109–28.

Spencer, B. P., 1928. *Wanderings in wild Australia.* London: Macmillan.

—— and F. J. Gillen, 1899. *The native tribes of central Australia.* London: Macmillan.

—— and —— 1904. *The northern tribes of central Australia.* London: Macmillan.

—— and —— 1927. *The Arunta.* London: Macmillan.

Steward, J. H., 1938. Basin-Plateau Aboriginal sociopolitical groups. *Bureau of American Ethnology*, Bulletin 120, Washington, D.C.

Stockton, E. D., 1971. Investigations at Santa Teresa, central Australia. *Archaeology and Physical Anthropology in Oceania*, 6 : 44–61.

Strehlow, T. G. H., 1965. Culture, social structure and environment in Aboriginal central Australia. *In* Berndt, R. M. and C. H. Berndt (eds), *Aboriginal man in Australia*, pp. 121–45. Sydney: Angus and Robertson.

Tindale, N. B., 1940. Distribution of Australian Aboriginal tribes, a field survey. *Transcripts of the Royal Society of South Australia* 64(1) : 140–231.

—— 1965. Stone implement making among the Nakako, Ngadadjara, and Pitjandjara of the great western desert. *Records of the South Australian Museum*, 15 : 131–64.

White, J. P., 1969. Typologies for some prehistoric flaked stone artifacts of the Australian New Guinea highlands. *Archaeology and Physical Anthropology in Oceania*, 4 : 18–46.

Woodburn, J., 1968. An introduction to Hadza ecology. *In* Lee, R. B. and I. Devore (eds), *Man the hunter*, pp. 49–55. Chicago: Aldine.

Yallop, C. 1969. The Aljawara and their territory. *Oceania*, 39 : 187–97.

Investigations of backed blade problems by statistical specification of distinctive features

R. H. PEARCE

Abstract

The presence of wide formal variations among backed blades, introduces problems in comparison and analysis. In several studies, metrical methods have been used to facilitate investigations.

Analysis of measurements of the backed blade industry from Bullsbrook indicates that slenderness is a useful criterion for categorisation.

Statistically significant correlations were found between butt trimming and relative thickness, also between dorsal trimming and four other attributes. Edge angle measurements indicate similarities of function or technique with other tool types.

The patterns may indicate cultural peculiarities, and they show that the attributes are potentially useful for analysis.

Descriptions of backed blades

Formal typology Backed blades have usually been reported in the Australian literature in terms of formal classes such as provided by McCarthy *et al.* (1946) or Campbell and Noone (1943). Explicit details of the industries are not often published, and it was noted by Mulvaney (1969 : 128) that class boundaries are indistinct. Comparison and analysis are difficult with a class showing wide formal variations.

Previous applications of statistics Length measurements have been recorded for several collections, for example McCarthy (1943 : 133; 1948 : 9), Coutts (1970) and Dickson (1973 : 11), while Moore (1970 : 54) has compared attributes between three sites, and ratios were calculated by Lampert (1971 : 42), Bindon (1973) and Hume (1965).

Factor analysis was used by Glover (1969), indicating that the ratio length to width was a useful criterion, and he also compared attributes between four sites, finding uniformity in the tradition (Glover 1967).

The analysis by Wieneke and White (1973) showed that formal properties were incidental to function and manufacture, and no significant means of metrical or formal classification were indicated.

Measurements of backed blades from Bullsbrook, Western Australia My examination of this industry at Bullsbrook, an open sandy site at the foot of the Darling Range about 40 km from Perth, has been reported elsewhere (Pearce, 1972). However, a summary is reproduced (Table 1), the data having been divided into groups A and B as the length : width ratio of the artifacts falls below/above 2.0. I have retained the same usage of the terms group A and group B as Glover

(1967) and Lampert (1971), for convenience in making comparisons. To avoid confusion I shall use the words 'group' or 'subgroup' when dealing with divisions based only on measurements. For divisions based on traditional morphological typology I shall use the terms 'type' and 'class'. The words category, division and set, will not be restricted.

For meanings of the terms backed blade, Bondi, geometric, and microlith, I shall for the present follow ordinary Australian usage (eg. McCarthy, 1967).

In the treatment which follows I have dealt only with those attributes which appear to be significantly correlated but are not necessarily governed by the nature of the stone. It is possible that they may be culturally significant.

The application of tests, and the use of measurements, serve firstly to make explicit certain features which may not be easily described otherwise, secondly as a check that suggested relationships do not arise by chance (within certain limits), and lastly to provide a measure of the degree of separation or association (whichever is applicable), between attributes. Such procedures may be of most value when comparing assemblages where the differences are small, as is evident between backed blade industries.

The term 'distinctive feature' is used in linguistics to denote a characteristic which is essentially due to its semantic influence, and similarly in anthropology to refer to a component which reflects the originator's cognition. When backed blade features believed to be independent variables, prove to be significantly correlated, then it is possible to suggest that they are 'distinctive features', although their actual meaning may require further data for elucidation. It is in this context that I suggest features discussed in this paper are 'distinctive'.

Analysis of the Bullsbrook data

Distinctiveness of groups Before further use can be made of the metrical categories A and B, it is necessary to examine the degree of difference between the two groups. Can the division be justified by showing that the parameters are significantly different?

The question may be approached by applying tests of correlation. Using parameters of the length : width ratios, the *t* coefficient is 16.9, and the probability is less than 0.001 that the groups A and B are random samples of a single population as far as this ratio is concerned. This is supported by the coefficient 6.3 obtained by using the thickness : width ratios from Table 1.

The mean values in Table 1 show that group A items on average are shorter, thicker, and wider than group B items, and suggest that the ratio length : (width plus thickness) might be an efficient indicator of differences.

Table 1 Summary of metrical data for Bullsbrook backed blades

Group A
Length/width up to 2.0 33 items

	Mean	s	Range
Mass (grams)	0.66	0.45	0.2 – 1.97
Length (mm)	16.6	3.5	10.8 –27.4
Width (mm)	9.6	1.9	5.7 –15.1
Thickness (mm)	3.9	1.4	2.1 – 7.8
Length/width	1.73	0.17	1.18– 2.0
Thickness/width	0.40	0.11	0.22– 0.72
Chord angle degrees	34	9	12 –49
Back angle degrees	73	11	50 –84
Single unworked dorsal facet		27%	
Chord use present		6%	
Backed from both faces		21%	
Backed left side		61%	
Butt trimmed		70%	
Step scars present		48%	

Group B
Length/width more than 2.0 90 items

	Mean	s	Range
Mass (grams)	0.50	0.50	0.10– 3.11
Length (mm)	19.7	5.1	12 –39.3
Width (mm)	6.76	2.11	3.4 –15
Thickness (mm)	3.28	1.43	1.7 – 6.5
Length/width	3.03	0.67	2.04– 5.42
Thickness/width	0.51	0.13	0.28– 0.84
Chord angle degrees	37	11	20 –72
Back angle degrees	72	11	35 –90
Single unworked dorsal facet		29%	
Chord use present		6%	
Backed from both faces		45%	
Backed left side		58%	
Butt trimmed		70%	
Step scars present		57%	

s = standard deviation

Relationships between metrical and formal categories In view of the close correspondence reported by Glover (1967 : 419) between metrical group A and geometric formal type, it is of interest to enquire if the same situation applies to Bullsbrook industries. The collection was inspected and typologically classified with the assistance of McCarthy's reference list (1967 : 45).

I found that group A contained 22 geometric forms and 11 Bondi forms, while group B contained 7 geometric and 83 Bondi forms. Combining them produces 29 geometrics and 94 Bondis.

Graphical presentation of results Two histograms have been drawn to show the frequencies of distribution of items, as the length : width ratio rises from 1.0 to 6.0. Fig. 1 applies to metrical groups A and B.

Fig. 2 applies to formal typology, showing the incidence of the geometric class as diagonal shading, while the Bondi class constitutes the remainder. In Fig. 2 there is a degree of overlap of formal types on both sides of the value 2.0 used for separating metrical groups, this shows how the frequency distributions differ between metrical groups and formal types for this length : width indicator.

There are two factors to bear in mind, firstly the criterion for dividing metrical groups is fixed arbitrarily at length : width 2.0, and secondly, the geometric-Bondi assessment is subjective, and is liable to vary between different observers. At present there appears to be no reason to alter the criteria of division, and the metrical method has the advantages of being objective, precise, and easy to operate.

The metrical and formal graphs of frequency distributions have somewhat similar shapes, suggesting that for this indicator or attribute (ie. length : width ratio), analogous categories may exhibit statistical properties with close correspondence. If the degree of correspondence could be specified, it should become possible to employ a few metrical processes on those industries for which only formal classifications have been published. Parameters of the Bullsbrook geometric and Bondi classes were calculated and correlation tests with metrical groups were applied, producing the coefficient 1.75 between geometric class and group A, and 0.26 between Bondi class and group B.

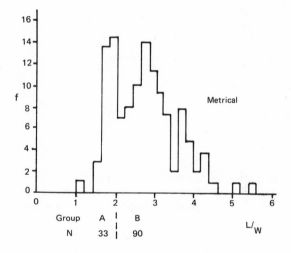

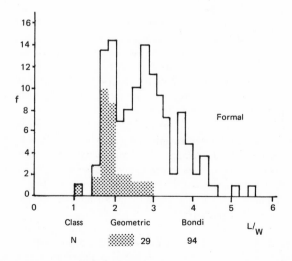

Figs 1 and 2: Metrical and formal histograms of the length/width distribution of Bullsbrook backed blades.

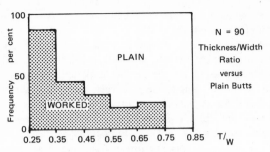

1. Percentage Plain Butts in each thickness/width class.

83	39	31	14	20	0	Plain butts % in class.
5	9	9	3	1	0	Plain butts in class.
6	23	29	22	5	5	Total in each class.

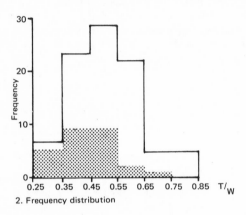

2. Frequency distribution

Fig. 3: Histogram of Group B.

In both cases the differences could arise by chance with a probability greater than 0.1. To this extent the respective formal-metrical categories are related. In other words the tests using slenderness as an indicator show that group A is closely related to geometric class and group B is very closely related to Bondi class.

For other backed blade industries the length : width distribution may be different, for example it is unimodal in the Sassafras industry (Hume, 1965 : 30), while elsewhere there may be more than two modes.

These data indicate that one of the interesting aspects of difference between industries from different sites or levels, is the extent by which the metrical groups are separated (such as Bullsbrook A and B), and this can be measured roughly by using the t test.

Relationships between attributes Previous workers concluded that backed blades comprised a single category, with no evidence of significant correlations between independent attributes (Wieneke and White, 1973). A different result may be obtained however, by examining another assemblage, or by using different attributes.

It has been shown (Pearce, 1973) that certain attributes of backed blades exhibit intersite variability, indicating heterogeneity of the tradition. I now propose to search the Bullsbrook industry for significant internal peculiarities, dealing mainly with the group B category.

The subgroup with 'unworked' butts In group B there are 27 items with plain (unworked or slightly worked) butts. Items in this subgroup are nearly all smaller in size (mean mass 0.42 gram) than the items with worked butts (mean mass 0.66 gram).

A similar relation between mass and butt trimming was found for Yarrar points by Flood (1970 : 45). The Bullsbrook case seems more relevant to hafting than to weight reduction.

The subgroup with plain butts is not distributed evenly through group B with respect to thickness nor to the ratio thickness : width. The thickest items tend to be most worked, the thinnest are least worked on the butts. The distribution of plain butts was examined using frequency counts in the upper and lower halves of the thickness : width range. The value 3.0 at first obtained for χ^2 is not particularly significant, so a more detailed analysis was attempted.

The frequency distribution of group B items is shown in Fig. 3 for increasing thickness : width ratio, in six categories. In each category the number of items with plain butts was counted and expressed as a percentage of the total in each category. The percentage is higher in the categories of low thickness : width ratio and lowest in the categories of high ratio, as shown in the graph (Fig. 3).

In order to examine the significance of this distribution, the Spearman Rho test was applied, comparing the rank order of percentages with the six thickness : width categories (Table 2).

Table 2 Percentage plain butts versus relative thickness

% Plain butt	Rank	Thickness : width	Rank	D	D²
83	6	0.3	6	0	0
39	5	0.4	5	0	0
31	4	0.5	4	0	0
14	2	0.6	3	—1	1
20	3	0.7	2	1	1
0	1	0.8	1	0	0

Rho = 0.94

With this value of rho, the observed distribution could occur by chance with a probability less than 0.05, and a real relationship between the two variables is indicated. Secondly the χ^2 test was applied, comparing observed with expected frequencies (Table 3).

Table 3 Relative thickness versus plain butts

| T/W ratio | Observed | | | Expected | |
	Plain	Worked	Total	Plain	Worked
0.3	5	1	6	1.8	4.2
0.4	9	14	23	6.9	16.1
0.5	9	20	29	8.7	20.3
0.6	3	19	22	6.6	15.4
0.7	1	4	5	1.5	3.5
0.8	0	5	5	1.5	3.5
	27	63	90		

$\chi^2 = 9.6$ df = 2

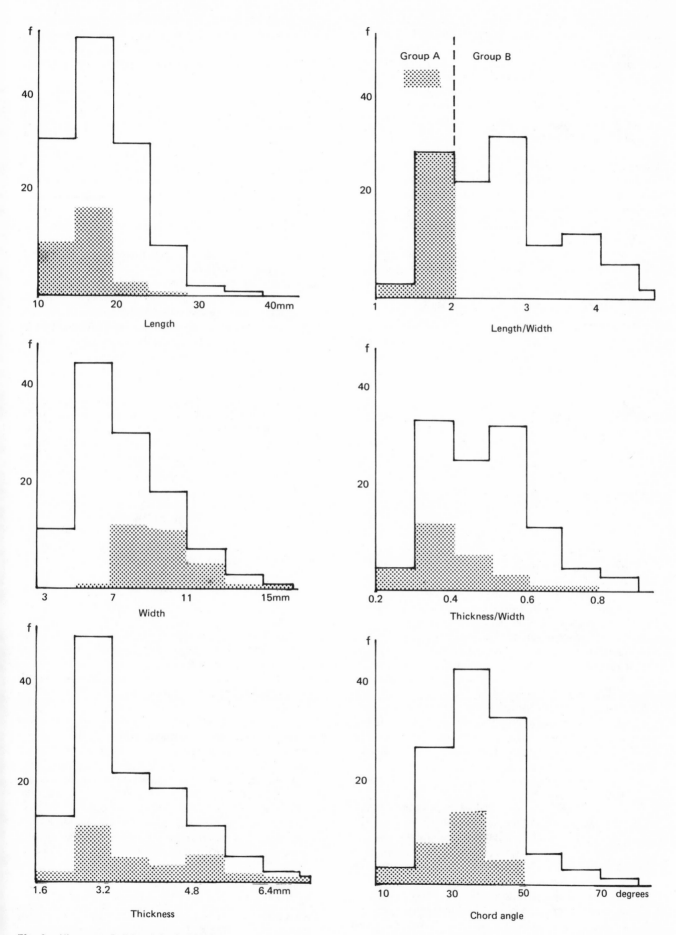

Fig. 4: Histogram, Bullsbrook backed blades.

This is significant at probability less than 0.01, and it is unlikely that the distribution arose by chance. Regression χ^2 is 10.15, and with one degree of freedom, probability is less than 0.005 that the differences between observed and expected frequencies are due to chance. It is concluded, that random dispersion does not account for the observed uneven distribution of plain butts, and that their higher incidence among items of small thickness : width ratio is a distinctive feature of the Bullsbrook industry.

Backing from both faces The set of implements worked from dorsal and bulbar faces contains a higher proportion of items made from quartz, more items with single dorsal facets, and has higher values of thickness : width and length : width ratios, than is found in the set without dorsal working (Table 4).

In each case the χ^2 values indicate probabilities less than 0.01 of occurrence by chance of the observed frequency distributions.

Table 4   Correlations with dorsal working

Subgroups:	With dorsal backing	Without dorsal backing	χ^2	Probability less than
Quartz items	14	4	7.3	0.01
Chert	28	44		
Single dorsal facet	20	6	11.8	0.01
Double facet	22	42		
Thickness:				
width > 0.5	26	15	7.3	0.01
< 0.5	16	33		
Length:				
width > 3.5	16	6	6.7	0.01
< 3.5	26	42		

Implements with a single dorsal facet were probably made in most cases from bladelets of triangular crossection, and they are on average slightly thicker than items with two or three facets, but they are not otherwise distinctive, except for dorsal backing.

Angles of edges The angles of backing, and of the sharp (chord) edges of the Bullsbrook items, were found to average 72° and 37° respectively (Table 1, group B). These values are close to the angle measurements reported by Gould et al. (1971 : 151) for ethnographic adzes and knives, as shown in Table 5.

Tests show that the small differences within each set are not statistically significant.

The data indicate that the method of trimming backed blades may be similar to that used for adze flakes, and that the sharp edge is potentially suitable for cutting purposes.

Backed blades have not been observed in use by Aborigines, but four kinds of use wear (cutting, scraping, piercing and graving) were recognised by McCarthy (1943 : 149) as occasionally occurring on different parts of Bondi points.

Many investigators have favoured the cutting function, and Moore (1970 : 59) reported that use wear of the sharp edge occurred on about 15% of items from ten sites. He also

Table 5   Comparison of edge angles

	Mean angle	Standard deviation	Range	N
Angle of backing				
Bullsbrook backed blade	72°	11	35–90	40
Ethnographic tula*	75.2°	11†	50–90	9
Ethnographic *purpunpa**	67°	13†	40–90	26
Chord angle				
Bullsbrook backed blade	37°	11	20–72	90
Ethnographic knife*	35°	11†	19–59	8
Ethnographic *Tjimari**	39.52°	9†	19–59	25

* Gould, et al., 1971 : 151
† Calculated from published groupings

recorded mean edge angles of three industries, as 33.2°, 36.5° and 40.75° (*ibid.*: 53).

In the Bullsbrook case there are 6% of items with use marks on the chord edge.

Resin stains have been recorded on eight backed blades, in each case along the backed margin, indicating hafting to facilitate use of the sharp edge (Mulvaney, 1969 : 263 one from Fromm's Landing, three from Graman, and Moore, 1970 : 59 four items from the Hunter Valley).

The comparison of sharp edge angles made in the present study tends to support the claims for a cutting function.

In considering functions there are questions raised by Coutts (1970 : 117) which still remain unanswered, showing that more data are required. (a) If backed blades were rejects from use, what were their original shapes? (b) If their present shapes were deliberately prepared for use, why are whole items so common on occupation sites?

Conclusions from Bullsbrook data

(a) The division based on slenderness is statistically significant and analytically useful.
(b) A significant relationship exists between thickness and butt trimming in group B.
(c) Items trimmed from both faces tend to be thick and long with respect to width, and to have triangular cross sections.
(d) The proportion of dorsal trimmed items is much higher in quartz (80%) than in chert (42%).
(e) Angle measurements indicate factors in common with certain other types of implement.

As there are no obvious ways in which the relationships could have been dictated by the physical nature of the stone, or by the methods of measurement, it may be suggested that the combinations of attributes represent particular cultural preferences. In addition they may reflect behaviour in different temporal phases, since Bullsbrook is rich in artifacts, and may have been occupied over several millennia.

Whatever may be the explanation for the relationships, it appears that certain attributes are suitable for analysis independently of formal typology.

Acknowledgments I wish to thank Mrs S. J. Hallam for comments on an early draft of this paper, Mr A. R. Pearce for drawing figures 1, 2 and 3, Mr A. Fewings for assistance with statistical procedures, and the A.I.A.S. for enabling me to present the paper. The author is solely responsible for all of the measurements, calculations, errors, omissions, and other deficiencies in this paper.

References

Bindon, P., 1973. Surface campsite collections from the A.C.T. *Australian Institute of Aboriginal Studies, Newsletter*, 3(6) : 4–12.

Campbell, T. D. *and* H. V. V. Noone, 1943. South Australian microlithic stone implements. *Records of the South Australian Museum*, 7 : 281–307.

Coutts, P. J. F., 1970. *The archaeology of Wilson's Promontory*. Canberra : Australian Institute of Aboriginal Studies.

Dickson, F. P., 1973. Backed blades and points. *Mankind*, 9 : 7–14.

Flood, J., 1970. A point assemblage from the Northern Territory. *Archaeology and Physical Anthropology in Oceania*, 5(1) : 27–52.

Glover, I. C., 1967. Stone implements from Millstream Station, Western Australia: Newall's collection re-analysed. *Mankind*, 6 : 415–25.

—— 1969. The use of factor analysis for the discovery of artefact types. *Mankind*, 7 : 36–51.

Gould, R. A., D. A. Koster *and* A. H. L. Sontz, 1971. The lithic assemblage of the Western Desert Aborigines of Australia. *American Antiquity*, 36 : 149–69.

Hume, S. H. R., 1965. *The analysis of a stone assemblage to determine change*. B.A. (Hons) thesis, University of Sydney.

Lampert, R. J., 1971. Burrill Lake and Currarong, *Terra Australis I*. Canberra: Australian National University.

McCarthy, F. D., 1943. An analysis of the knapped implements from eight elouera stations on the South Coast of New South Wales. *Records of the Australian Museum*, 21 : 127–53.

—— 1948. The Lapstone Creek excavation. *Records of the Australian Museum*, 22 : 1–34.

—— 1967. *Australian Aboriginal stone implements*. Sydney: The Australian Museum.

——, E. Bramell *and* H. V. V. Noone, 1946. The stone implements of Australia. *Australian Museum Memoir*, 9 : 1–94.

Moore, D. R., 1970. Results of an archaeological survey of the Hunter River Valley, New South Wales, Australia. *Records of the Australian Museum*, 28 : 25–64.

Mulvaney, D. J., 1969. *The prehistory of Australia*. London: Thames & Hudson.

Pearce, R. H., 1972. *A discussion of the Australian backed blade tradition*, Anthropology Department, University of Western Australia. Manuscript.

—— 1973. Uniformity of the Australian backed blade tradition. *Mankind*, 9(2) : 89–95.

Wieneke, C. *and* J. P. White, 1973. Backed blades: another view. *Mankind*, 9 : 35–58.

The cultural chronology of the Roonka Flat

A preliminary consideration

GRAEME L. PRETTY

Unto these of our Urnes none here can pretend relation, and can only behold the Reliques of those persons, who in their life giving the laws unto their predecessors, after long obscurity, now lye at their mercies. But remembering the early civility they brought upon these Countreys, and forgetting long passed mischiefs; we mercifully preserve their bones, and pisse not upon their ashes.

SIR THOMAS BROWNE, 1652

Introduction

Stone tools have always been first resorted to as sources of evidence for the cultural development of precivilised man. In our continuing usage of the terms Palaeolithic, Mesolithic and Neolithic to describe the subdivisions of man's cultural development as it has attained global spread, we reaffirm the usefulness of defining it in stone tool technical terms. Because stone tools are still the most widespread, plentiful and clearly identifiable of early man's residues and are so readily incorporated into the sediment patterns of the biosphere, they have seemed admirably fitted to play a primary role in stratigraphic and chronological studies.

Nevertheless, their longstanding employment by archaeologists has disclosed limits to their applicability. For example their range of original functions and sensitivity to chronology has been found unspecific when compared against that of the fired earth and metallic objects which in time replaced them. Furthermore, it has become a matter of relatively modern knowledge that the living cultural and technological systems which stone tool traditions have stood for were probably far more complex and changing than was previously allowed. This richer recent insight has come about primarily through advances in the stratigraphic interpretation of humanly enriched soils. It has also come about from better knowledge of the workings of hunter-gatherer societies based on observations of living specimens of these societies that have survived into the modern era.

Nowhere could knowledge of hunter-gatherer societies have better come from than Australia where these societies had preserved themselves in isolation and in their purest form until very recently. Paradoxically, nowhere was the vulnerability of hunter-gatherer societies better exemplified than in the Australia of a century ago, where the ephemeral and incidental handiwork of a race obsessed with the workings of the cosmos, came under the scrutiny of an incoming race whose interest in the cosmos was relatively detached, but whose passionate pride in making things was without parallel in the world of that time. In the mindless conflict which ensued, a great cosmology and fascinating ethology passed into history with the barest of notice. Now that Australia's history is becoming recognised as primarily the tale of tribal hunter-gatherer societies, we are having to carefully sift the slender store of evidence which has been preserved. It is further becoming clear that we may even have to resort to prehistory for the supply of suggestions as to what further may have been lost.

In Australia, the reconstruction of the prehistoric past has also been characterised by studies based on stone tools. Chronologies have been calibrated against them and complete lifeways have been defined in terms of them. Nevertheless, there is no reason against assuming that in Australia too the meticulous study of sites in the field will not fail to yield stratigraphic markers of complex and changing cultural systems. This implies that archaeologists should pay sustained attention to the unique characters of Australian soils and to the dissecting out and identification of the human traces and residues which they contain. As these soils differ significantly from those made familiar by the archaeological literature of other countries, field workers must of needs occupy themselves with their field interpreting as much as with the analysis of finds recovered from them.

This paper is a preliminary report of findings from excavations conducted in obedience to the above imperatives. The work has been carried out at a complex of open sites situated in the lower Murray River valley of South Australia.

The sites in their landscape

The sites so far investigated extend along a 16 km stretch of the Murray for an equal distance north and south of Blanchetown (34° 21′ S; 139° 36′ E). The area lies some 40 km downstream from the Big Bend where the Murray breaks its east–west course across south-eastern Australia and flows south into the ocean. For that particular portion, the river runs between high limestone cliffs marking the edges of an immense stretch of arid scrub-covered plain. To the east the plain extends hundreds of kilometres into Victoria but to the west it is broken 40 km distant by the line of scarps marking the Mount Lofty Ranges. Deep within its limestone walls the river flows sinuously between wooded flats and rush-filled lagoons. Although now vastly altered by 150 years of urban–industrial agriculture, enough survives to suggest that it was once most attractive for hunter-gatherer subsistence. Then the lagoons would have yielded birds, fish, molluscs and crustacea together with reeds and other edible-rooted plants. The flats would have yielded yams, fruits and herbs and furnished an environment for subterranean and arboreal game. The mallee scrub of the high plain beyond would have accommodated larger game animals, fowl and the large flightless birds. Such resources would have supplied not only food but all the raw materials—wood, bone, sinews, fibres, feathers and resin—of hunter-gatherer technology. The only essential material lacking in such an inventory is the silicious stone suitable for the manufacture of sharp tools. The Murray is singularly poorly endowed with this material. It was therefore an article of value, without doubt an item of trade and a substance to be substituted for where possible and used up completely when available. This same deficiency however makes the Murray region an ideal testing ground for the archaeological value of stone tool studies.

Tribal geography Despite the gaps in the source material for this area at the time of its colonisation by Europeans we know that the tribal owners called themselves Ngaiawang and admitted to some relationships with both their neighbours downstream, the Nganguruku, and, upstream to the north, the Ngawait (Radcliffe-Brown, 1918; Tindale, 1940). Discernible though lesser relationships seem to have been felt for a considerable distance further up river at least to a point beyond the Murray's junction with the Darling and some distance up the latter (Tindale, 1939). It has been stated that these river societies exhibited certain features that distinguished them from their neighbours on either side. There is evidence to suggest that this had much to do with their fairly fixed attachment to relatively circumscribed territories and a consequent localising of descent groups. In this way their social structure is thought to have absorbed some of the more obvious classificatory and structural features so well known of Australian social organisation (Radcliffe-Brown, 1930).

Sites north of the Roonka Flat Archaeological investigation has so far been confined to the river trench (Map 1) although certain sites have been located on the mallee plains. The first work carried out in the area was at Haylands Station in 1928 where cave paintings in a rockshelter were recorded and the floor test-excavated (Sheard, 1928). The present project had its first beginnings in 1962 when a rock shelter was test excavated at McBean's Pound. At this spot, the base of the Murray cliff is undercut into a series of shallow overhangs whose floors fall away to the flood plain beneath in a shallow sloping surface of soil and scree. The flood plain juts out as an irregular extent of relatively low lying soil subject to inundation. In places, where the plain is intersected by channels, silted-over fireplaces and shell refuse heaps are exposed. As a landscape association it is typical for this part of the Murray.

The Roonka Flat (Map 1) The Roonka Flat, immediately to the south of McBean's Pound on the same bank, presents a quite different appearance. Here the river, having veered around McBean's Pound across to the east bank cliffs and back to the west bank, strikes off again at a much shallower angle due to the elevated mass of the Roonka Flat. Thus, a large semicircular slab of ground some 350 ha in area (1·3 sq miles) emerges 5 m in height above the flood plain. This landscape prominence has successfully resisted all historically recorded floods. Evidently it has also resisted the floods of several previous millennia. Its eastern curving margin is marked by a low dune of sand still preserving the remnants of a summit at its mid-point. Behind the dune the ground falls away shallowly as the flat is traversed westwards, to be broken by distant line of gullied and gently rising slopes—remnants of the former cliffline. In front of the dune and hugging the margins of the high flat is a narrow strip of flood plain intersected with channels and a lagoon. This is called Cumbunga Flat.

Systematic survey of the flat, mapping of sites exposed on the ground and excavation at selected points have supplied an outline to its prehistoric cultural geography. At the northern end, where the flat, the flood plain and the rising ground meet, is a cluster of sites constituting a 'North Flat' group. The Roonka Station buildings are situated here, sheltered by the rising ground close behind. The rubble of hunter-gatherer stone cobble fireplaces can still be seen in and among the station buildings, although the main density is located a little to the south on both sides of a dry gully that cleaves into the rising ground. A flash flood at this spot in 1961 exposed inhumations and campsites. The area is now cultivated. A little to the west and further up the gully, the ground has been trenched and a series of stone cobble cooking structures have been unearthed. The broad extent of the Flat has now lost its woodland cover and is mostly meadow. A century ago the root systems of the trees furnished an environment for the relished Roongko grub—hence the name Roonka. The Roonka Flat Dune is strung out around the edge of this onetime woodland (Plate 1). It is replete with sites and has been trenched at several points, principally in the middle where erosion has been severest. It has been referred to as the 'Roonka Flat Dune' group.

The southern edge of the Roonka Flat falls away shallowly to the Cumbunga Flat flood-plain. The cause of this has been identified as a fossil lagoon and stream system anterior to the present day one and immediately adjacent. We have called this the Wetjungali system. It has the appearance of having long since silted in and is now discernible in faint outline only. To the west it is fed by another broad gully intersecting the slope that descends from the mallee plain. At its eastern end it leads into a shallow former stream line which runs along the base of the dune and follows its curve. A series of sites occur around the lagoon margin. They must be old as they are penetrated by the root systems of defunct box gums. They have been called the 'Wetjungali' group. Immediately south of the Wetjungali system and intersecting the level flood-plain is the still functional Cumbunga lagoon and creek system. Its margins are dotted with sites and many of the red gums along Cumbunga creek still bear the scars of bark removed for canoes. The Wetjungali and Cumbunga site complexes have been classed together as the 'South Flat' group. One site has been tested by excavation.

Across river from Roonka and surmounting the cliffs rising above the river valley is a series of ancient linear dunes trending inland. Blown swales within them have yielded stone tools and habitation residues of an ancient sort. One of them has been trenched. As they fall within the boundaries of Glenforslan Station, they will be referred to as the Glenforslan sites.

Setting aside the Glenforslan sites (which appear separate and older) the sites on the Roonka Flat itself appear to dispose into three major groups, the North, the Dune, and the South. Significantly, each of them straddles the full range of food sources, riverine, lacustrine, woodland and high mallee plain. There is reason to suppose that they could have extended across river to the flats and cliff overhangs of the east bank.

It is tempting to further suppose that each of them might be a separate hunting territory. Although the historic literature confirms the density of Murray valley hunting territories, we as yet have no way of evaluating their extent. It may be that careful archaeological mapping may supply the answer.

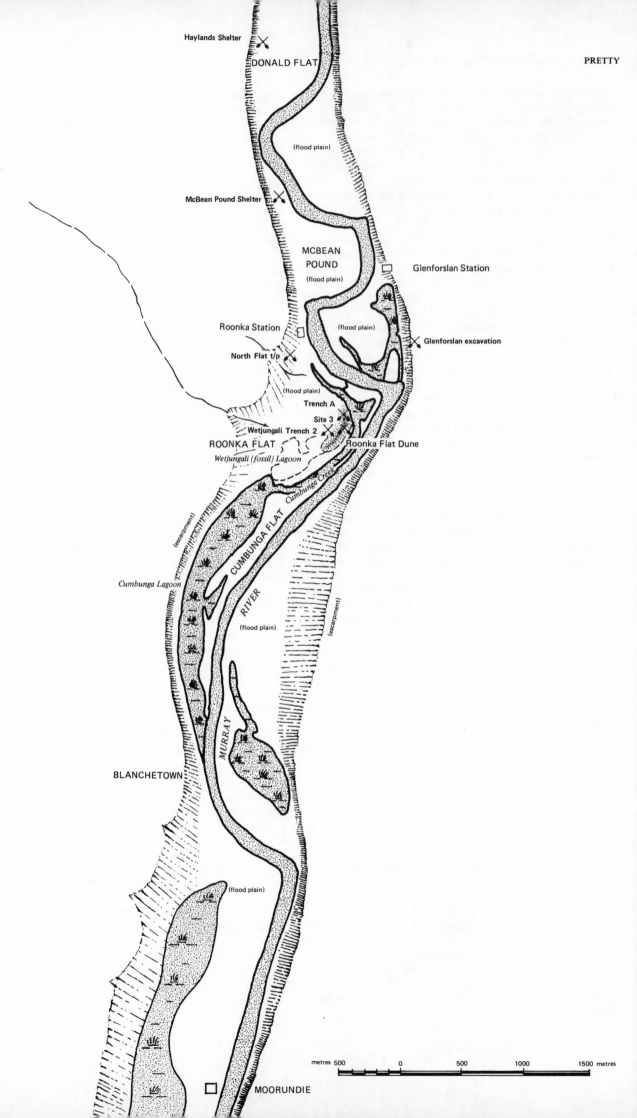

Haylands Shelter

DONALD FLAT

(flood plain)

McBean Pound Shelter

MCBEAN
POUND

(flood plain)

Glenforslan Station

(flood plain)

Roonka Station

North Flat t/p

Glenforslan excavation

(flood plain)

Trench A

Site 3

Wetjungali Trench 2

Roonka Flat Dune

ROONKA FLAT

Wetjungali (fossil) Lagoon

Cumbunga Creek

CUMBUNGA FLAT

Cumbunga Lagoon

RIVER

(escarpment)

(flood plain)

(escarpment)

MURRAY

BLANCHETOWN

(flood plain)

metres 500   0   500   1000   1500 metres

MOORUNDIE

Plate 1: Part of the Roonka Flat from the air. A: Trench A (far left middle-ground); B: Roonka Flat Dune; C: Stream bed of fossil Wetjungali system (marked by broken line); D: permanently inundated Cumbunga Stream system; E: main stream; F: East bank cliffs (Glenforslan dunes at top left outside picture).

South of the Roonka Flat   Leaving the Roonka Flat and, following the river south for 5 km, one comes to Blanchetown which used to be a river port and then the site of lock No. 1. Nowadays it is principally a holiday resort. Aboriginal campsites were frequently reported on both sides of the river at Blanchetown but all traces of them have disappeared.

From Blanchetown the river assumes a relatively straight course and flows close to the east bank cliff leaving a narrow low-lying and well wooded flat on the west bank. The former site of Moorundie lies 6 km south of Blanchetown on the west bank. It was abandoned in 1856 when Blanchetown was settled. It was at Moorundie in 1841 that the government of the then three year old colony established a station for the protection of Aborigines and to create peace between them and the settlers who were droving stock overland from New South Wales and Port Phillip. Most evidences of Moorundie's layout have long been obliterated but a recent examination suggests that it too could be usefully explored by excavation.

Map 1 (opposite): Murray Trench and Roonka Flat showing the major localities investigated, the location of the sites and the features referred to in the text.

Excavation of the Roonka Flat dune — methodology and stratigraphy

The most striking first impression of the Roonka Dune prior to excavation was the broad shallow depression scooped out of the middle of the dune. It was densely carpeted with human skeletal remains in varying states of fragmentation. Isolated finds of human remains and archaeological habitation residues had been common occurrences on the Flat since its severe gullying and loss of top soil in the 1956 flood. The greatest density however was found eroding from the dune. Even for the Murray, where archaeological residues have always been dense on the ground, it was evident that this was an extraordinary site. In the absence of any overall correlation between the ancient biological, cultural and ecological evidence for the region, it seemed likely that Roonka would be a promising locality for investigation. Recording such a wealth of evidence was of the highest priority and urgency because of its obvious vulnerability. The principal difficulties were in acquiring resources for undertaking the work.

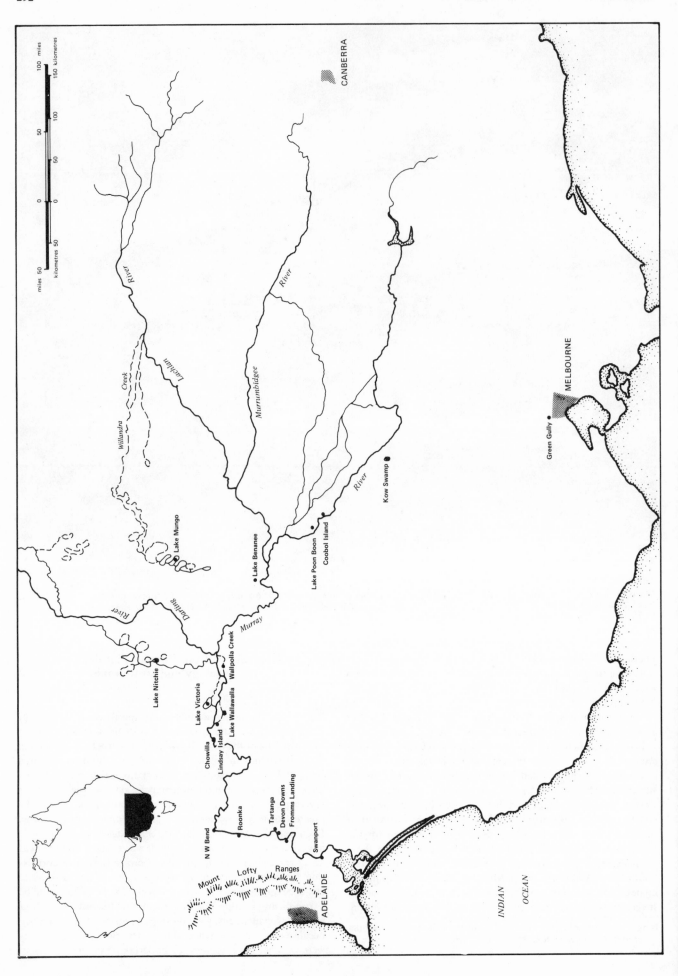

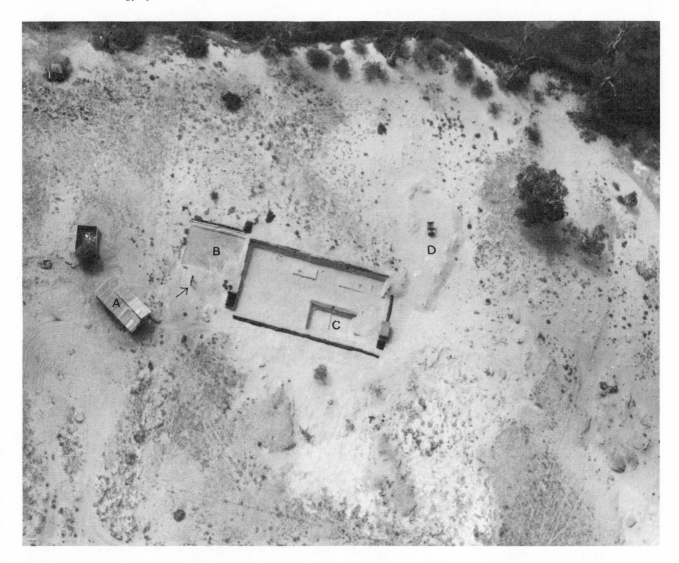

Plate 2: Trench A, Roonka Flat Dune from the air 1972. A: project workshed; B: supplementary trench OA; C: Sondage pit penetrating Layers 4–5; D: spoil heap (note mechanical dumper). Scale can be measured by the two adults standing below OA (see arrow). Left hand photograph margin indicates north.

Fortunately it was possible to assemble and commit a large team of volunteer fieldworkers. Excavation began in the Roonka Flat Dune in November 1968. Six trenches measuring 15 × 30 m were laid out, the surface debris collected, and one of the trenches (Trench A) selected for intensive study (Plate 2). At the moment of writing six further trenches have been sunk into the dune. In addition, a considerable proportion of the stray finds and features eroding out of the ground have been rescued as exposed.

This paper is based on material drawn primarily from Trench A although reference will be made to features excavated in other trenches where necessary. This presentation must still be regarded as provisional although the general outlines of the site's prehistory appear to have firmly emerged.

The skeletal material has been moving away from the centre of attention. It now ranks as one component only of a much larger range of archaeological phenomena which,

Map 2 (opposite): The Murray–Darling stream system in southeastern Australia showing location of sites referred to in the text.

taken together, make Roonka a singular specimen of an open station of ancient hunter-gatherer man. The succession of cultural events preserved within the site discloses a history that extends from colonist times back to the late Pleistocene.

Initial interpretation of the profile   Initial inspection of the exposed profile disclosed a series of three superimposed sands with well defined unconformities (Plate 3). The three components rested on a compact *terra rossa* subsoil which had resisted deflation. The top sand was faintly red, unfeatured and relatively sterile. Beneath it lay a broad band of greyish brown loam varying in thickness and densely intertextured with hunter-gatherer settlement debris—oven stones, broken shell and bone. The lowermost and thickest unit was also a sand, faintly reddish in colour. The majority of the inhumations seemed to emerge from this third layer. The most obvious problem presenting itself seemed to be clarification of the relation between the lower two sands. The settlement residues seemed complex stratigraphically with diverse and hopefully clearly identifiable settlement features and perhaps patterns of such features might be recoverable. For such reasons, combined with knowledge that a matrix as poorly consolidated as sand would readily diffuse traces of occupation as those of hunter-gatherers within it, it was resolved to excavate large areas and aim for the closest feasible stratigraphic control. For this reason the trench size was fixed at 15 × 30 m and the vertical units of excavation were fixed at 3 cm.

Field methodology To further ensure exact control over stratigraphic content a series of additional procedures were adopted. At the conclusion of excavation to each 3 cm level, all finds, features and unconformities were planned. To assist this, the greater area of the trench was subdivided into 12 quadrangles. The fixing of levels was accomplished with theodolite and a staff calibrated to 3 cm divisions. The soil was removed with trowels. No sieves were used. Spirit levels were employed to keep excavated surfaces true. All finds and features were photographed *in situ* and cross checked by theodolite plots. In the closing stages of excavation an additional refinement of recording was obtained by painting rubber latex over freshly cleared features. After strengthening with bandages and drying, the rubber pulled away as a sheet preserving an exact replica of the form, colour and texture of the features. It can be appreciated therefore that assured of a three dimensional grid of such closeness, an extremely precise picture of the soil's internal contents has been recovered.

The *rationale* behind this choice of methods supposes that the soil of any archaeological site will be the product of three processes. First there will be the agents of soil accumulation which include removal, redistribution and replacement as well as accumulation *per se*. Second there will be the periodic intrusion into this accumulation of living forms. Each of these will leave its traces and a proportion will survive. Man is one of them and for our purposes the main one. The third and final process is a geochemical one and is brought about by the interaction of the other two over time and in response to climate. Ideally, field archaeology is the careful recovery and identification of the products of all three processes in order to

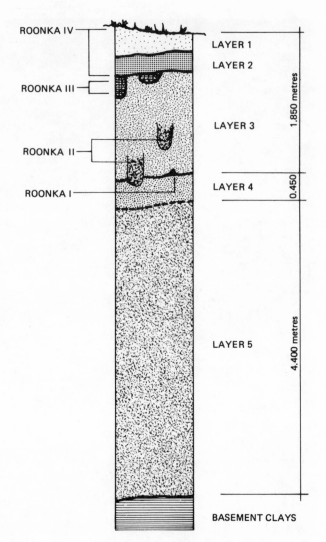

Fig. 1: Stratigraphic column, Trench A, Roonka Flat Dune. The cultural sequence is set out down the left of the column and the stratigraphic layering on the right.

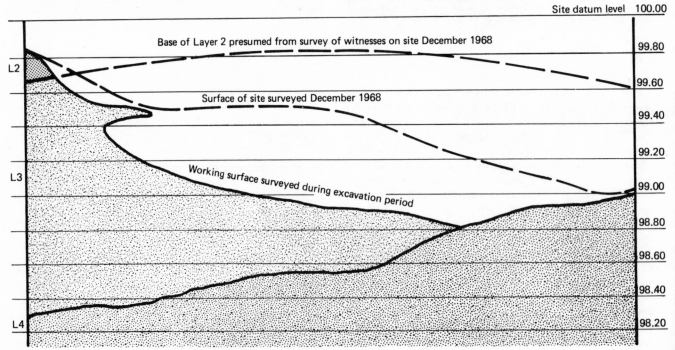

Fig. 2: Diagrammatic section EW through Trench A, Roonka Flat Dune showing form and rate of deflation of its mass throughout duration of excavation.

Plate 3: Trench A, Roonka Flat Dune at conclusion of excavation showing layering exhibited in profile. The figures denote numbered stratigraphic layers penetrated by excavation.

dissect out and study the traces left by one member of the living forms group, *viz.* Man. It can therefore be appreciated that stone tools, putting their intrinsic functional and industrial properties to one side, are of prime sequential value insofar as they can be validly related to stratified traces of past human events whether they be deliberate or merely residual in nature. The nature of these relationships can only be adequately determined in the field.

Stratigraphy   At the conclusion of excavation the following stratigraphic picture has emerged (Figs 1, 2 and Plate 3).

Layer 1 varies from 0·15 to 0·40 m. It is faintly reddish ferruginised sand composed of recent deflation products derived from adjacent erosion surfaces. It is archaeologically sterile.

Layer 2 is generally about 0·30 m thick, can increase to 0·75 m while at certain points it is completely removed.

Structurally it is highly complex being principally composed of small interleaved elements of aeolian origin. There is much redistribution of elements and whorling is apparent in cross-section. Its composition is primarily of humicified sand and carbon, intensely intruded by archaeological settlement debris including artifact material of urban-industrial origin. Within Trench A, this layer appears to exhibit three phases of development, although a short distance further south, at least six subphases can be distinguished. Layer 2 has now been identified as post-European colonisation in age and composed primarily of deflation products derived from a soil that had already been enriched by older human residues. This accounts for the obvious mixing of cultural debris from both traditions. It still remains to be determined whether the artifact content comes from on-the-spot or whether it too has been transported. Present indications are in favour of the former. There are no signs of wind deflated pavements buried in the profile and the artifactual debris, largely oven-stones, is

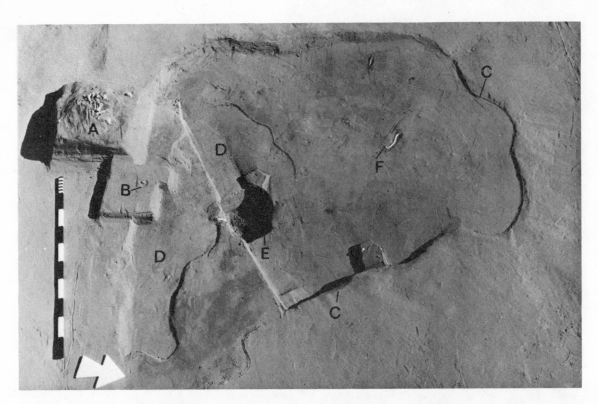

Plate 4: Feature 110 partially excavated to disclose internal structure. A: pedestal denoting top of Grave 73; B: human bone fragment thought to be in association with A; C: outline of Feature 110; D: outline of Feature 113 (afterwards Grave 80) within, showing its clarification in outline and part penetration in section (E); F: stray human clavicle dissociated and incorporated into general fill. Note darker ashy colour of fill.

fairly evenly mixed. There is some evidence for a relationship of inversion between the deflation products redeposited in Layer 2 and their presumably original superposition in similar undisturbed soils nearby. The exact mode of formation of Layer 2 however continues to be problematical.

Layer 3 varies from 0·85 to 1·40 m and is also relatively homogenous, faintly ferruginised sand, much intruded into by extraneous features. It appears to be of aeolian origin. There are some grounds for inferring that its original formation was marked by interruptions. Their presence can now be detected only from differential reduction of the erosion face at those levels. The lowermost few centimetres are also faintly distinguished by colour and texture from the remainder. There is some evidence for fluvial action but its role seems attributable to the subjacent soil. Grit and small iron-stone pebbles are increasingly met with as the surface of the underlying *terra rossa* is approached. The surface of the *terra rossa* basement beneath exhibits a pattern of guttering and solution pipe development which suggests fluvial scouring.

The features in Layer 3 derive from both subterranean fauna and man. The activities of the fauna are signified by burrows which were detected by the whitening effect left by carbonate accumulating differentially in their presumably less compacted interiors. Insect burrows, worm traces and vegetation root traces have been collected at all depths. Their specific identification remains to be confirmed.

The features of human origin fall into two kinds, settlement traces and inhumations. Representing the former are two large deep intrusions (F99, F110) which appear to derive from a previous settlement horizon of much broader extent

(Plate 4). They have been planed off to some depth and appear in profile as truncated remnants resembling pits. The inhumations are of two kinds, cylindrical shafts of a slightly oval section or shallow longitudinal pits. In their arrangement, orientation and contents they exhibit great variety that can be subdivided into two groups, those that relate to the overlying settlement zone and those that do not. These latter appear to be a distinct and earlier group.

No further traces of man have been found below the third layer.

Layer 4 is a *terra rossa* approximately 0·45 m thick. Its terminal surface erosion has been mentioned above. Its age and origin are uncertain although its integrity as a separate stratigraphic unit has been confirmed. Internally it has developed a columnar polygonal structure which has penetrated into the soil adjacent to it. There is evidence of calc migration along this structure. Except where inhumations from Layer 3 have penetrated, it exhibits no extraneous features.

Layer 5 is a sand of probable alluvial origin. Excavation has penetrated to a depth of 1·40 m and borings disclose that it continues in depth for a further 3 m before basal grey-green clays are encountered. Internally it is subdivided into parallel shallow sloping zones of calc enrichment alternating with fainter zones of dark mineral enrichment. At a depth of 0·45 m, strung diagonally across one corner of the trench, appeared a band of thinly distributed fine fragments of animal bone. A large tooth fragment has been tentatively assigned to the genus *Sthenurus*, a late Pleistocene antecedent to the modern kangaroo.

The stratified materials extend to a depth of 6·70 m of which the upper 1·85 m is humanly enriched.

Structurally the stratigraphy sub-divides into three:

(a) the accumulation of Layers 5 and 4 and their planation;

(b) the buildup of dune (Layer 3) on the surface so created and its enrichment by human occupance;

(c) the destabilising of the dune summit and deep erosion of Layer 3; followed by its replacement with Layers 2 and 1.

Culturally, four distinct phases have been distinguished. They have been named Roonka IV, III, II, and I in order of increasing depth in the profile.

Roonka IV, to which Layers 1 and 2 have been assigned, represents the site's history since the onset of European colonisation. Its commencement in this locality can be fixed at between 1841 and 1843.

The three prehistoric cultural phases preceding this are all enfolded within the dune remnant represented by Layer 3. Its reduction and invasion by recent deflation prevent any more than generalised reconstructions of its original profile. Within the remnant however, the excavation of features and traces of human workmanship and their stratigraphic analysis discloses three separate groups of events.

At the top of Layer 3 are occupance features and inhumations distinguished and linked by their content of ashy humic camp residues. One feature, Grave 48, deeply situated within this part of the sequence, has been radiocarbon dated to 3930±120 BP (ANU-407). This phase has been named Roonka III. It appears to be subdivisible internally into two subphases. It is presumed to have been brought to an end by the onset of European colonisation. Deeper within the profile and partly intruded into by Roonka III features are a group of dissimilar inhumational structures which share certain traits, principally, a total absence of any intrusive occupance residues. One of these, Grave 89, deep in the sequence, has been dated by radiocarbon to 6910±450 BP (ANU-1408). Another high in the sequence has been provisionally dated to c. 4000 BP. This assemblage of older features has been assigned to Roonka II. Some of them penetrate Layer 4. At the base of Layer 3, in between the Roonka II features, is a group of scattered hearths. They occur in adjacent trenches where they are accompanied by food refuse and cooking stone debris. One of the hearths has been dated to 18 050±340 BP (ANU-406). They thus represent a stratigraphically distinct and significantly more ancient phase. It has been called Roonka I.

Thus, Roonka III signifies a period when the site was intensively occupied by hunter-gatherer man. It appears to have had a complex history but its analysis is made difficult by severe losses of content from erosion. Its onset has been dated to c. 4000 BP by radiocarbon.

Its predecessor, Roonka II signifies a period when this part of the dune was used as a necropolis. It appears to have been so used from c. 7000 to c. 4000 BP.

Roonka I represents a vastly older occupation of the site. Then it seems to have been in occasional use as a hunter-gatherer open air encampment. It has been dated at c. 18 000 BP. There is no trace of man in the *terra rossa* basement soils.

The validity of this sequence has been established from a number of criteria—feature morphology and its associations within the broader soil–stratigraphic context, the cultural analysis of feature contents, geochemical alterations of feature contents, and relationships with feature assemblages from other sites investigated nearby. It must be stressed however

that confirmation of this sequence is still far from complete and a great deal of investigation has still to be done.

The value of the Trench A sequence is its supply of a time line and culture history against which the feature inventories from sites elsewhere on the flat may be compared and contrasted. The gap in between Roonka I and II marking the end of the Quaternary and spanning eleven millennia has set the direction of further work for example, the exploration of dunes of that age at nearby Glenforslan.

Each of the four phases will now be considered in detail.

Roonka IV

The most striking feature of Roonka IV is its accompanying effects on the landscape within and around the site. Severe deterioration has taken place (Plate 5). The severity of landscape destruction can be appreciated by studying a typical E-W cross-section of Trench A bearing a reconstructed outline of the original land surface for comparison against its present contour. Such a reconstruction can be reasonably validated from old Government survey books and aerial photographs. This shows that approximately two-thirds of the original soil volume within Trench A was removed prior to the beginning of excavation. Reference to Fig. 2 shows the rate at which erosion was continuing during the site's excavation in its initial stages, before it was protected by plastic sheeting (1970).

Close inspection of the profiles shows the recent erosion and deposition characterising Roonka IV to be subdivisible into two phases. One of these accounts for the present erosion surface and spillage of drift sand, while the earlier probably accounts for Layers 1 and 2. These latter layers are now both transected by the presently active erosion surface (Fig. 3). Presumably they represent an earlier spillage of drift from an erosion surface situated some distance further west. The stratigraphic relationships of Layers 1 and 2, faint reddish sand on top of redeposited humicified sands, are the reverse of those found elsewhere on the site where original soil contexts are undisturbed. It shows a classic instance of overturned stratigraphy.

The existence of undisturbed contexts complete with well-preserved archaeological features was not confirmed until the latter stages of excavation. This has clarified the age and cultural relationships of Layer 2, the period of European settlement. Previous to this, the well-defined unconformities, the artifact content and uninterrupted extent across the trench all pointed to the prehistoric and stratigraphic integrity of Layer 2. The inference seemed valid in spite of the evidence for deep contamination from industrial refuse of urban–industrial origin and the absence of clearly defined archaeological features. By the time clearly identifiable and undisturbed profiles had been located by trenching, the length of section visible for study and exhibiting Layer 2 in superposition amounted to 80 m. This provides a useful insight into the scale of stratigraphic disturbance on Australian open sites.

Landscape deterioration through man's agency is a familiar archaeological theme. In the instance of Roonka, the documentary source material is rich enough to suggest what course the process may have taken and what were the causes. It therefore justifies elaboration.

Early descriptions reveal something of the precolonist appearance of the Roonka Flat. The river flood–plain, intersected with its lagoons and creeks would have been fringed with huge red gums surrounded by expanses of rushes and

Plate 5: Roonka Flat Dune, South of Trench A during excavation showing extent and severity of deflation. Note distribution and proportions of surviving dune remnants.

reeds. In 1845 they were reported as being as 'thick as canes' and 6 feet above a man's head whilst on horseback (Hawker, 1845). The more elevated, better-drained mud flats were covered with thick bushy polygonum scrub. The high broad flat rising beyond would have borne a dense cover of box gums, oaks and sandalwood, with small woody bushes and natural grasses in between. In the sandier parts, the ground would have been covered by a thick carpet of Murray lily. The sand dune fringing the eastern margin of the high flats would have been stabilised by native pines and grasses. At

that time, the dune would have been sheltered from the prevailing south-westerly gales by the densely wooded flat behind. Protection from the occasional, but violent, valley winds was however, probably less adequate. The dune, then some 4 m higher than today would have provided an outlook across the valleyscape in all directions.

The name Roonka is generally thought to be derived from *roongko*, the Ngaiawang word for a grub found in the rotting timber of gum trees and greatly relished as food. The early survey books however, report the name as Cumbunga Flat,

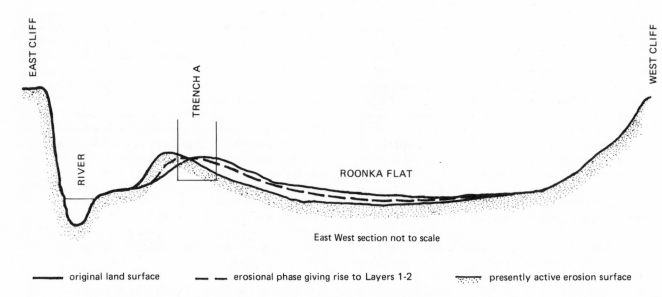

East West section not to scale

——— original land surface   — — erosional phase giving rise to Layers 1-2   ˗˗˗˗˗ presently active erosion surface

Fig. 3: Diagrammatic section EW across Murray Valley trench at a point passing through the Roonka Flat Dune showing extent and direction of dune remobilisation through Roonka IV up to the present time.

Cumbunga being an Aboriginal word of general application meaning reeds (N. B. Tindale, pers. comm.). The origin of this word has still to be determined and it is not recorded in vocabularies from this region.

The factors reducing the landscape to its present state emerge clearly from the historic sources.

As early as 1838, a little over a year after the colony's foundation, herds were being driven across the country to Adelaide from Sydney. The route followed was that of the first explorers and for a large extent followed the Murray. McBean's Pound immediately to the north of Roonka, was a natural enclosure and one of the major staging points for this traffic. The size of many of these herds was large varying from 7000 to 10 000 head, and a great deal of vegetable feed was eaten *en route*. Almost from the outset, losses of stock through spearing by Aboriginal hunters developed into hostilities. In 1841, in an attempt to end the conflict, a Government station was established on the Murray. The agent appointed to this station was E. J. Eyre who had recently distinguished himself as an explorer as well as having the ability to get onto terms of friendship and mutual respect with Aborigines. The station was at Moorundie, a short distance downstream from Roonka and which Eyre had discovered during one of his previous journeys. His three years at Moorundie were marked by a number of apparently highly successful diplomatic missions among the Murray tribes. His chief bequest, however, has been his published journals (Eyre, 1845) which are an outstanding document for the period with their sympathetic and detailed portrayal of the people on and around Roonka. Although Eyre left Moorundie in 1844, the station continued until 1856 so that colonists had confidence to commence pastoral settlement along the river.

In 1843 James Hawker took up land at Moorundie and recorded in his diary that he had entered into a pig 'speculation' on the River Murray, 'as that place seems calculated for breeding and rearing stock of this kind at a very trifling expense. The flats are covered with a root resembling a small yam of which the pigs are very fond' (Hawker, 4 March 1843).

In January 1844 Hawker extended his holding to the Roonka Flat which he stocked with 123 pigs. He built a hut of reeds and a number of styes but made no fences and the pigs ran wild, rooting out the bulbs growing on the flat. The pigs became so wild that he had great difficulty in catching them so he employed Aborigines to spear or net them. Shortly after Hawker's settlement on the flat, the adjacent land was taken up by Lachlan McBean and when Hawker departed in 1847, McBean absorbed the flat into his lease.

Although Hawker had departed, the pigs remained. In subsequent years their numbers were increased both naturally and by pigs from other farms which had been abandoned. Wild pigs continued to roam the river flats for almost a century, the last was captured at Roonka in the 1940s.

McBean occupied Roonka from 1844 on a squatter's occupation licence and then on a pastoral lease until a survey of the Pound and some of the river frontage was carried out in 1855. The remaining sections were surveyed in 1865. At that time, regulations decreed that when leased land was surveyed into sections it had to be offered for sale at public auction. This obliged the previous lessee to compete for land which he had established. Speculators were quick to find ways to take advantage of this, and although McBean was able to purchase some of the Roonka sections, others fell to seven different owners and their associates, most of whom were absentee investors and lessors of land.

During this period pastoral properties throughout South Australia were grossly overstocked and there is nothing to suggest that Roonka was any exception. All the box gums on the flat were ring-barked because it was believed more grass would grow if the trees were killed.

Even more drastic destruction of trees took place during the era of the river steamers which commenced to trade in 1853, reached their peak in the 1880s then gradually declined, unable to compete with railways. By 1910 few remained. During their 60 years of operation they were fuelled by the timber growing along the river and large numbers of men found employment in felling trees and carting them to loading points. One such a loading point was situated on the Roonka Flat. For this reason whole forests of native pines disappeared as well as any other trees which could be conveniently handled.

Land cleared by felling the trees was cultivated and this, compounded by the loss of grass cover through over-grazing, set much of the sand country drifting, buffeted by the strong south-westerly winds.

The 1860s brought a period of serious drought followed in 1870 by a record flood. This was a period of rural decline and the 1880s brought further economic depression plus a plague of rabbits in incredible numbers. Efforts to eradicate the rabbits by poison had little effect other than destroying enormous numbers of birds and other wildlife. When, in 1884, the Crown Ranger reported rabbits to be out of control on the flats, Roonka was riddled with burrows. At the same time it was stocked with goats, so that any vegetation escaping rabbits and near-starving stock, would probably have been devoured by goats whose feeding methods were particularly destructive, for example through digging out plant roots and stripping bark as well as leaves from trees. By 1882 McBean had managed to regain possession of all the freehold sections of his station but redivision began almost immediately. In 1885 the Flat was leased to an agent who sublet land to farmers without sufficient finance to lease a section for themselves. This resulted in over-stocking and intensive cultivation by tenants trying to wrest a living from too small a piece of land. After McBean's death in 1894 the freehold sections were again divided among separate owners and changed hands several more times.

In 1910 further landscape change was heralded when the Murray Water Agreement authorised the construction of a series of locks and weirs along the river. The first lock was commenced in 1913 and located at Blanchetown. The following years took their toll, 1914 with serious drought plus the disruption of World War I, and in 1917 there was another major flood which disrupted lock construction.

The Blanchetown lock was completed in 1922. As a consequence the river level was raised at Roonka by some metres, and the red gums which had escaped the ringbarker's axes or proved too large to fall victim to the woodcutters for the river boats, now slowly drowned; their giant skeletons still stud the lagoons and river banks.

The 1920s heralded another period of economic depression and at Roonka there was a sad parade of exploitation, mortgages and foreclosures. It was not until 1933 when the various deeds of ownership were re-absorbed into a single holding that the years of multiple occupation and over-exploitation came to an end. However, it was still necessary to continue grazing stock on the flat where little in the way of regeneration or rehabilitation could be undertaken. Another major flood in 1956 submerged the flat so that only the summit of the dune remained above water. The already weakened soil broke away under the force of the flood scarring large areas of the flat with a series of deep erosion gutters. These persist today.

Such processes as these caused the Roonka Flat to take on its present form. The high flat has been completely stripped of its trees and the original land surface blown or washed away to such a degree that it is now taxing the full resources of our survey team to record and reconstruct. The northern edge of the flat is still carved into deep channels caused by the great flood of 1956 and the Roonka dune along the eastern edge of the flat has broken down for most of its length and is migrating towards the river. The river flats to the south are permanently inundated for most of their extent by water banked up behind the Blanchetown lock.

It can thus be seen that a comparatively short span of time has brought about enormous alterations to the landscape.

Roonka IV also serves to remind us how archaeology requires resorting to a broad spectrum of historic source material in order to explain the picture presented by excavation.

Finally, we should learn from Layer 2 of Trench A at Roonka that caution is essential in the interpretation of archaeological stratigraphies in open sites. Although Layer 2 had been much intruded by artifactual debris of an obviously subsequent type, the assuming of a prehistoric status for this layer seemed justifiable until remnants of undisturbed soil marked by intact archaeological features were found nearby. Obviously similar mixing could take place in environments where two or more succeeding hunter-gatherer technologies had been in occupance. Failure to follow up artifactual recording and sampling by confirmation of undisturbed features and investigating their links with associated cultural residues could lead to erroneous conclusions.

Roonka III

The archaeological evidence for this phase is drawn from the following sources:

(a) the pre-European artifact residues in Layer 2;

(b) the two deep features (F99, F110) in Layer 3, considered to be remnants of a habitation zone, since removed and largely replaced by the events giving rise to Layer 2;

(c) a series of inhumations;

(d) a small yield of artifact residues in the upper levels of Layer 3 which appear to have migrated downwards from the prehistoric settlement zone.

It is now fairly evident that the chief obstacle to our understanding of the events representing Roonka III is the complete removal of the original land surface down to some depth during Roonka IV. The only remnant is represented at the top of Layer 3 in our profiles. At Site 3, some 60 m further south along the dune, the removal has been less severe and a greater proportion of its original profile preserved. This has revealed the probable fabric of the original undisturbed sediments.

Radiocarbon and dateable cultural items combine to extend the span of Roonka III from four thousand years ago up to the middle of the last century.

Study of all available material from Roonka III yields evidence for most aspects of hunter-gatherer habitation. It also supplies evidence for the ritual disposal of the dead in direct association with the camp. It does not however account for all the dead nor does it disclose traces of any other category of ritual. The evidence of habitation is comprehensive and includes hunting, gathering, eating and general technology. The evidence for disposal of the dead discloses at least one major change in mortuary procedures serving to subdivide the succession into two subphases. It further discloses a persisting tradition of deliberate choice in the persons to be buried at such a spot.

The subdivision of the inhumations on stratigraphic grounds has been recognised by separating the phase into subphases IIIa and IIIb. There is a possibility that this could be extended to three but the evidence needs further examination.

Roonka III features The range of clearly identifiable features is still limited. Four categories have been distinguished:

(a) Cooking structures

To date these consist of earth ovens, still partly enclosing heat-retaining stones and food residues. The general features of this cooking method, heating the stones in the pit, clearing out the coals and stones, returning the still hot stones packed in and around the carcass or vegetable bundle, sealing them under earth and ashes in order to steam cook, is well-known from the literature. Deflation has removed them completely from Trench A and the only remains are loose cobble detritus. A richer and more diverse inventory can be studied from Wetjungali 1—Trench 2, situated at a distance beyond the dune. Within this trench are 14 stone cobble cooking structures. They appeared to subdivide into two types, one with the cobbles forming an irregular oval surface with ash and charcoal wedged between, the other with the cobbles filling a shallow pit. The latter vary in shape, are surrounded by spillage and show some evidence of reuse (Plate 6). The shape of the oval cobble surfaces conforms to ethnographic descriptions of the ovens or kilns used by the Murray people for steaming vegetables (Angas, 1847, I: 89). While the structure and contents of the cobble-filled pits conform to the well documented hunter-gatherers' oven for the cooking of game, nevertheless it cannot be corroborated from the journals and observations of early settlers in the area. These features still have to be dated as the first samples were underweight, and further samples are being prepared. Preliminary assays suggest an order of age of 2–3000 BP which seem sufficient grounds for provisionally correlating it with Roonka III. Another group of stone cobble cooking structures has been investigated on the North Flat where they occur in association with inhumations. However they are still only partly excavated. Another group also has come to light in the Glenforslan sites on the east bank and are currently being investigated.

(b) Food residues

These usually occur in the form of isolated inclusions or lenses of freshwater mussel shells. They can be found in and around the stone cobble filled pits or mixed together with ash and fragments of burnt bone as an isolated lens and which therefore can be called a rubbish pit. Deflation has caused their almost complete removal in Trench A although they are thickly strewn as secondary detritus in the mixed layers. Their original disposition is best seen from Trench B at site 3. Here, deep within the undisturbed settlement-enriched horizon still preserved in Layer 3, there is a continuous sheet of freshwater mussel shells that dips along what

Plate 6: Feature 10 Trench 2, Wetjungali site 1. A stone cobble cooking structure, partly half-sectioned to show dispersed cobble throw out on all sides.

must have been an earlier contour of the dune. The mantle of soil covering this midden proved to contain a group of ashy hearths without any cobblestones and beneath it, thinly separated from the midden, a dispersed scatter of burnt mammal bone. The situation suggests an alternation in site use throughout the period of the profiles' development. Neither the hearths nor the distribution of mammal bones are continuous across the trench area but the midden layer is remarkable for its even spread. No samples of carbon have as yet been submitted for dating although the range of features so far recovered from both trenches suggest a correlation of the midden layer with the Roonka III also. Site 3 was selected for excavation because it looped out across the flood plain to where Cumbunga Creek enters the main stream, a situation which probably prevailed throughout Roonka III.

(c) Hearths

This identification has been based on small irregular areas of fine grey ash with an insignificant component of charcoal. They too are best studied from site 3 (*vide supra*). According to eye-witness accounts of Aboriginal camp life, hearths (by which term is meant fires maintained principally for warmth), were very economical of wood and consisted of little more than a single length of timber smouldering away to a fine ash.

No trace of postholes or other evidences of above-surface structures have been found anywhere. However, because the matrix is uncompacted sand any traces would have disappeared with the possible exception of the more recent ones near the surface of the dune. Unfortunately no traces seem to have survived.

No evidence of specific workshop locations has been found either. Presumably, in a region as poor in resources of stone as the Murray, all stone knapping would have taken place randomly in the camp.

(d) Inhumations

The most numerous and best-preserved of the features are inhumations. In Trench A those assigned to Roonka III amount to some 70 in number. As a group they are distinct because of the way in which the skeletons are arranged but primarily because they all have an infill containing habitation refuse from the contemporary settlement residues. The precise relationship of inhumations to settlement however is not simple. A proportion of them is sealed in by the faintly reddish sand of Layer 3 which would imply that both the campsite and grave were abandoned after burial. On the other hand actual settlement zone remnants outlined by sharp unconformities remain, and within them among inhumations a considerable quantity of burnt and broken human bone was found. Much of this appeared old and weathered when first excavated and included stray teeth, complete phalanges, calcaneums and pieces of bone small enough to have escaped destruction. It bears out Eyre's remark (Eyre, 1845, II: 350): 'The natives have not much dread of going near to graves, and care little for keeping them in order, or preventing the bones of their friends from being scattered on the surface of the earth. I have frequently seen them handling them, or kicking them with the foot with great indifference'.

In presenting an analysis of the inhumations there are many variables which seem to provide significant results. In a

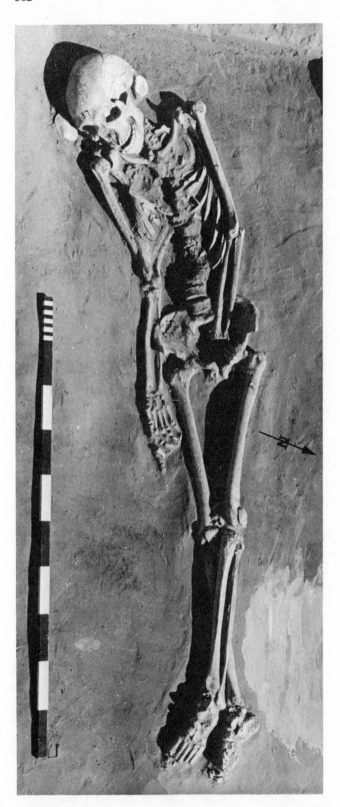

Plate 7: Grave 37, Trench A, illustrating the inhumational mode of full dorsal extension. In this instance the body has been twisted slightly to the right. The objects against left and right sides of the skull are mussel shell valves, apparently placed with deliberate care by the inhumers. The scale measures one metre. The arrow points north. This inhumational mode is most characteristic of Roonka IIIb although the one illustrated here is from a small group assigned to Roonka II.

preliminary paper of this sort we shall examine the following:

(a) Tomb morphology

Almost without exception the inhumations are primary interments in pits. The pits take the form either of shallow longitudinal trenches or vertical shafts having a faintly oval section. In a very few instances there is the suggestion of fire in the pit (Graves 48, 50, 87) but on the whole there is no evidence for cremation.

(b) Arrangement or position of the body

These appear to be three major variants:

(i) Extended (Plate 7). The body appears to be laid out supinely with limbs fully extended. In many cases the feet appear to have been lashed. The position of arms and hands varies, so does the orientation, which is generally to the western half-circle of the compass. There is one instance of a body prone in the ground.

(ii) Contracted (Plate 8). There is variation in degree of flexion although generally the body rests on its side. The degree of flexion can either be moderate or sharp. Orientation varies, but arrangement of the arms and hands is more constant.

(iii) Recumbent-contracted. This rather clumsy term applies to a singular group of inhumations where the body rests in a supine attitude but where the legs seem originally to have been drawn up but have since slumped to one side so as to give the body the posture of a person squatting or kneeling. This arrangement of the lower limbs is not constant, as in some cases they project forward from the body. Legs are however always folded under the thighs. Both orientation and arrangement of arms varies. These inhumations can be separated from the previous two forms on several grounds.

(c) Chronology

Seriation of graves in archaeology is always fraught with problems and Roonka proves no exception despite the care exercised in determining upper limits of the pits. There is some superposition of inhumations but it mainly applies to the superpositioning of Roonka III inhumations over and into those of Roonka II. Within Roonka III there is evidence for superpositioning of the extended inhumations above the recumbent-contracted, although no such clear relationship exists between the extended and the contracted forms. Because of this, and considering the evidence from drawn profiles that the recumbent-contracted inhumations are dug from a deeper level than either of the former, it seems safe to assume that they are the earlier of the three groups. It is less easy to decide on the relationships between the contracted and the extended forms. It is best to conclude that they were contemporaneous and alternative choices of burial as they do not appear to intrude one into the other or separate out on stratigraphic grounds. The inhumations assigned to Roonka III thus appear to subdivide into two subphases, illustrating a distinct change of burial mode. In the earlier phase (a), it appears that the body was always disposed in a recumbent-contracted position. Later, this was replaced by disposal of the body in either a contracted or extended attitude. The significance of this will be discussed later. In absolute chronological terms we can

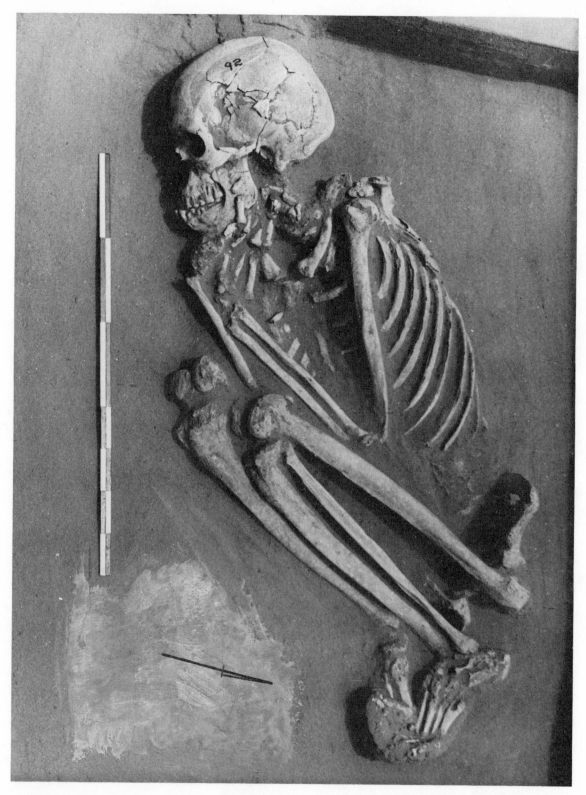

Plate 8: Grave 92 (Roonka IIIb) Trench A illustrating the inhumational mode of full contraction. The scale measures 500 cm. The arrow points north.

assign a date of 3930±120 to one of the recumbent-contracted inhumations (G48). This is one of the Roonka III series having clear evidence of fire contemporaneous with burial. We can also assign a terminal date of about 1840–1850 AD to three inhumations which contain trade articles of urban-industrial origin. Pending the outcome of further dating work this will serve for the moment as a chronological bracket for Roonka III.

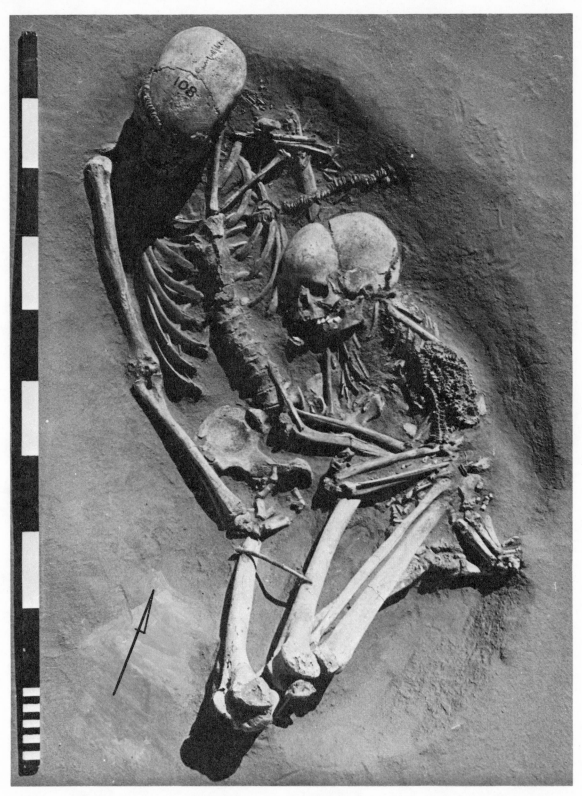

Plate 9: Grave 108 (Roonka IIIa) Trench A. A compound status grave illustrating the inhumational mode of recumbent-contraction. This is the richest and most carefully appointed of the Roonka tombs and is described fully in the text. Scale one metre. Arrow points to north.

(d) Matters of status and selection for burial

There is good evidence for status as a factor in burial choice at Roonka. It is most apparent in the presence of a number of status inhumations, often elaborately furnished, but whose minimum accompaniment is the body of a child deliberately placed with that of an adult. Status is also signified at Roonka by the actual presence of a burial as it seems that only part of the population received such care and that the remainder must have been disposed of in other ways.

Status inhumations are represented in all three types found in Roonka III—extended, contracted or recumbent-contracted. The most striking of them have elaborate suites of grave goods. Grave 108 (Plate 9) provides a good illustration. This is a deep cylindrical shaft tomb assigned to the earlier phase of Roonka III. The structure of the grave is interesting in that it develops from a deep oval shaft into a small chamber in which both the major and minor interments are comfortably disposed.

The pit is largely filled with the skeleton of a large and robust adult male in a recumbent position but with head and shoulders slightly elevated in relation to the rest of the body. The legs appear to have originally been flexed or drawn up, but have subsequently slumped to one side. The man is accompanied by a skeleton of a small child whose body has been arranged on its side with limbs moderately contracted. It rests on the man's left arm. The man's body has been attired and equipped with much evidence of concern for a splendid appearance. The head is encircled with a fillet or chaplet of wallaby teeth in two parallel strands. This has been carefully put together from matched pairs of mammal incisors each of which has been notched, presumably in order to give additional purchase to a plaited or knotted binding (Fig. 17). Along the midline of the body is a series of bone pins. At the breast is a triangular arrangement of four bone pins all complete with articular protuberances. (These are often found broken away and missing.) Over and behind the left shoulder is a dense mass of small bones (largely mammal tarsals) in position of articulation. The overall arrangement of these finds suggests that the body was garmented, most probably with a skin cloak, fixed at the left shoulder by an arrangement of fibulae presumably allowing the paws of the pelts to hang over the shoulder behind. The line of pins along the body's midline suggests the pinning together of such a cloak as a shroud which could conceivably have pulled the right arm to its present position hard against the chest. Harder to explain is the broad band of scattered small bones running along the left side of the body, resting on the body but extending beneath the child. They have been identified as coming from birds and the most satisfactory explanation is to suppose that the garment was fringed with a band of bird feathers, possibly still partly incorporated as part-limbs, as a form of edging decoration.

The child is without ornament except for the truncated skull of a bird, probably a pendant, in front of its chest and some traces of ochre staining on the feet. On its rib cage however, there is a coiled mass of string upon string of reptile vertebrae, presumably the remains of a necklace.

Finally, the most problematical find is a further band of wallaby incisors of similar arrangement to the chaplet, but fully extended as a strip across the man's left forearm. They rest on top of both the body and the fringe of bird bones, yet extend too far beyond the latter to permit their being considered attached to it in any way. Presumably they represent another headband, possibly, with the chaplet, components of a matched pair.

The following interpretation is provisional and may have to be revised. Nevertheless it is already obvious that this inhumation is a human event with many signs of broader cultural perspectives. It is without doubt the most striking and elaborate tomb yet unearthed in this country and its interpretation, with its implications of social status and ritual infanticide, open up a new dimension in the study of ancient Australian societies.

Grave 108 is not however unique. Grave 50 is comparably furnished differing only in that the adult body has been disposed dorsally in a fully extended position. It too is accompanied by the body of a child, also contracted on its side, and a similarly elaborate furniture made up principally of bone pins, bodkins, awls and traces of food offerings instead of the jewellery exhibited in 108. Grave 13 is similar to Grave 50 but the furniture is largely comprised of stone tools.

Status at Roonka is also reflected in the choice of persons qualifying for burial as contrasted with those who must have been disposed of in other ways. Although there appear to be more males than females, the proportion of adults (75%) to adolescents (10%) infants (15%) and aged is most marked. The percentage for the infants does not take into account the fact that about half of them are deliberate depositions in status graves. Evidently, primary interment in the dune was reserved for adults and persons of status only, the young and the very old were disposed of elsewhere. Such a pattern fits very closely to that disclosed for this region by historic ethnographic sources (*see for example* Angas, 1847, I: 60, 70, 75, 86, 94–95). These reveal that the old and infirm were abandoned to die and decay in the open while the very young were either disposed of immediately or enveloped in bundles and carried around for some time to desiccate. Final disposal was accomplished by placing the bundle in the cleft of a rock face or an old tree.

It appears that the inhumers of Roonka deliberately affirmed that grave furnishings are not confined to the status graves of Roonka III, although these contain the richest inventories. It would appear however that the recumbent-contracted graves in the primary phase of Roonka III were marginally better furnished than those that follow.

The finds from Roonka III Like previous excavations in this region the number of artifacts found at Roonka was very small. While Roonka seems to have more artifacts than most other sites in the Lower Murray, it is less productive than Devon Downs (Hale and Tindale, 1930).

We shall first consider the stone tools. Out of a total flaked stone assemblage of 532, 58 or some 10% have been utilised in some way. At this stage the small but additional component of glass has not been analysed because of certain difficulties in distinguishing fortuitous from deliberate utilisation. An

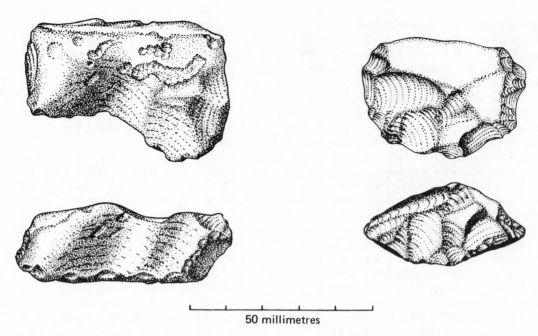

50 millimetres

Fig. 4: Stone tools: scrapers—flaked. l. to r.: find 409, find 4.

important factor governing the analysis presented here is the inference of the presence of certain *types* of tools from quite insignificant fragments that have survived. For example, although no ground stone axes have come from Trench A or elsewhere on the site, there are flakes of a fine grained volcanic stone characteristic of these tools. Thus their existence has been inferred. Such a mode of inference underlines the area's widely reported lack of stone suitable for implements.

The following stone tool types are represented:

(a) Scrapers

There are two major types based upon whether the edge is formed by percussion around the scar surface of a struck flake (Fig. 4) or whether it is formed by percussion around the surface of a high-backed or tabular block (Fig. 5).

There are two size and two edge morphology variants. On average the size varies from 3 cm to 1 cm. In conformity with standard terminology we shall refer to the smaller size variant as microlithic (Fig. 6). It is worth noting that the microlithic form is not found in the high-backed scrapers, only those made from struck flakes. The larger, heavier and 'macrolithic' high-backed scraper type familiar from Australian industries of Pleistocene date is also not represented in Trench A (although these tools have been found in the Glenforslan sites across river). The edge morphology can be either convex or concave and it appears on both the struck flake and the high-backed types. The function and mode of hafting of the scrapers prepared from struck flakes is well known from the ethnography (Roth, 1897: 101; Spencer, 1927, II: 501; Horne and Aiston, 1924: 89; Thomson, 1964: 416–19; Tindale, 1965: 133–39). Scrapers were mounted to hafts with vegetable resins and according to available evidence were used in wood working and shaping. The mode of hafting for the high-backed scrapers however has not been recorded although presumably they had comparable functions.

(b) Knives

There is only one specimen of this type (Fig. 7). It is a fragment of what was originally a struck scalar flake which has had a shallow acute edge formed along one margin by percussion flaking. It bears similarities to the resin-butted *tjimari* knife and now familiar to archaeologists from central Australia. There are no examples of dentate-edged flake tools at Roonka.

(c) Points

Two pirri points have been recorded (Fig. 8), one made from quartz and rejected prior to completion, the other made from chert and unifacially worked to a high median keel. The latter specimen was found in a grave.

(d) Microliths

These are best grouped with points. Three forms are represented—trapezoids, crescents and segments. All have been abruptly retouched around their thicker margins (see Fig. 9).

(e) Cores and debitage

The struck flake debitage much of it comprised of small pointed flakes should be considered within this category. Additional pointed flakes occur in the remainder of the debitage but without evidence of deliberate removal by percussion and appear to have been fragmented by pounding and shattering blows. They merit consideration as utilised flakes within this category because Eyre (1845, II: 306 and Pl. IV) illustrates a typical fighting spear which he describes as having its tip barbed bilaterally with a line of quartz and flint fragments set into gum. Specimens of such spears which have survived are equipped with unretouched pointed flakes similar to those presently classified as debitage from Roonka. The contents of certain graves testify to killing by spearing with bone tipped projectiles at this site and, although the stone debitage from grave pits has not yet been examined from such a viewpoint, it will be in the final analysis.

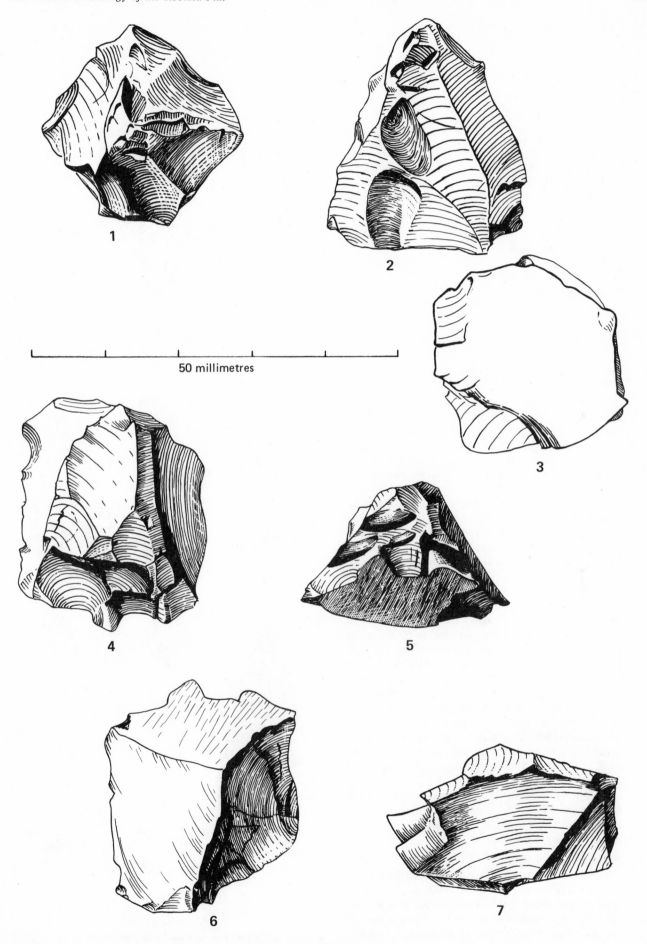

50 millimetres

Fig. 5: Stone tools: scrapers—high backed. 1–3 find 1696; 4–7 find 1273.

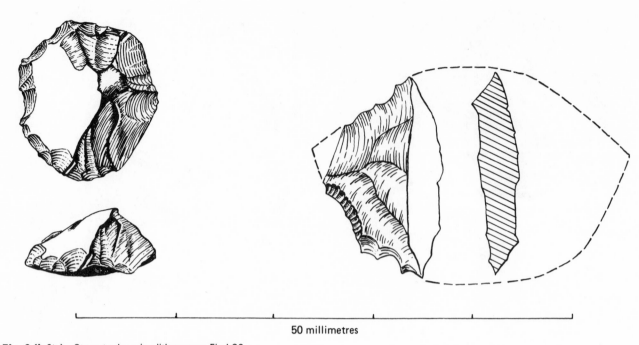

50 millimetres

Fig. 6 (left:)   Stone tools: microlith scraper. Find 36.
Fig. 7 (right:)   Stone tools: microlith knife blade—scalar. Find 1602.

The remainder of the debitage, in which is included a small group of microlithic polygonal cores (Fig. 10), is more interesting for its composition distribution. The largest component is quartz followed by cherts which vary from white-speckled to yellow through honey brown to dark red. Dark blue-grey flint is barely represented and is in the same proportion as quartzite. The distribution is interesting when compared with known sources of stone for this region. The quartz and perhaps some of the chert would have come from the Lofty Ranges, a comparatively short distance away. The yellow, brown and red cherts are well-known from from historic quarries in the Upper Murray area, near Renmark. The best known site for flint is the southern coastline some distance east of the Murray mouth. It was in widespread use for implements in the lower reaches of the Murray far to the south of Roonka. Quartzite came from the southern Flinders Ranges some distance to the north west. In the historic times, the tribes to the north west were disliked and avoided by the Murray people (N. B. Tindale, pers. comm., cf. his discussion of Ngadjuri expansion in *Aboriginal tribes of Australia* 1974: 214). The distribution of refractory stone therefore implied that most trade would have been to the west, followed by the upper Murray and then the southern Murray and the scrub country extending up towards the Flinders Ranges. There is a certain amount of indirect ethnographic evidence of similar broad cultural relationships that lends added support to this picture.

(f) Pounders and anvils
    These are very scarce and came only from the surface. Not one was recovered in the excavation. This leaves open the possibility that more may once have existed but have been removed by private collectors. There are two pounders and each has clear evidence of bruising, and one anvil (*see* Fig. 11). The anvil is characterised

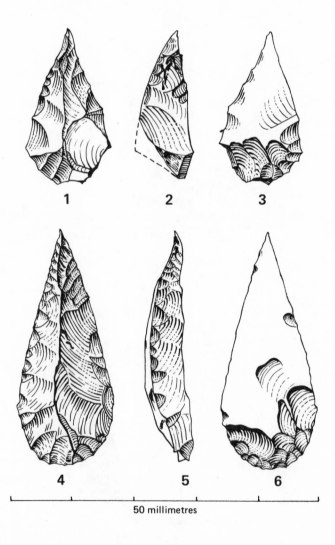

Fig. 8:   Stone points—projectile. above: find 5; below: find 24 (from Trench B).

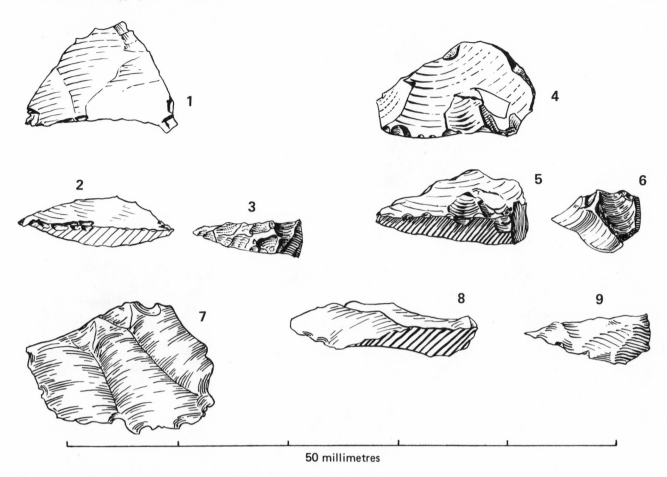

50 millimetres

Fig. 9: Stone microliths—geometric. 1–3 find 2450; 4–6 find 1323; 7–9 find 414.

by a shallow depression in its upper face. Nothing answering to the description of a grindstone has been found.

(g) Worked slate

One marginal fragment of a slate flensing tool together with fragments which could have come from another have been excavated (*see* Fig. 12). The distinguishing characteristics of these tools and their use along the Murray have been described by Basedow (1925).

(h) Ochres and colouring plasters

A considerable quantity has been recovered. They range in shade from red to yellow, thence to white. A slab of gypsum crystal and a quartz crystal should be considered under this category. The former is reported as having been useful for rain magic and the latter for the curing of illnesses (Eyre, 1845, II: 361).

(i) Oven stones

These constitute the greatest bulk of stone cultural detritus. Their function and distribution have already been discussed (*see* page 300).

Fifty-three bone tools were recovered and are the next most numerous component of the artifact assemblage. This is approximately half the number found at Devon Downs. In their range of differing forms the bone tools at Roonka are similar to those found at Devon Downs and Fromm's Landing (Mulvaney, 1960; Mulvaney, Lawton and Twidale, 1964). At Roonka however, the bone industry differs from the

other sites in its distribution and what it indicates about the functions of these instruments is most important. In each case it is the deliberate deposition of bone tools in graves that has provided such insights.

(a) Piercing instruments

The greatest number consist of mammal fibulae with their swelling articular terminus intact but the shaft of the bone tapers away gradually to a point (Fig. 13a–b). These are found in graves generally in the position of fastening pins although there is a suggestion that broken specimens could have been saved for this purpose rather than discarded. From the ethnographic literature we know that they were used as needles or bodkins, for example in the sewing together of pelts or cloaks (Eyre, 1845, II:310, Pl. IV, figs 9–12). But they obviously had many supplementary uses which the evidence of the grave implies. For example, bundles of pins thrust through the hair might pin down headdresses. We have one such a bundle in Grave 50. Alternatively, they might be used by mourners to lacerate themselves as an expression of grief and then cast into the pit during its filling. One of the pins at Roonka warrants such an interpretation (Fig. 13c).

Deserving to be grouped with the piercing instruments is another type best interpreted as awls where the point is abruptly tipped rather than tapering (Fig. 14). There are two at Roonka, one with a thin section made from a mammal fibula, the other much thicker sectioned and made from a metatarsal bone.

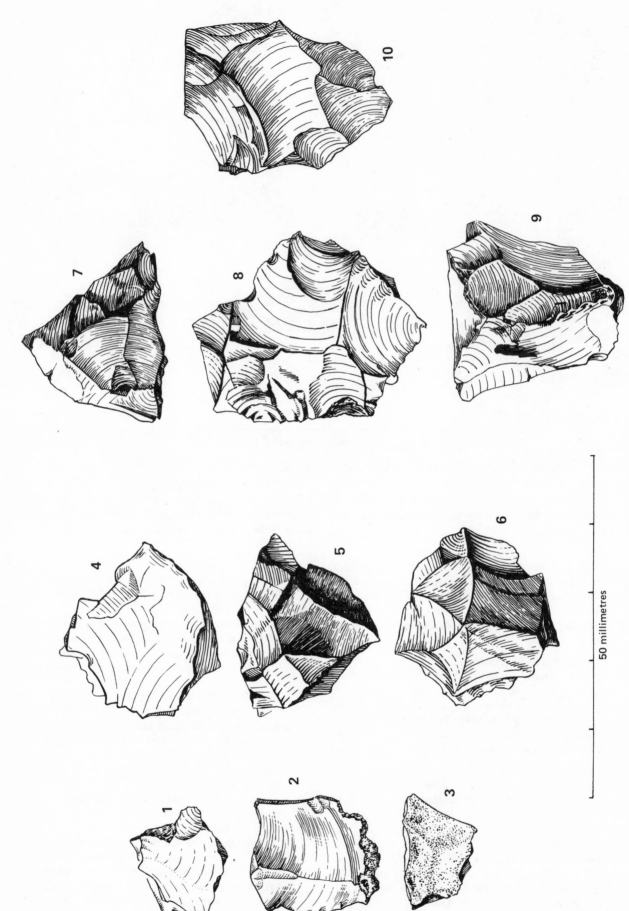

Fig. 10: Stone cores—polygonal. 1–3 find 1351; 4–6 find 1347; 7–9 find 1348.

50 millimetres

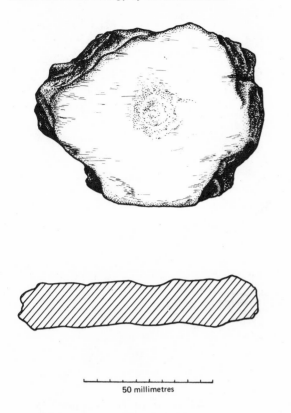

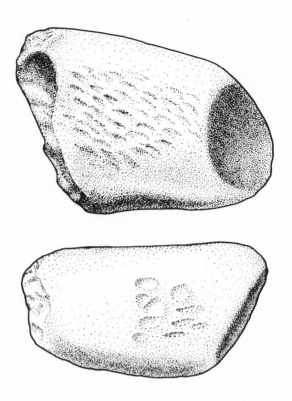

50 millimetres

Fig. 11: Stone anvil and pounder (surface finds).

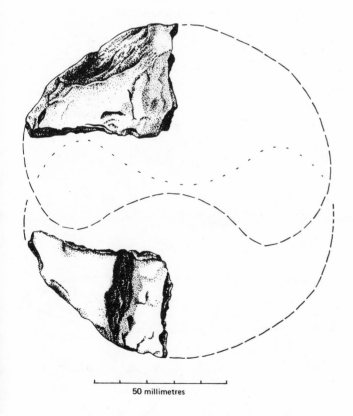

50 millimetres

Fig. 12: Worked slate—probably flenser (fragment) showing both faces. Find 914.

(b) Projectile points

Confirmation of their use is best had from Grave 45 which contains the contracted body of a man. The rib cage has been transversely pierced by a bone point, causing the shattering and displacement of ribs. The fragments of the bone tip remain in their original position. The reconstructed tip proves to be a shallow concave-sectioned instrument fashioned from a mammal long bone (fig. 15a). Two further possible projectile points came from the furnishment of Grave 13. The type is well represented but invariably broken, at Fromm's Landing, Devon Downs and Tartanga.

(c) Fusiform points

These are most commonly known by the name *muduk*, a word applied to them by Tindale (Hale and Tindale, 1930) who interpreted them as having been used as fish gorges. The fusiform points at Roonka (Fig. 16) do not fit easily into this interpretation however, nor is there any evidence for them in Eyre who describes the Ngaiawang as spearing or netting fish in the open river or in ponds left behind from floods. Some of these ponds were artificial and there is a possible instance of one at McBean's Pound where there is a small wall of stones blocking one of the major channels into a large lake that intrudes into the flood plain there. The fusiform points at Roonka seem better interpreted as projectile points because of their size and variation. One specimen (not however from Trench A) has one end shaped into a rounded butt similar to a pirri point. The question of *muduks* and projectile points will be explored more fully in the discussion (*see* pp. 321–22). For the moment, the most valid evidence of fishing tackle on the Murray is the pair of unbarbed bone hooks excavated by Gallus (Gallus and Gill, 1973).

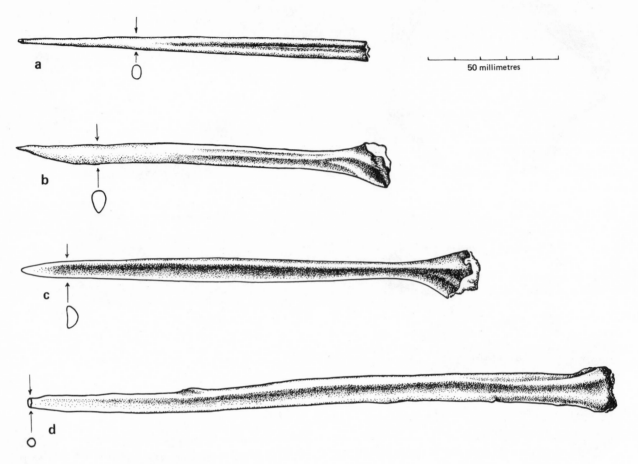

Fig. 13: Bone piercing instruments—tapering tip. a: S.A.M. No. A57275 (from North Flat); b: find 790; c: find 1693; d: find 2028b.

(d) Ornaments

These are from teeth as well as bone, and although still requiring further study, can be described as ornaments with reasonable confidence. The most singular of them is the double strand fillet of notched marsupial incisors encircling the adult's forehead in Grave 108 (Fig. 17). In addition to this are the bands across the chest of the adult in Grave 109, one of which appears to use broken lengths of bone as beads while the other appears to employ them as spacers. No references to these have been found in the ethnographic sources so far.

Preliminary consideration of the artifact assemblage for Roonka III yields little evidence for change over time. When the assemblage is then compared against the stratigraphy, while it helps to confirm the link between graves and settlement zones, thereby offsetting the invasive effects of Roonka IV, it still has little use as a direct index of cultural change. When, however, stratigraphy, artifacts and the ethnographic sources for this area are considered together, it becomes evident that there is a relationship between them which permits the reconstruction of certain patterns of cultural and behavioural change within an overall chronological framework.

Stratigraphic features, in addition to supplying patterns of broad change, can also supply evidence for events of brief duration. For example, study of the graves discloses such instances as: death through childbirth (Grave 110), by disease

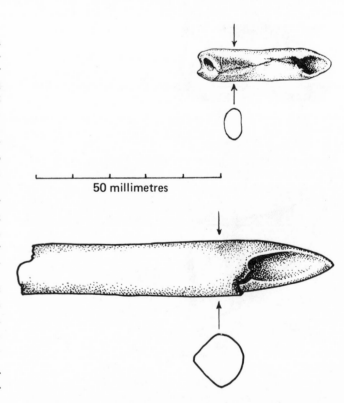

Fig. 14: Bone piercing instruments—abrupt tipped. Top, find 14; below, find 802.

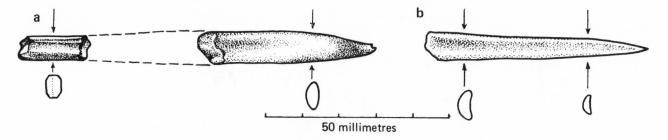

Fig. 15: Bone concave sectioned points—narrow tapering. a, find 400; b, find 2028a.

(Grave 19) and from the genetic abnormality of microcephaly (Grave 77). Grave 56 contains an adult male with jaw in correct position but with the skull missing. The bony structure of the face, broken away from the skull, has been placed in another part of the grave. This could confirm reports that Murray tribes-people robbed graves for skulls in order to use them when caulked and fitted with string handles as vessels for carrying water. There is also an instance from the north flat of possible homicide because a small bone has been inserted into the abdomen. This could be an example of the occasionally reported use by the Murray tribes of bones to commit murder by stealth (N. B. Tindale, pers. comm.). There is reason for claiming that much of ethnographic literature can be confirmed or given further elaboration by such means.

On the other hand, resorting to the ethnographic evidence helps elucidate the slenderness of the artifactual record. For example, it would appear that the staple components of a daily diet in this area consisted of fresh water mussels and steamed or roasted roots and yams:

'In this district the natives were very numerous, their encampments being scattered along the narrow strip of ground between the limestone cliffs and the water's edge: there they find plenty of food from the fish, mussels, crayfish, bullrush-root and other products of this larger river. We frequently came upon their ovens or cooking fires, resembling kilns, beneath which the roots of the bullrush were being steamed between heated stones.' (Angas, 1847, 1: 58.)

'The freshwater mussels found in the muddy flats of the river are much sought after by the natives, who cook them by burying them in the ashes of their wooden fires. The shells are used to scrape the fibres of the bullrush-root, after it has been well chewed, for the purpose of making cord for their mats and baskets.' (*Ibid*: 55.)

Eyre gives detailed descriptions of the complex range of nets and traps used to capture fish, bird life and game. Reviewing his account leaves a strong impression that such devices, used in conjunction with spears and wooden wedges, would have supplied all the daily wants of these Murray people.

The archaeological record, therefore, fits this picture very well consisting as it does of a primary food-extractive component of cobble ovens, shell residues, hammers, anvils, a miscellany of stone and bone projectile tips, plus a secondary fabricative component of chisels, spokeshaves, axes, skin flensers and a diverse kit of piercing instruments. There are certain features which do not comply, for example, the high-backed scrapers and the fusiform points which appear to suggest that some technological change must have occurred.

There are, however, many marked discrepancies between the two records that require careful examination. The absence of references in historic sources to the deeper graves, with their bodies in recumbent-contracted attitudes and their noticeably more lavish ornamentation can be understood if it is accepted that they are older. The absence of any reference to the status graves that appear as a continuous tradition throughout all of Roonka III is harder to understand. The ethnographic accounts do not resolve the apparent but inexplicable association of contracted with extended interments as contemporaneous and alternative choices of burial. On the other hand there are certain curious omissions from the archaeological record when it is matched against the ethnographic sources. For example, there is no evidence of the mourning helmets of gypsum plaster, specimens of which were collected from around Blanchetown in the 1870s, nor is there any evidence of wooden structures around the graves.

However, discrepancies of this minor order prompt further enquiry as to whether the ethnographic evidence itself might not benefit from re-evaluation in the light of certain major historical events. For example, there are several early references to 'burial grounds' and specific spots being reserved by Aborigines for burial of the dead. However, it is almost unknown for human remains to be discovered along the Murray today without campsite residues.

It is well known that in the early 19th century, between about 1820 and 1830, terrible epidemics of smallpox raged along the length of the Murray Valley. Their progress, the loss of life they caused and consequent disruption to customary practice have been documented by Stirling (1911). It is

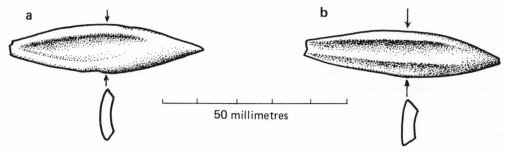

Fig. 16: Bone concave sectioned points—broad fusiform. a, find 15; b, find 2151.

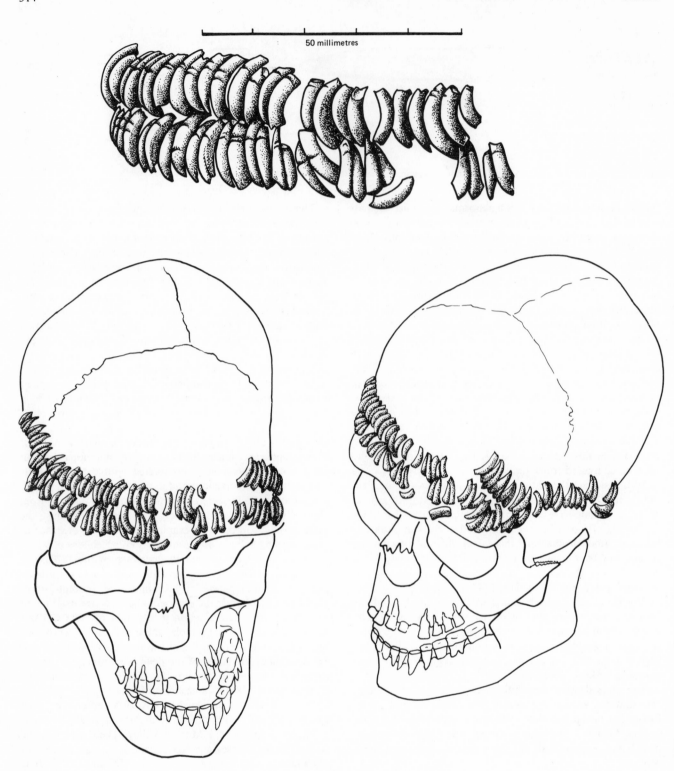

Fig. 17: Teeth pendant ornaments—notched. Find 2227. Lower section of figure is not to scale.

possible that the spectacular loss of life brought about by such a calamity might have suspended normal mortuary practices and caused the establishment of massed graves on a similar pattern to the plague-pits of post-mediaeval Europe. This would account for certain of the answers to queries from the first European observers who entered in on the region at least a decade after the plague had passed. It is a pity that no sites supporting this hypothesis have ever been reported in

the area. The identification of such a site, if only to ascertain its characters, would be of considerable significance.

In assessing early accounts of mortuary practices, we might also usefully consider the separateness and mistrust felt between the original observers and observed. We should ascertain the degree to which reported eye-witness accounts are the recounting of isolated instances or the record of systematic and sustained observation and study. We should ask whether the observers saw all that actually happened, saw only what their patience would permit or whatsoever their Aboriginal hosts were willing to disclose to them. It should not be forgotten that this was the period of initial encounter between two fundamentally different societies.

A third point to be considered is the rapidity with which European colonist enterprise disrupted and redistributed Aboriginal populations after settlement and the effect this had on ethnological observance. It therefore frequently happened that information was besought and recorded from informants who were themselves strangers to the area. For this reason, documentary analysis of the phase of first contact yields certain instances of diffusion whose isolation requires some extremely ingenious analysis.

In spite of the near removal of Roonka III as a stratigraphic feature in Trench A a substantial part of the cultural record survived. There are also certain factors that enable valid subdivision into chronological components. It should be noted that this has been drawn principally from study of archaeological structures and feature associations. The stone technology exhibits no evidence of significant or comparable change; this is consistent with the overall picture of its development elsewhere on the continent throughout this span of time.

Roonka II

Roonka II in Trench A is solely represented by graves and tombs. Twelve of them have been assigned to this phase. They are distinct partly by reason of stratigraphic zonation and contents but principally because they include a group of vertical shaft tombs. The singularity of these structures is thrown into sharp relief by the evidence (*see below*) that the disposition of the dead within them may have been a long drawn out process involving sustained attendance from the living. The dating of this phase is made difficult by the paucity of associated carbon but preliminary counts suggest a range from 4000 to 7000 BP. Considered together with its age, this mode of disposal makes a sharp break with the body of knowledge concerning Australian mortuary custom known from ethnographic sources. Considered with the additional evidence of variant ornament technology, it constitutes one of the strongest arguments for marked cultural change in ancient Australia. Stratigraphically, these 12 graves are disposed in the lower half of Layer 3, some penetrating the red brick earth of Layer 4. They were difficult to detect as, unlike the Roonka III inhumations, they were not outlined by their distinct fill of dark camp refuse stained soil. Fortunately, the penetration of some into Layer 4 gave rise to a fill studded with tiny crumbs of red clay. This gave the tomb fill a speckled appearance and enabled the full extent and shape of the structures to be determined with some degree of precision.

Their distinguishing from the Roonka III group, stratigraphically, goes further than the colour of the fill. It was observed for example that whilst none of the Roonka II graves penetrated either each other or those of Roonka III, some were penetrated by the latter. Although interference of earlier graves by later graves is a striking stratigraphic feature of the Roonka III pits, it is unknown for Roonka II. Perhaps Roonka II inhumations were marked on the original ground surface in some way.

A further distinguishing factor was the soil mineral speckling of bones, probably from manganese, which was a distinguishing feature of the Roonka II skeletons. It was not observed in the Roonka III group. The possession of such a surface patina by some supine inhumations in the same stratigraphic provenance suggested that these too should be assigned to Roonka II.

The distribution of the sexes within each of the two major inhumation groups is random thus ruling out any interpretation of a sex based dualism in favour of one based on social classifactory criteria. Considering the prevalence of dual subdivisions in Australian tribal societies, the eliciting of a dual aspect to ancient mortuary practice at this site is worthy of more than passing notice.

The shaft tombs The most noteworthy feature of Roonka II is the presence of shaft tombs. These exhibit a wide range of variability which suggests that a complex set of mortuary practices were in operation. Apparently the bodies were initially introduced fully erect into the grave. One of the shafts preserves this situation perfectly (Grave 51). It appears that the bodies then tended to slump into a mass in the bottom of the shaft. Various intermediate stages of the probable process have been preserved. The evidence further implies that for some reason at some stage or stages during that process the grave was revisited in order to manipulate and further arrange the body (Plate 10). This is clearly exhibited by the twisting of a body against its line of subsidence in one instance and in another by the recovery of bones, their sorting into groups and rearrangement on top of the still fully articulated lower part of the skeleton. It can only be assumed that the shaft was either left open or reinforced and resealed in some way. No traces of any internal structural material have however been identified.

Some of the shafts contained carbon. In at least three instances this assumed the form of a linear vertical intrusion alongside the body. It seems as if a burnt or smouldering stick had been thrust into the shaft. The quantity of carbon in all cases is extremely small and has created great difficulties in radiocarbon dating.

Some of the shafts contain associated objects. In two instances (one of them occurring in a trench adjacent to A) the adult is accompanied by an infant. One of these was transversely compacted, suggesting an already bundled and coffined corpse. Ornaments were found in two of the shafts, a point that makes their separate detailing worthwhile. Grave 63 contained the skeleton of an adult fully erect in the shaft but longitudinally compressed. This has caused the thorax and skull to sink below the level of the shoulders and the legs and feet to wedge themselves forward at a shallow angle against the shaft bottom. The skeleton of an infant adjacent to the left thigh was recovered. Two mandibular segments of a dasyurid (native cat) were in the pelvic region. They may have originally been higher up the body and fallen down. A neat attachment hole (Fig. 18a) has been drilled in the ascending ramus of each mandible.

Grave 89 contained the compressed and subsided skeleton of an adult in the bottom of a deep shaft. Three finds were discovered deposited with the skeleton which bore traces of red ochre. The most striking of them was a large thin disc of fossil oyster shell, similar to those in the fossil bearing cliffs nearby. At one point where the shell tapers to a hinge are two neatly drilled holes close together and side by side (Fig. 18b). A more curious object is a moderately large (15 cm × 9 cm) oval and flattened river pebble. Its most distinctive feature is the almost entire removal of its smooth cortex by systematic bruising. Only at a single point does a tiny scrap

Plate 10: Grave 104 (Roonka II) Trench A, showing the skeleton in a state of partial subsidence. Note the alignment of the thorax, twisted around almost 180° to present the dorsal aspect of the vertebral column facing the observer whilst leaving the arms in their near original position. The hole to be seen emerging just above the right hand denotes a near vertical shaft of charcoal and ash removed not long before the photograph was taken. Scale measured 500 cm.

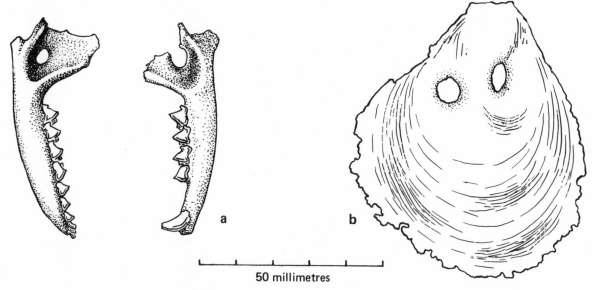

Fig. 18: Teeth and shell pendant ornaments—perforated.

of it remain. The bruised surface is fresh and unweathered and it is impossible to guess its function. At some distance above the skeleton but still well within the shaft was a simple bone pin made from a sharpened mammal fibula. It was pointing downwards at an angle implying that it had been dropped into the shaft in the course of its filling.

No associated objects come from the group of inhumations containing skeletons in full extension, save for Grave 106 where most of the ribs of the left thorax were prised apart from the breast bone by a large pointed bone dagger. It was fashioned from a large fibula sharpened at one end. Its length is 29 cm (Fig. 13d). Perhaps it was an instrument of autopsy as the vault of the thorax near the dagger tip yielded a broken tip of a concave-sectioned bone projectile point.

Roonka II raises a number of points of interest. Although the background of belief giving rise to the disposal of dead persons upright in shafts must be left to further conjecture, the evidence of selective factors reserving such forms of disposal to adults is clearly evident. Save for the deliberate deposition of infants with some, the interments are all mature adults.

An inspection of a specimen cross section of the E-W profile at any point shows how the volume of remaining soil increases constantly with depth so that far more surface area of Roonka II has been preserved than Roonka III. The bias this creates in the frequency of inhumations can be corrected by selecting the part of Trench A's eastern quadrangles which is up against the profile, so that it presents a constant volume with descending depth. This supplies the following inhumation tallies:

Roonka II   6   Roonka IIIa   8   Roonka IIIb   33

This shows that the site's use per unit of profile increased markedly in Roonka IIIb by comparison with Roonka IIIa and Roonka II. However the fact that this phase possesses two distinct forms of disposal, perhaps requires its further subdivision and may enforce a revision of the use per unit of profile.

The most interesting feature of the finds is the drilling of perforations in ornaments presumably for suspension or attachment in some way. This contrasts with the evidence of notching or simple removal of articular protuberances of bone elements to permit threading through the hollow tubular

bone bodies found in Roonka III. This in turn contrasts with the simple employment of complete and fractured pieces of bone inserted into squeezed balls of vegetable gum. This method is attested for the historic period by ethnographic sources and collections. There are no flaked stone tools in Roonka II although there are assemblages of a similar order of age from other excavated sites in the region.

Without doubt, the most noteworthy feature of Roonka II is the absence of any traces of associated settlement. Roonka II is the only assemblage of features so far recovered from Roonka that justly bears classification as a cemetery or necropolis. It may be that further radiocarbon dating will show links between Roonka II and some of the assemblages of settlement features distributed elsewhere on the Flat but so far no clear tie-ups can be demonstrated. For the present there is a gap in the evidence.

Phase II at Roonka has revealed a number of new and important insights into the society and thought of ancient Australian man. It will be interesting to see an analysis of the physical form of its members. Although supplying little or no direct information about stone tools, Roonka II supplies a number of features suggestive of cultural change.

Roonka I

Roonka I in Trench A is represented by four hearths positioned almost at the unconformity between Layers 3 and 4. Their principal claim for attention lies in the fact that charcoal from one of them was dated to 18 150±340 BP by radiocarbon (ANU-406). In Trench 0A, immediately adjacent, the same stratigraphic situation has yielded stone cobble cooking structures and a well defined living floor with freshwater mussel shells.

The living floor in Trench 0A   This assemblage of features was excavated throughout late August 1974. As in Trench A, it was penetrated by subsequent structures. No stone tools were found but the size and thickness of the mussel shells bore comparison with only one other locality, also currently under excavation and likely to produce a rich component of stone tools. It has been named the Glenforslan Sequence.

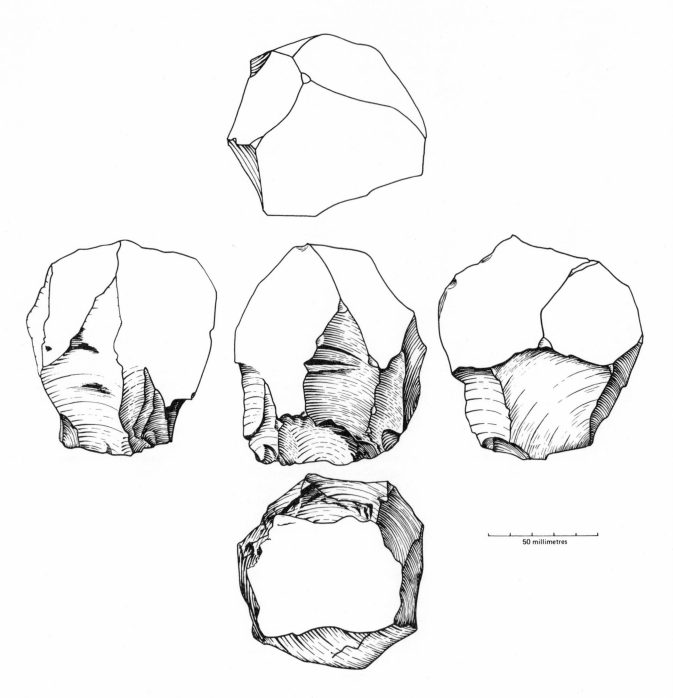

50 millimetres

Fig. 19: Stone chopper—high backed core. Surface find, East Bank, South Dune.

The Glenforslan Sequence The Glenforslan group is in E.W. linear dunes on the summit of the east bank cliffs over the river from the Roonka Flat and came to notice through the donation of an assemblage of stone tools by Mr R. E. Teusner of Tanunda. Mr Teusner had collected the tools from blown swales in these dunes.

Their principal component consisted of 'horsehoof cores', high backed blocks with a flat base formed into the shape of a disc by repeated blows which create a steeply retouched often step-flaked edge (Fig. 19). Included with them were one or two specimens of a more acutely-angled discoid tool made from a flake—the *karta* of Tindale (1937) (Fig. 20). The recovery of such associations of tools variously named *karta* (Tindale,

1941) or the 'Australian Core Tool and Scraper Tradition' (Bowler, Jones, Allen and Thorne, 1970) is of interest as such assemblages are widely considered to be late Pleistocene in age. Of additional interest is the fact that the stone materials of the Glenforslan assemblage, a pale creamy silicified limestone, is virtually unknown in the general Lower Murray Valley lithic tradition. The only other comparable specimen is a surface find from Wetjungali 1. This tool appears to be some sort of cleaver and is made from a large tabular block of silcrete alternately flaked along one edge. Another feature of the Glenforslan assemblage was encrustations of carbonate upon much of the implement surfaces.

The site is a series of deep blown swales in dunes. The

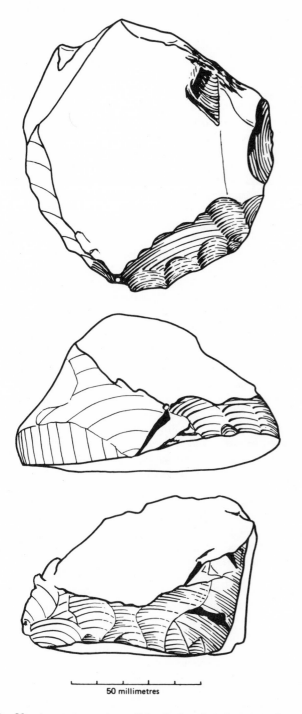

Fig. 20: Large stone scraper—flake. Surface find, East Bank, South Dune.

blown surfaces of the swales were strewn with further similar implements and debitage. One flaked quartz spheroid was found and collected. In addition to implements and debris there were a number of stone cobble cooking structures, shells and fragments of human bone. The shells attracted a lot of notice. Unlike the familiar ones from the Roonka Flat these were significantly thicker and larger. A short time afterwards, comparable specimens were found during excavation of Trench 0A.

The dunes differed from those on the Roonka Flat. Firstly they were less affected by erosion. Although the present vegetated surface itself bore evidence of prior stripping (for example perched root systems of trees) much of it was still present. The parallel E-W alignment of the dunes thus places them and their fellows firmly within the larger distribution of the great Australian dunefield. Fossil soils exposed in road cuttings through dunes a short distance away contain carbonates which appear to identify the Loveday soil (Firman, 1973) whose formation seals soils of an age in excess of 16 000 BP (Gill, 1973: 20–21). We identified similar soils though without carbonate, in the dunes containing human residue. It therefore seemed reasonable to suppose that assemblages deep within these dunes are late Pleistocene in age.

Tindale (1957) and Cooper (1959, 1961), the most assiduous students of these assemblages in South Australia, have drawn attention to the position of the sites on the summits of ridges overlooking Pleistocene valley basins. As the sites lie along the currently seafilled St Vincent's Gulf, their pre-Recent antiquity has been lent support. As in all cases, however, these sites had long since lost their mantle of soil so that only the implements exposed on the ground surface remained. Their age is necessarily uncertain. The situation of Glenforslan, with its commanding view over the deeply incised trench of the Murray compares closely with the St Vincent Gulf sites except that the covering mantle of soil remains.

The excavations in the Glenforslan dunes are at this stage insufficiently advanced to say much more. The trenches are rich in stone cobble cooking structures and no evidence of modern contamination has been found. Though the features and finds compare better with Roonka III than with those in the base of the blowouts the strong possibility remains that these excavations will relate to the antecedents to Roonka II.

Roonka I therefore, though distinct in the Roonka Flat Dune, remains shadowy and ill defined in its wider aspects. The excavations at Glenforslan show possibilities of filling such gaps, thus further enlarging upon the overall cultural perspectives of the Roonka Flat Sequence.

Discussion

A review of the data presented up to this point supplies a number of evidences and inferences which, put together, say something about the process of cultural change at Roonka. We can point to three principal aspects of cultural change:

First there is a considerable degree of chronological differentiation in mortuary practice. This is demonstrated by the cycle of dual disposal in Roonka II (notable for its distinctive mode of erect stance in shafts and their apparently curated decay and collapse) to Roonka IIIa, where the dualism is no longer evident and bodies are arranged in shaft bottoms recumbently but with legs drawn up against the body; thence finally to Roonka IIIb, with its restoration of dual modes but with differing manifestations.

There is also some chronological differentiation to be had from studying the rationale governing placement of sites in the dune. This can be gauged from the occasional open-camp aspect implied by Roonka I, the deliberate separation of settlement and necropolis implied by Roonka II, and the incorporating of inhumations into the settlement in Roonka III. In addition to varying chronologically, site function may have varied spatially throughout each cultural phase. Certainly this seems to be the case in Roonka III, where in addition to the phenomena and features recorded in the dune, there are a number of contemporaneous sites close by. Thus, in the dune, Phase III displays a limited range of food residues and a dispersed spread of cooking structures. In the open camps of the Wetjungali fossil system Phase III shows up as dense clusters of well-defined cobble ovens and almost no food refuse at all. In the McBean Pound rockshelter, the residues contemporaneous to Phase III, have a rich and diverse range of food residues while none of the related cooking structures have survived sufficiently intact for their structure or their distribution to be discernible. Overlooking the limited chronological span they represent, the Roonka III site patterns imply the feasibility of setting up hypothetical functional relationships as models for inquiry and instruments for predicating ongoing investigation. The limited span of time represented by Roonka III furthermore alerts us to the relevance of landscape transformations in major riverine systems and the necessity of introducing geomorphic considerations into the overall research strategy.

When we look at the inventories of stone tools, bone tools and ornaments we can see that all three streams differentiate at different rates in time and fail to show clear functional interrelations. However, they all show themselves to be substantially more sensitive as cultural markers than faunal residues.

To be properly evaluated the variations in these inventories have to be studied against a background of continuity of tradition. At Roonka this has two aspects.

First there is a continuity in the food processing technology. This to some extent mirrors the limited scale of change evident in stone and bone tool technology just as the comparatively more pronounced changes in costume ornament technology mirror marked changes in mortuary fashion. This devotion to matters of custom seems significant. We are obviously directed to consider a cultural perspective on ancient Australian society which our preoccupation with matters of industrial technology and resource processing ill-equip us to make good use of.

Second there appears to be a deeply based and unchanging exhibition of a social status or a rank-structure more important than the value of human life. It is hard to suppose a more satisfactory interpretation of the graves containing deliberately disposed infants.

There are however certain other problems which excavation has raised and identified but only partly resolved. Three deserve comment. First there are persisting difficulties in untangling the links that separate or relate the three principal inhumation forms in Roonka III. What relationships were there between the pits containing recumbent-contracted, true contracted and full dorsal extension inhumations? Were they contemporary or did they succeed each other in time? Radiocarbon may help to supply an answer. Second, the cultural detail of the settlement zone, originally part of Phase III and destroyed by the events bringing about Layers 1 and 2, is an obscurity that only further excavation could clarify. Finally, we await firm linkages between sites on the Flat, the flood-plain, the dune and cliff overhangs. Again, radiocarbon may hold the answers.

The most significant new insights to emerge are (a) the confirmation of late Pleistocene contexts surviving in the Lower Murray tract; (b) the discovery of a true necropolis in Roonka II with its suggestion of delayed and primary inhumations as contemporaneous modes and ornaments of a distinctly different workmanship and (c) the distinguishing of a new inhumational mode, the recumbent-contracted, in IIIa.

When we compare the sequence established at Roonka with the sites in the wider Murray region beyond (Map 2), three major groups emerge. Each is situated in its own distinctive landscape.

The first group includes the sites which like Roonka are enclosed within the Murray Trench—that part of the river tract between Chowilla, the North West Bend descending to Murray Bridge, where the river's flow is constricted by high cliffs. The sites investigated here are all downstream from Roonka. The first of them is the open-air site at Tartanga excavated by Tindale (Hale and Tindale, 1930) and the accompanying rockshelter at Devon Downs, almost directly opposite. Further downstream on the right bank is Fromm's Landing, a series of rock overhangs overlooking a lagoon-studded flood-plain. Two have been excavated by Mulvaney (Mulvaney, 1960; Mulvaney, Lawton and Twidale, 1964).

Downstream from Murray Bridge, the Murray's trench-like aspect gives way to an undulating plain. The river, prevented from dispersing into deltaic swamps by the force of the southern Indian Ocean, terminates in a series of broad shallow lakes and lagoons protected behind a long seawall of sandspits. In pre-European times it supported dense populations. A short distance downstream from Murray Bridge is Swanport. Here, in 1911, the demolishing of a dune for swamp reclamation uncovered a dense cluster of skeletons. Their rescue and provisional study was the subject of a paper by Stirling (1911).

The third group of sites is situated some distance upstream from Roonka. Here the river is a tangled skein of streams and lakes in a vast inland plain of ancient silts which it is reworking. Some of the streambeds are fossil and dry; so also are many of the lakes. Many of these relics still fill for short periods during high river flow. The closest group to Roonka is between Chowilla and Mildura, investigated by Blackwood and Simpson (1973). Not far away is Lake Nitchie where an isolated interment was recovered by Macintosh and his colleagues (Macintosh, Smith and Bailey, 1970; Macintosh, 1971). A number of sites extending for the full length of this tract have been investigated by Black (Sunderland and Ray, 1959). Beyond this and much further upstream is the group of burials recovered from Kow Swamp (Thorne, 1971; Thorne and Macumber, 1972) not far from the fossil site of Cohuna. Far to the north of this, in another relict system of connected lakes (the Willandra system) are the sites currently under investigation at Lake Mungo (Bowler, Jones, Allen and Thorne, 1970; Bowler, Thorne and Polach, 1972). The extent and uniformity of this plain have brought about a dispersed pattern of settlement very different from that at Roonka. Mungo and Kow Swamp however stand most apart from the other sites by their remoteness in time.

All these sites have produced inhumations. Most have been reported on in sufficient detail for comparisons to be made. It will therefore be useful to review them in the light of what has been learnt from Roonka.

Before doing so however some appreciation should be had of the rapid advances in our understanding of the Murray Basin's landscape evolution in the Quaternary, as a result of the past decade's research. This is important because the stratigraphies are becoming sufficiently understood to be used in field investigations.

The work of Butler (1950) demonstrated the existence of an ancient and deeply based Murray stream and sediment system aberrantly situated to that of today. This opened up the way for detailed investigations into streambed fluctuations and their causes. The work of Pels (1964, 1971) clarified this by demonstrating the river system's sensitivity to displacement and rejuvenation by minor tectonics and fossil climatic change. This has identified stream patterns intermediate between the very ancient and those of the present day. The value of relict lake systems and their aeolian deposited margin deposits for illustrating fossil climatic changes of late Quaternary age has been explained by Bowler (1971). Bowler has also drawn archaeologists' attention to the presence in these aeolian lake margins of human residues of late Pleistocene age. The effects of all these events on the Murray Trench discharge corridor to the sea (complicated as it is by tectonic movements emanating from the mountainous basin margins and from eustatic advances and regressions along the river tract) emerges from the work of Firman (1973). Gill (1973), drawing upon Firman's work and Lawrence's (1966) and combining them with his own fieldwork in the central Murray tract, has succeeded in blending events in the river tract, lake basins and dune plains on either side, into a unified picture of landscape evolution, changing in response to cyclic alternations of aridity and humidity and identifiable in the field from facies markers in surficial stratigraphies. This history has permitted insertion of the emerging human sequence into a context of environmental evolution.

We shall now return to the three major groups of sites and consider them in detail commencing with those closest to Roonka in the Murray Trench.

Tindale's excavations at Devon Downs trenched a rockshelter looking out over the east bank of the Murray (Hale and Tindale, 1930). A further trench was sunk at Tartanga, immediately upstream from Devon Downs, where a secondary lagoon displaced into the west bank flood-plain had left a narrow strip of land as remnant from the old riverbank. To Tindale there appeared good grounds for linking both sequences in a relationship of direct succession. Tartanga was posited as the earlier. Although subdivisible stratigraphically, the Tartanga cultural sequence was discussed by Tindale as a single formation. The Devon Downs sequence however appeared subdivisible into three components on a basis of unit tool traits. These subdivisions Tindale named in ascending order as Pirrian—where the sequence was characterised by small finely worked leaf shaped points; Mudukian—where the sequence was characterised by bone bipoints; and Murundian—a zone of somewhat indefinite artifactual character. Further support for the direct linking of both Tartanga and Devon Downs sequences from confirmatory radiocarbon tests was published by Tindale in 1957. The earlier date 6000 BP was reported from deep within the Tartanga sequence, while the other (4250 BP) was reported from deep in the Devon Downs sequence.

Further consideration of Tindale's reporting and its review in the light of what has been found at Roonka raises certain points in favour of revising his interpretaton.

Firstly, close inspection of the stratigraphic information suggests the possibility of two sequences overlapping instead of succeeding each other in time. The total depth of section opened up by trenching amounted to 4 m; another 1.5 m below this was explored by augering. The profile exposed in section subdivides into two principal soils well separated by a stratum of archaeologically sterile, unfeatured grey mud (Beds F-G). The full depth of profile rested on a basal red sand of undetermined depth. The most significant point of division is the grey mud unit represented by Beds F and G.

Above this break, in a zone Tindale called the 'Upper Beds', the soil is composed of sandy clays developing into unconsolidated sands. Below the break, in a zone called the 'Lower Beds', the soil matrix is sandy but consolidated to an advanced degree. Its fabric is stoney, and exhibits considerable geochemical differentiation of elements, eg. soil mineral oxidisation, ferric staining of intrusive matter and formation

of carbonate nodules. No doubt this has been made more complex by the enrichment products of contained faunal residues deposited through human settlement agencies. Considering these points, and looking beyond Tindale's zeal to discern bedding planes, we appear to have a soil unit of principally sandy composition but incorporating calc and ferric compounds between the grey muds and the red sand basement. Structurally it appears to have ascended through a profile consisting of a clay rich sandy basal zone and a body of ferric containing sands. Within its stratigraphic boundaries, the sands appear to have contained two minor zones of a greyish colour, one situated medially, and the other at the top of the bed just beneath the unconformity. Experience at Roonka suggests that these grey zones can denote occupance enrichment; Tindale's date of 6000 BP came from the lower zone.

The Tartanga sequence bears interpretation as a developing aeolian dune, similar to the Roonka Flat dune, but having its development interrupted by an event which submerged it under floodplain sediments thereby subjecting it to geochemical alteration, after which it resumed its previous mode of formation. The cause of its possible submergence is difficult to identify although the valley cliffs at this locality fall within a zone of recent faulting. Throughout all of its period of formation, save when it was submerged by silt, it was occupied by man. Firman (1973) dates the onset of the sedimentation of grey muds (Coonambidgal Formation) in the Lower Murray tract to 4080 ± 100 BP. This is of comparable age to the initial refilling stages of the rockshelters in the lower tract following upon what must have been a preceding scour of their previous contents. Stratigraphically it would appear, that whilst there is good reason to place the 'Lower Beds' at Tartanga immediately prior to the filling of the Devon Downs rockshelter, there is equally good reason to equate the 'Upper Beds' with the rockshelter fill in time.

We may enlarge on our view of the parallel histories of Roonka and Devon Downs–Tartanga by considering the technological evidence. Devon Downs and Tartanga still constitute our richest single source of stratified cultural evidence for the Murray area. They compares well on all grounds with Phases II–III at Roonka. Considering both sequences together shows them to be broadly similar in general terms although differing considerably in detail. Considering both sequences in their broadest terms it can be seen that in technology they are within the same time scale; 7000 BP to the onset of European colonisation at Roonka and 6000 BP to the same event at Tartanga and Devon Downs. The range of tools and instruments at both sites is similar— made of stone are flake scrapers, points, microliths and polygonal cores. Made of bone is an array of awls (varying from taper to abruptly finished) and projectile points.

The Roonka inhumations allow us to see the functions of tools more clearly and this enforces revisions of cultural detail for Devon Downs and Tartanga. At Roonka, concave-sectioned bone points bear identification as projectile tips, as also do bipoints. Tindale's identification of the Devon Downs bone bipoints as fish gorges has never carried a full weight of accord, qualified as it is by the extent of negative evidence against it. Ethnographic sources picture the Murray as a region deriving its fish by netting or spearing in the river or artificial ponds. The spears for which we have specimens or descriptions, include single and multipronged forms with plain or composite points including a proportion tipped with bone in both simple forward and reverse positionings. The archaeological validity of *muduks* as gorges is thus placed under considerable strain, faintly supported as it is by a single cited instance from a coastal habitat (Smyth, 1878, i, 391).

This instance describes an object similar to Tindale's muduk but fashioned from wood. No word confirming its presence could be obtained from the Murray vocabularies; Tindale was therefore obliged to name it with the nearest native generic word for 'bone', *muduk*. Although serving as an instance of what was fair archaeological reasoning for its time this insight of Tindale's does not appear to have stood the test of later evidence. It would be preferable for it to be, if not dropped, then put very much to one side for the present. The technical and evolutionary problems surrounding fish gorges in Australia are discussed fully by Anell (1955).[1]

Considering the evidence of point, barb and scraper traditions in stone and bone in parallel as representing food extractive and fabricative instruments respectively, it is striking to see how the internal differences between Tartanga and Devon Downs fade from view and the similarity between them and Roonka II–III, is sustained. A strong impression is left that there is an underlying similarity between both places over what the dating evidence shows to be a similar span of time.

There seems reason then to suppose that the sequence at Tartanga and its neighbour, Devon Downs, do not merge into each other as a continuum but overlap considerably. They may also reflect similar functional relationships between differently situated sites having functional contrasts. We have already noted this at Roonka where the comparison of the dune with the McBean Pound rockshelter shows marked differences between food refuse spectra; so also at Devon Downs the rockshelter fill is rich and diverse whereas the fill of the 'Upper Beds' at Tartanga, across the river, contained little more than ash and mussel shell debris. Their lack of artifact content no doubt explains the brief treatment they have received in the published report.

The argument for functional contrasts in differently situated sites is strengthened by considering the evidence from the inhumations. Three were excavated at Tartanga, all of them in the older consolidated unit ('Lower Beds'). All were introduced into settlement residues. Two of them were sufficiently complete to identify as primary inhumations, both of them laid out in full dorsal extension. All three remains of bodies were sub-adult. Four further inhumations were recovered from the Devon Downs trenches. Three were infants, the fourth a child aged about five years. The three infant interments were all primary inhumations and the third had disturbed and dissociated the fourth. Two of the graves were partly protected by cist-like structures of stone fragments. All were introduced into occupance debris.

Comparing this suite with Roonka, certain points emerge. Noticeably absent are any traces of inhumed adults or aged persons. It is as if the proportional paucity of infants and juveniles noted in the Roonka dune are now complemented by their proportional abundance at Devon Downs and Tartanga. It lends support to the notion that the age of the deceased determined where and by what means they were to be interred. The next point of note requires acceptance of the inference that the 'Lower Beds' at Tartanga are the stratigraphic and time correlates of Phase II in the Roonka

dune. This then could disclose Tartanga as a specimen of the open air encampment contemporary with the necropolis represented by Phase II in the Roonka dune. If both places do functionally complement each other it clarifies the pattern of site-inhumation relationships already suggested from Phase II at Roonka. The third point emerges from the previous one and draws attention to the apparent continuity of situating certain categories of inhumation within sites of occupance and extends this practice back from Roonka III times into Roonka II. It suggests, for example, that (should it be ever located) the settlement belonging to the necropolis marked by Phase III in the dune, is likely to contain sub-adult inhumations. It also suggests that certain missing components of the prehistoric population at Roonka may prove to have been interred in the floors of nearby cliff overhangs.

It is tempting to speculate on whether and where there could have been a dune necropolis at Tartanga correlating with the settlement zone represented by the 'Lower Beds'. On Tindale's 1930 plan (p. 147) there is a reference to a further site described as a 'burial ground (recent)' on the same side of the river as Tartanga and located a short distance downstream. Sheard (1927) in his preliminary notice of Devon Downs refers to the same site as being in an area of drifting sand where skeletal remains could be observed. Fortified by our experience of quite ancient remains in similarly unconsolidated sands at Roonka, it might well be queried whether this burial ground was necessarily wholly 'recent' after all?

Considering the possible sealed antiquity of its 'Lower Beds' and the curious possibility of its submergence, there seem good reasons for undertaking further investigation at Tartanga.

The comparison between Roonka, Devon Downs and Tartanga can be extended to the excavations at Fromm's Landing where there are several rockshelters first reported on by Sheard, Mountford and Hackett (1927). Grenfell Price and Mountford excavated a test pit in 1952 (Price 1952). Two of the shelters were excavated by Mulvaney and his collaborators between 1956 and 1963 (Mulvaney, 1960; Mulvaney, Lawton and Twidale, 1964). Mulvaney has devoted considerable discussion to the sedimentology and industrial traditions but, in considering the inhumations, he has confined himself to descriptions only. A review of his reports raises three points.

The first is the remarkable consistency of radiocarbon spans with Devon Downs and Phase III at Roonka. Level 9 at Devon Downs yielded a date of 4250±180 (Tindale, 1957), level 10 at Fromm's 2 dated at 4850±100 (NZ 364), level 16 at Fromm's 6, 3450±90 (NPL 63) and inhumation 48 at Roonka (calibrating the beginnings of Roonka III) at 3930±120 (ANU-407). This tends to support an equation between all of the four and establishes upper and lower chronological limits in which to compare and explore the detail of cultural traditions. It also tends to renew attention to wider geomorphic processes, considering the evidence now coming to hand of traces of human occupation within the valley with an antiquity greater than 5000 BP. Accepting the probability that the present valley floodplain sediments were laid down from about 4000 BP onwards and that it is likely they were preceded by a phase of stream rejuvenation and downcutting, it is possible to fit the scouring out of the rockshelters at Devon Downs and Fromm's Landing into a broader picture of geomorphic evolution. The bottoms of each of these shelters are so close to the historic uncontrolled mean river levels that it is readily conceivable that they would be emptied of their prior fill by a phase of high discharge.

---

1. N. B. Tindale told me that after publishing his 1930 report he obtained independent verification of the use of fusiform fishing toggles in the Lower Murray from Albert Karloan, a Jaralde. Karloan (1863–1943) informed Tindale that these fusiform points were also put to use as reverse barbs on spears.

If this correlation is shown to be valid, we should expect the rockshelter fill at McBean Pound to fit within the same time span.

The second point raised by Fromm's Landing is the comparative value of its industrial traditions. Mulvaney declares himself impressed more with the essential continuity of the tool traditions than by any variance attributable to distributional idiosyncracies deriving from trench sampling of the varying cultural samples present in any site. The usefulness of Fromm's Landing, as he sees it, is to demonstrate the parallel continuity of backed blade tradition developing from geometric microliths with a tradition of finely worked stone points. Considering the import of the Roonka-based interpretations of *muduks*, it appears useful to consider *pirris*, backed blades, fusiform bone points and concave-sectioned bone points as all variants of a single projectile point tradition. The usefulness of Roonka thus arises from its implanting of the rockshelter sequences into a longer and more ancient context of cultural change, altering perspectives and blunting the edge of internal differences in artifact distributions at individual sites.

The third point raised by Fromm's Landing relates to the disposal of the dead. These amount to five, one of them a desiccated infant's body swaddled in kangaroo skin and recovered from a cliff cleft. The other four were inhumations. Two of these were infants, one under stones as was noted at Devon Downs, but the other two were adults, both female. Both appear to have been manipulated into a position of contraction of the limbs with the body placed on its side. Both were resting at the bottoms of appreciable shafts.

Putting aside the confirmatory evidence of further infant inhumations similar to those discussed at Devon Downs, the presence of two adult females in such a context injures the hypothesis that adults were deliberately interred in places without infants. It is further to be observed that in Trench A at Roonka there was a similar small proportion of infant inhumations—by proportion amounting to almost 8% of the total. There is no satisfactory explanation for this aberration other than to suppose that, as with most other cultural continuities, compromises of custom inevitably occur. Looking beyond this, however, it is worth pointing out that interment in deep cylindrical shafts is a continuing tradition at Roonka and one which has escaped notice ethnographically and archaeologically.

In concluding the discussion on sites other than Roonka within the tract of the Murray Trench, a number of concordances can be stated. There is the similarity of the rockshelter fills at Devon Downs and Fromm's Landing evidenced by the industrial traditions, food residues and radiocarbon. The discontinuous and complementary distribution of inhumations between rockshelter fills and open air dunes implies that their explanation lies in a self conscious structuring of the societies they represent into distinct age statuses; it also adds to the inventory of forms of interment ascertainable from Roonka itself and shows a shift of inhuming localities as Roonka II gives way to Roonka III about 7000 BP. There is no trace of Roonka I or the Glenforslan assemblages at any other site and the introduction of this greater perspective, along with other evidences of cliff scouring and sedimentation renewal between 4000 and 5000 BP, suggests that the geomorphic events within the Murray Trench at this time would well repay further investigation.

Whereas the comparison of Roonka with other sites in the Murray Trench supports an inferred social structure based on age-statuses, Roonka's further comparison with Swanport downstream sees the same structure's repetition, shows it to possess a differing range of manifestations and confirms it from nineteenth century first-hand reporting.

Swanport is the only site we have on the Murray between its emergence from the high cliffs of the Trench and where it breaks up into terminal lakes. The original investigation of Swanport denies us radiocarbon dates or a cultural stratigraphy, although there is good material for dating the bone and careful drawings of the profile made at the time allow for certain stratigraphic inferences of a limited kind.

The substance of Stirling's enquiries (Stirling 1911) suggests that the archaeological residues at Swanport were buried in a gently sloping sandy rise. This at one time was vegetated and surmounted by a stand of native pines. Its situation, jutting out into the main stream, thereby banking up a lengthy reed swamp running parallel to the bank, guaranteed a commanding position over a broad range of the river's food resources. For these reasons, its classing as a cemetery by Stirling is curious, the more so when its associated residues are considered alongside the skeletal evidence.

The Swanport soil profile was distinguished by a well demarcated zone of occupance residues, principally shell and ovenstones, in a matrix of black sand. Above, was a thin band of undifferentiated sand sealed by grass, while below it the sand appeared as a broad band of reddish matter intertextured with discontinuous spreads of mussel shells. Beneath the reddish sand was a basement of travertine and calcareous marls. The inhumations all appeared to relate stratigraphically to the zone of occupance whose distinctive colouration outlined the shape of the pits.

In general stratigraphic appearances Swanport best compares with Roonka III, a link which obtains further support from the mention of certain skeletons resting on one side in a sharply contracted attitude. Stirling is moreover emphatic that no extended inhumations were present. His noting of bodies of infants occurring in the same pit as adults recalls the compound status inhumation familiar from Roonka.

The most characteristic and most frequently occurring inhumation practice at Swanport is without parallel at Roonka; the body was disposed in a sharply contracted position but sitting upright in the ground. This is highly significant for the present analysis because it is amply supported from the historic sources and sheds light on the hypothesised age statuses governing interment modes acknowledged as central to the argument of this paper. Stirling puts it down to the custom of smoke mummifying the corpses of people, deceased in their prime, prior to burial. Its distinctiveness appears to have been paid little attention hitherto. It is best exemplified, according to Stirling, by skeletons primarily inhumed but missing skeletal elements belonging to the body extremities, for example, finger and foot bones. Comparable instances have been reported from other localities around the Murray mouth, the Coorong and the Adelaide Plains.

Although standing apart from Roonka and typifying a site with a distinct cultural milieu, Swanport has a value for the analysis of Roonka because it is in an area for which there is ample historical source material. It verifies the historical accounts of the Lower Murray tribes whose distinctions in modes of disposing the dead depended on the age of the deceased at death. According to Angas (1847), for example, dead children were carried about in a desiccating state by the mother for some time prior to disposal. Adults were trussed into tight bundles and smoked on platforms for a period prior to burial. Old men's bodies were exposed on raised platforms and covered with bracken until they fell to pieces; old women were put up into the structures of trees there to decay and disintegrate. Angas is by no means the only observer to record this and the details of the modes, together with their supporting *rationale*, have been amply documented. For us it is sufficient to note the outcomes it would have upon archaeological inhumation patterns. Despite our lack of comparable source material from the region around Roonka, archaeologically we might reasonably assume a similar set of inhumational modes based on age-structure but with differing manifestations, for example the cist-like structures covering infant inhumations.

In addition to the testimony of written sources, the bones and their analysis supply further insights. The sum total of material rescued from Swanport is represented by the collection at present in the South Australian Museum. Unfortunately no field notes made at the time have yet been located. According to Stirling's computation, the maximum number of individuals amounted to 160. This includes a number which when first exposed were missing their crania. This absence was put down to prehistoric interference, for example the robbing of graves for skulls to be converted into water vessels. The actual tally of crania now in the collection amounts to 109. Stirling's foreshadowed systematic study of the population was never performed but the value of the collection, as a well defined population isolated in time and space, has long been known and it has been repeatedly studied by physical anthropologists (Campbell, 1925; Hrdlicka, 1928; Fenner, 1939; Brown, 1973; Howells, 1973). From the catalogues of Hrdlicka, Campbell, and Barrett with Kailis (Kailis, pers. comm.) it has been possible to subdivide the population into its age–structural components of infants (7), children (10), adolescents and adults (79) and aged (13). It is in the last named category that the authorities differ most in their assessments. The pattern is remarkable for the high proportion of adults as against the young and aged. Not only does it constitute inversion of the standard U-shaped curve of most biological populations (see for example Acsadi and Nemeskeri, 1970: 26) but it is closely similar to the age structure of the population excavated from the Roonka dune. It is strikingly evident that what we are confronted with on the Lower Murray sites is not population biology modified by chance but the operation of human custom.

Swanport has yielded extremely little in the way of artifacts. These are three bone awls made from kangaroo fibulae and one quartz flake described as a 'spearhead' but not available for study at present.

The Swanport evidence raises two further matters. Stirling's observation that the area occupied by inhumations was a confined part of the sandhill, suggests that it could have been marked out or reserved in some way. He reports no instances of graves intruding one into the other. This is unusual for the Murray, the only other reported instance being a necropolis represented by Phase II in the Roonka Dune. The second point of note about Swanport is the dune's former possession of native pines. These, before the spread of farming, were an identifying feature of Murray dunes, a proportion of which we know contained prehistoric inhumations. It is no doubt the favouring of these trees for domestic purposes in the last century that caused their eradication, the dunes remobilising as a consequence and producing the widespread exposure of their skeletal content. The presence of inhumations in association with camps in the clays of the Roonka Flat eliminates the obvious explanation that dunes were favoured for inhumation because they were easy to dig.

Swanport then, despite its disadvantages is clearly a settlement with important inhumation associations. It compares best with Roonka III. It could well do with further study. Bone dates for example could resolve some of the stratigraphic problems. It further isolates itself and its region from Roonka by distinct traits in inhumational practice. Reviewing Roonka in the light of Swanport shows that whereas both sites reflect similar age structures in their placement of inhumations there are two features of Roonka which remain unique—the status or compound inhumations and the dualism exhibited in disposal modes. It remains therefore to test this structure of inference further by looking at the sites and distributions reported from the Central and Upper Murray tracts.

The sites of the Central Murray tract (Map 2) comprise Lake Nitchie, Lake Victoria, Lindsay Island, Lake Walla-walla and Walpolla Creek. Further upstream are the sites of Lake Benanee, Lake Poon Boon and Coobool Island. The distribution of sites thus available for comparison extends to beyond Swan Hill.

Lake Nitchie is a late Quaternary relict lake bed discordantly aligned to the present Darling anabranch and occasionally filled by it during high rivers (Bowler, 1970). The discovery of inhumations eroding from a paleosol in its aeolian lunette margin invited their careful recovery for examination. The excavation of the best preserved of these by Macintosh has been detailed in reports (Macintosh, Smith and Bailey, 1970; Macintosh, 1971). Two aspects of the find have attracted wide notice.

Its most noteworthy feature was its yield of a lengthy necklace constituted from pierced teeth of the extinct (on the Australian mainland) marsupial carnivore *Sarcophilus* (Tasmanian Devil). The necklace was in position, slung from the neck of the entombed person and draped across the chest. This discovery cast a completely new light on Australian mortuary practice as it was understood. Although ethnographic accounts attest to disposal of personal possessions with the dead, no evidence of grave goods having any intrinsic cultural significance had yet emerged from inhumations in this country.

The next most noteworthy feature of Nitchie was the arrangement of the skeleton. Crammed into a narrow subcircular pit in a semi-recumbent attitude, the legs bent back on themselves sharply, feet introduced into a shallow extension to the shaft bottom, the whole body bearing marked evidences of downward compression, it appeared as a unique find among Australian reports on these matters up to that time. Subsequent dating work (Macintosh, 1971) established the skeleton's age as 6820 ± 200 BP.

The archaeological content of Roonka II confirms and elaborates on the Nitchie find in all three of its mortuary, technological and chronological aspects, supplying a broader based context for the find. There are differences however. At Roonka the tomb shafts were deeper and the better articulated skeletons were, if not erect, then wedged nearly vertical in the shaft in full extension or devolutions from it. In one instance the body had sunk down thrusting the knees forward, in another, the skeleton was half-squatting in the shaft. In each case the degree of vertical compression, forcing skull and thorax down below the level of the shoulders, is similar to that described at Lake Nitchie. It is difficult however to reconcile this with Macintosh's view that the Nitchie body was squeezed into a shallow pit which it was necessary to impact externally and alter for the feet's benefit at the bottom in order to accommodate the body satisfactorily. Nevertheless, the overall concordance of custom between the two sites is strikingly similar, as is the parallel presence of perforated ornaments in both places at a similar period in time. At Roonka, the perforated shell pendant in shaft tomb 89 has been dated to 6910±450 BP (ANU-1408). The report by Dortch and Merrilees (1973) of a fully worked and perforated bone bead from a context dated to 17 000 BP in the Devil's Lair Cave, situated on the far southwestern tip of the continent, identifies these ornaments as belonging to a long and developed tradition.

The principal source of information for the Central Murray tract is found in the report by Blackwood and Simpson (1973) detailing their rescue recoveries in the tract of river between Chowilla and Mildura. At the time of their work part of the river was destined for submergence through dam construction. Seventy-two inhumations were investigated and removed from eight points at four localities. The four localities investigated were Lake Victoria, Lindsay Island, Lake Wallawalla and Walpolla Creek. The hydrologic features are all fossil relatives of the present day Murray stream system.

The work on these sites has to be evaluated with the recognition that this was a rescue project. For this reason all inhumations recovered were identified from surface exposures, no sealing soil mantles were penetrated in order to uncover them. Even the relationships with Gill's work on the soil geology are difficult to establish with certainty since, no doubt, this synthesis was being formulated at the same time from fieldwork conducted in parallel. Arising from these circumstances, it does not appear to have been possible to pay attention to the morphology of the pits or structures out of which the skeletons were removed. Similarly, the stratigraphic relationships of associated occupance residues do not appear to have been ascertainable. Finally, the skeletons vary in their states of completeness, thus affecting the identifications of age and sex.

Nevertheless, a great deal has been learnt. Superpositioning of inhumations above and into each other was noted in many cases and several inhumations were dated by radiocarbon. Comparing the results with Roonka discloses similarity on three grounds.

First, there is an identical range of burial modes including recumbent-contracted and collapsed erect forms. This relates these sites to Roonka II–III and Lake Nitchie. Second, there are similar elements in the cultural stratigraphy of both sites. For example, the promiscuous intrusion of later into earlier graves can be recorded for the inhumers of skeletons in the modes of full dorsal extension, contraction, and recumbent-contraction. The collapsed erect interments are free from intermixture with each other as was found at Roonka. On the other hand, the apparent disregard for the previous dead exhibited by prehistoric inhumers is qualified by some instances of elaborate care in leaving previous inhumations undisturbed. This is also reported from Phase III at Roonka. Third and finally and to the extent of its completeness, there appears to be a similar age-mortality structure in the inhumed population as has been discussed in detail for the Lower Murray sites.

There are however contrasts and differences worthy of note. The nature of relationships between inhumations and sites of occupance does not emerge from Blackwood and Simpson's report, nor, from the data they present, does there seem any cause for positing such a relation. In this aspect their sites appear very different from the Lower Murray sites. A second noticeable contrast is the absence of grave goods or compound status inhumations. Fragments of a gypsum plaster 'mourning helmet' was found with one skeleton and food shells, thought to be deliberate depositions, were found with others, but there is nothing to compare with the stately arrays unearthed in certain of the tombs at Roonka.

Six radiocarbon assessments, mostly direct from the bone itself, attest to a similar range of antiquity as the Roonka inhumations. Actual age of changes in burial mode however seem to occur slightly earlier. Nothing older than 7000 BP was excavated.

The series recovered by Blackwood and Simpson is far exceeded by the recoveries of the late Murray Black from five well-spaced localities extending the full length of the Central Murray tract (Sunderland and Ray, 1959). The localities tested comprise Chowilla, Lake Victoria and the Rufus Creek leading into it, Lake Benanee, Lake Poon Boon and Coobool Island. Published information concerning provenances is scanty but enough data is available to draw some extremely tentative conclusions.

Inhumational modes range from full dorsal extension to moderate lateral flexion and contraction. They include one illustrated specimen of a recumbent-contracted skeleton and a possible instance of secondary disposal.

This range is shared with Blackwood and Simpson's sites together with a lack of associated settlements—in contrast with Roonka. They also share the presence of gypsum plaster helmet fragments. One exception to this is Chowilla where a mention of charcoal and ash in grave fills may denote an associated settlement.

In addition to these purely negative evidences, the Murray Black sites have one additional feature not detected by Blackwood and Simpson in their investigation. There is evidence for burning and scorching the body in the grave. In certain cases this affected the bones to the point of charring them. On the basis of Black's reports, the practice seems to have been distributed from Chowilla to as far as Lake Benanee, near the Murray's junction with the Murrumbidgee. Burning the body of a deceased person, extending to true cremation, is widely reported among the historic inventory of mortuary practices in Victoria and there is at least one confirmable instance of it at Roonka where it has been dated to 3930±120 BP. Its usefulness as a regional diagnostic indicator therefore appears valid.

The Murray Black collection, like Swanport, could well benefit from renewed attention. Judging from the photographs and information appearing in its published notice, a catalogue of the inhumations' cultural features could be put together to supplement the existing biological catalogue and, with bone dates, could elicit a valid chronology.

The artifact content of the Central Murray sites is meagre. Both Blackwood and Simpson, and Black, report gypsum plaster mourning helmets and their fragments. These have a wide distribution extending up the Darling a considerable distance. At present they are poorly fixed in time and space although one recovered from one of the Lake Victoria inhumations was dated to 750±170 BP. Black reports finding bone awls in some graves. Casey (1973) describes a collection of stone artifacts evidently collected by Gill and his associates from erosion surfaces in the area of their field surveys. Unfortunately no evidence of provenance is noted. The most interesting find is two unbarbed bone fishhooks reported by Gallus and Gill. Apparently they were associated with what could be a recumbent-contracted inhumation in the Walpolla Creek locality. Nothing however is known of its age.

With the exception of the sites investigated by Macintosh and Blackwood with Simpson, where the broad features of the Roonka tradition are repeated, we are not yet able to see a clear pattern emerging from the Central Murray inhumations. It would appear that all the principal inhumation modes (full extension, collapsed erect, recumbent-contraction and full contraction) are shared by Roonka and all the Central Murray sites.

It would appear, however, that there are differences of detail that justify the delineating of boundaries to separate provinces. It is possible to distinguish the Central tract of the Murray up to the Murrumbidgee junction from the Upper tract because it possesses the tradition of scorching the remains. Nevertheless on most other grounds (inhumation-encampment association, inhumation form and chronology, population age-structure) the supply of information remains too inadequate for delineating boundaries.

There are a number of factors not considered in this analysis, which further work could convert to use, such as orientation of the body, variations in the arrangement of arms, and the presence or absence of evulsed teeth. Renewed attention to the material already accumulated without recourse to extensive excavation of further sites could improve problems of delineation of boundaries.

In sum then, for that part of the river between Roonka and Swan Hill for which we have both distribution patterns and time depth, there appears to be a widespread sharing of traits, and some evidences of aberrant exotic instances from site to site. As is testified by the Aboriginal tales collected in the area, movement along the stream system for long distances was not unknown (Tindale, 1939) and must have had outcomes in social history. Viewed in such a context Roonka stands out most for its possession of a persisting tradition of status graves incorporating adults and deliberately deposited infants as part of the grave's furnishment. It also stands apart in the comparative richness of its grave goods. To clarify the situation any further it is obviously necessary to pay closer attention to the sites in the Central Murray and pursue the inquiry into the Upper tract of the Murray beyond Swan Hill and north across the tributary-crossed plain. At this moment the only sites in this area for which we have information are deeply based in much older environments of Quaternary age. The two sites of this age which have been investigated are Lake Mungo and Kow Swamp.

Lake Mungo is one of the late Quaternary environments whose human use in times of high lake fill was first reported by Bowler. Its yield of a fully cremated adult female has been abundantly detailed (Bowler et al., 1970; Thorne, 1971). It is however a single isolated find from an erosional residual and although reports of further finds have come to hand nothing about them has been published at the time of writing.

The principal significance of the cremation is its antiquity, which has been dated by radiocarbon to 24 710±1270/±1100 (ANU-G186) by Bowler, Thorne and Polach (1972). As a consequence, most attention has been paid to its physical morphology. Although considerable quantities of artifactual material and food residues are referred to in various communications, and references to what must be strings of open camps along lake strandlines, the specific relationship of these sites to inhumations has not been stated. The morphology of the excavated cooking structures is clearly described and interesting. They consisted of broad shallow pans of ash

and charcoal intermixed with food remains from a broad variety of mammals, birds and fish. Their content included discarded stone artifacts. The artifacts subdivide into untouched highbacked cores bearing a flat base and steeply retouched scrapers (Bowler et al. 1970).

The major series of Quaternary inhumations however comes from Kow Swamp, another Murray locality, situated upstream from Swan Hill in a relict lake associated with a fossil stream system (Thorne, 1971; Thorne and Macumber, 1972). The aeolian dune loams on the feature's eastern margin have yielded a number of primary inhumations and representative remains of several others. This site was badly disturbed by agricultural activity prior to investigation and the clarity of its site distribution patterns and cultural stratigraphy is unclear as a consequence. Again, as with Mungo, the physical morphology has claimed priority of attention over the archaeology. All the inhumations with one exception, KS9, appear to have either lost their sealing soil or are intrusive within the sediments they occupy. KS9 however is well sealed within the uppermost sandy unit. Its antiquity has been established as 9 300±220 by radiocarbon (ANU-619b). The range of forms assumed by the skeletons within the graves was highly variable. It includes full dorsal extension (including one instance where the body rested on its side), full contraction with the body resting on one side, and recumbent-contraction. There is one instance of a tightly contracted individual pronely forward in the ground. The excavators of Kow Swamp report artifacts, pieces of quartz and red ochre and food shells in the grave. Whereas they see its deliberate placement as feasible its status as grave goods is not admitted as certain. The possibility of its deriving from adjacent occupation refuse is thus opened up. There is no mention of ornaments of any kind.

In the absence of further sites of comparable age and paucity of published data, it is difficult to evaluate Kow Swamp. The need for more recent instances of inhumation traditions and settlement sequences in the immediate area is obvious.

Both Mungo and Kow Swamp extend beyond the chronological range of the Roonka inhumations. Being furthermore situated in abandoned relict environments as yet unconnected with more recent sequences for those localities, they make the positing of relationships with other traditions difficult. It would be most useful if sites representing more recent sequences could be found in the Upper Murray tract.

Reviewed from the context of other sites in the region the chronological differentiation exhibited in the Roonka sequence alters in perspective. Many of the inhumational forms, particularly the age-structuring of disposals, appear to have a wide distribution in space and when more is known about their chronological relationships it may be possible to review the validity of inferring contemporaneous dualism, and other sociostructural features, from this information also. Furthermore, the wider region contains further styles of inhumation which are not found at Roonka, or are barely represented there. The overall pattern of distributions discloses the Murray's subdivisions into at least three major inhumation provinces. The time-depth of these is unclear, so is its uncertainty as to what extent the provinces represent well established traditions or overlapping variants. Roonka appears to represent a tradition which practised at least three successive and differing inhumational modes over seven millennia while retaining certain unique and continuing preferences. These include compound or status graves characterised by the deliberate deposition of infants or small children with adults as part of the tomb's furnishment. Secondly there is a persisting and comparatively noticeable taste for elaborate tomb goods arranged with evident care and deliberation. Thirdly it retains certain unique features of tomb morphology, which include simple shafts and chambered pits.

The Lower Murray, characterised by Swanport, presents a different picture. Here the principal inhumational form is attributed to trussing and smoking of bodies prior to burial and inhuming them sitting upright. The Central Murray tract employs similar inhumational forms to Roonka but evidences a practice of scorching and burning of bodies prior to inhuming them. It has a distinct accompaniment in its possession of gypsum plaster helmets or 'widows' mourning caps'. The structures created for inhumations are very poorly known as are the nature of their relationships to sites of the living.

Penetrating in time to the period represented by Phase II at Roonka one detects substantial changes which in turn must have reflected a vastly different outlook on the part of the living. At Roonka we are presented with a marked dualism of treatment which must denote some duality of outlook and custom in the same society of that time. Its most striking manifestation is the interring of bodies erect in pits and thereafter curating them to a point of disintegration before sealing the pit. Further instances of this custom are cited from Lake Nitchie, Lindsay Island and Walpolla Creek, all of them relict streambeds of the Murray system in the vicinity of its junction with the Darling. It has its furthest echo in Southern Victoria, where at Green Gully just out of Melbourne a sealed inhumation dated to 6 460 ± 190 BP from the bone, was assessed by Macintosh as representing a deliberately put together compound of two separate individuals of differing sex, presumably re-assembled after what could only be a period of prior exposure (Macintosh, 1970). This extraordinary find, hitherto put to one side by archaeologists for its lack of relationships, now finds place in a fairly well defined chronological context, lending it a vastly extended distribution in its turn.

The antecedents to this milieu are at present unknown at Roonka itself although contexts likely to contain them are still under investigation at nearby Glenforslan. Should they yield the evidence it is hoped they contain, they should assist in linking up with Kow Swamp to carry the inquiry and its cultural outcomes into the Quaternary.

Penetrating beyond the differentiation in time and space thus made evident, discloses a residue of unchanging outlook and custom that may supply broader insights into ancient Australian society. Three points emerge.

First there is reason to suppose that prehistoric Murray societies subdivided their dead on an age basis and altered modes of disposal and funeral obsequies accordingly. This indicates recognition of social ranking on their part. Secondly, attention to the stratigraphy of graves at Roonka and Swanport suggests that at certain periods, more than one mode of disposal was employed and that, as persons of either sex were treated in dual ways, yet another form of rank or status was held applicable to that society. At other periods and places, however, a single form of disposal appears to have been mandatory. Third and finally, Roonka appears to be unique in its possession of compound graves characterised by the presence of infants, deliberately disposed among an accompaniment of goods placed as an offering within the tomb. This stands out from the evident preference for interring most other infants in other places in other ways.

At the core of the inhumation traits exemplified by Roonka there seems to be a fundamental recognition of a state of reciprocity existing between the dead and the living. There seems to be a recognition that the rites of disposal should ratify the anxiety felt by surviving relatives that would justify the relationship they bore to the deceased. It would appear to ratify an accord between the dead and the living. Looked at from another point of view one is struck by the fact that careful disposal is a rite accorded to those able to bear or beget. In other words reciprocity between living and dead is confined to that part of the population whose function it is to procreate. It lends support to the idea that social organisation, or the regulated traffic of men and women by their peers, is a very old fundamental and persisting feature of human culture on this continent.

Supposing that there is an element of reciprocity justifying the anxieties on the part of the living for the dead, it may contribute insights to some of the more striking and aberrant incidents preserved in the Roonka inhumation. It could help to explain the careful interment of a child mental defective, interment of a woman deliberately killed to conclude unsuccessful parturition, the interment of two young girls in a common grave, of three infants and a child in a mass grave. The same rationale could have operated inversely at Fromm's Landing, so that the interments of two adult females occur in contexts where interred infants are more usual. There is insufficient information to justify more than speculation at this stage but the inquiry should be pursued.

In small societies like those of hunter-gatherers, death is a disruption to the community which demands the earnest attention of all its members. The outreach of public business as against private life is far broader in these societies than our own society accustoms us to conceive as normal. Most members of hunter-gatherer societies are in regular face-to-face contact, most have their relationships to each and every one of their fellows regulated by classification and customary observance, most specify differentiated behaviours for the uninitiated and the aged. Although it is a truism that age and experience count high as agencies of authority in such societies, it appears nevertheless that authority stems from the ability of its possessors to articulate and communicate their experience rather than mere possession of advanced age itself. There is no simple equation between the two. Nevertheless, death represents an event which inspires such societies to act out their beliefs about themselves and their dead fellows in an intensely self conscious and highly charged way. Without doubt it constitutes a highly sensitive index of social and cultural change, and the most direct avenue into supratechnological matters open to archaeological analysis. It therefore follows that, provided the cultural stratigraphy and analysis can be rendered sufficiently precise, archaeology may be of much benefit to the continuing inquiry into the social life of ancient Australia. It could well be that Australia, with its long and continuous hunter-gatherer tradition implanted deeply and everywhere into its landscape, may prove well equipped to supply clear insights into the history and development of hunter-gatherer societies.

We have still however to assess these views by matching them against what can be learnt from the artifact traditions. These yield somewhat less by comparison. Firstly they are meagre in quantity. Stone tools are one member of a series of traditions which also include bone, shell and teeth. The stone tools are disclosed as one of several streams of evidence which differentiate in time at different rates and unconnectedly. It could be said that artifact traditions are of comparatively limited usefulness in the reconstruction of innovation and change, except insofar as they prove instrumental in bringing about total transformations in settlement and society. In Australia the full span of prehistoric industrial tradition can be classified as Stone Age, and culture and society at time of contact, supply no hints of a movement beyond hunter-gatherer modes of existence. Therefore the continuing usefulness of viewing Australian prehistory so strictly in stone artifact terms appears dubious. Devotion to stone tool technology for its insights into artifactual evolution and sophistication would appear a more profitable pursuit in other parts of the world. Furnished with insights into other avenues of prehistory, bequeathed us from the Murray stream system, one cannot but feel profoundly impressed by a society which counted physical expression of its social structure and world view as so much more precious than its technology that it evolved and transformed its customary modes over and over again through a period when its technology exhibits the most trifling of alterations. One is constrained to query how effective technology is as a means of arriving at an understanding of hunter-gatherer prehistory anywhere.

Conclusion

Returning to the subject matter of the symposium, there are a number of factors at Roonka which when put together, shed light on its portrayal of cultural change. The stone tools are a relatively minor factor.

Although not present in large numbers there are sufficient stone and bone tools (together with a quantity of debitage) to show some chronological differentiation. In the final outcome however they rank low in the list of discriminant factors. Instead, the governing factors giving rise to the cultural chronology has been a range of stratigraphically ordered soil features all of them identified as of human origin and preserving to varying degrees the signifying criteria of those behaviour sets that brought them into being.

These soil features, each of them artifacts of a unique set of events, have extended across a broad range. In their most miniscule form they can be of the most incidental sort—a small pocket of wind-redistributed sand appearing in cross-section as a whorl for example. At a somewhat more generalised level, features can exhibit distinct forms which characterise a specific activity, for example the burrows of animals or the hearths of man. At a more complex level of organisation, they can be deliberately made and filled structures, for example tombs with buried skeletons furnished with offerings and deposited goods. At an even more complex level again are structures and zones of human residue enrichment that denote generalised behaviour of a more sustained or recurring sort. At this level of complexity the intensity of human use has created a distinct stratigraphic soil layer with clearly defined margins that separate it from the soils that envelop it.

Considered from the point of view of their function, it is possible to rank all such soil phenomena (or at least those of them attributable to man) according to the degree that they exhibit conscious deliberate behaviour. At one end of the scale is for example, the making and filling of inhumations, in between is the instance of cooking structures. At the other end is the truly random and undirected behaviour signified by discarded food residues.

While no less classifiable as artifacts than stone tools themselves these behaviour traces (as they are for the moment best called) have an analytical advantage over stone tools in that, as time markers, their integrity is guaranteed by the degree to which they have been preserved intact in the soil. As such they are acutely sensitive registers of events having both human origin and fixed duration. Their function, duration and their succession in time (given the precision offered by today's excavation methods) can be fixed without any reference to the culture trait traditions which have so heavily influenced previous archaeological reasoning. A stone tool found during excavation is a record of at least two events, first the event of its manufacture (to which could be added the record of its subsequent modifications) and second the event that caused it to be placed in the precise locus of its unearthing. Its usefulness as a signifier of events in the distant past depends more on what is known about the latter than the former and while it is reasonable to suppose that the lapse of time between its manufacture and enclosure in the soil is never long viewed through an archaeologist's eyes, yet its unearthing and removal from the soil without prior determination of its links with some identifiable event causing it to have such a locus, deprives it of true stratigraphic meaning and withdraws any further inquiry back to the inferred moment of manufacture and to the general state of knowledge concerning its technological tradition.

This point is well worth careful consideration for two reasons. First it points to solutions for some of the longest standing problems of hunter-gatherer archaeology as a field discipline. This area of archaeology has always been limited in its findings by the technological limitations of hunter-gatherers themselves, in particular their limited powers of scarring the earth with sufficient permanency to satisfy the requirements of analysis. Hunter-gatherers on the whole left no permanent structures whose foundations required immersion in the soil, whose fabric decayed to form complete strata of human origin. Nor did they till the soil or excavate and throw up lasting earthworks. They did however dig pits, excavate graves and accumulate food refuse, often to landscape proportions, and it is these which have to furnish the basic data for comparison with the more numerous range of phenomena left by their successors. What they did bequeath, and in vast numbers, were their stone tools whose removal in the course of break-down of the features just outlined have caused them to survive in vast quantities and so to form the first resort of analysis by archaeologists. The vulnerability of soil features to break-down (and the difficulties of isolating and identifying them) have contributed to their being overlooked by archaeologists in favour of artifact and residue studies.

Undisturbed camps of hunter-gatherers have been rare and difficult to find, subject as they are to lateral spreading across the landscape and limited stratigraphic depth; sites of hunter-gatherers in caves have been more favoured because the confines of the overall structure have concentrated debris. On the debit side, however, this same constriction of movement in caves has tended to intensify human activity with the result that the cave floors are constantly mobilised, features are pulverised and there is a tendency for artifact residues to convect vertically in the soil. Thus the long attachment of archaeology to artifact studies has tended to favour this kind of site's investigation despite the implicit disadvantages it contains.

The result has been a prehistory more strongly marked by the stamp of technology than by any other form of behaviour. It is also a prehistory characterised more by the panorama of ordered seriated technological evolution than by the more erratic picture of advances and reversals familiar to us from better documented periods. Such a view of prehistory has tended to depend for subdivisions primarily upon technical alterations in the tools themselves with a secondary frame of reference drawn from variations in the pattern of soils as exhibited in excavated profiles.

This view of prehistory has often been admitted as gravely limited and a considerable amount of effort has been spent in reasoning the links between its technological, artistic and ecological manifestations in order to liberate it from solely artifactual confines. The chief obstacle has been the scarceness of sites where all three classes of evidence have been enveloped together within the same soil. It is only now becoming evident how better precision in the field and better dating methods can liberate archaeologists from the four walls of a trench to trace the scatter of surviving time-linked human phenomena across far greater distances than before.

In Australia the limitations imposed by lithic and ecological evidence have been painfully evident, so aware are we of the complexity of social systems and the wealth of philosophical and poetic cosmic thought that drew off much more time and energy from Aboriginal Man than the activities of hunting and toolmaking.

The work at Roonka has addressed itself to problems of this sort. The dissecting out of features complete with artifact content, their grouping and ranking into phases of strictly cultural origin, although carefully fitted between the ceilings and floors of pedological events has, nevertheless, been liberated from their controls. There is furthermore, a resulting inventory of events and actions whose contribution to the functioning of tools and instruments has contributed to the broader understanding of them as traditions.

Secondly, in addition to supplying solutions to long-standing problems of hunter-gatherer archaeology the careful attention to excavating for traces of stratified behaviour raises certain queries about current field practices in archaeology. The strength of the drive to recover artifact sequences or food residue sequences as prime objects of analysis has had profound effects on the style of contemporary archaeological work. It has given rise to a battery of sampling methods and extractive techniques which have reduced time spent in the field and postponed the main work of analysis to the laboratories. It has governed the methods and treatment given such residues and the form given to reports on their results. It has even influenced the choice of sites favoured for excavation. Fortified by the proven usefulness of statistical and clinal methods and the current popularity of deductive models of inference in archaeology, it has given the science a metric appearance and underpinned it with a tight network of applied scientific supports. It still seems doubtful however that it is telling us any more about Ancient Australian Man than his stimulus/response relationships to the food-bearing environment.

The principal value of the work at Roonka has been to demonstrate how a differing approach to fieldwork has disclosed human behavioural detail in correct chronological order without loss to either technological or ecological perspectives. The food shell component to cite an instance, is all in store and available for study.

We return to the concept of an archaeological site as a unique table of events preserved within the soils, investigation is first and foremost the exact recovery of all those events whose traces survive; and only after that do we infer their unique relationships to cultural traditions. If the clarity of these events fails to discriminate between the variations in their function, duration and chronological relationships then we are obliged to fall back upon formalised artifact traditions as a basis of comparison for the sequence of objects derived. As we are already familiar with the slowness with which these traditions changed throughout that vast segment of human history allocated to hunter-gatherers, our chances of penetrating beyond them to discern and monitor the changing pattern of lifeways they gave rise to, are very faint indeed. We are therefore reminded that the means of deriving a broad and comprehensive history from such a time and space depends on our skill in dissecting undisturbed traces of human events from the soil.

There are other features of the Roonka project which space and purpose require omitting. The human palaeontology and palaeodemography will be better known after Dr Prokopec has completed his study. The wider relationships of the open sites to the rock shelters, rock art sites, trackways and quarry sources now coming to light in the surrounding district are also receiving separate study. Similar attention will be paid to the sites and traces of the original European colonists whose activities help to explain the region's present day aspect. All these will be the subject of further communications.

This preliminary notice has sought to show how choice of a broader set of stratigraphic modalities than stone tools has yielded a valid and comprehensive human background to an important and ancient theatre of Australian history.

Acknowledgements This paper is the third of a series of notices of the excavations at Roonka, the previous two having been delivered at the 41st Congress of the Australian and New Zealand Association for the Advancement of Science, Adelaide, 1969 and the 28th International Congress of Orientalists, Canberra, 6–12 January 1971. On each of these occasions persisting doubts about the basic make-up of the site's stratigraphy have rendered it necessary to defer going into print on the results of the work. This present paper therefore celebrates the author's satisfaction that the archaeology is now sufficiently clear to commit preliminary notice of it to paper. The author tenders his thanks to all who were present on these occasions and contributed by their inquiries and observations.

The principal debt of gratitude however is due to the people who continue to carry out fieldwork, which has obliterated their weekends for the past six years. The following are singled out for special mention: Joy Chilman for her research into documentary sources for the area's history; Lloyd Chilman took most of the photographs; Bob Inns has served as identifier and recorder of the finds; Helen Tolcher has successfully accomplished most of the more difficult and vexatious excavation problems thrown up in the course of the work and much of the workshop tabulation; Vern Tolcher has borne the burden of all three-dimensional recording and supply of precise and beautifully drawn plans. Thanks are due to many many others too numerous to list here but the debt is recorded with sincere thanks.

Thanks are tendered to colleagues for advice and assistance which has hastened the way to the viewpoints submitted in this paper. Henry Polach and his staff in the ANU radiocarbon laboratory have taken an informed interest and supplied prompt assays. Ilmars Gemuts of Anaconda Australia drew attention to the significance of faulting in the Murray Trench landscape; John Firman of the South Australian Geological Survey has recurringly made himself available to discuss soil stratigraphic problems.

Grateful thanks are recorded to Professor Grahame Clark (University of Cambridge) and Professor Hallam Movius (Harvard University) for reading an earlier version of this paper and for supplying comments of such pertinence as to cause a resumption of fieldwork and a wealth of additional results. A special word of thanks is recorded to Dr Miroslav Prokopec (Institute of Epidemiology and Medical Hygiene, Prague) for his coming to Adelaide to study the palaeanthropology and share in the assessment of its value.

Thanks are offered to the successive owners of Roonka Station; Mr and Mrs S. B. Armstrong, Mr and Mrs P. Armstrong, and Mr and Mrs H. Sobey and to the owner of Glenforslan Station, Mr D. Byrne, for permitting the work's performance.

The excavations have been accomplished through funds furnished by the Board of the South Australian Museum, the Australian Institute of Aboriginal Studies, the South Australian Aboriginal and Historic Relics Advisory Board and private sources. The abiding interest of Dr W. Grant Inglis, Permanent Head, South Australian Department for the Environment is recorded with gratitude.

References

Acsadi G. and J. Nemeskeri, 1970. *History of human life span and mortality*. Budapest.

Anell, B., 1955. Contribution to the history of fishing in the South Seas. *Studia ethnographica Upsaliensa No. 9 Almquist & Wiksells*. Uppsala.

Angas, G. F., 1847. *Savage life and scenes in Australia and New Zealand: being an artist's impression of countries and people at the Antipodes*. 2 vols. London: Smith Elder.

Basedow, H., 1925. Slate scraping implements of the extinct Adelaide tribe. *Man*, 25 : 173–76.

Black, L., 1950. *Stone arrangements, being a continuation of a series on the customs of the Aborigines of the Darling River Valley and of central New South Wales*. Perth: Brokensha.

Blackwood, Sir R., and K. N. G. Simpson, 1973. Attitudes of Aboriginal skeletons excavated in the Murray Valley region between Mildura and Renmark. *Memoirs of the National Museum of Victoria*, 34 : 99–150.

Bowler, J. M., 1970. Lake Nitchie skeleton—stratigraphy of the burial site. *Archaeology and Physical Anthropology in Oceania*, 5(2) : 102–43.

—— 1971. Pleistocene salinities and climatic change: evidence from lakes and lunettes in south-eastern Australia. *In* Mulvaney, D. J. and J. Golson, *Aboriginal Man and Environment in Australia*. pp. 47–65. Canberra: Australian National University Press.

——, R. Jones, H. Allen and A. G. Thorne, 1970. Pleistocene human remains from Australia, a living site and human cremation from Lake Mungo, Western New South Wales. *World Archaeology*, 2(1) : 39–60.

——, A. G. Thorne and H. A. Polach, 1972. Pleistocene Man in Australia: age and significance of the Mungo Skeleton. *Nature*, 240(5375) : 48–50.

Brown, T., 1973. *Morphology of the Australian skull studied by multivariate analysis*. Canberra: Australian Institute of Aboriginal Studies.

Butler, B. E., 1950. A theory of prior streams as a causal factor of soil occurrence in the Riverine Plain of south-eastern Australia. *Australian Journal of Agricultural Research*, 1 : 231–52.

Campbell, T. D., 1925. *Dentition and palate of the Australian Aboriginal*. University of Adelaide, Publications under the Keith Sheridan Foundation, No. 1: Adelaide.

Casey, D. A., 1973. Aboriginal stone artifacts from the Murray River region between Mildura and Renmark, Australia. *Memoirs of the National Museum of Victoria*, 34 : 209–13, pl. 29.

Cooper, H. M., 1959. Large archaeological stone implements from Hallett Cove, South Australia. *Transactions of the Royal Society of South Australia*, 82 : 55–60, pls. 1–4.

—— 1961. Archaeological stone implements along the Lower River Wakefield, South Australia. *Transactions Royal Society South Australia*, 84 : 105–18.

Dortch, C. E. and D. Merrilees, 1973. Human occupation of Devil's Lair, Western Australia, during the Pleistocene. *Archaeology and Physical Anthropology in Oceania*, 8(2) : 89–115, pls. 1–4.

Eyre, E. J., 1845. *Journals of expeditions of discovery into Central Australia and overland from Adelaide to King George's Sound in the years 1840–41: sent by the colonists of South Australia with the sanction and support of the Government: including an account of the manners and customs of the Aborigines and the state of their relations with Europeans*. 2 vols. London: T. & W. Boone.

Fenner, F. J., 1939. The Australian Aboriginal Skull: its non-metrical morphological characters. *Transactions of the Royal Society of South Australia*, 63(2) : 248–306, pls. 10–11.

Firman, J. B., 1973. Reginal stratigraphy of surficial deposits in the Murray Basin and Gambier embayment. *Geological Survey of South Australia, Report of investigations No. 39*. Adelaide.

Gallus, S. A. and E. D. Gill, 1973. Aboriginal bone fishhooks with Aboriginal skeletons at Wallpolla Creek, W. of Mildura, Australia. *Memoirs of the National Museum of Victoria*, 34 : 215–16, pl. 30.

Gill, E. D., 1973. Geology and geomorphology of the Murray River region between Mildura and Renmark, Australia. *Memoirs of the National Museum of Victoria*, 34 : 1–97, pls. 1–11.

Hale, H. M., and N. B. Tindale, 1930. Notes on some human remains in the Lower Murray Valley, South Australia. *Records of the South Australian Museum*, 4(2) : 145–218.

Hawker, C. L., 1842–3. Diaries 18–19. South Australian Archives.

Horne, G. and G. Aiston, 1924. *Savage life in Central Australia*. London: Macmillan.

Howells, W. W., 1973. Cranial variation in Man, a study by multivariate analysis of patterns of difference among recent populations. *Papers of the Peabody Museum of Archaeology and Ethnology, Harvard University*, vol. 67. Cambridge (U.S.A.).

Hrdlicka, A., 1928. Catalogue of human crania in the United States National Museum collections. *Proceedings of the United States National Museum*, 71 : 1–140.

Lawrence, C. R., 1966. Cainozoic stratigraphy and structure of the Mallee region, Victoria. *Proceedings of the Royal Society of Victoria*, 79(2) : 517–53, pls. 53–56.

Macintosh, N. W. G., 1970. The Green Gully remains. *Memoirs of the National Museum of Victoria*, 30 : 93–100.

—— 1971. Analysis of an Aboriginal skeleton and a pierced tooth necklace from Lake Nitchie, Australia. *Anthropologie* (Moravske Museum, Ustav Anthropos, Brno, Czechoslovakia) 9(1) : 49–62, pls. 1–7.

——, K. N. Smith and A. B. Bailey, 1970. Lake Nitchie skeleton—unique Aboriginal burial. *Archaeology and Physical Anthropology in Oceania*, 5(2) : 85–101, pls. 1–4.

Mulvaney, D. J., 1960. Archaeological excavations at Fromm's Landing on the lower Murray River, South Australia. *Proceedings of the Royal Society of Victoria*, 72(2) : 53–85, pls. 6–8.

——, G. H. Lawton and C. R. Twidale, 1964. Archaeological excavations of rock shelter No. 6 Fromm's Landing, South Australia. *Proceedings Royal Society of Victoria*, 77(2) : 479–516, pls. 68–74.

Pels, S., 1964. The present and ancestral Murray River system. *Australian Geographical Studies*, 2(2) : 111–19, pl. 1.

—— 1971. River systems and climatic changes in south-eastern Australia. *In* Mulvaney, D. J. and J. Golson, *Aboriginal Man and Environment in Australia*, pp. 38–46. Australian National University Press, Canberra.

Price, A. G., 1952. St. Mark's College scientific work at Fromm's Landing. *Proceedings of the Royal Geographical Society of Australasia*, 43 : 25–27.

[Radcliffe]-Brown, A. R., 1918. Notes on the social organisation of Australian tribes. *Journal of the Royal Anthropological Institute*, 48 : 222–53.

—— 1930. The social organisation of Australian tribes, Part II. *Oceania*, 1(2) : 206–46.

Roth, W. E., 1897. *Ethnological studies among the north-west-central Queensland Aborigines*. Brisbane: Government Printer.

Sheard, H. L., 1927. Aboriginal rock carvings at Devon Downs, River Murray, South Australia. *Transactions and Proceedings of the Royal Society of South Australia*, 51 : 18–19, pls. 3–5.

—— 1928. Aboriginal rock paintings seven miles north of Blanchetown, River Murray, South Australia. *Transactions of the Royal Society of South Australia*, 52 : 231–34.

——, C. P. Mountford and C. J. Hackett, 1927. An unusual disposal of an Aboriginal child's remains from the lower Murray, South Australia. *Transactions and Proceedings of the Royal Society of South Australia*, 51 : 173–76, pls. 11–12.

Smyth, R. Brough, 1878. *The Aborigines of Victoria, with notes relating to the habits of the natives of other parts of Australia and Tasmania*. 2 vols. Victoria: Government Printer.

Spencer, W. B., 1928. *Wanderings in wild Australia*. 2 vols. London: Macmillan.

Stirling, E. C., 1911. Preliminary report on the discovery of native remains at Swanport, River Murray: with an inquiry into the alleged occurrence of a pandemic among the Australian Aboriginals. *Transactions of the Royal Society of South Australia*, 35 : 4–46, pls. 2–9.

Sunderland, S. and L. J. Ray, 1959. A note on the Murray Black collection of Australian Aboriginal skeletons. *Proceedings of the Royal Society of Victoria*, 71 : 45–48, pls. 6–7.

Taplin, G., 1874. *The Narrinyeri; an account of the tribes of South Australian Aborigines inhabiting the country around the Lakes Alexandrina, Albert and Coonong and the lower part of the River Murray*. Adelaide: J. T. Shawyer.

Thomson, D., 1964. Some wood and stone implements of the Bindibu tribe of Central Western Australia. *Proceedings of the Prehistoric Society*, 30 : 400–22.

Thorne, A. G., 1971. Mungo and Kow Swamp: morphological variation in Pleistocene Australians. *Mankind*, 8(2) : 85–89, pls. 1–3.

—— and P. G. Macumber, 1972. Discoveries of late Pleistocene Man at Kow Swamp, Australia. *Nature*, 238 : 316–19.

Tindale, N. B., 1937. Relationship of the extinct Kangaroo Island culture with cultures of Australia, Tasmania and Malaya. *Records of the South Australian Museum*, 6(1) : 39–60.

—— 1939. Eagle and crow myths of the Maraura tribe, lower Darling River, New South Wales. *Records of the South Australian Museum*, 6(3) : 243–61.

—— 1940. Results of the Harvard–Adelaide Universities Anthropological Expedition, 1938–1939; Distribution of Australian Aboriginal Tribes: A field survey. *Transactions of the Royal Society of South Australia*, 64(1) : 140–231, map.

—— 1941. The antiquity of Man in Australia. *Australian Journal of Science*, 3(6) : 144–47.

—— 1957. Culture succession in south-eastern Australia from late Pleistocene to the present. *Records of the South Australian Museum*, 13(1) : 1–49.

—— 1965. Stone implement making among the Nakako, Ngadadjara and Pitjandjara of the Great Western Desert. *Records of the South Australian Museum*, 15(1) : 1–164.

—— 1974. *Aboriginal tribes of Australia; their terrain, environmental controls, distribution, limits and proper names*. Berkeley: University of California Press.

The *bout coupé* handaxe as a typological marker for the British Mousterian industries

MYRA L. SHACKLEY

Abstract

The middle Palaeolithic of north-west Europe is characterised by diverse Mousterian industries, generally associated with *Homo sapiens neanderthalensis*. Within this technocomplex several variations exist, identified by distinctive tool assemblages representing separate cultural traditions. These variants, with a high concentration of sites in the Périgord area of southern France, are distributed throughout the rest of France and adjoining countries.

Recent work has suggested that *Homo sapiens neanderthalensis* reached Britain, his presence being recognised solely from a change in tool types, since skeletal evidence is sparse and poorly documented. The variant present is the 'Mousterian of Acheulean Tradition', which is related typologically to the older final Acheulean industries and is characterised by a high percentage of handaxes and varied racloirs. These handaxes, generally of discoid or cordate shape, include a distinctive form known as the *bout coupé*, which is triangular or D-shaped, very thin and well-refined, finished with a soft hammer and often made on a flake. The form links the British industries, often of a definite 'provincial' appearance, with the classic, better-made, French series, and provides a chronological and typological datum for the arrival of the tradition in Britain.

Bearing in mind the differential preservation of lithic material it is possible to use this form, and associated industries, to outline the distribution of Mousterian culture in Britain during the late stages of the last interglacial (Riss/Würm) and the early part of the last (Würm) glaciation. Concentrations of industries are associated with the 7.5 m raised beach, and are also found in association with faunal material at several cave sites.

This paper discusses the recognition, significance and chronology of the *bout coupé* handaxe.

Mousterian industries

Mousterian variants The earliest phases of the last (Würm) glaciation in Europe are characterised archaeologically by the immense Mousterian technocomplex, which lasted from about 70 000 to 35 000 BP. This complex probably had its roots in the last (Riss/Würm) interglacial, or perhaps even as far back as the Riss glaciation, and is represented archaeologically by a series of lithic industries found both in cave and open sites in Europe, Asia and Africa. The culture, generally associated with *Homo sapiens neanderthalensis*, contains the first manifestations of religious and artistic feelings, and of any systematic arrangements of the dwelling place. Recent work on Mousterian sites, both by excavating new sites and re-excavating old ones, has enabled detailed correlation; to be made between floral, faunal, sedimentological and archaeological evidence, especially in the cave sites of the Périgord (Dordogne, France). The lithic industries have been the subject of much recent quantitative work, enabling their division into sub-groups, namely the Ferrassie, Quina, Denticulate and Typical Mousterian industries, and the Mousterian of Acheulean Tradition (Bordes, 1953, 1961; Mellars, 1967, 1969). The relative chronology of these variants has been discussed by Mellars (1967) and Bordes (1973). Bordes uses technological and typological attributes to define his tool types, characterising assemblages by the relative proportions of the implements present, and the way in which those implements were made. Sixty-three different tool types are recognised, together with 21 varieties of handaxe, and further quantification is possible by the application of descriptive indices.

Controversy exists at present over the significance of the different industries. One school of thought, following Professor Bordes, views the industries as products of different cultural traditions (Bordes, 1973), with culture groups co-existing in the same areas but having different tool making traditions. The second view-point holds that the assemblage differences are the result of different activities, and that the tool assemblages themselves represent specialised activities or activity complexes (Binford and Binford, 1966, 1969).

The 'Mousterian of Acheulean Tradition' This subdivision of the Mousterian was first recognised by Peyrony (1930) and more closely defined by Bourgon (1957) and Bordes (1961). It is a cultural tradition descended from the Acheulean and bearing a complex relationship to the Micoquian and final Acheulean cultures. D. and A. Collins (1970) consider that it is the only Mousterian variant significantly present in Britain. Mousterian of Acheulean Tradition (often abbreviated to M.A.T.) assemblages are typified by cordiform handaxes, backed knives and a racloir frequency never greater than 50%, together with a comparatively high percentage of denticulate tools. The tradition is divided into Mousterian of Acheulean Tradition Type A (with a variable percentage of handaxes and racloirs, and many denticulates) and Mousterian of Acheulean Tradition Type B (with a low percentage of racloirs many Levallois points and backed knives). All known occurrences of Type B are stratigraphically later than Type A, for example at Le Moustier and Pech de l'Azé in the Dordogne. The two subdivisions should be considered as variants of a single evolving tradition.

D. and A. Collins (1970) created a number of metrical indices for the definition of M.A.T. handaxes, including an 'elongation index' (= 100 × breadth/length), which distinguishes M.A.T. handaxes from those of the Acheulean cultures. The M.A.T. handaxes from Le Moustier have elongation index values of about 73, whilst the Acheulean implements from Hoxne (Suffolk, England) have values averaging around 61. The boundary distinguishing the traditions would appear to fall at about 72.

Mousterian of Acheulean Tradition industries in Britain The British M.A.T. industries are characterised by the presence of flat semi-cordiform handaxes known as the *bout coupé* type (Roe, 1967). They may be triangular or D-shaped, and are always very well-refined, often by using a soft hammer. The Collins (1970) identify the same form as the 'Paxton' type, which has an angular butt and straight or convex sides. Even before the existence of definite British Mousterian industries had been confirmed the connection between the *bout coupé* axe and artifacts of Levallois facies had been realised, and Roe (1967) stated that 'there is a strong case for supposing that the distribution of *bout coupé* handaxes is mainly a reflection of the movement over open ground of Mousterian man'. Many of the *bout coupé* handaxes are unfortunately only stray finds, but wherever the form is associated with an implement assemblage that assemblage can be considered as Mousterian of Acheulean Tradition.

The *bout coupé* form acts as a cultural and typological 'marker' for the beginning of the British Mousterian industries, and enables correlations to be made between the rather crude provincial variant of the tradition present in Britain and the classic, better-made series occurring in France. The *bout coupé* provides a chronological and typological datum line for the arrival of Mousterian man. Smith (1926) and Calkin and Green (1949) illustrate the typical form of the implement, which is quite unmistakable with carefully flaked corners and a straight or slightly convex cutting edge. Occasionally a gently twisted profile occurs, although a straight edge is more common.

The Mousterian industries present in Britain are poor in comparison with Continental assemblages but there are several recognised M.A.T. sites, notably Oldbury (Kent), Kents Cavern (Devon) and La Cotte de St Brelade (Jersey). Recent work has located a further series associated with the 7.5 m (late Monastirian) raised beach in southern England, all of which include *bout coupé* axes. This trebles the number of acknowledged British M.A.T. sites, and in addition there are a number of occurrences of small artifact groups whose relationship to the main tradition is more nebulous, for example Fisherton (Wiltshire) or Bleak Down (Isle of Wight). The stratigraphy of the British M.A.T. cave sites is sparse and poorly developed when compared with the Continental material, and the implements are often thick, crude and 'provincial' in appearance. The lack of systematic early work on many of the important assemblages has led to the loss of much material, often unpublished.

Mousterian of Acheulean Tradition sites in Britain

Kents Cavern Kents Cavern (Fig. 1), a cave site in Devon, was first investigated on an unsystematic basis over fifty years ago, and has recently been re-excavated by Campbell and Samson (1971) who were only able to trace 46 accurately stratified implements, out of an original total of several thousand. These come from the level of loamy cave earth designated A$_2$, and were associated with faunal remains. The

extant industry includes four handaxes of *bout coupé* type, several racloirs, a denticulate tool and some flakes (Table 1). Despite the poverty of the assemblage both Campbell and Samson (1971) and the Collins (1970) considered that it could be classed as Mousterian of Acheulean Tradition.

Oldbury The Mousterian of Acheulean Tradition implement from Oldbury (Kent) is more extensive than that from Kents Cavern, and was analysed by the Collins (1970) using the method of Bordes. Some 43 handaxes, nearly all of cordiform or *bout coupé* type, were found (Table 1), together with 19 other retouched pieces and over 500 flakes. The handaxes were described using Collins's 'Elongation Index', and his 'CV' index $\left(CV = \dfrac{\text{Total concave sides}}{\text{concave + convex + straight sides}} \right)$. The CV values for all the Oldbury handaxes are greater than 75, which the Collins take as the boundary between M.A.T. axes and those produced by other cultural traditions. The Collins also attempt to quantify the presence of the *bout coupé* handaxe by calculating a 'Paxton' index, on the basis of the frequency with which the form occurs. The index value is highest at the chronologically late M.A.T. sites, such as Le Tillet (Bordes, 1961).

La Cotte de St Brelade This cave site on Jersey (Fig. 1) is the only British Mousterian site without *bout coupé* axes. There is a large tool assemblage (15 000 pieces) but the publication does not include any quantitative treatment and the verbal descriptions are non-standardised. The implements include a series of notched and denticulate tools, varied racloirs and some Levallois flakes. The handaxes seem mainly discoidal and the group includes some 10 000 non-Levallois flakes and about 250 cores, some of the 'tortoise' variety.

Despite the inadequate publication it is difficult to find another British Mousterian assemblage that shares these characteristics. The implement drawings include a series of tools very similar in type to the continental 'Faustkeilblätter', occurring mainly in the German Micoquian industries (Bosinski, 1967). Mellars (1967) has noted the occurrence of Micoquian tool forms in some of the French Mousterian of Acheulean Tradition assemblages, but they are not found in

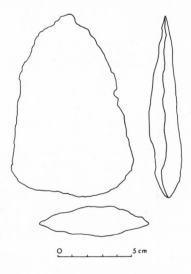

Fig. 1 : Typical outline shape of a *bout coupé* handaxe. Example from Fisherton, Wiltshire.

Table 1　Composition of British Mousterian of Acheulian Tradition industries

Site and grid reference	Publication	Associated Fauna • = present	Total implements ever recorded	Total now available	Number of axes	Number of retouched implements	Number of cores	Number of Levallois flakes	Flakes and waste
Oldbury (Kent) (composite assemblage) TQ 582562	Collins (1970)	•	c. 600	88	43	28	0	11	316
Kents Cavern (Devon) (A 2 cave earth) SX 93456415	Campbell & Sampson (1971)	•	c. 1000	45	5	14	0	15	25
Great Pan Farm (Isle of Wight) (composite terrace assemblage) SZ 507866	Poole (1925)	—	c. 5000	125	55	39	1 (tortoise)	17	3
Warsash (Hants) SU 507060		Group (1)	??	98	19	18	3 (tortoise)	47	11
(composite assemblage from 7.5 m terrace) SU 590057		Group (2)	??	42	0	3	1	24	10
Cams (Fareham, Hants) (composite assemblage from 7.5 m terrace) SZ 51287	Unpublished	—	c. 20	18	2 (frags)	6	1 (tortoise)	3	6
Bleak Down (Isle of Wight) (composite assemblage) SU 138302	Poole (1932)	—	13	13	8	3	1	1	0
Fisherton (Wilts) (from brickearth) ST 532479	Evans (1897)	•	2	0	0	2	0	0	0
Hyaena Den (Wookey, Somerset) ST 532479	Tratman et al. (1971)	•	11	11	9	0	0	0	2
Rhinoceros Hole (Wookey, Somerset) ST 532479	Unpublished Personal Communication	•	1	1	1	0	0	0	0
La Cotte de St Brelade (Jersey) Würm 'head'	Marett (1942) McBurney (1971)	•	c. 15,000	9,634	174	c. 3,600+	250+	??	??

the 'classic' Périgordian sites. Commont (1912) and Bordes (1953) note examples of this form from sites on the Younger Loess of northern France, where the M.A.T. variant present is different from that of the southern caves. The basal loessic industries do, however, include the *bout coupé* form as well, although it is absent from La Cotte. The presence of a quantity of naturally-backed knives and denticulate tools in the La Cotte assemblage strengthens the impression that it is to be classed as M.A.T., although the high racloir frequency is more typical of Quina Mousterian. However, the thick flake tools, transverse racloirs and plentiful limaces of the Quina facies are absent here.

Mousterian of Acheulean Tradition industries stratified in the 7.5 m raised beach A series of industries have been recognised from exposures of the 7.5 m raised beach along the south coast of England. At Warsash, near Southampton, a collection of 55 pieces was stratified within the beach gravels, including 17 handaxes, two of the *bout coupé* form, and four of the distinctive 'Wolvercote' type (Roe, 1964). Retouched Mousterian tools include a thick Quina-type scraper and a fine Mousterian point, together with numerous Levallois flakes and a tortoise core (Table 1). The material is hardly worn, with abrasion index values (Shackley, 1974) of less than 1. A further collection of at least 50 pieces was probably associated with the same beach remnant, but their stratigraphic context was less clear. Within this second group a further series of racloirs and Levallois flakes occurred. The calculated Mean Sea Level of 24.01' O.D.(7.31 m) to High Water Mark at the base of the terrace bluff falls within the limits estimated for the 7.5 m (late Monastirian) beach. The occurrence of the slipper-shaped 'Wolvercote' axes in association with the *bout coupé* form is interesting, since this is a form which occurs at Continental sites only in a restricted date range at the extreme end of the Riss/Würm interglacial and the beginning of the Würm. The Wolvercote form is related to the 'Faustkeilblätter' described above, and is of Micoquian origin. Both Wolvercote and *bout coupé* axes are found together in an unworn state, and their contemporaneity possibly suggests a certain degree of cultural mixing at the time.

A small Mousterian of Acheulean Tradition assemblage was recovered from a little further down the coast at Cams (Fareham), also stratified within the raised beach. The group includes two fragments of axes, three Levallois flakes, a tortoise core and six retouched flake tools, but the abrasion is differential and, therefore, throws some doubt on the typological unity of the group. A further fine series of Mousterian tools has been recovered from allied beach terrace levels at Christchurch (Hampshire), including an excellent series of *bout coupé* axes, illustrated by Calkin and Green (1949). However, the site of Great Pan Farm (Isle of Wight) has produced the best documented and preserved Mousterian assemblage in the area. Poole (1924) records 140 implements, together with a further 150 flakes, recovered from extensive beach gravel deposits which were worked commercially for road metal at the beginning of this century. Fortunately the deposit was dug by hand and the precise position of each implement recorded. Some 125 implements are still available for study, although the rest have been lost. Fifty-five handaxes, 39 retouched flake tools, 17 Levallois flakes and a tortoise core are included in the assemblage (Table 1). The Levallois flakes are rather large and flat, reminiscent of the Bakers Hole form (Wymer, 1968). With the exception of a

single chert handaxe all the implements are made of a speckled yellow-grey flint which does not occur in the immediate locality, since the gravels containing the assemblage are composed almost entirely of Greensand Chert. This seems to be deliberate selection of raw material on the part of Mousterian man. The implements are remarkable for their small size, few exceeding 10 cm in length, and for the presence of several very refined *bout coupé* axes. The group includes some naturally-backed knives, together with notched and denticulate tools. Both Poole (1924) and Roe (1968) suggested that an occupation site might be found nearby, but excavation made in the summer of 1971 by the writer showed no trace of this. No further implements were found, a fact not particularly surprising since only a small remnant of the original gravel survives, and the estimate of implement density was one tool per 200 tons of gravel. The main characteristics of the handaxes were summarised by Roe (1968) using a metrical analysis, who assigned them to the 'more pointed' variety of his Ovate Tradition (Group 6), the same group that contains the Mousterian of Acheulean Tradition axe assemblages from Oldbury and Holybourne.

The Basingstoke area of northern Hampshire has produced a series of unstratified finds of Mousterian cultural material, frequently associated with deposits of clay-with-flints. The sites are always at comparatively high levels (100–150 m O.D.) on the chalk downlands. At least one location (Holybourne) shows such a high concentration of 'stray' flints, that it appears to represent more than a random accumulation. The implements are all heavily weathered and covered with a thick chalk white patina, and a haze of frost cracks. Several fine Mousterian-type racloirs and cores have been found, together with a series of well refined *bout coupé* axes, very similar typologically to the material recovered from the raised beach deposits. Other minor British sites where the *bout coupé* axe form occurs include the Hyaena Den and Rhinoceros Hole (Wookey, Somerset), and the brickearth site of Fisherton (Wiltshire). At the Hyaena Den the implement types are rather more crude than those found at Oldbury, but the presence of the *bout coupé* axe form led the Collins (1970) to include the site in the Mousterian of Acheulean Tradition group. The Fisherton exposures of brickearth produced two splendid and beautifully refined *bout coupé* axes, neither of which can now be traced (Evans, 1897). The deposits contained extensive molluscan and mammalian remains and the site remains one of the few localities where there is any useful association between the axe type and a fauna. Further minor finds of *bout coupé* axes have been made at the Torbryan caves (Devon) and at Pontnewydd cave (North Wales), both with associated faunas.

There seems little doubt that the implements found stratified within the 7.5 m raised beach may be classed as Mousterian of Acheulean Tradition, since they all contain the characteristic *bout coupé* handaxes, backed knives and denticulates. There are, of course, variations within the beach assemblages and between them and the implements from inland sites such as Oldbury, and these are attributable both to normal inter-site variation and to the small size of the majority of the assemblages. The Levallois technique does not seem to be especially important in the British industries, and the paucity of material is most striking in comparison to the Continent. It is unfortunate that, with the exception of Oldbury and some of the Hampshire sites, no quantitative work has been done on these assemblages, since this means that the typological and technological indices of Bordes (1961) have not

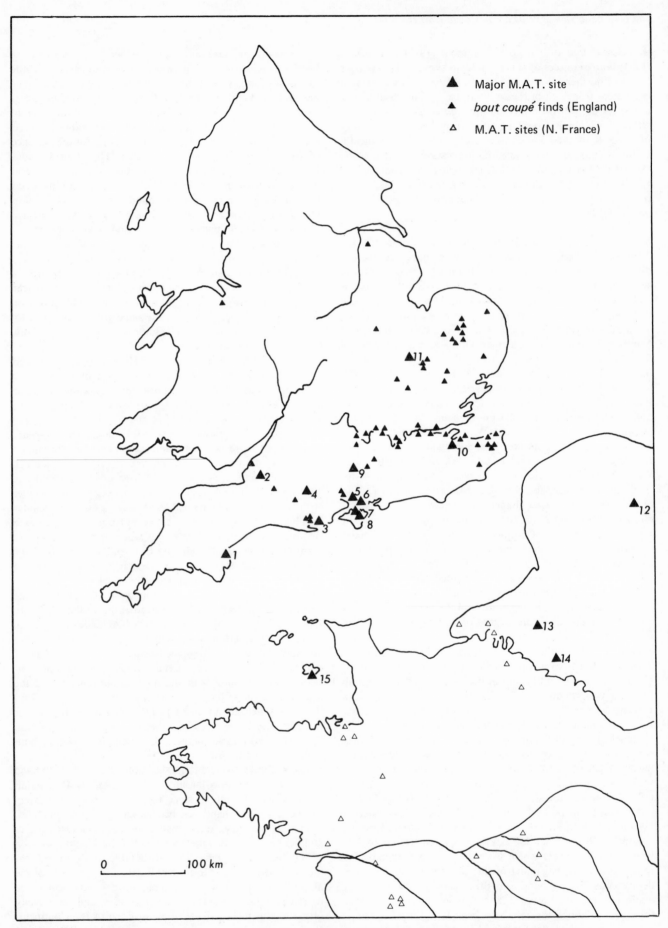

Fig. 2: Distribution of Mousterian of Acheulean Tradition sites in England and northern France. 1 : Kents Cavern (Devon) ; 2 : Hyaena Den and Rhinoceros Hole (Wookey, Somerset) ; 3 : Christchurch (Hampshire) ; 4 : Fisherton (Wiltshire) ; 5 : Warsash (Hampshire) ; 6 : Cams (Hampshire) ; 7 : Great Pan Farm (Isle of Wight) ; 8 : Bleak Down (Isle of Wight) ; 9 : Holybourne (Hampshire) ; 10 : Oldbury (Kent) ; 11 : Paxton (Huntingdon) ; 12 : Balve ; 13 : St Just ; 14 : Le Tillet ; 15 : La Cotte de St Brelade (Jersey).

Legend:

▲ Major M.A.T. site

▲ *bout coupé* finds (England)

△ M.A.T. sites (N. France)

0   100 km

been calculated. Both Mellars (1971, personal communication) and Collins (1971, personal communication) consider that the raised beach industries do belong to the British Mousterian of Acheulean Tradition, although certain features such as the comparative thickness of some of the handaxes make them distinctive. The attribution of minor sites such as Fisherton or the Hyaena Den to the Mousterian of Acheulean Tradition relies solely on the presence of the *bout coupé* axe.

Chronology of the Mousterian of Acheulean Tradition

Dating the continental Mousterian of Acheulean Tradition On the Continent the two major Mousterian of Acheulean Tradition variants (A and B) seem to have been made at different periods. The earlier (Type A) variant occurs at the beginning of Würm I, at the base of the Younger Loess in France. The later (Type B) variant is found close to the end of the Mousterian period in the late Würm II, which is the phase containing the classic Périgordian M.A.T. sequence. Bordes (1953) considers that the B variant always succeeds the Würm I/II (Brørup) interstadial and that it develops into the Périgordian at the end of the Würm II/III (Gottwieg) interstadial.

Dating British Mousterian of Acheulean Tradition Mellars (1971, personal communication) considers that the Hampshire material could belong equally well in either of the two M.A.T. variants, since the assemblages are not really large enough to be diagnostic. Typological relationships between some of the Hampshire implements and the Balve 4 and Karsten groups of Bosinski's Central European M.A.T. (Bosinski, 1967) suggest a pre-Würm I/II date. The Collins (1970) postulate a seriation trend for the M.A.T. on typological grounds, starting with the basal loessic industries such as Le Tillet 'Café au lait' series (Bordes, 1954) early in Würm I, and ending with the later material at sites like La Rochette (Delporte, 1963). Le Tillet is the only continental site on this seriation line which has the *bout coupé* handaxe form. The fact that this handaxe type is characteristic of the British M.A.T. industries suggests that they are early, and the slight admixture of Micoquian forms would again support a date at the beginning of Würm I, or even very late in the Riss/Würm interglacial.

Dating the British Mousterian of Acheulean Tradition on faunal grounds The faunal assemblages associated with M.A.T. industries, and with the *bout coupé* axe form, have a number of points in common. Mellars (1971) notes that the faunas associated with the typical Mousterian of Acheulean Tradition horizons in Périgord generally consist of bovids or red deer. In Britain the M.A.T. faunas tend to be rather cold-loving, although with a sufficient admixture of more warm-loving animals to suggest a mixed steppe-tundra/woodland type of environment. Both Kents Cavern and Oldbury have faunas which could fit equally well into an environment at the transition between glacial and interglacial conditions. Evidence from the first site points to a date soon after the beginning of Würm I, and from the second to a date near the Würm I/II interstadial. At Fisherton the faunal assemblage is complex, and the mollusca seem to represent the type of conditions that were present at the extreme end of the Riss/Würm interglacial, extending into the cool *Pinus* zone (h-i), (Evans, 1972, personal communication). This would

at first seem to be at variance with the mammalian evidence which indicates tundra, but a closer examination shows the presence of some steppe forms. A date close to the extreme end of the Riss/Würm or during the early stages of Würm I seems reasonable. Further examination of the Fisherton site is planned for 1977.

Stratigraphic dating of the 7.5 m beach There is a great deal of evidence to suggest that the 7.5 m (late Monastirian) raised beach dates to a period of high sea level during the Riss/Würm interglacial. The beach is found in a tectonically undisturbed context at La Cotte at 8 m O.D., and in numerous other locations in the north-western seaboards of Europe at between 7.3–8 m O.D. It has been dated by the Th/U method to about 80–100 000 BP. The beach deposits are frequently capped by head and 'brickearth' produced during the succeeding (Würm) glaciation. West and Sparks (1960) consider the date of the beach in the south of England, and the relationships between estimated Mean Sea Levels and the height of remnants. There is little doubt that the Hampshire fragments already mentioned form part of this beach (Zeuner, 1959), as does the Normannien II (late Monastirian) beach found in Normandy at the same height, the English Channel having been a stable area during the period. Since the industries are stratified *within* the raised beach they must either be contemporary with its formation or slightly pre-date it, and the fresh condition of the majority of finds makes the former hypothesis more likely.

Conclusion

Assigning the Hampshire Mousterian of Acheulean Tradition industries to the late Riss/Würm interglacial from their stratigraphic context makes it possible that the M.A.T. began earlier in Britain than was formerly supposed. The littoral distribution of the British M.A.T. sites is similar to that seen on the Continent, and it seems possible that the makers of the industry did not care to live at too high an altitude, nor too far from the sea or a major river. However, the stray finds of *bout coupé* axes at non-littoral sites presumably means that the hunting range of the groups extended into upland areas. It seems likely that the cultural horizons marked by the *bout coupé* handaxes and their associated industries are to be dated either to the extreme end of the Riss/Würm interglacial or to the beginning of Würm I. Their makers must, therefore, have arrived in Britain before the high sea level represented by the 7.5 m raised beach, if the Hampshire industries are contemporary with inland sites such as Oldbury. The Le Tillet type of M.A.T., with the *bout coupé* axe, ceased being made in France during Würm I. Industries derived from within the first weathering horizon of the Younger Loess series (Younger Loess I, Würm I/II) either have no handaxes, or have the occasional handaxe but not of *bout coupé* type. They appear to be a poor variety of typical Mousterian. The British M.A.T. industries, therefore, almost certainly pre-date Würm I/II, and can probably be assigned to a period either just before or just after the maximum cold of Würm I.

The Collins (1970) view Oldbury as fitting in the middle of their seriation line which started with Le Tillet, and the 'Paxton' stage at the beginning, but it seems likely that the more recently discovered Hampshire littoral industries are earlier than this, and that Oldbury is rather later. The scatter of *bout coupé* finds at isolated sites must, therefore, fit somewhere between the extreme end of the last interglacial and the

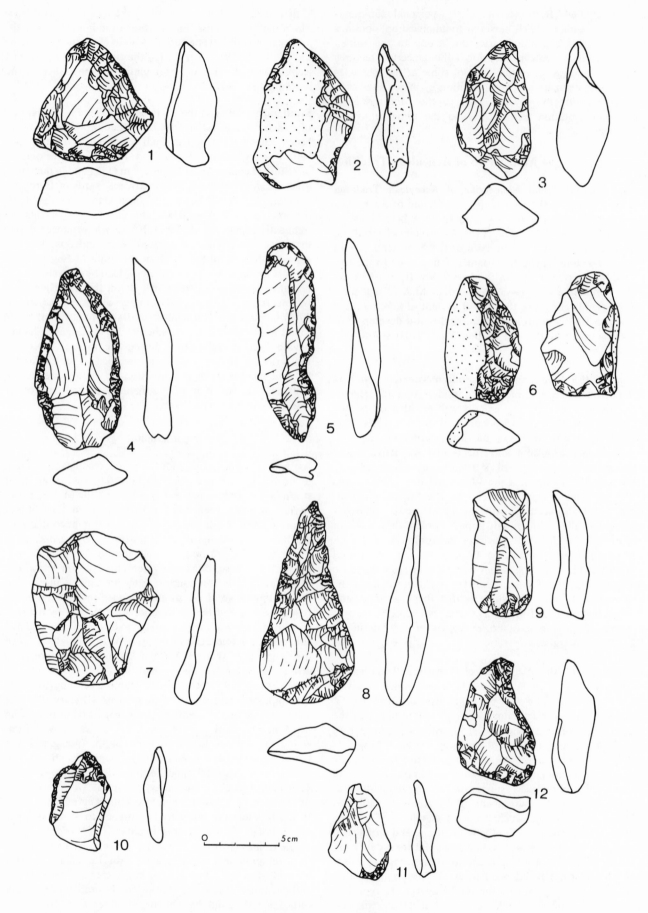

Fig. 3: A Mousterian of Acheulean Tradition assemblage from Warsash, Hampshire, including a Mousterian point (4), a backed knife (5), handaxes (1), (8) and (12), and an unretouched Levallois flake (7).

Würm I/II interstadial, probably at the beginning of the period rather than at the end. The arrival of the Mousterian tradition in Britain is marked by the *bout coupé* form, which also acts as an indicator of its distribution. The *bout coupé* handaxe horizon acts as both a typological 'marker' to separate the older Acheulean traditions from the new incoming Mousterian ideas, and serves to indicate the arrival

date of the new culture, possibly associated with *Homo sapiens neanderthalensis.*

Acknowledgements Thanks are extended to Mr A. M. ApSimon, Mr D. Collins, Dr P. A. Mellars and Professor F. Bordes for their criticism and help. Dr E. K. Tratman kindly informed the writer of the recent find of a *bout coupé* axe at Rhinoceros Hole (Mendip, U.K.) and Dr J. G. Evans provided information on the molluscan fauna from the Fisherton brickearths.

References

Binford, L. R. and S. R. Binford, 1966. A preliminary analysis of functional variability in the Mousterian of Levallois facies. *American Anthropologist,* 68(2) : 238–95.

—— and —— 1969. Stone tools and human behaviour. *Scientific American,* 220(4) : 70–84.

Bordes, F., 1953. Essai de classification des industries Moustériennes. *Bulletin de la Société Préhistorique Francaise,* 50 : 457–66.

—— 1954. Les Limons Quaternaires du bassin de la Seine. *Archives de l'Institut de Paléontologie Humaine* (Paris), Memoire 26.

—— 1961. Mousterian cultures in France. *Science,* 134 : 803–10.

—— 1973. *A tale of two caves.* New York : Harper and Row.

Bosinski, G., 1967. *Die Mittelpaläolithischen Funde im Westlichen Mitteleuropa.* Fundamenta. Reike A. Band 4. (Cologne).

Bourgon, M., 1957. Les industries Moustériennes et Pré-moustériennes du Périgord. *Archives de L'Institut de Paléontologie Humaine (Paris).*

Calkin, J. B. and J. F. N. Green, 1949. Paleoliths and Terraces near Bournemouth. *Proceedings of the Prehistoric Society,* 15 : 21–37.

Campbell, J. and G. Sampson, 1971. *Excavations at Kents Cavern, Devon.* University of Oregon, Anthropological Papers, 3.

Collins, D. and A., 1970. Excavations at Oldbury in Kent; Cultural evidence for Last Glacial Occupation in Britain. *Bulletin of the Institute of Archaeology* (University of London), 8–9 : 151–76.

Commont, V., 1912. Le Moustérien ancien à Saint-Acheul et Montières. Congrès Préhistorique de France (Comptes Rendus) 8th session: 297–320.

Delporte, H., 1963. Le Gisement de la Rochette. *Gallia Préhistoire,* 5 : 1–23.

Evans, A., 1897. *Ancient stone implements.* London.

Marett, R. R., 1916. The site, fauna and industry at La Cotte de St Brelade, Jersey. *Archaeologica,* 67 : 75–118.

McBurney, C. B. M. and P. Callow, 1971. The Cambridge excavations at La Cotte de St Brelade, Jersey—a preliminary report. *Proceedings of the Prehistoric Society,* 37(2) : 167–208.

Mellars, P. A., 1967. *The Moustérian succession in south-west France.* Unpublished Ph.D. thesis. University of Cambridge.

—— 1969. The chronology of Mousterian Industries in the Périgord region of south-west France. *Proceedings of the Prehistoric Society,* 25 : 135–71.

Peyrony, D., 1930. *Le Moustier.* Paris: Revue Anthropologie.

Poole, H. F., 1924. Paleoliths from Great Pan Farm, Isle of Wight. *Papers and Proceedings of the Hampshire Field Club and Archaeological Society:* 305–19.

Roe, D. A., 1964. The British Lower and Middle Palaeolithic: Some Problems, Methods of Study and Preliminary Results. *Proceedings of the Prehistoric Society,* 30 : 245–67.

—— 1967. A study of handaxe groups of the British Lower and Middle Palaeolithic periods using methods of metrical and statistical analysis, with a Gazetteer of British Lower and Middle Palaeolithic sites. Unpublished Ph.D. thesis, University of Cambridge.

—— 1968. British Lower and Middle Palaeolithic Handaxe Groups. *Proceedings of the Prehistoric Society,* 34 : 1–83.

Shackley, M. L., 1974. Stream abrasion of flint implements. *Nature,* 248 : 501–2.

Smith, R. A. 1926. *A guide to antiquities of the Stone Age in the Department of British and Medieval Antiquities* (3rd ed.). London: Trustees of the British Museum.

Tratman, E. K., D. T. Donovan and J. B. Campbell, 1971. The Hyaena Den (Wookey Hole), Mendip Hills, Somerset. *Proceedings of the University of Bristol Speleological Society,* 12(3) : 245–79.

West, R. G. and B. W. Sparks, 1960. Coastal interglacial deposits of the English Channel. *Philosophical Transactions of the Royal Society of London, Series B,* 243 : 95–133.

Wymer, J. J., 1968. *Lower Palaeolithic archaeology in Britain.* London: John Baker.

Zeuner, F. E., 1959. *The Pleistocene period.* London: Hutchinson.

Taxonomy at the service of prehistory

E. D. STOCKTON

Prehistory, despite its well-known limitations, is history. It is concerned with people, with change, with cause and effect. Its principal instrument of research is archaeology, but it cannot rest content with simply recording differences in technology in a stratified sequence. When faced with change, the prehistorian must ask what is the nature of this change— natural development, alien influence, replacement of one culture by another?—and whether the changes he detects in successive tool kits extend to the people as a whole. Likewise the record of similarities and differences in contemporary tool kits spatially separated must raise questions about cultural diffusion, and ultimately about ethnic expansion, trade, imitation, parallel development and so on. Within the evidence available (in the absence of documentation it is almost impossible to consider the impact of new ideas), the prehistorian feels impelled to seek causes for the cultural changes he has observed, eg. population pressures, environmental conditions. On the basis of stone artifacts, i.e. one segment of a total culture, he tries to reconstruct, however sketchily and tentatively, not only the sequential framework but also the interplay of causes in man's development.

It is understandable that the present day prehistorian shies away from the subjective, the intuition, the tentative conclusion. But subjectivity cannot be altogether excluded, either from the reconstruction of history or, as will be noted later, from the synthetic stage of classification. An analogy can be taken from the study of language, since on the one hand artifacts are being made to tell a story, and on the other a sentence is an artifact, i.e. a natural phenomenon (sound or line) artificially modified to serve a human need. As with tool types, traits of a language can be combined in seemingly infinite ways, but within the limits of culturally conditioned accidence, syntax and idiom. The study of contemporary languages is relatively simple, because the users can be consulted as to meaning and reasons for usage. With the study of an extinct language, extant only in written form, the scholar uses every objective means (e.g. statistically recording the recurrence of letters and words) to decipher the language and to observe regularities of grammar. He does not stop there: he is expected to hazard an idea of meaning, as it were to meet the ancient mind halfway ('What sort of thing would I want to scribble on this sherd—something like "10 jars of oil for 20 shekels"?'). Likewise the prehistorian does not rest content with a mass of statistical data or technical terms, but gropes by their means towards a perception of a human history.

To be more precise in the field of prehistory, it is from differences between artifact assemblages that the story begins to emerge. It is therefore crucial to prehistory that stone artifacts be so described and classified that differences through time and space can be specified and the nature of cultural change can be judged. Obviously there are many ways in which one can classify a group of objects. Any system will be determined by the purpose. The purpose of the prehistorian will be different from that of the anthropologist. For example, Big John at La Grange, Western Australia, the acknowledged expert in matters of local art and craft, when discussing the stone implements of his area made the primary division between 'secret' and 'non-secret' (he thumbed through McCarthy's book [1967] dividing the stone tools of a whole continent on the same basis), but the consideration which was important to him was hardly serviceable to the prehistorian. The latter cannot enjoy an 'inside' view of cultural objects, even if he possesses ethnographic data for recent items, because his terms of comparison must be the same for extinct cultures. A system of classification for the purpose of prehistory would need to possess, at least, the following characteristics.

Objective description

There would seem to be general acceptance for the ideal of describing artifacts by stone form and method of manufacture, and for this there exists an established nomenclature (cf. Casey, Crawford and Wright, 1972 : 102–10). Less happy are non-descriptive terms, i.e. those derived from place names, Aboriginal words and from (presumed or known) functions, because they do not facilitate comparisons between industries, whether within Australia or overseas. However in practice some terms have enjoyed long usage and are well defined, and hence are convenient short designations.

Precise differentiation

This is an aspect of proper description. Lack of precision in description of individual tool types tends to blur the changes observable between periods and regions. For example, in some excavation reports scrapers are seen as a continuous and major component of successive industries, creating an impression of cultural continuity. Undifferentiated use of the term 'scraper' is practically meaningless: J. de Heinzelin de Braucourt attacks English terminology in this regard as 'notoirement imprécise' (1962 : 27). The fact that half to three-quarters of an assemblage can be written off as scrapers itself suggests the need for further subdivision. Such was undertaken by Lampert at Burrill Lake (1971 : 16–28), starting from a definition of a scraper 'as a piece of stone with all or part of its margin unifacially and systematically retouched to form a working edge that could have been used for scraping'. Such a definition, which would be generally acceptable, would demand that the working edge be even, whether curved or straight, yet Australian usage often extends the term to implements with jagged edges (*ibid.* figs. 5, 11; Mulvaney, 1969: figs. 32, 37–7). Again, tulas and semi-discoids are commonly assimilated (eg. Campbell and Edwards, 1966 : 194–95), but it can be demonstrated that they are quite different tools (Stockton, 1971 : 50–51), with significantly different distributions, for example in south-east Australia semi-discoids are found but not tulas. It seems that the problem of precision is most likely to arise in non descriptive terminology.

Characterisation of whole assemblage

I feel that it is important that one assemblage be compared to another on the basis of all its components, rather than of one or a few; hence it, too, needs to be characterised by an objective description, in much the same way as a botanist characterises a plant community. The tendency has been to define an industry by a single cultural marker, eg. in south-east Australia the Capertian, Bondaian and Eloueran industries have been distinguished by the 'saw', the bondi point and the elouera adze-flake respectively. This procedure unduly highlights one tool as if it were the most important in the tool kit (which is not known), says nothing about similarities and differences between assemblages, and it easily happens that a surface site or an excavated level lacks a cultural marker. Mulvaney saw the need of coming to grips with whole assemblages when he proposed a sequence of non-hafted and hafted industries (1965), and more recently, a sequence of Early, Inventive and Adaptive phases of Aboriginal culture (1969); these proposals were not well received on account of their implications (White, 1969; Lampert, 1971 : 65–70) and they might be further criticised for not being descriptive of the industries themselves. The designation of the earliest Australian industry as the 'Core Tool and Scraper Tradition' (Bowler *et al.*, 1970 : 52) moves in the right direction, although core tools and scrapers are prominent in later industries as well.

In order to take a whole view of an assemblage, I believe one needs to be aware of the formal relationships between the components and that therefore a system of classification should not only divide the material into individual tool types but also group them into a hierarchical system according to various lines of relatedness, much like biological classifications into families, genera and species. It is open to question whether hierarchical ordering is an objective procedure, since one is swayed by intuition to consider one basis of relatedness before another, but it does make a mass of material more meaningful and workable for the investigator, and this is the ultimate purpose of classification.

For the purpose of comparing successive industries in various parts of Australia, I have gradually developed a method of classification which takes account of the following objective traits.

(a) Size of flaked material By the simple procedure of weighing and counting all flaked stone in each level of a stratified sequence, the mean weight of flake can be calculated and the figure is found for the most part to decrease progressively through time, and most markedly at transition points (Stockton, 1971 : 58; 1973 : 116). It is not appropriate to compare absolute figures between sites, because local supply has some bearing on flake size, but rate of variation

is comparable. This criterion is useful in assessing levels which produce small amounts of material and lack cultural markers.

(b) Stone type Selection of stone is naturally associated with tool type, eg. chert for backed blades, quartzite for leiliras, basalt for edge-ground axes. Where there is a variety of stone available, certain cultural importance attaches to the respective percentages of stone types at a given level, and this again is a criterion which can be applied to the total flaked material. In general terms, the percentage of chert and fine textured silcrete is found to be greatest at the height of the small tool tradition, least in the earliest and latest industries (Hughes, Sullivan and Lampert, 1973 : 224; Stockton, 1973 : 112–13).

(c) Stone form The primary division is between casual stones (pebbles, blocks, incidental flakes, whose immediate potential for use is realised by primary flaking, leaving shape amorphous) and flakes produced to desired shape and size and secondarily retouched or used. Blade tools may be differentiated from other flake tools, but the distinction does not seem to have as much importance as in upper Palaeolithic Europe, except to illustrate the peak sophistication of the small tool tradition. In general flake tools are characteristic of later industries.

(d) Type of retouch There appears to be chronological and therefore cultural development from crude knapping to pressure flaking, while the latter tends to show regional variation between steep retouch serially applied from a common edge (as in back-blunted and edge-trimmed tools) and surface retouch (as in tulas and bifacial/unifacial points). Examination of glass used casually by Australian Aborigines for scraping wood has convinced me that it is often difficult to distinguish use-wear and edge-trimming. Other kinds of retouch include grinding and polishing. Retouch from the edge across the face may be unifacial or bifacial, the latter including alternate flaking. The outline of a trimmed edge may be even (curved or straight), serrated or dentated (i.e. crudely jagged or finely toothed).

(e) Location of retouch Cultural significance can be detected in long sequences in the shift of attention from the working part of the tool (with intent to increase the efficiency of a sharp edge or point) to the body shape (with intent to increase control of handling, eg. backed tools). For convenience, these two types of technology are here called use-directed and control-directed.

The next stage, that of combining the above traits into temporally and culturally significant groups, demands an intrusion of subjectivity. I suggest that in these combined traits, as variously grouped in different tools and tool-kits, one can detect a number of ways in which the primitive toolmaker approached his task. I further submit that each culture can be characterised by the predominance of one or several of these 'approaches' (cf. Clark's modes, 1969 : 31).

Group 1. Core and thick flake tools The toolmaker takes a large stone of casual form (i.e. as shaped naturally or as a by-product of previous toolmaking) and modifies the potential working part for immediate use (cutting, chopping, sawing, piercing) with little or no modification of the body of the tool. This is an example of use-directed technology.

Included in this group are choppers (bifacial and unifacial) steep scrapers (with a working edge formed by the under surface and a flaked face more or less perpendicular to it, often showing minute step-flaking from plane use or rejuvenation), serrated flakes (with a series of projections produced by removing deep, high-angled flakelets at more or less regular intervals), and also edge-ground axes, millstones, hammerstones, anvils.

Convention applies the term core to a lump from which flakes have been removed, and while strictly speaking a core belongs to a flake industry, it can be included in this category as a casual stone potentially serviceable for producing flakes, and in fact some cores (eg. horsehoof cores) are used, and even primarily fashioned, for chopper and scraper functions.

Group 2. Edge-trimmed flake tools The toolmaker deliberately produces small flakes which are then trimmed or used in a way which results in a series of small facets along the sharp working edge. This again is use-directed technology. The trimmed edge may be straight (side scraper), convex (end/discoid/nosed scraper) or concave (notched scraper). The marginal trimming may also be intermittent, producing a series of fine regular teeth (dentated flake), or acutely angled—in both cases a cutting function may be suspected. Some flat points show edge-trimming, seemingly to modify the shape (for symmetry?) or to produce awls.

Group 3. Surface-trimmed flake tools This is basically a body-shaping technique (for hafting?) which also enhances the working part, so combining use-directed and control-directed technology. Included under this heading are unifacial/bifacial points, tulas and certain amorphous adze-flakes (Flood, 1970 : 37; Stockton 1971 : 50–52). This technique is found over a large part of central, northern and western Australia. Associated waste flakes are generally tiny, flat, often wide with practically no platform. Dortch describes associated core preparation by which the shape and dorsal surface is predetermined by longitudinal and centripetal (Levallois type) flaking of the core (1972b : 67–71). Because of prior preparation by surface flaking, leilira points and blades may be assimilated to this group (see also McCarthy, 1967 : 38).

Group 4. Back-blunted flake tools This technique is almost exclusively a body-shaping one, the sharp edge or point being more often left untrimmed. It is an example of control-directed technology. The intention is apparently to fit the tool for hafting. Included are backed points, geometric microliths and eloueras, all characteristic of later industries in south-eastern Australia, but also found in the south-west. Core preparation by faceted butt technique is the general association.

What follows is an application of the foregoing system both to fieldwork and to a reconstruction of Australian prehistory. The fieldwork can be summarised under the following headings.

(a) Central Australia: excavation at Kurringa (Santa Teresa) south of Alice Springs (Stockton, 1971)

Sequence: Phase I — Group 1 tools
Phase II — Groups 1 (reduced in size), 2, 3, 4, in equal proportions
Phase III — Groups 2 and 3

The latest phase (III) was apparently continuous with the middle phase, though poorer, but the middle phase represented a sudden technological jump from the earliest phase, occurring in a single level. In European terms, it was like a jump from the lower Palaeolithic to the upper Palaeolithic or even the Mesolithic. Without a bridging flake industry, comparable to the middle Palaeolithic, it was impossible to explain the development as a local one and natural to look for vectors of a new culture swamping the old. The same sudden transition is evidenced by stratified sequences elsewhere in Australia.

(b) Blue Mountains: excavation of six sites at altitudes deliberately chosen to correlate cultural and climatic data in a climate-sensitive area—occupation dating back to $22\,240 \pm 1000$ BP, with at least one break in occupation, i.e. between the Capertian and the Bondaian (Stockton and Holland, 1974).

Sequence: Earliest — Group 1 tools, found mainly
industry   on open sites
Capertian — Group 2 tools, in rock shelters, c. 12 000 to 6000 BP, evidence of very dry conditions.
Bondaian — Group 4 predominating, in in rock shelters, c. 3000 BP to European contact, climate probably moist becoming drier.

Subdivisions of Bondaian: Early—first backed blades, perhaps spasmodic occupation;
Middle—greatest variegation in tools and techniques, peak concentration of flakes, c. 1500–1000 BP.
Late—poorer lithic technology, fabricators, tools of organic material, bondi points persisting in some places. One of the most important results was the characterisation of the Capertian as a purely flake industry, dissimilar to the earlier industry in lacking large components, and to the Bondaian in lacking backed tools, but as an industry of flakes with retouch on the working part (use-directed technology) it stood intermediate between the two. It was now possible to suggest that the Bondaian could have developed in south-eastern Australia from the large tool tradition by medium of the Capertian. Recently Lampert has excavated in a rock shelter at Kangaroo Island, well-known for its archaic Kartan industry on open sites, a flake industry similar to the Capertian and dated like it to about 10 000 BP (Lampert, 1972 : 223–24).

(c) Surface surveys in the Kimberleys, western New South Wales (north–west of Darling, Hay–Maude), central coast of New South Wales (Stockton, 1972, also site reports lodged with the Australian Institute of Aboriginal Studies). All areas have Group 1 tools of a size and grossness indicative of the basal Australian industry, also Group 2 tools with some regional specialisation affecting certain tool types (e.g. dentated flakes and semi-discoids in inland Australia). In north-west Australia Group 3 predominates to the virtual exclusion of Group 4 (cf. Glover, 1967; Flood, 1974; Dorch, 1972a, 1972b); Group 4, but not Group 3, is found in south-east Australia; both groups co-exist in central Australia and western New South Wales (cf.

Mulvaney and Joyce, 1965; Gould, 1968; Stockton, 1971). Regionalisation, indeed polarisation, in recent assemblages is so marked between the north-west and the south-east as to suggest two technological provinces, each with its characteristic point and adze-flake association: the north-west with the unifacial/bifacial point and tula (Group 3), the south-east with the backed point and elouera (Group 4). In a broad band running diagonally across the continent the provinces overlap, possibly in different proportions and in different stratigraphic order, making for further sub-regionalisation.

Very tentatively and sketchily, a reconstruction of Australian prehistory is proposed on the basis of the above data and of sparse environmental evidence.

(1) The most primitive Australians employed Group 1 tools, i.e. hand-grasped artifacts fashioned from casual stones by use-directed technology for simple immediate ends. It seems that material culture was uniform across the whole continent, including Tasmania, except for variations due more to the available stone than to cultural differences (Mulvaney, 1969; 150–52). This industry flourished during the maximum of the last major glaciation, in a climate therefore relatively cold and possibly wet (cf. Bowler *et al.*, 1970). One presumes an abundance of mega-fauna, favouring a hunter-gatherer economy despite the primitive tool kit, but this was a diminishing advantage. Open-sited find spots may indicate that shelter was makeshift or non-existent, or simply that stone tools were fashioned and discarded at place of use in the field.

(2) Towards the end of the Pleistocene, severe and general aridity set in (cf. Bowler *et al.*, 1970) forcing human occupation from much of the inland. Isolated by desert barriers in haven areas (e.g. highland, coast), stone technology began to develop along different but parallel lines, later to result in the polarisation between the north west and south eastern provinces. It would be interesting to know if the later developments in the two provinces were prepared for by the corresponding flake industries, i.e. the Group 3 tools of the north-west arising out of flake production of the 'Levallois' type and the Group 4 tools of the south-east resulting from production of flakes by faceted butt technique. Regardless of conjectures, the Capertian industry in the south-east was characterised by Group 2 tools, i.e. deliberately produced flakes with use-directed retouch—such tools may have been hafted or held at finger-tip (as flaked stone or glass is held to trim wooden implements, even today). In notable contrast with the preceding industry, find spots of the Capertian are more often rock shelters, suggesting preference for permanent, substantial shelter. Such preference, together with the concentration of toolmaking and other activities at the camp-site, advances in tool technology including the use of smaller implements, and the presumed adaptation to a shrinking food supply, may be seen as related aspects of the total change in culture.

(3) Increased pluviation, from *c.* 7000 to *c.* 3000 BP, is inferred from the occupation of an inland rock shelter (Gould, 1968) and from apparent abandonment of highland sites (Tindale, 1961; McCarthy, 1964; Mulvaney and Joyce, 1965; Stockton and Holland, 1974 : 55, 60). Meanwhile sophisticated flake industries accenting control were developing in the north-west (Group 3) and in the south-east (Group 4), and with the opening up of vast areas of the continent, the two cultures expanded, met and mingled the mix giving rise to further cultural regionalisation. From slight indications in western New South Wales it appears that the south-east culture, more characteristic of a temperate climate, may have arrived first, subsequently to be replaced by the north-west 'desert-ranging' culture.

With the tailing-off of the wet, and despite the possibility of a minor cold period *c.* 3000–1500 BP (Costin, 1973), the south-east highlands were re-occupied about 3000 BP by the bearers of the Bondaian industry. The use of rock shelters was even more marked than before: the concentration of flaked stone at levels dating towards the end of the first millennium AD may indicate increasing preference for cave dwelling (due to cold?), more activity at the camp-site and/or larger population—these factors, coinciding with a peak sophistication in stone technology and the possible effect of a moist temperate climate on food supply, may point to a more settled way of life.

Over the last 1000 years south-east Australia has experienced a return to a warmer and drier climate, which may have reduced food resources and human population; smaller flake yields in the upper levels of cave sites may suggest lessened dependence/preference for permanent shelter, corresponding to European records that, at the time of contact, bark huts were the prevalent form of habitation; the tool kit tended to become simpler and more economic, with perhaps greater use of organic materials. All or some of these factors may be related to an increasing nomadic form of life. In the highland areas cultural changes were not so marked in the late Bondaian, possibly because the otherwise adverse conditions favoured mountain dwelling and demanded less adaptation. It is interesting that the bondi point certainly persisted in the Blue Mountains, by (possible) contrast to the coast, corresponding with the distribution of skin-cloak usage as reported by the early settlers.

Even in this century we have seen a final chapter in the continuing story of hunter-gatherer man in a marginal environment reacting to climatic change: the Petris' note that, prior to and unrelated to European pressure, tribal people have recently evacuated the Western Desert in the face of progressive desiccation (1970 : 267–75).

References

Bowler J. M., R. Jones, H. Allen and A. G. Thorne, 1970. Pleistocene human remains from Australia: a living site and human cremation from Lake Mungo, western New South Wales. *World Archaeology*, 2 : 39–60.

Campbell, T. D. and R. Edwards, 1966. Stone implements. *In* B. C. Cotton (ed.), *Aboriginal Man in South and Central Australia*, pp. 159–220. Adelaide: Government Printer.

Casey, D. A., I. M. Crawford and R. V. S. Wright, 1972. The recognition, description, classification and nomenclature of Australian implements. *In* D. J. Mulvaney (ed.), *Australian Archaeology: a Guide to Field and Laboratory Techniques*, 2nd ed., pp. 104–10. Canberra: Australian Institute of Aboriginal Studies.

Clark, G., 1969. *World prehistory: a new outline*, 2nd ed. Cambridge: Cambridge University Press.

Costin, A. B., 1972. Carbon-14 dates from the Snowy Mountains area, South-Eastern Australia, and their interpretation. *Quaternary Research*, 2 : 579–90.

Dortch, C. E., 1972a. Archaeological work in the Ord Reservoir area, East Kimberley. *Australian Institute of Aboriginal Studies Newsletter*, 3(4) : 13–18.

—— 1972b. An archaeological site in the Chichester Range, Western Australia: a preliminary report. *Journal of the Royal Society of Western Australia*, 55 : 65–72.

Flood, J. M., 1970. A point assemblage from the Northern Territory. *Archaeology and Physical Anthropology in Oceania*, 5 : 27–52.

Glover, I. C., 1967. Stone implements from Millstream Station, Western Australia: Newall's collection re-analysed. *Mankind*, 6 : 415–25.

Gould, R. A., 1968. Preliminary report on excavations at Puntutjarpa Rockshelter, near the Warburton Ranges, Western Australia. *Archaeology and Physical Anthropology in Oceania*, 3 : 161–85.

de Heinzelin de Braucourt, J., 1962. *Manuel de typologie des industries lithiques*. Bruxelles.

Hughes, P. J., M. E. Sullivan and R. J. Lampert, 1973. The use of silcrete in southern coastal N.S.W. *Archaeology and Physical Anthropology in Oceania*, 8 : 220–25.

Lampert, R. J., 1971. *Burrill Lake and Currarong: Coastal sites in southern New South Wales*. Terra Australis 1, Canberra: Australian National University.

—— 1972. A carbon date for the Aboriginal occupation of Kangaroo Island, South Australia. *Mankind*, 8 : 223–24.

McCarthy, F. D., 1964. The Archaeology of the Capertee Valley, New South Wales. *Records of the Australian Museum*, 26 : 197–246.

—— 1967. *Australian Aboriginal stone implements*. Sydney: Australian Museum.

Mulvaney, D. J., 1969. *The prehistory of Australia*. London: Thames and Hudson.

—— and E. B. Joyce, 1965. Archaeological and geomorphological investigations on the Mt. Moffatt Station, Queensland, Australia. *Proceedings, Prehistory Society*, 31 : 147–212.

Petri, H. and G. Petri-Odermann, 1970. Stability and change: present-day historic aspects among Australian Aborigines. *In* R. M. Berndt (ed.) *Australian Aboriginal Anthropology*, pp. 248–76. Nedlands: University of Western Australia Press.

Stockton, E. D., 1971. Investigations at Santa Teresa, Central Australia. *Archaeology and Physical Anthropology in Oceania*, 6 : 44–61.

—— 1972. A Central Coast Survey. *Australian Institute of Aboriginal Studies Newsletter*, 3(5) : 20–4.

—— 1973. Shaw's Creek Shelter: Human displacement of artefacts and its significance. *Mankind*, 9 : 112–17.

—— and W. N. Holland, 1974. Cultural sites and their environment in the Blue Mountains. *Archaeology and Physical Anthropology in Oceania*, 9 : 36–65.

Tindale, N. B., 1961. Archaeological excavation of the Noola Rock Shelter: a preliminary report. *Records of the South Australian Museum*, 14 : 193–96.

White, J. P., 1969. Back to 28,000 B.C. (review of Mulvaney, 1969). *Nation*, 23.8.69 : 23.

Adaptive significance of the Panara or grass seed culture of Australia

NORMAN B. TINDALE

Introduction

One of the relatively late accessions to the long lasting Aboriginal hunting cultures of Australia has been the intensive use, as food, of grass seed, after processing it by a special technique of wet grinding, followed by baking in hot ashes as a form of unleavened bread or cake.

One consequence of this development in the principal grassland areas of Australia seems to have been an increase in the number of people who have been able to link themselves together as a tribe, namely from a mean of around 450 to perhaps double that number. Among the people practising this way of life may be named as examples the Kamilaroi, Wadjari, Weraerai, Iliaura and Walpiri, and many of them have relatively large populations in comparison with other hunting tribes in Australia. There is evidence for the incipient development of grain storage, and in two situations a suggestion that the effectiveness of seasonal flooding of grassed plains had been modified by damming stream beds prior to the advent of summer rains, implying incipient interest in irrigation.

Examination of activities associated with other foods such as wild rice, water chestnuts (*Eleocharis*), and *Dioscorea* yams encourage a suggestion that many of the activities of northern Australian people were already akin to those associated with the earliest gardening cultures, lacking principally the idea of the deliberate preservation and sowing of new seed. Thus a suggestive subtitle for this paper could well have been 'Pre-Dawn of Agriculture in Australia'. A preliminary version of it was read under this title at a seminar in the University of Colorado in February 1970, and some details are given in Tindale (1974).

The distribution of the special upper and lower millstones, in some areas called [tjiwa] and [tjuŋguri], clearly register, in their form and wear, the activities associated with such types of grass seed preparation so that we have both archaeological as well as present day ethnographic evidence to suggest that a wet grinding practice spread both south and westward from the Gulf of Carpentaria, with general limits in southern New South Wales and a spread along the northern side of the Great Western Desert and then southward as far as the tribal territory of the Wadjari, inland on the Murchison River.

In extensive areas the name of the grass seed bread is [konakandi], literally 'dung food', an obvious reference to the appearance of the wet meal as it is moulded and placed to cook in the ashes of the fire. An important element in this economy is a set of shallow oval to elongate wooden dishes, often with riffled inner surfaces. Sets of these are used in the gathering, winnowing and cleaning of the seeds and in the holding of the wet crushed grain. In the northern part of the distribution of the technique the dishes are known as [pana] and some of the people are spoken of by other Aborigines as Panara, variously transcribed also as Bunara, Boonarra etc., and it is suggested that this term Panara might well be used in our discussions as a general term of reference for the peoples who use or practice this form of grain-using economy.

The grasslands people

When contemplating ecological controls that appear to be present in the economic life of the Australian Aborigines, it is to be noticed that while advanced agricultural economics tend to be concentrated on heavily watered and timbered areas, even though the forests have to be removed, the first choices of the Aborigines, their most attractive areas of living, have tended to be savannah woodland and open grassy plains where there is some water and much game. Both arid desert areas and dense rainforests are kinds of refuges, sought chiefly by those less well equipped, or whose physical type destines them to an inferior role.

In earlier papers (Tindale, 1937, 1940, 1959, 1960) I have commented on some of the geographical factors which seem to determine the distributions and limits of Australian Aboriginal tribes, and in a paper before a conference at the Australian National University in October 1973 and in a book (1976), I have drawn further attention to ecological controls evident in tribal limits.

The generally inverse relationship between rainfall and the size of tribal lands has been noticed in previous papers; also that the areas occupied tend to vary rather than the numbers of people who come to regard themselves as associated with a particular name-bearing unit of the kind which is commonly called a tribe in Australia. This mean number of people has been noticed to comprise about 450 persons.

Notwithstanding this general conclusion it cannot be denied that there are some named tribal groups whose population numbers have tended to be higher than this, so that, in certain areas over twice as many people constitute a tribe. These supposedly larger than usual aggregates are noticed to be present in predominantly grassland areas. For example they are present in a belt extending in a north-south direction in the flatlands west of the Great Dividing Range from southern New South Wales to near the coastlands of the Gulf of Carpentaria, and thence westward, generally south of the 16° south latitude nearly to the west coast of Australia, and thence southward on the interior plains as far south as the Murchison area of Western Australia.

Representative of tribes in these areas are the Wiradjuri, Kamilaroi, Kunggari, Iliaura, Walpiri and in the west the Wadjari. It has been observed that although these widely scattered peoples and others occupying the grassland belt differ widely in the details of their social organisations, as well as in their ceremonial observances, increase rites and initiation practices, they share in common the practice of harvesting and grinding up the various grass seeds, and in peripheral areas also other seeds, such as those of the coolibah (*Eucalyptus microtheca*, Myrtaceae) and *Tecticornia* (Chenopodiaceae). With these grains they prepare a form of unleavened bread using a wet-grinding process of preparing the meal. The technical processes have been illustrated in the 16 mm cine film which I made in August 1930 (Macdonald Downs Reel 2). This was published by the University of Adelaide. In this part of Central Australia the Iliaura tribespeople exploit many grass seed bearing plants. One of the principal ones is called by them otteta [ót:eta] and is a species of *Panicum*. This grass springs up and flourishes after northwest monsoonal rains, growing luxuriantly on plains where the storm showers flood the soil temporarily to a depth of a few centimetres. The seed heads are ready by late autumn. At this time the country is dry and the ground sunbaked. It is possible to gather some grain in ear but the Aborigines tend to rely on the activities of a species of ant which has the habit of carrying the seeds to their nests where they arrange them in a ring around the entrances to their holes.

Women take advantage of this to sweep the mixture of grit, chaff and seed into their wooden dishes. After preliminary cleaning by winnowing and rocking in the dishes to separate the grain from other particles the ears are hulled by treading the seed in a circular hole in the ground, conveniently placed near a tree so that the woman operator can support herself as she rotates her feet, right and left over the grain.

The husked grain is removed from the husking hole, is again winnowed to remove the bulk of the dross, and then subjected to further rockings in the dishes, some of which are furnished with longitudinal riffles which seem to expedite the separation of the grain from the rest of the contents. Following several stages of this preparation, the grain is milled.

A wet-grinding process is employed, using a large flat nether millstone which I have elsewhere, for convenience, called by the Pitjandjara name tjiwa [ťjiwa], and a smaller upper millstone called a tjungguri [ťjuŋguri]. The latter is usually, when new, about 5 cm thick, but in use it wears down to much less. In the milling process a small heap of grain is placed on the stone, moistened with a squirt of water from the mouth of the operator, and the mass pushed away to the distal end of the tjiwa under the slightly tilted upper stone. It is then dragged back again and the process repeated. Now suitably crushed the meal is shoved obliquely to the right over the lip of the stone into a wooden dish placed there for its reception. Sometimes this is done with the hand but may be done with the aid of the upper stone, the results of the latter action become registered in wear on the lip which develops because of the general concentration of work in the middle of the stone. Each woman has her own idiosyncrasies of working but the general record left on the stone mills is quite clear and serves to register the wet-grinding technique on the stone.

By the time that sufficient meal for a cake has been prepared some of the water in the meal has separated out and this is discarded as the meal is pressed into a loaf, or, as often happens is poured on to a layer of hot ashes and pressed together to form an elongate flattened loaf. Care is taken to ensure that no foreign matter becomes incorporated in the soft mass, the top surface of which is hardened a little by being exposed to the heat of small twigs held over it, until the surface becomes dry enough for ashes to be placed over it for the final baking. A brush of grass stems is used to expose the cooked but still tender hot loaf which is delicately tipped on to a wooden dish for final dressing and cooling. Important tools used by the women in addition to their digging stick are several wooden dishes, called [ṕana], a deeper wooden water holder, and a fire shovel for manipulating the ashes in which the bread is cooked.

During the harvesting period more grain than immediately needed may be gathered and is stored in such places as caves and hollow trees.

One of the more northern of the tribes who rely on grass seed for a considerable part of their diet is the Karawa whose country is situated around latitude 17°S in the country north of the Barkly tableland. I was able to work with a few of them in 1963. They call the grass seed food bodjan [bo:djan] and employ a flat nether millstone known as a jamara [ja:mara] and a flat hand stone called tungalan [tuŋalan]. Theirs is a wet-grinding technique.

Fourteen hundred and fifty kilometres to the south, among the Ualarai of the area around Walgett on the upper Darling River the Karawa name for the vital nether millstone used in the milling process has become the name for the grain that is harvested, namely jamara [ja:mara]. Mrs Langloh Parker (1905 : 105, 108, 114) tells us that in that matrilineally oriented society men played an important part in the harvesting of the grass seed and that the product, which she called *yammara*, was stored against future use. Women collected the ripening ears of grass while still green and they were piled into a brush enclosure and the whole set on fire. Women turned the pile to shake out the parched seeds, using long sticks. The seeds were then piled on possum skin rugs. Men took the part of removing the husks by treading them in a square hole in the ground. Other men worked a stick around in a circular hole filled with the trampled grain, causing the husks to work their way to the top. Further winnowing and the use of bark dishes, known as *wiri* and an especially large canoe-shaped bark vessel known as a *jubbil* completed the cleaning of the grain. Since there was a harvesting season the grain was stored in skin bags until required. Then the grain was prepared for eating by wet-grinding on millstones called dajurl [dajurl] and made into flat cakes to be cooked in the ashes of a fire.

Apparently similar methods were employed by the Wiradjuri and the Kamilaroi. The Kunggari, who originally lived along Nebine Creek in southern Queensland also milled their grass seeds and made a form of 'damper'. Harriott Barlow (1873 : 169, 174) names the food yielding grass as [í:li], her *eel-lee*.

As described by S. Hill (1901 : 25) the Maiawali of the upper Diamantina River in Queensland depended on grass seed milling. They called their grass [ṕapa] and it was prepared by the wet-grinding method.

Further to the west the seeds of the [kulaba], i.e. the coolibah or coolabah tree (*Eucalyptus microtheca*, Myrtaceae) which also were called [ṕapa], were collected in the manner used by the Ualarai. Great branches were heaped on hard ground and allowed to ripen and shed their seed, to be swept up, winnowed and milled. According to J. Coghlan (1898) the millstones used in the Glenormiston district (in the territory of the Wongkadjera), for the preparation of [ṗapa] seed bread were traded from a mine situated in Wakaja territory to the north. Permission had to be given by the occupiers of the mining area before slabs of stone could be removed. Relationship of mine to place of use may suggest a movement of such stones in a southward direction along the riverine corridors of western Queensland and seems to support the suggestive evidence of a vocabulary link between the Ualarai and Karawa mentioned in an earlier paragraph.

Simpson Newland (1889 : 22) described the gathering of grass seed among the Naualko (his Wampangee) giving a general name *parper* for the several grass seeds used and indicating the use of a wet grinding method. His name for the grasses evidently is the same as among the Maiawali, some seven tribes removed and 650 km to the north.

Among the Ngemba people in the heart of the western grass land plains of New South Wales millstones were in constant use in the wet-grinding process. Nether mills were known as jauai [j́auai], and the flat upper as marra [ṁar:a]. The latter is a word widely used elsewhere for the hand. R. H. Mathews (1904 : 203–381) tells of the native tradition that the ancestral being Baiame pounded nuts and ground grass seeds to make seed cakes at Bai, native name of a granite rock with a water supply near and west of the town now known as Byrock.

It seems that the Kamilaroi, Wiradjuri and the Ualarai are important examples of tribes in the south-eastern portions of the grasslands of Australia, the Walpiri and the Iliaura in the north and the Wadjari in the west, where the people have come to depend for a goodly part of their sustenance on natural grain crops.

The importance of the grass seed milling activities of people of the grassland areas was not appreciated in 1930 when I filmed the procedures during the University of Adelaide Expedition to Macdonald Downs. Lists of the grass seed foods were given in the reports of the expedition (Cleland, 1932). Campbell (pers. comm.) noted that the Iliaura, who are heavily dependent on konakandi had a higher percentage of dental caries than he had observed elsewhere up to that time. This may have been one of the more serious debilities experienced by people on adopting such a relatively soft carbohydrate diet.

In later years my continuing interest in the Iliaura led to the information that the most desirable grasses were most commonly found on mulga plains that became flooded for limited periods after heavy summer rains, and that it was proper to fill the runoff channels of creeks so that larger areas of ground would be flooded when the rains came. For many years there was no substantiation, but in 1963 a Wanji man from the Nicholson River country indicated that his people knew it was an advantage to get as large an area as possible flooded by these freshets, and at certain places where the country was suitable, they choked up the channels with stones, earth and other debris. Areas such as these were well known as grainfields and were visited at the proper times to gather the harvest. Even the suggestion of manipulation of water in the most rudimentary fashion in such areas may be worthy of attention, since it hints at the beginnings of agricultural irrigation.

Wet-grinding of grass seed, and associated activities, have attracted my increasing attention because of the emerging indications that there may be an important link between the grassland belts and the main areas of distribution of the characteristic large stone mills required for the preparation of konakandi. These mills are found in great numbers in a belt extending along the western flank of the Great Dividing Range, down the Diamantina but become increasingly rare and disappear in the lower Murray Valley where they are smaller and by their patterns of wear suggest that, like the ethnographically modern ones they were used for other purposes such as the dry pounding and ¢rushing of coarse *Acacia* and other shrub seeds, the pulping of other seeds and fruits and in the Western Desert the cracking of the hard seedpods of *Brachychiton* and kernels of the quandong (*Santalum acuminatum*).

Among the Iliaura, and especially among tribespeople further to the south-east, replacements even for the smaller tjungguri upper stones are so hard to come by that they are used on both faces until they are so thin that it becomes difficult for women to avoid wearing away the tips of their fingers. At this stage the stones are tilted and so develop series of slightly oblique facets by the confining of the areas of maximum friction to the left rear side as a woman elevates the right side to protect her fingertips. A sharp smooth edge often develops at the same time as the woman scrapes off the meal obliquely away to the right. Some women tend to use their hand for this purpose thus accounting for some of the differences registered in the stones. Extreme wear is a register of the relative remoteness and inaccessiblity of replacements since there is not a mine for such mills in every tribal area and the obtaining of new ones may involve intertribal contact, trade, and in some cases armed trespass.

Despite the comparative rarity of the gritstone slabs on which the Panara economy rests, a vast number of the mills have been transported from the principal known mines such as in the Flinders Ranges in South Australia, the Grey Range in western New South Wales and the Wakaja tribal area mentioned above.

There is a woman's lament which protests the inertia of men who will not make the travel effort necessary to obtain new stones for their wives.

Slabs of sandstone and sandy shales strongly bound with silica were mined and shaped for the milling of grass seeds and for the sharpening of stone axes. In the eastern grasslands men might travel great distances and undergo hardships and danger to obtain suitable stones. The precious nature of the mills is registered at Wertaloona, in the territory of the Jadliaura tribe in the Flinders Ranges where there are several camps within about two kilometres of the mine area which are strewn with partly trimmed slabs. On trails leading away east into the stoneless country small piles of partly finished slabs show where in the past carriers have had to revise the loads with which they had started back optimistically on their homeward journey.

The southern limits of the distribution of the special milling tools of this wet-grinding technique of seed preparation are reasonably well known and in the south-eastern parts of Australia, in the ethnographic present, correspond rather well with the known boundary of the grasslands at about 36° south latitude. In the north the technique seems to be practised today chiefly in areas south of about latitude 16°S.

What seem to be archaeological examples have been found as far north as latitude 12°S. in Arnhem Land and thus this form of food economy may have had a respectable antiquity in late Pleistocene history. C. White (1971 : 141) indicates a date of about 18 000 BP in Arnhem Land for portions of stones showing a flat, presumptively milling surface, which could have had such use. If so there may have been exploitation of grass seed during the height of the last great cold phase of the Wisconsin Ice Age. At such times the areas about 12°S may well have had a relatively dry climate similar to that now found further south where the grass seed techniques are still employed. It may be corrrect to assume that at that time the areas suitable for the dominance of grass did not reach much further south than the Tropic of Capricorn.

In earlier papers I have drawn attention to the strong limitations imposed on the spread of the post-Pleistocene types of diorite stone axes in the area south of Cloncurry, by the presence and absence of the tree hollow utilising *Trigona* bees which are in turn assisted in their distribution by the tree hollowing activities of species of termites, as well as the attractions of the large timber-boring species of the Cossid moth genus *Xyleutes*. Conversely there are encouragements, in the absence of such axes in the southern parts of the Western Desert, which seem to ensure the survival of the hand-held horsehoof core implement, which still serves as an unhafted adze, a necessary tool for making the upper and lower notches in the trunk of a large mulga when preparing to split off the billet for a spearthrower, one of the principal tasks for which an adze-like or axe tool would be essential in such desert areas.

In similar fashion I now ascribe to economic demand the limited distribution of the tjiwa mill. Their apparent absence from Pleistocene levels at Lake Menindee and at Mungo is thus a result of their former exclusion from what were then predominantly woodland areas rather than the open grasslands they are today. There has been a question whether the western Queensland and New South Wales grasslands were an artifact developed with the aid of the firestick of the Aborigines during the period of the Flandrian Recession or whether they have always been a feature of the Australian landscape. In the period of greatest Wisconsin cold, latitude 26°S or thereabouts might well have been the southern limit for the extensive presence of such grasslands. Archaeological studies have not yet proceeded far enough to demonstrate with certainty that during the times when the Kartan suites of implements were in exclusive use that grass milling was practised. At that time the relics which Mr Norman Blunden and I have found in the areas around Wellington and at Noola near Rylstone, consist of the tools similar to those found on Kangaroo Island, the type area of the Kartan Culture, including pebble side-choppers, side-choppers on angled cleavage blocks, discoidal *karta* block implements, together with a large (15 cm) diameter discoidal implement with two opposed deeply notched scraping grooves, heavy elongate chopping tools suitable for two-handed use with the adzing trims on the end, and as an addition many large grooved, and a few ungrooved so-called bogan picks. Most of these have come from monocultural Kartan sites found within the general triangle area with points at Brewarrina, Coolamon and Quirindi while working from Wellington. On one site only was there a superimposition of culture phases, and that just to the north of Wellington, is the north-eastern most site from which the characteristic implements of the suite called Pirrian have been found, in a rich assemblage. Indications having been gained that the bogan pick is an accompaniment of the Kartan culture suite, Norman Blunden (pers. comm., 9 March 1974) has suggested that the bogan pick could have been hafted and employed in the killing and

perhaps the opening up of the bodies of entrapped large Australian mammals such as the *Diprotodon* and the giant kangaroos. If his conclusions are valid that the pick was an accompaniment of the early Kartan it would have become less useful and ultimately forgotten as the need for it declined with the disappearance of these animals. He has noted that these implements have occurred in numbers of cases in situations where, as in constricted depressions, traps might have once been employed.

The above suggestion of possible Kartan period hunting activities recalls to mind that the *Diprotodon* giant marsupials that died by being bogged in the muds of Lake Callabonna, in the manner that cattle are today trapped in drying waterholes along the upper Victoria River in the Northern Territory, had as their last meals masses of twigs and similar shrubby vegetation, suggesting, either that they were shrubland and forest dwellers, or that there was little grassland as such in the vicinity of where they died. Lake Callabonna lies just north of latitude 30°S thus well above the present limits of grasslands.

Having concluded that there is some evidence to suggest that the people of the Kartan culture phase did not have particular interests in grass seed as a principal staff of life, I have accepted evidence suggesting that the Panara economy may well have accompanied the entry in northern Australia of the Tartangan stone implement culture phase which was first recognised in South Australia in 1930 and can be equated with the same tool making and using practices as became locked away in Tasmania after the separation of that island from the Australian mainland in a phase of the Flandrian Recession between 12 000 and 10 000 BP. While the Tartangan elements appeared in the north and extended to western New South Wales before 25 000 BP it seems likely that the absence then of grasslands did not immediately encourage the use of the large tjiwa millstone, the uses of which only spread south as the climatic conditions changed. If this view is correct we are in a position to see that the factors operating to control the southward spread of the tjiwa have been at work for a long time and it will be one of the interesting chores in the future to see at what rate and when the movements southward took place. It seems likely that the dramatic warming up of climate after 10 000 BP must have been a major stimulus to the initiation of a southward spread of the Panara economy, but the present day line marked by the Kamilaroi and Wiradjuri present day territories may have been attained only during the Peronian periods of the mid-Recent.

Some of the evidence for the assertions given in the above paragraphs has been set out in more detail in my book (1974). In this paper I have deliberately attempted to be provocative in speculations as to the significance of a suggested late Pleistocene incursion of a new technique of preparing carbohydrate foods, which seems to have had long-term effects in changing some of the social, as well as the implement-using patterns of those Aborigines who have come to exploit the expanding post-Pleistocene grasslands of Australia.

Addendum

A few additional references given by Etheridge (1918) have been found, and yield support to some of the conclusions set out in earlier paragraphs.

Explorer Sturt (1849 : 294) wrote of seeing ricks of panicum grass on the Darling River, below Bourke, where 'the whole ground where it lay resembled a harvest field'.

In similar vein Gregory (1837 : 131) refers to the harvesting of panicum grass on Cooper Creek. There the grass was cut down using stone knives, cuts being made part way down the stalk so that when the heads were beaten, the seed left the straw, which often accumulated in large heaps.

Gregory, in the same paper reported that Aborigines of the west coast, when digging up native yams 'invariably reinsert the heads of the yams so as to be sure of a future crop'. This record predates by nearly eighty years my own observations on a similar practice by women among the Walmbaria Aborigines of Flinders Island, Queensland.

References

Barlow, H., 1873. Vocabulary of aboriginal dialects of Queensland. *Journal of the Anthropological Society of Great Britain*, 2(2) : 166–75.

Coghlan, J., 1898. Foods of north west Aboriginals (Glenormiston, Queensland). *Science of Man*, 1(2) : 48.

Etheridge, R., 1918. *The dendroglyphs, or 'carved trees' of New South Wales*. Memoirs of the Geological Survey of New South Wales. Ethnological Series, no. 3. Sydney : Government Printer.

Gregory, A. C., 1887. Memoranda on the Aborigines of Australia. *Journal of the Anthropological Institute*, 16 : 131.

Hill, S., 1901. Ceremonies, customs and food of the Myoli tribe. *Science of Man*, 4(2) : 24–25.

Mathews, R. H., 1904. Ethnological notes on the Aboriginal tribes of New South Wales. *Journal of the Proceedings of the Royal Society of New South Wales*, 38 : 203–381.

Newland, S., 1889. Parkingees, or Aboriginal tribes on the Darling River. *Proceedings of the Royal Geographical Society of Australia*, 2(1887–1888) : 20–32.

Parker, K. L., 1905. *Euahlayi tribe*. London.

Sturt, C., 1849. *Narrative of an expedition into central Australia . . . during the years . . .* London: Boone.

Tindale, N. B., 1937. Prupe and Koromarange. *Transactions of the Royal Society of South Australia*, 62 : 18–28.

—— 1940. Distribution of Australian tribes. *Transactions of the Royal Society of South Australia*, 64(1) : 140–231.

—— 1959. Ecology of primitive aboriginal man in Australia. *In* Keast, A. *et al.* (eds), *Biogeography and ecology in Australia*, pp. 36–51. The Hague: W. Junk.

—— 1974. *Aboriginal tribes of Australia*. Berkeley: UCLA Press.

University of Adelaide, 1930. Macdonald Downs, Reel 2 (16 mm silent film). Adelaide.

White, C., 1971. Man and environment in Northwest Arnhem Land. *In* Mulvaney D. J. and Golson J. (eds), *Aboriginal man and environment in Australia*, pp. 141–157. Canberra: ANU Press.

The 'fabricator' in Australia and New Guinea

R. L. VANDERWAL

In the course of fieldwork in central coastal Papua in 1969 and 1970 I recovered, from a late period coastal site, a series of stone artifacts whose opposed edges are bruised and splintered (Vanderwal, 1973). They bore a striking resemblance to similar Australian artifacts which appear in the literature as fabricators, and are defined (eg. McCarthy *et al*; 1946:34) as tools used to make other tools. Recently, however, similar artifacts have been seen in the process of manufacture at Lake Kopiago in the Western Highlands of New Guinea (White, 1968). There the flint nodule is wrapped in bark, held vertically on an anvil and is pounded until several flakes have been removed. White describes the production of thin cores, bruised and battered on opposing ends, as the final result of the process. Suitable flakes are selected for later use while the bipolar core and reject flakes are discarded. White has therefore called into doubt the validity of the term 'fabricator' and that which it implies, suggesting instead the term scalar core, that is a waste product in the manufacture of small flakes. If, as previously assumed, the artifact was used to make other tools, White argues, there should be a direct correlation between them and (for example) Bondi points, which there is not (White, 1968:663); nor is there a correlation with any other of the sophisticated stone tools. White's is a working hypothesis which has largely been accepted (see Lampert, 1971:43-47); it is the purpose of this paper to firstly evaluate the merits of the hypothesis in the terms of the artifacts I collected in 1969-70, and to secondly re-examine the concept as it is applied to Australia.

My sample of bipolar artifacts came from the Uro'urina site on Yule Island. The site is by the sea and consists of an ellipsoid of debris, 87 m × 33 m, with a maximum surface relief of 1.6 m compared with the surrounding largely flat terrain. A total of 6 m² was excavated, demonstrating a maximum occupational deposit of 0.9 m. Large quantities of pottery, bone, shell and stone were recovered. The stratigraphy of the site was confusing; it was made up of numerous shell, ash and earth lenses while the only major division that could be made was between darker upper soils and lighter lower soils. However, analysis of the pottery component of the site failed to distinguish a cultural difference between the observed soil colours. A carbon sample (ANU 730) from a depth of 0.8 m dated at 720 ± 105 years BP.

The pottery at Uro'urina is identical to much of that from the lower levels at the Port Moresby Motupore site and radiocarbon dates are in close agreement (Jim Allen, pers. comm.). Allen considers that the later and descendant occupants of Motupore are directly ancestral to the ethnographic Motu.

Most of the stone recovered from the Uro'urina site is a high grade quartz, though there is the occasional chert artifact. Few of the artifacts were secondarily worked.

Yule Island had previously been settled by a pottery using people whose occupation spanned nearly 1000 years (Vanderwal, 1973), who usually inhabited coastal hill localities, and who over time had made themselves very much at home in their environment. Either locally or through trade they acquired a very high grade chert for making their tools (Vanderwal, 1973). But the coastal lowland dwellers who appeared at Uro'urina used pottery completely foreign in style and relied on an inferior stone for their tools—they were newcomers to the area. Innovations they introduced include the use of dog for food (Vanderwal, 1973) and a bipolar flaking technique.

White's observation of Duna (Lake Kopiago) flaking behaviour indicated that archaeologically there are three classes of artifacts associated with bipolar flaking: the core, waste flakes and unmodified but utilised flakes. Almost all the stone at Uro'urina is quartz. As it has been noted that the bipolar flaking technique is very useful in working quartz (see White, 1968:664 and Lampert, 1971:44) we have a good opportunity to test White's hypothesis (that 'fabricators' are in fact the end product in manufacturing flakes for use) by analysing the bipolar artifacts and the utilised quartz flakes that may have been derived from bipolar flaking at Uro'urina. In the analysis that follows it was reasoned that if flakes are being struck from a core by the bipolar method and if the purpose was to use suitable flakes so struck off, then particularly the mean length and possibly the mean width of the cores should be less than the same dimensions on the utilised flakes. Thus, it might be envisaged that as the core decreased in size with each successive attempt to make new flakes, the size of the flakes would similarly decrease but would normally range longer than the parent cores (see Dickson, this volume). Furthermore, the size of the *cores* would probably approach a normal distribution as a function of size below which suitable flakes cannot be obtained. Similarly the size of *utilised flakes* would probably be normally distributed as a function of selection for best size. Thus conceptualised, it was felt that a metrical comparison of these two kinds of artifacts would be useful by testing the distribution with the *t* statistic to evaluate the hypothesis in question.

From a total of 112 utilised flakes, 70 quartz ones were measured. All 40 of the complete bipolar artifacts were included in the analysis. The mean values for these measurements are seen in Table 1. In Table 2 it will be seen that in length the two artifact classes are significantly different with 99 % confidence. In breadth, however, the difference is not statistically significant. If we accept the model proposed above, that the length of flakes is expected to normally range longer than the bipolar core, then these results are broadly consistent with those expected in terms of White's hypothesis.

Table 1   Mean measurements on various artifact classes

		No.	Length	Breadth	Breadth/Length
(1)	Utilised quartz flakes	70	4·14 ± 1·26	2·87 ± 0·79	0·71 ± 0·11
(2)	Bipolar artifacts	40	3·39 ± 0·69	2·55 ± 0·61	0·76 ± 0·13
(3)	Sample utilised quartz flakes	18	3·85 ± 0·77	2·92 ± 0·59	0·76 ± 0·10
(4)	Chert utilised flakes	10	2·46 ± 0·57	1·72 ± 0·44	0·71 ± 0·14
(5)	Oposisi site chert sample	30	2·84 ± 0·54	1·82 ± 0·78	0·65 ± 0·16

White's data (White, 1968 : 663), however, indicates that the Uro'urina bipolar artifacts are considerably larger than those from Lake Kopiago. I thought at first the extraction technique may have accounted for the increased size range. A half inch screen was used on all but one of six 1 m² units at Uro'urina because the shell and cultural debris was too thick to permit economical use of a quarter inch screen. However, screen size was apparently not responsible for the larger Uro'urina bipolar artifacts; the narrowest two are 1.6 cm and next largest is 2.0 cm, well above the screen size (1.27 cm with a diagonal of 1.78 cm). There is additional evidence. Artifacts recovered from the quarter inch screened unit consisted of 69 waste flakes, 18 utilised flakes and 2 bipolar artifacts (included in the above sample). Comparison of the distribution (Table 1) between the two utilised flake samples shows that although those recovered from the quarter inch screen are slightly smaller, in length the two samples are statistically not significantly different. Table 2 furthermore shows that we can be 95% confident that a difference exists between the smaller sample of utilised flakes and the bipolar artifacts.

Table 2   t test significance levels between various artifact classes (Table 1)

	1	2	3	4	5	
1	X	·01	—	·01	·01	
2	—	X	—	·01	·01	
3	·01	·01	X	·01	·01	Length
4	·01	·01	·01	X	—	
5	·01	·01	·01	—	X	

Only a few utilised chert flakes were recovered, and no chert bipolar artifacts. The chert flakes are consistently smaller than those in quartz (Table 1), different at 99% confidence in all comparisons (Table 2). Two reasons might be suggested for the observed differences: (1) that chert was valuable enough to flake into the smallest possible usable pieces; and (2) that chert is naturally capable of finer flaking. Having seen and handled quantities of both chert and quartz artifacts, I suspected that natural flaking properties might be of greater significance. In devising suitable tests, I compared the Uro'urina quartz and chert flakes with a population of utilised flakes made by the people who lived at the hilltop site of Oposisi, who used only chert and who preceded the Uro'urina occupation on Yule Island by some 200 or 300 years (Vanderwal, 1973). Compared with all classes of Uro'urina quartz artifacts, the Oposisi chert sample differed significantly with a confidence of 99%. This difference is perhaps an indication of the natural flaking

properties of the stones, and almost certainly reflects the use requirements of size of quartz artifacts compared with those of chert. However when a comparison was made between the Oposisi and Uro'urina chert samples, it was found that in both length and breadth the two samples were found to be statistically indistinguishable from one another. The tests used, then, provide a clear demonstration that there are differences in the populations of chert and quartz artifacts, and it is suggested that these differences are due to the flaking characteristics of the two stones. The marginally shorter length of the Uro'urina chert might indicate scarcity.

It has thus far been suggested that the Uro'urina bipolar artifacts were manufactured in much the same way as those observed by White at Lake Kopiago, though the Uro'urina sample is considerably longer. It was then demonstrated that no known collection factor was responsible for the difference. Statistical comparison of chert and quartz flakes revealed a significant difference in their respective sizes, and it was therefore suggested that perhaps the size difference noted between our two bipolar samples is due to the flaking characteristics of the stone involved. These two samples, then, represent two extremes, one of which is made solely in chert, the other in quartz. They therefore provide good control points for further analysis.

From his observations amongst the Duna and a closely woven argument showing the lack of correlation between 'fabricators' and that which might have been fabricated, White (1968:664) has suggested that the Australian bipolar artifacts were, as at Lake Kopiago, scalar cores. In an attempt to review the application of a 'scalar core' hypothesis to Australian bipolar artifacts, I have here included for comparative study measurements made on bipolar artifacts from the New South Wales sites of Capertee 3, Bobadeen and Gymea Bay which White (1968:662) used in his analysis, and those from other sites reported by Lampert (1971), McBryde (n.d.), Flood (1973) and Wright (1970). The means and standard deviations for the samples are shown in Table 3, and significance levels for the t statistic are presented in Table 4. The following statements are tested: (1) there is no similarity between the Lake Kopiago and Uro'urina samples; (2) there is no similarity between the Australian samples on the one hand, and New Guinea samples on the other; and (3) there are no differences between populations in the Australian sample.

Of the three attributes used in the analysis (see Tables 3 and 4), I consider length to be the most diagnostic because, firstly, bipolar artifacts typically are bruised on those opposing ends which are furthest apart (White, 1968:662; Flood, 1973; Dickson, this volume), and secondly, from a purely practical point of view it would seem the maker would allow himself the

Table 3   Metrical data on Australian and New Guinean bipolar artifacts

	Site	No.	Length	Breadth	Breadth/ Length	Quartz %	Source
1	Yankee Hat	30	$1 \cdot 8 \pm 0 \cdot 3$	$1 \cdot 4 \pm 0 \cdot 4$	—	100	Flood 1973
2	Sassafras I	53	$1 \cdot 8 \pm 0 \cdot 5$	$1 \cdot 2 \pm 0 \cdot 3$	—	100	Flood 1973
3	Tidbinbilla	30	$1 \cdot 9 \pm 0 \cdot 5$	$1 \cdot 5 \pm 0 \cdot 4$	—	100	Flood 1973
4	Chambigne	24	$1 \cdot 9 \pm 0 \cdot 6$	$1 \cdot 8 \pm 0 \cdot 4$	—	?	McBryde n.d.
5	Seelands Upper	40	$2 \cdot 0 \pm 0 \cdot 5$	$1 \cdot 9 \pm 0 \cdot 4$	—	?	McBryde n.d.
6	Bobadeen	32	$2 \cdot 0 \pm 0 \cdot 5$	$1 \cdot 6 \pm 0 \cdot 5$	$0 \cdot 8 \pm 0 \cdot 3$	?	White 1968
7	Gymea Bay	42	$2 \cdot 0 \pm 0 \cdot 6$	$1 \cdot 8 \pm 0 \cdot 6$	$0 \cdot 9 \pm 0 \cdot 1$	<50	White 1968
8	Currarong	37	$2 \cdot 1 \pm 0 \cdot 8$	$1 \cdot 9 \pm 0 \cdot 7$	$0 \cdot 9 \pm 0 \cdot 2$	37	Lampert 1971
9	Seelands IIIA	12	$2 \cdot 1 \pm 0 \cdot 8$	$2 \cdot 1 \pm 0 \cdot 8$	—	?	McBryde n.d.
10	Wombah II	13	$2 \cdot 2 \pm 0 \cdot 4$	$2 \cdot 3 \pm 0 \cdot 4$	—	?	McBryde n.d.
11	Lapstone Creek	118	$2 \cdot 3 \pm 0 \cdot 6$	—	—	44	Wright 1970
12	Bendemeer I	12	$2 \cdot 5 \pm 0 \cdot 9$	$2 \cdot 3 \pm 0 \cdot 9$	—	?	McBryde n.d.
13	Green Gully	13	$2 \cdot 5 \pm 0 \cdot 7$	—	—	54	Wright 1970
14	Capertee 3	28	$2 \cdot 5 \pm 0 \cdot 6$	$2 \cdot 1 \pm 0 \cdot 8$	$0 \cdot 8 \pm 0 \cdot 1$	48	White 1968
15	Lake Kopiago	43	$2 \cdot 9 \pm 0 \cdot 3$	$2 \cdot 8 \pm 0 \cdot 7$	$1 \cdot 0 \pm 0 \cdot 2$	0	White 1968
16	Uro'urina	40	$3 \cdot 4 \pm 0 \cdot 7$	$2 \cdot 6 \pm 0 \cdot 6$	$0 \cdot 8 \pm 0 \cdot 1$	100	Vanderwal 1973

greater margin for his fingers between anvil and hammer. If length is accepted to be the most important attribute, examination of the Table 4 matrices will reveal that breadth reflects population differences in much less detail than length. Due to the small number of samples for which a breadth/length ratio could be statistically calculated, the value of that index for analyses such as this could not be determined. The matrix in which we are most interested, that of length, demonstrates in the terms of our hypotheses that while the two New Guinea samples are dissimilar from the Australian population, there is likewise no similarity between Lake Kopiago and Uro'-urina. While there are obvious differences between the smallest and largest artifacts in the Australian sample, there is a continuum of similarity when viewed as a whole.

As noted above, I consider the differences within the New Guinea samples to be largely a function of raw material. Accordingly, those Australian samples with larger quantities of quartz bipolar artifacts might be thought to exhibit a longer size range due to the unpredictable nature of the quartz cleavage planes. Conversely the bipolar flaking of chert would theoretically allow the production of much smaller cores because of greater assurance that usable flakes could be manufactured from a progressively smaller core. This, however, does not appear to be the case. Table 3 shows that the three sites in the sample with 100% quartz bipolar artifacts contain the smallest of such artifacts. Other sites in the Australian sample contain variable percentages of quartz artifacts. The Lake Kopiago sample is made entirely in a chalcedonous stone, is larger than any of the Australian bipolar artifacts populations and yet is smaller than the quartz artifacts from Uro'urina. So, it is only in two New Guinea samples where smaller bipolar cores appear to be derived from the more tractable stone.

The resolution of these differences probably lies in cultural factors. The only ethnographic example we have of bipolar flaking is from Lake Kopiago where the derived flakes were unretouched and sometimes mounted in a 'pitpit' handle (White, 1968:661). The range of usable artifacts struck from a bipolar core by a Duna speaker who attended this symposium

(see White and Modjeska, this volume), did not appear to be any different than that of the Uro'urina utilised flakes. Though this is little more than an impression, I would think that the Uro'urina and Lake Kopiago stone technologies were equally sophisticated, i.e., unretouched flakes were used to perform a variety of tasks. The only significant difference is the raw material and this may well be a function of availability rather than of preference.

One is tempted to make much the same statements about the Australian samples for, like the New Guinea stone technology that of Australia is impoverished where 'fabricators' are present (White, 1968: 662). Yet the normal range of such artifacts is significantly smaller than the New Guinea ones which suggests a different function for the derived flakes, perhaps one that requires smaller flakes. Lampert (1971:46) notes that such flakes, usually in quartz, were used to form rows of barbs on death spears, an interpretation supported by Flood (1973). If small quartz flakes are the most desirable, this might explain the smaller sizes of quartz cores and the continuum of similarity presented by the statistical analysis where greater or lesser infusions of chert artifacts are present. The people making these objects, however, might be expected to husband their energies toward economy of effort, so that even though the ultimate aim of bipolar flaking might have been the production of death spear barbs, other larger flakes almost certainly would have been used differently. Lampert (1971) and Flood (1973) note the presence of use-polished flakes and even cores. Dickson (this volume) has furthermore noted by experiment that stone can be pecked (as in axes and adzes prior to grinding), using it as the anvil in the incidental manufacture of bipolar artifacts. Hence, some of these artifacts might equally have been fabricators. This kind of pursuit, however, would certainly have been fairly rare. I, too, vote for death spear barbs or some similar object.

White's original hypothesis, that 'fabricators' are the core component of a bipolar flaking technique, has been supported by the analysis of quartz artifacts from the Uro'urina site. Though the raw material differed, it was thought that the stone technologies represented by the Lake Kopiago and by the Uro'urina samples were quite similar. Comparison with

Table 4 t test significance levels for samples listed in Table 3

	1	2	3	4	5	6	7	8	9	10	11	12	13	14	15	16
1	X	—	—	—	—	—	—	—	—	·05	·01	·01	·01	·01	·01	·01
2	—	X	—	—	—	—	—	—	—	—	·01	·01	·01	·01	·01	·01
3	—	·05	X	—	—	—	—	—	—	—	·05	·05	·05	·01	·01	·01
4	·05	·01	—	X	—	—	—	—	—	—	·05	·05	·05	·01	·01	·01
5	·01	·01	·05	—	X	—	—	—	—	—	·05	—	·05	·01	·01	·01
6	—	·01	—	—	—	X	—	—	—	—	·05	—	·05	·05	·01	·01
7	·05	·01	—	—	—	—	X	—	—	—	·05	—	·05	·01	·01	·01
8	·01	·01	·05	—	—	—	—	X	—	—	—	—	—	—	·01	·01
9	·01	·01	—	—	—	—	—	—	X	—	—	—	—	—	·01	·01
10	·01	·01	·05	·05	—	·01	·05	—	—	X	—	—	—	—	·01	·01
11	0	0	0	0	0	0	0	0	0	0	X	—	—	—	·01	·01
12	·01	·01	—	·05	—	·05	—	—	—	—	0	X	—	—	—	·01
13	0	0	0	0	0	0	0	0	0	0	0	0	X	—	·05	·01
14	·01	·01	—	—	—	·05	—	—	—	—	0	—	0	X	·05	·01
15	·01	·01	·01	·01	·01	·01	·01	·01	·01	—	0	—	0	·01	X	·01
16	·01	·01	·01	·01	·01	·01	·01	·01	·01	—	0	—	0	·05	—	X

several Australian samples (whose internal differences formed a continuum thought to be a function of greater or lesser infusions by cherty bipolar artifacts) suggested that there was little similarity in the function of the derived flakes. The most plausible interpretation seems to be that such flakes in New Guinea were multipurpose tools but that the need for small flakes suitable for (death) spear barbs in Australia resulted in a smaller core.

While the death knell for 'fabricator' was tolled several years ago, there is still the question of terminology. White (1968) introduced the term 'scalar core', and this was supported by Lampert (1971). Flood (1973) has subsequently suggested that 'scaled pieces' is a more meaningful term, as among other reasons it is a direct translation of the French term *pièces ecaillées* used in European prehistory to identify such objects. I personally have no stake in the issue, but would argue that we do not lose sight of the fact that they are all nothing more than 'bipolar artifacts'.

Acknowledgements My research on Yule Island was supported by the Australian National University while I was a research scholar in the Department of Prehistory, Institute of Advanced Studies.

References

Flood, J., 1973. *Investigations towards a prehistory of the south-eastern highlands of Australia*. Unpublished Ph.D. thesis, Australian National University, Canberra.

Lampert, R.J., 1971. *Burril Lake and Currarong*. Terra Australis, No 1. Canberra: The Australian National University.

McBryde, I. (n.d.) Archaeological investigations of a prehistoric midden site at Wombah, Lower Clarence River, New South Wales. Ms. with author, Australian National University, Canberra.

McCarthy, F.D., E. Brammel and H.V.V. Noone, 1946. *The stone implements of Australia*. Memoir of the Australian Museum, 9. Sydney: Australian Museum.

Vanderwal, R.L., 1973. *Prehistoric studies in Central Coastal Papua*. Unpublished Ph.D. thesis, Australian National University, Canberra.

White, J.P., 1968. Fabricators, Outils ecailles or scalar cores? *Mankind*, 6:658-66.

Wright, R.V.S., 1970. Flaked stone material from GGW-1. In the Green Gully Burial. *National Museum of Victoria Memoir*, 30:79-92.

The persistence of upper Palaeolithic tool-kits into the early south-east Spanish Neolithic

MICHAEL WALKER

Neolithic Attributes...?

Aceramic Neolithic assemblages from south-west Asia testify to societies practising agricultural cultivation at a time before they had ceramic technology. European assemblages with pottery, polished stone tools, and 'Neolithic' attributes are presumed to have acquired them by diffusion, and by extension are assumed to have practised agricultural cultivation and animal husbandry. Discovery of a wheat grain or grape pip at a site may be inflated into presumptive evidence that cultivation was the predominant economic activity. Some archaeologists hold that pottery alone is sufficient testimony to cultivation, on the ground that pots may be used for soaking or boiling grain—in which case, one wonders how aceramic Neolithic cultivators coped! Attention has recently been drawn to the need for looking carefully at the assumptions underlying archaeological deductions about the nature of man-animal and man-plant relationships from excavated materials (Higgs and Jarman, 1972; H. N. Jarman, 1972; Jarman and Wilkinson, 1972; M. R. Jarman, 1972).

The presumption of a single regional source for agricultural and ceramic technologies is untenable in the light of discoveries in eastern Asia and Meso-America. It is possible that in Neolithic south-west Asia and Europe there was repeated adoption and abandonment of domestication of particular animals and cultivation of particular plants at the onset of the Neolithic. Nor does it seem impossible that in late Palaeolithic times at least, there may have been selectivity in the choice of man-animal and man-plant relationships engaged in by human populations occupying perhaps even very similar habitats. In Europe the Neolithic seems to differ from that of south-west Asia in the greater frequency of cattle and pig (Murray, 1970). Hunting and even sporadic domestication of red deer may have occurred (M. R. Jarman, 1972). The Spanish Levantine rock paintings depict man-animal activities involving caprines, bovines, equines and cervines in such proximity with anthropomorphs as to suggest docility if not domestication (Walker, 1971). The proximity of men and mammals in the Saharan Tassili paintings is open to a similar interpretation. It has been proposed that Egyptian paintings of men and wild animals may indicate taming of local species (Clark, 1971) rather than hunting, although this perhaps does not imply that those species were domesticated and used for breeding. Hunting is not confined to Palaeolithic subsistence economies—there were wall-paintings of hunting scenes at Çatal Hüyük—and, of course, polished/ground stone tools are not confined to agricultural societies (thus, Australian ground edge axes). In the upper Palaeolithic of Europe there may have been seasonal movements reflecting

man-animal interdependencies (Davidson, 1972). When considering Neolithic sites, any or all of the following possibilities must be borne in mind; hunting, transhumance, pastoralism, cereal cultivation, and horticulture, along with the possibility that any or all may have been practised at permanently occupied settlements or seasonally or intermittently occupied sites, by one or both sexes. It is not wholly implausible (even if a nomadic 'symbiosis' between men and animal herds was practised, by which men followed docile large mammals ensuring selective slaughter and loosely guiding the herds to pastures and water) that the women, children, aged and infirm might have lived at a permanent base, especially if physiographical barriers effectively restricted their menfolk's wanderings to a range of, say, 100 km across, and even before domestication and animal husbandry were practised. Moreover, just as cultivation of plants may have been practised by aceramic societies, so ceramic-using groups may have engaged in mainly non-cultivating subsistence economic activities. Ethnographic parallels might be cited for that, as well as for yet more complex relations between cultivators and pastoralists living in geographical contiguity while sharing some elements of material culture.

With regard to short occupations, it may be remarked that in some regions (eg. south-east Spain) there may be two grain harvests a year, and animal fodder may mature in as little as three weeks. Impermanence of prehistoric settlements need not exclude agriculture therefore. On the other hand, pottery need imply neither cultivation nor permanency. A vessel may be made in a day. It may be stored when a dwelling is left, perhaps for re-use on a later visit as is common to-day in the summer mountain huts of shepherds. Spouted pots are found in Mediterranean, north African, and south-west Asian lands (including Neolithic south-east Spain, eg. the caves of Nerja, Hoyo de la Mina, l'Or), and to-day in south-east Spain farm-hands and shepherds carry unglazed, earthenware, spouted *botijos* when working outdoors. Wine is not carried in these usually, but in glazed, glass or leather vessels. The *botijo* keeps drinking water cooler than those, however, because solar heat is spent evaporating water which has permeated the unglazed fabric and thus does not heat up the water within. This was very likely recognised in antiquity, and may have accelerated ceramic technology in hot climates quite apart from the use of pots for grain preparation.

These heretical thoughts serve as a critical background to material to be presented which demonstrates that in south-east Spain later upper Palaeolithic man-animal activities predominated at the earliest stage of ceramic utilisation, when elements of the stone tool-kit underwent but trivial change.

South-east Spanish Neolithic

The choice of this part of Spain was determined partly by family considerations, partly by my interest in the mechanisms whereby the local Neolithic developed into metallurgical cultures of varying facies in the Spanish Levante and Andalusia (Maps k, l, m, o, p), where successive maritime influences had been invoked to account for them (Blance, 1960 and 1971). Between the Levante and Andalusia lie the basins of the rivers Segura and Vinalopó (Maps a, b, c), and a field survey of the antiquities of those basins seemed appropriate in order to throw light on regularities and discontinuities of spatial and temporal transformations of artifact types, assemblage compositions, and cultural complexes. My conclusions on the developments of the Neolithic and Copper Ages (Walker, 1973a) will be published elsewhere. However, it became clear that Neolithic origins and their relation to later upper Palaeolithic ('Mesolithic' or 'Epipalaeolithic' according to other writers) cultural complexes in south-east Spain suggested continuity of man-animal economic subsistence activities (Walker, 1971, 1972, 1973a) rather than Neolithic immigration by settled cultivators. Spanish Levantine naturalistic rock paintings show elements of material culture often termed 'Neolithic' (eg. barbed and tanged arrowpoints at Alpera and other sites). It is possible that such artifacts represent the tool-kits of hunters and gatherers, or, at least, large mammal-dependent activities, rather than cultivators engaged in animal husbandry. Other representations suggest pre-Neolithic artifacts (Walker, 1971, 1973a). The paintings show an inland, montane/rolling uplands distribution (Map h) reflecting the distribution of Palaeolithic (Map j) and pre-ceramic to ceramic transitional (Map i) sites. The coastal plains and rich earth of the lower valley systems have a much lower incidence of occupation. However, in fairness it must be pointed out that the alluvial *huertas*, sustaining a market garden economy today, were not formed until upland erosion commenced in Neolithic times, and were not available for settlement until perhaps 1000 BC or even later, and that the 10 m thick alluvial deposits of the lower reaches of the valleys may have obliterated earlier settlements, not to mention the removal by erosion of upland sites (Walker and Cuenca, in press and in preparation).

Division of peninsular Neolithic stone tools into 'Hispano-Mauritanian' (geometric, microlithic) and 'Ibero-Saharan' (bifacial arrowpoints), believed to follow one another chronologically both north and south of the Straits of Gibraltar, owes to Martínez Santa-Olalla (Martínez, 1946), but it is neither helpful nor accurate. Bifacial arrowpoints are uncommon in Tunisia and eastern Algeria, where the best embarkation points occur for crossings to Spain under sail (Jáuregui, 1949); and, although it is sometimes said that in Iberia they are commonest in the south-west, they are also present in the south-east. In south-east Spain it has been said that they are late elements at Neolithic cave sites (Plá, 1958). They are also widespread in Copper Age collective burials in caves and chambered tombs. However, at the Neolithic site of Coveta de l'Or (Alicante) they were found stratified deeply, and a case can be made for attributing them tentatively even to those earliest ceramic-using communities in the south-east engaged in activities with large mammalian fauna (*vide supra*). Jordá (1953) proposed two strands in the Levantine Neolithic: (a) backed bladelets with cardial impressed pottery derived from a so-called Levantine Epigravettian IIIA (*cp.* Jordá, 1954) of the later upper Palaeolithic, and (b) geometric microliths with plain pottery derived from a so-called Epigravettian IIIB of geometric facies. The Valencian Cueva de les Mallaetes was placed in the first, and the Cueva de la Cocina in the second. It is instructive to consider why this dual origin was advanced. An early element in the peninsular Neolithic, the so-called Cave Cultures, had been proposed much earlier by Bosch Gimpera (1932), and this was contrasted against traditions believed to have north African affinities supposedly present in regions near the Iberian littoral. At first sceptical of that, Martínez Santa-Olalla later put forward two successive waves of Neolithic colonisation from north Africa, the 'Hispano-Mauritanian' (eg. El Gárcel) and 'Ibero-Saharan', but later modified his stance by accepting the earlier presence in the peninsula of an indigenous, 'microlithicising' Neolithic. However, it was soon realised that regional ceramic variation within the peninsula might complicate the two-wave hypothesis (San Valero, 1948, 1950), and the discovery of Levantine geometric cave assemblages (Cocina and Llatas: Pericot, 1946; Jordá and Alcácer, 1949) suggested to Jordá that there were two, rather than just one, indigenous cultural strands. It is easy to knock holes in his proposal, but it is important to remember that whereas previous workers had considered the backed bladelet and geometric elements to be diachronic, Jordá regarded them as contemporaneous and indigenous. To some extent my own views are but an extension of Jordá's, with the difference that I would like to think that the tool-kit variations represent functional differences rather than exclusive societal traditions.

The arguments for two separate cultural strands in the later upper Palaeolithic of south-east Spain (manifested as backed bladelet and geometric assemblages respectively (Jordá, 1954)) are not strong. The triangles of the uppermost level at the Cueva de El Parpalló (Pericot, 1942) could be cited, but other elements of the assemblage (eg. shouldered points, awls, and burins) are found in post-Magdalenian complexes in France and Germany, and even backed bladelets may be found sporadically in such contexts. Probably closer to those, however, is layer 4 at the Málaga cave of Hoyo de la Mina (Such, 1920) where parrot-beak burins suggest an off-shoot of Magdalenian traditions. Magdalenian and backed bladelet ('Epigravettian') tools were found together at the Valencian Cueva de les Mallaetes (Jordá, 1954; Fletcher, 1956a, 1956b). As at other sites in eastern Spain, there were found painted and engraved stone plaques from the pre-ceramic layers at Mallaetes (*c.p.* Cueva de El Parpalló throughout the upper Palaeolithic succession; Balma de Sant Gregorí—Vilaseca, 1934; Cueva del Filador—Vilaseca, 1949; and Cueva de la Cocina). Filador demonstrates the impracticality of Jordá's scheme for classifying Epigravettian IIIA and IIIB tool assemblages. A rigorous application of the classification would demand that the lowest layer be IIIA, the next one up IIIB, and the succeeding levels IIIA once again. Maybe that is why Jordá discretely avoided making reference to the site in the article in which the scheme was put forward (Jordá, 1954).

Fortunately, there is no doubt that there are several south-east Spanish cave sites where there is a succession of levels from later upper Palaeolithic through to ceramic-using stages. The Cueva de les Mallaetes and Hoyo de la Mina are two of these. Another is the Valencian Covacha de Llatas, characterised by various kinds of geometric flint tools from its two lower pre-ceramic and its upper ceramic layers. As well as triangles and crescents, there also were retouched flint blades and backed blades. The pottery included incised and relief-

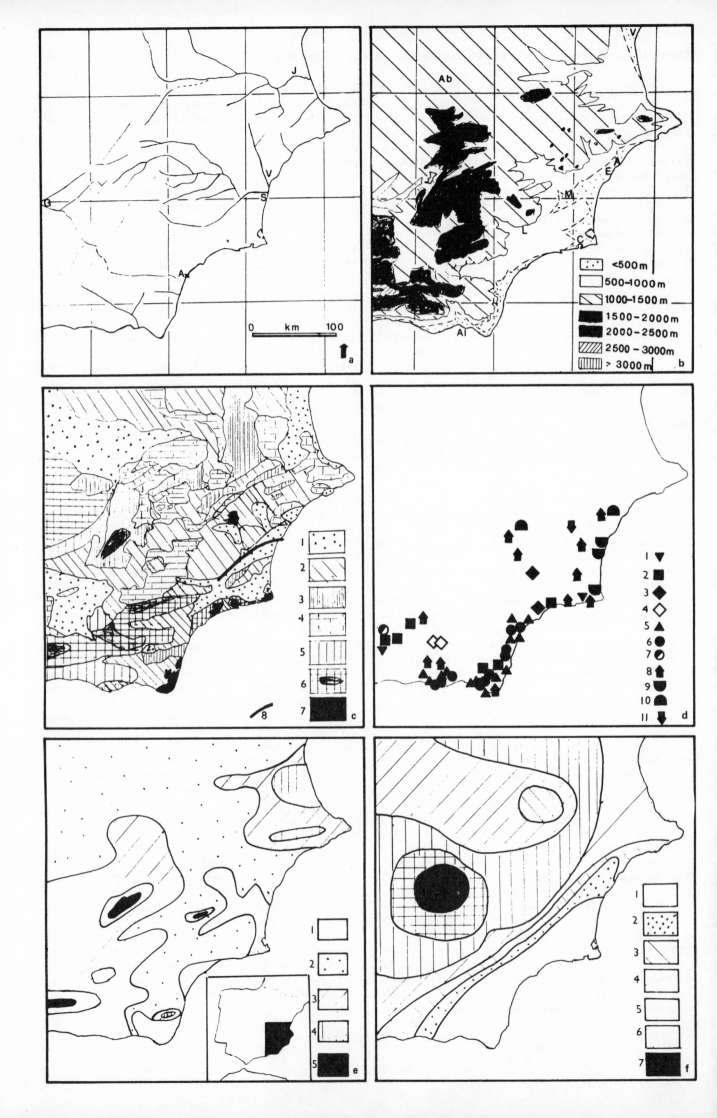

ornamented wares. Out of 5351 flint items, 400 (7%) were classifiable forms (Jordá and Alcácer, 1949). The Valencian Cueva de la Cocina (Pericot, 1946) is often cited in the context of the European 'Mesolithic' (thus Clark, 1958), and a re-assessment of the assemblage has been undertaken recently (Fortea, 1971) which subdivides it into two pre-ceramic and two ceramic-using phases. Flint triangles occur at all levels, although it should not be overlooked that small quantities of backed bladelets are also present throughout. Fortea regards the assemblage as more in the tradition of backed bladelet industries than of geometric ones. The earliest ceramic level contained a cardial impressed sherd, and the ceramic stages also provided a grinding stone and polished stone axe. The uppermost pre-ceramic layer contained engraved and painted plaques, as well as red ochre, and Pericot (1946 : 54) mentioned traces of paintings in red on the south wall of the cave, including an animal representation. It has been suggested that the Valencian geometric assemblages might be contemporary with those of Portuguese middens (Clark, 1958), a view with which I concur (Walker, 1971, 1972, 1973a). However, it is important to bear in mind that even at the Portuguese middens, backed bladelets were present in all layers at Moita do Sebastião (Roche, 1960). Radiocarbon dates for the Portuguese middens (Libby half-life) are as follows:

Pre-ceramic phases
Sa-16 Moita do Sebastião 7350±350 BP
(base of midden) (Delibrias *et al.*, 1964)
Sa-195 Cabeço da Amoriera 7030±350 BP (*ibid.*)
(lower layer)
Sa-197 Cabeço da Amoriera 6430±300 BP (*ibid.*)
(lower layer)

Ceramic phases
Sa-194 Cabeço da Amoreira 6050±300 BP (*ibid.*)
(upper layer)
Sa-196 Cabeço da Amoreira 5150±300 BP
(upper layer) (Delibrias *et al.*, 1965)

Those may be compared with Breton geometric sites such as Hoëdic dated by Gif-227 to 6575±300 BP (Delibrias *et al.*, 1966), as well as with Montclus (Gard) and Châteauneuf-les-Martigues (Bouches-du-Rhône) which span the period 7800–6000 BP, during which pottery makes its appearance in the succession (Escalon de Fonton, 1970), possibly even as early as 7520 BP at Châteauneuf-les-Martigues in layers F6 and F5, although the more recent determinations published (Evin *et al.*, 1973) suggest a rather later date (Ly-446 6430 BP, Ly-623 6070 BP, Ly-622 5910 BP) for pottery at that site. The earlier date may not be unthinkable, however, in the light of the radiocarbon date to be presented below from south-east Spain, and in the light of a date of 7555 BP from a ceramic-using stage at the Grotta della Madonna in Italy (Guilane, 1970). Only one south-east Spanish site, Coveta de l'Or (Alicante), has been dated hitherto by radiocarbon. The dates are (KN-51) 6510±160 BP and (H-1754/1208) 5265±75 BP (Schwabedissen and Freundlich, 1966; Schubart, 1965; Schubart and Pascual, 1966). At Coveta de l'Or there was no pre-ceramic horizon deep to the Neolithic. Hopf and Schubart have published cereal grains from the cave (Hopf and Schubart, 1965; Hopf, 1966) where *Triticum monococcum*, *Triticum dicoccum*, *Triticum aestivum*, and *Hordeum vulgare* were identified, and the suggestions proffered that either the cereals were imports from south-west Asia, or else that they were a product of local, unknowable palaeo-edaphic conditions. The grain occurs with cardial impressed pottery. Higher up in the sequence, plain wares predominate. Barbed and tanged bifacial flint arrowpoints and a sherd incised with two deer representations were found during excavation. The lowest deposits, however, were characterised by trapeze points, and —quite unlike El Gárcel—crescentic microlithic implements.

A comparison has been offered (Fortea, 1971) between the geometric flint types at the Cueva de la Cocina and those of the Portuguese middens. Phase I at Cocina, in particular, has been likened to the Moita do Sebastião assemblage by Fortea, whereas the Cocina II (also pre-ceramic) assemblage seems closer to that from Cabeço da Amoreira in terms of proportions of artifact types represented. Those observations strengthen the argument for close contemporaneity and dating of Cocina and the middens to between 7000–6000 BP in 'radiocarbon years'. Another cave which, like Cocina and Llatas, shows a transition from pre-ceramic to ceramic-using stages, is the Alicante Cueva del Lagrimal near Villena

---

Key to maps opposite

Map a   River systems
Az: Almanzora
G: Guadalquivir
J: Jucar
S: Segura
V: Vinalopo

Map b   Contours, cities
Ab: Albacete
A: Alicante
Al: Almeria
C: Cartagena
E: Elche
G: Granada
L: Lorca
M: Murcia
V: Valencia

Map c   Geology
1: alluvial spreads
2: Tertiary plateaux
3: Mesozoic folded ranges
4: Mesozoic limestone plateaux
5: Triassic folded relief
6: Metamorphic plateaux and (shaded) ranges
7: Volcanic cones
8: line of Guadalentin-Segura faulting
(acknowledgements: Cuenca, Fallot, Houston, Sole)

Map d   Inorganic resources
1: tin
2: copper
3: zinc
4: mercury
5: lead
6: silver
7: gold
8: iron
9: salt
10: fossil amber
11: 'jumellite'
(data from: Vila, Hernandez-Pacheco, Jimenez de Cisneros)

Map e   Rainfall (*after* Masachs)
1: below 300 mm p.a.
2: 301–500 mm p.a.
3: 501–800 mm p.a.
4: 801–1201 mm p.a.
5: above 1201 mm p.a.

Map f   Aridity (*after* Masachs)
1: very high temperatures, minimal rainfall (sub-desert)
2: high temperatures, low rainfall (very arid)
3: high temperatures, occasional rain (very arid)
4: hot, intermittent rain (arid)
5: warm, intermittent rain (some degree of aridity)
6: temperate, considerable precipitation (no aridity)
7: temperate. high rainfall (no aridity)

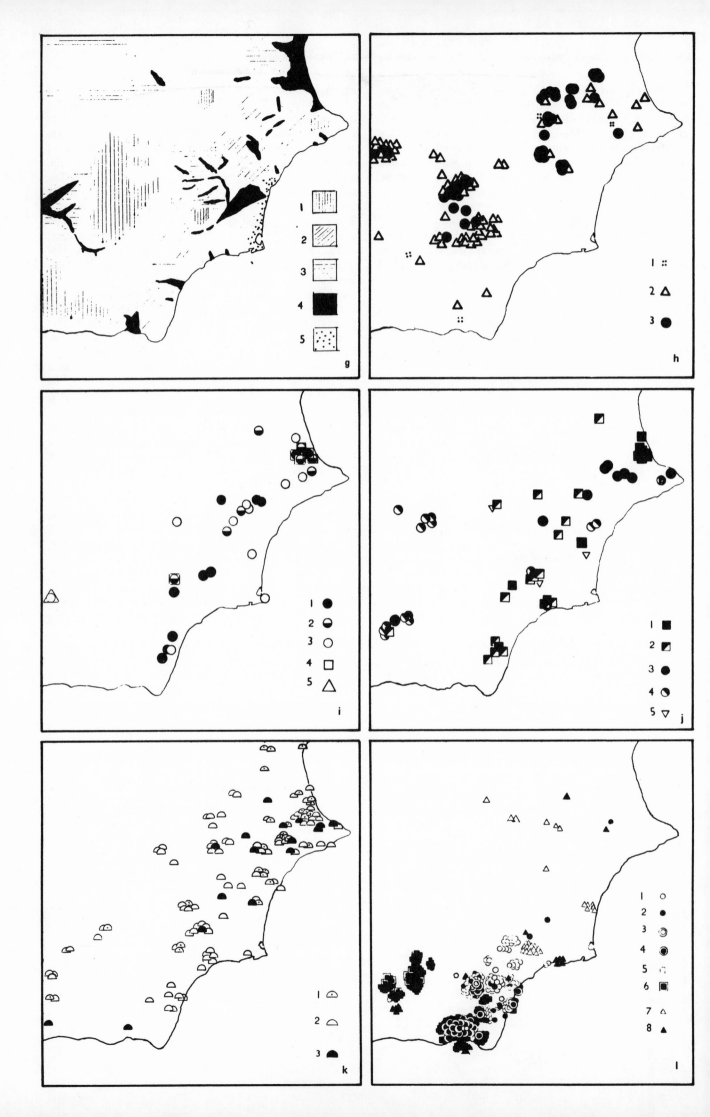

(Soler, 1968–69). Once again, the tool-kit shows no drastic changes between the respective stages. The lowest layer contained geometric and backed bladelet flint implements, though the geometric pieces are atypical. However, there are features of the assemblage which link it with other Neothermal Period sites in the south-east (Walker, 1973a). Next follows a ceramic layer in which geometric pieces are said to be more frequent, followed by a layer with still fewer backed bladelets, and containing bifacial flintwork, a polished stone axe, and copper implements. A transition from pre-ceramic to ceramic-using stages occurs, too, at the Cueva Ambrosio (Murcia) (Ripoll, 1960–61; Jiménez, 1947, 1962). Upper Palaeolithic material, including Solutrean, is separated by massive collapse from upper layers with 'Epipalaeolithic' flints. Extensive ceramic material comes from the upper levels and also from a second rock shelter nearby. Jiménez seems to suggest that, as at Hoyo de la Mina, there was a lower ceramic phase with a low incidence of pottery, followed by abundant sherds in the topmost levels. Some of the wares recall beaker pottery (*cp.* Savory, 1968) but the absence of metal at so large a site lends support to the opinion that it is wholly within the Neolithic. Mention may be made of the Alicante Cueva d'En Pardo shortly to be published by srta. Asquerina. There, Copper Age material, no doubt a funerary assemblage, lay above Neolithic strata with cardial impressed sherds and bifacial flint arrowpoints. Below those there was a sterile layer and then a backed bladelet assemblage at a deeper level. Other sites in the south-east are probably roughly contemporary with the 7000–6000 BP period also, *viz.* Cueva Pequeña and Cueva Grande near Villena (Alicante) (Soler,

1956, 1968–69), Cueva de la Palica near Antas (Almería) (Fortea, 1970), Cueva del Gato near Moratalla (Murcia) (Cuadrado Díaz, 1947), Cantos de la Visera near Yecla (Murcia) (Breuil and Burkitt, 1915), Cejo del Pantano (Murcia) (Martinez *et al.*, 1947,—but see Pericot, 1950 and Pericot and Cuadrado Ruiz, 1952, who believe it to be upper Palaeolithic), Los Mortolitos (Murcia) ('upper Palaeolithic'— Pericot and Cuadrado Ruiz, 1952), Cueva de la Fuente del Lentisco (Murcia) (material in Almería Provincial Museum, as for the other Totana sites, Cejo del Pantano and Mortolitos), Cañada de San Pedro near Zeneta (Murcia) (Fernández de Avilés, 1942, and also material in Almería Provincial Museum), El Moralico, near Vera (Almería) (material in Almería Provincial Museum), El Hacho (Almería) (material in Almería Provincial Museum), Doña Clotilde and Cocinilla del Obispo (Almagro, 1944, 1947) in the Sierra de Albarracín further north at the second site of which there was found a polished fibrolite axe.

Despite the evidence for a continuation from later upper Palaeolithic to Neolithic times, the Almerian site of El Gárcel near Antas (Siret and Siret, 1887; Siret, 1893; Gossé, 1941) has usually been cast in the role of the type-site of the earliest Spanish neolithic (eg. Savory, 1968). It was an agricultural settlement a few kilometres from the coast, now about +10 m above the bed of the Río de Antas on a fluvial terrace, but probably on the flood-plain of that river at the time it was founded. Underground silos were found, grain, and costrel shaped pottery said to be of north African affinity but also present at other Spanish sites such as the Cueva de Nerja in Málaga (Pellicer, 1962), from which a radiocarbon

---

Key to maps opposite

Map g   Vegetation zones
1 :   considerable stands of conifers and deciduous trees
2 :   uplands with *garrigue* landscape, scrub, and attempted vine-olive-esparto cultivation
3 :   uplands now or formerly capable of supporting cereals
4 :   *huerta* market garden crops: legumes, fruit, cereals, rice, etc.
5 :   saline soils, salt marshes, dunes

Map h   Rock paintings and markings
1 :   cup marks
2 :   schematic rock paintings of copper age
3 :   naturalistic rock paintings of later upper Palaeolithic to early ceramic-using times
Note that whereas the naturalistic art extends north in eastern Spain (Walker, 1971), the schematic paintings which overlap with it in the south-east largely are found further west in Andalusia, and by stylistic analogies with ceramic motifs can firmly be dated to the third-second millennia B.C., thereby suggesting a *terminus post quem* for the naturalistic paintings.

Map i   Later upper Palaeolithic/ceramic-using transition sites
1 :   pre-ceramic, later upper Palaeolithic sites
2 :   sites with pre-ceramic lower strata, ceramics in upper strata
3 :   sites with pottery of 'neolithic' attribution
4 :   upper Palaeolithic material present at a site with later assemblages
5 :   middle Palaeolithic material present at a site with later assemblages
(for details of sites, *see* Walker, 1973a)

Map j   Middle and upper Palaeolithic sites
1 :   securely attributed upper Palaeolithic sites
2 :   possibly upper Palaeolithic sites
3 :   securely attributed middle Palaeolithic sites
4 :   possibly middle Palaeolithic sites
5 :   possibly lower Palaeolithic find-spots
(for details, *see* Walker, 1973a)

Map k   Neolithic and Copper Age cave sites
1 :   caves with human remains
2 :   other caves with assemblages
3 :   'splendid' cave burial assemblages
(for details, *see* Walker, 1973a)

Map l   Burials under mounds
1 :   round graves
2 :   circular passage graves
3 :   'splendid' round grave assemblages
4 :   'splendid' circular passage grave assemblages
5 :   angular passage graves
6 :   'splendid' angular passage grave assemblages
7 :   other burials under mounds/cairns, e.g. cists, pithoi
8 :   burials under mounds/cairns of unknown type
(for details, *see* Walker, 1973a)

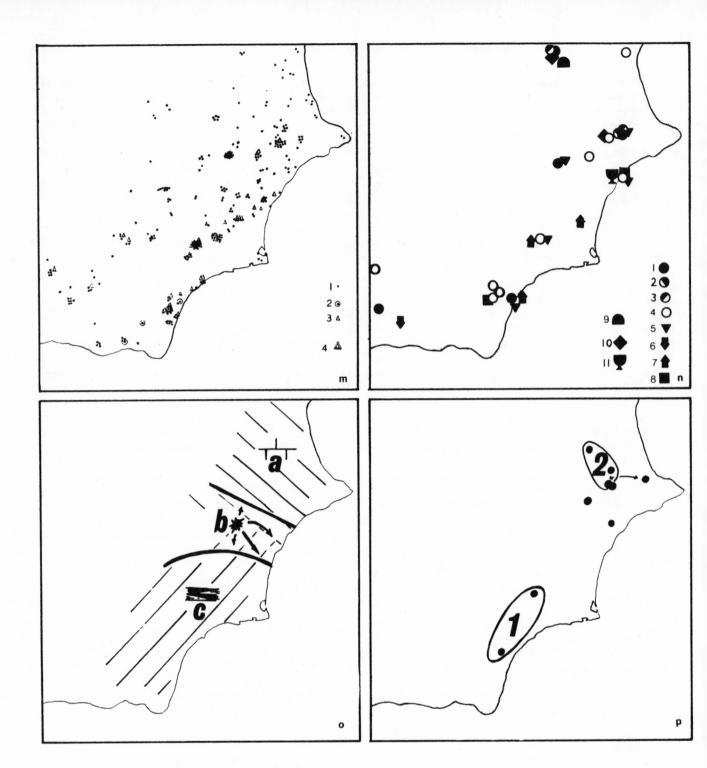

date of 5065±40 BP has been published (Pellicer and Hopf, 1970; Muñoz, 1970), and also from Coveta de l'Or (Llobregat, 1973). Copper slag and a violin idol from El Gárcel (Siret and Siret, 1887; Siret, 1893) suggest a date contemporary with the Aegean early Bronze Age, roughly 5500–5000 BP in 'radiocarbon' years. It is interesting to recall that a similar violin idol occurred at Hoyo de la Mina (Such, 1920). The evidence from Nerja, Hoyo de la Mina, and l'Or rather suggests that the Neolithic continued with no drastic changes until Chalcolithic times. The evidence from El Gárcel is totally lacking for any definitely Neolithic age; rather, the site is probably early Copper Age. The El Gárcel flint assemblage is of interest. Out of nearly 11 000 flint pieces (Gossé, 1941) almost 3000 were identifiable pieces, indicating a considerable efficiency in tool production, and a situation quite different from such early Neolithic sites as Llatas, Cocina, or (*vide*

infra) the Abrigo Grande. This is further circumstantial evidence in favour of separating El Gárcel from Neolithic assemblages. Polished stone implements and ochre were also found at El Gárcel. There was a high proportion of retouched blades. Unlike at the Neolithic sites these are large blades, not microlithic backed bladelets. Trapeze points were common, as at some of the Neolithic sites, and so, too, were curious transversely retouched blade fragments, reminiscent of the north African Capsian. However, the Capsian seems to have acquired Neolithic attributes very early, appearing about 7000 BP at the Haua Fteah in Cyrenaica (McBurney, 1967) and perhaps as early as 9000 BP in 'radiocarbon' years at Ai Naga in Algeria (Rahmouni *et al.*, 1970). Although El Gárcel rather seems to stand by itself in south-east Spanish prehistory, the following table shows that it is not really like the Capsian in respect of flint tool proportions:

Table 1   Percentage composition of assemblages from south-east Spain and north African sites: Selected stone tool types

Artifact	Cocina I + II	Abrigo Grande	Gárcel	El-Mekta	Sidi Mansour	Ain Khanga
Backed blade	0.0	2.8	28.2	2.6	0.3	2.0
Angle burin	0.6	0.0	3.3	6.4	1.5	4.0
Backed bladelet	2.6	56.4	4.5	25.7	21.0	28.0
Notched piece	19.0	9.9	4.1	23.7	6.0	3.5
Scalene triangle	10.0	0.0	{18.3}	4.8	6.5	15.0
Trapeze	21.0	0.0		4.8	16.5	3.0
Microburin	27.1	2.8	12.5	11.1	28.0	10.0

(Cocina data after Fortea, 1971 ; Gárcel data from Gossé, 1941 ; north African data from Balout, 1955)

Because of its importance in western Mediterranean prehistory, a few words are in order about the south-east Spanish Chalcolithic. In addition to authors mentioned earlier, intruders in south-east Spain have been postulated more recently, both for the Neolithic (Evans, 1958; Blance, 1960 and 1971) and also for the Chalcolithic (Blance, *loc. cit.*, 1961). The latter view has its opponents (eg. Renfrew, 1967), whilst other investigators, who also prefer to stress the divergence between peninsular Chalcolithic complexes and any particular regions where some artifactual parallels have been drawn in Egypt or south-west Asia, nevertheless prefer to keep an open mind (Savory, 1968 : 160). The statistical basis for Blance's justification of Neolithic invasions (Blance, 1960 and 1971) can be shown to be quite unsound (Walker, 1973a and forthcoming). The distinction between 'Almerian' and 'Millaran' complexes is regarded as illusory by Tarradell (1959), who sees no reason for not viewing all of the so-called Almerian Neolithic as Copper Age like the 'Millaran' itself.

Tarradell makes an exception for El Gárcel, calling it Neolithic. I can see no good reason for not including El Gárcel with the Chalcolithic; certainly the cross-dating with the early Aegean Bronze Age can be justified. Parallels suggesting contemporaneity between the Chalcolithic site of Terrera Ventura, near Tabernas (Almería), and late Linear Pottery-Gumelnita have been proposed (Topp, 1959; Topp and Arribas, 1965), and these also argue in favour of a fourth millennium chronology for the early south-east Spanish Copper Age. Artifacts from collective burials in south-east Spain (tombs and caves) occasionally have their parallels in south-west Asia and Egypt (Arribas, 1953; Savory, 1968; Walker, 1973a), often suggesting derivative, locally made items rather than imports brought by an invading cultural complex. Sporadic trading contacts suffice to account for their presence. Nor is there incontrovertible evidence for immigration by people of different physical type at any time (see Map p). A thriving fourth millennium early Copper Age

Key to maps opposite

Map m   Occupation sites of Neolithic, Copper and Bronze Ages
1 :   occupation site
2 :   large copper age settlement site
3 :   finds of 'Argaric' artifacts*
4 :   large 'Argaric' settlement site
* This category includes cist/pithos burials with 'Argaric' assemblages. since such burials are usually at open occupation sites.
(for details, *see* Walker, 1973a)

Map n   Plant cultigens from Neolithic, Copper and Bronze Age sites
1 :   *Triticum aestivum*
2 :   *Triticum dicoccum*
3 :   *Triticum monococcum*
4 :   'wheat' of unknown kind
5 :   *Hordeum vulgare*
6 :   *Macrocloa tenacissima*
7 :   *Linum usitatissimum*
8 :   *Olea europea*
9 :   *Vicia faba*
10 :   acorns
11 :   *Vitis vinifera*
In addition unclassified fruit stones are reported from several sites, in some cases *Prunus* sp. perhaps.
(for details, *see* Walker, 1973a, 1973b)

Map o   Ceramic zones
Based upon petrological inspection of thin sections of wares from neolithic, copper and bronze age sites, and on X-ray emission spectroscopy, three zones are tentatively proposed. Zone (a) employs crushed limestone filler, Zone (c) employs micaschist filler, whilst in Zone (b) wares of the other two types are mixed with wares containing phlogopite crystals from the lamproitic 'jumellite' source near Jumilla (Murcia). Trade in this material involved the middle-lower Segura region, but not the Guadalentin tributary system, and the Vinalopo valley also. It appears to have commenced in the third millennium B.C.
(for details, *see* Walker, 1973a)

Map p   Human types of the Copper/Bronze Ages
A study of about 370 skulls by principal components multiple factorial analysis and by *t*-tests of metrical data, and an inspection of non-metrical characters, suggests two groups, which are not necessarily genetically exclusive. Zone (1) is a homogeneous group including the later Copper Age/Bronze Age settlements of Argar and La Bastida. Zone (2), based mainly on perhaps slightly earlier upland zone cave burials in Valencia and Alicante shows a greater variation, though there is some homogeneity. It has been tentatively suggested that the upland communities might have diverged either/or due to founder effect and/or genetic drift due to emigration to the lowland 'Argaric' townships, which, being larger, might not have undergone changes due to those effects. The heterogeneity of the Zone (2) group argues against two genetically distinct populations, one lowland and 'Argaric', the other upland and 'Valencian' (*see* Walker, 1973a).

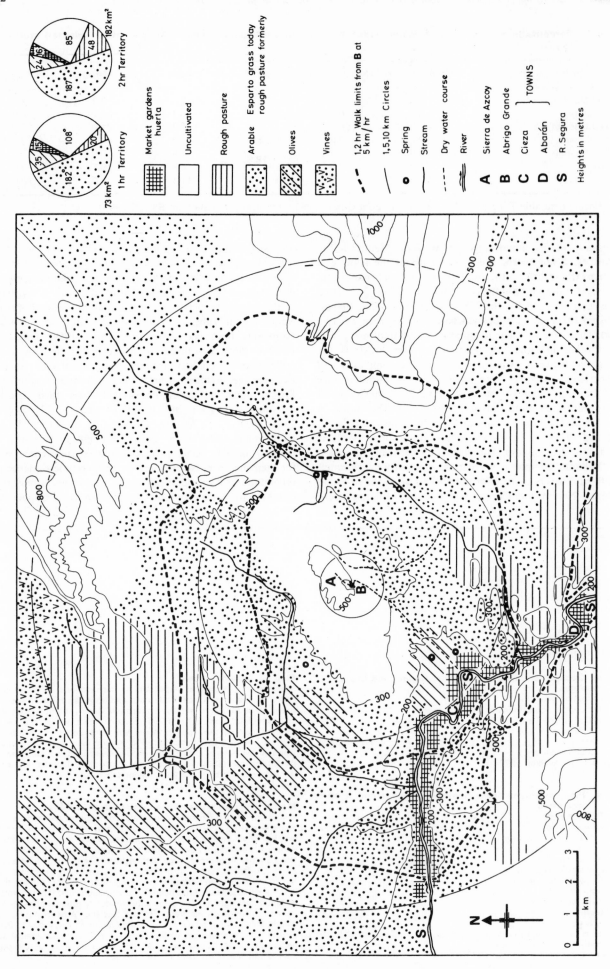

also accounts for the notable absence of Chassey-Cortaillod-Lagozza Neolithic assemblages in the south-east (although those are present in north-east Spain). Terrera Ventura was occupied from an early period with painted ware, through phases corresponding to incised 'Millaran' pottery, down to beaker times (Gusi, 1972, personal communication), and radiocarbon samples submitted before the recent excavations, extracted by me from earlier exposed cuttings, suggest a time-span between HAR-155 5370±350 BP (3420 BC) and HAR-298 3970±115 BP (2020 BC). Dr R. L. Otlet of A.E.R.E., Harwell (U.K.), who kindly supplied those dates, advises me that a bristlecone pine correction would suggest an absolute date for HAR-155 of about 4230 BC. It becomes clear that the south-east Spanish early Chalcolithic is contemporary with the developed Neolithic cultures of Catalonia, France, and northern Italy. It is hardly a matter for surprise if its main trading contacts were with the Chalcolithic societies of the eastern Mediterranean, rather than with the barbaric Neolithic world to its north. The dates previously available from Los Millares and Almizaraque at between 2200–2400 BC in 'radiocarbon' years, are now supported by HAR-521 which I submitted from 'Parazuelos' (Siret and Siret, 1887) in Murcia, viz. 4350±80 BP (2400 BC) or about 3050 BC when the bristlecone pine correction is applied. The flat and round based carinated vessels with broad, flared, curving rims found at 'Parazuelos' by the Sirets suggest an eastern Mediterranean inspiration ultimately. However, in my opinion, the south-east Spanish Chalcolithic was essentially a homespun affair, and its luxury items based on a local economy involving agriculture, pastoralism, vine and olive cultivation, and local metallurgy (Walker, 1973a), incorporating many traditions of the earlier Neolithic of the region (as at El Gárcel and other sites). Both the tell of Almizaraque (now 1.5 km inland) and the 'Parazuelos' site (now 4 km inland) were clearly coastal settlements, if not offshore islands, and were no doubt ports. Both sites are very close to copper ores, and also other metals (see Map d). About the time of their occupation alluvial aggradations in the middle reaches of the valleys were consolidating, and for the first time there were available for cultivation sufficiently large areas of soil to sustain large villages or small towns (Walker and Cuenca, in preparation), although the montane pastoral tendencies of the earlier Neolithic phase continued also.

The foregoing allows us to define the Neolithic chronologically (and see dates given below) as lasting between 7000–5250 BP in 'radiocarbon' years or 6000–4000 BC in absolute reckoning.

Key to map opposite

Map q   Site exploitation territory of the Abrigo Grande
The map indicates the 1-hour and 2-hour ranges from the site, the former being seen to approximate to a 5 km radius area. Present day land utilisation patterns are shown, although it is probable that in neolithic times almost the entire area was rough pasture, uncultivated land with more scrub and woodland than now (see text). The modern alluvial huerta soils were not present. The map appears truncated at the bottom, but that is because the relief becomes much steeper as the Segura is followed downstream, i.e south, from Abaran and its valley is greatly constricted. It is unlikely that such a region offered much scope for exploitation, and has therefore been omitted.

Abrigo Grande excavation

Near Cieza (Murcia) in a canyon called the Barranco de los Grajos which descends the Sierra de Azcoy (Map q) there are painted rock shelters bearing naturalistic and schematic figures, including anthropomorphs without weapons and which are possibly females engaged in some non-violent display, as well as a few zoomorphs (figs 1a,b). They were the discovery of a school-teacher, sr. Eduardo López Pascual (López Pascual, 1968; Beltrán, 1968a, 1968b, 1969; Walker, 1971, 1972). The zoomorphs are cervines, caprines, a possible suine, and four queer cross-hachured quadrupeds which suggest unfamiliarity on the part of the artist with his subject matter and which are almost without parallel in Levantine rock art. Written permission from Dr Martín Almagro Basch was telegraphed authorising my excavation of a rock shelter adjacent to the painted Levantine shelter. The rock shelter at which excavation was proposed contained a few paintings of different type (Fig. 2) from Levantine rock art, and I have named it the Abrigo Grande on account of its large size. The excavation material, deposited with the Museo Arqueológico Nacional, Madrid, is described in full with a complete inventory in an article submitted in 1971, following the 1970 excavation season, for publication in Noticiario Arqueológico Hispánico (Walker, in press). Illustrations of some of the material are given here (Figs 9, 10, 10a, 11, 11a, 12). The rock shelter contained four stratigraphical units, the upper two with pottery, the lower two without. The uppermost pre-ceramic unit comprised a thick layer of aeolian sand. The rock shelters face north and are out of the sun for all but an hour in the evening making ideal domestic quarters. Aeolian sands are found in many north-facing caves in Murcia and Alicante (Walker and Cuenca, in preparation), and are absent in caves of other aspects. It is believed by us that these sands are derived from the Meseta, and that they were removed by cyclonic wind activity over the peninsula following the northward retreat of the glacial anticyclonic north Atlantic winds after the Fenno-Scandian advance and the Younger Dryas (i.e. after 7250 BC). The cyclonic winds would have precipitated their Atlantic moisture over the western region of the peninsula, and then could pick up sand for deposition further to the south-east in the Peni-Baetic mountains. A radiocarbon date from a sample of material from both ceramic layers is as follows: HAR-179-(III) 7200±160 BP (5250 BC). This is beyond the bristlecone pine range, so the true age of the material is probably considerably earlier, perhaps 6000 BC. The estimation is reliable, based on 650 g dry weight of bone which yielded 62.7 cm CO_2 and gave a delta-^{13}C of 17.5. (By contrast, an attempt was made to date the pre-ceramic layers on a charcoal sample which weighed 160 g dry but yielded only 13 cm³ CO_2 and for which the delta-^{13}C was unmeasurable, rendering quite meaningless the estimation HAR-180 of 5120±620 BP: Dr R. L. Otlet, A.E.R.E., personal communication). A sherd of cardial impressed ware was found on the surface by a workman, and another impressed sherd occurred in the ceramic layers. The radiocarbon date of 7200 BP is in line with dates given above from southern France and Italy for impressed wares. There is no reason to reject the antiquity of the Abrigo Grande, therefore.

There follow tabular displays of the incidence and occurrence of the artifacts by cutting, by layer, by type, of the retouched pieces by tool type, of the breakdown of artifacts according to situation, proportions and weight partitioning, of the tools according to partitioning of angles of retouch facets, of the implements as pi-diagrams and histograms layer by layer, of the faunal remains by layer, the archaeological sections, and the illustrations of some of the finds (Figs. 5–12).

Table 2　Abrigo Grande: Distribution of lithic material* by cuttings

	Cutting I				Total
	Layer 1	Layer 2	Layer 3	Layer 4	
Flakes	567	238	808	391	2004
Blades	237	97	245	66	645
Lumps	8	4	11	10	33
Artifacts/cores	12	8	14	1	35
Limestone			3		3
	824	347	1081	468	2720
	Cutting II				
Flakes	585	335	485	196	1601
Blades	169	107	118	44	436
Lumps	19	7	7	5	38
Artifacts/cores	4	9	5	3	21
Limestone	1		1		2
	778	458	614	248	2098
	Cutting I/II Baulk				
Flakes	106	**	350	178	632
Blades	58		120	41	219
Lumps	5		11	6	22
Artifacts/cores	2		8		10
Limestone			3		3
	171		492	223	886
	Cutting III				
Flakes	788	**	**	**	788
Blades	286				286
Lumps	8				8
Artifacts/cores	15				15
	1097				1097

* Flint or chert, unless otherwise stated
** Corresponding layers were not present in the cutting

Table 3　Abrigo Grande: Distribution of lithic material by layer (unretouched pieces)

Layer			Type			Total
	Flakes	Blades	Lumps	Artifacts cores	Lime-stone	
1	1940	692	35	31	1	2699
2	573	204	11	17		805
3	1293	361	18	19	4	1695
4	587	110	15	4		716
Total	4393	1367	79	71	5	5915

Table 4　Abrigo Grande: Distribution of lithic material by cutting (unretouched pieces)

Cutting			Type			Total
	Flakes	Blades	Lumps	Artifacts cores	Lime-stone	
I	1372	426	11	25		1834
II	1601	436	38	21	2	2098
I/II	632	219	22	10	3	886
III	788	286	8	15		1097
Total	4393	1367	79	71	5	5915

Table 5　Abrigo Grande: Distribution of tool types by layer

Type		Layer			Total
	1	2	3	4	
Crescent	1				1
Backed bladelet	19	12	9		40
Retouched blade	1			1	2
Notched/serrated blade	2		1		3
Awl	2				2
End-scraper	2		1	1	4
Discoidal scraper				1	1
Pyramidal scraper	1		4	1	6
Pyramidal core	2	4	3		9
Notched flake	1	2			3
Notched flake-blade	1				1
Total	32	18	18	4	72*

* The total 72 (as against 71 in the earlier tables) is due to a double end-scraper on a notched blade classified separately in each category. Two microburins were found and are not included in the tables.

Table 6　Abrigo Grande: Faunal remains (brackets represent minimum numbers of individuals)

Vertebrate Fauna				
		Layer		
	1	2	3	4
Oryctolagus cuniculus	+(42)	+(16)	+(23)	+(2)
Sus scrofa	+(2)	+(1)	+(1)	+(1)
Cervus elaphus		+(1)	+(1)	+(1)
Equus caballus		? (1 ?)*	+(1)	+(1)
Caprinae	+(1)	+(1)		
Bos sp.	+(1)	? (1 ?)*		
Shells				
Rumina decollata	+(126)	+(31)		
Otala alonensis and Sphincterochila candidissima**	+(235)	+(102)	+(41)	+(100)
Pecten jacobaeus***		+(1)		+(1)
Littorina littoralis***			+(8)	+(7)
Donacilla cornea***	+(1)	+(1)		

* The doubtful identification of *Equus/Bos* refers to a single bone from layer 2.
** The two species were not clearly differentiated during excavation, except for a sample 660 mm square, which demonstrated that *O. alonensis* was commoner in layer 1 (80% : 20%), whereas in lower layers the two species were present in roughly equal proportions (*Otala* : *Sphincterochila* 55% : 45%).
*** These three marine species demonstrate that there was some contact, direct or indirect, with the sea coast 60 to 70 km distant.

There were no convincing burins in the lithic assemblage, although several flint spalls might have been from burins. However, as in no instance did the spalls have their own primary bulbs of percussion, it was impossible to say with certainty that the so-called burin blows had not been executed before the spall was struck off the core.

Retouch facets were classified (Fig. 7) and partitioning demonstrates two groups corresponding to backed blades and scrapers as determined subjectively. The subsidiary peak of the former group is no more than an indication of those members which had retouch backing in two opposite directions. The debitage was also examined (Fig. 7) and when compared with the retouched bladelets it was found that unretouched bladelets were longer and broader, with the unexpected finding that there was an under-representation of

Fig. 1a: Principal painted rock shelter at the Barranco de los Grajos (*Courtesy of Rosalie de Méric*). Note anthropomorphs, frequently with skirts, and without bows and arrows. Note one anthropomorph below cervine at right hand side of panel with implement (?) at his waist. Note small quadrupeds lacking clearly defined heads and with hachured bodies—sheep (?).

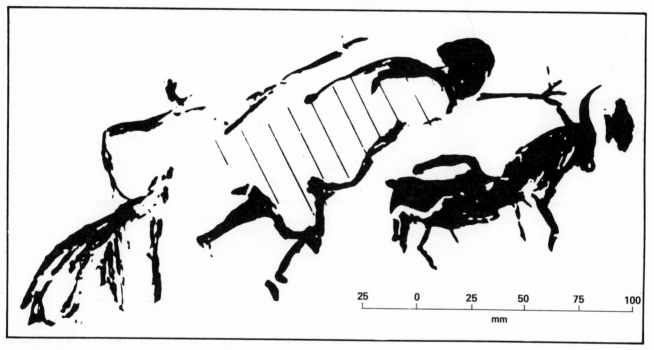

Fig. 1b: Same rock shelter at the Barranco de los Grajos, opposite wall. Much damaged panel of two skirted anthropomorphs one of whom is holding a caprine by its horn. Hachuring indicates missing area of rock due to damage by vandals. (*Courtesy of Rosalie de Méric*).

unretouched bladelets of short length, suggestive of a functional requirement for blades for subsequent retouching of a particular length and an effective technique for removing primary blades from the parent core such that there were few mistakes. Backing reduced the width of the blades and breakage, whether accidental or intentional, the length of the retouched artifact. When compared by layer (Fig. 6) there is a hint of relatively more pyramidal pieces in the pre-ceramic layers, and relatively more backed bladelets in the ceramic layers, but these differences are not of statistical significance. However, the greater density of artifacts in the thin layer 2 (Fig. 8) must also be borne in mind in evaluating the significance of that observation.

It must be emphasised that the most striking aspect of the excavated material is the preponderance of backed bladelet artifacts at a ceramic-using site. This is almost without parallel in the region. It is accepted that geometric microliths are common in the early Neolithic of south-east Spain, but the surprise find here of backed bladelets in profusion, with other forms attested to by a single crescent and two microburins only, demands a reconsideration of the place of microlithic flint implements in the early south-east Spanish Neolithic. Moreover, it is clear that the backed bladelets of the pre-ceramic layers are essentially similar to those of the ceramic ones, indicating a continuity of lithic traditions before and after pottery was adopted. It may be surmised

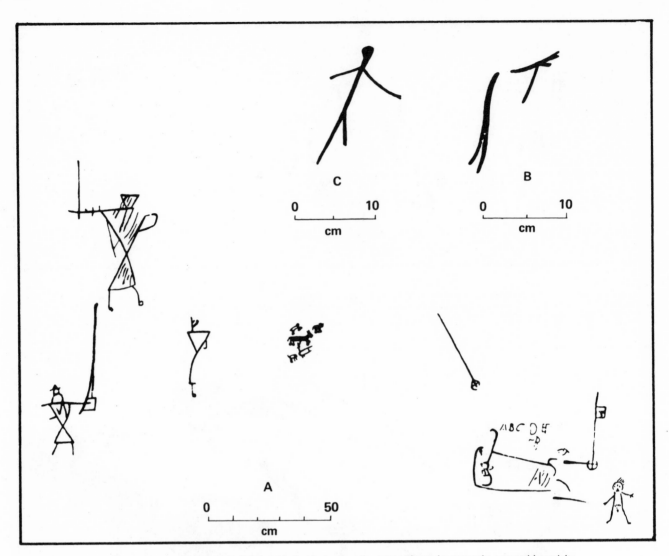

Fig. 2a: Abrigo Grande, parietal paintings. On left hand side in black are anthropomorphs and zoomorphs covered by calcite flow, on right are alphabetic letters and anthropomorph in red. These paintings are of unknown age.
Fig. 2b: Abrigo Grande, parietal painting in a niche at rear of cave of an anthropomorph in red.
Fig. 2c: Black anthropomorph in another rock shelter further up the Barranco de Los Grajos from the principal painted shelter and the Abrigo Grande.

that the introduction of pottery did little to alter the subsistence economic activities of the occupants of the rock shelter.

Before speculations are offered as to what those activities were, it is important to stress the similarities between the Abrigo Grande situation and those other sites, often excavated according to the methods of a previous generation, which, nevertheless, demonstrated a pre-ceramic to ceramic transition (Cocina, Llatas, Lagrimal etc.). Although attention has been drawn most frequently by other investigators to geometric traditions at such sites, from what has been said earlier, it is clear that there is a variety of lithic facies in fact, and even at Cocina backed bladelet traditions of flint working appear to have been important (Fortea, 1971). The Abrigo Grande excavation, therefore, confirms what was already long anticipated by many archaeologists, namely, that the roots of the earliest south-east Spanish Neolithic must be sought in the pre-ceramic societies of the region, and not in some distant land from which advanced 'colonists' might or might not have emanated. The onus is on those who believe that

the Neolithic of south-east Spain was due to an intrusive population to demonstrate that presumed region of origin where the Neolithic facies parallels the very varied aspect which it presents in south-east Spain. I can think of no ceramic-using cave-dwelling cultures with similar lithic tool-kits which might have colonised south-east Spain in the sixth millennium BC. The extra assumption that some supporters of 'colonists' invoke, namely that their culture was transformed or diminished following migration, is essentially unprovable, explaining away the differences rather than constructing working hypotheses which can be confirmed by analysis of assemblages or by predictive searches of geographical regions for 'intermediate' cultural steps. The possibility of such cultural impoverishment among Neolithic migrants is demonstrated by, for instance, the colonisation of Polynesia or New Zealand, but as a model for testing by prehistoric archaeologists it is just not amenable to the materialistic methodology which they rely upon. It cannot compete with simpler working hypotheses which explain the observations *without* invoking extra assumptions.

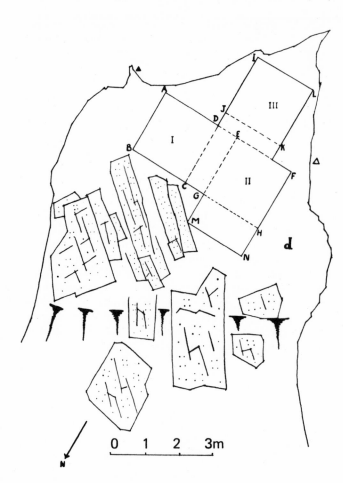

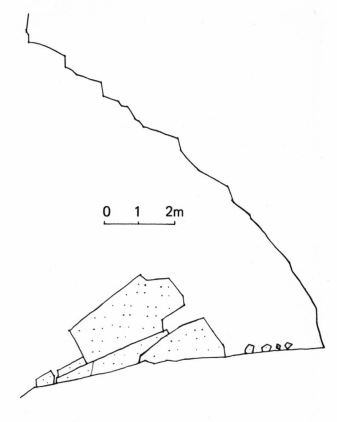

Fig. 3a: Ground plan of Abrigo Grande indicating position of cuttings. Letters correspond to letters on sections in Fig. 4. d = disturbed area. Solid triangle: painted figure of Fig. 2b; open triangle: painted motifs of Fig. 2a.

Fig. 3b: Elevation of cave before excavation.

One such is that there was a generalised hunter-gatherer-fisher society in the lands bordering the northern shore of the western Mediterranean basin in the sixth millennium BC which acquired the use of pottery and the technique of decorating it with *Cardium edule* impressions, which domesticated local species (*cp.* Murray, 1970 : 22–26) perhaps employing domesticates occasionally acquired from other Neolithic societies, which hunted local wild animals, and which occasionally acquired—whether by local domestication or acquisition from other Neolithic societies—*Triticum monococcum, T. dicoccum, T. aestivum,* and *Hordeum vulgare.* Such a picture may be equally difficult to prove definitively, but at least is somewhat simpler and involves less special pleading.

At least as far as concerns south-east Spain, there is one extra assumption which must be made, and that is that the differences in assemblage composition between the transitional pre-ceramic to ceramic sites represent functional differences rather than the hall-marks of synchronic but exclusive societies. This view, in the light of what has been said concerning a re-assessment of lithic assemblages from south-east Spain, seems rather more plausible than does the opinion of cultural diminution consequent upon migration. A 'cultural gavotte' of exclusive societies moving between, say, Mallaetes, Cocina, Llatas, l'Or, Sarsa, Ambrosio, Hoyo de la Mina, Lagrimal, Abrigo Grande, etc., seems perverse. Some sites

(eg. Filador, *vide supra*) would have had to be occupied by different groups at different times. What makes the 'gavotte' model so uninviting is that there is a uniformity of rock shelter art across the region. It is hard to imagine that the uplands between the Seguna and Júcar basins, and continuing further north up the Turia and into Teruel and Castellón, were really the scene of such 'toing and froing'. However, the Levantine rock art distinguishes the culture(s) of the eastern peninsular region from those of southern France or Italy, attesting to the largely indigenous roots of eastern peninsular rock shelter dwellers.

Since some Neolithic attributes (*vide supra*, also Walker 1971, 1973a) occur in the Levantine art, there seems no good reason to believe that some, if not all, of the paintings did not straddle the chronological period embracing the later upper Palaeolithic and the earliest ceramic-using societies of south-east Spain. Since both the painted sites and the occupation sites occur in the same geographical inland area and in the same habitat zone, it is not an unreasonable opinion. The occurrence of ochre in most levels at the Abrigo Grande (Fig. 5) may be testimony to the artistic endeavours of the occupants, both as represented by the single anthropomorph of Levantine type at the shelter itself, and the elaborate panels at the adjacent principal painted rock shelter. It is hard to see who else was living in the region in the later upper Palaeolithic and earliest ceramic-using times who might have executed the art if it was not the cave dwellers. Moreover, at the Barranco de los Grajos, there is some suggestion from the principal painted shelter (Fig. 1a) that one anthropomorph carries at his waist a hafted implement (axe?), and is it beyond possibility that the cross-hachured quadrupeds represent an unusual acquisition such as sheep (*cp.* Murray on turbary sheep in the French later upper Palaeolithic, 1970 : 22–26)?

To what extent can the Abrigo Grande be interpreted in terms of possible territorial exploitation (*cp.* Higgs and Vita-Finzi, 1972)? The large mammalian fauna (Table 6) represents insufficient individuals for an analysis based on faunal remains. However, all the species found except horse are depicted at the nearby principal painted shelter. A breakdown of land which can be reached within (a) 1 hour and (b) 2 hours from the site by walking has been attempted (and see Map q) as follows:

Table 7 Abrigo Grande: Land utilisation within 1 or 2 hour walk from site

	1 hour +	1-to-2 hours =	2 hour total
Huerta soils	3 km²	5 km²	8 km²
Uncultivated	22	21	43
Rough pasture	4	20	24
Arable upland	37	58	95
Olives	7	5	12
	73 km²	109 km²	182 km²

The tables require a few words of comment. Most of the *huerta* soils of today are between 3 and 5 km from the site

Table 8 Abrigo Grande: Percentage of land utilised in different ways within 1 or 2 hour walk from site

	Percentage of total land within		Total
	1-hour range	2-hour range	
	%	%	%
Huerta soils	4.1	4.4	8.5
Uncultivated	30.1	23.6	53.7
Rough pasture	5.5	13.2	18.7
Arable upland	50.5	52.0	102.5
Olives	9.6	6.6	16.2
	99.8	99.8	199.6

(Map q). They are probably too far away to give a useful yield (*cp.* Vita-Finzi and Higgs, 1970; Higgs *et al.*, 1967). In any case, the alluvial soils of which they are composed were probably not yet aggraded in the sixth millennium BC. Most of the arable upland is thin, poorly watered soil largely given over to *esparto* cultivation for the twine industry, and olives are also a relatively recent innovation in the uplands where they have required the sinking of costly artesian wells in order that large stands of trees could be made economic to farmers. Probably nearly all the land within the walking range of the site was rough grazing or uncultivated in the Neolithic. There

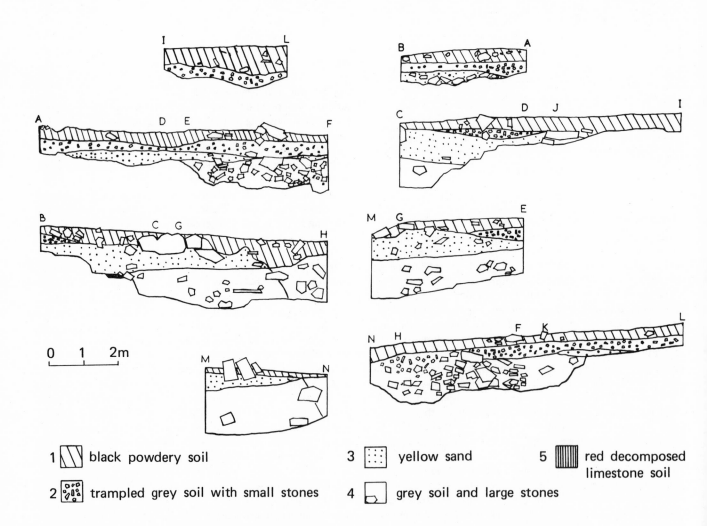

1 ◿◺ black powdery soil
2 ▨ trampled grey soil with small stones
3 ⬚ yellow sand
4 ▱ grey soil and large stones
5 ▥ red decomposed limestone soil

Fig. 4: Left hand side: transverse sections of cuttings, i.e. from side-to-side of cave. Topmost is at rear, bottom is at entrance of shelter. Right hand side: longitudinal sections of cuttings, i.e. from entrance to back of cave. Topmost is nearest east wall, bottom is nearest west wall of shelter. The rear of the cave is at the right of this group of sections. Note suggestion of disturbance of layers 1, 4 in the region of N–H, not clearly distinguished stratigraphically from either layer.

may have been more active springs (see Map q) than today, and perhaps more of the original climax vegetation based on pine and *Quercus ilex* rather than the present 'ruined' *garrigue* landscape of stunted sclerophyllous xerophytes. Tree cover may have been more prevalent than now (Map g), before overgrazing and deforestation for domestic and industrial purposes got under way. Nevertheless, it is likely that at all times the modern pattern of low precipitation and very high mean annual temperature (Maps e, f) prevailed, making agricultural cultivation difficult, and often necessitat-

ing the grazing and watering of herds over a considerable distance.

It is interesting to speculate as to the numbers of large wild mammals which might have occupied the territorial catchment area of the Abrigo Grande, using the foregoing figures. Red deer only will be used, as they are among the most frequently represented species at Levantine art sites (Table 9), although it is clear that different art sites have differing proportions of faunal representations. The data in the table are taken partly from my own investigations at sites in Murcia and Albacete,

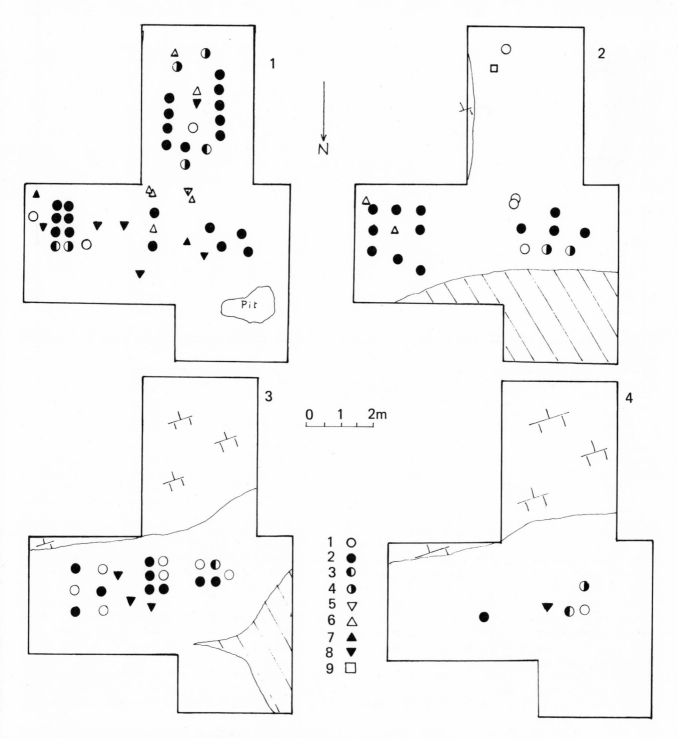

Fig. 5: Distribution of artifacts by layer according to their spatial situation. In the case of some of the smaller backed bladelets and ochre pieces, positions are only approximations. Hachuring indicates stratigraphical disconformity. Conventional limestone symbol indicates bedrock. 1 : flint pyramidal artifacts ; 2 : flint backed bladelets ; 3 : flint end-scrapers ; 4 : other retouched flint ; 5 : worked bone ; 6 : pottery ; 7 : pierced shell ; 8 : ochre ; 9 : rock crystal.

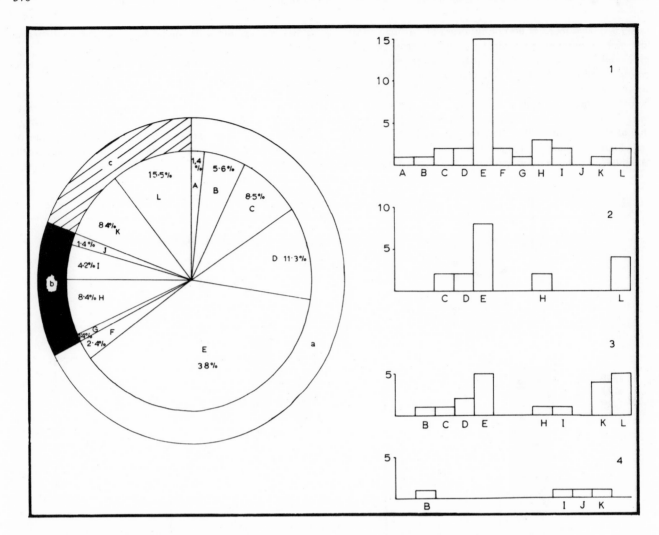

Fig. 6: Left hand pi diagram: assortment of retouched flint as percentages of implement types. Right hand histograms: assortment of retouched flint by layer as absolute numbers of implements. 1 : layer 1 ; 2 : layer 2 ; 3 : layer 3 ; 4 : layer 4.
a : backed bladelets ; c : pyramidal flint pieces ; b : other.
A : crescents ; B : bladelets with retouch on two margins ; C : backed bladelets with two rows of retouch but with flaking in same direction ; D : backed bladelets with two rows of retouch but with flaking in opposing directions ; E : backed bladelets with a single row of retouch facets ; F : awls ; G : serrated pieces ; H : notched pieces ; I : end-scrapers ; J : discoidal scrapers ; K : pyramidal scrapers ; L : pyramidal cores.
Comment : (a) some pieces with, say, a notch and end-scraper facets appear twice, so percentage total exceeds 100% ; (b) is there an inverse relation between pyramidal and backed flint pieces as the strata are ascended ?—it is not statistically significant, however.

and partly (Minateda, Cueva de la Vieja) from Breuil (Breuil, 1920; Breuil and Burkitt, 1915; Breuil and von Obermaier, 1912) owing to the deterioration suffered by many paintings due to maltreatment by tourists. Table 9 also demonstrates how exceptional is the principal painted shelter at the Barranco de los Grajos with respect to the proportions of zoomorphs and anthropomorphs respectively, reinforcing the opinion that the shelters of the canyon were employed for a different purpose from those of caves facing more or less southwards. Possibly the Barranco de los Grajos sites were domestic, perhaps largely used by women, whereas some of the other sites may have been male hideouts or hunting lodges. This is pure fancy, however.

To return to the red deer, if we accept Scottish red deer densities of one animal per 0.12 to 0.20 km² (Vita-Finzi and Higgs, 1970)—higher densities occur in regions more wooded

than Scottish moorland, incidentally—then there might have been between 608 and 365 animals in the 73 km² of Table 7. It is also likely that red deer were observed at all seasons of the year by Levantine artists, because they are often portrayed in full antler which is retained from late summer through till the spring, and that therefore deer slaughter might have been an all year round activity (not to mention occupation of rock shelters, which are exceedingly cold and draughty during the winter in the Peni-Baetic mountains!). A third assumption is that each adult red deer weighed between 150 kg (in adverse conditions) and 200 kg (in optimal conditions) (see Harris and Duff, 1970). An assumption of an annual kill of 0.167 of the herd size may be made, such that the herd neither diminishes nor expands in numbers. If 66.7% of each adult by weight were edible, and if the mean venison intake of each human per day were about 0.250 kg, then the size of the dependent human population might be calculated (Table 10).

Table 9 Levantine art sites: Numbers of animals of different types and of humans at sites in Murcia and Albacete

Art site	Mammals					Domesticated mammals?	Anthropomorphs		
	Cerv.	Capr.	Bov.	Equ.	Other		with bows	with skirts	others
Fuento del Sabuco	3	1		1	8		8	2	20
Cañaíca del Calar	3	1			5		2		
Solana de las Covachas	23	19			21	1?	16	3	2
Barranco de los Grajos	2	3			2	4?	1?	15	14
Minateda	39	27	7	10	64		59	9	71
Cantos de la Visera I	3	3	3	9	11				
Cantos de la Visera II	3	1	9		19				8
Cueva de la Vieja	18	11	4		16		28	2	25

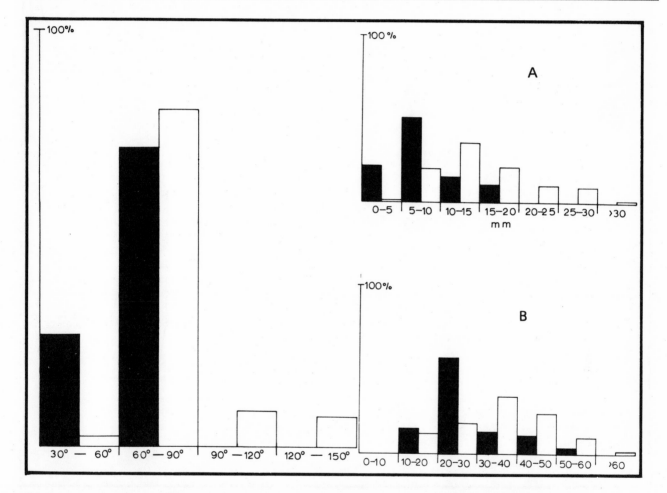

Fig. 7: Left hand histogram shows partitioning of angles between retouch facets and bulbar surface for retouched blades, flakes, and pyramidal artifacts. Black: flakes and pyramidal pieces worked into scrapers; White: backed bladelets. Right hand histograms: A, partitioning of breadth; and B, partitioning of length, for 50 backed bladelets (black) and a sample of 50 unretouched bladelets (white).

Table 10 Abrigo Grande: Population estimates based on venison diet—four possibilities

	Red deer density 0.12/km² 200 kg beasts	Red deer density 0.2/km² 200 kg beasts	Red deer density 0.12/km² 150 kg beasts	Red deer density 0.2/km² 150 kg beasts
Total deer wt in 73 km²	121 660 kg	73 000 kg	91 245 kg	54 750 kg
If only 0.167 of total wt taken, weight is	20 277 kg	12 167 kg	15 207 kg	9 125 kg
66.7% of wt taken is edible	13 518 kg	8 112 kg	10 138 kg	6 083 kg
If daily intake 0.25 kg, man-days	54 072 kg	32 448 kg	40 552 kg	24 332 kg
Man-years	148	89	111	67

Mean men/year = 104

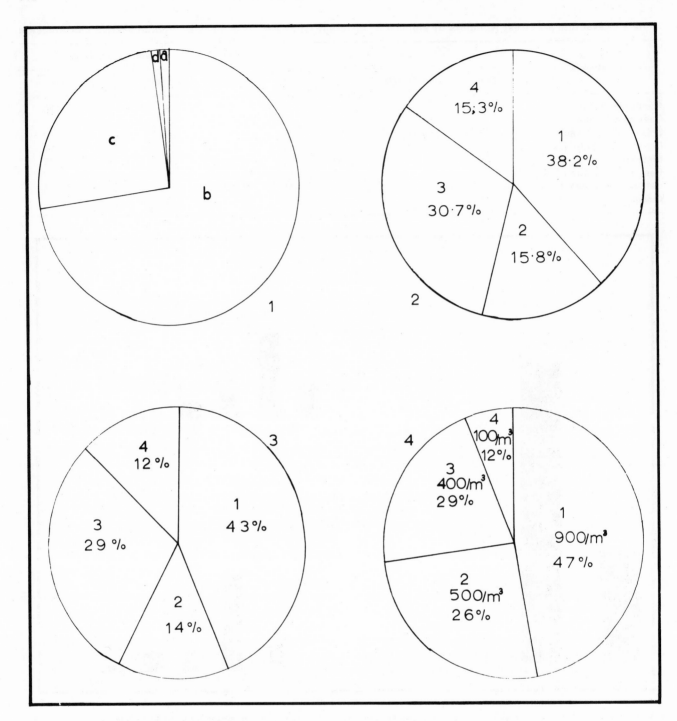

Fig. 8:
1. Pi diagram to show breakdown of lithic assemblage as proportion of total number of flints (5,915), where a: worked pieces; b: unworked flakes; c: unworked blades; d: unworked lumps and cores.
2. Breakdown of lithic assemblage as proportion of total weight (10,410 g) from each layer 1,2,3,4.
3. Breakdown of lithic assemblage as proportion of total numbers of flints (5,915) from each layer 1,2,3,4.
4. As for pi diagram 3, but with correction for volume of soil in each layer, giving approximate artefact densities per layer in absolute figures and as percentage of summed absolute densities, where the absolute densities are notional figures extrapolated for a representative cubic metre from the observed find numbers.

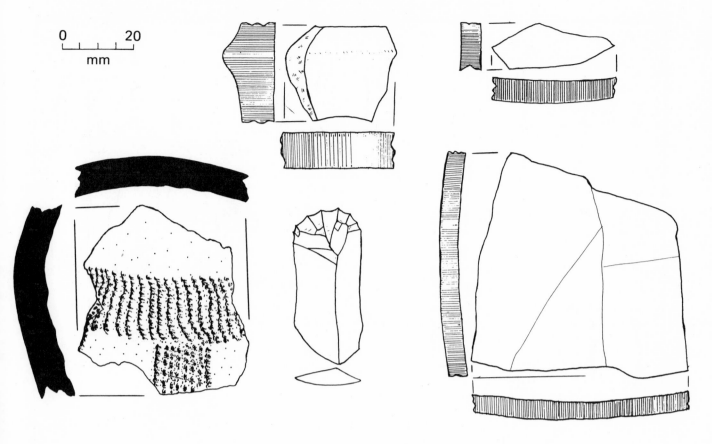

0   20
mm

Fig. 9: Artifacts found on surface before excavation.

Based on a high protein diet two and a half times the normal western European average for today, but perhaps not far removed from that of modern Eskimos (Weiner, in Harrison *et al.*, 1964 : 416), and supplemented by plant food, and protein from ibex, wild cattle, wild horse, boar, lagomorphs, birds, snails and frogs, a population of over 100 people might have been sustained by exploitation of an area not more than one hour's walk from the rock shelter. What direct evidence is there? Unfortunately, as has been said, there is none from the excavation material. However, the principal painted shelter (Figs 1a, 1b) depicts approximately 30 anthropomorphs, some of whom wear skirts, and none of whom appears to be armed with bows and arrows, except perhaps one which has an arcuate object held in both hands above its head. If these are female representations, then equal numbers of menfolk and children (or rather more children to allow for child mortality) would make a population of about 100 to 120 people an acceptable number. Possibly the artistic representation of a human group is better testimony even than an estimate of its numbers based on food debris, as the latter can be misleading in various ways. Ideally, it would be useful to have both testimonies.

If such numbers could be supported from so small a territory then what might the population density have been during the earliest ceramic-using period in south-east Spain? There is no reason why there may *not* have been tens of thousands of people in the region; we really have no idea. Certainly, a diet based on high fat and protein is nutritious and less susceptible to development of malnutrition than is one based on cereal grains principally. The former demands

some plant food and thus the intake of plant-derived vitamins. The latter is susceptible to crop failures and avitaminoses owing to inadequate alternative (ie: meat or fish) food sources. We have no evidence for cereal crops in south-east Spain before 6500 BP in 'radiocarbon' years. It is not until some time after 5000 BP that there is evidence for breeding of cereal varieties which had wide geographical employment in the region (Walker, 1973b). Distribution (Maps k, l, m) of burials and settlement sites from about that period not only show a greater density than for the earlier phase (Map i), but suggest that the valley alluvia were being utilised, and that the metal ores near the coasts (Map d) were being exploited. Chalcolithic settlements nevertheless have provided large quantities of mammal bones (Boessneck, 1969; von Driesch, 1969).

Following the cyclonic climatic phase mentioned earlier, the climate changed to the modern anticyclonic conditions. These are characterised by winds charged with Mediterranean moisture which precipitate their load on the Peni-Baetic mountains in winter and early spring. Most of the region suffers intense heat, aridity, and water deficit for most of the year (Maps e, f). This change may have led to closer man-mammal relationships either at or just before the earliest ceramic-using times. The reduction of the climax vegetation, leaching of the soil, scarcity of grassland, and drying up of springs would have been exacerbated by pasturing of animals, removal of young tree shoots, and the stripping of bark from trees. Under conditions of stress, gamekeepers in Scotland can feed wild red deer herds by hand, mingling among the animals. Domestication of mammals living in close proximity

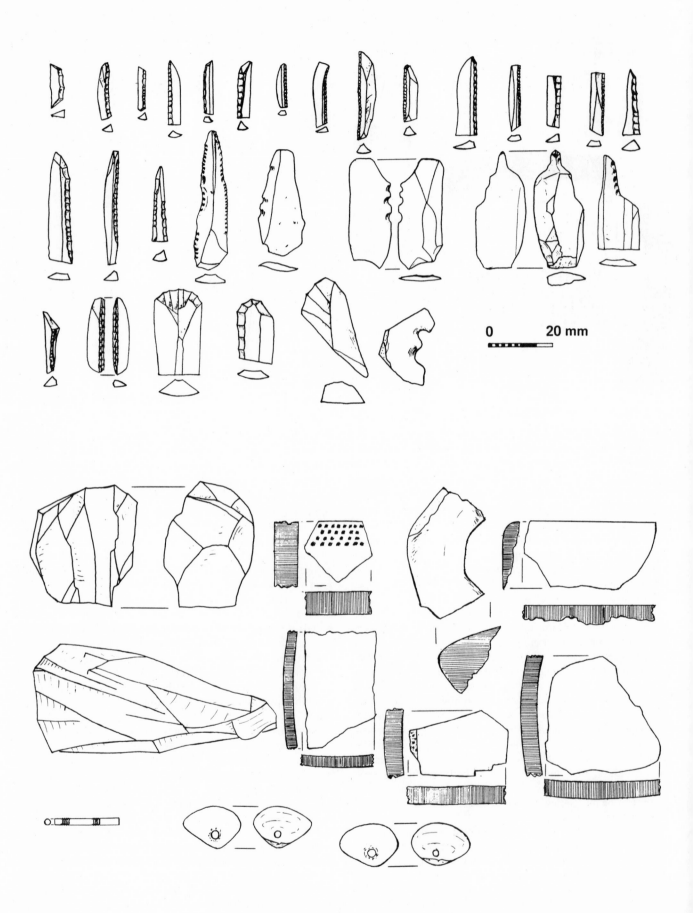

Fig. 10: Artifacts from layer 1 (ceramic phase).

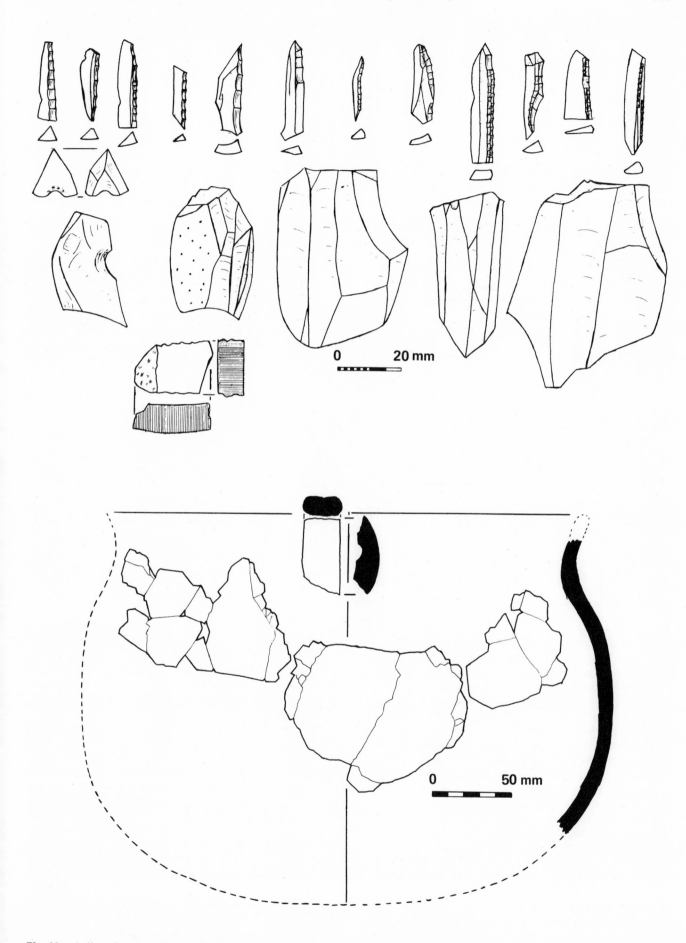

Fig. 11: Artifacts from layer 2 (ceramic phase).

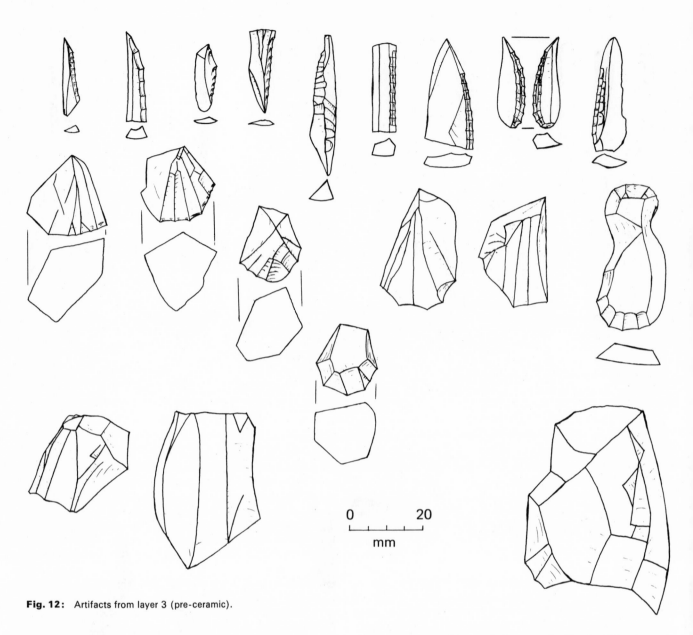

Fig. 12: Artifacts from layer 3 (pre-ceramic).

to men has been postulated by various writers for the European Neolithic (eg. Tringham, 1971) and the role of red deer in particular has been stressed by Jarman (Jarman, 1972). The relationship between modern Lapps and their reindeer herds may offer a parallel. Regulated slaughter would be undertaken to try to strike a balance between maintaining herd size in relation to available environmental resources and maintaining the population of the dependent human group, which would follow the herds and guide them to suitable pastures and water. The two aims may have become incompatible as human population expanded and the ecological characteristics underwent rapid change due to deforestation and lower precipitation. This might have necessitated long distance movement of perhaps domesticated animals by some, at least, of the members of the group and also the exploitation of food resources, particularly plants, near to base settlements. However the large-scale exploitation of the latter would have had to await the consolidation of fluvial alluvia brought down by winter hill=wash consequent upon the changed climatic pattern and the erosion of the top-soil it had induced.

The evidence for continuity of lithic implement forms at the Abrigo Grande, and other sites, supports the view that there was no sudden switch to agricultural cultivation of cereals at the time of the earliest ceramic-using societies. The continued use of upland caves suggests that the subsistence economy was geared to the same sort of exploitation which had occurred in the preceding phase.

Different sites, however, have different types of artifacts. At the Huesa Tacaña, a hill near Villena (Alicante), there are two caves (Soler, 1956, 1968–69) with different tool-kits, comprising respectively backed bladelet and geometric assemblages. Whilst it is not known if the two were contemporaneous, it is possible that they had different functions. Those functions might have been determined by differing available species at different times of the year, or they may have involved activities absolutely unrelated to food. Different rock shelters have different proportions of mammal species depicted (Table 9). The rolling uplands between the middle reaches of the Segura and the Júcar could support no doubt more equines and bovines than the upper reaches of the Taibilla (Fuente del Sabuco, Cañaíca del Calar, Solana de las Covachas) where deer and ibex predominate. However, at the Barranco de los Grajos and at several stations like it in

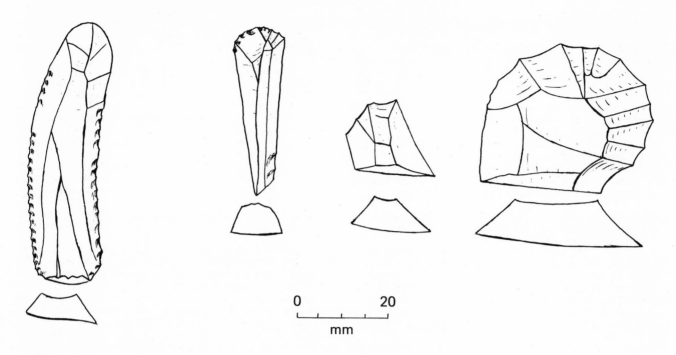

Fig. 13:   Artifacts from layer 4 (pre-ceramic).

the rolling uplands belt, deer and ibex form an important part of the art of course. There may have been specialisation with regard to different species, or groups of species, by different human groups, thus creating a need for differing tool-kits. We simply do not know. That the culture was integrated is testified to by the similarity of an anthropomorph with out-turned feet at Solana de las Covachas and others, with head-dresses, in similar attitudes at Cueva de la Vieja near Alpera, 150 km to the north, but still in our region. In both cases, those figures stand out from the other anthropomorphs in a marked way, as if they were accorded some special treatment. Further, at both shelters there are similar painted hafted barbed arrowpoints though at Alpera other representations suggest hafted microlithic arrowpoints too. There is no reason at all not to believe that such artifacts as bifacially worked flint arrowpoints with barbs and tangs or pottery were acquired as part and parcel of a general process

of cultural change in the sixth millennium BC in the western Mediterranean basin, and no reason to believe that initially such artifacts were used in south-east Spain in the context of a society practising cereal crop cultivation. The inland distribution of the earliest sites reinforces the opinion that the earliest ceramic-using phase in the region was not intrusive in the sense of colonisation of the peninsula by maritime agriculturalists, nor is there one whit of evidence for any such colonisation at any time. The development of cereal cultivation may quite well have been a necessary adaptation to changing environmental conditions and societal needs, and the technology involved may have been received from contact with other societies of the western Mediterranean region, who perhaps originally absorbed it from the Balkans or south-west Asia in order the better to dominate deteriorating surroundings and to maintain human population sizes which had grown during a preceding phase.

References

Almagro Basch, M., 1944. Los problemas del epipaleolítico y mesolítico en España. *Ampurias*, VI : 1–38.

—— 1947. El paleolítico español. In *Historia de Espana I : I*, Menéndez Pidal, R. (ed.), pp. 243–485. Madrid: Espasa-Calpe.

Arribas, A., 1953. El ajuar de las cuevas sepulcrales de los Blanquizares de Lébor (Murcia). *Memorias de los Museos Arqueológicos Provinciales XIV* : 78–126.

Balout, L., 1955. *Préhistoire de l'Afrique du Nord*. Paris: Arts et Métiers Graphiques.

Beltrán Martinez, A., 1968a. La cueva de los Grajos, y sus pinturas, en Cieza (Murcia). *Caesaraugusta*, XXXI–XXXII: 45–88.

—— 1968b. El arte rupestre levantino: cronología y significación. *Caesaraugusta*, XXXI–XXXII : 7–43.

—— 1969. *La cueva de los Grajos y sus pinturas, en Cieza, Murcia*. Monografías Arqueológicas VI, Seminario de Prehistoria y Protohistoria, Facultad de Filosofía y Letras, Universidad de Zaragoza. Saragossa.

Blance, B., 1960 and 1971. The origin and development of the early bronze age in the Iberian peninsula (Ph.D. thesis, 1960, Edinburgh University.) Published in German without revision in 1971 entitled *Die Anfänge der Metallurgie auf der Iberischen Halbinsel*. Studien zu den Anfängen der Metallurgie IV. Berlin: Romisch-Germanisches Zentralmuseum.

—— 1961. Early bronze age colonists in Iberia. *Antiquity*, 35 : 192–202.

Boessneck, J., 1969. Die Knochenfunde von Cerro del Real bei Granada (Prov. Granada.) *Studien über frühe Tierknochenfunde von der Iberischen Halbinsel* I : 3–42.

Bosch Gimpera, P., 1932. Etnologia de la península ibérica. Barcelona.

Breuil, H., 1920. Les peintures rupestres de la péninsule ibérique XI Les roches peintes de Minateda (Albacete). *L'Anthropologie*, 30 : 1–50.

—— and M. C. Burkitt, 1915. Les peintures rupestres d'éspagne VI. Les abris peints du Mont Arabí près Yecla (Murcie). *L'Anthropologie*, 26 : 313–28.

—— and H. von Obermaier, 1912. Les premiers travaux de l'Institut de Paléontologie Humaine II Travaux sur les peintures rupestres d'éspagne. *L'Anthropologie*, 23 : 1–27.

Clark, J. D., 1971. A re-examination of the evidence for agricultural origins in the Nile valley. *Proceedings of the Prehistoric Society*, 37(2) : 34–79.

Clark, J. G. D., 1958. Blade and trapeze industries of the European stone age. *Proceedings of the Prehistoric Society*, 24 : 24–42.

Cuadrado Diaz, E., 1947. Yacimientos arqueológicos albacetences de la cuenca del Río Taibilla. Appendix in *Excavaciones y trabajos arqueológicos en la provincia de Albacete de 1943 a 1946*. Informes y Memorias XV : 123–127. Madrid.

Davidson, I., 1972. The fauna from La Cueva del Volcán del Faro (Cullera, Valencia). *Archivo de Prehistoria Levantina*, XIII : 7–15.

Delibrias, G., M. T. Guillier and J. T. Labeyrie, 1964. Saclay natural radiocarbon measurements I. *Radiocarbon*, 6 : 233–50.

——, —— and —— 1965. Saclay natural radiocarbon measurements II. *Radiocarbon*, 7 : 236–44.

——, —— and —— 1966. Gif natural radiocarbon measurements. *Radiocarbon*, 8 : 74–95.

Driesch, A. von, 1969. Die Fauna des 'Cabezo Redondo' bei Villena (Prov. Alicante). In *Studien über frühe Tierknochenfunde von der Iberischen Halbinsel I*, J. Boessneck (ed.), pp. 43–87. Published by Institut für Palaeoanatomie, Domestikationsforschung und Geschichte der Tiermedizin der Universität München and Deutsches Archäologisches Institut, Madrid.

Escalon de Fonton, M., 1970. Définition de l'épi-cardial. In *Les civilisations neolithiques du Midi de la France*, 9–10. Carcassonne.

Evans, J. D., 1958. Two phases of prehistoric settlement in the western Mediterranean. *Thirteenth Annual Report and Bulletin for 1955–56*, University of London Institute of Archaeology, pp. 49–70.

Evin, J., G. Marien and Ch. Pacchiaudi, 1973. Lyon natural radiocarbon measurements IV. *Radiocarbon* 15(3) : 514–33.

Fernández de Avilés, A., 1941. Museo arqueológico de Murcia. *Memorias de los Museos Arqueológicos Provinciales 1940*: 70–77.

Fortea Péra, J., 1970. La cueva de la Palica. Serrón (Antas). *Trabajos de Prehistoria*, XXVII : 61–91.

—— 1971. *La cueva de la Cocina. Ensayo de cronología del epipaleolítico (facies geométricas)*. Servicio de Investigación Prehistórica, Diputación Provincial de Valencia, Serie de Trabajos Varios XLII. Valencia.

Gossé, G., 1941. Aljoroque, estación neolítica inicial, de la provincia de Almeria. *Ampurias*, III : 64–84.

Guilane, J., 1970. Sur l'épicardial languidocien. In *Les civilisations néolithiques du Midi de la France*, 13–16. Carcassonne.

Harris, R. A. and K. R. Duff, 1970. *Wild deer in Britain*. Newton Abbot: David and Charles.

Harrison, G. A., J. S. Weiner, J. M. Tanner and N. A. Barnicot, 1964. *Human Biology*. Oxford: Oxford University Press.

Higgs, E. S. and M. R. Jarman, 1972. The origins of animal and plant husbandry. In *Papers in economic prehistory*, E. S. Higgs (ed.), pp. 3–13. Cambridge: Cambridge University Press.

—— and C. Vita-Finzi, 1972. Prehistoric economies: a territorial approach. In *Papers in economic prehistory*, E. S. Higgs (ed.), pp. 27–36. Cambridge: Cambridge University Press.

——, C. Vita-Finzi, D. R. Harris and A. E. Fagg, 1967. The climate, environment and industries of stone age Greece pt. III. *Proceedings of the Prehistoric Society*, 33 : 1–29.

Hopf, M., 1966. Triticum monococcum L. y Triticum dicoccum Schübl. en el neolítico antiguo español. *Archivo de Prehistoria Levantina*, XI : 53–73.

—— and H. Schubart, 1965. Getreidefunde aus der Coveta de l'Or (Prov. Alicante). *Madrider Mitteilungen*, VI : 20–38.

Jarman, H. N., 1972. The origins of wheat and barley cultivation. In *Papers in economic prehistory*, E. S. Higgs (ed.) pp. 15–26. Cambridge: Cambridge University Press.

Jarman, M. R., 1972. European deer economics and the advent of the neolithic. In *Papers in economic prehistory*, E. S. Higgs (ed.), pp. 125–47. Cambridge: Cambridge University Press.

—— and P. F. Wilkinson, 1972. Criteria of animal domestication. In *Papers in economic prehistory*, E. S. Higgs (ed.), pp. 83–96. Cambridge: Cambridge University Press.

Jáuregui, J. J., 1949. Influencia de los vientos y corrientes de la cuenca occidental del mediterráneo en las relaciones iberoafricanas. In *Crónica. IV congreso arqueológico del sudeste español. Elche 1948*, 96–104. Cartagena.

Jiménez Navarro, E., 1947. Sobre el orígen del vaso campaniforme. In *Crónica. I congreso arqueológico del sudeste español. Albacete 1946*, 127–32. Albacete.

—— 1962. Excavaciones en cueva Ambrosio. *Noticiario Arqueológico Hispánico V* (1956–1961) : 13–48.

Jordá Cerdá, F., 1953. Notas sobre los comienzos del neolítico en nuestra península. *Archivum*, III : 259–71.

—— 1954. Graveteinse y epigraveteinse en la España mediterránea. *Ceasaraugusta*, IV : 7–30.

—— and Alcácer Grau, J. 1949. *La covacha de Llatas (Andilla)*. Servicio de Investigación Prehistórica, Diputación Provincial de Valencia, Serie de Trabajos Varios XV. Valencia.

Llobregat Conka, E. A., 1973. *Del fin del neolítico de cerámicas impresas al comienzo de la edad de bronce en la región valenciana*. Papeles del laboratorio de arqueología de Valencia IX. Universidad de Valencia.

López Pascual, E., 1968. El testimonio rupestre: nota acerca de las pinturas rupestres de Cieza (Murcia). *Geo y Bio Karst*, V : 468–69.

Martinez Santa-Olalla, J., 1946. *Esquema paletnológica de la península hispánica*. Madrid.

——, B. Sáez Martin, C. F. Posac Mons, J. A. Sopranis Salto and E. del Val Caturla, 1947. *Excavaciones en la ciudad del bronce mediterráneo II, de la Bastida de Totana (Murcia)*. Informes y memorias XVI. Ministerio de Educación Nacional, Comisaría General de Excavaciones Arqueológicas, Madrid.

McBurney, C. B. M., 1967. *The Haua Fteah (Cyrenaica) and the stone age of the south-east Mediterranean*. Cambridge: Cambridge University Press.

Muñoz Amilibid, A. M., 1970. Estado actual de la investigación sobre el neolítico español. *Pyrenae*, VI : 28.

Murray, J., 1970. *The first European agriculture, a study of the osteological and botanical evidence until 2000 BC*. Edinburgh: Edinburgh University Press.

Pellicer Catalá, M., 1962. *Estratigrafía de la cueva de Nerja*. Excavaciones arqueológicas en España XVI. Madrid.

—·— and M. Hopf, 1970. Neolithische Getreidefunde in der Höhle von Nerja. *Madrider Mitteilungen*, XI : 18.

Pericot Garcia, L., 1942. *La cueva del Parpalló*. Centro Superior de Investigaciones Científicas, Madrid.

—— 1946. La cueva de la Cocina (Dos Aguas). *Archivo de Prehistoria Levantina* II (1945) : 39–71.

—— 1950. El paleolítico superior del sureste. In *Crónica. I congreso nacional de arqueológia y del V congreso arqueológico del sudeste. Almería, 1949*, 57–62. Cartagena.

—— and J. Cuadrado Ruiz, 1952. Dos nuevas estaciónes solutrenses en Totana. In *Crónica. II congreso nacional de arqueológia. Madrid, 1951*, 89–92. Saragossa, 1952.

Plá Ballester, E., 1958. La covacha de Ribera (Cullera-Valencia). *Archivo de Prehistoria Levantina*, VII : 23–32.

Rahmouni, C., C. Roussillot and F. Armanet, 1970. Algiers radiocarbon measurements I. *Radiocarbon*, 12 : 353–57.

Renfrew, C., 1967. Colonialism and megalithismus. *Antiquity*, 31 : 276–88.

Ripoll Perelló, E. 1960–1961. Excavaciones en cueva Ambrosio (Vélez Blanco, Almería). Campañas de 1958 y 1960. *Ampurias*, XXII–XXIII : 31–48.

Roche, J., 1960. *Le gisement mésolithique de Moita de Sebastiño (Muge–Portugal)*. Lisbon: Instituto da Alta Cultura.

San Valero Aparisi, J., 1948. El neolítico y la península hispánica. *Actas y Memorias de la Sociodad Española de Antropología. Etnología y Prehistoria* XXIII (Homenaje a Julio Martínez Santa-Olalla III), 124–44.

—— 1950. *La cueva de la Sarsa*. Servicio de Investigacion Prehistórica, Diputación Provincial de Valencia, Serie de Trabajos Varios XII. Valencia.

Savory, H. N., 1968. *Spain and Portugal. The prehistory of the Iberian peninsula*. London: Thames and Hudson.

Schubart, H., 1965. Neue Radiokarbon-daten zur Vor- und Frühgeschichte der iberischen Halbinsel. *Madrider Mitteilungen*, VI : 11–19.

Schubart, H. and V. Pascual, 1966. Datación por el carbono 14 de los estratos con cerámica cardial de la coveta de l'Or. *Archivo de Prehistoria Levantina*, XI : 45–51.

Schwabedissen, H. and J. Freundlich, 1966. Köln radiocarbon measurements. *Radiocarbon*, 8 : 239–47.

Siret, H. and L. Siret, 1888. *Les premiers âges du métal dans le sud-est de l'Espagne*. 2 vols. Antwerp.

Siret, L., 1893. L'Espagne préhistorique. *Revue des Questions Scientifiques*, 2nd. ser. IV : 489–562.

Soler, Garcia, J. M., 1956. La cueva grande de Huesa Tacaña. In *Libro homenaje al conde de la Vega del Sella*, 123–31. Oviedo.

—— 1968–69. La 'cueva pequeña' de la Huesa Tacaña y el 'mesolítico' villenense. *Zephyrus*, XIX–XX : 33–56.

Such, M., 1920. Avance al estudio de la caverna 'Hoyo de la Mina'. *Boletín de la Sociedad Malagueña de Ciencias*, 3ª época no. 3 : 23–54.

Tarradell, M., 1959. El estrecho de Gibraltar. ¿Puente o frontera? (Sobre relaciones post-neolíticas entre Marruecos y la península ibérica.) *Tamuda*, VII : 123–38.

Topp, C., 1959. Some Balkan and Danubian influences to southern and south-eastern Spain. *Archivo de Prehistoria Levantina*, VIII : 115–23.

—— and A. Arribas, 1965. A survey of the Tabernas material lodged in the Museum of Almería. *University of London Institute of Archaeology Bulletin* 5 : 69–89.

Tringham, R., 1971. Hunters, fishers and farmers of eastern Europe 6000–3000 B.C. London: Hutchinson.

Vilaseca, S., 1934. L'estació taller de sílex de St. Gregori (Falset, Baix Priorat). *Memorias de la Academia de Ciencias y Artes de Barcelona*, XXIII : 415–39.

—— 1949. Avance al estudio de la cueva del Filador de Margalef (provincia de Tarragona). *Archivo Español de Arqueologia*, XXIII : 347–61.

Vita-Finzi, C. and E. S. Higgs, 1970. Prehistoric economy in the Mount Carmel area of Palestine: site catchment analysis. *Proceedings of the Prehistoric Society*, 36 : 1–37.

Walker, M. J., 1971. Spanish Levantine rock art. *Man*, NS 6 : 553–89.

—— 1972. Cave dwellers and artists of the Neothermal period in southeastern Spain. *Transactions of the Cave Research Group of Great Britain*, 14(1) : 1–22.

—— 1973a. Aspects of the neolithic and copper ages in the basins of the rivers Segura and Vinalopó, south-east Spain. D. Phil. thesis, Oxford University.

—— 1973b. T-tests on prehistoric and modern charred grain measurements. *Science and archaeology*, 10 : 11–32.

—— (in press). Excavaciones preliminares en el Abrigo Grande del Barranco de los Grajos, término de Cieza, Murcia, 1970: contribución al estudio del período neotermal en la península. Noticiario Arqueológico Hispánico.

—— and A. Cuenca Payá (in press). Comentarios sobre el cuaternario continental en el centro y sur de Alicante. Trabajos sobre Neogeno-Cuaternario, 2.

—— and —— (in preparation). Environment and habitat in SE. Spain: observations on the Pleistocene and recent fluvial aggradations and cave sediments.

Group definitions and mental templates

An ethnographic experiment

J. PETER WHITE, NICHOLAS MODJESKA and IRARI HIPUYA

Preface

This paper is written in two sections, each of which discusses the same problem. We have done this not from failure to reach agreement on the material but because it has seemed to us valuable to illustrate not only the different perspectives through which an archaeologist and a social anthropologist view the same material but also the complexities and difficulties that arise in cross-cultural experiments which try to investigate the ethnographic reality behind apparently simple archaeological concepts.

I

There are two concepts which are common in much archaeological thinking but have been explicitly tested only rarely. The first is that single classes of archaeological remains can be assumed to define 'cultural groups'. It is assumed that similarities between artifactual assemblages denote a common cultural tradition, while the presence of synchronic variation is taken to imply that different cultural groups are present (eg. Deetz, 1967:7; Collins, 1969; see also Binford, 1972).

Although the precise scale of group involved is often left unclear, we consider that in many cases (eg. the French upper Palaeolithic) it would be equated with a socially conscious, face-to-face one. Such an equation is difficult to test archaeologically but ethnographic examples may help to indicate under what conditions and at what levels the proposition may be true.

The second concept is that of a 'mental template'. The definition of this concept is not widely agreed upon and at least two levels of meaning can be found in the literature.

As defined by Deetz, a mental template is 'the idea of the proper form of an object [which] exists in the mind of the maker' (1967:45). An artifact is the result of this idea expressed in tangible form. From this we can argue, with Clarke, that 'repeated clusters of selected and correlated attributes constitute a metamorphosed message which still conveys information about the intentions of the fabricator' (1968:135).

But what precisely are these intentions? At one level, Clarke's statement is so obviously true as to be barely worth discussing. Quite clearly, any aspect of an artifact's form which is not determined by the raw material must derive from the maker's conscious *or unconscious* intentions and abilities, as Dunnell so clearly realises (1971:132). Further, if 'intentions' can be unconscious they can only be elucidated by observing recurrent attributes in the artifacts produced. Patterns of recurrent attributes however are the very stuff of archaeological research, and will be used irrespective of the nature of the 'intentional' dimension. At this level of meaning then it

seems that the concept of a mental template is unnecessary, at least for archaeologists, while it is exceptionally difficult to conceive how it might be tested anyway.

Mental templates however are understood by some authors to refer to *conscious* ideas and ideals of the artifact makers, so that their identification is equivalent to recognition of 'cognitive' or 'emic' types which are those that would be distinguished by the artisans (Spaulding, 1969:76; Rouse, 1972:52; Thomas, 1974:12-13). According to this view, if we identify mental templates through the patterning of attributes in archaeological materials we have in fact derived one aspect of the makers' taxonomic system. It is this proposition which has been vehemently rejected (eg. by Dunnell, 1971:134; Sheets, 1973:20) and quite clearly its testability cannot proceed through the archaeological data. Any relationship between artifact patterning and cognitive type can only be observed in situations where the makers' categories can be obtained through some means other than observation of their artifacts. Ethnographic situations which allow for the interviewing of artisans provide such a means, since conscious 'emic' types must be expressed in language (Rouse, 1972:52).

The ethnographic situation we have used to explore these problems occurs among makers of flaked stone tools in the Western Highlands of Papua New Guinea where fieldwork was conducted in 1973. We describe this situation, use it to formulate hypotheses and then test these experimentally.

'The Duna' comprise some 17 000 speakers of the Duna language who live in three main valley systems around Lake Kopiago in the Western Highlands (Sinclair, 1966; 1973). Culturally they are similar to the more numerous Huli to the south-east (Glasse, 1968) while to the west across the Strickland River and to the north and south live 'non-Highlanders' who are culturally very different, and whose languages, in some cases, do not belong to the Highlands Phylum. We worked almost entirely in one of the three Duna valleys, along the Tumbudu River, and among the 12 parishes which occupy the lower 30 km or so. (Map, Fig. 1).

Duna, like other Highlanders, are horticulturalists and pig raisers, and the bulk of their diet consists of sweet potato. They live in scattered houses which, prior to Christian mission influence, were occupied by men, or women and children, but not both. Most pigs also live with the women. Population density is low—our estimate is under 12 per km²—and declines rapidly as one moves west along the Tumbudu towards the Strickland River.

Political organisation is acephalous. The largest local political groups are formed of a few hundred people who occupy areas of territory believed to have been demarcated by the earliest ancestors. These groups are referred to as 'villages' in administration records and correspond to 'parishes' in the terminology of Hogbin and Wedgwood (1952-54). The effective unit for the initiation of warfare and the organisation of ceremonial distributions is a smaller group, based on non-unilineal descent, called a *damene* ('family' or 'related kind'). Members of any one *damene* will usually be found in several parishes, but the majority of male members of a politically functioning ambilineage will be found residing within only one parish. Men tend to live within the same local groups as their fathers, but most men will reside with their mother's group at some time during their lives and not a few will also live elsewhere. As men come and go ambilineages tend to coalesce and disperse within the larger local groupings, producing a complex and frequently shifting pattern of residence and descent.[1]

Duna stone technology is a very simple one and has been fully described elsewhere (White, 1969; White and Thomas, 1972). It consists of flaking nodules of flint or chert and using the unretouched pieces (*aré*) (either flakes or remnant cores) for a variety of tasks. Smaller pieces of stone are hafted in a simple stick for some tasks and these pieces, which are bound into the haft with plant fibre, are called *aré kou* (wrapped *aré*).[2] The common use of these tools was abandoned 10-20 years ago when steel axes and knives became generally available, but a few men still carry around some flakes with them, and many would use a stone flake if a steel knife was not to hand. All men with whom we worked could remember stone-age times and were able to make and use flaked stone tools, although some men were more apt at this than others. Even today *aré kou* are preferred to any available steel tool for the purpose of preparing cane for bindings, and we have only occasionally observed a knife being used for this purpose.

Duna classifications are, in general, simple, one-level categories. If verbal behaviour is any guide, classes of things exist *hangu hangu* 'another and another' i.e. separate and not hierarchically arranged. Thus there is no word in the language which can be translated as 'stones' or 'things made of stone'. Stone axes, *aré*, cult stones and 'stone things' (stone around the landscape) are separate and distinct classes and it certainly makes no sense to any Duna speaker to try and group them together. In other fields of classification too, such as the plant and animal worlds, Duna behaviour is such as to produce unrelated, non-taxonomic categories, and we suggest that Duna classificatory behaviour is in general far more referential than paradigmatic, i.e. it works by constant reference to objects in order to form groups rather than by setting up mental paradigms or systematic discriminations. Thus when NM first asked some Horaile men to arrange some *aré* into whatever groupings they liked, one of them remarked 'in the old days we didn't do that, we didn't know anything about putting them in different piles, we just looked for the good ones and used them'. So also in discussing *aré* there are several descriptive terms for various groups of stones, but little evidence that they form any *system* of classification, let alone one which is

commonly used. We might compare our own possible categories of green, yellow, red, etc. ball-pen casings, which we can certainly understand and operate, but which tell us nothing about how ball-pens are customarily classified in our society. Further, the *aré* situation is more complex in that any one piece of stone *can* be put into a number of cross-cutting categories. Thus we can set up the contrast sets:

1)
	aré	
aré kone	*aré kou*	*aré nguni*
('real' *aré*)	(*aré* which can be hafted)	(not sharp)

OR

2)
	aré	
aré kone	*aré yokona*	*aré nguni*
(real *aré*, light coloured)	(true flint, dark brown to black)	(weathered, decomposed)

While each of these sets can be formed in Duna, the first would be so in response to questions about *aré* as tools, the second to questions about *aré* as material for tools. Other sets may be formed in response to other questions. We would thus stress that there is no *single* idea behind Duna classifications and no single classificatory scheme inherent in Duna language (cf. Wallace, 1962).

In such a situation we might well expect very localised variation in man-made objects. If people work primarily through objects rather than classifications then it could be presumed that they learn primarily by copying the objects they see around them. We should thus find a series of diverging objectifications. Copying, and trial and error, rather than explicit teaching, are certainly the methods by which young Duna men learn about flaked stone.

This might be expected to be further reinforced by Duna attitudes about knowledge. Duna men are not intellectualists and do not spend their time discussing the meaning of things.[3] They assume that all people think the same way until faced with evidence to the contrary, in which case they remark: 'well they're other men, their ways are something else'. Duna men always insist on the particularistic nature of knowledge. What one man knows is not what another knows and, we suspect, the two cannot know the 'same' things. Only among the *damene* is there a claim for common knowledge, and men will claim that 'my *damene* thinks in one way only' whereas other men think differently—or rather 'other men are other men, you'll have to ask them'. Members of one *damene* however are simply *expected* to have one consciousness since they are all descended from the same ancestor and 'we all do as our fathers do'. But it would probably be more correct to say that in most matters of classification the group has no common pattern of expressed thought at all, so that there would be nothing to prevent localised variation in artifacts occurring.

The establishment of such highly localised artifact variations (even though the linguistic taxonomy does not vary) however would be strongly militated against by the nature of Duna residence. Not only do Duna men live in scattered homesteads and generally practise their technology in isolation, but they also change residences every few years. While these changes *usually* occur within parish borders this is by no means always true and many men live for at least part of their lives outside

---

1. To clarify this a little further: while members of an ambilineage will distinguish between true agnates ('put by men') and non-agnatic cognates ('put by women') the latter are in no way less 'real' or 'true' members of the lineage, so that men can claim to be members of several lineages (grandparents', etc.) and will assert whichever claim is convenient for their current political activity and residential propensity.

2. The Duna refer not to the hafting of the piece but the fact that it is wrapped in fibre — i.e. they stress the process of manufacture not the functionally different tool which is produced.

---

3. Cf. Fortune, 1935, v: 'The Manus delight in facts and argument . . . They debate questions about entirely useless matters from the love of truth!' No greater contrast with the Duna could be imagined.

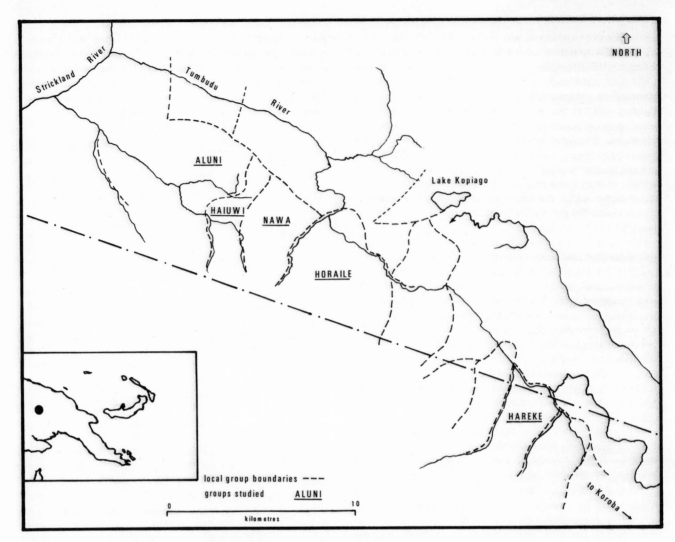

Fig. 1: Map of Lower Tumbudu River valley, showing local groups studied.

the parish in which they were born. Even those who remain within the parish however do not necessarily live in proximity to other members of their *damene*. Further, not only do *damene* and parish members alternate their residence within and between parishes over time, but this pattern appears to extend on a larger scale. Valley systems within Duna country do not set boundaries to residential mobility nor do language boundaries between the Duna and their neighbours. Some men from Haiuwi and Nawa (see map) for instance have lived even as far away as Koroba (50 km) while some trans-Strickland residence is also practised.

This combination of disinterest in classification and shifting residence suggests to us that not only is there no conscious mental template of *aré* among the Duna (*aré* simply are) but that we should not expect well-developed local traditions of artifact manufacture to exist. These conclusions may be re-phrased to give us two predictions.

The first is that we should find little or no variation between the artifacts selected for specific tasks in different parishes since residential movement will constantly militate against its development. Nonetheless we might expect whatever variation there is to increase with distance, i.e. to be inversely correlated with residential movement.

The second prediction is that at any one time within any parish we might expect to find considerable individual variation in the range of artifacts grouped in a particular class,

since artifacts are largely manufactured and used in isolation and are not tightly defined in Duna language.

A comprehensive test of these predictions would clearly involve observations of tools actually used by many men over some time, as well as an artificial test situation. It might be the case, for example, that the tools actually used for a task would be more similar metrically than those selected in an artificial experimental situation where an apparently appropriate taxon was employed, although our limited observations on the actual use of stone tools do not suggest that the difference would be marked.

The ideal situation is, however, impossible to attain among the Duna—or, we suspect, anywhere in the world—and our tests relied on an artificial situation in which men produced and classified flaked stone tools at our request. (We note in passing that all men who worked for us were paid at the same *per diem* rate of A30 cents for about an hour's work).

The experiment used to test the above predictions forms part of a larger project designed to elucidate the contribution of the three major sources of variation—technical competence, raw material differences and cognitive variability—to an assemblage of flaked stone tools. In a previous experiment in 1967 which made some discriminations between these sources, JPW nonetheless failed to make the contribution of each source clear (White and Thomas, 1972). In 1973 we have experimented with the *selection* as well as the *production* of stone tools. By presenting a number of men with the same assemblage to classify we have, we think, controlled almost completely the variables of raw material and technical competence and should be able to focus on cognitive variability within and between groups. It is of course likely that cognitive variability includes an appreciation of raw materials, which in turn may be influenced by technical competence, so that variations observed within and between groups will include these to some extent. But any variation will still be entirely in the sphere of personal evaluation rather than in those areas uncontrollable by the artisan.

For our experiment we selected a random sample of 122 stone flakes from the much larger number made by eleven men of Nawa parish on a particular day. These men were employed to make stone tools for one hour/day, during which time they usually produced 50–150 tools. Each man was asked to divide his output into *aré kone* and *aré kou*, and our sample was selected to be representative of the full range of variability, in terms of size, shape, colour and rock type, among the tools designated as *aré kou*. The sample was actually drawn from the output of four men. Measurements of the sample are given in Tables 5–7. It will be noted that the majority of specimens are small flakes (65% weigh less than 2.0 g) and have acute edge angles (58% less than 55°), while nearly half have length/breadth ratios of more than 2:1 (i.e. are blade-like).

This sample of *aré kou* was then presented by NM and IH to 63 men from five parishes (Northwest to Southeast: Aluni, Haiuwi, Nawa, Horaile, Hareke (see map). These men were not told that the flakes had been originally designated by their makers as *aré kou*, and each man was asked to sort the pile into *aré kou*, *aré kone* and *aré nguni*. A transcription of the instructions as given by IH to one man is given below.[4]

Although the instructions given to each man varied in minor ways, we do not think this affected the results. Our informants seldom expressed any uncertainty about what they were being asked to do, for it was common knowledge that we were interested in the discrimination of *aré kou* from other stones. It is worth noting that the experiment was carried out during the interviewing of each man about his technical aptitudes, residential mobility, trading expeditions, familiarity with quarry sites and other aspects of life history relevant to material culture. Sorting experiments and interviews were conducted in a semi-public context where there were always other men sitting around and, sometimes, discussing them. We did not attempt to conduct our experiments within an isolated laboratory-type situation but in one more nearly comparable with the situations in which most decisions are reached in Duna society. Although each man was told to use his own

judgment in sorting, there were occasional discussions over an individual piece.

Our conviction that, in general, the men who made the selections were operating according to the same understanding of our instructions is reinforced by the fact that four of the five parishes picked out a very similar percentage of the total (Table 1). We would attribute the difference at Horaile to the fact that people there are accustomed to using inferior materials and are therefore prepared to accept a wider range of pieces.

Table 1 *Aré kou* **selected**

	Aluni	Haiuwi	Nawa	Horaile	Hareke
No. of men	13	12	12	13	13
Total No. of *aré kou* selected	665	646	701	1035	628
Max. possible no. to select	1586	1464	1464	1586	1586
Percent selected	41·9	44·3	48·1	63·6	39·6
Range selected no.	31–74	35–70	40–73	41–95	18–75

Among the *aré kou* selected it is clear that a few specimens were highly favoured by nearly all men, and these must be considered as very close to an 'ideal' type. (Five specimens are illustrated in Fig. 2 upper row.) After the 'ideal' specimens were removed however there was much less agreement between individuals on which were the desirable *aré kou* as Table 2 shows.

Table 2 *Aré kou*—**agreement in selection within local groups**

		Aluni	Haiuwi	Nawa	Horaile	Hareke
Number of *aré kou* selected by:	all men	16	16	21	27	1
	all but 1 man	11	11	12	19	3
	all but 2 men	6	10	6	10	7
	all but 3 men	3	4	5	6	10

---

4. Irari's instructions to Lup (Piru), 23/10/1973.

Aiyu Lupko,	aré kou	hangu	doaino,		dina.	Aré kou
Now Lup	aré kou	only	place (*or* put),		(I say).	Aré kou

tsuwano		binia	hangu	doaino,	dina.	Eh . . . . .
shaver (*or* planer)		those	only	place,	(I) say.	Eh . . . . .

mini	dugu	tsia,	aré tsuwano	binia	hangu	doaino,	dina
forked	arrow	shaving,	aré shaver	those	only	place	(I) say

Nguni	binia,	nguni	aré	tsuwano	neyao	aka,	nguni	binia	hangu
Bad	those,	bad	aré	shaver	not	?	bad	those	only

waka	doaino
another place	put.

Aiyu,	ka	dapanda	kone,	dianua.
Now,	you	will choose	truly,	(he) says.

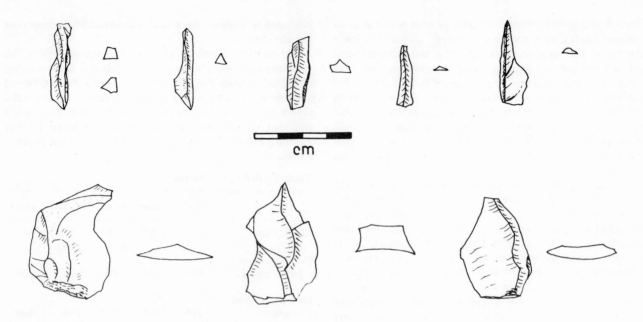

Fig. 2: *Aré kou.* (Upper) five selected by nearly all men in all local groups; (lower) three not selected by any men.

The one aberrant local group is Hareke. Several reasons may be involved. One obvious one is that our sojourn at Hareke was brief and people there were less cognizant of our work and less committed to it. This may have resulted in a less careful selection of material on the part of some men, although we are surprised that the results would be so random. Another possible reason is that Hareke men are used to working entirely in fine black flint whereas only about half the sample we are using here is of this material, the rest being off-white to brown chert. However, inspection reveals that Hareke men are not particularly biased towards black flint: of the 21 specimens listed in Table 2 only 7 are black, while 8 could be labelled off-white. Another possible reason concerns the size of the artifacts since an earlier experiment found that *aré kou* made at Hareke did tend to be larger than those from Aluni (White and Thomas, 1972). However we think this insufficient to account for so great a difference since there are other specimens not selected from the sample that would seem to us to have been more appropriate for selection if that were so.

There was a high degree of agreement on 'ideal' types between the local groups as Table 3 shows. It will be noted that while there is some divergence between Hareke and the other groups the degree of agreement is still high. No geographical trend is apparent in the variation between local groups.

Considerable numbers of stones were not selected by any men, and there is a wide measure of agreement between local groups in this also (Table 4). Three of these specimens are illustrated in Fig. 2 (lower).

Tables 5–7 set out some measurements of the tools preferred by the men of each parish.

In relation to tool weights (Table 5) there seem to be some minor differences between parishes, a few heavier specimens being preferred as one moves up-valley. The differences however are not statistically significant. This was tested by transforming data from Haiuwi, Horaile, and Hareke by natural logarithms and then after verifying that the shape of curves did not deviate significantly from normality and that variances were homogeneous, performing a one-way analysis of

Table 3 *Aré kou* selection—agreement between local groups

		Aluni	Haiuwi	Nawa	Horaile	Hareke
Total no. of *aré kou* selected*		27	27	33	46	25
	A	X	23	25	26	19
	H		X	25	27	19
No. of *aré kou* in	N			X	30	21
common	H				X	22
	H					X

* Number of *aré kou* selected by all men or all men but 1 at Aluni, Haiuwi, Nawa and Horaile; all specimens selected by 9 men or more at Hareke.

Table 4 *Aré kou* not selected

		Aluni	Haiuwi	Nawa	Horaile	Hareke
No. selected by no men		33	38	22	11	18
No. in common	A	X	29	19	11	13
	H		X	20	11	16
	N			X	11	11
	H				X	10
	H					X

variance. The variance ratio (F) of 0.8332 shows that a null hypothesis of no difference between means of the three groups is acceptable.

Table 6 shows no differences between preferred length/breadth ratios for the five parishes. Indeed, the similarities are so marked that statistical testing is unnecessary.

Table 5 *Aré kou* **preferred weights** (%)

gm	Aluni	Haiuwi	Nawa	Horaile	Hareke	All specimens
0·1–0·5	36	33	33	26	19	13
0·6–1·0	36	36	30	33	27	22
1·1–1·5	24	20	18	20	15	18
1·6–2·0	8	12	9	6	12	12
2·1–2·5	4	4	3	4	15	7·5
2·6–3·0	—	—	3	4	4	7·5
3·1–3·5	—	—	—	—	4	2·5
3·6–4·0	—	—	—	—	—	2·5
4·1–4·5	—	—	—	4	—	2·5
4·6–5·0	—	—	—	2	4	3·5
>5·0	—	—	—	—	—	9
mean	0·87	0·84	1·02	1·13	1·44	2·18
s.d.	0·57	0·52	0·89	0·95	1·23	2·04
N	27	27	33	46	25	122

Table 6 *Aré kou*: **preferred L/B ratios** (%)

L/B	Aluni	Haiuwi	Nawa	Horaile	Hareke	All specimens
<1·6	—	—	—	—	—	20
1·6–2·0	—	—	—	12	4	34
2·1–2·5	28	24	30	30	25	21
2·6–3·0	32	40	33	28	33	15
3·1–3·5	20	20	15	10	17	5
3·6–4·0	20	16	15	10	13	4
4·1–4·5	4	4	3	2	4	1
4·6–5·0	4	4	3	2	4	1
mean	3·1	3·1	3·0	2·8	3·0	2·2
s.d.	0·7	0·7	0·7	0·7	0·8	1·0
N	27	27	33	46	25	122

Table 7 *Aré kou*: **preferred angles** (%)

Angle	Aluni	Haiuwi	Nawa	Horaile	Hareke	All specimens
15–24	14	12	10	10	8	13
25–34	6	4	10	7	8	12
35–44	15	24	21	16	25	17
45–54	23	20	21	23	23	16
55–64	18	18	16	17	17	13
65–74	21	18	18	18	18	15
75–84	6	4	3	4	4	6
85–94	—	—	—	3	3	7
95–104	—	1	2	3	3	2
>104	—	—	—	—	—	1
mean	49·6	49·1	49·1	50·3	49·8	53·1
s.d.	18·1	17·6	17·5	18·3	17·7	22·3
N	53	51	62	77	48	219

The same is true of the similarity in edge angles (Table 7), which is probably related to function. We note that the range of acceptable angles is very wide and that the functions for which an *aré kou* serves can obviously be carried out by a wide range of angles. There is clearly however some preference for the middle range of angles—neither too fine and thus fragile nor too obtuse and thus insufficiently sharp.

Comparison with the results obtained in 1967 (White and Thomas, 1972:290-91) shows much greater similarity between all five parishes tested in 1973 than was observed previously between two of them (Aluni and Hareke). We would see this as stemming from the fact that in this experiment we are looking at *selection* whereas in the earlier one *performance* (flaking competence in relation to particular raw materials) was a major factor.

We may now return to the predictions made on the basis of ethnographic data and attempt to assess their accuracy. The first, that there would be little or no variation in artifact selection between parishes, has clearly not been falsified in the case of the adjacent parishes of Aluni, Haiuwi, Nawa and Horaile. The marked differences at Hareke were also expectable in terms of the prediction although we suggest that not all the observed variation is explicable within these terms. The other factors which may have exaggerated the variation have been outlined earlier. We can thus suggest that the current residential pattern does prevent the development of locally different artifact traditions and further, that socially conscious, face-to-face groups may well exist without developing such traditions even where such apparently important factors as styles of learning and conditions of artifact use would appear to favour such development.

The second prediction, that a wide range of artifacts would be approved of, has clearly been falsified in at least four cases. Although the artifacts that were manufactured and given to us as *aré kou* came in a wide range of shapes and sizes (cf. Fig. 1), there is clearly, within each parish except Hareke, a general agreement on the ideal form designated by the term *aré kou*. The pattern observed at Hareke conforms much more closely to that anticipated, but, as in the previous case, that this is due in part to extraneous factors must be considered possible.

In the four parishes of Aluni, Haiuwi, Nawa and Horaile we believe that our results suggest that operational criteria (the way in which *aré kou* are hafted and used) give rise to a 'covert category' (Berlin *et al*, 1968) which has been used by our workers but is not linguistically accessible. The 'emic' type *aré kou* then refers only to one level of the distinctions made by Duna speakers in relation to stone tools.

In conclusion, we would simply draw attention to the fact that an attempt to investigate either of the concepts discussed at the start of this paper opens up a wide range of problems. It might be convenient to believe that the Duna, because of the fluidity of their group compositions and residential practices and the apparent effects of these upon the formation and transmission of cultural traditions, are an ethnographer's (and archaeologist's) nightmare, but in fact we know of no good reason for suggesting that they are very exceptional.

Perhaps the problems lie in our over-precise and over-simplified ideas about the social structures, classifications and technological procedures of non-industrial societies?

J.P.W.

II

1. The determinants of form   'The determinants of form can be sought among the four concepts called Purpose (purposeful use or useful function), Idea (conception power or artistic volition), Material (nature's raw materials or characteristics of materials) and Hand (skill or technique)' (Kojiro, 1965:20).

Kojiro and his associates point out that these four concepts can be thought of as forming the vertices of a tetrahedron-shaped space, within which any form may be located according to the relative influence of each pole (Fig. 3). This admirably simple schematisation, which in fact corresponds closely to the archaeological concepts of artifact function, mental template, material and technological skill (see also Clegg, this volume), allows us in particular to distinguish clearly between the idea of an artifact as it exists in the mind of its maker and the purpose of the artifact (its function) which may or may not be optimally matched to the idea in any instance. Much archaeological discussion about mental templates has tended to confuse or equate the two, but in our experiment the distinction is a crucial one since purpose appears to be the principal factor reponsible for the nature of the ideas in the minds of the makers.

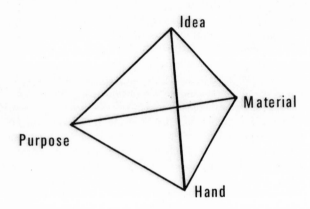

Fig. 3:   The determinants of form (*after* Kojiro).

A final point needs to be made in clarification of the concept of 'mental template'. Some writers (eg. Watson *et al.*, 1971) equate mental templates with 'shared ideas' as a part of what is called 'the normative view of culture'. Of course there is no necessary connection between ideas in an individual maker's mind and the norm commonly accepted within a culture. Ideas within minds can be as varied as external behaviour and the normative view of culture blinds us to the importance of variation in both realms.

Indeed, there are grounds for supposing that individuals' mental representations, because they are covert and unobservable, are much less socialised than the behaviour that follows from them. Therefore we should beware of conceptions of mental templates which stress their normative aspect as representations of the 'collective consciousness' (Durkheim and Mauss [1901–02] 1963 : 85) at the expense of an appreciation of their naturalistic aspect as individual, psychological phenomena. The normative aspect of mind has been particularly stressed in American ethnoscience and cognitive anthropology studies which have influenced the archaeologists' concept of mind. Heider's (1972) study of individual variation in Dani (New Guinea) colour terminology

has provided a much-needed corrective to the normative view within anthropology; perhaps the present paper can perform a similar function for archaeology. The concept of mind which archaeology is at present operating with is often too rigid and may be preventing the recognition of patterns in the search for the shape of the unseen. As Roger Brown has pointed out, at least one other conception of mind may offer attractive alternatives:

> For ethnoscience the mind seems to be a categorical grid imposed on reality, rendering some things equivalent and others nonequivalent. Since the cells of the grid are usually named, the design of the grid should be discoverable from inquiries about the meanings of words. For Piaget, intelligence is an activity; to think is to operate. Intellectual operations seem to him to be motoric operations that have been internalized ... The mind, for Piaget, is more transformer than template (Brown, 1964:251).

2. Procedures   As Deetz (1967) has observed, the accuracy with which a mental template is expressed depends upon the process by which an artifact is manufactured. Artifacts flaked from stone, because of the nature of fracture patterns and the impossibility of replacing removed material, cannot express mental templates as accurately as can pottery, for example. We therefore decided upon an experiment in which subjects would select 'good *aré kou*' from a standard assortment, working on the principle that men can judge forms more readily than they can create them. The selection of the standard assortment and the presentation of the test to our subjects is described above in JPW's section of the paper. Two further points should be noted:

(1) The inference of mental templates from the data of selection experiments depends upon the assumption that subjects actually pay attention to the task at hand and attempt to sort out 'good *aré kou*' just as they would in normal artifact-using behaviour. We have to assume that our subjects have understood the instructions and responded appropriately. We have no way of knowing whether some of our subjects have failed to 'choose truly' or perhaps even deliberately deceived us. In my judgment there was a lack of attentiveness on the part of certain men, but I doubt if any of them would think of deceiving us. Some estimate of the effects of inattentiveness might be made by retesting the same men at a latter date. However, because Duna do not understand the rationale of re-testing they are often annoyed by requests to repeat such experiments and any attempt to validate our findings in this way would probably fail.

(2). The mental templates inferred from our data are collective rather than individual representations. This is necessarily so because we have had to depend upon *agreement* in selections within and between groups as a measure of the favourable judgment of *aré kou* form. To employ Piaget's distinctions concerning the process of thinking, Duna thinking about the forms of artifacts is carried on mostly at the 'pre-operational intuitive' level. In sorting 'good *aré kou*' our subjects proceeded intuitively and apparently without any operational level concepts relating to size, weight, edge-angle, material or length/breadth ratio (Thomas' [1974] account of earlier experiments gives a contrary impression). That our subjects' sorting procedures were in fact internalised motoric responses (as Piaget believes) was suggested by the sorting behaviour of several men who picked up each stone in turn, found an appropriate edge and then gestured in the air with the stone to indicate the direction they would use it in cutting. This procedure was repeated each time before sorting the stone into its appropriate pile. The clearest evidence I have for the absence of operational level thinking comes from my complete lack of success in trying to get subjects to arrange their *aré kou* in order of magnitude from 'good' to 'bad/useless', a basic operational level ability. The notion of rank ordering has been presented to the Duna through political education programmes aimed at explaining the Australian-introduced system of preferential voting. Nevertheless, I was unable to convey to my subjects the notion of 'preferential voting for *aré kou*', and it was for this reason that agreement between subjects had to be taken as the measure of favourable judgment. It is relevant here to note that there is no simple way to ask questions in Duna equivalent to our 'Which is better?'. For Duna, an *aré* is either an *aré kou* or it is not. Categories or things are seen as unitary and internally undifferentiated. They are based upon the recognition of perceptual invariants which cannot, from their point of view, be broken down into sets of related attributes.

3. Results and interpretations JPW approaches the problem of mental templates by making two predictions to be tested against the data gathered in the experiment. His first prediction concerns population *variance* between local groups in the metrical attributes of the artifact assemblages selected. His second prediction concerns the amount of *agreement* in selection within local groups. No specific predictions are made concerning variance within groups or agreement between groups.

With respect to his first prediction, JPW argues that there will be little variance between local groups due to the effects of residential mobility in Duna society. Because men move around a lot, local traditions never have a chance to establish themselves. Rates of residential mobility in societies seem to have received little attention from archaeologists despite their obvious relevance for prehistory, and contemporary ethnographic records will be of central importance here. Assuming an ideal model of exogamous clans with patrilineal descent and patrilocal residence, one might expect male residential mobility to be zero. The Mae Enga, living some 140 km to the east of the Duna, approach such a situation, and Meggitt (1965:12) records an average number of domiciliary changes (presumably changes between clan-parish territories) of 0.2 moves per adult male (N=223). Considering only changes in parish of residence, I recorded 2.01 moves per adult male at Horaile (N=86). Although little comparable data can be found in the ethnographic literature, it seems reasonable to suppose that residential mobility in most societies is inversely correlated with population density (as is true in the above cases).

In order to assess the effects of mobility upon the formation of local traditions it would also be necessary to know how far people move over the landscape. Data derived from the residential histories of Horaile men are presented in Table 8. There are seven parishes separating Aluni from Hareke, and although a few Horaile men have made residential shifts of this magnitude during their lives, none of the Aluni men in our experiment had ever resided at Hareke, nor any of the Hareke men at Aluni. Of the ten Horaile men who had made moves over four or more parishes, four had moved as children, before the age at which familiarity with *aré* is acquired. Thus only around 7% of all men make moves of any great distance. On the other hand, there is considerable movement between adjacent parishes, and this movement could create an enchainment of local traditions leading to the kind of effect JPW postulates, a single homogeneous tool tradition throughout

Table 8 Residential mobility between parishes by Horaile men

	Number of parishes moved between					
	0	1	2	3	≥4	Total
No. of men	28	31	7	10	10	86

the continuously settled areas of the valley systems occupied by the Duna (in the northwest) and the Huli (in the southeast) and possibly beyond. A sophisticated model of this enchainment would be required if one wished to estimate the probabilities of divergence between the local traditions at each end of the chain.

All of the above reasoning is, however, based on an assumption that mental templates *qua* local traditions somehow form themselves autonomously in the minds of men who are in face-to-face contact with each other. But as Kojiro's tetrahedron shows us, ideas about the forms of object are influenced by Purpose, Material and Hand in a paradigm of mutual interaction. Alexander makes a similar point of criticising the widely accepted concept of 'image' (equivalent to 'idea' or 'mental template' in this discussion) proposed by Miller, Galanter and Pribram in *Plans and the Structure of Behaviour* (1960). Alexander writes:

> The 'image' is presented there as something present in every problem-solver's mind, and used by him as a criterion for the problem's solution .... In the majority of interesting cases I do not believe that such an image exists psychologically, so that the testing paradigm described by Miller *et al* in *Plans* is therefore an incorrect description of complex problem-solving behaviour. In interesting cases the solution of the problems cannot be tested against an image, because the search for the image or criterion for success is actually going on at the same time as the search for a solution (1960:196-97).

Again, it appears that our own mental images of mental templates are too rigid. Local traditions do not exist in an isolated noumenal realm; they are in constant interaction with Purpose, Material and Hand.

What are the likely influences of these factors? Purpose, particularly for *aré kou*, can be assumed nearly constant throughout Huli and Duna country and perhaps beyond. The Purpose of an *aré kou* is that it be of suitable shape for hafting onto a simple handle of wood or cane, and that the resulting composite tool be adapted to the task of shaving or planing long strips of fine rattan into uniform widths for the manufacture of armbands and other bindings. Hand, the factor of craftsmanship and technical skill, varies considerably between men within a single local group, but there is no reason to suppose that Aluni men are on average more or less clumsy than those from Hareke, or Duna than Huli. But subtle factors may be at work here. Although stone flaking techniques throughout the Papua New Guinea Highlands are all relatively rudimentary, we have insufficient data on the distribution of different techniques (eg. hand-held core *vs.* hammer and anvil) and their effects on the stone flaking process. Yet another intriguing possibility is suggested by my observation that 'big men' seem to produce 'big *aré*' (see Appendix). Men at Horaile assert that as one moves up-valley from the Strickland River, there are more people and they are physically larger. While I lack anthropometric data, population figures and my subjective impressions of physical types in the region agree with these assertions. It might then be

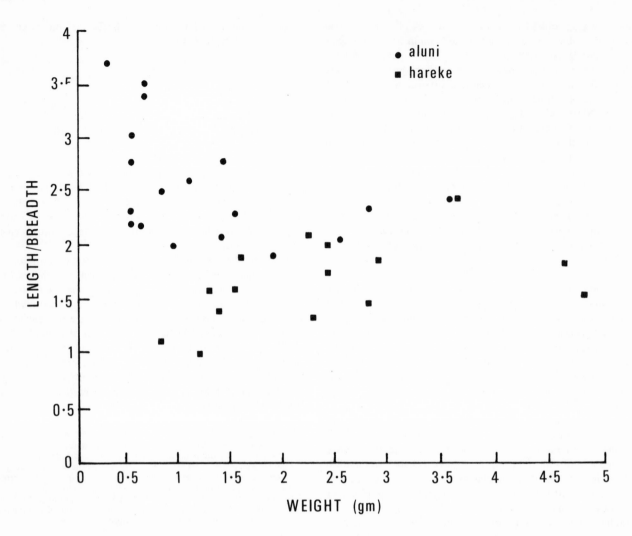

Fig. 4: Weight and length/breadth ratios of *aré kou* selected by four or more additional men from Hareke than Aluni and vice versa.

argued that the size of the maker influences the size of the tool, because the character of both 'hand' and 'purpose' (how the finished tool fits into the hand of the user) are thereby changed.

The tendency for Hareke men to select slightly larger *aré kou* than Aluni men could be explained in this way. But the most obvious variable influence is Material. There appear to be numerous local quarry sites along the Müller Range which bounds the study area on the southwest, and the qualities of stone found in these quarries show considerable variation. In making *aré kou* each man acquires a familiarity with the character of his local materials. His cumulative experience of what 'good *aré kou*' are like depends upon the results he obtains with his materials and determines the on-going development of his personal mental templates. Memory plays a role in perceptual structuring. Thus I think it likely that constancy of Purpose and (to a lesser degree) Hand are reponsible for the selection of metrically similar distributions of *aré kou* between parishes in our experiment, while variation in local materials result in slight differences in local mental templates which are responsible for variations observed. Because a man is accustomed to a particular kind of material, he tends to select examples of that kind while rejecting examples of different materials which may well be just as functionally useful. In order to test this, we have investi-

gated the attributes of those *aré kou* which had the highest *differential* rate of selection between the parishes of Aluni and Hareke (Figs. 4, 5; for procedures, see note 5). It is clear from the figures that Hareke men *do* prefer *aré kou* that are heavier and less blade-like than Aluni men. In each case also a striking feature of the selections is the resemblance of *aré kou* preferred to the kind of material available at local quarries within each parish, with Hareke men preferring dark grey stones and Aluni men a lighter brown to cream chert. We are not yet in a position to say whether or not the metrical differences observed are due to properties inherent in the materials.

JPW's second prediction concerns the amount of agreement in selection within local groups. Because most men work in the

---

5. Two analyses were performed in attempting to assess differences between groups. The data in Fig. 4 was derived by determining the number of times any particular *aré kou* was selected by the 13 men of each parish and investigating two characteristics of those preferred by 4 (or more) *more* men in one parish than the other. Thus an *aré kou* selected by 6 men at Aluni and 12 at Hareke is considered to be preferred by Hareke, while one preferred by 5 at Aluni and only 1 at Hareke is preferred by Aluni.

The data in Fig. 5 plots two characteristics of the *aré kou* preferred by all or all-but-one (i.e. 12 or 13) men at both Hareke and Aluni, but distinguishes between those selected by both groups and those selected by only one.

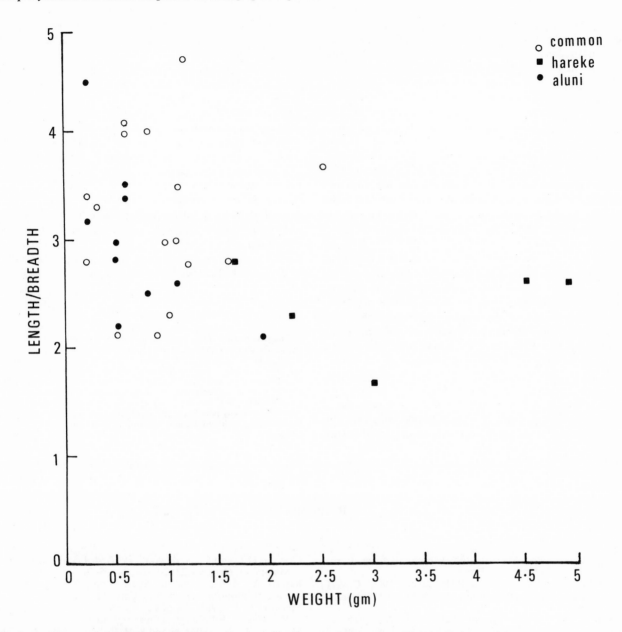

Fig. 5: Weight and length/breadth ratios of *aré kou* selected by all, or all but one, men at Aluni and Hareke.

isolation of their own homesteads, and because there is no formal teaching about *aré* or encodement of dimensions of form within their language, JPW predicts that there will be a large amount of disagreement between selections within local groups. He finds his prediction falsified in four cases out of five and suggests that despite the factors working against agreement, operational (i.e. functional or purposeful) criteria give rise to a covert category held in common by members of the group. This suggestion is in line with my own interpretation in terms of the interplay of Material (variable between groups but constant within them) and Purpose (constant between groups) in the formation of mental templates. I would suggest that even if the men of a local group operated their stone technology in total isolation from one another there would still be a strong tendency for them to arrive at similar mental templates, since both their Materials and their Purposes are constant.

N.M.

APPENDIX

A visit to a quarry In order to learn something of the Duna way of making flake-tools, I gathered together four men known to me well and set off for a quarry within the forests of the lower part of Horaile. None of the men had been to this place before and we stopped first at the house of one man's father-in-law to ask directions. We were directed along a path to the homestead nearest the quarry, and told that we would find the 'father of the place' at home. This man had lived with 'brothers' and 'fathers' in the immediate vicinity of the quarry for many years, and it would be a breach of etiquette not to visit him first. When we reached his homestead he gave us sugarcane to eat and then joined us on our trip. We reached a stagnant green pond at the bottom of a sinkhole within the forest. Green light filtered through the moss-laden trees, while a swarm of white butterflies danced in a beam of sunlight from a patch of blue sky overhead. The floor of the sinkhole about the pond was strewn with rubble—chunks of limestone and occasional nodules of chert and flint-like stones (called in Duna *aré kuani*, 'new, unripe flints'). Each man gathered nodules and found a place to work, either by himself or beside another man, facing in such a way that flying splinters of rock would not strike anyone. Some of the men gathered a number of small nodules. One man dug a huge nodule out of the ground, which he then hurled against an outcrop of limestone in order to break it open. One man used a hand-held core technique, another used a swinging stroke to break flakes from his core against a stationary anvil; the others selected hammers and anvils of varying sizes and kinds of rock. Sometimes a core would be wrapped about with a piece of leaf to control the splintering of fine pieces; but some men never seemed to use this technique. No one talked very much. The sinkhole echoed with the sounds of hammering and sharp reports as flakes were struck off their cores, sometimes accompanied by sparks and the smell of limestone. Most of the stone was grey to orangish chert, although a few of the nodules proved to contain black flint-like stone. Breaking open one such nodule a man exclaimed '*Aii! aré mindu kone, aré yokona!*' ('Aii! truly black flint, *yokona* flint!'). Occasionally the men showed each other especially good flakes they had struck off: '*Kepa! aré peli kone, naipi numbawan tru.*' ('Look! a really good flint, a firstclass knife.') I asked them to divide their outputs into *aré kone* ('true flints') and *aré kou* ('flints for wrapping onto a handle'). Each man kept his output beside him, carefully arranged on one or two leaves. After about an hour of intense

concentration on the task they began to lose interest. I gathered their outputs into labelled plastic bags and we returned home.

On this and following days my over-riding impressions were of the diversity of methods and materials, the variability in the assemblages produced and an elusive but somehow apparent individual style that characterised both the ways of working and the outputs of each man. 'Big men' (who were often both physically big and socially voluble) seemed to produce either bigger *aré* or larger piles of *aré* than anyone else. 'Thought men' respected for their ability to settle disputes and effect compromises) seemed to work more slowly and produce thinner flakes. 'Nothing men' (men of no particular merit) seemed to have problems with their techniques and their assemblages were often irregular. However, one 'nothing man' turned out to be a natural craftsman. Other men admired his flakes for their consistently good quality, yet he claimed that he had never before tried his hand at *aré pouya* ('flint husking').

N.M.

Acknowledgement This research was entirely financed by the Australian Research Grants Committee and, through the provision of research leave to JPW, by the University of Sydney. The Australian National University kindly allowed us to use their field house at Lake Kopiago and we were greatly helped by officers in several branches of the Government of Papua New Guinea, especially Tom Webster, A.D.O., Lake Kopiago. Richard Wright kindly advised us on statistical matters. Members of many parishes in the Tumbudu River valley were prepared to cooperate with our curious requests and we are grateful to them above all.

References

Alexander, C., 1964. *Notes on the synthesis of form*. Cambridge: Harvard University Press.

Berlin, B., D.E. Breedlove and P.H. Raven, 1968. Covert categories and folk taxonomies. *American Anthropologist*, 70:290-99.

Binford, L., 1972. Paradigms and Palaeolithic Research. *In* D.L. Clarke (ed.), *Models in archaeology*, pp. 109-66. London: Methuen.

Brown, R., 1964. Discussion of the conference, *American Anthropologist* (Special publication: Transcultural studies in cognition, A.K. Romney and R.G. D'Andrade, eds) 66, (3), Part 2: 243-53.

Clarke, D.L., 1968. *Analytical archaeology*. London: Methuen.

Collins, D., 1969. Culture traditions and environment of early man. *Current Anthropology*, 10:267-316.

Deetz, J., 1967. *Invitation to archaeology*. New York: Natural History Press.

Dunnell, R.C., 1971. *Systematics in prehistory*. Glencoe: Free Press.

Durkheim, E. and M. Mauss, 1901-2. De quelques formes primitives de classification: contribution à l'étude des representations collectives', *Année Sociologique*, VI (1901-02), Paris: 1-72. Translated by R. Needham as *Primitive classification*. London: Cohen and West, 1963.

Fortune, R.F., 1935. *Manus religion*. American Philosophical Society, Memoirs, 3. Philadelphia.

Glasse, R., 1968. *Huli of Papua*. Cahiers de l'Homme, No.8. Mouton,: The Hague.

Harris, M. 1968. Comments. *In* S.R. and L.R. Binford (eds) *New perspectives in archaeology*, pp. 359-61. Chicago: Aldine.

Heider, E.R., 1972. Probabilities, sampling and ethnographic method: the case of Dani colour names. *Man*, n.s., 7:448-66.

Hogbin, H.I. and C. Wedgwood, 1952-54. Local groupings in Melanesia. *Oceania*, 23: 241-76; 24: 58-76.

Kojiro, Y., 1965. *Forms in Japan*. Translated by Kenneth Yasuda. Honolulu: East-West Center Press.

Meggitt, M.J., 1965. *The lineage system of the Mae-Enga of New Guinea*. Edinburgh: Oliver and Boyd.

Miller, G.A., E. Gallanter and K.H. Pribram., 1960. *Plans and the structure of behaviour*. New York: Holt, Rinehart and Winston.

Rouse, I., 1972. *Introduction to prehistory*. New York: McGraw-Hill.

Sheets, P.D., 1973. The structure of an industry: a behavioural analysis of Mesoamerican chipped stone. Paper presented to Annual Meeting, American Anthropological Association, New Orleans.

Sinclair, J., 1966. *Behind the ranges*. Melbourne: Melbourne University Press.

—— 1973. *Wigmen of Papua*. Brisbane: Jacaranda Press.

Spaulding, A.C., 1960. Statistical description and comparison of artifact assemblages. *In* R.F. Heizer and S.F. Cook (eds) *The application of quantitative methods in archaeology*. pp. 60-83. Viking Fund Publications in Anthropology, 28.

Thomas, D.H., 1974. *Predicting the past*. New York: Holt, Rinehart and Winston.

Wallace, A.F.C., 1962. Culture and cognition. *Science*, 135: 351-57.

Watson, P.J., S.A. LeBlanc and C.L. Redman, 1971. *Explanation in archaeology*. New York: Columbia University Press.

White, J.P., 1969. Fabricators, outils écaillés or scalar cores? *Mankind*, 6:658-66.

—— and D.H. Thomas, 1972. What mean these stones? *In* D.L. Clarke (ed.) *Models in archaeology*, pp. 275-308. London: Methuen.

List of contributors

D. ALLBROOK, Department of Anatomy and Human Biology, University of Western Australia, Nedlands, W.A.

M. J. BARRETT, (formerly) Department of Oral Biology, University of Adelaide, Adelaide, S.A.

L. R. BINFORD, Department of Anthropology, University of New Mexico, Albuquerque, U.S.A.

F. H. BORDES, Laboratoire de Geologie, Universite de Bordeaux, 33405 Talence, France.

S. BULMER, Department of Anthropology, University of Auckland, New Zealand.

J. K. CLEGG, Department of Anthropology, University of Sydney, Sydney, N.S.W.

E. CROSBY, Department of Prehistory and Anthropology, Australian National University, Canberra, A.C.T.

P. J. F. COUTTS, Victoria Archaeological Survey, 213 Lonsdale Street, Melbourne, Vic.

F. P. DICKSON, 38 Trevellyan Street, Cronulla, N.S.W.

C. E. DORTCH, Western Australian Museum, Francis Street, Perth, W.A.

L. FREEDMAN, Department of Anatomy and Human Biology, University of Western Australia, Nedlands, W.A.

A. GALLUS, 2 Patterson Street, Nunawading, Vic.

A. K. GHOSH, Department of Anthropology, University of Calcutta, Calcutta, India.

J. GOLSON, Department of Prehistory, Research School of Pacific Studies, Australian National University, Canberra, A.C.T.

R. A. GOULD, Department of Anthropology, University of Hawaii, Honolulu, U.S.A.

S. J. HALLAM, Department of Anthropology, University of Western Australia, Nedlands, W.A.

B. HAYDEN, Department of Archaeology, Simon Fraser University, Burnaby, Canada.

I. HIPUYA, c/o Catholic Mission, Horaile, Lake Kopiago, Southern Highlands Province, Papua New Guinea.

G. LL. ISAAC, Department of Anthropology, University of California, Berkley, U.S.A.

R. M. JONES, Department of Prehistory, Research School of Pacific Studies, Australian National University, Canberra, A.C.T.

J. KAMMINGA, Department of Anthropology, University of Sydney, Sydney, N.S.W.

R. J. LAMPERT, Department of Prehistory, Research School of Pacific Studies, Australian National University, Canberra, A.C.T.

H. LOURANDOS, Department of Anthropology, University of Sydney, Sydney, N.S.W.

I. MCBRYDE, Department of Prehistory and Anthropology, Australian National University, Canberra, A.C.T.

F. D. MCCARTHY, 10 Tycannah Road, Northbridge, N.S.W.

N. MODJESKA, School of Behavioural Sciences, Macquarie University, North Ryde, N.S.W.

D. J. MULVANEY, Department of Prehistory and Anthropology, Australian National University, Canberra, A.C.T.

J. F. O'CONNELL, Department of Prehistory, Research School of Pacific Studies, Australian National University, Canberra, A.C.T.

R. H. PEARCE, 21 Davies Crescent, Kalamunda, W.A.

G. L. PRETTY, South Australian Museum, North Terrace, Adelaide, S.A.

M. L. SHACKLEY, Institute of Archaeology, 35 Beaumont Street, Oxford, England.

E. D. STOCKTON, St Patricks College, Manly, N.S.W.

N. B. TINDALE, 2314 Harvard Street, Palo Alto, California, U.S.A.

R. L. VANDERWAL, Department of History, La Trobe University, Bundoora, Vic.

M. J. WALKER, Department of Anthropology, University of Sydney, Sydney, N.S.W.

J. P. WHITE, Department of Anthropology, University of Sydney, Sydney, N.S.W.

R. V. S. WRIGHT, Department of Anthropology, University of Sydney, Sydney, N.S.W.

Author

Turner, R. 206
Tuttle, R. H. 14
Twidale, C. R. 309, 320, 322
Tylor, E. B. 263

Ucko, P. J. 1, 133, 171, 192

Vandermeersch, B. 37
Vanderwal, R. L. 103, 350, 351
Vicedom, G. F. 42, 155, 156, 157
Vilaseca, S. 355
Vita-Finzi, C. 169, 171, 368, 370

Waddell, E. 159
Walker, D. 150, 174
Walker, M. J. 354, 355, 357, 359, 361, 363, 367, 373
Wallace, A. F. 381
Warner, W. L. 193, 211
Watson, P. J. 155, 156, 157, 158, 159, 162, 386
Wedgwood, C. 381

Weidenreich, F. 146
West, R. G. 337
Wet, J. M. J. de 174
White, C. 40, 57, 172, 192, 205, 208, 209, 251, 256, 257, 259, 347
White, J. P. 42, 43, 44, 45, 53, 97, 98, 100, 121, 123, 128, 131, 136, 139, 142, 150, 154, 158, 159, 180, 192, 251, 270, 271, 282, 284, 341, 350, 351, 352, 353, 380–2, 384–7, 389
Whittelegge, T. 264
Wieneke, C. 282, 284
Wilkinson, P. F. 219, 354
Willey, G. R. 104, 171
Williams, W. T. 83, 85, 96
Witthoft, J. 209
Wright, R. V. S. 123, 125, 133, 139, 192, 243, 266, 340, 351
Wyndham, W. T. 234

Yellen, J. 171
Young, T. C. 154, 158

Zubrow, E. B. W. 162

Subject

abrasion 206, 207
Abrigo Grande 363–77
  excavation of 363–8
  technology of 363–4
Acheulian 8, 9, 37–8, 149, 332
  variation in 9
activity models see site use
adze, flake 61, 117, 121, 123, 127, 164–5, 167, 174, 178, 180, 189, 192, 193, 197, 207, 271–2, 286, 342, 348
  distribution of 193
adze, ground 25, 67–82, 83–96, 154, 155, 157
  edge angle 68
  function of 67–82, 155
agriculture 40, 154–60, 345
  incipient 345
  population growth 154
  preparign land 155, 157
  technology of 155–60
anvil, see hammer and anvil
archaeology 30, 33–6, 158–9, 164, 166–8, 169, 185, 187
  and behaviour 32–3
  interdisciplinary approach 169
  patterning in, 30, 33–6, (see also, patterning)
  visibility 33–6, 158–9, 164, 166–8, 185, 187
  of women 185, 187
Arnhem Land 205–12, 345, 347
  incipient agriculture in 345, 347
art 112, 201, 211, 237, 239, 241, 252–3, 254, 256, 355, 357 365–6, 367–71, 373, 377
artifact, conception of 133–44, 179, 243, 266–7, 380–90
artifact, cultural marker 5–6, 8, 147, 341, 320
artifact, disposal of 5, 33–6, 166, 182, 328
artifact, distribution 251–61
artifact, function 2–3, 5, 46, 52–3, 60, 85, 88, 90, 133–44, 148, 149, 151, 164–6, 178–87, 205, 212, 219, 220, 239, 256, 265, 321, 386,
  replication of 205–12
artifact homogeniety 85, 95–6
artifact patterning 5–6, 24, 30–1, 33–6
artifact variation 9–10, 60–6, 83, 85–96, 104, 269–81 (see also, cultural variation, technological variation)
Australopithicus, hand and toolmaking 16
awls 75, 214, 305, 355
axe 25, 37, 39, 60–1, 63, 64, 67–82, 83–96, 112, 119, 121, 123, 141, 148–50, 151, 152, 154, 155, 160, 164, 187, 192, 193, 194, 196, 197, 207, 242, 251, 253, 257–61, 306, 332–9, 348
  Acheulian handaxe 37–9

bout coupé handaxe 332–9
  function of 67–82
  grooved 112, 121
  ground 141, 154, 187, 192, 193, 194, 196, 197, 207, 251, 257, 306
  manufacture of 119, 259
axe/adze 40–58, 154, 159
  lenticular 57, 159

backed blades 38, 99, 123, 192, 229, 234, 255, 282–6, 323, 342, 355, 357, 365–66
  function of 282, 286
  manufacture of 282
  variation 284 (see also, bondi points)
Baliem Valley 154
bamboo knives, see knives, bamboo
Batari 43
bipolar core 97–103, 119, 121, 127, 350–3
bipolar flaking technique 98, 214, 350
Blue Mountains 342, 343
Bobadeen 351
Bondaian 229, 341, 342
bondi points 98, 99, 100, 101, 102, 192, 193, 255, 283, 343, 350
  distribution of 193 (see also, backed blades)
bone tools 193, 305, 306, 309, 311–13, 321, 325
boomerang 19, 193, 196
  for butchering 19
Bullsbrook 282–6
burials 288–329
  status in 304–5
burins 119, 123, 148, 185, 187, 192, 229, 271, 355
  function of 185
burning 7, 75, 155, 169, 170, 173, 175, 195, 197, 348
burrens 116, 192
Burrill Lake 206, 216–17
butchering 19, 25, 42, 164, 183
  boomerangs 19
  teeth 19
butt working 282–6

Callabonna, Lake 348
Capertee 351
Capertian 341, 342
Cathedral Cave 60–6
ceremonies 170, 201, 300, 346
change, see technological change